African American National Biography

African American National Biography

SECOND EDITION

HENRY LOUIS GATES JR.

EVELYN BROOKS HIGGINBOTHAM

Editors in Chief

VOLUME 6: HITE, MATTIE – JUST, ERNEST EVERETT

OXFORD

UNIVERSITY PRESS

OXFORD

UNIVERSITY PRESS

Oxford University Press is a department of the University of Oxford.
It furthers the University's objective of excellence in research, scholarship,
and education by publishing worldwide.

Oxford New York
Auckland Cape Town Dar es Salaam Hong Kong Karachi
Kuala Lumpur Madrid Melbourne Mexico City Nairobi
New Delhi Shanghai Taipei Toronto

With offices in
Argentina Austria Brazil Chile Czech Republic France Greece
Guatemala Hungary Italy Japan Poland Portugal Singapore
South Korea Switzerland Thailand Turkey Ukraine Vietnam

Oxford is a registered trademark of Oxford University Press in the UK and certain other countries.

Published in the United States of America by
Oxford University Press
198 Madison Avenue, New York, NY 10016

Library of Congress Cataloging-in-Publication Data
African American national biography / editors in chief Henry Louis Gates Jr., Evelyn Brooks Higginbotham. – 2nd ed.
p. cm.
Includes bibliographical references and index.
ISBN 978-0-19-999036-8 (volume 1; hdbk.); ISBN 978-0-19-999037-5 (volume 2; hdbk.); ISBN 978-0-19-999038-2 (volume 3; hdbk.);
ISBN 978-0-19-999039-9 (volume 4; hdbk.); ISBN 978-0-19-999040-5 (volume 5; hdbk.); ISBN 978-0-19-999041-2 (volume 6; hdbk.);
ISBN 978-0-19-999042-9 (volume 7; hdbk.); ISBN 978-0-19-999043-6 (volume 8; hdbk.); ISBN 978-0-19-999044-3 (volume 9; hdbk.);
ISBN 978-0-19-999045-0 (volume 10; hdbk.); ISBN 978-0-19-999046-7 (volume 11; hdbk.); ISBN 978-0-19-999047-4 (volume 12;
hdbk.); ISBN 978-0-19-992077-8 (12-volume set; hdbk.)
1. African Americans – Biography – Encyclopedias. 2. African Americans – History – Encyclopedias.
I. Gates, Henry Louis. II. Higginbotham, Evelyn Brooks, 1945-
E185.96.A4466 2012
920'.009296073 – dc23
[B]
2011043281

1 3 5 7 9 8 6 4 2
Printed in the United States of America
on acid-free paper

African American National Biography

Hite, Mattie (ca. 1890–ca. 1935), blues singer and musician, was born in New York City around 1890. Very little is known about her family or upbringing except that she may have been a niece of LES HITE, a 1930s saxophone player and big band leader. Mattie Hite, who might have also been known by the alternative first name of Nellie, was a blues and cabaret singer who worked at various jazz clubs in New York and Chicago and sang on more than a dozen albums between 1915 and 1932.

Hite began singing in Chicago in 1915 at the Panama Café for twelve dollars a week with other blues singers such as ALBERTA HUNTER and FLORENCE MILLS. She returned to New York City in 1919 to work at Barron Wilkins's Café. For the next twelve years, Hite supported herself from performances at a host of New York City nightclubs, including Edmund's Cellar (1920), Leroy's (1920), the Lafayette Theatre (1928), the Lincoln Theatre (1928), and the Nest Club (1929). The height of her career coincided with Prohibition (1920–1933), which prompted the creation of a number of smaller, concealed nightclubs called "speakeasies," where alcohol was available and jazz performers were quite popular. An accomplished performer, Hite broke many barriers for African American women singers, as her songs became known for their emotional depth and overall quality. Although she performed live far more often than she recorded, her contribution to the Jazz Age—between the end of World War I and the onset of the Great Depression—was substantial, and she directly influenced the following generation of jazz singers. Widely esteemed as a blues singer,

Hite was revered for her risqué words and exaggerated toughness in the barely integrated racial clubs and dance halls where the sad and reflective tone of the blues ruled the room. Hite's true skill was her full tone and warmth—her vocals invited a listener into a life of struggle and pain. However, she was not as financially successful as other singers such as BESSIE SMITH, ETHEL WATERS, Alberta Hunter, and MAMIE SMITH.

In late 1920s New York City Hite joined other singers in a number of revues that sometimes ran at Broadway and Off-Broadway venues for a few weeks at a time, including *Hot Feet* (1928), *Tip Top* (1928), *Chocolate Blondes* (1929), *Temple of Jazz* (1929), and *Desires of 1930* (1930). These revues might feature songs, sketches, and short dances, often based upon a comedic theme. Drawing in bigger crowds and more attention, Hite's following grew, which meant more opportunities to be recorded. Hite appeared on a handful of jazz recordings with piano accompaniment, including a 1920 album with Julian Motley (on the Victor label), a 1923 recording with FLETCHER HENDERSON (on the Pathe label), and one with Cliff Jackson (on Columbia) in 1930. She was listed on fewer than a dozen albums during her life, but reappeared on reissues and newer collections, such as the multivolume set *The Female Blues Singers*, (volume 9, on the Document label). One significant recording that helped Hite build her popularity was her 1924 version of "St. Joe's Infirmary," a blues tune that was later popularized by CAB CALLOWAY. Hite's emotional tone makes the listener feel the *blues* within the song. The song is a narrative ballad about a dead lover, and she croons the lyrics in a raspy and weary-sounding voice:

Let her go
Let her go
God bless her …
I may be killed on the ocean
I may be killed by a cannonball
but let me tell you, buddy
That a woman was the cause of it all.

Hite's last documented performance was a 1932 revue at the Lafayette Theatre in New York City; after that, her whereabouts and the details of her life are largely unknown. In a 1960 article in *Jazz Review Magazine*, the author James Johnson called Hite "one of the greatest cabaret singers of all time" (Mar./Apr. 1960, 13).

FURTHER READING

Harris, Sheldon. *Blues Who's Who* (1979).

JAMES FARGO BALLIETT

Hobson Pilot, Ann (6 Nov. 1943–), harpist, was born Ann Stevens Hobson in Philadelphia, Pennsylvania, the younger of two daughters of Grace Stevens Smith and Harrison D. Hobson. Her father was a social worker and her mother an accomplished pianist and a Philadelphia public school teacher. Her older sister, Harriet Hobson, was a child prodigy who began piano studies at age two, performed in piano recitals by age four, and by high school gave up the instrument.

When Hobson was five, her family moved to Germany where her father, a U.S. Army lieutenant colonel, was stationed in Giessen and Mannheim after World War II. Hobson's musical training began at age six with her mother's lessons on piano and music fundamentals. She attended the U.S. Army school, and her musical talent was further nurtured by German piano teachers and the rich musical and cultural heritage of Germany. The Hobsons spent four years in Germany.

Hobson and her family returned to Philadelphia in 1953, and she continued piano studies with her mother. She also was enrolled at the Philadelphia Girls School. Hobson became upset when her mother interrupted her practice to correct her mistakes, and she consequently took a dislike to practicing. Her mother terminated her piano lessons when Hobson was fourteen, citing her own lack of interest in the instrument. This suited Hobson, as by this time she was motivated to find another instrument her mother was unfamiliar with.

The public schools in Philadelphia at this time had a fine instrumental music program. But there were already too many students studying the flute, violin, and cello at the Philadelphia Girls School, and only the harp was available. Because she had a strong piano background, Hobson was encouraged by the school's chairman to take up the harp. She did so, and soon found that she excelled at playing it.

Hobson gained valuable experience performing as harpist in churches in Philadelphia after only one year of study. She attended the Philadelphia High School for Girls, graduating in 1961. Her first professional job as a harpist was at age seventeen performing at Philadelphia's Latin Casino, where she played five days a week following performances by Peggy Lee and JOHNNY MATHIS. She made considerable money at these gigs and continued gaining experience by playing in the Philadelphia All-City High School Orchestra and later in the all-black Philadelphia Concert Orchestra.

In her senior year in 1960, Hobson came into contact with the principal harpist of the Philadelphia Orchestra, Marilyn Costello, who also taught in the Philadelphia public schools and later at the Curtis Institute of Music. Costello became her mentor and harp teacher. Costello was responsible for training many of the harpists of the world's major orchestras, including those of the Berlin Philharmonic, the Metropolitan Opera, and the National and St. Louis symphony orchestras. Therefore, being recognized by her as a major talent was important.

In 1960 Hobson, through the encouragement of Costello, auditioned for Carlos Salzedo, founder and director of the Maine Harp Colony in Camden, Maine, and considered one of the most eminent performers and instructors on the instrument. But he refused to admit black students and, though impressed by Hobson, would not make an exception for her. After graduating from high school, Hobson enrolled at the Philadelphia Musical Academy and continued studies with Costello. After Salzedo's death in 1961, the Maine Harp Colony, renamed the Salzedo Harp Colony, admitted Hobson for the summer of 1962. Her instructor was Alice Chalifoux, the harpist of the Cleveland Orchestra and director of the Harp Colony. She would have a profound influence on Hobson's development and eventual career. Hobson continued study with Chalifoux when she transferred from the Philadelphia Musical Academy in her junior year on a full scholarship to the Cleveland Institute of Music, where she graduated in 1966 with a BM.

During her senior year at the Cleveland Institute, in 1965–1966, Hobson became substitute second harpist for the Pittsburgh Symphony Orchestra. In the fall of 1966 she became principal harpist of the National Symphony Orchestra in Washington,

D.C., becoming also its only black member. The original one-year position was extended to three years. In 1969, with the encouragement of the Boston Pops conductor Arthur Fiedler, she auditioned for the position of principal harpist of the Boston Pops, a position which included duties as assistant principal harpist of the Boston Symphony Orchestra. She was selected over thirty other candidates for those positions. She held the position of assistant harpist of the Boston Symphony Orchestra until 1980, when she became its principal harpist.

In 1971, along with her flutist and cellist colleagues of the Boston Symphony Orchestra, Hobson founded the New England Harp Trio. She was also a member of the contemporary music group Collage, the Boston Symphony Chamber Players, and the Ritz Chamber Players. She made her Tanglewood solo debut on July 1972 with the Boston Symphony Orchestra performing Mozart's Concerto in C for Flute and Harp. After that time, she performed numerous times as soloist at Tanglewood. On many occasions she performed the Concerto for Harp and Orchestra by Alberto Ginastera with the Boston Symphony Orchestra and Boston Pops.

In August 1980 she married R. Prentice Pilot, a jazz bassist and music teacher in Boston public schools. They had a daughter, Lynn, who studied the flute and viola but became a doctor of naprapathy in Chicago. Pilot was originally from Chicago, where he received his BM in Music Education from Roosevelt University. In 1972 he relocated to Boston for graduate study at the New England Conservatory of Music. He has worked as an administrator and music teacher in both Chicago and Boston and played the string bass with the Boston Pops Orchestra. Ann Hobson Pilot served on the harp faculty of the Philadelphia Musical Academy; the Ambler (1968–69), Marlboro, Newport (1993), and Sarasota (2000, 2003, 2006) music festivals; the New England Conservatory of Music (beginning in 1971); Tanglewood Music Center (beginning in 1989); and Boston University (beginning in 2002), including its Tanglewood Institute (beginning in 2002). She conducted master classes in the United States and in the People's Republic of China and organized harp clinics for young students. She also served on the board of trustees at the Longy School of Music (1993–1996) and on the board of directors at Holy Trinity School, Haiti (1993–1996).

Hobson Pilot enjoyed an extensive career as a soloist with major symphony orchestras including the Springfield and Utah symphony orchestras (1998), the Orchestra of Port-au-Prince in Haiti, the London Symphony (1993), the New Zealand Symphony Orchestra (1993), the National Symphony Orchestra of South Africa (1997), the Symphony by the Sea in Salem and Byfield, Massachusetts (2007), and orchestras in other countries. She has also performed with Claudia Arrau, Leonard Bernstein, Rafael Frühbeck de Burgos, Charles Dutoit, Arthur Fiedler, James Galway, James Levine, JESSYE NORMAN, Seiji Ozawa, John Williams, and others. She recorded the harp concertos by Beethoven, Norman Dello Joio, Alberto Ginastera, Kevin Kaska, and William Mathias. Her 1991 album for Boston Records, titled *Ann Hobson Pilot, Harpist*, included sonatas and partitas by Johann Sebastian Bach and works by Claude Debussy, Gabriel Fauré, Paul Hindemith, Albert Hay Malotte, Gabriel Pierné, Maurice Ravel, and Carlos Salzedo. She also released several albums devoted to contemporary music, including *Contrasts*, with Leone Buyse on flute, which included Joseph Castaldo's *Contrasts* for solo harp (1956); John Heiss's *Four Lyric Pieces* for solo flute (1962); Geoffrey Dana Hicks's *A Dream* for alto flute and harp (1994); Katherine Hoover's *Kokopeli* for solo flute (1990); David Noon's Sonata da Camera for flute and harp, Opus 89 (1986); Vincent Persichetti's Serenade no. 10 for flute and harp (1957); and Charles Rochester Young's *Song of the Lark* for flute and harp (1989).

She and her husband initiated a concert series beginning with the 1993/1994 concert season in St. Maarten, where they had a home, and St. Croix, with emphasis on African American composers and musicians, chamber music, and jazz. They both were prominent members of several outreach programs in the United States dedicated to exposing black and other minority students to classical music. Free instrumental instruction forms part of the programs, which include the Boston Symphony Orchestra's Cultural Diversity Committee (beginning in 1991); the Boston Music Education Collaborative; and Boston's String Training and Educational Program (STEP) (beginning in spring 1993).

In 1997 Hobson Pilot traveled to Johannesburg, South Africa, in search of the roots of the harp and performed WILLIAM GRANT STILL's *Ennanga* with the National Symphony of Johannesburg. Her trip was documented in the 1998 video *Ann Hobson Pilot: A Musical Journey*, which premiered in 1998 on PBS.

Hobson Pilot received several awards and honors, including those from the Professional Arts Society of Philadelphia (1987), an honorary doctorate of fine arts from Bridgewater State College (1988), Sigma Alpha Iota's Distinguished Woman of the Year Award (1991), the Philadelphia College of Performing Arts, School of Music Alumni Achievement Award (1992), and the Distinguished Alumni Achievement Award, Cleveland Institute of Music (1993). In 2000 she was honored by the Boston Pops for her contributions to music education.

FURTHER READING

Dyer, Richard. "Striking a Note for Diversity; BSO's Pilot Looks for Ways to Aid Other Black Musicians," *Boston Globe*, 5 June 1992: 25.

Handy, A. Antoinette. "Ann Hobson-Pilot, Harpist," in *Notable Black American Women* l.2, ed. Jessie Carney Smith (1996).

"An Interview with Harpist Ann Hobson Pilot of the Boston Symphony and R. Prentice Pilot of the Boston Pops" *Reunion* (Sudbury) (1 Nov. 1994).

Koch, John. "Ann Hobson Pilot," *Boston Globe Magazine* (2 July 2000).

Thomas, Cullen F. "Hobson, Pilot Ann," in *Current Biography Yearbook* (2003).

BARBARA BONOUS-SMITH

Hodges, Augustus M. (18 Mar. 1854–22 Aug. 1916), journalist and writer, was born Augustus Michael Hodges in either Brooklyn, New York, or Virginia, the eldest child of Sarah Ann Corprew and Willis Augustus Hodges, the latter an abolitionist leader, Reconstruction politician, and journalist. Hodges's parents often divided their time between their home states of Virginia and New York, and as their exact whereabouts during the time of Augustus's birth are unknown, biographers dispute his birthplace. Biographies of Hodges published during his lifetime say he graduated from Vineland High School in New Jersey, but Hodges once said that he lived in Virginia from age fourteen to twenty-eight. As a young adult, Hodges taught school in Kempsville, Virginia, the township where he cast his first vote. After graduating from the Hampton Normal and Agricultural Institute in 1874, two years before his classmate BOOKER T. WASHINGTON received his diploma, Hodges was elected to the Virginia House of Delegates in 1877 but was denied his seat by the Democratic Party. He remained in Virginia for five more years before moving to Brooklyn in 1882, where he resided until the end of his life.

In 1885 Hodges married Anna Kennedy, an Irish immigrant, and the couple had three children. His family life inspired his writing, which was prolific during the latter part of the nineteenth century. Irish immigrants in general were especially sympathetic to the political and social plight of African Americans and so could be allies in the quest for full American citizenship. In his regular column in the *Freeman* of Indianapolis, Hodges wrote under the moniker "B. Square." In addition to his *Freeman* column, "B. Square's Bluster," Hodges wrote short essays, fiction, poetry, fables, and stories for children. His work appeared in many of the leading African American newspapers and magazines, including the Baltimore *Afro-American*, the *Christian Recorder* of the African Methodist Episcopal (AME) Church, and the *Colored American*. He started his own newspaper, the *Brooklyn Sentinel*, in either 1889 or 1890.

Hodges was known to be active locally. In 1888 he helped found the Charles Sumner Club, named after the Massachusetts senator who was badly beaten in 1854 for delivering an antislavery speech. The club established a free reading room, with its books and newspapers being donations from its three hundred members, including Hodges's aunt, Catherine Corprew. In addition to weekly debates on such topics as the success of the Union after the Civil War, the club not only sponsored a free night school managed by Hodges's brother Willis Jr. but also registered voters for the Republican Party. Hodges also served on the governing board of the Criterion Building Association that was created in 1888 to help African Americans purchase real estate. Politically and journalistically active, Hodges also worked day jobs as a clerk, messenger, and at the navy yard—where he was appointed to the construction department in 1889.

After writing as a staff correspondent for the *Freeman* for five years, Hodges, Willis Jr., the prominent journalist IRVINE GARLAND PENN, and others founded the Augustus M. Hodges Literary Syndicate in 1894. The stated goal of the syndicate was to provide all publishing venues, black and white, with stories about African American heroes and heroines. The syndicate was also a savvy business move by Hodges to gain more financial control over his material. Hodges used his column to counter the ire of publishers who said they were insulted that Hodges demanded remuneration for his labor as a writer. He replied, "An author may be able to live upon fame but his family needs food" (*Freeman*, 27 June 1896). The Augustus M. Hodges Literary Syndicate was a practical solution Hodges posed to the so-called race problem, approached from a number of different angles by prominent writers of the nineteenth century. FREDERICK DOUGLASS, who appeared frequently in the pages of the *Freeman*, defined the existence of color prejudice not as a "race problem" but as a national problem. Booker T. Washington insisted that the problem could be solved by ensuring African Americans succeeded economically by receiving an education in agriculture. Throughout his career, Hodges echoed the sentiments of both Douglass and Washington when offering his solution: increased wealth through the establishment and patronage of African American businesses. This solution also appeared thematically in Hodges's allegorical short fiction, in such stories as "Afro-Baba and the Forty Merchants," in which the character Afro-Baba receives the respect and honor of Anglo-Saxon when he learns the magic words "Open Business" (Hodges, *Freeman*, 10 Feb. 1894).

In 1896, when Hodges began serializing his father's previously unpublished autobiography in the *Freeman*, he began receiving up to thirty letters a day from readers across the United States—some as far away as California. That same year, Hodges's wife died, and Catherine Corprew helped him to care for his three children. The response he received from women interested in his newfound bachelorhood prompted him to publish the short story "The Stepmother's Side of the Story, or The Second Wife's Tale of Woe" in 1897, after which Hodges received a letter that accused him of flirting. He replied angrily that he intended never to remarry, although he did, in 1901, to a schoolteacher from Kentucky named Caroline.

Hodges's publications tapered off as the first decade of the twentieth century progressed. He moved to Manhattan to live with his daughter a year before his passing. With the exception of Bettye Collier-Thomas's compilations of Christmas stories, Hodges's extensive body of work was not reprinted. However, his poetry, serialized novels, humorous and educational short stories, and political essays were of great literary value to post-Reconstruction era readers who subscribed to newspapers to get B. Square's views on topics ranging from Hodges's awkward bike-riding skills to the frustrations of being ignored by party leaders after voting the Republican ticket. He died in 1916 at Brooklyn's Kings County Hospital at age sixty-two.

FURTHER READING

Collier-Thomas, Bettye, ed. *A Treasury of African American Christmas Stories*, 2 vols. (1997, 1999).
Gatewood, Willard B., Jr., ed. "Introduction," *Free Man of Color: The Autobiography of Willis Augustus Hodges* (1982).
Penn, I. Garland. *The Afro-American Press and Its Editors* (1891, repr. 1969, 1976).
Wolseley, Roland E. *The Black Press, U.S.A.* (1990)

JENNY HEIL

Hodges, Ben (c. 1856–1929), also known as "Nigger Ben" or "Nigga Benjy," cowboy, cattle rustler, card cheat, and con artist, was born Benjamin F. Hodges in Texas, the son of an African American buffalo soldier assigned to the Ninth Cavalry stationed in San Antonio and a Hispanic mother, neither of whose names is known. Nothing is known about Hodges's family, childhood, or education, or indeed of his life before he arrived in Dodge City, Kansas.

Hodges arrived in the newly established town of Dodge City in 1872 with a herd of Texas cattle. Robert M. Wright, author of *Dodge City*, indicates that Hodges, then in his late twenties, was one of the earliest Texas drovers to arrive in Dodge City. Although not as famous as some of the town's other residents, notably Wyatt Earp, Bat Masterson, and Doc Holliday, Hodges was one of the most colorful characters ever to come up the Western Trail. Hodges had abandoned the itinerant life of a cowboy for the possibilities of Dodge City.

Dodge City, a town established by the Atchison, Topeka & Santa Fe Railroad in 1872, was Hodges's home. Describing Dodge City, Robert Wright, a contemporary of Hodges's, noted "People of all sorts, sizes, conditions, and nationalities; people of all color, good, bad, and indifferent, congregated here, because it was the big door to so vast a frontier" (p. 152). Cowboys eager for action transformed Dodge City into a frontier Babylon where saloons, dance halls, brothels, and gambling dens proliferated. Annual cattle drives fueled the town's growth. By 1877 drovers from Colorado, New Mexico, Texas, and the Indian Territory brought more than 200,000 Texas longhorns to Dodge City by way of the Western Trail.

Although he lacked money after arriving in Dodge City, Hodges secured a position as a local handyman. His notorious adventures as an artful dodger began with a visit to the Wright, Beverly & Company store where he overhead a group of ranchers mention the existence of an old Spanish land grant. One local rancher, noting that the rightful owners were being sought in Texas, mockingly asked Hodges if he was a potential heir. Instead of being insulted, Hodges put his mixed ancestry to good use by returning to San Antonio to learn more about the lucrative land grant. A short time later Hodges returned to Dodge City, where his contrived story persuaded some residents to accept the merits of his claim. By producing a document resembling a power of attorney authorizing Hodges to negotiate for all of the heirs, Hodges also convinced a local attorney to represent his interests. The support enabled Hodges to secure loans from local business leaders and bankers to help prosecute his claim. Some ranchers, hoping to appease Hodges in the event that he proved successful in his bid for the ancient claim, lavished him with gifts. Some residents, notes the historian Harry E. Chrisman, supported Hodges for the fun of it. Unfortunately for Hodges, his case was eventually dismissed when Print Olive, a rancher who had previously threatened to hang Hodges for cattle rustling, revealed the huckster's checkered past.

Hodges also launched other schemes. When a local fire destroyed the Wright, Beverly & Company store, Hodges learned that the four-ton safe had tumbled into the basement, landing on its doors. Hodges recognized the significance of this immediately; he knew that Texas cattlemen deposited precious legal documents and land claims in the vault. Luckily for Hodges, he had recently learned that thirty-two sections of land were currently open for settlement in Gray County. Moving quickly, Hodges wrote a letter to the land commissioner in Garden City, Kansas, the location of a newly built land office. Hodges, believing that the legal documents deposited in the safe had been destroyed, informed the land commissioner that he had recently purchased the thirty-two sections of available land in Gray County, Kansas. He noted that because of the recent fire his legal papers were currently unavailable, and he presented a number of signed affidavits to convince the gullible commissioner to issue him a letter of credit until his legal documents could be salvaged from the store's charred ruins.

The resulting document identified Hodges as the rightful owner of the thirty-two sections of land in Gray County. In addition, the letter of credit noted that he owned a large Mexican land grant in New Mexico that contained profitable gold and silver mines. The impressive collection enabled Hodges, who now dressed in the garb of a cattle baron, to bargain for cattle herds. Although Hodges had arranged for the delivery of thousands of head of cattle, a dramatic spike in the price of cattle killed his scheme when he was unable to meet the terms of the negotiated contracts. In a desperate attempt to raise the funds necessary to secure his cattle, Hodges even contacted Omaha bankers and eastern investors. When the scheme finally dissolved, Hodges's reputation was known in cattle, financial, and railroad circles from San Antonio to Kansas City.

Hodges's other schemes included securing a VIP pass from local railroad barons by convincing them that he owned large numbers of cattle that needed to be shipped by rail. His attempt to secure an appointment as Dodge City's livestock inspector failed, however, when local ranchers informed Governor Edmund N. Morrill that Hodges was one of the region's "cleverest cow thieves." Apparently the petitions of support gathered from the town's saloonkeepers, soiled doves, and gamblers failed to persuade the governor.

The enterprising Hodges became a legend in livestock circles after a storm scattered a herd belonging to John Lytle and Major Conklin. When a local agent informed Dodge City residents that his company would issue receipts, redeemable in cash, to those who helped retrieve the company's cattle and horses, Hodges forged receipts for several hundred cattle and a great many horses. He then headed to Kansas City to meet with Major Conklin, the partner responsible for reimbursing those who possessed valid receipts. Conklin, a penny-pincher who was unaware of Hodges's reputation, offered the con man a reduced price, a new outfit of clothes, ten dollars in spending money, and a week's board at a local hotel. Hodges received the royal treatment for one month until he left town after discovering that the other proprietor, John Lytle, was on his way. When the business partners finally reunited at the Saint James Hotel, Conklin pulled out a stack of forged receipts and boasted about swindling an ignorant black cowpoke named Ben Hodges. The other cattlemen, having heard of Hodges's exploits, burst into laughter.

A bold attempt at rustling a herd of dairy cattle nearly cost Hodges his life when authorities arrested Hodges because circumstantial evidence hinted at his involvement in the herd's disappearance. Robert M. Wright posted bond for Hodges. Wright, who remarked that he liked watching good con men at work, later recalled that "my sympathies went out to him, as he had no friends and no money, and I set about his discharge on my firm belief of his innocence" (Wright, 275). Hodges's courtroom performance was brilliant. Perhaps the penalty of death for cattle rustlers provided the inspiration that Hodges needed to develop tall tales regarding his ties to Spanish nobility and New Mexico landholdings. His theatrical performance resulted in so many explosions of laughter from the jurors that the judge finally prohibited any further outbursts.

The jury later returned a verdict of not guilty, thereby saving Hodges's life. Ironically, the pilfered cows had returned to their owners a few days later when a storm scattered them from the isolated canyon that Hodges had driven them to. Wright ended his brief written account of Ben Hodges's exploits by noting, "I could fill a large book with events in the life of this remarkable fellow" (Wright, 277).

Although frequently described as a deadbeat and general high-hander, according to historical records Hodges, a fluent Spanish speaker, was liked by Dodge City residents, who relished his quick wit and colorful scams. Later in his life Hodges relished his status as a Dodge City celebrity. The local children visited him often to hear his fanciful stories and tall tales of the Old West. Local residents even outfitted a shack for the indigent Hodges to live in. Although poor, Hodges managed to eke out a living by selling geese and vegetables that he grew on a small plot of land.

The pioneering black cowboy and notorious Western swindler died in Dodge City at Saint Anthony's Hospital. The town's inhabitants buried Hodges in Dodge City's Maple Grove Cemetery near his old acquaintances, where even in death they could keep an eye on him. His tombstone reads, "Ben Hodges, Self-styled Desperado, a Colorful Pioneer, 1856–1929."

It has been estimated that of the approximately thirty-five thousand cowboys working the Western cattle trails from the mid-1860s until the beef bonanza crashed by the late-1880s, about a quarter, or eight or nine thousand, were African American. Many of the black cowboys, notably BILL PICKETT, NAT LOVE, and BOSE IKARD—who often had to cope with bad horses that white cowhands frequently shunned—became particularly good riders, ropers, cooks, wranglers, and top hands. In the Kansas cow towns where segregation still flourished, blacks were often forced to bunk in local stables. Even the town's brothels were segregated. Only the gambling parlors, eager to relieve the recently paid cowboys of their earnings, allowed African Americans. Despite Jim Crow's presence, many black cowboys felt that they enjoyed better treatment on the open range, where they ate, slept, and worked alongside whites who respected their abilities and skills.

FURTHER READING

Billington, Monroe Lee, and Roger D. Hardaway, eds. *African Americans on the Western Frontier* (1998).

Chrisman, Harry E. *Lost Trails of the Cimarron* (1961).

Cromwell, Arthur, Jr., ed. *The Black Frontier* (1970).

Haywood, C. Robert. "'No Less a Man': Blacks in Cow Town Dodge City, 1876–1886," *Western Historical Quarterly* 19.2 (May 1988).

Wright, Robert M. *Dodge City, the Cowboy Capital, and the Great Southwest in the Days of the Wild Indian, the Buffalo, the Cowboy, Dance Halls, Gambling Halls, and Bad Men* (1913).

JON L. BRUDVIG

Hodges, Johnny (25 July 1907–11 May 1970), jazz musician, was born Cornelius Hodges in Cambridge, Massachusetts, the son of John Hodges and Katie Swan. The family moved to Boston when Cornelius was an infant, and he grew up in a rich musical environment. His neighbors included HARRY CARNEY, the future baritone saxophonist for the DUKE ELLINGTON band, and both his mother and sister played piano. Katie Hodges taught him enough piano so that he could play at house hops, and throughout his career he often worked out musical ideas at the keyboard.

During his early teens Hodges began to play both soprano (curved) and alto saxophone. He met SIDNEY BECHET in 1920 when the soprano saxophonist came to Boston with a burlesque show, and Bechet and LOUIS ARMSTRONG through their recordings became Hodges's chief influences. He gained early experience playing in groups led by Bobby Sawyer and the pianist Walter Johnson, and he began to visit New York City on weekends, playing with the pianist LUCKEY ROBERTS's society band, with WILLIE "THE LION" SMITH at the Rhythm Club, and in various cutting contests. But his most important early experience was with Bechet, who adopted Hodges as his protégé and introduced him to the straight soprano saxophone. At Bechet's Club Pasha, Hodges played soprano duets with his mentor and often led the group when Bechet was late or absent.

From 1925 until 1928 Hodges spent time in both Boston and New York, playing with groups led by Lloyd Scott and CHICK WEBB. Duke Ellington's early group, the Washingtonians, spent summers in New England, and at times Hodges heard them in person. Ellington heard Hodges in both Boston and New York. Twice Ellington invited him to join the band, but Hodges felt he needed more experience. Finally, in 1928, on Webb's recommendation and after Otto Hardwick (Ellington's alto and soprano saxophonist) had been injured in an automobile accident, Hodges joined Ellington for a stay that, with only one interruption, lasted until his death.

Hodges immediately became a star attraction, and Ellington often turned to him for compositional and melodic ideas, contrasting his smooth tone with the "jungle" sounds of JOE ("Tricky Sam") NANTON, BUBBER MILEY, and COOTIE WILLIAMS. During the 1930s Hodges developed the sensuous, deeply lyrical sound that became his trademark, "a tone so beautiful," Ellington later wrote, "it sometimes brought tears to the eyes." His playing sounded like "poured honey" that could "melt the melody to smoldering." Hodges's deeply sensual sound is evident in such specialties as "Warm Valley" and "Passion Flower" and in the later Ellington compositions "Isfahan," "Come Sunday," "Star-Crossed Lovers," and BILLY STRAYHORN's masterpiece, "Blood Count." But Hodges's playing stayed rooted in the blues, clearly so on such pieces as "Jeep's Blues" and on the sextet album he recorded with Ellington in 1959, *Back to Back*. His solos never failed to convey a propulsive sense of swing. Pieces like "The Jeep Is Jumpin'," "Things Aint What They Used to Be," and "On the Sunny Side of the Street" are forever marked as swinging Hodges vehicles.

By 1940 Hodges had tired of the burden of playing lead and solos on both alto and soprano saxophones, and he decided to concentrate on the alto. He also began a long series of recordings with small groups drawn largely from Ellington's band. He recorded nine sextet sessions in 1938 and 1939 under the name of Johnny Hodges and His Orchestra, with Ellington on piano, and in 1947 he recorded with the Johnny Hodges All-Stars. In 1948, while Ellington was in Europe convalescing from surgery, Hodges, Strayhorn, the vocalist Al Hibbler, and five others enjoyed great success in a seven-week engagement at the Apollo Bar on 125th Street. Hodges also recorded with an octet in Paris in 1950.

By 1951 economic conditions had deteriorated for big bands. Even Ellington, one of the few leaders who held a band together without interruption, was forced to cut salaries. A dispirited Hodges and several others struck out on their own and Hodges signed a contract with the impresario Norman Granz for Verve Records. Immediately he had a huge recorded hit with "Castle Rock," a piece with a strong rhythm and blues feeling that featured the new group's manager, Al Sears, on tenor saxophone. The band enjoyed continued success; a summer 1954 session, *Used to Be Duke*, is particularly noteworthy. But Hodges disliked the responsibilities required of a bandleader and in 1955 he returned to Ellington.

Hodges continued to record with smaller groups, including a septet featuring Strayhorn on piano, for which he recorded, because of contractual reasons,

under the pseudonym "Cue Porter," in 1958, an early 1959 sextet with Ellington, and 1959–1960 sessions with a ten-piece orchestra. In 1961 he toured Europe with an octet from the band while Ellington worked on the film *Paris Blues* (1961) in France. Hodges recorded one of his best albums, *Everybody Knows Johnny Hodges* in 1964, with both a big band and a smaller group. Ellington crafted the beautiful "Isfahan" movement of the *Far East Suite* with Hodges in mind. Although his health deteriorated during the 1960s, Hodges continued to play inspirationally. He died in New York City.

Although some found him personally brusque and aloof, in truth Hodges was painfully shy. In fact he often mediated disputes between band members. He was a dedicated family man. After a failed early marriage he married Edith Cue Fitzgerald, a dancer in the Cotton Club chorus, in 1957. The couple had two children. Never a good sight reader (Harry Carney and BARNEY BIGARD often had to guide him through new orchestrations during rehearsals), Hodges possessed a powerful sense of swing, a fluid, graceful way of phrasing, and among the most softly beautiful sounds in jazz history.

FURTHER READING

Ellington, Duke. *Music Is My Mistress* (1973).
Tucker, Mark, ed. *The Duke Ellington Reader* (1993).
Obituary: *New York Times,* 12 May 1970.

DISCOGRAPHY

Dance, Stanley. *The Complete Johnny Hodges Sessions, 1951–1955* (Mosaic Records, 1989).
This entry is taken from the *American National Biography* and is published here with the permission of the American Council of Learned Societies.

RONALD P. DUFOUR

Hodges, Sylvester (30 Apr. 1942–), civil rights activist and school board president, was one of six boys born in Montrose, Arkansas, to Chester and Maggie Hodges. His family moved from Arkansas to Oakland, California, in 1946. Sylvester attended Prescott Elementary, Lowell Junior High School, and McClymonds High School. He married Lola Ingram in 1965, and the couple had one son.

Hodges became a passionate reader while serving in the U.S. military. He was influenced by *The Autobiography of Malcolm X* and was particularly interested in the changes in Malcolm's strategic thinking that took place immediately before his death in 1965.

Hodges's first foray into electoral politics occurred when he attended Merritt College in Oakland during the late 1960s, the same school at which the Black Panthers were organizing at the time. There were no African Americans in student government positions, although African Americans made up a large portion of the student body. The white student leadership believed that Hodges was conservative, and they agreed to run him for vice president on their slate. From this position he was able to assist in the election of other African American candidates.

He graduated from California State University, Hayward, (CSUH) in 1969, where he was named to the CSUH Sports Hall of Fame as Most Valuable Wrestler. He worked first for the Oakland Public Schools and then for the recreation department in San Mateo County. He developed an advocacy organization of one hundred East Oakland parents while his son was attending E. Morris Cox Elementary School. Hodges ran for a seat on the school board and was defeated by the nationally prominent African American minister J. Alfred Smith. When Smith resigned from the board because his school board duties interfered with his church responsibilities, Hodges won the citywide election called to fill Smith's vacated seat. He served on the board from 1985 to 1997. Geoffrey Pete, the owner of Geoffrey's Inner Circle (later Planet Soule) and a cofounder of both the Oakland Black Caucus and Niagara Movement Democratic Club, said of Hodges, "He was the most influential individual in terms of integrating the economic landscape in Oakland" (interview).

Hodges's greatest contribution was his successful strategy to prevent the takeover of the Oakland school district by the State of California in 1988. While African Americans made up 12 percent of the U.S. population, only 2 percent of elected officials were black, and many of those were school board members. In 1988 Oakland became one of the first school districts in America to be confronted with possible takeover of the local school district by state government. The underrepresentation of African Americans gave added significance to the elimination and disempowerment of urban school boards that began in this period—the state government had far less representation of African Americans and Latinos than the local Oakland government. A powerful array of state politicians initiated a loan of $10 million to the district without the request of the school board, arguing that the loan would be necessary given the district's midyear budget projections. This loan would have placed Oakland under the fiscal control of the state for thirty years. Hodges believed that local control was fundamental to the economic and educational civil rights agenda he was pursuing. His school board

colleague Darlene Lawson argued that the takeover attempt was a camouflaged effort by white businesses to return the school district to its segregated, white-controlled past. "It seems to me it's a power trip for the downtown business interests, who are mostly white" (Lawson, 3). Hodges and Lawson together arranged a form of financing called certificates of participation, which precluded the need for a state loan and prevented the takeover.

In the subsequent decade, Hodges, as chair of the Budget and Finance Committee of the board, led the district to achieve Standard & Poor's highest bond rating. Because the district maintained local control for an additional fifteen years after 1988, the African American majority was able to pursue such important initiatives as increased African American employment and contracting, the rejection of the racially insensitive Houghton Mifflin social studies textbooks, and the affirmation of African American language rights (known as the Ebonics debate). Soon after Hodges retired from the board, the district went into significant debt and was taken over by the State of California in 2003.

Oakland's school history is full of struggles over racial justice. It was Oakland that served as the testing ground for the racially skewed IQ test developed by the eugenics supporter Lewis Terman, and a hundred years later it was Oakland that asserted the language rights of African Americans. Under Hodges's leadership, Oakland became the first and perhaps only African American school district to prevent state takeover, even temporarily. In the period that followed, Philadelphia, Chicago, Detroit, Baltimore, Chester, Pennsylvania, and many other districts lost local control. After his retirement from the Oakland school board, Hodges served as president of the PAUL ROBESON Centennial Committee.

FURTHER READING
"Battle Lines Drawn on State Control of Oakland Schools," *Los Angeles Times*, 11 Sept. 1989.
Epstein, Kitty Kelly. *A Different View of Urban Schools: Civil Rights, Critical Race Theory, and Unexplored Realities* (2006).
Scott, Jack. *The Athlete Revolution* (1982)
KITTY KELLY EPSTEIN

Hogan, Ernest (1865–12 May 1909), vaudeville comedian and songwriter, was born Reuben Crowder (or Crowders) in Bowling Green, Kentucky. He left home as a child to join a traveling production of *Uncle Tom's Cabin*. Assigned the standard role for a young African American performer, Crowder appeared as an unnamed "pickaninny," singing and dancing in company numbers. He spent his teens and early twenties touring with minstrel shows. By 1891, inspired by the success of Irish comedians, he had taken on his stage name and co-founded Hogan and Eden's Minstrels, a Chicago-based company that toured the Midwest.

In the mid-1890s Hogan left the relative obscurity of the minstrel stage, moved to New York City, and secured his first vaudeville bookings, billing himself as "The Unbleached American." A compact, handsome man, Hogan was a tremendously animated stage presence, noted for his strong voice, mobile facial expressions, and a flawless sense of comic timing. Like most minstrel players, he was a song and dance man. His specialty was eccentric dance, a pre-tap style that emphasized improvisational leg movements. He wrote his own material and interspersed the verses with dance steps, the most famous of which involved a forward hop followed by crablike backward steps. He was said to capture the audience from the minute he hit the boards and called out his famous greeting, "Is everybody happy?"

Hogan quickly became a leading figure in New York's black theatrical set, a small but dynamic group that included BERT WILLIAMS and other show business pioneers. In 1895 he published his first song, "La Pas Ma La," which introduced a dance step of the same name. The following year he and Williams put out "Ninth Battalion on Parade." Hogan went on to write or co-write many other songs. None, however, proved as popular as the second he published in 1896, "All Coons Look Alike to Me." The song, often remembered only for its title, tells the tale of a hard-luck black man, a stock character taken from the minstrelsy tradition, who has recently been jilted by his girlfriend, a strident, equally caricatured figure. The lines of the chorus are set to a catchy tune, the first ever published as "rag," and consist of the girlfriend's parting words:

All coons look alike to me
I've got another beau, you see,
And he's just as good to me as you, nig!
Ever tried to be.

Despite a low-profile premiere, rendered by the black-face comedienne May Irwin in an all-white show, the song was a runaway hit. Sheet music sales eventually ranked among the highest of the decade. By 1900 "coon songs" had become a vaudeville staple. The word "coon" became a firmly established and ever more commonplace racial slur, and Hogan became the subject of increasingly harsh criticism within the black community.

In the short term, however, the success of "All Coons" strengthened Hogan's position. In 1897 he appeared as the featured comedian with Black Patti's Troubadours, the famous company led by Mme. SISSIERETTA JONES; Hogan wrote the script for the comedy half of the show and several of its musical numbers. Early in 1898 a chance meeting with the composer WILL MARION COOK led to Hogan's participation in *Clorindy, or the Origin of the Cake Walk*, the first black musical production to appear in a Broadway venue. The poet PAUL LAURENCE DUNBAR wrote the book and lyrics for the show, which featured Cook's ragtime orchestra. *Clorindy* opened on 5 July 1898 at the Casino Roof Garden as the final part of an evening of vaudeville; the music, dancing chorus line, and lengthy cakewalk finale made it an instant hit. As master of ceremonies Hogan was the lead player, appearing in nearly every scene; he also edited the script (to Dunbar's chagrin, reportedly).

Hogan had now secured star status, but his next few years were far from smooth. Following a brief engagement as the lead, and the only black, performer in the 128-member *Captain Kidd* company, he returned to Black Patti's Troubadours. His part in the tour ended abruptly in New Orleans as a result of an altercation with a white box office agent, whom Hogan knocked to the ground. Hogan had to be rushed out of the city overnight; back in New York, he immediately signed on as director of entertainments in the Curtis Minstrels. The production was slated to tour Australia and New Zealand but instead was stranded twice, first in rural Australia and again in Honolulu. Acting as director and booking agent, Hogan reorganized the performance, made arrangements with local theaters, and continued to play the lead. Rave reviews followed the show as it worked its way home. A mix of success and trouble followed Hogan to New York where, on the night of 1 August 1901, he narrowly escaped the mob violence (one of the worst race riots in the city's history) that had broken out near his home in the black residential district of downtown Manhattan.

Hogan then embarked on another big-time circuit tour. Audiences greeted his appearances with great enthusiasm, often demanding encores after every number. Critics were equally lavish in their praise, routinely comparing his performance favorably with anything on the bill that night or in the course of the season. Also in 1901 Hogan became one of city's first prominent African Americans to purchase a house in Harlem. He continued touring and sometimes appeared in group shows (among them the 1902 Smart Set musical *Enchantment*, in which he played alongside the minstrel star Billy McClain).

In 1905, now at the height of his career, Hogan mounted two highly successful productions. The first, billed (somewhat disingenuously) as the "first syncopated music concert in history," was performed by the Memphis Students, a new group he and his then wife, Louise Hogan, had assembled. Featuring performances by Hogan, ABBIE MITCHELL, and the Russian dance specialist Ida Forsyne, the production played a run of one hundred shows at Hammerstein's Victoria Theater on Broadway, one of the country's top vaudeville houses. Next Hogan arranged his first true star vehicle, the musical *Rufus Rastus*. Hogan wrote the book, co-wrote the music with Thomas Lemonier, and played the title character, a struggling vaudevillian working a series of day jobs and dreaming of success. Hogan's rendering of the protagonist, at once wistful, resentful, and comically ironic, was considered the crowning achievement of his career. The New York run of *Rufus Rastus* was followed by a two-year tour.

In 1907 Hogan and Bert Williams spearheaded the formation of the Colored Actors' Beneficial Association, the first African American actors' union. At the time, Hogan was also planning a follow-up to *Rufus Rastus*. The new show, *The Oyster Man*, drew upon an impressive pool of talent: the composer Will Vodery, the lyricists Henry Creamer and Lester Walton, and the writer-comedians Flournoy Miller and Aubrey Lyles. The show seemed poised for success. Hogan's health, however, was in decline, and he deteriorated rapidly as the show made its preview tour. *The Oyster Man* disbanded in March 1908, Hogan having appeared only once in its brief New York City run. In June, Hogan's show business contemporaries staged a testimonial in his honor, but he was too ill to attend. Ernest Hogan died of tuberculosis.

In a lifetime spent almost entirely onstage, Hogan proved that he could do it all: sing, dance, write, direct, and produce. Among his fans he numbered many of his most prominent contemporaries, including JAMES WELDON JOHNSON, Flournoy Miller, EUBIE BLAKE, and LUCKEY ROBERTS, who called Hogan "the greatest performer I ever saw" (Stearns, 120). If Hogan was widely admired for his accomplishments, however, his role in spawning the "coon song" craze was equally deplored. The year before he died Hogan told a friend, the entertainer Tom Fletcher, that he wished he had never written the song that made him famous. The mixed legacy of Hogan's career has continued to be debated. His talents have not. Ernest Hogan's early death left a gap in the New York theatrical community that had developed with him as a principal figure.

FURTHER READING
Fletcher, Tom. *One Hundred Years of the Negro in Show Business* (1954).
Hill, Errol G., and James V. Hatch. *A History of African American Theater* (2003).
Johnson, James Weldon. *Black Manhattan* (1930).
Sampson, Henry T. *The Ghost Walks: A Chronological History of Blacks in Show Business, 1865–1910* (1988).
Southern, Eileen. *A Biographical Dictionary of Afro-American and African Musicians* (1982).
Stearns, Marshall, and Jean Stearns. *Jazz Dance: The Story of American Vernacular Dance* (1968).
Woll, Alan. *Black Musical Theater: From Coontown to Dreamgirls* (1989).

JOANNA WOOL

Hogan, Moses (13 Mar. 1957–11 Feb. 2003), composer, pianist, and conductor, was born Moses George Hogan in New Orleans, Louisiana, one of six children of the New Orleans natives Moses and Gloria. Hogan was raised in a home of working-class parents. His father served in the military during World War II and his mother worked as a nurse. Their work ethic and support of Hogan's musical talent fostered his commitment to developing his musicianship at an early age. By the age of nine he was already an accomplished pianist. Marie Moulton, Hogan's first piano teacher, remained an influence throughout his life.

Hogan utilized his music skills at the New Zion Baptist Church where his uncle, Edwin Hogan, was the organist and choir conductor. Edwin Hogan became a model of how to balance keyboard skills, compositional facility, and choral conducting. It was at the New Zion Baptist Church that Hogan gained his initial understanding of choral singing and the genre of concert spirituals. The choral community in New Orleans, including the choirs in predominantly African American churches, embraced a wide range of choral repertoire. In addition to gospel, Hogan was regularly exposed to sacred choral genres including masses, cantatas, hymns, and the genre in which he would leave his legacy: spirituals.

In addition to his piano teacher, his uncle, and his church, Hogan's life work was shaped by the historic and musical setting of New Orleans itself. He was one of the first graduates of New Orleans Center for Creative Arts (NOCCA) in 1975, along with the jazz musician Branford Marsalis, and continued his music education at Oberlin Conservatory of Music in Oberlin, Ohio. There Hogan honed his piano and vocal accompanying skills with the renowned piano teacher Joseph Schwartz, earning a BM in Piano Performance in 1979. After Oberlin, Hogan briefly pursued study of piano performance and vocal accompanying at the Juilliard School in New York City. During his solo piano career, he won several competitions, including first place at the 28th annual Kosciuszko Foundation Chopin Competition in New York. After studying and performing in New York, Hogan returned home and worked at Louisiana State University in 1985 and 1986, where he accompanied students taking voice lessons with the opera singer MARTINA ARROYO.

In 1980 Hogan founded the New World Ensemble, where he was able to fully utilize his musicianship as a conductor, composer, and pianist. The New World Ensemble was a volunteer choral group in New Orleans made up of local music educators selected by Hogan. The choir sang a wide range of repertoire, including concert spirituals. During the ensemble's tenure Hogan noticed two things: that spiritual singing was becoming increasingly influenced by the gospel style of singing and that the popularity of spirituals was decreasing. He then committed to continuing the tradition of choral concert spiritual singing by composing new arrangements of spirituals.

In 1993 Hogan began as artist-in-residence at Dillard University, where he stayed on the faculty for fourteen years. While in New Orleans, Hogan established the Moses Hogan Chorale, a volunteer touring chorus. This choir performed internationally from 1991 until 1999, presenting popular choral pieces in addition to concert spirituals. Hogan arranged and published concert spiritual arrangements for the choir with the Hal Leonard Corporation. In 1991 the Moses Hogan Chorale became the first southern African American community chorus to perform at Carnegie Hall for the American Choral Directors Association conference. This ensemble also recorded two albums of spirituals with the guest countertenor soloist Derek Lee Ragin. Hogan's pairing of a solo countertenor with chorus was unprecedented for concert spiritual recordings. The international tours of the Moses Hogan Chorale brought Hogan acclaim and respect. His opportunities covered three fronts: Hogan was in demand at choral clinics to discuss the history and singing of concert spirituals with choral directors and choirs; as a composer, with commissions from the St. Olaf Choir, the American Cancer Society, and PBS for its 1995 documentary *The American Promise*; and as a conductor, directing the Mormon Tabernacle Choir.

Inspired by the success of the Moses Hogan Chorale and with the encouragement of the seasoned concert spiritual arrangers Wendell Whalum and Jester Hairston, Hogan made the decision to become an ambassador for concert spirituals. In 1998 he founded a new ensemble, the Moses Hogan Singers. This group was a smaller, nationally auditioned ensemble composed of twenty-eight professional singers whose mission it was to perform concert spirituals. The Moses Hogan Singers made their debut at Alice Tully Hall and also performed at the Kennedy Center and Sydney Opera House. Their debut album, *Give Me Jesus*, was recorded for EMI with the renowned soprano BARBARA HENDRICKS in 2002. Hogan also launched his own record label, MGH Records, on which he released *The Moses Hogan Choral Series 2002*. During the height of the Moses Hogan Singers' fame, Hogan published a volume of ten spiritual arrangements for solo voice and piano titled *The Deep River Collection* which expanded Hogan's influence to the solo singer in addition to choral ensembles. Hogan also edited a groundbreaking anthology of choral concert spirituals, published as the *Oxford Book of Spirituals* in 2002. His final arrangements were recorded on the 2003 album *This Little Light of Mine*. Hogan's professional memberships included Phi Mu Alpha Fraternity and the American Society of Composers, Authors and Publishers (ASCAP).

Though piano was Hogan's instrument, he single-handedly established concert spirituals into standard choral repertoire and introduced professional choral spiritual singing to the world, revitalizing a tradition that by the 1980s had become somewhat ossified. His arrangements became staple pieces for high school, church, community, and professional choirs, known for their harmonic and rhythmic complexity. With his choirs as his muse, Hogan was precise in his arrangements of spirituals to ensure that they would remain true to his intent. Respected by his singers, Hogan was active in music until his death in Louisiana of a brain tumor.

FURTHER READING

Hogan, Moses. *The Deep River Collection* (2000).
Hogan, Moses. *Feel the Spirit* v. 1 (2003).
Hogan, Moses. *Feel the Spirit* v.2 (2003).
Hogan, Moses. *The Oxford Book of Spirituals* (2002).
MARTI K. NEWLAND

Holder, Geoffrey (20 Aug. 1930–), dancer, painter, choreographer, actor, author, photographer, director, musician, and costume and set designer, was born in Port of Spain, Trinidad. He was one of four children of middle-class parents of Irish, French, and African descent.

Holder was educated at Queen's Royal College in Port of Spain. His grandfather, Louis Ephraim, was a French painter whose influence led both Holder and his older brother Boscoe to begin experimenting with oils. Geoffrey began teaching himself to paint at age fifteen when he was forced to stay home from school due to a prolonged illness. He also learned much from Boscoe, who was a pianist, painter, and dancer. When Boscoe moved to England, Geoffrey took over as director of his brother's dance company while continuing to create new paintings and display work at gallery exhibitions. Holder's work was displayed at the public library in Trinidad for several years while he was still in his teens. His first one-person show in the United States was at the Barone Gallery in New York City in 1954.

Holder's first professional dance performance was with Boscoe when they toured the West Indies and Puerto Rico. After an invitation to audition for Agnes de Mille, Geoffrey moved to New York in 1953 to develop his painting and dance career. He did not receive the dance sponsorship, but he instead taught at the KATHERINE DUNHAM School of Cultural Arts. His Broadway debut was made in Truman Capote and Harold Arlen's *House of Flowers* in 1954. The six-foot-six Holder appeared as a dancer, soloist, and choreographer in productions including the role of Lucky in the all-black cast of the revival of *Waiting for Godot* in 1957. He held the position of premier danseur at the Metropolitan Opera House in productions of *Aïda* and *La Périchole* in the late 1950s. Holder wrote and starred in the original musical *Josephine Baker* on Broadway in 1964. In 1968 Holder designed the costumes, sets, and choreography for a Brazilian-themed ballet, *Jeux des dieux*, for the Harkness Ballet. In 1975 Holder's work on *The Wiz* won him the Tony Award for costume design as well as best director of a musical. His close friendship with the dancer ALVIN AILEY allowed him to collaborate on many projects, including set design and costumes for the Dance Theatre of Harlem's *Firebird*, which remains part of the company's permanent repertoire. Holder staged an original special concert, *The Boys Choir of Harlem and Friends*, on Broadway in 1993.

Holder's stage career also brought him into contact with movie directors and casting agents. His first movie role was in 1957 in *Carib Gold*, and in 1962 he was cast in *All Night Long*, a jazz and dance retelling of Shakespeare's *Othello*. Holder also appeared in *Doctor Doolittle* (1967), *Everything You Always Wanted to Know about Sex (But Were Afraid to Ask)* (1972), *Live and Let Die* (1973), *Swashbuckler* (1976), *Annie* (1982), *Boomerang* (1992), and *Goosed* (1999)

Holder's memorable deep voice was featured in a series of commercials for the soft drink Seven Up. The commercials were an instant hit and earned the advertising industry's top award, the Clio. He continued to do voice-overs for commercials and was a featured voice artist on a musical CD for children titled *The Dream Dragon*. Holden was also the narrator for *The Pebble and the Penguin* (1995) and the 2005 movie version of *Charlie and the Chocolate Factory*. His television work includes productions of *The Bottle Imp* (1957), *Aladdin* (1958), *Androcles and the Lion* with Noel Coward (1967), *The Man Without a Country* (1973), and the role of the Cheshire Cat in the Public Broadcasting Service's *Alice in Wonderland* in 1983. With the choreographer and dancer MERCEDES ELLINGTON, Holder starred in the 2000 television show *Harmony in the Kitchen*, demonstrating the creation of various dishes from Trinidad.

Holder's publications include *Caribbean Cookbook* (1974) and *Black Gods, Green Islands* (1959), an illustrated text on the folklore of Trinidad. As an artist, Holder works in oil and enjoys drawing. Two of his large murals hang in the Trinidad Hilton Hotel and another mural is located at the University of the West Indies. He continues to display his work at exhibitions and gallery shows. His impressionistic style, he says, is influenced by the French and English heritage of Trinidad and Martinique.

Holder's place in the history of popular culture rests in his commercial advertisements, but his real contributions to the arts are in costume and set design, set direction, and innovations in dance in the theater. His skill as a painter won Holder a Guggenheim Fellowship in 1957. Holder's paintings and drawings hang in the collections of the Museum of the City of New York, the Corcoran Gallery, the Leonard Hana Collection, and the Barbados Museum. He received the Trinidad government's Hummingbird Medal for his contributions to the arts, the Medal of Liberty from the City of New York, and an honorary doctorate from North Carolina Central University in 1986.

Holder married the dancer CARMEN DE LAVALLADE in 1955. They met while working and

Holder proposed to de Lavallade after only four days into rehearsals. Their only child, a son, was born in 1957.

FURTHER READING
Holder, Geoffrey. *The Art of Geoffrey Holder* (forthcoming).
Dunning, Jennifer. *Geoffrey Holder: A Life in Theatre, Dance, and Art* (2001).

PAMELA LEE GRAY

Holiday, Billie (7 Apr. 1915–17 July 1959), vocalist and lyricist, was born Eleanora Fagan in Philadelphia, to a nineteen-year-old domestic worker, Sadie Fagan, and Clarence Holiday, a seventeen-year-old guitarist who would later gain fame as a member of the FLETCHER HENDERSON Orchestra.

Shortly after giving birth, Sadie Fagan returned to her home in Baltimore with her newborn daughter in tow. During her youth in this gritty, working-class port town, the young Holiday would encounter two things that influenced her for the duration of her life: the criminal justice system and music. By the time she entered Thomas E. Hays Elementary School, Holiday was the stepdaughter of Philip Gough, who had married her mother on 20 October 1920. A tomboy, the future singer enjoyed playing stickball and softball with the boys in the neighborhood, and she loved the movies. These two forms of recreation, sports and film, helped to inspire the nickname by which she would become famous: Billie. Billie Dove was a popular film star of the day whom Holiday greatly admired. As a child, she began to sing popular blues songs around the house and in her neighborhood.

After her mother divorced Gough, Holiday was placed in the care of a neighbor while Sadie sought work elsewhere. Perhaps in an effort to protest her mother's absence, she began to skip school, and by January 1925 her truancy found her before the juvenile court. After finding Sadie Gough unfit as a mother, the judge sent Holiday to the House of the Good Shepherd for Colored Girls, a home run by Catholic nuns. While there Holiday was baptized. After a nine-month stay she was released in care of her mother, and the two moved into a small apartment about two blocks away from Sadie's new business venture, a small eatery. Sadie spent long hours at work, and the young Holiday was often left alone. On Christmas Eve 1926 Sadie came home from work to find her neighbor, Wilbert Rich, having sex with her daughter. Rich was arrested and charged with rape; Billie was sent, once again, to the House of the Good Shepherd. Rich was indicted on six counts of

Billie Holiday, nicknamed "Lady Day" by Lester Young, recorded over three hundred songs, setting the standard for both jazz and American popular singing in general. (Library of Congress.)

rape, but only found guilty of one. He served three months in prison. After she was released, Holiday never returned to school. Instead, she began to work in her mother's restaurant and in a local brothel. Her work at the brothel first involved only cleaning the white marble steps, running errands, and doing light cleaning in exchange for the opportunity to listen to the Victrola, but biographers agree that she eventually worked as a prostitute, a kind of "pretty baby" who also sang for the entertainment of the clientele. While at the brothel, she discovered the records of BESSIE SMITH and LOUIS ARMSTRONG, both of whom profoundly influenced her unique singing style. Other early influences were ETHEL WATERS and the Gregorian chant Holiday had heard at the House of the Good Shepherd.

In 1928 Holiday's mother moved to New York, settling in Harlem, and the following year she sent for her teenage daughter. By May 1929 both mother and daughter had been arrested for prostitution, caught in a raid on a Harlem brothel. Holiday spent one hundred days in the penitentiary workhouse on Welfare Island (formerly Blackwell's Island, now

Roosevelt Island). Upon her release she determined never again to work as a maid or a prostitute. She began singing in small clubs in Brooklyn and later in Harlem, soon moving to the more renowned Harlem clubs like Small's Paradise. Beginning her apprenticeship and advanced musical education, Holiday spent every waking hour with other musicians. In 1933 she was discovered by the young producer and aspiring impresario John Hammond, who heard her at a Harlem club called Covan's. He immediately wrote about her for a London-based jazz publication, *Melody Maker*, and later produced her first record, "Your Mother's Son-in-Law" and "Riffin' the Scotch," with Benny Goodman. She was eighteen years old. The following year Holiday met the tenor saxophonist LESTER YOUNG, with whom she had an immediate affinity.

In 1934 Holiday made her film debut in a DUKE ELLINGTON short, *Symphony in Black*, in which she sang "Saddest Tale," a slow blues. Holiday is riveting on film, but she made only one other, *New Orleans* (1947), with Louis Armstrong, playing a singing maid. Starting in 1935 Holiday recorded a number of sides with the gifted pianist TEDDY WILSON. Some of the best of these featured Benny Goodman on clarinet, ROY ELDRIDGE on trumpet, and BEN WEBSTER (with whom Holiday had a brief and tumultuous affair) on saxophone. In the mid-1930s Joe Glaser, who managed Louis Armstrong, began to manage Holiday, and she began to get more work and greater exposure. He arranged for her to sing with the Fletcher Henderson Orchestra, one of the most popular big bands of the day. With the Henderson outfit, Holiday made a number of radio broadcasts, gaining exposure to a national audience. In the spring of 1937 she joined BUCK CLAYTON and her good friend Lester Young, as well as the blues belter JIMMY RUSHING, in the Count Basie Orchestra; before long, she was on the road with the band. Basie gave her extraordinary freedom to stretch out musically and to cultivate her own style. She recorded for Columbia with members of the Basie outfit, especially Lester Young, but never with the entire orchestra. During this time, Lester Young gave Holiday the nickname "Lady Day," and she dubbed him "Prez." Life on the road was especially difficult for Holiday, as she faced firsthand the racism of the Jim Crow South. At one point she was encouraged by club owners to wear dark makeup so that Southern white audiences would not think she was a white woman singing with black musicians. By 1938 Holiday was no longer singing with the Basie Orchestra; she said she left because she was not paid enough.

When the white bandleader Artie Shaw heard that Holiday had left Basie, he offered her a job. She became one of the first black artists to join an all-white band. She traveled with Shaw throughout the country; although life on the road, with its constant confrontations with racial prejudice, proved to be more than Holiday wanted to handle. In New York, the owner of the Lincoln Hotel where she was performing with the Shaw band asked that Holiday take the service elevator. Although she had been thinking of leaving Shaw for some time, this proved to be the straw that broke the camel's back.

Fortunately John Hammond brought her an offer that would change the direction of her career and in so doing make an indelible mark on the history of popular music. With Hammond's assistance, Holiday opened at Café Society, a new nightclub in Greenwich Village. Founded by Barney Josephson, the club not only presented racially mixed bands, but also had an integrated audience, making it unique in New York nightlife. It eventually became one of the favorite nightspots of bohemian intellectuals and political activists, as well as socialites looking for the thrill of something new.

During her tenure at Café Society, Holiday further shaped her style, both her singing and her visual presentation. A dramatic performer, she used each song as an opportunity to connect with her audience through a narrative that seemed almost personal. Here she began to sing the torch songs with which she would be identified throughout the rest of her career. She worked with smaller bands, including one led by Teddy Wilson. But most significantly, it was at Café Society that Holiday introduced "Strange Fruit," a song written by Abel Meeropol as a protest against the practice of lynching. She often closed her performances with dramatic renditions of this song, after which she would leave the stage and refuse to return for an encore, and included it in her repertoire throughout her career. When her record company, Columbia, refused to record it, she sought out the independent record producer Milt Gabler, who arranged for her to record the song with his label, Commodore Records. With "Strange Fruit," Holiday came to the attention of a whole new audience of artists, activists, and intellectuals. She also came to the attention of the FBI when she began to sing what was also considered a political song, "The Yanks Aren't Coming." The recording of "Strange Fruit" marked the second stage of Holiday's career. From 1945 to 1950 Gabler recorded Holiday classics such as "Don't Explain," "Lover Man," and "My Man" on Decca, while also recording more blues- and jazz-oriented fare like "Fine and Mellow" and "Billie's Blues" for Commodore.

Holiday left Café Society to become the queen of Fifty-second Street, where the most important jazz clubs were located. During this time she was first arrested for possession of heroin, and in 1947 she was sent to the Federal Reformatory for Women at Alderson, West Virginia, where she served nine and a half months. It is said that she never sang a note while there. Upon her release Holiday was denied her cabaret card and thus was unable to perform in jazz clubs where liquor was sold. A number of significant jazz artists fell prey to this law and found their livelihood severely limited. Limited in her club appearances, Holiday began singing in large halls. Shortly after her release from Alderson she appeared before a wildly enthusiastic audience at Carnegie Hall on 27 March 1948.

From the time of her first arrest in 1947 until her death in 1959, Holiday would be harassed and haunted by law enforcement for possession and use of narcotics. She sometimes beat the charges, but they inevitably took their toll on the sensitive singer. She was arrested in May 1947 in Philadelphia, in January 1949 in San Francisco, in February 1956, again in Philadelphia, and, even as she lay on her deathbed in New York in 1959, a guard was placed outside her hospital room.

In 1952 Holiday signed with Verve Records. She began working with Norman Granz, who had helped to ensure the financial and critical success of ELLA FITZGERALD and Frank Sinatra, and hoped to do the same for Holiday. Granz surrounded her with major jazz talent and recorded her in the small jam-session atmosphere in which she thrived, using such musicians as OSCAR PETERSON, Ray Brown, Ben Webster, Jimmy Rowles, Benny Carter, and Harry Edison. In recordings of these sessions, one can hear the grain of her voice, and at times her songs are like recitations and incantations. Holiday's choices are thoughtful and original, and, as always, she makes every note count.

The album *Lady in Satin*, recorded in 1958, is perhaps one of Holiday's most controversial recordings. Critics disagree in their appraisals; gone is the youthful Holiday of the early Columbia sides and the fully mature singer-actress of the torch days. In her place is a woman looking back on some of her earlier material, reinterpreting it through the lens of a life that had been difficult but full, an artist wholly committed to her form.

Holiday died in New York from heart, kidney, and liver ailments, along with lung blockage, the unfortunate but inevitable consequence of decades of substance abuse. She was forty-four years old. She had been married twice, once to Jimmy Monroe and then to Louis McKay. She had no children.

Holiday recorded more than three hundred songs and set the standard for jazz singing in particular and American popular singing in general. She paved the way for the sophisticated black songstresses who followed her, but who have rarely matched her level of artistry or originality. Billie Holiday is undoubtedly one of the most important artists of the twentieth century, and her singular sound and distinctive approach to timing and phrasing, along with her iconographic life and image, have influenced not only other musicians, but poets, painters, novelists, and critical theorists.

FURTHER READING

Holiday, Billie, with William Dufty. *Lady Sings the Blues* (1956).

Clarke, Donald. *Wishing on the Moon: The Life and Times of Billie Holiday* (1995).

Gourse, Leslie, ed. *The Billie Holiday Companion: Seven Decades of Commentary* (1997).

Griffin, Farah Jasmine. *If You Can't Be Free, Be a Mystery: In Search of Billie Holiday* (2001).

Nicholson, Stuart. *Billie Holiday* (1995).

O'Meally, Robert. *Lady Day: The Many Faces of Billie Holiday* (1991).

Obituary: *New York Times*, 18 July 1959.

DISCOGRAPHY

Billie Holiday: The Complete Billie Holiday on Verve, 1945–1959 (PolyGram Records).

Billie Holiday: The Complete Commodore Recordings (GRP Records).

Billie Holiday: The Complete Decca Recordings (GRP Records).

Billie Holiday: The Legacy (1933–1958), (Sony).

Lady Day: The Complete Billie Holiday on Columbia, 1933–1944 (Sony).

FARAH JASMINE GRIFFIN

Holland, Annie Welthy Daughtry (c. 1871–6 Jan. 1934), educator and promoter of public education for blacks, was born in Isle of Wight County, Virginia, on land adjacent to the Welthy (also spelled Wealthy) plantation, the daughter of Sarah Daughtry and J. W. Barnes. (Her parentage, incorrectly reported in some earlier sources, has been confirmed by her death certificate.) Her grandfather Friday Daughtry had been born and raised a slave but during the 1860s was freed by the Welthy family. Annie had been named after Annie Welthy of the Welthy plantation. Sometime between 1872 and 1879 her mother divorced her father. Her mother later remarried, and the family moved to

Southampton County, Virginia. In 1880 Friday Daughtry brought Annie back to Isle of Wight, where she lived with her grandmother Lucinda and worked on the farm while studying at the county school. In 1883, at the age of eleven, she enrolled as an eighth-grade student at Hampton Institute, an agricultural and industrial school for blacks founded in 1868 at nearby Hampton, Virginia. To help pay for her second year of study she spent the summer of 1884 in New York working for a wealthy white family. She had to leave school before the end of the following summer, however, owing to a bout with malaria, which left her unable to work, as well as her grandfather's financial troubles; failing health had made it difficult for him to continue to pay her tuition. She then returned to Isle of Wight where for two years after taking the teachers examination and receiving a second-grade certificate, she taught in the county elementary school. In 1888 she left her teaching post and went to work in New York but soon returned because of the illness of her grandmother. Just before her grandmother died in 1888 she married Willis B. Holland, a Hampton graduate and educator; they would have at least one child, a daughter.

In 1897 the Hollands moved to Franklin, Virginia, where he served as principal of Franklin Public School and she as his assistant, a position she held until early 1899. Later that same year she asked to be transferred to the countryside, both for reasons of health and because she believed that education for blacks was particularly lacking in rural areas. After completing the teacher training course at the Normal Institute in Petersburg in 1903, Holland passed the examination for a five-year teaching certificate. She then taught in the rural schools until 1905, when she succeeded her husband as principal of the Franklin school after he went into insurance and real estate.

In 1911 Holland moved to Gates County, North Carolina, to become county supervisor of rural schools. From her base at the Gates Institute in Sunbury, she supervised industrial classes in twenty-two schools. In 1912 she moved up the road to Corapeake, near the Virginia border. In 1914 she returned to Hampton Institute, where she attended a ten-day summer normal course in agriculture. The following year she was named state home demonstration agent for North Carolina, a post that carried the dual role of state supervisor of the Anna T. Jeanes Fund. The Jeanes Fund, which sent hundreds of teachers around the South beginning in 1907, was a private trust designed to promote the development of public education for rural blacks.

Now in charge of roughly four dozen county supervisors Holland traveled throughout the state, organizing meetings and fund drives and teaching demonstration classes. Her 1916 schedule required her to visit ten eastern North Carolina counties extending from Virginia to South Carolina. In 1917 she concentrated her efforts on the Piedmont counties, where she taught vegetable canning, nutrition, sewing, and gardening, as well as reading and writing, and also encouraged the homemakers clubs to raise and sell poultry and livestock. Between 1916 and 1917, under Holland's supervision, Jeanes Fund teachers reportedly made more than three thousand visits to more than a thousand schools in thirty-five counties. They worked to improve the physical appearance and structure of many schools, some of which extended their school term from four to five months. Holland's position was jointly funded by the Jeanes Fund and the North Carolina Colored Teachers' Association until 1921, the year the North Carolina General Assembly established the Negro Division of Education, whereupon the post was incorporated into the state educational organization. Holland's title was changed to state supervisor of Negro elementary schools, and from then on the position was paid, in part, with state funds. She continued to travel around the state, organizing reading circles and clubs designed to assist in the education of black students.

In 1923–1924, from out of the Community Leagues that Jeanes teachers had helped to develop, Holland began to organize parent-teacher associations. In 1927 she founded the North Carolina Congress of Colored Parents and Teachers. The National Congress of Colored Parents and Teachers, conceived by black Americans and founded in 1926, was a national parent-teacher association concerned with child welfare, improving the quality of life of black families, and developing effective communication between parents and teachers. The North Carolina congress held its first annual meeting at Shaw University in Raleigh, North Carolina, on 14 April 1928. During its first year (1928), the state PTA established 784 local associations comprising 15,770 members, and within two years the group had raised more than $115,000. Jeanes teachers and the PTA, under Holland's supervision, installed libraries, erected new buildings, and extended school curricula to include dental hygiene and health.

Holland died at a doctor's office in Louisburg, North Carolina, soon after collapsing while addressing a group of black teachers. More than 800 persons attended a memorial for her in Raleigh. She was buried in Franklin, Virginia. In 1938, the tenth anniversary of the North Carolina Congress of Colored Parents and Teachers, a tree was planted in her memory at Shaw University. A women's residence hall at North Carolina Agricultural and Technical State University in Greensboro is named in her honor.

Holland is reported to have been a kind as well as devoted worker in the cause of educating rural blacks in North Carolina. Her organizational abilities and happy disposition helped to unite white and black interests, parents, and professionals in working toward the goal of quality education for all children; and through her activism and commitment she forced the issue of funding to the state and national levels. The success of education for North Carolina's rural blacks can be explained, in part, by the cooperative impulse of Annie Holland, an able educator who devoted her life to teaching teachers.

FURTHER READING

Papers related to Holland's tenure as state supervisor can be found at the North Carolina Department of Archives, Raleigh.

Brown, Hugh Victor. *A History of the Education of Negroes in North Carolina* (1961).

Gavins, Raymond. "A Sin of Omission," in *Black Americans in North Carolina and the South*, eds. Jeffrey J. Crow and Flora J. Hatley (1984).

This entry is taken from the *American National Biography* and is published here with the permission of the American Council of Learned Societies.

DEBI HAMLIN

Holland, Brian (15 Feb. 1941–), songwriter, record producer, recording engineer, and singer, was born and raised in Detroit, Michigan, where he attended Davison Elementary, Cleveland Intermediate, and Wilbur Wright High School. Holland began his career in the music industry as a singer. In 1958 Kudo Records released Holland's debut single, "(Where's the Joy?) In Nature Boy"; "Shock," on the record's flip side, was cowritten by BERRY GORDY JR. The following year, Gordy founded Motown, and Holland, a recording engineer, was one of Motown's first employees. During the company's early days, Holland was a member of the Satintones, Motown's first vocal group, and the Rayber Voices, Motown's backup vocal group on records by Marv Johnson and others.

Holland began writing and producing songs with Robert Bateman, and they were the successful production duo known as Brianbert. Their initial success was the Marvelettes' "Please Mr. Postman" (1961), which was Motown's first number one pop hit and second record to sell one million copies. In 1962, after Bateman left Motown, Holland, teamed with LAMONT DOZIER and Freddie Gorman, continued to write and produce songs for the Marvelettes. One year later, Holland's older brother, Eddie, replaced Gorman, and the songwriting as well as record producing trio known as Holland-Dozier-Holland (HDH) was formed. Brian Holland and Lamont Dozier were primarily responsible for writing the melodies and tracks while EDDIE HOLLAND wrote most of the lyrics.

HDH's debut single was the Marvelette's "Locking Up My Heart" (1963); it was followed by HDH's first hit record, Martha [Reeves] and the Vandellas' "Come and Get These Memories" (1963). For the next five years, HDH was Motown's preeminent songwriting and production team as they created hit records such as "You Lost the Sweetest Boy" (1963) for MARY WELLS, "Mickey's Monkey" (1963) for the Miracles, "Can I Get a Witness" (1963) for MARVIN GAYE, "(I'm a) Roadrunner" (1966) for JUNIOR WALKER and the All Stars, and "This Old Heart of Mine (Is Weak for You)" (1966) for the Isley Brothers. HDH, noted for creating a variety of hits for most of Motown's artists, achieved even greater success with the Four Tops and the Supremes. Among the multiple hits written by HDH for the Four Tops are "I Can't Help Myself (Sugar Pie, Honey Bunch)" (1965) and "Reach Out I'll Be There" (1966) while HDH's numerous hits for the Supremes include "Baby Love" (1964) and "Stop! In the Name of Love" (1965). During the 1960s, HDH wrote and produced an abundance of Motown singles that reached the top forty charts; indeed HDH created at least seventy singles that were top ten hits, and more than twenty number one hits. Holland also served as head of Quality Control at Motown.

HDH left Motown in 1968. Eddie Holland created several record and publishing companies, and Brian Holland and Lamont Dozier joined him in those ventures. They wrote and produced hits for Freda Payne, the Chairmen of the Board, the Honey Cones, and others. During the early 1970s, Brian Holland returned to singing and recorded duets with his brother and Dozier as well as solo; the most notable is the Brian Holland-Lamont Dozier single "Don't Leave Me Starvin' for Your Love" (1972), where Holland sings lead. In 1974 Dozier left to concentrate on his singing career, and ten years later, Brian and Eddie Holland formed the Holland Group and HDH records. More than two decades later, HDH reunited in order to create the score for *The First Wives Club—the Musical* which debuted in July 2009 at the Old Globe Theater in San Diego, California.

Brian Holland's musical talents have garnered national and international acclaim. *Pop Annual 1955–1999* (sixth ed., 2000) ranks Holland second in its "Honor Roll of [the Top 200] Songwriters." As a member of HDH, he received the Recording Industry Academy of Arts and Sciences' Trustees Grammy Award (1998), the Broadcast Music, Inc. (BMI)'s Icon Award (2003), the British Academy of Composers and Songwriters/Performing Rights Society's Special International Ivor Novella Award, and the National Academy of Popular Music's Johnny Mercer Award (2009). The three men were inducted into the National Academy of Popular Music/Songwriters Hall of Fame (1988), the Rock and Roll Hall of Fame (1990), and the Hollywood Rockwalk (2003).

FURTHER READING

Dahl, Bill. *Motown: The Golden Years* (2001).

Gordy, Berry. *To Be Loved: The Music, the Magic, the Memories of Motown: An Autobiography* (1994).

"Holland-Dozier-Holland." In *Contemporary Black Biography*, ed. Ashyia Henderson, vol. 36 (2002).

Singleton, Raynoma Gordy, with Bryan Brown and Mim Eichler. *Berry, Me, and Motown: The Untold Story* (1990).

LINDA M. CARTER

Holland, Edward "Eddie" (30 Oct. 1939–), songwriter, record producer, and singer, was born and raised in Detroit, Michigan. He graduated from Wilbur Wright High School and attended college until 1958, when he became involved in the music industry. Holland met BERRY GORDY JR., who was a songwriter for JACKIE WILSON, and consequently Holland recorded demos of Gordy's songs. Gordy produced Holland's Mercury single, "You" (1958). The following year, Gordy founded Motown records and released Holland's next single, "Merry Go Round" (1959), which was written by Gordy. More singles followed, including "Jamie" (1961), which reached number six on Billboard's R&B list and number thirty on Billboard's pop list; and "Leaving Here" (1964), which reached number twenty-seven on Billboard's R&B list. During the interim between the latter two singles, one album, *Eddie Holland* (1962), was recorded. Although two additional singles were released in 1964, Holland was no longer interested in singing. One year earlier, Holland; his younger brother, BRIAN HOLLAND; and LAMONT DOZIER formed their own songwriting and production team at Motown known as Holland-Dozier-Holland (HDH) with Eddie Holland as the principal songwriter.

From 1963 to 1968, HDH was responsible for numerous Motown hits. HDH's first hit record was Martha [Reeves] and the Vandellas' "Come and Get These Memories" (1963). The prolific trio wrote subsequent hits for Martha and the Vandellas such as "(Love Is Like a) Heat Wave" (1963) and "Nowhere to Run" (1965), and HDH also generated hit records for the Marvelettes, the Miracles, MARVIN GAYE, Junior Walker and the All Stars, and the Isley Brothers. HDH, as Motown's most consistently successful songwriting and production team, reached their zenith with the Four Tops and the Supremes as they created both groups' biggest hits. HDH wrote and produced such Four Tops' hits as "Baby I Need Your Loving" (1964), "I Can't Help Myself (Sugar Pie, Honey Bunch)" (1965); "Reach Out I'll Be There" (1966), "Standing in the Shadows of Love" (1967), and "Bernadette" (1967). Among the Supremes' HDH records are five consecutive number one hits: "Where Did Our Love Go" (1964), "Baby Love" (1964), "Come See about Me" (1964), "Stop! In the Name of Love" (1965), and "Back in My Arms Again" (1965). Motown, in recognition of HDH's phenomenal success with the Supremes, released the tribute album, *The Supremes Sing Holland-Dozier-Holland* (1967). In addition to his work as a member of HDH, Eddie Holland cowrote a number of hit records for the Temptations with Norman Whitfield and other Motown songwriters; these records include "The Girl's Alright with Me" (1964), "Girl (Why You Wanna Make Me Blue)" (1964), "Ain't Too Proud to Beg" (1966), "Beauty Is Only Skin Deep" (1966), "(I Know) I'm Losing You" (1966), and "Loneliness Made Me Realize It's You That I Need" (1967). Holland assumed even more responsibility at Motown in 1967, when Gordy named him head of the artist and repertoire department. One year later, HDH left Motown after Gordy and HDH could not agree on royalties.

Holland then founded Invictus Records and Hot Wax Records as well as two publishing companies: Gold Forever Music, Inc., and Holland Dozier Holland Music, Inc. Along with his brother and Dozier, Holland wrote and produced hits for Clarence Carter, the Chairman of the Board, Freda Payne, the Honey Cones, and others. Dozier left the partnership in 1974 and resumed his singing career; one decade later, the Holland brothers established the Holland Group and HDH records. *Heaven Must Have Sent You: The Holland-Dozier-Holland Story* was released by Hip-O Universal in 2005. The box set of three compact discs contains sixty-five songs that offer the first comprehensive compilation of HDH music. The three men collaborated on the score for *The First Wives Club—The Musical*; the stage adaptation of the film and novel premiered in July 2009 at the Old Globe Theater in San Diego, California.

Pop Annual 1955–1999 (sixth ed.; 2000) ranked Eddie Holland third in its "Honor Roll of [the Top 200] Songwriters." Eddie Holland, Brian Holland, and Lamont Dozier were inducted into the National Academy of Popular Music/Songwriters Hall of Fame (1988), the Rock and Roll Hall of Fame (1990), and the Hollywood Rockwalk (2003). HDH received the Recording Industry Academy of Arts and Sciences' Trustees Grammy Award (1998), the Broadcast Music, Inc. (BMI)'s Icon Award (2003), and the National Academy of Popular Music's Johnny Mercer Award (2009).

FURTHER READING

Dahl, Bill. *Motown: The Golden Years* (2001).

Henderson, Ashyia, ed. "Holland-Dozier-Holland." In *Contemporary Black Biography*, vol. 36 (2002).

Whitall, Susan. "Motown Songwriters Are Back in the Groove." *The Detroit News Online*, 2 Aug. 2005.

LINDA M. CARTER

Holland, Endesha Ida Mae (29 Aug. 1944–25 Jan. 2006), civil rights activist, educator, scholar, and dramatist, was born Ida Mae Holland in the Delta town of Greenwood, Mississippi. She was the youngest of four children of Ida Mae, a strong-willed, independent woman and midwife, who raised her children as a single parent. Holland never knew the true identity of her biological father.

Holland received her early education in Greenwood, Mississippi, but had dropped out of school before she reached the ninth grade. At the age of eleven, Holland experienced an incident that would change her life. She was sexually assaulted while babysitting for a white family. By the age of twelve, the young and rebellious Holland was working as a prostitute. She later noted, "I was always big for my age. But after the rape—and that White man gave me $5—I knew I was a woman. And since I didn't want to go to the cotton fields and work all day, I figure this was a way that I could make money. And I started turning tricks ($5 for Black men, $10 for White)" (*Ebony*, 126).

Around 1959, Holland married Ike, and by the age of sixteen she had been arrested numerous times for shoplifting, fighting, and soliciting. In 1962, just as she was spiraling out of control, she discovered the civil rights movement and, more importantly, the office of the Student Nonviolent Coordinating Committee Office (SNCC). Holland remembered, "I saw and heard things in that office that I had never seen or heard before.... I had never heard of people talking about civil rights of voter registration" (*Ebony*, 126). Holland became a volunteer within SNCC, and soon a key speaker for SNCC, Holland traveled extensively across the country for the civil rights cause, encouraging African Americans about the importance of the vote. She met and worked with prominent leaders of the movement, including MARTIN LUTHER KING JR.

During one spate of activism in 1965, the home of Holland's mother was firebombed and her mother killed. This act of violence formed an important turning point in Holland's life. She later recalled, "It was like for the first time the importance of what I was doing was really clear to me. And I knew that I had to do more with my life" (*Ebony*, 127).

Holland was at another crossroads in her life, and by the age of twenty, she had married, had a son, Cedric, and divorced. She married two more times, and these marriages also ended in divorce. Holland wanted a change in her life, and with the assistance of her movement friends she got her GED, and then pursued a college education. Holland received a full scholarship to the University of Minnesota, and in 1966 she enrolled as a full-time student. In 1979 she graduated with a B.A. degree in African American studies. Preoccupied with her activism, it took Holland thirteen years to complete her studies for her degree. By 1984 she had received her master's degree and in 1985 the PhD, both in American studies. Holland's experiences in the civil rights movement became the foundation for her dissertation, "The Autobiography of a Parader Without a Permit."

In 1983 she met Dr. MAULANA KARENGA, founder of the Kwanzaa holiday and scholar of African history. Shortly thereafter Holland added the name "Endesha" to demonstrate her ethnic pride. The name comes from Swahili and means "driver"—that is, she who drives herself and others forward. A strong influence, Karenga helped Holland to understand her life and uniqueness within the context of her own personal history. The name "Endesha" describes the next chapter of Holland's life as a motivator for the downtrodden, invisible people with whom she came in contact. She tirelessly encouraged and supported her many acquaintances in their efforts to change their lifestyles and get a formal education. Holland knew firsthand the importance of education. Her compelling story helped others to achieve greatness despite the odds.

While in Minnesota Holland remained a community activist. To aid female ex-offenders in the Minnesota area, she started a group in the 1970s called Women Helping Offenders, which offered training in job skills and life skills and encouraged women to earn their high school diplomas.

With her life taking a new direction and her academic accomplishments in hand, Holland accepted a teaching post at the State University of New York at Buffalo in American studies. She taught at Buffalo from 1985 to 1993, and she had such an effect on the community and the university that she was known as the down-home, electrifying, approachable professor. During her time at Buffalo she authored the series of plays that proved to be her life's work.

On 18 October 1991 Holland returned to Greenwood, Mississippi, for a visit. Mayor Ray Mabus dedicated a day in her honor, calling it the "Endesha Mae 'Cat' Holland Day" because of her academic achievements and her many prestigious honors, which included a nomination for a Pulitzer Prize for her play *From the Mississippi Delta*, in 1988. Holland's *Freedom on My Mind*, a documentary, received an Academy Award nomination and her other plays included the *Reconstruction of Dossier Ree Hemphill* (1980), *Requiem for a Snake* (1980), *Second Doctor Lady* (1980), *Fanny Lou* (1984), and *Miss Ida B. Wells* (1984). Holland was introduced to the field of playwriting when she mistakenly took an advanced course for playwrights, taught by Dr. Charles Nolte, instead of an acting class while an undergraduate student at the University of Minnesota. Holland received numerous awards and accolades for her creative works, and she held memberships in several organizations, including the Dramatist Guild and the Black Theater Network. Her plays were inspired by her life in Mississippi, her mother, and her friends down in the Delta. *From the Mississippi Delta* was performed throughout the United States and in London. It opened off-Broadway in late 1991. Her plays were produced by notables including Woodie King Jr., Susan Quint Gallin, and OPRAH WINFREY.

During the 1990s, Holland was diagnosed with ataxia, an incurable, degenerative neurological disorder. Holland's motor coordination was compromised by this neurological condition, and it caused her to have bouts of depression. In 1993 Holland left New York for southern California, where she took a post at the University of Southern California's School of Theater. She retired in 2003 and died three years later in Santa Monica. Her personal collection is part of the Givens Collection at the University of Minnesota Library.

FURTHER READING

Holland, Endesha Ida Mae. "The Autobiography of a Parader Without a Permit" (1984).

Holland, Endesha Ida Mae. *From The Mississippi Delta: A Memoir* (1997).

Seo, Diane. "The Long March of Endesha Ida Mae Holland," *Los Angeles Times*, 8 May 1994.

Whitaker, Charles. "Endesha Ida Mae Holland: From Prostitute to Playwright." *Ebony* (June 1992).

Obituary: *The New York Times*, 1 February 2006.

VIVIAN NJERI FISHER

Holland, Jerome Heartwell (Brud) (9 Jan. 1916–13 Jan. 1985), educator, diplomat, and administrator, was one of thirteen children born to Robert and Viola Bagsby Holland in Auburn, New York. Most of the children did not survive childhood. One of his younger siblings affectionately called him "Brudder," later shortened to "Brud," which he was called by relatives and friends throughout his life. His father was a gardener and handyman for several families in Auburn. "Brud" Holland began to work with his father at age eight to support their poor family. He determined early in life that education was the key to success.

Holland was a stellar basketball and football player. He played four years on the varsity football team for Auburn High School and twice earned statewide honors. His high school coach years later referred to him as the best all-around athlete ever to play for Auburn. Holland entered Cornell University's College of Agriculture in 1935. Despite his football exploits, he was not offered a scholarship. Holland paid his own way through college, by living in the basement of a fraternity house, where he stoked the furnace, hauled ashes, and waited tables. He later refused an offer of financial assistance. At six feet tall and 215 pounds, he played both offense and defense. He was considered one of the best collegiate defensive ends of his era and dazzled spectators with his blazing speed on the end around play on offense. He became an All-American in 1938 and 1939.

Holland graduated with honors in 1939 from Cornell University with a B.S. in Sociology. He sought a career in business, but because of racial discrimination, he never received an interview from a corporate recruiter. Instead, he accepted a position teaching sociology and coaching football at the historically black Lincoln University in Pennsylvania while completing a master's degree in Sociology at Cornell. He received his M.S. in 1941 with a thesis on "The Role of the Negro Church as an Organ of Protest." From 1942 to 1946 Holland was the director of personnel for Sun Shipbuilding and Drydock Company in Chester, Pennsylvania. In 1946 he became director of the division of political and social science at Tennessee Agricultural and Industrial State College, a historically black school in Nashville, Tennessee. While there, he drew on his experience as personnel director for the shipbuilding company and had completed a doctorate in sociology by 1950 at the University of Pennsylvania. The title of his dissertation was "A Study of Negroes Employed by the Sun Shipbuilding and Drydock Company during World War II and Their Problems in the Post-War Period." In 1948 he married his fellow educator Laura Mitchell, who taught at nearby Fisk University. They had two children, Lucy and Joseph. An earlier marriage, which also produced two children, Jerome and Pamela, ended in divorce.

From 1951 to 1953 Holland served as a consultant to the Pew Charitable Trusts, when the governor of Delaware asked him to rescue Delaware State College, a historically black school that had recently lost its accreditation. He had helped the school regain its accreditation by 1957 and placed it on sound academic footing. Hampton Institute selected him as its president in 1960. There, he doubled the size of the physical plant and made its endowment the largest among historically black colleges and universities. In the tradition of Hampton's founder, Samuel Chapman Armstrong, and its most famous graduate, BOOKER T. WASHINGTON, Holland advocated education and economic development as the best means to achieve racial equality in the United States In 1965 he was inducted into the National Football Hall of Fame. His book *Black Opportunity*, published in 1969, urged African Americans to work within the system for economic gains, rather than relying on separate group economic development. This approach put him at odds with critics of the American economic system, especially the Black Panther Party, which seized Hampton's administration building in 1969 and demanded Holland's resignation. The occupation ended peacefully since Holland had the support of most Hampton faculty and students. A year later, however, he did step down as president, having served a decade in office.

In 1970 President Richard M. Nixon appointed Holland U.S. Ambassador to Sweden, a position that had been vacant for almost fifteen months after the United States recalled its ambassador to protest Sweden's condemnation of the war in Vietnam. When Holland and his family arrived in Sweden, they were met at the airport by demonstrators who protested his presence. Some held placards that announced "Go home, murderer, you are not welcome!" Opponents of America's role in Vietnam dubbed the U.S. Embassy in Sweden "Uncle Tom's Cabin." When Holland rode to the palace to present his credentials to the king of Sweden, he encountered racial slurs and shouts of "Yankee, go home!" As he traveled about the country, angry protesters often threw eggs and Ping-Pong balls at him and his entourage. After two months of such treatment, Holland met with a group of protesters, who seemed to be misinformed about the conditions of African Americans, whom they characterized as completely downtrodden and without hope for change. Gradually, the country began to accept Holland, although it still strongly opposed the Vietnam War.

Holland enjoyed a number of firsts in his life. In 1965 he became the first African American to serve on the board of an Ivy League university when Cornell appointed him to its board of trustees. In 1972, after his return from Sweden, he became the first African American elected to the board of the New York Stock Exchange. Holland served on the board of directors of numerous corporations during the 1970s when corporations, which had no black directors prior to the 1960s, began to appoint African Americans to their boards. According to a 1973 *Black Enterprise* magazine survey of black directors of major corporate boards, Holland held a record eight board memberships. In 1979 President Jimmy Carter named Holland chairman of the board of the American National Red Cross, making him the first African American to hold that position. A fellow of the American Academy of Arts and Sciences, he was the recipient of more than twenty-four honorary degrees. In 1985 President Ronald Reagan posthumously awarded him the Presidential Medal of Freedom, the nation's highest civilian award for exceptional meritorious service. Several facilities have been named after him, including the high school stadium in Auburn, New York, an international living center at Cornell University, the Health, Physical Education, and Recreation Center at Hampton University, and the laboratory for biomedical sciences of the American Red Cross in Rockville, Maryland.

Jerome "Brud" Holland, who fulfilled his dream of being a part of American corporate life despite early racial discrimination and who was always determined to pay his own way, died of cancer at age sixty-nine.

FURTHER READING

The Jerome Heartwell Holland Papers, 1953–1985, are in the Kroch Library of Rare Books and Manuscripts at Cornell University. Materials from his years as president at Hampton University, 1960–1970, are in the Hampton University Archives.

Obituary: *New York Times*, 14 Jan. 1985.

ROBERT L. HARRIS JR.

Holland, Justin (26 July 1819–24 Mar. 1887), guitarist, teacher, composer, arranger, and civil rights advocate, was born in Norfolk County, Virginia, to Exum Holland a farmer. His mother's name is not recorded.

Justin Holland recognized at an early age that rural Virginia offered few opportunities for an ambitious young African American. Born on a farm in Norfolk County to free parents in 1819, Holland was only fourteen when he set out for Boston. Massachusetts was the first state to abolish slavery (in 1783), and Boston had a small but comparatively thriving black population. Holland found work that provided, in his words, "a good living" in nearby Chelsea and became immersed in the energetic cultural life of the city. He had shown a knack for music from a young age, but farm life provided little opportunity to develop musical talent. Now, inspired by the performances of Mariano Perez, one of the numerous Spanish guitarists riding the crest of a guitar craze that swept America in the 1830s, Holland began studying the instrument that would make him one of the most celebrated African American musicians of the nineteenth century.

According to JAMES MONROE TROTTER, a nineteenth-century biographer of black musicians, Boston offered "the amplest facilities for the study of music. ... There the doors of the conservatories and other music schools ... are thrown open to all. ... A love of the 'divine art' pervades all classes in Boston; and there the earnest student and the skillful in music, of whatever race he may be, receives ready recognition and full encouragement" (Trotter, p. 287). Holland never attended a conservatory in Boston, but he found two outstanding teachers,

Simon Knaebel and William Schubert. Knaebel, who taught music theory and arranging, was a member of Edward "Ned" Kendal's renowned brass band. Schubert was a leading guitarist and guitar instructor. Holland also studied flute with a man named Pollack.

While his music instructors were first-rate, Holland felt his education was otherwise deficient. In 1840 he sent a letter to Oberlin Collegiate Institute in Ohio, one of the few colleges that readily accepted black students. "I ... have strove in vain to obtain a decent education," he said in the letter, addressed to Oberlin's president. "I feel & see the importance of a decent education & would gladly make any sacrifice in my power if I could thereby obtain what I wish" (Clemenson, p. 3). Holland had saved $200 for his education, but after receiving a catalog from the college, he realized he could not yet afford to attend Oberlin. He continued to save, and the following year he applied to the school and was accepted. He studied music at Oberlin for a year and then moved to Mexico to study Spanish so that he could read the works of guitar masters such as Dionisio Aguado and Fernando Sor in their original language. Two years later he returned to Ohio.

Holland briefly attended Oberlin again. Soon afterward he married, and in 1845 the couple settled in Cleveland, where he set up shop as a teacher of guitar, flute, and piano. Cleveland, while only having 7,500 residents in 1840, was a rapidly growing city with an appetite for culture. It also was generally accepting of African Americans. "The feeling towards them [African Americans] in Cleveland ... is very kind, and they do better there than in most places," wrote abolitionist and Transcendentalist philosopher James Freeman Clarke. Holland's timing also was very good. A rage for the six-string Spanish guitar, sometimes known as *la guitaro-manie* from a series of illustrations by the French artist and guitarist Charles de Marescot, swept America in the early 1830s. By the 1840s the instrument was firmly established as a popular alternative to the piano for amateur musicians, and good guitar teachers were in high demand. Given his talent, training, and credentials, Holland's race was only a secondary consideration, if an issue at all, for many serious white guitar students. It did not take long to build a loyal following among the elite families of the city.

Holland was the leading guitar teacher in Cleveland, but it was through his transcriptions and arrangements for guitar that he gained a national reputation. He had more than three hundred published arrangements for guitar to his credit. His arrangements include guitar solos, duets, and accompaniments for solo voice, for several voices, or for a chorus. He frequently adapted themes from popular operatic works such Rossini's *William Tell*, Donizetti's *La Fille du Regiment*, and Verdi's *Rigoletto* and wrote many guitar accompaniments for the popular sentimental ballads of the day. Though he thought of himself principally as a transcriber and an arranger, he composed a number of original guitar solos that are well crafted and engaging.

Most of Holland's compositions and arrangements were published by S. Brainard's Sons, a Cleveland firm that marketed Holland's works through its widely read monthly publication, *Brainard's Musical World*. He also was published by other leading houses including J. L. Peters & Co. in New York and the John Church Company in Cincinnati. Holland also wrote a teaching method for Brainard, *Holland's Comprehensive Method for the Guitar* (1874), which was widely recognized as one of the best American guitar method books of the age. Two years later, Peters published a more condensed tutor, *Holland's Modern Method for the Guitar*.

Trotter believed that Holland achieved nationwide success not by overcoming prejudice, but only because most guitarists were unaware of his ethnicity: "It is almost certain, that had it generally been known, as it was not outside of Cleveland, that this gifted and accomplished musician was a member of the colored race, his success would have been much curtailed, so greatly has the senseless, ignoble feeling of color-phobia prevailed in this country" (Trotter, p. 126). Holland and his publishers, however, did not go to great lengths to disguise his race. In fact, his guitar method book prominently featured his portrait. While it may be going a step too far to say that Holland triumphed over the deep-seated prejudices of the era, guitarists apparently were more concerned with the quality of the music they performed than with the color of its arranger.

As a black man navigating the largely white, middle-class world of Cleveland's amateur guitar community, Holland was always conscious of the image he presented. "I ... decided that in my intercourse as a teacher I would preserve the most cautious and circumspect demeanor," he wrote in a letter to a friend. His publisher, Brainard, described him as "a refined and educated man of very modest and unpretending character." But though Holland

kept a low profile, he was nonetheless a prominent local leader in the civil rights movement. He helped to organize and actively participated in local, state, and national conventions where issues affecting African Americans were addressed. He was appointed an assistant secretary of the 1848 National Negro Convention held in Cleveland, and he was a secretary of Colored Americans of Cleveland. Holland came to be an advocate of emigration, and in 1859 he was appointed secretary of the Central American Land Company, an organization formed to purchase land in Central America to be colonized by black Americans. The effort collapsed when the governments of potential host countries opposed the project. Holland briefly emigrated—living in the West Indies for two years during the Civil War—but he returned to Ohio when commercial opportunities failed to materialize.

Holland was an active Mason and was a member of Cleveland's Excelsior Lodge No. 11. Black Masonic lodges—so-called Prince Hall lodges, after one of the first black freemasons—provided an important social and business network. Black Masons also hoped that membership in this influential international fraternal organization would be a channel for overcoming social discrimination. Toward that end, the Prince Hall Grand Lodge of Ohio commissioned Holland, who could correspond in Spanish, French, German, Italian, and Portuguese, to obtain official recognition from foreign Masonic organizations. By 1877 Holland had succeeded in gaining recognition from the Grand Orient of Peru, the League of German Grand Lodges, the Grand National Orient of the Dominican Republic, the Grand Orient of France, the Grand Orient of Italy, and the Grand Orient of Hungary. He also was appointed the U.S. representative of the Grand Lodges of France and Peru, and a sketch of his life was published in the Austrian freemason periodical, *Der Freimaurer*. In the United States, however, white Masons steadfastly refused to acknowledge the legitimacy of black lodges. Holland believed strongly that freemasons had an obligation to uphold the highest moral and ethical standards, and he resigned from the organization when he uncovered corruption in the Cleveland lodge.

Cleveland, which initially attracted Holland because of its liberal attitudes, became increasingly intolerant over time. As a result, Holland's children, Justin Minor, Catherine, and Claire, moved to New Orleans. Justin Minor Holland also gained recognition as a guitarist, composer, and arranger, though he principally supported himself as a bricklayer and, later, a clerk in the U.S. Customs Office. Justin Holland died at his son's home.

FURTHER READING

Bone, Philip J. *The Guitar and Mandolin: Biographies of Celebrated Players and Composers* (2nd ed., 1954; repr. 1972).

Clemenson, Barbara. "Justin Holland: Black Guitarist in the Western Reserve." *Western Reserve Studies Symposium* (1989).

Trotter, James. *Music and Some Highly Musical People: Containing brief chapters on: A Description of Music, the Music of Nature, a Glance at the History of Music, the Power, Beauty, and Uses of Music. Following which are given sketches of the lives of remarkable musicians of the colored race. With portraits, and an appendix containing copies of music composed by colored men* (1878).

DAVID K. BRADFORD

Holland, Milton Murray (1 Aug. 1844–15 May 1910), Civil War soldier and Medal of Honor recipient, was born in Austin, Texas, the son of slaves Jack and Emily Holland. Milton had three known brothers, Toby, William, and James, all part of "the third generation of African-Americans born as slaves" on the Holland Family Plantation run by Bird Holland, later the Texas secretary of state (Arlington National Cemetery). Perhaps because of his light complexion and the fact that he was later freed and sent to school in the North, Bird Holland may have been the real father of Milton, as well as his brothers William and James, a fact speculated upon by some historians. Bird Holland would later free Milton, William, and James and send them north to Ohio in the late 1850s. Here, Milton Holland attended the Albany Manual Labor Academy, an educational institution that accepted blacks and women. This school was the forerunner of the Albany Enterprise Academy, a school owned and operated by African Americans, established after the Albany Manual Labor Academy was purchased by the Disciples of Christ Christian Church and subsequently refused to accept black students. In Albany, Holland would have learned reading and writing, arithmetic, geography, and might have even taken higher level classes in algebra, bookkeeping, history, philosophy, and astronomy. That Milton Holland benefited from his schooling in Albany is evident in the insightful letters he wrote during the Civil War, as well as his successful business career afterward. The beginning of the

Milton Murray Holland, c. 1900. (Library of Congress./The Washington Bee newspaper.)

Civil War found Milton Holland in Albany, Ohio. Holland was excited about the prospect of fighting for the Union cause, later commenting that "There is a brighter day coming for the colored man, and he must sacrifice home comforts if necessary to speed the coming of that glorious day" (Levstik, 13), but he could not yet serve in the army because of his skin color. Instead, he served in a private militia unit, the Attucks Guards, formed in Albany by its African American residents, many of them students, standing ready to defend Ohio if the need arose. Although the details of the actions he may have taken part in are unknown, Milton Holland soon got a chance to experience the war firsthand when he was employed as a servant by Nelson Van Voorhees, a junior officer in the 3d and 18th Ohio regiments, colonel of the 92d Ohio Regiment by 1863, and future congressman. This arrangement was traditional in the army long before the Civil War; just as George Washington had his own valet, WILLIAM LEE, during the American Revolution, so, too, did many Union and Confederate officers have their own personal servants. However, Milton Holland would soon gain the chance to become a real soldier in the Civil War, not just an officer's servant, and proved to be an accomplished "Black Warrior" and one truly "worthy of freedom" (Arlington National Cemetery).

By 1863 the war was grinding on, and the Union army needed increasing numbers of soldiers to continue the fight against the Confederacy. Previously, black soldiers had been denied the right to fight due to mainly political concerns. Now, however, the tide of public opinion in the North at last had turned; once lukewarm to the idea of an all-black regiment, the Ohio governor David Tod now changed his mind and authorized the formation of the state's first black regiment, the 127th Ohio Regiment. Authorized in August 1863, Camp Delaware was set up to accept new recruits and begin the regiment's training. Later, when officially accepted as a unit in the federal army, the regiment was redesignated the 5th U.S. Colored Troop (USCT) Regiment. While the recruiting was slow at first, Milton Holland did his part, later telling readers of the Athens, Ohio, *Messenger*: "You will be reminded of the company of colored soldiers raised by myself in the county of Athens (Ohio) and taken to Camp Delaware, 25 miles north of Columbus, on the Olentangy. It has since been mustered into the service in the 5th Regt. U.S. Colored Troops" (Levstik, 11). Serving as a sergeant in Company C, Holland was one of several noncommissioned officers in the regiment, along with JAMES H. BRONSON, ROBERT PINN, and POWHATAN BEATTY, who would later prove to be effective and courageous battlefield leaders. While all the USCT regiments were led by white officers, and though fewer than 100 blacks during the entire war were commissioned as officers, the backbone of these regiments, as has always been the tradition in the army, were the "noncoms," the sergeants who knew the men in their companies and kept them organized and effective on a daily basis.

Once the 5th USCT was fully organized and trained, it departed Ohio for the war in October 1863. The regiment was first stationed in Virginia as part of General Edward Wild's African Brigade, serving with several other USCT regiments. Holland and the men of the 5th USCT experienced minor fighting in the swamps of the Tidewater region, all the while honing their skills as soldiers. As with all armies, there were highs and lows in combat; Holland, writing from Norfolk, Virginia, on 19 January 1864, recounts how "Our 4th sergeant, Charles G. Stark, is said to have killed a

picket guard while in the act of running away," but later in the letter bitterly relates that "One of the boys belong to Co. D was captured and hung. He was found by our cavalry pickets yesterday and is to be buried today ... the soldier was found with a note pinned to his flesh. Before this war ends we will pin their sentences to them with Uncle Sam's leaden pills" (Levstik, 12; letter dated 19 Jan. 1864). Later, the regiment was transferred to the front lines before the Confederate capital of Richmond as part of General Benjamin Butler's Army of the James. The men of the 5th USCT distinguished themselves in battle on 15 June 1864, taking part in the storming of Petersburg Heights. In this battle, Holland's Company C was among those deployed as skirmishers, moving in advance of their regiment to form a line of battle; he would later write of "the enemy pouring a galling fire of musketry, grape, and canister into ranks slaying many," and told of a rebel officer racing up and down the enemy lines on a "white charger ... shouting from the top of his voice to stand, that they only had niggers to contend with." However, Holland and the men of the USCT prevailed as "the black column rushed forward, raising the battle yell, and in a few moments more we mounted the rebel parapets. And to our great surprise, we found that the boasted Southern chivalry had fled. They could not see the nigger part as the man on the white horse presented it" (Levstik, 15). While casualties in this engagement were light, bigger things were to come.

Late September 1864 found the 5th USCT and Milton Holland stationed opposite Confederate fortifications just south of Richmond at New Market Heights. This strategic bluff and the enemy post, Fort Harrison, that held it was one of four key points in the Confederate line. In the early hours of 29 September Butler's Army of the James and its USCT regiments were on the move, part of a plan to take these strategic forts and perhaps put an end to the siege of Richmond. The resulting Battle of New Market Heights was an epic one in the history of the USCT; though this battle accomplished little, the men of the USCT achieved the only success in a battle that lasted two days and cost the Union 5,000 casualties, capturing Fort Harrison. The enemy defense of Fort Harrison was fierce, and Holland and the men of the 5th USCT paid dearly for every inch of ground they gained. When white officers, including the 5th's commander, Colonel Shurtleff, were shot down, black sergeants quickly took control of their companies and led them forward throughout the battle. When the day was over, Fort Harrison was captured and fourteen black soldiers of the USCT had earned the Medal of Honor, among them Sergeant Milton Holland and three other company sergeants. Indeed, General Butler was so moved by the inspired leadership of the sergeants Holland, Bronson, Pinn, Beatty, as well as that of JAMES DANIEL GARDNER and EDWARD RATCLIFF, that he caused "a special medal to be struck in honor of these gallant colored soldiers" (*Official Records*, 168). This medal was indeed "struck"; made of Tiffany silver and depicting a black soldier charging an enemy parapet, it was first called the Colored Troop Medal and later the Butler Medal. The creation of such a medal as a result of individual combat gallantry by Holland and five other men is unique in American military history, the only such award ever designated for black soldiers. While Holland surely wore the Medal of Honor, presented on 6 April 1865, and the Butler Medal proudly, the latter was prohibited from being worn on USCT soldiers' uniforms after Butler was relieved of his command following the bungled invasion of Fort Fisher, North Carolina, in early 1865.

Following this action, Milton Holland continued to serve with the 5th USCT through the remainder of the war, seeing action at the Battle of Fair Oaks, the assault and capture of Fort Fisher, and the capture of Wilmington, North Carolina, before being mustered out of service in North Carolina on 20 September 1865. Ironically, his former master, Bird Holland, was killed while fighting for the Confederacy in 1864. In his postwar civilian life, Milton Holland would be equally distinguished, graduating with a law degree from Howard University in 1872 and working for the government in Washington, D.C., as an auditor. In 1892 he founded the Alpha Insurance Company in Washington, one of the first black-owned insurance companies in the United States. After his death due to a heart attack, Milton Holland was buried in Arlington National Cemetery, remembered as a successful businessman, gallant soldier, and the first African American from Texas ever to win the Medal of Honor.

FURTHER READING

Arlington National Cemetery. "Milton M. Holland, Sergeant Major, United States Army," available online at http://arlingtoncemetery.net/mholland.htm.

Combs, Issa Lara. "Albany School Pioneered in African American Education," available at http://www.seorf.ohiou.edu/~xx057/albany.htm (1994).

Levstik, Frank R., ed. "From Slavery to Freedom: Two Wartime Letters by One of the Conflict's Few Black Medal Winners," *Civil War Times Illustrated* 11.7 (Nov. 1972).

United States Government Printing Office. *The War of the Rebellion: Official Records of the Union and Confederate Armies* (1893, series I, vol. 42, part III).

                                            GLENN ALLEN KNOBLOCK

Holland, William H. (1841–27 May 1907), slave, Union soldier, state legislator, teacher, and school superintendent, was one of three brothers born in Marshall, Texas, either to Emily and Jack Holland and later purchased by Captain "Bird" Holland, or to Captain "Bird" Holland himself and a slave.

Despite indeterminable origins, Holland's father purchased the freedom of the three men and sent them to Ohio in the 1850s, where each of them went to Albany Enterprise Academy, a school for blacks. In addition to reading and writing, students there were exposed to a range of subjects, including algebra, geometry, geography, history, chemistry, and astronomy. One of the school's first trustees was THOMAS JEFFERSON FERGUSON.

At the age of twenty-three, Holland fought on the side of the Union to end slavery by joining the 16th U.S. Colored Troop (USCT) on 22 October 1864. The 16th was a Tennessee contingent which opened its ranks to include black men from various states, including Ohio. Holland and his regiment successfully fought to repel Confederate soldiers, led by John Bell Hood, at Overton Hill in Nashville, Tennessee, around 14 December 1864.

After serving his country, Holland enrolled in English classes at Oberlin's preparatory department, a private secondary school, in 1867. After attending two nonconsecutive years, he dropped out and returned to Texas to become an educator.

After the Civil War, Holland used his education, wartime experience, and political talent to join with many other black Texans to frame the political future of blacks in the state. They, along with blacks from other states, were able to take advantage of the void left when white former Confederates boycotted the constitutional conventions ordered by President Andrew Johnson in 1868 because blacks were allowed to participate. As a result, individuals like Holland were able to shape their states' constitutions in ways that addressed, as much as possible, their political concerns regarding topics like lynching, due process, and black suffrage. In 1873 Holland served as a committee member at Brenham's Colored Men's Convention, but three years later, in 1876 (and again in 1880), he was chosen as a black Republican delegate to the national convention.

Holland went on to serve as a state representative for Waller County in Texas' 15th District. He fought to have a share of Texas's federal land grants used to establish an agriculture and mechanics school for blacks since one already existed for whites. His bill became law in 1876 with the political help of the wealthy African American state senator WALTER M. BURTON, who was well respected among his white counterparts. In honor of his efforts, Holland became known as the "Father of Prairie View University" (later Prairie View A&M University), which opened in 1879. Holland succeeded in convincing Texas to establish a school for African Americans who were deaf, mute, or blind (the Deaf, Dumb, and Blind Institute for Colored Youth) in 1887. He served for thirteen years as the school's first superintendent.

Holland was married to Eliza H. James, a deaf instructor who also worked at the institute. They had two daughters. Holland died at the age of sixty-six.

FURTHER READING

Brewer, John Mason. *Negro Legislators of Texas* (1970).

Pitre, Merline. *Through Many Dangers, Toils, and Snares: The Black Leadership of Texas, 1868–1900* (1985).

Prather, Patricia Smith. *From Slave to Statesman: The Legacy of Joshua Houston, Servant to Sam Houston* (1993).

Rice, Lawrence. *The Negro in Texas* (1971).

TERESA A. BOOKER

Holley, Major (10 July 1924–25 Oct. 1990), bassist, known as Mule, was born Major Quincy Holley Jr. in Detroit, Michigan, the son of Major Quincy Holley, a minister and bass singer. The name of his mother, a pianist, is unknown. He first studied violin around the age of six with a German teacher named Mr. Hilken, and at first his parents only allowed him to listen to classical music. At age thirteen he heard on the radio the sound that would eventually draw him to play the string bass—- SLAM STEWART's bowed bass solo on "Champagne Lullaby."

Holley attended Cass Technical High School in Detroit from 1938, where he studied the tuba. Among his classmates were the vibraphonist MILT JACKSON, the tenor saxophonist Lucky Thompson, the trumpeters DONALD BYRD and HOWARD McGHEE, and the bassist PAUL CHAMBERS. His

first professional work came in 1937–1938, on violin, for Leroy Smith's group the Ink Spots.

Holley joined the navy in 1942 and trained at the Great Lakes Naval Training Station in Chicago, joining several other outstanding musicians. After a year he was accepted into the "A" band, where he played sousaphone and learned to double on bass. His bunkmate was Willie Smith, swing alto saxophonist and arranger for the JIMMIE LUNCEFORD band. He also met the trumpeter CLARK TERRY, who became a longtime friend and colleague. Terry originally dubbed Holley the "pack mule" because of all the instruments he carried, and the nickname "Mule" stuck. Later, Holley was transferred to San Diego, where he met CHARLES MINGUS. He attended informal bass classes taught by Mingus out of his home and also met the bassist OSCAR PETTIFORD and the tenor saxophonist ILLINOIS JACQUET. While in the navy Holley gravitated toward the bass as his primary instrument, although he continued to double on tuba. The Canadian Bobby Rudd was instrumental in strengthening his bass technique. Bill Doggett, the pianist in LUCKY MILLINDER's band, taught him bass line technique based on chord progressions. Between 1943 and 1945 Holley also became familiar with a new instrument, the electric Fender bass.

After his discharge at the end of World War II Holley embarked on a freelance career. He played at Birdland and the Alvin Hotel in New York City and made his first recordings in 1950 as part of a duo with the pianist OSCAR PETERSON. He performed with such figures as CHARLIE PARKER, COLEMAN HAWKINS, Al Haig, ART TATUM, and EARL BOSTIC. He landed steady work with the tenor saxophonists WARDELL GRAY and DEXTER GORDON, as well as a stint on baritone saxophone for the rhythm and blues guitarist and singer T-BONE WALKER.

In 1951 Holley traveled to England, where he worked for five years as a freelance bassist and studio musician. His first work in England was with the pianist Lennie Felix at the Astor Colony restaurant and with the tenor saxophonist Ronnie Scott. He also performed with Tubby Hayes, Jimmy Deuchar, Joe Harriot, Vic Ash, and Ray Ellington and on the British television show *Son of Fred* with Reggie Owen. While in England Holley married for the first time. Although little information is available about his wives, Holley mentioned in an interview with Bob Rusch that he had several unsuccessful marriages. He returned to the United States in January 1956, although he traveled back to England to perform on several occasions.

For a while Holley concentrated on freelancing in New York City as a studio and club musician. In 1957 he worked with a group led by Illinois Jacquet, and in 1958 he recorded on tuba with Michel LeGrand alongside the legendary tenor saxophonist BEN WEBSTER. He went to Detroit briefly during this time, where he performed with Coleman Hawkins and ELLA FITZGERALD. In 1958 and 1959 he performed and recorded in Brazil with Woody Herman's orchestra. Following his return to the United States he played with a group headed by the saxophonists Al Cohn and Zoot Sims (former Herman band members) from 1959 to 1960.

The 1960s brought continued success to Holley. He maintained an active studio career, worked with the pianists Bill Evans and TEDDY WILSON during 1961–1962, and played with DUKE ELLINGTON's band for eight months in 1964. Holley also performed with the legendary multi-reed instrumentalist RAHSAAN ROLAND KIRK in 1965, which resulted in the album *Here Comes the Whistleman* (1967). While with Ellington Holley began drinking heavily. Personal problems exacerbated the situation; Holley lost his wife and house as well as other material possessions. He ultimately sought treatment and later became a volunteer for several drug and alcohol rehabilitation programs in New York City. As part of his efforts he created Piano Playhouse, an open performance forum at Jacques' on Sunday afternoons in Greenwich Village.

By 1966 electric bass had begun to play a greater role in Holley's career. Holley taught electric bass at the Berklee College of Music in Boston from 1967 to 1970. In New York he appeared regularly with Jaki Byard at Bradley's. He also performed with the singer ARETHA FRANKLIN and introduced her to Columbia Records.

But Holley maintained an active double bass career, working with notable musicians such as the COUNT BASIE Band, Benny Goodman, ROY ELDRIDGE, Lee Konitz, Roland Hanna, Frank Sinatra, QUINCY JONES, and Buddy DeFranco. Holley was the house bassist at Jimmy Ryan's in New York City in the 1970s. Throughout the 1980s he appeared as a sideman at numerous international jazz festivals. He toured Europe with the singer HELEN HUMES and a group called the Kings of Jazz and returned to Sao Paulo to lead his own group for a short time in the late 1980s. One of his last performances was in the summer of 1990 at the North Sea Festival, where he played with DOROTHY DONEGAN and Ellis Marsalis. He died in Maplewood, New Jersey.

Holley was a dependable sideman on cello, electric bass, baritone saxophone, and tuba in addition to the double bass. When soloing on double bass, he often hummed or sang wordlessly along in unison, a technique employed earlier by Slam Stewart. His 1986 album with Stewart, *Shut Yo' Mouth*, exemplified this style. Throughout his career he played with musicians associated with traditional jazz, swing, bop, cool jazz, modal jazz, avant-garde jazz, rock, soul, and rhythm and blues. Versed in these varied styles of music as well as in multiple instruments he was able to remain an active freelance musician in a rapidly changing international musical environment. His willingness to help others was displayed by his affiliations with rehabilitation programs and the National Association for Jazz Education.

FURTHER READING
Arnaud, Gérald, and Jacques Chesnel. *Masters of Jazz* (1992).
Floyd, Samuel A., Jr. "The Great Lakes Experience; 1942–45," *Black Perspective in Music* 3, no. 1 (Spring 1975).
Richards, Martin. *Jazz Journal International* 40, no. 4 (1987).
Rusch, Bob. *Cadence* 15, no. 7 (1989).
Obituary: *New York Times*, 27 Oct. 1990.
This entry is taken from the *American National Biography* and is published here with the permission of the American Council of Learned Societies.

DAVID E. SPIES

Holley, Susie Catherine (2 Apr. 1896–2 Feb. 1981), educator, organizer, and fund-raiser, was born Susie Catherine Miller in Goshen, Albemarle County, Virginia, to the Reverend and Mrs. R. L. Miller. Educated in the Virginia public schools, she completed her high school training and received her bachelor's degree in Sociology with honors at Virginia Theological Seminary in Lynchburg, Virginia. She later studied guidance and sociology at Atlanta University. Holley married the Reverend R. L. Holley, dean of languages at Virginia Theological Seminary; they would have two children.

The couple moved to Birmingham, Alabama, where the Reverend Holley was a pastor, then relocated to Live Oak, Florida, where he became dean of religion, then president, of Florida Baptist Institute in 1926 (later Florida Memorial College), a high school and junior college operated by the Baptist General Convention of Florida since 1879. Susie Holley taught sociology there and served as field director and promotional secretary for eastern and midwestern states. During the 1920s Holley formed the Famous Female Quartet of Florida Memorial College at Live Oak, Florida, which traveled to twenty-seven states and performed for churches, conventions, hotels, and civic organizations, raising substantial donations for the institution. Holley advanced African American education in Florida by soliciting contributions to benefit educational programs and strengthening college curriculums. Money raised from her ventures aided Florida Memorial College's administration, increased classroom resources, and provided financial aid to students.

In 1941 Florida Baptist Institute of Live Oak merged with St. Augustine's Florida Baptist Academy to form the Florida Normal and Industrial Institute. Her role in the merger yielded her appointment as promotional secretary for the institute, and she began a "watch care" initiative, routinely supervising the successful degree completions of students she recommended to the college. Holley's work among Baptist women resulted in her election as the first vice president of the Women's Convention Auxiliary to the National Baptist Convention USA. Holley worked with other churchwomen at Baptist General Convention of Florida to organize a campus "love gift day," also known as Donation Day, first held on 21 November 1957. Their efforts succeeded in collecting canned goods and other food, equipment, and money with a value of more than $3,000. She also collected cash donations of $2,163.20 to purchase items for the college dining hall in 1957.

She mobilized statewide groups of women subdivided by regions to promote Donation Day sponsored by the Women's Auxiliary of the Baptist General Convention of Florida and the Progressive Missionary and Educational Baptist State Convention of Florida. Holley resigned from her position as promotional secretary of Florida Normal and Industrial Institute in 1949 to accompany her husband to Fort Lauderdale, Florida, following his retirement from the presidency of the institution to become the pastor of Piney Grove First Baptist Church, where he remained until his death in 1959. During the 1950s Holley, assisted by Mrs. Alfred Holt of Fort Lauderdale, organized Cradle Nursery, a day care center located in a room at Piney Grove Baptist Church. The success and popularity of this program overwhelmed the church's facilities, which motivated Holley to mobilize other women, including Ruth Black Moore and

Mary Moen of the Pilot Club and Ethel McClane of the Community Service Council. Holley and McClane led a successful campaign, acknowledging Cradle Nursery as a United Way agency and raised funds for the construction of a building housing the program on Sixth Court and Thirteenth Avenue in Fort Lauderdale. Holley was president of Cradle Nursery for a decade and also served on its board of directors. The facility was renamed the Susie C. Holley Cradle Nursery in honor of Holley's contributions.

Holley worked with missionary societies and initiated the first adult education program at the First Baptist Piney Grove Church, teaching migrant parents to read and write. She worked on behalf of Provident Hospital, Broward County's first and only black hospital. She also served the First Bethlehem District and in the Florida East Coast District as director of leadership education for the Women's Convention Auxiliary to the Baptist General Convention and later became its president. As a member of the board of trustees and vice president of the Women's Convention Auxiliary to the National Baptist Convention USA, Holley secured more than a half-million dollars in pledges to Florida Memorial College for the Florida Memorial College Development Program.

Holley served three years on the National Church Women United Assignment Race Task Force, which sought to expedite compliance with the 1954 Brown v. Board of Education Supreme Court decision outlawing school segregation. The City of Fort Lauderdale recognized Susie C. Holley as Woman of the Year in 1955. In December 1964 Florida Memorial College conferred upon her the honorary doctor of humanities degree. In 1970, under her leadership, the permanent headquarters of the Women's Convention Auxiliary to the Baptist General Convention headquarters was built in Fort Lauderdale and in 1971 furnished by the women of the Baptist General Convention.

Throughout the 1970s Holley worked as a volunteer for many local and national organizations, including the Bi-racial Committee, the United Fund, and the Personnel Committee for the Economic Opportunity Program. Holley also served on educational boards, including the Nova University Chartered Alumni, the League of Women Voters, the Fort Lauderdale Historical Committee, the Committee on Quality Education for Broward County, the State Board of Directors for Church Women United, and the Juvenile Court Board of the City and Board of the Fort Lauderdale

Chain of Missionary Assemblies. In 1979 the National Council of Christians and Jews honored Susie C. Holley along with the CBS News anchorman Walter Cronkite.

Holley served on Florida Memorial College's board of trustees as chairman of the executive committee, and her fund-raising activities for the institution yielded more than $1.6 million in 1979. She received more than fifty community service honors and awards during her lifetime. Holley died on 2 February 1981, and on 4 November, Florida Memorial College held a groundbreaking ceremony for a building that was completed in 1984 and aptly named the Susie C. Holley Religious Center. In the early twenty-first century Holley's impact continued to be noted by the women of First Baptist Piney Grove Church, who annually observed Susie C. Holley Day. Donation Day was also annually observed at Florida Memorial College (which became Florida Memorial University in 2005) in her honor. In summarizing her life, Holley stated, "if one would ask where my deepest dedication and conviction lie, I would say in devising and promoting opportunities for youth to become trained and inspired in Christian principles and standards through Christian higher education."

FURTHER READING
Colburn, David R. *Racial Change and Community Crisis: St. Augustine, Florida, 1877–1980* (1985).
McKinney, George Patterson, and Richard I. McKinney. *History of the Black Baptists of Florida, 1850–1985* (1987).

ROSE C. THEVENIN

Holliday, Jennifer Yvette (19 Oct. 1960–), singer, recording artist, and actress in musical theater and television, was born the oldest of three children in Riverside, Texas, to Omie Lee, a pastor, and Jennie Thomas Holliday, a schoolteacher. Jennifer was raised by her mother, who encouraged and supported her young daughter's interest in music. Later, her mother would remarry and have more children.

As a teenager, Holliday sang in Houston's Pleasant Grove Baptist Church. It was when she was seventeen and singing in the choir that a dancer in the touring company of *A Chorus Line* named Jamie Patterson heard her and recognized her potential as a vocalist. He bought her a ticket to go to New York to audition for the director VINNETTE CARROLL's revival production of the musical *Your Arms Too Short to Box with God.* Carroll was impressed and

Holliday won a part. In 1981, her work in the production earned her a nomination for a Drama Desk award for Best Featured Actress.

Holliday's big break on Broadway came in December 1981, when she and Cleavant Derricks, a former cast mate from Carroll's production, were cast in the musical theater production of *Dreamgirls.* At the Imperial Theater on Broadway, Holliday assumed the role of Effie Melody White. Originally, the role was intended for the actress Nell Carter, but Carter had declined the role. Instead, Holliday appeared alongside Cleavant Derricks, Loretta Devine, and Sheryl Ralph Lee in the premiere production. *Dreamgirls* won six Tony Awards in 1982 and ran an estimated 1,522 performances during its four-year stint. Holliday won numerous accolades for her portrayal of Effie: a Tony Award for Best Leading Actress in a Musical, a Drama Desk Award for Best Leading Actress; and a Theatre World Award for Outstanding Broadway Debut.

The role of Effie also provided Holliday with two songs that remained in her repertoire for her entire career: "I Am Changing" and her signature song "And I Am Telling You I'm Not Going," written by Tom Eyen and Henry Krieger. During the 1982 Tony Awards telecast she delivered a show-stopping performance of the latter, an aria-like piece about love, devotion, and commitment, which won her both further acclaim and a wider national audience. The song was popularized further by her subsequent chart-topping recording of the single. It reached #1 on *Billboard*'s R&B Singles chart and #22 on the *Billboard* Hot 100 chart and earned her a Grammy for Best Female Performance in Rhythm and Blues in 1982.

Following her crossover from musical theater actress to recording artist, Holliday recorded another hit titled "I Am Love," which reached #2 on the *Billboard* R&B chart. In 1985 three more hits followed. "Hard Time for Lovers" and "No Frills Love" were especially popular as dance tracks, establishing Holliday as an enduring club favorite, and she was a featured singer with the hard rock band Foreigner on their single "I Wanna Know What Love Is." In the midst of her success as a recording artist, she returned to musical theater in *Sing, Mahalia, Sing* in 1986. She followed her tenure in this production with another recording project, *Get Close to My Love* (1987), but the album's major single, "Heart on the Line" failed to crack the R&B top fifty.

In 1990 Holliday underwent drastic weight loss as the result of a gastric bypass procedure and intermittent issues with diet and depression.

Subsequently, she was vocal about her health challenges. She admitted that she had attempted suicide on her thirtieth birthday, unable to cope with her fluctuating weight loss. After Holliday's recovery from that attempt, she spoke openly about her bouts with depression, in order to remove the stigma from those suffering from the illness. The National Mental Health Association welcomed her as a spokeswoman for issues regarding the symptoms and causes of depression.

In January 1991 Holliday met the pianist Billy Meadows while she was performing in a nightclub. They married two months later, but divorced in December after only nine months. In this year of tumult, she recorded the album *I'm on Your Side*, the title track of which reached the R&B Top Ten.

Holliday was remarried in 1993 to the Michigan minister Reverend Andre Woods. Her husband was allegedly unfaithful and swindled her out of her money. Four months after her mother's death from cancer, the marriage ended and they divorced in 1995. Her mother's illness and her marital troubles fueled her 1994 gospel album, *On and On*, which did well on the gospel charts and earned her a Grammy for Best Inspirational Performance in the gospel category for her rendition of the track "Come Sunday."

Throughout the 1990s and 2000s Holliday was a staunch supporter of the Lesbian, Gay, Bi-sexual, Transgender (LGBT) community. Through the scheduling efforts of Scott Sherman and the sponsorship of the Atlantic Entertainment Group, she lent her strength to numerous LGBT fund-raisers and pride appearances.

In 2000 Holliday released another album, *Breaking Through*, featuring the single "A Woman's Got Power," which reached #7 on the U.S. dance chart. She experienced a resurgence of popularity with a dance remix of her signature song, "And I Am Telling You I'm Not Going" in 2001, which hit #6 on *Billboard*'s U.S. dance chart. In addition, she sang "America the Beautiful" on the first broadcast of the World Wrestling Entertainment pay-per-view after the terrorist attacks of 11 September 2001.

Holliday made appearances on television shows such as *Touched by an Angel*, *Hang Time*, and *Ally McBeal*, in which she played the recurring role of choir director Lisa Knowles. She also starred in the independent film *The Rising Place* (2001). She received acclaim from the NAACP, as a recipient of the Image Award, and honors from *Time* magazine as Performer of the Decade. Holliday frequently appeared on the Trinity Broadcasting Network television station to talk about her life and spiritual journey. When she was awarded an honorary doctor of music from Berklee College of Music in Boston, Massachusetts, she acknowledged Texas congresswoman Barbara Jordan as her childhood hero. Holliday attributed her vocal style to her gospel roots and to the influence of artists such as ELLA FITZGERALD, ETTA JAMES, and Tony Bennett.

FURTHER READING

Bailey, Peter A. "Dreams Come True on Broadway for Young Stars in *Dreamgirls*." *Ebony* 37 (May 1982): 90.

Jones, John Bush. *Our Musicals, Ourselves: A Social History of Musical Theater* (2003).

Warner, Jay. *On This Day in Black Music History* (2006).

Woll, Allen L. *Black Musical Theater: From Coontown to Dreamgirls* (1989).

ALISHA LOLA JONES

Holloman, John Lawrence Sullivan, Jr. (22 Nov. 1919–27 Feb. 2002), physician, medical administrator, and activist, was born in Washington, D.C., the son of Dr. John Lawrence Sullivan Holloman Sr., minister of the Second Baptist Church, and Rosa Victoria Jones, a homemaker. Little is known of his early education, but John L. S. Holloman Jr. attended Virginia Union University, as had his father, graduating in 1940 with a bachelor of science degree. Three years later, he would matriculate at the University of Michigan Medical School, earning his MD in 1943. Entering the armed services in that year, Holloman served in the medical corps for the duration of World War II and was honorably discharged on 2 November 1946 with the rank of captain. He married Charlotte Patricia Wesley, a concert pianist, who was the daughter of the historian and minister Dr. CHARLES HARRIS WESLEY. The couple would go on to have four daughters and one son.

Taking advanced medical courses at the Cornell University School of Medicine, and first being assigned to Bellevue Hospital in New York City, Holloman soon established a long-standing private medical practice in the city. He also helped found the Medical Committee for Civil Rights, which focused on pressuring the American Medical Association (AMA) to end its discriminatory practices and policies. The committee's early meetings were held at his office, and he became its co-chair in 1963. He took the lead in organizing a mass demonstration at the AMA National

Convention in Atlantic City, New Jersey, protesting the AMA's support of medical associations that would not admit black patients. This took place on 12 June 1963. He assumed an active role in the civil rights marches of the 1960s, primarily as an attending physician to the marchers. During the Selma march of 1965 he was particularly instrumental in much of the medical planning and administration. Holloman, as president of the Medical Committee for Human Rights, the successor organization to the Medical Committee for Civil Rights, in 1965 was at the forefront of the efforts to dispatch volunteers to investigate hospitals and hospital systems throughout the South that were discriminating against African American patients and physicians. As a result of their findings—and of demonstrations and pickets (including a major one conducted by Holloman himself on the headquarters of the Department of Health, Education, and Welfare in Washington, D.C.)—the Title VI process for institutions receiving Medicare funding from the federal government was enacted into law. Holloman's subsequent consultant's oversight of the Office of Equal Health Opportunity assured that compliance with and implementation of Title VI stipulations were quickly put into place and that segregation within the health services sector soon became a thing of the past. He served as president of the National Medical Association from 1966–1967 and continued to be a persistent critic of certain longstanding AMA practices, and closely watched that organization for any civil rights violation.

Holloman also served as vice president for the Health Insurance Plan of New York from 1972 until 1974, and became nationally known as the director of the New York City Public Hospital Corporation from 1974 until 1977. He took a year away from administrative tasks to teach at the University of North Carolina at Chapel Hill as a visiting public health professor (1977–1978), then served on the professional staff to the U.S. Congressional Ways and Means Committee (1979–1981), and still later as medical officer to the U.S. Food and Drug Administration (1980–1985). Holloman held a position on the board of trustees for the State University of New York (SUNY) from 1966 until 1995 and chaired the trustee board for his alma mater, Virginia Union University, from 1961 until 1976, taking a pivotal role in spearheading the most successful capital fund-raising campaign in the university's history. In 1983 Virginia Union University awarded him the honorary degree of doctor of the sciences.

During the 1990s he was an ardent supporter of the Clinton administration's initiative to devise a national health insurance program—an idea he had indeed advocated many years earlier—and was in the vanguard of warning of the disproportionate effect of the AIDS epidemic on minorities. From 1981 until 2002 he held the post of associate director of health services at the William Fitts Ryan Community Health Center in New York. He held membership in Alpha Phi Alpha Fraternity, Boule, the board of the Health Manpower Development Corporation, and the New York City H.I.P. Automated Multiphasic Health Testing Center. Holloman died of a stroke in Queens, New York.

FURTHER READING

Holloman Family Papers, 1915–1975 (Collection No. 41) are located at the Martin Luther King Jr. Memorial Library, Washingtoniana Division, Washington, D.C., Community Archives.

Coombs, Orde. *The Making of a Black Middle Class Family: The End of an Era* (1975).

Harris, Janette Hoston. "In Memoriam: Charles Harris Wesley," *Journal of Negro History* 83.2 (Spring, 1998).

Morais, Herbert M. *The History of the Afro-American in Medicine* (1976).

Rangel, Charles. "Recognizing the Life of the Late Dr. John Holloman," address in the House of Representatives, *Congressional Record*, 7 Mar. 2002.

Smith, David Barton. "Healing a Nation: How Three Graduates of the U-M Medical School Wrote Their Own Chapter in the History of Civil Rights in America," *Medicine at Michigan* 2.2 (Summer, 2006).

Obituary: *New York Times*, 2 Mar. 2002.

RAYMOND PIERRE HYLTON

Holloway, Josephine Amanda Groves (19 Mar. 1898–7 Dec. 1988), field adviser, district adviser, and camp director of Girl Scouts, USA, and social worker, was born in Cowpens, South Carolina, the seventh child of ten born to John Wesley Groves, a Methodist minister, and Emma Mae Gray.

The Groves family relocated to Greenwood, South Carolina, to provide better educational opportunities for their children. Holloway attended the Brewer Normal School in nearby Beaufort. Encouraged by one of her teachers, she enrolled in Fisk University in Nashville, Tennessee, in 1919. Declaring a major in sociology, Holloway doggedly pursued her college education. She wound the campus clocks and worked in the dining hall to augment her meager funds, and overcame a bout of influenza as she strove to complete her degree. In June 1923 she earned her degree in Sociology.

Following her graduation from Fisk, Holloway returned to South Carolina to find work. In 1923 she accepted a position working with young girls at the Bethlehem Center in Nashville, Tennessee. Bethlehem Centers, associated with the Methodist Church, provided social services and after-school activities for adults and children. The next year, Holloway organized the area's first African American Girl Scout troop. Juliette Gordon Low, the founder of the Girl Scouts, provided a training session to scouting enthusiasts at the George Peabody College for Teachers in Nashville in 1924; Holloway attended the event. She brought her new knowledge and excitement back to the Bethlehem Center and organized the troop. Unfortunately, the Girl Scout Council refused to charter it; only white troops received such recognition.

On 30 June 1925 she married her fellow Fisk alumnus Guerney Holloway, a boys' worker at the Bethlehem Center whom she had started dating while at college. They had three daughters: Nareda, Josephine, and Weslia.

The mores of the times, however, stymied Holloway's career plans. She left her position after the center's director informed her she would not have adequate time to be both wife and counselor. Holloway's replacement showed little interest in the Girl Scouts and let the troop fold. She left the center, but did not lose her determination to serve others and further her own career. Holloway resumed her education, enrolling in Tennessee A&I State College in Nashville, and received a B.A. in Business in 1927. That same year she became assistant registrar for her alma mater, Fisk. She held the position until 1934, when she joined the Tennessee Department of Welfare. She wasted little time in pursuing her mission, the reestablishment of a black Girl Scout troop.

Holloway faced strong opposition from the Girl Scout Council. Scouting had begun in Tennessee in 1917, and in 1926 the Nashville Council was chartered. Consistent with the rules of segregation, the council and official Girl Scout troops were open only to whites. Undaunted, Holloway created an unofficial Girl Scout troop, even designing distinctive gingham uniforms for them. Her husband purchased official Girl Scout handbooks for the troop, which the local council had forbidden her to buy. The girls learned the Girl Scout Promise and Scout laws so they would be ready to become invested as official members of Girl Scouts of America if, and when, the organization desegrated.

In 1943 Girl Scouts of America, Troop 200, became a reality. Forty girls, including the Holloways' three daughters, were inducted into the official organization. The council president Juli Mosely credited Holloway with training the girls so well that no grounds existed to block their membership. Tennessee now had official black Scouts and white Scouts, but functioning independently of one another, according to the laws of segregation.

The Tennessee Girl Scouts, having allowed a black troop, now needed black volunteers and professionals, and Holloway was brought on as a member of their professional staff. In the fall of 1944, in this two-tier system, Holloway assumed the role of professional organizer and field adviser, responsible for some two thousand black members and other personnel. Later that year she became a district director and camp director. The Holloway family donated land to provide camp experience to the black Girl Scouts. Recognizing her unflagging service to the organization, in 1951, the council named the facility Camp Holloway. She retired from the Girl Scouts in 1963.

Before her death at age ninety, Holloway received the SOJOURNER TRUTH Award from the Nashville Chapter of Business and Professional Women, and the Zeta of the Year Award from her sorority, Zeta Phi Beta. During the nation's 1976 bicentennial, the Girl Scouts of America officially recognized her as one of the country's unsung leaders, a "Hidden Heroine."

FURTHER READING

Perry, Elisabeth Israels. "'The Very Best Influence': Josephine Holloway and Girl Scouting for Nashville's African American Community," *Tennessee Historical Quarterly* 52 (1993): 73–85.

Smith, Jessie Carney. "Josephine Holloway," in *Notable Black American Women, Book II*, ed. Jessie Carney Smith (1996).

PEGGY J. HARDMAN

Holloway, Tommie Lee (24 Dec. 1924 – 10 Nov. 2008), World War II soldier and Silver Star recipient, was born in Brunswick, Georgia, the son of Tom and Mary Lee Holloway. His father worked as a fireman and engineer for the Atlantic Coast Line railroad. Tommie attended Brunswick public schools and later enrolled in the Civilian Conservation Corps at Waycross, Georgia, on 8 April 1941, serving for one year prior to enlisting in the U.S. military during World War II.

Holloway was inducted into the army at Fort Benning, Georgia, on 9 April 1943. Though the details of Holloway's early military career are not completely known, he was eventually assigned to the 471st Amphibious Truck Company and was trained as a "duck" driver. This famed vehicle of World War II, which received its nickname from its manufacturer designation (DUCKW), was a specially designed truck that could operate on both land and sea. First used in 1942, the duck became an instrumental vehicle for both the army and marines in helping to land men and supplies ashore during amphibious operations, as well as helping to act as seagoing ambulances in the evacuation of casualties from invasion beaches to hospital ships. Vehicles such as this were generally crewed by two or three men, including a driver, an assistant driver, and (for those ducks specially fitted) a machine gun operator. Drivers like Tommie Holloway were not only trained on how to drive their ducks, but how to perform field maintenance and, if the need should arise, emergency repairs. Time and circumstances would eventually demonstrate that Holloway was one of the most skilled and brave (and lucky) of all the duck drivers to see combat action.

The service of African Americans such as Holloway, WAVERLY WOODSON, and GEORGE WATSON was important during World War II, but their stories have seldom been told. What is not commonly known is that of the just over one million African Americans that served in the army during the war, only a small percentage would be allowed to serve in actual combat units. Because of the continued racial stereotypes held by army brass that black soldiers were inferior soldiers to whites, they were instead largely assigned to segregated service companies in the Quartermaster Corps, transportation units, field artillery and antiaircraft battalions, port companies, or construction companies, to name just a few. These units were vital to the war effort, but their members have seldom received their due because they were often stationed behind the front lines or in recently secured areas and were not directly or continually exposed to enemy fire. Even trained black combat troops were stationed stateside until increasing political pressure resulted in their eventual use beginning in 1944. As for service companies, they would experience a wide variety of overseas postings beginning in 1942, and a number of units, such as Tommie Holloway's 471st Amphibious Truck Company, would soon prove their skill and bravery under the most severe combat conditions. By their fine performance under fire, these black soldiers would prove their worth to army brass and thereby contributed to the army's eventual decision to end its segregationist policies during the Korean War.

On 18 August 1944, Private Tommie Holloway and the men of the 471st departed the United States, bound for the Pacific. After undergoing further amphibious training in Hawaii, they were soon assigned to the 5th Marine Division, a unit that was also going into combat for the first time, and the invasion of the island of Iwo Jima in February 1945. The 5th Marines, including the men of the 471st, hit the beaches of Iwo Jima on D-Day, 19 February 1945, under heavy machine gun and mortar fire. The invasion of Iwo Jima was one of the toughest of the Pacific island invasions on the road to defeating Japan, and the 5th Marines and their elements suffered more casualties than any other unit. Private Tommie Holloway's duck was loaded with a 155 mm Howitzer, ammunition, and its gun crew, and made the beach under heavy fire; as he was driving his vehicle over the sand to an artillery battery to unload, his windshield was hit by sniper fire, but still Holloway continued onward. After unloading his cargo, Holloway and his assistant driver started to return to the beach but were soon caught in a traffic jam. Under heavy fire, Holloway and his assistant driver took cover on the beach near their duck. When a Marine officer approached them and asked them to deliver small arms ammunition to an infantry company, Holloway quickly agreed to do so. While attempting to deliver the ammunition, Holloway's duck again took heavy fire from an enemy pillbox, and the driver's cabin was hit several times by machine gun fire. Once again, Holloway had to take cover, but after darkness set in he successfully delivered the ammunition and returned to the landing beach to await further orders. However, when the morning came he found his duck so badly shot up he had to perform makeshift repairs to enable him to get back out to the ammunition ship. With his duck patched up, Holloway continued to deliver ammunition to the soldiers on the beach at Iwo Jima for the next two days, often under heavy fire. After two days, Tommie Holloway's duck was so damaged it was nearly inoperable.

For his actions at Iwo Jima on 19–21 February 1945, Private Tommie Holloway was subsequently awarded the Silver Star, the army's third-highest combat decoration. He was one of seventeen black soldiers in amphibious truck companies to earn the Silver Star in the Pacific during the last year of the war. Following this action, Tommie Holloway, now promoted to corporal (technician 5th grade), continued to serve with the 471st in the Pacific until his return stateside on 1 January 1946. He subsequently received an Honorable Discharge from the army at Fort McPherson, Georgia, on 21 January 1946, but immediately reenlisted for a three-year term of service in the Army Reserve.

On 14 May 1948 Holloway married Janie B. Maxwell, with whom he would have four children, Tommie Lee Jr., Catherine, Marsha, and Christine. He had one daughter, Cynthia, from a previous relationship. After his discharge from the army, Tommie Holloway and his family resided in Brunswick, Georgia, where he would reside for the remainder of his life. A quiet and modest man, Tommie Holloway was not one to speak of his military service, and few in his family knew the full extent of his heroism until after his death. Holloway worked at several manufacturing jobs in the years before he retired and joined the First Jordan Grove Missionary Baptist Church in 1948, serving as an assistant Sunday school teacher and deacon. Upon his death Tommie Lee Holloway was interred at the Memory Gardens Cemetery, Brunswick, Georgia.

FURTHER READING

The author kindly acknowledges the assistance of Mrs. Janie B. Holloway in the preparation of this article. She provided copies of her husband's military service records and background information.

Converse, Elliot V., Daniel K. Gibran, John A. Cash, Robert K. Griffith, and Richard H. Kohn. *The Exclusion of Black Soldiers from the Medal of Honor in World War II* (2008).

GLENN ALLEN KNOBLOCK

Hollowell, Donald Lee (19 Dec. 1917–27 Dec. 2004), lawyer and civil rights activist, was born in Wichita, Kansas, to Ocenia Bernice (Davis), teacher, baker, and domestic worker, and Harrison Hannibal Hollowell, custodian and prison guard. Donald Hollowell married Louise Thornton in 1943.

In 1935, Hollowell left high school and enlisted in the army with the all-black 10th Cavalry, one of the regiments also known as the Buffalo Soldiers. During his time with the army, Hollowell earned his high school diploma. In 1938, he enlisted in the army reserves and enrolled in Lane College, an all-black college in Tennessee. After the Japanese attacked Pearl Harbor in 1941, Hollowell reenlisted in the army, earning the rank of captain, and served in the European theater.

Hollowell was shaped by his experiences with segregation and discrimination in the army when he was stationed at bases in Georgia, Texas, Louisiana, and Virginia. While finishing at Lane College in 1946, he attended the Southern Negro Youth Congress in South Carolina, which examined how to broadly attack racial discrimination. After graduating from Lane in 1947, Hollowell enrolled in Loyola University Law School to obtain his law degree, with the intent of fighting discrimination. He graduated in 1951.

In 1952, Hollowell moved to Atlanta, Georgia, with his wife, and established a new law practice. One of Hollowell's early clients was Horace Ward, who sued the University of Georgia for admission after his application was rejected in 1952. The school, like many across the region, was segregated and did not admit African American students. The NAACP Legal Defense and Educational Fund, Inc., challenged this policy, and NAACP lawyers, including THURGOOD MARSHALL and ROBERT L. CARTER, partnered with Hollowell on Ward's case. Ultimately, in 1957, the case was dismissed on a technicality, and Ward went on to earn his law degree from Northwestern University, joining Hollowell's law firm in 1960. Hollowell's firm would eventually employ the prominent African American lawyers Howard Moore Jr. and William H. Alexander.

In 1960, Hollowell represented MARTIN LUTHER KING JR. and other protestors, mostly students, who were arrested during sit-ins at Rich's department store in downtown Atlanta during a wave of direct action protests in the city. While the students were freed, King was sentenced to hard labor at the maximum security Reidsville prison because of an earlier traffic violation. Hollowell helped secure King's release.

In 1960, HAMILTON HOLMES and CHARLAYNE HUNTER (Hunter-Gault), with the help of Hollowell and Ward, along with then–law clerk VERNON JORDAN, and national NAACP lawyers, including CONSTANCE BAKER MOTLEY, sued the University of Georgia for admission. Hunter and Holmes were successfully admitted in January 1961, though not without strife. A riot broke out on campus, and when Governor Ernest Vandiver threatened to cut off state funding to an integrated University of Georgia, Hollowell helped obtain a temporary restraining order against Vandiver. Beginning in 1961, Hollowell, along with the attorneys, C. B. King, Constance Baker Motley, and William Kunstler, defended protestors, including Martin Luther

King Jr., arrested during the Albany Movement in Albany, Georgia.

In 1962, Hollowell's firm began defending Preston Cobb, a fifteen-year-old who was five days away from execution by electrocution for the murder of a white man in Monticello, Georgia. Cobb was finally released in 1968 after seven years on death row. In 1965, Hollowell, along with Moore, assisted legal challenges to Taliaferro County's segregated public schools.

In 1964, Hollowell ran for superior court bench in Fulton County, but lost the election, in part due to low African American voter turnout. In 1966, Hollowell left his law practice after being appointed by President Lyndon Johnson as Southeast regional director of the Equal Employment Opportunity Commission. Hollowell was the first black appointed as regional director of a major federal agency. This agency, created through the Civil Rights Act of 1964, investigated and helped reconcile complaints of discrimination in employment. In 1976, Hollowell was promoted to the commission's regional attorney, retiring in 1985. Hollowell also served as president of the Board of Directors of the Voter Education Project in Georgia from 1971 to 1986.

Hollowell died in 2004 in Atlanta of heart failure. He was one of the most important legal advocates for civil rights in Georgia. As Charlayne Hunter-Gault recalled in her autobiography, *In My Place*, the chant of student protestors in Atlanta was, "King is our leader, Hollowell is our lawyer, and we shall not be moved" (p. 157). To honor Hollowell's contributions, both Emory University and the University of Georgia established professorships in his name.

FURTHER READING

Hunter-Gault, Charlayne. *In My Place* (1993).

Pratt, Robert. *We Shall Not Be Moved: The Desegregation of the University of Georgia* (2005).

Obituary: *New York Times*, 2 January 2005.

KRISTAL L. ENTER

Holly, James Theodore (30 Oct. 1829–13 Mar. 1911), black emigrationist, missionary, and bishop, was born free in Washington, D.C., the son of James Overton Holly, a bootmaker, and Jane (maiden name unknown). At fourteen he and his family moved to Brooklyn, New York, where he worked with his father. By 1848, while clerking for Lewis Tappan, an abolitionist, Holly became interested in the antislavery movement. In 1850 he and

his brother Joseph set up as "fashionable bootmakers" in Burlington, Vermont, where both became involved with the growing debate over black emigration. James supported the American Colonization Society and Liberia, while Joseph believed that freed slaves should not have to leave the United States.

In 1851 Holly married Charlotte Ann Gordon (with whom he would to have five children) and moved to Windsor, Canada West (now Ontario), to coedit HENRY BIBB's newspaper *Voice of the Fugitive*. During his three years in the Windsor-Detroit area, Holly worked for the unsuccessful Refugee Home Society, ran the Amherstburg Emancipation Convention in 1851, and used the *Voice* to argue that emigration was the only solution for the problems of African Americans. He abandoned Roman Catholicism for the Protestant Episcopal Church, becoming a deacon in 1855 and a priest in 1856. Holly's new occupation, together with his devotion to the creation of a black nationality, set the course for his adult life.

While teaching grade school in Buffalo, New York, Holly was a delegate to the first National Emigration Convention in 1854 in Cleveland, Ohio. The next year, while representing both the National Emigration Board and the Board of Missions of the Protestant Episcopal Church, he visited Haiti to negotiate an emigration treaty and to locate a possible site for an Episcopal mission. Unsuccessful in both ventures, Holly settled in New Haven, Connecticut, where he taught school and served as priest of St. Luke's Church from 1856 to 1861. After participating in the 1856 National Emigration Convention, Holly traveled extensively to advocate African American emigration to Haiti. His lecture *Vindication of the Capacity of the Negro Race for Self Government and Civilized Progress*, published in 1857, proclaimed black pride and urged immigration to Haiti, a place of "far more security for the personal liberty and general welfare of the governed ... than exists in this bastard democracy [the United States]." He also cofounded the Convocation of the Protestant Episcopal Society for Promoting the Extension of the Work among Colored People, a group whose goals included encouraging blacks to join the church and the emigration movement.

Convinced that free blacks needed white allies to support mass departure for Haiti, Holly corresponded in 1859 with Congressman Francis P. Blair Jr. about U.S. government aid for emigration. He also petitioned, unsuccessfully, the Board of Missions of the Episcopal Church to underwrite him as a missionary to Haiti. In 1860 Holly worked for the Scottish journalist and abolitionist James Redpath, the official Haitian commissioner of emigration. As an agent for the Haitian government, Holly lectured frequently in New England, New Jersey, and Pennsylvania and organized the New Haven Pioneer Company of Haytian Emigrants. In 1861 Holly and 101 recruits moved to Haiti. As one colonist wrote home, "I am a man in Hayti where I feel as I never felt before, entirely free."

The initial year in Haiti proved to be disastrous for Holly's settlement. The rainy season brought fevers, fatalities, and then desertions. Among those who died were Holly's mother, his wife, two of their children, and thirty-nine others. Only Holly and a few followers remained on the island. In 1862, by then a Haitian citizen dedicated to the "regeneration and purification" of the Black Republic through the establishment of the Episcopal Church in Haiti, Holly returned to the United States. He hoped this trip would secure financial support from the General Convention of the Protestant Episcopal Church to establish a Haitian mission station. His request failed, but the American Church Missionary Society did agree to pay his salary in Haiti. In 1865 the Board of Missions of the Protestant Episcopal Church began minimal sponsorship of Holly's mission in Haiti, an arrangement that continued until 1911.

Holly hoped to replace Haiti's dominant Roman Catholicism with a national Episcopal church. In 1874 he became bishop of the Orthodox Apostolic Church of Haiti and was consecrated missionary bishop of Haiti at Grace Church, New York City. As the first black bishop of the Episcopal Church and as head of the Haitian Episcopal Church, he attended the Lambeth Conference in London in 1878. Recognizing education and good health to be important concerns of the church, Holly worked zealously to establish schools and medical institutions in Haiti. But fires and political upheaval hampered his efforts, and his overall church membership never exceeded a few thousand.

Although an infrequent visitor to the United States after 1861 (he made only seven trips in fifty years), Holly never lost interest in African Americans. He and his second wife, Sarah Henley, whom he married in 1862, sent nine sons to the United States for schooling. Holly also corresponded extensively with American blacks and published frequently on religious, political, and social issues in the *A.M.E. Church Review*.

While other emigration advocates of the mid-1800s spoke of leaving the United States but stayed, Holly spoke of leaving and actually left. Until his death in Port au Prince, Haiti, Holly never abandoned his belief that emigration was the only way for African Americans to improve their lives.

FURTHER READING

Holly's papers are in the Archives and Historical Collections of the Episcopal Church in Austin, Texas.

Dean, David M. *Defender of the Race: James Theodore Holly, Black Nationalist and Bishop* (1979).

Holly, James Theodore. "Vindication of the Capacity of the Negro Race for Self Government and Civilized Progress," in *Negro Social and Political Thought, 1859–1920: Representative Texts*, ed. Howard Brotz (1966).

Miller, Floyd J. *The Search for a Black Nationality* (1975).

This entry is taken from the *American National Biography* and is published here with the permission of the American Council of Learned Societies.

DAVID M. DEAN

Holman, M. Carl (27 June 1919–9 Aug. 1988), civil rights leader, English professor, editor, and award-winning poet and playwright, was born Moses Carl Holman in Minter City, Mississippi, and was raised from age three in St. Louis, Missouri. He attended St. Louis public schools, where his devotion to education was formed. He graduated from high school in 1936.

In 1942 he graduated magna cum laude from Lincoln University in Jefferson City, Missouri, and earned a master's degree from the University of Chicago in 1944; he later received a creative writing scholarship to attend Yale and obtained another master's degree (1954). Holman's love of the written word had been shaped early on, and he was known to write anywhere and everywhere he could. In 1938 the nineteen-year-old Holman had become the first black person to win one of the annual scriptwriting awards sponsored by the popular *Dr. Christian* radio program and received a $350 prize. The play aired later that year and met with praise.

He began teaching English and the humanities at Clark College (later Clark Atlanta University) in Atlanta in 1948, where he realized his calling for instructing others. In the early 1950s he joined Whitney Young in forming the Atlanta Committee for Cooperative Action, which he eventually headed. Later, in support of the 1960s student movement in Atlanta, the group helped negotiate a plan to desegregate the city's stores and hotels and open up new job opportunities for blacks.

As the civil rights movement gathered momentum among Atlanta's black students, Holman became an unofficial adviser to young leaders of the movement, as student activists routinely went to him to test their ideas and proposals for action. The group's critical analysis of the status of blacks in Atlanta, "A Second Look," stirred the community to long overdue changes. The *Atlanta Inquirer*, a weekly black journal at Clark College that reported on civil rights issues in the South, was founded in response to complaints that civil rights activities in the area were covered unfairly. Holman agreed to edit the paper, and it quickly achieved a reputation for in-depth, hard-hitting reporting on discrimination and deprivation. Soon Holman met and married his wife, Mariella; they had two sons, Kwasi and Kwame, and a daughter, Kinshasha. The two were married until his death.

In 1962 he was appointed to the staff of the U.S. Commission on Civil Rights and moved to Washington, D.C. President John F. Kennedy named him deputy staff director in 1966. Addressing the final session of the 1966–1967 Hungry Club Forum of the Butler Street YMCA in Atlanta, Holman said that blacks must press their roles in the decision-making process, "whether or not someone extends us an invitation to do so." Later he was also known to have said, "We've got too many problems to argue about who gets the credit. Save your energy and do something."

In 1968, a year in which *Ebony* magazine listed Holman as one of the one hundred most influential black Americans, he joined the National Urban Coalition, an organization formed after the riots of 1967. Initially serving as vice president of programs, he became president in 1971, the first black to head the organization. Holman advocated for programs in housing, education, employment, and economic development. He was instrumental in developing such programs as the Minority Contractors Assistance Project and the "Counterbudget," a book-length proposal to establish new, more humane national priorities through reform of the federal budget process. During Holman's tenure the coalition opened up new lines of communication in many urban areas. It brought together mayors, police chiefs, and civic leaders for the 1970 Mid-America Criminal Justice Seminar. In cooperation with the Conservation Foundation, he played a key role in drawing representatives from many national organizations for the 1971 National Conference on Public Transportation.

In later years Holman worked for the development of the "Just say YES to a Youngster's Future" program, which helped minorities and girls develop math, science, and computer skills. He was appointed to the Task Force on Women, Minorities, and the Handicapped in Science and Technology and was selected to serve on the National Low Income Housing Preservation Commission.

Holman was the recipient of numerous awards during his career. These include first prize in the National Community Theatre Festival, for his play *The Baptizin'* (1971); the John B. Fiske Poetry Prize; the Rosenwald Fellowship, established to help African Americans get professional educations; the John Hay Whitney Fellowship, which provided fellowships to the racially and culturally deprived; and the Blevins Davis Playwriting Prize.

Moses Carl Holman died of a heart attack at the age of sixty-nine. A poet and playwright and a devoted civil rights activist, he never sought glory out front in the movement but was content to labor in the background, working diligently on race relations. He treated everyone he met, no matter how young or old, as an equal, and he expected no less from anyone else. He holds a firm place in history as a leader and teacher.

FURTHER READING

Additional information on Moses Carl Holman can be found at Inman Page Library, Lincoln University, Jefferson City, Missouri. The Archives Department of Clark Atlanta University contains further documentation as well as a surviving copy of the radio play for "Dr. Christian."

David, Jay, ed. *Growing Up Black: From Slave Days to the Present: 25 African-Americans Reveal the Trials and Triumphs of Their Childhoods* (1992).

Obituaries: *New York Times* and *St. Louis Post-Dispatch*, 11 Aug. 1988.

CHESYA BURKE

Holman, Steve (2 Mar. 1970–), track and field athlete, was born Clyston Orlando Holman III in Indianapolis, Indiana, the elder of the two sons of Clyston Orlando Holman Jr., a Baptist minister, and Janet Mullins, a high school guidance counselor. In 1972, when Steve was two, the Holmans moved from Indianapolis to Richfield, Minnesota, a suburb of Minneapolis. Steve's early childhood was marked by his tendency to run fast—in the house, outside with his friends (despite outrunning them), and to the local corner store.

He received his early education in the public schools of Richfield, Windom, and Elliot elementary schools, East Middle School, and Richfield Junior High School. As a freshman at Richfield High School, Steve, at five feet three inches and ninety pounds, ran cross-country and later track, winning the Minnesota high school state titles in the 800- and 1,600-meter runs in both 1987 and 1988. In 1988 he set a state record in the 800-meter run, a record that was not broken until 1996.

In 1988 Holman entered Georgetown University, where he majored in English while running cross-country and track. During his first year at Georgetown he ran third leg on the four by 800-meter relay at the National Collegiate Athletic Association (NCAA) indoor track and field championships and placed third in the USA Track & Field (USATF) juniors outdoor championships for the 1,500-meter. In 1990 he placed fifth in the USATF outdoor championships and third in the Olympic Festival, again for the 1,500-meter. In 1991 Holman was ranked fifth in USATF outdoor and sixth in NCAA indoor mile. Also known in the running world for his writing, Holman began writing "The Bell Lap," a column for runnersworld.com. Overall the 1990s marked a productive period of running and writing for Holman, who also served during this time as chairman of the USATF athletes advisory council.

In 1992 after receiving a B.A. in English from Georgetown, Holman set aside plans to attend law school after winning the NCAA 1,500-meter outdoor title with a time of 3:38.39, coming in second in the Olympic trials 1,500-meter, and earning a spot on the U.S. Olympic team for the 1992 Barcelona Summer Olympic Games. That year he also ran personal bests in both the 1,500-meter and the mile. He was ranked number two in the United States, with a 3:34.95 best in the 1,500-meter and a 3:52.73 best in the mile. For the U.S. track and field community, Holman was the long-awaited embodiment of their desire for a world-class middle-distance runner.

Ranked number two in 1993 by the Track and Field National Federation and at the top of his game, Holman ranked fourth in the world in the indoor mile. Beginning with his appearance in the 1992 Olympics, Holman became known for dominating American milers, consistently running well on the ultrafast European circuit. Holman was ranked fifth in the world in the mile in 1994 and fourth in 1995. In 1996 he won the U.S. indoor mile and ranked thirteenth in the Olympic trials, with an overall rank of number two in the United States.

In August 1997 he ran a career-best 3:31.52 at a meet in Belgium, making him the third-fastest American ever in the 1,500-meter. He was the outdoor national champion in the 1,500-meter in 1999 and placed ninth in that year's world championships. In 2000 he placed fifth at the Olympic trials and was ranked fifth in the United States, with the best performance by an American of 3:33.59 in Zurich. His bests include 1:44.98 in the 800-meter, 3:31.52 in the 1,500-meter (the third-fastest American in history), 3:50.40 in the mile, 4:57.14 in the 2,000-meter, and 7:43.21 in the 3,000-meter indoors.

In 1999 Holman married, and he and his wife, Teresa, had a daughter, Chloe, in 2002. In 2001, one year after he placed fifth at the Olympic trials in the 1,500-meter and after having battled a string of injuries and training burnout, Holman, without making any official declaration, retired from world-class miling. That same year he took a job as a writer at the Minnesota State Senate and was inducted into the Minnesota Track and Field Hall of Fame. In 2002 Holman entered the Wharton School of Business at the University of Pennsylvania, earning an MBA in 2004. In 2005, *Black MBA Magazine* recognized Holman as one of the "Top 50 Under 50" for his work as Senior Manager of IRA Services at Vanguard.

Consistently America's fastest 1,500-meter runner of the 1990s, Holman began marathon training in 2003 and ran 2:30:47 in the 2003 Twin Cities Marathon, his first marathon, and 2:35:15 in the 2004 New York Marathon.

FURTHER READING

Ashe, Arthur R., Jr. *A Hard Road to Glory, a History of the African-American Athlete: Track and Field* (1988, 1993).

Nance-Nash, Sheryl. "Top 50 Under 50," *Black MBA Magazine: The Official Magazine of the National Black MBA Association, Inc.* 10.2 (Summer 2006): 26.

Shropshire, Kenneth L. *In Black and White: Race and Sports in America* (1996).

TERESA GILLIAMS

Holmes, Eugene Clay (12 Oct. 1905–5 July 1980), chair of the Howard University Department of Philosophy following ALAIN LOCKE, worked with Locke to interweave philosophy with his

Eugene C. Holmes of the Howard University Department of Philosophy, 1942. (Library of Congress/Office of War Information.)

understanding of the black experience. Holmes is sometimes described as one of the only two Marxist philosophers of African descent in the United States (along with C. L. R. James), from the 1930s until ANGELA DAVIS began teaching philosophy in the 1960s.

He was born in Paterson, New Jersey (McClendon, p. 37), to Samuel and Arabella Holmes, who had been born, like their own parents, in Virginia. Samuel Holmes worked as a bartender and later as a hotel waiter; Arabella washed laundry, sometimes on her own, sometimes as a commercial employee, retiring a few years earlier than her husband. Growing up in nearby Passaic and later in Pleasantville, Atlantic County, Holmes had a brother, Lawrence, one year older, and sister, Gladys, two years younger (Census, 1910 and 1920).

At the age of twenty-five, Holmes continued to live with his parents, working as a waiter (Census, 1930), while pursuing higher education at New York University, earning a bachelor's degree in 1932. The same year he published "JEAN TOOMER: Apostle of Beauty" in the August issue of *Opportunity* and was hired as an instructor at Howard University, beginning a lifelong association with the Howard faculty. Adding to initial interest in literary criticism a focus on philosophy, he earned a master's degree from Columbia in 1936 and was promoted

to assistant professor at Howard in 1937. That year he published "Problems Facing the Negro Writer Today" in *New Challenge*, asserting that "The problems of the Negro writer, whether he wills it or not, are bound up with the fight against fascism and the protection of the cultural rights of minority groups" (Gates, p. 394).

Between 1933 and 1937, Holmes married Margaret Cardozo, one of three Cardozo sisters who ran a highly respected beauty salon in Washington, D.C. They were granddaughters of FRANCIS L. CARDOZO, the secretary of state and state treasurer of South Carolina during Reconstruction who subsequently left the state for the District of Columbia, and cousins of ESLANDA CARDOZO GOODE ROBESON. Another sister, Catherine, married the Howard University historian Harold O. Lewis (Susannah Walker, "'Independent Livings' or 'No Bed Of Roses?' How Race and Class Shaped Beauty Culture as an Occupation for African American Women from the 1920s to the 1960s," *Journal of Women's History* 20 no. 3 [2008]: 60–71), while Emmeta married the Howard professor Granville Huxley (Ruth Edmonds Hill, ed., *Black Women Oral History Project, Vol. 6*, 1991, p. 65). In 1937 Margaret Cardozo Holmes opened Cardozo Hairstylists, the first beauty salon owned by an African American woman in West Hyannisport, Massachusetts (*Contributions of Black Women to America: The Arts, Media, Business, Law, Sports*, 1982, p. 343).

Columbia awarded Holmes a Ph.D. in 1942, but he was not promoted to full professor at Howard until 1946. His doctoral dissertation, "Social Philosophy and Social Mind: A Study of the Genetic Methods of J. M. Baldwin, G. H. Mead, and J. E. Bodin" offered a critique of the pragmatism represented by John Dewey, denouncing the appearance of democratic opposition to monopoly capitalism that this philosophy had acquired by attaching itself to the populist and progressive currents in American politics (McClendon, p. 38). It provided a foundation for the Marxist perspective in his later work and his critique of class distinctions within African American culture.

From 1932 to 1959, Holmes contributed articles on various topics to journals such as *International Literature, Science and Society, Opportunity, American Teacher, American Journal of Physics*, and *Philosophy and Phenomenological Research*, including "The Negro as Capitalist," "Pushkin in America," and "Philosophical Problems of Space and Time." During the same period, he contributed to *The New Masses* a review of C. S. Johnson's "Negro College

Graduate" and an article "Mrs. James Crow: D.A.R." and wrote a series for the *Chicago Defender*, "Anti-Semitism." In 1942 *The Crisis* proudly observed that Holmes "has for more than a year been contributing editor of the recently published *Dictionary of Philosophy*" (April 1942, p. 108). In 1945 Holmes wrote a laudatory review for *The Journal of Negro Education* of Ralph Korngold's *Citizen Toussaint*, a biography of Toussaint Louverture "rich in historical detail and social meaning," which made it "probably the most authentic one we have."

During the 1950s Holmes studied the philosophy of science, which required mastery of higher mathematics, physics, and the concept of space/time developed in Albert Einstein's theory of relativity. He published three articles applying dialectical materialism to space and time, perhaps the only professionally trained black philosopher to do so. Holmes was a coeditor with RAYFORD W. LOGAN and G. Franklin Edwards of *The New Negro Thirty Years Afterward*, containing a series of papers presented at Howard's Sixteenth Annual Spring Conference of the Division of Social Sciences, and published by Howard University Press in 1955. Among the papers was Holmes's "Alain Locke—Philosopher," a tribute to the Howard philosophy professor widely remembered as the architect of the New Negro Movement and an influence on the Harlem Renaissance.

Locke was a mentor and, until his death in 1954, a profound influence on Holmes, who succeeded Locke as department chair and wrote many biographical articles about his predecessor. Among the more prominent of these were "Alain Leroy Locke" in 1955, "Alain Locke—Philosopher, Critic, Spokesman" in 1957, "Alain L. Locke and the Adult Education Movement" in 1965, and "Alain Locke and the New Negro Movement" in 1968.

A member of the "faculty of the left" of the 1930s and 1940s, Holmes often wrote on African American culture for Communist Party–affiliated publications under the name Eugene Clay (Smethurst, pp. 34, 37) and was influential in bringing the poet STERLING BROWN to the attention of left literary publications (Smethurst, p. 231). Holmes participated as a member of Howard's Division of Social Sciences in the 1953 Spring Conference on "Academic Freedom in the United States"—a direct response to the anticommunist hysteria of the time. Holmes gave a closing address, "The Social Responsibility of the Scholar," which is seldom quoted. Howard's president, MORDECAI WYATT JOHNSON, presented "The Social Responsibility of the Administrator,"

asserting "There is only one effective defense against revolutionary Communism in America and the world. It is the responsible discharge of the obligation to change whatever basic condition hurts human life" (Rayford W. Logan, *Howard University: The First Hundred Years 1867–1967*, 1969, p. 440).

Holmes was listed in the House Committee on Un-American Activities (HUAC) report, "The Communist 'Peace' Offensive: A Campaign to Disarm and Defeat the United States" (issued on the auspicious date 1 April 1951), as a sponsor of the Scientific and Cultural Conference for World Peace, 25 to 27 March 1949, in New York City, organized by the National Council of the Arts, Sciences and Professions (p. 104). LANGSTON HUGHES was described in the same report as one of three sponsors affiliated with "from seventy-one to eighty Communist-front organizations," Paul Robeson (the son of Holmes's wife's cousin) was affiliated with "from fifty one to sixty," and W. E. B. DUBOIS with "from eleven to twenty," as were Albert Einstein (p. 107) and Holmes himself (p. 108). Holmes was also listed among the signators to a statement of "Greeting from American sponsors to World Congress for Peace" held 20–25 April 1949 in Paris, "firmly united in the common determination that peace must prevail in the world" (p. 111).

In a 1965 paper, "A General Theory of the Freedom Cause of the Negro People" (*American Philosophical Association*, Dec. 1965), Holmes dissected the philosophy of Plato, Cicero, St. Paul, St. Augustine, St. Thomas Aquinas, and John C. Calhoun, rejecting them all as reactionary due to their reliance on, or acceptance of, the master/slave relationship. Acknowledging Calhoun as the only philosopher produced by the antebellum American South, Holmes proceeded to support the militant tactics of the Student Nonviolent Coordinating Committee and the Mississippi Freedom Democratic Party, observing that "much of America is a wasteland because of the ghetto-like practices of educational segregation" (McClendon, p. 46). The same year *Freedomways* published "W. E. B. DuBois: Philosopher," emphasizing DuBois as a materialist philosopher in the social sciences (vol. 5, no. 1, Winter 1965).

Holmes retired from Howard as an emeritus professor in 1970. About a year earlier, C. L. R. JAMES had returned to the United States and began teaching at Howard. It was not an auspicious time for black Marxists. James's student, John H. McClendon, described African Studies at Howard by that time as "a hot bed for all kinds of degenerate, backward, right-wing forms of Pan-African nationalism" (McClendon, p. 7), anathema to James, and undoubtedly a disappointment to Holmes. He spent his last years in West Hyannisport, Massachusetts, dying of cancer 5 July 1980 at Cape Cod Hospital. A student of Holmes, Percy E. Johnston, organized the *Afro-American Journal of Philosophy* in 1982.

FURTHER READING

Gates, Henry Louis, and Gene Andrew Jarrett. *The New Negro: Readings on Race, Representation, and African American Culture, 1892–1938* (2007).

McClendon, John H. *C. L. R. James's Notes on Dialectics: Left Hegelianism or Marxism-Leninism?*

McClendon, John H. "Eugene C. Holmes: A Commentary on a Black Marxist Philosopher." *Philosophy Born of Struggle* (1983).

Smethurst, James Edward. *The New Red Negro: The Literary Left and African American Poetry, 1930–1946* (1999).

CHARLES ROSENBERG

Holmes, Hamilton (8 July 1941–24 Oct. 1995), orthopedic surgeon and one of the two black students who desegregated the University of Georgia, was born Hamilton Earl Holmes in Atlanta, Georgia, the son of Alfred "Tup" Holmes, a businessman, and Isabella Holmes, a grade school teacher. His influences in civil rights were strong; his father, grandfather Hamilton Mayo Holmes, and uncle Oliver Wendell Holmes filed suit to desegregate Atlanta's public golf courses in 1955. The resulting 1956 Supreme Court decision on their cases made the golf courses the first integrated public facilities in Atlanta. His mother had been part of a program that integrated blind or partially sighted children into mainstream classrooms.

Hamilton, nicknamed "Hamp," was a successful student at Henry McNeal Turner High School in Atlanta. Though shy, occasionally stuttering when he spoke, he was president of his junior and senior class, co-captain of the football team, captain of the basketball team, and valedictorian of his senior class. When the Turner Wolves football team won the homecoming game, Holmes presented the game ball to Charlayne Hunter, Turner's Homecoming Queen of 1958–1959, who would later integrate the University of Georgia with Holmes and become noted journalist CHARLAYNE HUNTER-GAULT.

In 1958 Jesse Hill Jr., an Atlanta civil rights leader, began compiling a list of accomplished high school seniors in Atlanta's black high schools as potential college integrators. He found Holmes and Hunter in 1959. Holmes suggested that they apply for admission to the University of Georgia (UGA). While readying his application papers, Holmes attended Morehouse College in Atlanta. For a year and a half UGA's registrar office denied admission to Holmes and Hunter for a variety of reasons, including that the dormitories were full. During admissions interviews, Holmes was asked if he had ever visited a house of prostitution, a "tea parlor," or "beatnik places."

On 2 Sept. 1960 attorney Donald Hollowell filed suit with the federal district court in Athens, claiming that they had been denied admission to UGA on account of their race, in violation of the 1954 U.S. Supreme Court decision that declared racial segregation unconstitutional. Just before the December 1960 trial UGA registrar Walter Danner wrote that Hunter would be admitted the following fall, while Holmes had been rejected for being "evasive" during the interview, and that there had been "some doubt as to his truthfulness." A similar reason had been given eight years before in Horace Ward's rejection from UGA's law school. Ward assisted in Holmes's and Hunter's trial, as did Donald Hollowell, VERNON JORDAN, Gerald Taylor, and CONSTANCE BAKER MOTLEY.

On 6 January 1961 while Georgia's then-governor Ernest Vandiver was promising that "no, not one" black student would attend UGA under his authority, federal judge William A. Bootle declared that Holmes and Hunter were "fully qualified for immediate admission."

On 7 January 1961 escorted by Ward, Holmes registered at UGA. At the entrance to campus some students burned crosses and hanged a black effigy named "Hamilton Holmes." Hunter also enrolled. During their first week tension culminated in a riot on campus, which had been so well planned that students vied for dates to the event. Following the riot Holmes and Hunter were temporarily suspended. Yet no subsequent acts of violence ensued. Once, when Holmes had parked his car near the Kappa Alpha fraternity house, he returned to find it blocked by another car and by a crowd of fraternity brothers. Holmes found a flashlight in his car and held it in his pocket, pretending it was a gun. The students moved the blocking car.

While Hunter received considerable media attention, Holmes retreated into solitude, studying, playing basketball at an all-black YMCA, eating his meals at Killian's Four Seasons—the small restaurant operated by the family with whom he boarded in Athens—and faithfully returning to Atlanta every weekend to visit a steady girlfriend, his friends, and his family. "I haven't actually cultivated any close friendships," Holmes told the author Calvin Trillin. Holmes excelled scholastically at UGA, making the Phi Kappa Phi honor society. Yet his morale reached a particularly low point his junior year. "I'm just counting the days" until graduation, he told Trillin his senior year.

In 1963 Holmes graduated with a bachelor of science degree cum laude and became the first black medical student at Emory University in Atlanta. In 1967 he received his medical degree. That same year he married Marilyn Elaine Vincent; they had two children. In 1969 he became a major in the U.S. Army, serving in Germany. After his discharge from the army in 1973 he became assistant professor of orthopedics and associate dean at Emory University School of Medicine. At Grady Memorial Hospital in Atlanta he served as senior vice president of medical affairs, medical director, and head of orthopedic surgery for the Grady Health System. Though his years at UGA seem dismal he later became a supporter of his alma mater. In 1981 he helped plan UGA's bicentennial celebration, and two years later he became the first black trustee to the University of Georgia Foundation. In 1985, as part of UGA's bicentennial, the Holmes-Hunter lectureship was established, and Holmes attended each year, joined by Hunter-Gault in 1992. He died in his sleep in Atlanta, two weeks after having quadruple bypass surgery.

FURTHER READING
Hunter-Gault, Charlayne. *In My Place* (1992).
Trillin, Calvin. *An Education in Georgia: Charlayne Hunter, Hamilton Holmes, and the Integration of the University of Georgia* (1964; repr. 1991).
Obituary: *New York Times*, 28 Oct. 1995.
This entry is taken from the *American National Biography* and is published here with the permission of the American Council of Learned Societies.

MARY JESSICA HAMMES

Holmes, Isabella Snowden (1810–27 May 1874),

anti-slavery activist, was born in Portland, Maine, the daughter of the Reverend SAMUEL SNOWDEN and his first wife, Nancy Marsh, from Monmouth, Maine.

Isabella grew up as a free black woman in a home in which her father was both a well-known preacher and an anti-slavery activist. When she was eight years old, Isabella moved to Boston with her family when her father was called to pastor the growing African American congregation which was then a part of the Bromfield Methodist Episcopal Church. Her father often assisted runaway slaves, and her home was a refuge for those from the South seeking asylum.

Isabella eventually married Henry Holmes, a barber in Boston. They had at least one child, Emily Otis, who was born c. 1833 and married Charles H. Stephens from Newport, Rhode Island, on 29 October 1854. Nothing more is known about Emily and Charles and their lives.

Although not a lot is known about Holmes's life, she did become involved in a number of anti-slavery activities and other efforts to improve the quality of life of her people, as did her younger half-brother, Isaac H. Snowden. A number of activities in which she was involved are reported in the *Liberator*, William Lloyd Garrison's anti-slavery newspaper based in Boston.

As early as 1838 Mrs. Isabella Holmes appears on a list of donors for the Samaritan Asylum for indigent children established in Boston in 1833 to care for poor black children in the city. On 1 February 1843, a large meeting of the "colored citizens of Boston" was held to consider a number of items, including their lack of support for opposition to the state law which forbade "persons of different colors to intermarry," and their censure of the "oppressive customs of some of the railroad corporations of the State." Isabella Holmes was one of three women and four black men to be appointed to obtain signatures to the various petitions which were passed that evening (*Liberator*, 10 February 1843). Shirley J. Yee, in her book, *Black Women Abolitionists* (p. 130), reports that Eunice R. Davis was a member of this committee, along with two other black women whose names she does not list (p. 130). Davis was a Native American.

In July of the same year Isabella Holmes was the only woman to serve on a committee for the New-England Freedom Association to plan the annual 1 August celebration of the emancipation of British slaves (*Liberator*, 28 July 1843). One year later in August, 1844, Isabella Holmes was again one of three black women chosen to serve on a committee to plan an evening in honor of well-known abolitionist David Ruggles (*Liberator*, 31 August 1844). As late as 1861 Mrs. Isabella Snowden Holmes is listed as one of the contributors to the Twenty-Seventh National Anti-slavery Subscription Anniversary (*Liberator*, 15 February 1861).

There is a slight possibility that Isabella Holmes was also a member of the Boston Female Anti-Slavery Society (BFAAS). Although there seems to be no existing documentation of her membership, Eunice R. Davis, who served with Isabella Holmes on both the committee to gather petition signatures in 1843 and the committee to plan an evening to honor David Ruggles in 1844, was an active member of that Society, and it seems feasible that Isabella Holmes might have been among the handful of Methodist women who were members. On the other hand, since her father and brother Isaac were both strong supporters of William Lloyd Garrison, and since a schism eventually occurred within the BFAAS over support for Garrison and his politics (with the majority being anti-Garrison), she may have chosen not to join the Society in the first place. The fact that she is listed as making a donation to the Samaritan Asylum (noted above) separately from the BFAAS may also be an indication that she was never a member of the Society.

Isabella Holmes is most remembered in contemporary literature, however, for providing refuge for runaway slaves after her father's death. As noted previously, her father Samuel was well-known for providing such refuge; the *Liberator* reported on 3 January 1851 that thirteen slaves arrived on the Snowden doorstep seeking refuge on 8 October 1850, the day of his death. Though "Father Snowden" was no longer able to assist these slaves, Holmes apparently welcomed them, as Francis Jackson reports that "Isabella S. Holmes (Father Snowden's daughter)" was reimbursed for expenses relating to the provision of room and board to runaway slaves in both November and December of 1850 (p. 8). One of those slaves was Henry Williams, whose escape to Canada with the assistance of the writer Henry Thoreau is described in *To Set This World Right: The Antislavery Movement in Thoreau's Concord* by Sandra Harbert Petrulionis (p. 93).

In 1854, Holmes's brother, Isaac Humphrey Snowden, sailed to Liberia to become a physician for those African Americans emigrating to that country from America as a part of the colonization movement. The following year he returned to America and sailed back to Liberia with his mother, Lydia, his wife, Caroline, and their daughter, Lydia Elizabeth, and Caroline's sister, Mrs. Eliza Williams. In 1856 their half-sister, Mary Jane Holmes Triplett, and her two daughters, Anna Maria Holmes and Helen Lorinda Triplett, emigrated to Liberia as well. By the end of 1860 Isabella's half-brother, Charles, had also emigrated to Liberia with plans to bring his wife, Isabella, and their two children, Isabella E. R. B. and Thomas C., as soon as a suitable home could be built. Charles, however, died in March, 1860, and his family remained in Newport, Rhode Island, where they were living at the time.

Isabella Holmes seems to have been the only known living sibling of Isaac who did not emigrate to Liberia. Her husband, Henry, was still alive at the time the others emigrated. He did not die until sometime between 1860 and 1865. Isabella died in 1874 in Boston of softness of the brain.

FURTHER READING

Jackson, Francis. *Account Book of Francis Jackson, Treasurer; the Vigilance Committee of Boston* (Facsimile copy, 1924).

Petrulionis, Sandra Harbert. *To Set This World Right: The Antislavery Movement in Thoreau's Concord.* (2004).

Records of the American Colonization Society online at http://www.footnote.com/documents/27399185/american_colonization_society/.

Wesley, Dorothy Porter, and Constance Porter Uzelac, eds. *William Cooper Nell: Nineteenth-Century African American Abolitionist, Historian, Integrationist* (2002).

Yee, Shirley J. *Black Women Abolitionists: A Study in Activism, 1828–1860* (1992).

PATRICIA J. THOMPSON

Holmes, Larry (3 Nov. 1949–), world heavyweight boxing champion, was born in Cuthbert, Georgia, the fourth of twelve children of John Henry Holmes, a sharecropper, and Flossie Holmes. Shortly after the family moved to Easton, Pennsylvania, in 1956, his father left for another woman and the children were raised on welfare by their mother. To bring in money, Larry would go to grade school and then shine shoes until ten o' clock at night. The family struggled in poverty but held together.

Holmes was good at sports from an early age. At age ten he began boxing in Police Athletic League fights, displaying endurance and strength but little skill. In seventh grade he excelled at football, but after an altercation with a teacher who disliked him and an ultimatum from the school, Holmes dropped out and went to work in a car wash. He had frequent street brawls and brushes with the law. Continuing to work at various menial jobs, Holmes, at age sixteen, became involved with the twenty-two-year-old Millie Bowles, with whom he had two daughters.

Ernie Butler, a former professional fighter, came to Easton and opened a gym. Holmes met him by chance one day and Butler began to give him a thorough training in the technique of boxing. He began to fight in amateur tournaments and train at Gleason's Gym in New York, and by 1971 he was winning Golden Glove and AAU bouts. Butler drove Holmes to MUHAMMAD ALI's training camp in Deer Lake, Pennsylvania. Ali let him stay and gave him new equipment, and Holmes studied Ali's art in sparring sessions.

Holmes made it to the finals of the 1972 Olympic trials but lost to Duane Bobick by being disqualified for clinching. He turned professional on 21 March 1973 with a four-round decision over Rodell Dupree that paid him $63. Six weeks later Holmes beat Art Savage by a technical knockout in the third round, then whipped Curtis Whitner on a first-round TKO in June. Three consecutive six-round decisions were followed by TKOs of Kevin Isaac, Howard Darlington, Bob Mashburn, and Joe Hathaway. Holmes briefly joined the camp of top contender Earnie Shavers, where he met promoter DON KING and trainer Richie Giachetti. He signed a contract with them, but was little aided by King. In 1974 Holmes was hired as a sparring partner by JOE FRAZIER, but he lasted only one day as Frazier fractured one of his ribs. Ali soon hired Holmes back to help prepare for his title shot against GEORGE FOREMAN.

Holmes's own career resumed with little fanfare. He fought at a dizzying pace in 1975, knocking out Charlie Green, defeating Oliver Wright by TKO, knocking out both Robert Yarborough and Ernie Smith in the third round, and stopping Obie English. He scored a sixth-round TKO of Rodney Bobick on the undercard of the famed Ali-Frazier "Thrilla in Manila." Holmes fought twice in eleven days in December, dropping Leon Shaw in the first round and stopping Billy Joiner in the third.

Larry Holmes was not known for a knockout punch, but his speed, boxing skills and relentless jab wore opponents down and often led to the knockout. He scheduled three fights in 1976 and won them all, including a ten-round decision over Roy (Tiger) Williams, once a fellow sparring partner with Ali. After a very long wait, Holmes finally got his shot on 25 March 1978. In an elimination bout against feared puncher Earnie Shavers, Holmes turned in a near perfect effort, stinging Shavers with his jab and winning all twelve rounds.

Holmes's WBC title matchup against KEN NORTON on 9 June 1978 was one of the classic fights in Heavyweight history. Norton, the champion, was favored. Holmes moved well and hammered Norton with the left jab to lead the early rounds of the fight, but the middle rounds became hotly competitive. After a wild fifteenth round, Holmes won a split decision by one point and became champion of the WBC, returning home to screaming crowds in Easton. He successfully defended his WBC title against Alfredo Evangelista, Ossie Ocasio, and Mike Weaver before again taking on his friend Earnie Shavers in Las Vegas in 1979. Shavers unleashed a devastating right hand to the jaw that dropped Holmes briefly to the canvas in the seventh round before Holmes came back to win by a eleventh-round TKO. Now he would face the legend to whom he had so often been unfavorably compared.

On 2 October 1980, hoping to capture the Heavyweight title for an unprecedented fourth time, an aging and impaired Muhammad Ali entered the ring at Caesars Palace in Las Vegas to fight his old sparring partner. Ali had no chance from the outset and Holmes tried not to embarrass his mentor. He pulled punches and repeatedly backed away from a cornered Ali, and the fight was stopped in the eleventh round.

Despite a falling-out with trainer Giachetti, Holmes rolled on. He hired veteran trainer Eddie Futch and defeated Trevor Berbick and former champion LEON SPINKS. On 6 November 1983 he went down once in a fight against Renaldo Snipes but came back to win. He stopped an overly hyped but powerful Gerry Cooney and won an easy fight over Randall "Tex" Cobb, then scored decisions over Lucien Rodriguez and Tim Witherspoon and a hard fought fifteen-round decision over Carl "The Truth" Williams. A win next over Michael Spinks would tie the 49-0 career record of the late Rocky Marciano. Weary of the prefight hype, Holmes attracted criticism when he said, "Marciano couldn't carry my jockstrap." But on 21 September 1985, with Giachetti back in his corner, he lost a narrow fifteen-round split decision to Spinks, only to do so again on 19 April 1986 before retiring.

Returning in 1988 to face young champion MIKE TYSON, Holmes was knocked out in the fourth round. He upset the undefeated Ray Mercer in 1992, but then lost a title fight against EVANDER HOLYFIELD and did so again against Oliver McCall three years later. Holmes's last fight of record was a ten-round decision over Eric (Butterbean) Esch on 27 July 2002. Larry Holmes retired to Easton to pursue successful business ventures and fight occasional exhibitions. "The Easton Assassin," who was inducted into the International Boxing Hall of Fame on 8 June 2008, won 69 of his 77 professional fights, 44 by knockout, and his 20 successful defenses of the Heavyweight title from 1978 to 1985 were second only to the record of JOE LOUIS. He married Diane Robinson on 23 December 1979 and they raised four daughters, Belinda, Misty, Lisa and Kandy, and a son, Larry, Jr..

FURTHER READING

Holmes, Larry, with Phil Berger. *Larry Holmes: Against The Odds* (1999).

Remnick, David. "The Sporting Scene," *New Yorker*, August 11, 1997, p. 25.

DAVID BORSVOLD

Holsey, Lucius Henry (3 July 1842–3 Aug. 1920), minister and denominational leader, was born near Columbus, Georgia, the son of James Holsey, a plantation owner, and Louisa, a slave. When his father died in 1848, Lucius was sold to his white cousin, T. L. Wynn, who lived in Hancock County, Georgia. After Wynn's death in 1857, he became the slave of Richard Johnston, a professor at Franklin College (now the University of Georgia) in Athens. He was spared the rigors of labor in the fields by working as a house servant and carriage driver. While he received no formal education, he was able to teach himself to read and write. With the outbreak of the Civil War, Johnston left Athens and took Holsey back to Hancock County. In November 1863 Holsey married Harriet Anne Turner, a slave who once belonged to George Foster Pierce, a bishop of the Methodist Episcopal Church, South (MECS). The couple had nine children.

Following emancipation in 1865, Holsey managed a farm near Sparta, Georgia. During that period he was instructed in theology by Pierce, who wished Holsey to become an evangelist among freed African Americans. Licensed by Pierce as a Methodist preacher in February 1868, Holsey served briefly in the Hancock County circuit. In 1869 he moved to Savannah, Georgia, where he took charge of the Andrew Chapel. He later served as the minister of Trinity Church in Augusta, Georgia, from 1871 until 1873. His principal contributions to his church, however, were as an organizer rather than as a pastor. He was a delegate to the first General Conference of the Colored Methodist Episcopal Church (CMEC), which convened in Jackson, Tennessee, in December 1870. The CMEC, which became the Christian Methodist Episcopal Church, had been established by the MECS to provide a separate, autonomous denomination for the approximately twenty thousand African Americans who remained affiliated with white Southern Methodism after the Civil War. When the second General Conference of the CMEC met at Holsey's church in Augusta in March 1873, the gathering elected him the fourth bishop of the fledgling denomination.

Holsey, then barely in his thirties, proved to be a dynamic leader who strengthened the institutional structures of the CMEC during the next four decades. He recognized that education was one of the chief needs of the former slaves who made up the membership of the CMEC. Since he knew that most white southerners had little desire to lift African Americans out of their traditionally subordinate social position, he sought funds from white Methodists not to educate the general black population, he said, but to provide training for black clergy and teachers to shape the moral values of their people. Persistent in this effort, he raised sufficient money to open the Paine Institute (later Paine College) in Augusta, Georgia, in 1884. Although overall control of Paine remained solidly in white hands throughout Holsey's lifetime, the school provided an arena in which black and white Methodists were able to interact on an approximately equal plane. Holsey was influential as well in the founding of several other church-related institutions: Lane College in Jackson, Tennessee; the Holsey Normal and Industrial Academy, a secondary school in Cordele, Georgia; and the Helena B. Cobb Institute for Girls in Barnesville, Georgia.

Holsey held a number of prominent honorary positions within the CMEC over the course of his lengthy career. He represented the denomination at the first two Ecumenical Methodist Conferences, in London in 1881 and in Washington, D.C., in 1891, and he served as secretary of the College of Bishops of the CMEC for twenty-five years. He was also instrumental in the establishment of the CME Publishing House and helped launch a denominational newspaper, the *Gospel Trumpet*, in 1896. In addition, he edited *The Hymn Book of the Colored M.E. Church in America* (commonly known as the "Holsey Hymnal") in 1891 and *A Manual of the Discipline of the Colored Methodist Episcopal Church in America* in 1894. He was the senior bishop of the CMEC at the time of his death in Atlanta.

Holsey was the principal spokesperson of his denomination during its formative years. His social philosophy was at first conservative, for his commitment to education and racial uplift enabled him to take advantage of white paternalism in the aftermath of the Civil War. However, toward the end of his life, the dramatic increase of racism in the South led him to advocate the value of racial separatism. Between the Civil War and World War I he played a key role in the successful growth and development of the CMEC and was recognized as one of the most prominent African American religious figures of the late nineteenth century.

FURTHER READING

Holsey, Lucius Henry. *Autobiography, Sermons, Addresses, and Essays* (1898).

The Autobiography of Bishop L. H. Holsey (1988).

Cade, John Brother. *Holsey—The Incomparable* (1964).

Eskew, Glenn T. "Black Elitism and the Failure of Paternalism in Postbellum Georgia: The Case of Bishop Lucius Henry Holsey," *Journal of Southern History* 58 (Nov. 1992).

Hildebrand, Reginald F. *The Times Were Strange and Stirring: Methodist Preachers and the Crisis of Emancipation* (1995).

This entry is taken from the *American National Biography* and is published here with the permission of the American Council of Learned Societies.

GARDINER H. SHATTUCK

Holstein, Casper (1876–1944), philanthropist, activist, and numbers banker, was born in the Danish Virgin Islands. Holstein emigrated with his mother to the United States when he was nearly 12 years old. Little is known about his early childhood in the Virgin Islands. He attended high school in Brooklyn, New York, and enlisted in the U.S. Navy in 1898. He was stationed, for a time, on the islands of his birth. After completing his tour of duty he settled in Harlem in New York City. Holstein began working as a porter and bellhop at a Wall Street brokerage firm. As he swept floors and carried packages he also observed the intricacies of the stock market. He had ambitions that stretched far beyond his work as a porter.

Holstein had arrived in Harlem when the numbers game known as *Bolito* was a waning but still-popular recreational pastime for blacks in that neighborhood. This was an illegal gambling game in which players would place bets with "numbers banks." Players would bet by choosing a series of three numbers and giving them to number runners who would turn them over to the numbers bank. In winning bets, the numbers chosen by players matched those that were randomly selected through various systems by the numbers bank. Many players were suspicious of the randomness of the number selection and led to a lack of faith in number bankers and the numbers game itself. Holstein, like many other Harlemites, saw this pastime as a means of getting rich.

According to legend, Holstein, who had faithfully saved copies of daily newspapers, was reading the papers at work one day when he noticed the clearinghouse totals consisted of two sets of numbers that varied daily. Holstein suddenly had an idea that would forever change the numbers game. He devised a system in which the winning combination of numbers in a game would be chosen in a standardized way from the clearinghouse totals. In his system he would choose two numbers from the first set of numbers and one from the second to determine the winning number combination. Before Holstein revolutionized the numbers system, winning numbers were chosen randomly from racetrack totals or selected in drawings by the numbers bankers. After his epiphany, Holstein saved six months' worth of his meager wages; then he went into business as a numbers banker. Players were impressed with his system, since it guaranteed legitimate winning number combinations. In addition, players could check the winning numbers for themselves, free of dubious middlemen. With six-hundred-to-one odds for winners, Holstein quickly amassed a small fortune. Within a year, he owned three luxury apartment buildings in Harlem, a fleet of expensive cars, a Long Island home, thousands of acres of farmland in Virginia, and the infamous Turf Club, which also served as the headquarters of his numbers business.

With his growing wealth, Holstein became deeply involved in philanthropy and political activism in both Harlem and the Virgin Islands. He often wrote about what he considered to be the unjust situation in the U.S.-occupied Virgin Islands in the *Negro World*, a well-circulated publication of MARCUS GARVEY's Universal Negro Improvement Association (UNIA). The United States had purchased these islands in 1917 to build bases that would give U.S. military forces quick access to the Panama Canal. In 1925 he wrote an article for *Opportunity* magazine, a publication of the Urban League, detailing and protesting the abusive treatment of Virgin Islanders at the hands of the U.S. Navy.

Although members of Harlem's elite generally looked down on Holstein because of how he made his money, he often attended events hosted by the very people who disdained him. In 1925 he attended the first Opportunity Awards dinner and soon became an important figure during the Harlem Renaissance: At this inaugural event he donated the money to make the 1926 Opportunity Awards possible.

Well known in Harlem circles for other philanthropic endeavors, Holstein was a Black Elk and contributed heavily to their lodges. He was one of the largest individual contributors to the Universal Negro Improvement Association, and he took impoverished children up the Hudson River for an annual summer retreat. He aided black colleges, building dormitories and financing scholarships. He also established a hurricane relief fund for the Virgin Islands and founded a museum. With the numbers racket growing in popularity—in part because of his system of picking winning numbers—Holstein was worth nearly a million dollars by 1926. Holstein's wealth and local fame, however, did not come without a high cost.

Although numbers bankers were not the brutally violent types found in downtown New York City among the Italian and Irish gangsters of the 1920s, the numbers business was no doubt a competitive and cutthroat industry. Holstein faced competition from numbers luminaries such as STEPHANIE ST. CLAIR, who ran a prosperous business prior to Holstein's entry into the numbers racket. Although St. Clair and Holstein were rivals, they did not interfere with each other's businesses.

By the late 1920s, however, the downtown mafia had become aware of the enormous profits being made by the Harlem bankers, and they began to threaten Holstein and others. As a result, the number of black bankers dropped dramatically in Harlem. Yet Holstein was steadfast and ignored these threats.

On 23 September 1928 Holstein left his Harlem apartment and walked toward his limousine waiting outside. He was immediately kidnapped by white gangsters and held for a $50,000 ransom. This case was highly publicized and put a spotlight on the numbers racket. It also exposed the country to the wealth of upper-class blacks in Harlem—a phenomenon that had been unknown to most people outside that neighborhood. Within a few days Holstein was left on a street corner beaten and bleeding. The events of the kidnapping remained murky. He never identified his abductors and denied that any ransom had been paid. Unable to sustain his numbers operation in the

face of the mob's massive organization and use of gun violence, he quietly scaled down his business. Holstein eventually dropped out of the numbers game completely, as local, state, and federal investigations into the mob, their illegal businesses, and the numbers racket, gained intensity in the early 1930s.

Holstein was arrested in 1935 under a federal warrant from the Samuel Seabury Commission for illegal gambling and policy violations. He proclaimed his innocence and said his arrest was in direct connection to his political activism on behalf of the Virgin Islands. He spent nearly a year in prison and returned to Harlem penniless as the white mob took over the remainder of his numbers business. Holstein died in 1944.

At a time in America's history when African Americans had few legal pathways to wealth, Holstein built a business empire via illegal means. However, he used his wealth in many altruistic ways—mainly for the benefit of blacks in America and abroad.

FURTHER READING

Anderson, Jervis. *This Was Harlem: A Cultural Portrait, 1900–1950* (1982).

Lewis, David Levering. *When Harlem was in Vogue* (1997).

Schatzberg, Rufus. *Black Organized Crime in Harlem, 1920–1930* (1993).

Schatzberg, Rufus, and Robert J. Kelly. *African American Organized Crime: A Social History* (1997).

Wilson, Sondra K., and National Urban League. *Opportunity Reader: Stories, Poetry, and Essays from the Urban League's Opportunity Magazine* (1999).

H. ZAHRA CALDWELL

Holtzclaw, William Henry (June 1870–27 Aug. 1943), educator, writer, and publisher, was born William Henry Harrison Tecumseh Zachary Taylor Holtzclaw in Roanoke, Alabama, the oldest of twelve children born to Jerry Holtzclaw, a farmer, and Addie Holtzclaw, a food preparer. Despite their poverty the Holtzclaw family had a strong craving for education. Although Holtzclaw's father had little education, he taught him the basic principles of reading, writing, and arithmetic. Knowledge of arithmetic enabled Holtzclaw to calculate his daily pay for picking cotton. Before he was old enough to attend school himself, Holtzclaw often followed his older sister to school, where he so impressed the teacher that he was invited to become a kind of honorary student. Much later, at his father's urging, Holtzclaw applied for admission to Tuskegee Institute and was accepted in 1889.

There he established a close relationship with BOOKER T. WASHINGTON, the Institute's famed director, and became a great inspiration to him. During Holtzclaw's first year at Tuskegee, he worked in Washington's office during the day and attended school at night. His duties consisted of running errands, folding circulars, affixing stamps, and performing other odd jobs.

Following his father's death in 1893 Holtzclaw returned to Roanoke, Alabama, to care for the family and work on the farm. He and his two brothers shared the responsibility of farm life. Holtzclaw began teaching school in numerous locations in order to earn money to pay his father's unpaid debts. His first teaching assignment was in Whitesburg, Georgia, where he earned $46 for four months' work. During the remaining eight months Holtzclaw participated in local politics. The Honorable Bob Sewell, a powerful and influential leader in the black community, appointed Holtzclaw as his private secretary, a position that provided Holtzclaw with experience in planning, organizing, and carrying out political activities. After working with Sewell for a short time Holtzclaw was convinced that white men in the Republican Party were insincere. This insincerity played a major role in Holtzclaw's decision to give up politics. In an effort to persuade others to follow him, Holtzclaw wrote a series of articles that were published in a local newspaper under the pseudonym "Clodmocher." He appealed to black Republicans to break away from white Republicans who were perceived as insincere. In many Republican gatherings, this series of articles became the main topic for discussion.

Holtzclaw remained determined to complete his education at the Tuskegee Institute. When his mother, Addie, married Floyd Joiner, Holtzclaw and his brother Sidney returned to Tuskegee. He became a substitute teacher in the evening program at Tuskegee, earning $8 per month. During his last year at Tuskegee he received many offers for work as a teacher—including one from Tuskegee—but decided to teach in the state of Mississippi. Nevertheless, before finalizing his decision, Holtzclaw conferred with Mr. William J. Edwards (a visiting alumnus at Holtzclaw's graduation ceremony) concerning his plans to establish a school similar to the one founded by Edwards in Snow Hill, Alabama. Edwards was interested in Holtzclaw's plans and invited him to teach a class in

printing at Snow Hill until his plans in Mississippi were finalized. The class provided a profitable print shop that serviced Snow Hill Institute and white merchants in Alabama. Holtzclaw also organized the Farmer's Conference to help raise the standards of black farms and farming at the Institute. He organized the Black Belt Improvement Society to encourage economic self-sufficiency among rural blacks through the sale of land to farmers.

Holtzclaw believed that "God sent me to Utica [Mississippi] to lift the black man's burden. In my feeble way, I have lightened it, but I still have not lifted it. I will keep my boots on until He calls me" (Holtzclaw, R. Fulton, 228). Determined as he was to found a public school to train blacks to read, write, compute, and develop farmland communities, he began to teach about twenty students under a tree. In 1903 Holtzclaw founded his school in a rented log cabin, which served as his family's home and the home for two of the first boarding students. The school was chartered in the state of Mississippi as the "Utica Normal and Industrial Institute for the Training of Colored Young Men and Women." From 1903 until 1910 the school operated in the town of Utica near St. Peter Missionary Baptist Church. Around 1907 he sought property to relocate the school in order to move away from the distractions of the town and to be near subterranean water. By 1910 Holtzclaw and friends had raised $25,000 to purchase 2,000 acres of land located five miles south of Utica, Mississippi. Holtzclaw sold 400 acres of the land to five teachers, and purchased the property's plantation mansion for his family. Holtzclaw's mother, Addie, graduated from Utica at age ninety-four and all of his children graduated and taught at the Utica Institute.

In 1915 Holtzclaw wrote *The Black Man's Burden*, his autobiography. The book, which included an introduction by Booker T. Washington, won praise throughout the United States and Canada. Its publication made Holtzclaw one of the first African Americans in Mississippi to publish a book. In 1917 Holtzclaw received an honorary master of arts degree from Alabama Agricultural and Mechanical Normal Institute, and began to publish a weekly newspaper that featured news of interest to the community. In 1925 he organized the Utica Institute Jubilee Singers, and the group toured New York and New England to help raise funds for the Institute and to purchase a bus to travel. Holtzclaw founded the Mississippi Association of Teachers in Colored Schools and was a member of the Mississippi Educational Journal Board of Directors. After his death in Utica in 1943, Holtzclaw's son, William Holtzclaw Jr., succeeded him as principal of Utica Institute. In 1946 Holtzclaw Jr. and his mother, Mary Ella Holtzclaw, agreed to donate the school and property to Hinds County, which changed the school's name to Hinds County Agricultural High School, Colored.

FURTHER READING

Holtzclaw, William H. *The Black Man's Burden* (1971)
Holtzclaw, William Henry. *A Negro's Life Story* (1908).
Holtzclaw, R. Fulton. *William Henry Holtzclaw: Scholar in Ebony* (1977).

MARY L. YOUNG

Holyfield, Evander (19 Oct. 1962–), boxer, was born in the mill town of Atmore, Alabama, the youngest of eight children born to Annie Holyfield, who later moved with the family to Atlanta. Life was difficult for Annie, who bore the burdens of being a single parent and only possessed a grade-school education. She worked many hours to support her family and ensure that Evander and his siblings never felt deprived in the housing projects. One of Evander's brothers, Bernard Holyfield, became a well-known actor and dancer.

Holyfield's mother constantly reminded him that if he believed in God, worked hard, and never despaired he would be able to achieve anything he desired. Despite his intense religious upbringing Holyfield never wanted to be a clergyman, but aspired instead to be a football player for the NFL's Atlanta Falcons, a fireman, or a boxer. It was his mother who introduced him, when he was eight years old, to boxing at the Warren Memorial Boys' Club in southeast Atlanta. She felt it would be a productive activity and keep him out of trouble. Initially, boxing did not appeal to Holyfield (he did not like the idea of being punched), but he was interested in hitting the speed bag. Carter Morgan, the club's boxing coach, only agreed to allow him to hit the speed bag if he joined the boxing team.

Reluctantly, Holyfield complied and embarked on his boxing career. He won his first fight at age eight. Seeking to build his confidence, Morgan would frequently tell Holyfield that if he persisted at boxing, one day he would become the heavyweight champion of the world. When the boy drew attention to the fact that he was only eight years old and weighed sixty-five pounds, Morgan assured him that he would not always remain at that age and weight.

For the next three years Holyfield went undefeated at the club. His mettle and self-confidence

were initially tested when at eleven years of age he was defeated by his first white opponent, Cecil Collins. This was a double blow as it was not only his first loss but it was at the hands of a white. He returned home crestfallen and bitter, and informed his mother that he wanted to quit the team and sport. His mother calmly advised her son to never quit, but told him that he could indeed leave the boxing team—but only after defeating Collins.

Holyfield entered the second encounter, but again lost. He remained on the team and patiently waited for the rematch to redeem himself. The third time he boxed Collins, Holyfield won. While continuing his boxing, Holyfield attained perfect attendance at high school and began working. His first job was as a vendor at the Fulton County Stadium in Atlanta. He also pumped gas at an airport and served as a lifeguard.

The teenage Holyfield was a prolific and fearless amateur boxer with a 169-11 record. At Fulton High School he also played football, though mostly as a benchwarmer. At the school's last game he impressed the public and coach with his determination and skill in blocking, but he did not change his plans to focus on a career in boxing after he graduated in 1980.

In 1983 Holyfield was chosen for the U.S. Pan-American Games team in Venezuela. He triumphantly returned home with a silver medal. In the next year, Holyfield won the National Golden Gloves Championship and made his debut on the U.S. Olympic Team. Weighing in at 175 pounds, Holyfield fought in the light heavyweight division and was heading for a victory, but was disqualified by the referee for landing a late blow to his opponent, Kevin Barry of New Zealand. In an unorthodox reaction among athletes in this position, Holyfield calmly accepted the controversial ruling, which many present thought was a mistake. Video footage of the fight suggested that Holyfield was robbed of a victory.

After the catastrophic bout at the Olympics, Holyfield, at age twenty-one, decided to become a professional. He made his professional debut by defeating Lionel Byarm. Holyfield subsequently won four fights in the junior heavyweight division. As his weight increased, Holyfield moved to the new cruiserweight division, which had a limit of 190 pounds. He dominated this category and won his first world title, the WBA (World Boxing Association) and IBF (International Boxing Federation) Junior Heavyweight (Cruiserweight) Championship, beating Dwight Muhammad Qawi in a bruising fifteen-round bout on 12 July 1986. On 9 April 1988 Holyfield knocked out Carlos DeLeon in the eighth round and won the WBC (World Boxing Council) Junior Heavyweight title. That year Holyfield decided to make another move upward, and entered the keenly contested heavyweight division.

In February 1990 Buster Douglas defeated MIKE TYSON to become the world's heavyweight champion. His next challenger would be Holyfield. On 25 October 1990 the much anticipated battle resulted in Holyfield knocking out Douglas in the third round. Finally Morgan's prophecy and Holyfield's childhood dream had been fulfilled.

The scheduled fight between Holyfield and Tyson in November 1991 was initially postponed because Tyson had injured his rib during training. The fight was rescheduled for 1992 but later cancelled when Tyson was convicted of raping a beauty contestant that year. He served three years in an Indiana prison. Holyfield survived three title defenses, but on 13 November 1992 was defeated by RIDDICK BOWE. This was Holyfield's first loss after twenty-nine professional bouts. Almost a year later, on 6 November 1993, in a rematch lasting twelve rounds, Holyfield reclaimed the heavyweight title from Bowe. In 1994 Holyfield again lost the title, this time to the faster-fisted Michael Moorer. Holyfield briefly retired in April 1994 following a minor heart complaint, but in December 1994 returned to the sport.

The much anticipated clash between Tyson and Holyfield finally occurred on 9 November 1996. Holyfield, viewed by many as the underdog and past his prime, won the WBA version title by knocking out the highly favored "Iron Mike" in the eleventh round. In the rematch of June 1997 Tyson again suffered at the hands of Holyfield, and in the third round the sporting world was horrified and shocked to see Tyson bite off a piece of Holyfield's ear. Tyson was disqualified for his conduct, and Holyfield retained the title and won the $35 million prize. On 8 November 1997 Holyfield defeated Moorer and won the IBF title. However, he could not repeat this performance in the encounter with Lennox Lewis, but held on to the prestigious IBF and WBA titles after a twelve-round draw in March 1999. However, in a rematch in November 1999 he lost both titles to Lewis. In August 2000 Holyfield defeated John Ruiz to regain the WBA title and become the first boxer to win the heavyweight championship for a fourth time. In March 2001 Holyfield lost the rematch to Ruiz. A few

months later, in December, another Holyfield-Ruiz encounter ended in a draw after a grueling twelve-round bout.

In December 2002, in a bid to regain the coveted IBF title, Holyfield lost a twelve-round decision to Chris Byrd. Likewise, in October 2003 Holyfield was soundly defeated in the ninth round by James Toney. Almost a year later, in November 2004 at Madison Square Garden, Holyfield, at forty-two years of age, took a beating from Larry Donald. Subsequently, the New York State Athletic Commission placed Holyfield on an indefinite medical suspension. After his retirement from the sport, Holyfield stayed involved through the establishment of the Holyfield Foundation, which assisted community groups and boxing clubs. His lifetime ring earnings have exceeded $100 million.

In early 2007 a steroid scandal threatened to sully the image of Holyfield. The *Times Union* of Albany revealed that Holyfield, using an alias, was on the customer list of Applied Pharmacy in Mobile, Alabama. Federal agents swooped down on this pharmacy, which had been accused of distributing illegal drugs to men and women in the sporting arena. Holyfield was not charged in the investigation, but he later admitted that he might have unknowingly used a drug from the pharmacy, in 2004, to deal with a hormonal problem.

Throughout Holyfield's career, the four-time world heavyweight champion was known for his public effort to promote Christianity. During prefight interviews Holyfield, whose nickname is "The Real Deal," often sported a baseball-style cap with the words "Jesus Is Lord" emblazoned on it. His boxing robe and shorts bore the inscription "Phil. 4:13," referring to the New Testament Epistle to the Philippians, which states, "I can do all things through Christ who strengthens me."

FURTHER READING

Holyfield, Evander. *Holyfield: The Humble Warrior* (2006).

Sugar, Bert Randolph. *Boxing's Greatest Fighters* (2006).

Thomas, James. *The Holyfield Way: What I Learned about Courage, Perseverance, and the Bizarre World of Boxing* (2005).

JEROME TEELUCKSINGH

Homer, LeRoy (27 Aug. 1965–11 Sept. 2001), air force pilot and first officer of United Airlines Flight 93 on 11 September 2001, was born LeRoy Wilton Homer Jr. in Long Island, New York, one of nine children of Ilse and LeRoy Homer. On 11 September

2001 Officer Homer, along with Captain Jason M. Dahl, piloted United Airlines Flight 93, which was hijacked by four terrorists while coming from Newark en route to San Francisco. Overwhelmed by the terrorists, Flight 93 eventually crashed outside Stonycreek and Shanksville, Pennsylvania, leaving no survivors.

Homer grew up in Long Island, New York, with nine siblings, seven of them girls. As a child, he had a deep passion for flying. He would read literature on aviation, assemble model airplanes, as well as collect aviation memorabilia. Homer's father would often take him to the town of Islip's MacArthur Airport to view the takeoffs and landings. He was only fifteen when he started flight school, learning his trade in a Cessna 152. He worked part-time jobs to help pay for flying instructions. By the time he was sixteen he had completed his first solo flight, and he earned his private pilot's certificate in 1983.

In 1983 he entered the U.S. Air Force Academy. He was a member of Cadet Squadron 31 as an upperclassman. Upon graduating in 1987 he obtained the rank of second lieutenant and specialized in flying Lockheed C-141B Starlifters, an outstretched low-level, night-flying cargo plane used by the U.S. Air Force. In 1988 he was assigned to the Eighteenth Military Airlift Squadron stationed at McGuire Air Force Base in New Jersey. While on active duty during the early 1990s, he served the country in the Gulf War–Operation Desert Storm (1990–1991) and Desert Shield in Somalia (1992–1993). During American military operations in the Persian Gulf region, Homer flew the C-141B Starlifter from bases in Europe to the Middle East. In 1993 he was named the 21st Air Force Aircrew Instructor of the Year by the U.S. Air Force.

Homer continued his military career in the U.S. Air Force Reserve, receiving the rank of major. He started out as an instructor pilot with the 356th Airlift Squadron at Wright-Patterson Air Force Base in Ohio. He then served as academy liaison officer, recruiting individuals into the U.S. Air Force Academy, as well as the Air Force Reserve Officers' Training Corps. In 1995 Homer was honorably discharged from active duty.

In 1995 he began to fly commercial planes for United Airlines. His first assignment was as second officer aboard a Boeing 727. Homer then met Melodie Thorpe through an acquaintance. After carrying on a brief long-distance telephone relationship, the two of them finally met and were engaged on Valentine's Day in 1997. Homer and Thorpe were married in 1998. In 2000 they had their first and only daughter, Laurel. By 1996 he had been promoted to first officer aboard a mammoth Boeing 757/767.

On 11 September 2001 the United States came under siege by a series of coordinated terrorist suicide attacks by Muslim extremists affiliated with al-Qaeda. That morning, nineteen Muslim terrorists hijacked four commercial airliners. The airliners were en route to California from Logan International, Dulles International, and Newark airports. There was a trained pilot with each team of hijackers.

The terrorists ambushed the planes by using pepper spray and box cutters to ward off and, in some cases, eventually kill passengers and flight attendants. The first plane, United Airlines Flight 175 (a Boeing 767), crashed into the North Tower of New York City's World Trade Center at 8:46 A.M. The second plane, American Airlines Flight 11, another Boeing 767, crashed into the South Tower at 9:02 A.M. The third hijacked plane was American Airlines Flight 77, a Boeing 757 that crashed into the Pentagon in Washington, D.C., at 9:37 A.M.

The fourth hijacked plane, United Airlines Flight 93, was a Boeing 757 piloted by First Officer Homer, along with Captain Jason M. Dahl. The plane's crew had been overwhelmed by four terrorists while flying from Newark en route to San Francisco. At 10:03 A.M. the plane crashed in a field near the rural Somerset County town of Shanksville, Pennsylvania, leaving no survivors.

The black box recordings from Homer's United Airlines Flight 93 revealed that both the flight crew and passengers on board attempted to forcibly regain the plane from the hijackers, causing the terrorists to miss their original target, the U.S. Capitol. In addition to the nineteen hijackers, 2,973 people (mainly civilians) died on 11 September; another twenty-four were missing and assumed dead.

Homer received many posthumous awards and honorable mentions for his actions aboard Flight 93, including honorary membership in the historic Tuskegee Airmen, the Southern Christian Leadership Conference's Drum Major for Justice Award, the Westchester County Trailblazer Award, and the Congress of Racial Equality's DR. MARTIN LUTHER KING JR. Award.

WILLIAM BANKSTON

Honeywood, Varnette (27 Dec. 1950–12 Sept. 2010), artist, was born in Los Angeles, California, the younger of two daughters of Lovie Honeywood;

information about her father is unavailable. Her regular visits to relatives in rural Progress, Mississippi, and Louisiana would provide a foundation for her artwork, as would the teachers and her close-knit family who encouraged her artistic talent. Her sense of identity was honed in her youth as her family experienced prejudice upon their move into a mixed Los Angeles neighborhood. In the 1960s, she became active in civil rights protest demonstrations and rallies.

Originally aspiring to become a history teacher, Honeywood was a history major at Spelman College before switching to art. Her years at Spelman were influential to her development as a painter. Spelman's all-female atmosphere was nurturing and had a long-standing reputation for producing African American scholars and artists. While there she networked with artist-professors such as Kofi Bailey and SAMELLA LEWIS. Honeywood graduated with a BFA in 1970 and went on to earn a master's degree in education from the University of Southern California (USC) in 1972.

After meeting African students while visiting her older sister, Stephanie, at UCLA and then going to Lagos, Nigeria, for the World Black and African Festival of Art and Culture in 1977, Honeywood started to collect African textiles such as Ghanaian kente cloth and Nigerian resist-dyed fabrics and to incorporate African pictorial symbols into her work. "The important thing is that we draw on Africa for inspiration in symbolism and technique...," Honeywood said, "The exciting thing is that the African American artists are coming into their own. I think it's time we recognize our own visual history" (Benberry, 78).

Honeywood became a director of art programs at USC and worked with underprivileged children until 1979, when funding was cut. It was then that she made the decision to become a full-time professional artist. Establishing her studio on the top floor of her parents' home, she was featured in Carroll Parrott Blue's 1979 documentary, *Varnette's World: Study of an Artist*. Honeywood saw an opportunity to market her work and, with her sister, created Black Lifestyles, a family-run business selling reproductions of her works in greeting cards and prints.

Her paintings are characterized by the use of bright, bold, expressive colors and a graphic collage style that has been compared to that of other African American artists such as ROMARE BEARDEN, ARCHIBALD J. MOTLEY JR., and JACOB LAWRENCE.

They are extensions of herself and interpretations of her experiences. "What I paint are visual statements of Black life. I am recording endangered scenes. Rituals and traditions that will one day be no more. If we don't record our triumphs and struggles, who will?" (Honeywood, 122). She follows in the footsteps of other African American female artists such as ELIZABETH CATLETT and LOIS MAILOU JONES by drawing upon African American life for inspiration.

Traditional quilt designs also figure prominently in Honeywood's work. Although not a quilter herself, she grew up surrounded by quilts made by her grandparents and great-aunt. Patterns such as the double wedding ring, broken dishes, and kente-reminiscent strip designs can often be found in her works such as *A Century of Empowerment*, commissioned in 1985 for *Essence* magazine's fifteenth anniversary. Many of these quilt designs also have their roots in traditional African patterns. Honeywood creates a blend of these art forms in her paintings.

Her use of quilts in her work draws comparisons to the quilt paintings of African American artist FAITH RINGGOLD. Both women draw upon what Arna L. Bontemps Jr. describes as a form of continuity of tradition as "it is not illogical to assume that Black women in America continued to manifest a strong aesthetic affinity for tactile perception and sculptural form" (Robinson, 85).

In 1985, Honeywood received a career boost when comedian BILL COSBY featured her works in the set design for his long-running hit television show *The Cosby Show*. The multiculturalism movement of the 1980s and 1990s helped to bring her to the forefront of artists considered "Afrocentric" and created an increased demand for her work. In 1992, when she was an artist-in-residence at Spelman College, she had a one-woman retrospective of her work at her alma mater.

Her work can be found in many private collections. Widely traveled, she visited many locations in the African diaspora, such as Senegal, Nigeria, and São Paulo and Bahia in Brazil. It is this sense of a greater community that inspired her work: "Meeting Black artists from around the world was enlightening. The similarity in our experiences and goals as artists showed me that I had made the right choice: to paint what I feel is valid. It made me realize that our legacy as an African people is still with us in our culture today." She died in Los Angeles at the age of 59.

FURTHER READING

Benberry, Cuesta. *Always There: The African-American Presence in American Quilts* (1992).

Freeman, Roland. *A Communion of the Spirits: African-American Quilters, Preservers, and Their Stories* (1996).

Honeywood, Stephanie. "Varnette Honeywood: Art that Hits Home," *Essence* (August 1983).

Lewis, Samella. *African American Art and Artists* (2003).

Robinson, Jontyle Theresa. *Bearing Witness: Contemporary Works by African American Women Artists* (1996).

Von Blum, Paul. "Kuumba: The African Art of Varnette Honeywood," *Z Magazine* (July 2000).

LAWANA HOLLAND-MOORE

Hood, James Walker (30 May 1831–30 Oct. 1918), bishop of the African Methodist Episcopal Zion Church and grand master of the Prince Hall Masonic Lodge, was born in Kennet Township, Pennsylvania, the son of Levi Hood and Harriet Walker. James and his eleven siblings lived so close to the Delaware border, where most blacks were still enslaved, that he could say he "slept in Pennsylvania and drank water from a Delaware spring" (Martin, 23–24). Levi Hood was a minister of the Union Church of Africans in Delaware and used his small farm in Pennsylvania as a stop on the Underground Railroad for escaping slaves. Harriet Walker had been a member of RICHARD ALLEN's Bethel Church in Philadelphia, which in 1816 became the mother congregation of the African Methodist Episcopal (AME) Church. Though not an ordained minister, the public role that she played in her husband's church as an exhorter was unique for its time and inevitably influenced young James's progressive attitudes about the role of women.

Though James and his family were free, African Americans in Pennsylvania were largely barred from voting and faced segregation and discrimination in most areas of public life. His parents were able to secure the most rudimentary education for James by allowing him to work for a nearby Quaker family on the condition that they provide him with food, clothing, and at least six weeks of academic instruction each year. By age thirteen he had spent a maximum of two years at a rural school. He credits his mother for imbuing him with a love of learning and oratory that inspired him to continue his education independently and with the aid of tutors, so that by the age of fifteen he was able to give his first public address in a refined manner. Later in life Hood's intellectual attainment was recognized by honorary doctorates from Livingstone College, which he helped to found, and Lincoln University.

In 1852 Hood married Hannah L. Ralph and the two moved to Philadelphia, where he found work as a porter, waiter, and steward, but even then his strongest desire was to become a minister. After his wife's death in 1855 he relocated to New York City and joined a branch of the Union Church of Africans in lower Manhattan. The pastor of the congregation, the Reverend William Councy, was so taken with Hood's ability and sincerity that he awarded him a license to preach in 1856. When he moved to New Haven, Connecticut, the following year and discovered that there was no Union Church of Africans in the city, Hood joined the fledgling African Methodist Episcopal Zion (AMEZ) Church, known locally as "Allenites." In order to distinguish the two organizations with such similar names and theologies, the former group added "Zion" to its title in 1848 and its members became known as "Zionites." Hood would spend the rest of his life building and expanding the influence of the AMEZ.

Hood married Sophia J. Nugent, daughter of a Washington, D.C., deacon, in 1858. They would have four children before her death in 1875. At first Hood supported his growing family by working at the Tontine Hotel in New Haven to supplement his meager income as an AMEZ minister. In 1859 he was dispatched to serve two congregations in Nova Scotia, Canada, that were forty miles apart. The AMEZ churches there were so poor that Hood had to find work digging potatoes. The local black community was heavily influenced by the Baptists and not receptive to the Methodist liturgy, hierarchical structure, and strict prohibitions against alcohol and tobacco. Though Hood made little progress during his three years in Canada, his tenacity brought him to the attention of AMEZ leaders who quickly advanced him first to deacon and then within a year to elder. As president of the Board of Officers of the Home and Foreign Mission Board at the height of the Civil War, Hood argued that more attention needed to be paid to the spiritual and political well-being of the vast majority of black people in the South.

In 1864, after a brief appointment to a congregation in Bridgeport, Connecticut, Hood followed the advancing Union army to New Bern, North Carolina. While military battles were still being fought around them, representatives of the northern AME and AMEZ churches were waging their own battle for the souls and denominational affiliations of the newly freed black majority. Only 12 percent of the four million slaves at the start of the Civil War belonged to any church, and most of the two hundred thousand black Methodists under the control of the white Methodist Episcopal Church, South were now free to choose their alliances. Harry V. Richardson states that "The A.M.E.'s had only 19,963 members, and the "A.M.E.Z.'s had only 4,600" members nationally in 1860 (Richardson, 146). Both organizations recognized the tremendous opportunity for growth that existed among the majority of African Americans who were unchurched.

Against two competitors from the AME Church, Hood won the loyalty of Andrews Chapel in New Bern, a crown jewel among black churches in the state. The congregation then changed its name to St. Peter's AMEZ Church and elected Hood as its pastor.

Hood moved quickly and effectively to add more churches to the ranks of the AMEZ in the state and to establish his efforts in North Carolina as a model and springboard for further missionary activity throughout the South. His phenomenal trailblazing and demonstrated organizational skills allowed him to be elevated to the position of bishop in 1872. By 1874 he had overseen the creation of 366 churches with a net increase of over twenty thousand new members to the AMEZ Church.

During Reconstruction, Hood was a delegate to the Black or Freedman's State Convention in Raleigh, North Carolina. The body elected Hood as president, and he proceeded to articulate its demands for the "right to the jury-box, cartridge box, and ballot box." A white newspaper wrote that Hood and other African Americans would get these rights in one box, a "coffin box" (Martin, 69). At the Reconstruction State Conventions from 1867 to 1868 Hood was one of only thirteen black delegates. He represented Cumberland County and fought for new homestead laws (land apportionment), public education, and women's rights. He became assistant superintendent of education and supported legislation to make the University of North Carolina part of the public education system. He defended the potential of black students by arguing that two-and-a-half centuries of slavery, which he described as "the most degrading vassalage," made it impossible for former slaves as a whole to "compare favorably with the Anglo-Saxon in point of intellectual culture" (Hildebrand, 52). Hood worked for the Freedmen's Bureau, was a deputy collector for the Internal Revenue Service,

and was a delegate to the 1872 Republican National Convention that nominated President Ulysses S. Grant to his second term of office. He was also a founder of the AMEZ newspaper, *Star of Zion*, and one of its leading contributors. In politics and temperament Hood was forceful but cautious. His positions fall somewhere between those of the conservative BOOKER T. WASHINGTON and the radical W. E. B. DuBois.

As grand master of the North Carolina Grand Lodge of PRINCE HALL Masons, Hood contributed to the burgeoning intellectual and fraternal life of black North Carolinians. Hood's first exposure to freemasonry occurred in New York, where he was made superintendent of the southern jurisdiction.

Hood established the King Solomon Lodge No. 1 shortly after his arrival in New Bern. He simultaneously built churches and lodges in Fayetteville, Wilmington, and Raleigh that united in 1870 to become the North Carolina Grand Lodge. By 1874 eighteen chapters were set up around the state with a combined roll of almost five hundred members. Because of pioneers like Hood there would be over 117,000 Prince Hall Lodges in the United States by the turn of the century with nearly two-thirds of the members located in southern states. Hood was also instrumental in founding a ladies' auxiliary to the Prince Hall Lodge called the Order of the Eastern Star.

The two most significant issues that confronted the AMEZ church during Hood's forty-four years as a bishop were merger negotiations with the AME Church and controversies surrounding the ordination of women. In 1886 the AME and AMEZ were close to an agreement; only terminology and personalities divided them. Some Zionites thought the term "African" should be dropped because it implied that the denomination was racially exclusive. AME Bishop HENRY McNEIL TURNER retorted that "Greek Orthodox," "Roman Catholic," and "Anglican" or "Church of England" all make reference to national or geographic locations. Bishop Hood proposed a reasonable compromise in "United African Methodist Episcopal Church," but a final solution eluded them. Merger discussions between the two bodies continue periodically to the present day.

When Bishop Hood ordained JULIA FOOTE a deacon at the New York Annual Conference in 1894 she became the first ordained female Methodist. There was concern in some quarters but no crisis. However, the ordination of the Reverend Mary J. Small, wife of AMEZ Bishop John Small, to the position of elder in 1898 raised a firestorm because it placed women in high managerial positions and opened the door to women becoming bishops. Hood argued that God created woman from Adam's rib to indicate that "she is to stand beside him as his equal" (Martin, 170). With the help of other progressives Hood was able to block a resolution prohibiting the ordination of women, but the general practice of limiting women to lay positions continued. Ironically, the Reverend Mary Small later defeated Bishop Hood's third wife, Keziah Price McCoy (whom he married in 1877 and with whom he had two children) for the presidency of the Woman's Home and Foreign Missionary Society.

In 1916 the AMEZ adopted a policy that made seventy-four the mandatory retirement age for all bishops; Hood, who was already eighty-five, was forced to step down. When he died at his home in Fayetteville, North Carolina, two years later he left a legacy that included five books, including *The Negro in the Christian Pulpit: Two Characters and Two Destinies* (1884), a collection called *Sermons* (1908), and the historical work *Sketch of the Early History of the African Methodist Episcopal Zion Church* (1914). Moreover, the foundation he played such an important role in building left the AMEZ and the Prince Hall Lodges vital and permanent fixtures in African American religious and civic life.

FURTHER READING

The main body of papers covering Bishop Hood's life and career is located in the AMEZ denominational archives at the Bishop W. J. Walls Heritage Center at Livingstone College in North Carolina, the Woodruff Library at Atlanta University, and at the Schomburg Center for Research in Black Culture of the New York Public Library.

Hackett, David G. "The Prince Hall Masons and the African American Church: The Labors of Grand Master and Bishop James Walker Hood, 1831–1918," *Church History* 69.4 (December 2000).

Hildebrand, Reginald F. *The Times Were Strange and Stirring: Methodist Preachers and the Crisis of Emancipation* (1995).

Martin, Sandy Dwayne. *For God and Race: The Religious and Political Leadership of AMEZ Bishop James Walker Hood* (1999).

Richardson, Harry V. *Dark Salvation: The Story of Methodism As It Developed among Blacks in America* (1976).

SHOLOMO B. LEVY

Hood, Walter (24 June 1958–), landscape architect and educator, was born in Fort Bragg, North Carolina, where his father was a career army serviceman, and grew up in Charlotte, North Carolina. In 1981 he earned his B.S. degree in Landscape Architecture at North Carolina A&T State University, where he came under the mentorship of Charles Fountain. Fountain impressed upon Hood the need to judiciously balance a love of art with a strong sense of social responsibility and emphasized that, as a minority landscape architect, he should seek novel ways to improve environmental conditions for marginalized populations. Hood's attraction to graduate study at the University of California, Berkeley, where he earned master's degrees in Architecture and Landscape Architecture in 1989, was a logical consequence of Fountain's influence. Garrett Eckbo was also a major source of inspiration for Hood and also emphasized the social responsibility of landscape architects. Although Eckbo had retired from teaching at Berkeley before Hood began his graduate study, Hood worked for Eckbo's architectural landscaping firm while he was a graduate student.

Eckbo introduced the concept that music and painting could serve as primary sources of inspiration for socially engaged landscape architects. The abstract paintings of the Russian artist Wassily Kandinsky, for instance, are critical to understanding Eckbo's impact on Hood. Eckbo loved Kandinsky paintings, particularly a series of "improvisations," highly abstract compositions inspired by the artist's experience of listening to music by the composers Arnold Schoenberg and Aleksandr Scriabin. While Kandinsky's abstract paintings were inspired by classical music performances that evoked particular colors, hues, and saturations, Hood paralleled Kandinsky's transformation of music into visual forms by drawing upon his own memories of hearing blues and jazz in North Carolina, and he let them inspire his landscape designs. In fact the word *improvisation* was at the forefront of Hood's descriptions of his work; he titled his 1993 book *Blues and Jazz Landscape Improvisations*. For Hood, improvisation in landscape architecture entailed avoiding rigid categories of how a landscape should look and favoring what a particular landscape was like in daily motion, a lively and messy amalgam of unpredictable social and natural interactions.

This spirit of improvisation was illustrated by projects Hood completed in the San Francisco Bay Area, where he worked as a professor of landscape architecture at the University of California,

Berkeley, and as head of the Hood Design firm in Oakland. Hood designed Splash Pad Park, a successful marketplace that was once a traffic island adjacent to I-580, an Oakland freeway. He is widely acclaimed for the landscaping at the M. H. de Young Memorial Museum in San Francisco's Golden Gate Park National Recreation Area, in which he integrated the park seamlessly with the museum by using plantings around the museum that mimic plants found in the area (for example, tree ferns and eucalyptus) and that suggest the textile designs in the museum's collection.

FURTHER READING
Hood, Walter. *Urban Diaries* (1997).
Barton, Craig Evan, ed. *Sites of Memory: Perspectives on Architecture and Race* (2001).

NORMAN WEINSTEIN

Hooker, Earl (15 Jan. 1930–21 Apr. 1970), blues guitarist, was born Earl Zebedee Hooker Jr. in Clarksdale, Mississippi, the son of Earl Hooker Sr. and Mary Blare, Delta farmers. Because Earl Sr. played several instruments, including the guitar, and Mary had once worked as a vocalist with a touring variety show, Earl Jr. and his twin sister were exposed to music at an early age. Earl Jr. taught himself to play guitar by age ten, and a year later, after a move to Chicago, he began taking formal lessons at the Lyon and Healy music school, learning not only guitar but also banjo, mandolin, piano, and drums. His primary mentor was an older Arkansas-born guitarist, ROBERT NIGHTHAWK, an established blues professional who taught Hooker to play electric bottleneck style.

In his teens Hooker performed on the streets, at times with another Mississippi transplant, Ellas McDaniel, later known as BO DIDDLEY. By 1947 he was working with Nighthawk, touring the South and doing radio shows on KFFA in Helena, Arkansas, WDIA in Memphis, and other stations. In 1949 Hooker relocated to Memphis, where he eventually teamed up with the pianist IKE TURNER—also a Clarksdale native—and toured the South with Turner's band. In the late 1940s and early 1950s he also worked with the harmonica virtuoso SONNY BOY WILLIAMSON on the popular *King Biscuit Time* show broadcast on station KFFA.

Working in Florida with his own band in 1952 Hooker recorded several blues tunes, including "Sweet Angel" and "On the Hook," issued on the Rockin' label, and "Race Track" and "Blue Guitar Blues," issued on King. In 1953 he teamed up in Memphis with the pianist Pinetop Perkins and the guitarist Boyd Gilmore to do some session work for the Memphis Recording Service, but nothing was issued at the time. By the mid-1950s Hooker was touring the Midwest with the Chicago-based guitarist and singer OTIS RUSH. As Rush later recalled, "Earl Hooker ... stayed with me for six months, longer than anybody in the world that I ever heard of him playing with." Hooker by then had developed a marked preference for working with his own band.

Through the 1950s and early 1960s Hooker worked mainly around Chicago, recording a series of singles for various small-time Chicago labels: Argo, C. J., B+B, Chief, Age, Checker, and Mil-Lon. The best of these were for Mel London's Chief and Age labels, which included collaborations with the harmonica player and vocalist JUNIOR WELLS and the vocalists Lillian Offitt and Ricky Allen. Hooker himself never became a confident blues vocalist, perhaps because of his long battle against tuberculosis. He concentrated instead on playing guitar, eventually mastering not only blues but also other styles—jazz, rock, even country and western. Stranded once in Waterloo, Iowa, he played guitar with an all white "hillbilly band" for six months, discovering in the process that his comparatively thin singing voice adapted comfortably to songs by such country stars as Hank Williams and Ernest Tubb.

During the early 1960s Hooker was hospitalized several times as his tuberculosis worsened, but he never quit playing entirely, even if it meant doing hospital benefit concerts. By the mid-1960s he was back on the Chicago and midwestern club circuits, working with various artists—including the blues singer Little Junior Parker—and recording an instrumental album in Wisconsin. In 1965 he formed a band to back his cousin, the singer Joe Hinton, and toured with the band in Europe, where he appeared on a London television show with the British rock group The Beatles. Returning to Chicago he continued to work clubs with his own band through 1969, also playing at Theresa's, a landmark South Side blues club, with the Junior Wells band. The albums he recorded for Bluesway, Arhoolie, and Blue Thumb during this period brought him newfound recognition, and in 1969 he recorded a blues-rock collaboration with Steve Miller in California, raising the possibility of additional crossover work. That same year, after Hooker returned from a European tour with the American Folk Blues Festival, he put together yet another group, the rock-influenced Electric Dust Band. Although he appeared to be on the brink of crossover success, his chronic illness forced him to enter a municipal tuberculosis sanatorium in Chicago, where he died. He was survived by his wife, Bertha Nixon.

During his twenty-five-year career Hooker played with most of the major blues artists of his era, including B. B. KING, MUDDY WATERS, Bobby Bland, and Jimmy Witherspoon. He also led several exotically named bands of his own: the Roadmasters, the Soul Twisters, the Invaders, and his final group, the Electric Dust Band. Known more as a guitarist rather than a singer, Hooker recorded with a long lineup of blues vocalists: Lillian Offitt, Harold Tidwell, Junior Wells, A. C. Reed, and Andrew Odum, among others.

While Hooker's guitar work was influenced by blues, jazz, and country players ranging from the slide specialist Robert Nighthawk to the country pickers Merle Travis and Joe Maphis, he distilled his many sources into his own easily recognizable sound. Known to his peers as "Zeb," from his middle name, he was the undisputed master of the slide, ultimately surpassing the skill of his mentor Nighthawk. Hooker was also one of the first blues guitarists to master the wah-wah peddle and the double-necked guitar. He influenced many other blues guitarists, as well as crossover rockers such as Ike Turner, JIMI HENDRIX, Elvin Bishop, and George Thorogood.

Despite his chronic illness Hooker had terrific drive when on stage, dazzling audiences with both his technical skill and his showmanship—playing the guitar with his teeth, for example, or behind his back. At the time of his death Hooker was considered by many other musicians to be the best guitarist in Chicago. But his death cut short the events that might have extended his fame beyond the inner circle of musicians who constituted his most enthusiastic legion of fans.

FURTHER READING

Danchin, Sebastian. *Earl Hooker, Blues Master* (2001).
Harris, Sheldon. *Blues Who's Who: A Biographical Dictionary of Blues Singers* (1989).
Obituary: *Living Blues* 1, no. 2 (Summer 1970).
This entry is taken from the *American National Biography* and is published here with the permission of the American Council of Learned Societies.

BARRY LEE PEARSON AND
BILL MCCULLOCH

Hooker, John Lee (22 Aug. 1917?–21 June 2001), bluesman, was born near Clarksdale, Mississippi, on a large farm owned by his parents, William Hooker, a preacher as well as a farmer, and Minnie Ramsey. The fourth boy of ten to thirteen children, some of whom died in childbirth, Hooker's earliest musical experiences involved singing spirituals in the church where his father preached, though he resented both the enforced, backbreaking labor and the church singing on which his father insisted. When blues singer-guitarist Tony Hollins, who later recorded in 1941 and 1952, began courting Hooker's sister Alice, Hooker was enthralled by his musical performances. In fact, he acquired his first significant blues influence from Hollins, who gave him an old, beat-up guitar, which Hooker's father allowed him to keep even though the preacher dubbed it "the Devil" because of its secular lure. A Gypsy woman at a carnival told the young Hooker he would be famous all over the world, but he had little reason to dream that an illiterate African American boy from Mississippi would actually fulfill her prophecy, especially since his father would not even allow him to play the guitar in the house. As Hooker reached adolescence, his mother and father separated, and Minnie began a relationship with the sharecropper Will Moore. Unlike his brothers and sisters, young John Lee went to live with his mother and Moore, largely because Moore was also a guitar player and encouraged his stepson's playing. With a new Stella guitar, music lessons, and spiritual support provided by his stepfather, Hooker drew on the repertoires of Moore and his associates, the Delta blues giant CHARLEY PATTON and the Texan BLIND LEMON JEFFERSON. Excluded from work with Moore at country suppers, dances, and fish fries because of their violent ambience, Hooker ran away to Memphis around 1931, working both outside music and with gospel groups like the Big Six, the Fairfield Four, and the Delta Big Four. After a year Hooker arrived in Cincinnati, where his playing began to get wider public exposure. Some three years later he moved to Detroit, setting the stage for his emergence as a recording artist. At Henry's Swing Club, Hastings Street nightspots, and Lee's Sensation Bar, Hooker began establishing a reputation as an up-and-coming bluesman. The record store owner Elmer Barbee discovered Hooker and took him to Bernie Besman, a record distributor and owner of the Sensation label, who recorded four tunes by Hooker on 3 November 1948. The release on the Modern Records label of "Sallie Mae" and its B-side, "Boogie Chillun," a boogie in

John Lee Hooker performed as a surprise guest during a Tom Petty concert at the Fillmore Theater in February 1997. (AP Images.)

using such monikers as John Lee Booker, John Lee Cooker, Birmingham Sam and his Magic Guitar, Boogie Man, Delta John, Texas Slim, and Johnny Williams to disguise the fact that he was violating his contracts to record with different labels. These pseudonyms were superficial masks at best; Hooker's blues and boogie style is too deeply distinctive to deceive any but the most uninitiated and tone-deaf ear.

These early recordings are often considered Hooker's best. Playing alone on his electric guitar, he creates a stark world as a deep, Delta blues feeling passes through the alembic of his genius. Hooker can be both deeply traditional and spontaneously original, his deep and haunting voice moaning at times in unison with stark, jagged guitar lines and then pulsing into insistent, rhythmic action as his boogie rumbles sensually into place as a relief to the fierce isolation of his blues. The whispers and cries of his rich, baritone voice and the hammered chords and nervous rambling of his idiosyncratic guitar style are so individual that they sometimes render intensely personal to Hooker songs that were composed by other performers such as ROOSEVELT SYKES, PERCY MAYFIELD, Charles Calhoun, and SONNY BOY WILLIAMSON. His duet and group recordings are somewhat less successful, since Hooker's creative approach to musical structure could befuddle all but the most sympathetic of backup musicians.

By 1955 Hooker had moved on to Chicago and the Vee-Jay label, owned by the African American entrepreneurs Vivian Carter and Jimmy Bracken, who had previously struck gold with JIMMY REED. The Vee-Jay years produced such hits as the oft-covered "Dimples" and "Boom Boom," as well as remakes of some of his earlier hits, and found Hooker frequently accompanied by bands in an attempt to update and commercialize his sound; even the pop-soul group the Vandellas provided backing vocals at one session. With recordings for Riverside, Fortune, Prestige, Atco, Galaxy, and Stax in between sessions for Vee-Jay in the 1955–1964 period, Hooker was a high-profile bluesman, both for the African American market and the emerging "folk blues" audience of the early 1960s.

The "folk" and "rock" portions of Hooker's career began with appearances at the Newport Folk Festival in 1959 and 1960, when he began performing on acoustic guitar to match his new white audience's sense of what an "authentic" blues performer should sound like. His overseas appearance in 1962 with the Rhythm and Blues USA tour in England and Germany helped introduce Hooker to an

a groove that Hooker had learned from his stepfather Will Moore, provided Hooker with a smash hit and initiated a marathon series of recordings on both Modern and Sensation. A number of his hits became blues standards, including his version of Tony Hollins's "Crawling King Snake," "Hobo Blues," and "I'm in the Mood." During this time Hooker had three wives: Alma Hopes, to whom he was married for a few months in the early 1940s and by whom he had a daughter, Frances; Sarah Jones, with whom he lived for about one year; and Maude Mathis, whom he met in 1944 and to whom he stayed married until they divorced in 1971. They had five children: Diane, John Lee Jr., Karen, Robert, and Zakiya. He was also married briefly to the Canadian Millie Strom in the late 1970s. Hooker continued to record for Modern until 1954; however, always on the lookout for moneymaking opportunities, he also recorded for the King, Regent/Savoy, Staff, Regal, Gone, Acorn/Chance, Chess, Deluxe, Gotham, JVB, Savoy, and Specialty labels, becoming one of the most recorded blues performers of all time. He is also one of the most pseudonymously recorded bluesmen of all time, international audience and instituted a new phase of his career, during which both his early recordings, which had generated a number of African American imitators, and his newer folk performances were copied by white electric blues bands such as Canned Heat and ZZ Top in America and the Animals and the Groundhogs in England. This set the stage for frequent American and European tours, appearances on the *Dick Cavett Show* (1969), *Midnight Special* (1974), and *Don Kirshner's Rock Concert* (1978), and, increasingly, recordings featuring white admirers among his accompanists. Highlights from this period include recordings with his cousin EARL HOOKER (1969) and the blues-rock group Canned Heat (1970), who provided sympathetic accompaniment and increased Hooker's visibility through joint touring in 1970. An appearance in the *Blues Brothers* movie (1980), recordings with Hank Williams Jr. (1984), and a contribution to the soundtrack of *The Color Purple* (1985) acknowledged his status as an elder statesman of the blues and set the stage for the album *The Healer* (1989), which featured Carlos Santana, Los Lobos, and Bonnie Raitt and won several Grammy awards, as did his last album of new recordings, *Don't Look Back* (1997). After the release of *The Healer*, Hooker became a staple of pop culture, appearing in advertisements and in videos on MTV, and collaborating on *The Hot Spot* movie soundtrack (1990) with MILES DAVIS. Increasingly fragile toward the end of his life, Hooker died in his sleep at his home in Los Altos, California.

John Lee Hooker is one of the great performers in the history of American music, and though his influence can be heard in the music of several successive generations, his primary importance still rests in his expression of the deepest human emotions in music of surpassing originality and beauty. Appropriately, he was one of the original performers inducted into the Blues Foundation's Blues Hall of Fame in 1980 and was inducted into the Rock and Roll Hall of Fame in 1991.

FURTHER READING

Fancourt, Leslie. *Boogie Chillun: A Guide to John Lee Hooker on Disc* (1992).

Murray, Charles Shaar. *Boogie Man: The Adventures of John Lee Hooker in the American Twentieth Century* (2000).

Obrecht, Jas, ed. *Blues Guitar: The Men Who Made the Music: From the Pages of Guitar Player Magazine* (1993).

Obituary: *The Guardian* (U.K.), 23 June 2001.

DISCOGRAPHY

Complete John Lee Hooker, 1948–1951 (vols. 1–4, Body and Soul 3057012, 3063142, 3067872, 3074242).
Ultimate Collection, 1948–1990 (Rhino 70572).
The Vee-Jay Years, 1955–1964.

STEVEN C. TRACY

hooks, bell (25 Sept. 1952–), intellectual, feminist, educator, cultural critic, social activist, and poet, was born Gloria Jean Watkins in Hopkinsville, Kentucky, to Veodis Watkins, a custodian, and Rosa Bell Watkins, a housekeeper. One of seven children, hooks grew up in a poor family in which poetry was a well-respected art form. On stormy nights the Watkins family would host talent shows in their living room. As a youth, hooks would recite poems by such authors as LANGSTON HUGHES and JAMES WELDON JOHNSON. By the age of ten, hooks was already writing and reading her own work.

Hooks attended BOOKER T. WASHINGTON Elementary, a segregated black school. Her teachers, mostly single black women, nurtured and fostered her young mind. With the integration of public schools in the 1960s, however, black students were bused to white schools. Hooks soon learned that the white teachers at CRISPUS ATTUCKS High School valued obedience from black children rather than intellect (Burke, B., 2005). When hooks ventured outside her mostly black town she was greeted with prejudice and marginalization. Her views on gender and race were shaped by such experiences. These memories would later heavily influence and inform her cultural critiques.

Despite the discriminatory treatment she received from her teachers, hooks graduated in 1968 and earned a scholarship to Stanford University. While there, she worked as a telephone operator. Though the job left little time for writing, her coworkers—a group of working-class black women—were supportive of hooks in the way her teachers had been in Hopkinsville. As an undergraduate at Stanford, hooks met poet and novelist NATHANIEL MACKEY. The pair subsequently lived together for more than ten years. In 1973 hooks received a B.A. in English. She then went on to the University of Wisconsin, where she received her M.A. in English in 1976. Before receiving a Ph.D. in literature in 1983 from the University of California, Santa Cruz, hooks worked at the university as a lecturer in English and ethnic studies.

The name hooks eventually assumed was her great-grandmother's. She changed her name as homage to female legacies and rendered it in lowercase to accentuate the substance of her work, rather than her identity. She adopted the name bell hooks in 1978 with the release of her first book, *And There We Wept*, which was a chapbook of poems published by Golemics. She has used the alias ever since.

Hooks's *Ain't I a Woman?: Black Women and Feminism* (1981), the first in a series of studies marking the historic ties between black women and feminism, was published by South End Press. This was followed by *Feminist Theory: From Margin to Center* (1984) and *Talking Back: Thinking Feminist, Thinking Black* (1989). In *Talking Back* hooks coined the phrase "white supremacist capitalist patriarchy," which was referenced by a number of authors, including James D. Anderson, Eithne Quinn, Carolyn Moxley Rouse, and William H. Watkins. From 1985 to 1988 hooks taught African American studies and English at Yale University.

In 1992 a *Publishers Weekly* poll called hooks's *Ain't I a Woman?* "one of the twenty most influential women's books in the last 20 years," and hooks was awarded the Writer's Award from the Lila Wallace-Reader's Digest Fund in 1994. She was chosen as one of the *Utne Reader*'s "100 Visionaries Who Could Change Your Life" in 1995.

As a cultural critic, hooks explored the interconnectedness of race, class, gender, and sexuality throughout her work. She wrote more than thirty books, including three children's books and numerous essays on the arts and pop culture, including *Black Looks: Race and Representation* (1992), *Art on My Mind: Visual Politics* (1995), and *Reel to Real: Race, Sex and Class at the Movies* (1996).

Hooks was a favorite speaker on college campuses and the community forum circuit. She joined the faculty of Oberlin College in 1988 and joined the City College of New York in the Women's Studies and English departments in 1995. She even appeared in such films as *Black Is, Black Ain't* (1994), *Give a Damn Again* (1995), *Cultural Criticism and Transformation* (1997), and *My Feminism* (1997).

Hooks was nominated for a National Association for the Advancement of Colored People Image Award in 2001 and the Hurston Wright Legacy Award in 2001. Her children's book *Homemade Love* (2002) was awarded the Bank Street College Children's Book of the Year. The *Atlantic Monthly* referred to hooks as "One of our nation's leading public intellectuals." bell hooks went from bearing the brunt of marginalization to being a recognized critic of it. In 2004 she joined the faculty of Kentucky's Berea College as the Distinguished

Professor in Residence. In 2009 hooks published *Belonging: A Culture of Place*, an examination of black rural life and identity in the 20th century.

Inspired by such thinkers as feminist SOJOURNER TRUTH, Brazilian educator Paulo Freire, theologian Gustavo Guitierrez, playwright LORRAINE HANSBERRY, writer JAMES BALDWIN, and civil rights leaders MALCOLM X and MARTIN LUTHER KING JR., hooks was also heavily influenced by her experiences with Buddhism. She once said, "My cause is the cause of justice it has no race no gender no class because my mission as a thinker as an activist is to be part of the struggle to end domination wherever it arises" (*blackademics online,* 15 Dec. 2006).

FURTHER READING

Florence, Namulundah. *Bell Hooks' Engaged Pedagogy: A Transgressive Education for Critical Consciousness* (1998).

Freelon, Pierce. Interview with bell hooks. *Blackademics,* 15 December 2006.

Leatherman, Courtney. "Gloria Watkins: The Real bell hooks," *The Chronicle of Higher Education,* 19 May 1995.

Mayo, Kierna. "bell hooks," *Emerge* (March 1997).

NICOLE SEALEY

Hooks, Benjamin Lawson (31 Jan. 1925–15 Apr. 2010), minister, judge, and executive director of the NAACP, was born in Memphis, Tennessee, to Robert Britton Hooks, a photographer, and Bessie White Hooks. He was the fifth of seven children. Hooks hailed from one of the most prominent African American families in Memphis; his grandmother Julia Britton Hooks was the first black to attend Berea College. At age sixteen Hooks enrolled at his father's alma mater, Le Moyne College in Memphis, but he was drafted and enlisted in the army before he could complete his degree. After serving from 1943 to 1946 in Italy, Hooks returned to the United States and enrolled at DePaul University Law School. He completed his law degree in 1948 and opened a private practice in Memphis, only the second African American to practice law in the city. Hooks married Frances Dancy, a childhood acquaintance, on 20 March 1951; the couple had one adopted daughter, Patricia Louise Hooks Gray.

Hooks juggled several entrepreneurial ventures with his legal practice. In 1952 he opened a grocery store with his brother Robert. Four years later he organized a federal savings and loan association with his law partner A. W. Willis. He subsequently launched a fast food chain, Mahalia Jackson Chicken, which featured the gospel singer MAHALIA JACKSON as its primary spokesperson. Mahalia Jackson Chicken had twenty-seven stores in seven states by the early 1960s, but it foundered in the wake of mismanagement by its parent company, Minnie Pearl Chicken, and filed for bankruptcy in 1969. Yet Hooks remained convinced that his entrepreneurialism represented a model for blacks to emulate, because he believed that black-owned businesses played a critical role in the struggle for racial equality.

Given his enterprising spirit it is perhaps ironic that Hooks rose to prominence through his groundbreaking legal career rather than as a result of his business exploits. He became the first African American to serve as public defender in Memphis, in 1961. Failed bids for state office did not dim Hooks's star, and in 1965 Tennessee Governor Frank Clement appointed him criminal court judge in Shelby County—another first for an African American in Tennessee. Hooks's appointment to the bench made him the first black judge in the South since Reconstruction. He brokered changes in the jury pool selection process and promoted the practice of suspending sentences for first-time offenders. Hooks's ties to the core leadership of the civil rights movement strengthened during his tenure on the bench, especially after MARTIN LUTHER KING JR. was assassinated in Hooks's hometown on 4 April 1968. Hooks quietly but forcefully advocated for change within the judicial system, and his efforts caught the attention of regional and national leaders.

In 1972 President Richard Nixon appointed Hooks to be a commissioner of the Federal Communications Commission (FCC). This appointment—another first for an African American—thrust Hooks into a growing debate about the dearth of black actors and entertainers, and he championed the few African Americans who graced the small screen. He also fought for minority ownership of radio stations and television licenses. As Equal Employment Opportunity chairman of the FCC, Hooks pushed for affirmative action programs that changed the face of the entertainment industry. By the end of his brief tenure at the FCC, minority employment in the entertainment industry had increased fivefold.

Hooks's success in advocating for minority rights at the FCC won him an even more prestigious role: the NAACP board elected Hooks executive director on 6 November 1976, replacing the retiring ROY WILKINS. But Hooks's tenure had a rocky start. The chairperson of the NAACP Board, Margaret Bush Wilson, attempted to dismiss Hooks in 1983 after the two disagreed over policy matters. But the majority of the sixty-four-member NAACP board backed Hooks rather than Wilson, and he emerged from the clash with firm command over the organization. Hooks parlayed his power into efforts to make the NAACP more relevant to a nation that thought the civil rights movement was past its prime. At times, he succeeded. NAACP marches against South Africa played a key role in swinging American opinion against that nation's racist policies and may have contributed to the eventual collapse of the apartheid system. Hooks led the NAACP in its stand against the appointment of CLARENCE THOMAS to the U.S. Supreme Court and in its denunciation of the judicial system after the 1992 RODNEY KING verdict. But the 1980s were the decade of Reaganism, and Hooks's NAACP found itself marginalized by the Republican administration and largely ignored by the youngest generation of African Americans. He felt overburdened with his role as executive director and chafed at the notion that the NAACP had grown stale. Even so, Hooks guided the nation's largest civil rights organization through budgetary crises and internal conflicts, leaving the NAACP on solid financial and organization footing when he resigned in 1992. The organization awarded Hooks its highest honor, the Spingarn Medal, in 1986.

Throughout his professional career Hooks served in a role he had held since his days as a young lawyer: Baptist minister. Hooks felt a desire to enter the ministry as a teenager, though his father pushed him to pursue a legal career. But a nagging sense of calling—and an open pulpit—led Hooks to begin serving Greater Middle Baptist Church in Memphis in 1956, a position he continued to hold nearly fifty years later. He took on another church, Mount Moriah Baptist Church in Detroit, in 1964. Hooks served both churches for thirty years, flying to each city on alternating weekends, before resigning from Mount Moriah in 1994. Hooks's faith propelled many of his more high-profile activities. He couched much of his oratory in the cadence of black preachers, and he often relied on the language of spirituals in his speeches and sermons. Hooks's faith in institutions—the legal profession, the judiciary, and the NAACP—seems a bit anachronistic in twenty-first-century America, but it resonates with his abiding connection to that most important of black institutions, the church. He died in Memphis at the age of 85.

FURTHER READING

Benjamin Hooks donated his papers to the Benjamin L. Hooks Institute for Social Change at the University of Memphis. Significant excerpts of his speeches can be found there, as well as in the *Crisis*, the NAACP's official magazine.

Hooks, Benjamin L., with Jerry Guess. *The March for Civil Rights: The Benjamin Hooks Story* (2003).

Warner, Ede, Jr., and Bernard L. Brock. "Benjamin Lawson Hooks," in *African-American Orators: A Bio-Critical Sourcebook*, ed. Richard W. Leeman (1996).

Obituary: *Commercial Appeal*, 15 Apr. 2010.

SETH DOWLAND

Hooks, Mathew "Bones" (3 Nov. 1867–2 Feb. 1951), a cowboy and town founder most famous for honoring enduring pioneers with single white flowers, was born in Orangeville, Texas, the eldest son of two former slaves, Alex and Annie Hooks. While still at the Hooks Plantation, located outside of Texarkana, Alex had learned to read and write (his owner taught him in defiance of the law and used him as a bookkeeper), which helped him avoid the economic toils so many penniless freedmen faced in the postbellum South. In Orangeville, Alex Hooks became a preacher and prominent educator in that tiny town's black community, and the Bible, accordingly, played a dominant role in the education of his five sons and three daughters. Wiry, skinny Mathew Hooks soon went by the nickname "Bones" and developed such rugged attitudes and salt-of-the-earth perseverance as would enable his successes in the Lone Star State. Among them were an uncompromising abstinence from alcohol and cigarettes, a knack for understatement, and a penchant for backbreaking labor. He learned to handle draft animals and maneuver a butcher's wagon before he turned seven, which was when the Denton-County cattleman D. Steve Donald employed him to drive an oxcart back to his ranch north of Dallas. The cowboys on the trek were impressed, and Donald rehired Bones for four successive summers as he returned for more cattle-buying trips. Then, at age eleven, Bones Hooks stayed in Denton for good.

In 1870s Texas, cattle-ranching remained the way of the future. The heyday of the cotton plantations had passed and the state's economy now reverted to the free-roaming herds of mustangs and longhorn cattle that had been wandering its prairies since the time of the Spanish Empire. The East and West of the United States hungered for beef, and ranchers in the North bought up cattle for their own herds. Stock prices consequently skyrocketed and ranchers hired vaqueros to brand about 5.7 million cattle and herd them out of state between 1866 and 1885. The droves at times lasted three to four months and spanned up to twelve hundred miles. Between 4 and 25 percent of Texas's cowboys were African American (estimates vary), and it was on the DSD ranch that Mathew Hooks, too, learned the tricks of this trade.

By the time he reached his teens, Bones was no longer bucked by any bronco. The lightweight boy broke horses often without bridle or saddle and mastered even supposedly untamable "outlaws." The demand for mustangs was high—several hundred could form the *remuda* that accompanied a cattle drove—and Hooks earned a respectable income. The affection he felt for the mighty animals, many of whom he named after their peculiarities ("Fox Trot"), other animals ("Coyote"), or girls who caught his attention ("Miss Sally Chisum"), made Mathew the ideal wrangler. He cared for the cowboys' steeds on many a roundup, staying faithful all the while to his trusty mule, "Dinamite." When Donald expanded his business into Oklahoma Indian Territory, his vaqueros no longer worried solely about rattlesnakes and stampedes—they now also feared "Indian raids." As he explored the territory west of his ranch, toward Henrietta, Donald lost sixteen-year-old Bones to J. R. Norris of JRE Ranch by the Pecos River. Mathew and Dinamite beat one of Norris's cowboys in an impromptu race and Bones signed up with his stunned new employer for the price of five horses and a fresh pair of boots. He set Dinamite free on the prairies.

Bones's new home then still seemed as unruly as a pitching mustang. Native Americans and large herds of buffalo competed with the cowboys and their longhorn cattle over the dried-up grass of the Panhandle plains. Yet the buffalo were slaughtered and the U.S. military muscled the original Americans out of their home. As new towns sprouted out of the desert ground, Bones Hooks shunned their saloons as dens of alcoholism and other sinful distractions. He preferred Clarendon, a five-year-old community that took pride in its strict Methodist Christianity. Yet in the early 1880s, several years after the end of Reconstruction, not even this town easily accepted a black resident. In spite of the racism he encountered (the men would not eat at the same table with him and enjoyed firing blanks at his feet), Bones admired the pioneers and the resilience of those who refused to quit. The women, in particular, were on his side, and he was in awe of their determination to church work, voting the town dry, and raising children—whom he helped care for—under adverse circumstances. The cowboys, too, he eventually befriended on many a trail on which water was so sparse that thirst kept Bones awake some nights and the steady southwesterly winds provided the only means of orientation in the endless open. During these years, Hooks worked for almost every notable ranch in the area, including the largest, XIT, and his connections across the Panhandle once even saved his life. A team of rustlers who had Bones in their employ as a wrangler got surrounded by vigilantes and was hanged on the spot. Hooks escaped certain death— with the noose already around his neck—only because "Skillety Bill" of Frying Pan Ranch put in a good word for him. Bones worked in North Texas and Oklahoma for a while until memory of the incident faded. A different fellow cattle thief would become a judge in later years and encounter Hooks again, in a courtroom, where they would conceal their secret in winking complicity.

In spite of his run-in with the makeshift authorities, Hooks himself joined the vigilantes upon his return to the Panhandle. Among the twelve to fifteen hasty executions performed in his time, one particularly memorable incident had Bones holding the horses, as usual, while the self-appointed judges sentenced a rustler to death by hanging, the common outcome of such "trials." The "convict" asked to have the sentence executed only by someone who had never stolen cattle or horses. None was able to step forward and the thief was let go.

Yet the days of collective rounding up of cattle, branding of calves, and herding of longhorns to Kansas, during which Bones Hooks and countless cowboys from neighboring ranches freely collaborated, were numbered. The debilitating winter of 1886 and the subsequent drought coincided with an outbreak of tick fever and decimated thousands of cattle. In those years, a final, manmade trend delivered the fatal blow to the huge, unimpeded droves so distinctive of previous decades: ranchers and farmers had proceeded to fence in their property with barbed wire. Ultimately, Mathew Hooks would need a new profession.

A brief intermission had Bones sell his own livestock and invest the profits in a grocery store in Wamba near Texarkana, but the "White Caps of Sand Gall Gizzard" scared him out of town. Back in the Clarendon area by 1887, Hooks—only twenty years old—returned to training horses for the changing cattle industry, whose surviving ranchers now owned far larger estates and relied more heavily on the railroad. In 1896 Hooks helped out on his last trail. By then, he had also ventured into self-employment. Earlier in the decade, the expert broncobuster had started a horse-training and -selling business with his white friend Tom Clayton, who managed the financial side. Their partnership was close and warm though not always free from racial tensions and ended abruptly when Tommy was crushed by his falling horse in 1894. Bones stayed with the drove's *remuda*, but sent a bouquet of Clayton's favorite white flowers after his dying friend. The courier could only hand it to Tommy's mother, who placed it on her son's coffin. It was after this tragic turn that Bones started honoring other hardy Texan individualists with white flowers.

As racial tensions increased in the segregating nation even for the fifty or so blacks living in the Panhandle, Bones made Clarendon somewhat of a safe haven by establishing a black church there in 1894. Despite adamant support among white Texans for the Democratic nominee, William Jennings Bryan, Hooks not only voted for William McKinley in the 1896 presidential elections, he also wagered (and won) money on the Republican candidate.

In 1900, at age thirty-three, Bones Hooks settled down. He married Indiana ("Anna") Crenshaw, one of very few black women in the Panhandle, and heeded her advice to seek a safer career in Amarillo. There, the couple worked for the Elmhurst Hotel and in ensuing years Bones became the first black juror in Potter County and joined many associations of former cowboys, where he was famous for his chili-cooking skills. In 1909 he accepted a job offer from the Santa Fe Railroad and would travel as far as San Francisco and Chicago as a Pullman Porter. In 1910, forty-three-year-old Hooks overheard a conversation among traveling ranchers about an untamable horse in Pampa, Texas. Bones bet money he could handle him, got off the train in Pampa, took off his porter's uniform, and rode the steed into submission. Though now famous on the trains, Bones never joined ASA PHILIP RANDOLPH's efforts at forming an effective union of Pullman Porters. In 1920 he buried his wife and remarried two years later, but the marriage to Minnie (née Bishop), who brought a daughter, Georgia, to the relationship, did not last. He divorced her in 1930. That same year, at age sixty-three, he also retired from the railroad on a disability pension.

Bones devoted the rest of his life to community service. In September 1930, he bought a sizable portion of land outside of Amarillo and established a black community at North Heights. A park dedicated there in 1932 was later renamed the Mathew Hooks Memorial. In his spare time, Hooks educated impoverished and orphaned boys in his Dogie Club, some of whom he would recruit as Selective Servicemen in World War II. The Panhandle Plains Museum is among the many historical clubs he founded, and before his life was over, he had sent five hundred white flowers as "Guerdons of Honor" to soldiers, U.N. delegates, and even a U.S. President (Franklin Delano Roosevelt).

An illness Bones contracted in 1949 bankrupted the eighty-one-year-old pioneer. Since he had no family, friends immediately raised money to pay for his care. Mathew "Bones" Hooks died at age eighty-three, after a full life that is often forgotten in such tales from the West as focus on white cowboys. His fellow pioneer John Trolinger honored their interracial friendship by placing a single white flower on Bones's coffin.

FURTHER READING

The Panhandle Plains Museum at West Texas A&M University in Canyon, Texas, houses the papers of Mathew Hooks.

Crimm, Ana Carolina Castillo. "Mathew 'Bones' Hooks: A Pioneer of Honor." In Sara R. Massey, ed., *Black Cowboys of Texas*, pp. 218–245 (2000).

Todd, Bruce G. *Bones Hooks: Pioneer Negro Cowboy* (2005).

MATHIAS HANSES

Hope, Elmo (27 June 1923–19 May 1967), jazz pianist and composer, was born St. Elmo Sylvester Hope in New York City. His parents, whose names are unknown, were from the West Indies. He studied the European piano tradition and often practiced with his boyhood friend BUD POWELL. Hope was giving recitals at the age of fifteen, but he and Powell as teenagers recognized the barriers to African Americans pursuing concert careers in classical music, and they turned to jazz.

By the mid-1940s Powell was widely acclaimed as the greatest pianist in the bop style. Hope would remain a permanently obscure figure for diverse reasons, of which probably the most important was an incapacitating addiction to heroin. His uncompromising personality and complex musical style also seem to have been factors in limiting his achievements.

Early in his career Hope often performed in unknown bands at low-class venues, and his most stable affiliation was with the trumpeter Joe Morris's rhythm and blues band from 1948 to 1951. Over the next five years notable activities were restricted to his occasional appearances in the studio. In June 1953 he recorded with the trumpeter CLIFFORD BROWN, who at this session used two of Hope's compositions, "Carving the Rock" and "De-Dah." That same month Hope recorded as the leader of a trio that included the bassist PERCY HEATH and the drummer PHILLY JOE JONES, both of whom had also worked with Morris. Further sessions as a leader came in 1954 and 1956, the latter date including the tenor saxophonists HANK MOBLEY and JOHN COLTRANE. With the tenor saxophonist Frank Foster, Hope co-led a session released under Foster's name as *Wail, Frank, Wail* (1955), and he recorded as a sideman with the alto saxophonists Lou Donaldson, in 1954, and JACKIE MCLEAN, in 1956.

At some point—probably in 1956—Hope spent several months in jail on Riker's Island in New York, presumably for a narcotics conviction. In 1957, having lost his New York City cabaret card and the consequent right to perform in local nightclubs, he accepted an invitation to tour with the trumpeter Chet Baker to Los Angeles. The job offered potential venues for work and also the possibility that the not yet excessively smoggy climate would ease the effects of Hope's emphysema.

Hope had been married at some earlier point, and a son had died; no other details are known. In 1957 he met his second wife, Bertha (maiden name unknown), a pianist, while he was accompanying SONNY ROLLINS at the Hillcrest in Los Angeles. In October he recorded as the leader of a quintet that included the tenor saxophonist Harold Land. In March 1958 Hope joined the bassist Curtis Counce's group and recorded with Counce the following month.

In 1959 Hope worked briefly with the vibraphonist LIONEL HAMPTON in Hollywood. Together with the bassist Scott LaFaro and the drummer Lennie McBrowne, he accompanied Rollins at the Jazz Workshop in San Francisco. Land then took over from Rollins, leading the group for two weeks at the Cellar in Vancouver. In August 1959, as a member of a quintet under Land's leadership, Hope recorded one of his two finest albums, *The Fox,* presenting four of his own compositions, "Mirror-Mind Rose," "One Second, Please," "Sims-a-Plenty," and "One Down." Hope married Bertha in 1960; they had three children. Early that year, with the bassist Jimmy Bond and the drummer Frank Butler, he recorded his second great album, *Elmo Hope Trio,* including a representative sampling of his compositions: "B's A-Plenty," "Barfly," "Eejah," "Boa," "Something for Kenny," "Minor Bertha," and "Tranquility."

Having found no more than the occasional opportunity to work on the West Coast, Hope returned to New York City, even though he was still without a cabaret card. In the 1960s, as Hope's health declined, he led further recording sessions that resulted in seven albums, all offering additional examples of his talents as a composer and an interpreter of bop. None of these is up to the high standard of the earlier albums, but the quirky brilliance of Hope's playing shines through, for example, in his rendering of DIZZY GILLESPIE's "A Night in Tunisia" from one of his last sessions in 1966. That same year Hope last performed in public in a concert at New York City's Judson Hall. In May 1967 he was hospitalized for pneumonia, and a few weeks later he died suddenly in New York City of a heart attack.

Hope was one of the most esoteric of bop musicians. His piano style was too personalized to have served as a model for other players, and his roughly seventy-five bop themes have yet to enter the repertoire of jazz standards, both because of their difficulty and because Hope evidently discarded notated versions once the music had been learned. These compositions range in character from a tortuous nervousness to an introspective, semilyrical romanticism. Some are extraordinarily creative. "Minor Bertha," for example, is notable not merely for the use of a 35-bar theme, with phrases of 9 plus 9 plus 8 plus 9 measures in place of the conventional 32 bars (8+8+8+8), but much more importantly for the quality of the repeated 9-bar-long segment, in which Hope elides together uncommon rhythms and purposefully weak harmonic relationships to confuse and to soften transitions from one phrase to the next. "One Down" offers another excellent example of his manner of restlessly spinning out ideas, while pieces like "Barfly" and the drumless but not entirely tranquil "Tranquility" transfer this approach into a ballad setting.

In a description cast negatively though nonetheless accurately, Alan Groves writes: "Hope's scores are complex, original, with typically involved chord sequences, all personally idiosyncratic.... Such music ... is not direct, does not swing violently, and Hope is withdrawn, oblique, and almost ignores the rhythm section at times. Listened to casually, it makes no impression." Hope constantly challenges his audience, but rewards are there if one wishes to make the effort to listen carefully.

FURTHER READING
Groves, Alan. "The Forgotten Ones: Elmo Hope," *Jazz Journal International* 36 (June 1983).
Obituary: *Jazz Journal* 20 (July 1967).
This entry is taken from the *American National Biography* and is published here with the permission of the American Council of Learned Societies.
BARRY KERNFELD

Hope, John (2 June 1868–20 Feb. 1936), educator, was born in Augusta, Georgia, the son of James Hope, a wealthy white Scotsman who came to America in 1817, and Mary Frances Butts, who was born a slave in 1839. John's great-grandmother, Mary, had been raped by a Georgia planter at the age of sixteen and gave birth to John's grandmother, Lethea. She in turn had seven children by a neighboring slave owner, including John's mother, Mary "Fanny" Frances. As a young woman, Fanny became a housekeeper in the home of a prominent white physician, Dr. George M. Newton. Shortly after joining the household, Fanny became pregnant with the first of two children she had with Dr. Newton before his death in 1859. James Hope, a business associate of Dr. Newton's, then invited Fanny into his home. They lived openly as husband and wife and had four children, the third being John Hope.

In referring to the relationship between Thomas Jefferson and his slave Sally Hemings, essayist Shelby Steele suggests that many slave women belonged to an invisible "companion class" to white men of power and wealth. This state of affairs marked John Hope's life in two important ways: in all outward appearances, John was white; but, having been raised in the bosom of the black community, he thought of himself as an African American and was determined to improve the lot of "his people." John was only eight years old when his father died, and though his mother retained the house they lived in, the rest of the estate went to his father's white relatives or was mishandled by the executors of the will. Consequently, John grew up in the South during Reconstruction in a family with little financial means. He attended the Fourth

John Hope, educator, president of Morehouse College and Atlanta University. (University of Massachusetts, Amherst.)

Ward Colored School, a single structure housing the primary, intermediate, and grammar schools. The school was poorly financed and offered only a rudimentary curriculum, but the students there were fortunate to have motivated and highly trained teachers. John worked hard for average grades, and when he graduated from the eighth grade he decided to forgo high school; thus, at the age of thirteen it seemed that he had reached the end of his formal education.

For five years John worked as a wine steward and bookkeeper at Henson's Restaurant, a black-owned establishment in Augusta that excluded black patrons because its owner wanted to cater to a white clientele. John detested this policy, and the experience helped shape his attitude about intraracial bigotry among blacks. Equally profound was the religious conversion that John and his mother underwent in 1886. The Reverend John Dart, a young evangelist from Providence, Rhode Island, who became the pastor of Union Baptist Church, so moved John and his mother that they publicly confessed their sins, foreswore drinking, smoking, and card playing, and were baptized in the Savannah River.

It was Dart who persuaded John, at age eighteen, to attend Worcester Academy in Massachusetts. John worked at odd jobs to pay his tuition and suffered many economic privations, but he endured them all to graduate first in his class in 1890. That September he enrolled at Brown University in Providence, Rhode Island, expecting to pursue a career in the ministry. As in prep school, John worked at local restaurants to meet his expenses. He also wrote articles for the *Brown Daily Herald*. The most popular social organizations on campus were the Brown fraternities. However, they had a "gentleman's agreement" not to admit persons of color. John was very familiar with "passing," the practice of some African Americans with very light complexions to pass for white, and he even knew family members who were passing. In 1893 he was invited by a friend to join an all-white fraternity on the tacit understanding that he would keep his black identity a secret. John indignantly refused. In later years, if people appeared to be confused about his race, John would proudly inform them that he was a "colored man."

Still deeply religious, John attended services at the black Pond Street Baptist Church on the west side of the city. There he cofounded a small literary club called the Enquirers, which sponsored social events and read works by PHILLIS WHEATLEY, FREDERICK DOUGLASS, and other African Americans. In this way John began to develop his leadership abilities and to create a more vibrant black community than the one he found on the campus of Brown University. By his senior year he had achieved a stellar academic record and was chosen to give the student address on Class Day in June 1894. His speech was titled "Brown University," but his remarks were an uncritical recitation of the virtues of what he called a "superior Western Civilization." The faculty advisory committee was so taken with John's performance that the afternoon before commencement the chairman, Professor Appleton, offered John a position that they had secured for him at the *Providence Journal*. When John told them that he wanted to return to the South and work in the black community, they regarded his decision as a foolish waste of talent.

In the fall of 1894, Hope began his teaching career at Roger Williams University in Nashville, Tennessee. Four years later he became a professor of classics at Atlanta Baptist College, founded by white missionaries in a church basement in 1867 as Augusta Institute, a seminary for the training of black men. When Hope arrived in Atlanta with his wife, LUGENIA BURNS HOPE, there was only one other black professor on the faculty. The dominant model for black higher education had been set by Samuel Armstrong at Hampton Institute in Virginia and his protégé, BOOKER T. WASHINGTON, who established Tuskegee Institute in Alabama. Both institutions stressed industrial training and character development as their primary missions. In fact, Hope was sitting in the audience at the famous 1895 Atlanta Cotton States and International Exposition when Washington offered the following compromise on the race question: Negroes would not press for social or political equality as long as white society assisted them in their quest for economic and moral development.

Hope had great personal admiration for Washington and well understood the challenges of raising funds to support black education, yet he vehemently disagreed with Washington's philosophical approach to education and civil rights. At one of his first public speeches Hope asked rhetorically, "If we are not striving for equality, in heaven's name for what are we living" (Davis, 87). Hope's open dissent on this issue aligned him with W. E. B. DuBois, a close friend, and WILLIAM MONROE TROTTER, who formed the Niagara Movement in opposition to Washington. When Hope became the first black president of Atlanta Baptist College in 1906, he seized the opportunity to provide an alternative vision of black higher education, emphasizing classical training and preparation for professional occupations.

During Hope's twenty-five-year tenure as president of Atlanta Baptist College, the institution changed its name to Morehouse College, its all-male student enrollment increased fivefold, and its faculty and academic curriculum were of the highest caliber. Hope managed to accomplish so much because, unlike Washington or DuBois, he developed a leadership style that allowed him to speak forcefully on racial issues without alienating white supporters. While president of Morehouse, he played an active role in the NAACP, was a representative at the first "Amenia Conference" of African American leaders in 1916, attended the Pan-African Congress in Paris in 1919, served on the board of the National Urban League, and was a president of the Association for the Study of Negro Life and History. Hope's crowning academic achievement was the role he played in the creation of the Atlanta University Center in 1929. Under this arrangement, Morehouse and Spelman Colleges would continue their undergraduate programs while Atlanta University supplied graduate studies in several academic disciplines. In 1931 Hope was unanimously elected president of Atlanta University, where he served until his death in 1936.

FURTHER READING

The John and Lugenia Burns Hope papers are stored at the Atlanta University Center Archives.

Davis, Leroy. *A Clashing of the Soul: John Hope and the Dilemma of African American Leadership and Black Higher Education in the Early Twentieth Century* (1998).

Torrence, Ridgely. *The Story of John Hope* (1948).

SHOLOMO B. LEVY

Hope, Lugenia Burns (19 Feb. 1871–14 Aug. 1947), clubwoman, community organizer, and reformer, was born Lugenia D. Burns in St. Louis, Missouri, the daughter of Ferdinand Burns, a well-to-do carpenter, and Louisa M. Bertha. Burns was raised in a Grace Presbyterian, middle-class family. Her father's sudden death forced her mother to move the family to Chicago to maintain their class standing and provide Lugenia, or "Genie" as she was called, with educational opportunities absent in St. Louis. From 1890 to 1893, while her older siblings worked to support the family, Burns attended high school and classes at the Chicago School of Design, the Chicago Business College, and the Chicago Art Institute.

Burns quit school abruptly to help support the family as a bookkeeper and dressmaker. After several years she became the first African American secretary to the board of directors of King's Daughters, a charitable organization serving teenage working girls, the sick, and the poor. She also worked as the personal secretary to the director of the Silver Cross Club, which ran cafeterias for Chicago businessmen and -women, and she was the person in charge of workers for the Warne Addressing Establishment.

Burns's interest in charity and reform work paralleled Chicago's reform movement of the 1880s and 1890s. Her work as a clubwoman with King's Daughters and the Silver Cross Club introduced her to intellectuals from the University of Chicago, African American intellectuals such as PAUL LAURENCE DUNBAR, and the social worker Jane Addams. These mentors helped her to see how to use community organizations to fight crime and poverty and establish her identity as a social reform worker.

In Chicago Burns met Georgia-born JOHN HOPE, a theology student from Brown University. They were married on 29 December 1897 and moved to Nashville, Tennessee, where he became an instructor at Roger Williams University and taught classes in arts and crafts and women's physical education. In 1898 Hope moved to the Deep South when her husband joined the faculty at Atlanta Baptist College (later Morehouse College). He became its first African American president in 1906. The Hopes lived and worked in Atlanta, Georgia, for forty-nine years and had two sons. In Atlanta Hope soon joined a group of women working to establish day care centers in the West Fair community. The Neighborhood Union, the first female social welfare agency for African Americans in Atlanta, was born in 1908. During the twenty-five years that Hope headed the Neighborhood Union, African American women of the community developed employment and probation services, health and recreation campaigns, cleanup campaigns, fresh-air work, lecture courses, classes, clubs, and reading rooms. They used scientific reform techniques to conduct investigations of schools, sanitation, and vice in order to improve community life and encourage community responsibility.

Together with the sociology department at Morehouse College, Hope helped improve the quality of African American social work. The techniques developed through Atlanta's Neighborhood Union were used by other communities to help shape their social programs. As an affiliate of the National Urban League, the Neighborhood Union became the model for urban reform recommended by the league. In 1916 Hope also helped found the Atlanta branch of the National Association of Colored Women's Clubs.

During World War I the YMCA's Atlanta War Work Council for African American soldiers was directed by the Neighborhood Union, which asked for greater access to the city's public facilities, more recreational centers, and increased police protection. Success resulted in Hope's appointment in 1917 as director of the hostess house program for black soldiers at Camp Upton, New York, sponsored by the YWCA. Hope thought that African American service during World War I would lead to improved racial conditions in postwar America. When, in fact, discrimination and segregation worsened after the war, she organized African American women to pressure the YWCA to adopt more interracial policies and leadership.

From 1920 to 1940 Hope served as an assistant to MARY MCLEOD BETHUNE, director of the Negro Affairs Division of the National Youth Administration (NYA), helping to implement NYA programs in African American communities. In 1927 she served on Herbert Hoover's Colored Advisory Commission, established to investigate catastrophic flooding in Mississippi. Hope lectured on the national level for the National Council of Negro Women and helped organize the National Association of Colored Graduate Nurses. In 1932 she became the first vice president of the Atlanta chapter of the NAACP.

Hope demonstrated her remarkable organizational skills through the implementation of Atlanta's Neighborhood Union of which, from 1908 to 1935, she was founder, president, and chair of the board of managers. By dividing the city into zones, the zones into neighborhoods, and the neighborhoods into districts, her organizational plan called for direct community involvement. She worked tirelessly to provide health care for children and adults in African American communities and to improve the level of public school education. She was coordinator of the Gate City Free Kindergarten Association in 1908 and chair of the Women's Civic and Social Improvement Committee for better black schools in 1913. She informed and educated African Americans about government and citizenship using the citizenship schools of the NAACP, provided adequate and safe recreational facilities for children, and persuaded the YWCA to organize African American branches in the South on the basis of equality. She capitalized on her middle-class status, prestige, and influence to muster the support needed to help African Americans in Atlanta move progressively into the twentieth century. Lugenia Hope died of heart failure in Nashville, Tennessee.

FURTHER READING

Rouse, Jacqueline A. "The Legacy of Community Organizing: Lugenia Burns Hope and the Neighborhood Union," *Journal of Negro History* 69 (1984).

Rouse, Jacqueline A. *Lugenia Burns Hope: Black Southern Reformer* (1989).

Torrence, Fred Ridgely. *The Story of John Hope* (1948).

Obituaries: *Pittsburgh Courier* and *Chicago Defender*, 30 Aug. 1947.

This entry is taken from the *American National Biography* and is published here with the permission of the American Council of Learned Societies.

THEA GALLO BECKER

Hopkins, Claude (24 Aug. 1903–19 Feb. 1984), jazz bandleader and pianist, was born Claude Driskett Hopkins in Alexandria, Virginia, the son of Albert W. Hopkins and Gertrude D. (maiden name unknown), supervisors of a school for orphaned boys in Blue Plains, Virginia. Around 1913 the family moved to Washington, D.C., where his father became postmaster at Howard University and his mother became matron of a Howard dormitory. After public schooling Hopkins enrolled at Howard, where he excelled in athletics and scholarship. Concentrating on music theory and classical piano while beginning preparations for medical study, he earned a B.A. in music. Despite his parents' preference he chose to become a musician, having already worked casually in nightclubs and theaters during his college years.

Hopkins had heard the Harlem stride piano style on piano rolls by JAMES P. JOHNSON and FATS WALLER, and like other distinguished jazzmen, including Waller himself, Hopkins learned Johnson's test piece, "Carolina Shout," by playing the roll slowly and imitating the fingering. In New York City he worked for a few months with the clarinetist Wilber Sweatman. The banjoist ELMER SNOWDEN reported that Hopkins was in his big band, replacing Bill Basie (COUNT BASIE) as Snowden's pianist at New York's Bamville Club in 1925.

In the summer of 1925 Hopkins led a band in Atlantic City. When the job ended, he brought his five-piece band to the Smile Awhile Café in Asbury Park, New Jersey, where they won a job by outplaying Basie's group at an audition. Their performance at the café of a novelty version of "St. Louis Blues," featuring the trumpeter Henry Goodwin as a "preacher" and the other two wind players as the "sisters" of the congregation, secured the band a place in the *Revue Négre*. The revue traveled to Europe with JOSEPHINE BAKER as its star and the reed player SIDNEY BECHET added to Hopkins's instrumentalists. Hopkins had recently married Mabel (maiden name unknown), and she was taught to dance in the chorus so she could join the tour. Hopkins, an inveterate womanizer, had an undisguised affair with Baker while in transit to France. The *Revue Négre* debuted in Paris in October 1925 and toured in Belgium and Germany, finishing in Berlin in March 1926. Baker left for the *Folies Bergères* in Paris, and most of Hopkins's

sidemen took other jobs. Struggling to fulfill commitments and keep a band together, Hopkins spent the next year performing in Europe. He and his wife returned to the United States in March 1927; they had one child.

In Washington, Hopkins formed a seven-piece band, including the trombonist Sandy Williams, the saxophonists Hilton Jefferson and Elmer Williams, and the guitarist Bernard Addison. The band returned to the Smile Awhile Café and tried to break into the New York scene but failed. Hopkins then worked on his own. He wrote for and led a band in another musical revue, *The Ginger Snaps of 1928*, which toured the Theater Owners' Booking Circuit (TOBA), a circuit of theaters presenting African American performers. He returned to Washington after the show failed.

Hopkins led a band at the Fulton Gardens in Brooklyn for the balance of 1928 and into 1929, and he recorded two titles with CLARENCE WILLIAMS's Blue Five on 20 September 1928. He then replaced the pianist Charlie Skeets at a dime-a-dance hall in Manhattan; the band included the clarinetist EDMOND HALL. After taking over the band's leadership from Skeets, Hopkins secured a job in January 1930 at the Savoy Ballroom, where his understated approach to big-band jazz gave him a musical identity distinct from the typically extroverted bands that played at this venue. After the first night the Savoy manager Charlie Buchanan suggested a more hard-hitting approach; but Hopkins persisted, and as it turns out, the Savoy dancers loved his style. The band stayed there for most of 1930 and then moved to the more prestigious Roseland Ballroom.

Hopkins held residencies at Roseland from 1931 to April 1934 and broadcast nationally from the ballroom on the CBS radio network. In the spring of 1932 Hopkins began to take leaves from Roseland for extensive touring and for performances at Harlem theaters, including the Apollo. His band performed in the movies *Dance Team* (1931) and *Wayward* (1932). Hopkins wrote the band's theme song, "I Would Do Anything for You," featuring the trumpet playing and smooth-toned singing of Ovie Alston; this was their first recording, made on 24 May 1932. The same session featured the arranger JIMMY MUNDY's "Mush Mouth." By 1933 Hopkins had hired a "freak" attraction, the singer Orlando Robeson, whose falsetto ballad singing was featured on "Trees," heard in the band's film short *Barber Shop Blues* (1933) and on record in 1935.

Hopkins's touring and Harlem theater engagements continued for a year after the band left

Roseland, during which time he recorded "Three Little Words" and "Chasing All the Blues Away" (1934). In a move away from its focus on dance music, the band played for shows at the Cotton Club from March through December 1935 while also appearing in the movie short *Broadway Highlights*, filmed at the Cotton Club. Hopkins's last movie short, *By Request*, dates from late that same year.

When his club residencies in New York ended Hopkins took his band on North American tours from 1936 to 1940. His sidemen during this period included the trumpeter JABBO SMITH (1936–1937) and the trombonist VIC DICKENSON (1936–1939). Finally the band seems to have grown stale, and opportunities for work diminished. Hopkins disbanded in 1940 and declared bankruptcy a year later in 1941.

Hopkins had already written for other bands; ANDY KIRK's big band recorded his arrangement of "A Wednesday Night Hop" in 1937. In 1941 Hopkins's former arranger and trombonist, Fred Norman, procured some assignments for Hopkins as a commercial arranger, but he disliked this job and went to work at the Eastern Aircraft defense plant in New Jersey in 1942. In 1944 he formed a big band at the new Club Zanzibar in New York; he stayed there, directing and arranging, until 1947. He toured until 1949 as the leader of a small group, and he participated in USO tours, playing at veterans' hospitals in 1949 and 1950. He formed his own touring variety show, but this venue was unsuccessful.

After a period in Sheraton Hotel lounge bands Hopkins worked alongside the trumpeter DOC CHEATHAM and the trombonist Vic Dickenson in the pianist and promoter George Wein's band at Mahogany Hall in Boston (1951–1953). Hopkins worked with the trumpeter RED ALLEN at the Metropole Cafe in New York until 1960. He spent the next six years working at the Nevele, a Catskill resort in Ellenville, New York, with the trumpeter Shorty Baker, a drummer, and a singer. Back in New York City he joined the Jazz Giants, a six-piece group featuring the cornetist Wild Bill Davison; they toured for three years and recorded an album in Toronto in 1968. In the 1970s Hopkins mainly led his own groups or performed as a soloist, but early in the decade he also worked with the trumpeter ROY ELDRIDGE at Jimmy Ryan's Club in New York. In 1972 he recorded the unaccompanied stride piano albums *Crazy Fingers* and *Soliloquy*. From 1974 he made annual tours of European festivals. Hopkins's health started to fail while he was in Europe in 1979. He died in a nursing home in the Riverdale section of New York City.

Studio recordings by Hopkins's big band are routinely criticized as undistinguished, unoriginal, and unmemorable. The solo albums of 1972 are offered as his finest recorded legacy, presenting in high fidelity the prewar Harlem stride piano style. Without arguing with this general assessment, one might make an exception for "Three Little Words" from the session of 6 April 1934. Hopkins's rollicking stride piano solo, underpinned by soft saxophone chords, gives way to his heavily percussive accompaniment to the saxophones' smooth statement of the melody; from there the band moves into tight ensemble work. With these segments glued together by a wonderfully bouncy rhythm section, one can begin to understand why Hopkins's somewhat unusual blend of stride and swing and soft pop was such a favorite of the Savoy and Roseland dancers.

FURTHER READING

Bernhardt, Clyde E. B., and Sheldon Harris. *I Remember: Eighty Years of Black Entertainment, Big Bands, and the Blues* (1986).

Dance, Stanley. *The World of Swing* (1974).

Vaché, Warren W. *Crazy Fingers: Claude Hopkins' Life in Jazz* (1992).

Obituary: *New York Times*, 23 Feb. 1984.

DISCOGRAPHY

Fernett, Gene. *Swing Out: Great Negro Jazz Bands* (1970).

Selchow, Manfred. *Profoundly Blue: A Bio-Discographical Scrapbook on Edmond Hall* (1988).

This entry is taken from the *American National Biography* and is published here with the permission of the American Council of Learned Societies.

BARRY KERNFELD

Hopkins, Esther (16 Sept. 1926–), chemist, patent attorney, and legislator, was born Esther Arvilla Harrison in Stamford, Connecticut, the only daughter of George Burgess Harrison and Esther Smalls Harrison. Her father was a chauffeur and custodian at a church and her mother worked in domestic service. Neither of her parents had an advanced education—her father had some high school education and her mother attended only primary school. She started school at the same time as her older brother, having tested into kindergarten at the age of three and a half. She and her brother continued to go to school together through elementary school. In high school Esther was on the pre-college track, taking all the science courses available to her. She had determined to become a brain surgeon after meeting a female brain surgeon in one of the offices her father cleaned. She was impressed by this woman and decided to attend Boston University as the doctor had done.

Harrison attended Boston University (BU) in 1943 as a pre-med student, with her hardworking parents sacrificing to pay the tuition bills. Although she had a scholarship to cover many of her bills, she had to live off campus because the university would not allow African Americans to live in the dormitories. She majored in chemistry rather than biology because she loved the style of reasoning involved. In 1947 she graduated Phi Beta Kappa and applied to Boston University School of Medicine. She was not granted admission because at that time there were only two slots in medical school for black students and one was reserved for a veteran and the other for a person with an advanced degree. She was devastated that her dream could not be fulfilled and did not apply to any other medical schools because she feared the results would be the same. Frustrated that she could not pursue her original career choice, she chose to apply for graduate studies in physical organic chemistry at Howard University. She became the first graduate student of LLOYD FERGUSON, a well known African American chemist, and graduated with an M.S. degree in 1949. Her first job was at Howard Medical School in the department of physiology where she discovered that, ironically, she did not like working with patients. Her next job was teaching chemistry at Virginia State College in Petersburg, a black college. She had trouble teaching students who did not seem to be motivated to earn. In 1952 she married a Liberian student named John Payne Mitchell, whom she had met at BU. They had one child, Susan Weamah Emma, but divorced shortly thereafter.

Hopkins unsuccessfully pursued a career at American Cyanamid Corporation after a series of positions with small chemical companies. In 1959 she married Thomas Ewell Hopkins, a social worker, and they had one son, Thomas Ewell Hopkins Jr. Realizing that she had no future as a chemist in corporate America without a PhD, she began graduate studies at Yale University in 1961. She received a traineeship (tuition and stipend) from the U.S. Public Health Service for graduate studies. This stipend and her husband's salary gave them just enough to live on. Her thesis adviser was Dr. Jui H.

Wang, and the title of her thesis was "Catalysis of Phosphoryl Group Transfer by Metal Ions," which she completed in 1967. She approached Cyanamid for a position but there was none at her level. She obtained a position at Polaroid Corporation owing to previous networking with a vice president of that corporation who had come to Yale looking for minority scientists. Her twenty-two-year career at Polaroid began as an analytical chemist working with photographic coatings.

While still at Polaroid she decided to study law on the advice of a colleague. She began attending night classes at Suffolk Law School in 1974, and applied for and received a career exposure experience in the patent department of Polaroid, where she worked while studying law. In 1977 she received her J.D. degree from Suffolk and spent her last eleven years at Polaroid in the Patent Department until her retirement in 1989. She then took a position as deputy general counsel for the Massachusetts Department of Environmental Protection and served in this position until 1999. She ran for selectman in her hometown of Framingham, Massachusetts, and lost the first time but won the second time she ran, in 1999, becoming the first African American woman to be a selectman in Framingham history. She ended her career as chairman of the board of selectman, another first for an African American.

Hopkins was also active with American Chemical Society as a local and national officer and trustee, beginning in 1970. In 1985 she was appointed to be a trustee of Boston University. In 1995 she received the Distinguished Alumni Award from Boston University and in 2003 she established a charitable gift annuity at BU, the proceeds of which will fund awards to members of underrepresented minorities studying science and technology. She was named Woman of Achievement in 1979 by the Massachusetts Business and Professional Women's Association. In 1988 she received the Henry Hill Award of the Northeastern Section of the American Chemical Society. She was a member Phi Beta Kappa, Sigma Xi, Sigma Pi Sigma, Beta Kappa Chi, and Alpha Kappa Alpha.

FURTHER READING

Ambros, Susan A., Kristin L. Dunkle, Barbara B. Lazarus, Indira Nair, and Deborah A. Harkins. *Journey of Women in Science and Engineering: No Universal Constants* (1997).

Davis Marianna W., ed. *Contributions of Black Women to America* vol. 2 (1982).

Hass, Violet B., and Carolyn C. Perrucci, ed. *Women in Scientific and Engineering Professions* (1987).

Warren, Wini. *Black Women Scientists in the United States* (1999).

JEANNETTE ELIZABETH BROWN

Hopkins, Lightnin' (15 Mar. 1912–30 Jan. 1982), blues singer and guitarist, was born Samuel Hopkins in Centerville, Texas, the son of Abe H. Hopkins, a musician, and Frances Sims. His father died when Hopkins was an infant, leaving the family to survive in the stark farmlands of the East Texas Piney Woods. Hopkins's sister and four brothers were musicians. He learned to play the organ at church at his mother's urging, but he was drawn to the guitar through the playing of his older brother, John Henry. He was forbidden to touch John Henry's guitar, however, so he built his own out of a plank of wood, a cigar box, and chicken wire. He continually pestered John Henry to allow him to play the real guitar and often borrowed it on the sly. After discovering Hopkins skillfully playing the instrument, an impressed John Henry gave it to him. The eight-year-old quit school and took to the road, working odd jobs and playing music wherever he could. In the summer of 1920 he traveled to Buffalo, Texas, and attended a performance by the blues legend BLIND LEMON JEFFERSON at a church picnic. Jefferson allowed the green but undaunted Hopkins to accompany him on guitar during his set, which included "I Walk from Dallas" and "You Ain't Got No Mama Now (Black Snake Moan)."

Hopkins's greatest vocal influence was his cousin Alger "Texas" Alexander, a singer and harmonica player with whom he often performed in the streets and bars of Houston and other Texas towns. During a long, arduous itinerancy from the 1920s to the early 1940s, Hopkins traveled throughout the South, accumulating a large repertoire of traditional and original blues songs while also earning money through farm labor and gambling. As he later described, he spent time in prison as well: "One time I had to cut a man that kept fooling with me, and that put me in the county farm up at Houston County. Several times I had them chains around my legs for stuff I'd got into" (McCormack, 315).

Hopkins's original music sprang from his experiences of survival as a black man in a chronically poor region. He was the embodiment of the country blues, the music of hard labor and raw hands, of plaintive voices rising from field workers singing to ease the burn of the sun. The everyday tragedies of a downtrodden life—empty pockets, straying women, fraternal violence, death—were the subjects of his songs, and his deep, unpolished singing voice perfectly suited their evocation.

A brilliant storyteller, Hopkins became known for the nuances he added to a song each time he sang it. His dramatic, often extemporized delivery recalled the African "good talkers" who rambled West African towns, fusing autobiography, folk tale, and social commentary for rapt audiences. The arpeggio wail of his acoustic guitar between verses enhanced the emotional power of his music; his playing style, as described by the music writer Wolfgang Saxon, alternated "ominous single-note runs on the high strings with a hard-driving bass in irregular rhythms that matched his spontaneous, conversational lyrics" (*New York Times*, 1 Feb. 1982).

Hopkins was called into the army during World War II, but the night before he was scheduled to report he was stabbed by a disgruntled gambling partner. After recovering, he returned to occasional farmwork and his music, once again performing with Alexander in Houston. In 1942 he married Antoinette Charles, who is believed to have been his third wife. He had four children, but some or all of these may have been from his previous marriages.

In 1946 Hopkins was discovered by a talent scout on Houston's Dowling Street. The woman had been sent in search of an "authentic" country-blues musician by Aladdin Records as part of an ongoing trend of transporting Texas artists to Los Angeles in the hope of creating a new, popular blues form "designed by sound engineers for the thump and screech of a juke box" (McCormack, 316). Hopkins was at the time playing with Wilson "Thunder" Smith, a barrelhouse pianist; the two, along with the pianist AMOS MILBURN, were taken to Hollywood to record at the RKO studios. Hopkins's free spirit and his penchant for altering his songs, however, did not suit the hit-making aspirations of Aladdin's producers. He made a handful of recordings and accepted the nickname "Lightnin'"—placed on him for his association with Thunder Smith as well as for the often frantic speed of his guitar playing—but he was unhappy in Hollywood and unwilling to change for the sake of wider success. He returned to Houston in 1947 and resumed his life in its familiar black wards.

Bill Quinn of Houston-based Gold Star Records approached Hopkins soon after the musician returned from California, and he subsequently recorded several singles for the label. The classic

"Short-Haired Woman" (written after Hopkins saw a woman stumble and lose her wig on a bus) backed by "Big Mama Jump" (1947) sold more than forty thousand copies. Later that year came "Baby Please Don't Go," which reached sales of eighty thousand copies, and "Tim Moore's Farm," a protest song based on Hopkins's experience working for a brutal white farmer. These early efforts exemplify his emotive guitar playing and the boogie-woogie style of many of his songs.

In 1949 Gold Star dropped Hopkins after he made some recordings for another label while in New York City. (Hopkins was not trustful of contracts; after a record company made money by releasing versions of his songs without his knowledge, he insisted on being paid in cash each time he recorded.) Throughout the 1950s he issued hundreds of records, taping as many as three albums in a week. Among his best works during this period are "Coffee Blues" (1950, Jax); "Policy Game" (1953, Decca); "Lonesome in Your Heart" (1954, Herald); and "Penitentiary Blues"/"Bad Luck and Trouble" (1959, FW). He recorded on many labels, including Time, RPM, Ace, Kent, Mercury, TNT, and Harlem. There was surprisingly little repetition within this musical output because of Hopkins's endless improvisations. At times his flowing style was also altered by producers who attempted to impose structure on his songs by adding bass and drums.

While Hopkins's records often sold well, his lifestyle was not conducive to holding onto money, and he constantly found himself in financial need. In 1959 music researcher Sam Charters "rediscovered" Hopkins and introduced him to a national audience through the release of *The Roots of Lightnin' Hopkins* on Folkways Records. Hopkins immediately became a presence on the folk music circuit, playing at the 1959 University of California Folk Festival in Berkeley and at Carnegie Hall and the Village Gate in New York City the following year. Other aficionados of the blues recorded Hopkins, including Chris Strachwitz, whose Arhoolie Records helped make classic blues performers such as Hopkins popular among white college students. (On Arhoolie, Hopkins recorded "California Showers" in 1961.) He recorded with his guitar-playing brothers John Henry and Joel Hopkins, as well as with BROWNIE MCGHEE, BIG JOE WILLIAMS, and SONNY TERRY, on *Wimmin from Coast to Coast* (1960, World Pacific). He also appeared on radio and television programs and was featured in two short Les Blank films, *The Sun's Gonna Shine* (1967) and *The Blues According to Lightnin' Hopkins* (1968).

Throughout the 1960s, Hopkins recorded and toured, although he remained apprehensive about new situations and preferred not to be away from Houston for long periods. In 1970 he suffered a neck injury in an auto accident that temporarily limited his travels. He eventually resumed his wide-ranging performances, however, which included sets at jazz festivals in Germany and the Netherlands in 1977 and a return to Carnegie Hall in 1979. Just months after undergoing surgery for cancer of the esophagus, he made his last public appearance at the nightclub Tramps in New York City. He died in Houston.

Hopkins is remembered for his rich contribution to the country-blues idiom. His unique lyrical style made him hard to imitate, a fact that may have lessened his influence on rock and roll musicians when compared to that of bluesmen such as MUDDY WATERS and JOHN LEE HOOKER. But the immense volume of his work—no blues artist was recorded more in his era—and the honesty of his poetic vision have afforded generations of listeners a window into the vibrant, often tragic world of the twentieth-century rural South.

FURTHER READING
Charters, Sam. *The Country Blues* (1959).
Loder, Kurt. "Lightnin' Hopkins, 1912–1982: A Classic Blues Life," *Rolling Stone*, 18 Mar. 1982.
Obituary: *New York Times*, 1 Feb. 1982.
This entry is taken from the *American National Biography* and is published here with the permission of the American Council of Learned Societies.

GRAHAM RUSSELL HODGES AND
JAY MAZZOCCHI

Hopkins, Linda (14 Dec. 1924–), blues singer and musical theater performer, was born Helen Melinda Mathews in New Orleans. Her father was a Baptist minister. Hopkins found her inspiration to sing at an early age through two legendary mentors. The first was MAHALIA JACKSON, who lived nearby in New Orleans and sang the gospel at Hopkins's father's church. Hopkins became a protégé of Jackson's, and with her encouragement joined the gospel group the Southern Harp Spiritual Singers. She sang with them for eleven years and did her first recordings with them in 1947 for King Records.

Hopkins started singing secular songs in the early 1950s, mostly in the blues idiom. She worked with some of the seminal producers and songwriters of the decade: Jerry Leiber and Mike Stoller, Ralph Bass, Johnnie Otis, and Herb Abramson. She recorded scores of songs for several labels, including Savoy, Atco, Federal, King, and later for RCA, Columbia, and DRG. She was on the best-selling charts only once, with "Shake a Hand", a duet with JACKIE WILSON, which reached #21 on the R&B chart on the Brunswick label in 1963. She honed her singing and recording skills during this period, and performed with many of the greats of the blues, rhythm and blues, and rock 'n' roll genres. She also toured as a featured singer in LOUIS ARMSTRONG's band.

In the late 1960s Hopkins began studying acting with the method acting teacher Stella Adler. The study led to a turning point in her career direction with a featured role in the Broadway show *Purlie* in 1970. The next year Hopkins had a featured role in director Tom O'Horgan's *Inner City*, for which she was awarded both a Tony and a Drama Desk Award. Although she would continue performing in nightclubs and recording, the theater now became the focus of her career.

Hopkins had performed a tribute to BESSIE SMITH in her nightclub act for many years. After several years of workshops, she developed this tribute into a one-woman *tour de force*, which became the Broadway smash hit of 1975, *Me and Bessie*. Hopkins then toured throughout the United States with the show, which won a Drama Desk Award in 1976.

Hopkins was one of television star Johnny Carson's favorite singers, and she became a nearly ubiquitous presence on his *Tonight Show*, singing more than 100 times during Carson's three-decade run. Only the blues great JOE WILLIAMS had more appearances on the show. She also sang on the *Ed Sullivan Show*, the *Merv Griffin Show*, the *Dinah Shore Show*, and the *Mitzi Gaynor Show*.

In 1989 Hopkins starred in the Broadway production of *Black and Blue*. The show was built around her and the singers RUTH BROWN and Carrie Smith, and also featured the work of choreographers Cholly Atkins and FAYARD NICHOLAS, the dancers BUNNY BRIGGS, JIMMY SLYDE, and SAVION GLOVER, and the musicians Grady Tate, Roland Hanna, and Jerome Richardson. The show ran on Broadway for over two years, toured Europe twice, won Tony Awards and a Grammy Award, and was turned into a PBS television special directed by Robert Altman.

Hopkins was known as one of her generation's most ebullient and dynamic of performers, and at the age of eighty-two continued to entertain throughout the world. In 1998 the producer Mel Howard built a blues review around her, *Wild Women Blues*, which toured Europe several times, most, playing Paris for a month in 2006. The cast album of *Wild Women Blues* was released in 2003.

FURTHER READING
Palmer, Robert. *Baby, That was Rock & Roll: The Legendary Leiber & Stoller* (1978).

BARRY MARSHALL

Hopkins, Pauline Elizabeth (1859–13 Aug. 1930), novelist, journalist, and editor, was born in Portland, Maine, the daughter of Northrup Hopkins and Sarah Allen. She grew up in Boston and graduated from Girls High School. At age fifteen Hopkins won the first prize of ten dollars in gold for her essay, "The Evils of Intemperance and Their Remedy," in a contest sponsored by WILLIAM WELLS BROWN. At twenty Hopkins wrote the play *Slaves' Escape; or, The Underground Railroad* and played the lead role alongside other family members in the Hopkins Colored Troubadours. The production received favorable reviews; in tours around the northeastern United States, the play varied in length from four acts to three and was sometimes titled *Peculiar Sam; or, The Underground Railroad*. The Colored Troubadours also put on a variety of musical performances, and Hopkins was noted for her singing; indeed, she was once referred to as "Boston's Favorite Colored Soprano" (Shockley, 23). During her career as a performer in the 1880s, she wrote a second play, *One Scene from the Drama of Early Days*, based on the biblical story of Daniel in the lion's den; however, no-record exists confirming that this play was ever produced.

To support herself financially, Hopkins trained and worked as a stenographer in the 1890s. During this period she also delivered lectures on subjects in black history, such as Toussaint-Louverture. Hopkins rose quickly to prominence in 1900 with the publication of her novel *Contending Forces: A Romance Illustrative of Negro Life North and South*, along with her work on one of the first journals owned and operated by African Americans, the *Colored American Magazine*. Both *Contending Forces* and the *Colored American* were published by the Colored Co-operative Publishing Company, and the novel was offered free to new subscribers of the magazine. As a cooperative venture, the *Colored American* stood out from its predecessors in African American publishing and from mainstream white magazines, and Hopkins became an active cooperative member, contributing both fiction and nonfiction, serving as editor of the Women's Department from 1901 to 1903 and later as literary editor in 1903. Indeed, Hopkins's writings appeared so often in the magazine that she sometimes used her mother's maiden name, Sarah Allen, or left her work unsigned, as in the case of her two series of biographies, "Famous Men of the Negro Race" and "Famous Women of the Negro Race." Hopkins also helped found the Colored American League in 1904, an organization that solicited support for the magazine, and she gave lectures throughout the United States to this end.

It is unclear what other roles Hopkins may have played throughout her tenure at the *Colored American* (1900–1904), or why she is listed as editor in chief on a single issue of the magazine (March 1904), but her editorial influence is undeniable. In addition to her own writing, she published works by WILLIAM BRAITHWAITE, BENJAMIN BRAWLEY, JAMES D. CORROTHERS, and ANGELINA WELD GRIMKÉ. Most of the literary pieces represented were in the protest tradition; like many African American intellectuals of her era, including W. E. B. DuBois, Hopkins believed that literature could and should be used as a political tool. This belief is evident in *Contending Forces* and in her three novels serialized by the magazine, *Hagar's Daughters: A Story of Southern Caste Prejudice, Winona; A Tale of Negro Life in the South and Southwest*, and *Of One Blood; Or, the Hidden Self*. In these novels Hopkins drew on the popular traditions of her day, combining romance and suspense with history in complex plots of miscegenation under slavery and interracial marriage in the post–Civil War era. Response to her direct treatment of these themes was mixed, as it was for her contemporary, CHARLES W. CHESNUTT. Issues of passing and interracial relationships were more readily accepted as worthy of literary consideration a few decades later in the works of NELLA LARSEN, LANGSTON HUGHES, and JESSIE FAUSET, among others.

Indeed, Hopkins's willingness to articulate the difficult racial issues of her day certainly led to her departure from the staff of the *Colored American* in 1904, when the magazine was purchased by a supporter of BOOKER T. WASHINGTON. The new publishers changed the course of the magazine's mission, conforming closely to Washington's accommodationist views, which were anathema to Hopkins. A 1912 article in the African American journal *Crisis* reveals that Hopkins's unwillingness to accommodate the sensibilities of white financial supporters of the *Colored American* led to her

resignation, and contemporary feminist critics also cite Hopkins's gender as a likely factor. Very few women, black or white, held positions of influence in the publishing world in the early twentieth century, and there is some evidence that several of her male contemporaries resented Hopkins's leadership role. Though she ostensibly left because of poor health, Hopkins's work was soon in print again, in her article "The New York Subway" (Nov. 1904) for *Voice of the Negro*. The *Voice* also published her series "The Dark Races of the Twentieth Century" (Feb.–July 1905).

Gender was assuredly a factor in Hopkins's inability to obtain steady work in the publishing industry after she left the *Colored American*. In 1905 she formed her own publishing company, P. E. Hopkins and Co., but probably due to lack of financial backing, the house released only one work, her pamphlet *A Primer of Facts Pertaining to the Early Greatness of the African Race*. She resumed her career as a stenographer and surfaced again briefly in the public eye in 1916, when she cofounded another magazine, *New Era*. Coedited by Walter Wallace, a former colleague on the *Colored American*, the new magazine resembled its predecessor (when under Hopkins's direction) in its mission and organization. *New Era* expressed great ambition in its commitment to uplift of the race, and included a wide range of journalistic writings, including history, essays, fiction, and a biography series explicitly described as a "sequel" to Hopkins's series for the *Colored American*. She also authored and printed the first installments of another serialized novel, *Topsy Templeton*, but the magazine folded after only two issues.

Little is known of Pauline Hopkins after the collapse of *New Era*. She was working as a stenographer at the Massachusetts Institute of Technology when she died from injuries suffered in an accidental fire at her home in 1930. Single throughout her life, she supported herself and, at times, her mother, through her work as a writer, editor, and stenographer. In her introduction to the first collection of essays on Hopkins, the literary critic NELLIE Y. MCKAY stresses that "there is a need for a full-scale biographical project to fill in the large empty spaces surrounding [Hopkins's] life" (Gruesser, 18). Hopkins was certainly as prolific as any of her male contemporaries, including Charles Chesnutt and W. E. B. DuBois; her frank discussion of miscegenation and her insistence on the rewriting of African American history prefigured themes and concerns that captured international attention during the Harlem Renaissance.

FURTHER READING

Hopkins's manuscripts are housed at the Fisk University Library in Nashville, Tennessee.

Gruesser, John Cullen, ed. *The Unruly Voice: Rediscovering Pauline Elizabeth Hopkins* (1996).

Johnson, Abby Arthur, and Ronald Mayberry Johnson. *Propaganda and Aesthetics: The Literary Politics of Afro-American Magazines in the Twentieth Century* (1979).

Shockley, Ann Allen. "Pauline Elizabeth Hopkins: A Biographical Excursion into Obscurity," *Phylon* 33 (1972): 22–26.

ALICE KNOX EATON

Horace, Lillian B. (c. 1886–6 Aug. 1965), writer and teacher, was born Lillian B. Ackard in Jefferson, Texas, the second of Thomas Armstead and Macey Matthews's two children. Two years after Lillian's birth her parents moved to Fort Worth, where Lillian developed a love for life and learning in the supportive environment of family members and friends. After her graduation from I. M. Terrell High School, twelve-year-old Lillian took courses from 1898 to 1899 at Bishop College in Marshall, Texas, a college (later defunct) established in 1881 for black Baptists by the Baptist Home Mission Society. As she noted in her diary, there she experienced a "spiritual awakening," "learn[ed] to study," and "learn[ed] more of people." In 1900, the year that her mother died, Lillian married David Jones; she was fourteen. The couple had no children, and they divorced in 1919.

Though her marriage dissolved, Lillian Jones flourished academically and professionally, dotting her diary with expressions like "joy" and "how glad" when referring to her educational pursuits. Like many young black southern women of her time, Jones began her teaching career before she graduated from college. She taught in Tarrant County, Texas, schools for six years, one in Handley and five in Mansfield. In 1911 at age twenty-five she returned to Terrell High School, her alma mater, to teach English. There she served as dean of girls and created the school's library by asking students and friends to donate books. Later, in 1924, she launched the *Terrellife* newspaper and pioneered the school's journalism and drama departments.

In 1914 she entered Prairie View A&M, writing in her diary, "Thrilled could not believe [I] was going." She graduated as valedictorian. Although she and other Prairie View students were introduced to BOOKER T. WASHINGTON's pragmatic philosophy of education and accommodation, Jones, like many talented black Texans, was determined to acquire more advanced education than the South had to offer. She demonstrated her commitment by enrolling in summer extension courses at the University of Chicago in 1917, 1918, 1919, 1928, and 1940, at the University of Colorado at Boulder in 1920, and at Columbia University. From 1921 to 1922 she worked and studied at Simmons University, a state school established by black Baptists in 1879 in Louisville, Kentucky. There she also served as dean of women and earned a bachelor's degree.

Driven by a strong sense of social responsibility and an appreciation for familial and personal connections, Jones returned to Texas. She was connected to every major institution that shaped the African American community at the turn of the twentieth century. In addition to being a devout Baptist, she was a teacher, a pioneering librarian, and a journalist. She was also a member of the Texas Commission on Inter-racial Cooperation (TCIC; founded in 1920), the Zeta Phi Beta sorority, Heroines of Jericho, Eastern Star, the Alphin Art and Charity Club, and the Progressive Woman's Club.

In 1916 Jones self-published her first novel, *Five Generations Hence*. Though it was all but unknown until an excerpt was republished in the 1995 anthology *Daring to Dream: Utopian Fiction by United States Women before 1950*, historians now honor *Five Generations Hence* as the earliest novel on record by a black woman from Texas. Like many African American writers of the post-Reconstruction era, Jones used her novel for a sociopolitical purpose. She and her contemporaries criticized the exclusion of blacks from American life and argued for their inclusion by creating characters who embodied middle-class values, piety, and production.

Jones's novel is nonetheless unique in its call—before the Harlem Renaissance and before MARCUS GARVEY—for a transcontinental dialogue between Africa and America, one that hinged on economic self-sufficiency and most particularly on the noble ideas and deeds of intelligent black women. Jones's heroine is Miss Grace Noble, a teacher and leader in a rural black community in Texas who responds to an awesome sense of social responsibility to educate the young black masses about her. When the novel opens Grace Noble is taking a stroll in the woods with her students, whose educational and social welfare is always on her mind. Their plight weighs so heavily on her that she takes to the woods, where she has a messianic wilderness experience. She loses consciousness during an agonizing dialogue between herself and the divine. The vision that she has ultimately leaves her full of hope for the future. Seven chapters later the reader learns what that vision is: American blacks will return to Africa "five generations hence."

In 1930 Jones wedded Joseph Gentry Horace of Groveton, Texas, a man as committed as she was to educational advancement. Joseph Gentry Horace graduated from Bishop College in 1935, accepted a call to the ministry in 1937, and moved to Evanston, Illinois, where he enrolled in the University of Chicago, completed his bachelor of divinity degree in 1942, and eventually accepted a ministerial position, at Second Baptist Church, which is still located at the address recorded on the front cover of Lillian Horace's diary: "1717 Benson Ave, Evanston, Illinois." J. Gentry Horace, the eighth pastor of the historic church, which was established in 1870 by a former slave, is credited with marshaling Second Baptist through the latter years of Great Depression and World War II. His contributions were later commemorated by the "J. Gentry Horace Leadership Award for Freedom," one of two major service awards sponsored by Second Baptist Church.

Lillian Horace, a multidimensional preacher's wife, clearly enjoyed social, professional, and intellectual activities. She participated in the Texas Library Association (1933), nourished her appreciation for travel; attended the "Second Annual Conference of Parents and Leaders of Parent-Teacher Associations" (1936); served as Chaplain of the National Association of Colored Women's Clubs (1937); attended the organization's 50th-year anniversary (1946); and began working on her second novel, *Angie Brown*. Notwithstanding her and J. Gentry's professional and intellectual productivity, their marriage ended in 1946, when J. Gentry Horace confessed his love for another woman. J. Gentry and Lillian Horace had no biological children but adopted a daughter whom Lillian raised to adulthood.

Lillian Horace was deeply disappointed by the divorce and "struggled to readjust." In 1947 she journeyed to California, where she remained for six months and continued to pursue her desire to write and even contemplated marrying a third time. By 1948 she had finished her first draft of *Angie Brown*. The following year she attempted, unsuccessfully, to have the book published by Lemuel L. Foster in New York. Departing from her earlier dreams of Africa, Horace used *Angie Brown* to showcase the strength of the everyday woman and to suggest that although black women endured the double burden of "being a woman" and "being a Negro," they should strive to be strong. The novel also reveals the importance of black female bonding and cross-generation ties in black women's survival. In call-and-response fashion, the novel's younger woman benefits from the older woman's past, while the older woman draws pleasure and inspiration from shaping the younger woman's future. Reflecting the importance of oral tradition, the novel's women use stories to transmit wisdom and history. Horace also used *Angie Brown* to argue that economic progress, not social progress alone, was key to black advancement. Accordingly the novel's protagonists are depicted as savers and sound-minded investors despite living in a community where education stopped at the seventh grade. Perhaps Horace could not find a publisher because the end of her story was out of step with the changing times: Angie Brown remarried and opened a "colored motel."

In addition to her creative works Horace authored the biography of Lacey Kirk Williams, an influential Baptist minister born in 1871 who left his ministerial post at Mount Gilead Baptist Church, Fort Worth, Texas, in 1916 to become pastor of Chicago's Olivet Baptist Church—with twelve thousand members, the largest black church in the country. Horace's biography of Williams, *"Crowned with Glory and Honor": The Life of Reverend Lacey Kirk Williams*, was published around 1941 and was republished in 1978.

Horace died in Fort Worth. Thanks to her published and unpublished works, which were rare among black women of her generation, Horace's life and literary contributions promise to thrive in the annals of African American women's history.

FURTHER READING

Horace's papers are held by the Tarrant County Black Historical and Genealogical Society, Fort Worth, Texas.

"Berkeley, Calif." *Chicago Defender*, 11 Aug. 1934: 18.

"Bishop College to Hold Confab for PTA Leaders." *Chicago Defender*, 18 Apr. 1936: 12.

Calvary Missionary Baptist Church. "A Church Pressing On and Upward." Available at http://www.cmbc-ch.org/new_history.htm.

"Celebrating 133 Years of Faith, Freedom and Fellowship." Available at http://secondbaptistevanston.org/default.asp?page=133anniverary.

"Federated Clubs." *Chicago Defender*, 17 Aug. 1946: 17.

Kessler, Carol Farley. *Daring to Dream: Utopian Fiction by United States Women before 1950* (1995).

"Texas Librarians Hold Annual Meeting." *Chicago Defender*, 13 May 1933.

Winegarten, Ruthe. *Black Texas Women: 150 Years of Trial and Triumph* (1995)

KAREN KOSSIE-CHERNYSHEV

Hord, Noel Edward (10 July 1946–), footwear industry executive and humanitarian, was born in Kokomo, Indiana, to Reverend Noel Ernest Hord and Jessie Mae (Tyler) Hord. Noel was the fourth of five children with one older brother, Fred, two older sisters, Katherine and Gloria, and one younger brother, Ken.

Noel graduated from Wiley High School in 1964 and began his career in footwear as a teenaged stock-boy in Terre Haute, Indiana. In the early 1960s there were few opportunities for a young black man to advance in retail industries. Many whites were still uncomfortable with the idea of a black man waiting on a white woman in a venue like a shoe store. However, Noel's likeability and popularity opened doors. He was initially given permission by a "progressive" employer to sell shoes to men. Once he was on the sales floor, former white classmates from his integrated high school requested that he wait on them. In a bold move for the time, he was eventually allowed to sell shoes to both men and women. Given the climate of the day, Noel's long-term ambitions were understandably modest: eventually, he hoped to manage a shoe store.

Hord married Cora Eileen Ritchie on his twentieth birthday, 10 July 1966. She was three years his senior and a graduate of Indiana State University. After his junior year as a student at Indiana State University, Noel had left school and opted to sell shoes. Working for the Wohl Shoe Co. in 1967, Hord found he had a natural instinct for sales. It was during that time that Noel noticed that many of his white counterparts were enrolling in Wohl's management training program and he decided to do the same. He moved into his first management job in Gary, Indiana, in 1969. His oldest child, Michelle Denise, was born shortly after the move. His son, Noel Daniel, was born a few years later in 1973. With a young family to support, Hord was more focused on his career than ever before. He became the first black executive to be promoted to Wohl's corporate headquarters in St. Louis, Missouri, where he was responsible for sixty-five specialty shoe businesses under the name of Franklin Simon.

He then went on to become vice president and general manager of the entire women's shoe operations at J. L. Hudson in Detroit, Michigan. In 1980 Hord received the James C. Taylor Personnel Award in recognition of his outstanding work in human resources and career development.

In 1984 Noel moved from Detroit to Connecticut to join Fisher Camuto, Inc., as vice president of operations for the wholesale division of Nine West, a women's shoe manufacturer. He became senior vice president in 1986 and general manager in 1987, and was soon promoted again to executive vice president and general manager of the Nine West Division. In 1988 he became president of the Enzo Angiolini division, and in 1991 became group president of both the Nine West and Enzo Angiolini divisions. During his time there the company prospered, even as the shoe industry stumbled nationwide. Analysts at the time said that the introduction of casual workdays and an aging consumer market contributed to a decline in shoe sales in the early 1990s. But Nine West's revenues defied the national slump, jumping approximately 17.3 percent per year during that period.

In May of 1993 Hord left Nine West Group to take over as president and chief executive officer (CEO) of U.S. Shoe Corporation's Footwear division in Ohio. In February 1994, less than a year after moving to Ohio, Noel's wife, Cora, died suddenly.

In 1995 Noel came back to the East Coast when Nine West purchased U.S. Shoe. He was named president and chief operating officer (COO) of the $1.4 billion company that dominated the $14 billion women's retail shoe market. It was the largest non-athletic shoe company in North America. As the president and COO of the newly renamed "Nine West Group," Hord was principally responsible for the supervision and coordination of the company's retail and wholesale operations along with its administrative and operational functions. In 1999, before online shopping became mainstream, Noel joined Dunk, Inc., as president and CEO Dunk marketed and sold athletic apparel and footwear over the Internet with superstar product endorsers such as SHAQUILLE O'NEAL.

Noel continued his prominence in the footwear industry as president and COO of BCBG Max Azria and New York Transit, Inc., respectively.

In addition to building a successful career, Hord was dedicated to giving back to the black community. This tradition of service could be traced back to his parents, who were able to leverage their leadership of the Second Baptist churches, first in Terre Haute, Indiana, and later in Shelbyville, Indiana, into opportunities to work as civil and social activists. In 1993 Noel and his wife, Cora, had founded the Hord Foundation, Inc. This organization focused on granting minority students educational scholarships. By 2004 the Hord Foundation had granted more than $2 million in scholarship money. In 2007 the state of Connecticut honored the foundation with its coveted MARTIN LUTHER KING JR. community service award. In 1993 Hord also cofounded Concerned Black Men of Action for Youth in Danbury, Connecticut. He was the first president of that organization, which focused on mentoring black youth. Noel was also active in the Urban League's National Black Executive Exchange Program. This effort sponsored visiting professionals and mentor programs at the country's leading black universities and colleges. In May 2001 Hord was awarded the Presidential Medal Award from Western Connecticut State University for outstanding leadership and contribution to the university and community of Danbury.

In June 2002 Noel married Tamar Christopher and together they continued his work of service to the black community.

FURTHER READING

The information for this entry was obtained through personal interviews by the author with its subject.

MICHELLE D. HORD

Horn, Shirley (1 May 1934–20 Oct. 2005), jazz singer and pianist, was born Shirley Valerie Horn in Washington, D.C., the eldest child of Ernest Horn, a general accounting office clerk, and Grace Saunders Horn, a devoted homemaker with a taste for recordings by big bands and popular singers; she had gone to school with BILLY ECKSTINE. A self-described "mama's child" and "homebody," daughter Shirley lived in Washington with pride for her entire life, settling within blocks of her childhood home. Her two younger brothers did the same, a testament to their strong upbringing and familial bond.

Although Horn's later popularity would be centered on the quiet intensity of her vocals, her musical education and early performance experiences focused almost exclusively on the piano. Even as a toddler she was entranced by the old upright in the parlor of her grandmother, a church musician who played by ear. Horn started playing around the age of four and undertook formal lessons a year later.

Throughout junior high and high school her piano studies took her to Howard University's Junior School of Music, where she worked every day after school with Dr. Gladys Hughes. Horn's favorite classical composers were Rachmaninoff and Debussy, perhaps the source for her lightness of touch, sensitive pedal work, and shimmering chord voicings. Outside the classical realm the jazz pianist ERROLL GARNER would become her greatest influence. Horn provided accompaniment for many school activities—classes, assemblies, and musicals— as well as Sunday school and church. Initially unbeknownst to her parents, the teen also began to appear at the Merryland Club, rendering light classics for the dinner clientele. Always shy about her voice, she received the bribe of a teddy bear from a gentleman customer to sing "Melancholy Baby." The rest, as they say, was history. Offered scholarships to continue her studies at Juilliard and Xavier University, Horn ultimately did not attend, a decision motivated primarily by her mother's desire to keep her close to home. Without regret Horn kept performing and turned increasingly towards jazz. She often said that OSCAR PETERSON became her Rachmaninoff, and AHMAD JAMAL her Debussy. Sitting in at the 7th and T Cocktail Lounge,

Shirley Horn, left, and trumpeter Miles Davis during a recording session at Clinton Studio in New York, in August 1990. (AP Images.)

a well-known after-hours spot near the Howard Theater, gave her the opportunity to impress many jazz luminaries; she would eventually become the house pianist. In 1954 Horn established her own trio, the opening act for major touring artists at Olivia's Patio-Lounge. She made her first recording in 1959 in a trio accompanying the violinist STUFF SMITH, a friend of her father's. Unfortunately the date was falsely credited to another pianist. Horn did not receive proper credit until Smith's recordings were reissued by Mosaic in 1999.

John Levy, a pioneering African American artists' manager, took on Horn's representation and helped bring her into the spotlight. Her first recording as a leader, *Embers and Ashes* (1960), already displayed her penchant for glacially slow ballads and whisper-soft vocals. (Unfortunately, this extremely rare LP remains out of print and the masters appear to be lost.) It opened many doors. After the legendary trumpeter MILES DAVIS heard the album, he personally invited Horn to open for him at New York's Village Vanguard, thus establishing an important musical friendship. QUINCY JONES, who attended the Vanguard dates, would produce and arrange the music for her two records on Mercury: *Loads of Love* (1963) and *Shirley Horn with Horns* (1963). For both of these Horn was pressured into abandoning the piano to be a "stand-up singer," a move she attributed to her gender and the expectations for vocal stars at that time. One final major label recording followed, for ABC-Paramount, called *Travelin' Light* (1965).

Despite her growing career Horn gave up touring to be with her family. She married Sheppard Deering, a Metro mechanic, in 1956, and their daughter Rainy was born in 1958. She continued to perform in local clubs such as the One Step Down and, for a time, operated a club of her own, the Place Where Louie Dwells. In 1968 Horn sang the theme songs for the films *For Love of Ivy* (which starred SIDNEY POITIER and ABBEY LINCOLN) and *A Dandy in Aspic*, both written by Quincy Jones. In the late 1970s she recorded for the independent Danish label Steeplechase.

Horn's "rediscovery" at the North Sea Jazz Festival in 1981 intersected with a resurgence of interest in veteran jazz artists and singers in particular. She was signed to Verve Records in 1987 and made over a dozen albums for the label. This not only reestablished her as a major talent but also proved crucial in revitalizing Verve; the label had only recently resumed releasing new material. Three of her albums hit number 1 on *Billboard*'s jazz sales charts: *Here's to Life* (1992) a lush orchestral affair with string arrangements by Johnny Mandel; a live album, *I Love You, Paris* (1992); and a grooving RAY CHARLES tribute, *Light out of Darkness* (1993). Miles Davis performed as a guest on *You Won't Forget Me* (1990) shortly before his death, and Horn would win a Grammy for Best Jazz Vocal Performance in 1998 with *I Remember Miles*, a tribute to her former mentor.

Throughout these recordings Horn demonstrated her remarkable ability to stretch the tempo of ballads to create a sense of timelessness, to tease the romantic sentiment of the popular song into sexy pillow talk or wispy expressions of pathos. She also possessed a down-home sense of swing informed by the blues. Considered by many to be the premier singer-pianist in jazz of her time, Horn paid particular attention to her vocal settings. She enjoyed enduring relationships with the sidemen who served in her trio and thought of them like family, in particular, the electric bassist Charles Ables and the drummer Steve Williams, who both played with Horn for well over twenty years. Their performances together are beautifully documented in the Gene Davis film *Shirley Horn Sings and Plays: Here's to Life* (1992).

In 2002 Horn's right foot was amputated owing to complications from diabetes; the operation left her unable to perform the delicate pedal work that her piano playing required. Undeterred, she continued singing and reconfigured her trio to include the pianist George Mesterhazy. She died in Washington from complications related to diabetes, including a number of strokes. Among her numerous awards and honors, she received a total of nine Grammy nominations and was named a National Endowment of the Arts Jazz Master in 2005.

FURTHER READING
Levy, John, with Devra Hall. *Men, Women, and Girl Singers* (2000).
Stokes, Royal. *Living the Jazz Life* (2000).
Pellegrinelli, Lara. "Around the Horn with Shirley," *Jazz Times* (May 2001).
Obituaries: *New York Times* and *Washington Post*, 22 Oct. 2005.

LARA PELLEGRINELLI

Horne, Frank (18 Aug. 1899–7 Sept. 1974) optometrist, educator, administrator, and poet, was born Frank Smith Horne in Brooklyn, New York, the son of Edwin Fletcher and Cora Calhoun Horne. He attended the College of the City of New York (now

City College of the City University of New York), and after graduating from the Northern Illinois College of Ophthalmology and Otology (now Illinois College of Optometry) in 1922 or 1923, he went into private practice in Chicago and New York City. He also attended Columbia University and later received a master's degree from the University of Southern California (c. 1932). He was married twice, to Frankye Priestly in 1930 and to Mercedes Christopher Rector in 1950, ten years after his first wife's death.

In 1926 Horne was forced to leave his optometry practice and move to the South owing to poor health. He became a teacher and track coach at Fort Valley High and Industrial School (renamed Fort Valley Normal and Industrial in 1932 and now Fort Valley State University) in Fort Valley, Georgia, and within a decade he had risen to the position of dean and acting president. After 1936 he held a number of governmental administrative positions and was a member of President Franklin Roosevelt's "black cabinet." He was assistant director of the Negro Affairs division of the National Youth Administration in Washington, D.C., from 1936 to 1938 and worked in various capacities for the U.S. Housing Authority, including in the Housing and Home Finance Agency and the Office of Race Relations in Washington and New York City, from 1938 to 1955. He also served as the executive director of the New York City Commission on Intergroup Relations from 1956 to 1962 and as a consultant for the New York City Housing Redevelopment Board on race relations from 1962 to 1974. He was a founding member of the National Committee against Discrimination in Housing in 1950.

As a poet Horne is best known for *Letters Found near a Suicide*. Submitted pseudonymously by "Xavier I," the eleven-poem composite won second prize in the poetry category of the Amy Spingarn Contest in Literature and Art sponsored by *Crisis* magazine in 1925. Beginning with "To All of You," the poems in the series address individuals who have played significant roles in the speaker's life. "To Jean," for instance, addressed to a romantic rival, begins:

When you poured your love
like molten flame
into the throbbing mould
of her pulsing veins
leaving her blood a river of fire
and her arteries channels of light,
I hated you.

In 1929 Horne published seven more poems in the series in *Crisis* as *More Letters Found near a Suicide*, and the expanded version was published in 1963 as the initial section of *Haverstraw*, his only volume of poetry. The title poem of the collection, also a composite, is subtitled "Lyrics for the halt" and concerns Horne's attempt, after a crippling illness, "to learn to walk again … / all tensed and trembling."

Although *Letters Found near a Suicide* and other sporadically published poems, including "On Seeing Two Brown Boys in a Catholic Church" and "Nigger, a Chant for Children," form the basis of Horne's literary reputation, he also contributed fiction, essays, and numerous reviews to black-oriented periodicals. "The Man Who Wanted to Be Red," an allegory for children on the absurdity of race, was published in *Crisis* in 1928, and "I Am Initiated into the Negro Race," detailing his experiences with segregation upon his arrival in Georgia, appeared in *Opportunity* the same year. The Fort Valley High track team was the subject of "Running Fools: Athletics in a Colored School," published in *Crisis* in 1930; "To James," one of the poems in *More Letters Found near a Suicide*, is addressed to James Collins, the school's star sprinter. Horne's essay "Concerning White People," three vignettes framed by the ironic assertion "There is one thing that white people clearly understand … and that is the working of the Negro mind," won honorable mention in the *Opportunity* literary contest in 1934. "The Industrial School of the South," a two-part series published in *Opportunity* in 1935, is a testament to his emulation of BOOKER T. WASHINGTON's educational model, but later essays, including "Providing New Housing for Negroes" (1940) and "War Homes in Hampton Roads" (1942), both in *Opportunity*, and "Interracial Housing in the United States" (1958), in *Phylon*, signal Horne's increasing advocacy of a federal role in public housing.

A significant if minor figure in the Harlem Renaissance, Horne created a perhaps more lasting legacy in his tireless efforts as a public official to improve housing conditions for African Americans across the nation. In 1954 the composer Earl Kim adapted Horne's most famous work as *Letters Found near a Suicide* for baritone and piano.

FURTHER READING
Brown, Sterling. *Negro Poetry and Drama* (1937).
Primeau, Ronald. "Frank Horne and the Second-Echelon Poets of the Harlem Renaissance," in *The Harlem Renaissance Remembered*, ed. Arno Bontemps (1972).

Obituary: *New York Times*, 8 Sept. 1974.

HUGH DAVIS

Horne, Lena (30 June 1917–9 May 2010), singer and actress, was born Lena Calhoun Horne in the Bedford-Stuyvesant neighborhood of Brooklyn, New York, the only child of Edna Scottron and Edwin "Teddy" Horne. Besides the extremely light-skinned Edna, only Horne's equally fair grandmother, Cora Calhoun Horne, was present at her birth, misleading the hospital staff into expecting a white baby, not the "copper-colored" child who was in fact born. The character of Horne's middle-class family was best embodied by her grandmother, an outspoken suffragist and member of the NAACP (in which she enrolled Horne at age two), and her uncle, Dr. FRANK HORNE, an educator and occasional adviser to President Franklin D. Roosevelt. After the Hornes divorced in 1920, Edna pursued a mediocre performance career with the

Lena Horne. The singer and actress signed a contract with MGM Studios that had a clause explicitly excluding her from the stereotypical roles previously doled out to African American women. (Library of Congress.)

Lafayette Players, while Edwin, by most accounts a racketeer, moved to Pennsylvania. Horne accompanied Edna on her travels throughout the South, but eventually she settled with her grandmother in Brooklyn. When Horne was fourteen, Edna returned from a Cuban tour with a new husband, Miguel Rodriguez; now unwelcome among the black bourgeoisie of Brooklyn, the family moved to the Bronx. In 1933 Edna arranged for her daughter to become one of ETHEL WATERS's chorus girls for the white audiences of Harlem's Cotton Club. Horne soon dropped out of school, abandoning her dream of becoming a teacher to pursue a career as an entertainer. The gig at the Cotton Club was far from glamorous and required little but scant clothing, but over time Horne performed with the likes of BILLIE HOLIDAY, DUKE ELLINGTON, COUNT BASIE, and CAB CALLOWAY. She also earmarked a portion of her twenty-five-dollar weekly wage for singing lessons. Horne, as well as many early critics, never maintained that she had a natural singing voice, but it responded tremendously to formal training.

At age seventeen Horne appeared briefly on Broadway, playing the Mulatto Girl in a voodoo scene from *Dance with Your Gods* (1934). The show ran for only a couple of weeks, and Horne continued at the Cotton Club for another year. Despite some friction with the club's white management, Edna and Miguel secured Horne's release to join NOBLE SISSLE's orchestra in Philadelphia, performing under the ostensibly more elegant pseudonym Helena Horne. Touring eventually brought them through Pittsburgh, where her father, Edwin, was now managing a hotel; he and Horne reunited, and a year later she married one of his friends, Louis Jones. Nine years her senior and with no career prospects of his own, Jones's indulgent spending strained the marriage, yet the couple had two children in three years, Gail (1938) and Teddy (1940). Horne continued looking for work in show business, landing a role in the "quickie musical," *The Duke Is Tops* (1938); salary was delayed for the all-black cast, souring her first Hollywood experience. She then earned a coveted role in the Broadway revue *Blackbirds of 1939*, but the production lasted only nine performances. Despite the esteem she had gained over four years of working clubs and fronting orchestras, along with film and stage work, Horne had not yet found her breakthrough gig. For a while she settled into domesticity; but in 1940 she separated from Jones and moved to New York, planning to get a foothold on her career and send for her children shortly.

In December of that year, her manager burst into a movie theater where Horne was enjoying the afternoon and implored her to audition for Charlie Barnett's band that same day. Barnett awarded her the job halfway through her first song, making her one of the first black women to sing lead with a white band. Her career hit full stride when she and Barnett recorded "Haunted Town" and "Good for Nothing Joe." But her personal life suffered. Jones had granted her full custody of Gail, but only occasional visitation rights with Teddy.

Soon Horne was appearing at the Apollo Theater and Carnegie Hall, and in 1941 she began singing regularly at the Café Society Downtown, where she reportedly met WALTER WHITE and PAUL ROBESON on the same night. Their commitment to civil rights made a lasting impression on Horne, and when she was offered top billing at a Los Angeles club, White convinced her that she might be on the cusp of a larger accomplishment for African Americans as a whole. So in 1942 Horne left her boyfriend, the boxer JOE LOUIS, and moved to Los Angeles with Gail and a cousin, Edwina, who had been caring for her.

After a short singing stint at the Trocadero Club, Horne signed a seven-year contract with MGM which had an explicit clause that she would not play the stereotypical roles previously doled out to African Americans—thus paving the way to more dignified roles for other black actresses. But she lost her first role, a speaking part in *Thank Your Lucky Stars,* to Ethel Waters, because her skin was too light on film and any makeup bore too close a resemblance to blackface. She did receive a bit part in *Panama Hattie* (1942) that established the routine for most of her subsequent MGM films: Horne would appear in an evening gown, lean against a pillar, and sing in a single scene that could easily be deleted for southern theaters. But in 1943, when MGM gave her the lead in the all-black musical *Cabin in the Sky,* response was so positive that Twentieth Century–Fox leased her for one picture, the BILL ("Bojangles") ROBINSON musical *Stormy Weather* (1943). Horne sang the title track, and it remained her calling card throughout the rest of her career.

While filming *Stormy Weather,* Horne met Lennie Hayton, the white musical director who eventually worked on such hits as *Singin' in the Rain* and *Hello, Dolly!.* Meanwhile, she continued at MGM, appearing in *I Dood It* (1943), *As Thousands Cheer* (1943), *Broadway Rhythm* (1944), *Two Girls and a Sailor* (1944), and *Ziegfeld Follies*

(1946). Horne divorced Jones in 1944 and married Hayton in Paris in 1947, though the news was withheld until 1950. She had also become a World War II pinup girl and sang for the troops at American military bases. One story holds that at Fort Riley, Kansas, she spotted German prisoners of war with better seats than the African American soldiers, so she swept right past them and sang to the blacks in the back row.

Largely because of her connection with Paul Robeson, Horne was periodically blacklisted in Hollywood during the McCarthy witch hunts. She shifted her career back to the clubs and within a few years could command $12,500 per week. Horne appeared on television specials hosted by Ed Sullivan and Steve Allen and in 1956 was offered her first speaking role in a movie with whites, *Meet Me in Las Vegas.* The next year she recorded *Lena Horne at the Waldorf-Astoria,* perhaps her most successful album. She appeared in her first starring role on Broadway, the wildly successful *Jamaica* (1957), but lost the leading role of the "mulatto" Julie in the movie *Show Boat* to Ava Gardner, who, it turns out, ended up wearing the "Light Egyptian" blush that Max Factor had designed especially for Horne.

In the 1960s Horne increasingly involved herself in civil rights, on occasion working with JAMES BALDWIN, HARRY BELAFONTE, LORRAINE HANSBERRY, and Robert F. Kennedy. She participated in the March on Washington in 1963 and frequently raised money for civil rights organizations around the country. Hayton's death in 1971 had been preceded by Edwin's and Teddy's, both in 1970. Having lost the three men closest to her in less than two years, Horne retreated from the public eye; but she resumed performing a couple of years later and collaborated with Tony Bennett in a 1974 Broadway show. In 1978 Horne played the good witch in *The Wiz,* a black version of the *Wizard of Oz* with DIANA ROSS and MICHAEL JACKSON. She was lauded with an honorary doctorate from Howard University in 1979, and that same year she put on a television special with Belafonte.

In 1981 Horne staged her most triumphant professional performance, the one-woman show *Lena Horne: The Lady and Her Music.* The pinnacle of the show came when she sang "Stormy Weather" twice, first as she had sung it in Hollywood almost forty years earlier, and then in the more fully matured and regal style of her current voice. *The Lady and Her Music* ran to 333 performances before touring in America and Europe for two years; it won a Tony Award, a citation from the New York Drama Critics Circle, and two Grammy awards. Horne died of heart failure in New York City at the age of 92.

FURTHER READING
A collection of Lena Horne's papers is housed at the Schomburg Center for Research in Black Culture of the New York Public Library.

Horne, Lena, with Helen Arstein and Carlton Moss. *In Person: Lena Horne* (1950).

Horne, Lena, with Richard Schickel. *Lena* (1965).

Buckley, Gail Lumet. *The Hornes: An American Family* (1986).

Haskins, James, and Kathleen Benson. *Lena: A Personal and Professional Biography of Lena Horne* (1984).

DAVID F. SMYDRA JR.

Horse, John (1 Jan. 1812?–1882), Seminole Maroon leader and Mexican army officer, also known as Juan Caballo, John (or Juan) Cavallo, John Cowaya, John Coheia, Gopher John (beginning in 1826), and Juan de Dios Vidaurri (during and after 1856), was born in the Florida Alachua savanna west of Saint Augustine. His father is believed to have been of mixed American Indian and Spanish heritage and his mother of African and American Indian descent. Until his early thirties he was considered a Seminole slave. His surname is a translation of that of Charles Cavallo, his Indian owner. Cavallo might also have owned Horse's mother and been his father.

The Seminole Maroons were mostly runaways from South Carolina and Georgia plantations, together with slaves captured by Seminoles from Florida plantations and some free blacks. Some were considered Seminole slaves, but servitude among the Seminoles was based upon tribute and deference. Typically Seminole slaves gave their owners a small annual tribute of crops or livestock in exchange for protection against reenslavement by whites. The Maroons lived apart from the Seminoles in communities headed by their own principal men, and they controlled most aspects of their daily lives. Little is known of Horse's early years, but during that period the Seminole Maroons endured the traumas of the East Florida annexation plot (1812–1813), the destruction of the so-called Negro Fort at Prospect Bluff on the Apalachicola River (1816), the First Seminole War (1818), the annexation of Florida by the United States (1821), and forced removal to a reservation south of Tampa under the terms of the Treaty of Moultrie Creek (1823).

By 1826 Horse was living in his owner's village on Thonotosassa Lake, twelve miles from Fort Brooke, near Tampa Bay. He took to visiting the military post, and the wily teenager played a prank on one of the officers there, tricking him into paying for two gophers (edible terrapins) multiple times. The officer gave Horse the nickname Gopher John, by which he became known to U.S. army officers on the frontier for the next fifty years. Horse continued to frequent Fort Brooke for several years, interacting with the officers there by running errands and serving as a guide on hunting trips. He also raised livestock and came to own ninety head of cattle and other property.

Horse's life soon would change dramatically as Indian and Maroon resistance to the removal policies of Andrew Jackson culminated in the Second Seminole War, 1835–1842. As leader of the Oklawaha Maroons, Horse actively opposed the U.S. forces in Florida at the beginning of the war. But offered the promise of freedom he agreed to surrender and remove west with the Seminoles in March 1837. The American commander reneged on his promises, however, and in early June, Horse and the Seminole leaders Osceola and Coacoochee (Wild Cat) carried off the hostages they had surrendered under the terms of the truce. Horse and Coacoochee were captured in October and imprisoned at Fort Marion in Saint Augustine, but the two led a daring and successful escape during the night of 29–30 November.

On 25 December 1837 Horse led the Maroons and Coacoochee, Alligator, and Sam Jones led the Seminoles in the battle of Okeechobee, the most important engagement in the most serious and protracted of all "Indian" wars. But Okeechobee proved to be the pinnacle of Seminole and Maroon resistance to removal. Again promised freedom Horse surrendered with Alligator and his band in April 1838 and immediately boarded transports at Tampa bound for the West. He returned to Florida the following year in the new role of U.S. government agent. Between 1839 and 1842 Horse served as a paid guide, interpreter, and intermediary who persuaded 535 Indians to sue for peace and remove west.

By 1840 Horse had married Susan July, the daughter of July, a Seminole Maroon guide and interpreter killed in Florida, and Teena, who removed to the Indian Territory. The couple remained together until his death more than forty years later. They had one son who grew to adulthood, Joe Coon. Susan and Joe Coon both died soon after John Horse.

In 1842 Horse was described as "a fine looking fellow of six feet, as straight as an Indian" (Porter, *The Black Seminoles*, 37). He was powerfully built and sported silver armlets, sashes, and leggings and the plumed turban favored by the Seminoles. His long, dark hair always was groomed. He became known on the frontier as an excellent marksman and horseman with a liking for strong liquor. He came to speak at least five languages: Afro-Seminole (an English-based Creole spoken by the Maroons), Hitchiti and Muskogee (spoken by the Seminoles), Spanish, and later in Mexico, Kickapoo.

Horse left Florida for good in the summer of 1842, sailing to the Indian Territory via New Orleans. He and his family made their home on the Deep Fork of the North Canadian River. Upon the death of Charles Cavallo in Florida, Horse had become the property of the Seminole chiefs. In February 1843, for services rendered to the Seminoles during removal, the chiefs declared him to be free. As a free black in the Indian Territory, Horse was in grave danger of being kidnapped by Creeks or whites and returned to slavery. Some of the Seminoles also resented his serving as a government agent in Florida and his growing influence within the tribe. Consequently he spent much of his time at Fort Gibson, serving as an interpreter for those Seminoles residing around the post.

In April 1844 Horse accompanied a Seminole delegation, headed by Coacoochee, to Washington. He had been back at Fort Gibson only a few days when a Seminole shot at him with a rifle, wounding him slightly and killing the horse he was riding. He and his family were forced to move from the Deep Fork to Fort Gibson and reside there for the next three and a half years. Besides the horse shot under him, Horse already had acquired over fifty head of stock, a wagon, tools, and farming implements on the Deep Fork. These too were lost.

In January 1845 the Seminoles, the Creeks, and the United States signed a treaty aimed at uniting the two tribes. Because of their minority status Seminole interests would be buried beneath those of the Creeks, creating a source of contention in the future. For now, though, the Seminoles agreed to settle on their assigned lands. For sixty days, from February until early April, Horse drove his wagon pulled by three yoke of oxen in the train that removed the Seminoles and their belongings from their camps near Fort Gibson to the Little River country. But his position remained precarious. During the removal Seminoles made a second attempt on his life, and again he was forced to seek refuge at the post. In April he traveled to Washington, seeking permission to resettle in Florida. He spent the next year in the nation's capital working on behalf of his people. Horse succeeded in securing the protection of the Maroons by the military at Fort Gibson and the referral of their case to the president. He then returned to the Indian Territory.

In June 1848 Attorney General John Mason decided that the Maroons should be returned to the Seminoles. Ordered to leave the post in early January 1849 Horse led his family and followers from Fort Gibson to Wewoka Creek, where they established a community some distance from the Seminoles. The settlement was situated just north of the present-day town of Wewoka, Seminole County, Oklahoma.

Horse's sister, Juana, already had suffered two of her children being sold to a Creek by her Seminole owner. Fearing that he, his family, and his fellow Maroons would be kidnapped and sold or reenslaved and subjected to Creek slave codes, Horse entered into an alliance with the disaffected Coacoochee that resulted in bands of Maroons and Seminoles quitting the Indian Territory in November 1849. They traveled through Texas to Coahuila in northern Mexico, where legal servitude had been abolished in 1829.

Naming Horse's followers Mascogos, the Mexicans in 1852 gave the Maroons, the Seminoles, and a band of Southern Kickapoos separate land grants at Nacimiento, near Múzquiz, to establish military colonies. In exchange for land, tools, and livestock, the immigrants agreed to protect the Mexican interior by engaging in campaigns against Apache and Comanche raiders. The Mexican authorities viewed John Horse as the undisputed head of the Mascogos and referred to him as El Capitán Juan Caballo.

During the early 1850s Horse became extremely unpopular with Texas settlers on the border, being regarded as impudent and boastful of having killed many whites in Florida. To the delight of local residents and the border press he was expelled from Fort Duncan while laying claim to a horse that had been taken from him and sold. Then, while attending a dance in Piedras Negras, he became involved in a brawl and was shot and wounded by a Texan. The slave catcher Warren Adams rushed across the border with his henchmen and took Horse back to Eagle Pass in handcuffs. Coacoochee crossed over from Mexico and paid $500 in twenty-dollar gold pieces for the return of his friend and ally. As a warning to Adams, the coins were stained with human blood.

Beginning in 1856 John Horse sometimes was referred to as Juan de Dios Vidaurri. This name may have derived from a godfather, following Horse's Catholic baptism. That same year smallpox claimed the life of Coacoochee and many other Seminoles. Disillusioned with Mexico the remaining Seminoles returned to the Indian Territory between 1859 and 1861. To prevent attacks by Texas filibusters, in 1861 Horse and most of the 350 Mascogos moved to the Laguna de Parras in southwestern Coahuila.

In 1864 the Maroons experienced conflict resulting from the French invasion of Mexico under Emperor Maximilian. The group retained a tradition that Horse persuaded the invaders not to burn their dwellings. It has been said that he joined the Mexican army to fight against the French and that his exploits were so successful that he was commissioned a colonel. He did become known on the border as El Coronel Juan Caballo, but more likely the title derived from service against Indian raiders. As further reward, the Mexican government gave him a silver-mounted saddle with a gold-plated pommel in the shape of a horse's head. Horse used that saddle when riding his favorite horse, a white with blue eyes named American.

In 1865 John Kibbetts and a large number of Maroons felt it safe to return to Nacimiento. In the late 1860s American officials suggested that they return to the United States as part of a policy aimed at relocating border Indian bands hostile to white settlers. During the summer of 1870, the Nacimiento Maroons crossed the border and made camp on Elm Creek at Fort Duncan. In August the able-bodied men enrolled in the U.S. army as a new unit that came to be known as the Seminole Negro Indian Scouts. Horse crossed over to Fort Duncan from Parras in December, but he never served with the scouts. Some of his supporters followed in late 1872 and early 1873, but most chose instead to return to Nacimiento.

After Horse returned to Texas, there was contention among the Maroons as to who should be considered their leader. In December 1873 the 130 Maroons at Fort Duncan elected Kibbetts headman over Horse by a majority of seventeen votes. Kibbetts's success may be explained by most of Horse's supporters having returned to Nacimiento. The aging but knowledgeable and experienced Horse thereafter assumed a patriarchal role and offered counsel on important issues affecting the Maroons in Texas. The Kibbetts-Horse group removed to Fort Clark in early 1876 and built a settlement on Las Moras Creek, which became the scouts' home base. Horse and his family made their home just above the fort's graveyard, on the west side of the creek.

Local whites feared that the Maroons would acquire land outside Fort Clark and also accused them of stealing cattle and other property. During the evening of Friday, 19 May 1876, Horse was attacked while returning to the Maroon village from a saloon in neighboring Brackettville. Hired assassins ambushed Horse and Titus Payne just south of the post hospital. Horse was on horseback, while Payne walked alongside. Payne was killed instantly, and four bullets tore through Horse's leg and body, but his mount, American, although wounded in the neck, carried him to safety.

That incident and subsequent attacks on other group members caused Horse and other leading Maroons to rejoin their kinsmen at Nacimiento. In the late 1870s and early 1880s the Mascogos and Mexican Kickapoos faced a grave crisis when their title to land at Nacimiento was contested and they faced eviction. They determined to send a representative to state their views before the Mexican president Porfirio Díaz. Consequently Horse, possibly accompanied by one or two other Maroons, set out for Mexico City during the first week of August 1882. The outcome is unknown, as Horse died before he could reveal the details of his mission. Accounts vary as to the circumstances of his death. Some say that he was murdered in a cantina during the return journey, but more likely he died of a sudden bout of pneumonia in a military hospital in Mexico City in the early afternoon of 9 August.

A decade after Horse's death the Mexican government reaffirmed the Mascogos' and Mexican Kickapoos' title to land at Nacimiento. Descendants of the Seminole Maroons still reside on that land in the early twenty-first century.

FURTHER READING

Foster, Laurence. *Negro-Indian Relationships in the Southeast* (1935; rpt. 1978).

Littlefield, Daniel F., Jr. *Africans and Seminoles: From Removal to Emancipation* (1977; rpt. 2001).

Mulroy, Kevin. *Freedom on the Border: The Seminole Maroons in Florida, the Indian Territory, Coahuila, and Texas* (1993; rpt. 2003).

Porter, Kenneth W. *The Black Seminoles: History of a Freedom-Seeking People*, eds. Alcione M. Amos and Thomas P. Senter (1996).

Porter, Kenneth W. *The Negro on the American Frontier* (1971).

This entry is taken from the *American National Biography* and is published here with the permission of the American Council of Learned Societies.

KEVIN MULROY

Horton, George Moses (1797?–1883?), poet, was born in Northampton County, North Carolina, a slave of William Horton; the names of his parents are unknown. As a boy he moved with his master's household to Chatham County, where he tended cows on the farm. Horton's teenage pleasures, he later wrote, were "singing lively tunes" and "hearing people read" (Horton, iv), and he taught himself to read, first learning the alphabet from an old spelling book. He acquired an extraordinary vocabulary and the forms, topics, and styles of his verse from reading the New Testament, Wesley's hymnal, and books given to him by University of North Carolina (UNC) students.

In his early twenties, now the slave of William's son, James Horton, George avoided the manual labor he disliked by walking eight miles from the farm to Chapel Hill on weekends to sell fruit and his poems. From about 1830 on, he hired his time from successive masters and lived on the university campus, earning his living as a professional poet and college servant. In about 1818 Horton married a slave woman surnamed Snipes with whom he had two children, a daughter, Rhody, and a son, Free Snipes.

During his early poetic career Horton composed verses in his head while plowing the fields—he could not write until about 1832—and dictated these love lyrics and acrostics to student customers who paid him twenty-five to seventy-five cents for each poem. He sold a dozen verses a week in this way for many years, until he found a benefactor, Caroline Lee Hentz, a poet and novelist. Mrs. Hentz inspired, copied down, and edited the verses Horton dictated. She had two of his poems published in the Lancaster, Massachusetts, *Gazette* (1828), and she probably transcribed the twenty-one verses for Horton's first book, *The Hope of Liberty* (1829). In the summer and fall of 1828 the New York *Freedom's Journal* published a few of Horton's poems along with editorials appealing for contributions for his manumission. In the same months, the Raleigh *Register* printed his poems, and with influential friends of the poet, such as the UNC president Joseph Caldwell and John Owen, the governor of North Carolina, the *Register* campaigned for Horton's freedom. Money to buy the poet's freedom was to come from sales of *The Hope of Liberty*, but this historic volume earned scarcely any profit for its author and failed to generate enough funds to purchase his freedom.

Horton continued to earn three to four dollars a week from sales of his love poems, while he hired his time for twenty-five cents a week, gaining a substantial profit. His fame spread when *The Hope of Liberty* was reprinted in Philadelphia and Boston (1837–1838), and periodicals in the North and South published his verses in the 1840s. The first stanza of "On Liberty and Slavery" aptly describes his plight and illustrates his style:

> Alas! and am I born for this,
> To wear this slavish chain?
> Deprived of all created bliss,
> Through hardship, toil and pain!

In 1843 his new master, Hall Horton, a tanner and farmer of Chatham, raised the slave's hire fee to fifty cents, adding to other troubles. Horton's need to acclimate himself at age forty-six to a new young master, the death a few years earlier of his mentor, president Joseph Caldwell, the rise of pro-slavery sentiments and repressive legislation in North Carolina, and the pain of almost half a century in bondage all motivated Horton to try again to buy his freedom.

On 3 September 1844 Horton wrote an appeal to the abolitionist William Lloyd Garrison, who ten years earlier had printed Horton's "On Liberty and Slavery" in the *Liberator* (29 Mar.). Horton entrusted the mailing of this letter to the new UNC president, David L. Swain, who filed it among his papers. A year later the poet and his supporters circulated a subscription list in Chapel Hill for his new volume, *The Poetical Works* (1845). Even with the sales of this book of forty-four poems Horton could not accumulate sufficient funds to purchase his freedom, perhaps because some of his income went for drink. During the next fifteen years Horton continued to hire his time and survived as a poet, servant, odd-jobs man at the university, and part-time farm laborer.

In 1849 the Raleigh *Register* (29 Dec.) published Horton's spirited defense of American over foreign literature. In 1852 Horton wrote a letter begging David Swain to purchase him for $250 to alleviate his arduous eight-mile commute from the farm to Chapel Hill and promising to pay back Swain from sales of his poetry books. President Swain filed this letter, too (with a later appeal from Horton), and advised him to write to Horace Greeley. Horton wrote to Greeley in September 1852, asking for $175 "to remove the burden of hard servitude…. I am the only public or recognized poet of color in my native state or perhaps in the union, born in slavery but yet craving that scope and expression whereby my literary labor of the night may be circulated throughout the whole world." He added a poem, "The Poet's Feeble Petition," and entrusted the letter for mailing to David Swain, who again buried it in his papers. The slave would wait another dozen years for emancipation.

In his sixty-second year Horton delivered an oration, "An Address. The Stream of Liberty and Science. To Collegiates of the University of N.C. by George M. Horton the Black Bard" (1859). He spoke to freshman students, several of whom copied down parts of the "Address" as Horton rambled on. This chaotic twenty-nine-page manuscript reveals Horton's privations and need for liberty, and it includes visions of Judgment Day and a reborn world; fatherly advice to students, love, of knowledge and learning, and political opinions, including a prescient fear of the approaching bloody "dissolution of national union." Horton's voice sounds estranged and embittered, hopelessly resigned to his bondage. The slave's life in Chapel Hill became even more difficult after 1860; with the university depleted of students and resources by the Civil War, Horton lost the market for both his services and his poems.

On 17 April 1865 the Ninth Michigan Cavalry Volunteers entered Chapel Hill, and Horton found a patron in Captain William H. S. Banks. The twenty-eight-year-old Banks and the sixty-eight-year-old poet traveled in North Carolina with the Volunteers, going to Greensboro and Lexington in May, to Concord in June, and back to Lexington, where, on 21 July, Banks was released from service; then Banks and Horton journeyed to Raleigh. As he walked and camped some three hundred miles during three summer months, Horton composed ninety new poems for his third volume, which Banks got published in Raleigh as *Naked Genius* (1865). In *Naked Genius*, Banks solicited sales agents for a new book by Horton, "The Black Poet," but it was never published, and Banks soon abandoned Horton in Raleigh.

Few facts document the poet's last eighteen years. Probably in the winter of 1865–1866 he traveled to Philadelphia, Pennsylvania, where, on 31 August 1866, the Banneker Institute interviewed him, "a poet of considerable genius" (Stephen B. Weeks, "George Moses Horton: Slave Poet," *Southern Workman* [Oct. 1914], 576). The *Christian Recorder*

(10 Nov. 1866) published his poem "Forbidden to Ride on the Street Cars," a protest against Philadelphia's segregated streetcars. The *African Repository* (Jan. 1867) printed his "Song for the Emigrant" and noted that Horton had immigrated to Liberia. The *Repository* (Feb. and Mar. 1867) reported that fourteen persons from Philadelphia had been sent by the Pennsylvania Colonization Society on the trader *Edith Rose* from New York to Grand Bassa County, Liberia. They had sailed on 5 December 1866, arrived at Monrovia on 7 January 1867, and continued to Bexley a few days later. A "List of Emigrants for Liberia" describes Horton as sixty-eight years old, a tanner, and a Methodist, who could read and write. Later communiqués from the Philadelphia emigrants fail to mention Horton.

Collier Cobb, the head of the department of Geology at UNC, wrote in 1929 that he had "called on Poet Horton in Philadelphia in 1883, the very year in which he died." "I called him 'Poet,' which pleased him greatly," wrote Cobb in a letter to Victor Palsits, "and he told me that I was using his proper title." No other mention of Horton's presence or death appears in census or death records, periodicals, or archives after 1867.

Poet Horton lived in slavery for sixty-eight years. Although JUPITER HAMMON had been the first African American to publish a poem in 1760 and PHILLIS WHEATLEY had been the first black person to publish a volume of poetry in 1773, Horton is the first African American poet whose work centers on the struggle for freedom. He was also the first African American to publish a book in the South, the only slave to earn a significant income selling his poems, and the only poet of any race to produce a book of poems *before* he could write. In recent years Horton has been honored by the founding of the George Moses Horton Society for the Study of African American Poetry (1996). He was inducted into the North Carolina Literary Hall of Fame in 1996 and the following year he was named Historic Poet Laureate of Chatham County.

FURTHER READING

Horton's letters and "An Address" are in collections of the University of North Carolina, Chapel Hill. Cobb's letter to Victor Paltsis is in the Schomburg Center for Research in Black Culture of the New York Public Library.

Horton, George Moses. *The Poetical Works of George M. Horton, the Colored Bard of North Carolina, to Which IS Prefixed the Life of the Author, Written by Himself* (1845).

Pitts, Reginald H. "'Let Us Desert This Friendless Place': George Moses Horton in Philadelphia—1866," *Journal of Negro History* 80 (Fall, 1995).

Sherman, Joan R., ed. *The Black Bard of North Carolina: George Moses Horton and His Poetry* (1997).

JOAN R. SHERMAN

Horton, Walter (6 Apr. 1918–8 Dec. 1981), blues harmonica player and vocalist, known variously as "Big Walter," "Shakey," "Mumbles," and "Tangle-eye," was born in Horn Lake, Mississippi, just south of Memphis, Tennessee, the son of Albert Horton Sr. and Emma McNaire. When Horton was five his father bought him a harmonica, or mouth harp, and he began teaching himself to play. The guitarist Johnny Shines first encountered Horton around 1930 and recalled that he was a serious musician, constantly working on new techniques, even as a preteen. After Horton's father got a job as a handyman with the city of Memphis, his family moved there, giving Horton ample opportunity to further his musical education.

Various stories, some passed along by Horton himself, have him recording with the Memphis Jug Band as early as 1927 or 1928, but evidence suggests otherwise. It is more likely that he simply played with the group or with various members, such as the harmonica player Will Shade. After his father's death Horton became active as a Memphis street musician to help support his mother. In his early teens he played with the guitarist Floyd Jones, working crowds in Church Park, since renamed in honor of the composer W. C. HANDY. Through the 1930s Horton also played with the guitarists Little Buddy Doyle (with whom he also may have recorded), Homesick James, BIG JOE WILLIAMS, Shines, David Honeyboy Edwards, and other blues musicians, sometimes on the road, sometimes in Memphis.

From the mid-1930s through the late 1940s Horton alternated between the life of a traveling musician and various nonmusical jobs—cook, cabdriver, ice hauler. Working with Edwards in Jackson, Mississippi, in 1940, Horton supposedly became one of the first musicians to play amplified harmonica. Around 1949 he hooked up with the guitarists EDDIE TAYLOR and Jones for a stint in Chicago.

By 1951, however, Horton was back in Memphis, broadcasting over WDIA radio with the pianist Willie Love, the guitarist JOE WILLIE WILKINS, and the drummer Willie Nix, catching the attention of Sam Phillips, who had recently opened the Memphis Recording and Sound Service. Phillips, who would later found the Sun label, was then recording southern blues talent for two West Coast labels owned by the Bihari brothers and for the Chicago labels owned by the Chess brothers. Phillips recorded Horton and the guitarist-percussionist Joe Hill Louis in January and February 1951. The resulting single, issued on the Bihari-owned Modern label, featured "Little Boy Blue," a reprise of a ROBERT LOCKWOOD JR. blues, and "Now Tell Me Baby." Inexplicably Horton was identified only as "Mumbles" on the release.

A June session with a more conventional blues band produced Horton's second record, this one on the RPM label, also owned by the Biharis. Again Horton was identified as "Mumbles." A 1952 record for Phillips, featuring Horton and Jack Kelly, was credited to "Little Walter" and "Jackie Boy." Horton recorded for Sun in 1953, accompanied by the guitarist Jimmy DeBerry, a longtime sideman. These sessions produced some fine music—the title "Easy" became a classic, for example—but none of the Sun material was released at that time.

In 1953 Horton rejoined Taylor in Chicago. Their musical reunion lasted only a few weeks, though, because when the harp player JUNIOR WELLS was drafted for military service, Horton was invited to take his place in the MUDDY WATERS band. Because of health problems, especially the aftereffects of pneumonia and alcohol-related disabilities, which plagued him throughout his life, and also because he was said to be undependable, Horton did not have a long run with Waters, though he did record with the band in 1953 and 1954.

After backing Shines at a session for the JOB label Horton recorded under his own name for Chicago's States label at a 1954 session supervised by the bass player, songwriter, and arranger WILLIE DIXON. The session yielded "Hard Hearted Woman," issued in 1955, probably Horton's best-known song. In 1956 he again collaborated with Dixon for the Cobra label, producing "Have a Good Time," featuring OTIS RUSH on guitar. As with "Hard Hearted Woman," it is now considered a classic recording, but at the time it did little to advance Horton's career. That same year he backed fellow Muddy Waters bandmate JIMMY ROGERS on his hit "Walking by Myself."

Through the 1950s into the 1960s Horton continued club work with artists including Shines, Rogers, and Johnny Young. In 1964 he recorded an album, *Shakey Horton: The Soul of Blues Harmonica*, for

Argo, a Chess subsidiary. The album was coproduced by Dixon and included fine musicians, such as the guitarist BUDDY GUY, but there was little commercial interest in it.

In Chicago, as earlier in Memphis, Horton's innovative techniques exerted a strong influence on other harp players. Horton always bragged that he had taught every player from SONNY BOY WILLIAMSON to LITTLE WALTER JACOBS to Carey Bell. "To me, it sounded like another one of his stories," said Charlie Musselwhite, a harmonica player who often worked with Horton in Chicago, "but as the years went by, I kept hearing it from other people—that it was true. And now … I do believe it. He might not have taught them every note they played, but he got them going." Musselwhite, who considered himself one of Horton's students, said Horton was seldom willing to explain particular techniques; he preferred to teach by example: "I remember going over to his house one day, just for a harmonica lesson. We just ended up talking mostly, and drinking, and going around to see old friends and things, and just having little jam sessions here and there—in the alley, in the liquor store, in different people's homes."

During the mid-1960s Horton became a regular on the blues revival festival circuit, touring Europe in 1965, 1967, and 1970. He also continued to work the club scene and recorded as a sideman for Vanguard, Testament, and Arhoolie. He toured and recorded with Willie Dixon's Chicago Blues All Stars and in 1972 was featured on an Alligator album, *Big Walter Horton with Carey Bell*. Bell was Horton's protégé. The album also featured Horton's longtime companion Taylor. Other session work followed in the 1970s, including records with Johnny Winter and Muddy Waters, along with more club and festival dates. But he was showing the effects of his chronic health problems, domestic strife, and heavy drinking. After a return from Europe in 1981 he began drinking and was later found dead in a Chicago neighbor's apartment, the victim of heart failure and acute alcoholism. His wife, Anna Mae Horton (they married probably in the early 1960s; her maiden name is unknown), and five children survived him.

Although Horton was not particularly successful as a vocalist or recording artist, his instrumental skills were unsurpassed. He had what fellow musicians called "deep tone" and could play in up to five different "positions," or keys, on a single harmonica. Long-time musical partner Dixon, in his book *I Am the Blues*, wrote, "Little Walter was a very good player, but Big Walter … was a helluva harmonica player." Horton's musical career was littered with obstacles: alcoholism, poor health, partial paralysis (the result of several shooting scrapes), and a reputation for being undependable. But when he was on, said Musselwhite, "there'd be no stopping him. There'd be chorus after chorus of just brilliant playing—things you'd never, ever heard before, even from him."

Horton will be remembered in pop culture for a brief appearance in the film *The Blues Brothers*. In his lifetime he was a true "blues brother" to musicians like Taylor, Jones, Rogers, Young, and Shines. From their perspective he was the best of all harmonica players. As Shines put it in Peter Guralnick's *Feel Like Going Home*, "This harmonica blowing is really a mark for Walter—it's not something he picked up, he was born to do it." Along with John Lee Williamson, the older Sonny Boy Williamson, and Little Walter, Horton is now recognized as one of the architects of modern blues harmonica. Horton was inducted into the Memphis-based Blues Foundation Hall of Fame in 1982.

FURTHER READING
Leadbitter, Mike, ed. *Nothing but the Blues* (1971).
Obituary: *Living Blues* 52 (Spring 1982).

DISCOGRAPHY
Big Walter Horton with Carey Bell (Alligator 4702).
Leadbitter, Mike, and Neil Slaven. *Blues Records 1943–1966* (1968).
Oliver, Paul, ed. *The Blackwell Guide to Blues Records* (1989).
Shakey Horton: The Soul of Blues Harmonica (Argo 4037).
Walter "Mumbles" Horton: Mouth Harp Maestro (Flair V2-86297).

This entry is taken from the *American National Biography* and is published here with the permission of the American Council of Learned Societies.

BILL MCCULLOCH AND
BARRY LEE PEARSON

Horton, William R., Jr. (12 Aug. 1951–), convicted felon, was born in Chesterfield, South Carolina, the son of William Horton Sr., a city trash collector, and Sara Horton, a domestic worker. The Horton home was in constant upheaval, and Sara, Willie, and his two sisters suffered abuse at the hands of a father whose violent streak was exacerbated by alcohol and drug abuse. An older brother, Charles, had moved north to find industrial work in Lawrence, Massachusetts, and by the mid-1960s Sara and the girls had relocated to New York. Willie, by then a tall, muscular teen, remained in South Carolina and moved in with his grandparents. Already viewed as something of a troublemaker, Horton dropped out of Grady High School in order to pursue steady employment. Much of the rest of Horton's free life would be marred by violent, criminal outbursts.

Trouble marked his remaining years in South Carolina as he served two separate sentences for breaking and entering at the state reformatory in Columbia. An attack on a cab driver landed Horton in an adult penitentiary for two years, after which he joined his mother's new family in New York. Unable to reconcile differences with Sara's new husband, Willie joined his brother Charles and his wife, Helen Mays, in Lawrence, Massachusetts, in 1971.

It seemed for a time that Willie would settle down. He found work as a machinist making brake linings and began dating Catherine Mays, Helen's sister. The couple began living together in 1973 and had a daughter, Tara, the following May. Unfortunately, Horton's increasing restlessness spoiled this newfound domestic tranquility. He was unable to hold down a steady job and, following in his father's footsteps, sought comfort in vodka, marijuana, and other drugs, many of which he began peddling on the streets of Lawrence and the surrounding communities.

On 26 October 1974 Horton and two friends, Alvin Wideman and Roosevelt Pickett, robbed the Marston Street Mobil station. In the course of the robbery, they murdered the seventeen-year-old attendant, Joseph Fournier, stabbing the boy nineteen times before dumping his body in a trash can. After an investigation led to the three men's arrest, it was determined that the robbery had been Horton's idea and that he had wielded the murder weapon. Although Horton vociferously denied these charges, all three men were swiftly convicted on the count of first degree murder and sentenced to life in prison without parole.

The story of Willie Horton might have ended there but for a signal piece of state legislation signed by Republican governor Francis Sargent in 1972. The Correctional Reform Act had been adopted, ostensibly, to help reintegrate inmates into society. It established incentives for good behavior in the form of furloughs supervised by outside sponsors. Despite the emphasis on reintegration, inmates serving life sentences were not exempted from the program in the hope that it would help reduce in-house disciplinary problems. Throughout his remaining years in the Massachusetts system, Willie Horton would repeatedly apply for one of the coveted furloughs.

After a series of transfers between maximum and medium security facilities, Horton arrived at the minimum security Northeast Correctional Center at Concord in September 1984. Despite a number of infractions, including repeated marijuana busts, Horton was granted his first trip outside the prison in August 1983. When his first sponsor, an anonymous woman listed in public records only as Sponsor A, ended her relationship with Horton, he secured a second sponsor in the person of Helen Mays, his sister-in-law. Under her limited supervision Horton found himself back in familiar territory, surrounded by familiar people, and facing familiar temptations. On 6 June 1986 Horton fled after being released for a weekend furlough. His escape would have national repercussions.

For the next ten months Horton moved down the East Coast, settling at last in Oxon Hill, Maryland. There, on 3 April 1987 he entered the home of Cliff Barnes and his fiancée, Angela Miller. Incapacitating Barnes and raping Miller, Horton was finally apprehended after attempting to flee in a stolen vehicle. A Maryland judge sentenced him to two consecutive life terms plus eighty-five years, refusing to return Horton to Massachusetts lest he be furloughed again.

Horton's escape became one of the central issues of the 1988 presidential campaign. The Democratic candidate, Michael Dukakis, was the governor of Massachusetts and a strong advocate of the furlough program. In 1976 he vetoed a bill that would have made first degree murderers ineligible for furloughs and when questioned by one of his primary challengers, Al Gore, then a senator from Tennessee, about the program Dukakis repeatedly maintained its effectiveness.

Although Gore had not specifically targeted the Horton case, the Republican campaign picked up the issue upon Dukakis's nomination as the Democratic presidential candidate. The Republican candidate, George H. W. Bush, repeatedly mentioned Horton in his speeches while campaign manager Lee Atwater bragged that he would make Horton a household name before the elections were complete. Focus group discussions confirmed that the Horton issue could swing white voters into Bush's camp by playing on their fear of violent crime. For many of the same voters the name Willie

Horton became synonymous with a violent stereotype of black America.

Starting on 21 September 1988 the Americans for Bush, an arm of the National Security Political Action Committee, began running an ad titled "Weekend Passes," featuring a mug shot of Horton. In early October the Bush campaign began running its own ad, "Revolving Door," attacking Dukakis's support of the furlough program. The ads stirred controversy and were deemed racist by the Democratic vice presidential candidate Lloyd Bentsen and the civil rights leader JESSE JACKSON. Though Atwater would later apologize for some of his remarks during the campaign, the effectiveness of the attacks on Dukakis was indisputable. They effectively painted him as a hardcore liberal who was soft on crime, a candidate incapable of protecting white America from a growing menace symbolized by Willie Horton. Bush won the election handily.

On 18 April 1996 Horton was transferred to the Maryland House of Correction Annex, a maximum security prison in Jessup, Maryland.

FURTHER READING

Anderson, David C. *Changed American Justice* (1995).

Horton, James Oliver, and Lois E. Horton. *Hard Road to Freedom: The Story of African America from the Civil War to the Millennium* (2002).

Mendelberg, Tali. *The Race Card: Campaign Strategy, Implicit Messages, and the Norm of Equality* (2001).

NATHAN M. CORZINE

Hose, Sam (c. 1877–23 Apr. 1899), laborer and lynching victim, was born Samuel Wilkes near Macon, Georgia. The names of his parents, who were probably farmers or sharecroppers, have not been recorded, but it is known that his father died when Samuel was a child. Samuel, his mother, his sister, and his brother then moved a few miles south to Marshall, in present-day Crisp County in Georgia, where they earned a reputation for honesty and hard work. Samuel learned to read and write and was considered in the town to be an intelligent young man, but there were few opportunities in Marshall for African Americans other than to work as a laborer picking peanuts or cotton.

Sometime before 1896, when Samuel was nineteen years old, his sister married and his mother became seriously ill, leaving Sam to be the sole breadwinner in the family, since his brother was severely mentally handicapped. Wilkes worked for around two years as a laborer on the Jones family farm near Marshallville, Georgia, but he fled to Atlanta following an incident in 1896 or 1897 in which he was accused of assaulting a fellow employee, an older African American woman. It may have been around this time that Sam Wilkes adopted the surname Hose, which is in some accounts rendered as "Holt."

In late 1897 Hose began working as a laborer for Alfred and Mattie Cranford on their farm in Palmetto, Coweta County, Georgia, just southwest of Atlanta. Little is known about Hose's life there until the afternoon of 12 April 1899, when he appears to have killed Alfred Cranford with an axe. Hose promptly fled to his mother's home on the Jones farm seventy-five miles away, but he was captured by the Jones brothers thirteen days later, on Sunday, 23 April, following the most extensive manhunt in Georgia history. Although his captors had hoped to receive the $1,600 in rewards offered by Georgia Governor Allen Candler and the *Atlanta Journal Constitution* among others, a mob took Hose from the Joneses and brought him to Newnan, the county seat of Coweta County.

As had been predicted—indeed, urged—by the *Journal Constitution*, Sam Hose was then tortured and mutilated before a crowd of more than two thousand spectators (some reports claim four thousand), many of whom had arrived on specially arranged trains from Atlanta. The crowd included many of the community's most respected and respectable citizens, most of whom had probably attended church that morning. What followed can hardly be characterized as Christian, though in his autobiography W. E. B. DuBois pointedly described the scene as a crucifixion. The leaders of the mob chained Hose to a pine tree, cut off his ears, fingers (which were severed one by one and shown to the crowd), and genitals, poured kerosene on his body, and set him ablaze. The torture lasted almost half an hour before Hose died. "Such suffering has seldom been witnessed," one newspaper reported (quoted in Litwack, 281). The spectators then dismembered what remained of the victim's body for souvenirs; when there were no body parts left they contented themselves with pieces of the pine tree and chains. Some of these were kept as mementoes, others were sold. A piece of bone went for twenty-five cents, a slice of liver (cooked) went for a dime. Some reports allege that a piece of Hose's heart was delivered to the avowedly pro-lynching Governor Candler.

There are two widely divergent accounts of what happened on 12 April 1899 in the Cranfords' farmyard to provoke such a seemingly extraordinary response. The version given by the Cranford family and relatives appeared in most Georgia newspapers at the time and was reported in highly salacious detail. One such account contended that Hose "crept into [the Cranfords'] happy little home" while they were at supper and "with an ax knocked out the brains of the father, snatched the child from its mother, [and] threw it across the room" (cited in Dray, 4). Hose then allegedly raped Mrs. Cranford.

Detective Louis P. Le Vin of Chicago, however, hired by IDA B. WELLS-BARNETT to investigate Hose's lynching, concluded that Hose had killed Alfred Cranford in self-defense. According to witnesses, Hose admitted that he had quarreled with his employer a week earlier when Cranford denied his request for extra money to pay for a visit to his ailing mother. In Hose's account Cranford, who was known to have a volatile temper, borrowed a revolver the following day and threatened to kill Hose if he caused any more problems. Hose claimed to have been chopping wood in the farmyard on the afternoon of 12 April when Cranford again confronted him about their earlier quarrel and drew his gun to shoot. Hose admitted that he then attacked Cranford with his ax before escaping into the woods, but stated that he did not know if he had killed his employer. Hose also insisted—and continued to insist throughout his ordeal and torture—that he did not rape or in any way assault Mrs. Cranford, who had remained in the farmhouse throughout the confrontation. Detective Le Vin concluded that Hose probably was innocent of the charge of rape. He noted that Mrs. Cranford had made no mention of any such assault when she ran to the home of her father-in-law to tell him of the attack on her husband. Family relatives and the press, Le Vin believed, were responsible for spreading the rumor that Hose was guilty of rape.

These competing interpretations of Cranford's death were never adjudicated in court by a judge and jury of Samuel Hose's peers. The lynch mob did bring Hose to the Cranford home so that Mrs. Cranford could identify him as her assailant, but she was too ill to do so. Mrs. Cranford's mother, however, identified Hose as the perpetrator, which was sufficient proof for the mob—even though she had not witnessed the crime. For those who lynched Sam Hose the law and matters of due process simply did not matter. A Newnan newspaper declared shortly before Hose's capture that in the Cranford case "the provocation is so unbearably aggravating" that "people cannot be expected to

wait with patience on the laggard processes of the courts" (quoted in Dray, 5).

This demand for instant "justice" was hardly new in American history, but lynch law took on a new-and-radically different character in the post-Reconstruction South. In earlier times lynching had had no specific racial character, but from the 1880s to the 1920s it became something that white people in the South, and especially in the Deep South, did to African Americans. Between 1882 and 1930, 90 percent of the estimated 2,800 Southern lynch victims was black; 94 percent of those black victims were lynched by whites. Like segregation and voter disfranchisement during the same time period, lynching functioned to keep black people in their place. "The real purpose" of the Hose lynching, wrote Ida B. Wells-Barnett, "is to teach the Negro that in the South he has no rights that the law will enforce" (*Lynch Law in Georgia*, 1899, 1).

Wells-Barnett's investigation of the Hose affair also revealed that it was not an isolated incident but was in fact only one of twelve lynchings and attempted lynchings in the vicinity of Palmetto, Georgia, in a six-week period beginning in mid-March 1899. The first nine victims had been arrested in February of that year for their alleged roles in a series of arsons in Coweta County. The nine men, who had no previous convictions and were probably innocent, languished in jail for nearly a month, chained together, until a masked mob of more than a hundred heavily armed men broke into the jail to lynch them. The mob fired a volley of shots into the cells, killing five of the prisoners instantly and wounding two of the others. A *New York Times* report suggested that Alfred Cranford may have been one of the leaders of the masked mob. Relations between the races were thus already volatile by the time of Cranford's killing. Hose's death did not, however, appease the white citizens of Coweta County. In the week that followed, mobs forced hundreds of African Americans off their land, burned down a black church, and burned and tortured at least two other black men—Elijah "Lige" Strickland, a well-known local preacher, who was accused of conspiring with Hose, and Albert Sewell, who allegedly threatened revenge for Hose's murder.

The Sam Hose lynching was widely publicized. In addition to the lurid—and generally approving—coverage of the affair in the white-owned Georgia press, northern newspapers such as the *New York Times* provided extensive and more critical coverage, while African American newspapers like the *Richmond Planet* recorded the compelling evidence of Hose's innocence that emerged following Detective Le Vin's investigation. Bishop ALEXANDER WALTERS of the African Methodist Episcopal (AME) Church spoke for many religious leaders in condemning the Hose lynching and in advocating "manly resistance on the part of Afro-Americans themselves" to prevent further atrocities ("Race War Predicted," *New York Times*, 27 Apr. 1899, 2). The Hose lynching also left a deep impression on ROBERT CHARLES, who decided thereafter to arm himself and who later provoked a bloody race riot in New Orleans in 1900.

The most dramatic effect of the Sam Hose lynching, however, was on W. E. B. DuBois, then teaching at nearby Atlanta University. DuBois was engaged in a social-scientific investigation of race relations in America, and he still believed that southern whites would ultimately accept full equality for the Negro. Not fully aware of the details of the Hose lynching, DuBois set off to discuss the affair with Joel Chandler Harris, an editor of the *Atlanta Journal Constitution* who had popularized for a white audience the Uncle Remus stories. En route to Harris's office, DuBois saw Sam Hose's knuckles hanging on display in a butcher's window. "Something died in me that day," DuBois later wrote in his autobiography (*Dusk of Dawn: An Essay toward an Autobiography of a Race Concept*, 1940, 67). The barbarity of the Sam Hose lynching convinced DuBois that rational arguments and precise social-scientific data were inadequate tools in the black struggle for equality. The lynching of Sam Hose was thus one of the more significant factors in DuBois's founding of a national civil rights organization, the National Association for the Advancement of Colored People (NAACP), which in the 1920s helped to reduce dramatically the number of lynchings in the South.

FURTHER READING

Dray, Philip. *At the Hands of Persons Unknown: The Lynching of Black America* (2002).

Litwack, Leon F. *Trouble in Mind: Black Southerners in the Age of Jim Crow* (1998).

Tolnay, Stewart E., and E. M. Beck. *A Festival of Violence: An Analysis of Southern Lynchings, 1882–1930* (1995).

STEVEN J. NIVEN

Hosier, Black Harry (c. 1750–1806), lay preacher, itinerant minister, early Methodist leader and guide, was born a slave, perhaps in the area of Fayetteville,

North Carolina. There have been variations of his last name circulating throughout history: Hoosier, Hossier, and Hoshier in particular. Apparently he was often called "Black Harry" because of his purely African lineage. Little is known about his early life, his parentage or his family, and there is no record of the exact month and day of his death. He may have been enslaved by a Henry (or Harry) Dorset Gough in the Baltimore area. Hosier's tremendous power as a preacher, however, is well documented, beginning around 1780. Hosier preached in the Carolinas, the Middle Colonies and into the New England area. His fame as a circuit preacher emerged alongside several luminaries of early Methodism: Francis Asbury, Freeborn Garretson, Thomas Coke, Jesse Lee, Richard Whatcoat, and John Walker. These ministers, as well as the prominent Philadelphia physician Benjamin Rush, extolled Hosier's preaching in superlative terms, placing him among the best in the nation and the world.

Hosier's message was typical of early evangelicals, including Methodists. He spoke of the humanity's sinfulness and the need for redemption through faith in Jesus Christ. Hosier was illiterate and preferred not to formally educate himself. He believed his powerful memory of scripture and songs and ability to deliver rousing sermons was as an exercise of faith in God. While accompanying Francis Asbury as a preacher, Hoosier also served as Asbury's guide through the colonies. In addition to Asbury, Hosier also traveled with Thomas Coke, another early Methodist leader. His service as Coke's guide helped lay the foundation for the Christmas Conference in 1784, which established the Methodist Episcopal Church as a denomination independent from the Church of England. He assisted Jesse Lee in establishing one of the earliest African American Methodist congregations, Zoar Methodist Church in Philadelphia. Scholars raise the possibility that he might have known another prominent early African American Methodist clergyman, HENRY EVANS, who established Methodism in Fayetteville, North Carolina. It is documented that he knew PRINCE HALL, who established the first organization of African American Freemasons, the Prince Hall Masonic Order. Scholars note that Hosier helped recruit African Americans to Methodism, perhaps much more successfully than his white counterparts. Yet it is clear that he preached to many whites as well. Asbury, for example, knew that the knowledge Hosier was conveying through his preaching would attract a substantial audience composed of both blacks and whites.

Interestingly, despite Hosier's fame as a great pulpiteer and his impressive ministerial associations, he was only licensed to preach—he had never been ordained as deacon or elder in the Methodist Church. In 1805 there was a petition drive in Philadelphia to have him ordained, but it was unsuccessful. Perhaps certain personal factors contributed to his being denied ordination. Sally Lyons once accused him of improper conduct, but he was cleared of the charge. While there is no firm evidence, rumors circulated that Hosier had bouts of alcoholism. Even if such rumors were true, they did not obstruct his duties. Lyons's charge and the rumors of alcoholism may have helped keep Hosier from full ordination, but it is also known that Methodist authorities (and those of other denominations at the time) simply refused to ordain black men into the ministry.

During his preaching career Hosier constantly traveled up and down the East Coast. However, during the last years of his life, he focused his attention on the middle states of Pennsylvania and Maryland. The exact date of his death remains unknown, but he was buried on 18 May 1806.

Hosier is a prime example of an early black Christian who won recognition during the Revolutionary era and into the early nineteenth century for his tireless work preaching Christianity to both whites and blacks.

FURTHER READING

Aaseng, Nathan. *African-American Religious Leaders* (2003).

Smith, Jessie Carney, ed. *Notable Black American Men* (1999).

SANDY DWAYNE MARTIN

Hoskins, Dave (3 Aug. 1925–2 Apr. 1970), baseball player, was born David Taylor Hoskins in Greenwood, Mississippi, to unknown parents. Information about Dave's early life is inconsistent and sketchy, including the year of his birth, which may have been earlier than 1925, and his name, which is listed in his death record as "David Will" though he went by David Taylor during his baseball career. Most sources say his family moved to Flint, Michigan, in 1936, but his obituary listed him as a graduate of G. H. Jones Industrial School in Highlandale, Mississippi. Some sources listed him as a four-sport star at Northern High School in Flint, though he does not appear in the school's

annuals. Hoskins married a woman named either Cora or Josephine, and they had four children.

Tall and lanky (6'1", 180 pounds), Hoskins played baseball in the Flint City Leagues, usually as a right-handed pitcher, but he was also known as an impressive left-handed batter. In 1944 Hoskins began playing professional baseball when he signed with the Homestead Grays of the Negro League. He pitched for the Grays for one season before an arm injury forced him to move to the outfield. Hoskins had three impressive seasons with the Grays, batting .355, .341, and .317, respectively. In 1945 the Boston Red Sox invited Hoskins to a tryout, but an injury prevented him from attending.

Hoskins played briefly for the Ethiopia Clowns before joining SATCHEL PAIGE on one of his barnstorming tours in 1947. While on tour, Hoskins picked up many pitching pointers from Paige. In 1948 Hoskins returned to pro ball when he joined the Grand Rapids, Michigan, Jets of the Central League, becoming the first black player in that league. Despite being treated poorly by fans and opponents, he had an impressive .393 batting average. The next season, on the recommendation of Paige, the Cleveland Indians signed Hoskins to a minor league contract and assigned him to their Class-A affiliate in Dayton, Ohio. During the 1950 season, Hoskins suffered a head injury when he was hit with a fastball. The injury led to his decision to switch back to pitching full time to minimize his plate appearances. In 1951 Hoskins moved up to Wilkes-Barre, Pennsylvania, of the Eastern League, where he had a 5-1 record as a starting pitcher.

In 1952 Dick Burnett, owner of the Dallas Eagles of the Texas League, was looking for a player who could help his team not only win ball games but also help create a draw for the black entertainment dollar. The Eagles had a player agreement with the Indians, who suggested that Hoskins was ready to play at the Class-AA level. As a pitcher, Hoskins possessed a mediocre fastball, an excellent curveball, a good changeup, and excellent control of all of his pitches. He debuted with the Eagles on 13 April 1952, a 4-2 win over Tulsa, becoming the first black player in the Texas League. While his teammates and fans in Dallas readily accepted him, Hoskins faced some adversity when the team was on the road. Before a June 1952 game against Shreveport, Hoskins received three separate death threats. Hoskins never told the manager for fear he would be benched for the game. He pitched in the game without incident and beat the Sports 3-2.

The 1952 season was Hoskins's best professional season as a pitcher. He finished with a 22-10 record, a 2.12 earned run average (ERA), and a .328 batting average, third in the league. He was a unanimous Texas League All-Star selection and had the Eagles' only two wins in the playoffs against Oklahoma City. During his year with the Eagles, record attendance figures followed Hoskins, with some people saying he single-handedly saved the league. Before 1952 attendance figures averaged 2,000–3,000, but Hoskins regularly drew 6,000–7,000 fans at games he was scheduled to pitch. Not only did he desegregate the Texas League, he also desegregated Burnett Field, the home stadium of the Eagles, when that team had to open the grandstands to African American spectators because of his popularity.

His success in Dallas led the Indians to call him up to the major league club in 1953. Hoskins made his major league debut on 18 April 1953, losing 7-6 to the Chicago White Sox. The Indians used Hoskins as a relief pitcher and spot starter, and he compiled a 9-3 record for the season. During the 1954 season, Hoskins bounced between the Indians and their minor league affiliate in Indianapolis of the American Association. He played only fourteen games in the majors, with a 0-1 record, and pitched his last big league game on 21 September 1954. The Indians won the World Series that year, and though Hoskins was inactive for the playoffs, his teammates voted him a full share of the World Series money allotted to the players.

Hoskins spent the 1955 season pitching for Indianapolis, compiling an 8-10 record, before the Indians released him the following spring. He played for the San Diego Padres of the Pacific Coast League in 1956, with a record of 7-4, and the Louisville Colonels of the American Association in 1957, with a record of 10-11. In 1958 Hoskins returned to Dallas, a city he apparently thrived in as he had his second best professional season, compiling a 17-8 record. He played part of the 1959 season in Dallas before a mid-season trade sent him to the Houston Buffs. Hoskins started the 1960 season, his last professional season, with the Montreal Royals of the International League, but he was released in June. Hoskins's career record as a pitcher, not including his time in the Negro League, was eighty-nine wins and sixty losses.

After baseball, Hoskins returned to Michigan where he used his World Series earnings to buy a farm just outside Flushing. He put his baseball life behind him to work his farm and take care of his family until he died of a heart attack. In 1983

Hoskins was inducted into the Flint Greater Hall of Fame and in 1987 the Greater Flint Afro-American Hall of Fame. Throughout his life and baseball career, Hoskins was considered an intelligent, soft-spoken man able to handle the pressures (and media attention) of being a pioneering black baseball player in the South.

FURTHER READING

Adelson, Bruce. *Brushing Back Jim Crow: The Integration of Minor-League Baseball in the American South* (1999).

Moffi, Larry, and Jonathan Kronstadt. *Crossing the Line: Black Major Leaguers, 1947–1959* (1994).

Obituary: *Flint Journal*, 3 Apr. 1970.

MICHAEL C. MILLER

House, Callie Delphia (1861?–6 June, 1928), washerwoman, seamstress, organization founder, lecturer, and leader, was born into slavery in Rutherford County near Nashville, Tennessee. She had at least one sister, Sarah, and a brother, Charles. Her parents were slaves. Her father, Tom Guy, apparently served in the Union army. The 1880 Census lists her mother, Ann Guy, as a widowed washerwoman. Callie Guy had only a primary school education, probably attending Freedman's Bureau and church schools, but exhibited a high degree of literacy as an adult.

In 1883 she married William House, a laborer in Rutherford County, and bore six children, five of whom survived to adulthood. In the 1890s she was a widow, taking in laundry like her mother and other impoverished black women in the South.

About this time, a new idea for political action surfaced in Rutherford County and other communities where former slaves lived. Traveling agents began selling a pamphlet called the "Freedmen's Pension Bill: A Plea for American Freedmen." Ten thousand copies of the pamphlet, at one dollar each, sold in 1891, and several editions were produced thereafter. The author, Walter Vaughan, former editor of the Omaha *World*, a native of Selma, Alabama, and a white Democrat, had used his political contacts to get a pension bill for former slaves, patterned after the idea of the widely accepted Union veteran's pensions, introduced in the U.S. Congress.

House and other African Americans had Union veterans in their families and they knew pensions were possible, although black widows and children had difficulty obtaining them because they lacked legal documentation of their marriages and births.

This idea of pensions for ex-slaves captured House's imagination.

The legislation Vaughan had persuaded his Republican Nebraska congressman, William J. Connell, to introduce, in 1890, established a payment formula later used by the Ex-Slave Mutual Relief, Bounty and Pension Association. The measure called for a pension of fifteen dollars per month and a one-time payment of five hundred dollars for each former slave of seventy years and older. For younger former slaves the bounty and pensions were reduced in increments for each decade under age seventy.

Former slaves and such persons as "may be charged by laws of consanguinity with the maintenance and support of freedmen who are unable by reason of age or disease to maintain themselves," were eligible (Berry, 34). Thus relatives who cared for a freedman could, upon providing satisfactory proof to the secretary of the interior, also receive the pension.

Under the bill, former slaves included those freed by Lincoln's Emancipation Proclamation, by state constitutional amendment, or "by any law, proclamation, decree or device." The plan appeared uncomplicated, requiring only that a claimant had been enslaved. Under the proposal, anyone alive before 1861 was presumed to be a slave in the South unless proof to the contrary was presented.

Vaughan's motivation for promoting his scheme had little to do with an altruistic interest in aiding former slaves. Rather, he wished to enhance the South's meager resources for business and industrial development. Money to former slaves would to some extent ameliorate the devastation of the South caused by the Civil War, especially since Congress denied pensions to ex-Confederate soldiers. In his pamphlet, Vaughan grieved over the South's defeat, and expressed nostalgia for slavery times. House and other former slaves rightly rejected him and his motives.

House, however, paid careful attention to Vaughan's detailed description of his efforts to lobby Congress for former slave pension legislation. She knew from her rudimentary education that citizens had the right to petition the government but she had no idea how it was done. Isaiah Dickerson, a Rutherford County African American teacher and minister, was a traveling agent for Vaughan until he left over disagreements about the purpose and management of the enterprise. He thought that, with the right leadership, the former slaves might be successfully organized.

House created an organization that combined political advocacy and service goals. She added chapters that would provide mutual aid in the form of medical and burial assistance, and would collect petitions to Congress signed by the former slaves when they were literate and by others for them when they were not. The movement offered a democratic structure in which local people had control and a voice at a time when black men were becoming disenfranchised throughout the South.

Using the contacts Dickerson had gained from his work with Vaughan, House and Dickerson traveled throughout the former slaveholding states to enroll members and organize local chapters through the black churches. In the years before his death in 1909, Dickerson's experience was invaluable to House. They went on the road organizing chapters of the Ex-Slave Mutual Relief, Bounty and Pension Association, receiving immediate and enthusiastic responses from African Americans. At the grassroots level, the former slaves, who were among the poorest citizens in the nation, embraced what was essentially a poor people's movement. Old and disabled by so many years of manual work, poor diet, and no medical care, these people understood and supported the association's demand for pensions to compensate years of unpaid labor. The effort also was endorsed and supported by local ministers, and the association's membership grew rapidly. The federal government calculated that by 1915 it had grown to almost 300,000 dues-paying members.

Soon after House began the Ex-Slave Association work, she and her children and her brother and his family moved to Nashville, which she made her home for the remainder of her life. Despite organizing work, she still described herself as primarily a washerwoman and seamstress. House's sister and her family continued to live in Rutherford County.

The Ex-Slave Association held annual conventions attended by delegates from the South and from wherever former slaves lived. House used sophisticated political strategies in her attempt to gain pensions for the former slaves. The chapters sent thousands of petitions to Capitol Hill and hired lobbyists who succeeded in having the pension bill introduced repeatedly in the Congress and considered in the pension committee but never voted out for floor debate. House also hired prestigious counsel and financed a lawsuit in federal court demanding that cotton tax proceeds in the federal treasury be handed over to the former slaves. The suit went all the way to the Supreme Court but could not overcome the principle of sovereign immunity.

Despite the movement's work, most black leaders were focused on the failing effort to gain federal aid to education and a voting rights bill. With the exception of FREDERICK DOUGLASS, established political leadership opposed the pension bill and distanced themselves from this poor people's movement and its poorly educated non-elite leader, Callie House. The federal Pension Bureau and Post Office Department tried to destroy the movement by denying the association the use of the U.S. mails. When the work continued, they jailed Callie House. Fearing anarchy and riot when the hundreds of thousands of former slave petitioners understood they would never receive pensions, federal officials accused her of using the mails to defraud. Ignoring the right to petition the government for any purpose, they convinced an all-white, all-male jury in Nashville that House was guilty simply because she had organized to do something that the government would obviously never do—provide pensions to former slaves.

Despite her imprisonment—one year in the Missouri State Prison in Jefferson City, since there was no federal prison for women at the time—the chapters of the organization survived and continued to offer mutual assistance to former slaves into the 1920s. After her release from prison, House died at her Nashville home from uterine cancer.

The former slave pension movement lived on as some of its agents joined MARCUS GARVEY's Universal Negro Improvement Association. QUEEN MOTHER MOORE came from the New Orleans Garvey chapter. The federal government prosecuted Marcus Garvey using the same postal fraud statute it had employed against Callie House.

The modern reparations movement can be traced through the Garveyites, Nation of Islam, and MALCOLM X back to the Ex-Slave Association. When Callie House called for pensions as reparations in 1900, only 21 percent of the African American population, or about 1.9 million persons, had been born in slavery. Their numbers, like veterans covered by the lucrative Union pension provisions, were slowly diminishing by death. But those former slaves still alive were not able to gain pensions despite their years as unfree laborers and small number. Modern reparation movements such as N'COBRA and the Restitution Study Group seek recompense for African Americans beyond those whose ancestors had been slaves, but they are all, in a sense, the children of Callie House.

FURTHER READING

Berry, Mary Frances. *My Face Is Black Is True: Callie House and the Struggle for Ex-Slave Reparations* (2005).

Bittker, Boris. *The Case for Black Reparations* (1973).

Winbush, Raymond A. ed. *Should America Pay? Slavery and the Raging Debate on Reparations* (2003).

MARY FRANCES BERRY

House, Son (21 Mar. 1902?–19 Oct. 1988), blues musician, was born Eddie James House Jr. in the Mississippi Delta plantation community of Riverton, north of Clarksdale in Coahoma County, Mississippi, the son of Eddie House and Maggie (maiden name unknown). His parents worked as farm laborers in Mississippi and Louisiana. In later interviews, House said his father was also a musician who performed on weekends until he put secular music aside and joined the Baptist Church. House, also active in the church, showed little interest in secular music as a youth. He supposedly preached a sermon while still in his mid-teens and later became a Baptist pastor.

Following his parents' separation and then his mother's death, House turned to a life of rambling. He traveled through Mississippi, Arkansas, and Louisiana, taking seasonal work on farms and cattle ranches, and serving as a pastor in Lyon, Mississippi, near Clarksdale. When he was about eighteen, he married Carrie Martin, a woman fourteen years his senior (assuming he was born in 1902 and not earlier, as some researchers suspect). They left Mississippi and moved to northern Louisiana. Although the chronology is uncertain, owing to his own varying accounts, House spent some time, perhaps six months, as a steelworker in St. Louis. After returning to Louisiana, probably around 1926, he and his wife separated. House moved back to the Clarksdale area.

By 1927 the church no longer dominated his life, although it would remain a source of inner conflict until his death. Inspired by the guitarist Willie Wilson, whom he met in the town of Mattson, below Clarksdale, House decided to take up guitar. Accounts vary as to his musical education. On at least one occasion he said he learned from Wilson; at other times he insisted he was self-taught. According to the researcher Dick Waterman, House bragged that he bought a guitar on a Wednesday and was playing that weekend. Whatever the case, he was a quick study, picking up repertoire and technique from local musicians, particularly Reuben Lacey, and playing house parties by 1928. At a house party near Lyon that year, he shot and killed a man, supposedly in self-defense, and was incarcerated. After about two years, however, his case was reconsidered, and he was set free on condition that he leave the Clarksdale area.

He then settled in Lula, Mississippi, where he came in contact with CHARLEY PATTON, often regarded as the father of Delta blues, and was soon performing with Patton and Patton's partner, Willie Brown. In the spring of 1930, when H. C. Spier, a representative of Wisconsin-based Paramount Records, contacted Patton about a recording session, Patton suggested that the session also include House, Brown, and the barrelhouse pianist Louise Johnson (probably Patton's girlfriend at that time). The four blues artists and the gospel singer Wheeler Ford drove to Grafton, Wisconsin, for what would be one of the most important sessions in blues history. For House, the 28 May 1930 session was distinguished by three songs, each long enough to take both sides of a 78rpm record and each considered a classic: "My Black Mama," "Preachin' the Blues," and "Dry Spell Blues." Paramount listed several other sides for House, but only one of them, "Walking Blues," was ever recovered. House claimed he received forty dollars for the session, which he considered reasonable.

Returning to Mississippi, House continued to associate with Patton and Brown. With Patton's death in 1934, House and Brown became a duo. Working out of Robinsonville, Mississippi, they ranged as far as Memphis, encountering and influencing a young ROBERT JOHNSON along the way. In 1934 House married Evie (maiden name unknown).

In August 1941 the folklorist Alan Lomax recorded House, accompanied by Brown on guitar, Fiddlin' Joe Martin on mandolin and washboard, and Leroy Williams on harmonica, at a country store near Lake Cormorant. Lomax, who was working on a survey of African American music for the Library of Congress, returned the following summer for a second solo session with House.

Around 1943 House moved to upstate New York in search of steady work. He eventually settled in Rochester and got a job as a Pullman porter on the Empire State Express, one of the top passenger trains of that era. (House later confided that he lied about his age to get the job, fueling speculation that he was born earlier than his listed birth date.) During this time, he made music when he visited Brown in Mississippi or when Brown came to Rochester, but after Brown's death around 1952 he gave it up.

In 1964 Dick Waterman and two other blues enthusiasts traced House to Rochester and urged him to try for a second musical career. Although his guitar playing was affected by a senile tremor, his voice remained exceptionally strong, and he made his return that year, appearing on the festival circuit and recording for Blue Goose, a Washington, D.C., label. Signing on with Waterman's booking agency, Avalon Productions, he toured with fellow blues rediscoveries MISSISSIPPI JOHN HURT and SKIP JAMES; appeared at major festivals, including the Newport Folk Festival, the Philadelphia Folk Festival, and the Ann Arbor Blues Festival; and recorded for several labels, most notably Columbia in New York City, where he was produced by John Hammond. He toured Europe several times through 1970 and was the subject of a short film. By 1971, though, his health was failing and he curtailed his appearances. In 1976 he moved to Detroit, where he died twelve years later in Harpers Hospital. He was inducted into the Memphis-based Blues Foundation Hall of Fame in 1980.

With his highly rhythmic, fully supportive slide guitar playing and his impassioned vocal style, House was one of the seminal figures in Mississippi Delta-style blues, ranking with such greats as Patton and TOMMY JOHNSON. Although he never truly reconciled his church background with his music, he merged the traditions of the folk sermon and the blues singer, preaching the blues with great depth of feeling and a riveting onstage delivery. According to some sources, he actually did preach in country juke joints on occasion as Saturday night became Sunday morning—then would pick up his guitar and return to "jooking."

FURTHER READING

Lester, Julius. "I Can Make My Own Songs," *Sing Out* 15.3 (July 1965), 38–45.

Lomax, Alan. *The Land Where the Blues Began* (1993).

Obituary: *Living Blues* 84 (Jan.–Feb. 1989), 48–50.

DISCOGRAPHY

Dixon, Robert M. W., and John Godrich. *Blues and Gospel Records: 1902–1943* (1982).

Leadbitter, Mike, and Neil Slaven. *Blues Records, January 1943 to December 1966* (1968).

Oliver, Paul, ed. *The Blackwell Guide to Blues Records* (1989).

Oliver, Paul, ed. *Blues Records, 1943 to 1970: A Selective Discography*, vol. 1 (1987).

This entry is taken from the *American National Biography* and is published here with the permission of the American Council of Learned Societies.

BILL MCCULLOCH AND
BARRY LEE PEARSON

Houser, N. B. (14 Feb. 1869–28 Aug. 1939), physician, drug store owner, and investor, was born Napoleon Bonaparte Houser near Gastonia, in Gaston County, North Carolina, the son of William H. Houser, a brick mason and contractor, and Fannie Houser, a housekeeper. The elder Houser's $600 in real estate and $200 in personal property, according to the 1870 U.S. census, made him one of the wealthiest black businessmen in the Charlotte, North Carolina, area. The young Houser attended Charlotte public schools and worked as a farmhand on his father's farm from the age of nine until fourteen. At fourteen he began to work at his father's brick factory, and at age sixteen became his father's personal secretary.

In 1881 Houser entered the Presbyterian-affiliated Biddle University in Charlotte, and in 1887 attended the Leonard Medical School at Shaw University in Raleigh, North Carolina. After finishing medical school in 1891, he received his medical license from the North Carolina Medical Board and began his medical practice in Charlotte. From 1891 until 1901 he consulted with Biddle University, supervised Samaritan Hospital for three years, and served one year as president and two years as the secretary of the North Carolina Colored Medical Association—an organization he helped found. Around 1890 he married his first wife, Maggie (whose maiden name is unknown), a North Carolina native.

Houser moved his medical practice from Charlotte to Helena, Arkansas, in June 1901, following a visit to his brother, Charles, who was working there as a brick mason. According to a 1911 profile, Houser saw Helena's "climate, fertile soil and teeming population of the race" as "a veritable Promised Land" (Hamilton, 356). Helena, a booming Arkansas Delta river town on the Mississippi River, was full of opportunities. It was at the center of a regional economy dominated by cotton and hardwood timber, and it was the county seat of Phillips County, which in 1900 had a mostly rural agricultural population that was over 78 percent black. At the same time, increased racial tension in North Carolina generally, and Charlotte specifically, likely also pushed Houser to pursue new opportunities and leave his home state. In the spring of 1899 North Carolina

had passed a Jim Crow railroad bill that insulted the values of middle-class blacks like Houser, who believed that hard work, education, and, ultimately, success would earn respect and insulate their class from white racism. Then in 1900, as Democrats campaigned for a disfranchisement amendment, white supremacy clubs sprang up throughout the state. With the amendment's overwhelming support, especially in Houser's home county of Mecklenburg, Charlotte's luster was lost.

Houser apparently moved to Helena without his first wife, Maggie, and soon married another North Carolina native, Annie S. Alston, on 18 January 1902 in Helena. Their union produced one daughter, Willie Henry Houser, who was born around 1914. Houser prospered as one of the few black doctors in Helena. In 1904 or 1908 he opened the Black Diamond Drug Store in downtown Helena with $7,500 in capital. By 1911 he reported that the drug store did $2,000 in sales each month. In 1910 he became president of the Helena Negro Business League. Houser invested considerably in rental property and purchased stock in the Phillips County Land Investment Company, and the Mound Bayou Oil Mill Manufacturing Company. He was also active in the social life of fraternal organizations. One contemporary biography claimed, "the doctor is a member of all the fraternities" (Hamilton, 358). His memberships included the Prince Hall Masons, Odd Fellows, Knights of Pythias, and the Little Rock, Arkansas–based Mosaic Templars of America.

In 1920, just after the October 1919 Elaine Race massacres tore at Phillips County's social fabric, Houser left Helena and resumed his medical practice in Charlotte. Upon his death, the *Charlotte Observer* described his practice as "one of the largest practices of any negro doctor in the Carolinas" (9 Aug. 1939).

FURTHER READING

Greenwood, Janette Thomas. *Bittersweet Legacy: The Black and White "Better Classes" in Charlotte, 1850–1910* (1994).

Hamilton, G. P. *Beacon Lights of the Race* (1911).

Richardson, Clement. *National Cyclopedia of the Colored Race* (1919).

Smith, C. Calvin. "Serving the Poorest of the Poor: Black Medical Practitioners in the Arkansas Delta, 1880–1960," *Arkansas History Quarterly* (1998).

Strong, Charles Moore. *History of Mecklenburg County Medicine* (1929).

Obituary: *Charlotte (N.C.) Observer*, 29 Aug. 1939.

BLAKE WINTORY

Houston, Charles Hamilton (3 Sept. 1895–22 Apr. 1950), lawyer and professor, was born in the District of Columbia, the son of William LePre Houston, a lawyer, and Mary Ethel Hamilton, a hairdresser and former schoolteacher. Houston graduated Phi Beta Kappa from Amherst College in 1915. After a year of teaching English at Howard University in Washington, D.C., he served during World War I as a second lieutenant in the 351st Field Artillery of the American Expeditionary Forces. Having experienced racial discrimination while serving his country, Houston "made up [his] mind that [he] would never get caught ... without knowing ... [his] rights, that [he] would study law and use [his] time fighting for men who could not strike back." He entered Harvard Law School in 1919, where he became the first African American elected as an editor of the *Harvard Law Review*, and in 1922 he earned an LLB cum laude. In 1922–1923 he studied for the doctorate in juridical science, becoming the first African American to be awarded the SJD at Harvard. Following an additional year of study with a concentration on civil law at the University of Madrid, Houston passed the bar examination for the District of Columbia in 1924. In that year he married Margaret Gladys Moran. They divorced in 1937, and Houston married Henrietta Williams, with whom he had one child.

Houston practiced law as a partner in the District of Columbia firm of his father (Houston & Houston; later Houston, Houston, Hastie & Waddy) from 1924 to 1950, with occasional leaves of absence. He also taught law and became an academic administrator at Howard University Law School, serving on its faculty from 1924 to 1935. His accomplishments at Howard were remarkable. From 1929 to 1935 he provided leadership during the transformation of the then-nonaccredited evening school to a highly respected, full-time, American Bar Association–accredited day law school that enjoyed membership in the Association of American Law Schools. Directing the work of the law school as vice dean and chief administrative officer (1930–1935), Houston inspired the faculty and students with a sense of urgency and a spirit of boldness regarding the duty of African American lawyers as advocates of racial justice. Houston expounded a philosophy of "social engineering," which was grounded in the beliefs that law could be used effectively to secure fundamental social change in society and that the law was an instrument available to minority groups who were unable to use fully the franchise or direct action to achieve

recognition of their rights and equality. Among his students during this period were OLIVER HILL, William Bryant, and THURGOOD MARSHALL, each of whom would become distinguished civil rights litigators and the latter two of whom would achieve national renown as federal jurists.

Houston's civil rights advocacy primarily focused on achieving recognition of African Americans' equal rights under law through the elimination of legally enforced racial discrimination. He argued that the status of African Americans as an oppressed minority necessitated the "complete elimination of segregation" through a protracted struggle including a legal campaign supported by a "sustaining mass interest," with "leadership ... develop[ing] from the aspirations, determinations, sacrifices and needs of the group itself." He served as the first full-time, salaried special counsel of the National Association for the Advancement of Colored People (NAACP) from 1935 to 1940. He proposed in 1934 and thereafter implemented a strategy for overturning the "separate but equal" precedent of *Plessy v. Ferguson* (1896) to the end that racial discrimination and segregation might be declared unconstitutional by the U.S. Supreme Court. In recognition of courts' reliance on *stare decisis* and of widespread racism, Houston developed a long-range strategy of building favorable precedents over time until a direct attack on segregation per se could be made based upon such precedents rather than following one proposed earlier by Nathan Margold to make an immediate attack on segregation. Houston's strategy was implemented by the NAACP and later its Legal Defense and Educational Fund under Thurgood Marshall's direction. While the NAACP and its Legal Defense Fund were concerned about various manifestations of racial discrimination, a special grant from the American Fund for Public Service was primarily devoted to funding cases involving discrimination in education because of its relation to the fundamental problem of white supremacy. According to Houston in 1935, "Apparent senseless discriminations in education against Negroes have a very definite objective on the part of the ruling whites to curb the young and prepare them to accept an inferior position in American life without protest or struggle."

As special counsel and later adviser to Thurgood Marshall, Houston emphasized for the sake of "effectiveness" both the importance of the use of African American lawyers and the commitment to a program of "intelligent leadership plus intelligent mass action." Houston worked with local African American attorneys and argued before the U.S. Supreme Court *Missouri ex rel. Gaines v. Canada* in 1938, the first major Supreme Court case in the groundwork laid for *Brown v. Board of Education* (1954), which declared segregation in public schools unconstitutional. He thereafter shaped with Marshall many of the essential legal precedents leading to *Brown*, including *Sipuel v. Oklahoma State Board of Regents* (1948), *McLaurin v. Oklahoma State Regents* (1950), and *Sweatt v. Painter* (1950). For African Americans in the Consolidated Parent Group of the District of Columbia, Houston initiated litigation against inequality in public schools, which under JAMES NABRIT was later transformed and ultimately led to *Bolling v. Sharpe* (1954), the companion case to *Brown* declaring segregation in the district's public schools unconstitutional.

Houston's historical significance is chiefly derived from his role as strategist, legal counsel, and adviser in the struggle against racial discrimination in public education. It is noteworthy, however, that while he was among the first to emphasize the importance of training lawyers to change law and to participate in dissent regarding fundamental policy and practice of the government, he recognized that the judicial process was slow and not designed to change, but rather to uphold the status quo. Because of these "limitations," he cautioned those who would rely on the courts alone and encouraged African Americans to "do [their] own fighting and more of it by extra-legal means"; that is, boycotts, demonstrations, and the like.

Houston's contributions to eliminating legal validation of racial discrimination extended into other areas, particularly the struggles for fairness in employment, housing, and the rights of the accused. He served, for a time, on the President's Fair Employment Practices Committee and in 1944 successfully argued before the U.S. Supreme Court in *Steele v. Louisville and Nashville Railroad* as well as *Tunstall v. Brotherhood of Locomotive Firemen and Engineers* the duty of fair representation regardless of race or union affiliation. In regard to housing discrimination, Houston assisted the NAACP in its preparation for *Shelley v. Kraemer* (1948) and was chief counsel before the U.S. Supreme Court in the companion case, *Hurd v. Hodge* (1948), in which the Court barred racially restrictive covenants in the states and the District of Columbia. With respect to the rights of persons accused of crimes, Houston litigated *Hollins v. Oklahoma* (1935) and *Hale v. Kentucky* (1938), in which the U.S. Supreme Court overturned the convictions and death sentences of African American defendants who had been tried by juries from which African Americans had been excluded on the basis of race.

An active participant in the civil rights struggle of African Americans beyond the courtroom, Houston engaged in a variety of expressions of political activism during his lifetime, including marching during the 1930s for the freedom of the SCOTTSBORO BOYS, writing a regular column of political commentary in the *Afro-American*, and testifying before Congress against lynching and other forms of racial injustice. His analysis and experiences compelled him in 1949 to urge African Americans not simply to be "content … with … an equal share in the existing system," but to struggle to establish a system that "guarantee[d] justice and freedom for everyone."

Charles Hamilton Houston's grueling pace in the struggle for racial justice eventually resulted in a heart attack from which he died in Washington, D.C. He was buried in Lincoln Memorial Cemetery in Suitland, Maryland.

FURTHER READING

Letters and papers of Houston may be found in the records of the NAACP and the William L. Houston Family Papers in the Library of Congress, in the records of the Fair Employment Practices Committee at the National Archives, and in the Charles H. Houston vertical file, the Consolidated Parent Group Records, and the C. H. Houston Collection at the Moorland-Spingarn Research Center, Howard University.

Kluger, Richard. *Simple Justice* (1976).

McNeil, Genna Rae. *Groundwork: Charles Hamilton Houston and the Struggle for Civil Rights* (1983).

Segal, Geraldine. *In Any Fight Some Fall* (1975).

Tushnet, Mark. *The NAACP Legal Strategy against Segregated Education, 1925–1950* (1987).

Obituaries: *Afro-American*, 29 Apr. 1950; *Pittsburgh Courier*, 6 May 1950.

This entry is taken from the *American National Biography* and is published here with the permission of the American Council of Learned Societies.

GENNA RAE MCNEIL

Houston, Drusilla Dunjee (20 June 1876–8 Feb. 1941), author, journalist, self-trained historian, and teacher, was born Drusilla Dunjee, most likely in Harpers Ferry, Virginia, although a few sources say that she was born in Winchester, Virginia.

She was the daughter of Lydia Ann (Taylor) and John William Dunjee, a Baptist minister who built black churches across the South as a member of the American Baptist Home Missionary Society. Raised in a prosperous, middle-class home, Dunjee and her family were part of a pioneering group of African Americans who headed west after the Civil War in search of a freer life and greater opportunity. Her keen intellect and interest in ancient Africa were cultivated early on by her father's library and prominent circle of associates, among whom were FREDERICK DOUGLASS and BLANCHE K. BRUCE. These influences encouraged Houston's passion for learning and life-long interest in African culture.

When she was twenty-two Drusilla eloped with Price Houston, a businessman and storekeeper more than ten years her senior. After the birth of their first daughter, the two settled in McAlester, Oklahoma, where Houston owned and operated a school for girls named the McAlester Seminary from 1898 to 1910.

As a devout Baptist and schoolteacher, Houston's duties were typical of those performed by black churchwomen who trained young women for spiritual and educational leadership. Among the thousands of black migrants who settled the Oklahoma Territory before it achieved statehood in 1907, Houston became an active and engaged resident of Oklahoma City, spending much of her early married life building church schools and administering to institutions that served black youth, including Oklahoma Baptist College for Girls and the Oklahoma Vocational Institute of Fine Arts and Crafts, a private school that she founded sometime between 1923 and 1925. The institute featured courses in law, civil service business, academic preparation, journalism, fine arts, elocution, music, painting, domestic art, and printing. The positive effect of Houston's public work in education reflected a larger tradition of volunteer service by black women who for over a century provided the black community with nearly all of its social services.

By 1900 the proliferation of black newspapers and magazines allowed black women writers like Houston to make meaningful contributions to the field of journalism as essayists, columnists, and guest editors. Raised in a newspaper family, Houston and her brother ROSCOE DUNJEE followed the tradition begun by their father, who published the *Harper's Ferry Messenger* during Reconstruction. In 1915 Houston's younger brother Roscoe purchased a small printing plant from which he published a weekly newspaper, the *Black Dispatch* of Oklahoma City.

Supporting her brother's efforts to maintain the publication during its early years, Houston served as a contributing editor and regular feature writer for close to three decades, reporting little-known facts on people and events in black history and offering commentary on social issues relevant to the black community. Many of these stories chronicled her early research on the Cushite Empire, the indigenous groups of ancient northeast Africa (now Ethiopia) who shared cultural links with black groups across the Arab world, including Persia, Babylonia, and India. Houston argued that these ancient Ethiopians were among the early builders of human civilization. Her articles were frequently syndicated to other black newspapers by the Associated Negro Press and consequently gained for Houston a national reputation and wide black readership.

Although rarely counted among the ranks of notable black women writers of the 1920s and 1930s, Houston was an early researcher and self-trained expert on the history of ancient Africa. Her best-known work, *Wonderful Ethiopians of the Ancient Cushite Empire, Volume I*, was published in 1926. An examination of the links between the native people of the Upper Nile Valley in Egypt and Ethiopia with those in Arabia, Persia, Babylonia, and India, *Wonderful Ethiopians* was the initial book of a planned multivolume study, the first of its kind, attempting to place Africans at the center of both African and world history. Recognizing the physical and cultural connections of African people across the world, Houston was not the first to use history as a medium to refute the notion that Africans had no history before the arrival of Europeans. However, she is one of the few women and the only one of her generation to document this history in such depth. Her mastery of facts and data on ancient Africa relied on references from multiple disciplines including geology, ethnology, geography, archaeology, linguistics, and history. With her focus on Africa as the cradle of civilization, Houston attempted to correct the distorted and negative manner in which people of African descent were commonly portrayed. At a time when young black writers were rediscovering their African roots, Houston's work became a source of racial pride and positive affirmation for those receptive to the flourishing art and ideas of the Harlem Renaissance and the New Negro movement.

Favorably reviewed by most of the major black newspapers and journals of the day, *Wonderful Ethiopians* was the only volume, of the three Houston completed, ever published. The other volumes included *Wonderful Ethiopians of the Americas* and *Wonderful Ethiopians of Western Europe*. Sources suggest that financial hardship, a lack of research assistance, failing health, and Houston's position outside academic circles were among the reasons she was unable to publish the remaining volumes. Though a path-breaking study for its time, the book encountered criticism for its uncritical writing style, lack of citations, bibliography, and index; the latter two have been added since its original publication. Still one of few available texts written on ancient African civilizations, *Wonderful Ethiopians* is part of a larger body of works that continues to inform the research of contemporary Pan-African scholars.

Houston died in Phoenix, Arizona, having lived with tuberculosis for many years. Still a relatively unknown figure in African American history, Houston's life and writings have become the subject of renewed interest by scholars wishing to examine her accomplishments in the fields of journalism, literature, and history.

FURTHER READING

Houston, Drusilla Dunjee. *Wonderful Ethiopians of the Ancient Cushite Empire* (1926).

Brooks-Bertram, Peggy. *Uncrowned Queens: African American Women Community Builders of Western New York Volume I* (2002).

Des Jardins, Julie. *Women and the Historical Enterprise in America: Gender, Race, and the Politics of Memory, 1880–1945* (2003).

Taylor, Quintard. *In Search of the Racial Frontier: African Americans in the American West, 1628–1990* (1998).

DE ANNA J. REESE

Houston, Joshua (1822–8 Jan. 1902), the self-reliant bondsman of the legendary Sam Houston, was born to a slave mother and reared on the Temple Lea Plantation in Marion, Perry County, Alabama, three years after the territory gained statehood. Joshua stood out at an early age. Although a field hand, the boy began learning blacksmithing and other skills. With the aid of the Lea family Joshua also began reading. The remarkable youngster garnered a reputation early on as a precocious and assiduous child. Barely eighteen, he carried this reputation with him when moved to Texas.

In 1834 Joshua's owner, Temple Lea, died and willed the twelve-year-old Joshua to his teenage daughter Margaret Moffette Lea, who six years later at the age of twenty-one married and became the third wife of the forty-six-year-old Sam Houston. Houston, the former general who led the Anglo-American victory against General Antonio López de Santa Anna's six-thousand-man Mexican army at the Battle of San Jacinto in April 1836, had an unusual capacity for social reform and racial tolerance. As a teenager he had spent two years with Cherokee Indians, and he considered the eastern Tennessee band his surrogate family. For most of his military and political life he worked to protect the precarious rights of Indian groups. A slaveholder, he opposed corporal punishment for slaves and promoted literacy among them.

Houston immediately recognized Joshua's talents, cultivated them, and continually rewarded the industrious slave. Houston resumed Joshua's education and also continued his apprenticeships in blacksmithing, carpentry, wheelwrighting, and horse training. Recognizing Joshua's trustworthiness, Houston assigned him numerous responsibilities. As a skillful carpenter Joshua helped construct the Houston family homes of Cedar Point near Houston and Raven Hill outside Huntsville in Walker County. Occasionally Joshua managed the family household when Sam and Margaret Houston were away. Mostly, however, Joshua became Sam Houston's driver. Joshua chauffeured Houston on the East Texas campaign circuit during his presidential reelection bid in 1840, on road trips to Tennessee to visit Houston's dear mentor and friend Andrew Jackson, and in Austin during his short stint as governor. Joshua chauffeured other dignitaries as well, and frequently he traveled alone, running errands for the Houston family. He drove full-time for a stagecoach company in the 1850s, giving his owner half of his wages. He had enormous respect for Sam Houston and sought to pattern his own life after Houston's.

Like his mentor and master, Joshua Houston had a full personal life. In the late 1840s he began an affair with a nearby slave. Joshua and Anneliza lived together as man and wife and had three children—Julie, Joe, and Lucy. The relationship at some point changed because both Joshua and Anneliza went on to marry other people. Anneliza and the children moved to Crockett, Texas, in Houston County and lived on the Hall family's Bluff Plantation. At some point, probably after Anneliza moved to Crockett, Joshua began a relationship with the slave Mary

Green, also of the Huntsville area. They had two children, Ellen and Joshua Jr.; Mary died while giving birth to Joshua Jr. during the Civil War. Joshua married his third wife, Sylvester Baker, in 1863 or 1864 and had three more children, including daughter Minnie and son Samuel W. Like thousands of slave couples, Joshua and Sylvester legalized their nuptials after the Civil War.

Joshua Houston saw Emancipation and Reconstruction as pivotal periods of black agency. In 1862 Sam Houston, who as governor opposed secession, freed Joshua and all his other slaves. Ill and poor, Sam Houston died months later in 1863, leaving his widow with expenses. Hearing of Margaret Houston's financial woes, Joshua offered her two thousand dollars in gold—his life savings. She refused the offer and encouraged him instead to use the money for his family.

He took her advice, buying property, building a home, and opening a prosperous blacksmith shop. During the beginning years of Reconstruction he also concentrated his efforts on promoting the ideal of self-sufficiency in the black community. With his own funds and the help of like-minded freedmen, such as the businessman and property owner Memphis Allen, Houston organized a number of institutions for Huntsville blacks. In 1867 Houston and others founded the Union Church, the first black-owned institution in Huntsville, where Baptists and Methodists worshipped together. Houston believed that education was a weapon against racism and helped form a school for black youths—for which they paid a modest tuition—inside the sanctuary. Houston also entered local politics, serving as an alderman and county commissioner. Elected county commissioner for two terms, he used his accommodationist-activist approach to secure money for the building of a second school, the Bishop Ward Normal and Collegiate Institute, in 1883. Lack of funds, however, prevented the institution's success and led to its closing five years later.

Joshua Houston's propensity for hard work and academic excellence lived on in his offspring. His son, the educator Samuel Walker Houston, who attended Atlanta University with JAMES WELDON JOHNSON, became one of the leading pioneers of black education in Texas as the founder of the Sam Houston Industrial and Training School, the first institution in Huntsville to offer African Americans a high school education. Without question Joshua Houston's commitment to educational advancement and agency revealed the strength and vision

of the freed community following slavery. At the same time his conduct as a slave challenged notions of black inferiority. Surrounded by his grateful and loving family, Joshua Houston died in 1902 in Huntsville and was buried only a few yards from his former owner.

FURTHER READING

Kreneck, Thomas H. "Houston, Sam," in *The New Handbook of Texas*, vol. 3, ed. Ronnie C. Tyler (1996).

Ledé, Naomi William. *Samuel W. Houston and His Contemporaries: A Comprehensive History of the Origin, Growth, and Development of the Black Educational Movement in Huntsville and Walker County* (1981).

Monday, Jane Clements. "Houston, Joshua," in *The New Handbook of Texas*, vol. 3, ed. Ronnie C. Tyler (1996).

Prather, Patricia Smith, and Jane Clements Monday. *From Slave to Statesman: The Legacy of Joshua Houston, Servant to Sam Houston* (1993).

Seale, William. "Houston, Margaret Moffette Lea," in *The New Handbook of Texas*, vol. 3, ed. Ronnie C. Tyler (1996).

BERNADETTE PRUITT

Houston, Kenneth Ray (12 Nov. 1944–) pro football player, was born in Lufkin, Texas, to Herod and Ollie Houston. His father was the owner of a dry cleaning business and his mother was a housewife. He was the third of four children (two boys and two girls). He first got involved in sports as a sophomore at Dunbar High School in Lufkin, Texas (which he attended from 1959 to 1962), where he played both basketball and football.

After graduating from Dunbar High School in 1962, Houston was recruited to attend Prairie View College in Texas, where he played center and linebacker on the school's football team, ran track, and was on the swimming team. During Houston's junior year his father suffered a stroke and Houston considered dropping out of school, but was persuaded by his family to continue. The Prairie View football team won the national championship in 1963 and 1964, and despite the fact that he stood six-foot three-inches tall and was only about two hundred pounds, Houston was named to several All-American teams as a linebacker.

In February 1967 Houston married Gustie Rice, who was an optical engineer for NASA as well as an assistant principal for the Houston, Texas, school district; they would have two children. In 1967

Houston was drafted by the Houston Oilers in the ninth round of the American Football League (AFL) draft. Tom Williams, who at the time was the track coach at Grambling University and a scout for the Oilers, had spotted Houston and liked his speed. Williams suggested that the Oilers play Houston at safety, and he proved to be a natural at that position. In his third game as a starter against the New York Jets, Houston scored two touchdowns, one on a forty-three-yard interception return and the other on a forty-five-yard run after picking up a blocked field goal attempt. His best season with the Oilers may have been in 1971 when he intercepted nine passes and set a single season record by returning four for touchdowns.

In 1972 he was traded to the Washington Redskins for five players. His most memorable play as a Redskin took place in a Monday night game, broadcast on national television in 1973, when he tackled Walt Garrison on the one-yard line to preserve a victory against the arch-rival Dallas Cowboys on the last play of the game. He retired after the 1980 season. During his fourteen-year pro football career, Houston played in ten Pro Bowls, from 1968 until 1979, and in two AFL All-Star games.

During his career he earned a reputation as a bruising tackler with excellent speed, quickness, and size for a safety. He intercepted forty-nine passes and returned a record nine for touchdowns and recovered twenty-one fumbles, returning one for a touchdown. He also returned a punt and a blocked field goal for touchdowns. He played in 183 consecutive games, the most ever by a defensive back.

In 1999 he was ranked sixty-first on the Sporting News's list of the 100 Greatest Football Players and was selected for the National Football League's 1970s All-Decade Team and the 75th Anniversary All-Time Team. He was elected to the Pro Football Hall of Fame in 1986. Houston would later credit that one play when he tackled Garrison on the one-yard line during that Monday night game in 1973 as the catalyst that got him elected to the Hall. He was also elected as one of the seventy greatest Redskins in 2002. In 1980 the National Football League Players Association awarded him the Byron Whizzer White Award for Humanitarian Service.

After retiring as an active player in 1980, Houston served as head football coach at Wheatley High School and Westbury High School in Houston in 1981. He also coached the defensive backs for the Houston Oilers from 1982 until 1985, and was the defensive backfield coach for the University of Houston football team from 1986 until 1990. He went back to school in 1973 to get a masters degree in counseling, and beginning in 1990 he counseled children who were in hospitals, homebound, or who were placed with agencies by the state of Texas for the Houston Independent School District. He sponsors Hall of Fame golf tournaments every year to benefit the Texas Childrens Hospital in Houston, Texas.

FURTHER READING

Beall, Alan. *Braves on the Warpath: The Fifty Greatest Teams in the History of the Washington Redskins* (1988).

Jains, Robert. "Whatever Happened to … Ken Houston" (capitalnewsservices.net) (2005).

Taylor, Levine, and Konoza. *Washington Redskins 1937–1986 Official 50th Anniversary Team Yearbook* (1986).

Whittingham, Richard. *Hail Redskins: A Celebration of the Greatest Players, Teams and Coaches* (2004).

ROBERT JAINS

Houston, Ulysses L. (Feb. 1825–2 Oct. 1889), Baptist minister and politician, was born a slave in Beaufort, South Carolina, to Jack and Dora (Pooler) Houston. His master, James B. Hogg, was a deacon in the First Baptist Church of Savannah, Georgia, and brought him to live in Savannah at an early age. Houston, raised as a house slave, was baptized at the age of sixteen on 27 June 1841 and became an active member of the First African Baptist Church in Savannah.

Houston hired out his own time in Savannah, earning fifty dollars per month as a carpenter and working as a butcher in a wholesale meat business. Sailors in the Marine Hospital in Savannah taught him to read and write while he was employed there. Houston married his first wife, whose name is unknown, in 1848. In addition to singing in his church's choir, Houston was appointed as a deacon 3 November 1851 and licensed to preach in April 1855. A presbytery of white Baptist ministers appointed by the Savannah Baptist Church ordained Houston as a minister on 12 May 1861.

In October 1862 Houston became pastor of the First Bryan Baptist Church, the ninth pastor of the African American congregation, and like many African American preachers, he began a career in politics and education. He was part of the delegation of Savannah black ministers that met with General William T. Sherman and Secretary of War

Edwin Stanton on 23 December 1864 to discuss the needs of the newly freed black population. The following April, Houston helped to establish a short-lived settlement on Skidaway Island for former slaves, capitalizing on Sherman's plan to give land to black freedmen. Houston's influence continued to rise and in 1868 he was elected to the state's general assembly by the voters of Bryan County. Although white legislators in the Georgia legislature voted in September of that year to prohibit Houston and the other newly elected African Americans from taking their seats, the state supreme court reinstated the legislators the following year. During his two years as a legislator Houston supported educational legislation and successfully introduced a bill requiring equal facilities for all races on public transportation, though he stopped short of calling for full integration.

In 1870 Houston ran for reelection to the Georgia legislature, but lost. Meanwhile some members of First Bryan Baptist Church, resentful of Houston's frequent absences from Savannah, led a campaign to elect Alexander Harris, an influential deacon in the church, as pastor. At that time First Bryan Baptist Church elected its pastors on a yearly basis and Harris successfully kept Houston off the ballot and won the election. Without a congregation Houston founded both the Zion Baptist Church in Liberty County and the Ogeechee Baptist Church in Chatham County. On 1 February 1870 Houston married Henrietta (her last name is unknown) in Atlanta, Georgia. The 1870 census lists four children under the age of eight in Houston's household, though it is not known if they were all his children.

In 1871 the controversy at First Bryan Baptist Church came to a dramatic climax. Some members of the congregation, feeling cheated at the initial vote to expel Houston because a majority of the members were absent, petitioned the church council for a recount. The church reinstated Houston on 31 December 1871. Harris filed a complaint against the church with the Chatham County Superior Court, and the Savannah police arrested Houston for disturbing the peace following a confrontation with Harris during an evening church service. The next day trustees of the congregation bailed him out of jail and the court dismissed the charges a few days later, declaring that the court had no jurisdiction in church affairs. Houston remained pastor of First Bryan Baptist Church until his death.

In the later years of his life Houston remained active in both the church and in civic service. In addition to his duties as pastor he served as moderator of the Zion Baptist Association for seventeen years, and was elected vice president of the Georgia Baptist State Convention for four successive terms. He also was one of the oldest Masons in Georgia and was a member of the Eureka Lodge No. 1, A.F. & A.M., in Savannah. Houston's great influence in the community was evidenced after his death by the petitions from Savannah longshoremen and other black societies asking to hold his funeral on a Sunday, when more might attend. Delegates from Georgia, Florida, and South Carolina attended the funeral and coverage of the event appeared in both the white and black newspapers in Savannah. Houston is buried in Laurel Grove South cemetery in Savannah, Georgia.

FURTHER READING

Foner, Eric. *Freedom's Lawmakers: A Directory of Black Officeholders during Reconstruction* (1996).

Simms, James M. *The First Colored Baptist Church in North America* (1888).

Obituaries: *Savannah Morning News*, 5 Oct. 1889; *Savannah Tribune*, 12 Oct. 1889.

ELIZABETH A. RUSSEY

Howard, Clara Ann (23 Jan. 1866–3 May 1935), teacher and missionary, was born in Greenville, Georgia, and raised in Atlanta. Nothing is known of her parents, her childhood, or her early life. Howard became a member of Atlanta's Friendship Baptist Church, which was organized in 1866 as the city's first independent black Baptist congregation. Unable to buy property, the congregation worshipped in a donated boxcar that would serve as the first classroom of what later became Atlanta University (later a part of the Atlanta University Center). Membership of Friendship Baptist Church grew rapidly, and the congregation moved to a larger building on the corner of Hayes and Markham streets and then later moved to a site on Northside Drive.

Friendship Church assumed a major role in promoting black education in the city. A contractual agreement was made between Friendship's leaders and what would become Atlanta University to share the donated boxcar for church services and educational purposes. In 1879 Morehouse College moved to Atlanta from Augusta, Georgia, and set up classes in the new Friendship Baptist Church as did the Atlanta Baptist Female Seminary (later Spelman University) in 1881. By the late 1870s Atlanta University had begun granting bachelor's degrees and supplying black teachers and librarians to the public schools of the South. In 1929 Atlanta University joined with Morehouse College and Spelman College in a university plan known as the Atlanta University System.

Howard was one of the first students to enter Atlanta Baptist Female Seminary after its founding on 11 April 1881. She graduated as valedictorian of her class in 1887 and was one of the school's first six graduates. Atlanta Baptist Female Seminary had been founded with the help of the African American pastor Frank Quarles; the First Baptist Church of Medford, Massachusetts; the Woman's American Baptist Home Mission Society; and Harriet E. Giles and Sophia B. Packard, two white New England Baptist missionaries and teachers who were graduates of Oread Institute in Worcester, Massachusetts. At the time of its founding, Oread was the only college in America founded exclusively for women. Among Oread's graduates was Laura Spelman, the future wife of John D. Rockefeller. In 1882 Giles and Packard met with Rockefeller who pledged $250 to the seminary. Two years later, Rockefeller visited the school, settled the debt on the property, and renamed it Spelman Seminary in honor of his wife and her family, longtime activists in the antislavery movement. Rockefeller's gift precipitated a flurry of interest from other benefactors, and their investments allowed the school to flourish. Spelman conferred its first high school diplomas in 1887, established its missionary training department in 1891, and in 1901 granted its first college degrees.

After Howard's graduation from Spelman, her first teaching job was 200 miles from Atlanta; but she later returned to teach in that city's public schools. Believing that she was needed more urgently in Africa, Howard applied for a missionary assignment. On 9 September 1889 she was appointed to the Congo by the Women's Baptist Foreign Missionary Society, an organization formed in the 1870s by women of Northern Baptist churches. Howard sailed from Boston on 3 May 1890 and arrived in the Congo the following month. She was the second Spelman graduate to go to Africa—NORA GORDON had arrived in 1889. Howard was stationed in the Lukunga region of the western Congo and assumed responsibility for the primary school, which eventually grew to 100 pupils.

In 1895 continuing bouts with malaria forced Howard to return to America. Her health was slow in returning and most sources indicate that she resigned from the Mission Society on 3 May 1897.

She joined the faculty of Spelman Seminary in 1899 and later worked as matron or supervisor in the school's student boarding department. She died in 1935. Spelman College dedicated the Howard-Harreld dormitory on 23 November 1969 in honor of its first seminary graduate and Claudia White Harreld, its first college graduate.

FURTHER READING

Hartshorn, W. N., ed. *An Era of Progress and Promises, 1863–1910* (1910).

Read, Florence Matilda. *The Story of Spelman College* (1961).

SYLVIA M. JACOBS

Howard, Elston (23 Feb. 1929–14 Dec. 1980), baseball player, was born Elston Gene Howard in St. Louis, Missouri, the son of Wayman Hill Howard, a high school principal, and Emmaline Webb, a dietician. A three-sport star in high school, Howard received twenty-five scholarship offers to play intercollegiate football and basketball. Instead, inspired by JACKIE ROBINSON's recent breaking of the color ban in organized baseball, Howard signed in 1948 to play with the Kansas City Monarchs of the Negro American League.

While with the Monarchs, a team that eventually graduated far more players to the major leagues than any other Negro League club, Howard caught the attention of the New York Yankees' scouts, and in 1950 he signed a contract to play with Muskegon, Michigan, in the Class A Central League. After an army hitch in 1951–1952, Howard spent 1953 with the Kansas City Blues of the Class AAA American Association. He had a strong season and decided to play winter baseball in Puerto Rico as a prelude to making the Yankee roster. But during spring training the Yankees switched him from the outfield to catcher under the tutelage of the Hall of Fame receiver Bill Dickey and then assigned him to Toronto of the Class AAA International League. Howard quickly mastered his new position. Named the league's Most Valuable Player for 1954 after hitting .330 with 22 home runs and 109 runs batted in (RBIs), he joined the Yankees in 1955, the first black to play for baseball's most storied franchise. To those who charged that his promotion had been delayed because of race, Howard replied only, "I am playing for the greatest baseball team in the history of the game."

Howard's successful pioneering was based on temperament as well as talent. Indeed, it was likely his ingratiating personality and gentleman's demeanor as much as his athletic ability that prompted the Yankees to select him to integrate the club. Still, his early years with the Yankees were trying. While not directed toward him personally, the racist attitudes and epithets of the general manager George Weiss and the field manager Casey Stengel were hard for the mild-mannered and soft-spoken Howard to endure. He knew that the Yankees had been severely criticized since the early 1950s for fielding lily-white teams and that his presence was especially conspicuous in contrast to the significant number of black players on the crosstown Brooklyn Dodgers and New York Giants. The failure of the Yankees to promote other African Americans did not help matters; six years later, there were only two other blacks, one of them a Panamanian, on the club. Moreover, because Stengel considered him the consummate utility player, Howard bounced between three positions during his first five years with the Yankees. While serving as backup to Yogi Berra, the team's fixture at catcher, Howard played mostly in left field and occasionally at first base. Things changed when Ralph Houk, a former catcher, replaced Stengel as manager after the 1960 season.

In 1961, at age thirty-two, rather old for the position, Howard finally became the team's regular catcher. Perhaps not coincidentally, he hit a career-high .348 with 21 home runs and 77 RBIs. The next year 21 homers and 91 RBIs brought him little national recognition, but in 1963, following injuries to the sluggers Mickey Mantle and Roger Maris, Howard assumed leadership of the Yankees. Refusing to allow racist hate mail to mar his performance, he was voted the league's Most Valuable Player after batting .287 with 28 homers and 85 RBIs. After hitting .313 with 84 RBIs in 1964, his batting skills deteriorated badly, and in early August 1967 the Yankees traded him to the Boston Red Sox, then involved in a close pennant race. Although he hit only .147 for the Red Sox (.178 overall), Howard played a major role in the team's league championship by providing leadership and effectively handling the young pitching staff. He also caught six of seven games in Boston's loss to St. Louis in the World Series.

Howard retired as a player after the 1968 season, returning to New York as the first black coach in the American League. He coached first base and worked with catchers, and he was frequently mentioned as a possible manager. He resigned after the 1978 season, perhaps because of resentment at never having the opportunity to manage a major

league team. Out of baseball in 1979, he rejoined the Yankees in the following year as an administrative assistant to the principal owner George Steinbrenner.

In 14 seasons, 12.5 of them with the Yankees, Howard never led the league in any offensive category and posted solid albeit unspectacular statistics—a lifetime .274 batting average, 167 home runs, 619 runs, 762 RBIs. But the true indicator of his excellence—his ability to play several positions and his defensive prowess as a catcher as well as his knack for handling pitchers—is his being named 9 times to the American League All-Star team. He also won the Gold Glove for fielding twice, in 1963 and 1964. He appeared in 10 World Series, 9 with New York, earning the Babe Ruth Award as the outstanding player in the 1958 series after leading the Yankees to a 3-game comeback win over the Milwaukee Braves. In 1963 he became the first African American to be named Most Valuable Player in the American League.

Howard married Arlene Henley in 1954; they had three children. When Howard died unexpectedly in New York from myocardinitis, Yankee executives departed from convention in praising the man more than the player. Executive vice president Cedric Tallis declared that the self-effacing Howard "was one of the most popular Yankees of all time." Owner George Steinbrenner said, "If indeed humility is a trademark of many great men, with that as a measure, Ellie was one of the truly great Yankees." In 1984 the Yankees retired Howard's uniform number (32) and placed his name on the center field honor plaque at Yankee Stadium.

FURTHER READING
Forker, Dom. *Sweet Seasons: Recollections of the 1955–64 New York Yankees* (1990).
Howard, Arlene, and Ralph Wimbish. *Elston and Me: The Story of the First Black Yankee* (2001).
Rust, Art, Jr. *"Get That Nigger off the Field"* (1976).
Obituaries: *New York Times*, 15 Dec. 1980; *Sporting News*, 3 Jan. 1981.
This entry is taken from the *American National Biography* and is published here with the permission of the American Council of Learned Societies.
LARRY R. GERLACH

Howard, Milton (1821?–18 Mar. 1928), Civil War soldier, cabinetmaker, and fifty-two-year employee of the Rock Island (Illinois) Arsenal, was born free but was kidnapped by slave traders at around the age of five along with his mother, father, brother, and a sister (all of whose names are unknown) from their home near Muscatine, Iowa. He was first sold as house slave to a man named Pickett from Alabama, and later to an Arkansas planter whose last name he took for a surname; he was generally known as "Milt." Reports of his age vary greatly: census, military, and burial records indicate he was born between 1821 and 1845.

Howard and another house slave were married in a formal ceremony at the Pickett Plantation, a privilege that was customarily afforded only to house servants. Several children were born to the couple, but all family ties were severed when Howard was sold to the Arkansas planter whose surname he was given. Nothing else is known about this first family. He would eventually marry two more women and father six more children from those marriages.

After trying several times to escape from the Howard farm, he finally succeeded in the early 1860s. The journey to freedom was torturous. Chased by baying bloodhounds through the wild hill country of Arkansas and southwestern Missouri, he would later tell how he hid underwater for hours, breathing through a hollow reed until it was safe to continue his trek. Aided by the Underground Railroad he finally made it to safety in the North, and was living in MacGregor, a Mississippi River town in Northeast Iowa, when the Civil War broke out in 1861.

He fought on the Union side during the Civil War, enlisting 21 January 1864 in Clayton County, Iowa, and serving with distinction as a private with the U.S. Colored Troops, 60th Infantry F. Howard saw action in the battles of Arkansas Post, St. Charles, Moon Lake, and Big Creek. He was twice wounded at Big Creek—once in the thigh by a musket ball and then in the head by buckshot. Later he was injured when a heavy artillery gun carriage ran over his right leg. As a result of his injuries, he walked with a stiff limp for the rest of his life. He mustered out of the army 15 October 1865 at Devall's Bluff, Arkansas, and once again headed north, free this time, and with a canteen and musket of his own.

He settled in his hometown of Muscatine after the war, working for room and board as an apprentice cabinetmaker. He remarried and fathered two sons, Edward and Warren. Nothing is known about his second wife, who predeceased him.

Howard began his long career at the Rock Island Arsenal around 1870 when he was hired to do janitorial and maintenance work. One of his first assignments was to help tear down some of the buildings that had once held Confederate prisoners of war. Located in the Mississippi River, between Davenport, Iowa, and Rock Island, Illinois, Arsenal Island was home to a prison camp widely known and feared by Southern troops. Over the course of the war, the camp housed more than twelve thousand captured Confederate soldiers. Nearly two thousand men died, most of them victims of a smallpox epidemic that swept the camp, pneumonia, or dysentery; they were buried in the Confederate cemetery on the island. The twelve-acre prison camp included eighty-four wooden barracks, each measuring twenty-two feet by one hundred feet, and a hospital surrounded by a twelve-foot-high fence. The last building was demolished in 1909.

Howard was recognized in the 1880s for saving the life of Arsenal Commander General D. W. Flagler. According to arsenal accounts, the general was ice-skating when the ice broke, plunging him into the frigid water. Howard saw the general struggling, weighed down by his waterlogged woolen clothing, and ran to his rescue.

Following the death of his second wife, Howard met Lena, a beautiful young woman whose last name is now unknown, at a church gathering in Muscatine. The couple wed in 1893 and moved from Muscatine to Davenport, some twenty miles upriver. By then Howard was in his sixties and she was twenty-three. The couple had two sons together, William and Rayfield, and two daughters, Eugene (Jean), and Pearl. The neighborhood near their home at 1531 Judson Street, Davenport, was culturally rich with people from many countries. Howard learned to speak many languages and became a close friend to many. A family member once recalled how he would translate so that two of his friends, one German and one Italian, could speak to one another.

In June 1920, during a grand outdoor ceremony with bands playing, Howard received a gold medal from Colonel Harry B. Jordan in recognition of fifty years of service to the Rock Island Arsenal. The following year he traveled to Aberdeen, Maryland, a gift from Colonel D. M. King in honor of exemplary service to his country. Howard retired from the arsenal in 1922 after fifty-two years of service, though he remains a presence there today, the subject of an exhibit at the Rock Island Arsenal Museum.

Howard died as he arrived for services at Third Missionary Baptist Church, Davenport, a church he and several other former slaves had founded. In death his life drew the attention of the *Davenport Democrat and Leader*, which published the story of his passing on the front page of its 19 March 1928 edition.

Pearl's sons, Howard and Glenn Perkins, would continue their grandfather's legacy of service at the arsenal. Howard, a management analyst, became the arsenal's first Equal Employment Opportunities Officer. Glenn, the family genealogist, worked as a plating room foreman at the arsenal and served eight years as president of the local chapter of the NAACP.

Photographs of Milton Howard reflect a man of great dignity who did not let injustice or hardship lessen his character. He met each challenge as it came, always overcoming, moving forward, one step at a time, living a life of great substance, worthy of remembrance.

FURTHER READING

Information relating to Howard is available at the Rock Island Arsenal Museum, Rock Island, Illinois.

"Arsenal Workman Sold in Slavery as a Child." *Arsenal Record*, 27 Aug. 1918.

Lindburg, Beverley. "An American Odyssey: The Remarkable Saga of Milton Howard," *The Leader*, 21 Feb. 2003.

"Milton Howard: Slave, Soldier, Hero & Centenarian." *The Target, Rock Island Arsenal*, 2 Feb. 1977.

Obituary: *Davenport Democrat and Leader*, 19 Mar. 1928.

BEVERLEY ROWE LINDBURG

Howard, Perry Wilbon (14 Jan. 1877–1 Feb. 1961), Republican politician and lawyer, was born in Ebenezer, Mississippi, the first of seven sons of Perry W. Howard Sr., a farmer and successful blacksmith, and his wife, Sarah. Both parents were former slaves. The only black family in Ebenezer, the Howards received sympathy from whites in the community, who respected their ambition, hard work, and frugality. Perry attended the Holmes County public schools before entering Alcorn A&M in 1891. He did not graduate but later earned his B.A. from Rust University, now Rust College, in Holly Springs, Mississippi, in 1899. He then served for one year as president of Campbell College, a small African Methodist Episcopal (AME) Church school in Jackson, Mississippi. He studied mathematics at Fisk University in Nashville and was chair and professor of mathematics at Alcorn A&M until 1905. In 1904, while still at Alcorn, he earned a law degree from the Illinois College of Law in Chicago

(now DePaul Law School) and was admitted to the Mississippi bar the following year.

In 1907 Howard married Wilhelmina Lucas of Macon, Mississippi, a Fisk graduate who taught in the literary department at Tuskegee Institute and the music department at Alcorn. The Howards had three children, but only two survived into adulthood. Howard was one of only twenty-four black lawyers practicing in Mississippi at the turn of the twentieth century, a period recognized by the historian RAYFORD W. LOGAN as the nadir of southern race relations, when African Americans suffered from segregation, disenfranchisement, and the ever-present fear of lynchings and racial violence. Whites did not seek the services of black lawyers and, since the state precluded African Americans from serving on juries, many blacks believed they would be given a fairer hearing if white lawyers represented them before white juries.

Howard's law practice, located in the center of Jackson's black business district, does not appear to have been profitable, but he compensated for this by serving as national chief counsel for the Elks and as president of the Mississippi Beneficial Life Insurance Company. Moreover, he worked as an officer for the Mississippi Negro Business League, the state affiliate of the National Negro Business League; became the first secretary and, later, president of the National Negro Bar Association; and was a trustee at Mississippi Utica Normal and Industrial Institute, a school designed after BOOKER T. WASHINGTON's Tuskegee model. (Howard, although he had received a liberal education at Fisk, was a staunch advocate of Washington and industrial education.)

That politics became Perry Howard's passion is no understatement. Early in his political career Howard was a protégé and political ally of CHARLES BANKS. Banks, a businessman and Booker T. Washington's chief lieutenant for Mississippi, was the most powerful African American in the state. To some extent whites accepted, and even encouraged, Howard's power and autonomy within the Mississippi Republican Party. On one occasion the Ku Klux Klan even burned a cross on the lawn of Howard's white opponent to warn voters not to vote for the opponent. Because of Howard's political influence in the state, the Republican president Warren G. Harding appointed him special assistant to the attorney general for the United States in 1921, making him the highest-paid African American working in the federal government. Howard moved to Washington, D.C., and lived there for the rest of his life, never again voting in Mississippi, though remaining an active force in the state's political life.

That same year, he joined one of Washington's leading black law firms, Howard, Hayes, and Davis (which became Cobb, Hayes, and Howard in 1935). Howard, JAMES A. COBB, and George E. C. Hayes all had strong political connections the Republican Party. Hayes had worked as the general counsel at Howard University, and Cobb had worked as a municipal judge for some years before joining the partnership. Thus, unlike a number of other black law firms that practiced only criminal law, Howard's firm branched out into municipal law, a more profitable area. The law firm also argued civil rights cases before the federal courts.

Except for 1920, Howard served as a Mississippi delegate to every Republican National Convention (RNC) from 1912 to 1960, an era in which the white supremacist Democratic Party ruled the state's political life. Although there was a movement within the Republican Party to make its southern wing as lily-white as the Democrats, in 1919 Howard led a large contingent of African Americans to the Republican National Committee meeting in St. Louis and to the Republican National Convention in Chicago in 1920, seeking recognition for his black-and-tan faction of the party. Both times he was defeated in his effort to be chosen as the Republican national committeeman for Mississippi by the forces of Michael J. Mulvihill, the white national committeeman from Vicksburg. However, in 1924 Howard successfully unseated Mulvihill at the national convention in Cleveland after Mulvihill refused to appoint any blacks to significant positions within the party. Howard thus became one of the first African Americans to serve on the RNC in the twentieth century. His position brought along with it little more than prestige and patronage power, and even then the patronage most often went to white Democrats and very rarely to blacks.

Within a year of his election to the RNC, Howard became embroiled in controversy, which followed him throughout much of his public career. In 1925, when the Federal Bureau of Investigation and the Post Office Department uncovered widespread political corruption in Mississippi, Howard's political machine was accused of selling offices. Lesser postal positions allegedly went for up to $1,500, while more lucrative positions, such as U.S. marshal, postmaster, and revenue collector, went for as much as $2,500. Investigators also charged Howard with illegally soliciting campaign funds.

Many people understood that Howard, more than any other Republican in Mississippi, controlled the party's appointments. Although the case was never proved in court, many observers presumed that Howard received most of the graft.

Howard, however, denied any wrongdoing and asserted that white supremacists, lily-white Republicans, and disappointed office seekers were out to get him. Despite Howard's denial, the chief examiner for the Justice Department recommended that the patronage charges against Howard be turned over to a grand jury and that Howard be fired from his appointed position for illegally soliciting campaign contributions. U.S. Attorney General John Garibaldi Sargent, however, did not act on these recommendations, and the FBI agents who conducted the investigation against Howard were either quietly reassigned or fired. Howard's behavior did not differ much from that of white politicians engaged in the business of patronage politics. Nonetheless, in 1929, after Howard had gone to trial twice, and with the prospect of a third trial, President Herbert Hoover's administration forced him to resign from his government post.

Black Mississippians criticized Howard for spending so much time away from his state. They contended that he rarely visited Mississippi after moving to Washington, that he made no effort to expand the black electorate in the Magnolia State, and that conditions for black Republicans were virtually the same as they had been under white national committeemen. Several national black leaders also criticized Howard for joining southern whites in opposing the Dyer federal antilynching bill in 1922 and for opposing the formation of the Brotherhood of Sleeping Car Porters (BSCP), a group of black Pullman car porters trying to unionize. Although Howard had worked as a Pullman porter during his college years, when black porters attempted to unionize, he wrote a solicitous letter to the Pullman Company agreeing to help them resist the effort. Eventually the company paid Howard to try to derail the movement. While Howard never denied being a paid agent for Pullman, he claimed that he opposed the black union effort because communists inspired it and black workers were about to destroy what he believed was their "amicable" relationship with the Pullman Company.

Both of Howard's allegations were spurious. A. PHILIP RANDOLPH, the leader of the BSCP, was a socialist, but also a vigorous anticommunist, and he called on President Calvin Coolidge to replace Howard with a black leader more representative of

African American thinking. W. E. B. DuBois also criticized the Coolidge administration for allowing Howard to accept a fee from the Pullman Company while officially holding a governmental position. Randolph prevailed upon the white Wisconsin representative Victor L. Berger to investigate Howard's activities and ascertain if they warranted his removal from office. Other African American leaders, including JAMES WELDON JOHNSON, felt that Howard was an "Uncle Tom" who supported Pullman only because they paid him. Despite these criticisms, Howard kept his seat on the RNC until 1960. At that time he was eighty-three years old and the committee's ranking member. Perry Howard died in Washington the following year, after a very long career.

FURTHER READING

Jackson, David H., Jr. *A Chief Lieutenant of the Tuskegee Machine: Charles Banks of Mississippi* (2002).

Lisio, Donald J. *Hoover, Blacks, and Lily-Whites: A Study of Southern Strategies* (1985).

McMillen, Neil R. *Dark Journey: Black Mississippians in the Age of Jim Crow* (1990).

McMillen, Neil R. "Perry W. Howard, Boss of Black-and-Tan Republicanism in Mississippi, 1924–1960," *Journal of Southern History* 48.2 (May 1982).

Mollison, Irvin C. "Negro Lawyers in Mississippi," *Journal of Negro History* 15 (Jan. 1930).

Obituary: *New York Times*, 2 Feb. 1961.

DAVID H. JACKSON JR.

Howard, T. R. M. (4 Mar. 1908–1 May 1976), physician, civil rights leader, and entrepreneur, was born Theodore Roosevelt Howard in the town of Murray, Calloway County, Kentucky, to Arthur Howard, a tobacco twister, and Mary Chandler, a cook for Will Mason, a prominent local white doctor and member of the Seventh-day Adventist Church (SDA). Mason took note of the boy's work habits, talent, ambition, and charm. He put him to work in his hospital and eventually paid for much of his medical education. Howard later showed his gratitude by adding "Mason" as a second middle name.

Theodore Howard attended three SDA colleges: the all-black Oakwood College in Huntsville, Alabama; the predominantly white Union College in Lincoln, Nebraska; and the College of Medical Evangelists in Loma Linda, California. While at Union College he won the American Anti-Saloon League's national contest for best orator in 1930.

During his years in medical school in California, Howard took part in civil rights and political causes and wrote a regular column for the *California Eagle*, the primary black newspaper of Los Angeles. He was also the president of the California Economic, Commercial, and Political League. Through his work with the league and in his newspaper columns Howard championed black business ownership and the study of black history, and he opposed local efforts to introduce segregation. After a residency at City Hospital No. 2 in St. Louis, Missouri, Howard became the medical director of the Riverside Sanitarium in Nashville, Tennessee, the main SDA health-care institution serving blacks.

Howard married the prominent black socialite Helen Nela Boyd in 1935. The Howards were married for forty-one years and had one adopted son, Barrett Boyd. Howard also fathered several children outside of his marriage, most of them by different women.

In 1942 Howard took over as chief surgeon at the hospital of the Knights and Daughters of Tabor, a fraternal organization in the all-black town of Mound Bayou, Mississippi. While there he founded an insurance company, restaurant, hospital, home construction firm, and large farm where he raised cattle, quail, hunting dogs, and cotton. Howard also built a small zoo and a park, as well as the first swimming pool for blacks in Mississippi. In 1947 he broke with the Knights and organized a rival organization, the United Order of Friendship, and opened its Friendship Clinic.

Howard rose to prominence as a civil rights leader after founding the Regional Council of Negro Leadership (RCNL) in 1951. His compatriots in the council included MEDGAR EVERS, whom Howard had hired as an agent for his company, the Magnolia Mutual Life Insurance Company, and AARON HENRY, a future leader in the Mississippi Freedom Democratic Party. The RCNL mounted a successful boycott against service stations that denied the use of restrooms to blacks, distributing twenty thousand bumper stickers with the slogan, "Don't Buy Gas Where You Can't Use the Restroom."

The RCNL organized yearly rallies in Mound Bayou for civil rights, which drew as many as ten thousand people, including the budding activists FANNIE LOU HAMER and AMZIE MOORE. RCNL rally speakers included the U.S. congressmen WILLIAM LEVI DAWSON and Charles Coles Diggs, the Chicago alderman ARCHIBALD CAREY JR., and the NAACP attorney THURGOOD MARSHALL. One of the entertainers was MAHALIA JACKSON.

In 1954 Howard hatched a plan to fight a credit squeeze by the white Citizens Councils against civil rights activists in Mississippi. At his suggestion the NAACP encouraged businesses, churches, and voluntary associations to transfer their accounts to the black-owned Tri-State Bank of Memphis.

Howard moved into the national spotlight following the murder of EMMETT LOUIS TILL in August 1955 and the trial in September of his killers J. W. Milam and Roy Bryant. Howard was heavily involved in the search for evidence and gave over his home to be a "black command center" for witnesses and journalists. Visitors noticed the high level of security, including armed guards and a plethora of weapons. Howard himself evaded Mississippi's discriminatory gun-control laws by hiding a pistol in a secret compartment of his car. Emmett Till's mother, MAMIE TILL MOBLEY, and Charles Diggs stayed at Howard's home when they came to testify in the trial. Like many black journalists and political leaders, Howard alleged that more than two people took part in the crime. After an all-white jury acquitted Milam and Bryant, Howard gave dozens of speeches around the country, talking about Till's murder and other examples of racial violence in Mississippi. The speaking tour culminated in a rally at Madison Square Garden in New York City. Before a crowd of twenty thousand Howard shared the stage with ADAM CLAYTON POWELL JR., A. PHILIP RANDOLPH, Eleanor Roosevelt, and AUTHERINE LUCY, the first black student to attend the University of Alabama. He also had a highly visible public dispute with J. Edgar Hoover, whom Howard accused of slowness in finding the killers of blacks in the South.

In the final months of 1955 Howard, his wife, Helen, and their son were increasingly subjected to death threats and economic pressure. As a result the Howards sold most of their property and moved to Chicago. In early 1956 the *Chicago Defender* gave Howard the top spot on its annual national honor role. That same year he founded the profitable Howard Medical Center on the South Side and served for one year as president of the National Medical Association, the black counterpart of the American Medical Association. Howard also became medical director of S. B. Fuller Products Company, founded by SAMUEL BACON FULLER, one of the richest black men in the country.

In 1958 Howard ran for U.S. Congress as a Republican against the powerful incumbent Democrat William Levi Dawson, an African American and close ally of the Chicago mayor Richard A. Daley. Although Howard received much favorable media publicity and the support of black leaders opposed to the Daley machine, Dawson overwhelmed him at the polls. Howard was unable to counter either Dawson's efficient political organization or rising black-voter discontent with President Dwight D. Eisenhower's civil rights record.

Shortly before the election Howard helped found the Chicago League of Negro Voters. The league generally opposed the Daley organization and promoted the election of black candidates in both parties. It nurtured the black independent movement of the 1960s and 1970s that eventually propelled four of Howard's friends to higher office: RALPH METCALFE, Charles Arthur Hayes, Gus Savage, and HAROLD WASHINGTON. In the two decades following Howard's failed congressional bid he had little role as a national leader, but he remained important locally. In 1965 he chaired a Chicago committee to raise money for the children of the recently assassinated leader MALCOLM X, and later he was one of the founders of Operation Push. As a doctor he also became well known as a leading abortion provider and was arrested in 1964 and 1965 but never convicted. Howard regarded this work as complementary to his earlier civil rights activism.

Howard was a big-game hunter and made several trips to Africa for such hunting. His Chicago mansion, which he often opened for tours, included what he called a safari room filled with trophies. The Howards' New Year parties were a regular stop for Chicago's black social elite. In 1972 Howard founded the multimillion-dollar Friendship Medical Center on the South Side. The hospital, which was at the time the largest privately owned black clinic in Chicago, boasted a staff of 160, including 27 doctors. Howard died a few years later in Chicago after many years of deteriorating health.

FURTHER READING

Howard's papers are housed at the Eva B. Dykes Library, Oakwood College, Huntsville, Alabama.

Beito, David T., and Linda Royster Beito. "'The Most Hated, and the Best Loved, Man in Mississippi': The Eventful Life of Dr. T. R. M. Howard," *A.M.E. Church Review* 4 (Spring, 2001).

Beito, David T., and Linda Royster Beito. "T. R. M. Howard: Pragmatism over Strict Integrationist Ideology in the Mississippi Delta, 1942–1954," in

Before Brown: Civil Rights and White Backlash in the Modern South, ed. Glenn E. Feldman (2004).

Beito, David T., and Linda Royster Beito. *Black Maverick: T. R. M. Howard's Fight for Civil Rights and Economic Power* (2009).

Dittmer, John. *Local People: The Struggle for Civil Rights in Mississippi* (1994).

LINDA ROYSTER BEITO

DAVID T. BEITO

Howell, Abner Leonard (9 August 1878–?), football player, was born in Mansfield, Louisiana, to Paul C. and Mary Howell. Little is known of their early lives, but in the late 1880s Howell's parents decided to leave Louisiana, seeking a new life in the American West. In 1888 the Howell family and their six children (Abner was the only boy) reached Dodge City, Kansas, and then traveled together to Trinidad, Colorado. Under unknown circumstances, the family split up; Paul Howell went ahead by train, reaching Salt Lake City, Utah, in 1888. Mary and the children remained in Colorado until 1890, when they were able to join Paul in Salt Lake City, where he had been hired as the city's first black policeman. Although Paul and Mary Howell did not join the Church of Jesus Christ of Latter Day Saints (LDS), which was based in Salt Lake City and commonly known as the Mormon Church, Paul was reportedly present at the official dedication ceremonies at Salt Lake City's LDS Temple in April 1893. The Howell children were not raised as Mormons, but as a young adult Abner Howell converted to the LDS Church. In Howell's later writings, he happily recalled his association with future LDS president Heber Grant, who frequently allowed young Abner into a local baseball stadium to watch games in which Grant sometimes took part as a second baseman. Young Howell knew Grant well enough to be selected as one of the porters who accompanied Grant's large Mormon Church mission to Japan in 1901, although Howell accompanied the group only as far as its American departure point at Portland, Washington.

In the late 1890s Howell attended Salt Lake City public schools, where he was among the few black students. An athletically gifted student, he joined the Salt Lake City YMCA on 1 September 1898 and also played football for the exceptionally talented Salt Lake City High School team, which often played college teams. On Thanksgiving Day in 1900 some five thousand fans watched as Howell led his team to a 34–0 victory over a team from East Denver, Colorado. By this time, intercollegiate sports were becoming more popular; football had eclipsed rowing and baseball, and universities and colleges vied to attract talented players to their institutions. In 1901 the University of Michigan was anxious to gain national recognition through its athletic and academic programs. It hired a full-time football coach, Fielding Harris Yost, the former West Virginia University football star and coach at San Jose State College and Stanford University. While in the West, Yost apparently learned about Howell's outstanding skill on the football field, and invited him to attend Michigan and play football for the "Wolverines," as the team was called. Howell already had a job in Salt Lake City as the YMCA's athletic director, but he resigned and moved to Ann Arbor, where he enrolled in the University of Michigan Law School.

Howell played fullback for Michigan during the 1902–1903 and 1903–1904 seasons. Under Coach Yost, the team won the national collegiate football title four consecutive years between 1901 and 1904. When Howell began playing for Michigan, the Wolverines were renowned for their "point-a-minute" offense, in which Howell played a central role. However, Howell was excluded from official team photographs. His name does not even appear in a 1974 book devoted to the history of black athletes at the university. Coach Yost was known to harbor racist feelings, but he permitted Howell to play because his exceptional athleticism made the Michigan team virtually unbeatable. Yost remained as football coach at Michigan until 1926 and then served as Michigan's athletic director until 1941. With the sole exception of Howell, Yost reportedly excluded all other black student-athletes from playing football for the university until 1932.

Howell did not graduate from law school. On 1 August 1903 he married Nina Stevenson in Detroit in an LDS Church ceremony. The couple had seven children and raised them in the Mormon faith. At the outset of the Great Depression Howell and his family moved to Salt Lake City. There Heber Grant, now president of the LDS Church, helped arrange employment for Howell with the LDS as a construction worker on local church buildings. Howell soon became a leader of organized labor groups in Salt Lake City, and he also emerged as a civic leader. He served on the board of the local LDS Welfare Council, on the executive board of the local Boy Scouts of America Council, and on the board of directors of the Salt Lake City Community Chest. He also worked for two years as the doorman for the Utah State Senate at the State Capitol Building, which opened in Salt Lake City in 1916.

Howell's first wife, Nina, died 1 February 1945. Later that year he married Martha Perkins, who died in 1954. According to his own account, Howell occasionally encountered discrimination from other Mormons in the South during the 1950s. After his second wife died, Howell moved to Los Angeles, California, as one of his sisters lived in the area. During the late 1950s he regularly gave lectures at the University of Southern California and at the LDS Temple in Los Angeles, which opened in 1956. The exact date and place of his death are unknown.

FURTHER READING

Behee, John. *Hail to the Victors! Black Athletes at the University of Michigan* (1974).

Gems, Gerald R. "Football and Cultural Values," *College Football Historical Society* (August 1997).

University of Michigan. *Catalogue of Graduates, Non-Graduates, Officers, and Members of the Faculties, 1837–1921* (1923).

Young, Margaret Blair, and Darious Aidan Gray. *The Last Mile of the Way* (2003).

LAURA M. CALKINS

Howlin' Wolf (10 June 1910–8 Jan. 1976), blues singer and musician, was born Chester Arthur Burnett to Leon "Dock" Burnett, a farm laborer, and Gertrude Jones in White Station, Mississippi. Gertrude's father was Native American, and it was apparently he who gave the nickname "Wolf" to his grandson. Dock had been doing farm work in the Delta every spring, and he left the family and moved there permanently when Chester was a year old. Chester sang with his mother in church. A religious fanatic, Gertrude showed signs of mental instability, often singing and attempting to sell original spirituals in the streets. She cast out her son when he was just ten years old. The young Chester trudged miles over frozen ground with only burlap to cover his bare feet and eventually reached the home of his great-uncle, Will Young. Young already had an extended family residing with him, and he put the large boy to work for long, hard hours on the family farm. After three years Chester fled the constant whippings and neglect to find his father.

Chester moved in with his father's family on the Young and Morrow Plantation in Ruleville, Mississippi, near the Will Dockery Plantation. Dock Burnett had remarried, and the presence of an extended family provided a nurturing

environment for his oldest son. After a good crop in 1928, Dock bought his son a guitar. It was on the Dockery Plantation that Chester first heard and met CHARLEY PATTON, who has been called the father of the Delta blues. Patton took the young Wolf under his wing and shared his knowledge of different guitar tunings and slide guitar techniques. Patton employed a strong and percusive guitar attack, virtually reinventing 4/4 time with his emphasis on the second and fourth beats; people came from miles around to see and hear him perform. Known for his guitar showmanship, Patton played the guitar behind his neck and between his legs, and he threw it up in the air and caught it, never missing a beat. Wolf picked up Patton's guitar tricks and developed many others of his own. Patton sang in a rough, raspy voice, as did many of the evangelical preachers of the time. Wolf incorporated this into his vocal stylings and used techniques similar to those of the various throat singers around the world who sing more than one note at a time.

In 1933 Wolf's family moved across the river to Arkansas to escape the harshness of Mississippi and eventually settled on the smaller Phillips Plantation north of Parkin, on the Saint Francis River. Wolf traveled the Delta during the 1930s, and he sang and played guitar often in the company of such notables as ROBERT JOHNSON, SON HOUSE, Willie Brown, and Rice Miller (SONNY BOY WILLIAMSON). It was Miller who taught Wolf how to play harmonica. Wolf tried out many nicknames, such as John D. and Big Foot Chester, before he settled exclusively on Howlin' Wolf. He returned every spring to help his father plow, and he worked at farming much of the time. In 1939 Wolf and his girlfriend Elven Frazier had a son, Floyd.

Wolf was drafted into the army in 1941 and stationed in Seattle. His time in the army was the low point in his life. He developed a nervous condition because of his near illiteracy, and he had difficulties adapting to army discipline. He was honorably discharged in 1943, and his veteran's status served him well later in life when he could receive dialysis at Veterans Administration hospitals across the country while touring.

Wolf returned to farming and sang and played at night. He married Katie Mae Johnson in 1947, and he brought his son Floyd to live with him and his wife. In 1948 Wolf and his family moved to West Memphis, Arkansas. Thousands of African Americans were migrating out of the Delta, put out of work by mechanical harvesters. Many moved north to Chicago and Detroit.

Technological modernization was also beginning to affect music. As MUDDY WATERS was electrifying the blues in Chicago, Wolf began doing the same in West Memphis. Wolf formed a band with the finest musicians available, with Matt Murphy, Willie Johnson, and occasionally Pat Hare on guitars, Junior Parker and James Cotton on harmonica, IKE TURNER on piano, and Willie Steele on drums, frequently augmenting this lineup with saxophones.

In 1949 Wolf approached the radio station KWEM in West Memphis about doing a fifteen-minute radio show. He had subbed for Sonny Boy Williamson on his famous *King Biscuit Boy* radio program on KFFA and recognized the benefits of promoting his upcoming performances. That he went out and procured his own sponsors further demonstrated Wolf's determination. Wolf would work the door at his live performances, and he demanded professionalism from his musicians; he would not tolerate drinking or tardiness. He was known as a tough taskmaster and levied fines for mistakes but also paid salaries and ultimately unemployment compensation for his musicians. At six feet four inches and close to 300 pounds Wolf was an intimidating presence both on and off the stage, but he adopted a paternalistic role toward his band.

West Memphis was a bustling boomtown. Whereas Memphis, Tennessee, across the river had a curfew, West Memphis was called a blues Las Vegas, a wild and wooly place with music and gambling all night. Wolf's band dominated the scene. He wowed crowds throughout Arkansas, Mississippi, Tennessee, and Louisiana with his powerful performances, putting all of his energy into his stage act, often even getting down on all fours and howling like a wolf.

The legendary producer Sam Phillips, who later discovered Elvis Presley, heard Wolf on the radio and said, "This is for me. This is where the soul of a man never dies." Phillips produced "Moaning at Midnight" and "How Many More Years" in 1951, and they were released on Chess Records. By this time Wolf's band was pared down to Willie Johnson on guitar and Willie Steele on drums, with either Ike Turner or Albert Williams on piano. They exploded with a primitive yet modern sound. "Moaning at Midnight" began with an unearthly moan as Willie Johnson played a hypnotic guitar line. Whether they vamped over eerie one-chord grooves or rocked out on jump blues and boogie forms, Johnson's distorted guitar wove sophisticated

dominant jazz chords and struck brilliant single-string solos over a rollicking piano and bashing drums. This foundation supported Wolf's powerful vocals and harmonica playing. An accomplished Delta-style guitarist, Wolf all but abandoned his guitar and focused on his vocals and harmonica. His harmonica prowess has long been underrated. Heavily influenced by Sonny Boy Williamson, Wolf used his limited technique to profound advantage. He had a strong vibrato and a rhythmic, tasteful sound that was the perfect complement to his rasping, commanding voice.

Competing for Wolf's recording output with the Modern and RPM Record labels, Leonard Chess drove to Memphis and persuaded Wolf to move to Chicago. The huge city was a hotbed of the blues, with most of the city's African Americans living on the South and West sides. Wolf took great pride in driving his own car to Chicago with cash in his pocket, something that many of his predecessors—including Muddy Waters, who barely scraped together enough money for the train fare to move north—had not been able to do. Wolf's move was at a great sacrifice, however, because neither his band nor his family accompanied him. His wife died of cancer soon afterward. Willie Johnson and the piano player Hosea Kennard eventually joined Wolf, who sent for the young West Memphis guitarist HUBERT SUMLIN to join him. Except for a short stint with Muddy Waters, Sumlin stayed in Wolf's band until Wolf died. For twenty-five years they had a close, though often tempestuous, father-son relationship, and Sumlin was Wolf's most sympathetic accompanist.

Wolf's reputation and records preceded him to Chicago, and though Waters helped Wolf get established, the two became arch competitors vying for top dog in Chicago blues. They both enjoyed big hits with songs written by WILLIE DIXON, who would get one of them interested in a particular song by claiming that it was meant for the other. Wolf recorded a string of hits, including "No Place to Go," "Evil," his first Dixon song, and his masterpiece "Smokestack Lightning," a stark, desperate plea for a train to stop and let him ride. Wolf knew what he was singing about. Many of the repetitive themes in his songs, such as women doing him wrong, money or the lack thereof, and having no place to go, were no doubt formed by his early abandonment by his mother. Wolf was cautious and suspicious for the rest of his days.

Though the blues started to fall from favor among young African Americans, Wolf continued to thrive with his constant performances in Chicago clubs and tours around the United States and Europe. He enjoyed a resurgence of hit records in the early 1960s, mostly penned by Willie Dixon. "Wang Dang Doodle," "Spoonful," "300 Pounds of Heavenly Joy," and "Little Red Rooster" remain blues standards. The Rolling Stones recorded "Little Red Rooster" and insisted that Wolf appear along with them on the popular television show *Shindig* in 1965.

Wolf took great pride in improving himself, and he studied music and attended night school to advance his reading and writing. He married Lillie Handley in 1963 and relished his home life. He was a good husband and stepfather to Lillie's two daughters, and unlike many of his fellow bluesmen he handled his money wisely. His neglect of his own son, Floyd, was ironic considering his own earlier experiences.

In addition to clubs Wolf performed at many colleges and festivals, including the Newport Jazz Festival and the Ann Arbor Blues Festival. In 1970 he recorded *The London Howlin' Wolf Sessions* in England, accompanied by Eric Clapton, Steve Winwood, and Bill Wyman and Charlie Watts of the Rolling Stones. The record succeeded both musically and commercially and introduced him to many white fans.

Though plagued by health problems in his later years, Wolf continued to perform until he died. He could no longer roam the stage, crawl across the floor, or play much harmonica, but he continued to put his all into every song that he sang. A larger-than-life bluesman and a one-of-a-kind performer, Wolf provided a link between the stark music of the Mississippi Delta and modern music and thereby helped lay the foundations of rock and roll.

FURTHER READING

Guralnick, Peter. *Lost Highway: Journeys and Arrivals of American Musicians* (1979).

Humphrey, Mark. *Nothing but the Blues: Bright Lights, Big City* (1993).

"Interview with Howling Wolf." *Living Blues Magazine* 1.1 (1970).

Palmer, Robert. *Deep Blues* (1981).

Rowe, Mike. *Chicago Blues: The City and the Music* (1973).

Segrest, James, and Mark Hoffman. *Moanin' at Midnight: The Life and Times of Howlin' Wolf* (2004).

MARK S. MAULUCCI

Hubbard, James H. (22 July 1838–c. 1912), minister and activist, was born to free parents, Ann Maria (Booth) and her husband, who was surnamed Hubbard, in Baltimore, Maryland. Little is known of them, but his mother was apparently widowed when Hubbard was young, and she turned to her extended family and to the church for support. Through aid from her brother Edward Booth, who had grown wealthy as a trader in the West Indies and then California, Hubbard attended the Allegheny Institute between 1851 and 1853. At this radical experiment in black higher education— funded by the white abolitionist Charles Avery and later renamed Avery College—Hubbard was probably taught by former Oberlin professor Philotus Dean and by one of the first black college teachers in the nation, Martin Henry Freeman; he also met future luminaries including BENJAMIN TUCKER TANNER and THOMAS MORRIS CHESTER.

Drawn by family ties and the promise of the West, Hubbard moved to California in June 1854. He worked a variety of jobs in both Sacramento and Nevada County, often living with his mother or uncles. At an African Methodist Episcopal (AME) revival in Nevada County in September 1855, he converted to the AME Church and soon became a protégé of the powerful AME minister THOMAS M. D. WARD. Although he was not officially licensed to preach until 1860 or 1861, Hubbard did church work in Nevada City, Grass Valley, Marysville, and Sacramento throughout the rest of the 1850s. Like most AME activists in northern California, he also engaged in the movements surrounding the State Colored Conventions—especially the fights for equal education and black testimony rights. In September 1859 he married Josephine Carson, a Missouri-born resident of Sacramento. Over the next two decades, the couple had six children.

Hubbard was ordained as a deacon in 1865 and an elder in 1869. His ministry continued to focus on northern California (Grass Valley, Marysville, Chico, Stockton, Sacramento, and San Francisco) and to include activism. He also worked for a time as the secretary of the AME's California Conference. Beyond Ward, his circle included BARNEY FLETCHER, JEREMIAH BURKE SANDERSON, THOMAS DETTER, PHILIP BELL, JENNIE CARTER, and several other black leaders of northern California.

Shifts in the AME hierarchy in the early 1870s led to Hubbard's transfer to the Missouri conference, where, between 1873 and 1876, his charges included Kansas City and Leavenworth, Kansas. He drew praise from both congregants and church leaders; Alexander Wayman, who had called Hubbard "a fine scholar and an excellent preacher" in a 10 August 1872 piece for the *Christian Recorder*, noted in the 13 April 1876 *Recorder* that, though the Kansas City church had just been destroyed by fire, "with such a leader" as Hubbard, the congregation "must succeed" in its efforts to rebuild.

When the Missouri Conference split, Hubbard worked with Bishop James A. Shorter to organize the Kansas Conference and then served as the Conference Secretary for several years during the 1880s. Most of his charges during this time were in Kansas—Wyandotte, Fort Scott, Atchinson—though he also worked actively in Denver, Colorado. His sermons and short essays occasionally appeared in the *Recorder* during this period, and his experiences on the frontier led to his appointment as the Presiding Elder of the Denver District in 1884. In a speech published in the 13 September 1884 *Christian Recorder*, he told the Denver congregation that "the presiding elder is not supposed to be a boss, but a Christian minister having the work at heart," and, to that end, he actively ministered to AME congregations in Denver, Colorado Springs, Pueblo, and Leadville for the next two decades. When Bishop John M. Brown separated Colorado from the Kansas Conference in 1887, Hubbard again aided in the key work of reorganization. Horace Talbert estimated that, in Hubbard's seven years as presiding elder, he traveled "not less than ten thousand miles a year through the thinly settled Districts of the extreme West" and that "the revival spirit ... constantly abides with him" (Talbert, 145). While most of his children lived in California, Hubbard reportedly stayed in Colorado until his death, though the details of the final years of his life remain hazy.

FURTHER READING

Beasley, Delilah. *Negro Trail Blazers of California* (1919).
"Rev. James H. Hubbard of the Colorado Conference." *Christian Recorder*, 14 July 1887.
Talbert, Horace. *The Sons of Allen* (1906).

ERIC GARDNER

Hubbard, Philip Gamaliel (4 Mar. 1921–10 Jan. 2002), inventor and educator, was born in Macon, Missouri, to Philip Alexander Hubbard, a draftsman, and Rosa Belle (Wallace) Hubbard, a teacher who later worked as an elevator operator and freelance dressmaker. Hubbard's parents selected his middle name in recognition of Warren Gamaliel Harding's inauguration as U.S. president on the day he was born. Hubbard's father died eighteen days after he was born, and his mother was left to care for him and his three brothers. The family was close-knit, and Hubbard and his siblings were cared for by relatives while his mother taught school. When he was four years old his mother sacrificed her teaching career and moved the family to Des Moines, Iowa, in hopes of better educational opportunities for her sons. An avid reader from an early age, Hubbard thrived at Nash Elementary School, where he won a spelling bee competition in the sixth grade. He went on to be a stellar student at Washington Irving Junior High and North High School, where he engaged in many extracurricular activities including football, band, chorus, orchestra, glee club, and the Iwakta (biology) club. He graduated from high school in 1939 as a member of the National Honor Society. After working for a year shining shoes to save money for college, he enrolled at the University of Iowa in 1940. His affiliation with the university would span more than a half-century.

With $252.50 in savings, Hubbard enrolled in the College of Engineering. He selected engineering because of its intellectual stimulation. He also believed that engineering would provide him the best combination of a rewarding career and less racial discrimination than was prevalent in most other professions at the time. Hubbard was further inspired by an African American engineer living in Des Moines named Archie Alexander, a former All-American football player at the University of Iowa who befriended him while he was in high school.

Although the university provided him with an excellent educational opportunity, Hubbard and other African Americans were not accepted as full citizens of the university community and had to fend for themselves for housing and social support. Hubbard lived with an African American couple he knew prior to coming to college and helped to coordinate many social events for the African Americans at the university. Despite the adverse circumstances he excelled in the program, earning membership as well as leadership positions in the engineering (Tau Beta Pi), chemistry (Phi Lambda Upsilon), and electrical engineering (Eta Kappa Nu) honorary societies for students.

On 11 May 1943 Hubbard's educational career at Iowa was briefly halted as he was called to active duty in the U.S. Army during World War II. Prior to reporting for duty, on 3 May, he married his fiancée of two years, Wynnona Marie Griffin. They eventually had five children. While in the army Hubbard studied electrical engineering at Pennsylvania State University. He received U.S. Army certification in May 1944 and was selected by his fellow officers to receive the award for outstanding leadership. Hubbard had hopes of becoming an officer and took the officer candidate examination. He scored a perfect 150 on the exam but was told only that he would be placed in an officer selection pool. This upset Hubbard and prompted him to inquire about being discharged from the army. He found that the only way he could be honorably discharged was by making significant contributions to the war effort. He requested and received a letter from the dean of the College of Engineering at the University of Iowa indicating that his skills were needed for classified war research at the university. He received an honorable discharge on 23 January 1945.

Back in Iowa Hubbard was able to apply many of the courses he had taken in the three years prior to his army service and obtained a B.S. degree in Electrical Engineering with honors in 1946. Remaining at the university he received an M.S. in Mechanics and Hydraulics in 1949 and worked as a research engineer at the Iowa Institute of Hydraulic Research to help with living expenses. His appointment as a research engineer was the beginning of many firsts for Hubbard at the University of Iowa.

Hubbard pursued a Ph.D. while working, and completed his doctoral studies in engineering in 1954. His dissertation research was a significant contribution to the field of hydraulics engineering and garnered national as well as international attention. The device he invented as a basis for his dissertation, a hot-wire and hot-film anemometer, was highly sought after because of its ability to measure and analyze water turbulence. He also developed other devices that detected the pressure and velocity of water in certain situations. With such knowledge and skills Hubbard was quickly propelled to international expert and scholar status. He received national and international honors for his research, speaking regularly and conducting research all over the world. As a result of the high demand for the devices he had developed, he formed the Hubbard Instrument Company and Hubbard Consultants. His clients included the U.S. armed forces, General Electric, General Motors, the Iowa State Highway Commission, Johns Hopkins University, and the National Bureau of Standards.

After completing his dissertation Hubbard had several attractive career opportunities. He chose to remain at Iowa, accepting a position as assistant professor of mechanics and hydraulics in the College of Engineering in 1954. He was the first African American tenure-track professor at the university. He was promoted to associate professor in 1956 and professor in 1959, making him the first African American full professor at the university.

In 1966 Hubbard was appointed dean of academic affairs, making him the first black administrator at any of Iowa's three state universities. He launched a campaign for equality for minority students and advocated for diversity among the faculty. He also poured himself into many community activities, notably his participation in the fair and open housing campaign in Iowa City. He worked diligently to eradicate the housing discrimination that had been prevalent during his college years. He spoke at community functions urging business leaders to approve a strengthened fair housing ordinance for Iowa City, which the city adopted on 18 August 1964.

In 1971 the University of Iowa named Hubbard vice president of student services, making him the highest-ranking minority member in Iowa educational circles and the first black vice president at a Big Ten university. In fall 1987 Hubbard and others founded Opportunity at Iowa, a program designed to attract and retain minority students and faculty. On 31 December 1990 Philip G. Hubbard retired at age sixty-nine. As a lasting memorial to him, Union Field was renamed Hubbard Park on 6 December 1991. Dr. Hubbard died at the age of 80 on 10 January 2002.

FURTHER READING

Philip G. Hubbard's papers are housed at the Special Collections Department, University of Iowa Libraries, Iowa City.

Hubbard, Philip G. *My Iowa Journey: The Life Story of the University of Iowa's first African American Professor* (1999).

JAMES BETHEA

Hubbard, William DeHart (25 Nov. 1903–23 June 1976), the first African American to win an individual Olympic Games gold medal, was born in Cincinnati, Ohio, the son of William A. Hubbard. Olympic historians know nothing of his father's occupation nor his mother's full name at the time of her marriage. After excelling in both academics and athletics at Walnut Hills High School between 1918 and 1921, Hubbard entered the University of Michigan. As a freshman he tied the school record in the 50-yard dash, set a school record of 24 feet 6¾ inches in the long jump, and won two U.S. National

Amateur Athletic Union (AAU) Championships in the long jump (24 feet 5½ inches) and triple jump (48 feet 11½ inches). He won All-American honors in 1922, and until his graduation in 1925, his exploits reserved for him recognition as the greatest combination sprinter-jumper of the 1920s.

Hubbard was a compact, 150-pound world-class sprinter, and no one before his time nor during his career was able to "run off" the wooden toeboard with the same speed as "King Hubbard." His speed and technique not only won him American, world, and Olympic honors, but he was the precursor of the even greater sprinter-jumpers of the next generation. The British expert Colonel F. A. M. Webster watched Hubbard, his speed, and jumping prowess and called Hubbard "a regular pinch of dynamite." Hubbard won AAU long-jump titles six times between 1922 and 1927, "an astonishing achievement," wrote the historian Roberto L. Quercetani. "His style included a run of less than 30 meters, a remarkable acceleration and a single, fast kick of the lead leg."

Hubbard qualified as an American Olympic team member for the 1924 Games in Paris; despite an injured leg, he won the gold medal with a 24 foot 5⅛ inches leap. Returning home to his studies and his athletics, Hubbard dominated the jumps and sprints at the prestigious National Collegiate Athletic Association (NCAA) Championships. He had won the 1923 NCAA jump title, and at the 1925 competition he literally hurled himself out of the sand pit with a world record leap of 25 feet 10⅞ inches, having already won the 100-yard dash. The Associated Press release on 13 June 1925 shouted, "Hubbard approaches 26 feet, a long jump record that may stand for all time."

In 1926 Hubbard ran 100 yards in 9.6 seconds, tying the world record. He had recently graduated from Michigan, "one of only eight blacks in a class of 1,456" (Ashe, 79). Injuries plagued Hubbard, slowing him down so much that at the 1928 Olympic Games in Amsterdam he finished in eleventh place. His athletic career was finished, and with a degree in physical education, Hubbard accepted a position with the Cincinnati Recreation Department. For fifteen years he supervised African American athletic leagues in that city and persisted in efforts to improve housing for blacks. In 1943 Hubbard moved to Cleveland and served as race relations adviser to the Federal Housing Authority, remaining in that position for many years. Hubbard died in Cleveland. His wife, Audrey, and three children survived him.

FURTHER READING
Ashe, Arthur R. *A Hard Road to Glory: A History of the African American Athlete*, vol. 2 (1988): 78–79.
Mallon, Bill, et al. *Quest for Gold* (1984), 309–310.
Quercetani, Roberto L. *A History of Modern Track and Field* (1990): 73.
Webster, F. A. M. *Athletics of To-Day* (1929): 206–207.
Obituaries: *New York Times*, 25 June 1976; (*London*) *Times*, 26 June 1976.

This entry is taken from the *American National Biography* and is published here with the permission of the American Council of Learned Societies.

JOHN A. LUCAS

Hudson, Hosea (12 Apr. 1898–1988), union leader and Communist Party organizer, was born in Wilkes County, Georgia, the first of two sons of Thomas Hudson and Laura Camella Smith, sharecroppers. After three years of a stormy marriage, Laura left Thomas and took their two children a few miles west to Oglethorpe County to live with her parents George and Julia Smith, her sister Georgia Mae, and her brother Ned.

Life in a poor sharecropping family in the Georgian Black Belt was difficult, and several terrifying episodes left Hudson traumatized at an early age. Not least of these occurred when a lynch mob of men on horseback came to Hudson's home one night and demanded the surrender of Uncle Ned, who, accused by one of the men of "talking about" his sister, was being framed by a white employer who owed Ned money. Luckily, Hudson's grandmother was able to ease the situation temporarily when she recognized three of her white half-brothers in the mob; soon a heavy thunderstorm dispersed the crowd, leaving the family thoroughly frightened but unhurt. Other similar experiences, combined with the unfair business practices of the landlords who took much of the family's yearly harvest, made sharecropping life extremely difficult but gave Hudson a keen awareness of the social and economic issues that shaped the Deep South.

At the age of nineteen Hudson married Lucy Goosby, and together they had a son, Hosea Jr., in 1920. They began sharecropping on their own, but in the fall of 1922 a family crisis and a boll-weevil infestation that destroyed their crops prompted Hudson to seek employment in Atlanta, where he heard that he could make a staggering five dollars a day. Temporarily leaving his wife and child with her parents, Hudson moved to the city to become a railroad laborer, but he soon resented the long hours and exhausting conditions working the coal chutes.

A year later Hudson rejoined his family and moved to Birmingham, Alabama, where he became both a skilled iron molder at the Stockham foundry and a successful quartet singer. As a member of the L&N quartet (named after the local Louisville and Nashville Railroad) he was known as one of the best bass singers around and enjoyed a devoted following. Wanting to make a career of his talent, Hudson pleaded with a local radio station to give the quartet a spot, and the station manager, despite his reluctance to broadcast a black group, was so impressed by the quartet's singing that he put it on the air every Sunday afternoon. However, after the group performed a popular hit for a transatlantic New Year broadcast several months later, the station began "losing" their paychecks and refusing to pay them for their services, so they quit. Regardless, the group was the first black quartet broadcast in the city, and according to Hudson, "I was the man that made the breakthrough for Negro talents to be on the air" in Birmingham (Painter, 80).

Throughout the 1920s Hudson remained relatively uninvolved in politics, but as the Great Depression began to aggravate the already difficult living conditions of poor blacks, his resentment of the injustices suffered by his people intensified. In the summer of 1931 Hudson met Al Murphy, a young black worker and member of the Communist Party USA (CPUSA), who invited him and a handful of other workers at the foundry to a meeting to discuss politics. At the end of the meeting Hudson and his companions immediately joined the party, and Hudson was elected the unit organizer for the Stockham plant.

Like many other blacks at the time, Hudson was impressed both with the CPUSA's staunch support of the SCOTTSBORO BOYS and with the party's program, which demanded, among other things, "full economic, political, and social equality to the Negro people and the right of self-determination to the Negro people in the Black Belt of the South." The Scottsboro Boys, nine young black men falsely accused of raping two white women on a freight train in Alabama in 1931, were represented in court by the Communist-led International Labor Defense (ILD), which argued that the plight of the boys fit into a larger framework of racial oppression and class rule in America. After the conviction of the nine men by an all-white jury in 1933—which seemed to confirm the position of the ILD—support

for the Communist Party grew rapidly, particularly among southern blacks.

Within a year of joining the party Hudson was fired from his job at the Stockham plant because of his Communist Party membership, and he was forced to earn a living by accepting odd jobs around Birmingham and by molding iron under assumed names. Still, much of the burden of supporting the family during this time fell to Lucy, who resented that Hudson put his work for the CPUSA above the interests of their family. As the Depression worsened, Hudson worked with the party to set up committees to help secure welfare payments for laid-off workers and protect them against evictions.

Leaving the South for the first time, Hudson traveled to New York in 1934 for ten weeks to attend the CPUSA national training school, where he studied Marxist theory and learned to read and write. After spending a few years in Atlanta organizing for the Communist Party and doing other community work, Hudson returned to Birmingham in 1937. There he founded the Right to Vote Club, which sought to educate blacks and other poor people about how to register to vote by providing them with information on the procedural and legal requirements of voting. Free community workshops taught people the ways in which Alabama and other states disenfranchised voters by using literacy tests, employment requirements, poll taxes, and other unfair practices to obstruct working-class participation in elections. Although the Right to Vote Club never became a mass organization, falling apart in 1940 because of internal quarrels and disunity, it helped bring to light the racist and undemocratic nature of elections in the South and succeeded in quadrupling the number of black voters in Jefferson County between 1938 and 1940 (Kelley, 184).

While in Birmingham, Hudson also worked for the Works Progress Administration (WPA), set up by President Franklin D. Roosevelt to provide jobs to communities hit hard by the Great Depression. Along with a few other comrades Hudson joined the Workers Alliance, a national organization that represented WPA workers in Birmingham. After the local leadership, appalled by the presence of assertive, militant blacks in their organization, quit in disgust, Hudson helped transform the conservative, predominantly white union into an integrated labor union heavily influenced by Communist thinking. In 1937 Hudson was elected vice president of the Birmingham and Jefferson county branches of the Workers Alliance, and he served in this post until 1939 when the WPA laid off most of the union membership.

When World War II broke out and the economy shifted to the war effort, Hudson resumed iron molding and became involved in the United Steelworkers of America (USW). Upon being approached by several co-workers who had heard of his successes in the Workers Alliance and wanted his help in lobbying for better wages, Hudson recommended that they start a union. After obtaining a USW charter, Local 2815 was established, and Hudson was elected president. Under his leadership working conditions in his foundry were improved, and wages increased from 30 cents to 90.5 cents for unskilled labor and $1.04 for molders (Hudson, 78). During this time Hudson was also a delegate to the Birmingham Industrial Union Council and the vice president of the Alabama People's Educational Association, the renamed state section of the CPUSA, which had been reorganized nationally as the Communist Political Association.

Hudson's rigorous political life took a toll on his family, and the anti-Communist hysteria of the postwar era imposed a series of hardships on him. His marriage of thirty years ended in 1946 when he accused his wife of infidelity, and in 1947 he was fired from his job and blacklisted for being a Communist, stripped of his positions in the USW, and expelled from the Birmingham Industrial Union Council. Forced to conceal his identity until 1956, he lived in Atlanta and New York City and eventually moved to Atlantic City, New Jersey, where he worked as a janitor, a CPUSA liaison, and a community activist.

Returning briefly to the South in 1964, Hudson was impressed with the dramatic social changes that had occurred in his absence, including the gradual abandonment of Jim Crow laws, the rise in economic well being for some blacks, and the emergence of an influential black political leadership. Despite these achievements Hudson remained intensely critical of life in the South:

> In the meanwhile, the sufferings and oppression of the vast mass of Black, Chicano and Puerto Rican people remain at an increasingly unbearable level. Unemployment, lack of housing, ghetto misery, arrests, frame-ups, the murder of innocent men and women—all these increase, and only basic changes in the structure of society will solve these terrible conditions (Hudson, 128).

While always striving toward the greater goal of workers' revolution, Hudson centered his effort, often at the expense of a healthy family life, on alleviating the day-to-day misery of the oppressed.

Though his career was not as visible on the national stage as those of such prominent members of the Communist Party as A. PHILIP RANDOLPH, PAUL ROBESON, RICHARD WRIGHT, and CLAUDE MCKAY, Hudson's life illustrates both the personal and the professional difficulties faced by workers and organizers at the local level. He remained an active organizer and outspoken proponent of Communism until the end of his life, and although his legacy remains largely uncelebrated, two autobiographies have slowly helped him gain the recognition he deserves. The city of Birmingham proclaimed 26 February 1980 as Hosea Hudson Day, and Hudson was given the key to the city in honor of his outstanding civil rights work. Hudson moved to Gainesville, Florida, in 1985, where he died three years later.

FURTHER READING

Hudson, Hosea. *Black Worker in the Deep South: A Personal Record* (1972).

Kelley, Robin D. G. *Hammer and Hoe: Alabama Communists during the Great Depression* (1990).

Painter, Nell Irvin. *The Narrative of Hosea Hudson: His Life as a Negro Communist in the South* (1979).

BRYNLEY A. LLOYD-BOLLARD

Huff, Edgar R. (1920–2 May 1994), Marine Corps noncommissioned officer and veteran of World War II, Korea, and the Vietnam War, was born in Gadsden, Alabama. His parents' names are unknown, but his father was a veteran of World War I who died in 1926, and his mother worked as a domestic. When she became ill in 1935 Edgar dropped out of school to support his family by working at a steel mill. Like many black families living in Alabama during this era of Jim Crow segregation, the Huffs lived in constant fear of the Ku Klux Klan (KKK). In recounting how a neighbor was kidnapped by the KKK and nearly beaten to death, Huff would later recall that "Whenever the Ku Kluxers would come, I would be terrified.... I just don't see how black people survived down there in those days" (Terry, 148). In the early days of World War II Huff was told by a white co-worker, an ex-Marine, that the Marines were now accepting black recruits. Six feet six inches tall and over two hundred pounds, the strapping Huff was a catch for any of the branches of the armed forces; he chose the Marines for the simple reason that "I heard the Marines were the toughest outfit in the world, and I knew they couldn't be tougher than what I was going through. So I decided to join" (Terry, 141). Huff was accepted in the Marine

Corps on 26 June 1942, one of the first fifty African Americans ever to serve in the Marines.

When Huff entered the Marine Corps he was joining one of the most tradition-bound services in the armed forces, and one entirely white in its composition. While blacks had served in the navy over the years—by 1933 reduced to duty strictly as stewards and mess attendants serving officers—the Marines did not even have this experience. The idea of blacks serving in the Corps was not only opposed by many officers, it was to them downright bewildering; Marine officers simply had no idea how they should "handle" these black recruits. But the black recruits would serve, even if by government mandate, and a facility for their training was established at Montford Point Camp, close to Marine headquarters at Camp Lejeune, North Carolina. These first black recruits arrived in camp on 26 August 1942 and were trained by white drill instructors in the ways of the Marine Corps. For Huff, the experience was both eye-opening and lonely, and the tough Marine would remember that "when I went to bed the first night, I heard this music. I started crying, wondering what my mama was doing. So I asked this boy, why in the world is they playing that song. They told me that was 'Taps.' I had never heard a bugle before in my life" (Terry, 142). As part of Battery A of the Fifty-first Composite Defense Battalion, Huff and his fellow recruits completed their training by late November 1942 and were full-fledged Marine privates.

Soon after completing boot camp, Huff received word from his white commanding officer, the well-regarded Colonel Samuel Woods Jr., that his mother was very ill and that he would be allowed to go on furlough to see her. Huff had little money to his name, but Woods gave him bus fare to return home. As with many of the new black Marines, Huff soon found that the idea of a black serving in the Marines was unacceptable to many whites; in uniform while at a bus station in Atlanta, Huff was accosted by Marine MPs and asked why he was wearing "that uniform." Huff replied that he was a Marine, but was rudely rebuffed with the comment that "there ain't no damn nigger Marines," and was promptly hauled off to jail (Terry, 142). Ignored by the MPs, his pleas for assistance unheeded by a Marine captain and navy chaplain who visited the jail on other matters, Huff remained incarcerated for five days before he was able to convince someone to contact Colonel Woods. Upon doing so, Huff was quickly released and returned home, having spent Christmas 1942 in jail. Many black Marines experienced similar episodes while on furlough or liberty in the unfriendly South.

An imposing figure and model soldier, Edgar Huff was chosen in early 1943 to serve as a drill instructor at Montford Point for future black recruits. Huff and eight other men now took over the training duties formerly performed by white drill sergeants, and from then to the end of the war, all recruit training for black Marines was performed by black non-commissioned officers. Trained by such outstanding men as Huff, GILBERT JOHNSON (who married Huff's sister), Alvin Ghazlo, and others, black Marines would prove to be effective and courageous soldiers in the fierce Pacific battles that would take place on Saipan, Peleliu, Iwo Jima, and Okinawa, living up to the Corps' proud fighting tradition.

Huff quickly became an outstanding drill instructor and became the field sergeant major in charge of all recruit training at Montford Point. But as his brother-in-law Gilbert Johnson had done before him, Huff headed to the war in the Pacific in 1944, serving as first sergeant in the Fifth Marine Depot Company and seeing action on Saipan and Okinawa; he was posted to China after the war ended.

In 1947, Huff married a young woman named Beulah (whose maiden name is now unknown); they had one son, Edgar Jr. But Huff's service in the Marines was far from over: he returned to Montford Point Camp and headed the recruit training there. Later, he served in the Korean War, from 1951 until 1952, as a gunnery sergeant in the Second Battalion, First Marine Division, taking part in the action in the "Punch Bowl" area, one of the epic battlegrounds in the war on the Thirty-eighth parallel in North Korea, near the coast in a shallow circular depression in what is otherwise a rugged mountain area. Here, from June–September 1951, Chinese and American armies fought a series of battles to gain control of the strategic ground; the casualties were heavy in battles at such legendary locales as Heartbreak Ridge. The UN offensive in the Punch Bowl area was the last of the war, such action and the resulting casualties being deemed too high a price to pay. After his second wartime hitch, Huff served as first sergeant in a weapons company of the Eighth Marines in the Second Marine Division, and was later assigned to duty as guard chief at the Naval Air Station at Port Lyautey, Morocco, in 1955. On 31 December 1955 he was promoted to the rank of sergeant major, the first African American ever to hold this position in the Marine Corps. Huff would subsequently serve at a number of bases throughout the United States, as well as overseas in Okinawa.

Huff served in yet a third war when he did two tours of duty in Vietnam from 1967 until 1968 and 1970 until 1971 as part of the Third Marine Amphibious forces. While stationed in Da Nang during the Tet Offensive in January 1968, the old Marine earned a Bronze Star and Purple Heart for rescuing his radio operator while under enemy fire. Huff would later comment that "Hell, he was one of my men. Black or white, I would have done the same even if I got shot to hell in the process" (Terry, 147). Before his retirement from the Marines on 30 September 1972, Huff had proven his valor and leadership time and again for thirty years, earning the Bronze Star twice, the Purple Heart three times, as well as three Navy Commendation Medals, the Navy Achievement Medal, and the Combat Action Ribbon.

Upon retiring, Edgar Huff and his family moved to Hubert, North Carolina, close to Montford Point and Camp Lejeune. Later in life Huff would readily acknowledge that prejudice was rife in the service and that "over the years, I was so unhappy sometimes in the Marines, I didn't know what to do" (Terry, 144). Huff died in 1994. His skill and leadership in training the first black Marines, and his subsequent years of leadership, established not only his own legacy but also a tradition of black service in the Corps that continues to this day.

FURTHER READING

Shaw, Henry, Jr., and Ralph Donnelly. *Blacks in the Marine Corps* (2002).

Terry, Wallace. *Blood—An Oral History of the Vietnam War by Black Veterans* (1984).

GLENN ALLEN KNOBLOCK

Huff, Leon (8 Apr. 1942–), songwriter, pianist, producer, and record company executive, was born in Camden, New Jersey. His father was a barber and a blues guitarist, and his mother played gospel piano. Along with his songwriting and business partner Kenny Gamble, Huff was largely responsible for creating a popular musical style, known as Philadelphia soul, that was for a time nearly ubiquitous in American popular culture. Although Huff grew up playing drums at Camden High School and regularly made the Camden All-City Orchestra until his graduation in 1960, it was his piano playing that gained him entrance into the music business.

In the early 1960s Huff traveled to New York City and began playing piano on some of the legendary producer Phil Spector's recording sessions, including the session for the Ronettes' "Baby I Love You." He had the unique opportunity to observe the development of Spector's orchestral "wall of sound" production style, which influenced Huff's own stylistic approach as a producer. Huff became a regular at New York's famed Brill Building, working on sessions with some of the era's most prolific songwriters, including the teams of Jerry Leiber and Mike Stoller and Ellie Greenwich and Jeff Barry. During the early 1960s Huff traveled back and forth from New York to the Philadelphia area, which was another major center for teen-oriented pop music, thanks to Cameo-Parkway Records and the television show *American Bandstand*. Huff met Gamble by chance in the elevator of the Schubert Theatre in Philadelphia, which housed several music studios. Huff soon joined Gamble's band, Kenny Gamble and the Romeos (which also included their later collaborator Thom Bell, who is credited with introducing the falsetto sound of Philadelphia doo-wop into the slick productions of Philadelphia soul). The group worked on the weekends and even toured with CHUBBY CHECKER, who was a popular act at the time.

In 1967 Gamble and Huff started Gamble Records, and in 1968 they wrote the hugely successful "Only the Strong Survive" with the singer JERRY BUTLER, who later worked with them at Philadelphia International. In 1969 they founded Neptune Records, which was distributed through Chess Records. Neptune boasted such successful artists as the O'Jays, the Three Degrees, and Billy Paul, all of whom became important to Gamble and Huff's careers later on. Unfortunately, Leonard Chess's death in 1969 left them without a distributor.

Their new label, Philadelphia International Records, partnered with Columbia Records (CBS) from 1971 to 1983. Philadelphia International Records quickly became a formidable rival of the long-established, since 1959, Motown Records, to which it was only second as a black-owned record label. Through Philadelphia International, Gamble and Huff introduced what became known as Philadelphia soul into American popular music. Philadelphia soul is also popularly known as the "Sound of Philadelphia," which was also the name of one of Gamble and Huff's top groups (recording under the acronym TSOP). John A. Jackson describes Philadelphia soul as "a multilayered,

Leon Huff (second from right) in June 2006 with (from left) Berry Gordy Jr., Kenny Gamble, and Chubby Checker after the Rhythm & Blues Foundation's Fourteenth Annual Pioneer Awards in Philadelphia. (AP Images.)

bottom-heavy brand of sophistication and glossy urban rhythm and blues, characterized by crisp, melodious harmonies backed by lush, string-laden orchestrations and a hard driving rhythm section" (Jackson, ix). The sound developed around the same time as disco and was similar to disco (particularly MFSB's "Love Is the Message"), but Philadelphia International's productions were more musically complex and had more staying power than many disco tunes. Gamble and Huff wrote over three thousand songs and were responsible for many top-forty hits in the late 1960s and the 1970s. The gold or platinum singles they penned include "Back Stabbers" (1972) and "Love Train" (1972) by the O'Jays, "If You Don't Know Me by Now" (1972) by Harold Melvin and the Blue Notes, "When Will I See You Again?" (1973) by the Three Degrees, "Cowboys to Girls" (1973) by the Intruders, "Me and Mrs. Jones" (1974) by Paul, "Wake Up Everybody" (1975) and "The Love I Lost"

(1976) by Harold Melvin and the Blue Notes, "If You Don't Know Me by Now" by Harold Melvin, "Ain't No Stoppin Us Now" (1979) by McFadden and Whitehead, and "Turn off the Lights" (1979) by TEDDY PENDERGRASS. Many of their songs are imprinted in the American popular consciousness and endured (through sampling, covers, and use in film) well past the end of the twentieth century, making Gamble and Huff one of the great American songwriting duos.

At the height of their success, Gamble and Huff were investigated by the U.S. government as a part of the Project Sound investigation, which sought to uncover cases of payola or pay-for-play arrangements in which record companies paid radio disc jockeys to play their records. Project Sound disproportionately targeted black record companies and black music industry figures, leading to much speculation that it was racially motivated. Gamble and Huff were both indicted in June 1975. In April

1976 charges against Huff were dropped. (Gamble worked out a plea bargain in which he admitted minor wrongdoing.)

By the early 1980s the Philadelphia sound faced declining commercial fortunes. In 1983 CBS Records ended its affiliation with Philadelphia International Records, dealing a major blow to the label. Soon thereafter Gamble and Huff dissolved the label, thus dropping their top-selling artist and friend Pendergrass, who had been paralyzed in a major car accident not long before. This was difficult for Pendergrass; he felt betrayed by Huff and Gamble. Throughout the 1980s and 1990s Philadelphia International Records stayed in business but never again attained its 1970s glory. In 1995 Gamble and Huff were inducted into the National Academy of Songwriters Hall of Fame.

Gamble and Huff were often described as opposite personalities. In addition to his songwriting prowess, Gamble was an outgoing person and a natural businessman, whereas Huff was primarily a musician and was often described as reserved, gruff, and media shy.

In the early twenty-first century the city of Philadelphia used its 1970s musical heritage to promote and refashion its image, and in 2002 Gamble and Huff were asked to create an official theme song for the city. In 2006 they opened a gift shop in Philadelphia, selling merchandise with themes based on their former musical glory. Huff had three daughters, Erica, Inge, and Bilail, and a son, Leon Jr., who was also involved in the music business.

FURTHER READING

Hunter, Al. "Philadelphia to Market Itself with Music," *Philadelphia Daily News* (Oct. 2002).

Jackson, John A. *House on Fire: The Rise and Fall of Philadelphia Soul* (2004).

Olsen, Eric. "Billy Paul Wins $500K in Dispute with Gamble and Huff," Blogcritics.com, http://blogcritics.org/archives/2003/05/01/104924.php (May 2003).

Perrone, Pierre. "How We Met: We Were So Hot, at One Point We Had Ten Records in the Top One Hundred; Kenny Gamble and Leon Huff," *London Independent on Sunday* (July 2006).

PAUL DEVLIN

Huggins, Ericka (5 Jan. 1948–) educator, human rights and community activist, was born Ericka Jenkins in Washington, D.C., to Cozette Jenkins, a secretary for the State Department, and Gervazae Jenkins, a clerk at the Pentagon. In high school Ericka was conscious of the inequality and discrimination African Americans experienced and participated in community service projects. Her first opportunity to partake in the excitement of the civil rights movement was with the 1963 March on Washington, which her parents did not want her to attend. Yet at age fifteen her rebel spirit was awakening as she defied her parents and stood among the multitude of marchers. She recalled that the powerful voice of LENA HORNE singing the word "freedom" inspired her. The historic march cemented her determination to serve people for the rest of her life.

After high school Ericka was one of the first women to attend Lincoln University after transferring from Cheney State College, both in Pennsylvania. While working toward a degree in special education she met John Huggins, whom she married in 1968. At Lincoln she joined the black student organization at a time when young people across the nation protested segregation and America's involvement in Vietnam. Urban black communities exploded in flames as people expressed dissatisfaction with the limited gains of the civil rights movement. College did not offer the kind of grassroots activism she desired, so in 1968 Ericka and John left Lincoln and drove to California, where they joined the Black Panther Party (BPP).

Like the Hugginses, BPP founders HUEY NEWTON and BOBBY SEALE had also felt a void in campus activism. When created in 1966 in Oakland, California, the BPP adopted traditions of armed self-defense, though women were not initially trained to use firearms. Although the popular media-driven image of the BPP is one of gun-toting fanatics, the initial impetus for the organization was to protest police brutality in the black community. Moreover, the Panthers designed programs to counteract the forces of capitalist exploitation by providing crucial services to impoverished blacks. High levels of community involvement allowed them to establish a wide array of services including free breakfast programs for children, senior and teen programs, and health clinics, all of which Huggins helped to develop in California.

Huggins's membership in the BPP proved to be both challenging and satisfying. In December 1968, Huggins gave birth to a girl, Mai. Unfortunately, in January 1969, the murders of John Huggins and Alprentice "Bunchy" Carter, another leader in the Los Angeles chapter of the BPP, violently interrupted their lives. It happened during a shoot-out after a Black Student Union meeting at UCLA involving members of MAULANA KARENGA's US, a Los Angeles-based cultural nationalist organization with whom the Panthers had conflict. Though Panthers accused US members of the murder, it was later revealed that the FBI's COINTELPRO (counterintelligence program) was responsible for the incident.

After spending the night in police custody and learning about her husband's death, Huggins returned to John's family in New Haven, Connecticut, determined to continue their fight for black liberation. Ericka agreed to start a BPP chapter in New Haven where she taught political education classes and established a community school on behalf of the Party. Three months after her arrival in New Haven, police arrested her and thirteen other Panthers on charges of conspiracy, murder, and kidnapping for the death of a man police claimed was an FBI informant that had infiltrated the party.

Huggins remained a strong role model for the women detained in Niantic prison as they all awaited the trial of the New Haven Fourteen. While imprisoned she found peace through meditation, a practice she shared with other inmates and maintained throughout her life. Letters from all over the country, including *New York Times* writers and ANGELA DAVIS, applauded her strength and bravery as a revolutionary woman. When charges against twelve of the defendants were dropped, she and Seale, chairman of the BPP, stood trial as co-defendants. After a hung jury and the prosecution declined a retrial, the two were acquitted in May 1971. Immediately after, Huggins watched sadly as Seale was handcuffed and extradited to stand trial as a member of the Chicago Eight.

Upon returning to Oakland, the BPP chair ELAINE BROWN appointed Huggins to the party's central committee. Huggins was also editor of the Black Panther Intercommunal News Service until appointed director of the BPP's Oakland Community School (OCS), a position she occupied from 1973 to 1981. The OCS, which started as a home school for Panther children, grew in response to parental requests for a larger facility that other community children could attend. At its height it accommodated 150 children, with hundreds, including many unborn, on the waiting list.

Under Huggins's leadership the California Department of Education and the California state legislature recognized the school for excellence. As a teacher of English and creative writing, Huggins

set an example for her students with the publication of *Insights and Poems* (1975), co-authored with Newton. In 1976 she became the first African American woman elected to the Alameda County Board of Education and maintained memberships in professional alternative school associations.

When FBI and police attacks, internal divisions, and paranoia took a toll on the party in the late 1970s, Huggins stayed on, dedicating thirteen years of her life to the BPP. She maintained a spiritual balance and used her commitment to the children to persevere. After leaving the party in 1981, she continued her mission to educate. She directed alternative schools, taught women's studies in various universities throughout California, and served as a consultant on student resiliency to various school districts.

Like HARRIET TUBMAN, MAYA ANGELOU, ELLA BAKER, and so many of the anonymous women who struggled for human rights and freedom, Huggins worked to improve the quality of life for the generations of slave descendants. She merits a place on the roster of African Americans who sacrificed themselves for the greater good of their communities.

FURTHER READING
The papers of the Black Panther Party, including mid-1970s interview with Huggins, are a part of the Dr. Huey P. Newton Foundation Inc. Collection, housed in the Department of Special Collections in the Cecil H. Green Library at Stanford University.

Brown, Angela D. "Ericka Huggins," in *Black Women in the United States: An Historical Encyclopedia* (1992).

Brown, Elaine. *A Taste of Power: A Black Woman's Story* (1992).

Foner, Philip S., ed. *The Black Panthers Speak* (1995).

LeBlanc, Angela. "Surviving Revolution: A History of the Community Programs of the Black Panther Party for Self-Defense, 1966–1982," Ph.D. diss., Stanford University (2000).

Matthews, Tracye. "No One Ever Asks, What a Man's Role in the Revolution Is": Gender and the Politics of the Black Panther Party, 1966–1971. Jones, Charles E., ed. *The Black Panther Party Reconsidered* (1998).

S. SHERRIE TARTT

Huggins, Hazel Renfroe (1905–15 Aug. 2005), art educator and art collector, was born in Chicago to Eugene Renfroe and Bertha Wiley and grew up on the South Side with her brothers Everett and

Earl. She graduated from Bowen High School and received a teacher's certificate from Chicago Normal College, becoming an elementary art teacher in the Chicago public schools. African American teachers were a rarity in mainstream public schools, and Huggins broke into a segregated teaching field, advancing from teacher to district supervisor of arts. To enhance her qualifications for the supervisor position, she returned to school to obtain her bachelor's degree, graduating from the University of Chicago in 1933. In 1956 she received her master's degree in art education from the Illinois Institute of Technology.

When Huggins entered the teaching profession, American public schools were barely one hundred years old and still in the developmental stages. Indeed art and music were not part of the curriculum in early state-funded American schools. But in 1830 the Massachusetts abolitionist and education advocate Horace Mann said that art would be academically and morally valuable for students. Elizabeth Palmer Peabody then advanced the cause of art education by founding the first kindergarten in 1859. In 1833 the National Education Association developed a separate art department to authorize training and teaching and to install an art-based curriculum within schools. Of course the very act of creating an art department generated debate, which was a necessary component in creating diverse academic programs. By teaching art Huggins furthered a progressive educational initiative to implement and advance the humanities within the public school sector.

Although art in the schools was further legitimized with the creation of the National Art Education Association in 1949, advances in art education slowed during the 1950s, when cold war politics and the United States' so-called space race with the Soviet Union dominated the decade. The National Defense Education Act called upon schools to emphasize math and science and to downplay the importance of art.

Throughout these developments and changes Huggins, as an art educator, joined a seemingly ongoing discussion about education procedures and theories. She enriched this discussion with her research and her collections of African and black American art. While working on her graduate degree during the 1950s, Huggins had traveled to Europe, where she realized the influence of Africans in the art world. She became an ardent collector and scholar of black American art, educating others on past and contemporary black artists.

Huggins introduced black American artists into the Chicago school system's general curriculum, teaching students about artists such as the landscape painter HENRY OSSAWA TANNER and SCIPIO MOORHEAD, an African slave trained to paint and mentioned in the poem "To S.M., a Young African Painter, on Seeing His Works," by the poet and former slave PHILLIS WHEATLEY. The artists of the Harlem Renaissance, such as LOIS MAILOU JONES, WILLIAM H. JOHNSON, and SARGENT CLAUDE JOHNSON, were prominently featured in her lessons as well as the later Federal Arts Project (FAP) and Works Project Administration (WPA) artists CHARLES WHITE and DOX THRASH, the self-taught artist HORACE PIPPIN, and the sculptor ELIZABETH CATLETT.

Black American art soon became a tradition with not only its own school of criticism but its own collections, such as the Harmon Foundation Collection. The Harmon Foundation, established in 1922, recognized achievement in the fine arts as well as other fields. One of its most impressive shows was the 1944 Portraits of Outstanding Americans of Negro Origin exhibit that traveled throughout the country. Many of the works in the Harmon Collection have been displayed in the National Portrait Gallery. Two other such prominent collections were the Walter O. Evans Collection of African American Art from the Civil War to the 1930s and 1940s and the Paul R. Jones Collection, housed at the University of Delaware.

Married and divorced twice, Huggins had no children, though she was a major figure in the lives of her many nieces and nephews. She was known in Chicago as the one who brought art by black Americans into the domain of area schools, enriching and motivating thousands of students. An opera lover, bridge player, and member of civic and philanthropic organizations, she spent her life in Chicago as a leading member of society, and it was only when she reached her late nineties that her participation in civic activities began to wane. On her one hundredth birthday she received a congratulatory letter from U.S. senator BARACK OBAMA of Illinois, who commemorated what "you have done and experienced in your lifetime ... two world wars, Prohibition and the Great Depression, the Roaring Twenties and the prosperity of the '50s. You have seen Neil Armstrong walk on the moon and the epic struggle of the Civil Rights movement." Never content to be a mere witness, Huggins lived and participated in society with vigor, serving as a role model, motivator, and educator.

FURTHER READING

Bearden, Romare, and Harry Henderson. *A History of African-American Artists: From 1792 to the Present* (1992).

Bontemps, Arna Alexander. *Forever Free: Art by African American Women* (1980).

Cederholm, Theresa Dickason. *Afro-American Artists: A Bio-Bibliographical Directory* (1992).

Davis, Lenwood G., and Janet L. Sims. *Black Artists in the United States: An Annotated Bibliography of Books, Articles, and Dissertations on Black Artists, 1779–1979* (1980).

Hyland, Douglas K. S. *The Harmon and Harriet Kelley Collection of African American Art* (1994).

Perry, Regenia A. *Free within Ourselves: African-American Artists in the Collection of the National Museum of American Art* (1992).

ROBIN JONES

Huggins, Nathan Irvin (14 Jan. 1927–5 Dec. 1989), educator and historian, a leading scholar in the field of African American studies, was born in Chicago. Huggins was the son of an African American father, Winston J. Huggins, a waiter and railroad worker, and a Jewish mother, Marie Warsaw. When his father left the family, his mother moved her two children to San Francisco. Two years later she died, and fourteen-year-old Nathan and his sister were on their own. He divided his time between attending high school and working as a warehouseman, longshoreman, and porter. Drafted near the end of World War II, he completed high school in the army and used the GI Bill of Rights to enter the University of California.

His studies at Berkeley, particularly the classes in the history of the South, slavery, and Reconstruction taught by Kenneth M. Stampp, exposed him to a revisionist view of the past that demolished many of the myths he had been taught about the historical experience of blacks in American society. This exposure to the relevance of the past reinforced his enthusiasm for the study of American history, including the lives of peoples ordinarily left outside the framework of the American experience. After obtaining his bachelor's degree from Berkeley in 1954, Huggins remained uncertain about his academic future. Outside of the historically black colleges and universities, few job prospects existed in the 1950s for a black Ph.D. in history. Hoping to enhance his chances, he elected to go to Harvard for his doctorate. As a graduate student he worked to establish his identity as a historian rather than as an African American historian. The state of "Negro

history" in the 1950s forced him to establish his academic credentials in other areas.

Under the direction of Oscar Handlin, Huggins wrote his dissertation on Boston charities and received his doctorate from Harvard in 1962. He would subsequently teach at California State College at Long Beach, Lake Forest College, the University of Massachusetts at Boston, and Columbia University before returning to Harvard in 1980 as the W. E. B. DuBois Professor of History and of Afro-American Studies and the first permanent director of the W. E. B. DuBois Institute for Afro-American Studies. His published works include *Harlem Renaissance* (1971), an intellectual and cultural history of "the capital of the black world" in the 1920s and early 1930s; *Protestants against Poverty: Boston's Charities, 1870–1900* (1971), his doctoral dissertation, which examined how the values of charity workers reflected nineteenth-century Protestant culture; *Slave and Citizen: The Life of Frederick Douglass* (1980), an interpretive biography; and *Black Odyssey: The Afro-American Ordeal in Slavery* (1977). After her husband's death, Brenda Smith Huggins edited a collection of his essays and commentaries on his life and scholarship, *Revelations: American History, American Myths* (1995).

Huggins's most important contribution to the historical literature on African Americans was his examination of the Harlem Renaissance. In this pathbreaking and ambitious book his aim was to evaluate the literary outpouring by black writers in the 1920s and how they sought to free themselves from the patronizing and distant philanthropy of the elite literary establishment. Black writers responded to the call by LANGSTON HUGHES "to express our individual dark-skinned selves without fear or shame" ("The Negro Artist and the Racial Mountain," *Nation*, 23 June 1926). That would enable them to discover who they were and what role and responsibilities, if any, they had in the society in which they lived and worked. In this book, not a celebration but a critical appraisal of their aspirations and literary output, Huggins found that the quality of the literature they produced varied enormously, but what set them apart was a sensitivity to the unique opportunity to assess their role as black intellectuals. Placing the Renaissance firmly within the context of the American experience, Huggins examined the tension between white and black identity, how Harlem served the exotic fantasies of whites, the relationship of black writers and artists to their culture, and the masks that both whites and blacks wore in adapting to the mores, tensions, and compulsions of black-white relations.

It is common enough to think of oneself as part of some larger meaning in the sweep of history, a part of some grand design. But to presume to be an actor and creator in the special occurrence of a people's birth (or rebirth) requires a singular self consciousness. In the opening decades of he twentieth century, down to the first years of the Great Depression, black intellectuals in Harlem had just such a self-concept. These Harlemites were so convinced that they were evoking their people's "Dusk of Dawn" that they believed that they marked a renaissance.

Although Huggins appreciated the unique quality of the history of African Americans, he insisted on teaching and writing about that history as an intimate part of American history, as a central theme in the American experience. As director of the DuBois Institute he sought to establish at Harvard the legitimacy and intellectual respectability of African American studies. He remained adamant, at the same time, in opposing efforts to reduce the complexities, ambiguities, and paradoxes of the black experience to a therapeutic search for "a usable past" or a political agenda. The distinctiveness of the American experience, Huggins thought, rested in large measure on its African American component. Consistent with that belief, Huggins envisioned a curriculum in both the public schools and colleges that would reflect the racial and cultural diversity of the United States.

Huggins served the historical profession in a variety of capacities. For the Organization of American Historians he was a member of the Program Committee (1972), the Executive Board (1979–1981), and the Frederick Jackson Turner Prize Committee (1986–1987). He also sat on the editorial board of the *Journal of American History* (1987–1989), *American Historical Review* (1978–1982), and *Journal of Ethnic History*. He served as a juror for the National Endowment for the Humanities; as a member of the Smithsonian Council, the USIA Panel on International Educational Exchange, and the Bradley Commission on History in the Schools; and as an adviser to the Children's Television Workshop and to numerous historical documentaries. He was a Guggenheim fellow, a Rockefeller Foundation humanities fellow, a Fulbright-Hayes senior lecturer, and a Ford Foundation travel-study fellow.

In his book *Black Odyssey*, Huggins wanted to explore slavery as the enslaved experienced it, "to understand the past through them, to see history through their eyes, making them essential witnesses to the events historians discussed." It was necessary to describe the brutality and oppression, as that was clearly a part of the historical record, but it was imperative as well to utilize a variety of sources to underscore the resiliency of enslaved blacks and the ways in which they chose both to resist and transcend their condition.

Many slaves lived their lives without much that we would call resistance. They died whole persons nevertheless, able in their souls to meet their God without shame. No black American, and certainly no white American, has cause to apologize for them. Modern history knows of no more glorious story of the triumphant human spirit.

Near the end of his life Huggins wrote an essay, "The Deforming Mirror of Truth," that would be published in the reissued edition in 1990 of *Black Odyssey*. He addressed the paradox of a nation based at its founding on black unfreedom, on the most enormous of human inequities, in which the nation's leaders were usually slaveholding champions of liberty and freedom. He called for a national history that incorporates the slave experience not as some kind of aberration but as an integral part of the American experience. "Such a new narrative would bring slavery and the persistent oppression of race from the margins to the center, to define the limits and boundaries of the American Dream. Such a new narrative would oblige us to face the deforming mirror of truth." To Huggins, the extraordinary advances made from the 1960s to the 1990s had not simply integrated African Americans into American history, it had transformed and redefined that history.

FURTHER READING

Blight, David W. "Nathan Irvin Huggins, the Art of History, and the Irony of the American Dream," *Reviews in American History* 22, No. 1 (Mar. 1994): 174–190.

Obituary: *New York Times*, 7 December 1989.

LEON F. LITWACK

Hughes, Albert and Allen Hughes (1 Apr. 1972–),

filmmakers and film producers, were born in Detroit, Michigan, the twin sons of an African American father and a white Armenian mother, Aida Hughes. Though information about their father is limited, the Hughes Brothers, as they are most well known commercially, have suggested in interviews that he was or tried to be a pimp. Their parents divorced when the brothers were two years old. In 1981 Aida moved her young sons to Pomona, California, a suburb near Hollywood. With little more than a fast food restaurant worker's income, Aida supported her family while simultaneously putting herself through college. She eventually established her own business to rehabilitate injured workers and satisfied her activist spirit by becoming president of the Pomona chapter of the National Organization for Women.

To keep her boys out of trouble, Aida lent her company's video camera to her sons to occupy their time, creating a tremendous fascination in the boys with moviemaking. The brothers soon began to fashion short subjects on topics like the doings of the neighborhood drug dealer, as well as recreations of their favorite films, like Brian De Palma's *Scarface* (1983) and the Bruce Lee classic *Enter the Dragon* (1973). Their approach to the technical needs for their films further showcased their youthful ingenuity—they used VCRs for editing purposes and a boom box for sound effects.

The Hughes's love for film entered their formal education as well when one of their high school teachers challenged them to construct a short film for a class assignment. Honoring the proposal, the twins presented a visual manual that instructed viewers on *How to Be a Burglar*. Soon filmmaking took precedence over school, and the brothers dropped out of high school in the eleventh grade. They began showing their work on the local cable access channel, and one of these films, *The Drive-By*, drew the attention of an agent. As a result they moved into music video production, making videos for artists as diverse as rock and metal groups like Korn to rap and hip hop artists such as TUPAC SHAKUR, Digital Underground, and Tone-Loc. Yet despite the appeal of working in music video, the Hughes Brothers sought to extend their storytelling capabilities beyond the brevity of video to feature films.

The twins released their debut film *Menace II Society* in 1993. Made for a reported $2.5 million and written in collaboration with the screenwriter Tyger Williams, *Menace II Society* tells the story of Caine, a young man coming to terms with the violent and nihilistic behavior that has permeated his Watts neighborhood. An homage to the gangster films of old Hollywood and the style of acclaimed directors such as Martin Scorsese, *Menace II Society*, which showcased the talents of flourishing and veteran actors such as Tyrin Turner, Larenz Tate, Jada Pinkett, CHARLES DUTTON, and SAMUEL L. JACKSON, premiered at the prestigious Director's Fortnight program sponsored by the Cannes Film Festival, grossed $28 million domestically, and was heralded as a powerful and realistic portrait of urban youth and society. The film's success led to a number of crucial developments in the Hughes Brothers' careers. They secured a two-picture deal with the Walt Disney Corporation and started their own boutique record label (Underworld Records) with Capitol Records specializing in R&B and hip-hop music. Because the twins divided the responsibilities on set with Albert focusing more on the technical aspects of the production while Allen worked closely with the actors, they were allowed by the Directors Guild of America to share directing credit on their films (DGA rules traditionally prevent directors from sharing credit for a film).

The Hughes Brothers soon made their sophomore film *Dead Presidents* (1995). Based on an account from Wallace Terry's oral history on African American Vietnam veterans called *Bloods*, the film depicts a soldier who, after returning home from the war to little fanfare and even less opportunity for employment, participates in an armored car heist, with disastrous results. Unfortunately the film did not enjoy the success of its predecessor, earning $24 million and less than stellar reviews from critics.

It would be four years before the twins expressed themselves again cinematically with their documentary *American Pimp* (1999). Though they had originally planned to translate ROBERT "ICEBERG SLIM" BECK's underground classic, *Pimp: The Story of My Life*, from text to screen, the Hughes Brothers decided instead to focus on the philosophy and business acumen of the contemporary pimp. Consisting of interviews with pimps from diverse backgrounds and experiences, the film was nominated for the Grand Jury Prize at the Sundance Film Festival that year.

The twins followed *American Pimp* with an adaptation of Alan Moore and Eddie Campbell's graphic novel *From Hell* (2001). The story of a police inspector investigating a series of brutal murders committed by Jack the Ripper in Victorian England, the film, starring Johnny Depp and Heather Graham, was the most mainstream undertaking in the twins' young career. While hardly an enormous success, *From Hell* grossed $75 million worldwide and received fairly decent reviews from critics.

Following *From Hell*, the Hughes Brothers acted as executive producers on projects as diverse as the "turntablism" documentary, *Scratch* (2001), to the science fiction television crime drama *Touching Evil* (2004). In 2005 they broke with tradition and worked separately when Allen directed *Knights of the South Bronx*, a cable television movie about a businessman who teaches chess to inner-city children.

Never married, Albert and Allen Hughes, the fathers of a daughter and a son respectively, added a dazzling blend of ferocity, carnage, and societal critique to the annals of film that will inform a generation of filmmakers to follow.

FURTHER READING

Massood, Paula. *Black City Cinema: African American Urban Experiences in Film* (2003).

Terry, Wallace. *Bloods: An Oral History of the Vietnam War by Black Veterans* (1984).

Watkins, S. Craig. *Representing: Hip Hop Culture and the Production of Black Cinema* (1998).

MARK D. CUNNINGHAM

Hughes, Cathy (22 Apr. 1947–), radio and television broadcasting entrepreneur and entertainment personality, was born Catherine Elizabeth Woods in Omaha, Nebraska, the eldest of four children of William Alfred Woods and Helen Jones Woods. Both of Hughes's parents had notable accomplishments. William Woods was the first African American to receive an accounting degree from Nebraska's Creighton University. Helen Woods was a trombonist with Mississippi's Piney Woods orchestra at Piney Woods Country Life School, an African American boarding school founded by her father, LAURENCE C. JONES, in 1909. This female orchestra, called the International Sweethearts of Rhythm, famously ran away from Piney Woods in pursuit of musical creative freedom; they sought to play swing music, not gospel. Her mother also earned a master's degree in Social Work.

Hughes spent her childhood in a low-income housing project. She was the first African American to attend Omaha's Duchesne Academy of the Sacred Heart Catholic girls' school. She was also an avid listener of the radio during the early days of black radio, which began broadcasting in 1949. Hughes married Alfred Liggins Sr. when she became pregnant at age sixteen; their son, Alfred Jr., was born in 1963. The marriage was short-lived and soon Hughes found herself a single mother. Although she did graduate from high school and attended Nebraska's Creighton University (and then the University of Nebraska) as a business administration major, she did not complete her degree. In 1969 Hughes took her first job in radio. While still a student, she performed general tasks at KOWH, a

black radio station in Omaha. Through her work at KOWH, she came to the attention of Tony Brown, the founder of the School of Communication at Howard University in Washington, D.C.

In the 1970s she married second husband Dewey Hughes and began a career at Howard University that led to her pioneering activities in broadcasting. Hughes advanced quickly at Howard. In 1973 she became sales director at the university radio station, WHUR-FM, and increased the station's revenue from $250,000 to $3 million in a single year. In 1975 Hughes became the first female and the first African American female vice president and general manager of a Washington, D.C., radio station. At WHUR, Hughes was credited with creating a timeless and widely popular radio format called "the Quiet Storm," which used smooth-voiced deejays playing love songs for several hours (Jones, *Essence*, Oct. 1998, 174). From 1978 to 1980 Hughes served as president and general manager at WYCB-AM, a Washington, D.C., gospel station, where she gained hands-on experience in how to build a radio station.

In 1980 Hughes and her husband, Dewey, a broadcast journalist, bought their own radio station, WOL-AM, to offer programming content for African Americans. She had been turned down by 32 banks before the thirty-third bank granted her approximately $1 million in loans to fund the new station. Soon after Radio One was operational, Hughes's second marriage ended, and she was once again a single mother.

Although Hughes was chief executive officer of Radio One—a position she would hold until 1997—by 1983 she was close to financial ruin; she and her son, Alfred, even lived at the station for a while. Radio One began turning a profit, however, in 1986 on the strength of a successful talk show hosted by Hughes. The show established her as an outspoken black activist and passionate advocate for African Americans, for which she has received both criticism and praise.

In 1987 Hughes paid $7.5 million for her second station, D.C.'s WMMJ-FM, which would become the first East Coast FM station with an "urban adult contemporary" format. From there, Radio One continued to grow and expand. Key to the growth of Radio One was the Federal Communication Commission's 1992 passage of the "duopoly rule," which allowed one individual to own two stations each of AM and FM frequency in the same market. After the FCC ruling, from 1992 to 1998 Radio One purchased multiple stations in black urban markets for around $132.2 million. In 1995 Radio One purchased yet another station in Washington, D.C.: WYKS for $40 million. At the time, this was the largest transaction between two black companies in broadcasting history.

On 6 May 1999 Radio One went public, and Hughes became the first black woman to lead a publicly traded company on the New York Stock Exchange. Radio One raised $172 million in its initial public offering. In 2004 Radio One continued its leadership in the broadcasting industry with the acquisition of a 51 percent share in TOM JOYNER's Reach Media and TV One, a cable and satellite television network, in partnership with Comcast. TV One broadcasted in 37 cities with African American adults being the target audience. The program *TV One on One*, hosted by Hughes, began broadcasting on TV One. With WOL-AM as the leading talk-radio station in Washington, D.C., in 2006 Radio One began syndication of the 24-hour black news talk format.

Involved in many community activities, Hughes served on the boards of the Baltimore Development Corporation, the Broadcasters Foundation, the National Urban League, the Maryland African American Museum Corporation, the Baltimore Museum of Art, and the Piney Woods School (the school founded by her grandfather). She also served as a Lincoln University trustee.

Hughes received numerous awards and honors in recognition of her accomplishments. These include an honorary doctorate from Sojourner Douglass College in Baltimore; the Living Vision Scholarship Fund, 1995; the National Association of Broadcasters' Distinguished Service Award, 2001; and the Golden Mike Award from the Broadcasters' Foundation. Turner Broadcasting awarded Hughes the Trumpet Award, and award given to honor the achievements of African Americans. Hughes was also inducted into the Maryland Chamber of Commerce Business Hall of Fame.

As chairperson and founder of Radio One, Hughes and her son, Alfred C. Liggins III (who served as chief executive officer and president), jointly owned 71 percent of the company's stock. She amassed a personal fortune estimated at approximately $300 million. Radio One became the country's seventh largest radio broadcasting company and the largest African American-owned radio broadcasting company. Radio One also grew to be the sixteenth-largest media company in the country. Through her influence in broadcasting, Hughes provided an indispensable voice for African Americans in the mediums of television and radio.

FURTHER READING

Clarke, Robyn D., and Derek T. Dingle. "The New Blood: Meet the Latest Movers and Shakers in the Exclusive B. E. 100s Community," *Black Enterprise* (June 1999).

Jones, Charisse. "Owning the Airwaves—Cathy Hughes Buys Radio Stations for African-American Programming," *Essence* (Oct. 1998).

TERRI L. NORRIS

Hughes, Langston (1 Feb. 1902?–22 May 1967), writer, was born James Langston Hughes in Joplin, Missouri, the son of James Nathaniel Hughes, a stenographer and bookkeeper, and Carrie Mercer Langston, a stenographer. Left behind by a frustrated father who, angered by racism, sought jobs in Cuba and Mexico, and also left often by a mother searching for employment, Hughes was raised primarily in Lawrence, Kansas, by his maternal grandmother, Mary Langston. In 1915 he went to reside with his mother and stepfather, Homer Clark, in Lincoln, Illinois, later moving with them to Cleveland, Ohio. Hughes spent the summers of 1919 and 1920 with his father in Mexico, writing his first great poem, "The Negro Speaks of Rivers," aboard a train on his second trip. By the time he entered Columbia University in September 1921, Hughes already had poems published in *Brownies' Book* and the *Crisis*. He left Columbia after one year, traveled as a dishwasher and cook's assistant on freighters to Africa and Holland and at Le Grand Duc in Paris, and later worked as a busboy in Washington, D.C. With financial help from the philanthropist Amy Spingarn, he entered Lincoln University in 1926 as an award-winning poet who had taken first place in an *Opportunity* contest and second and third places in a contest in the *Crisis* the year before. By the time he graduated in 1929, he had published two volumes of poetry, *The Weary Blues and Other Poems* (1926) and *Fine Clothes to the Jew* (1927), and had helped to launch the daring African American literary journal *Fire!!*. He had also completed a reading tour in the South with the writer and anthropologist ZORA NEALE HURSTON, had become friends with other leading lights of the Harlem Renaissance, and had interested white socialites, artists, and patrons in his work.

For developing his artistic and aesthetic sensibilities, however, Hughes credited those people he dubbed admiringly as the "low-down folks." He praised the lower classes for their pride and individuality, that "they accept what beauty is their own without question." Part of the beauty that attracted him most was their music, especially the blues, which Hughes had heard as a child in Kansas City, as a teen in nightclubs in Chicago, Harlem, and Washington, D.C., on his trips through the South, and even as a young man in Europe. To Hughes the blues were, as he wrote in "Songs Called the Blues" (1941), songs that came out of "black, beaten, but unbeatable throats." They were the sad songs of proud and wise people who, through the mixture of tears and laughter (often their response on hearing the lyrics) demonstrated a vivacity, wisdom, and determination. This inspired Hughes to attempt to capture the pulse and spirit of the blues tradition as a way of interpreting his people both to the rest of the world and to themselves. Hughes was galvanized by the music of his people, whether blues, jazz, or religious. The music provided him with themes, motifs, images, symbols, languages, rhythms, and stanza forms he would use in his writing throughout his career. As early as 1926, he was trying to schedule blues music as part of his poetry readings; in 1958 he recorded his poetry to the accompaniment of jazz groups led by RED ALLEN and CHARLES MINGUS. At Hughes's funeral, a program of blues was performed.

At the beginning of his writing career, Hughes was encouraged by the writer and editor JESSIE FAUSET, W. E. B. DuBOIS, JAMES WELDON JOHNSON, one of the judges who awarded Hughes his first poetry prizes and later anthologized some of Hughes's work, and ALAIN LOCKE, whose 1925 issue of the *Survey Graphic*, later revised into the groundbreaking volume *The New Negro* (1925), included some of Hughes's work. Through both the intellectual leadership of the highbrows and the invigorating atmosphere provided by the "low-down" folks in Harlem, Hughes found himself encouraged and gaining in fame. Vachel Lindsay's praise in 1925 of poems left by his plate in the Wardman Park Hotel in Washington by a "busboy poet" precipitated a flurry of interest and brought Hughes a wider audience for his poetry. But it was the arts patron Carl Van Vechten who gave Hughes's career its biggest boost in the white world by taking Hughes's first book to Knopf and establishing contacts for Hughes that would serve him personally and professionally. Hughes repaid Van Vechten's assistance most directly with his support of and contributions to Van Vechten's novel *Nigger Heaven*; the two remained friends until Van Vechten's death in 1964.

At the end of her review of *The Weary Blues* in the *Crisis* in 1926, Fauset said of Hughes that "all life is his love and his work a brilliant, sensitive interpretation of its numerous facets." Not all reviews of Hughes's first book were so laudatory. Although the white press largely responded positively to Hughes's poetry, some black reviewers, seeking middle-class respectability from their "Talented Tenth" writers rather than Hughes's more realistic portrayal of the range of African American life, reacted negatively. They particularly opposed the blues and jazz poems of the opening section of the book. In his review in *Opportunity* in February 1926, the poet COUNTÉE CULLEN characterized the book as "scornful in subject matter" with "too much emphasis here on strictly Negro themes." Hughes naturally identified with the black masses, but at the same time he aligned himself with the modernist predilection for experimentation and frank treatment of themes previously banished from polite literature. Thus Hughes was both avant-gardist and traditionalist in his approach to his art. Surely he must have appreciated Locke's review in *Palms* in 1926, which stated that some of the lyrics "are such contributions to pure poetry that it makes little difference what substance of life and experience they are made of." Clearly, however, the substance of life and experience of which they were made also was paramount to Hughes. The lives and dreams of African Americans found intimate expression in Hughes's poems, such as the heritage-laden "The Negro Speaks of Rivers," "Mother to Son," with its doggedly determined narrator, "To Midnight Nan at Leroy's," with its evocation of Harlem nightclub life, and the longingly hopeful "Dream Variation." The volume was an auspicious beginning that established Hughes's ideological and artistic leanings and conflicts that recurred amplified in his later work.

The responses to *Fine Clothes to the Jew* were even more extreme. Hughes realized that the book was, as he told the *Chicago Defender*, "harder and more cynical." He braced himself nervously for the reviews, encouraged by positive responses from Amy and Arthur Spingarn and GEORGE SCHUYLER. Again many black critics believed that Hughes had presented a cheap, tawdry portrait, far from the respectable African American they longed to see in their literature. The "poet 'low-rate' of Harlem" the reviewer for the *Chicago Whip* dubbed him; "Sewer Dweller," sneered the headline of the *New York Amsterdam News* review; "piffling trash," pronounced the historian J. A. ROGERS in the *Pittsburgh Courier*. Attacks on the short-lived *Fire!!* and Van Vechten's *Nigger Heaven*, which Hughes supported and for which he wrote blues lyrics following a lawsuit against Van Vechten for copyright infringement, compounded Hughes's embattled aesthetic consciousness at this time. However, Hughes continued undeterred, in spite of the volume's failure to sell well. In winter 1927, Alain Locke introduced Hughes to "Godmother" Charlotte Mason, an elderly, wealthy widow with a newfound interest in African American authors, who became his benefactor, offering both financial support and opinions about his work. After reading and lecturing in the South in summer 1927, during which he met up with Hurston in Biloxi, Mississippi, Fauset in Tuskegee, Alabama, and BESSIE SMITH in Macon, Georgia, Hughes returned to Harlem and the directive of Mason to write a novel, *Not without Laughter* (1930).

Initially Hughes and Mason got along well, but the artistic and social demands she made on him were at times stultifying, and even the stipend she provided placed him in uncomfortable surroundings that impeded his artistic progress. The social "upward mobility," the economic support for his mother and half brother Gwyn Clark, the free apartment, the patron-funded trip to Cuba—all were mixed blessings. After their relationship was ruptured in 1930, Hughes, hurt and angry, wrote about the situation in the poem "The Blues I'm Playing" (1934) and in the first volume of his autobiography, *The Big Sea* (1940). Winning the Harmon Foundation Prize in 1930 brought him welcome cash, and he occupied some of his time by collaborating with Hurston on the play *Mule Bone* and traveling to Haiti, but the break with Mason was both psychologically and physically trying for Hughes.

Hughes dedicated *Not without Laughter* to his friends and early patrons, the Spingarns; his *Dear Lovely Death* was privately printed by Amy Spingarn in 1931. At the same time he was losing Godmother, difficulties with Hurston concerning *Mule Bone* put a chasm between them and a distrust of Locke, who was vying for Godmother's favor, separated Hughes from him as well. Hughes avoided dealing with these personal difficulties by going first to Florida, then Cuba, and on to Haiti, where he met with the Haitian poet Jacques Roumain, who, inspired by Hughes, later wrote a poem titled "Langston Hughes" and received a letter of support from Hughes when he was sentenced to prison for alleged procommunist activity. Hughes, of course, had always identified with the masses, and he had a distinct influence on writers like Roumain and Nicolás Guillén, whom Hughes had inspired in 1929 to employ the rhythms of native Cuban music in his poetry. A 1931 reading tour partially sponsored by the Rosenwald Fund reintroduced Hughes to the rigid segregation and racism of the South, as did the much-publicized trial of the SCOTTSBORO BOYS. Hughes, the poet who initially had not been radical enough for the Marxist *New Masses* but who later published poems in that journal while at Lincoln, now began writing more controversial and directly political poems, such as "Christ in Alabama," which caused a furor that swelled his audience and increased sales of all his work.

In June 1932 he left for the Soviet Union with a group interested in making a film about race relations in America. Although the film, proposed by Soviet authorities and backed by the black communist JAMES W. FORD, was never made, Hughes's travels in the Soviet Union showed him the lack of racial prejudice he longed for and a peasant class that he sought out and admired. Both *The Dream Keeper* and *Popo and Fifina*, children's books, were released to acclaim while he was in Russia. After visits to Japan, where Hughes was both questioned and put under surveillance because he was a "revolutionary" just come from Moscow, and Hawaii, Hughes returned to the wealthy arts patron Noel Sullivan's home in Carmel, California, where he worked on the short-story collection *The Ways of White Folks* (1934), which was published shortly before his father died in Mexico.

Hughes's interest in drama, as shown by his collaboration on *Mule Bone*, finally bore fruit with the 1935 production of his play *Mulatto* at the Vanderbilt Theater on Broadway and the Gilpin Players' 1936 production of *Troubled Island*. He received financial support from a Guggenheim Fellowship in 1935 and worked in Spain as a correspondent for the *Baltimore Afro-American* in 1937. Following the death of his mother in 1938, Hughes founded the Harlem Suitcase Theatre that same year, the New Negro Theatre in Los Angeles in 1939, and the Skyloft Players in Harlem in 1942. During this period he had plays produced in Cleveland, New York, and Chicago, among them *Little Ham* (1936), *Soul Gone Home* (1937), *Don't You Want to Be Free?* (1938), *The Organizer* (with music by JAMES P. JOHNSON, 1939), and *The Sun Do Move* (1942), and he collaborated on a play with ARNA BONTEMPS, *When the Jack Hollers* (1936). His experience with Hollywood, writing the script for *Way Down South* (1939), was a bitter disappointment. Still, Hughes managed to establish his importance as an African American dramatist and continued to write plays and libretti for the rest of his career.

The year 1939 found Hughes back in Carmel working on his autobiography, *The Big Sea*, which dealt with his life up to 1931. Positive response to the work was overshadowed by fevered excitement over RICHARD WRIGHT's *Native Son*, but Hughes did receive a Rosenwald Fund Fellowship at a point when his repudiation of his poem "Goodbye Christ" had turned some of his leftist friends against him. The Rosenwald money allowed Hughes to focus on writing rather than on financial matters. His blues-inflected *Shakespeare in Harlem* (1942) picked up where he had left off with *Fine Clothes to the Jew* in 1927 and provoked the same divided response as the earlier volume. Following an invitation to the writers' colony Yaddo, where he met Carson McCullers, Katherine Anne Porter, and Malcolm Cowley, he contacted the *Chicago Defender* about being a columnist and was hired. In 1943 Hughes created the beloved comic character Jesse B. Semple ("Simple"), the assertive and lively "low-down" hero who appeared in many of his *Defender* columns over the next twenty years. Also in 1943 he published the prose poem *Freedom's Plow* (introduced with a reading by Paul Muni, with musical accompaniment by the Golden Gate Quartet and later performed publicly by Fredric March) and *Jim Crow's Last Stand*, a leftist, patchwork book of poetry.

In 1945 Hughes began to work on lyrics for Elmer Rice's *Street Scene*, with music by Kurt Weill, which opened to strong reviews in 1947. Hughes, however, opted to work as a visiting writer-in-residence at Atlanta University that year, seeing his book of lyric poems *Fields of Wonder* released to mixed reviews and the publication of his translation, with Mercer Cook, of Roumain's *Masters of the Dew*. Receiving a regular salary from Atlanta and one thousand dollars from a National Institute and American Academy of Arts and Letters Award in 1946, plus royalties from *Street Scene*, provided him more financial stability, thus leaving time for him to edit with Bontemps a reissue of James Weldon Johnson's *Book of American Negro Poetry*. He was also able to publish a translation (with Ben Frederic Carruthers) of Nicolás Guillén's *Cuba Libre* and prepare another collection of poetry, *One-Way Ticket*

(1949). A return to jazz- and blues-saturated poetry, this volume contains Hughes's celebrated "Madam" poems and the song "Life Is Fine," trumpeting perseverance and optimism. When the opera *Troubled Island* opened in 1949, Hughes was busy trying to find a publisher for the second volume of his autobiography and a new volume of poems. The production of *The Barrier* (1950), an opera based on the play *Mulatto*, yielded little money, though the collection of Simple stories *Simple Speaks His Mind* (1950) sold thirty thousand copies and received general critical acclaim. Hughes was becoming better known, and translations of his work and critical essays were appearing.

Yet as success loomed, Hughes's masterful jazz-imbued *Montage of a Dream Deferred* (1951), a book-length poem in five sections depicting the rhythms of bop, boogie, and blues of the urban African American experience in the context of continued deferment of the promises of American democracy, was critically panned. However, his short-story collection *Laughing to Keep from Crying* (1952) fared better with critics. Prolific throughout his career in multiple genres, Hughes began work on a series of children's books for Franklin Watts, which released *The First Book of Negroes* (1952), *The First Book of Rhythms* (1954), *The First Book of Jazz* (1955), *The First Book of the West Indies* (1956), and *The First Book of Africa* (1960). He also published other historical nonfiction works, *Famous American Negroes* (1954), *Famous Negro Music Makers* (1955), *A Pictorial History of the Negro in America* (with Milton Meltzer, 1956), *Famous Negro Heroes of America* (1958), *Fight for Freedom: The Story of the NAACP* (1962), and *Black Magic: A Pictorial History of the Negro in American Entertainment* (with Meltzer, 1967). The quality and success of these books established Hughes's importance as a popular historian of African American life. The second volume of his autobiography, *I Wonder as I Wander* (1956), emphasized Hughes's determination to survive and prosper, undaunted by the adversity and suffering he had faced in his travels in this country and around the world.

Nevertheless, Hughes found himself increasingly under the siege of McCarthyism and was forced to appear in March 1953 before Joseph R. McCarthy's Senate subcommittee, not to defend his poetry but to repudiate some of his zealous leftist activities and work. Hughes's Simple stories continued to draw positive critical response and pleased his readers, although the Simple collections, *Simple Takes a Wife* (1953), *Simple Stakes a Claim* (1957),

The Best of Simple (1961), and *Simple's Uncle Sam* (1965) did not sell well. The play *Simply Heavenly* began a reasonably successful run in 1957, landing on Broadway and on the London stage. That same year his translation of *Selected Poems of Gabriela Mistral* appeared, followed in 1958 by his selection and revision of his writings, *The Langston Hughes Reader*, and in 1959 by *Selected Poems of Langston Hughes* and his rousing play *Tambourines to Glory*, which he had converted into a novel of the same title in 1958.

Certainly by the 1960s Hughes was an elder statesman of his people and a literary celebrity, adding to his publications stagings of his dramas, recordings, television and radio shows, and appearances at conferences (in Uganda and Nigeria and at the National Poetry Festival in Washington, D.C., in 1962), jazz clubs, and festivals. He received honorary doctorates from Howard University in 1963 and Western Reserve University in 1964. The poetry was still flowing, with *Ask Your Mama* (1961) and *The Panther and the Lash* (1967) demonstrating that Hughes's satiric and humanitarian impulses were undiminished, as were his dramatic juices, evidenced by the critical success of the gospel play *Black Nativity* (1961). Always eager to help younger writers, he edited *New Negro Poets: USA* (1964).

Indeed, the final years of his life were filled with activity: the production of his play *The Prodigal Son* (1965), a two-month State Department tour of Europe lecturing on African American writers, work on *The Best Short Stories by Negro Writers* (1967), and trips to Paris (with the production of *Prodigal Son*) and to Africa (as a presidential appointee to the First World Festival of Negro Arts), along with readings and lectures, filled his days. In the midst of this frenetic life, Hughes was admitted to the hospital with abdominal pains, later found to be caused by a blocked bladder and an enlarged prostate. Despite a successful operation, his heart and kidneys began to fail, and Hughes died in New York City.

Langston Hughes praised the "low-down folks" in the essay "The Negro Artist and the Racial Mountain" (*Nation*, 23 June 1926) for furnishing "a wealth of colorful, distinctive material" and for maintaining "their individuality in the face of American standardizations." Hughes's own life and career might be viewed in the same light. The variety and quality of his achievements in various genres, always in the service of greater understanding and humanity, and his specific commitment to depicting and strengthening the African American

heartbeat in America—and to helping others depict it as well—gave him a place of central importance in twentieth-century African American literature and American literature generally. Hughes sought to change the way people looked not only at African Americans and art but also at the world, and his modernistic vision was both experimental and traditional, cacophonous and mellifluous, rejecting of artificial middle-class values, and promoting emotional and intellectual freedom. He demonstrated that African Americans could support themselves with their art both monetarily and spiritually. Hughes published more than forty books in a career that never lost touch with the concerns of sharecroppers and tenement dwellers as it provided inspiration for not only African American writers but for all working people.

FURTHER READING

Hughes's papers are in the James Weldon Johnson Memorial Collection, Beinecke Rare Book and Manuscript Library, Yale University.

Berry, Faith. *Langston Hughes: Before and Beyond Harlem* (1983).

The Langston Hughes Review (1982–present).

Mikolyzk, Thomas A., ed. *Langston Hughes: A Bio-Bibliography* (1990).

Nichols, Charles, ed. *Arna Bontemps–Langston Hughes Letters, 1925–1967* (1980).

Rampersad, Arnold. *The Life of Langston Hughes*, vol. 1 (1986) and vol. 2 (1988).

Tracy, Steven C. *Langston Hughes and the Blues* (1988).

Obituary: *New York Times*, 24 May 1967.

This entry is taken from the *American National Biography* and is published here with the permission of the American Council of Learned Societies.

STEVEN C. TRACY

Hughes, Louis (1832–19 Jan. 1913), author, businessman, and nurse, was born into slavery near Charlottesville, Virginia, the son of a white man and a black woman, possibly John and Susan Hughes. When he was about six years old, Hughes was sold with his mother and two brothers to Dr. Louis, a physician in Scottsville, Virginia. When Dr. Louis died, young Hughes was sold with his mother and brother to Washington Fitzpatrick, also of Scottsville, who soon sent him, then about eleven years old, to Richmond on the pretense of hiring him out to work on a canal boat. Parting with his mother at such a young age was difficult; even more difficult was his realization that he would never

Louis Hughes, former slave, businessman, and nurse. (University of North Carolina at Chapel Hill Libraries.)

see his mother again. For Hughes this experience became the central symbol of the fundamental inhumanity of the system of slavery, a symbol to which he returns at key points in the autobiography that is the sole source for most of the information on his life, *Thirty Years a Slave* (1897). George Reid owned Hughes for a brief time after his arrival in Richmond; however, Reid sold Hughes because of the latter's frequent illnesses. Edmund McGehee, under whose ownership Hughes remained for the next two decades, purchased the young boy in November 1844. McGehee relocated Hughes to Pontotoc County, Mississippi, where he presented Hughes to his wife as a Christmas gift. In August 1850 McGehee sent Hughes to Memphis, Tennessee, to assist in the construction of a new house, in which Hughes would soon be established as butler and body-servant. Among Hughes's duties were the tasks of "working with medicine, giving it and caring for the sick" (Hughes, 2002, 57), an occupation to which Hughes would return years later following his escape from enslavement. While serving at

the new house in Memphis Hughes met his future wife, Matilda. Matilda was born on 17 June 1830 in Fayette County, Kentucky, and was purchased by McGehee in 1855. Hughes and Matilda were married three years later, on 30 November 1858. The ceremony was held in the McGehee house parlor and presided over by the McGehee's parish minister, a rare privilege among the enslaved and proof of the couple's high status in the household. A year later Matilda gave birth to twins.

But while Hughes expressed his appreciation for McGehee's acknowledgment of the sanctity of marriage, he emphasized the limitations of McGehee's humanitarianism and the harshness of everyday life for himself and his wife. Hughes had tried to escape twice before his marriage and was severely punished after the second unsuccessful attempt. After their children were born, Matilda made her own desperate attempt to change her situation because she felt she was being forced to neglect them. She left with the twins and returned to Forrest's slave market, presenting herself to be sold again. Matilda was returned to the McGehees, who, according to Hughes, "beat her by turns" (Hughes, 2002, 78). The twins died six months later, weak from insufficient care. "Things continued in this way," Hughes reports, "until about June, 1862," when the McGehee family fled from advancing Union forces and Hughes was sent to the family plantation in Bolivar, Mississippi. After this forced separation from his wife, Hughes was reunited with her in 1863 when he was sent to a family farm in Panola County, Mississippi.

The couple did not succeed in escaping from enslavement until close to the end of the Civil War. Before that time, after the outbreak of the Civil War, Hughes had made two more unsuccessful escape attempts. The first of these efforts, in the winter of 1862–1863, ended when Hughes was captured by Confederate soldiers. A few months later, Hughes and Matilda tried to escape with another couple, but all were recaptured. Shortly after that, in the spring of 1863, the couple was sent with most of McGehee's other slaves to Alabama to be leased out to the state-run saltworks on the Tombigbee River, where Hughes and his wife remained for two years, and where Matilda gave birth to their daughter Lydia. Finally, on 26 June 1865, Hughes successfully escaped to Union-occupied Memphis. With the help of two Union soldiers, Hughes returned to Mississippi for Matilda and Lydia. They finally arrived in Memphis and their long-sought freedom on the Fourth of July 1865, which was after General Robert E. Lee's surrender at Appomattox

Courthouse, but before they would otherwise have been freed.

After about six weeks in Memphis, the family moved to Cincinnati, Ohio, in August 1865, where Matilda hoped to find relatives. She was reunited with her mother and one of her sisters, and the family lived for a few months in Hamilton, Ohio. But they were determined to go to Canada, "as we regarded that as the safest place for refugees from slavery" (Hughes, 2002, 141), and so they traveled north through Detroit and entered Windsor, Ontario, Canada, on Christmas Day 1865. Hughes and Matilda secured positions at a hotel and remained there until the following spring, when Hughes returned to Detroit in hope of earning higher wages. Following two years of working first as a waiter in Detroit and then on a steamboat, Hughes secured a position in a Chicago hotel, where he worked until 1868. During this time Hughes also attended night school. In Chicago he met John Plankinton, who offered Hughes a position in his new hotel in Milwaukee, Wisconsin. The Plankinton House was opened in September 1868, and Hughes's family, now enlarged by the recent birth of twins, was soon settled in what would be their permanent home. Sometime later Hughes rediscovered his brother, from whom he had been separated since childhood, living in Cleveland, Ohio. He looked forward to a life "in which the joys of social intercourse had marvelously expanded" (Hughes, 2002, 147).

In Milwaukee, Hughes established himself as an enterprising businessman and a leader of the city's small African American community. In 1869 he was one of the founders of St. Mark's African Methodist Episcopal (AME) Church, a congregation in which the Hughes family remained prominent and active members. After a year's work at the Plankinton House, Hughes and his wife began to supplement their income with an independent laundry service. By 1874 their laundry work had increased so significantly that Hughes left the hotel to develop the growing family business. In the 1880s, though, Hughes returned to his earlier interest in caring for the sick and established himself as a nurse, his last and fondest professional enterprise. In his work as a nurse, Hughes traveled the country, going first to New Orleans and eventually as far as California and Florida.

While the events of his life make for a rich story of individual determination, religious faith, and familial devotion, Hughes's life, like so many others of the time, would have remained unknown had he not written the autobiography for which he is remembered. The book was copyrighted in 1896 and published by the South Side Printing Company in Milwaukee. Scholars disagree about whether Hughes wrote it himself or with the help of another person, but the book clearly represents Hughes's perspective on his many experiences. In addition to relating the dramatic story of his life in and escape from slavery, Hughes presents a panoramic view of the South—including descriptions of various locales, agricultural methods and commerce, and southern society—as well as a revealing glimpse into post-emancipation life for African Americans in both the South and the North. By arranging for the independent publication of his narrative, Hughes freed himself "to write about his experience in the South and the North in his own way," and the story that he tells "identifies Hughes in several ways as more representative of the African American rank-and-file, both before and after slavery, than [FREDERICK] DOUGLASS or most of the other celebrated fugitive slaves whose antebellum narratives have dominated our understanding of what slavery was like" (Andrews, 9).

Matilda died on 7 October 1907, and Hughes followed some years later on 19 January 1913. Before his death, his church published a history that included prominent attention to the Hughes family, and at his death, Hughes's status in the larger community was acknowledged in the form of obituaries in various Milwaukee newspapers.

FURTHER READING

Hughes, Louis. *Thirty Years a Slave: From Bondage to Freedom; The Institution of Slavery as Seen on the Plantation and in the Home of the Planter; Autobiography of Louis Hughes* (1897, repr. 2002).

Andrews, William L. "Foreword," *Thirty Years a Slave: From Bondage to Freedom; The Institution of Slavery as Seen on the Plantation and in the Home of the Planter; Autobiography of Louis Hughes* (2002).

Ash, Stephen V. *A Year in the South: Four Lives in 1865* (2002).

Stevens, Michael E. "After Slavery: The Milwaukee Years of Louis Hughes," *Wisconsin Magazine of History* 86 (Autumn, 2002): 40–51.

JOHN ERNEST

Hughes, Revella (2 July 1895–24 Oct. 1987), musician, singer, and educator, was born Ravella Eudosia Hughes in Huntington, West Virginia, the daughter of George W. Hughes, a postman, and Annie B. (maiden name unknown), a piano teacher and seamstress. At age five Hughes began studying piano with her mother and, at eight or nine, violin with a musician friend of her father's. She attended Huntington's segregated public schools. Disturbed when she was racially harassed, her parents sent her to Hartshorn Memorial College (later part of Virginia Union University) in Richmond, which she attended from 1909 to 1911, graduating with a degree in music and elementary studies. She attended Oberlin High and Conservatory, graduating in 1915. In 1917 she earned a bachelor of music in Piano from Howard's Conservatory of Music, where she studied piano with LeRoy Tibbs and voice with the conservatory director LULU VERE CHILDERS. Hughes then taught violin and piano at the Washington Conservatory of Music from 1917 to 1918 and voice, piano, and violin at North Carolina State College. In 1919 she became director of music at A&M College in Orangeburg, South Carolina.

During the early 1920s Hughes pursued a career as a lyric soprano, performing classical art songs, arias, art songs by black composers, and spirituals in New York, New Jersey, and New England. Her vocal gift was recognized by ROLAND HAYES, who arranged for her to study voice with George Bagby. She lived in New York with family friends, the family of ADAM CLAYTON POWELL SR. Hughes was featured in Bagby's Sunday morning Memorial Concerts at the Waldorf-Astoria. She also studied with Walter Kiesewetter. She appeared with HENRY THACKER BURLEIGH, PAUL ROBESON, and MARIAN ANDERSON in separate concerts in 1920. Hailed as a fine lyric soprano, Hughes was dubbed the "Sepia Lily Pons" and the "Colored Nightingale" by the African American press.

Hughes turned to musical theater, appearing onstage in *Dumb Luck* in 1922 and joining *Shuffle Along* the same year, singing "I'm Just Wild about Harry" and "Gypsy Blues." Hughes became the first female Broadway choral director when NOBLE SISSLE and EUBIE BLAKE asked her to direct the chorus of the show's Chicago road company. In 1923 she appeared in Fess Williams's *And the Band in Padlox* at Chicago's Regal Theatre. She later played the lead in JAMES PRICE JOHNSON's *Runnin' Wild*, the show that introduced the Charleston, and in Will Vodery's *Swing Along*. She was one of the Four Bon Bons, a quartet including GEORGETTE HARVEY, Musa Williams, and Lois Sparker that first appeared in *Runnin' Wild*. The group disbanded after two years when Hughes

became ill and needed surgery. After recovering, Hughes performed as a solo entertainer in black theaters, such as the Lafayette and the Alhambra in New York, the Regal and the Metropolitan in Chicago, and the Howard in Washington, and on the B. F. Keith vaudeville circuit. She appeared with DUKE ELLINGTON, CAB CALLOWAY, CLAUDE HOPKINS, FATS WALLER, and Blake. She also recorded for Black Swan and appeared briefly on radio over WHN.

When her mother became ill in 1932, Hughes returned to Huntington to care for her. She worked as supervisor of music of Negro schools and taught elementary school music at Douglass High School for eleven years. While at Douglass, she organized a 128-piece band in 1938–1939 and directed the orchestra and an award-winning fifty-voice choir. Praised for her outstanding work, Hughes received a citation from the Cabell County Board of Education. She was also briefly the director of the piano and violin departments at West Virginia State College. Hughes remained active in Huntington, leading her Society Syncopators, which played dances and society functions throughout West Virginia. During school summer vacations, she attended Northwestern University's Graduate School of Music Education, earning a master's of music education degree from Northwestern University in 1942, the year her mother died. She briefly pursued doctoral studies at Columbia University, though she never finished the degree.

After her mother's death, Hughes returned to New York and show business. In 1949 she adopted the name Camella Dasche and performed on the Hammond organ in nightclubs and lounges in the eastern cities of Baltimore, Philadelphia, Albany, Troy, Monticello, and Harlem, New York. She was known for "swinging the classics," a blend of the classical piano and jazz she called "informal music" because, as a classically trained pianist, she did not improvise but performed from written arrangements that she memorized. She rearranged classical, jazz, and Latin American pieces and spirituals, exaggerated the rhythm, and enhanced the harmony. Hughes entertained the U.S. armed forces during the 1950s, performing at the Salvation Army Servicemen's Center. In 1953 she toured Europe and the Middle East for fourteen weeks with the Wandering Gypsies in the Gypsy Markoff Celebrity Show, a USO show sponsored by the Entertainment Department of the U.S. Air Force. She played the Hammond organ and piano and was musical director. In 1957 she made a second tour of Europe. After returning to the United States, she resumed playing in clubs. In February 1956, while appearing with Markoff's All-Girl Revue in the Beverly Hotel Supper Club Room in New York, Hughes met the heiress Evelyn V. "Sally" Adams, the granddaughter of the Adams chewing gum company founder Thomas Adams Jr. In July Adams invited Hughes to Europe. The two became lifelong friends, sharing Adams's residence. Hughes retired in the late 1950s but continued performing, playing organ for services at Norman Vincent Peale's Marble Collegiate Church. In 1961 Hughes inherited Adams's $1 million estate.

Honored at age eighty-five by Sarah McLawler's third Women's Jazz Festival, Salute to Women in Jazz, in 1980, Hughes performed on the Saturday of the festival. She appeared at the jazz festival the following year. She was also honored by the Bramwell Mapp Scholarship Fund at the Waldorf-Astoria in 1982 and received Howard's Alumni Achievement Award in 1987. She died in Manhattan.

Though largely forgotten in the last thirty years of her life, Hughes was an important figure in art music, musical theater, and jazz. During the late 1910s and early 1920s, she was among the ranks of a generation of pioneering African American concert singers. As a musical theater actress, she appeared in several important, trendsetting African American musicals. Although she did not improvise in the strict sense, she was one of the few women who pursued and sustained a career as a jazz and nightclub instrumentalist.

FURTHER READING

Hughes's papers are at the Moorland-Spingarn Research Center at Howard University, Washington, D.C., and at Marshall University in Huntington, West Virginia.

McGinty, Doris Evans. "Conversation with Revella Hughes: From the Classics to Broadway to Swing," *Black Perspective in Music* 16 (1988).

Nettles, Darryl Glenn. *African American Concert Singers before 1950* (2003).

Obituary: *New York Times*, 27 Oct. 1987.

DISCOGRAPHY

Turner, Patricia. *Dictionary of Afro-American Performers: 78RPM and Cylinder Recordings of Opera, Choral Music, and Song, 1900–1949* (1990).

This entry is taken from the *American National Biography* and is published here with the permission of the American Council of Learned Societies.

GAYLE MURCHISON

Hughes, Samuel Thomas (20 Oct. 1910–8 Aug. 1981), baseball player, was the youngest of twelve children born in Louisville, Kentucky, to Henry Hughes and Mary Susan Cowhard. As a youngster, Sammy worked with the Missionary Society of his family's church home, Ebenezer Baptist. Dropping out of school after the eighth grade, Hughes began his professional career in 1929 at age nineteen with the Louisville White Sox. In 1931 he hit .421 but did not have enough at-bats to qualify for the league lead.

After spending his first three seasons with his hometown team, the smooth-fielding second baseman joined the Washington Pilots in 1932. In 1933 he moved to the Nashville Elite Giants where he remained with the organization through several franchise moves during the 1930s.

From 1935 to 1940, while playing with the Elite Giants of Nashville, Columbus, Washington, and Baltimore, Hughes earned batting averages of .355, .353, .319, .302, .345, and .254. In early 1937 Hughes played in the California Winter League, accumulating a .384 average in seven consecutive seasons. In the 1940–1941 seasons, he led in homers with four in ten games played. He was in the top 10 in homers with 17 in 294 at-bats. Lured to Mexico in 1941, the crack second sacker recorded a .324 average with the Torreon Cotton Dealers.

With his strong arm, agile fielding and wide-ranging defensive skills, the 6'2" lanky journeyman was arguably one of black baseball's best second basemen during the 1930s and early 1940s. Hughes was a steady contact hitter who excelled at the hit-and-run. An outstanding bunter, he was a consistent number-two batter in the Elites lineup.

Hughes's sixteen-year career had him appearing in more East-West All Star games than any other second baseman, garnering the most votes (among second basemen) in 1936, 1937, 1938, and 1940. Hughes averaged .238 at the plate in six yearly outings facing All Star pitching.

In 1942 Hughes hit a team best .309 average, beating out notables ROY CAMPANELLA and Wild Bill Wright. He also led the league with eleven doubles. In August, Hughes along with Campanella and David Barnhill received an offer to tryout with the Major League's Pittsburgh Pirates. An apparent publicity ploy, the opportunity did not materialize. Moreover, Hughes and Campanella were fined and suspended by Elite's owner Tom Wilson for not getting consent to leave for the tryout.

During World War II, Hughes served three years in the United States Army with the 196th Support

Battalion, which invaded New Guinea. After being honorably discharged, he returned in 1946 to the Elite Giants, where he finished his career with a .277 batting average.

Hughes is credited with an overall lifetime average of .296 in the Negro Leagues and a .353 average in exhibition play against white major leaguers. After retiring from baseball, Hughes worked for the Pillsbury Milling Company in Los Angeles. In 1956 he married Thelma Smith. The couple had one child, a daughter Barbara. Hughes died at age seventy in his home in Los Angeles.

FURTHER READING

Lester, Larry. *Black Baseball's National Showcase* (2001).

Riley, James A. *The Biographical Encyclopedia of The Negro Baseball Leagues* (1994).

BYRON MOTLEY

Huiswoud, Otto Eduard Gerardus Majella (28 Oct. 1893–20 Feb. 1961), American Communist Party activist, was born in Paramaribo, Suriname, the son of Rudolf Francis Huiswoud, a freed slave and tailor, and his wife, Jacqueline Hendrietta (Bernhard). After attending Catholic schools, in 1913 at age nineteen he became a scullion on a banana boat and immigrated to the United States.

During the First World War Huiswoud joined the Harlem Socialist Party (SP) along with other "New Negro" radicals including Grace Campbell, LOVETT FORT-WHITEMAN, CHANDLER OWEN, A. PHILIP RANDOLPH, and RICHARD B. MOORE. In general the American SP ignored the oppression of black people, at worst supporting segregation and at best arguing that blacks were subject only to class and not race oppression. However, the Harlem branch, uniquely among Socialists, attempted to develop a Socialist program to deal with black oppression, in part owing to the work of the pioneer black Socialist HUBERT HARRISON (who had left the SP by the time Huiswoud joined).

The Bolshevik Revolution in November 1917 reverberated throughout the international Socialist movement, which was already reeling from the war and the capitulation to pro-war sentiment among many Socialist leaders. In 1919 Huiswoud joined the Communist movement in the United States, becoming the first important black member of the Communist Party (another Caribbean immigrant, Arthur P. Hendricks from British Guiana—now Guyana—was also active in the proto-Communist left wing within the Socialist Party but died before the final split). At the same time, Huiswoud also became active in the African Blood Brotherhood (ABB), a militant pro-Bolshevik black nationalist organization founded by CYRIL V. BRIGGS in 1919. By the mid-1920s several leaders of the New York ABB, including Briggs, Moore, and Huiswoud, had become the leading Communists in Harlem.

Huiswoud quickly became important in the Communist Party's work directed at recruiting black workers and intellectuals. In April 1921 the party leadership created a Negro Committee consisting of Huiswoud, Lovett Fort-Whiteman, and Joseph Zack. In 1922 Huiswoud (using the pseudonym "J. Billings") was an official American delegate to the Fourth Congress of the Communist International (Comintern). There Huiswoud articulated the party's position at the "Negro Commission" that "although the Negro Problem as such is a fundamentally economic question, it is aggravated and intensified by the friction which exists between the black and the white races" (*Fourth Congress of the Communist International*, London, 1923, session 22). However, another, unofficial, American delegate to a large degree upstaged Huiswoud. The Jamaican-born poet CLAUDE MCKAY argued that black oppression was racial as well as economic and that many American leftists were themselves prejudiced and not willing to deal with black oppression. Both McKay and Huiswoud met with Vladimir Lenin—who was quite ill—during the congress. The resolution on the "Negro Question" from the congress made black liberation an important goal of world communism. Reflecting the Caribbean background of many black American Communists, the resolution also placed the issue within the context of anticolonialism.

In the mid-1920s Huiswoud continued his party activities. He joined the Central Executive Committee in 1923. In 1925 he helped organize the American Negro Labor Congress (ANLC). In September 1926 he married Hermine Alicia Dumont, a British Guiana–born stenographer and activist. Huiswoud also attended printing school in New York City during this period.

In 1928 the Sixth Comintern Congress voted that black Americans in the South were an oppressed nationality and that the party should fight for "self-determination for the black belt," which meant national independence for blacks in the South. With the exception of Harry Haywood, none of the leading black Communists supported this position at first. Nonetheless, the Sixth Congress elected Huiswoud as an alternative member of its executive committee. In 1929 the Comintern criticized

Huiswoud and the party leadership for opposing the new line. Huiswoud's disagreement, while not causing a break with the party, did dampen his success and authority.

In 1929–1930 Huiswoud was active in the Caribbean. In 1930 he was the Communist representative to MARCUS GARVEY's Convention of Negro Peoples of the World in Jamaica, where he debated Garvey on black nationalism. Because of his labor and Communist-organizing, he was expelled from a number of Caribbean countries at this time. For the remainder of the 1930s he filled a number of international assignments for the Comintern, including studying at the Lenin School in Moscow; working for the Comintern's labor arm, the Profintern; helping the South African Communist Party; and editing the Profintern's *Negro Worker*, which was aimed at black workers.

He also faced regular state harassment and repression in Europe, the United States, and the Caribbean. In 1934 Huiswoud and his wife were arrested by Belgian authorities for possession of Communist propaganda and mailing lists, and were deported to the Netherlands. In 1939 Huiswoud returned to New York City, but in January 1941 he went back to Suriname for health reasons and was promptly arrested by Dutch authorities and interned until October 1942; no formal charges were brought nor was representation provided. When he attempted to return to the United States after the Second World War, U.S. authorities would not allow him to do so, and he settled in the Netherlands with his wife. There he continued to be active in Caribbean nationalist and leftist politics, leading the Ons Suriname (Our Suriname) organization in the late 1950s. Otto Huiswoud died in Amsterdam in 1951.

FURTHER READING

Blakely, Allison. *Blacks in the Dutch World: The Evolution of Racial Imagery in a Modern Society* (1993).

Gertrudis van Enkevort, Maria. *The Life and Work of Otto Huiswoud: Professional Revolutionary and Internationalist*. Ph.D. thesis, University of the West Indies (2001).

James, Winston. *Holding Aloft the Banner of Ethiopia: Caribbean Radicalism in Early Twentieth-Century America* (1998).

Naison, Mark. *Communists in Harlem during the Depression* (1984).

Solomon, Mark. *The Cry Was Unity: Communists and African Americans, 1917–36* (1998).

Obituary: *The Worker*, 31 Dec. 1961.

J. A. ZUMOFF

Hulett, John (19 Nov. 1927–21 Aug. 2006), civil rights activist, sheriff, and probate judge, was born in Gordonville in Lowndes County, Alabama, to Jim Hulett and Daisy (Baker), both farmers. Before 1950 John Hulett was eager to travel outside the Black Belt to see more of America. After graduating from Central High School in Gordonsville around 1945 and already planning to be a policeman, he took classes in law enforcement at Stanford University, the University of Wisconsin, and the University of Alabama in preparation for his future career. Upon his return to Alabama in 1950 he settled in Birmingham and began working for the Federal Rural Housing Alliance as a housing consultant. Hulett traveled throughout six southern states, helping to provide homes for the poor in rural areas. While in Birmingham he also became affiliated with the organized labor movement working to secure jobs for African Americans in the city. During this time Hulett also conducted voter registration drives in a mostly African American suburb of Birmingham named Prattsville.

Hulett returned to Lowndes County in 1955. There he continued his work with the Federal Rural Housing Alliance, building and repairing homes for the poor. He also immediately began to encourage local residents to register to vote. No African American had registered to vote in Lowndes County, Alabama, since the end of Reconstruction in 1877. Hulett was determined to change that fact.

In February 1960 Hulett married Eddie Mae Aaron, of whom little is known except that she was also involved in the Lowndes County voting rights campaign. The couple had eleven children.

Hulett was assisted in his efforts to organize black voters by two major events: passage of the Civil Rights Act of 1964 (which desegregated public facilities) and the Voting Rights Act of 1965 (which made it possible for African Americans in the South to register and to vote without fear and intimidation). These two laws were especially important for Lowndes County, considering it was the fifth-poorest county in the nation during the 1960s and one of the most dangerous in terms of violence against African Americans and civil rights activists. Two white civil rights workers, Viola Liuzzo from Detroit and Jonathan Daniels from New Hampshire, were killed in Lowndes County in 1965.

In early 1965, after consulting with MARTIN LUTHER KING JR. and his organization, the Southern Christian Leadership Conference (SCLC), Hulett went back to Lowndes County energized and ready to register residents to vote. But of the thirty-seven African Americans he took with him in March of that year to the Hayneville, Alabama, courthouse to register, only Hulett and another organizer, Sidney Logan Jr., were allowed to do so. In response, Hulett and seventeen other local activists created the Lowndes County Christian Movement for Human Rights (LCCMHR) in March 1965. Hulett was elected chair of the LCCMHR, which worked closely with STOKELY CARMICHAEL (Kwame Ture) and other activists in the Student Nonviolent Coordinating Committee (SNCC) to register as many black residents of Lowndes County as they could throughout the spring and summer of 1965. When the Voting Rights Act was finally passed in August of 1965 they were able to register hundreds more.

Because of the high number of African Americans registering to vote, Hulett, with SNCC's guidance, decided to start a third political party in order to run their own candidates for local offices in the 1966 elections. Despite many setbacks, including intimidation and unfair laws, the Lowndes County Freedom Organization (LCFO) was created in March 1966. Hulett resigned as chair of the LCCMHR and was appointed president of the LCFO. Needing a symbol that would help African American voters recognize the party at the voting polls, the LCFO chose a black panther as its party symbol. Because of this, the LCFO came to be known as the Black Panther Party even before the Oakland, California, Black Panther Party was founded in October 1966.

The election took place in November 1966 but none of the LCFO candidates was elected. The LCFO, with Hulett as its president, ran three candidates in the following election in 1968 but again failed to win any seats. By 1969 the LCFO lacked the funds to remain an effective political party. Late in 1969 the LCFO merged with the National Democratic Party of Alabama (NDPA). The NDPA was a black political party whose founders were Alvis Howard Jr., Dr. John L. Cashin, and Charles Morgan.

In 1970 Hulett became the first African American elected sheriff of Lowndes County, Alabama. He served in that position for twenty-one years, after which he became the county's first African American probate judge, an elected position that he held for six years. He retired in 1998 because of failing health, but even in retirement Hulett continued to do good for his community by helping to clean up the neighborhoods and roads in Lowndes County and helping older residents gain access to affordable medication.

Hulett, who died in Mosses, Alabama, inspired many people, including the founders of the NDPA which eventually helped elect him sheriff, and the California-based Black Panther Party whose founders, HUEY NEWTON and BOBBY SEALE, adopted the Black Panther logo of the Lowndes County Freedom Organization. One of Hulett's sons, John Hulett Jr., carried on his father's work, and was elected probate judge of Lowndes County in 2001.

FURTHER READING

Carmichael, Stokely, and Charles V. Hamilton. *Black Power: The Politics of Liberation in America* (1967).

Frye, Hardy T. *Black Parties and Political Power: A Case Study* (1980).

BERGIS K. JULES

Hull, Agrippa

Hull, Agrippa (1759–1848), Revolutionary War soldier, was born free in Northampton, Massachusetts, of unknown parentage. He was taken to Stockbridge, Massachusetts, at the age of six by Joab, an African American former servant to Jonathan Edwards. When Hull was eighteen years old, in May 1777, he enlisted to fight in the Revolutionary War as a private in General John Paterson's brigade of the First Massachusetts Regiment of the Continental army. Free blacks had been allowed by the Continental Congress to enlist in the army since January 1776, but each unit commander determined whether or not he would accept African American recruits.

Hull served as General Paterson's personal orderly for two years. He then attended General Tadeusz Kosciuszko, the Polish volunteer in the American cause, as an orderly for four years and two months. As an orderly, Hull performed a variety of personal and military duties for the generals, including serving as a surgeon's assistant in South Carolina in 1781. Hull was with Kosciuszko during battles from Saratoga, New York, through the campaign in the South and served with the general until the end of the war. When the Continental army was disbanded at West Point in the summer of 1783, Hull received a discharge signed personally by George Washington, the commander in chief, a document he prized for the rest of his life.

After the war Hull returned to Stockbridge, Massachusetts, where he eventually owned a small plot of land. As was the case for many free African Americans in New England after the Revolution, Hull was on the economic margins of society, and he eked out a living from a variety of sources. He farmed his land, performed odd jobs around Stockbridge, and occasionally served as a butler and a majordomo to the local gentry.

However marginal his economic position, Hull was very much a part of town life in Stockbridge. The prominent Stockbridge resident and novelist Catharine Maria Sedgwick, whose family was friendly to Hull, called him "a sort of Sancho Panza in the village." He acquired a reputation for understanding the supernatural and was considered something of the town "seer."

Hull married twice and adopted at least one child. His first wife (whom he married sometime before 1790) was Jane Darby, a fugitive slave from Lenox, Massachusetts, whose master, Mr. Ingersoll, tried to seize her after she had married Hull. After Jane Darby died, Hull married Margaret Timbroke. Sometime after the Revolutionary War, Hull adopted the daughter of Mary Gunn, a runaway slave from New York.

Like most Revolutionary War veterans, Hull was proud of his military service. When General Kosciuszko returned to the United States in 1797 after fighting for Polish independence, Hull traveled to New York to meet with him, and during this trip Kosciuszko directed the Ohio land granted to him by Congress to be sold to pay for a school for African Americans.

One of only several dozen African Americans who applied for Revolutionary War pensions, Hull received a veteran's pension from Congress, which he sought to have mailed to his home in 1828. Hull enlisted the help of Charles Sedgwick, who wrote to Acting Secretary of State Richard Rush for assistance with Hull's claim. Hull enclosed his discharge paper as proof of his service but worried that it might not be returned.

Slavery was outlawed by 1790 under the Massachusetts state constitution, but racial divisions in society persisted. Within a restrictive system of racial hierarchy, Hull used his good standing in the community of Stockbridge and his good humor to question the limitations of race. The town historian, Electa F. Jones, who knew Hull, recorded several anecdotes that reveal Hull's racial attitudes. For example, on one occasion he proclaimed: "It is not the *cover* of the book, but what the book *contains*…. Many a good book has dark covers."

That Hull was a respected member of Stockbridge society by the end of his life in the 1840s is evidenced by two main facts. The historian Francis Parkman recorded his impressions of Hull after a visit to Stockbridge in 1844, declaring that Hull "looked on himself as father to all Stockbridge." Hull's respectability was also portrayed visually in 1844 in a daguerreotype photograph by Anson Clark, which was copied as an oil painting in 1848. The photograph and painting present an image of Hull as a distinguished, formally dressed old man staring out resolutely and grasping a cane firmly in his left hand. The oil painting of Hull, one of the few formal portraits of an African American Revolutionary War veteran, hangs in the Stockbridge Public Library.

Hull died in Stockbridge. His position in the Continental army was more distinguished than that of most African Americans who were allowed to serve, and as the orderly to generals, he witnessed some of the most important fighting of the war. Hull carried with him for the rest of his life the legacy of his important service to the revolutionary cause, which enhanced his pride as a free African American man. He stands as an extraordinary example of early African American military service and as a typical example of the free African Americans who carved a place for themselves in New England society between the Revolutionary War and the Civil War.

FURTHER READING

Some materials are available in the Agrippa Hull Collection in the Stockbridge, Massachusetts, Public Library.

Bradley, Patricia. *Slavery, Propaganda, and the American Revolution* (1998).

Jones, Electa F. *Stockbridge, Past and Present* (1854, repr. 1994).

Kaplan, Sidney, and Emma Nogrady Kaplan. *The Black Presence in the Era of the American Revolution* (1989).

This entry is taken from the *American National Biography* and is published here with the permission of the American Council of Learned Societies.

SARAH J. PURCELL

Hull, Gloria Thompson (Akasha) (6 Dec. 1944–), poet, writer, and educator, was born Gloria Therese Thompson in Shreveport, Louisiana, one of three children of Robert Thompson, a disabled part-time laborer, and Jimmie (Williams)

Thompson, a housekeeper. Gloria grew up poor in a three-room shotgun house where the family was always strapped for cash. Her mother earned three dollars a day and the family kept a running tab with the corner grocer. Living in the segregated South added the sting of Jim Crow racism, and Gloria endured traumatic incidents like being run off the road by white policemen.

Although neither of her parents finished grammar school, her mother loved the poetry of PAUL LAURENCE DUNBAR and would often recite his work verbatim. Her mother's love of words and language resonated with the young Gloria, who wanted to become a journalist. At BOOKER T. WASHINGTON High School she wrote for her school newspaper, the *Booker T. Washington Roaring Lion*, and graduated in 1962 as class valedictorian. She earned a scholarship to Southern University in Baton Rouge, where she majored in English and wrote for her college newspaper. Between her junior and senior years at Southern, Thompson spent the summer of 1965 at Yale University working with the New Haven Human Relations Council. That summer she decided to visit New York City and the Columbia School of Journalism, where she had a positive interview with the assistant dean. However, family finances led her parents to encourage her to become a teacher.

She graduated summa cum laude from Southern University in 1966 and won a National Defense Education Act fellowship for graduate study in English literature at the University of Illinois, Urbana. She married Prentice R. Hull, her college sweetheart, on 12 June 1966. Prentice Hull had graduated from Southern University in 1965 with a B.S. in Chemistry and was pursuing a Ph.D. in Chemistry at Purdue University in Lafayette, Indiana. After spending one semester at Urbana, Gloria Hull relinquished her fellowship and followed her husband to Purdue, where she became a teaching assistant and new mother (to a son, Adrian Prentice Hull). However, she did not relinquish her academic career, earning her master's degree in English from Purdue in 1968 and beginning work on her doctorate.

While she was completing her PhD, Hull, her husband, and her son moved to Delaware, where her husband had gotten a job at the University of Delaware (Newark). Hull became an instructor of English there in 1971 as she completed her dissertation. She earned her Ph.D. in English from Purdue in 1972. She became an assistant professor of English at the University of Delaware in 1972 and associate professor in 1977.

During this period Hull's interest in black women's literature began to expand. She became involved with the black feminist group the Combahee River Collective, which she describes as "an association of fifteen to twenty African American women committed to consciousness-raising and organizing" (Hull, 25). Hull eventually worked on the group's Feminist Reprints Committee, where she met ALICE WALKER, who became a major influence. As Hull explained to the *Monterey County (CA) Weekly* (29 Jan. 2004), "She [Walker] was the first to teach a women's studies course in literature [at Wellesley College] in the '70s, and a few of us followed suit." While attending the annual meeting of the Modern Language Association in 1974, Hull also met BARBARA SMITH, who would become a collaborator.

In 1979 Hull decided to take a year's sabbatical leave from the University of Delaware to spend time in Washington, D.C. The year was one of deep, significant spiritual change for Hull. As a child she had attended Zion Baptist Church in Shreveport, and then Sunday chapel at Southern University. Now she was voraciously reading spiritual material on metaphysics, Jungian psychology, Eastern spiritual philosophies, and Afro-Catholic practices (Santeria). Most significantly, Hull read TONI CADE BAMBARA's novel *The Salt Eaters* (1980). With its themes of politics and healing, the novel helped Hull to realize the purpose of her life's work—prompted by a question in a poem by AUDRE LORDE—to express a black feminist vision that encompasses and harmonizes politics, spirituality, and creativity, in order to "evolutionize the world."

Hull also realized that this black feminist vision needed to be represented with greater inclusivity at the university level, where it was missing from black studies and women's studies curricula. She helped found the field of black women's studies and, with Patricia Bell Scott and Barbara Smith, published the groundbreaking book *All the Women Are White, All the-Blacks Are Men, but Some of Us Are Brave* (1982). The curriculum guide, which asserted that black female voices had been marginalized by the civil rights and women's movements, won the 1992 National Institute of Women of Color Award.

Hull returned to the University of Delaware after her sabbatical, where she was an associate professor of English until 1986 and full professor from 1986 to 1988. During this period Hull also spent two years as a Fulbright lecturer at the University of the West Indies, and she published prolifically. Perhaps due to her mother's love of Paul Laurence Dunbar, Hull focused on the works of Dunbar's wife ALICE DUNBAR-NELSON, publishing *Give Us Each Day: The Diary of Alice Dunbar-Nelson* (1984); *Color, Sex and Poetry: Three Women Writers of the Harlem Renaissance* (1987); and *The Works of Alice Dunbar-Nelson* (1988). Another significant change occurred in Hull's personal life. She and her husband divorced in 1983, and Hull embraced a lesbian lifestyle and identity that coincided with her professional interest and her personal healing from childhood emotional and sexual abuse.

She was a visiting scholar at Stanford University in 1987–1988 and then moved to California to accept a position as professor of women's studies and literature at the University of California, Santa Cruz (1988–2000). She was chair of the Women's Studies Department there from 1989 to 1991 and also published *Healing Heart Poems, 1973–1988* (1989).

By 1991 Hull had begun to synthesize all that she had experienced, seeking to write a book about what she saw as the rise of a black feminist consciousness that had erupted in the 1980s, as evidenced by her personal life as well as by the social, literary, and academic changes that occurred during that decade. The result was her book *Soul Talk: The New Spirituality of African American Women* (2001). A subheading on the book's cover describes the work as "a transformative paradigm featuring conversations with Alice Walker, Toni Cade Bambara, LUCILLE CLIFTON, Dolores Kendrick, SONIA SANCHEZ, Michele Gibbs, Geraldine McIntosh, Masani Alexis DeVeaux, and Namonyah Soipan." *Soul Talk* was the first book she published as Akasha Gloria Hull, having changed her name legally in 1992. Previous titles were reprinted with the name change. "Akasha" is reportedly a Sanskrit word, meaning sky, space, the "hidden library" of mystical knowledge that is encoded in a non-physical plane of existence and accessed through deep meditation.

Hull became professor emerita of women's studies and literature at UC Santa Cruz in 2000 and ceased teaching full-time that year to focus on her writing. Living with her partner in the Monterey/ Salinas area of northern California, Hull continued to lecture and consult in the areas of inclusion and diversity. In May 2003 Hull delivered the inaugural black feminist studies lecture at UC Santa Barbara, presented by the Department of Black Studies, titled "Creativity, Black Feminist Roots, and Human Revolution." Her short story "Plum Jelly in Hot Shiny Jars" was published in the 2003 anthology *Age Ain't Nothing but a Number: Black Women Explore Midlife.*

FURTHER READING

Hull, Akasha Gloria. *Soul Talk: The New Spirituality of African American Women* (2001).

Masters, Ryan. "Word Warrior: Local Poet Helped Forge Links between Feminism, Black Power, and New Literature," *Monterey County (CA) Weekly*, 29 Jan. 2004.

SHARON D. JOHNSON

Humes, Helen (23 June 1909–13 Sept. 1981), jazz, blues, and rhythm and blues singer, was born in Louisville, Kentucky, the daughter of John Henry Humes, a railroad worker who became one of the first African American attorneys in Louisville and then worked in real estate, and Emma Johnson, a schoolteacher. "Well, I was born June 23, 1909, but I put it June 23, 1913. And everybody that's been writing books and things, they got 1913," Humes explained to Helen Oakley Dance (12 May 1981). Her mother sang in a Baptist church choir and played piano at home. Humes sang with her mother and then took piano lessons as well. At Central High School her classmates included the jazz trombonist DICKY WELLS, the drummer Bill Beason, and the trumpeter Jonah Jones. At age seventeen, before finishing her schooling, Humes traveled to St. Louis to make her first blues records for the Okeh label, pairing "Black Cat Blues" and "A Worried Woman's Blues" in April 1927. Further sessions in New York in November produced "If Papa Has Outside Lovin'," "Do What You Did Last Night," "Everybody Does It Now," and other titles.

Like many famous individuals who are interviewed regularly, Humes developed a story of her life from which the same anecdotes were repeatedly published, including the false account of a fourteen-year-old blues singer. When retelling these anecdotes, Humes routinely contradicted herself; consequently the details of affiliation, location, and chronology are difficult to determine, but there seems to be no confusion over the essential outline of her story.

After graduation from Central High School, Humes worked for her father and took a two-year business course that led to a position as a secretary in a bank, but she quit to work as a waitress. She went to Buffalo on vacation and stayed for two years, singing at the Spider Web Club with the saxophonist Al Sears's band and at the Vendome Hotel in a band that included the violinist STUFF SMITH (probably in 1935). After working as a cook in a restaurant in Albany, probably in 1936, she returned home for a few months. She rejoined Sears in 1937 at the Cotton Club in Cincinnati, where COUNT BASIE heard her sing and asked her to join his band. The pay was low, and she did not want to travel, so she decided to stay with Sears. Later that same year Sears himself decided to travel, and Humes went with him to New York City, where the jazz promoter John Hammond heard her singing at Vernon Andrade's Renaissance Ballroom. Hammond soon organized the trumpeter Harry James's first sessions, using sidemen from the Basie and Benny Goodman bands, and Humes sang on several tracks, including "(I Can Dream) Can't I?" (December 1937), "Song of the Wanderer" (January. 1938), and "It's the Dreamer in Me" (January 1938).

On 3 March 1938 BILLIE HOLIDAY left Basie, and Hammond contrived to have Humes compete in the Apollo Theater's renowned amateur contest as a means of getting her into Basie's band. Humes finished second to an ELLA FITZGERALD imitator, but when that unidentified woman proved unsuitable at an audition, Basie hired Humes. For three years their careers ran together. Humes participated in Basie's rise to fame during a stand at the Famous Door on Fifty-second Street and in his subsequent extensive touring. She joyfully recalled doubling as the band's cook during tours of the South, where the difficulty in finding restaurants that would serve African Americans made her culinary talent especially useful and appreciated.

Although membership in Basie's greatest band was the most significant affiliation of Humes's career, her best recordings were made elsewhere. It was impossible for Basie to assign blues songs to her when he had the magnificent blues singer JIMMY RUSHING in the band. The significant exception is "Blues for Helen," recorded on 3 June 1938 with Basie's sextet, including the trumpeter BUCK CLAYTON and the clarinetist LESTER YOUNG. It was not issued until two decades later, when Hammond put the performance into the 1960 *Spirituals to Swing* album, splicing in a fake spoken introduction and applause at the end to make it appear as if it were part of his famous From Spirituals to Swing concert of 23 December 1938. In her work with Basie, Humes sang ballads and pop songs in arrangements that were unfortunately lugubrious, saccharine, or childish. Superior examples of her ballad and swing style from this period included amateur low-fidelity recordings of "Stardust" and

"Exactly like You," made while she sang with DON BYAS at Minton's Playhouse in Harlem in May 1941, one month after she tired of touring and left Basie. "Stardust," the writer Eric Townley claimed, is "the greatest vocal version of [Hoagy] Carmichael's song" (*Jazz Journal International*, Nov. 1981).

After she left Basie, Hammond secured a job for Humes at Café Society, where from 1941 to 1943 she sang to the accompaniment of the boogie-woogie piano trio of ALBERT AMMONS, MEADE LUX LEWIS, and PETE JOHNSON; the pianist ART TATUM (who, Humes reported, characteristically played too many notes); the pianist TEDDY WILSON's band; and the clarinetist Edmond Hall's group. In 1942 she also sang at the Three Deuces, at the Village Vanguard with the pianist Eddie Heywood, and on a midwestern tour with the trombonist Ernie Fields's band.

In 1944 Humes moved to California, where initially the pianist Connie Berry accompanied her at the Streets of Paris in Hollywood. After working in another all-woman group, she sang with the all-star swing and bop conglomerate Jazz at the Philharmonic. In 1945 Humes recorded "Be-baba-leba," which became a hit in the emerging rhythm and blues field. Accompanied by DIZZY GILLESPIE's big band, she sang in the movie *Jivin' in Bebop* (1947). In August 1950 a live recording of a performance in Los Angeles with Roy Milton's band yielded another rhythm and blues hit, "Million Dollar Secret." In October she was reunited with Basie, now leading a small group, for the film shorts *(If I Could Be with You) One Hour* and *I Cried for You*; these performances were used in mid-1950s compilation films, including *Harlem Jazz Festival* and *Stars over Harlem* (both 1955). Accompanied by DEXTER GORDON's band in November 1950, Humes made further rhythm and blues recordings, including "Helen's Advice" and "Airplane Blues." Humes's voice was also featured in three movie soundtracks: *Panic in the Streets*, *My Blue Heaven* (both 1950), and *The Steel Trap* (1952). During these years Humes rejoined Jazz at the Philharmonic several times, including concerts in the Northeast in 1946 and a Hawaiian tour in 1951. She married Harlan O. Smith, a navy man, in 1952; they separated permanently in 1960.

In 1956 Humes toured Australia with the vibraphonist Red Norvo, and she recorded with his group in March 1958. She then recorded her first albums under her own name, which became classics, *Helen Humes: 'Tain't Nobody's Biz-ness if I Do* (1959), *Songs I Like to Sing* (1960), and *Swingin' with Humes* (1961), and she performed at the Newport

(1959) and Monterey (1960, 1962) jazz festivals. She toured Australia again in 1962 and Europe with the *American Folk Blues Festival* and *Rhythm and Blues USA* (1962–1963). In 1964 she worked in Australia for ten months. She resumed working in the United States, mainly in Los Angeles, until 1967, when her mother became terminally ill. Humes returned home to Louisville and quit singing to stay with her father and work in a munitions factory. The jazz writer Stanley Dance persuaded Humes to sing with Basie's reunion band at the Newport festival on 3 July 1973. Five days later she began a European tour, during which she recorded the album *Helen Comes Back* in France. The year 1974 witnessed her return to Newport, another European tour, another French album, *Sneaking Around*, and a brief stand at the Half Note in New York. After her father's death, she began an engagement at the Cookery in New York on 31 December 1974. Receiving rave reviews, Humes returned to the Cookery regularly through the late 1970s. In 1975 she recorded yet another fine album, *The Talk of the Town*, featuring the tenor saxophonist and clarinetist Buddy Tate, the pianist Ellis Larkins, and the electric guitarist George Benson. That same year Humes sang in "The World of John Hammond" on the PBS television series *Soundstage*, and she performed at the Nice Jazz Festival in France. In 1976 she sang in a tribute to LOUIS ARMSTRONG in Rotterdam. She was a guest with Basie's big band on a National Education Television show filmed in San Francisco in 1978, and she returned to the festival in Nice that year. She recorded the album *Helen Humes and the Muse All Stars* in 1979. In 1980 she performed in Japan, in New York, and at Ronnie Scott's club in London. She died in Santa Monica, California.

Humes's voice was centered on a trebly, sweet sound, but it also conveyed gutsiness and had a raspy edge that separated her approach from that of mainstream popular singers and made her suitable for and convincing in the musical context of African American jazz and rhythm and blues bands. Humes repeatedly professed a preference for pop songs, but her finest work is founded on her sparky, clearly enunciated, joyful approach to blues singing, of which a definitive example is "I Don't Know His Name" on *The Talk of the Town*.

FURTHER READING

A tape and a transcript of Helen Oakley Dance's interview with Humes on 12 May 1981 are in the oral history collection at the Institute of Jazz Studies, Newark, New Jersey.

Balliett, Whitney. *American Singers: Twenty-Seven Portraits in Song* (1988).

Harris, Sheldon. *Blues Who's Who: A Biographical Dictionary of Blues Singers* (1979).

Obituaries: *New York Times*, 14 Sept. 1981; *Jazz Journal International* 34 (Nov. 1981): 22–23.

DISCOGRAPHY

Sheridan, Chris. *Count Basie: A Bio-Discography* (1986).

This entry is taken from the *American National Biography* and is published here with the permission of the American Council of Learned Societies.

BARRY KERNFELD

Hundley, Mary Gibson (18 Oct. 1897–1 Jan. 1986), educator and civil rights activist, was born Mary Gibson in Baltimore, Maryland, the daughter of Malachi Gibson, a lawyer and graduate of Howard University, and Mary Matilda Syphax, a teacher. Gibson was the granddaughter of William Syphax, the first superintendent of Colored Public Schools in Washington, D.C., and Georgetown after the Civil War and, according to family tradition, a descendant of George Washington Parke Custis, grandson of Martha Custis Washington. She attended the M Street School (which relocated and changed its name to Dunbar High School in 1916) in Washington, D.C., and went on to Radcliffe College in Cambridge, Massachusetts, where she was the first black student to come from a southern segregated public school. At Radcliffe she was one of a handful of black students, all of whom lived off campus. She enjoyed easy relations with her classmates, writing songs for her class and serving as an accompanist for college musical productions, and relished the opportunity to concentrate in English and study with leading professors in the field. But her college experience was clouded by financial difficulties and by what she later called "the persecution" at the hands of Dean Bertha Boody, who insisted that she work her way through college as a maid. Gibson's refusal to do this would have led to her withdrawal from college but for the intervention of President LeBaron Russell Briggs, who arranged a loan for her. Mary graduated cum laude in 1918. She later pursued graduate study in French at Middlebury College, from which she received an AM in 1929; she had earned another from the Sorbonne in 1928.

Mary Gibson married William Miles Brewer, a Harvard graduate, in 1924 and divorced him in 1935.

Three years later she married Frederick F. Hundley, a public school art teacher who died in 1955. Neither marriage produced children. She began her teaching career in Baltimore and then moved back to her alma mater, Dunbar High School, where she taught French, English, and Latin from 1920 to 1955. Her pupils remembered her as a demanding but fair teacher whose high standards brought out the best in generations of students. She believed that teaching was a "noble profession," developing "ideals of freedom, tolerance, opportunity, democracy, and citizenship" in future citizens. But a good teacher, she wrote, "must do other things as well." These "other things" for Hundley included organizing after-school enrichment programs, the Coleman and Margaret Jennings Clubs (social service clubs), Le Cercle Français, and the Junior Auxiliary of the Freedmen's Hospital, which provided voluntary nursing aides. As a member of the Guidance Committee and chair of the College Bureau from 1943 to 1949, she was credited with inspiring many students to enroll in Ivy League and other colleges. In 1955 she transferred to Eastern High, an integrated school, where she taught English and Latin, and from 1959 to 1964 she tutored French at Howard University, joining twenty-five of her former pupils on the faculty.

Hundley's pride in Dunbar High School and the achievements of its alumni prompted her to write *The Dunbar Story, 1870–1955* (1965), a chronicle of the school, its faculty, and its alumni. Dunbar was the first college preparatory school for African Americans in the nation, and its roster of notable alumni includes the civil rights lawyer CHARLES HOUSTON, the judge and Harvard law professor WILLIAM H. HASTIE, the U.S. senator EDWARD BROOKE, the scientist CHARLES DREW, the university professor EVA DYKES, the gynecologist LENA EDWARDS, Secretary of Health, Education, and Welfare ROBERT WEAVER, and other leading clergy, teachers, administrators, and doctors. In its heyday, 80 percent of the students went on to college. Ironically, its success was dependent on a racially segregated education system, and when, after integration in 1955, it became a high school in a deprived neighborhood, the proportion of students attending college dropped to 23 percent. From 1973 to 1977 Hundley led the Dunbar Alumni Association in an unsuccessful campaign to prevent the demolition of the original school building.

In 1941 the Hundleys purchased and moved into a house in Washington, D.C., with a restrictive racial covenant. Their white neighbors brought suit against them and won the case in December 1941. The Hundleys were enjoined from occupying their house and were evicted in July 1942. The judgment was reversed on appeal in December 1942. The landmark case of *Hundley v. Gorewitz* was one of those cited in *Shelley v. Kraemer* (1947), a U.S. Supreme Court case that established that covenants restricting use and ownership of property to whites violated the equal protection clause of the Fourteenth Amendment and affirmed the right of minorities to live in neighborhoods without regard to race.

Hundley was active in many African American organizations, including the Links, the Women's Auxiliary of the Freedmen's Hospital, the NAACP, and the Phillis Wheatley Branch of the Washington Young Women's Christian Association. She was a member of the American Association of University Women, the International Federation of University Women, and the Radcliffe Club of Washington, D.C. She also was active in St. Luke's Episcopal Church and in Washington, D.C., organizations that provided guides and interpreters for foreign visitors. From 1974 to 1979 she was a docent at the Renwick Gallery of the Smithsonian Institution.

Although in 1946 she wrote frankly to Dean Mildred Sherman about the prejudice she had encountered in the Radcliffe Club of Washington, D.C., and was critical of the then "unfavorable local conditions" for black students at Radcliffe, she always remained fiercely loyal to her college. In 1979 she received the Radcliffe Alumnae Recognition Award, which honored her dedicated service as an educator and courageous citizen. She died in Washington, D.C.

FURTHER READING
Hundley's papers are at the Schlesinger Library, Harvard University, Cambridge, Massachusetts.
Hundley, Mary Gibson. *The Dunbar Story, 1870–1955* (1965).
Obituaries: *Washington Post*, 3 Jan. 1986; *Washington, D.C., Afro-American*, 11 Jan. 1986.
This entry is taken from the *American National Biography* and is published here with the permission of the American Council of Learned Societies.
JANE KNOWLES

Hunster, Richard L. (July 1862–23 Jan. 1928), photographer, was born in Madison, Indiana, one of six children of Alexander A. Hunster, a barber, and Catherine Campbell Hunster. The Hunsters were both free blacks whose families had left the South in the mid- to late 1830s.

When Richard was only a few years old, the Hunsters moved to Portsmouth, Ohio, where his father was employed as a barber aboard an Ohio River steamboat. There is limited information available about Hunster's early life, but his family apparently lived comfortably in Portsmouth. Hunster and his siblings attended school, although their education was probably limited to the elementary grades. Growing up in a town along the river and having a father who worked on a steamboat, Hunster no doubt visited the Portsmouth wharf regularly and marveled at the big paddle wheelers that plied up and down the Ohio River. These childhood images of steam rising from the water and thick black smoke filling the air were probably the impetus for his fascination with steamboats, which became the subject of many of the photographs he took later in life.

With the death of Alexander Hunster in 1877, the family's financial responsibilities shifted to Catherine Hunster, who soon had to sell the family home and some of its furnishings. She eventually began working as a seamstress. Within a few years, Hunster left home to support himself. Where he initially lived and worked is unknown, but by 1882 he had found work in Cincinnati as a porter.

Hunster's early years in Cincinnati must have been difficult ones as he was continually moving from one boarding house to another, never staying in one location for more than a year. Finally in the late 1880s he gained steady employment as an artist, and his situation in Cincinnati began to improve. One of his employers was a photographer named Isaac Benjamin. Benjamin was primarily a studio photographer, but he was also a partner in a business that specialized in reproducing photographs on china. Whether Hunster worked in the studio or in the china business has not been determined; but either way, his employment with Benjamin certainly exposed him to photography as a career.

By 1896 Hunster had received enough training to begin taking photographs professionally on his own. While he always managed to purchase the necessary equipment and supplies he needed to operate his business, he never made enough money at photography to afford a studio of his own. The apartment he rented served as both residence and workplace. While portraiture was his primary source of income, he became best known for his photographs of Cincinnati steamboats.

The steamboat was a great asset to the growth and development of Cincinnati. When the first steamboat arrived in Cincinnati in the early nineteenth century it not only revolutionized the way people traveled but it also had a tremendous effect on the economy. By the mid-nineteenth century Cincinnati had become one of America's largest inland ports. At this time Hunster's parents were living in Cincinnati, and there were more than 3,600 annual steamboat arrivals in the city. In contrast, at the close of the nineteenth century there were about 1,500 annual steamboat arrivals. By the time Hunster stopped taking photographs there were fewer than 600. Hunster was obviously aware of the gradual disappearance of the steamboat from the river. His interest in them was such that from 1896 to about 1924, he set about visually recording on film as many of the remaining Cincinnati steamboats as he could. In addition he sought out and purchased photographs of steamboats from the past as well. Some of these older images dated back to the 1860s. With the photographs he took himself and the copies he made from the ones he collected, Hunster began to sell steamboat pictures to collectors and rivermen.

While he photographed all types of steamboats, Hunster particularly favored taking images of the packet boats that carried passengers and freight between Cincinnati and other ports along the Ohio and Mississippi rivers. Similar to the packets were the excursion boats, and he photographed several of the ones that carried passengers between the Cincinnati Public Landing and Coney Island Amusement Park. Hunster also shot views of the towboats that transported bulk cargoes such as coal and gravel by barge to the various terminal facilities along the river.

Hunster's pictures varied from simple scenes of a steamboat lying cold at the wharf to more dramatic scenes of a steamboat under way with a billowing cloud of smoke coming from its smokestacks. Still others were haunting images of the lifeless remains of a steamboat hull following the tragedy of a fire or some other disaster. On occasion Hunster would board one of the boats to take a posed picture of the crew usually around the dinner table. Whenever Hunster was asked to take one of these group portraits, it provided him with an excellent opportunity to bring a selection of his steamboat pictures to sell to the crew.

Hunster was not the only photographer in the steamboat picture business. There were a number of photographers up and down the Ohio and

Mississippi rivers who also dealt in this trade. Hunster, however, was probably the only black photographer engaged as such. Like these other photographers, he had a wide selection of postcard views for sale. He also sold enlargements. His prices were considered reasonable. While he was selling his postcard views for a nickel apiece, other photographers were selling theirs for two to three times this much. Since Hunster's financial resources were limited, he kept his business practices simple. While other photographers had printed or typed lists of the steamboat views they had for sale, Richard laboriously wrote his picture lists out by hand, customizing each list to a particular customer's request. Many photographers had their names stamped or embossed on their photographs, but for the most part Hunster chose not to identify himself on his photographs. In some cases he scratched his initials or a date on a negative, but this was the exception rather than the rule. Such anonymity would have caused Hunster's work to be long forgotten if it had not been for the steamboat historian and riverboat pilot Captain Frederick Way Jr.

Way had begun collecting steamboat pictures as a teenager. Over the years he purchased many steamboat photographs but, unlike most collectors, he generally identified the photographers who took them. Way corresponded with Hunster on a regular basis and he purchased many of Hunster's photographs. In adulthood, Way began to sell copies of the photographs he had amassed over the years just as Hunster had done earlier. He became a recognized authority on steamboat history and periodically would write in various publications about Hunster's collection. Without the identifications that Way put on the Hunster photographs in his own collection, the photographer behind these images would simply remain a mystery.

Richard Hunster stopped taking photographs around 1924. His last known job was as a porter at the Palace Hotel. When Hunster died in Cincinnati, his negatives and equipment were apparently discarded. What remains are the hundreds of Hunster steamboat pictures scattered about in collections, including the Inland Rivers Library at the public library in Cincinnati, that help students and researchers alike understand and appreciate the history of steamboats.

FURTHER READING

Kesterman, M'Lissa. "Richard L. Hunster and His Photographs of Cincinnati Steamboats," *Queen City Heritage* 57.2/3 (Summer/Fall 1999).

Way, Frederick, Jr. "The Best of Hunster," *S & D Reflector* 23.2 (June 1986).

Way, Frederick, Jr. "Steamboat Pictures," *Waterways Journal* 49.27 (5 Oct. 1935).

M'LISSA KESTERMAN

Hunt, Gilbert (1780?–1863), blacksmith and hero of the 1811 Richmond Theatre fire, was born a slave at the Piping Tavern near the Pamunkey River in King William County, Virginia. The names of his parents are unknown, though his mother appears to have been a slave of the keeper of the Piping Tavern. What little is known of Hunt's life comes from a brief biographical sketch published in Richmond, Virginia, on the eve of the Civil War by Philip Barrett, a white journalist. A transcription of Hunt's reminiscences accounts for much of this sketch of the "meritorious old negro" (5), in which Barrett urges his fellow, predominantly white citizens of Richmond to be profoundly grateful for Hunt's long years of service to the community. Hunt, in Barrett's view, was a man of "high integrity" whose bearing and words betrayed his "true, generous-hearted, disinterestedness" (4).

Hunt arrived in Richmond in the first decade of the nineteenth century, brought there by his new master, the Piping Tavern keeper's son-in-law, who taught him the trade of carriage making before selling him to another master, who apprenticed Hunt as a blacksmith. While resident in Richmond, Hunt married a fellow slave, whose name is unknown. On the evening of 26 December 1811 Hunt was having supper at his wife's home when her mistress told him of the outbreak of a major fire at the Richmond Theatre and that her daughter was among those in attendance. Hunt then ran off to the theater to rescue the mistress's daughter, who had taught him to read and write.

On arriving at the theater, packed to overflowing for an evening performance, he found the building in flames and saw "terrors" that, in Barrett's account, "roused the selfishness of human nature to its utmost strength" (23). Seventy-two people died in the blaze, including the Virginia governor George Smith and the president of the Bank of Virginia, though the victims included people of all classes and of both races and genders. Many were overcome by smoke and fire, while others plunged to their deaths leaping from the burning building. A subsequent investigation found that the death toll would have been much higher had it not been for Hunt's role in catching twelve young white women thrown out of a theater window by James McCaw, a burly white doctor. According to Barrett, Hunt "possessed naturally a powerful frame, and by wielding the sledge hammer, his muscles had become almost as strong and as tough as the iron he worked" (27). Hunt, who also saved Dr. McCaw from a collapsing wall, said little about his actions, but characteristically he expressed regret that he had arrived too late to rescue his mistress's daughter.

Richmonders were also indebted to Hunt's role in developing and securing the city's defenses during the war of 1812. Working seven days a week for more than eighteen months at his master's foundry shop, he kept four forges going at the same time to cope with the demands of securing the American home front. Escaping to the relative safety of the countryside, Hunt's master left his young slave in charge of his family home and workshop, which built carriages and mounted cannon on them, shoed horses, and made guns and pickaxes for the army, as well as grappling hooks for American naval vessels at Norfolk. Although Richmond did not fall, Hunt later recalled that "no American would have fought more" to defend the city and even his master's property than he, "for he never treated me like a servant, but rather like a member of his own household. He never spoke a cross word to, nor struck me a lick during his whole life" (8).

Hunt's blacksmithing skills and his celebrated heroics at the Richmond Theatre also made him a valuable member of the city's fire brigade, notably during a major blaze at the state penitentiary in 1823. Hunt used a wide array of tools to help break the jailhouse bars and release the more than 224 prisoners from the burning building. He also freed several of the prisoners (temporarily) from their shackles, many of which he had made himself in his master's foundry. Hunt then returned to his foundry with a contract for new shackles for the prisoners.

In December 1829, six years after the Richmond penitentiary fire, Hunt unlocked his own shackles, having earned enough money as a blacksmith to purchase his freedom and set up business on his own. Public records note that the blacksmith later owned at least two slaves, perhaps including his wife and children. The historian CARTER G. WOODSON's research suggests that around 2 percent of free blacks in the South at that time owned slaves. Though matters were different in other states, Virginia law allowed free blacks to purchase fellow family members.

Like other free blacks at the time, Hunt also contemplated emigration, and he in fact went to Liberia in 1830. He traveled well into the interior, witnessing with horror the sight of African slaves chained like cattle and bound for Cuba, but he also learned much from the indigenous people, many of whom he found to be hospitable and generous. Hunt was particularly struck by a native blacksmith who sat cross-legged like a tailor, "his anvil, bellows, [and] hammers all around him." "Even in this position," Hunt recalled," he could beat me working all to pieces" (14). Defrauded by some Liberian natives whom he later described as "perfect African Yankees," Hunt returned to the United States in 1831, where he became a vocal critic of black emigration schemes (16).

Gilbert Hunt remained in Richmond for the next three decades, continued his thriving blacksmith business, and became increasingly active in the Baptist church. When he died in his adopted city at the age of eighty, hundreds of mourners of both races attended his funeral. For African Americans his legendary strength and heroism foreshadowed the exploits of JOHN HENRY, among others, but it was Hunt's humility and loyalty to his masters and former masters, as well as his undoubted courage, that endeared him to Richmond whites.

FURTHER READING
Information about Gilbert Hunt and antebellum
    African American life in Richmond can be found at
    the Valentine Museum in Richmond, Virginia.
Barrett, Philip. *Gilbert Hunt: The City Blacksmith* (1859).
STEVEN J. NIVEN

Hunt, Henry Alexander, Jr. (10 Oct. 1866–1 Oct. 1938), educator and government official, was born in Sparta, Hancock County, Georgia, the son of Mariah and Henry Alexander Hunt Sr., a tanner and farmer. Mariah, who exhibited some of the fundamentals of an education and had studied music, was a freewoman of color; Henry Sr. was white. Available evidence suggests that the couple lived together before the Civil War but maintained separate households afterward. Henry Jr. was the fifth of eight racially mixed children. At age sixteen, having completed the formal education available to him in Hancock County, he followed his older sister and enrolled at Atlanta University. A popular campus leader, Hunt was captain of the baseball team, moot court judge, and president of the Phi Kappa Society. In addition to his college course, Hunt learned the builder's trade and, during vacations, worked as a journeyman carpenter to earn money for his education. He graduated with a

Henry Alexander Hunt Jr., educator and principal of the Fort Valley Normal and Industrial School. He implemented a curriculum based on manual and agricultural training. (University of Massachusetts, Amherst.)

B.A. in 1890. Hunt's first job after college was as a teacher in Jackson, Georgia; before completing the term there, he moved to Charlotte, North Carolina, where he became principal of a grammar school. In November 1891 Hunt joined the faculty of Biddle (later Johnson C. Smith) University, where for more than thirteen years he served as superintendent of the industrial department and proctor over the boys, who reportedly idolized him. In 1893, while in North Carolina, Hunt married Florence S. Johnson, his college sweetheart and sister of EDWARD A. JOHNSON, the first black assemblyman of New York. The like-minded, devoted couple would have three children.

In February 1904 Hunt became the second person to serve as principal of the Fort Valley High and Industrial School (FVHI). At the time, many of FVHI's administrators, teachers, and students as well as black trustees favored the school's developing liberal arts curriculum, but Hunt—and the white philanthropists who helped fund the school—favored simple agricultural and manual training, the approach taken at both the Hampton Institute in Virginia and Tuskegee Institute in Alabama. In 1906 William Taylor Burwell Williams, a black school inspector for the General Education Board (GEB), reported that there was some "very positive opposition to Mr. Hunt" among "the colored trustees and a set of the young men teachers of the school." In June of that year, believing that such resistance threatened the effective and rapid development of industrial education, the white philanthropists, using their power as a majority of the board of trustees, removed virtually all black trustees who opposed Hunt's educational blueprint. The board named new trustees who held to BOOKER T. WASHINGTON's model of industrial education, among them William H. Spencer, a leading black educator in Columbus, Georgia, and EDWARD R. CARTER, pastor of the Atlanta Friendship Baptist Church and one of the most influential black ministers in Georgia. Hunt's brother-in-law, Warren Logan of Tuskegee, was also named to the board. In addition, black board president Lee O'Neal, pastor of Usher's Temple Colored Methodist Episcopal Church, was demoted to vice president and replaced by Theodore J. Lewis, a white man from Philadelphia Pennsylvania.

At the same time, the FVHI faculty was undergoing its own purge. As the historian James D. Anderson later observed, Hunt succeeded in weeding out black teachers who opposed his educational plan. In his 30 June 1908 report to the trustees, Hunt recommended a decrease of "our teaching force for the coming year," noting that "decreased contributions" made the recommendation "not only wise but imperative." In his fifth annual report to the board in 1909, Hunt announced that "our classes are now more closely graded and more attention has been given to the work of accurate records of the student's standing with the result that they are applying themselves more assiduously to their studies than in other years." By 1913 the FVHI program comprised a grammar school and a high school as well as industrial training classes for men that focused on agriculture, carpentry, and bricklaying. Women typically studied cooking, laundering, sewing, and dressmaking; both genders were instructed in basketry and chair caning. In 1914 a black GEB inspector described FVHI as "the most thorough-going industrial school in Georgia."

Between 1904 and 1938 FVHI changed from being an ungraded school to a graded grammar school, high school, and junior college. Also under Hunt's leadership the school undertook a major construction program and increased its enrollment from about 145 students in 1904 to about one thousand in 1938, including 103 junior college students as a result of the institution gaining junior college status by 1928. In 1932 the name was changed to the Fort Valley Normal and Industrial School (FVNI). Hunt's official title, however, remained the same.

The school's first sustained financial support, other than that from local sources, came from the American Church Institute for Negroes of the Protestant Episcopal Church. Support from the American Church Institute began as early as 1913, but FVHI did not officially come under the institute's auspices until 1918. Even then, the Fort Valley school could not be described as a sectarian institution. From 1918 to 1938 the school imposed no religious requirements.

Hunt and his teachers brought scientific farming methods to many farmers in the so-called Black Belt of Georgia. The agricultural instruction and demonstrations at the school and community outreach programs were, in general, deeply constructive forces. Because of this work Hunt gained state and national prominence, and in August 1918 Georgia governor Hugh M. Dorsey appointed him supervisor of Negro Economics. Through this position he oversaw state efforts to deal with problems relating largely to agricultural labor. Hunt believed in frankness. Speaking on the subject of the "rural conditions of labor" at the Tenth Anniversary Conference of the NAACP held in June 1919, he explained that blacks had trouble finding jobs away from southern farms because of bias against them. "In going over this country," he said, "I have yet to find a place where there is not prejudice against the Negro." Hunt also argued, however, that black leaders should bear some of the blame: "I believe that when our ministers and leaders in our lodges give a little less attention to exploiting the people, taking care of the sick and burying the dead, when they give more attention to the development of the living, helping those who are living to see and understand and to know their rights and privileges, I believe we shall make progress by leaps and bounds."

However overly optimistic Hunt was in assessing the situation of rural black southerners, his naiveté was not born from an ignorance of causes, and he never ceased to search for solutions. In November 1933, at the recommendation of Henry Morgenthau Jr., governor of the newly activated Farm Credit Administration (FCA), President Franklin D. Roosevelt appointed Hunt as Morgenthau's assistant, thus becoming the FCA's "Negro adviser" in its attempts to address the economic problems faced by black farmers. Hunt's primary function was to keep black farmers informed about credit opportunities available through the federal government. Although he was headquartered in Washington, D.C., most of his time was spent on the road, traveling from state to state to advise black farmers about FCA services and to help them form credit unions.

Hunt learned early on that the problems caused by a lack of information were greatly exacerbated by artificial barriers placed by race. Black farmers, for example, could not join the white loan associations that extended credit under the New Deal's decentralized program. Moreover, black farm owners, just as other black farm operators, were at a disadvantage because local appraisers often discriminated against them when setting a value on property to be used as collateral. Nonetheless, Hunt's educational campaigns—he used various methods, including the mass media and public forums—brought about a widespread awareness of the national program. In addition, as a result of their participation in Hunt's educational campaigns, black agricultural agents and vocational agricultural teachers became better-informed public servants of black farmers. The outcome was largely positive. As Hunt's secretary, Martha B. Goldman, informed Lawrence A. Oxley, chief of the Division of Negro Labor in the Department of Labor, in 1936: "Thousands of colored applicants are receiving Farm Credit Administration loans freely from the Federal land banks, the production credit associations, and the emergency crop loan office committees, and these loans are being repaid by the colored farmers without trouble and without delay."

Hunt was also primarily responsible for the establishment of the Flint River Farms, a farm cooperative community located near the town of Montezuma in Macon County, Georgia. The community, made up of 146 units and a similar number of families, was one of thirteen such cooperatives established exclusively for black farmers during the New Deal. In addition, Hunt had a great deal of success getting black workers in various fields and groups of blacks who had "a common bond of occupation" to form credit unions.

During his five-year tenure at the FCA, Hunt had to contend with some serious problems as principal of FVNI. The institution suffered a budget deficit after employing twenty-five new teachers in 1937. Albert J. Evans, a local merchant and chairman of the finance committee, threatened to resign from the board of trustees if the deficit continued. Hunt was being pressured as well by Bishop Robert W. Patton, director of the American Church Institute for Negroes, who objected to Hunt's "absentee management" while away in Washington. In August 1938 Patton wrote to Bishop Henry T. Mikell of the Atlanta diocese and chairman of the board of trustees to say he believed the institute needed new leadership. " Mrs. Hunt is the real Principal of that school," Patton alleged, "and she acts under general instructions from Hunt. Neither of them is what they used to be. The school is being run by the Hunt oligarchy, and that means tyrannous[ly], like other Negro schools, not of the Institute type." Before any action could be taken, however, Hunt died in Washington, D.C. His death marked the passing of a powerful influence in the black education movement in North Carolina and Georgia during the late nineteenth and early twentieth centuries.

FURTHER READING

Letters from Hunt are in various collections, among them the George Foster Peabody Papers, the Booker T. Washington Papers, and the NAACP Papers, all in the Library of Congress.

Alexander, Adele Logan. *Ambiguous Lives: Free Women of Color in Rural Georgia, 1789–1879* (1991).

Day, Carolina Bond. *A Study of Some Negro-White Families in the United States* (1932).

DuBois, W. E. B. "The Significance of Henry Hunt," *Fort Valley State College Bulletin: Founder's and Annual Report I* (Oct. 1940): 5–16.

Obituary: Woodson, Carter G. "Henry Alexander Hunt," *Journal of Negro History* 24 (Jan. 1939): 135–36.

This entry is taken from the *American National Biography* and is published here with the permission of the American Council of Learned Societies.

DONNIE D. BELLAMY

Hunt, Ida Alexander Gibbs (16 Nov. 1873–19 Dec. 1957), Pan-Africanist, feminist, writer, educator, was born in Victoria, British Columbia, the third of four children of Mariah A. (Alexander) Gibbs, originally of Kentucky, and MIFFLIN WISTAR GIBBS, originally of Pennsylvania. Ida Gibbs's father was the self-educated, wealthy son of free Philadelphia blacks who was himself notable for his many accomplishments: he founded the

first African American owned newspaper; made a fortune selling boots and prospecting equipment to miners during the Gold Rush in San Francisco, California; was the first black elected municipal police judge in Little Rock, Arkansas; and served six years as United States Consul in Madagascar under Presidents McKinley and Roosevelt. Ida Gibbs's uncle JONATHAN C. GIBBS was at one time secretary of state in Florida during Reconstruction. Growing up in an atmosphere of educational and financial success may have influenced the Gibbs children to achieve in higher education and in the political arena. Upon reaching adulthood, Ida Gibbs indeed became a woman of firsts and a person of influence.

Gibbs was one of the first African American women to graduate from Oberlin College in Ohio (in 1884) along with such other notable African Americans as MARY ELIZA CHURCH TERRELL and ANNA JULIA COOPER. Oberlin College had been established in 1833 by liberal Congregationalists; it was one of the first coeducational institutions in the country, and one of the first to open its doors to students of all races.

After graduation Ida Gibbs taught at various institutions, including the State Normal School in Huntsville, Alabama, and later at the M Street High School (now PAUL L. DUNBAR High School) in Washington, D.C. In between, she studied for and received a master's degree from Oberlin (1889–1892).

Appointed by President McKinley in 1898, Ida Gibbs's father, Mifflin Gibbs, served as U.S. consul in Tamatave, Madagascar. He was one of a small number of blacks to win a diplomatic position when Republicans regained political control after President Cleveland was defeated. Gibbs's secretary, a young man named WILLIAM HENRY HUNT, took over for Gibbs as consul in 1901. He and Ida were married in 1904. The couple spent the next twenty-seven years abroad: in Madagascar (1904–1906), France (1906–1926), the West Indies (1927–1928), St. Michaels Island (1929), and Liberia (1931–1932), before returning to Washington, D.C., in 1932.

It was in France that Ida Gibbs Hunt began her mission to promote human rights and social justice. She joined countless organizations, committees, and movements that supported the causes of peace, women's suffrage, and civil rights. She was active in the Red Cross, the Femmes de France, the Club Franco-Etranger, and most notably, the Pan-African Congress. The Pan-African Congress was a gathering of politicians, lawyers, and social activists dedicated to promoting the interests of Africans and people of African descent worldwide. Hunt participated as assistant secretary for the first Pan-African Congress, hosted in Paris in 1919, and attended the second in 1921. In 1923 she served as co-chair with W. E. B. DuBois and presented a paper, "The Coloured Race and the League of Nations," at the third Pan-American Congress in London.

Back in the United States, Hunt joined a group of other influential black women in founding the first YWCA in the District of Columbia, and was a member of the Washington Welfare Association, and the Women's International League of Peace and Freedom.

In addition to her national and international committee work, Hunt was the author of numerous journal and newspaper articles, writing about the issues she championed. One famous example is an article printed in *The Journal of Negro History* (January 1938) titled "The Price of Peace," in which she wrote, "Nearly two decades after the great holocaust to end war we still have wars and rumors of war. Men delve in science and art; they construct beautiful edifices and surround themselves with ease and luxury; and then, like children who build houses of blocks, tear them down in a great game called war."

Hunt died at home in Washington, D.C., on 19 December 1957. She was 85 years old. She and her husband had no children, but she left behind as her legacy a lifetime of concern for her fellow man in the activities she participated in and the words she wrote.

FURTHER READING

Hunt, Ida Gibbs. "The Price of Peace," *Journal of Negro History*, vol. 23, no. 1 (Jan. 1938).

Justesen, Benjamin R. "African-American Consuls Abroad, 1897–1909." *Foreign Service Journal* (Sept. 2004).

Smith, Jessie Carney. "Ida Alexander Gibbs Hunt," *Notable Black American Women, Book II* (1996).

JOLIE A. JACKSON-WILLETT

Hunt, Richard (12 Sept. 1935–), sculptor and printmaker, was born in Chicago, Illinois, to Victoria Inez, a librarian and beauty shop owner and Cleo Howard Hunt, a barber. Hunt's father was born in rural Georgia, his mother in Tennessee. His parents were part of the Great Migration, the early twentieth century exodus of over one million African Americans out of the violent and limiting South to locations where greater economic opportunity and social equality were more likely. His parents met in Chicago, where their families had relocated, and married in 1934. The family lived mostly on the south side of Chicago. Between the ages of nine and eleven, Hunt and the family lived in the small town of Galesburg, Illinois. Hunt's mother sang both professionally and in church. Her idol was MARIAN ANDERSON, and she named Hunt's younger sister after the noted gospel singer. She encouraged her son's early interest in art; when he was twelve she enrolled him in the Junior School of the Art Institute of Chicago to supplement the arts education he received in public school. He studied at the Art Institute for five years.

In 1948 Hunt enrolled in the Junior School of the Art Institute of Chicago. A year later Shirley Walters, a teacher at Englewood High School, urged her pupil to try a sculpture class at the Art Institute. He followed her advice, and soon his interest shifted from painting and drawing to sculpture—and Hunt also decided to take metalworking classes. In 1950 Hunt set up a clay modeling studio in his bedroom. In 1951 he became an assistant in the zoological laboratory at the University of Chicago where he worked until 1957. In January 1953 Hunt saw the work of Julio González in the Museum of Modern Art exhibition, *Sculpture of the Twentieth Century*, held at the Art Institute. In a 1979 interview with Dennis Barrie for the Smithsonian Archives of American Art, Hunt described how the innovative, Spanish-born artist González and his "direct-metal" approach of "drawing in two dimensions and taking away the paper" inspired him. Despite the danger, Hunt began welding in the basement of his parents' house using found materials and equipment he managed to obtain. That June he graduated from high school. He continued his training at the School of the Art Institute that September with the help of a scholarship from the Chicago Public School Art Society. During his senior year at the Institute, he received the James Nelson Raymond Travel Fellowship. He graduated with a BAE in June 1957 and studied in England, France, Spain, and Italy that fall and winter. While in Europe he was drafted into the U.S. Army. Hunt requested and received a deferment on his draft date so that he might complete his study and prepare for a major exhibition at the Charles Alan Gallery in New York. In Florence he did a series of cast bronzes. In November, while in Rome, he married Betty Scott whom he had met at the Art Institute. Following his well-reviewed solo exhibition, Hunt served in the U.S. Army Medical Corps from 1958 to 1960.

Hunt's early metal works were organic, abstract, and geometric soldered constructions that were in Hunt's words, "a way of practicing welding" and moving from the monolithic to developing a unique relationship with space. The works ranged from small sculptures less than a foot tall to those having human scale. Some of their titles included *Man on a Vehicular Construction* (1956), *Icarus* (1956), *Wing Bloom* (1956), and the *Form Carried Aloft* (1960). The works Hunt created in his early twenties met with enormous success. The Museum of Modern Art acquired *Arachne* in 1956 when he was twenty years old and still a student. The Whitney Museum of American Art added Hunt's *Extending Horizontal Form* to its collection in 1958. These works resembled plant-like creatures in motion.

While stationed in San Antonio, Texas, Hunt was able to get a studio outside the army base where he could weld. Hunt participated in numerous exhibitions while in the service. Once discharged in 1960, Hunt considered moving to New York but decided against it. Instead he began teaching in the fall of 1960 at the University of Illinois, Chicago, and the School of the Art Institute. In 1961 he established a studio in Chicago and a year later was hired full time at Illinois where he taught sculpture. After two years, when the income from the sale of his sculptures equaled his teaching salary, he decided to dedicate all of his time to sculpting. A Guggenheim Fellowship in 1962 made his transition to full-time sculptor that much easier. That year his daughter Cecilia Elizabeth was born. In 1963 the influential art critic Hilton Kramer ranked Hunt among the most gifted sculptors in the world. He taught at Yale University and California Arts Institute in 1964. In 1965 Hunt taught at Purdue University, received a Ford Foundation Fellowship, and studied and worked at the Tamarind Lithography Workshop in Los Angeles. In 1966 he and Betty divorced.

While in Italy, Hunt had spent considerable time in Florence working with bronze, casting, and investigating the classical contributors to Western sculpture. In his 1979 Smithsonian interview, he expressed his dissatisfaction with casting. He felt it was an intermediary, technical step that distanced him from his initial artistic conceptualization. Casting did however offer him another important way to develop sculpture. One of Hunt's early pursuits was to reconcile "the organic and the industrial," and to juxtapose "what is experienced

in nature" with the energy and dynamics of the city. Hunt's work was delicate but massive, inert but in motion, and both primeval and futuristic. Uninterested in a unified style, Hunt worked in welded and cast steel, bronze, aluminum, and copper; in a general sense, he enjoyed experimenting with the possibilities of welded metal.

Hunt's contribution to public art began with *Expansive Construction*, a nine-foot-tall welded bronze and copper work for Louisiana State University in Baton Rouge in 1960. In 1968 he completed an eight-foot-tall aluminum sculpture for Ridgewood High School in Northridge, Illinois. In 1969 he completed his first major commission—*Play*, a Cor-ten steel 12'×12'×12' outdoor sculpture for the John J. Madden Mental Health Clinic in Hines, Illinois—through the project architect Walter Netch, who had been collecting Hunt's work privately. His first major bronze commissions were installed at the University of Chicago and the University of California at Los Angeles.

From the late 1960s to 2007, Hunt completed more public sculpture than any other American artist. Thirty of these works may be found throughout Chicago. A map by the Cultural Affairs Department of the City of Chicago directed tourists to his installations and sculptures both inside and on the grounds of office buildings, libraries, apartment buildings, and university campuses. Among the most famous are *Jacob's Ladder* (1977), which can be found at the Carter G. Woodson Regional Library, *Sea Wall* (1971), which houses an aquarium at the Kundstadter Children's Center, *Sculptural Enlightenment* (1995) at Roosevelt University, and *Freeform* (1993) at the State of Illinois Center. Other important works can be found at the following institutions: Howard University, the National Gallery, the National Museum of American Art, and the Hirshhorn Museum and Sculpture Garden in Washington, D.C.; the Frederik Meijer Gardens and Sculpture Park in Grand Rapids, Michigan; Century City Plaza in Los Angeles; the Storm King Art Center in Mountainville, New York; the National Museum of Israel in Jerusalem, and Hunt's memorial to MARTIN LUTHER KING JR. in Memphis, *I Have Been to the Mountain* (1977).

Hunt exhibited extensively. Among his most important solo exhibitions were those at the Milwaukee Art Center (1967), retrospectives at the Museum of Modern Art where some of his prints were exhibited and the Art Institute of Chicago sponsored by the Johnson Publishing Company (both 1971), the U.S. Information Service and the

Los Angeles Museum of African American Art traveling tour of West Africa (1987–1988), the Studio Museum in Harlem (1997), and the Charles H. Wright Museum of African American History in Detroit (1998). Also of importance was the 1993 traveling exhibition, "Two Sculptors, Two Eras" curated by SAMELLA LEWIS in which Hunt's work was compared to that of RICHMOND BARTHÉ.

Hunt received thirteen honorary degrees. He was one of the first artists to serve on the National Council on the Arts (1968–1974). He served on two dozen boards of major arts festivals, educational associations, and arts societies. Especially noteworthy was his service to the American Council for the Arts (1974–1997), the Advisory Committee of the Getty Center for Education in the Arts (1984–1988), the International Sculptor Center where he served as director (1984–1996), and the National Board of Directors of the Smithsonian Institute (1994–1997). In 1998 he was elected to the American Academy of Arts and Letters. Among his numerous fellowships, prizes, and awards, he was the 2005 recipient of the Hoffman Prize awarded by the National Academy of Design. He was in residence at numerous art programs including those at Cornell and Harvard and Michigan State universities.

Hunt was described as a "mainstream" artist—an artist for whom the pursuit of art was more significant than the exploration of racial identity. This is a narrow reading of Hunt's exploration of abstraction and an odd commentary on his early success. It detaches Hunt's work from an African tradition of organic abstraction and segregates his investigation of nature and transcendence. It also short circuits Hunt's sculptural trailblazing. He was less defined by the mainstream than he defined by the mainstream.

Hunt reported to Barrie that he saw within his work the "roots and resonances of the African American experience," and he stated that it was his "intention to develop the kind of forms nature might create if only heat and steel were available to her." Looking at the images of works completed between 2000 and 2007 at his website, his sculptures dance, reach, and punctuate the space with a lyrical and joyous energy.

In the *Sculpture of Richard Hunt*, the catalog of his 1971 MOMA exhibition, he wrote:

> To a great extent the success of an artist in today's society might still be a matter of building a better mouse trap. There is danger in being drawn into the whirlpool of day-to-day relations. In this respect, the problem is to keep one's head in the clouds but one's feet on the ground. I think that artists who posit, as a first condition of a contemporary culture, the fostering of art, dream in vain and ask too much. To work, in relative freedom, within its complicated framework is enough.

If Hunt's work and contribution can be simply summed up, it would be in the phrase *relative freedom*, a phrase that speaks to proportion, music, connectedness, autonomy, and breathing space.

FURTHER READING

Amaki, Amalia, ed. *A Century of African American Art: The Paul R. Jones Collection* (2004).

Castro, Jan Garden. "Richard Hunt: Freeing the Human Soul." *Sculpture* (May/June 1998).

Fine, Elsa Honig. *The Afro-American Artist: A Search for Identity* (1982).

Hunt, Richard. Studio home page. Available online at www.richardhunt.us/pages/2000.html.

Lewis, Samella. *Art: African American* (1990).

Richardson, Julieanna L. HistoryMakers Video Oral History Interview with Richard Hunt. Available at www.thehistorymakers.com.

Riedy, James. *Chicago Sculpture* (1981)

MONIFA LOVE ASANTE

Hunt, William Henry (29 June 1869–19 Dec. 1951), foreign service officer, was born near McMinnville, Tennessee, to parents whose names are unknown. His mother was illiterate and poor. His father was a white southerner who gave the family only his name. Hunt never saw him. Hunt's mother died when he was twenty-one. They were so poor that Hunt did not wear shoes for the first several years of his life. Later in his life Hunt observed that he had begun with a "three and two count" against him from the umpire of fate. Poverty forced Hunt to drop out of elementary school in Nashville just months after starting. He worked as a janitor, bellhop, and Pullman porter and developed an interest in the wider world.

Contacts Hunt made through work helped him acquire formal education. Employment as a traveling companion for a wealthy invalid at the end of the 1880s carried him through many countries in East Asia, the Middle East, and Europe. While working as a Pullman porter on the Canadian Pacific Railroad a few years later, he became acquainted with Alfred Oren Jower, the headmaster of the Lawrence Academy, a prep school in Groton, Massachusetts. Jower helped him gain admission at Lawrence in the fall of 1890. Hunt graduated in 1894 and entered Williams College in Massachusetts the same year with a scholarship. However, he left after only one year because of what he viewed as the racism there. He moved to New York City, where he worked first as an assistant in a chemical laboratory and later as a messenger for a Wall Street brokerage firm. At the same time he took an active interest in Congregational Church social concerns. Among the notable figures he met in the course of these activities were the conservationist Gifford Pinchot and Seth Low, the president of Columbia University.

The path to Hunt's foreign service career opened suddenly as a result of the appointment of MIFFLIN WISTAR GIBBS as U.S. consul at Tamatave, Madagascar, in 1897. Hunt was introduced to Gibbs by his daughter Ida, whom Hunt had met some years earlier, and she persuaded her father to accept Hunt's request to accompany him on his mission. In Madagascar Hunt first worked as a consular clerk. He was appointed vice consul in 1899 and consul in 1901 when Gibbs resigned because of illness.

During a leave of absence to the United States in 1904, Hunt married IDA GIBBS HUNT. She subsequently accompanied him to all of his posts during his long career as a U.S. consul. After serving at Tamatave (later Toamasina) until 1906, he was appointed consul at St. Etienne, France, a rare assignment since black officers were assigned almost exclusively to African or Caribbean posts. Hunt's good relations with the French in their protectorate of Madagascar may partially explain this good fortune. He served at St. Etienne until 1926, when that post was closed. While there he became well known and liked in local society. He became fluent in French, was elected honorary head of several social and cultural organizations, and was prominent in relief efforts during World War I. From France, in the period before the war, he visited North Africa, where he later recalled taking his first airplane flight. This probably placed him among the first of his race to experience this new technology. After his long service in France he was assigned to Guadeloupe in the West Indies then in 1929 to St. Michaels, the Azores. In December 1930 he was appointed secretary in the diplomatic service. His final appointment was as consul at Monrovia, Liberia, in January 1931. In August 1932 he was assigned temporarily to the State Department, from which he retired in December of the same year.

Hunt's career held him apart from the growing civil rights struggle in which so many of the notable black leaders he knew were engaged. In addition to the geographical separation, his official status carried the restrictions placed on all foreign wervice officers. Some of his letters and reports suggest that he accepted the common European assumptions about the backwardness of the colonized peoples. However, since the students he had met during his prep school summers in Boston included such future civil rights leaders as W. E. B. DuBois, JOHN HOPE, and CLEMENT GARNETT MORGAN, there can be no doubt that he was conscious of the critical thinking on national liberation and racial equality. Moreover, his collected papers include materials concerning the Niagara Movement, the NAACP, the Association for the Study of Negro Life and History, and Pan-African activities. Ida Hunt, working with DuBois, led the planning for the Third Pan-African Congress, which met in London in 1923. After retirement Hunt resided in Washington, D.C., continuing the public silence to which he had become conditioned by three decades of government service. He died in Washington.

FURTHER READING

Hunt's papers are in the Moorland-Spingarn Research Center, Howard University, Washington, D.C. Other vital materials on his career are in the records of the Department of State.

This entry is taken from the *American National Biography* and is published here with the permission of the American Council of Learned Societies.

ALLISON BLAKELY

Hunter, Alberta (1 Apr. 1895–17 Oct. 1984), singer, was born in Memphis, Tennessee, the daughter of Charles Hunter, a sleeping-car porter, and Laura Peterson, a maid. Hunter attended public school until around age fifteen. Her singing career began after she went to Chicago with one of her teachers. Hunter stated at times that she was eleven or twelve years old when she tricked the teacher into allowing her to ride with her by train on a child's pass. However, other accounts suggest that she may have been in her mid-teens. Until she was able to support herself as a performer in Chicago's South Side clubs, she lived with a friend of her mother's.

Throughout her career, Hunter worked hard to keep her personal relationships out of the limelight. Her sudden marriage in 1919 to Willard Saxbe Townsend was most likely a cover for her lesbianism, although she claimed to love him. The marriage was never consummated, but Townsend did not apply for a divorce until 1923. Hunter's biographer, Frank Taylor, states that sexual abuse in her childhood may account for her abhorrence of any man who attempted to become intimate. Her close relationship with her mother probably was her most enduring alliance. She is known to have had female traveling companions during her sojourns abroad, but there is scant written evidence of her openly acknowledging her homosexuality in the press, although language in her autobiography implicitly suggests her preference for women.

Hunter's first singing job was in a bordello. From there she moved to the small clubs that catered mainly to sporting men—black and white. In 1914 she was tutored by Tony Jackson, a prominent jazz pianist, who helped her to expand her repertoire and to compose her own songs.

The next move put her in the company of and competition with other aspiring young women such as MATTIE HITE, Cora Green, FLORENCE MILLS, and BRICKTOP Smith. The Panama Club, owned by Isadore Levine and I. Shorr, was one of a number of white-owned clubs with white-only clientele that were gaining popularity in Chicago, New York, and a few other cities. Hunter claimed that her act was in the upstairs room where the music and the action were "kind of rough and ready." The barrelhouse upstairs contrasted with the ballads and fox-trot songs that Mills and others performed downstairs. In this setting Hunter developed as a blues singer for a cabaret crowd that was dramatically different from the audiences in black theaters and clubs. During the second decade of the twentieth century, she and the other women who performed in these surroundings shaped the blues into an insurgent song form that attracted an increasing number of white patrons: "The customers wouldn't stay downstairs. They'd go upstairs to hear us sing the blues. That's where I would stand and make up verses and sing as I go along." Hunter's appeal was based on her extraordinary gift for improvising lyrics to titillate and satisfy the white audience's appetite for ribald or humorous material. Other songwriters, recognizing her ability to promote a song by adding her unique melodic and textual twists, brought their new songs to her. This source of income added to her security as a performer and allowed her to support her mother, who had moved to Chicago.

Hunter moved from one small club to another from 1916 until 1920. She considered herself as having arrived when she got a contract at the Dreamland Café, where the fabulous KING OLIVER Band, with the young LOUIS ARMSTRONG, was playing. Her performances at the Dreamland garnered praise from the local black press, and by 1921 she was recording for the Black Swan label. Her first release—"How Long, Sweet Daddy, How Long?"—established her as a blues singer of substantial quality. By the end of 1922 Hunter had already recorded fourteen blues and torch songs. The Black Swan numbers were recorded with the Dreamland orchestra or the FLETCHER HENDERSON Orchestra. The material was rather trite and reflected the label's hesitancy to record what it considered raw blues.

In mid-1922 Hunter switched to the Paramount label, for which she recorded her own creation, "Down-Hearted Blues," which was to become famous when BESSIE SMITH recorded it a year later for Columbia Records. She was called "The Idol of Dreamland" by Paramount Records when it advertised her releases in the *Chicago Defender*. She cut two sides with EUBIE BLAKE on piano around the same time, including "Jazzin' Baby Blues," a light fox-trot rather than a blues. In 1923, while still working for Paramount, she also recorded for Harmograph Records under the pseudonym May Alix. Hunter was listed as Alberta Prime, accompanied by DUKE ELLINGTON and SONNY GREER, on the Biltmore label by the end of 1924. On Gennett she assumed her sister's name, Josephine Beatty, accompanied by Armstrong and the Red Onion Jazz Babies. There is no question that Hunter is the artist on these numbers because her phrasing and expressiveness are evident. From 1921 until 1929 she recorded at least fifty-two songs under her name and various pseudonyms. Her accompanists included some of the finest jazz artists of that era: Armstrong, Henderson, Blake, Ellington, FATS WALLER, and BUSTER BAILEY.

Hunter's career received a decided boost from the record advertisements that appeared in the black press. Unlike most of her blues singing peers, she seldom appeared in vaudeville. She was the darling of the cabaret set who enjoyed their blues in intimate club settings undisturbed by the lively crowds on the Theater Owners' Booking Association circuit. In 1923 she was the star of a touring musical revue, *How Come*, but she quit the company to return to New York after five months. Other shows in which she was featured were *Runnin' Wild* and *Struttin' Time*. In late 1924 she performed along with black artists such as NOBLE SISSLE, Blake, and Fletcher Henderson for a benefit sponsored by the NAACP in New York.

Hunter, augmented by two male dancers and a pianist, presented her new act, Syncopation DeLuxe, in February 1925. It opened at New York's Loewe's Theatre and moved to the Waldorf-Astoria in April. She had the only black act on the eighteen-act bill, according to the *Chicago Defender*. She toured the Orpheum circuit in the West and the Keith circuit in the East during that year and went back to New York in January 1926 to record her first release on the Okeh label. In June she and Samuel Bailey formed a duo, which toured on the Keith circuit.

Hunter's first European tour came at the end of 1927 and proved an overwhelming success with appearances at London's Hippodrome, Monte Carlo, and the Casino de Paris. She signed with the London cast in mid-1928 for Jerome Kern's *Show Boat*, in which she created the role of Queenie opposite PAUL ROBESON's Joe. The show remained in London at Drury Lane for nearly ten months, earning accolades for the two actor-singers. When *Show Boat* closed, Hunter toured the nightclub circuit in France, Denmark, and Germany.

On her return to New York in 1929, Hunter recorded on the Columbia label and formed another song-and-dance act with two young male dancers. Chicago continued to have its pull because of her early successes and her mother's presence, so she often moved between the two cities. New York, however, was where she recorded and performed regularly in clubs. She left again for Europe in 1933. That tour included Holland and a stint as a replacement for JOSEPHINE BAKER at the Casino de Paris. Londoners were particularly fond of Hunter's interpretation of ballads, and she did nightly broadcasts while there. Her first European film, *Radio Parade of 1935*, was produced in England. She was cast as a singing star in an episode depicting African dancers and drummers, but she had no speaking part.

Hunter frequently worked abroad during the 1930s. Her itinerary expanded to include the Middle East, Egypt, and Russia by the mid-1930s. Toward the end of the decade, however, the spread of fascism made Europe less receptive to black performers. She returned to Chicago in 1938, where she broadened her radio audience. She also tried serious drama with a role in *Mamba's Daughters*. From that point she performed mainly in small clubs in Chicago, Detroit, and the Great Lakes region. She made few recordings, and by the end of 1940 she was not to be recorded again on an American label for another forty years. By this time the music scene was dominated by the big swing bands, and opportunities were few for African American women to record with the major white bands that garnered most of the recording contracts.

Ironically, World War II gave her another performing opportunity when she was attached to a USO unit. Her efforts to entertain the troops ended with a command performance for General Dwight D. Eisenhower in June 1945. After the war Hunter officially retired from the stage and stayed home to care for her ailing mother. She earned a nursing certificate at an age when most women were retiring from the profession. Her habitual lying about her age and her youthful appearance fooled the authorities and enabled her to serve in that capacity until she was eighty-two.

Although she had declared that she would not return to the stage, Hunter was enticed to try the cabaret scene again in the fall of 1977 by the Greenwich Village club owner Barney Josephson. This appearance revived her singing career, but this time she concentrated on singing the blues for young patrons who were delighted by the octogenarian's naughty ad-libs. Energetic and bubbly with a wry sense of humor, Hunter embarked again on songwriting and recording with the assistance of Columbia Records producer John Hammond. Together, they produced her album *Amtrak Blues*, which included her compositions: the title song and revivals of the 1920s' "I Got a Mind to Ramble" and "I'm Having a Good Time." She also recorded her songs for the soundtrack of *Remember My Name* (1977) and an album of new and old blues, *The Glory of Alberta Hunter* (1981). Hunter appeared in clubs, documentaries, and in commercials, on television talk shows, and at jazz festivals and concerts until her death in New York.

FURTHER READING

Harrison, Daphne Duval. *Black Pearls: Blues Queens of the 1920s* (1988).

Taylor, Frank C., with Gerald Cook. *Alberta Hunter: A Celebration in Blues* (1987).

Obituary: *New York Times*, 19 Oct. 1984.

This entry is taken from the *American National Biography* and is published here with the permission of the American Council of Learned Societies.

DAPHNE DUVAL HARRISON

Hunter, Charles Norfleet (c. 1851–4 Sept. 1931), North Carolina political activist, journalist, civil servant, and publicist, was born into slavery in

Raleigh, North Carolina, around 1851, the son of enslaved artisan Osborne Hunter and Mary Hunter, also enslaved. From about age four, Charles Hunter was trained to be a house servant in the home of their slave master, William D. Haywood. Somewhat later Hunter became a servant for Richard H. Battle. However, his intimate relationship with the Haywood family remained a feature of his life well after slavery.

When freedom came, Hunter and many fellow former North Carolina slaves faced profound changes. By 1867, young Hunter allied himself with prominent black Union League politicians George W. Brodie and James H. Harris and like them was gradually able to gain clout through affiliation with the Republican Party. He worked as a temperance advocate in the late 1860s and early 1870s, and by 1879 Hunter, together with his brother Osborne and others, led a group called the NCIA (North Carolina Industrial Association) which aimed to advance progress in "industry and education" among blacks. The organization published a periodical focusing on industrial training titled the *Journal of Industry*.

During the 1880s Hunter pursued a number of jobs as an educator, acting as principal of Raleigh's Washington Graded School, and as a civil servant, working as a clerk in the Raleigh Post Office and as a letter carrier. Losing his postal patronage position after Grover Cleveland's election, Hunter returned to education, serving as superintendent of two Goldsboro black schools. By 1881, however, as the black-led North Carolina State Teachers Association protested against racial and sectional bias in textbooks, Hunter, a naïve believer in fair play, found himself blindsided by the Dortch Act of 1883, which separated educational tax allocations by race, thereby institutionalizing a system of school-house inequality. While Democratic forces hoped that this would force support for their party, Hunter and other black leaders saw this as a move toward racial segregation in education. This led him to lobby for and achieve the union of two previously separate units, one white and one black, the former committee chaired by his associate, Charles Brantly Aycock. After writing "Some of the Evils of Reconstruction," published in the African Methodist Episcopal (AME) Church's *Quarterly Review* in January 1888, Hunter found himself popular among white Democrats yet opposed by entrenched black leaders who he chided as being corrupt remnants of the Reconstruction era. While lauding his brother

Osborne and a handful of other worthy black role models, Hunter's criticisms brought a charge from AME Bishop HENRY M. TURNER of defamation; other African Americans followed suit. A Democratic statewide electoral victory in 1888 and disfranchisement in 1889 left Hunter again jobless; he was unable to reclaim his postmaster position which he had capably filled it in the past. Meanwhile, an exodus of 50,000 black migrants fled the Old North state for safer climes.

By the 1890s new forces came to prominence within North Carolina, most notably a coalition of populists, represented by separate but closely articulated alliances of white and black farmers and by 1894 a fusionist movement of populists and Republicans. Between that date and 1897 fusionists brought about substantial changes in governance in North Carolina, reversing some of the most retrograde measures instituted by previous Democratic administrations, and helped create space for substantive black empowerment. During this period Hunter found himself out of step with the African American majority who clamored for greater inclusion in the democratic political process, while he continued to eschew politics in favor of conciliation. Fusion was characterized by unprecedented alliances between African American politicians and a coalition linking Republicans and populists. Though each maintained its distinct identity, the two collaborated on strategy, avoiding contests pitting the two parties against one another, thereby successfully keeping Democrats at bay in 1894 and 1896 state elections.

Hunter's relationship to this movement was complex and contradictory. Though he might have felt sympathetic to its perspective and aims, he often worked against it, publicly and privately, verbally and in his own voting. He analogized fusionism to reconstruction, claiming that it would be as short-lived and in his mind as counterproductive to black interests. He also occasionally voted Democratic as well as Republican, making him extremely difficult to target. His stances show a preference for cultivating and maintaining white goodwill over black empowerment via using the franchise. Built upon preventing vote splitting between Republicans and Populists at the polls, the fusion alliance led to victories in the North Carolina statewide elections of 1894 and 1896. The fact that the fusionist alliance aided 1,000 black elected or appointed officials, including Congressman GEORGE H. WHITE, effectively caused Hunter to seem out of step during this era.

At the same time, Democratic party strategy had consistently relied upon appeals to segregation and racial fear, precipitating the horrific white supremacy campaign of 1898–1900. This retrenchment of racial attitudes was spearheaded by Hunter's associates, *Raleigh News and Observer* editor Josephus Daniels, and gubernatorial candidate Charles B. Aycock. Both strove to incite white rage against blacks. Democrats retaliated against fusion by neutralizing the Republicans in a September 1898 pogrom that exaggerated black electoral influence. Democrats devised a suffrage amendment to disfranchise blacks, combined with a series of acts of terror, climaxing in the 11 November 1898 Wilmington Race Riot in which fusionists were overturned at the ballot box, blacks were brutalized into submission, and the Fourteenth and Fifteenth Amendments nullified in a "Wilmington Declaration of Independence." The unkindest cuts of all came from Daniels who wrote, "There is no half-way ground in a revolution such as we have passed through; no election law can permanently preserve white supremacy" (Haley p. 120), while Aycock went on record with the argument, "We say the Negro is unfit to rule. We carry it one step further and convey the current idea when we declare he is unfit to vote" (Haley p. 120). Grievously hurt by these betrayals, Hunter waxed surprisingly sanguine about the past failure of the power structure to grant the freedmen the support they deserved. He tried every means he could muster to forestall black disfranchisement yet was imprisoned in his own contradictions and compromises, even desperately voting for Democrats like the treacherous segregationist Aycock out of belief in the firm bonds of their friendship.

Hunter stood by as respected black elected officials James H. Young, Abe Middleton, James E. Shepard, Willie Lee Persons, John T. Howe, Isaac Smith, John Dancy, and George White were vilified by Aycock as "nigger savages, lusty brutes and rascals." While Democrat mobs used arson and murder to advance their agenda, Hunter sought to keep in the good graces of the leaders of the disfranchisement campaign, even supplying copies of his own earlier writings and granting them carte blanche in their utilization. On 6 January 1899, Democrats introduced a proposed amendment in the state legislature outlining voting qualifications which included a grandfather clause that capitalized on the willingness of some educated black elites to accept restricting the franchise to the literate. A month later these distinctions disappeared, as the measure was passed over opposition. The campaign was predicated upon the notion that black folk were uneducable, a slap in the face to the work to which Hunter had devoted his life. Marshalling evidence supporting a belief in the salutary gains made by African Americans since emancipation, Hunter failed to recognize that the objective of North Carolina's Democrats was total nullification of the Thirteenth, Fourteenth, and Fifteenth Amendments; his naiveté proved exceedingly costly.

By August 1900 a Democratic suffrage amendment effectively disfranchised blacks. The tragic turn of events led Hunter to exit the state for Washington, D.C., then Trenton, New Jersey. Though he carried with him letters from influential North Carolinians attesting to his gifts as an educator, in Trenton Hunter was unable to secure employment in any fields other than farm work, waiting tables, and laboring in coal yards and sewers. At length he became a partner and of the Inter-state Real Estate and Employment Agency before returning to North Carolina in 1902.

From Spring 1901 to 1902 Hunter struggled to survive in Washington and New Jersey, then returned to North Carolina where he played a more subdued role in politics. In the early twentieth century, black disfranchisement proceeded apace, expanding to include men of education as well as those who lacked it. Under these circumstances, he and his black colleagues found themselves in untenable positions, equivocating on issues that were used to further degrade and marginalize their fellows while seeking to secure jobs from and curry favor with segregationist Democratic elites. Yet Hunter was also capable of paradoxical positions such as the moment in 1907 when, employed as a traveling agent by the cautious North Carolina Mutual Insurance Company, he spoke out against the savage repression visited against black populations in the state. At the same time he was among a group of African Americans who secured a grant to create an exhibit on black progress in America as part of the Jamestown Tercentennial. However, Hunter never extricated himself from the entangling alliances he had forged with the likes of white supremacist campaigners Josephus Daniels and Charles Aycock, lauding the former when he was named Woodrow Wilson's Secretary of the Navy in 1912 and extolling the late latter leader's virtues despite ceaseless calumnies leveled at the African American people.

Hunter's career revolved around appeals to the "better class of whites" in a vain hope that it might become possible to create circles of common purpose based on Christian ethics. To some degree this was a class-based strategy, positing the existence of an educated elite with interests that transcended race who would be able to uplift North Carolina. Hunter pursued this strategy as an educator and visionary, as editor of the Raleigh *Independent* newspaper, through participation in annual Emancipation Day festivities, conferences with scores of men of power and prestige, creating networks that spanned not only length and breadth of his state but eventually reached all the way to the nation's capital. A survey of his life reveals a man of uncommon tenacity, tremendous self-confidence, unusual optimism, and seemingly limitless energy. He was as active in local, regional, and national politics in the last decade of his life as when he set out on his career, more than seven decades before.

Having institutionalized his state fair and newspaper, and having carved out a place of passion, if not always percipience, Hunter died underappreciated on 4 September 1931.

FURTHER READING

Haley, John. *Charles N. Hunter and Race Relations in North Carolina* (1987).

Lewis, Earl. "Invoking Concepts, Problematizing Identities: The Life of Charles N. Hunter and the Implications for the Study of Gender and Labor," *Labor History* 34, issues 2 and 3, summer 1993.

DAVID H. ANTHONY III

Hunter, Clementine (Dec. 1886?–1 Jan. 1988), folk artist, was born Clemence Reuben at Hidden Hill Plantation near Cloutierville, Louisiana, the daughter of John Reuben and Antoinette Adams, plantation workers. Her exact birth date is unknown. Most sources agree that she was born in either late December 1886 or early January 1887.

Leaving Catholic school in Cloutierville at a young age because she disliked the discipline of the nuns, Reuben, now called Clementine, became a cotton picker and field hand at several plantations in the Cloutierville area. In her adolescence her father moved the family to Melrose Plantation, about fifteen miles south of Natchitoches, Louisiana, in the central part of the state.

Melrose Plantation had been established in 1796 by MARIE-THERESE COINCOIN, a freed female slave, who became one of the most successful plantation and slave owners in the United States. After the Civil War ownership of the plantation was transferred to white families, and it became a successful cotton and pecan plantation. Cammie Garrett Henry, the owner from the 1920s until her death in 1948, took over management of the plantation after the death of her husband and encouraged the development of the arts within the community. Reuben was one of the many African American employees who worked on the plantation. In the late 1920s she became a servant in the big house built by the descendants of Coincoin. Reuben's first two children resulted from a common-law relationship with Charlie Dupree from about 1906 until his death in 1914. In 1924 she married Emanuel Hunter; the union produced five children, two of whom died at birth. Emanuel Hunter died in 1944 at Melrose Plantation.

During her employ in the house, Hunter met many painters and writers who were guests of Cammie Henry. In the early 1940s, using discarded paints left by one of the artists, Hunter—then in her late fifties—created her first works on window shades, cardboard, and shoe-box tops. François Mignon, a writer and librarian living on the plantation, recognized her talent in capturing scenes of plantation life and encouraged her experimentation with paints.

With encouragement and supplies from Mignon and his friends, Hunter began a career that spanned almost the next half century. Her paintings captured scenes of everyday plantation life as seen from the perspective of an insider. She documented the routines of life on a large southern plantation as few others were able to accomplish.

The subjects of her titled paintings are classifiable into four categories: plantation work, such as *Picking Cotton, Wash Day*, and *Gathering Pecans*; recreation, such as *Fishing, Saturday Night at the Honky Tonk*, and *Playing Cards*; religion, such as *Black Jesus, The Nativity*, and *Baptizings*; and still lifes and special themes, such as *Zinnias, The Masks*, and *Uncle Tom in the Garden*.

Hunter's works were repetitious in theme, but no two paintings were ever exactly alike. Many of the plantation tasks depicted in her works, such as manual cotton and pecan harvesting, disappeared after World War II, when mechanization of agriculture developed and blacks migrated in large numbers from the South to the North in search of better-paying, often industrial, jobs. Hunter claimed that she was unable to paint a subject simply by looking at it; instead "it had to come to her head" before she was able to put it in a picture.

Having no formal art instruction, Hunter was self-taught and painted in two dimensions without the perspective of depth. Frequently she would paint an object smaller and place it in the sky in order to show its background position. Her colors were intense and often directly out of the oil paint tubes; any mixing was done on a homemade plywood palette and stirred with her brushes.

In addition to her paintings, Hunter also produced quilts with illustrations sewn onto the fabric. Using a technique taught to her by her mother, she would cut pieces of fabric into designs and sew them together to produce a picture similar in style to her paintings of plantation life.

A significant aspect of Hunter's painting style was the evolution of her signature. Her earliest works were unsigned. From the late 1940s until the mid-1950s, a reversed C became the identifying mark of her work. Hunter said that the reason for using the mark was that the plantation owner, Cammie Henry, also had the initials C. H., and she wanted to make sure people did not confuse her works with Miss Cammie's. Once the C was reversed, over the years it then moved over to touch the H. At the end of her career the H was completely inside the reversed C. Dating Hunter's paintings can be approximated according to the nature of the signature.

Hunter's largest and most encompassing work was a mural of plantation life completed in 1955 around the walls of the second floor of the African House, one of the original structures built by the family of Marie-Therese Coincoin. It depicts many of the activities of Melrose, including church scenes, cotton picking and ginning, a wedding, a funeral, baptizing, and cooking, as well as the major structures on the plantation.

In 1955 the Delgado Museum (now the New Orleans Museum of Art) featured Hunter in its first one-person show by a black artist. The show yielded stories in such magazines as *Look* and *Ebony* and brought Hunter national recognition. Robert Bishop, director of the Museum of American Folk Art in New York City from 1977 to 1991, called Hunter "perhaps the most celebrated of all southern contemporary painters ... [who] knows well the black life she so touchingly portrays" (Bishop, 171). Clementine Hunter's paintings not only artistically captured scenes of rural plantation life but also documented as cultural history a part of American life that disappeared in the

mid-twentieth century. She died in Natchitoches, Louisiana, at age 101.

Hunter's works were widely exhibited and her paintings held in many major collections, including the Riverside Museum in Baton Rouge, Louisiana, the Museum of African-American Life and Culture in Dallas, Texas, and the New Orleans Museum of Art. A traveling retrospective of her work was organized in 2000 by the curator Shelby R. Gilley.

FURTHER READING

Gilley, Shelby R. *Painting by Heart: The Life and Art of Clementine Hunter, Louisiana Folk Artist* (2000).

Wilson, James L. *Clementine Hunter, American Folk Artist* (1988).

Yelen, Alice Rae. *Passionate Visions of the American South: Self-Taught Artists from 1940 to the Present* (1993).

Obituary: *(Baton Rouge) Morning Advocate*, 2 Jan. 1988.

This entry is taken from the *American National Biography* and is published here with the permission of the American Council of Learned Societies.

THOMAS N. WHITEHEAD

Hunter, Ivory Joe (1914–1974), singer, songwriter, and pianist, was born in Kirbyville, Texas, in 1914. It is not known whether "Ivory Joe" was his given name or simply an early nickname; it was the name by which he was always called. One of fourteen children, Hunter developed musical interests early in life, influenced by his parents: his father David Hunter—a preacher—also played guitar, and his mother, whose name is not known, sang gospel. In addition, Hunter's siblings all displayed musical talent, so it is not surprising that Ivory Joe learned to play piano at an early age. He soon found himself traveling a circuit of vaudeville, tent, and club shows around the Texas countryside, playing a popular brand of post–FATS WALLER boogie-woogie blues. He was good enough at nineteen to make his first recording (in 1933), a version of the timeless blues classic "Stagolee," as part of the Lomax brothers' Library of Congress project. While the Lomax cut remained unreleased, Hunter's increasing musical eclecticism led him to explore other styles, including variants of jazz and pop music, which combined with his burgeoning, style-blending songwriting skills to make him unique among his many contemporaries.

Hunter's successful experience led to a radio-programming job at station KFDM in Beaumont, Texas, and later to regular gigging as a musician in Houston, where he was nicknamed "rambling fingers" by his fellow pianists Charles Brown and AMOS MILBURN. With the outbreak of World War II, however, Hunter joined many musicians (and African Americans more generally) in relocating to Los Angeles, where the wartime economy presented opportunities otherwise unavailable. Hunter started Ivory Records, his own label, whose handful of releases—including those by Leroy Carr and Hunter's own combo, Johnny Moore and the Three Blazers—helped mark the development of rhythm and blues. Regional success and Pacific Records, another short-lived label, followed.

Hunter signed with King Records in 1947 and enjoyed his first taste of national recording success two years later, with four R&B hits in 1949 and 1950, including the chart-topping "I Almost Lost My Mind," recorded for MGM. He also recorded "Jealous Heart," a country hit, in 1949, signaling both the popularity of country repertoire with R&B performers and Hunter's specific later success with country material.

Hunter kept busy in the first half of the 1950s, recording more than a hundred songs for MGM, and later Atlantic, at the dawn of rock and roll. He toured steadily, particularly in the South, where he was very popular. Hunter's nuanced style, easygoing manner, and bespectacled appearance precluded stardom within the young, energetic rock-and-roll market. Nevertheless his keen ability to blend black and white musical styles, as well as his established reputation as both performer and songwriter, ensured that Hunter maintained his presence in the recording world.

Although Hunter tried his hand at a few uptempo dance numbers, his greatest success of the period—and his career—came in 1956 when the bluesy "Since I Met You Baby" topped the R&B charts for three weeks and became his only top-40 pop hit. Later covered by a multitude of pop, R&B, and country artists, "Since I Met You Baby" is perhaps the definitive Ivory Joe Hunter release, an insistent, emotive track with clear musical antecedents in pop, blues, jazz, and country. Although Hunter had other minor hits during the Atlantic years, the creative and commercial accomplishment of "Since I Met You Baby" could not help but overshadow the rest of his (often compelling) catalog.

Hunter left Atlantic in 1958, signing with Dot Records, a Nashville-based label best known for its flagship star Pat Boone, whose contrived covers of LITTLE RICHARD and FATS DOMINO won him (and the label) great ignominy in rock-and-

roll history. Boone also covered "I Almost Lost My Mind," taking the song higher on the charts than Hunter's original. Despite this unsavory reputation, Dot signed several R&B artists during this period, including ARTHUR ALEXANDER, himself a country-R&B alchemist, and Hunter, who recorded his final major hit, the loping "City Lights," for Dot in 1959. Soon after "City Lights," which was written by the country star Bill Anderson, Hunter's fortunes faded, and his releases (for Dot, Vee-Jay, Smash, and Capitol) stopped appearing on any listings whatsoever.

Hunter did not fade completely out of sight, however, and the veteran entertainer soon found a new home as a regular performer on the Grand Ole Opry. The appearances, along with the burgeoning country-soul genre popular in southern music during the 1960s, provoked a series of country recordings from Hunter; though artistically satisfying, these later releases had little commercial impact. Even the 1970s *The Return of Ivory Joe Hunter*, with a hot Memphis-based soul ensemble featuring ISAAC HAYES and the Memphis Horns, failed to reignite Hunter's career. He continued to make concert appearances, including a celebrated set at the Monterey Jazz Festival, and his many songs remained popular choices for cover versions, including the country star Sonny James's country number-1 version of "Since I Met You Baby" in 1970.

After Hunter was diagnosed with lung cancer in 1973, the Grand Ole Opry threw a benefit concert featuring George Jones, Tammy Wynette, Isaac Hayes, and others; Elvis Presley sent his best wishes, and Hunter himself performed from a wheelchair. He died in 1974 while living in Memphis.

Hunter's legacy is both obvious and underexplored. Certainly his catalog of thousands of songs, with his long career as a live performer, makes him an obvious inclusion in any history of R&B or of American popular music in general. Still, Hunter's greater importance arguably lies in his symbolic bridging of both eras and genres within pop traditions, representing American musical expression at its innovative, desegregated best. With admirers as famous as Elvis Presley, yet with roots firmly in the black clubs of rural Texas, Ivory Joe Hunter was a prolific, prodigious testament to black American creativity.

FURTHER READING
Dahl, Bill. "Ivory Joe Hunter," in *All Music Guide to Rock: The Definitive Guide to Rock, Pop, and Soul*,

3d ed., eds. Vladimir Bogdanov, Chris Woodstra, and Stephen Thomas Erlewine (2002).

Staff of the Country Music Hall of Fame. *Night Train to Nashville: Music City Rhythm and Blues, 1945–1970* (2004).

CHARLES L. HUGHES

Hunter, Jane Edna (13 Dec. 1882–19 Jan. 1971), autobiographer and black women's rights activist, was born Jane Edna Harris in Pendleton, South Carolina, the daughter of Edward Harris and Harriet Millner, sharecroppers. Following her father's death due to jaundice when she was ten years old, Jane and her three siblings were distributed briefly among the homes of various relatives. His death and the ensuing dispersal of her nuclear family were especially difficult for Jane, in part because she had customarily been "father's ally in his differences with mother" (*A Nickel*, 12) but also because she now had to forgo formal schooling to earn her keep in Anderson, South Carolina, as a live-in nursemaid and cook. Although treated so poorly by her mistress that white and black neighbors alike protested, she was taught to read and write by the eldest daughter.

Harris entered Ferguson Academy (later Ferguson-Williams College) in 1896, graduating four years later. Sometime later that year or early the following spring, yielding to her mother's exhortations, Harris entered into a loveless marriage with Edward Hunter, forty years her senior. Soon after the wedding and with her husband's blessing, she moved to Charleston, South Carolina, where she received formal training in nursing from the Cannon Street Hospital and Training School for Nurses. She also took a year of advanced training in the Dixie Hospital and Training School for Nurses at Hampton Institute in Hampton, Virginia, in 1904. These years of schooling helped Hunter recognize the employment difficulties facing even highly trained young African American women.

Upon her arrival in Cleveland, Ohio, on 10 May 1905, Hunter faced a dilemma that redirected her life. Her autobiographical account covers those first hours in the city spent searching for living quarters and stresses "the conditions which confront the Negro girl who, friendless and alone, looks for a decent place to live in Cleveland" (*A Nickel*, 67). Although Hunter had moved continually throughout the South, she had never arrived in a new location without an extended family member or a new employer to greet her. During this turbulent period, Hunter was forced to resort to menial cleaning positions while continually attempting to secure employment as a nurse. As Adrienne Lash Jones pointed out, the obstacles faced by Hunter were not only the initial racial barriers created for black nurses by a white medical community but also the very social structure of a city in which "the YWCA residence was not open to black women" (40). Despite eventually developing a clientele of wealthy white patients for whom she served as massage therapist or private-duty nurse, during periods of temporary unemployment she would invariably have to seek out cleaning or laundry jobs.

Constantly aware that "[a] girl alone in a large city must needs know the dangers and pitfalls awaiting her" (*A Nickel*, 77), in September 1911 Hunter brought together seven of her closest friends to discuss means to alleviate the difficult living conditions for single black women. Agreeing to pay a nickel each as weekly dues and electing Hunter as president, these eight women founded the Working Girls' Home Association. Despite opposition, largely from other African Americans who believed that this self-segregating organization would further hinder efforts to bring about complete racial integration in such institutions as the YWCA, Hunter's group flourished. In 1912 it changed its name to the Phillis Wheatley Association to commemorate PHILLIS WHEATLEY, the African American poet.

The following year, after electing an interracial board of trustees, the organization leased a twenty-three-room house. Although many detractors argued that there would be little demand for the Phillis Wheatley Home, "weeks before the formal opening, fifteen young women had already taken up residence" (*A Nickel*, 106). Hunter's vision for the Wheatley Home had been that it would become not merely a boardinghouse but an establishment dedicated to training black women in various professions; her dream had reached fruition. Hunter remained the driving force behind the Phillis Wheatley Association, first arguing against a merger with the YWCA in 1916 and then securing donations to purchase both a new seventy-two-room Phillis Wheatley Home in 1917 and an adjacent two-story building in 1919. In 1925 Hunter passed the Ohio bar, having completed her studies at the Cleveland Law School, and promptly began soliciting funds for an even larger home, a plan she accomplished two years later with the erection of an eleven-story building.

For more than thirty years Hunter helped oversee the Phillis Wheatley Association while dedicating herself and her superb fund-raising skills to various peripheral black women's enterprises. Although she officially retired in 1947, she found severing her bonds from her life's work extremely difficult. In 1960 she was found mentally incompetent and was placed in a rest home in Cleveland, where she remained until her death.

Her autobiography, *A Nickel and a Prayer* (1940), carefully chronicles the laborious stages leading to the creation of the association. Although the publication received little attention, the few reviews it garnered were glowing. In her lifetime she received recognition for her efforts from various sources, but "perhaps her most meaningful honor was from Tuskegee Institute, which conferred a master of science degree, in recognition of her achievements in the development of the social and vocational program conducted at the Phillis Wheatley Association" (Jones, 124).

Hunter devoted herself to the welfare of others and particularly to the assistance of single black women, first in her early pursuit of a nursing profession and then in her role in the foundation and enlargement of the Phillis Wheatley Association in Cleveland, Ohio. This organization fulfilled her dream of providing housing for single black workingwomen and helping them develop their autonomy by training them in various professions.

FURTHER READING

Hunter's collected papers and those of the Phillis Wheatley Association are housed at the Western Reserve Historical Society in Cleveland, Ohio.

Hunter, Jane Edna. *A Nickel and a Prayer* (1940).

Barton, Rebecca C. *Witnesses for Freedom: Negro Americans in Autobiography* (1948).

Dannett, Sylvia G. L. *Profiles of Negro Womanhood* (1964).

Jones, Adrienne Lash. *Black Women in United States History*, vol. 12: "*Jane Edna Hunter: A Case Study of Black Leadership, 1910–1950*" (1990).

This entry is taken from the *American National Biography* and is published here with the permission of the American Council of Learned Societies.

CHRISTOPHER J. NEUMANN

Hunter, John McNeile (23 Jan. 1901–July 1979), physicist, was born in Woodville, Texas, the oldest son of John Alexander Hunter and MARY EVELYN VIRGINIA (Edwards) HUNTER. His father, a former school principal, had moved to Texas from Louisiana soon after his marriage to Edwards, who had been one of his students. His mother was a teacher, home demonstration agent, and administrator. The young family only stayed in Woodville for about a year before moving again, first to La Porte and later to Jennings Island, Texas, where Hunter's father secured a ninety-nine-year lease on a property and began developing a ranch. Hunter's father taught Hunter and his brother at home for the first five grades. Once he was officially enrolled in classes at La Porte, Texas, Hunter had to cross two-and-a-half miles of open water to reach the classroom. He completed his secondary education at Prairie View State Normal and Industrial College (later Prairie View A&M University, part of the Texas A&M University system), where he simultaneously received his high school diploma and teaching certificate.

Two of Hunter's teachers encouraged him to apply to the Massachusetts Institute of Technology (MIT) in Boston, but he lacked the foreign languages necessary for admission to the undergraduate program. Determined nevertheless to secure a higher education, Hunter enrolled at the University of Kansas to complete the necessary requirements. Two years later he transferred to MIT, where he completed a B.S. in Electrical Engineering in 1924. Hunter had planned on a career in teaching in his field, but soon discovered that only one black college, Howard University, offered faculty positions in electrical engineering. He therefore turned to physics and enrolled at Cornell University, in Ithaca, New York, where he completed his M.S. in 1927 and his Ph.D. in 1937. Hunter was the third African American to receive a Ph.D. in physics.

In 1925 Hunter accepted a position at Virginia State College (later University) in Petersburg, Virginia—the institution he would make his home for the rest of his professional life. It was in Virginia that he met and, in 1929, married his wife, Ella Louise Stokes, a mathematician. At the beginning he taught both mathematics and physics, as the university lacked faculty in both departments. In 1932 he became the college's youngest dean when the acting dean went on leave to complete his graduate work. Hunter worked in administration throughout his career, serving as acting dean or dean in 1932, 1934–1935, and 1957–1967; he also served as chief assistant to the college president for several years in the 1950s and director of graduate studies from 1939 until 1965.

Hunter was deferred from military service in World War II both because of his marital status—by then the Hunters had a daughter, Jean Evelyn—and because his expertise was considered critical. During the war, Hunter trained over a hundred students in the use of military radio and radar. He also served as the director of an army engineering training program that instructed approximately 450 recruits in surveying, map-reading, and basic engineering concepts. Late in life Hunter would recall the relative luxury of earning a government salary at a black state college—during the war he made more than the college president.

Aside from his administrative duties, the bulk of Hunter's career was spent strengthening scientific training at black colleges and universities, particularly in his own areas of physics and mathematics. Virginia State, Fisk University, and Howard University were the only southern institutions offering a physics curriculum to African Americans for most of Hunter's career. He strongly believed in the importance of separate disciplinary departments such as physics, chemistry, and biology rather than the more typical arrangement found in "departments of science." He personally taught physics to over four thousand students, including sixty-five physics majors, and served as the primary adviser for eleven Ph.D. students.

For many years Hunter was deeply involved with the National Institute of Science (NIS), which was formed in 1943 to improve the teaching of science on black college campuses. In the organization's first year, Hunter served as the regional director for the East, which included twenty-eight colleges and universities in Virginia, Maryland, Pennsylvania, the District of Columbia, Delaware, and North Carolina; from 1944–1945 he served as its president. His leadership of this organization afforded him the opportunity to tour the dismal teaching conditions in science departments across the South. Later in life, Hunter's enthusiasm for this organization—and black scientific organizations generally—would wane. Although he thought separate organizations were necessary in the Deep South, he found them redundant in areas such as Virginia where he found himself welcomed in both black and white scientific organizations. Hunter let his membership in the NIS lapse in 1957. In an oral history conducted in 1972, Hunter reflected, "Throughout my life as a teacher I have sought to be an American teaching physics.... This doesn't mean that we shouldn't introduce people like PERCY JULIAN ... to our students. But it means that to develop to the highest level we have to adopt the American civilization and contribute to its development."

Hunter was a fellow of the American Association for the Advancement of Science and a member of a number of scientific organizations, including the American Association of Physics Teachers, the American Physical Society, Sigma Xi, Sigma Pi Sigma (the physics honor society), and Kappa Mu Upsilon (the mathematics honor society). He was one of the organizers of the Physics Club of Richmond, Virginia, where for many years he and his wife were the only African American members. Hunter's personal memberships included the Episcopal Church, Kappa Alpha Psi, and Sigma Pi Phi. He retired from college administration in 1967 but continued to teach and advise the college for several years. In 1973 he received a Distinguished Service Citation from the American Association of Physics Teachers. He died in Petersburg.

FURTHER READING

Hunter discarded his personal papers after being unable to find an archive or library willing to take them. Little information about his life is available in print, but a detailed oral history is on deposit as part of the Black Oral History Program (1972), Special Collections, in the John Hope and Aurelia E. Franklin Library, Fisk University, Nashville, Tennessee.

"AAPT Distinguished Service Citations for 1973." *Physics Teacher* 12 (May 1974).

King, William M. "Hubert Branch Crouch and the Origins of the National Institute of Science," *Journal of Negro History* 79 (1994).

AUDRA J. WOLFE

Hunter, Mary Evelyn Virginia (11 Aug. 1885–4 Mar. 1967), teacher, home demonstration agent, and administrator, was born in Finchburg, Alabama, to Elijah E. and Frances (Moore) Edwards. Mary Evelyn V. Edwards was the fifteenth of their seventeen children, and she worked as a bookkeeper at her father's store, sawmill, and gin. She was a senior in the local high school when she married J. A. Hunter, the high school principal. The couple moved first to Woodville, Texas, and then relocated to La Porte, Texas, where they leased a ranch on Jennings Island. They had two sons, JOHN MCNEILE HUNTER in 1901 and Ira T. Hunter in 1905. M. E. V. Hunter taught school, and after her husband's death in the early 1910s, she began taking courses at Prairie View State Normal and Industrial College (later Prairie View A&M) to gain teaching credentials. She ultimately earned a B.S. from that school in 1926, and then became the first African American women to earn an M.A. in Home Economics Education from Iowa State College, in Ames, Iowa, in 1931. She pursued advanced coursework at Ohio State University from 1937 until 1939, and was awarded an honorary LLD from Texas College in Tyler, Texas. She dedicated her fifty-year career to improving the lives of rural African Americans.

In 1915 Hunter, by then a widow, became the first African American employee of the Texas Agricultural Extension Service (TAEX), when white officials created the Negro Division that year, and employed two men and a woman to implement the service. Hunter began her professional career at a time when few rural African American women had access to higher education or the opportunities to apply their knowledge. Her experiences highlight the pressures that minority professionals had to overcome in the segregated South during the early twentieth century. Clarence Ousley, TAEX director, told Hunter and the two other African American agents hired to begin the TAEX's Negro Division that "if we succeeded others would be added to the force and if we failed that there would be no other Negro agents employed in the near future." Hunter recounted that the three "accepted this challenge with the determination to win and establish for ever in the minds of those in authority that some Negroes will plan and develop large organizations if permitted to do so" (Hunter, TAEX Historical Files).

Over the next sixteen years Hunter increased the division's home demonstration staff, which worked with women and girls to improve nutrition, sanitation, and home and farm management, from one in 1915 to twenty-three in 1931, and expanded services from informal community gatherings in freedmen communities to a formal club organization with nearly thirty thousand dues-paying women and girls. Hunter attributed such success to her tireless dedication to the "promotion of human happiness" accomplished by giving "freely of her time, energy, and money" (Hill, 134). By 1931 her peers considered Hunter "the most proficient state agent that we have in the entire system of Extension work for Negroes in the South" because of her "initiative, good judgment, tact, a strong personality, and ... enthusiasm" (Hill, 137).

Hunter, who taught adults reading and writing in Alabama prior to her marriage, excelled at informal education because she devised practical solutions that relatively illiterate rural blacks could use to improve their lives. For example, during her years with the Negro Division of the TAEX, she devised the "Steps in Canning" program, to convince farm women and children to diversify their diets. She directed them to put up 240 cans of vegetables so that they would have at least one can for each day of the year not supplied by their gardens. She urged families to raise at least 104 chickens so they could have two meals based on poultry a week, year round. She advocated home building and land acquisition and improvement with simple practical directions, tying home and farm management to sound financial management that challenged the prevailing credit system, the crop lien. Ultimately, she believed in professional service organizations, and to that end she had created a state organization for African American girls by 1925, and for women by 1927. She consistently raised the standards for extension agents, both county agricultural and home demonstration agents, and wrote a guide that helped standardize and improve performance.

In addition to mobilizing rural women, girls, and her male and female colleagues, Hunter took advantage of opportunities afforded by related professional and special-interest organizations. Through the Texas Commission on Inter-racial Cooperation she publicized home demonstration work and gained support for it and other services among rural African Americans. Additionally, she held membership in the Colored Teachers State Association of Texas, the National Association for Teachers in Colored Schools, and the Texas Federation of Colored Women's Clubs. Such visibility allowed her to lecture to biracial audiences on rural reform and to influence policy making. For example, she advocated for a state home for delinquent girls and was instrumental in 1927 in developing legislation that authorized the school, eventually known as Crockett State School.

In 1931, after sixteen years as home demonstration agent, district agent, and state supervisor of home demonstration in the segregated division of TAEX, Hunter moved to Virginia to serve as professor of home economics and head of the Division of Home Economics at Virginia State College for Negroes (later Virginia State University). In 1925 one of her sons, John McNeile Hunter, had secured an appointment to teach at the college, and she joined him there (her other son, Dr. Ira T. Hunter, practiced dentistry in Tyler, Texas, until his death in 1972). She continued her work with rural community reform during her twenty-five years in home economics education and administration. Hunter raised professional standards by emphasizing research and professional growth for home economists through graduate training. She remained committed to lifelong learning and interracial cooperation, evident through the program in adult education that she began at Virginia State as a result of the Chesterfield County Field Laboratory project in the 1940s. She retired in 1954, and died twelve years later in Petersburg, Virginia.

FURTHER READING

Papers produced by and associated with Hunter's career are housed in the Texas Agricultural Extension Service Historical Files, Cushing Memorial Library and Archives, Texas A&M University, College Station, Texas; the Agricultural Extension Service Files, Special Collections, John B. Coleman Library, Prairie View A&M University, Prairie View, Texas; and The Mary Evelyn Victoria Hunter Papers (1931–1963), Special Collections and Archives, Johnston Memorial Library, Virginia State University, Petersburg, Virginia.

Brandenstein, Sherilyn. "Mary Evelyn V. Edwards Hunter," *New Handbook of Texas* 3 (1996).

Hill, Kate Adele. *Home Demonstration Work in Texas* (1958).

Hunter, John McNeile. Oral History Interview. Black Oral History Collection. Special Collections, John and Aurelia Franklin Library, Fisk University, Nashville, Tennessee (1972).

Potts, L. A. *Biography of Mrs. M. E. V. Hunter* (MS, Special Collections, Johnston Memorial Library, Virginia State University, 1958).

Reid, Debra A. *Reaping a Greater Harvest: African Americans, the Extension Service, and Rural Reform in Jim Crow Texas* (2007).

Winegarten, Ruthe. *Black Texas Women: A Sourcebook* (1996).

DEBRA A. REID

Hunter-Gault, Charlayne (27 Feb. 1942–), broadcast journalist, was born in Due West, South Carolina, the oldest child of Althea Ruth (Brown) and Charles S. H. Hunter Jr. Her family life was nourishing despite the frequent absences of her father, a U.S. Army chaplain who was away more than he was home, serving tours of duty in Korea and other countries. Charlayne's mother, a teacher, passed on her love of learning. Hunter worked on the *Green Light*, the school paper at Atlanta's Turner High School, and decided that she wanted to get the best possible training to become a journalist. The University of Georgia had the best journalism program in the state but at the time did not admit blacks. At the urging of the NAACP and with the assistance of the attorneys CONSTANCE BAKER MOTLEY and DONALD HOLLOWELL, Hunter and her fellow Turner High student HAMILTON HOLMES, who aspired to become a physician, applied to the University of Georgia in July 1959. However, frustrated by the state's and the university's delaying tactics, Hunter enrolled at Wayne University (later Wayne State University) in Detroit, while continuing her fight for admission to the University of Georgia.

That university's administrators would not admit Hunter, saying that as a transfer student from Wayne University, she would lose academic credits. The decision to keep her out of Georgia was overturned in federal court after her lawyers discovered that a white transfer student was admitted to the school during the same period. On 9 January 1961 she and Hamilton Holmes became the first two black students enrolled at the University of Georgia, thereby integrating the formerly all-white institution.

The going was rough. During her first nights on campus, white students "welcomed" Hunter with chants of "Nigger Go Home" as they hurled rocks and bottles through her dormitory window. She recalled going days when not a soul would speak to her.

Hunter had never seen a black reporter who wrote for a white newspaper, but saw several during her time at Georgia, as they were covering her admission. Buoyed by her dream of joining them, she endured the taunts, insults, and slurs from white students who did not want black students at "their school." While at Georgia, she worked part-time for the *Inquirer*, founded by JULIAN BOND and other African American college students in Atlanta. During one summer she interned at the *Louisville (Ky.) Courier-Journal*, where she honed her craft.

Hunter survived racist taunts and a term on academic probation to graduate, with Holmes, in 1963 with a bachelor's degree in Journalism. Among the few white students who befriended Hunter was Walter Stovall, her first husband, with whom she had a child, Suesan. They amicably divorced after a few years of marriage.

After college Hunter went to work as a "Talk of the Town" reporter for *The New Yorker* magazine, under the editorship of William Shawn. There the young intern spent the mornings doing clerical work and the afternoons working on her stories. One of the first pieces she submitted for publication was a personal memoir about her summers in Harlem called "115th between Lenox and 5th." In 1967 Hunter accepted a Russell Sage Fellowship to study social science at Washington University in St. Louis, Missouri, where she also edited articles for *Trans-Action* magazine.

After she covered the 1968 Poor People's Campaign in Washington, D.C., she took a job as a reporter and anchorwoman with Washington television station WRC. A year later she joined the staff of the *New York Times*, where she worked for ten years, including two years as the newspaper's Harlem bureau chief. In 1971 she married the investment banker Ronald Gault, and gave birth to a son Chuma, her second child.

In 1978 Hunter-Gault joined the *MacNeil/Lehrer Report* on PBS, and was promoted to national correspondent in 1983 when the show went to a one-hour format. In 1995 it became the *NewsHour with Jim Lehrer*. During her time at PBS she also anchored the award-winning *Rights and Wrongs*, a television newsmagazine on human rights. Hunter-Gault joined National Public Radio in 1997 after twenty years with PBS. In April 1999 she joined CNN and later became the network's Johannesburg bureau chief and correspondent. Her numerous honors include two Emmy Awards and two Peabody Awards—one for her work on "Apartheid's People," a *NewsHour* series on life during apartheid in South Africa, and the second for general reporting on Africa in 1998. She was also the recipient of the 1986 Journalist of the Year Award from the National Association of Black Journalists, the 1990 Sidney Hillman Award, an American Women in Radio and Television Award, a *Good Housekeeping* Broadcast Personality of the Year Award, a Tom Paine Award, Amnesty International's Media Spotlight Award, and an African-American Institute Award for outstanding coverage of Africa. In 2000 the Africa-America Institute honored her with the Chairman's Award for Excellence in Media for her balanced reporting on Africa. She also held more than two dozen honorary degrees and wrote occasionally for several other publications, including *Essence*, *Life*, *Change*, and *Ms*. In 2011, Hunter-Gault participated in a series of events commemorating the 50th anniversary of her role in integrating the University of Georgia. In that year she also donated her papers to the UGA's Richard B. Russell Library for Political Research and Studies.

FURTHER READING

Hunter-Gault, Charlayne. *In My Place* (1993).

Pratt, Robert A. *We Shall Not Be Moved: The Desegregation of the University of Georgia* (2002).

Trillin, Calvin. *An Education in Georgia: Charlayne Hunter, Hamilton Holmes, and the Integration of the University of Georgia* (1963).

JAMES MICHAEL BRODIE

Hunton, Addie Waites (11 June 1875–21 June 1943), activist, teacher, and author, was born Addie D. Waites in Norfolk, Virginia, the daughter of Jesse Waites, an oyster and shipping business owner, and Adelina Lawton. Addie attended public school and belonged to the African Methodist Episcopal (AME) Church. Her mother died when she was a young child, and she was sent to live with an aunt in Boston. She attended Boston Girls' Latin (High) School and in 1889 became the first African American woman to graduate from the Spencerian College of Commerce in Philadelphia, Pennsylvania. She taught for a year in Portsmouth, Virginia, before moving to Normal, Alabama, to teach and later become principal of the State Normal and Agricultural College.

In 1893 Waites returned to Norfolk, where on 19 July she married WILLIAM ALPHAEUS HUNTON of Chatham, Ontario. He had moved to Norfolk in 1888 to become the first African American professional youth secretary in the international Young Men's Christian Association (YMCA), and in 1891 he had been appointed administrative secretary of the Colored Men's Department of the International Committee. The Huntons left Norfolk for Richmond, Virginia, then moved to Atlanta in 1899 and had two children.

Hunton worked as a secretary and bursar at Clark University in Atlanta from 1905 to 1906. When race riots erupted in Atlanta in 1906 the Huntons moved to Brooklyn, New York. Her husband's career as a YMCA official inspired Hunton to travel with him as his secretary when he attended YMCA conferences. Gradually she became as well known in YMCA circles as her husband was. While in Atlanta, she began to speak publicly against segregation and, beginning in 1904, penned numerous articles on issues relevant to women and, specifically, the African American woman. In 1907 the National Board of the Young Women's Christian Association (YWCA) appointed her secretary of the South and Middle West regions, which she toured through 1908. In 1909 Hunton left for Europe with her children to continue her education. She traveled first to Switzerland, then to Germany, where she studied at the Kaiser Wilhelm University in Strasbourg. When Hunton returned to the United States in 1910, she resumed her work with the YWCA, studied at the College of the City of New York, and cared for her husband, who was suffering with tuberculosis.

After Hunton's husband died in 1916, she volunteered for service in World War I, working in

Brooklyn canteens designated for Negro soldiers. In June 1918 she became one of three African American women invited to France as YWCA welfare workers. For the next fifteen months she worked with two hundred thousand racially segregated African American troops. Her first assignment was near the Loire River at Saint-Nazaire, a supply and transport center. Desiring to improve on the standard canteen and movies offered at YMCA huts, Hunton introduced a literacy course and a Sunday evening discussion program, each of which gained popularity with African American servicemen, many of whom felt lonely and demoralized by segregationist practices.

Hunton's second assignment, in January 1919, took her to Aix-les-Bains in southern France, where she helped establish a wide range of activities, including religious, educational, athletic, and cultural events for African American troops. Her final assignment was Camp Pontanezen in Brest, the last YMCA hut for African Americans in France, which Hunton closed on 3 August 1919.

Upon her return to the United States, Hunton coauthored *Two Colored Women with the American Expeditionary Forces* (1920) with another YMCA volunteer, KATHRYN M. JOHNSON, who, like Hunton, served overseas longer than any other African American woman. Their book exposed not only the racial discrimination endured by black troops during World War I but also the discrimination perpetrated by white YMCA workers against Hunton and Johnson.

Hunton concentrated her postwar career activities on fighting racism and improving the lives of African Americans and women. She served in numerous leadership positions on national boards, councils, and organizations, including the Council on Colored Work of the YWCA National Board, the International Council of the Women of Darker Races (as president), and the Empire State Federation of Women's Clubs (as president). In 1895 Hunton was a founder and organizer of the National Association of Colored Women, and she was the state organizer for the Georgia Federation of Colored Women's Clubs.

Hunton had been active in the NAACP almost from its beginning, working as a chapter organizer, lecturer, field worker, field secretary, and vice president. In 1919, working through the NAACP, she addressed the first meeting of the Pan-African Congress in Paris, where she stressed the importance of women in world affairs. She also served as an organizer for the Fourth Pan-African Congress

held in New York in 1927. Her interest in peace efforts led her to become president of the Circle for Peace and Foreign Relations. In 1926 she traveled to Haiti to observe American occupation of the country, doing so as a member of a six-woman committee for the Women's International League for Peace and Freedom of which she was an executive board member. The committee's observations and findings were published in the book *Occupied Haiti* (1927), in which Hunton coauthored a chapter with the book's editor, Emily Greene Balch. The book condemned American occupation and called for an independent Haiti, although Hunton's chapter was specifically on race relations. Her last public appearance occurred at the 1939 New York World's Fair, where she presided over a ceremony honoring outstanding African American women. She died of complications resulting from diabetes in Brooklyn, New York.

Addie Hunton dedicated her life to those causes she believed would promote a better life for women and African Americans. She advanced the cause of women's rights as an ardent suffragist, author, and teacher. She wrote and lectured on the need for day-care facilities for working mothers and shelters for homeless children. She worked tirelessly with soldiers facing discrimination overseas and raised America's consciousness of race and the cause of peace well after World War I had ended.

FURTHER READING
Hunton, Addie W. *William Alphaeus Hunton: A Pioneer Prophet of Young Men* (1938).
Hunton, Addie W., and Kathryn M. Johnson. *Two Colored Women with the American Expeditionary Forces* (1920).
Rice, Anna V. *A History of the World's Young Women's Christian Association* (1947).
This entry is taken from the *American National Biography* and is published here with the permission of the American Council of Learned Societies.

THEA GALLO BECKER

Hunton, Alphaeus (18 Sept. 1903–13 Jan. 1970), Pan-Africanist and labor leader, was born William Alphaeus Hunton Jr. in Atlanta, Georgia, to ADDIE WAITES HUNTON, a leading clubwoman and feminist, and WILLIAM ALPHAEUS HUNTON Sr., founder of the Negro YMCA. Alphaeus was the couple's second surviving child. After the Atlanta riot of 1906 the Huntons moved to New York. Alphaeus grew up in Brooklyn, where he attended public schools with his sister Eunice Hunton (Carter), who became a prominent clubwoman and lawyer. Alphaeus and Eunice lived for two and a half years in Germany with their mother.

In 1921 Hunton entered Howard University in Washington, D.C., earning a B.S. in 1924. He pursued his graduate studies at Harvard University, earning an M.A. in English literature in 1926. Beginning in 1933 Hunton worked toward his Ph.D. at New York University while teaching English literature at Howard as an assistant professor. He received his doctoral degree in 1938. The effects of the Depression upon African Americans, especially those he saw in Washington, D.C., shocked him and prompted his involvement in an array of left-wing and progressive causes, particularly the National Negro Congress (NNC).

In 1938 Hunton became chairman of the NNC's labor committee in Washington. The committee began a union-organizing campaign among domestic workers in 1940 and followed this campaign with one to demand better wages for black laundry workers. Hunton and the labor committee helped win appointments for three African Americans to the local Unemployment Compensation Committee. Under Hunton's leadership the NNC helped win the right for African Americans to register for jobs in the local Works Progress Administration (WPA) in 1938 and organized mass protests to demand jobs for African Americans in the city's public transit system in 1940–1941. Hunton helped to organize Howard University's Local 440 of the American Federation of Teachers (AFT) in the late 1930s. As America prepared for war in 1940, Hunton organized a mass campaign for black people to be hired at the all-white Glen L. Martin aircraft factory in Baltimore. During the course of the Glen Martin campaign Hunton led at least one street demonstration in Baltimore. He organized groups of African American men to apply daily for jobs at the Glen Martin plant.

In 1943 Hunton, who was separated from his wife, Margaret Reynolds, whom he had married in the early 1930s, decided to leave Washington. More pressingly, the Dies Committee, the Special Committee for the Investigation of Un-American Activities headed by U.S. Representative Martin Dies, and the Federal Bureau of Investigation had been harassing him about his suspected Communist affiliation.

MAX YERGAN, an old family friend, and PAUL ROBESON, co-chairs of the Council on African Affairs (CAA) in New York City, hired Hunton as education director of the CAA in May 1943. By autumn Hunton had divorced Reynolds, married Dorothy Williams, moved to Brooklyn, and begun work introducing Africa to African Americans. Along with other CAA leaders, including Robeson, Yergan, ADAM CLAYTON POWELL JR., and MARY MCLEOD BETHUNE, Hunton lobbied the State Department and later the United Nations for an end to colonialism in Africa. He organized conferences on Pan-Africanism, including a meeting in 1944 that brought trade union and civil rights leaders together with AMY JACQUES GARVEY and W. E. B. DuBois.

Hunton helped scholars with their research. He met with future leaders of new African nations such as Kwame Nkrumah of Ghana. The CAA published a monthly bulletin, *New Africa*, about current events on the continent and a regular newsletter, *Spotlight on Africa*. Hunton wrote articles and sent letters to any newspaper that would print them. One of the first of many pamphlets and articles that Hunton wrote for the CAA was *American Labor and the Future of African Workers*, published in 1946. In this widely circulated pamphlet he explained his own philosophy: "it is the responsibility as well as to the interest of … organized labor to see that the Africans and other colonial peoples are enlisted as our full and equal allies in defeating the fascist enemy, and that they are made full and equal partners in building a post-war world of peace and security." Other publications by Hunton include *Stop South Africa's Crimes: No Annexation of S.W. Africa* (1946), *Africa Fights for Freedom* (1950), and *Resistance against Fascist Enslavement in South Africa, with a Postscript for Americans* (1953).

The CAA and Hunton neglected no part of the continent in educational efforts and especially focused attention upon the Dominion of South Africa. Hunton's greatest concern after the end of World War II was the rise of apartheid and intensified labor oppression in South Africa. In 1946, 60,000 South African gold miners went on strike against British-owned companies. The Boer government and British mine operators responded quickly. Within one week of the strike's beginning, government police had murdered twelve miners. Hunton was a key organizer of the mass antiapartheid movement in the United States. He synchronized memorial services for the dead strikers in several cities and led pickets of the South African consulate in midtown Manhattan. He wrote *Stop South Africa's Crimes* and in 1946 helped publish *Seeing Is Believing*, a book of covertly obtained photographs from South Africa, and *8 Million Demand Freedom: What about It, Gen. Smuts?* (1946), by I. B. Tabata. As famine crippled South Africa even as the miners' strike began, Robeson and Hunton raised thousands of dollars and collected food for famine relief. On one Sunday when the council asked churchgoers in New York to bring donations to services, the CAA collected 22,000 cans of food and $5,000.

Hunton became executive director of the CAA after Max Yergan resigned amid scandal and recriminations. In addition to its antiapartheid organizing, the CAA mounted effective public campaigns around other issues, including the partition of the former Italian colonies in East Africa by the NATO powers in 1949. Hunton stood beside Robeson at the performer's concert in Peekskill, New York, when Robeson returned to the Upstate New York town following an early visit during which he had been attacked by local right-wing activists. Hunton picketed Winston Churchill when that leader visited New York a few days after his famous "Iron Curtain" speech in Missouri in March 1946. Hunton was an enthusiastic supporter of the Stockholm Petition against atomic weapons and of the Socialist Norman Thomas's campaign for the presidency in 1948.

Hunton, DuBois, and Robeson found themselves spokesmen for anti-colonialism, voices generally at odds with the U.S. government during the cold war. The CAA and its officers were repeatedly investigated by the FBI and accused of subversion. Although Hunton's membership in the Communist Party was a closely held secret (and was not revealed until after his death in 1970), he made no secret of his sympathies. In 1951 Hunton was brought before the House Un-American Activities Committee, and after refusing to testify against other citizens he was sent to prison. The federal judge Sylvester Ryan sentenced Hunton to six months in prison for contempt of court. He served three months in the federal house of detention in New York City and just under three months in a federal penitentiary in Virginia.

When Hunton was released he threw himself back into the work of the nearly defunct CAA, briefly reviving the organization until August 1953 when the U.S. attorney general Herbert Brownell petitioned the Subversive Activities Control Board (SACB) alleging that the CAA was an agent of a foreign power and among the top twelve subversive organizations in the country. The foreign power about which Brownell worried, Hunton discovered,

was the African National Congress. The Internal Revenue Service, the New York Joint Legislative Committee on Charitable Organizations, and the Federal Bureau of Investigation also pursued the CAA, effectively closing down the organization, which formally closed in 1955.

Hunton found work in the fur district and in an electronics factory doing semiskilled work. In 1957 he published *Decision in Africa: Sources of Current Conflict*, for which DuBois wrote the foreword. After the Guinean president Sekou Toure offered Alphaeus and Dorothy Hunton jobs, the couple moved to Guinea in 1960. Shortly afterward DuBois and his wife, SHIRLEY GRAHAM DuBOIS, moved to Ghana, where they launched the *Encyclopedia Africana* with the help of the Ghanan president Kwame Nkrumah. DuBois wanted Alphaeus Hunton to be his aide and successor. The Huntons moved to Ghana. Alphaeus Hunton traveled throughout Africa to forge ties with scholars and to court government funds for the encyclopedia project. After DuBois's death in 1963 Hunton became responsible for the project. Alphaeus and Dorothy Hunton were expelled from Ghana when a military coup ousted Nkrumah in 1966.

President Kenneth Kaunda of Zambia offered Hunton a writing job with the Kaunda Foundation. The Huntons also traveled around the world. Hunton contracted incurable cancer in 1969 and returned to Zambia, where he is buried. At a memorial service in New York City later that year John Mwanakatwe, then Zambia's minister of finance, called Alphaeus Hunton the "man who endeavored in his own quiet way to show the extent to which the roots run so deep, which connect Blacks of America to the Blacks of Africa" (*Muhammad Speaks*, 15 Jan. 1971).

FURTHER READING

Hunton's papers are held by the Schomburg Center for Research in Black Culture, New York Public Library, New York City.

Hunton, Dorothy K. *Alphaeus Hunton: The Unsung Valiant* (1986).

Lynch, Hollis. *Black American Radicals and the Liberation of Africa: The Council on African Affairs, 1937–1955* (1978).

Obituary: *New York Times*, 16 Jan. 1970.

CHRISTINE LUTZ

Hunton, William Alphaeus (31 Oct. 1863–29 Nov. 1915), organization leader and community leader, was born William Alphaeus Hunton in Chatham, Ontario, the sixth of the seven children of Stanton Hunton and Mary Conyers. Stanton Hunton had been born a slave. After purchasing his freedom he made a fortune as a bricklayer and landlord in the frontier town of Chatham. Stanton Hunton, along with one of William Hunton's older brothers, had conspired with John Brown in 1859. The Huntons continued their struggle against segregation in Chatham after the Civil War. William's mother, Mary Conyers, a free black who had moved to Canada from Ohio, was active in social work with runaway slaves until her premature death in 1869. After her death William was raised by his elder sister Victoria and his fiercely religious father.

In the early 1880s Hunton attended Nazrey Educational Institute in Chatham and the Wilberforce Collegiate Institute of Ontario. He left college and taught public school for a year, in 1884–1885. In that latter year he moved to Ottawa, where he worked in the Department of Indian Affairs and joined the Young Men's Christian Association (YMCA).

Though many African Americans had already established informal branches of the YMCA in the United States, the international committee of North American YMCAs was searching for an educated African American man to centralize what was called "colored work" and to establish permanent, affiliated Negro branches in the United States. The international committee offered William Hunton a job as a branch secretary, or executive director, in Norfolk, Virginia. In 1888 William Hunton became the first black YMCA branch director in the South and the director of the first affiliated Negro YMCA.

Two years after his arrival in the United States, Hunton began to court ADDIE WAITES HUNTON. In 1893, after the international committee of the YMCA put Hunton in charge of the YMCA's work with African Americans and authorized him to establish formal Negro YMCA branches around the country, the couple married. Within two years Hunton had launched drives in more than two dozen cities around the country. He met potential board members at church meetings and colleges, and he spoke before businessmen and other potential donors. About one-third of his time was devoted to fund-raising. Unless an independent branch had a board of directors and raised enough money to hire a trained branch secretary, the YMCA would not permit that branch to affiliate or to call itself a YMCA. Hunton insisted that Negro branch YMCAs meet the same criteria as did white branches.

The international committee hired Hunton as a field secretary in 1890; he was the first African American executive of the YMCA. By 1896 Hunton had helped forty-one Negro branches affiliate with the YMCA. He was a mentor to numerous younger men who themselves became leaders: JESSE EDWARD MOORLAND, JOHN HOPE, GEORGE EDMUND HAYNES, CHANNING HEGGIE TOBIAS, and MAX YERGAN. Hunton and Moorland began to hold annual retreats for the colored men's department. They invited African American branch secretaries to meet on the Delaware coast for training, fun, and solidarity. By 1903 more than one hundred men from eighteen states were attending the retreat annually.

In 1899 the Huntons moved to Atlanta where they had two children who survived infancy, Eunice Roberta Hunton (later Carter) in 1899 and William Alphaeus Hunton Jr. in 1903, who attended his father's retreats when he was a small boy. Hunton became increasingly confident about protesting segregation within and outside the YMCA; he refused to honor legally mandated segregated seating at a Nashville YMCA youth conference, for instance. In 1899 he joined Henry Hugh Proctor, William Henry Crogman, W. E. B. DuBois, and John Hope in petitioning the Georgia state legislature for equal enfranchisement. He raised the funds for the first Negro Young People's Christian and Education Congress, held in Atlanta in 1902. Five thousand youth attended. William Hunton's intervention with city fathers caused them to suspend trolley segregation during convention week.

Hunton continued to travel for the YMCA. He supervised a staff around the country and represented the YMCA at conferences. He attended the YMCA's golden jubilee in London in 1894, and then he traveled to Belgium and Scotland. Seven years later Hunton went to Japan, Hawaii, and China.

In September 1906 race riots broke out in Atlanta. Over three days at least two dozen African Americans were killed. The Huntons lived on Houston Street, close to where the riot began. Only one white neighbor offered to help the Huntons if the riot reached their street. Addie Hunton concluded, "We, as colored people, had really no rights as citizens whatsoever" (133). The family moved to Brooklyn, New York, in 1907.

Despite moving north William Hunton did not stop traveling through the South. He was determined to create safe spaces in which to train young men as race leaders. Hunton organized the first of the King's Mountain conferences, meetings of African American youth in North Carolina under the auspices of the YMCA. The circle of those he mentored expanded to include Mordecai Johnson. By January 1913, when the YMCA held a ceremony honoring William Hunton's twenty-five years of service, almost every African American college in the country had established a YMCA student branch. Nearly fifty cities had African American branches, and most of the city branches were fully equipped.

In 1913 the Huntons attended the tenth World's Student Christian Federation Conference, held at Lake Mohonk in Upstate New York. At this meeting Hunton called for "a glorious morning when man shall not judge his fellow man by color, race, tradition or any of the accidents of life, but by righteousness and truth and unselfish service to humanity" (Hunton, 119–120). Shortly afterward the couple met with LUGENIA BURNS HOPE and John Hope to plan another Negro Young People's Congress. The Hopes and Addie Hunton realized that William Hunton was ill—and indeed Hunton had contracted tuberculosis.

For two years Addie Waites Hunton dropped most of her own activities and sat by her silent husband's bedside. William Alphaeus Hunton Sr. blessed his children and died while holding his wife's hand. Memorial services were held for Hunton throughout the remainder of 1916 and in 1917 by blacks and whites around the country. By establishing the Negro YMCA, Hunton had provided a nonsectarian organization through which African Americans could network and train for leadership during the worst of the segregation era in the United States.

FURTHER READING

Hunton, Addie Waites. *William Alphaeus Hunton, a Pioneer Prophet of Young Men* (1938).

Mjagkij, Nina. *Light in the Darkness: African Americans and the Y.M.C.A., 1852–1946* (1994).

Obituary: *New York Times*, 6 Dec. 1916.

CHRISTINE LUTZ

Hurley, Ruby (7 Nov. 1909–9 Aug. 1980), NAACP activist, was born in Washington, D.C. Little information about Hurley's early life and education is available. She attended Miner Teachers' College and Terrell Law School. Almost all of Hurley's working life was devoted to the NAACP. However, her first job out of school was working for the Federal Industrial Bank, a Depression-era institution that served African Americans. While working for the bank in Washington, D.C., Hurley became involved in the effort to find a concert venue for the singer MARIAN ANDERSON. When Anderson was denied permission to perform at Constitution Hall in 1939, due to the segregation policies of the Daughters of the American Revolution, who owned the hall, Hurley served on the committee that sought and eventually secured another site (the Lincoln Memorial). This well-known story accounts for Hurley's entry into civil rights activism.

In the wake of the Anderson incident, some blacks in Washington decided to re-establish the NAACP branch in that city, and Hurley was one of the principals involved in getting the branch chartered. Within a couple of years, she had attracted the notice of the NAACP national staff through her acquaintance with the prominent NAACP activist and jurist WILLIAM HASTIE. He recommended her to the NAACP, since the national organization sought a youth council field secretary. Hurley eagerly sought this opportunity and in 1943, she was appointed to the position.

During the 1940s Hurley traveled and organized extensively to mobilize African American youth across the country. Her efforts focused particularly on college campuses, especially but not exclusively historically black colleges. The number of youth and college branches grew significantly under her guidance, with total youth membership rising from about 15,000 in 1945 to 25,000 in 1947. Hurley worked to organize youth conferences and regional meetings that addressed a wide range of topics, from employment issues to educational discrimination to juvenile delinquency. She also organized efforts to provide services and support to soldiers and veterans returning from the war. Her efforts in helping African American youth network with one another would pay important dividends in the years to come.

In 1951 Hurley was assigned a new position. She was initially given the task of setting up a base in the South from which to direct regional activities for the NAACP, specifically to generate interest and enroll new members and chapters in the organization. For several years southern NAACP branch officers had requested a full-time staff person to oversee NAACP work in a regional context. Hurley's assignment was originally intended to be temporary but once she had set up her headquarters in Birmingham, Alabama, it quickly became clear that there was an ongoing need for a full-time representative of the national office to remain in the area. In 1952 her appointment as the regional secretary of the Southeast Regional Office became permanent. The states in her district included Mississippi, Alabama, Georgia, Florida, Tennessee, and North and South Carolina.

Hurley spent the early 1950s engaged in the difficult, arduous, and frequently dangerous work of visiting towns and communities throughout the Deep South, explaining the program of the NAACP, encouraging the formation of branches, and investigating a variety of issues which were of concern to the Association. She undertook this work at a time when there were very few civil rights workers in the field and when reprisals for blacks challenging the status quo could be severe. But Hurley reported on numerous occasions that the African Americans among whom she organized at the local level were tired of the conditions under which they had been forced to live and work. Hurley found a receptive audience in most of the locales she visited, which provides evidence of the gathering momentum that would eventually be expressed through the civil rights activities of the post-1954 era.

It was also her responsibility to represent the national office to local branches; this relationship was a complex and not always amicable one. Hurley showed considerable tact in negotiating the conflicts between the New York office and local branches. She played a crucial role in helping the national leadership understand what might or might not be practicable to expect from local members and encouraged local branches to remember both the big picture and the extent to which NAACP resources were spread thin. She also served as a support person to THURGOOD MARSHALL and other members of the NAACP legal team, who needed assistance in securing witnesses, acquiring affidavits, and explaining to local branches why legal action seemed so slow in coming to fruition.

Events in the Deep South began to accelerate after 1955. In August of that year, EMMETT TILL was lynched in Money, Mississippi. Hurley, accompanied by the new NAACP field secretary in Mississippi, MEDGAR EVERS, was on the scene quickly. In order to secure affidavits from black sharecroppers in the area, Hurley disguised herself as a fieldworker and went onto the plantations, a dangerous operation under the circumstances. She also assisted in protecting the prosecution's most important witness, Mose Wright, who was Emmett Till's grandfather. The Till case was a pivotal moment in American

race relations, but it was part of a day's work for Hurley. She traveled throughout remote parts of the Deep South, seeking affidavits in cases of abuse, and encouraging local blacks to resist discrimination in all the myriad forms it took.

In 1956 the NAACP itself came under attack by Southern legislatures. In the wake of the U.S. Supreme Court's *Brown* decision, a number of Southern states sought to prohibit the NAACP from operation within their borders. Alabama succeeded in outlawing the NAACP in 1957, forcing Hurley to make an almost overnight move to Atlanta. The rapid pace of events forced Hurley to leave many of her possessions behind; typical of her style, she continued to write humorous letters to the New York office as she undertook the move. Hurley stayed in Atlanta for the rest of her career but it took the NAACP years to recover from the attacks by Southern politicians.

By 1960 the civil rights movement had exploded onto the national stage. The NAACP, with Hurley as its most important representative in the South, faced a difficult situation. It hoped to remain center-stage in the unfolding events, many of which it had laid the groundwork for in the previous decades of work. Yet the young people who seized the initiative after 1960 favored more confrontational and controversial tactics than did the NAACP leadership. Hurley was on the scene of many protests and sit-ins, helping to coordinate legal and logistical support, despite her misgivings about the methods being used. When the NAACP was called upon to raise bail money, Hurley was usually the person expected to serve as an immediate resource. Yet she remained critical of the approach many young activists employed. She also complained frequently about the lack of respect young people had for the long years of work the association (and she) had put in.

Hurley was at the center of an extraordinary number of initiatives. Into the 1970s the NAACP continued to seek school integration; Hurley often accompanied NAACP lawyers as they made court appearances throughout the South. She noted that despite the challenges of the 1950s and 1960s, the association remained on the scene and on task far longer than most of the other civil rights organizations of the 1960s. It is striking that despite Hurley's long career with the NAACP, she was not promoted higher into the leadership of the national organization. Although Hurley's name is not as familiar as that of some of the NAACP leaders of the time, her contributions to the association and to the civil rights era should not be overlooked.

FURTHER READING

"Inside the NAACP: Ruby Hurley's South," *Look* (Aug. 1957).

Papers of the NAACP. Manuscript Division, Library of Congress. Washington, D.C.

Raines, Howell. *My Soul Is Rested: The Story of the Civil Rights Movement in the Deep South* (1977).

                                    CAROLINE EMMONS

Hurston, Zora Neale (15 Jan. 1891–28 Jan. 1960), writer and anthropologist, was born Zora Lee Hurston in Notasulga, Alabama, the daughter of John Hurston, a Baptist minister and carpenter, and Lucy Ann Potts. John Hurston's family were Alabama tenant farmers until he moved to Eatonville, Florida, the first African American town incorporated in the United States. He served three terms as its mayor and is said to have written Eatonville's ordinances. Zora Neale Hurston studied at its Hungerford School, where followers of BOOKER T. WASHINGTON taught both elementary academic skills and self-reliance. Growing up in an exclusively black community gave her a unique background that informed and inspired much of her later work. Much of the chronological detail of Hurston's early life is obscured by the fact that she later claimed birth dates that varied from 1898 to 1903. Most often she cited 1901 as her birth year, but the census of 1900 lists a Zora L. Hurston, born in 1891, as the daughter of John and Lucy Hurston. According to Zora Neale Hurston's later accounts, she was nine years old when her mother died, and, when her father remarried, she left Eatonville to be "passed around the family like a bad penny." At fourteen, she reported, she joined a traveling Gilbert and Sullivan theater company as maid and wardrobe girl. After eighteen months on the road, she left the company in Baltimore, Maryland. There Hurston worked in menial positions and studied at Morgan Academy, the preparatory school operated by Morgan College.

After she graduated from Morgan Academy in 1918, Hurston moved to Washington, D.C. She worked in a variety of menial positions and was a part-time student at Howard University from 1919 to 1924. At Howard, Hurston studied with ALAIN LOCKE and LORENZO DOW TURNER, who encouraged her to write for publication. Accepted as a member of Stylus, the campus literary club, she published her first short story, "John Redding Goes to Sea," in its literary magazine, the *Stylus*, in May 1921. Three years later

CHARLES S. JOHNSON's *Opportunity*, a major literary vehicle for writers of the Harlem Renaissance, published two of Hurston's stories, "Drenched in Light" and "Spunk." In these early stories she staked out a perspective characteristic of her later African American folktales. They celebrate the lives of ordinary black people who had little interaction with or sense of oppression by a white community.

In 1925, after winning an award for "Spunk," Hurston moved to New York City, where she joined other writers and artists of the Harlem Renaissance. As secretary and chauffeur to novelist Fannie Hurst, Hurston also gained access to contemporary white literary circles. In September 1925 she began studying at Barnard College on a scholarship. Nine months later Hurston, AARON DOUGLAS, LANGSTON HUGHES, and WALLACE THURMAN launched a short-lived, avant-garde magazine, *Fire!!*. Against the claim of older African American mentors, such as W. E. B. DuBois and Alain Locke, that a black writer was obliged to express a racial consciousness in the face of white hostility, they held that the creative artist's obligation was to give voice to the vitality of an African American culture that was more than simply a reaction to white oppression. Hurston's short story "Sweat" is the most important of her published essays and short stories in this period.

At Barnard, Hurston became a student of the noted anthropologist Franz Boas. "Papa Franz," as she called him, encouraged Hurston's interest in the folklore of her people. Her first field research took Hurston to Alabama to interview a former slave, CUDJO LEWIS, for CARTER G. WOODSON's Association for the Study of Negro Life and History. Her article "Cudjo's Own Story of the Last African Slaves," which appeared in the *Journal of Negro History* (1927), was marred, however, by plagiarism from Emma Langdon Roache's *Historic Sketches of the Old South*. When Hurston received a B.A. from Barnard in 1928, she was the first African American known to have graduated from the institution.

In 1927 Hurston married Herbert Sheen, a medical student with whom she had begun a relationship in 1921 when they were both students at Howard University. Four months after their marriage, however, Hurston and Sheen parted company, and they were divorced in 1931.

Hurston's literary career illustrates the difficult struggle of an African American female writer for support and control of her work. From 1927

Zora Neale Hurston in the mid-1930s. Hurston published two important anthropological studies of African American and Caribbean folklore, as well as the well-known novel *Their Eyes Were Watching God*. (Library of Congress.)

to 1932 Hurston's field research was sponsored by a wealthy white patron, Charlotte Louise Mason. With that support, Hurston made her most important anthropological forays into the South, revisiting Alabama and Florida, breaking new ground in Louisiana, and journeying to the Bahamas. Working in rural labor camps and as an apprentice to voodoo priests, she collected an anthropologist's treasure of folklore, children's games, prayers, sermons, songs, and voodoo rites. Yet the hand that sustained was also the hand that controlled. Mason insisted that Hurston sign a contract that acknowledged the white patron's ownership of and editorial control over the publication of Hurston's research.

In the spring of 1930, Hurston and Langston Hughes collaborated in writing a play, *Mule Bone*. Only its third act was published, but in 1931 Hughes and Hurston quarreled over its authorship. When she claimed that its material was hers, he accused her of trying to take full credit for the play. The two authors never resolved their differences in the matter, but it seems clear that Hurston's anthropological research supplied the material to which Hughes gave dramatic form.

By the mid-1930s Hurston had begun to reach her stride. Her first novel, *Jonah's Gourd Vine*, was published in 1934. Its protagonist, John Buddy "Jonah" Pearson, is a folk preacher whose sermons display Hurston's mastery of the idiom. Indeed, the folk material threatens to overshadow the novel's characters and plot. Like her other work, the novel was also criticized for ignoring the effects of racial oppression in the South. In 1934, after a semester of teaching at Bethune-Cookman College in Daytona Beach, Florida, Hurston received a Rosenwald Fellowship and enrolled for graduate work in anthropology at Columbia University. Briefly in 1935–1936 she was employed as a drama coach by the Works Progress Administration (WPA) in New York. Hurston never completed a graduate degree, but she received Guggenheim field research fellowships for the 1935–1936 and 1936–1937 academic years. Her first major anthropological work, *Mules and Men*, appeared in 1935. It mined the rich lode of her research in southern African American folklore in the late 1920s and early 1930s. The Guggenheim fellowships took Hurston to Jamaica and Haiti to study Caribbean folk culture. Those studies produced her second major anthropological work, *Tell My Horse*, in 1938.

Now at the peak of her productive years, Hurston published her second major novel, *Their Eyes Were Watching God*, in 1937. Written in eight weeks, during which Hurston was recovering from a passionate romantic relationship, *Their Eyes Were Watching God* is the most successful of her novels artistically. Its heroine, Janie Starks, is a free-spirited woman who pursues her dream of emotional and spiritual fulfillment. Janie and her third husband, Tea Cake, like most of Hurston's folk subjects, enjoy their laughter and their sensuality even in their poverty. In her own life, however, Hurston was less successful in love. In 1939, after a year as an editor for the Federal Writers' Project in Florida and a year of teaching at North Carolina College in Durham, Hurston married Albert Price III, a WPA playground director who was at least fifteen years her junior. After eight months they filed for a divorce. There were attempts at a reconciliation, but the divorce became final in 1943.

Hurston's subsequent fiction was less successful artistically. *Moses, Man of the Mountain*, published in 1939, depicted the leader of the biblical exodus and lawgiver as a twentieth-century African

American witch doctor. In 1942 Hurston published her autobiography, *Dust Tracks on the Road*. It was the most successful of her books commercially. As autobiography, however, it was an accurate portrait not of Hurston's life but of the persona she wanted the public to know: an ambitious, independent, even "outrageous" woman, with a zest for life unhindered by racial barriers. Yet her life became increasingly difficult. Arrested on a morals charge involving a retarded sixteen-year-old boy, Hurston was eventually cleared of the accusations. The African American press gave graphic coverage to the sensational nature of the case, and the publicity had a devastating effect on her career. Hurston's efforts to win funding for a field trip for research in Central America were frustrated until she received an advance for a new novel. In 1947 Hurston left the United States for the British Honduras, where she did anthropological research in its black communities and completed *Seraph on the Suwanee*, her only novel whose characters are white. Published in 1948, *Seraph on the Suwanee*'s portrait of Arvay Henson Meserve as a woman entrapped in marriage might have found a more receptive audience two decades earlier or two decades later.

By 1950 Hurston's failure to find a steady source of support for her work forced her to take a position in Miami as a domestic worker. There was a stir of publicity when her employer found an article in the *Saturday Evening Post* written by her maid. During the 1940s and 1950s, however, Hurston's essays were more likely to appear in right-wing venues, such as the *American Legion Magazine* or *American Mercury*, rather than the mainstream press. By then her celebration of African American folk culture and her refusal to condemn the oppressive racial climate in which it was nurtured had allied Hurston with forces hostile to the civil rights movement. A 1950 article titled "Negro Votes Bought" seemed to oppose the enfranchisement of African Americans. Four years later, in a letter to the editor of a Florida newspaper, which was widely reprinted, Hurston attacked the U.S. Supreme Court's decision in *Brown v. Board of Education* on the grounds that it undervalued the capacity of African American institutions to educate African American people and of African American people to learn apart from a white presence.

Throughout the 1950s Hurston worked intermittently as a substitute teacher, a domestic worker, and a contributor to a local newspaper, but she was ill and without a steady income. She spent much of her time writing and revising a biography of Herod the Great, but both the subject and the language of the manuscript lacked the vitality of her earlier work. Even after a stroke in 1959, Hurston refused to ask her relatives for help. She died in the county welfare home at Fort Pierce, Florida. After a public appeal for money to pay for her burial, Hurston was laid to rest in Fort Pierce's African American cemetery. In 1973 the writer ALICE WALKER placed a granite tombstone in the cemetery, somewhere near Hurston's unmarked grave.

FURTHER READING
Material from Hurston's early career is scattered in collections at the American Philosophical Society Library, the Amistad Research Center at Tulane University, Fisk University's Special Collections, Howard University's Moorland-Spingarn Research Center, the Library of Congress, and Yale University's Beinecke Library. The Zora Neale Hurston Collection at the University of Florida includes letters and manuscripts from her later years.
Davis, Arthur P. *From the Dark Tower: Afro-American Writers, 1900–1960* (1974).
Gates, Henry Louis, Jr., and K. A. Appiah, eds. *Zora Neale Hurston: Critical Perspectives Past and Present* (1993).
Hemenway, Robert E. *Zora Neale Hurston: A Literary Biography* (1977).
Newson, Adele S. *Zora Neale Hurston: A Reference Guide* (1987).
Sundquist, Eric J. *The Hammers of Creation: Folk Culture in Modern African American Fiction* (1992).
Turner, Darwin T. *In a Minor Chord: Three Afro-American Writers and Their Search for Identity* (1971).
Walker, Alice. "In Search of Zora Neale Hurston," *Ms.* (Mar. 1975), 74–79, 85–89.
Wall, Cheryl A. *Women of the Harlem Renaissance* (1995).
Obituary: *New York Times*, 5 Feb. 1960.
This entry is taken from the *American National Biography* and is published here with the permission of the American Council of Learned Societies.

RALPH E. LUKER

Hurt, Mississippi John (3 July 1893?–2 Nov. 1966), blues singer and guitarist, was born John Smith Hurt in the hamlet of Teoc, Carroll County, Mississippi, the son of Isom Hurt and Mary Jan McLain, farmers. When he was two his family moved to Avalon, a town between Greenwood and

Grenada, Mississippi, where he remained for most of his life. He attended St. James School, dropping out after the fourth grade to help support the family. Inspired by a local guitarist, William Hilliard, who often stayed at Hurt's house, he picked up Hilliard's guitar one evening and began to make music when he was only eight years old.

Hurt's son John Jr. claimed that his father told him years later that his musical ability had come to him "in a dream … his mama sat up in bed, said, 'Oh, my son done started playing the guitar.'" Taking this as a sign of his talent, his mother bought him a secondhand guitar for a dollar and a half, and from around 1904 on he was playing local parties, picnics, and dances, as well as "serenading" local residents. He often worked with fiddlers, playing square dance music for both black and white audiences.

Along with his casual weekend music events, Hurt worked a variety of jobs: farming, maintaining river levees, and, for a brief period, lining track. Around 1923 he began to play dances with a gifted Carroll County fiddler. "There was a white dude called Willie Narmour," his son recalled. "He drew the bow on the fiddle and they played 'Carroll County Blues.' Man, you talking about fun. Then daddy, he never said a bad word, but he'd say, 'Hot dog, let's get down.'"

Hurt's association with Narmour led to his initial recording session. Through a fiddling contest, Narmour won the opportunity to record for Okeh Records; Recording director T. J. Rockwell, in Avalon to pick up Narmour, asked about other local musicians, and Narmour recommended Hurt. Supposedly they roused Hurt in the middle of the night, and after an impromptu audition Rockwell arranged to record Hurt in Memphis on 14 February 1928. Hurt cut eight sides, from which the ballad "Frankie" and the flip side "Nobody's Dirty Business" were released, and enjoyed moderate success.

Ten months later, at Rockwell's invitation, Hurt traveled to New York City by train and recorded twelve additional titles in two sessions on 21 and 28 December 1928. These included ballads, spirituals, and dance tunes as well as blues. Rockwell requested at least four "old-time tunes." Supposedly Hurt's first releases were listed as old-time music rather than as race records, demonstrating his ambivalent songster status and appeal to white listeners. Hurt later recalled that the guitarist LONNIE JOHNSON served as producer and chaperon during the New York sessions.

Hurt returned to Avalon and to his wife, Jessie Lee Cole, whom he had married in 1927 and with whom he had fourteen children, and resumed the life of a farmer and laborer. Despite his interest in more recording, he would not record again for thirty-five years.

In the 1950s, when two of Hurt's 1928 recordings, "Frankie" and "Spike Driver Blues," were included in a Folkways Records anthology of American folk music, a new audience had a chance to hear his music. By the early 1960s record collectors and blues researchers were actively hunting for blues artists who had recorded in the 1920s and 1930s. Hurt's "rediscovery" by Washington, D.C., blues enthusiast Tom Hoskins was the result of one of a half dozen fruitful searches.

Hurt could still play, his repertoire seemingly frozen in time. Hoskins persuaded Hurt to come to Washington, where he stayed with Richard K. Spottswood, an avid researcher and record producer. On 15 and 23 July 1963 Hurt recorded eighty-one songs and three folktales in Coolidge Auditorium at the Library of Congress. Public interest in his rediscovery and his music led to stories in *Time*, *Newsweek*, and the *New York Times* and appearances at the Newport Folk Festival in 1963, 1964, and 1965. Hurt relocated his family to Washington, where he became the resident artist at a club, Ontario Place. His presence in Washington sparked a local "blues revival," according to one of his musical cronies, Maryland blues singer Archie Edwards, who recalled, "You'd see people coming out of music stores with guitars—you'd say, 'Uh-oh, John has done spread an epidemic.'" Hurt signed with Dick Waterman's booking agency, Avalon Productions, which took its name from the town where Hurt grew up. Enjoying several years of fame, he appeared on NBC television's *Tonight Show*, made festival appearances, and recorded for Piedmont and Vanguard. He preferred the country life, however, and as soon as he could afford it, returned to Avalon. Hurt died in nearby Grenada.

One of the success stories of the 1960s, Hurt was lionized as the embodiment of what a folk artist should be: a friendly, gentle, deeply religious man who made countless friends and left a lasting impression on musicians and audiences alike. At heart he was a simple country person whose life was twice interrupted by celebrity, first as a rural musician who happened to be recorded in the late 1920s and then as a blues-revival hero in the 1960s. His complex three-finger guitar style, which he referred to as "cotton picking," seemed closer to East Coast tradition than that of Mississippi. Perhaps it represented an older, pre-Delta blues strain, or maybe it was simply idiosyncratic. Regardless, it was effective in supporting his varied songster repertoire, which spanned the nineteenth and twentieth centuries. His vocal approach was unforced, almost reserved, in contrast to the impassioned vocals of many Delta artists and was equally accessible to black and white audiences, whether at country dances in the 1920s or on the 1960s festival and coffeehouse circuit.

FURTHER READING

Seeger, Peter. "An Interview with Mississippi John Hurt," *Broadside*, 10 May 1967, 24 May 1967, and 7 June 1967.

Traum, Happy. *Finger-Picking Styles for Guitar* (1966).

DISCOGRAPHY

Dixon, Robert M. W., and John Godrich. *Blues and Gospel Records: 1902–1943* (1982).

This entry is taken from the *American National Biography* and is published here with the permission of the American Council of Learned Societies.

BILL MCCULLOCH AND
BARRY LEE PEARSON

Hutson, Bill (6 Sept. 1936–), painter, graphic artist, and archivist, was born William Richard Hutson in San Marcos, Texas, to Mattie Lee (Edwards) Hudson, a homemaker and employee at Texas State University, and Floyd Waymon Hudson, a laborer, bandleader, and pianist. He grew up with three siblings, Floyd Waymon Jr., Ellen Ruth, and Clarence Albert. When his father died in 1942 his family moved in with his grandmother. In 1949 he entered San Marcos Colored High School. With no art classes at school or in the segregated community, he took a drawing correspondence course in 1951 from Art Instruction, Inc. of Minneapolis, Minnesota, working odd jobs to cover costs. His mother died in 1952 at thirty-nine following a long illness, and Hutson moved to San Antonio with his siblings to live with aunts Jewel Littlejohn and Milber Jones in the East Terrace Housing Project, his uncle Wilbur Edwards adding support. There, Hutson enrolled at Phillis Wheatley High School.

Hutson's older brother Floyd encouraged his interest in photography and helped him build a darkroom in a storage area of their aunts' apartment. In 1954 he graduated from high school and joined the Air Force the same day, and was stationed in New Mexico. Working as a radar operator and technician, he was quickly promoted to sergeant,

and in 1956 began keeping a journal and taking drawing classes at the University of New Mexico. Completing his military obligations in 1957, he moved to California, where he was exposed to fine art museums, galleries, and full-time artists, and for unknown reasons, destroyed his diary. He studied design at Los Angeles City College from 1958–1959, at Los Angeles Trade Technical College in 1959, and at San Francisco Academy of Art from 1960 to 1961, where he focused on drawing and design.

In San Francisco he began collecting ephemera on African American artists and taking photographs of his travels, and started a new journal. Evicted from his room in 1961, he lost most of the artwork produced since 1959 and spent days in the reading room of Lawrence Ferlinghetti's City Lights bookstore until he worked briefly installing exhibitions at the San Francisco Museum of Modern Art. He also assisted his former San Francisco Academy of Art teacher Frank N. Ashley, one duty being reading Giorgio Vasari's book *Lives of the Artist* aloud while Ashley painted. He and Lenard Poreade collaborated with Ashley on a series of still life, cityscape, and seascape paintings that were sold in lots to hotels and signed P.A.H. (their initials).

Moving to Paris in 1963, he created abstract, low-relief collage paintings of fabric soaked in gesso and glue solutions with oil and varnish applied to unprimed canvas. In 1964 Hutson relocated to Amsterdam and married Sandra McDonald-Taylor, of whom little else is known. He also completed *Diary Series*, a group of brush-and-ink drawings later purchased by the Boysmans-Van Beunigen Museum in Rotterdam. The following year he had a one-man exhibition at John Bowles Gallery of large, canvas-based constructions, and had his first major show at the Stedelijk Museum in Apeldoorn, Holland. Hutson settled in London and worked as a bookcover designer for Triden Publishing Company. In 1966 he and his wife divorced.

Returning to Paris in 1967, Hutson painted in oils and experimented with acrylics on unstretched canvas and cloth. He was commissioned to do an etching of a Bateke mask for Editions George Visat printmaking workshop in 1969 facilitated by Roberto Matta-Echaurren. On Matta-Echaurren's advice, he went to Rome in 1970, where he met Wifredo Lam and began using invented signs and symbols inspired by African philosophy in his paintings.

Back in the United States in 1971, he met Alvin Loving, ROBERT BLACKBURN, and MEL EDWARDS in New York before a short stay in Chicago, where he received the Cassandra Foundation Award for his achievements in the Arts. In 1973 he taught at the Southwest Crafts and Creative Arts School in San Antonio before receiving a National Endowment for the Arts fellowship in painting in 1974.

He served as graphic arts adviser in the audio/visual research division of the National Museum of Art in Lagos, Nigeria, between 1974 and 1976, and resided in Senegal from 1976–1977 before returning to New York and affiliating with the Robert Blackburn Printmaking Workshop. In 1979 he was visiting artist at Louisiana State University, Baton Rouge, for one semester before serving as an adjunct lecturer at Hunter College of the City University of New York (CUNY) from 1979 until 1983. During this time at CUNY he participated in the Creative Artists Public Service Program (CAPS) in 1980. He also traveled to the Ivory Coast and Mali. He went on to become an assistant professor at Ohio State University between 1984 and 1987, worked as a visiting critic in painting at the Maryland Institute College of Art in 1988, and was a visiting artist and instructor at Johns Hopkins University in 1989.

Subsequently he began traveling extensively, conducting research, taking photographs, and collecting materials on artists of the African diaspora. As a result of his research, he went to France, Gabon (for lectures), the Netherlands, Senegal, and Spain from 1993–1998; Cambodia, Canada, France, Germany, Laos, Portugal, India, Spain, Thailand, and Vietnam from 1999 until 2001; and France, India, Myanmar (Burma), the Netherlands, and Thailand in 2002.

In 2004 he curated the traveling exhibition "Something to Look Forward To" that presented abstract art by twenty-two African American artists over age sixty. The following year he was named the Jennie Brown & Betsy Hess Cook Distinguished Artist-In-Residence at Franklin and Marshall College in Lancaster, Pennsylvania.

He was a guest speaker and instructor for numerous institutions including the University of Paris-Sorbonne Nouvelle; École Nationale d'Art et Manufacture, Libreville, Gabon; City University of New York; the Detroit Institute of Arts in Michigan; Maryland Institute College of Art and the Johns Hopkins University, both in Baltimore, Maryland. Hutson regularly pursued art information and resource materials in conjunction with personal work, and his exhibition opportunities led him to many countries around the world.

Hutson had more than thirty solo exhibitions at such venues as the Olmstead Gallery at Pennsylvania State University in Harrisburg, Studio Museum in Harlem, New York, and Louisiana State University in Baton Rouge.

Sites of the more than fifty group exhibitions in which he participated include the Cleveland Institute of Art in Ohio, Bronx Museum of Art in New York, and Museo Civico D'art Contemporanea Di Gibellina in Palmero, Italy. Hutson's work is in the collections of the Schomburg Center for Research in Black Culture in New York, Newark Museum in New Jersey, San Francisco Museum of Modern Art in California, the Paul R. Jones Collection at the University of Delaware in Newark, and in numerous corporate and private collections in North America, Africa, Asia and Europe.

FURTHER READING

Franklin and Marshall College. *Something to Look Forward To* (2004).

Logan, Fern. *The Portrait Series: Images of Contemporary African American Artists* (2001).

Studio Museum in Harlem, *Bill Hutson: Paintings, 1978–1987* (1987).

AMALIA K. AMAKI

Hutson, Jean Blackwell (7 Sept. 1914–4 Feb. 1998), librarian, archivist, bibliophile, and college professor, was born Jean Blackwell in Summerfield, Florida, to Paul O. Blackwell and Sarah Myers. Her father was a commission merchant who operated a farm, buying and shipping produce. Her mother taught elementary school. At age four she moved to Baltimore, Maryland, her mother's hometown. Paul Blackwell remained in Florida and visited the family over the years. Blackwell was a very precocious child and a voracious reader. She graduated as valedictorian from Baltimore's Frederick Douglass High School in 1931. The prestigious secondary school gave her a love of black history, which was taught by Yolande DuBois and MAY MILLER, daughters of two famous black leaders, W. E. B. DuBois and KELLY MILLER. She met the poet and writer LANGSTON HUGHES, with whom she shared a lifelong friendship, and the composer and pianist EUBIE BLAKE.

The Great Depression thwarted Blackwell's original career goal of psychiatry. Instead, she spent three years at the University of Michigan, after which her mother persuaded her to transfer to Barnard College. In 1935 Blackwell became the second black female graduate of Barnard; ZORA NEALE HURSTON was the first. Blackwell received a B.A. in English; the next year she received an M.A. from

Jean Blackwell Hutson, chief of the New York Public Library's Schomburg Collection, with Langston Hughes. (Schomburg Center for Research in Black Culture, New York Public Library.)

the Columbia School of Library Service and earned a teacher's certificate from Columbia University in 1941. In 1939 she married ANDY RAZAF, a song lyricist and FATS WALLER collaborator. The marriage ended in divorce after eight years.

Blackwell began her professional career in the New York Public Library from 1936 to 1939, when she left briefly to work as a high school librarian in Baltimore. Around 1947 she returned to the New York Public Library's Division of Negro Literature, the forerunner to the Schomburg Center, under the direction of ARTHUR SCHOMBURG. She remembered that "he arranged the books according to their color and size. So working late one night, I decided to rearrange them according to the Dewey Decimal System. When he discovered what I had done the next day, he was so angry that he fired me. I was immediately banished from the Library." Her clash with Schomburg in her first position in the New York Public Library system resulted in her reassignment to a succession of branch libraries in the Bronx and Manhattan. She also worked at several branches in the central Harlem

area. She returned to the Schomburg Collection in 1948 as curator, succeeding Dorothy Williams and LAWRENCE REDDICK. Jean Blackwell married John Hutson, a coworker, in 1952, and they adopted a baby girl. Her husband died in 1957, leaving Jean Blackwell Hutson a widow and single parent. Despite these personal tragedies, she persevered in her professional life, and under her guidance the Schomburg Collection thrived. *The Dictionary Catalog of the Schomburg Collection of Negro Literature and History* was published in 1962; two supplements and a microfilm copy made the holdings known to libraries throughout the world. During that same year Hutson became an associate adjunct professor in the history department of City College of New York, where she taught black history for almost ten years. During her tenure at the college she met President Kwame Nkrumah of Ghana while he was a student in New York City. At his urging, Hutson and his daughter spent the academic year 1964–1965 developing the African Collection at the University of Ghana.

Because of the deterioration of the 135th Street Branch Library, which had moved to the 136th Street former site of the mansion of A'LELIA WALKER's Dark Tower in 1941, Hutson began lobbying for a new building to protect the collection. With her help the Schomburg Corporation was established to raise funds and lobby for a new building. Hutson organized the corporation, lobbied politicians, and rallied the black community to preserve this heritage of their African descent. The Schomburg Collection had grown rapidly and became internationally known during the civil rights and Black Power movements of the 1960s. In 1951 the branch was renamed the Countée Cullen Branch Library after the famous poet, teacher, and friend and neighbor of the library.

Through Hutson's marketing efforts on behalf of the Schomburg collection and her speaking with various politicians and organizations, the Schomburg began to receive private and New York City and State grants. In 1965 annual city funding from the North Manhattan Project resulted in the first budgetary increase for the collection since 1948. The Ford Foundation provided a grant in 1967. The first National Endowment for the Humanities (NEH) grant provided for an inventory of the collection, the first one that had been conducted in twenty-five years. Another NEH grant enabled the massive clipping file to be microfiched and made available to the world. In recognition of her diligence and attention to the collection, Hutson's title was changed from curator to chief of the Schomburg Collection. In 1972 the Schomburg Collection was transferred to the Research Libraries Division of the New York Public Library, becoming one of four research centers within the system, and renamed the Schomburg Center for Research in Black Culture. Finally, a grant from the federal government financed the construction of a new, climate-controlled building, designed by the black architect Max Bond. In the spring of 1980 Hutson was promoted to Research Libraries Assistant Director of Collection Management and Development for Black Culture. The new block-long facility opened in September 1980 at its new address, 515 Lenox Avenue, now Malcolm X Boulevard, between 135th and 136th Streets.

Throughout her career Hutson was active in numerous civic, social, professional and cultural organizations, including Delta Sigma Theta Sorority, the American Library Association, the African Studies Association, the NAACP, and the Urban League. Hutson was a founding member of the Black Academy of Arts and Letters and served as the first president of the Harlem Cultural Council. Her community service often benefited the Schomburg. For example, the collection received entire archives, manuscripts, photographs, or organizational records from the Harry A. Williamson Masonry Collection, the *New York Amsterdam News*, the Kurt Fisher Haitian Historical Documents, the PHILIPPA DUKE SCHUYLER family, and the Melville J. Herskovits African Art collection. She persuaded her old friends, the authors RICHARD WRIGHT and Langston Hughes, to donate their correspondence and manuscripts to the Schomburg.

A bibliography of Hutson's writings is included in *Nine Decades of Scholarship: A Bibliography of the Writings, 1892–1983, of the Staff of the Schomburg Center for Research in Black Culture*. They include her foreword to ROI OTTLEY and William J. Weatherby's *The Negro in New York: An Informal Social History* (1967) and the 1978 entry on the "Schomburg Center for Research in Black Culture," published in the *Encyclopedia of Library and Information Science*.

Hutson received many honors during her lifetime, including a doctorate of humane letters from King Memorial College in Columbia, South Carolina. The Jean Blackwell Hutson Library Residence Program, University Libraries, at the State University of New York College at Buffalo offers a two-year post–master of library science position. Barnard College awarded its Medal of Distinction to Hutson in 1990, and Columbia University's School of Library Services honored her in 1992.

As an eightieth birthday tribute, the Schomburg Center celebrated Hutson's contributions during Heritage Weekend in January 1995 by naming the Jean Blackwell Hutson General Research and Reference Division in her honor. The division houses more than 150,000 volumes; the Schomburg Center itself provides access to more than 5 million items, all held under ideal environmental conditions.

Hutson died at Harlem Hospital on 4 February 1998. She worked at the Schomburg for thirty-two years, from 1948, when she was named curator there, until her retirement in 1980. Under her stewardship the Schomburg became the most comprehensive collection in the world of materials that document the history and culture of people of African descent. The collection includes not just materials about African Americans but covers the breadth of the African diaspora. Founded at the height of the Harlem Renaissance, the Schomburg's collections and exhibits have provided creative impetus to such important black artists as SPIKE LEE and ALEX HALEY and have made the production of numerous books, films, and documentaries possible.

FURTHER READING

Dodson, Howard, and Staff, Schomburg Center. *The Legacy of Arthur Alfonso Schomburg: A Celebration of the Past, A Vision for the Future* (1986).

Johnson-Cooper, Glendora. "African-American Historical Continuity: Jean Blackwell Hutson and the Schomburg Center for Research in Black Culture," in *Reclaiming the American Library Past*, ed. Suzanne Hildenbrand (1996).

Schomburg Center for Research in Black Culture. *Jean Blackwell Hutson: An Appreciation* (1984).

Schomburg Center for Research in Black Culture/St. Philip's Episcopal Church. *A Memorial Tribute to Jean Blackwell Hutson: September 7, 1914–February 4, 1998.*

Obituary: *New York Times*, 7 Feb. 1998.

SHARON HOWARD

Hutto, J. B. (26 Apr. 1926–12 June 1983), blues singer and guitarist, was born Joseph Benjamin Hutto in Elko, South Carolina, the son of Calvin Hutto and Susie Johnson, farmers. He spent his first three years on a farm but grew up primarily in Augusta, Georgia, where his family moved in 1929. Raised in a religious family, he and his siblings developed an early interest in spirituals, forming a family gospel group known as the Golden Crowns, which sang in two Augusta churches.

The family moved to Chicago sometime in the 1940s, and Hutto began working as a painter and plumber. Not yet twenty-one, he also began sneaking into clubs, he recalled later, to see blues artists such as BIG BILL BROONZY, MEMPHIS MINNIE, and MEMPHIS SLIM. With his gospel experience, Hutto was comfortable as a vocalist and was soon singing and playing drums in a band led by Johnny Ferguson, a guitarist who played in what musicians called "Sebastapol" tuning—to an open D or E chord. Given a chance to play Ferguson's guitar during breaks, Hutto began to develop his own open-tuned slide style.

In the late 1940s Hutto put together a four-piece band, the Hawks, and began playing at house parties, which he called "basement jumps," and West Side taverns such as the 1015 Club and the Globetrotter Lounge in Chicago. In the early 1950s he married Lulubelle Wade Black. Although they had no children of their own, he helped raise her two children from a previous marriage and stayed with her the rest of his life. After a stint with the military during the Korean War, Hutto returned to the West Side tavern scene in 1954, and the following year he signed with Chance Records, a small Chicago label. Hutto and the Hawks recorded nine sides, six of which were issued, including "Now She's Gone," "Lovin' You," and the aggressively erotic "Pet Cream Man." Although Chance folded soon after their release, these initial 78 rpm records gave strong indication that Hutto was coming into his own as an artist. By the late 1950s, however, he was out of the music business, disillusioned by too many ten-dollar-a-night club bookings and an incident in which a club patron supposedly broke his guitar by using it to assault her husband.

After working as an undertaker for a time, Hutto moved to the city's South Side, and by the mid-1960s he had returned to music. Playing three nights a week with a new incarnation of the Hawks at Turner's Blue Lounge, Hutto came to the attention of three documentary record producers: Sam Charters, Pete Welding, and Robert Koester. In December 1965 he recorded several songs for Charters, works that eventually made their way onto volume one of the historically significant *Chicago/The Blues/Today* series on Vanguard. In June 1966 he teamed up with the harmonica virtuoso WALTER HORTON, the guitarists Johnny Young and Lee Jackson, and the drummer Fred Below to record for Welding's Testament label. Six months later he recorded for Koester's Delmark label. Because of sound problems and illnesses, the Delmark session took two years to finish, but the resulting album was a critical success, helping spread Hutto's name beyond the city's tavern circuit.

By 1969 Hutto was living in Harvey, Illinois, after touring in California and was becoming a regular on the U.S. festival circuit and in blues and rock venues across the country. He led his first European tour in 1972. In 1975, after fellow Chicago slide guitarist HOUND DOG TAYLOR died, Hutto took over Taylor's band, the Houserockers. Two years later Hutto moved to Boston and formed yet another version of the Hawks. Despite an ongoing battle with diabetes, Hutto continued to tour and record through the late 1970s, working more and more with young, white sidemen. At the same time he began teaching two teenage nephews, James Young and Ed Williams, to carry on his music. Diagnosed with cancer in the early 1980s, Hutto moved back to Harvey, where he later died. In 1985 he was inducted into the Blues Foundation's Hall of Fame in Memphis, Tennessee.

Although he was in his twenties before he began playing guitar, Hutto developed a slashing slide attack that was partly his own and partly derived from his most important influence, ELMORE JAMES. He also became a capable songwriter. For those who saw him in the late 1960s and early 1970s, though, Hutto is best remembered for his energetic showmanship. A small, seemingly shy man off the bandstand, he was transformed during performances into what the author Bruce Cook described as a "roaring, howling Mr. Hyde, big-mouthing his blues in memorably earthy style" (142). In midsong, he would sometimes lead his band in a near-religious procession around a club, working and reworking every last nuance from a musical groove. While Hutto was not a stylistic influence in the manner of MUDDY WATERS or James, his music was carried on by his nephew's group, Lil' Ed (Williams) and the Blues Imperials.

FURTHER READING

Cook, Bruce. *Listen to the Blues* (1973).

Forte, Dan. "J. B. Hutto," in *Blues Guitar: The Men Who Made the Music*, ed. Jas Obrecht (1990).

Obituary: *Living Blues* 57 (Autumn, 1983).

DISCOGRAPHY

Leadbitter, Mike, and Neil Slaven. *Blues Records 1943–1966: A Selective Discography*, vol. 1, A–K (1987).

This entry is taken from the *American National Biography* and is published here with the permission of the American Council of Learned Societies.

BILL MCCULLOCH AND
BARRY LEE PEARSON

Hutton, Bobby (24 Apr. 1950–6 Apr. 1968), original member of the Black Panther Party. The youngest of seven children, he was born Bobby James Hutton to Dollie Hutton. His family moved from Arkansas to California when he was three years old, and following a tumultuous period in and out of school "Little Bobby" was, at age sixteen, the youngest recruit, in October 1966, of the newly formed Black Panther Party for Self-Defense (BPP). Founders HUEY NEWTON and BOBBY SEALE had supervised Hutton at the North Oakland Neighborhood Anti-Poverty Center, a government-funded agency that employed local youth to work on community service projects. Hutton served as the Black Panther Party's first treasurer until his premature death in 1968 at the hands of the Oakland police.

The BPP officially set up its first office in northern Oakland in January 1967 and began to recruit young black males, publicizing a ten-point platform whose first tenet read: "We want freedom. We want power to determine the destiny of our Black Community." Their all-black revolutionary garb of leather jackets and berets was amplified by their openly brandished weapons. A key component of the Black Panther strategy was a policing of the police—a deliberate inversion of the power politics endemic to what was for many African Americans, especially among the urban poor, a racist police state. This defiance extended to the legislature; Hutton was arrested in May 1967 when he led a protest by armed Panthers to the California state capitol in Sacramento to challenge the Mulford Act, a bill that would prohibit the carrying of loaded firearms in public places. The protest sparked a media frenzy, and the group was ultimately arrested under the felony charge of conspiracy to disrupt a legislative session.

The following year, on 6 April, two days after the assassination of MARTIN LUTHER KING JR., Bobby Hutton was killed by an Oakland police officer under suspicious circumstances. Accounts of the confrontation, which has been described both as a shoot-out and as an ambush, vary primarily with respect to who shot first but also whether Hutton was shot and killed while attempting to flee or in cold blood as he tried to surrender to police. What is generally accepted is that shots were fired and that a ninety-minute gunfight ensued wherein tear gas was fired into the house, forcing both Hutton and fellow Panther ELDRIDGE CLEAVER to leave the house and surrender. What is unknown is the extent to which the police may have been complicit in the possible planning of an ambush, or the details surrounding the actual shots fired that ended Hutton's life. The Black Panther Party maintained that an unarmed Hutton, shot at least seven times, was deliberately and brutally murdered by Oakland police as he stepped into their searchlight in surrender.

Following Hutton's death, eight members of the Black Panther Party were held on felony charges that varied from concealed weapons to attempted murder. Many blamed the police for excessive gun use in the confrontation and abuse of power—yet another example of what the Panthers had been fighting against since their inception. A grand jury concluded that the killing was justifiable and that Hutton had been trying to escape police custody.

Hutton immediately became a martyr for the cause of black power. The ambiguities and misinformation surrounding his death came to symbolize the racism within the criminal justice system he had stood so fervently against in his short years. More than two thousand mourners attended Hutton's funeral, and his death became a rallying cry of protest that propelled the Black Panther Party into the 1970s, a decade that would become fraught with internal upheaval. Bobby Hutton's life is celebrated annually in Oakland, and his legacy serves to inspire young African Americans to become involved in their communities, assuring that his death was not in vain.

FURTHER READING

Foner, Philip S., ed. *The Black Panthers Speak* (1995).

Jones, Charles, ed. *The Black Panthers Reconsidered* (1998).

Pearson, Hugh. *The Shadow of the Panther: Huey Newton and the Price of Black Power in America* (1994).

TIFFANY T. HAMELIN

Hyers, Anna Madah (c. 1853?–1930?), concert soprano, was born in Sacramento, California, the eldest of four daughters of the amateur musicians Sam B. Hyers and his wife. Anna's exact date of birth and death cannot be confirmed but most agree that she was born either in 1853 or 1855. At an early age she showed her prodigious talent. Her parents provided basic music training, and both of their daughters, Anna and EMMA LOUISE HYERS, later studied piano and voice formally with the German professor Hugo Sank and the former Italian opera singer Madame Josephine D'Ormy. On 22 April 1867 the Hyers Sisters made their professional debut at the Metropolitan Theater in Sacramento, and for the next four years they toured the California circuit and were well received by the public at each stop. Anna was said "to possess a pure, sweet soprano voice, very true, even, and flexible, of remarkable compass and smoothness" (Trotter, 162; Jackson, 550) when described by music critics and the press. Anna's "effortless high E-flat, and her birdlike trills" caused her to be likened to Jenny Lind, and recognized as one of America's first black *prima donnas* (Story, 33).

The Hyerses retired from the stage after their debut to continue study in preparation for making a cross-country tour. On 12 August 1871 the sisters returned to the concert stage and gave their first major recital at the Salt Lake Theater, accompanied by baritone Joseph LeCount, tenor Sam Hyers, and an accompanist. A succession of highly successful concerts in principal cities throughout the West—Saint Louis, Chicago, and Cleveland—gained them widespread recognition. After their triumphant tour in the West, Sam Hyers, manager of the group, expanded it to include the tenor Wallace King, baritone John Luca, and piano accompanist A. C. Taylor. Continuing the tour eastward, the troupe performed in New York City and in Brooklyn, drawing large, cultivated, and enthusiastic audiences, and were considered "a revelation" (Trotter, 172). The Hyerses were celebrities following their concerts in Massachusetts, Rhode Island, and Connecticut, and in 1872 they were invited to sing at the World Peace Jubilee in Boston. By 1875 Sam Hyers had formed the Hyers Sisters Concert Company, which was supported by Napier Lothian, director of the Boston Theater Orchestra, and with whom they gave sacred music concerts.

During the 1870s several black artists attempted to deviate from the minstrel tradition and incorporate more accurate aspects of black American culture into the content of the performance. Sam Hyers, as business manager, enlarged the company in order to produce drama as early as 1876. The company's first production was written especially for the sisters to perform on stage and was titled *Out of Bondage* (1877), a three-act musical drama adapted by Sam Hyers. This was followed by *Urlina: or The African Princess* (1877; copyright notice filed in 1872 by E. J. Getchell); *Colored Aristocracy* (1877),

in three acts; and *The Underground Railroad* (1879), in four acts. Black novelist PAULINE HOPKINS had written the latter two musical dramas. During this period the Hyerses toured nationally as the first and only black repertory company under the Redpath Lyceum Bureau. In 1883 they joined the Callendar Consolidated Spectacular Minstrel Festival at the Grand Opera House in New York and for a short period toured the nation with the minstrel troupe. This form of entertainment was popular then and was one of the few sources of consistent income for black musicians. The Hyers Sisters rejoined and expanded their own musical company with other notable talents such as BILLY KERSANDS, Celestine O. Brown, Don S. King, and pianist-composer Jacob Sawyer, among others. The company produced two musicals, *The Blackville Twins* (1887) and *Plum Pudding* (1887). Beginning in 1894 the sisters appeared in separate ventures and Anna joined John W. Isham's minstrel production "Octoroons" to sing opera excerpts in the show. By the turn of the twentieth century, she had joined the M. B. Curtis All-Star Afro-American Minstrels tour through the United States and Australia. After returning to the United States in the early 1900s, Anna appeared with Isham's Oriental American Company until 1902. Anna became the wife of a Dr. Fletcher of Sacramento and retired. She remained musically active in church and died in the 1930s.

FURTHER READING

Green, Mildred Denby. "Concert Music," in *Black Women in America—An Historical Encyclopedia*, vol. 1 (1993).

Jackson, Jacquelyn. "The Hyers Sisters," in *Notable Black American Women*, ed. Jessie Carney Smith (1992).

Southern, Eileen. *Biographical Dictionary of Afro-American and African Musicians* (1982).

Story, Rosalyn M. "Pioneers and Pathfinders," in *And So I Sing: African-American Divas of Opera and Concert* (1990).

Trotter, James M. *Music and Some Highly Musical People* (1878, rpt. 1969).

RICHLYN FAYE GODDARD

Hyers, Emma Louise (c. 1855?–189?), pioneer concert contralto, was born between 1853 and 1858 in Sacramento, California. Early on she revealed musical talent and studied music first with her parents, who were amateur musicians. She and her sister, the soprano ANNA MADAH HYERS, studied with opera singer Madame Josephine D'Ormy and piano and voice formally with Hugo Sank. They made their professional debut in their early teens, giving a joint recital, as the Hyers Sisters, to critical acclaim at the Metropolitan Theater in Sacramento on 22 April 1867. Writers praised young Emma Louise's beautiful contralto, one calling it "a voice of great power and depth … with a dark, rich timbre … that Miss Louise is a natural wonder, being a fine alto-singer, and also the possessor of a pure tenor voice" (Trotter, 162–163).

After their professional debut, the sisters retired from the stage for further study. Assisted by baritone John LeCount; their father and tenor Sam B. Hyers, and a piano accompanist, the sisters set out in 1871 to form a touring company, performing widely in the western and northern areas of the United States. The group worked its way eastward and performed at Steinway Hall in New York. It was, however, their successful appearance in 1872 at Patrick Gilmore's World Peace Jubilee concerts in Boston that solidified their fame, and by 1875 the Hyers Sisters Concert Company had been formed. Over the years popular musicians who belonged to the company included, at one time or another, the two Luca brothers, John and Alexander; tenors Wallace King and Sam Lucas, both of minstrel fame; piano accompanists A. C. Taylor and Jacob Sawyer; and violinist Claudio Jose Brindis de Salas. When the company gave concerts, talented local artists frequently made guest appearances.

In 1876 the Hyers Sisters Concert Company, under the management of their father, changed its format to become a musical-comedy company. Its first production was staged in Lynn, Massachusetts, on 20 March 1876, titled *Out of the Wilderness* and written especially for the company by Joseph Bradford. Over a period of a dozen or more years, they staged half a dozen musicals in repertory, including *Out of Bondage* (1876), a three-act musical adaptation of the Bradford play; *In and Out of Bondage* (1877), a three-act musical drama adapted by Sam Hyers; *Urlina or The African Princess* (1877, copyright notice filed in 1872 by E. S. Getchell); and both *Colored Aristocracy* (1877), a musical drama in three acts, and *Peculiar Sam: or, The Underground Railroad* (1879), a four-act musical drama, were written by black novelist, PAULINE HOPKINS. All of the Hyers's productions had racial themes; generally, the musicals began with slavery scenes, then traced the characters' adventures as they moved to freedom and a more rewarding life. For a short period during the early 1880s, Emma and Anna performed on the minstrel stage but resumed

touring with their own comic opera troupe. The Hyers produced the *Blackville Twins* (copyright notice filed in 1883 but not staged until 1887), a three-act musical drama adapted by Sam Hyers from the musical comedy by Scott Marble, with music by Fred V. Jones; and *Plum Pudding* (1887), a three-act comedy by G. M. Spence. By the fall of 1886 the Hyers had reorganized their dramatic company and were touring again with the *Out of Bondage* show. During the early 1890s the names of the Hyers Sisters appeared less frequently in the press; in April 1893 a press notice stated that they were leaving the stage and would appear only for special engagements. Thereafter no press notices to the Hyers as a duo appeared. All that can be confirmed regarding the remaining years of Emma's life is that in 1894 she performed with an *Uncle Tom's Cabin* company, and that she died shortly before 1900 in her native Sacramento, California.

FURTHER READING
Green, Mildred Denby. "Concert Music," in *Black Women in America—An Historical Encyclopedia*, vol. 1 (1993).
Jackson, Jacquelyn. "The Hyers Sisters," in *Notable Black American Women*, ed. Jessie Carney Smith (1992).
Southern, Eileen. *Biographical Dictionary of Afro-American and African Musicians* (1982).
Story, Rosalyn M. "Pioneers and Pathfinders," in *And So I Sing: African-American Divas of Opera and Concert* (1990).
Trotter, James M. *Music and Some Highly Musical People* (1878, rpt. 1969).

RICHLYN FAYE GODDARD

Hyers, May C. (June 1858–14 Feb. 1920), the first solo black female recording artist, was born in Chatham, Ontario, Canada. Little is known of her early life, including her maiden name, prior to her marriage around 1877 to fellow entertainer Sam B. Hyers (1830–1896). The marriage was Sam B. Hyers's second. His first, to Annie B. Hyers (maiden name unknown), had produced two daughters, Anna Madah and Louis Emma, who as the Hyers Sisters would earn fame in the 1870s as pioneers of black musical comedy theatre. May C. Hyers and Sam Hyers had two children, Mary Catherine Bohee and Chonita Hyers Dorsey.

From 1895 to 1896 Hyers, who used the stage name "Quagga," toured with her husband's "Colored Musical Comedy Co[mpany]." Following Sam B. Hyers's death in 1896, his company was taken over by L. Milt Boyer, who continued under the original banner of S. B. Hyers, with May C. Hyers as his principal star.

Hyers became the first black woman to make solo recordings (phonograph cylinders) for the Kansas City Talking Machine Company. In June 1898 Boyer stated, "May C. Hyers is singing better than ever. She is at present engaged, under my management, with the Kansas City Talking Machine Co." (L. Milt Boyer, *New York Clipper*, 11 June 1898). Hyers indeed made a series of recordings on wax cylinders, which sold at fifty cents each, or five dollars per dozen. A flyer for the cylinder company, which also offered an etched portrait of the singer, falsely (and perhaps mistakenly) claimed her to be one of the "Hyers Sisters": "Miss May C. Hyers (one of the Hyers Sisters) possesses a marvellous, rich and powerful contralto voice of rare brilliancy. She is so well known to the music loving public that we need not more than announce her name as being the maker of the list of records enumerated below. These records have been made by the use of a new process which we control exclusively and they possess the sweetness of voice which is so lacking in many records made by the female voice. They are suitable for either horn or tube use, as the enunciation is perfect."

The *Phonoscope* described this "new process" as follows:

Mr. H. W. Schroeder, of Kansas City, has hit upon an idea, perfected it and made successful records of a woman's voice. May C. Hyers, known as the "Black Patti," sang several solos into the phonograph, which were afterwards reproduced with good results. The method by which Mr. Schroeder has regulated the diaphragm to a woman's voice is very simple. Near the base of the horn, which conveys the voice into the machine, is a valve operated by an air bulb connected with it by a small hose. The bulb is held in the singer's hand and when she reaches particularly high notes in her song she presses the bulb, which opens the valve, allowing part of the volume of sound to escape. Thus the excessive vibration of the diaphragm is reduced and the needle properly records the tones (*Phonoscope* 2:5 [May 1898], 12).

Two different flyers of the Kansas City Talking Machine Company provide details on no less than sixty-one cylinders, numbered 200 up to 260. Hyers's repertoire is truly amazing, ranging, as it does, from "The Flag That Never Knew Defeat" to "Hot Coon from Memphis" to the "Toreador Song" from Bizet's opera "Carmen"—which makes her also the first black person to record classical music. No doubt the selection of titles reflects the popular tunes of the day as offered by the traveling troupes. It is impossible to determine the number of titles sold. Not one copy of any of the cylinders is known to have survived in either public or private collections. If found the cylinders will probably reveal piano accompaniment.

After those recordings, however, Hyers left few traces. In 1899 the "Boyer bros. 'Uncle Tom's cabin' Co. opened a new season with the Mobile Pickaninnies, Tennessee Jubilee Quartet, May C. Hyers, and others" (*New York Clipper*, 18 Nov. 1899). Four years later it was reported that "Madame Flowers, in duet with May C. Hyers are successful everywhere" as members of Grahams's Southern Specialty Co. (*New York Clipper*, 4 Apr. 1903, p. 136). After retiring from the stage, Hyers lived in Chatham, Ontario, until she passed away at age sixty-one. Her surviving relatives were her two daughters, Chonita and Mary Catherine (who had toured with her), a brother, and three sisters.

FURTHER READING

Photos of May C. Hyers and Bohee Hyers were deposited by May's granddaughter, Adrienne Dorsey Wheeler, at the Chicago Black Music Research Library. Photos of her stepdaughters, the Hyers Sisters, are deposited at Howard University Moorland—Spingarn Research Center. For biographical data on the Hyers family in California see

Abajian James de T. *Blacks in Selected Newspapers, Censuses, and Other Sources: An Index to Names and Subjects*, 7 volumes (1985–).

Abbott, Lynn, and Doug Seroff. *Out of Sight. The Rise of African American Popular Music 1889–1895* (2002).

Lotz, Rainer E. "Female Black Recording Pioneers," in *IAJRC [International Association of Jazz Record Collectors] Journal*, Vol. 40, No. 2, Summer 2007.

Sampson, Henry T. *Blacks in Blackface: A Source Book on Black Musical Shows* (1980).

Sampson, Henry T. *The Ghost Walks: A Chronological History of Blacks in Show Business, 1865–1910* (1988).

Southern, Eileen. "An Early Black Concert Company: The Hyers Sisters Combination," in *A Celebration of American Music. Words and Music in Honor of H. Wiley Hitchcock*, Richard Crawford, R. Allen Lott, and Carol J. Oja, eds. (1990).

RAINER E. LOTZ

Hyman, Flora "Flo" (31 July 1954–24 Jan. 1986), volleyball player, was born Flora Jean Hyman in Inglewood, California, to George W. Hyman, a railroad janitor and supervisor, and Warrene Hyman, the owner of the Pink Kitty Café. As a child Flo was self-conscious about her rapid growth—she stood six feet tall in junior high school—although her mother, who was also tall, encouraged her to be proud of her height and precocious athletic talent. Though she could have starred in basketball or track, in her sophomore year she took up volleyball, a game played primarily by affluent whites in nearby Redondo Beach, not by African Americans in working-class Inglewood.

In 1974 the strength and athleticism Hyman showed as a high schooler playing for the South Bay Spoilers earned her a place on the U.S. national volleyball team. That same year, the University of Houston volleyball coach Ruth N. Nelson awarded her the first athletic scholarship ever awarded to a woman at the college; Hyman characteristically refused to accept the full amount of the award so that some of her teammates might also benefit. She studied mathematics and physical education and received several honors, most notably the 1976–1977 Broderick Sports Award from the Association of Intercollegiate Athletics for Women. In 1977, after being acclaimed the nation's top collegiate player and one of the world's outstanding players, Hyman decided to forgo her senior year to practice and play full-time for the U.S. national team in preparation for the 1980 Olympics. Under Dr. Arie Selinger, a demanding but inspirational coach, Hyman hoped that the United States could match the sport's most dominant nations, though unlike Japan, the Americans lacked major corporate sponsorship, and unlike China, they lacked state support and a talent pool of 10 million players. Indeed, while basketball's WILT CHAMBERLAIN had vigorously promoted volleyball, most Americans ignored the sport, and the television networks showed no interest in broadcasting any women's team events. The American team made up for these deficiencies with a strong sense of camaraderie, which was sorely tested when the United States withdrew from the 1980 Moscow Olympics to protest the Soviet Union's invasion of Afghanistan. The Americans' absence from Moscow denied the team a major stage upon which to display its talents, but the global volleyball community took note of Hyman's skills at the 1981 World Cup, where she was selected the tournament's outstanding player, and at the world championships in 1982, when she led the United States to the bronze medal.

American sports fans began to pay attention, too. At six feet five inches tall, Hyman was the nation's most intimidating offensive player, able to spike a volleyball as fiercely and accurately as her contemporary, JULIUS ERVING of the Philadelphia 76ers, dunked a basketball. On defense, her rangy, angular frame was initially a handicap, but she overcame her reluctance to throw her body to the floor when required and soon mastered the backcourt as well. According to sports journalist George Vecsey, Hyman was also one of the most charismatic athletes of her generation. Yet if Hyman's dominance in women's volleyball in the 1980s was as great as MICHAEL JORDAN's ascendancy in basketball a decade later, her celebrity and financial rewards never came close to those of even journeymen NBA players.

Buoyed by corporate sponsorship and the patriotic fervor that accompanied the 1984 Olympics in her hometown of Los Angeles, Hyman led the U.S. women to unprecedented public acclaim and a silver medal. Having devoted ten years of her life to volleyball—often cutting short the brief vacations she allowed herself—Hyman earned plaudits for her dominating performance and for her magnanimous praise of the gold medal–winning Chinese team. Hyman made the most of the fame that the Olympics had granted her, joining the civil rights leader CORETTA SCOTT KING, the astronaut Sally Ride, and the vice presidential candidate Geraldine Ferarro at a women's rights rally during the 1984 elections.

American interest in women's volleyball proved fleeting, however, and Hyman returned to Japan, where she had begun to play professional volleyball for the Daiei team in 1982. By 1986 she had transformed Daiei, a struggling minor league team sponsored by a supermarket chain, into a leading force in Japan's major volleyball league. Hyman remained a fierce competitor, though her coaching skills and ability to read the game now mattered as much as her play on the court. Indeed, to many it seemed fitting that Flo Hyman's final words were an exhortation to a teammate, uttered shortly before she collapsed near the end of a match in Matsue City, Japan, in late January 1986. Hyman died later that evening from what was first reported as a heart attack, but later announced as complications resulting from Marfan syndrome, a hereditary disorder that often leads to a fatal rupturing of the aorta. Hyman displayed one manifestation of the syndrome, her height, but did not suffer the more telling signs of the disorder, notably curvature of the spine or breastbone. As a consequence her condition was never diagnosed, though her death helped to publicize Marfan syndrome and has encouraged athletes and others at risk from the disorder to be tested. Hyman, who never married, was buried at Inglewood Park Cemetery in her hometown, and was survived by her father, who died three years later, and eight siblings. Her posthumous awards have been many: she was inducted into the Volleyball Hall of Fame in 1988 and named by USA Volleyball as the MVP for the years 1978–2002. She was also the first woman admitted to the University of Houston's Hall of Honor in 1998.

Flo Hyman typifies the new generation of women athletes who emerged in the 1970s and 1980s. They were the first beneficiaries of Title IX, federal legislation passed in 1972 which prohibited sex discrimination in college athletic programs that received federal funding. Indeed, in 1985 Hyman and basketball player CHERYL MILLER testified on Capitol Hill in support of strengthening Title IX. Hyman's open determination to win also reflected broad changes in American gender roles. Female athletes had always exhibited strength, power, and endurance, but now they began to celebrate those attributes, as well as the more traditionally accepted virtues of speed, skill, and grace. As Hyman put it in an interview with the *New York Times* in 1983, "Pushing yourself over the barrier becomes a habit.... If you want to win the war, you've got to pay the price" (Vecsey, S3). Her widely admired resolve and sportsmanship makes it fitting, therefore, that the Women's Sports Foundation established in 1987 an annual Flo Hyman Award to the female athlete who best exemplified over the course of her career Hyman's "dignity, spirit, and commitment to excellence."

FURTHER READING
Demak, Richard. "Marfan's Syndrome: A Silent Killer," *Sports Illustrated* (18 Aug. 1986).
Vecsey, George. "America's Power in Volleyball," *New York Times*, 2 Oct. 1983.
Obituary: *New York Times*, 25 Jan. 1986.

STEVEN J. NIVEN

Hyman, John Adams (23 July 1840–14 Sept. 1891), North Carolina senator and U.S. congressman, was born a slave near Warrenton, Warren County, North Carolina. Nothing is known about his parents or his childhood. In 1861 Hyman worked as a janitor for a jeweler who with his wife taught Hyman to read and write. When that was discovered, the jeweler and his wife were driven from Warrenton, and Hyman was sold and sent to Alabama. Following the Civil War and his emancipation, having been at least eight times "bought and sold as a brute," as he described it, Hyman in 1865 returned to Warren County, where he was a farmer and store manager. Sometime between 1865 and 1867 he became a trustee of one of the first public schools in Warren County.

Hyman's formal political career began in September 1866, when at the age of twenty-six he was a delegate to the Freedmen's Convention of North Carolina. In that body he served on the Committee on Invitations, whose purpose was to ensure that influential public officials and private citizens were invited to participate in the convention. In 1867 Hyman was a delegate at the Republican State Convention and was appointed to the state executive committee. That year he served as a registrar for Warren County, organizing and assisting in black voter registration.

In 1868 Hyman was elected to the state constitutional convention. He also served as a state senator from 1868 to 1874, representing the Twentieth Senatorial District in Warren County. He was a strong advocate for black civil rights throughout his term. He opposed Andrew Johnson's leniency toward ex-Confederates, particularly his unwillingness to require ratification of the Fourteenth Amendment before states could be readmitted to the Union. In 1872 Hyman voted against the conviction of North Carolina governor William W. Holden, who was impeached for ordering the arrest of Ku Klux Klan members suspected of lynching and terrorizing blacks. Hyman, however, offered no opinion for his position. His senate career was tarnished by charges of fraud and corruption related to the selection of a penitentiary site in Warrenton and the Milton S. Littlefield–George Swepson railroad bond scandal between 1868 and 1871.

In 1872 Hyman ran for Congress but was defeated by Charles R. Thomas. In 1874 Hyman successfully won the congressional seat for the gerrymandered Second District, which included Warren County, defeating G. W. Blount by seven thousand votes. As congressman from the district referred to as the "Black Second," Hyman was a strong advocate for black civil rights. He submitted at least "fourteen petitions to Congress," asking for continuing aid to agencies assisting the freedmen (Reid, 231). He also supported relief efforts for Cherokee Indians. Hyman's congressional career ended in 1876, when he failed to gain the Republican nomination.

Hyman left Washington, D.C., in 1877, but that year President Rutherford B. Hayes appointed him special deputy collector of internal revenue for the Fourth Congressional District of North Carolina, a position he held from 2 July 1877 to 30 June 1878. By 1878 he had mortgaged or disposed of nearly all of his land to cover debts incurred while living in Washington. Hyman operated a liquor store in Warren County, joined the Colored Masons of North Carolina, and was a member of the Warrenton Negro Methodist Church, where he served as superintendent of the Sunday school. In 1879 the church leaders asked him to leave, accusing him of misappropriation of Sunday school funds and disapproving of his selling liquor.

Shortly afterward Hyman went to Washington, D.C., where he served as an assistant mail clerk until 1889. He then worked for the Agriculture Department in the seed dispensary. Hyman died of a stroke in Washington, D.C. His wife and four children survived him.

Hyman was one of five blacks elected to the North Carolina senate in 1868 and the first black and only Republican to represent the state in the Forty-fourth Congress of 1874. Though he gave few speeches, his presence in the political arena reflected Republican hopes for the reconstructed South. He gained political notoriety during an era of unprecedented racial violence in the Tarheel State. His brief success may have offered hope to newly freed blacks, indicating that they could realize, even for a brief time, the freedoms the Constitution guaranteed all persons. Although marred by corruption, Hyman's political prominence did represent, to a degree, triumph for some Reconstruction efforts in North Carolina.

Hyman's life illuminates a different interpretation of Reconstruction that contradicts the view held immediately afterward and well into the twentieth century. His career reflects the struggles of many black political leaders during an era in which North and South failed to thoroughly support the efforts of former slaves to obtain full civil rights and unconditional economic participation. Given that Hyman had been a slave for twenty-five years, his success is significant in that he surmounted adverse odds and held a visible presence in North Carolina politics. His life is symbolic of black achievement even as blacks struggled to obtain complete citizenship as guaranteed in the U.S. Constitution.

FURTHER READING

Foner, Eric. *Reconstruction: America's Unfinished Revolution, 1863–1877* (1988).

Poore, Benjamin Perley, comp. *The Political Register and Congressional Directory* (1878).

Reid, George W. "Four in Black: North Carolina's Black Congressmen, 1874–1901," *Journal of Negro History* 64 (Summer, 1979).

Obituary: *Washington Post*, 15 Sept. 1891.

This entry is taken from the *American National Biography* and is published here with the permission of the American Council of Learned Societies.

DEBI HAMLIN

Hyman, Phyllis (6 July 1949–30 June 1995), jazz, rhythm and blues, and popular music singer, songwriter, and stage and film actress, was born in Philadelphia, Pennsylvania, the oldest of seven children of Beatrice Lively, a homemaker, and Philip H. Hyman, a barber. Hyman grew up in the St. Claires Village Projects in the section of Pittsburgh called Northview Heights. Naturally gifted, Hyman enjoyed singing as a young girl, sang in school and in church, and was encouraged by her mentor and favorite teacher at Phillip Murray Elementary School, Eleanora Ferrell Lesesne. She was greatly influenced by JAMES BROWN and NANCY WILSON, her future mentor.

Attending Carrick High School, Hyman found another mentor in music teacher and jazz pianist David Tamburi, and gained valuable experience singing in the Pittsburgh public schools All-City Choir and performing with the Souls of Ebony trio at various music festivals and nightclubs She graduated from Carrick High School in 1967.

On a music scholarship, she studied at Robert Morris Business College in Coraopolis, Pennsylvania, to become a legal secretary but continued singing in her spare time at local nightclubs. Beautiful, statuesque, and six feet two inches tall, Hyman would have easily passed as a fashion model. After graduating from college, she was employed by General Electric as a file clerk, then at Westinghouse as a legal secretary, and later worked three years at Neighborhood Legal Services. But she still aspired to a career in music.

After leaving her secretarial position in 1971, she became part of Dick Morgan's R&B sextet, New Direction, and toured with them for six months in the Bahamas, Chicago, Las Vegas, Miami, and Puerto Rico. After the tour, New Direction disbanded and Hyman moved back to Pittsburgh, before relocating to Miami to pursue a full time musical career. In 1973, while performing on a cruise ship, she met Larry Alexander, a Jamaican

Phyllis Hyman gestures in a Manhattan apartment on 3 March 1976, as she speaks about her rapidly rising singing career. (AP Images.)

singer who later became her husband. In January 1974 in Miami, Hyman formed a band titled Phyllis Hyman and the P/H Factor. Alexander contacted the music producer George Kerr about Hyman, and Kerr flew from New York to hear her sing at Miami's Love Lounge. He convinced her to accept a recording contract with Kerr's Desert Moon Production and to dismantle the P/H Factor. With the availability of more singing opportunities in New York, Hyman and Alexander relocated there at the end of 1975. Alexander relinquished his singing career and became Hyman's full-time manager. At Kerr's studios in New York City, Hyman recorded eight songs, with the disco tune "Leavin' the Good Life Behind" released as a single on the Private Stock Records label.

She had frequent gigs, singing her original songs at upper west side clubs in New York, especially at Rust Brown's restaurant at 96th Street. By her second week there, she was performing nightly to packed houses with established musicians such as Cuba Gooding from Main Ingredient, George Harrison, AL JARREAU, and STEVIE WONDER in attendance. Her success at Rust Brown's led to performances at the legendary supper club, Mikell's, at 97th Street and Columbus Circle. Representatives from Arista, Atlantic, CBS, and Warner Bros. recording companies were in the audience. In late 1975, the jazz composer and arranger Onaje Allen Gumbs attended one of Hyman's performances there, and,

greatly impressed by her talent, he urged drummer and record producer Norman Connors to visit the club. After hearing her, Connors offered her a spot on his 1976 album *You Are My Starship*; Hyman recorded the 1972 hit "Betcha by Golly Wow," which made it to the top of the R&B charts, bringing her to the attention of Buddah Records. After signing with them, she released the album *Phyllis Hyman* (1977) which won World Records' Best New R&B Vocalist of 1977. In 1978, she released the R&B hit "Somewhere in My Lifetime" on the album with the same name in collaboration with Herbie Hancock. The following year in 1979 the disco dance hit "You Know How to Love Me" was issued on the album with the same title. In 1979, Buddah was acquired by Arista Records and Hyman produced several hit recordings under this label. Through the efforts of Arista's president Clive Davis, Hyman teamed up with Barry Manilow in 1979. Other hit albums by Hyman included *Can't We Fall In Love Again?* (1981) and *Goddess of Love* (1983).

Hyman married her manager Larry Alexander in 1978 and they settled in Miami before relocating back to New York. She was later cast as Etta in the hit Broadway musical *Sophisticated Ladies*, which premiered in March 1981 at the Lunt-Fontanne Theater in New York City. It led to appearances on the Mike Douglas and the Johnny Carson shows. She received a Tony award nomination in 1981 for Best Supporting Actress in a Musical and received the Theatre World Award for Best Newcomer. She performed in the musical until 1983 and this, along with her recordings, brought Hyman more popularity

A conflict arose between Hyman and Arista Records and they did not renew her contract in 1982. Hyman earned a living by singing at nightclubs, performing background and voice-over vocals, and singing in television advertisements for American Airlines, Bain de Soleil, Burger King, Clairol, MasterCard, Sassoon Jeans, and Welch's Grape Drink. She also became the spokeswoman for Clairol's *Born Beautiful* products, ambassador for Revlon's *Polished Amber* makeup, and promoter for Fashion Fair Cosmetics.

During this time Hyman and Alexander were experiencing marital problems which led to their separation in 1982 and divorce in 1986. In 1986, Hyman signed with Philadelphia International Records (PIR) and released some of her greatest albums: *Living All Alone* (1986) and *Prime of My Life* (1991), which included the number one rap hit "Don't Wanna Change the World." Top ten hits on the album included "When You Get Right Down to It," "I Found Love," and "Living in Confusion." She also performed in several films and movie sound tracks, such as *Lenny* (1974); *Children of Sanchez* (1978); *The Fish That Saved Pittsburgh* (1979); *Too Scared to Scream* (1985); *School Daze* (1988); *Norman the Doorman* (1989); and *The Kill Reflex* (1990); and on Barry Manilow CBS television special, *Swing Street*, in 1987.

In 1988 Hyman was invited as guest artist of the International Tokyo Music Festival. By 1989, personal problems had taken hold of her life. She gained weight, became insecure, was addicted to alcohol, plagued by financial problems, and worried about growing old and not attaining the fame she felt she deserved. Despite this, she continued performing as many as 120 concerts annually and recording. Deeply affecting Hyman in 1993 were the deaths of her mother (22 May 1993), grandmother, and her friend Linda Creed (co-composer of her early hit "Betcha by Golly Wow") within a month of each other. Some believed that these events may have pushed her over the edge, along with her involvement with the AIDS crisis. In 1995 she released her last album, *I Refuse to Be Lonely*, on the PIR label.

She was scheduled to appear at the Apollo Theater in New York City on 30 June 1995 as the opening act for the musical group, the Whispers. When her assistant Lenice Malina arrived at her apartment at 211 West 56th St around 2 P.M., Hyman was found unconscious in bed. Next to her were bottles of pills, vodka, and suicide letters. She was rushed to Roosevelt Hospital, where she died. The previous week, a heavier, sad, and despondent Hyman had appeared on *The Arsenio Hall Show* where she openly spoke of her loneliness, despondency, and depression.

Many questioned why she killed herself, but no specific reason was found. Numerous tributes were made in her honor, such as the All Stars Project Phat Friend Award, which was renamed in her honor in 1996 to the Phyllis Hyman Phat Friend Award for adult community heroes who administered valuable youth services in New York. The Whispers paid tribute to Hyman in the musical biography on Hyman's life titled *Thank God! The Beat Goes On*. Written by Loren Dean Harper and Barry Singer and produced by Michael Gardner with additional music by David Whitfield, it premiered at New York's Beacon Theatre in October 1997. Hyman recorded some of her best performances shortly before her death and some newly recorded songs and albums were released posthumously.

Hyman was an exceptionally gifted singer. Her distinctly beautiful, emotional, and dexterous contralto voice commanded international attention and won high acclaim. Remembered as a humanitarian who cared about those around her and was generous to those in need, Hyman actively participated in AIDS benefit concerts, spent time with AIDS patients at New York hospitals and hospices, and was deeply affected by their plight. She was an active woman's advocate and helped raise social awareness on woman's issues, especially battery and rape. Described as fun-loving, a perfectionist, and a no-nonsense person, Hyman's shocking and unexpected departure left an emptiness in the music world for some time.

FURTHER READING

Ali, Michael. "The Life & Times of Jazz Great Phyllis Hyman." *Oakland Post*, 16 July 1995.

"Fans and Friends Mourn Tragic Death of Singer." *Jet* 88 (July 24, 1995):52–61.

Grimaldi, Michael. "Phyllis Hyman Biography." *Phyllis Hyman Internet Newsletter*, online at http://members.tripod.com/~lowando/biog.html.

Manheim, James M. "Phyllis Hyman." *Contemporary Black Biography*. Vol. 19. (1999.)

"Phyllis Hyman Remembered." *A Touch of Classic Soul: the Music You Love From Back in the Day* 1 (no. 1, January, 2006). Online at http://blog.myspace.com/blog/rss.cfm?friendID=84388226.

Obituaries: Harrington, Richard. "Phyllis Hyman Is Dead at 45; Singer Was a Favorite in Washington." *Washington Post*, 1 July 1995;

"Phyllis Hyman, Jazz Singer, 45." *New York Times* July 1, 1995, online at http://www.nytimes.com/1995/07/01/obituaries/Phyllis-hyman-jazz-singer-45.html.

BARBARA BONOUS-SMIT

Ice Cube (15 June 1969–), hip-hop artist, actor, record executive, and movie executive, was born O'Shea Jackson in Los Angeles, California, to Hosea and Doris Jackson. Both his parents were employed at the University of California at Los Angeles, his father as a machinist and groundskeeper and his mother as a clerk. Though Jackson was raised in South Central Los Angeles, he was bused to the suburbs of the San Fernando Valley to attend William Howard Taft High School. While in high school Jackson grew fascinated with hip-hop culture; he began writing raps in earnest in ninth grade, after winning an informal contest with a classmate to see who could compose the better rhyme. Fascinated with the pimp-turned-author ICEBERG SLIM (ROBERT BECK), Jackson adopted the name Ice Cube.

In the mid-1980s Ice Cube and two friends, K-Dee and Sir Jinx, formed a group, C.I.A. (Criminals in Action). A local disc jockey, ANDRÉ "DR. DRE" YOUNG, took an interest in the trio. He helped the group land gigs at various Los Angeles–area nightclubs, particularly in the Compton area. With Young as a mentor, the trio gained a reputation as an entertaining live act. Its routine consisted of performing raunchy parodies of popular hits of the day. In 1987 C.I.A. convinced Alonzo "Lonzo" Williams, the owner of a Compton club, to record and release their music on vinyl. Ice Cube and Young wrote raps for Ruthless Records, a label founded by a former drug dealer named Eric "Eazy-E" Wright.

In 1987 Ice Cube graduated from high school, and moved to Phoenix, Arizona, to pursue an architectural drafting degree at the Phoenix Institute of Technology. He returned to Los Angeles the following year and discovered that Young and Wright had recorded a song he had written titled "Boyz-N-The Hood." The single was a huge local hit and the trio—along with MC Ren, DJ Yella, and, for a brief moment, Arabian Prince—formed the group N.W.A., or Niggaz With Attitude. N.W.A.'s debut album, *Straight Outta Compton* (1988), represented a startling shift in the evolution of hip hop. Dark, unapologetically violent, and proud, it laid down the foundation for a subgenre of hip-hop that became "gangsta rap."

Though Ice Cube's lyrics and boisterous attitude made him one of N.W.A.'s featured stars, he quit the group in 1989 after an angry dispute over royalties with Jerry Heller, the group's manager, and Young. Ice Cube formed a new record label, Street Knowledge, and temporarily relocated to New York City to collaborate with the Bomb Squad, a production team notable for its work with Public Enemy. In 1990 he released *Amerikkka's Most Wanted*, a commercial and critical success that separated him from the music of N.W.A. Later that year Ice Cube also released the *Kill at Will* EP, a nuanced and occasionally introspective release that suggested a nascent political awareness.

In 1991, Ice Cube starred in JOHN SINGLETON's *Boyz n the Hood*. Although Ice Cube had little acting experience, he earned critical praise for his portrayal of a conflicted drug dealer named Doughboy. The film was a surprise critical and commercial success, and Singleton earned two Academy Award nominations. During the film's production in South

Central, Ice Cube befriended Craig "Kam" Miller, a rapper and former gang member active in the local Muslim community. Miller introduced Ice Cube to Khallid Abdul Muhammad, the charismatic head of a local mosque. Later that year Ice Cube released *Death Certificate*, a furious and vulgar album that arguably represented his attempts to make sense of his own seemingly limitless rage. In an unprecedented move, *Billboard*, the leading music industry trade magazine, condemned the album. Despite Ice Cube's frequent calls for unity and empowerment within the African American community, he also espoused deeply intolerant attitudes toward Korean Americans ("Black Korea") and Jewish Americans ("No Vaseline").

The controversy that ensued only boosted Ice Cube's profile, especially with N.W.A. in disarray. In 1992 he was the sole rapper on the Lollapalooza package tour, winning him a devoted following among the tour's predominantly white attendees. He released his next album, *The Predator*, at the end of 1992. The album, which formalized his association with the Nation of Islam, became his most popular release to date. Critics, however, found it wanting. Many speculated that the Los Angeles riots, which had occurred that spring, had dissolved the prophetic bravado that was at the heart of Ice Cube's first striking material. Additionally, the sound of West Coast "gangsta rap" had changed following the 1992 release of Dr. Dre's solo debut album, *The Chronic*. Observers noted that its new melodic, laidback sound (known as "G-funk"), and hedonistic lyrics offered a stark contrast to Ice Cube's gritty realism. His next album, *Lethal Injection* (1993), would be his last solo effort for nearly five years. In the interim, he produced albums for other groups who had emulated him, Da Lench Mob and Kam, and formed a group with the rappers W.C. and Mack 10 called Westside Connection. In 1992 he married Kim Jackson, with whom he had four children.

Ice Cube devoted much of his time in the 1990s to film projects. Following the success of *Boyz*, his work in the movies *The Glass Shield* (1994) and *Higher Learning* (1995) was also well received critically. He also began directing music videos and writing screenplays. In 1995 he wrote, produced, and starred in *Friday*, a surprising hit comedy about two friends who become indebted to a local drug dealer. In 1998 he founded Cube Vision, a film production company. In 2002 Cube Vision produced *Barbershop*, a comedy that cemented Ice Cube's reputation as both a versatile actor and an adroit executive. A string of family-oriented films such as *Friday*

after Next (2002), *Barbershop 2* (2004), and *Are We There Yet?* (2004), capitalized on Ice Cube's skill as a comedic actor—a truly unlikely metamorphosis for one of the most eloquent, beloved and controversial outlaws in hip-hop history. His work in comedy continued with films such as *First Sunday* (2008), *Longshots* (2008), *Janky Promoters* (2009), *Lottery Ticket* (2009) and a television version of *Are We There Yet?* (2009-10). In addition, Cube released his ninth studio album, *I Am the West*, in 2010.

FURTHER READING

Bogdanov, Vladimir, ed. *The All Music Guide to Hip-Hop: The Definitive Guide to Rap and Hip-Hop* (2003).

Chang, Jeff. *Can't Stop Won't Stop: A History of the Hip-Hop Generation* (2005).

Light, Alan, ed. *The Vibe History of Hip Hop* (1999).

McIver, Joel. *Ice Cube: Attitude* (2002).

Nashawaty, Chris. "They Call Him Mister Cube," *Entertainment Weekly* (15 Nov. 2002).

HUA HSU

Iceberg Slim. *See* Beck, Robert "Iceberg Slim."

Ice-T (16 Feb. 1958–), hip-hop artist and actor, was born Tracy Marrow in Newark, New Jersey, to Solomon Marrow and Alice (maiden name unknown) but relocated to the Crenshaw district of South Central Los Angeles, California, following the untimely deaths of his parents due to heart failure. There he was raised by an aunt. Unfocused and undisciplined, Marrow drifted into a life of crime and violence as a member of the Crips street gang. He attended Crenshaw High School, where he became known for entertaining his classmates with impromptu performances of rhyming poetry. In high school he began going by the name "Ice-T," a moniker inspired in part by the onetime pimp, novelist, and poet Iceberg Slim. Marrow had memorized much of Iceberg Slim's work and frequently recited it to listeners. In 1979 Marrow left school to join the U.S. Army. He served in the military until 1981. Upon his discharge he sought a career in the music and recording industries. The early 1980s represented a transitional phase for rap music. Ice-T, like other rap artists on both the East and the West Coasts, charted a new direction for hip-hop, moving it away from its origins as party music into areas of sophisticated social criticism and trivial exploitation of gratuitous sex and violence. In 1984 Ice-T landed a small role in *Breakin'*, the cult-classic small-budget film about rap artists.

Ice-T performed "There Goes the Neighborhood" during his appearance on "The Arsenio Hall Show" at Paramount Studios in Los Angeles, July 1992. (AP images.)

Three years later he released his debut album on Sire Records, *Rhyme Pays*, an effort frequently credited as the first successful West Coast hip-hop record. Also in 1987 Ice-T cut the title track to the hit film *Colors*, a movie that portrayed violence and street life in South Central Los Angeles through the eyes of two policemen. Ice-T's song, also called "Colors" and marked by the performer's signature baritone growl, characterized much of his future work and brought Ice-T to the attention of a larger audience. Basically a form of thinly veiled artistic reportage, Ice-T's "gangster" style hip-hop made free and often gratuitous use of violent imagery, misogynistic appraisals of women (often invoked only as objects of sexual interest), and expressions of intense dislike for uniformed authority figures. His next album in 1988, *Power*, released under his new Rhyme Syndicate label, was a record that followed this "gangster" mold. Songs such as "The Syndicate," "Power," and "Grand Larceny" pretended to realistically portray the lives and attitudes of the streetwise and criminally inclined. Although Ice-T

held that the album was implicitly antigang, many observers criticized the record's profane language, sexist imagery, and violence. Even the explicitly antidrug "Pusher/I'm Your Pusherman" failed to quiet accusations that Ice-T was advocating the "gangster life" to his listeners. *Power*, like *Rhyme Pays*, went gold, and the effort went far in establishing Ice-T as a dominant figure on the West Coast hip-hop scene. In 1989 he advanced this status by responding to the criticisms surrounding hip-hop with *The Iceberg/Freedom of Speech … Just Watch What You Say*. With quick-witted and fearless cuts like "Freedom of Speech," "Peel Their Caps Back," "The Iceberg," and the heavy-metal inflected "The Girl Tried to Kill Me"—not to mention its provocative cover art featuring a drawing of a young black man with gun barrels inserted into his mouth and both ears—the album represented what commercial hip-hop had become by the late 1980s: deep-grooving and inventive if occasionally offensive.

In 1991 Ice-T produced what many considered his signature rap album, *O.G.: Original Gangster*. The record included the rampaging title track to the crime film *New Jack City* (in which Ice-T also played a supporting role), the self-aggrandizing "O.G. Original Gangster," and the horror-metal stomp "Midnight." Besides being a staple of early nineties West Coast hip-hop, *Original Gangster* introduced a musical act called Body Count, a heavy metal band that Ice-T had cut a single with previously. In 1992 Ice-T released an entire album with Body Count. One song, "Cop Killer," set off a firestorm of controversy that eventually led Ice-T to split with his record label, Warner Brothers. "Cop Killer" was protested by the National Rifle Association (NRA) as well as by a number of political and social interest groups. The controversy led to a highly publicized media battle between Ice-T and Darryl Gates, the outgoing chief of the Los Angeles Police Department. Many critics of hip-hop music used "Cop Killer" as an excuse to criticize the genre for its corrosive effects on young people and society in general. The familiar counterprotest that the song was merely intended as reportage of a particular point of view largely fell on deaf ears. Ice-T's antigang advocacy work likewise proved unconvincing. Time Warner eventually removed the song from the album and ironically replaced it with "Freedom of Speech." The controversial "Cop Killer" outcry signaled the end of Ice-T's run as a staple on the hip-hop scene. Though he cut more albums, including others with Body Count, none attracted the attention of his earlier efforts.

Throughout his career Ice-T appeared in a number of films and television programs, including *Tank Girl* (1995), *Johnny Mnemonic* (1995), and *Leprechaun in the Hood* (2000). His most familiar role, however, was that of Detective Fin Tutuola on television's *Law and Order: Special Victims Unit*, a long-running and highly successful police drama. Ice-T released his eighth album, *Gangsta Rap*, in 2006, and appeared in his first reality TV show, *Ice-T's Rap School*, on VH-1 the same year. In 2011 he and his wife appeared in another reality TV show, *Ice Loves Coco*, on the E! network.

In 2004 Ice-T married Nicole Austin, a model. He had three children, each with a different woman with whom he was involved before his marriage.

FURTHER READING

Ice-T. *The Ice Opinion: Who Gives a Fuck?* (1994).

Ro, Ronin. *Gangsta: Merchandizing the Rhymes of Violence* (1996).

Rose, Tricia. *Black Noise: Rap Music and Black Culture in Contemporary America* (1994).

JASON PHILIP MILLER

Ifill, Gwen (29 Sept. 1955–), journalist, television news correspondent, and author, was born in Queens, New York, the fifth child of Eleanor Ifill, a homemaker, and O. Urcille Ifill Sr., an African Methodist Episcopal minister. Due to her father's occupation, Ifill grew up with a strong religious background and moved around often in the northeastern United States. Both of her parents emigrated to the United States, her mother from Barbados and her father from Panama. Ifill went to high school in Buffalo, New York. In the *Washington Post*, Ifill commented to Howard Kurtz, "We were very conscious of the fact that we didn't have any money. I make more money in a week than my father made in a year." Ifill's love of journalism was fueled at an early age by her parents, who would insist that their children gather around the television nightly watching the national news. Later, Ifill went on to attend Simmons College in Boston, where she majored in Communications, graduating with her bachelor's degree in 1977. From an internship as a senior at the Boston *Herald-American*, Ifill became a food columnist. Ifill is quoted on the *PBS NewsHour* Web site saying, "I always knew I wanted to be a journalist, and my first love was newspapers."

Ifill stayed at the *Boston Herald American* until 1980. In 1981 she began working for the *Baltimore Evening Sun* where she focused on politics by covering City Hall. After three years there, Ifill began a career at the *Washington Post*, which moved her to Washington, D.C. In 1988, while at the *Post*, Ifill was promoted to the national news desk, where she covered the Republican National Convention. Ifill credits her experience with a political paper for teaching her what she knows today about the intricacies of politics. In 1991, Ifill began working at the *New York Times* as a reporter based out of D.C. She began her first assignment on the campaign trail of the Democratic presidential candidate Bill Clinton. Due to her mother's illness and having to move her closer to her home in Washington, Ifill felt that she could not adequately attend to all her duties, so she resigned in 1994.

Much sought after as a reporter, Ifill received job offers from three major news networks; she finally accepted an offer from NBC news and became the congressional correspondent at their Washington Bureau. During her tenure at NBC news, Ifill reported on the congressional budget gridlock of 1995, the Whitewater investigations, and President Clinton's impeachment hearings, as well as appearing as a guest on shows such as *Meet the Press*, *Washington Week*, *Nightly News with Tom Brokaw*, and *Today*.

She began working at PBS in 1999. In 1999 she became senior correspondent on *The NewsHour with Jim Lehrer* and has been moderator and managing editor of *Washington Week* since 1999. At *NewsHour*, she is responsible for interviews with key figures in political offices and sometimes fills in as news anchor for Jim Lehrer. With this position, Ifill is the first woman and African American to ever moderate the show. In 2004 and then in 2008, Ifill moderated the vice presidential debates, the first between Republican Dick Cheney and Democrat John Edwards, the second between Republican Sarah Palin and Democrat Joe Biden. Ifill also authored the book *The Breakthrough: Politics and Race in the Age of Obama*, which was published in 2009. The fact that she was working on that book during the presidential campaign prompted some Republicans to accuse her of a bias toward presidential candidate Senator BARACK OBAMA (D-IL) ahead of the 2008 debate. She denied the charge, making clear that her book was an analysis of the role of race and politics in the twenty-first century, not a pro-Obama discourse. Upon its publication in 2009, most commentators agreed that it was not partisan; the *USA Today* reporter Bob Minzesheimer described the book as "less about Barack Obama's victory than a generational

Gwen Ifill questions Attorney General Eric Holder during a NAACP Legal Defense and Educational Fund luncheon at the National Press Club in Washington on May 13, 2009. (AP Images.)

shift among black politicians and voters, black and white."

Ifill is a member of several organizations including Harvard University's Institute of Politics and the Committee to Protect Journalists; she also chairs the Robert F. Kennedy Memorial Journalism Awards. She has been honored by the Radio Television Digital News Foundation (2006), Harvard's Joan Shorenstein Center (2009), The National Association of Black Journalists (2009), Boston's Ford Hall Forum (2009), and was included in *Ebony* magazine's list of 150 Most Influential African Americans (2009) for her work in journalism. Ifill has received fifteen honorary degrees. When reflecting on her lack of anonymity as a television reporter, Ifill told the *Christian Science Monitor*, "I can't stress how important it is that young people know that anything is possible for them, and that if it means that a little black girl sitting in her living room somewhere sees me on TV and thinks 'maybe I could do that,'

then I feel like my day's work is done. I want to be that kind of example" (Lamb).

FURTHER READING

"Gwen Ifill." *PBS NewsHour*. http://www.pbs.org/ newshour/aboutus/bio_ifill.html.

Howard, Kurtz. "A Steady Faith in Herself; 'Washington Week' Host Followed Her Own Path." *Washington Post*, 1 Oct. 1999, C1.

Lamb, Gregory M. "Ifill Brings Grace, Warmth to PBS Talk." *Christian Science Monitor*, 26 May 2000, 13.

Minzesheimer, Bob. "Ifill's *Politics and Race* Goes beyond Obama." *USA Today*, 19 Jan. 2009.

ELIZABETH OKIGBO

Iginla, Jarome (1 July 1977–), hockey player, was born Jarome Arthur-Leigh Adekunle Tij Junior Elvis Iginla in Edmonton, Alberta, to Elvis Iginla, a lawyer originally from Nigeria, and Susan Schuchard, a teacher whose family moved from

Jarome Iginla, center, playing against Dallas Stars' goalie Andrew Raycroft, right, and Brenden Morrow during a 2011 Flames' game in Calgary, Alberta. (AP Images.)

Medford, Oregon, to Canada in the 1960s mainly due to their opposition to the Vietnam War. His parents divorced when he was not yet two years old. Following the separation in 1978, mother and son resided with Iginla's grandparents, Rick and Frances Schuchard, who assisted in raising him. In his early teens Iginla developed into a gifted multisport athlete, excelling in both hockey and baseball, but eventually decided to focus exclusively on hockey.

As a member of the St. Albert Raiders, Iginla led the Alberta Midget League in 1992–1993 with eighty-seven points. His stellar play continued in the Canadian Junior League with the Kamloops Blazers where he was an integral part of their success. The Blazers won back to back Memorial Cups (1994–1995), the premier North American junior hockey tournament. For his performance in that championship, Iginla was honored with the 1995 George Parsons Trophy for sportsmanship. On 8 July 1995 Iginla was the eleventh player selected in the first round of the NHL Entry Draft by the Dallas Stars, who traded him later that year to the Calgary Flames. He finished his junior career in 1996 playing

one final season for the Blazers, and although the team fell short in their playoff run, Iginla won the Four Broncos Memorial Trophy for most valuable player. Iginla's offensive skills were further showcased in the 1996 Junior World Championships held in Boston, where his prolific goal scoring propelled the Canadian team to a gold medal victory.

Nineteen-year-old Iginla made an immediate impact for the Calgary Flames as a novice right winger in the 1996–1997 NHL season, finishing second in the voting for the prestigious Caldor Trophy awarded to the best rookie of the year. The year 2002 turned out to be a breakthrough year for Iginla, who reached several professional and personal milestones. He became the first black player to win the Art Ross Trophy as the National Hockey League's top scorer, the Maurice "Rocket" Richard Trophy for most goals, and he was runner up for the Hart Trophy given to the league's MVP. Iginla was lauded as a national hero when as a member of the Canadian Olympic hockey team in the 2002 Salt Lake Winter Games he netted two goals as Canada defeated the United States 5–2 to win its first gold medal since 1952.

Iginla's prominent role in Canada's victory compounded by his ascendancy as one of hockey's most talented young stars drew the attention of fans throughout North America and provided a forum for a dialogue on the dearth of minority players in professional hockey. Neither Iginla nor his mother shied away from the subject matter, noting that while he faced little in the way of open discrimination, he did encounter naysayers who doubted that a black player could become a bona fide star in the NHL. In interviews following the Olympics, he acknowledged childhood heroes like goaltender GRANT FUHR, and left-winger TONY McKEGNEY, for inspiring him; and put the spotlight on pioneers like WILLIE O'REE, who finally desegregated the NHL on 18 January 1958, lacing up his skates for the Boston Bruins.

In 2004 Iginla repeated his previous scoring domination, winning a second Art Ross Trophy, and more than justified his elevation to the captaincy of the Calgary Flames by leading his team to the Stanley Cup finals, losing a hard-fought seven-game series to the Tampa Bay Lightning. That year, Iginla married his long-time girlfriend, Kara Kirland, whom he met when they were both twelve years old. The couple has three children, Jade, Tij, and Joe, the youngest, who was born in 2008.

Inginla played his 1,000th NHL game as a Calgary Flame on 5 February 2010 with his family in attendance. Later that month he made his third appearance as an Olympian earning his second gold medal with team Canada. At the outset of the 2010–2011 season Iginla had scored thirty goals nine times in his career and was on his way to reaching the five-hundred goal mark, a feat achieved by only forty-one players.

Despite his many hockey achievements, friends and peers are quick to draw attention to Iginla's professionalism on and off the ice, and to his generosity. Since 2002 he has spent part of his off-season mentoring young hockey players for the Jarome Iginla–Cassie Campbell Hockey School, and is a longtime supporter of organizations such as Kid Sport, the British Columbia SPCA, and Doctors without Borders.

FURTHER READING

Farber, Michael. "The Great Iginla," *Sports Illustrated*, 31 May 2004.

Harris, Cecil. *Breaking the Ice: The Black Experience in Professional Hockey* (2004).

Zernike, Kate. "Olympics: The Pioneer a Humble Iginla Raises His Profile," *New York Times*, 23 Feb. 2002.

DÁLIA LEONARDO

Ihetu, Richard "Dick Tiger" (14 Aug. 1929–14 Dec. 1971), boxer, was born in Amaigbo, Nigeria. There is little information on either his mother or father, although it is known that Ihetu spent his early years working on his father's farm in rural Nigeria. Both to escape the drudgery of agricultural work and to earn extra money, the young Ihetu was soon engaged in street fights in the local market village. His determination and power eventually brought him to the attention of British soldiers stationed nearby. By 1952 they had taken the young man under their wings and were providing him with more substantial training in the art of boxing. He turned professional that same year.

From 1952 through 1954 Ihetu (now fighting under the more colorful name of "Dick Tiger") fought exclusively in Nigeria. He rattled off ten straight victories but then met his match in Tommy West, whom he fought for the Nigerian Middleweight Championship in 1953, losing by a technical knockout. In a rematch in 1954 West again won, this time on points. After four more victories in Nigeria, Tiger moved to England in 1955 to seek better fights and richer paydays. His first few months in England were hardly auspicious. From December 1955 through March 1956, Tiger lost four consecutive decisions. For the next three years, Tiger, now fighting exclusively in England, put together a respectable record of nineteen wins, four losses, and a draw. In 1958 he won the British Empire Middleweight Championship by knocking out Pat McAteer in nine rounds.

Having accomplished what he could in England, in 1959 Tiger made his American debut. Again the immediate results were not impressive. In his first fights in the United States, Tiger managed just five wins, two losses, and a draw. There were signs of promise, however, as he split a pair of fights with the future middleweight champion Joey Giardello. In 1960 his career took another slip when he lost his British middleweight belt to Wilf Greaves in a fight in Canada. Perhaps the loss sparked something in Tiger, but whatever the motivation he became a terror in the middleweight and light-heavyweight ranks for the next seven years.

He began his climb to the top by knocking out Greaves in a rematch and regaining the British title, then won all four of his fights in 1961. He continued his march in 1962, winning his first two fights, including a decision over the dangerous contender Henry Hank. That victory earned him a shot at the rugged middleweight champion of the world Gene Fullmer. A crude fighter who was not above engaging in questionable tactics, Fullmer made nearly every one of his fights a contest of endurance. In October 1963 Tiger earned a decision after fifteen grueling rounds. The fight was so close, however, that a rematch was inevitable and so the two men went at each other again in February 1963. This time the bout ended in a draw, making a third match all but a necessity. In August of that year, Tiger and his arch-nemesis met for the final time, this time fighting in Nigeria. Tiger did not leave the matter up to the judges, subjecting Fullmer to a beating until the referee stepped in and stopped the fight in the eighth round. Fullmer announced his retirement shortly thereafter.

Tiger did not enjoy his new status as world champion for long. In December 1963 he fought a familiar foe—Joey Giardello. The result was a points victory for Giardello, a decision that left Tiger frustrated and bitter. A loss to the streaking Joey Archer in October 1964 seemed to suggest that perhaps Tiger was losing his edge. But he quickly rebounded with two wins in 1965, including a victory over the dangerous RUBIN "HURRICANE" CARTER. This earned him a rematch with Giardello, and Tiger exacted his revenge by decisioning the champion over fifteen rounds. The roller-coaster character of his career continued, however, as he lost the middleweight title to Emile Griffith in April 1966.

Unable to secure a rematch with Griffith, Tiger then announced that he would henceforth campaign as a light heavyweight. In December 1966 he decisioned Jose Torres for the world light-heavyweight championship and then defended his new crown three times in 1967. In May 1968 Tiger put his title on the line against the vicious punching of Bob Foster. In four rounds, Foster accomplished what no other fighter could ever do: put Dick Tiger down for the count. The four-round knockout loss to Foster effectively ended Tiger's days as a top contender. He fought just four more times over the next three years, showing that he still retained some skills by outpointing the world middleweight champion Nino Benvenuti in a non-title bout. In July 1970 he entered the ring for the last time against his old enemy Emile Griffith, who was by that time also going downhill as a fighter. Griffith won a decision. The next year, Tiger announced his retirement from the ring. He finished with a record of sixty-one wins, seventeen losses, and three draws.

Unfortunately, retirement was not a happy time for the still young man. Although he had made good money during his career he saw all of it go up in flames. During the mid-1960s Tiger was a staunch partisan for the cause of Biafra, the secessionist state that announced its separation from Nigeria in 1967. In 1966 he demonstrated his great commitment to the Biafran cause when he officially returned his Order of the British Empire medal to the British government in protest of its support of Nigeria in the brewing conflict. The war between Nigeria and Biafra, which lasted until 1970, resulted in untold numbers of deaths. For Tiger, the result was the loss of nearly all of his investments in Nigeria and Biafra. After his retirement, he even briefly served as a security guard at the Metropolitan Museum of Art in New York City. In 1971 doctors diagnosed him with serious liver problems and it was suspected that he had developed cancer of the liver. Wishing to spend his last days in his home country, Tiger traveled to Nigeria, where he died. In 1991 he was inducted into the International Boxing Hall of Fame and is recognized as one of the finest African boxers of the twentieth century.

FURTHER READING

Ifaturoti, Damola. *Dick Tiger: The Life & Times of Africa's Most Accomplished World Boxing Champion* (2002).

Makinde, Adeyinka. *Dick Tiger: The Life and Times of a Boxing Immortal* (2005).

MICHAEL L. KRENN

Ikard, Bose (1847?–4 Jan. 1929), cowboy and traildriver on the Goodnight-Loving Trail and close associate of the cattleman Charles Goodnight, was born a slave in Summerville, Mississippi, and later moved to Parker County, Texas, with the family of his owner and probable father, Dr. William Ikard. Bose Ikard's mother was named King and was also William Ikard's slave. Though the Texas Historical Commission lists Ikard's birth as 1843, and Ikard's own headstone lists 1859, a probable year of birth was 1847, the same year as that of William Ikard's "legitimate" son, with whom Bose was largely raised.

Ikard's association with Goodnight arose from their proximity as neighbors in Parker County, working in the same industry. With a move from Mississippi to Texas in 1852 the Ikard family became part of the primary industry of the region, cattle. The sale of one female slave, possibly Ikard's mother, to another neighbor, Oliver Loving, for a thousand dollars' worth of cattle established the family business, which later became well known throughout the region. Loving and Goodnight pioneered what would become a major cattle-driving trail of the time, moving steers and cows from ranches to markets farther north and west. Ikard's serendipitous location during these critical years of the cattle industry (cattle trails ran for only twenty-four years, from 1866 to 1890) included him in the history of this soon-to-be famous cattle trail, the Goodnight-Loving.

Though the Civil War set the Ikard family's slaves free, Bose, like so many other freed slaves, remained where he had been raised, on the ranch working with cattle. In June 1866, with a letter of recommendation from William Ikard, Bose began work as trail-driver in the Goodnight-Loving Trail's first year. As was true of the larger cattle industry in the mid- to late nineteenth century, there were many black cowboys working on this trail; however, due in part to the itinerant nature of the work, records were sparsely kept, and Jim Fowler is the only other black man named in the historical record for work on the Goodnight-Loving.

While the cattle trails ran only for a relatively brief period, it was a time of exceptional freedom and possibility for young men, black, white, or Mexican, to find skilled work in this field and make a decent living outside of the otherwise narrow social mores of the late nineteenth century. It is estimated that up to one-third of the cowboys working these trails were of African or Hispanic descent; the timing of Emancipation after the Civil War made this opening industry ideally suited to freed slaves with few family ties. NAT LOVE's memoirs of this period, for example, provide an exceptional first-hand account of a black cowboy's experience.

Ikard and Goodnight began a friendship in 1866 that lasted until Ikard's death. Ikard rode the Goodnight-Loving Trail from 1866 until 1869; many stories about him from this time are related by Charles Goodnight in his own memoirs.

Between trips on the trail, sometime in the late 1860s, Ikard married a woman named Angeline (no last name recorded, born into slavery in Texas, 19 Aug. 1853). By most accounts they had six children, of whom five survived to adulthood. Angeline died in 1902 at age forty-nine.

Historical accounts convey that Ikard intended to settle in Colorado near Goodnight when he retired from the trail. However, Goodnight advised Ikard against it, owing to the sparse black population in the Rocky Mountain area, and recommended that Ikard return to Parker County, Texas. He did so and took up farming there. Few records except census reports exist of his life after leaving his cowboying career. He is listed as "farmer" in 1880 U.S. census reports of the area.

Ikard's neighbors in Weatherford, Texas, remembered him as a handyman, someone who did yard work and ran errands. Unknown to them, Charles Goodnight sent Ikard money occasionally and maintained intermittent contact all through their lives. Bose died in Austin of influenza, and his body was brought back to Weatherford for burial. The obituary published for him at the time omits any mention of his days on the historical Goodnight-Loving Trail, of his adventures therein, or of his character. However, when Charles Goodnight learned of Ikard's death, he contacted local authorities. A new obituary was published in the Weatherford paper under a headline: "Chas. Goodnight Erects Monument To Negro Friend Buried Here." The epitaph Goodnight requested to be engraved on the gravestone reads "Served with me for four years on the Goodnight-Loving Trail, never shirked duty or disobeyed an order, rode with me in many stampedes, participated in three engagements with Comanches, splendid behavior— C. Goodnight."

The novel and movie *Lonesome Dove*, by Larry McMurtry, is loosely based on the lives of Charles Goodnight and Oliver Loving; the character Joshua Deets, portrayed by DANNY GLOVER in the film, is based on Bose Ikard. Ikard was inducted into the Texas Trail of Fame in 1997.

FURTHER READING
Durham, Philip, and Everett L. Jones. *The Negro Cowboys* (1965).
Haley, J. Evetts. *Charles Goodnight: Cowman and Plainsman* (1949).
Massey, Sara. *Black Cowboys of Texas* (2000).
                                    LIZ STEPHENS

Iman (25 July 1955–), model and cosmetics-company founder, was born Iman Abdul Majid in Mogadishu, Somalia, the second of five children born to Mohamed, an Ethiopian-born Arabic teacher and diplomat, and Marian Abdul Majid, a Somalia-born midwife. "Iman," a name generally given to a boy, means "to have faith in Allah." As the first girl born to her father's family in three generations, Iman appeared as a gift from Allah.

Very much a "daddy's girl," Iman worshipped her father. A fighter against sexism, Mohamed adhered to the theory that girls should be treated well at home to enable them to surmount any restrictions that society might try to place upon them. Accordingly, Iman was sent to boarding school because her father felt that such an environment offered girls the best education.

To his delight, Iman did well in her studies of Arabic, Italian, geography, and mathematics. She eventually left boarding school to join the family in Saudi Arabia, where her father had received a diplomatic posting from the Somali government. The move to such a conservative country came as a shock. While Iman and her sisters never wore veils, they did have to leave the room whenever a man came to visit. Iman felt suffocated and, as a result, her father sent her to a new school in Cairo, Egypt, where attitudes and official policies toward women were more liberal.

Iman thrived in Cairo until 1969, when the Somali communist revolution began with the assassination of President Abdirashid Ali Shermarke. Iman would later mark that point as the end of her childhood. Her parents returned immediately to Somalia and Iman and her brothers were quickly withdrawn from their schools. The situation they met was far worse than they had imagined. The friends of Mohamed Abdul Majid were executed, jailed without charge, or put under house arrest. The Abdul Majid family existed in a state of purgatory, waiting for death and violence to arrive on their doorstep. Iman later recalled that she went to bed every night not knowing if it would be the last time that she kissed her father. Meanwhile, Marian Abdul Majid, careful not to trigger suspicion with bank withdrawals, sold every personal possession of value to pay for an escape.

Iman wound up in Kiev in the Soviet Union for six months while attending a school that gave ideological and military training. While learning how to clean and load a gun, she decided that communism did not work well in Russia and could never work in Somalia despite the best efforts of the new Somali government to impose it. In 1970, when Iman had returned to Somalia, the Abdul Majids fled in the middle of the night in a rusted Volkswagen van to Kenya. Iman hid in the back with her baby sister with a blanket over their bodies. She walked across the border on foot. Mohamed stayed in Somalia with Iman's younger sister, who had polio. They joined the rest of the family a few months later. The family, now destitute, relied on a cousin for housing and food.

By 1975 Iman had married, although nothing is known of her first husband, and she had begun studying political science at the University of Nairobi. The fashion photographer Peter Beard spotted her walking down the street and sought to capture her unusual look of Somali, Muslim, and dispossessed. Iman agreed to sit for Beard for the money needed to pay her tuition. The subsequent photographs, artful nudes, were sent to the renowned Wilhelmina model agency in New York, which accepted her without having met her in person. Iman needed her husband's permission to leave Kenya but, with the marriage failing, it did not seem likely that she would receive it. So she fled Kenya with forged papers, arriving in Manhattan in 1975. The tale put out by her agents, with whom she colluded, was that Beard had discovered a peasant goatherd who spoke no English. Iman, noted for her stoicism and pride as well as her ability to speak five languages, found the tale to be both sexist and racist yet she agreed to it because it was excellent publicity, and she needed publicity to succeed as a model.

Iman's timing proved excellent. Fashion loved her, but African Americans were not so welcoming. Accustomed to West African features, blacks were stunned by Iman's East African appearance. Magazines like *Essence* dismissed Iman for looking like a white woman "dipped in chocolate." Ignoring the criticism, Iman demonstrated a strong sense of racial pride. Touted as the successor to Beverly Johnson partly because the fashion industry could only envision one black star model at a time, Iman made it a point to refer business to Johnson. The two models subsequently became friends.

Iman worked constantly. A star on the catwalk as well as in the pages of magazines, she showed a theatrical flair with her tall hair that accentuated her East African background. Photographers loved her. Iman was determined to secure the big, lucrative advertising assignments, particularly the campaigns that had never used solo black models before: Calvin Klein, Valentino, Versace, and Revlon. Much of the money went to her family. Iman paid for the education of all of her siblings and took enormous pride in having the ability to do so. However, she continued to fret about offending the Muslim sensibilities of her parents, now living in Virginia.

Iman retired from modeling in 1989 and moved to California to pursue an acting career. She had minor roles in a number of films, including *Out of Africa* (1985), *No Way Out* (1987), *Surrender* (1987), *Star Trek VI: The Undiscovered Country* (1991), and *Exit to Eden* (1994), among others. She made numerous television appearances, often as herself, as well as playing characters in episodes of *Miami*

Vice (1985 and 1988), *In the Heat of the Night* (1988), and *Dream On* (1993). She also appeared in digital form, as the voice of a character in the video game *Omikron: The Nomad Soul* (1999).

While Iman had numerous film and television appearances during the 1990s, she had far better luck in business. In 1994, tired of being unable to find make-up to match her complexion, she created her own range for all women of color, whether black, Latino, or Asian. The result was IMAN Cosmetics, Fragrances & Skincare.

A political activist and Democrat, Iman made the documentary *A Journey Home: Somalia* in 1992 to explain that the anarchy in the country came as the result of looting militias rather than indigenous brutality. She continued her involvement with African issues, organizing "Keep a Child Alive," a response to the AIDS pandemic in Africa. She also refused to join a DeBeers jewelry initiative in 2001 because of the company's controversial eviction of Bushmen from land with a diamond mine.

Iman met the English singer and actor David Bowie in Los Angeles in October 1991. They married in Lausanne, Switzerland, the following year. She had three children, a daughter Zulekha from her second marriage to the basketball player Spencer Haywood in the late 1970s, and two children with Bowie, a daughter Alexandria Zahra and a stepson.

FURTHER READING.

Iman. *I Am Iman* (2001).

Craig, Maxine Leeds. *Ain't I a Beauty Queen: Black Women, Beauty, and the Politics of Race* (2002).

Hunter, Margaret L. *Race, Gender, and the Politics of Skin Tone* (2005).

Rooks, Noliwe M. *Hair Raising: Beauty Culture and African American Women* (1996).

CARYN E. NEUMANN

Imes, Elmer Samuel (12 Oct. 1883–11 Sept. 1941), physicist, was born in Memphis, Tennessee, the son of Benjamin A. Imes, a minister, and Elizabeth Wallace. Imes attended school in Oberlin, Ohio, and the Agricultural and Mechanical High School in Normal, Alabama. Imes then enrolled at Fisk University in Nashville, Tennessee, where he received his B.A. in Science in 1903. Upon graduating, Imes accepted a position at Albany Normal Institute in Albany, Georgia, where he taught mathematics and physics. He returned to Fisk in 1910 and for the next five years worked toward an M.S. in Science while serving as an instructor in science and mathematics. After receiving his master's degree in 1915, Imes entered the University of Michigan's doctoral physics program, where he worked closely with Harrison M. Randall, who had recently returned from Germany. Randall had studied the infrared region of the spectrum in Friedrich Paschen's spectroscopy laboratory at Tübingen University.

For the next three years Imes investigated the infrared spectrum of three diatomic molecules: hydrogen chloride (HCl), hydrogen bromide (HBr), and hydrogen fluoride (HF). Experimental and theoretical work had already shown that the molecular vibrational spectrum is quantized. Imes and Randall were interested in obtaining definitive evidence that the rotational spectrum was also quantized. In 1918 Imes received his Ph.D. and published his dissertation in a long article in the *Astrophysical Journal* (50 [1919]: 251–276). This work had a major impact on atomic physics: "In 1919, Randall and Imes published a single work that opened an entirely new field of research: the study of molecular structure through the use of high resolution infrared spectroscopy. Their work revealed for the first time the detailed spectra of simple-molecule gases, leading to important verification of the emerging quantum theory and providing, for the first time, an accurate measurement of the distances between atoms in a molecule" (Krenz, 12). Another view of Imes's research was presented by Earle Plyler in a 1974 speech at Fisk: "Imes' work formed a turning point in the scientific thinking, making it clear that quantum theory was not just a novelty, useful in limited fields of physics, but of widespread and general application."

Imes's results were immediately recognized by quantum scientists in both North America and Europe. In the two decades after its publication the paper was extensively cited in research papers and reviews on the rotational-vibrational spectra of diatomic molecules. Within a very short time, discussions of his work and his precision spectrum of HCl was incorporated into the standard textbooks on modern physics. Imes's experimental results also provided the first evidence for the existence of nuclear isotopics. This was shown by examining the doublet structure in his absorption band structure of HCl at 1.76 microns. This feature was interpreted to mean that two isotopes of chlorine were present.

As a black scientist holding a doctorate degree, Imes found his employment opportunities essentially limited to teaching at a black southern college or to seeking a position within industry or the federal government. For the next decade Imes lived in and around New York City, where he was employed as an engineer and applied physicist. Imes's applied research and engineering activities resulted in four patents, each in the general area of measuring the properties of magnetic materials and the construction of instruments to conduct such tests. In 1920 Imes married NELLA LARSEN; they had no children. His own scholarly and literary interests, as well as his marriage to Larsen, one of the better-known writers of the Harlem Renaissance, allowed him to associate with many members of the "Negro" intellectual and power elite, including W. E. B. DuBois, CHARLES S. JOHNSON, ARNA BONTEMPS, LANGSTON HUGHES, AARON DOUGLAS, WALTER WHITE, and the white arts patron Carl Van Vechten. Many of these people would reappear in Imes's life in the 1930s as members of the Fisk University faculty or through some other strong connection to the institution.

In 1930 Imes was appointed chair of and professor in the physics department at Fisk, a position he held until his death. Imes initially devoted much of his time to the reorganization of the undergraduate physics curriculum and made preliminary preparations for the initiation of a full-fledged graduate program centered on research in infrared spectroscopy. Both Imes and his students were involved in several research projects; they used both X-rays and magnetic procedures to characterize the properties of materials and in the study of the fine structure of the infrared rotational spectrum of acetylene. Imes spent at least one summer at New York University carrying out experiments on magnetic materials, and he returned to the University of Michigan several summers to continue his research in infrared spectroscopy. He was active in three professional societies: the American Physical Society, the American Society for Testing Materials, and the American Institute of Electrical Engineers. Because of segregationist laws in the southern states he would only attend national meetings of these organizations when they were held in large northern cities or in Canada.

Imes felt that the students at Fisk, as well as his friends and colleagues, should be exposed to the general outline and themes of science. To this end he developed a course, Cultural Physics, and wrote a rather large manuscript to be used for the course. In addition to his duties as chair, Imes did detailed work on the planning and design of a new science building, and he carried out extensive correspondence with other researchers, equipment designers, and equipment manufacturers. Imes was heavily involved in the general academic and social life of the university. He operated film equipment for various university clubs, participated in both the planning and execution of the Annual Spring Arts Festival, and served on various scholarship and disciplinary committees. One of his major concerns was the education and training of his students; several of them enrolled in graduate studies in physics at the University of Michigan.

Imes's marriage ended in 1933 when Larsen divorced him on the legal grounds of "cruelty." The couple had already been separated for a number of years, mainly because of her desire to pursue a writing career in New York. Imes died in New York City.

Throughout his career Imes was held in high regard by his scientific colleagues. They immediately grasped the significance of the work he did at the University of Michigan showing that both the vibrational and rotational energy levels of molecules are quantized. His experiments also provided a precise set of data that could be used to make a critical test of the emerging quantum mechanics that was being formulated in Europe. Understood but never openly articulated during his lifetime was the fact that Imes's race had placed limitations on what he could achieve in science in America.

FURTHER READING

Imes's papers are located at Fisk University Library, Special Collections, the Carl Van Vechten Personal Collection, New York Public Library, and the James Weldon Johnson Collection, Beinecke Library, Yale University.

Krenz, Gary D. "Physics at Michigan: From Classical Physics to Nuclear Research, 1888–1938," *LSA Magazine* 2 (Fall 1988): 10–16.

Obituary: Swann, W. F. G. *Science* 94 (1941): 600–601.

This entry is taken from the *American National Biography* and is published here with the permission of the American Council of Learned Societies.

RONALD E. MICKENS

Innis, Roy (6 June 1934–), civil rights activist and black nationalist, was born Roy Emile Alfredo Innis in St. Croix, U.S. Virgin Islands, to Georgianna Thomas and Alexander Innis, a policeman. His father died when Innis was six years old, and in 1946 Innis relocated with his mother to New York City, where he attended Stuyvesant High School

Roy Innis, national chairman of the Congress on Racial Equality, speaks at the National Press Club in Washington, 5 January 2005, where he announced his support for Supreme Court nominee Samuel Alito. (AP Images.)

before joining the U.S. Army at the age of sixteen in 1950. Innis served for two years and was honorably discharged at the rank of sergeant after it was discovered that he had lied about his age to enlist. He returned to New York, where he completed his high school work and received his diploma. Innis matriculated at the City College of New York, where he earned a bachelor's degree in Chemistry. He found employment with the Vicks Chemical Company in New York City and married a woman named Violet (her maiden name and their wedding date are unknown); they had three children. That marriage ended in divorce. In 1963 Innis joined the Congress of Racial Equality (CORE) and began his long and often-controversial life in the civil rights movement. He rose quickly through the ranks of the Harlem branch in spite of his black nationalist philosophy, which was quite at odds with the organization's more moderate base, and he was named chairman in 1965. That same year Innis married Doris Funnye, a CORE member; they had eight children. Just two years later Innis ascended to the post of associate national director of CORE. This latter promotion was achieved in part through Innis's own maneuverings. He and the important and influential Harlem chapter had engineered the installation of FLOYD McKISSICK as national chairman, and it was McKissick who subsequently—and over the loud protests of CORE moderates—elevated Innis. In 1968 McKissick abandoned his post, and Innis assumed the role of national chairman. The evolution of CORE from a nonviolent, multiracial protest organization to one of black

nationalism and militancy was complete. In that same year tragedy struck close to Innis when his son Roy Innis Jr. was shot by a deranged man while playing in the street.

Many observers publicly lamented that CORE had ceased to be a significant national civil rights entity, and indeed its membership did dwindle following Innis's assumption of leadership. However, the organization remained highly active, if with a revised focus and new goals. During the early 1970s Innis and other members of CORE toured Africa, meeting with a number of national leaders. Controversy surrounded Innis when in 1973 he met with and praised Idi Amin, president of Uganda, making him an honorary CORE member. In 1978 Innis was charged with having misappropriated what were supposed be charitable funds, though the case was eventually settled. Whispers of budget allocations for CORE shell programs continued to dog him and the organization throughout the 1980s.

In 1982 Innis lost another son, Alexander, to gun violence. The young man was slain in Harlem, apparently following a dispute with three men on the street. Such a history of personal tragedy may help to explain Innis's and CORE's turn throughout the 1980s toward a number of criminal legal affairs and so-called victims' rights campaigns, including a highly publicized media defense of Bernhard Goetz, a white New Yorker who in 1984 had gunned down a number of young black assailants on a city subway car. Along with widespread accusations that Innis was running CORE as his personal fiefdom came calls that his politics, always somewhat radical, had taken a turn toward the conservative and authoritarian.

The rest of the 1980s saw the fulfillment of the latter charge for CORE. Innis supported the presidential campaign of Ronald Reagan over the Democratic challenger Walter Mondale in 1984, arguing that African Americans had been bamboozled into habitually supporting the Democrats, who had little or nothing of their interests at heart. He ran for a seat in Congress in 1986 in Brooklyn as a Democrat (by necessity, he said) but promised to caucus with the Republicans if he won. He went down in a decisive defeat. Meanwhile legal problems and accusations swirled around Innis and CORE.

Outside the roles of civil rights activists and observers, it is likely that Innis achieved his greatest popular recognition in the late 1980s, when a pair of on-air affrays brought him to the attention of the wider public. The first took place in 1988 during a recording of the *Morton Downey Jr. Show*, a television show that many critics considered exploitative and sordid, when Innis shoved the seated Reverend AL SHARPTON, causing him to fall backward in his chair. No charges were filed. A second, perhaps more famous incident occurred later that same year when Innis was featured on an installment of Geraldo Rivera's program *Geraldo* with a group of neo-Nazi skinheads. Innis rose from his chair, walked to the seated Tom Metzger, a white supremacist, and began to strangle him. Predictably, and no doubt to the delight of the show's producers and sponsors, a fight broke out that soon spilled over into the studio audience.

In 1993 Innis challenged the incumbent DAVID DINKINS in the New York City mayoral Democratic primary. But by this time Innis had become well known to New Yorkers as a Republican in Democratic cloth (an ideological affiliation Innis himself did nothing to disguise). So while his conservative positions—his anti–gun control stance, for instance—won him some support among white conservative New Yorkers, African Americans stayed away in droves, and Innis again was dealt a crushing defeat.

After 1993 Innis remained national chairman and director of CORE. The organization's principal focus was crime and its effect on the African American community, something Innis understood intimately. There was some suggestion in 1994 that Innis might run for governor of New York against the incumbent Mario Cuomo, but the campaign never materialized. In 1998 Innis joined the Libertarian Party, and in 2000 he was New York state chair for the presidential campaign of ALAN KEYES, another notable and often-controversial black conservative.

FURTHER READING

Meier, August, and Elliot Rudwick. *CORE: A Study in the Civil Rights Movement, 1942–1968* (1975).

JASON PHILIP MILLER

Irvin, Monte (2 Feb. 1919–), baseball player, was born Monford Merill Irvin in Halesburg, Alabama, the seventh of ten children of Cupid Alexander Irvin and Mary Eliza Henderson, sharecroppers. When his father challenged a white sharecrop boss, the family had to flee, first to Albany, Georgia, and then to Bloomfield, New Jersey. The Irvins ended their flight in Orange, New Jersey. There Monte attended integrated schools. But the restaurants were segregated, and movie theaters confined blacks to the balcony. Like PAUL ROBESON and JACKIE ROBINSON, with letters in football, track, basketball, and baseball, Irvin earned a reputation as his high school's greatest athlete. On graduation night, however, Monte and his date, along with two other black couples, could not eat at a local restaurant near school because of their color.

Sports provided opportunity. A scout from the University of Michigan offered Irvin a football scholarship. Unfortunately he lacked the funds to reach Ann Arbor, losing a splendid opportunity to play in the same backfield with Tom Harmon and Forest Evashevski. He settled on Lincoln University in Pennsylvania, where he befriended his lifelong friend, the late Max Manning. Less than two years later Irvin left to play baseball with the Newark Eagles. Having used a pseudonym, Jimmy Nelson, during his high school and college days in order to maintain his amateur status, Irvin was now free to play under his real name.

From 1937 to 1948, with time out for military service during World War II (1943–1945), Irvin played for the Newark Eagles in the Negro National League. After he learned to pull the ball by watching Joe DiMaggio, Irvin became one of the dominant hitters in the Negro League. Regarded by many as one of the best young black players, he hit .422 in 1940 and .395 in 1941 to capture the batting crown. When the Eagles' matriarchal owner Effa Manley refused Irvin's request for a monthly salary raise of $25, Irvin bolted for Mexico, where in only 68 games he batted .398, banged out 30 home runs, and won the triple crown. In 1942 he married Dee (maiden name unknown); they had two daughters, Pamela Irvin Fields and Patricia Irvin Gordon.

Though statistics are not always available or reliable, it is clear that Irvin could play with the cream of white ballplayers. In 1941 he and his teammate Max Manning were driving through Daytona Beach, Florida, when a white policeman stopped them. "Where are you goin'?" the policeman barked. "Home," a nervous Manning replied. "Home! Don't you know how to say 'sir'?" Manning froze in anger. "Yes, sir," Irvin volunteered quickly. "What's wrong with your buddy? Can't he say it?" As the officer began to unbuckle his billy club, Irvin explained that they were learning to play baseball; they wanted no trouble. This traumatic incident, recalled in an interview nearly sixty years after it happened, revealed Irvin's survival skills. Irvin suffered further indignities after he went off to war in 1943. A company commander warned Irvin and his fellow black soldiers not to fraternize with British women—or else. These absurd orders made a person feel "like you were nothing," Irvin later said. The war left Irvin with shattered nerves.

When he returned to civilian life he opted for more seasoning in the Negro League. In 1946 Irvin, LEON DAY, LARRY DOBY, and Max Manning led the Newark Eagles to a Negro League World Series victory over SATCHEL PAIGE's Kansas City Monarchs. While the team rode through Mississippi in an air-conditioned bus, white farmers jeered at them as "jigaboos." Irvin captured the irony. The farmers were broiling in the southern heat while the Eagles rode in comfort. So laughter eclipsed anger.

Based on his prewar accomplishments and sterling skills, Monte Irvin—not Jackie Robinson—should have been the first to break baseball's color line. Irvin was outstanding in every facet of the game: hitting, hitting with power, running, fielding, and throwing. According to his daughter Pamela, her mother intercepted a letter from Branch Rickey soliciting Irvin's services for the Brooklyn Dodgers. Aware of her husband's war-induced trauma, Dee Irvin wanted to spare her husband the ordeal awaiting Jackie Robinson. Even after the former UCLA star Robinson signed with Brooklyn, Rickey pursued Irvin. When the Eagles owner Effa Manley insisted on monetary compensation, the always provident if not parsimonious Rickey broke off negotiations.

Irvin signed with the New York Giants, who paid Manley a bargain-basement sum of five thousand dollars for his services in 1949. Farmed out to Jersey City in the Triple-A International League, Irvin hit a hefty .373 before reaching the parent club. Once established as a major leaguer, and nicknamed "the Sepia Slugger" (JOE LOUIS's moniker as well), Irvin proved his mettle. In 1949 he played in only 38 games, too short a span to shine. In 1950, the first year in which he played more than 100 games, he hit .299 and smacked 15 home runs. Over eight years he hit .293 during the regular season and .394 in two World Series, in 1951 and 1954. Arguably Irvin enjoyed his best season in 1951 when he hit .312, slammed 24 home runs and 11 triples, stole 12 bases, and knocked in 112 runs while leading the New York Giants to a miracle come-from-behind pennant over Jackie Robinson's Brooklyn Dodgers. Irvin was the first African American to win an RBI crown and play in an all-black outfield in the majors, flanked by WILLIE MAYS and HANK THOMPSON. With the national spotlight on him in 1951 Irvin excelled in the World Series. In game one he stole home. He wore out Yankee pitching with 11 hits in 24 plate appearances for a gaudy .458 average. Lamentably, his teammates could not match his performance as they bowed to the Yankees four games to two.

In 1952 disaster struck during spring training when Irvin suffered an ankle fracture, and he sustained recurring ankle problems in August later the same year. He still hit .310 over 46 games that season, and he returned to stellar form in 1953 when he hit a career high .329 with 21 homers and 97 RBIs. But advancing age and a weakened ankle took their toll. Playing three more seasons, Irvin never again hit better than .271.

After retirement Irvin worked for Rheingold Beer in promotions and public relations. He scouted for the New York Mets from 1967 to 1968, just prior to their miracle World Series victory over the heavily favored Baltimore Orioles. From 1968 to 1984 he labored as a special assistant to the baseball commissioner Bowie Kuhn during a turbulent era marked by free agency and other volatile issues. As the only black administrator in the commissioner's office, Irvin lobbied quietly behind the scenes to secure justice for his fellow Negro Leaguers. After his election to the Hall of Fame on 6 August 1973, he steered RAY DANDRIDGE, MARTIN DIHIGO, RUBE FOSTER, JUDY JOHNSON, and JOHN HENRY LLOYD through the portals of baseball immortals.

FURTHER READING

Irvin, Monte, with James A. Riley. *Monte Irvin: Nice Guys Finish First* (1996).

Overmyer, James. *Queen of the Negro Leagues: Effa Manley and the Newark Eagles* (1998).

Peterson, Robert. *Only the Ball Was White: A History of Legendary Black Players and All-Black Professional Teams* (1970).

JOE DORINSON

Irvis, K. Leroy (27 Dec. 1916–16 Mar. 2006), teacher and legislator, was born Kirkland Leroy Irvis in Saugerties, New York, the older of Francis H. and Harriet Ten Broeck Cantine Irvis's two children. Francis was self-employed, and Harriet was a homemaker. Shortly after his birth, the family moved to Albany, New York. While Irvis's father instilled in his children the value of education, his mother taught them the importance of art and human emotion. Her lessons would inspire Irvis to become a renowned wood sculptor and published poet. He graduated from Albany High School with honors in 1934 and went on to attend New York State College for Teachers (later SUNY), where he graduated summa cum laude in 1938 with an AB in History.

The harsh realities of racism that his parents tried to shield from him as a child would meet him head on as an adult. Denied teaching positions upon graduation, Irvis went back to the New York State College for Teachers and earned an M.A. in 1939. Still unable to find a teaching job in Albany, he called on family friend and civil rights activist and suffragist DAISY LAMPKIN for help. Lampkin arranged for Irvis to get a teaching position in Baltimore, where he stayed in the home of THURGOOD MARSHALL, whom he met through Lampkin. Irvis taught in the segregated Baltimore school system until World War II broke out. An avid builder and flyer of model airplanes, Irvis started his own model airplane club called the Prop Busters in Baltimore in 1939 when refused admission into a white club. When Irvis, an aviation enthusiast, tried to enlist in the armed forces and was denied entrance into the Army Air Corps by a recruiter because of his race, he became a civilian flying instructor in the War Department. When army officials discovered that Irvis had his Model Flyer's License, they recruited him to teach black women how to cut, rivet, measure, and drill metal to build bombers. The assignment lasted two years, and then Irvis, tired of the racism and discrimination he faced in Baltimore, went back to Albany. There he met Katharyne Anne Jones, who would become his first wife. They married in April 1945. The couple had no children. Jobless once again, Irvis once more turned to Lampkin, who set him up in Pittsburgh as the assistant to the labor secretary at the Urban League. Irvis and his wife arrived in Pittsburgh in 1945 and settled in the Hill District. Irvis quickly moved up the ranks in the Urban League, eventually heading the public relations division. In 1949 he led pickets of downtown Pittsburgh department stores to protest their refusal to hire black clerks. The demonstrations gained national attention as among the first of their kind but angered the leadership at the Urban League. Many of the owners of the downtown stores were major contributors to the Urban League and disapproved of Irvis's actions, as did Pittsburgh's mayor at the time, David L. Lawrence. Irvis was fired from the Urban League for leading the demonstrations.

In 1951 Irvis enrolled in the University of Pittsburgh School of Law. He did well there, was selected as a member of the law review, and graduated Phi Beta Kappa in 1954. He then became the first African American appointed law clerk at the Common Pleas Court. In 1957 he became assistant district attorney, and in 1958 he won election to the Pennsylvania State House of Representatives, representing Pittsburgh's Hill District, with the support of his former critic Mayor Lawrence, who admired Irvis's integrity. The following year Katharyne died unexpectedly from complications from a heart defect. Following her death, Irvis threw himself into his legislative work and won re-election to the house for fifteen consecutive terms. In his thirty years in the Pennsylvania legislature, Irvis sponsored or co-sponsored key civil rights legislation that included bills dealing with fair housing and employment, consumer protection, education, health, prison, and governmental reform. His most noted achievements included the sponsorship and passage of legislation creating the Pennsylvania Higher Education Equal Opportunity Program, the Pennsylvania Human Relations Commission, the Pennsylvania Higher Education Assistance Agency, the Minority Business Development Authority, the House Ethics Committee, and the Pennsylvania Council on the Arts. Irvis is also credited with the creation of the Community College System in Pennsylvania. He also spearheaded legislation that mandated PKU, or phenylketonuria, tests be administered to all newborns in Pennsylvania. The test, which detects an enzyme imbalance that can cause brain damage, became used nationwide. Irvis also initiated Act 101, which provided scholarships for disadvantaged youth to attend college. The legislation helped more than 32,000 Pennsylvanians attend college. During his tenure he authored or sponsored over 1,600 pieces of legislation and prided himself on his ability to rise above partisan politics and work with legislators on both sides of the aisle.

In 1974 Irvis married his second wife, Cathryn Lucille Edwards, a political organizer who founded the Black Women's Political Crusade (in Pennsylvania), served on the boards of numerous civic organizations and supervised Speaker Irvis's Pittsburgh office as its voluntary director. Together they had two children. During his third term in the legislature, Irvis became the Democratic Caucus chairman. He continued to rise through the ranks of leadership, and in May 1977 the house unanimously elected him speaker—making him the only black to hold the position in the United States at that time. In January 1979 the Democratic Caucus elected Irvis to serve as the Democratic leader for the 1979–1980 session. He was re-elected to the same post for the 1981–1982 session. In that latter year Irvis was elected a member of the Democratic

National Committee, and he would serve as a delegate to five Democratic National Conventions. He again served as speaker of the house from 1983 until his retirement in 1988.

Following his retirement Irvis wrote *This Land of Fire*, a book of original poems published by Temple University Press. He also was an accomplished sculptor and painter, working primarily with oil and wood. His African-styled masks were displayed in exhibits throughout the country. In 2003 the South Office Building within the Pennsylvania Capitol Complex in Harrisburg was renamed the Speaker K. Leroy Irvis Office Building. Irvis died of cancer in Pittsburgh at the age of eighty-nine.

FURTHER READING

Toler, Sonya M. "Irvis Honored by County Democrats," *New Pittsburgh Courier*, 24 Oct. 2004.

York, Jennifer. *Who's Who Among African Americans 17th ed.* (2004).

Obituary: *Pittsburgh Post-Gazette*, 17 Mar. 2006.

MICHELLE K. MASSIE

Isaac, Ephraim (29 May 1936–), was born in Nedjio, Ethiopia, to a Yemenite Jewish father, Yishaq, prominent in the Dire Dawa Jewish community as a silversmith, and an Ethiopian Christian mother, Ruth, who later converted to Judaism. He received his early education in Ethiopia and in 1937 came to the United States, where he dedicated his life to scholarship on Africa and became the founder and first professor of Afro-American Studies at Harvard University.

Professor Ephraim Isaac earned his secondary education in Ethiopia and was later given a scholarship to go to college in the United States. He earned B.A. degrees in philosophy and chemistry in 1958 from Concordia College in Minnesota. During this time, he was President of the Ethiopian Student Association in North America. He later received an M.A. from Harvard Divinity School and a doctorate in Near Eastern Languages and Civilizations from Harvard University.

Professor Isaac was one of the founders and first professor of Afro-American Studies at Harvard University, a department created in 1969. He lectured at Harvard between 1968 and 1977, teaching almost half of all students enrolled in the Afro-American program. One of his students, CORNEL WEST, later emerged as one of the leading public intellectuals of the late twentieth century and, like Isaac, was tenured at Harvard and Princeton. During his tenure at Harvard (1969–1977), Isaac was voted the best teacher each year by his students in the Afro-American department. Isaac later transferred to Princeton in 1979 as a fellow at the Institute for Advanced Study. He eventually became Visiting Professor at Princeton and taught the university's first Swahili class.

Apart from Harvard and Princeton, Professor Isaac lectured at various institutions including the University of Pennsylvania, Howard University, Hunter College, and Hebrew University in Jerusalem. In 2009 he was Director of the Institute of Semitic Studies at Princeton. He published in the *Journal of Afroasiatic Languages*, chaired the Board of the Horn of Africa Peace & Development Committee, and was President of the Yemenite Jewish Federation of America and Fellow of The Dead Sea Scrolls Foundation. He is also the author of numerous scholarly works, focusing primarily on Classical Yemenite Jewish and Ethiopic religious literatures.

His most famous works include investigations into some of the oldest known manuscripts to man, *The Book of Enoch* (Doubleday, 1983), translated from a fourteenth century Ge'ez manuscript, and *An Ethiopic History of Joseph* (Sheffield Press, 1990). In 2009 he worked on translating *Enoch* from fragments of the Dead Sea Scrolls with faculty members at the Princeton Theological Seminary. The Scrolls have been said to provide some of the missing links in theology and history between the Old and New Testaments.

In the span of his teaching career, Dr. Isaac received many honors, including an Honorary D.H.L. from John Jay College, CUNY, the Peacemaker in Action Award of the Tanenbaum Center for Inter-religious Understanding (2002), and the United Nation Association of Ethiopia Certificate of Appreciation (2000). In recognition of his accolades and historic role at Harvard, Harvard University endowed a prize in his name— the "Ephraim Isaac Prize for Excellence in African Studies"—in 1998. The prize is awarded annually to a graduating Harvard senior in the African Studies Department who has demonstrated overall excellence as well as exceptional capability in African languages.

Prior to his scholarly career, Ephraim Isaac was widely known in Ethiopia as the founder of the National Literacy Campaign that helped over one million Ethiopians become literate during the 1960s.

It has been speculated that the expert on Ethiopian history is a speaker of seventeen languages, and the first translator of Handel's Messiah into Amharic, the official language of Ethiopia. His field is marked by an effort to study Semitic languages, whose roots are in Ethiopia, with a history that goes back at least three thousand years. Ethiopia has a rich collection of manuscripts written in Ge'ez, the classical language of Ethiopia. The country's rich history is also woven with the legends of Israel's King Solomon and the Queen of Sheba, the lost Ark of Covenant said to rest in Axum, and the birthplace of the first recorded upright human being (Lucy). Professor Isaac's work has continued to make profound connections between Ethiopia and other cradles of civilization in Africa, which have in turn spawned a literature on the relationship among Christianity, Islam, and Judaism. In 2005 Dr. Isaac was also instrumental in helping settle a dispute between archbishops of the Ethiopian Orthodox Church and led a nonpartisan council of elders to break a political deadlock in Ethiopia concerning the life imprisonment of thirty-five opposition members sentenced for spurring election protests.

Issac married Sherry Rosen, a former lecturer at Rutgers University. They have three children: Devorah Esther, Raphael Samuel, and Yael Ruth. In 2009 Issac became the director of research at The Jewish Theological Seminary in New York. Professor Isaac is recognized as an advocate of civil rights in Ethiopia, where he is also hailed as a respected mentor to other scholars in recognition of his lifetime achievements and devotion to community service.

FURTHER READING
Bernal, Martin. *Black Athena* 3 vols. (1987–2006).
Heisey, Nancy R. "The Influence of African Scholars on Biblical Studies: An Evaluation." *Journal of Theology for Southern Africa* Vol. 101, July 1998, pp. 35–48.
Little, David. *Peacemakers in Action: Profiles of Religion in Conflict Resolution* (2007).
Quirin, James. "Case and Class in Historical North-West Ethiopia: The Beta Israel (Falasha) and Kemant, 1300–1900." *The Journal of African History* Vol. 39, No. 2, 1998, pp. 195–220.
Wilford, John Noble. "Scholars Clash over Origins of Dead Sea Scrolls." *The New York Times*, 21 Nov. 1989.

ADEBE DERANGO-ADEM

Isley, Ernest "Ernie" (7 Mar. 1952–), musician and songwriter, was born in Cincinnati, Ohio. He is the fifth of six sons born to O'Kelley Isley Sr., a former vaudevillian, and Sallye Isley, a church pianist and organist. In 1959, when Ernie Isley was seven years old, his older siblings, RONALD, O'Kelley, and Rudolph, recorded the Isley Brother's first hit record, "Shout," and the family moved to Englewood, New Jersey. In 1964, when Ernie Isley was eleven years old, JIMI HENDRIX was hired as the Isley Brothers' guitarist. During Hendrix's two-year stint with the band, he lived in the Isleys' home; thus Ernie Isley had ample opportunity to watch Hendrix play the guitar. Isley attended Englewood Junior High School, Dwight Monroe High School, and C. W. Post College Campus of Long Island University.

Although Isley's first appearance with his brothers was in 1966 as the group's drummer, and he played bass on the Isley Brothers hit "It's Your Thing" in 1969, he officially joined the group in 1973 as the group's guitarist (acoustic and electric). Isley's younger brother, Marvin, and Chris Jasper also joined the Isleys in 1973. That same year, the Isleys released the *3 + 3* album, which includes the hits "Summer Breeze" and "That Lady." In 1975 the group garnered additional success with *The Heat Is On*, an album that contains the hit singles "Fight the Power" and "For the Love of You." The aforementioned "That Lady" and "Fight the Power" along with "Harvest for the World" (1976), "Voyage to Atlantis" (1977), "Footsteps in the Dark" (1977), "Don't Say Goodnight" (1981), "I Once Had Your Love" (1981), "Choosey Lover" (1983), and "Caravan of Love" (1985) are among the hit songs cowritten by Ernie Isley for the Isley Brothers or Isley-Jasper-Isley.

The latter group formed when Isley, Jasper, and Marvin Isley left the Isley Brothers in 1984. The following year, the trio recorded the previously mentioned hit single "Caravan of Love." Isley-Jasper-Isley recorded three albums before the group disbanded in 1987. Then in 1990, Ernie Isley released his solo album, *High Wire*, a display of his virtuosity as a guitarist. One year later, Isley returned to the Isley Brothers; the group then consisted of Ronald, Ernie, and Marvin Isley. In 1992 the Isley Brothers (current and former group members) were inducted into the Rock and Roll Hall of Fame. The Isleys released another highly successful album, *Mission to Please* (1996), before Marvin Isley retired from the group in 1997. Ronald and Ernie Isley continued to tour and generate chart-topping albums including *Eternal* (2001), which includes the hit single "Contagious"; *Body Kiss* (2003), which features the hit single "What Would

You Do"; and *Baby Makin' Music*, which contains the hit single "Just Came Here to Chill."

In 2010 Ernie Isley appeared in the "Experience Hendrix Tour," which featured various guitarists paying tribute to Jimi Hendrix.

FURTHER READING
Gulla, Bob. *Icons of R&B Soul: An Encyclopedia of the Artists Who Revolutionized Rhythm* (2007).
Wilner, Paul. "Isley Brothers: A Family Affair." *New York Times*, 13 Mar. 1977.

LINDA M. CARTER

Isley, Ronald (21 May 1941–), musician and member of the Isley Brothers, was born in Cincinnati, Ohio, one of six brothers in a musical family: father Kelly sang professionally and mother Sallye was a church pianist. Both parents often accompanied four of their sons (Vernon, Rudolph, O'Kelly, and Ronald, then barely a teenager), as they formed a musical group in the early 1950s. Called the Isley Brothers, the group would lead Ronald and his siblings on an enormously successful, five-decade-long journey through African American music.

Initially, the Isley Brothers sang gospel, with Vernon Isley handling the duties of lead vocalist. In 1955 Vernon died in a bicycling accident, and Ronald—who possessed a bright, clear tenor—became the group's lead singer from that day forward. In 1957 the Isleys recorded a string of doo-wop singles, none of which achieved much success. Signed to RCA Records in 1960, they recorded "Shout," a semi-improvised, gospel-inflected dance tune that—although a commercial failure initially—eventually became a standard among dance bands. In 1962, while recording for Wand Records, the group released a jubilant version of the Top Notes' "Twist and Shout," a chart success that later gained increased prominence due to the success of the Beatles' 1963 cover version. The group formed their own label in 1964, T-Neck Records, following the path of SAM COOKE and other black artists who sought to avoid the pitfalls of commercial exploitation through the creation of their own distributive and promotional apparatus; even though they would only record one album on T-Neck in the 1960s, the label would be their home throughout the 1970s and early 1980s.

In 1965 the group signed with Tamla, a subsidiary of Detroit's mighty Motown Records, currently at the height of its chart dominance. Despite scoring a top-20 pop hit with "This Old Heart Of Mine," a sleek product of the Holland/Dozier/Holland songwriting and production team, the Isley Brothers soon felt that Motown's strict formula, which had produced only one hit for them, limited their creative energy. Seeking financial and creative autonomy, the group left Tamla in 1969, and relaunched T-Neck.

For the next fifteen years, the Isley Brothers evolved into one of the era's most consistently successful rhythm and blues groups. Adding younger brothers Marvin and Ernie, the expanded family group recorded a string of smash hits that followed the decade's musical path from soul to funk to disco, trading in their matching suits and processed hair for bright costumes and Afros. "It's Your Thing," a strong groove accentuated by lyrics of affirmation and self-worth, went to number 2 on the pop charts in 1969, the highest position on that listing the Isleys would ever achieve. In 1973 they found success with a reworking of one of their previous singles called "That Lady, Pt. 1," a blending of distorted rock guitar and the deep dance grooves that came to characterize the funk movement of the 1970s. In the second half of the decade, with the rise of disco, the group found success with a series of dance-oriented singles that topped the R&B charts, even while receiving little pop airplay. The resegregation of American radio during the late 1970s arguably was a widespread consequence of the divergence between perceived white and black niche markets, not limited merely to any particular act but affecting nearly all black artists, even one as prominent as the Isley Brothers.

In the 1980s the Isleys continued to record, for Epic and then Warner Bros. Records, and while they remained popular, their reign over major popular music popularity charts had ended. Group upheaval and personnel changes compounded their diminishing commercial power. In 1984 Ernie and Marvin left to form their own group; in 1986 O'Kelly died of a heart attack, and soon after Rudolph became a minister. Ronald became the last Isley standing; the 1989 album *Spend the Night* was essentially a solo effort, produced with his future wife, Angela Winbush, whom he married in 1993. The group briefly reunited in 1990, and in 1996, when the group—now made up of Ronald, Ernie, and Marvin—released *Mission to Please*, on which they collaborated with young artists like R. Kelly, Babyface, and Keith Sweat, three artists who exhibited the influence of the Isleys' classic recordings. *Eternal* (2001) and *Body Kiss* (2003) continued the same pattern, with R. Kelly providing increasing collaboration and support. In 1992 the group was inducted into the Rock and Roll Hall of Fame.

It was during the 1990s that Ronald Isley—the one remaining link with the original Isley Brothers—truly became the group's star. Their albums billed them as "The Isley Brothers featuring Ronald Isley," and—with the help of R. Kelly—Ronald developed the character of "Mr. Biggs," a flashy player who would make appearances on a variety of recordings during the period. They became one of the groups sampled most often on hip-hop recordings, and Ronald himself was utilized as a guest artist on hip-hop and R&B albums (one particularly interesting example was Ronald's shimmering vocal on "One Day," a track by the Houston gangsta rappers UGK). He showed off a different side of his musical personality in 2003 with *Here I Am*, an acclaimed album of songs written by the legendary pop tunesmith Burt Bacharach, who also produced and arranged the album.

The history of the Isley Brothers was, in its way, a history of black music from the 1950s onward. They began as a gospel quartet, stopped off in doo-wop, found their first success in the exuberant world of dance-band R&B, and recorded at Motown during its height. In the 1970s they became superstars of Black Power funk and disco (and, with T-Neck Records, owned and controlled their music), and continued to record, established as legends worthy of respect and admiration among another new generation. And Ronald Isley stood at the center of all of it.

FURTHER READING

Ankeny, Jason. "The Isley Brothers," in *All Music Guide to Soul*, ed. Vladimir Bogdanov (2003).

CHARLES L. HUGHES

Isom, Roger G. (10 Sept. 1965–), U.S. naval officer and submarine commander, was born in Monticello, Florida, one of nine children of John and Mary Isom. The farm the Isoms lived on consisted of sixty-eight acres, a portion of which was once sharecropped by Roger's grandfather. His father was an army veteran, as were six of his siblings. Ironically, when his mother asked Roger early on to consider attending the U.S. Naval Academy, he flatly refused. However, Isom later noted that "when my turn came to join the Army, I looked at the Navy instead, partly to compete with my older brother, and just to be different. I went to the Navy recruiter and said what can you do for me, I want to be an astronaut" (author's interview,

4 Mar. 2007). He subsequently enlisted in the navy in June 1983.

From his earliest navy days, Isom both aspired to and was placed in positions of leadership. Despite the fact that he had never been far from home and never traveled on an airplane, he was placed in charge of six recruits that made the flight from Jacksonville, Florida, to boot camp at San Diego, California. Upon completing boot camp, Isom attended the rigorous Broadened Opportunity for Officer Selection and Training Program (BOOST) and came through with flying colors, being recruited by the naval academy as part of the class of 1988. At the academy he continued to develop his leadership abilities and attained the highest level of leadership for a midshipman, that of brigade commander. When he graduated with merit in 1988 with a B.S. in Aerospace Engineering, he was the only African American midshipman to do so that year. Isom attributes much of his success at Annapolis to those he met at the academy and in the community, stating that "I had a big support network there consisting of many that helped me, white and black. One was a white family, the Mazzos, that took me into their home via the Naval Academy Midshipman Sponsor Program and treated me like family. From growing up in the south, I had perceptions and stereotypes about whites that were changed forever.... I also joined the Asbury United Methodist Church and developed a powerful relationship here with my first 'girlfriend,' Edna Booth.... She was eighty-five years old and took me under her wing. She made me study and was hard-core!" (author's interview, 4 Mar. 2007). Before her death in 2001, Booth received a special recognition award from the naval academy for her years of being a midshipman sponsor. Another vital and lasting part of Isom's support network was his future wife, Lisa Lewis, an assistant educator at Ediborough Preschool in Severna Park, Maryland. After their marriage in 1991, the bonds of family grew even stronger with the addition of two children, Roger Jr. and Brittany. Because of these relationships, Isom said he "became comfortable talking about diversity and had my eyes opened.... This really helped me in the navy" (author's interview, 4 Mar. 2007).

Ironically, prior to joining the Submarine Force, Isom had spent just one hour on a submarine; with the original intent of being a pilot and astronaut, Isom took his first flight at Pensacola but the experience made him physically uncomfortable. Seeking other options but viewing submariners as guys who were "bubbleheads, not very cool," and men "more into books and nuclear power" (author's interview, 4 Mar. 2007), Isom's mind was changed by his company officer Bob Brennan and submariner BRUCE GROOMS. As a future member of the Centennial 7, Grooms would make history as one of the few African Americans ever to command a submarine (the Centennial 7 has become the official designation for the first seven African American submarine commanders in the Submarine Force's first one hundred years). However, while in the pipeline to command, Grooms served as a mentor to several of those following, including Isom and RICHARD BRYANT. Isom later recalled that "all these guys [the Centennial 7] were examples contrary to my stereotypes about submariners and inspired me to look at the submarine service…. The more I looked, the more I embraced their heritage and I liked the brotherhood" (author's interview, 4 Mar. 2007).

Isom's first assignment in February 1990 was on board the USS *John Marshall*, followed by several other submarine assignments, where he usually took on engineering duties. Assigned in 1993 to the Naval Reserve Officer Training Corps (NROTC) unit at Hampton University, a historically black university, in Hampton Roads, Virginia, Isom served as company officer and instructor, a tour of duty he called "a great experience and great opportunity…. I loved the different setting, and teaching and demonstrating that, as an African American, you can be a success in the Navy as an officer. I also tried to show them as a submariner, that we're cool, we're warriors and it was a good way to go…. This was good for me both in my development as a leader, and for promoting diversity in the Navy…. We're not there yet but it's getting better" (author's interview, 4 Mar. 2007). During this period, Isom also earned a master's degree in Engineering Management at Old Dominion University in 1995.

After completing advanced submarine officer training and getting further sea experience on the USS *Baltimore* and later aboard the USS *Newport News* during a six-month deployment to the Mediterranean and Arabian Gulf, Isom went back to the naval academy to serve a tour as company officer as his mentor Bruce Grooms had done earlier. He also received the NAACP's ROY WILKINS Award for his navy diversity initiatives and also received the naval academy's 2001 Captain Frank Adams Junior Officer Leadership Award. In October 2001, Isom was named executive officer of the USS *Cheyenne* under Commanding Officer Chaz Doty. During this tour the ship was on an extended nine-month deployment that included three months of service in the Middle East in support of Operation Iraqi Freedom. It was *Cheyenne* that was tasked to fire the first naval missiles in this war and when she returned home Isom and the crew received a hero's welcome. Isom called this "a rewarding deployment and one in which I gained the most experience … after eighty-eight straight days at sea the brotherhood that developed among the crew was incredible" (author's interview, 4 Mar. 2007).

Upon the end of this tour, in 2003–2005, Isom completed a Pentagon assignment in Washington, D.C., as a maritime operations officer, followed by further schooling to complete his tour as a joint service officer. He then attended the prospective commanding officer instruction, taking "very intensive training" onboard submarines in preparation for gaining his own command. Part of this included duty on Richard Bryant's USS *Miami*. All this training finally paid off for Commander Isom when, on 3 August 2006, he was named the skipper of USS *Wyoming*'s Gold crew (all "missile boats," which are those submarines that carry strategic missiles and make what are called deterrent patrols, have two crews, designated "Gold" and "Blue," and therefore also two captains, which enable the boat to be constantly on station with a freshly rested and trained crew), becoming just the ninth African American ever to command a submarine, and the second, after MELVIN WILLIAMS JR., to command a Trident submarine.

Following his father's motto "let's do it together," he worked tirelessly to promote diversity in the navy and to cement the bond between him and his crew wherever he served. Above it all, this "skinny kid" from the Florida panhandle, descended from poor sharecroppers, remained in awe of where his life took him and sometimes, late at night, he could be seen by his crew taking a stroll through *his* boat to drink in the experience.

FURTHER READING

The primary source material for this article comes from the author's interview via telephone with Commander Roger Isom on 4 Mar. 2007 and subsequent e-mail exchanges.

Knoblock, Glenn A. *Black Submariners in the United States Navy, 1940–1975* (2005).

GLENN ALLEN KNOBLOCK

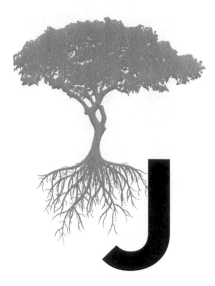

Jack, Beau (1 Apr. 1921–9 Feb. 2000), lightweight boxing champion, was born Sydney Walker in Waynesboro, Georgia. Little is known about his parents because shortly after his birth he was sent to live with and be raised by his grandmother, Evie Mixom, in Augusta, Georgia. It was from his grandmother that he acquired the nickname "Beau Jack," a moniker that stuck with him for the rest of his life.

As a young boy in Augusta, Jack worked a variety of small jobs, including shining shoes. He quickly discovered another way of supplementing his household's meager income, entering the rough-and-tumble world of "battle royals." These sporting contests were organized by well-to-do local whites for their entertainment. A group of African American men (and often boys) ranging from half a dozen to ten or more would be thrown into a roughshod boxing ring and made to fight until the last man was standing. In some cases, to add to the chaos, the fighters were blindfolded. These were no-holds-barred affairs, because the participants understood that only the winner would be awarded the money that was thrown into the ring by the spectators. Jack, despite his young age and small size, typically ended up on top in these contests by staying out of the way of the most brutal fighting while watching the other fighters pummel themselves into exhaustion or senselessness. At that point Jack would leap into the fray and down the last few opponents.

It was at one of these events in 1936, held at the Augusta National Golf Club (which was the home of the Masters Tournament), that Jack came to the attention of a group of wealthy whites, including the championship golfer Bobby Jones. Jack impressed the group with his nonstop punching style and ability to absorb punishment. When Jack again proved victorious he was rewarded with a job shining shoes at the golf club. In addition the men invested money to fund a professional boxing career for young Jack. With no professional boxing scene worthy of mention in Georgia, Jack was sent off to Massachusetts where he began to train in earnest for his boxing debut.

In May 1940 Jack fought his first professional bout. He did not exactly set the boxing world on fire, winning just two of his first six bouts, with three losses and one draw. From late 1940 through late 1942, however, Jack burst into boxing prominence. He fought forty-three times between August 1940 and November 1942, winning thirty-nine fights (twenty-five by knockout), losing just three, with one draw. Fighting almost exclusively in New York City, Jack developed a rabid following among fans who appreciated his attacking style. In December 1942 he challenged Tippy Larkin for the New York lightweight title (which at the time was considered nearly the equivalent of a world championship). Jack electrified the New York crowd by crushing Larkin in three rounds.

Through 1943 and into 1944 Jack fought some of the toughest opponents in the lightweight division. He beat the former champion Fritzie Zivic (generally considered one of the dirtiest fighters in the history of the sport) twice. He also defeated the still dangerous HENRY ARMSTRONG, who for a time in the 1930s simultaneously held the featherweight, lightweight, and welterweight boxing crowns. Jack fought another former lightweight champion Sammy Angott to a ten-round draw and defeated tough Al "Bummy" Davis. Jack was best known, however, for his fights with the "Philadelphia Bobcat," Bob Montgomery. Like Jack, Montgomery fought at full speed, and their fights became classics. In May 1943 Montgomery beat Jack in fifteen grueling rounds for the New York lightweight title. A rematch was inevitable, and when the two men met again in November 1943 Jack came out on top after fifteen exciting rounds. With one victory for each man, the clamor for a third fight could not be ignored. In March 1944 the familiar opponents faced off again. The fight once more went the entire fifteen rounds, and Montgomery emerged as the victor. All told, Jack headlined in the fights that drew the five biggest crowds to Madison Square Garden in 1943.

Jack and Montgomery saved their most famous fight for August 1944—and the lightweight title was not even on the line. By the time of the fight both Jack and Montgomery had been inducted into the U.S. Army. To raise money for the war effort the two men agreed to a fourth bout and encouraged those in attendance to buy war bonds. Nearly sixteen thousand people turned out for the fight, among them some of New York City's elite. Before the evening was through Jack had won a ten-round decision over his old adversary, and he and Montgomery had raised nearly $36 million in war bond sales.

Jack did not return to professional boxing until after World War II concluded, fighting just once in 1945, in December. In 1946 he was more active, becoming the only man ever to knock out Sammy Angott. An old leg injury began to hamper his movement in the ring, however, and he ended 1946 with a loss on points to a journeyman fighter. Eventually Jack went into the hospital for knee surgery. He began his comeback from the injury in February 1947 by taking on the tough contender Tony Janiro. It was quickly evident that Jack had attempted to return to the ring too quickly after his surgery. In the fourth round Jack backed away from Janiro and then crumpled to the canvas in agony, his kneecap having broken. Jack was taken from the ring on a stretcher.

Jack did not fight again until nearly ten months later and was soon back in the thick of the lightweight division. He broke Johnny Bratton's jaw in a January 1948 fight and beat another very good fighter, Johnny Greco, a few months later. In May

of that year he revenged his loss to Janiro with a ten-round decision. These fights set up a July 1948 match with the new king of the lightweight division, the heavy-hitting Ike Williams. Williams in 1947 had secured his hold on the lightweight crown by knocking out Jack's old nemesis Bob Montgomery. The fight with Williams provided brutal evidence that Jack's free-for-all fighting style was taking a toll on his body and stamina. In the sixth round of a lopsided bout Williams became the first man to score a knockout over Jack.

The decisive loss to Williams marked the end of Jack's career as a serious contender for a world championship, and Jack never again fought in a title bout. Nevertheless he continued to fight through 1951. Despite a knockout victory over the badly faded former lightweight champion Lew Jenkins in 1950, Jack lost every fight he had against a quality opponent. Johnny Greco and KID GAVILAN both beat Jack in 1949, Ike Williams defeated him in a nontitle contest in 1951, and the contender Gil Turner (who was in only his second year as a professional boxer) decisioned Jack in April 1951 and then knocked Jack out in a return match one month later. Following that defeat Jack announced his retirement from the ring.

Even though Jack had fought twenty-one headline matches in Madison Square Garden (fights that brought in more than 350,000 spectators and more than $1.5 million), Jack left the sport with little or no money. Jack blamed much of his financial trouble on unscrupulous managers and promoters, but he himself had taken the same freewheeling approach to financial matters that he had taken in the ring. It was rumored that he had fathered at least fifteen children during his lifetime, and some of his money went to support them.

In 1955 Jack returned to the fight game. After two victories against journeymen fighters and a draw against a faded Ike Williams, Jack fought his last bout in August 1955. Appropriately it was in the town where his boxing career got its start, Augusta. The opponent was familiar, and so was the outcome. Ike Williams left no doubt about the winner of this fight, stopping Jack in the ninth round.

Announcing his second retirement from boxing, Jack searched for some other means of support. He tried a variety of ventures, including owning a restaurant in Augusta, serving as a referee in wrestling matches, and even trying his hand at farming. Each of these attempts ended in financial disaster, and Jack eventually moved to Miami, where he took up his old profession of shining shoes. Jack became a familiar figure at his shoeshine stand at the Fountainbleau Hotel, and he also occasionally trained young fighters. In 1991 Jack was inducted into the International Boxing Hall of Fame. He died at the age of seventy-eight.

FURTHER READING
Heller, Peter. *In This Corner ... ! Forty World Champions Tell Their Stories* (1973).
Obituary: *New York Times*, 12 Feb. 2000.

MICHAEL L. KRENN

Jackman, Harold (1901–8 July 1961), teacher, model, dramatist, and collector of African American artifacts, was born in London to a West Indian mother and a British father, of whom little is known. It is believed that his mother was black and his father was white. Nor is it known when Jackman came to the United States, but he was raised in Harlem, New York, and graduated from DeWitt Clinton High School, where he befriended the poet COUNTÉE CULLEN. Jackman earned a B.A. degree from New York University in 1923 and an M.A. from Columbia University in 1927. For more than three decades he taught social studies in the New York Public Schools.

Aptly described as "the non-writer whom everyone adored," Jackman inspired tributes from those prominent Harlem Renaissance personalities with whom he socialized (Griffin, 494). Cullen, for example, dedicated an early version of his poem "Advice to Youth" (1925) to Jackman. In the same year, Winold Reiss's portrait of Jackman, titled *A College Lad*, was published on the back cover of an issue of *Survey Graphic*, whose subject matter was "Harlem: Mecca of the New Negro." Lewis incisively discusses the significance of the debonair "New Negro" and infers that Jackman, "one of Harlem's handsomer, more polished boulevardier bachelors" (Lewis, 115), appropriately exemplified this new identity. Bruce Kellner suggests, however, that Jackman was included in *Survey Graphic*, "less for his achievements than for his good looks" (Kellner, 189). Jackman worked as a model from the 1920s until the 1950s, most notably for Ophelia DeVore's Grace Del Marco (GDM) modeling agency. Thinly disguised characterizations of Jackman appeared in Carl Van Vechten's *Nigger Heaven* (1926) and WALLACE THURMAN's *Infants of Spring* (1932).

Jackman contributed significantly to the establishment and the promotion of African American theater. When, at the suggestion of Ernestine Rose, a librarian at the 135th Street branch, and W. E. B. DuBois, an ensemble of African American performers and playwrights established the Krigwa Players Little Negro Theater in 1926, Jackman was a founding member. He directed GEORGIA DOUGLAS JOHNSON's *Plumes* for the company's second season. Jackman helped establish the Harlem Experimental Theater Company in 1929 and was an active member of the American Theater Wing Stage Door Canteen in the 1930s and 1940s.

Jackman's friendship with Countée Cullen is of interest to scholars who study the influence of gay culture on the Harlem Renaissance because it exemplifies a typical combination of overt heterosexual and covert homosexual identities. During this period many gay African American men publicly socialized with women and privately associated with a network of gay men who shared a "positively defined same-sex interest" (Schwartz, 13). According to ARNA BONTEMPS, Jackman and Cullen were often referred to as the "David and Jonathan of the Harlem Twenties" because of their close friendship (Bontemps, 12). The homoerotic dimension of their friendship, however, was obscured by their obvious heterosexual behavior: Jackman frequently escorted single women to social events, and he was briefly married to Yolande DuBois, the daughter of W. E. B. DuBois. Shortly after the wedding on 9 April 1928, Jackman accompanied Cullen on a trip to Europe without Yolande, an incident that scholars conjecture confirms Cullen's homosexual orientation and suggests an intimate physical relationship with Jackman. Jackman and Cullen remained friends until Cullen's death in 1947.

By the end of the 1920s Jackman began sending his African American memorabilia to Atlanta University; he later urged friends such as LANGSTON HUGHES, Owen Dodson, Dorothy Peterson, and Van Vechten to contribute to this collection. On Cullen's death Jackman requested that the collection be named the Countée Cullen Memorial Collection—the name it bore until it was renamed the Countée Cullen-Harold Jackman-collection on the latter's death. Van Vechten and Jackman also gathered African American artifacts for the JAMES WELDON JOHNSON Memorial Collection at Yale, which includes Jackman's 1928–1930 correspondence with Cullen; for the Fisk University Library, and for the Schomburg Collection at the New York Public Library.

Jackman was associate editor of *New Challenge*, a literary magazine from 1935 to 1937 (Griffin, 495). He also worked as a contributing editor to and advisory editor of *Phylon*, a journal published by Atlanta University, from 1944 until his death in 1961. He was survived by his brother, Bertram, and his sister, Ivie Jackman, who instituted the Harold

Jackman Memorial Committee, which continued his commitment to conserving African American cultural artifacts.

Jackman contributed significantly to African American culture through his support of African American literature and art. His obituary in the *New York Times* paid tribute to his more than thirty years' service to the New York Public Schools, to his art patronage, and to his membership in social organizations such as the NAACP, the National Urban League Guild, the American Society on African Culture, and the Ira Aldridge Society.

FURTHER READING

The Harold Jackman Papers are in the Beinecke Rare Book and Manuscript Library, Yale University, New Haven, CT. Further materials on Jackman can be found in the Claude McKay Papers (Beinecke) and the Countée Cullen Papers, Amistad Research Center, Tulane University, New Orleans, Louisiana.

Bontemps, Arna. "The Awakening: A Memoir," in *The Harlem Renaissance Remembered: Essays Edited with a Memoir*" (1972).

Griffin, Barbara L. J. "Harold Jackman: The Joker in the Harlem Renaissance Deck," *CLA Journal* (June 2003).

Hawkswood, William G. *One of the Children: Gay Black Men in Harlem* (1996).

Kellner, Bruce. *The Harlem Renaissance: A Historical Dictionary for the Era* (1984).

Lewis, David Levering. *When Harlem Was in Vogue* (1981).

Schwarz, A. B. Christa. *Gay Voices of the Harlem Renaissance* (2003).

Obituary: *New York Times*, 10 July 1961.

DENNIS GOUWS

Jackson, Ada B. (11 July 1897–3 June 1989), community-and political activist, civil rights leader,-and women's rights advocate, was born in Savannah, Georgia. Jackson's father, whose name is not known, was freed from slavery by the Union army during the Civil War; nothing is known of her mother. Jackson's lifelong commitment to racial equality and social justice began when she was a child in Georgia. At a young age Jackson witnessed a family of eight being dragged from their home by a Ku Klux Klan mob and lynched. That experience shaped the course of her life.

Jackson left the South to attend the only historically black college in Oklahoma, the Colored Agricultural and Normal University (later Langston University). It is believed that she graduated, but the date of her degree and her course of study cannot be confirmed. After working briefly as a teacher, she moved north to Brooklyn, New York, with the Great Migration. In New York City, she joined the Young Women's Christian Association (YWCA), the NAACP, and became active in her church, Bethany Baptist, and the community more generally. At some point—whether before or shortly after moving north—she married a man whose name is now unknown. She was a mother of four, two of them adopted. Jackson fought to improve the neighborhood schools, chairing the local group Parents United Against Bigotry in the Schools, as well as the Parent-Teachers Association. She monitored conditions in area health centers as a member of the Bedford District Health Committee. During World War II, Jackson demonstrated her commitment by working with the Red Cross and War Bond campaigns at the same time that she led the Brooklyn Interracial Assembly in its protests against racial discrimination in the press and police brutality, and sponsored lectures in her home on African American history. Jackson's work in the community garnered her recognition and respect. Not only did the *Brooklyn Eagle*, the borough newspaper, name her one of Brooklyn's four "Fighting Ladies" during World War II, but she was also repeatedly asked to assume leadership roles, including serving as president of the Brooklyn chapter of the National Council of Negro Women (NCNW).

Jackson's civic activism drew her increasingly close to formal politics. In the mid-1940s she served on a local political education committee and then moved fully into the political arena when a citizens' group asked her to run for elected office. In 1944 Jackson ran for the New York State Assembly on the Republican Party and American Labor Party (ALP) primary ballots. During a voter registration rally with First Lady Eleanor Roosevelt, Jackson stated her commitment to full postwar employment and highlighted the importance of women exercising their political voice through the ballot. The progressive newspaper the *People's Voice* strongly endorsed Jackson's campaign, noting that she truly understood the needs of her community. Although she lost in the November election, Jackson's efforts in electoral politics were only beginning.

In 1946 Jackson again entered the Republican and ALP primaries for New York State Assembly. Her loss in the primary election against her Republican Party opponent, Maude Richardson, marked Jackson's last moments with the GOP. Railing against the party's racist practices, Jackson moved squarely into New York City's politically progressive coalition, running only on the ALP ticket from that point forward. Her defeat in the general election did not dampen her commitment to social change through the political process, nor did it mute her protests against injustice.

Even as the cold war escalated, Jackson sought political office a third time in 1947, running for the New York City Council. Activists including Paul Robeson, Lena Horne, Dorothy Parker, and the liberal paper *PM* supported her candidacy. Jackson's move to the left politically was evident in her platform, which called for the restoration of price controls and rent controls, the establishment of public day-care centers, the elimination of racial discrimination in employment and public housing, and a repeal of the anti-labor Taft-Hartley Act. Although her campaign generated a great deal of excitement among her Brooklyn neighborhood and political progressives, Jackson suffered yet another setback at the polls.

Community residents and the city's progressive activists were determined to see Jackson in office, so in 1948 they urged her to run for the U.S. House of Representatives. She was the first African American to run for U.S. Congress from Brooklyn. Two months before the election, Jackson roused a crowd of forty-eight thousand during a Progressive Party rally at Yankee Stadium. On the dais with strongly identified leftists, including the presidential candidate Henry Wallace, the actor Paul Robeson, and U.S. Congressman Vito Marcantonio, Jackson accused the Democratic presidential incumbent, Harry Truman, of misleading African American voters. She also reminded the crowd that the Democratic Party was dominated by southern racists. She then turned her attack on Thomas Dewey, the New York governor and Republican presidential candidate, referring to him as a silent reactionary. Despite the enthusiasm of local and national supporters, Jackson and the Progressive Party went down to defeat. The tide was turning even in New York City; the days were numbered for self-identified leftists in electoral politics.

Not one to give up easily, Jackson gave electoral politics one last try. In 1949 she ran on the ALP ticket for Brooklyn borough president. She was soundly defeated, even losing in her district by a wide margin. This was more than a defeat; it was an unmistakable message that Jackson and her politically progressive agenda had lost favor even in her own community.

After her final campaign, Jackson remained active. Not only was she an officer in the progressive Congress of American Women (CAW) but she also served as the ALP's delegate to the Women's International Democratic Federation Congress in Moscow in late 1949. From the Soviet Union, Jackson proceeded to China. Speaking at a conference with women from twenty-three African and Asian countries, she explored the concerns women had about their status, world peace, and child care.

Because of her outspoken stances and her activism, Jackson fell victim to red-baiting in the early 1950s. One of her organizations, the CAW, was branded a communist front by the U.S. attorney general and by the House Un-American Activities Committee (HUAC). Jackson's commitment to social and economic justice and her untiring efforts to improve the quality of life and the dignity of African Americans in Brooklyn meant little in the face of anti-communist witch-hunts. Jackson had fallen out of the news by the mid-1950s and her great work was largely hidden from history thereafter. Ada B. Jackson died in Brooklyn.

FURTHER READING

Newspaper clippings on Jackson's activities can be found at the Brooklyn Public Library and the Schomburg Center for Research in Black Culture in New York City.

JULIE GALLAGHER

Jackson, Al, Jr. (27 Nov. 1935–1 Oct. 1975), drummer, producer, and member of Booker T. and the MGs, was born in Memphis, Tennessee. Little is known of his mother, but his father Al Jackson Sr., led one of Memphis's most popular big bands, and it was with his father that Al Jr. first played professionally, beginning as a drummer at age ten. This apprenticeship proved fulfilling for the young musician: he got to play the jazz of his musical idols, and his tenure with his father won him gigs with the prominent dance groups led by Ben Branch and Willie Mitchell, respectively. These bands, which bridged the gap between postwar jazz and 1950s R&B, performed regularly in black clubs around the region, like the Flamingo Room and Plantation Inn. Aside from his steady gig, playing with the highly talented Mitchell soon brought Jackson into contact with Booker T. Jones, a prodigious keyboardist who—while still in high school—joined Mitchell's band.

In 1962 Jones was working sessions for an upstart Memphis R&B label called Stax, and he called Jackson to drum on a date behind the rocka-billy star Billy Lee Riley. Two early Stax mainstays, the guitarist Steve Cropper and the bassist Lewie Steinberg, completed that band. For reasons that are now unclear, the Riley session disintegrated, and the four talented players started jamming on a restless blues driven by Jones's humming organ. Recognizing the foursome's impromptu magic, Stax chief Jim Stewart decided to record the group's jam session. The instrumental became "Green Onions," released under the name Booker T. and the MGs in the fall of 1962. The song reached number 1 on the R&B charts and number 3 on Pop, marking the first time Stax achieved such crossover success.

Jackson initially expressed reluctance about leaving his well-paying job with Willie Mitchell to become a regular Stax employee, but the quick success of "Green Onions" quieted any fears he might have had. For the next five years, Booker T. and the MGs, with Jackson's solid drumming at its core, became the bedrock of the popular "Stax sound," both on their own recordings (the group charted several major hits, including "Boot-Leg," "Chinese Checkers," and "Hip Hug-Her") and as the backing band on nearly every release by Stax's legendary roster of artists, including classics by OTIS REDDING, Sam & Dave, Carla Thomas, WILSON PICKETT, and many others. As soul music became the dominant form of black popular music during the 1960s, with Memphis one of its primary centers, Jackson helped define Stax's trademark style. Based around spare, churchy arrangements that contrasted with the Phil Spector-esque "Wall of Sound" style favored at labels like Motown, Stax usually built tracks around Jackson's steady percussion, which provided a firm foundation for the pulsating polyrhythm of Jones's organ, Cropper's guitar, or the "Memphis Horns." According to Cropper, it was he and Jackson who took charge of finding each song's funky base (Bowman, 98). In addition, the half-white/half-black band offered a model for the interracial atmosphere of southern soul, which was far more integrated than its northern counterparts. Stax ascended rapidly, with Al Jackson behind the drum-kit. The label made a triumphant tour of Europe in 1966, and later brought "Memphis soul" to the burgeoning counterculture with Otis Redding's performance at the Monterey Pop Festival. During this period, all four MGs became members of the Stax "Big 6," a production pool and creative decision-making body that also included the songwriters and musicians ISAAC HAYES and David Porter.

The late 1960s saw a series of changes at Stax. Otis Redding's death and a number of poor business deals led new president Al Bell to push Stax in a different direction, one that emphasized the ambitious rhetoric of "Black Power" independence that Bell actively promoted. The MGs slowly disintegrated owing to a variety of factors ranging from interpersonal turmoil to the label's new management. Jones left in 1970 and Cropper soon followed. They continued recording sporadically, but their heyday as one of soul's premier ensembles was over. Production and songwriting duties moved away from the "Big 6," toward newly prominent songwriters and producers like Don Davis, the "We Three" team, and the group of musicians located at Muscle Shoals Sound Studio in northern Alabama. Still, Jackson continued at Stax in multiple capacities, including relatively regular production duties for new stars the Soul Children.

In 1970, while still working full time at Stax, Jackson started playing sessions for Willie Mitchell, now the house producer at Hi Records, another Memphis soul label about to break through with AL GREEN, Ann Peebles, and others. Mitchell's productions exhibited lush orchestrations and rich polyrhythms, and he found the perfect percussive firmament for these hit recordings with his old friend and band-mate Jackson. Jackson became one of Hi's primary drummers as its records climbed the charts.

In 1975, just as Jackson and "Duck" Dunn hoped to reform the MGs for a comeback album, a domestic disturbance between Jackson and his wife, Barbara (née Griffin, a former Flamingo Club singer), resulted in Barbara's shooting Al five times in the back as he left their Memphis home. Jackson recovered but only two months later he was the victim of another shooting, this time by an unidentified assailant. That attack was fatal. Initially believed to be a robbery, soon rumors began to circulate, implicating everyone from rogue elements in the Memphis police to Barbara Jackson herself. In fact, police later questioned Barbara, her friend and fellow singer, Denise LaSalle, and LaSalle's boyfriend in connection with the attack, but no one ever stood trial for Jackson's killing.

Less than a year after Jackson's death, Stax too met its end, felled by flawed economics and the departure of some of its most important talent. Jackson's death thus became both a senseless tragedy and a symbolic death-knell for a great American record label. His involvement with dozens of classic recordings (on both Stax and Hi) makes him one of the most important session musicians in twentieth-century American music.

FURTHER READING

Bowman, Rob. *Soulsville U.S.A.: The Story of Stax Records* (1997).

Bush, John. "Al Jackson, Jr.," in *All Music Guide to Soul*, ed. Vladimir Bogdanov (2003).

Guralnick, Peter. *Sweet Soul Music: Rhythm and Blues and the Southern Dream of Freedom* (1986).

DISCOGRAPHY

Booker T. and the MGs. *Time Is Tight: Anthology* (Stax Records, 4424).

Various Artists. *Royal Memphis Soul* (Hi Records, 11).

Various Artists. *The Stax Story* (Stax Records, 4429).

CHARLES L. HUGHES

Jackson, Allen F. (1897–9 Oct. 1970), civil rights activist and the first black physician in Hartford, Connecticut, was born in Washington, DC. The names of Jackson's parents are unknown, but census records indicate they were also born in Washington, DC. He grew up and attended public school in Washington, DC, and in 1922 he graduated from the Howard University School of Medicine. It is possible that he did not complete an undergraduate degree, since at that time a high school diploma plus only two years of college—and knowledge of mathematics, English, and Latin, were required for admission. During the year 1923, Jackson traveled to Hartford, Connecticut, where he worked as both a surgeon and physician until his death.

When Dr. Jackson began practicing medicine in 1923, he was considered Hartford's first black physician. In the United States, there were only several thousand black physicians at the time, many of whom were scorned by those outside their community. Around 1927, Jackson's name began appearing more frequently in the Hartford newspapers because of his participation in community activities concerning either medicine or politics. For example, he volunteered as an examiner in Hartford during the National Negro Health Week, a major campaign for the prevention of tuberculosis in which doctors were needed to provide free examinations. Also, he was a member of the committee organized to welcome to Hartford Republican U.S. Representative OSCAR DEPRIEST, the only African American in Congress, at that time. The 1930 census indicated that Dr. Allen Jackson had married and was living with Gladys S. Jackson (maiden name unknown), but they did not have any children together and eventually divorced. After his divorce, he married a woman named Ada Waldo Jackson; this marriage was also childless.

Starting in 1940, Dr. Jackson became a member of many civil rights organizations, such as the NAACP. In 1940, he was also cochairman of the Greater Hartford Drive of the United Negro College Fund. The goal of the campaign was to raise $25,000 to help provide African Americans with the funds for a higher education. Three years later, he became a member of the National Board of Directors for the NAACP, while maintaining his position as president of the local chapter in Hartford. In 1956 Dr. Jackson went to the Democratic National Convention as the first black delegate from Connecticut. During that same year, Dr. Jackson was mentioned in the *Journal of the National Medical Association* for his reappointment to the Connecticut Commission on Civil Rights by Governor Abraham Ribicoff. Five years earlier, he had been appointed by Governor Chester A. Bowles to that position, where he helped on various matters including reducing discrimination in housing and work areas.

For the last decade of his life, Dr. Allen Jackson continued to receive praise for all of his hard work and contributions toward the advancement of African Americans. For example, he served as a national vice president for the NAACP and received a Certificate of Appreciation from that organization in 1962. However, in 1963, he was found guilty of three counts of tax evasion and he was fined a total of $3,000, despite his protests that he was innocent. All through the trial, Dr. Jackson continued to be a member in various organizations, including the Faith Congregational Church, Old Timers Club, the New England Welfare League, the Shanti Club of New Haven, the New Nutmeg Lodge 67, IBPOE (The Improved Benevolent and Protective Order of Elks, a primarily African American fraternal and charitable organization), the Gillison Council 75, and the Omega Psi Phi and Carpe Diem fraternities.

After practicing medicine in Hartford for around forty-seven years, Jackson died in Mount Sinai Hospital on 9 October 1970. On 24 October 1972, a memorial was held in honor of Dr. Jackson and two other black civil rights activists. Dr. Allen Jackson played a key role in the advancement of African Americans in Connecticut and throughout the country.

FURTHER READING

Barker, R. G. "Jackson Heads Connecticut Commission." *Journal of the National Medical*

Association 48 (1956): 202. Available at: http://www.ncbi.nlm.nih.gov/pmc/articles/PMC2641100/pdf/jnma00721-0054b.pdf (accessed 20 March 2011).

"DePriest Will Speak Here On August 18; Negro Congressman from Illinois to Give Address at Parsons's in Afternoon." *Hartford Courant,* 26 July 1929, p. 25.

"Health Week To Be Held for Negroes; Intensive Campaign, with Tuberculosis Prevention Chief Object, Outlined by Committee" *Hartford Courant,* 2 Apr. 1927, p. 3.

U.S. Federal Census (1930). *Hartford, Connecticut;* Form 15-6; Enumeration District g-69.

Obituary: *Hartford Daily Courant,* 11 Oct. 1970.

CONSTANCE KY

Jackson, Angela (25 July 1951–), poet, fiction writer, and dramatist, was born in Greenville, Mississippi, to George and Angeline Jackson. Her family moved from the South to Chicago, Illinois, when she was a child, and she remained there during her studies, graduating from Northwestern University with a B.A. in 1977. In 1970 Jackson became involved with Chicago's Organization of Black American Culture (OBAC) and attended the writers' workshop run by HOYT FULLER, coordinator of OBAC and editor of *Black World.* Jackson, who became the coordinator of the OBAC in 1976 (a role she occupied until 1990), was influenced by its focus on the black aesthetic and dedicated her first book of poetry, *Voo Doo/Love Magic* (1974), to her family, Fuller, and OBAC. Her second collection, the chapbook *The Greenville Club,* was published in *Four Black Poets* (1977), a collection that Alvin Aubert argues is characterized by an "inevitably intense fusion of the sensibilities of the inner and outer, the private and public human being" (157). It reflects her own life in its focus on Chicago residents who relocated from Greenville, and, according to Aubert, it possesses a "precision of language, of articulateness, that invites repeated reading," engaging readers and giving them the sense of "having participated in a significant act of language … grounded in particular human experiences" (157). Both *Voo Doo/Love Magic* and *The Greenville Club* reflect the goals of the OBAC in Jackson's experimentation with language and form to articulate African American identity.

Her achievement in writing during the 1970s was marked by the awards she received: *Black World*'s Conrad Kent Rivers Memorial Award (1973), Northwestern's Edwin Schulman Fiction Prize, and the Academy of American Poets Prize (1974). During the 1970s and 1980s Jackson received tremendous support from her readership, critics, and the literary community. Both the Illinois Arts Council and the National Endowment for the Humanities awarded her fellowships in these years, literally demonstrating their support for her work. Jackson's third book of poetry, *Solo in the Boxcar Third Floor E* (1985), was awarded the American Book Award from the Before Columbus Foundation and was followed by two more volumes, *The Man with the White Liver* (1987) and *Dark Legs and Silk Kisses: The Beatitudes of the Spinners* (1993). While her early poetry earned her awards and established her reputation as a new voice in the 1970s, her poetry published in the 1980s and 1990s was critically praised, marking her achievements and solidifying her reputation as a central figure in contemporary African American literature. Jackson received many awards in the 1980s and 1990s that reflect the quality of her work in these volumes: the DuSable Museum Writers' Seminar Poetry Prize (1985), Pushcart Prize for Poetry (1989), Chicago Sun-Times/Friends of Literature Book of the Year Award for Poetry (1994), Carl Sandburg Award from the Chicago Public Library (1994), ETA Gala Award (1994), and Illinois Authors Literary Heritage Award (1996). Her 1998 collection of poetry, *And All These Roads Be Luminous: Poems Selected and New,* which was nominated for the National Book Award, represents her work from the 1960s to the 1990s. As the title suggests, it is an offering of both selected poems from her earlier volumes and new work, so in a sense it is representative of the trajectory of her contributions to a twentieth-century American literary tradition. While *And All These Roads Be Luminous* represents the emergence and development of a significant contemporary African American poet, Jackson has also worked across genres, composing short stories, a novel, and plays. Her short stories have been published in numerous venues, including *Chicago Review, First World, Black World, Story Quarterly,* and *TriQuarterly. Treemont Stone* (1984), a novel, reflects her experimentation in form and language. In different media Jackson creates a pastiche of forms and questions conventions. For example, in the poem "The Race of Memory," from *Dark Legs and Silk Kisses,* the speaker begins with the prose lines "I collect the race of memory, even in my stance, quiet, octave quiet. Not even one thread will quiver, no bough of silver break" and ends with the enjambed lines "Alive and weaving well. / Glorious in heaven / and earth. / At last. / Think of the Sun." In this poem and throughout her poetry she works at reconfiguring language and the forms of poetry and prose. While Jackson performed her poetry in the 1970s and 1980s in Chicago and as a participant in poets-in-the-schools programs, her adaptation of her poetry in the plays *Witness!* (1978), *Shango Diaspora: An African-American Myth of Womanhood and Love* (1980), *When the Wind Blows* (1984), and *Comfort Stew* (1997) are significant contributions to American drama and specifically to the literary scene in Chicago in the late twentieth century, as they were all produced there.

A prolific writer, Jackson has also been actively involved with universities across the country, as writer-in-residence at Stephens College (1983–1986) and Columbia College (1988–1992); Christa McAuliffe Visiting Professor of Diversity at Framingham State College (1994); and visiting professor and professor of writing at Howard University (1994, 1995–1997). Jackson directed the OBAC from 1976 to 1990, served as a member of the Illinois Arts Council literature panel between 1979 and 1981 and again in 1992, and was a member of the ETA Playwright Discovery Initiative from 1991 to 1998. She has demonstrated her commitment to her art as well as to artistic communities. In the piece "In Memoriam: GWENDOLYN BROOKS (1917–2000)," Jackson describes Brooks as an "amazing amalgam of the sublime artiste and the people's poet," concluding that "in this sense she was an essentially African-American poet" (*Callaloo* 23.4 [2000], 1166). In his review of *Four Black Poets*, Aubert writes, "There is a quality in Angela's style that is reminiscent of Gwendolyn Brooks's, at times in the sonar-rhythmical inventiveness of the senior Chicago poet but more often in subtler ways that let us know it *is* inventiveness, thus original" (158). Jackson's description of Brooks, "whose word was poetry itself," can be read as representative of what is at stake in her own legacy. Receiving the Shelley Memorial Award of the Poetry Society of America in 2002 indicates Jackson's solid presence in not only a twentieth-century American literary tradition but also an emerging tradition in the twenty-first century.

FURTHER READING

Aubert, Alvin. Review of *Four Black Poets, Black American Literature Forum* 12.4 (1978).

Dictionary of Literary Biography, vol. 41: *Afro-American Poets since 1955*, eds. Trudier Harris and Thadious M. Davis (1985).

LISA K. PERDIGAO

Jackson, Bessie. *See* Bogan, Lucille.

Jackson, Bo (30 Nov. 1962–), baseball and football player, was born Vincent Edward Jackson in the steel town of Bessemer, Alabama, the son of Florence Jackson and A. D. Adams. Vincent and his nine brothers and sisters were so poor that a mixture of grits and margarine was often their only meal of the day, if they ate at all. His frustration over this poverty, a severe stutter, and his father's absence led Vincent to such antisocial behavior that his older relatives nicknamed him "Bo," short for "boar hog," because he was as wild as one. A fear of jail finally motivated him to change, and he channeled his energy into sports. During his senior year at McAdory High School, Bo played four different positions on the football team, set state records in several track events, and tied a national high school baseball record with twenty home runs in twenty-five games. The New York Yankees selected him in the June 1982 draft and offered him a $250,000 signing bonus, but he chose college instead, driven by his mother's proclamation that "you can have money for a short time, but education is for your whole life."

Jackson enrolled at Auburn University in Alabama because the football coach agreed to let him start as a freshman and play multiple sports. In his first year Jackson rushed for 829 yards and scored nine touchdowns, including one that gave the Tigers their first victory in ten years over their rival, the University of Alabama. Jackson, Auburn's first three-sport letterman since the 1950s, became the school's all-time leading rusher in football, hit .400 in baseball, and nearly qualified for the 1984 Olympic track team. He also met his future wife, a graduate student in counseling psychology named Linda (whose maiden name is unknown), with whom he had three children. In his senior year Jackson overcame multiple injuries to rush for more than 1,700 yards and win the Heisman Trophy, college football's highest honor.

Jackson was drafted by both the Tampa Bay Buccaneers of the National Football League and the Kansas City Royals of Major League Baseball, and in a controversial decision he chose to sign with the Royals, stating that baseball was his favorite sport. It is also probable that Jackson simply did not want to play with the Buccaneers, one of the worst teams in the league. In his very first major league at bat, on 2 September 1986, Jackson got an infield hit off the future Hall of Fame pitcher Steve Carlton. During the remainder of that season and the next, Jackson showed both tremendous promise and maddening inconsistency, breaking the team record for home runs by a rookie (one 475-foot blast was the longest in the history of Royals Stadium) but also striking out far too often, including a record-tying five times in one game.

The possibility of a football career resurfaced when the Oakland Raiders drafted Jackson in 1987. After intense negotiations he agreed to play for them once the baseball season had ended. Some critics and fans were displeased when he referred to this decision as "adding another hobby to my off-season curriculum." This was all but forgotten, however, after a game against the Seattle Seahawks on 30 November 1987. During the *Monday Night Football* broadcast seen by millions around the country Jackson scored three touchdowns: a pass reception, a ninety-one-yard run from scrimmage (the eighth-longest in league history), and a play in which he literally ran over the highly touted Seattle rookie linebacker Brian Bosworth. He ended the season with an average of 6.8 yards per carry, nearly twice the league average, and legends such as GALE SAYERS, O. J. SIMPSON, and JIM BROWN proclaimed that he would be a sure Hall of Famer if he concentrated on football.

Jackson continued to improve in both football and baseball in 1988. Injuries and strikeouts still plagued him on the baseball diamond, but he threw out eleven base runners from center field and also became the first player in Royals history to hit twenty-five home runs and steal twenty-five bases. His second football season was also good, if not as spectacular as the first. In 1989, however, Jackson became a national phenomenon. After being named to his first All-Star Team in baseball, he was named the game's MVP, after hitting a 448-foot home run in his first at bat. His rising popularity also helped the Royals draw their biggest crowds ever that year. He then joined the Raiders for eleven games and rushed for nearly a thousand yards, including another spectacular ninety-yard run. Although there had been other two-sport athletes before him, only the 1930s golfer and track star Babe Didrikson Zaharias had truly excelled in more than one sport, and her deeds were largely overlooked by a press and public that had little interest in female athletes. Jackson, on the other hand, was a full-fledged star who rivaled MICHAEL JORDAN as the country's most popular athlete. Nike's hugely successful ad campaign featured him playing more than ten sports and made the words "Bo knows" a national catchphrase. At the same time, however, many people still thought that he should focus on just one sport.

In 1990 that decision was made for him. After he finished the baseball season with twenty-eight home runs and a career low in strikeouts, he rushed for nearly seven hundred yards and was selected to play in the Pro Bowl, thus becoming the first all-star in two professional sports. During the NFL playoffs, however, he suffered a hip injury that led to a condition known as avascular necrosis. This caused the cartilage and bone to deteriorate so much that doctors were forced to give him a prosthetic hip in early 1992. He retired from football, and the Royals released him from his contract, believing that he was also finished in baseball. After intense rehabilitation, however, Jackson returned to baseball in 1993 with the Chicago White Sox. He hit a home run in his very first game and helped the White Sox win their first division title in ten years, but the team was not convinced that he had good chances for a long-term recovery, and he was released again. Jackson played one final season with the California Angels (later the Anaheim Angels) in 1994 and hit a career-high .279 before his still-deteriorating condition forced him to retire for good.

Several months after announcing his retirement Jackson graduated from Auburn with a degree in family and child development, after which he established several businesses in Chicago and Alabama. He led a nonprofit youth program and the Sports Medicine Council, and he acted in several Christian television programs. His brief but spectacular career encouraged numerous other athletes to try their hand at both baseball and football, although only DEION SANDERS has come close to Jackson's level of success. Jackson was one of the first African American athletes to enjoy fame as a major corporate pitchman, helping to pave the way for stars like TIGER WOODS and LeBron James. In 1998 he was inducted into the College Football Hall of Fame, and two years later ESPN selected him as the seventy-second greatest athlete of the twentieth century; some argued that if the main criterion were potential rather than actual results, Jackson would have been at the very top of the list. This sentiment was echoed by Jackson's Kansas City Royals teammate George Brett, who boasted that "if he set his mind to anything, athletically, he could do it. He's just the best athlete I've ever seen" (Jackson, iii).

FURTHER READING

Jackson, Bo, and Dick Schaap. *Bo Knows Bo: The Autobiography of a Ballplayer* (1990).

Gutman, Bill. *Bo Jackson: A Biography* (1991).

DAVID BRODNAX SR.

Jackson, Daniel (7 Sept. 1870–18 May 1929), politician, businessman, and underworld boss, was born Daniel McKee Jackson in Pittsburgh, Pennsylvania, to Emmeline (maiden name unknown) and Emanuel Jackson. Emanuel was the owner of a successful funeral home that served the small African American population of Pittsburgh. Daniel, along with his sister Elizabeth and his brother Charles, grew up in the house that their father had built near the banks of the Allegheny River in 1861. Daniel Jackson attended Pittsburgh public schools and Western Pennsylvania University (later the University of Pittsburgh) before joining his father and brother in the family business.

When Jackson was twenty-two his father moved the funeral home to the South Side of Chicago, setting up shop on Twenty-sixth and State streets. In the 1890s the South Side was a diverse neighborhood with a tiny but growing number of black residents. The energetic and charismatic Jackson soon became a fixture in the intertwined worlds of vice and politics, rubbing elbows with figures like William Hale Thompson, the future mayor of Chicago, and Robert Motts, the owner of the Pekin, the city's preeminent black theater. The Emanuel Jackson Funeral Home lay within the boundaries of the Second Ward, a district fast becoming known as a place where ambitious blacks could make their mark on local politics, and Jackson longed to join the few powerful black men who had the ear of Chicago's established politicians. Precedent had already been set in the nearby First Ward where enterprising men like Edward H. Wright and William "Mushmouth" Johnson gained influence by delivering the black vote to mayoral candidates in exchange for political appointments and the freedom to run their saloons without police interference.

But Jackson aspired to more than just behind-the-scenes power. In a city where the black vote was courted by both the Republican and the Democratic parties, he quickly made himself known as a staunch Republican, frequently writing vituperative letters to the *Broad Ax*, a black Democratic weekly that he called "too vile to occupy a place in the toilet room" (*Broad Ax*, 16 Feb. 1901). In 1900 he received a nomination for county commissioner at the Republican convention but lost the election after several newspapers highlighted that he was the only black candidate.

Undaunted, Jackson served the rapidly enlarging black community of the South Side in other ways. Between 1900 and 1930 migrants from the South increased the African American population of Chicago from just over 30,000 to more than 200,000. Many blacks settled in and around the Second Ward, which became known as Bronzeville, the center of a thriving political and social world dominated by African Americans. After his father's death Jackson took over the Emanuel Jackson Funeral Home and continued to diversify his business activities. When Robert Motts died in 1910, Jackson married his sister Lucy Motts and became owner of the Pekin Theater, which he renamed the Beaux Arts Club. He ran gambling games out of this and other locations, where interested individuals could find a rousing game of craps or poker or could pay to pick the winning number in "policy," a lottery-like sweepstakes.

During William Hale Thompson's run for mayor in 1915, Dan Jackson accelerated the meteoric rise that would make him boss of the Second Ward. Thompson, an acquaintance of Jackson's since the 1890s, assiduously courted the black vote. Jackson helped secure 80 percent of the Second Ward's vote for Thompson, who became mayor shortly thereafter. In return Thompson turned a blind eye to extralegal activities on the South Side, allowing new gambling parlors, cabarets, and saloons to flourish unmolested. Jackson was now head of a syndicate that collected protection money from local business owners who faced the threat of a newly energized police force if they did not pay up. By 1921 the *Chicago Daily News* estimated that Jackson's vice syndicate, now also profiting from the illegal trade in alcohol made possible by Prohibition, collected $500,000 each year in the Second Ward.

Jackson's success provoked the ire of journalists and city politicians. His Tia Juana wheel, a large wooden barrel from which the winning numbers in policy were drawn each week, ran out in the open and drew huge crowds of spectators. The Beaux Arts, rumored to be the site of a "black and tan" club where interracial couples could meet for liaisons, was the source of outraged articles in not only the *Daily News*, a close follower of Jackson's activities, but also the *Chicago Tribune* and the *New York Times*. Press attention to the club and other aspects of the South Side's vibrant nightlife resulted in a state attorney's investigation into graft throughout

Chicago. As a result of this investigation the police captain Stephen K. Healy and OSCAR DE PRIEST, Chicago's first black alderman, were indicted for conspiring to allow gambling and prostitution. Jackson, however, escaped the investigation unscathed and went on to open one of Chicago's largest gambling resorts, the Racetrack, in 1922.

When William Hale Thompson failed to run for mayor in 1923, Jackson's luck seemed to have run out. Using the chorus from the popular song "Bye, Bye Blackbird" as a campaign slogan, the Democratic Party ran a successful campaign encouraging whites to elect William E. Dever as the new mayor, arguing that ousting the Republican Party would reduce the number of blacks in Chicago. Not surprisingly Jackson was unable to form the type of mutually beneficial arrangement with Dever that he had had with Thompson. Jackson's gambling parlors had to operate undercover, and his ability to collect protection money from the other establishments in his syndicate was weakened considerably. Dever authorized frequent police raids on speakeasies and gambling halls in Bronzeville, attempting to give his administration a reputation for being tough on crime.

Jackson vowed to do what he could to get Dever out of office. When William Hale Thompson ran for mayor again in 1927, Jackson delivered 91.7 percent of the Second Ward's black vote to his old ally. Shortly thereafter Thompson rewarded him with a rich banquet of political spoils. In 1928 Jackson cast a vote for Herbert Hoover as a delegate to the National Republican Convention in Kansas City. Later that year the Republican voters of the Second Ward elected Jackson to the position of ward committeeman, fulfilling his lifelong dream of holding elective office, and Governor Len Small appointed him to the Illinois Commerce Commission.

Despite the evident return to good fortune that Jackson experienced with Thompson's reelection, 1928 was a difficult year for him. His increased visibility had unpleasant consequences: a special grand jury indicted him in September 1928 on charges of protecting gambling, and gunmen held him up on the steps of city hall that summer, escaping with $25,000 in cash that he was carrying in his pockets. In the fall his good friend and Harlem businessman CASPER HOLSTEIN was kidnapped and held for ransom, and his wife, Lucy, passed away. Jackson died a few months later, after being stricken suddenly with influenza at his brother's home.

Although Jackson was a leading figure in Chicago's seamy underworld, many people loved and admired him for his generosity. He paid rent for friends and acquaintances, furnished coal for the needy during Chicago's brutal winters, and gave freely to the NAACP. One black journalist said shortly after his death, "While Jackson was in power the colored people always had a friend to go to" (Gosnell, 132). The *Chicago Defender* estimated that 6,000 people came to his Pittsburgh funeral, eager to pay their respects to "Fighting Dan." At a time when many blacks suffered the horrors of disenfranchisement, Daniel Jackson represented a new, indefatigable breed of urban black politician: shrewd, resourceful, and determined to amass power by any means necessary.

FURTHER READING

Allswang, John. *A House for All Peoples: Ethnic Politics in Chicago* (1971).

Bukowski, Douglas. *Big Bill Thompson, Chicago, and the Politics of Image* (1998).

Drake, St. Clair, and Horace R. Clayton. *Black Metropolis: A Study of Negro Life in a Northern City* (1945).

Gosnell, Harold F. *Negro Politicians: The Rise of Negro Politics in Chicago* (1935).

Ianni, Francis A. J. *Black Mafia: Ethnic Succession in Organized Crime* (1974).

Lombardo, Robert M. "The Black Mafia: African-American Organized Crime in Chicago 1890–1960," *Crime, Law, and Social Change* 38 (2002).

Schatzberg, Rufus, and Robert Kelly. *African-American Organized Crime: A Social History* (1996).

KIMBERLY SIMS

Jackson, Dinnah (c. 1740–after June 1818), property owner and matriarch of eighteenth-century free black Albany, New York. Records indicate that Jackson was the first African American to own property in Albany. In January 1779 she bought a city lot on the South side of lower Second Street. We know little of her origins; however, by the time of this fortuitous purchase she had married Jack Johnson, a free man of color from Albany. They had two sons, Jack and Lewis. In 1790 Dinnah Jackson worked as the housekeeper at the Masonic Lodge and at Saint Peter's Episcopal Church. Exactly how she was able to purchase her property is unclear, but she may have been extremely frugal and resourceful, or perhaps she had an unknown benefactor.

In the eighteenth and early nineteenth centuries people lived near their work, and most free blacks lived near one another for support and companionship. Unlike many other northern cities, no segregated free black communities are identified in colonial and Revolutionary Albany, New York, thus making Jackson even more of a pioneer. Scattered among the white Albanians, free blacks began to establish a community. The free blacks living on Ferry Street probably worked on the ferry and at the east side Hudson River water industries. Other free blacks on Maiden Lane, situated near the seat of government (city hall and the state capitol) on the west side, served the governor, his officials, and their families. Along the outer edge of North Market Street, free blacks served the merchant class. Finally, those in southern Albany lived near the homes of one or more prominent white Albany families, "Cherry Hill" (Johannes Van Rensselaer's residence), the Robert Yates House, and General Philip Schuyler's mansion to serve them and their families.

Sometime between 1779 and 1800 a second Jackson family, headed by Abraham Jackson, owned property in Albany. Abraham's wife was Diana, an emancipated slave formerly owned by an Albany merchant. Abraham and Diana owned their home on Bassett Street. The Albany city directory indicates that at least three of Abraham and Diana's Bassett Street neighbors were free black watermen: Bristol (Bristow), John Johnson, and Patrick Cole. Jack and Dinnah Jackson lived around the corner on South Pearl Street. Jack may have passed on as early as 1788; a state census for that year lists only a "Widow Jackson" living with her son in the area known as the Second Ward. In 1802 Albany taxed "Dian" or Dinnah Jackson for two properties, a house on Orange Street and a town lot nearby. By 1809 Dinnah's neighbor Abraham Jackson leased space on a Quay Street dock to work with the boatmen and ferrymen. A salesperson, Abraham sold produce and other goods. He was also a longshoreman (dockworker), who loaded and unloaded boats and ferries. Many of the boatmen and ferrymen were also free blacks according to the city directory. Two of them were Jack Jackson and Lewis Jackson, possibly Dinnah's sons; they lived in northern Albany.

In her declining years, probably outliving all her children (her two sons are absent from the record and either died or moved away), Jackson moved in with her grandchildren. Jackson's will dated June 1818 revealed six grandchildren as her only heirs. First, to her namesake Dinnah she left a bedstead with bedding, furniture, clothes, money, and five town lots in Arbor Hill. The very poor could not afford a bed off the floor (bedstead), other furniture, and more than one suit of clothes. Second,

Jain (Jane) received furniture, clothing, and one-half of another lot. Third, John Jackson received an additional Arbor Hill land lot. Finally, three young grandchildren, Elizabeth, Hannah, and Harrah, received money.

By the time she died, perhaps from exhaustion and overwork, Jackson owned at least twelve town lots in Albany. Though they were not huge plots, simply owning land made her a leader in the city's black community. Perhaps the grandchildren and other family members continued Jackson's legacy; *The 1820 Albany City Directory* listed fourteen Jackson households. Some lived in Dinnah Jackson's Arbor Hill, others in the South End, where they worked as a ferryman, a musician, a victualler, and a laborer. The women in these households may have worked as maids and housekeepers for the more prominent white city dwellers. Together with their children, these Jacksons represented fifty-seven free black persons.

The local artist James Eights, who captured her likeness on canvas in his 1850 painting *The East Side of North Market Street in 1805*, immortalized Jackson, matriarch of Albany's eighteenth-century free black community. In the painting Jackson is standing on Market Street near her Maiden Lane home, a residence she remained in until at least 1814. In the painting, she appeared to be under five feet tall. Dinnah was portrayed here as a handsome African American woman, medium dark skinned in complexion, pressed and tightly curled black ear-length hair with an hourglass figure (that is, a rather small waist and somewhat larger, but well proportioned breasts and hips). Her facial features are indistinguishable. Mrs. Jackson is wearing a blue-green ankle-length gown, with a loosely fitted bodice, natural waist, bell-shaped skirt, short-sleeves, above the elbow, and a modest oval neckline. She struck a natural pose, standing between two hitching posts, with the left hand on her hip, right arm at her side, and her feet shoulder width apart, on a beautiful spring day. As the community's matriarch, she ruled over thirty-nine other Jacksons, Lattimores, and Schuylers—the elite of free Afro-Albany. The total free black population in 1815 Albany was about eight hundred in a city of approximately thirty-five thousand people.

FURTHER READING
Bielinski, Stefan. "The Jacksons, Lattimores, and Schuylers: First African American Families of Early Albany," *New York History* (Oct 1996).

KAREN E. SUTTON

Jackson, Eliza Belle Mitchell (31 Dec. 1848–
7 Nov. 1942), teacher, organizer of schools, homes
for orphans and senior citizens, and social clubs,
was born in Perryville and grew up in nearby
Danville, Kentucky, the daughter of Monroe and
Mary Douglas Mitchell. Her father, who had been
enslaved, hired his time and earned money as a
carpenter, eventually purchasing his freedom and
then his wife's. Mitchell attended a school for free
colored children, permitted even before 1860, then
at age eleven was taken to Xenia, Ohio, by her
mother, where she attended the public school for
three years. She had at least two sisters, Mary and
Martha, recorded in the 1860 census. The family
home had several neighbors recorded as black or
mulatto, all presumably free, or they would only
have been counted in the slave census. Several
neighbors with no record of "color" would presumably have been considered to be white. At the age
of twelve, Mitchell made a profession of faith in the
Methodist church.

In the fall 1865, Mitchell was invited by Reverend
John G. Fee, superintendent of activities and services of the Baptist-affiliated American Missionary
Association (AMA) and Freedman's Aid Society
at Camp Nelson, Kentucky, to join the teaching
staff. He believed that an African American teacher
would serve as a role model; nevertheless, teachers, army officers, and chaplains (including units
from Maine and Illinois) objected to the young
lady eating in the common boarding hall. Fee
responded, "I will suffer my right arm torn from
my body before I will remove the young woman.
The young woman is fitted for her position; she
is modest and discreet; she is a Christian, and as
such Christ's representative: What I do to her I do
to him." Nineteenth-century accounts record that
two women, a Mrs. Colton and her daughter, also
welcomed her. While Fee was absent on personal
business, the camp commander asked her to leave.
AMA later sent a committee to Camp Nelson and
required all teachers "to sign a paper declaring they
would not make complexion a condition of association among teachers." The entire series of events
was known as the "Belle Mitchell Incident."

Mitchell returned to Danville, but the AMA soon
invited her to teach children of black soldiers at the
First African Baptist Church School in Lexington.
In 1867, she taught at Howard School in Richmond,
Kentucky, then in 1868 enrolled at Berea College
(founded by Reverend Fee). Just short of graduation, she married Jordan Carlisle Jackson, a veteran of Company E, 5th U.S. Colored Cavalry, on
23 February 1871. Jackson had been enslaved at birth,
28 February 1848 in Fayette County Kentucky, and
taught himself to read and write. During the couple's marriage he operated a funeral business and
livery stable described by Booker T. Washington
as "the finest in Central Kentucky." Although some
sources refer to 1874 Berea graduate John Henry
Jackson as Jordan Jackson's son by a previous marriage, Jordan Jackson was twenty-six when John
Henry Jackson graduated from Berea, making such
a connection highly unlikely.

The newly married Belle Jackson returned to
teaching school in Lexington. The Jacksons were
active members of St. Paul AME Church. They
had two children, Minnie and Mitchell Jackson,
and at least two granddaughters, Sadie Mae and
Myrtle Bell Yancey. There are conflicting references
as to whether Minnie, born in 1877, was adopted;
Mitchell, born in 1894, likely was.

As president of the Kentucky Association of
Colored Women, E. Belle Mitchell Jackson was
instrumental in establishing the PHYLLIS WHEATLEY
branch of the YWCA in Lexington. In 1892 she
led a small group of African American women
in establishing the Colored Orphan Industrial
Home, which provided food, clothing, and shelter
to children who had lost their parents. The group
also developed a retirement home, a hospital, and a
lending institution. Jackson was elected president of
the Ladies Orphans Home Society, which managed
the home, and she served on the board of governors for nearly fifty years. The home had a training
program intended for all colored youth, not only
resident orphans, modeled on industrial training
programs of the Hampton and Tuskegee Institutes.
Skills emphasized included blacksmithing, sewing,
chair-caning, cooking, carpentry, painting, gardening, and laundry work.

In 1900 the Jacksons lived with their chil-
dren Mitchell and Minnie at 242 Short Street in
Lexington. They also hosted two boarders, Doly
Sandusky and a woman named Rowe. In 1910, at 314
E. Short Street—where the family remained until
and sometime after Jordan Jackson's death—the
household included their married daughter Minnie
Yancey and her daughters, Sadie Mae and Myrtle
Bell Yancey, Mitchell Jackson, a ward named Cora
Frazer, and Belle Jackson's 83-year-old mother,
Mary E. Mitchell. At this time, Belle Jackson was
a partner in the business of Jackson and Hathaway,
advertised in the *Lexington Standard* (27 January
1900) as "The Only Colored Milliners in Lexington,"
offering hats and bonnets at 38 W. Main Street.

Jordan C. Jackson died of interstitial nephritis 4 October 1918, in Lexington, leaving all of his property to his wife, who survived him by an additional twenty-four years. Belle Jackson died in Lexington at her home on 277 E. 5th Street. Her death certificate erroneously recorded her year of birth as 1870, a date well after some of the most poignant incidents in her life. In fact, at her death she was just a few years short of one hundred.

FURTHER READING

Johnson, William Decker. *Biographical Sketches of Prominent Negro Men and Women of Kentucky* (1897/1973).

Sears, Richard D. *A Utopian Experiment in Kentucky: Integration and Social Equality at Berea* (1996).

Smith, Jessie Carney. *Notable Black American Women, Book 2* (1992–2003).

CHARLES ROSENBERG

Jackson, Emory Overton (8 Sept. 1908–10 Sept. 1975), journalist, newspaper editor, and civil rights activist, was born in Buena Vista, Georgia. In 1919 he moved with his parents and six siblings to Birmingham, Alabama. There he attended the city's first, oldest, and once the South's largest high school for African Americans, Industrial (now A. H. Parker) High School. After graduation Jackson returned to Georgia—not to his hometown of Buena Vista but to Atlanta, the home of his college of choice, the historically black Morehouse College. At Morehouse he majored in labor relations. He also laid the foundation for his future career by writing for the school newspaper, the *Maroon Tiger*. He graduated from Morehouse in 1932, two years into the Great Depression.

After graduating from Morehouse, Jackson did not immediately enter the newspaper business. Instead he returned to Alabama and taught school at Carver High School in Dothan and at Westfield High School in Jefferson County. He also served in the U.S. military during World War II. In 1941, however, Jackson became the managing editor of the *Birmingham World*, Alabama's oldest (but now defunct) African American newspaper. He would hold that position until his death in 1975.

As the managing editor of the *Birmingham World* Jackson turned the paper into his own personal sword of justice. He did so in conjunction with his active membership in various civic organizations, including the Jefferson County Progressive Democratic Council and the civil rights threesome of the Alabama Movement for Human Rights,

the Birmingham Urban League, and the National Association for the Advancement of Colored People (NAACP). He was an active member of the National Newspaper Publishers Association, an organization of black publishers, and the Birmingham Press Club. He also served on the board of directors of the Alabama chapter of the Society of Professional Journalism (Sigma Delta Chi).

Under Jackson's leadership the *Birmingham World* carried out the twofold mission of spotlighting the plight of southern blacks and ending racial discrimination against them. To do this Jackson wrote various columns for the paper. His most effective one was called "The Tip Off." Started in 1943, "The Tip Off" served as Jackson's primary tool for promoting his view of the world and how the plight of African Americans should be improved. It also helped to earn him the description as "one of the most vigorous, persistent, and courageous advocates in the South for full civil rights for his people" (quoted in *Birmingham World*, 12 Feb. 1963).

Fearless, Jackson constantly demanded that Birmingham's city hall hire black policemen and firemen. He also called for blacks to be placed on the boards of education and libraries. Those demands were virtually unheard of in the Deep South, especially Birmingham, once called "the most segregated city in America." Regarding education, Jackson worked behind the scenes to support strongly AUTHERINE LUCY FOSTER's successful enrollment as the first African American student at the University of Alabama in 1956. Jackson constantly called for vast improvements in black schools by using his newspaper to protest against the inadequate textbooks, limited community support, and faulty curriculum found there. He also urged job training for youth and the importance of informing them of job opportunities.

Additionally, Jackson stressed the need for African Americans to be more economically self-reliant. He often did so by highlighting black-owned businesses and their owners in the newspaper and by stating that African Americans need a "Dr. King of economics." (Like Jackson, MARTIN LUTHER KING JR. was a "Morehouse man.") To Jackson, African Americans would never obtain what he called the "trinity of first-class citizenship" until they had the necessary three ingredients: education, the dollar, and the ballot.

Called the "Black Moses of the Black Press" and the "Sapient Warrior from the Red Hill," Jackson waged a long, courageous, and often lonely fight for civil rights in Birmingham and throughout the South. Morehouse College rewarded him for his diligent efforts by conferring on him an honorary doctor of laws (LLD) degree at its June 1965 commencement.

Widely known and respected in the Birmingham civic, religious, and business community, Jackson never hesitated to criticize any and all persons and agendas that he felt sought to defame, damage, or destroy the African American community anywhere in America, most especially the South, particularly Birmingham. He therefore not only used the *Birmingham World* as a sword of justice against white supremacy and conservative groups and their proponents but also against ineffective, if not nonexistent, black leadership in the areas of business and education, the church and the community, and even fraternal orders.

Often Jackson found himself the target of threats against his life. One of the most spine-tingling episodes came when he was stuck on an elevator with two white police officers. Both of them pulled their guns and threatened to kill Jackson—"blow out his brains." Calmly Jackson told them: "Who are you trying to kill, me or my influence? Pull the trigger and you'll kill me, but my influence will do the same to you." Dumbfounded, the two officers re-holstered their guns and Jackson walked away. Such incidents were the reason that Jackson never married. In his words, "a woman ought to be a wife and not a widow."

Shortly before his death Jackson was in Washington, D.C., at the historically black Howard University. He helped to establish Howard's communication department's hall of fame for black publishers, editors, and journalists. Dying two days after his sixty-seventh birthday, Jackson was described by the noted black publication *Jet* as "frequently called the champion of protest and advocacy journalism on behalf of America's Blacks as well as the most influential writer and speaker on Southern politics of his generation." During his life, injustice, near and far, found him a force to be reckoned with.

FURTHER READING

The Emory Overton Jackson Papers are located in the Department of Archives and Manuscripts, Linn-Henley Research Library, Birmingham Public Library, Birmingham, Alabama.
Jackson, J. D. "Emory O. Jackson, 'The Black Moses of the Black Press,' and the Explosive Year of 1963," *Vulcan Historical Review* 3 (Spring 1999).
Obituaries: *Birmingham News*, 12 Sept. 1975; *Jet* (25 Sept. 1975).

J. D. JACKSON

Jackson, Fay M. (8 May 1902–3 June 1979), journalist and founding editor of *Flash* newsweekly, was born in Dallas, Texas, the daughter of Charles T. Jackson, a concrete mason, and Lulu Beatrice (maiden name unknown), a seamstress and musical actress. When Jackson was sixteen, her family moved to Los Angeles. She graduated from Los Angeles Polytechnic High School in 1922. She then enrolled at the University of Southern California and studied journalism and philosophy. Outside the classroom, she became the first president of the Epsilon chapter of Delta Sigma Theta in 1924 and was among the sorority's six charter members. In 1924 Jackson married John Marshall Robinson Jr., a Little Rock, Arkansas, native and medical student at the University of California, Berkeley; they had one daughter before they divorced in 1931. Jackson graduated from the University of Southern California in 1927. She earned a B.A. in Journalism and Philosophy.

Around 1928 Jackson founded *Flash* newsweekly magazine and coedited the publication with James McGregor. *Flash* covered the black socialite and intellectual scene in California and was a western contemporary of the NAACP's *The Crisis* and the Urban League's *Opportunity* magazine on the East Coast. In addition to literature, poetry, and culture, *Flash* covered sports, education, and local, national, and international news of interest to blacks to make up for the lack of coverage in the mainstream media. The magazine published articles such as "The Dilemma of the Negro Actor," about the stereotyped roles Hollywood studios assigned blacks, and "The Color Fad," about prominent whites who packed black nightclubs, the West Coast equivalent of "slumming" at Harlem's Cotton Club.

In the 1930s Jackson worked for CLAUDE BARNETT, founder of the Chicago-based Associated Negro Press (ANP), serving as the news service's Hollywood correspondent. The move distinguished Jackson as the first black journalist to cover the West Coast entertainment industry. Jackson gained a reputation as charismatic and friendly, and she had access to the leading movie studios and to entertainers and artists, notably PAUL ROBESON, HATTIE MCDANIEL, and the blues singer ALBERTA HUNTER. Jackson's dispatches served at least sixteen ANP client newspapers, and her work appeared in about two hundred newspapers.

In 1937 Barnett sent Jackson to London, England, to cover the coronation of King George VI. The assignment distinguished Jackson as the sole black foreign correspondent covering the event and it was her first overseas assignment. In covering the coronation Jackson focused on more than the pomp and glamour. Observing the royal family, she noted that the abundant ruby and diamond jewelry worn by the royals came from South African mines, where blacks "scratch[ed] for basic needs in housing, employment and human dignity," Jackson's granddaughter told the *Los Angeles Times* in 1988. Jackson wrote that the jewels and much of the British Empire's wealth was the result of colonialism, which was a controversial statement for the times. While abroad Jackson interviewed Haile Selassie of Ethiopia, the writer H.-G. Wells, and the prime minister of Ireland, Eamonn De Valera. When Jackson returned to the United States, CHARLOTTA BASS, editor of the *California Eagle* of Los Angeles, hired her to serve as political editor of that publication. One memorable Jackson article concerned a prominent black doctor in Glendale, California, who slept with a gun at his feet as protection from menacing Ku Klux Klansmen. In 1940 Jackson founded the *California News*, a weekly.

Jackson was also in demand as a writer and producer of African American history scripts for Los Angeles black radio programs, and she was a personal publicist for artists and entertainers, including ETHEL WATERS. Jackson challenged the social etiquette of that era by wearing tailored suits, carrying a briefcase, and cropping her hair into a short wavy bob. When her friend ETTA MOTEN—Barnett's wife and a performing artist—suggested that she stop wearing boyish clothes, Jackson answered that she functioned in a man's world of business, contracts, and negotiations and did not want her femininity to be a distraction. According to her granddaughter Dale Pierson, Jackson enjoyed a reputation as a tough businesswoman.

In the 1950s Jackson converted to Catholicism and began to study the life of Saint Francis of Assisi. She was a founding member of the Our Lady of Africa Guild and spent the last decades of her life serving charitable, religious, and civil rights organizations, among them the Los Angeles Civic League, of which she was a founding member. The league fought to end housing segregation, employment discrimination, and inequities in public policy. During the 132nd anniversary of the black press in 1959, Jackson received a citation for Historical Services as a Foreign Press Correspondent.

Jackson continued to speak and write for civic and social organizations during the final two decades of her life. She devoted much of her time to her only daughter, Joan Robinson Pierson, who became one of Los Angeles's first policewomen and probation officers and a regional director of the Product Safety Commission of the U.S. Department of Commerce.

Jackson died shortly after learning about the death of her daughter, who was killed in an airplane crash. Dale Pierson has worked to preserve Jackson's legacy by maintaining memorabilia—letters, poems, diaries, photographs, and rare publications—at the family home in South Central Los Angeles.

FURTHER READING
Danky, James P., and Maureen E. Hady, eds. *African-American Newspapers and Periodicals: A National Bibliography* (1988).
McMillan, Penelope. "Granddaughter Keeps Memory of Pioneering Black Journalist Vivid," *Los Angeles Times*, 15 Sept. 1988.
Pierson, Dale, and Kedric Beasley. *Ebony Renaissance 2000* (2000).
Watts, Jill. *Hattie McDaniel: Black Ambition, White Hollywood* (2005).

WAYNE DAWKINS

Jackson, George (23 Sept. 1941–21 Aug. 1971), radical black nationalist and anti-prison activist, was born George Lester Jackson in Chicago, Illinois, the second of the four children of Robert Lester Jackson and Georgia (maiden name unknown). George Jackson attended St. Malachy, a Catholic school located in what he later described as the "heart of the ghetto," from kindergarten through ninth grade (Jackson, *Soledad Brother*, 5). In 1956 Robert Jackson transferred his postal job to southern California, and he took young George with him—in large part to remove him from his increasing involvement in local gangs and from his minor scuffles with police. The two drove from Chicago to Watts, California, and were soon joined by the rest of the family.

In Watts, George Jackson engaged in an escalating series of petty thefts and acts of rebellion against local police officers, and he was arrested three times over the next two years. He spent several months in a correctional facility, the Paso Robles School for Boys, after attempting to break into a department store. Finally, in September 1960 Jackson was arrested for robbing a gas station with two other men. Upon the advice of his lawyer he pleaded guilty and, under new sentencing guidelines, received an indeterminate sentence of one year to life.

In February 1961 Jackson entered the Soledad Correctional Training Facility, where he spent fourteen months before being transferred to the infamous San Quentin State Prison, allegedly for frequent violations of prison rules and for what one official called his "surly and intractable" attitude (*New York Times*, 20 Sept. 1971). Jackson remained at San Quentin until early 1969; he spent much of this time in solitary confinement. As he put it wryly, "Just because I want to be my black self, mentally healthy, and because I look anyone who addresses me in the eye, they feel I may start a riot anytime" (*Soledad Brother*, 184–185). His prison record at San Quentin contained a long line of serious charges, including stabbing a fellow inmate and assaulting a guard, but Jackson insisted that these and other infractions were invented by malicious white prison officials who feared and resented his revolutionary politics and his refusal to bend to the system.

In fact, the endless months and years alone in his cell allowed Jackson ample time to read and study, which he did obsessively. He devoured the writings of Karl Marx and Mao Zedong, as well as books on Pan-Africanism, history, economics, and political theory, and he studied several languages, including Spanish, Chinese, Swahili, and Arabic. Jackson also joined the Black Panther Party, and whenever he was not in "the hole," he spent hours in conversation with fellow black prisoners in an effort to radicalize them and teach them to see themselves as political prisoners within a corrupt racist and capitalist system. Jackson fostered increasing consciousness and outspokenness about the links among the mass imprisonment of African Americans, the abuses and excesses of capitalism that worked against African Americans, and white European and American imperialism and colonialism in the so-called Third World.

In early 1969 Jackson was transferred from San Quentin back to Soledad. That summer a white corrections officer was beaten to death by prisoners, seemingly in retaliation for the shooting deaths of three African American inmates. Officials immediately accused Jackson, Fleeta Drumgo, and John Clutchette of killing the guard and sent them to the maximum-security block of San Quentin to await trial. There the so-called Soledad Brothers became the center of an international movement to free them and also to raise awareness about racism in the U.S. prison system. The African American

activist and communist ANGELA DAVIS, already embroiled in controversy over the rights of avowed communists to teach in California's public universities, achieved even greater notoriety when she became a vocal defender of the Soledad Brothers.

In August 1970 George Jackson's younger brother, seventeen-year-old Jonathan, rushed into a Marin County courthouse and demanded, at gunpoint, the release of the Soledad Brothers and all "black political prisoners." With the help of two coconspirators he took hostage a judge, a district attorney, and two jurors. In their attempt to escape Jonathan Jackson and three others were shot to death.

The episode brought greater attention to the plight of George Jackson, as did the publication in October 1970 of *Soledad Brother: The Prison Letters of George Jackson*. Indeed, he briefly became a household name; the *New York Times* ran several profiles of him, and the *New York Review of Books* excerpted two of his letters. *Soledad Brother* was a powerful testament to Jackson's will to survive and to his sense of resigned outrage not only at the prison system but also at what he called capitalist, white "Amerika." As he wrote: "Big Brother. He is rather transparent. I have his number. I know he's a punk, he can't stop me" (*Soledad Brother*, 302).

The book was an eloquent if incomplete and scattered record of his treatment behind bars; it revealed the development over time of an increasingly sophisticated and blistering critique of American capitalism and imperialism. Jackson's letters to his family, to his lawyers, and to comrades like Angela Davis exposed the inhumane treatment of African Americans and the often horrifying conditions in prison, as well as the intransigent parole board in California that kept him imprisoned longer than his crime merited. He recalled: "I had been accused of being a Muslim, Communist, agitator, nationalist, loan shark, thief, assassin, and saboteur. Nothing was ever settled, nothing was really exchanged except hostility" (*Soledad Brother*, 317). With the publication of his letters Jackson's status as a Black Power icon and as a hero to radicals was indelibly etched into the American political landscape.

On 21 August 1971 George Jackson was shot to death in prison. The assistant warden of San Quentin claimed that he was killed during an escape attempt, but many, including Jackson's mother, believed that he had been assassinated. His funeral was held at the St. Augustine Episcopal Church in West Oakland, California. A crowd of nearly five thousand attended, and the Black Panther leader HUEY NEWTON gave the eulogy, vowing, "[W]e will raise our children to be like him" and "slit every throat that threatens our freedom" (*New York Times*, 29 Aug. 1971).

Reaction to Jackson's shooting and rumors surrounding the manner of his death reached beyond the confines of California and even the United States. The writer JAMES BALDWIN commented from Europe that he did not believe the official account of Jackson's death. In London a group of fifteen hundred marchers appeared at the U.S. Embassy, demanding an investigation into the incident. Some speculate that the September 1971 inmate uprising at the Attica Correctional Facility in western New York was set in motion when Attica's African American prisoners held a day of silence and fasting and wore black armbands in George Jackson's memory.

Just before his death Jackson had completed a second book, *Blood in My Eye*, containing letters as well as essays on revolution, white imperialism at home and abroad, the war in Vietnam, and the importance of creating a new, international black consciousness. The book was published posthumously in 1972. His writings have endured as an influential example of black revolutionary thought in the United States. George Jackson is buried in Mount Vernon, Illinois.

FURTHER READING

Jackson, George L. *Blood in My Eye* (1972).

Jackson, George L. *Soledad Brother: The Prison Letters of George Jackson* (1970).

Durden-Smith, Jo. *Who Killed George Jackson?* (1976).

STACY BRAUKMAN

Jackson, George Washington (1854–21 June 1940), educator and writer, was born in Lee County, Alabama, the seventh of thirteen children of the Reverend Anderson Jackson and his wife, Clara. Anderson Jackson was a slave preacher who after Emancipation was a popular evangelist and one of the founders of the Colored Methodist Episcopal Church. George Washington Jackson learned how to read and write early in life and assisted his father with correspondence and notes.

Jackson attended a night school for blacks organized by the white teacher of the community day school. Jackson's father was regarded with favor by his former owner and was given his own house apart from the other black farm workers who remained on the plantation after Emancipation.

Thus Jackson and his siblings were raised mostly in seclusion from other children.

When Jackson was sixteen he passed the teaching examination and began his first teaching job at the public school in Russell County, Alabama. The following year Jackson taught at the school in Lee County. In 1876 after teaching one year in Lee County, Jackson moved with his brother William to Corsicana, Texas, to find their father's brothers, who reportedly lived in Navarro County. William returned home in 1878 to take care of the family following the death of their father. Jackson stayed in Texas to teach. His first year was spent teaching in Wadesville at the Colbert Community School. In 1879 Jackson entered Fisk University in Nashville, Tennessee.

Jackson returned to Corsicana in 1882 to become principal at the City Colored School, later known as the Fred Douglass School. Under Jackson's leadership the school was recognized as one of the leading African American educational institutions in the state of Texas. The city of Corsicana was one of the first to erect a brick schoolhouse for the black population. The school recruited teachers from all over the United States, including Tennessee, Georgia, Alabama, Kansas, Virginia, New York, Louisiana, Ohio, Michigan, Illinois, and Texas. In three years the school advanced from being only an elementary school to being a high school as well. The first graduates were awarded their diplomas in 1889. High school courses were taught by the principal himself, as was required by the state. By 1902 the Fred Douglass School had grown to include three high school teachers, including Jackson.

Jackson became an ardent advocate of BOOKER T. WASHINGTON's industrial training program at the Tuskegee Institute. Jackson approached the superintendent with the proposal of starting a similar program. With the approval of the school board and the superintendent Jackson raised the money from private citizens to build a girls' industrial cottage and a boys' industrial workshop. Ann Ayers and B. H. Earl from Tuskegee were hired to be teachers in the program.

Some members of the Corsicana community were opposed to the industrial education program because it took time away from reading and writing. A series of town hall meetings were held to discuss the issues. Jackson brought several influential speakers with him to speak at the meetings. Not long after, opposition to the program had shrunk. Within a few years the program had become a success. Girls were being trained in cooking and sewing, and boys were being trained in construction and home repair. By the time that Jackson retired in 1927, more than a hundred students had successfully completed the industrial education program. Following his retirement Jackson wrote a history of the Grand United Order of Odd Fellows, a secret society, in Texas. He also wrote a brief autobiography and a book of rhymes called *School Room Helps for Teachers and Parents* (1912).

When the Fred Douglass School burned down and a new building was erected in 1925, the school was renamed G. W. Jackson High School. In his forty-five years of service to the school district of Corsicana, Jackson guided the school from a one-room frame building to one of the most progressive and best-equipped schools for blacks in the state. In his autobiography Jackson wrote that there were three essentials to a good school: a good faculty, receptive students, and proper equipment. Jackson was able to accomplish all of these goals and have the good fortune of living in a community that wanted to see progress and success for all of its citizens, regardless of race.

FURTHER READING

Jackson, G. W. *A Brief History of the Life and Works of G.-W. Jackson* (1938).

Powell, Jimmie Dee Vellow. "History," *Navarro County Scroll* 15 (1970).

Powell, Jimmie Dee Vellow, and Wyvonne Putman. "Fred Douglass–G. W. Jackson High School," *Navarro County Scroll* 23 (1977).

MARK L. MCCALLON

Jackson, Giles Beecher (10 Sept. 1853–13 Aug. 1924), attorney, businessman, civic leader, and a confidant of U.S. presidents and of BOOKER T. WASHINGTON, was born Giles in Goochland County, Virginia, one of four children of the slaves Hulda and James Jackson. Little information is known about Giles's father; however, his mother was born into slavery in Spotsylvania County, Virginia, and later became the property of Charles G. Dickerson, a Goochland County gentleman farmer. During the Civil War young Giles was the body servant to Dickerson, his master and a colonel in Fitz Lee's Cavalry, and he also attended the horses and uniforms of General Robert E. Lee. He followed his master into battle, which led to his being captured near the end of the war. Jackson recounted his story in an issue of the *New York World* in 1915. Seized by Union troops in Caroline County, and again at City Point near Petersburg, Virginia, he was brought before General Ulysses S. Grant, commander of the Union forces, who allowed Jackson's release back to his master.

Immediately after the war, in 1865, Jackson was employed on the estate of the Stewart family, who were wealthy newspaper publishers, at Brook Hill near Richmond. He was taught the basics of reading and writing by his future wife, Sarah Ellen Wallace, herself in the employ of Virginia's elite at Brook Hill. Later Jackson was privately educated by both black and white citizens. After his marriage on 17 November 1874 in Washington, D.C., Jackson took odd jobs in Richmond to support a family that eventually grew to fourteen children. To settle a dispute over political boundaries in Richmond, Jackson drew a map showing the boundaries of the all-black enclave in which he lived. He appealed directly to General Grant while Virginia was still under military command a number of years after the end of the Civil War. Grant ended the argument by both parties by writing "Jackson's Ward" across the map handed to him by Jackson, saying, "I know only one of your number, and know him to be honest because I twice held him a prisoner of war and each time he had begged to be sent back to his people and master" (*New York World*, 30 May 1915). And "Jackson Ward" (its name having been slightly modified) it remained, named after Giles Jackson, and becoming a citadel of black business in the United States.

Jackson "read the law," a custom in Virginia, under the tutelage of William H. Beveridge, a Richmond lawyer who noticed Jackson's intellect after hiring him to do menial work. Subsequently, on 30 November 1887, six days after the death of his mother, Jackson became the first African American attorney to be allowed to practice before the Virginia Supreme Court, the equivalent of "passing the bar." It was Beveridge's influence during that time that resulted in Jackson's emergence as a public-spirited citizen and that fired his ambition for business, commerce, and politics.

Jackson became a successful lawyer in the black Richmond community, relocating his office and growing family to the upscale Jackson Ward neighborhood as he rose in national prominence, and distinguished himself in law and in business. He could practice law in any State of Virginia court and in all the lower courts of the City of Richmond and the nearby County of Henrico. Because of segregated practices, African American attorneys-at-law were restricted, for the most part, to the lower courts for civil actions, and generally to police court in criminal cases. Jackson, like his colleagues, filed papers for his clients, but usually did not prosecute action in higher courts, a privilege that other lawyers enjoyed. Jackson's nemesis in Richmond's police court was Justice John W. Crutchfield, a judge with no legal background who had a notorious distaste for lawyers, and was a fearful force with whom to be reckoned. However, Jackson, shrewdly diplomatic, often won the cases for unfortunate miscreants, most of whom were accused of drunkenness and other minor offenses. Jackson was so concerned for men and women of his race that he sometimes lost diligently acquired properties put up as bail bond for those charged with various crimes.

Jackson had a penchant for wide-brimmed hats that became his trademark. He was short of stature and gained weight through the years which gave him a pudgy profile. An old Civil War wound on his forehead from a Union bullet left a scar. Jackson was a leading member of the Grand United Order of True Reformers, a fraternal society. When the True Reformers opened a bank, Jackson wrote its articles of incorporation. With Jackson as the best publicist for black business, the Tuskegee Institute president, Booker T. Washington, selected him as an aide-de-camp when Washington organized the National Negro Business League in Boston in 1900. Serving as a vice president during its first three years, Jackson revealed in a 1901 letter to Washington that he was "regarded by the local newspapers as a kind of bureau of information as to the acts and doings of the colored people of our City and State" (Booker T. Washington Papers, Library of Congress). Ever the Washington supporter, Jackson organized thirty or forty League branches in a single year. He supported Washington also in his efforts to abolish Jim Crow laws in Virginia in the early 1900s. In 1901 Jackson was granted the honorary title of colonel by President Theodore Roosevelt and took part in the presidential inaugural parade. This commission was renewed in 1905 by Roosevelt so that Jackson could take command of the Third Civic Division, a cavalry of African Americans, at Washington, D.C., during the second presidential inaugural ceremonies.

In Richmond, Jackson purchased various properties near and in Jackson Ward, and his East Broad Street law offices in the early 1900s were near the judicial buildings in the hub of town. When the Virginia state General Assembly resolved in 1901 to commemorate the third centennial of the founding of the-first English-speaking colony in the New World, Jackson conceived and successfully promoted the idea for a separate, concurrent Negro Exhibit at the Jamestown Exposition of 1907. Jackson, like many of his African American contemporaries, felt that black achievement in and out of slavery had been ignored. To this end Jackson drafted provisions for a company he founded called the Negro Development and Exposition Company of the United States of America (NDEC). Initially he worked from his law office located in the Swann Hotel in 1903, but later moved to a building on East Broad Street, which housed a ground floor bakery in which he had invested. After securing a charter for the company and setting up a national group of advisers, directors, and officers of both races, black and white, Jackson, was appointed director general by President Theodore Roosevelt in 1903. He zealously promoted the concept of a Negro exhibition, undaunted by mistrust on the part of many blacks and by critics of separatism such as W. E. B. DuBois, T. Thomas Fortune, and William Monroe Trotter, who dismissed a separate exposition as accommodating to Jim Crow. Fully supported by Booker T. Washington, the NDEC petitioned the U.S. Congress for an appropriation of $1.2 million, funds the NDEC needed to reach its goal. Ultimately the organization received an appropriation from the Treasury Department of only $100,000, which was supplemented by small contributions from the State of North Carolina and a few other jurisdictions. Despite this shortfall, Roosevelt lauded the tremendous success of the enterprise during a visit to Richmond in 1905, when the president stopped his carriage in front of NDEC headquarters and congratulated Jackson and the representatives of the "colored race" on their efforts. On 10 June 1907, while at the Jamestown Exposition with Mrs. Roosevelt, the president viewed the Negro Exhibit, the only display he saw. For the second time, Roosevelt honored Jackson and the NDEC officers by congratulating them on the "unmistakable evidences of progress … shown by the exhibits" (*Final Report of Jamestown Tercentennial Commission*, 148). From three thousand to twelve thousand people visited it each day and went away astounded at the achievements of thrift and industry. Jackson and his co-author D. Webster Davis subsequently produced *The Industrial History of the Negro Race of the United States* (1908), detailing the 1907 Negro Exhibit effort and devoting chapters to business, the arts, and inventors and other topics. The book was utilized as a-school text in Virginia, West Virginia, and North Carolina.

The Negro Exhibit was viewed by less than 1 percent of African Americans during its three-month existence, however, and Jackson felt that most members of his race should see evidence of their progress and the fruit of their labors in their three centuries of steady upward mobility. He campaigned diligently to have the exhibit moved to a permanent location, where the public would know it as a "National Museum for Colored People." Jackson approached city, state, and federal authorities; however, he ran into local political opposition and was forced to abandon the idea.

Jackson labored earnestly for the betterment of his race, founding business league chapters, helping to establish fraternal orders, writing articles of incorporation, and publishing a newspaper, the *Negro Criterion*, to promote the Negro Exhibit and black business. During World War I Jackson was appointed chief of the Negro Division of the U.S. Employment Service in Washington, D.C., but resigned when his commission ended on 30 June 1919. He returned to his more profitable Richmond law practice. Colonel Jackson, the title he preferred, spent the last four years of his life campaigning the U.S. Congress for his initiative *To Create a Negro Industrial Commission*, introduced on 15 May 1920 by Representative Caleb R. Layton of Delaware.

Year after year Jackson requested support from governors, national religious and political organizations, and senators and representatives, urging them to endorse his bill that would ameliorate interracial labor troubles and promote better working conditions for blacks. Jackson sent a written appeal to President Warren G. Harding on 15 March 1921, and twice met with President Calvin Coolidge requesting a recommendation to Congress of the initiative. Both leaders agreed to look into the issue, but committed themselves no further. Representative Layton re-introduced the bill as H.R. 2895 on 13 April 1921. The bill was referred to the House Committee on the Judiciary, which held a hearing on 23 January 1923. Jackson and a supporter H. H. Price of Richmond rendered statements. Representative Israel M. Foster of Ohio filed the bill again, now H. R. 3228, on 23 December 1923, the year his detractors imitated this effort by introducing at the U.S. Senate a similar bill for a commission on the racial question, thus two bills were pending before Congress for the same purpose. The drafters of the Senate bill were prominent African American leaders in Washington, D.C., who may have believed that they, as university professors and businessmen, held more influence and power and could circumvent any pitfalls that Jackson might encounter with his proposal.

Nonetheless, on 24 May 1924, Jackson and that bill's supporters testified at the Senate hearing before a subcommittee of the Committee on the Judiciary. Jackson stated that he wondered about a "danger of confusion" between his plan, reported favorably by the House committee two days prior on 22 May 1924 (Richmond [VA] *Times-Dispatch*, 23 May 1924), and that of the Senate bill. His effort to create a commission to improve the race problem was filed again on 2 June 1924, now H.R. 936.

This new effort apparently was too much for Jackson. He became ill several weeks later while attending the Republican Convention in Cleveland, Ohio, recovered briefly, then died of cardiac asthma complicated by acute nephritis. Neither the House or the competing Senate bill ultimately survived. The Elks, of which Jackson was a Grand Exalted Ruler at one time, contemplated placing a statue in his memory in front of the State House in Richmond. The statue was never erected. Decades later the Association for the Study of Negro Life and History, Incorporated, dedicated a bronze tableau in Jackson's honor and placed it at the renowned Consolidated Bank and Trust Company in Richmond.

FURTHER READING

Giles B. Jackson's papers are in the personal collection of Patricia Carter Sluby. Some materials related to Jackson appear in the Booker T. Washington Papers, Library of Congress, Manuscript Division.

Hamm, J. R. *Proceedings of the National Negro Business League* (1901).

Ives, Patricia Carter. "Giles Beecher Jackson," *Negro History Bulletin* 38.8 (1975).

Ives, Patricia Carter. "James and Hulda Jackson of Goochland County, Virginia," *National Genealogical Society Quarterly* 67.2 (June 1979).

"The Negro Exhibit." Final Report of Jamestown Tercentennial Commission (1907). *New York World*, 30 May 1915.

United States Congress, House, Committee of the Judiciary, *To Create a Negro Industrial Commission*, Hearing, 67th Congress, 4th Session, H.R. 2895, 25 Jan.-1923.

PATRICIA CARTER SLUBY

Jackson, J. J. (8 Apr. 1941–17 Mar. 2004), radio and video disc jockey, was born John Julian Jackson III (although some sources give his birth name as "John Jay Jackson") in New York City, the son of John J. and Elma V. Jackson. Little is known of his family, but they apparently moved to Boston early in his life, as J.J. was raised in the Roxbury section of that city, and attended Boston public schools. He briefly joined the military, and then returned to Boston, and worked for a time in the fledgling computer industry. But he already knew that he really wanted to work in radio.

Jackson learned that Tufts University, where he was not a student, operated a radio station that permitted community volunteers to broadcast. His first on-air radio job, therefore, was at Tufts station WTUR, in nearby Medford in the late 1960s. While working there, he met Joe Rogers, a Tufts student who became the first announcer at a new Boston FM station, WBCN. In mid-March 1968, the former classical music station had become part of a growing movement on the FM dial known as "underground radio," and what they began to play was called "progressive rock." WBCN featured long album tracks as opposed to the hit singles that top-40 radio stations played, and where top-40 was often bland and repetitive, progressive music tended to address controversial themes such as racism or the war in Vietnam. Boston had a large college-aged population, and there was a demand for a station that played cutting-edge bands like the JIMI HENDRIX Experience, Jefferson Airplane, and the Doors. At first, WBCN's hours in its new format were limited to late evenings, but within a few months, the station had expanded and more announcers were needed.

Jackson's friendship with Joe Rogers helped him to meet Sam Kopper, the program director of the new station, who hired J.J. Although most of the announcers on album rock stations were white, Kopper had no hesitation about hiring Jackson as his first African American announcer (personal e-mail to author from Sam Kopper). He was given the mid-day shift; by 1970, he was doing afternoons and also helping with public service, keeping tabs on news events that affected the local black community. But it was in the area of live music that he became especially well known. Boston had a number of rock clubs like the Boston Tea Party, where the biggest names came to perform, and Jackson attended some of those shows, introducing acts like Led Zeppelin, the Who, and Jimi Hendrix. On FM stations, announcers had more freedom to choose the music they played, and they often praised bands they liked. Jackson's listeners were exposed to a number of up-and-coming bands that he believed in, and later, groups like Led Zeppelin, whom he had helped when they first played in Boston, came to think of him as a friend.

In early 1971 Jackson decided to take up a new challenge, moving to Los Angeles and another album-rock station, KLOS, where he did the afternoon shift. Just as WBCN had changed its format, so KLOS was now creating a new identity, having changed over from top-40 KABC-FM to the album-oriented rock that was so popular. With his deep voice and his encyclopedic knowledge of music, Jackson soon became a fixture in Los Angeles, making appearances and emceeing at clubs as he had done in Boston. His voice had become so familiar that he was chosen to voice the ubiquitous but unseen DJ in the 1976 movie *Carwash*. Jackson remained at KLOS for nine years, leaving for another Los Angeles station, KWST-FM, in February 1980.

A new opportunity presented itself in New York. The cable network Music Television (MTV) was about to make its debut, and Jackson was chosen as one of the five so-called "VJs" ("video jockey" was derived from radio's "disc jockey" or DJ). He was the only one who was black, and indeed was one of the-few black faces on the channel at all during its early years, when programming rarely included African American artists. Jackson had done some reporting about music for Los Angeles television station KABC-TV in the late 1970s, but a channel devoted entirely to music videos and music news was something quite different. When MTV went on the air on 1 August 1981, critics did not know if it would succeed, but the new channel carved out a niche, attracting a dedicated audience of young rock music fans.

As MTV became more popular, the role of the VJs was expanded. Originally, each VJ taped a week's worth of "intros" and "outros," where they announced the song and sometimes commented about the artist. These taped segments were mixed in with the music videos (Bernstein, 100). But as MTV became more popular, Jackson was soon doing much more than introducing the videos or announcing where the performers were playing; he was interviewing rock stars like Peter Townshend of the Who, Mick Fleetwood of Fleetwood Mac, or the members of Kiss. He was also sent to cover major events, such as July 1985's Live Aid benefit concert in London, England, which raised money for famine relief in Africa. When MTV put on a new program, he would sometimes be the host, such as in March 1986, when the network broadcast the first episode of *120 Minutes*, a show devoted to alternative rock. Being a VJ in New York City was quite different from his album rock radio days. Working in a visual medium, he now had to be more style conscious, because MTV was not just a source for the latest music; it had become a source of the latest fads and trends, and viewers often emulated their favorite VJs. Jackson seemed to find this phenomenon surprising. He wasn't accustomed to fans emulating, or even noticing, what he was wearing (Bernstein, 100).

At MTV, he was older and more experienced than his colleagues, and while this was considered a blessing by the other VJs, who often looked to him as a mentor, the network wanted young viewers and came to believe the VJs should also be young. In June 1986, when MTV saw that its ratings were slumping, the management decided it was time to bring in some new and younger hosts. Jackson was fired, replaced by another black VJ, "Downtown" Julie Brown. Jackson ended up back on the West Coast, doing commercial voice-over work both because his voice was still very identifiable and because he still had many friends there from his radio days. He found work in San Diego at KSON, and then for such Los Angeles stations as KROQ and KEDG. He also did some announcing on local cable TV. By late 1994, he had gotten into radio syndication, hosting "The Beatle Years," which was heard nationwide on about two hundred stations. In 2000 he returned to KLOS to do a once-weekly show. He also continued doing syndicated programs, including the popular "Super Stars Concert Series" for Westwood One.

Unknown to most of his fans, Jackson had begun having health problems, and required heart surgery. He quit smoking, lost weight, and made changes in his diet, but in March 2004, on his way home from dinner with a friend, he had a sudden and fatal heart attack. Many friends and colleagues packed the funeral home to pay tribute to him, remarking on how he often mentored younger announcers, and praising him for inspiring them to go into broadcasting. Afterwards, the Los Angeles media historian Don Barrett set up a Web site to commemorate the many achievements of the man his colleagues sometimes called "Triple J,"—J. J. Jackson, an album rock pioneer and television's first black VJ.

FURTHER READING

Barrett, Don. *Los Angeles Radio People* (1997).

Bernstein, Fred. "A Hard Day's Night with MTV Video Jocks." *People*, 17 October 1983.

Bieber, David L. "Rock Solid Radio," *Boston* magazine (June 1970).

Pareles, John. "MTV Makes Changes to Stop Ratings Slump," *New York Times*, 12 June 1986.

Sokolsky, Bob. "J. J. Jackson Dawns on the Colorful '7th Day,'" *Press Enterprise* (2 May 2000).

Span, Paula. "Music Meets TV and Kapow; MTV, the Rock Video Cable, Turns a Stylish 4," *Washington Post*, 1 Aug. 1985.

Obituaries: *Hollywood Reporter*, 19 Mar. 2004; *People*, 5 Apr. 2004.

DONNA HALPER

Jackson, Jay (10 Sept. 1905–Apr. 1953), cartoonist and illustrator, was born Jay Paul Jackson in Oberlin, Ohio. He was the fourth child and only son of Nellie Curry and Franklin R. Jackson. Jay Jackson tried his hand at a variety of trades before discovering his aptitude for cartooning. At the age of thirteen he joined the workforce, pounding railway spikes for a railroad company located just outside of Columbus, Ohio. He then worked as a steelworker in Pittsburgh, Pennsylvania, and had a brief career as a boxer while Ohio Wesleyan University in Delaware, Ohio, from 1925 to 1926. During his time at Wesleyan, an instructor redirected his interests toward the field of advertising.

At the age of nineteen, Jackson wed his first wife, Adeline C. Smith (?–1924) and started a successful sign-painting business. However, this success cost him his health. Jackson suffered a severe case of lead poisoning caused by the lead-based paints he worked with. After recovering enough to return to work, Jackson moved his family to Chicago in 1928, where he worked as a poster artist for the Warner Brothers chain of theaters until 1933. He rose swiftly through the ranks of artists to the position of First Poster Artist and then on to shop foreman.

Jackson suffered a series of personal tragedies with the death of his father, his first child, and his wife, which left him a single father at the age of twenty-two. He found escape from his depression through his illustrations and cartoons and he supplemented his income by freelancing cartoons and illustrations to the Pittsburgh Courier newspaper (1926–1950), the digest-size Abbott's Monthly (1928–1934), and the New York Amsterdam newspaper. It was because of his association in the late 1920s with publisher ROBERT SENGSTACKE ABBOTT that Jackson's art began to appear in the Chicago Weekly Defender in 1928. He joined the staff of the Chicago Defender in 1933, where he served as editorial and features cartoonist for twenty years.

The talented Jay Jackson was commissioned to paint a mural for an exhibit called Old Mexico at the Century of Progress at the 1933 Chicago's World Fair. He took over drawing the long-running comic strip, Bungleton Green, the same year.

While serving in the position of staff artist for the Chicago Defender, Jackson met his second wife, a Defender office worker by the name of Eleanor K. Poston from Nebraska. They were married in 1935. Along with Jackson's daughter from his first marriage, Carrie Lou (1924), over time the family grew to include Helen, Julie, and Jay Jr.

During his prolific career, Jay Jackson developed and illustrated a number of comics including As Others See Us, a cartoon that lovingly poked fun at the lifestyles and foibles of African Americans during the roaring twenties and in its own way, offered correction. Similar to the comic strip, *Joe Palooka*, Cream Puff was a coming-of-age story of an ambitious young boy from the South who heads North with big plans to do great things. Along the way, he becomes a prizefighter, poised to become the World Heavyweight Champion. But sinister forces are determined to prevent an African American from attaining the title. In the mid-1930s, Jackson took over from cartoonist Henry Brown as illustrator of the Chicago Defender's flagship comic strip, Bungleton Green, a cartoon originally created by Defender editorial cartoonist, Leslie Rogers in 1920. Destined to become one of the longest running comic strips featuring a black lead character, *Bungelton Green* could be compared in style and genre with Billy De Beck's *Barney Google*. The strip ran for forty-four years and was illustrated by six different Chicago Defender cartoonists, the last of whom was CHESTER COMMODORE, before the strip was retired in 1964.

Another cartoon drawn by Jay Jackson that appeared in the Defender included, Speed Jackson, an adventure strip about an African American soldier of fortune who fought Nazis and Italian fascists. The comic equated America's segregation to Nazi ideology. Girlie Gags was a single-panel cartoon that featured attractive pin-up girls of a type similar to E. Simms Campbell's *Cuties* comic. Jackson also drew So What?, a single-panel humor comic, and The Ravings of Prof. Doodle, which can be best described as an etiquette comic, instructing readers on proper public behavior. A large, quarter-page comic filled with activity and illustrated by Jackson was Homefolks. Each comic was about a specific theme or event, filled from top to bottom with drawings of different people and sometimes animals commenting on the action or about to become an unwilling part of it. Occasionally Jay

Jackson himself made a cameo appearance in his comics, often sitting at his drawing table, while his character frolicked around him.

Jackson drew comics and story illustrations for a number of other publications besides the Chicago Defender such as art to complement the story serial Tisha Mingo. His art appeared in the Sci-Fi magazine Fantastic Adventures (1938–1948), in the romance and gossip magazine, Tan Confessions, and in a series of humorous advertisements for Murray Pomade and photorealistic images of African Americans for Pepsi Cola. In 1948 Jackson worked for the Johnson Publishing Company as the art director before relocating to Los Angeles, California, where he lived for the remainder of his life.

In addition to his studies at Ohio Wesleyan University (1925–1926), Jackson studied at the Chicago Art Institute and the Los Angeles Art Institute as well as under Saturday Evening Post cover illustrator Norman Rockwell in 1949. Jackson was a member of the National Association for the Advancement of Colored People and the American Newspaper Guild.

FURTHER READING
Jackson, Tim. *A Salute to Pioneering Cartoonists of Color*, http://web.mac.com/tim_jackson.
Obituary: *The Chicago Defender*, 8 May 1953.

TIM JACKSON

Jackson, Jesse L., Sr. (8 Oct. 1941–), civil rights leader, was born Jesse Louis Robinson in Greenville, South Carolina. His mother, Nancy Burns, was only sixteen years old when Jesse was born, and she was not married to Jackson's father, Noah Robinson. On 2 October 1943 Jackson's mother married Charles H. Jackson, a janitor, who adopted Jackson and gave him his name. In the course of his career, Jackson has frequently used the fact that he was born out of wedlock to a teenage mother to try to inspire young people to believe that no matter what their backgrounds they can "be somebody." At Greenville's Sterling High School, Jackson was a good student and an outstanding athlete. After graduation from high school, he accepted a football scholarship at the University of Illinois but left after a year. Jackson attributed his departure to the school's racist sports policy, stating that he could not play quarterback because it was a "whites only position."

Enrolling in 1961 at North Carolina Agricultural and Technical State University (A&T), an historically black college in Greensboro, Jackson became the

Jesse Jackson, campaigning for the passage of the Hawkins-Humphrey Bill for full employment, 15 January 1975. Civil rights activist, minister, and occasional Democratic presidential candidate, Jackson remains one of America's most recognizable and sometimes controversial voices for equal justice under the law. (Library of Congress/Thomas J. O'Halloran, photographer.)

school's star quarterback, head of his fraternity, and president of the student government. He was also a leader of the campus chapter of the Congress of Racial Equality (CORE), one of the leading national civil rights organizations in the 1960s. At age twenty-three he led demonstrations protesting segregation at Greensboro lunch counters and helped to organize a student civil rights group, the North Carolina Intercollegiate Council on Human Rights. Thus, from his high school and early college days, Jackson displayed the talents and ambition for leadership that were to characterize the rest of his life. Equally clear at this time was Jackson's intention to use those talents and ambitions in the cause of civil rights, which he has continued throughout his career. In 1962 he married Jacqueline Lavina Davis, a student from Fort Pierce, Florida. In the course of their marriage the Jacksons had five children. (In 1996 his oldest son, JESSE LOUIS JACKSON JR., was elected to the U.S. Congress from Chicago.) In 1964 Jackson graduated from North Carolina A&T with a B.A. in Sociology and moved to Chicago to attend

seminary. He had entered the ministry while in college, but he was not ordained into the Baptist clergy until 1968. Jackson enrolled in the Chicago Theological Seminary in 1965 and continued his civil rights activism, working for the Coordinating Council of Community Organizations, an umbrella association of Chicago civic and civil rights groups. Within a year Jackson had become director of the Coordinating Council. He dropped out of seminary to join the voting rights protests in Selma, Alabama, then being led by JOHN LEWIS of the Student Nonviolent Coordinating Committee (SNCC) and MARTIN LUTHER KING JR. of the Southern Christian Leadership Conference (SCLC). King was a strong-willed and gifted leader, and he surrounded himself with men of similar abilities, including RALPH ABERNATHY, ANDREW YOUNG, HOSEA WILLIAMS, and WYATT TEE WALKER, among others. Viewing King as a hero and role model for activist ministry, Jackson desperately wanted to be a part of his inner circle. Within a year Jackson attained his goal when he was appointed national director of Operation

Breadbasket in 1967. Headquartered in Chicago, Operation Breadbasket was the northern arm of the largely southern-based SCLC. Modeled after a similar organization in Philadelphia, Pennsylvania, led by Leon H. Sullivan, Breadbasket targeted and protested against businesses with discriminatory employment and contracting practices.

Operation Breadbasket thrived in Chicago under Jackson's leadership. The organization led highly visible boycotts against some of the city's leading businesses, sometimes resulting in employment opportunities for black workers and contracts for black entrepreneurs. Breadbasket's success made Jackson an influential figure in Chicago politics and enhanced his stature in SCLC's inner circle. That Jackson, considerably younger than the other SCLC leaders, could so quickly be placed in charge of SCLC's northern operations is testament to both his talents and his ambitions. Jackson was with King at the time of his assassination in Memphis in 1968 and claimed to have cradled the dying leader on the balcony of the Lorraine Motel, although the others present dispute this claim. Indeed, it was this dispute about Jackson's role at the time of King's death that initiated tensions between him and the SCLC leadership and that would eventually lead to Jackson's suspension and ultimate resignation from the organization. Mistrust of Jackson was reinforced when, against the explicit wishes of the King family and SCLC staff, he appeared the day after the assassination before the Chicago City Council and on national television in clothing that he claimed bore King's blood.

At the time of his death King was in the final stages of planning the Poor People's Campaign—marches, demonstrations, and other protest activities designed to highlight the extent of poverty in America and to secure for the poor federally guaranteed jobs and income. Jackson, along with SCLC leaders JAMES BEVEL and Bernard Lafayette, had initially questioned the strategy and clarity of planning for the Poor People's March on Washington in internal SCLC deliberations. After King's death, however, he skillfully used the media and effectively stole the spotlight from Abernathy, King's designated successor, on the day of the national demonstration.

Undoubtedly Jackson believed that he was better equipped to succeed King than Abernathy, and shortly after the Poor People's Campaign concluded, he asked the SCLC board to give him a higher position in the organization. The board refused. Sensing that Jackson was turning Operation Breadbasket into an autonomous organization, in 1971 the SCLC board asked Jackson to move Breadbasket to Atlanta, SCLC's national headquarters. Jackson refused. Later in the year the board suspended Jackson for sixty days because of alleged irregularities in the handling of Breadbasket funds. At this point Jackson resigned from SCLC and created Operation "PUSH" (People United to Save Humanity) and named himself president. Operation PUSH (which in personnel was essentially Operation Breadbasket with a new name) continued Breadbasket's economic protests and boycotts, but it also began to engage in political protests and organizing. Jackson also established PUSH-EXCEL to encourage high performance by black schoolchildren. Adopting the self-styled characterization of the "country preacher," he traveled the country preaching moral responsibility, especially regarding sex during the teen years, out-of-wedlock childbearing, and the use of illegal drugs.

In 1972 Jackson made his first foray into national Democratic Party politics, cochairing an alternate delegation to the Democratic National Convention. Charging that the regular delegation headed by Mayor Richard J. Daley of Chicago had excluded minorities and women, Jackson played a major role in persuading the convention to oust the Daley delegation and replace it with the one he cochaired. In 1984 and again in 1988 Jackson ran for the Democratic nomination for president. He gained widespread support from black voters and Latinos, bringing significant numbers of new registrants into the Democratic Party. The excitement of his candidacy was felt largely in the Democratic primaries in 1984. He won in the District of Columbia and Louisiana, beating both the perceived front-runner Walter Mondale, a former vice president, and Senator Gary Hart, and in Maryland he came in second, ahead of Hart. Jackson's performance at the primary level won him delegates to the 1984 Democratic National Convention, but with little support from the larger white electorate, he did not come close to winning the nomination. More important, however, was the popular acknowledgment of Jackson as the leading African American in the Democratic Party. In both the 1984 and 1988 elections he stood out as one of the party's leading advocates for liberal and progressive causes. He also established the Rainbow Coalition Inc., as a progressive, liberal adjunct to the Democratic Party. By the 1980s public opinion polls showed that blacks and whites alike perceived Jackson to be the preeminent African American leader.

Jackson also achieved international recognition as a "citizen diplomat," visiting countries in the Middle East, Latin America, and Africa. Pursuing conflict mediation, he negotiated the release of American prisoners of war in Syria and Yugoslavia and the release of political prisoners in Cuba. In the 1990s he called attention to the need for African American economic empowerment. He established the Wall Street Project to facilitate access by blacks and other minorities to investment capital, credit, and contracts and to help them secure positions as executives and board members in major American financial and corporate institutions. Unlike the economic empowerment strategy of Operation Breadbasket, the Wall Street Project relied on negotiations between elite power brokers, rather than mass boycotts and protests. The peripatetic Jackson, however, continued to lead demonstrations for causes that included not only civil rights but also the environment, women's rights, and workers' rights. In addition, he hosted *Both Sides*, a Sunday afternoon news talk program on CNN. In 1995 Jackson's Operation PUSH and his Rainbow Coalition were merged. The new organization, with Jackson as president, was called the Rainbow/PUSH Coalition.

Jackson's popularity and moral authority as a leader were undermined early in 2001 when the tabloid press revealed that he had fathered a child with Karin Stanford, a member of his staff who had written a book about his involvement in international affairs. The revelation of this extramarital relationship diminished Jackson's credibility, especially given the allegations of financial irregularities regarding his organizations' payments to his mistress and their child. He also lost his television talk show on CNN as a result of the affair.

According to a national survey conducted in 2000 by the Joint Center for Political and Economic Studies, Jackson had declined considerably in influence. The Joint Center's poll revealed Jackson with an 83 percent favorable to 9 percent unfavorable rating among blacks. In a 2002 poll the Joint Center found that Jackson's favorable rating among blacks had dropped to 60 percent, while his unfavorable rating had increased to 26 percent. By 2003 black scholars and commentators on African American politics were increasingly talking and writing about the "end of the Jackson era." And, in a move widely viewed as an attempt to displace Jackson as the preeminent African American leader, AL SHARPTON, a Jackson protégé, announced he was running for the 2004 Democratic Party presidential nomination.

From a historical perspective, it cannot be denied that Jesse Louis Jackson Sr. held sway over the minds and hearts of African Americans in the post–civil rights era. During the 1980s and 1990s, at a time of declining civil rights gains, Jackson championed a spirit of protest that spoke to national and international human rights concerns, thus positioning himself as the most visible African American leader since Martin Luther King Jr. A 2000 poll of black political scientists asked them to list and rank the greatest black leaders of all time. Specifically they were asked to list in "rank order the five African Americans who, in your historical judgment, have had the greatest impact, for good or ill, on the well being and destinies of the African people in the United States" (Smith, 128). Of the ten greatest leaders, Jackson was the only living person on the list. He ranked number seven behind Martin Luther King Jr., W. E. B. DuBois, MALCOLM X, FREDERICK DOUGLASS, BOOKER T. WASHINGTON, MARCUS GARVEY, and THURGOOD MARSHALL, but ahead of IDA B. WELLS-BARNETT, MARY MCLEOD BETHUNE, FANNIE LOU HAMER, and ADAM CLAYTON POWELL JR. As one respondent in the poll wrote, "History will be very kind to him" (Smith, 133).

FURTHER READING

Frady, Marshall. *Jesse: The Life and Pilgrimage of Jesse Jackson* (1996).

Morris, Lorenzo, ed. *The Social and Political Implications of the 1984 Jesse Jackson Presidential Campaign* (1990).

Reed, Adolph. *The Jesse Jackson Phenomenon: The Crisis of Purpose in Afro-American Politics* (1986).

Smith, Robert C. "Rating Black Leaders," *National Political Science Review* 8 (2001): 124–138.

Stanford, Karin. *Beyond the Boundaries: Jesse Jackson in International Affairs* (1996).

ROBERT C. SMITH

Jackson, Jesse Louis, Jr. (11 Mar. 1965–), civil rights activist and U.S. congressman, was born to the civil rights leader REV. JESSE JACKSON and Jacqueline Davis Jackson in Greenville, South Carolina. Jackson had an older sister, Santita, and younger siblings, Jonathan, Yusef, and Jacqueline. As a child, he was active, assertive and intelligent.

Believing their sons "needed a more regimented form of discipline" (*Chicago Magazine*, May 1996, 58), in 1977 the Jacksons sent Jesse Jr. and Jonathan to a military school, LeMans Academy in Indiana, where Jesse Jr. was a student for two years. While traveling with the Reverend Jackson in Africa, the Middle East, and Europe on civil rights missions, the children were introduced to celebrities, including Pope John Paul II and Nelson Mandela, so they were familiar and comfortable with leadership and celebrity from an early age.

Jackson Jr. finished high school in 1984 at St. Albans School in Washington, D.C., a school known for educating the children of public figures. He excelled in both academics and athletics, and was active on the debate and football teams. After rushing for one thousand yards and thirteen touchdowns, he received scholarship offers from Notre Dame, Michigan, and the University of Southern California, but decided to attend North Carolina Agricultural and Technical State University, the historically black institution where his parents had met.

At North Carolina A&T, Jackson focused on his studies and graduated in three years, magna cum laude with a B.S. degree in Business Management in 1987, partly in order to help out with his father's 1988 presidential campaign. He and his siblings introduced their father during the 1988 Democratic National Convention, when Jackson Jr.'s remarks favorably impressed the delegates.

In 1987 Jesse Jackson Jr. also met Sandra Stevens, who was working for Michael Dukakis's rival presidential campaign. They married in 1991 and had two children, Jessica Donatella and Jesse L. Jackson III.

After finishing a master's degree in Theology in 1990 from the Chicago Theological Seminary, Jackson pursued law studies and graduated from University of Illinois Law School as a top student in 1993. Instead of practicing law, however, in 1993 Jackson became a field director for his father's National Rainbow Coalition, a prominent civil rights organization. There he used his computer and organizational skills to modernize the organization and take advantage of the Internet and Web sites. One of the projects he implemented was a program to register a million new voters. In addition, he designed a voter education program aimed at helping potential voters understand the importance of their vote in affecting political change, how to use technology to participate more efficiently in politics, and how to enhance the ability of candidates to win elective office.

In 1995, when U.S. representative Mel Reynolds of Illinois's Second District resigned in a scandal, Jackson ran for Congress in Chicago. His opponents belittled him as "daddy's boy," but Jackson used his ties advantageously, since he had met every president since Jimmy Carter and such world leaders as Israeli prime minister Yitzhak Rabin and Palestinian leader Yasser Arafat. Using his youth as the symbol of a new generation of political activism, he targeted voters aged eighteen to forty-five, and in the process registered five thousand new voters in thirty days. He won the election with three-quarters of the vote.

Jackson's congressional platform focused on the revitalization of the South Side of Chicago and its industrial legacy. He campaigned to assist residents who could not afford to move for better employment. He supported building a third Chicago airport, claiming that it would bring a quarter-million new jobs to the region. On the other hand, he opposed cutting Medicare and Medicaid spending.

In the House of Representatives Jackson earned respect for never missing a vote and gained a reputation for sticking to principles rather than compromising with either party, while being willing to work across partisan lines. For example, he opposed the Africa Growth and Opportunity Act proposed by Representative CHARLES RANGEL because liberal trade would benefit large corporations more than poor Africans. Jackson believed that Democrats, including presidential candidates, shifted in an unacceptably conservative direction to gain votes from moderates. He felt that when President Bill Clinton first ran for president in 1992, his call for strong investment in projects would improve the lives of ordinary Americans. But once in office, Clinton became the "Deficit Reduction President," cutting back on programs that helped needy Americans. Jackson later held that Al Gore was a conservative choice for vice president and that Gore's presidential running mate in 2000, Joseph Lieberman, was even more conservative. Despite sometimes sharp confrontations with fellow Democrats, few publicly criticized Jackson.

Since 2005, Jackson has proposed a series of amendments to the U.S. Constitution to "recognize that the Constitution … is an evolving document that [needs] to provide every American with economic security" (Nichols, 11). Among those that he supported were amendments guaranteeing an individual's right to vote, equal rights for women and minorities, education, universal health coverage, employment protection, affordable housing, environmental protection, and progressive taxation. In 2001 Jackson helped establish the National Center on Minority Health and Health Disparities (NCMHD) to address and alleviate the problem of relatively high occurrences of certain diseases such as diabetes, hypertension, and cardiovascular diseases among African Americans, compared to whites and other demographic groups.

Jackson was an outspoken critic of the 2002 invasion of Iraq because he believed it was based on unsubstantiated claims that the government of Iraqi president Saddam Hussein had developed so-called weapons of mass destruction. In 2003 Jackson, JOHN CONYERS, Dennis Kucinich, and three other Democratic representatives filed suit in Boston against launching an unconstitutional war; a district court judge rejected their suit because it was a political question beyond the judiciary's resolution.

In January 2005 Jackson attacked Chicago mayor Richard M. Daley as corrupt and formed an exploratory committee the following year for the 2007 Chicago mayoral race. He insisted he could have beaten Daley, but, with Democrats taking control of the House in November 2006, he claimed that he would be too busy to run for mayor. In the same election in which Daley was reelected in 2007, Sandra Jackson was elected to the Chicago City Council. Jackson exemplified strong leadership against injustice and inequality by shifting politics toward achieving community and social goals.

FURTHER READING

"Jesse Jackson, Jr.," *Contemporary Black Biography* 45 (2004).

"Jackson, Jesse L., Jr.," *Newsmakers 1998* 3 (1998).

Nichols, John. "Jesse Jackson Jr.: A Different Vision," *The Nation* (18 Sept. 2000).

Smith, Jessie Carney, ed. "Jesse L. Jackson, Jr.," *Notable Black American Men Book II* (2006).

RICHARD SOBEL

Jackson, Jimmy Lee (Dec. 1938–26 Feb. 1965), civil rights activist, farmer, and lumber worker, was born in a farmhouse near Marion, Alabama, the eldest child of Viola Lee Jackson and her husband (whose name is unknown), farmers. Jimmy Lee's childhood was not unlike those of his parents and grandparents, who lived close to the land. From an early age he learned to navigate his way through the piney woods near his Perry County home and to fish in nearby streams. He attended the segregated Baptist Academy for Negroes and later Lincoln High School, both in Marion, where he was viewed as an average student when it came to academics. Shy and something of a loner Jackson did not particularly stand out among his peers,

though—as was true with many of them—school was a diversion from his daily chores on the farm. For Jimmy Lee these chores ranged from looking after his parents' poultry and livestock to cutting pulpwood with his grandfather and other relatives. He particularly enjoyed working as a logger, but the pay was miserly. When Jackson graduated from high school in 1957 he thus decided to leave Perry County and make a living in Fort Wayne, Indiana, where he intended to stay with relatives who had migrated there several years earlier.

Only two weeks after Jackson had arrived in Indiana, however, his father was killed in an automobile accident and Jackson was forced to return to Alabama to manage the family farm. In addition to his farming and logging duties Jackson became active in his local church, Saint James Baptist, and in the Rising Star Association, the leading fraternal organization in Perry County, in which his maternal grandfather, Cager Lee, was a prominent member. The Rising Star Association served primarily as a dues-paying benevolent association that raised money to send promising students to college.

By the early 1960s, however, under the leadership of ALBERT TURNER, a labor leader and bricklayer, the Rising Star Association in Marion became the focal point of civil rights activism in Perry County. The organization's primary goal became to increase voter registration. As of 1962 only 150 of the county's 5,000 eligible African American voters were registered. Intimidation by white registrars ensured that no black voters had enrolled since 1954. But in a watershed show of defiance in December 1962, Jimmy Lee Jackson along with his mother, his eighty-year-old grandfather, and more than 300 of Perry County's black citizens lined up to register at the county courthouse in Marion. The white registrars initially frustrated this effort by arriving at the courthouse late and by taking two hours to test the eligibility of the first man in line, whom they failed. Jackson then helped draft a letter to a federal judge in Alabama requesting that he intervene to secure the constitutional rights of Perry County's black citizens. After several court challenges forty of the would-be registrants, including Viola Jackson, were admitted to the voting rolls by July 1963. Jimmy Lee Jackson attempted to register to vote five times but was rejected each time.

When not involved in civil rights work Jackson earned six dollars a day cutting pulpwood and worked with his mother and teenage sister Emma Lee on the family's two-acre farm. His labors barely kept the Jacksons afloat. They were among the poorest families in one of the poorest regions of the wealthiest nation in the world. The Jackson home had no electricity or running water and had only the most basic of furniture. His poverty did not cause Jimmy Lee Jackson to question his faith, however. He remained actively involved in local church affairs, and in August 1964 he was elected the youngest deacon in the history of Saint James Baptist.

Although civil rights efforts in Marion stalled around that time, they revived in January 1965 when MARTIN LUTHER KING JR. and the Southern Christian Leadership Conference (SCLC) launched a major voting rights campaign in Alabama. At that time only Mississippi had a worse rate of black voter registration, and the SCLC hoped to provoke the federal government into passing a meaningful voting rights law. In addition the Student Nonviolent Coordinating Committee (SNCC) increased its presence in the Alabama Black Belt by sending a full-time organizer to Perry County. After King and 3,000 demonstrators were jailed on 1 February 1965 in nearby Selma, Jackson and others in Marion engaged in a series of protests, culminating in the arrest two days later of more than 700 children, including Emma Lee Jackson, who had marched around the Marion courthouse.

Demonstrations continued over the next two weeks in both Selma and Marion. At a rally in Selma on 17 February the Dallas County sheriff James G. Clark imprisoned Jimmy Lee Jackson's mother after first punching her in the mouth. After her release that evening she joined her son and her father at an overflow meeting at Zion's Chapel in Marion. Around a hundred of the 300 assembled protestors then attempted to march in orderly pairs toward the Marion jailhouse, where an SCLC organizer was being held, only to find their path blocked by armed state troopers and sheriff's deputies. The Marion police chief T. O. Harris then demanded that the protestors disperse.

Before they had a chance to do so the town's lights went out, and state troopers began attacking protestors and journalists with nightsticks. In the melee several protestors tried to escape, among them Jimmy Lee Jackson, who bolted to a small café nearby, where he was joined by his grandfather, mother, and sister, among others, all of whom were pursued by the troopers and a crowd of angry local whites. Cager Lee had been savagely beaten, but his grandson's efforts to get him to a hospital were thwarted by troopers who forced Jackson and Lee back into the café. The troopers smashed the

lights in the café and began clubbing the protestors indiscriminately; for the second time that day a white police officer beat Viola Lee Jackson to the ground, this time with a nightstick. He then continued to beat her as she lay on the ground.

The official report of that night's events, written by white law-enforcement officers, claimed that Jimmy Lee Jackson threw a bottle at one of the officers. None of the black witnesses in the café confirmed that report, but they did agree with the troopers that Jackson lunged at his mother's assailant and then was beaten to the ground by that trooper. When Jackson tried to rise, another trooper pushed him back down, while a third raised his pistol and shot Jackson in the stomach at point-blank range. Bleeding heavily, he struggled to ward off further blows and dragged himself out of the café and into the street, where he collapsed.

Jackson's colleagues attempted to get him to Marion's Perry County Hospital, but according to several witnesses he was turned away because of his race. A white doctor at the hospital later denied that Jackson had been turned away—which would have been illegal under the 1964 Civil Rights Act—and claimed that he had given Jackson emergency treatment. Because of an alleged lack of blood at Perry County Hospital, three hours elapsed before Jackson received the blood transfusion that he required, thirty miles away at Selma's Good Samaritan Hospital. Under the care of the hospital's Roman Catholic nuns Jackson briefly improved and talked with visitors, among them Martin Luther King Jr., who prayed with him. Jackson was also visited by state troopers, who issued him with a warrant charging him with assault and intent to murder. One week after the shooting Jackson went into shock and died the following morning. Hospital officials recorded that the delay in giving Jackson a transfusion had aggravated the infection of his wounds. His killer, who insisted that he acted in self-defense, was never convicted of any wrongdoing.

Jackson's death provoked little response in the national media, who paid more attention to the attacks that same evening in Marion on several journalists, whose cameras were broken and sprayed with paint by local whites. But his death angered thousands of previously silent African Americans in Perry County and galvanized the efforts of the SCLC and SNCC in Selma and Marion. On 3 March 1965 a total of 4,000 mourners attended two memorial services for Jackson. At the first, in Selma, the Reverend RALPH ABERNATHY

JACKSON, JOSEPH HARRISON 253

hailed Jackson as a martyr for racial justice in the line of CRISPUS ATTUCKS, Abraham Lincoln, and MEDGAR EVERS. At the second, at Zion's Chapel in Marion, the Reverend King gave an eloquent eulogy for Jackson, the first person to die in an SCLC campaign. Albert Turner, who had brought Jackson into the movement, was so distraught that he proposed carrying the dead man's body to the steps of the state capitol in Montgomery. The SCLC leadership agreed instead to follow JAMES BEVEL's suggestion of a march from Selma to Montgomery to honor Jimmy Lee Jackson and to confront the man most responsible for the mood of violent white resistance that had resulted in Jackson's death: Governor George Wallace.

Four days after Jackson's funeral the world watched aghast as television cameras recorded the vicious beating of more than 500 peaceful protestors as they attempted to march from Selma to Montgomery. "Bloody Sunday" was followed three days later by the murder in Selma of the Reverend James Reeb, a white Bostonian. Unlike Jackson's funeral, which was ignored by national politicians, Reeb's funeral was attended by Senator Edward Kennedy and Vice President Hubert Humphrey. Jimmy Lee Jackson's friends and fellow activists resented that his earlier death had not provoked a similar outcry or response—and speculated that it was because he was black. The death of both men finally spurred President Lyndon Johnson and congressional liberals to action. On 15 March 1965 Johnson addressed Congress and the nation to demand the passage of the Voting Rights Act. Its passage three months later ensured that the United States would, after 189 years, finally become a democracy.

FURTHER READING

Garrow, David J. *Protest at Selma: Martin Luther King Jr. and the Voting Rights Act of 1965* (1978).

Mendelsohn, Jack. *The Martyrs: Sixteen Who Gave Their Lives for Racial Justice* (1966).

STEVEN J. NIVEN

Jackson, Joseph Harrison (11 Sep. 1900–18 Aug. 1990), president of the National Baptist Convention, USA, Inc., was born in Rudyard, Mississippi, to Henry Jackson and Emily Johnson Jackson. Jackson received a bachelor of arts degree from Jackson College in Jackson, Mississippi, in 1926, the same year that he married Maude Thelma Alexander. The couple had one daughter, named Kenny in honor of her state of birth, Kentucky.

In the following decade Jackson began his extensive educational training. He earned a bachelor of divinity from Rochester Colgate School of Divinity in New York in 1932 and a master of arts degree from Creighton University in Omaha, Nebraska, in 1933. Jackson engaged in post-baccalaureate study in Nebraska, Pennsylvania, and Chicago, and would later receive an honorary doctorate of divinity from his alma mater, Jackson College.

On 27 May 1934, the Reverend Jackson was installed as pastor of the Monumental Baptist Church in Philadelphia, Pennsylvania. During this time he was selected as the executive (corresponding) secretary of the Foreign Missions Board for the National Baptist Convention, USA, Incorporated, and vice president of the World Baptist Alliance.

He resigned from the Monumental Baptist Church 1941 to accept the pastorate of the Olivet Baptist Church in Chicago, Illinois. Olivet, founded in 1850, was the oldest and most prestigious Black Baptist Church in the city. In 1953 Jackson was elected president of the National Baptist Convention, becoming leader of the nation's largest African American religious organization (approximately five million members at that time). Under Jackson's direction, the convention focused on foreign missions (most likely influenced by his service on the Foreign Missions Board). In 1956 he authored a book regarding missions titled *The Story of a Preaching Mission in Russia*.

Prior to his election to the presidency, Jackson had sought to establish term limits for the office of the president, but after his election to the post, his position on the matter changed. In 1957 he failed to deliver on his promise to resign, but his supporters suspended the convention's rules and he was reelected to the office through a voice call vote.

Though Jackson was a supporter of the 1954–1955 Montgomery Bus Boycott, he was critical of later civil rights efforts during the 1960s that emphasized the use of non-violent mass demonstrations of disobedience. His disagreement with this method of social activism was rooted in his religious belief that breaking the law was morally wrong and a sin. Rather than engage in social activism, Jackson focused his efforts on encouraging African American economic empowerment. His trademark slogan, "From Protest to Production," emerged from this desire. His opposition to civil disobedience resulted in periodic protest demonstrations outside his Olivet Baptist Church. It also resulted in numerous challenges to his leadership as president of the National Baptist Convention.

In 1960 Jackson again met opposition to his reelection as president of the convention. A group of religious leaders, including the REVEREND MARTIN LUTHER KING JR. and the REVEREND MARTIN LUTHER KING SR., sought to oust Jackson through their support of the Reverend Dr. Gardner C. Taylor of Concord Baptist Church of Christ in Brooklyn, New York. As during the events of 1957, Jackson's supporters again suspended the rules and moved for a voice vote to elect him president. This strategy resulted in bedlam in the convention and Jackson retreated from the hall. Nonetheless, Jackson's political maneuvering and support from the board of directors resulted in his retention of the presidency.

Just a year later Jackson faced another challenge to his leadership. At the National Baptist Convention in Kansas City, Missouri, Jackson was reelected in a disputed vote that resulted in a riot. The riot led to the death of a clergyman when opposition ministers attempted to overrun the convention stage. After the 1961 riot the Baptist Convention split into two organizations, resulting in the founding by Jackson's rivals of the Progressive Nation Baptist Convention.

Jackson initiated a foreign mission finance campaign in the Republic of Liberia that same year by establishing a land investment program in which the convention purchased over 100,000 acres in the country for farmland development and settlement. As a result of this campaign, the Republic of Liberia honored Jackson by making him a Royal Knight, and he received another honorary doctoral degree from Bishop College in Monrovia, Liberia. In the United States, Jackson advanced his land investment program by establishing the National Baptist Freedom Farm, an agricultural development community of 400 acres in Somerville, Tennessee.

Jackson's opposition to the growing tide of civil rights activity made him a controversial figure within the black religious community. In 1961 he denounced the sit-in movement, and in 1963 he denounced the planned March on Washington. His disagreements with Martin Luther King Jr. were highly publicized during this era and resulted in condemnation of his views from other religious leaders of the time as well as from civil rights organizations such as the Congress of Racial Equality, the Student Nonviolent Coordinating Committee, and the NAACP.

Despite these domestic disputes, Jackson engaged in ecumenical and international conversations. He was an attendee at the Second Vatican Council in Rome and met personally with Pope John XXIII. Between 1964 and 1980 Jackson authored several books, including *Many but One: The Ecumenics of Charity* (1964); *Unholy Shadows and Freedom's Holy Light* (1967); and *Nairobi, A Joke, A Junket, or a Journey? Reflections upon the Fifth Assembly of the World Council of Churches, November 27–December 8, 1975* (1976); as well as a work focusing on the history of the convention, *A Story of Christian Activism: The History of the National Baptist Convention, U.S.A., Incorporated* (1980).

In 1982 Jackson retired from his position as president of the National Baptist Convention; however, he remained politically active and supported the reelection of President Ronald Reagan in 1984. When he died in 1990, he had served for forty-nine years as pastor of the Olivet Baptist Church. By that time, Jackson had become internationally recognized as a captivating orator. During his lifetime Jackson was well traveled, with mission and speaking engagements in over fifteen countries and four continents.

FURTHER READING

Estell, Kenneth. *Reference Library of Black America*: Volume 5 (1994).

Salzman, Jack, David Smith, and Cornel West. *Encyclopedia of African-American Culture and History: Volume 3* (1996).

Williams, James. *The Negro Almanac: A Reference Work on the African American* (1989).

Williams, Michael, and Kibbi Mack. *The African American Encyclopedia* (2001).

J. "LUKE" WOOD

Jackson, Leo Albert (10 Mar. 1920–19 Apr. 1996), World War II veteran, city councilman, and judge, was born in Lake City, Florida, the youngest of fifteen children of William and Hattie (Howard) Jackson. He spent his early years in Orlando, Florida. Courage was his touchstone for life. When he was seven, an armed mob with torches came to his home looking for one of his older brothers on trumped-up charges. His mother sent him out the back door into the darkness to call together armed family members while she led the mob by a circuitous route to the brother's home. The family members Jackson brought escorted the brother to jail and successfully prevented the brother's lynching.

Jackson earned a B.A. from Morehouse College in 1943 and an M.A. in Business Administration from Atlanta University in 1946. On 7 September 1945 he married his college sweetheart Gilberta Jackson in Atlanta, Georgia. They had two children. The family moved to Cleveland in the 1940s so Jackson could attend law school at Cleveland-Marshall College of Law. He worked at the Veterans Administration during the day and attended classes in the evening, earning a J.D. in 1950. He had applied to transfer to the University of Georgia Law School, which, rather than admit him to the all-white school, gave him a scholarship to study in Cleveland. He later said that if they were going to discriminate against him, they were going to pay for it.

The Jacksons made their home in Cleveland's Glenville area, and Jackson became active in community organizations. He was a champion of civil rights and a forceful advocate for the enforcement of housing codes and the provision of police protection for the residents of Glenville. In 1957, against what was characterized as overwhelming odds, he was elected to represent Ward Twenty-four on the Cleveland City Council, where he served for fourteen years. Jackson's uncompromising stands, often against powerful vested interests, quickly won him the sobriquet "Leo the Lion Hearted." Ohio governor Michael DiSalle appointed Jackson from 1959 to 1963 to his advisory group, known as his "kitchen cabinet."

In 1963 Governor DiSalle offered Jackson an appointment as a Cleveland municipal judge at a salary considerably higher than his councilman's salary. Feeling that his work on the council was not finished, Jackson declined the appointment. He was featured in *Ebony* in February 1963 as "the lawyer who turned down a judgeship." Later he declined an appointment as a department head for the mayor of Cleveland "because my people still need me in Council" (Sanders, 15). In 1966 President Lyndon Johnson appointed him to the planning committee of the White House conference "To Fulfill These Rights." In 1968 Jackson was elected a delegate to the Democratic National Convention and was a member of the Electoral College from Ohio.

In public speeches Jackson said that his one "overriding idea" was "the equal and just application of the law to all persons" ("Response," 30 Jan. 1987). His sense of equality was exemplified by his conduct in daily life. One day when he was parked outside of city hall, a police officer issuing tickets recognized his name and began to walk away. Jackson insisted that he be given a ticket along with the other illegally parked drivers.

In 1970 Jackson became the first black elected to the Ohio Court of Appeals when he defeated an appointed incumbent by a wide margin. Serving for three six-year terms, he was chief judge in 1976 and again in 1981. He sat by special assignment on the Ohio Supreme Court. He authored more than nine hundred opinions, including fifty-one concurring opinions and eighty-eight dissents. Jackson worked hard to follow the intent of statutes and their precedents. Yet he was skeptical of both reference books and later cases, always carefully tracing precedent back to its original source before accepting it as binding. He was a kind, congenial, and friendly person who made a distinguished appearance upon the bench. Yet in matters of right and wrong he was fiercely independent, and his strongly reasoned dissents were characterized by their courage and tenacity. As the judges of his court noted in an In Memoriam statement, he paid close attention to the record in each case and was "universally respected for his integrity and his legendary willingness to denounce evil as he saw it, wherever and whenever he found it."

For Jackson, there were no small cases and no unimportant people. Every case deserved his best efforts. In his speeches he often quoted President Abraham Lincoln: "I know how I would feel if I were in their place." While voting to affirm the overwhelming majority of the criminal convictions that came before him, in some noteworthy dissents he also held the police and the prosecutors to high standards, insisting that they, too, must follow the law. In one case the majority kept changing its opinion as Jackson's dissent pointed out its errors, causing lengthy delays after oral argument. Jackson took the unusual step of releasing his dissent to the public before the majority opinion was released in order to force the majority to decide the case. Colleagues who did not understand his firm commitment to equal justice once chided him for being overly aggressive in protecting the rights of a white woman. He responded, "If I can't protect the rights of Mrs. Colizoli, then what chance do I have of protecting the rights of Mrs. Smith, Mrs. Jones or Mrs. Jackson?" A man who had been the subject of discrimination his whole life, Jackson rose above it while fighting prejudice for the sake of future generations. He often said that "they" could try to do what they wanted with respect to him, but he would fight every kind of discrimination against his children, grandchildren, and future generations.

Jackson worked hard on the court of appeals and loved his work because it was a way to help people. In 1981, even though the judge had no Republican opposition, the Democratic county prosecutor ran an assistant county prosecutor against Jackson in the Democratic primary. The effort was unsuccessful, and Jackson won by a wide margin. He retired in 1986 to spend more time with his wife, who was ill. Jackson died of a heart attack in the Cuyahoga County Courthouse en route to a photography session with all the judges of the Eighth District Ohio Court of Appeals. On the bench Jackson's ideals were captured by the words of the nineteenth-century lawyer Rufus Choate, whom Jackson often quoted: "If a law is passed by a unanimous legislature, clamored for by the general voice of the public and a cause is before him on it, in which the whole community is on one side and an individual nameless and odious on the other, and he believes it against the Constitution, he must so declare it or there is no judge." As long as Jackson sat on the bench there was a judge and justice in Cuyahoga County, Ohio.

FURTHER READING

Jackson's papers are at the Western Reserve Historical Society, Cleveland, Ohio.

Bennett, Lerone, Jr. "Lawyer Who Turned Down a Judgeship," *Ebony* (Feb. 1963).

Sanders, Charles. "Why Negro Rejected Cleveland Cabinet Post, Turned Down $16,000 Plum," *Jet* (11-Apr. 1963).

"A Tribute to Judge Leo A. Jackson," *Cleveland State Law Review* (1987).

RICHARD L. AYNES

Jackson, Lillie Mae Carroll (25 May 1889– 5 July 1975), civil rights activist, was born in West Baltimore, Maryland, the seventh of eight children of Amanda (Bowen) and Charles Henry Carroll, who claimed to be a descendant of Charles Carroll of Carrollton, Maryland, one of the signers of the Declaration of Independence. Amanda was the daughter of John Bowen, who claimed to be an African chief. Educated in the Baltimore city public schools, Lillie Jackson graduated in 1908 as a teacher from the Colored High and Training School.

On 8 September 1910 she married Keiffer Albert Jackson, a native of Carrollton, Mississippi, who worked as a traveling exhibitor of religious and education films. For the first eight years of their marriage he and Lillie Jackson traveled throughout the country as he showed his films in churches and schools and she sang and lectured. Their three daughters, Marion, Virginia, and Juanita, would later say that they were born "on the road"—Marion and Juanita in Hot Springs, Arkansas, and Virginia in East St. Louis, Illinois. A son, Bowen, was born after they had resettled in Baltimore. In 1918 or 1919 Lillie Jackson had a mastoidectomy that brought her close to death and resulted in a deformity on the left side of her face. Thankful nonetheless for having her life spared, she vowed to devote her life to God's work, joined the Sharp Street Methodist Church, and served for several years as chair of its board of trustees.

Lillie Jackson's social activism began during the Great Depression, when, because of racism, blacks found it even harder than whites to find jobs. She thus became a catalyst at the fore of the civil rights struggle in Maryland. Her daughter Juanita had graduated from the University of Pennsylvania in 1931, and in October of that year Lillie Jackson assisted Juanita in organizing the City-Wide Young People's Forum as an organization for social education, uplift, and protest. She created an adult advisory committee to gird the forum and bring it respect at a time when blacks shunned the appearance of militancy.

Lillie Jackson helped the Young People's Forum launch a "buy where you can work" campaign that targeted job discrimination by the A&P food stores, about eleven in all, throughout the black northwest Baltimore area. She demanded that store managers hire black clerks. As the forum's picket lines spread to other stores, mothers, some with their children, joined the protests. A&P began hiring blacks.

As late as 1933 the lynching of a black man, George Armwood, took place on Maryland's Eastern Shore. Another example of Baltimore's Jim Crow character was department stores that permitted blacks to enter but required them to use a side or back door. Blacks were allowed to buy clothes but could not try them on. They were barred from entering theaters, restaurants, and, of course, the tax-supported University of Maryland. Public recreation facilities were similarly segregated.

As a result of Lillie Jackson's dynamic leadership of the A&P boycott, CARL MURPHY, publisher of the *Afro-American* newspaper, asked her to become chair of the reorganization committee of the Baltimore NAACP branch. The branch's membership, which had been limited to the elite (namely, doctors, teachers, lawyers, and other educated and professional blacks), had fallen to about 10 Jackson launched a membership drive among the masses that quickly registered 2,000. Walking the streets collecting memberships, she reportedly preached,

"We're all equal in God's sight. The NAACP is God's organization." By 1946 the Baltimore branch's membership had risen to a peak of 17,600, making it the largest local unit in the association. She was elected to the NAACP National Board of Directors in 1948.

Along with her preaching against racial discrimination, her unbending opposition to dancing, smoking, and drinking and her other demonstrations of moral rigidity made her a colorful legend in Maryland. She believed in social protest as a weapon. She loved the masses and promoted humble people to the board of directors of the NAACP branch. She encouraged a few more whites to serve the cause, even though they often did so secretly for fear of ostracism, and other whites simply contributed money to the branch's work.

Lillie Jackson actively involved her family as tools of integration. Notably, Juanita, after she obtained her law degree in 1950 from the University of Maryland Law School, headed the Baltimore branch's legal redress committee. Juanita, who gave her paying legal cases to other lawyers to entice them to contribute their services to the NAACP, also worked without pay.

Jackson's most profound contribution to the development of the modern civil rights movement was the inspiration and support she provided to the launching of the NAACP's court challenge to the constitutional foundation of the "separate but equal" doctrine established by the Supreme Court in *Plessy v. Ferguson* (1896). From 1935 to 1938, just out of law school, THURGOOD MARSHALL served as attorney for the newly organized NAACP branch. Joining forces with CHARLES HAMILTON HOUSTON, his mentor and former Howard Law School professor, Marshall in 1935 won admission for Donald Gaines Murray to the University of Maryland Law School. It would require six more cases, which were all won in the Court of Appeals of Maryland, to desegregate all of the university's professional schools. Nevertheless, the significance of *Murray v. University of Maryland* was that it was the test case that led to the NAACP's landmark victory in 1954 in *Brown v. Board of Education*, where the Supreme Court overturned *Plessy* by ruling that segregation in public schools was unconstitutional.

Under Jackson, the NAACP launched an attack on unequal teachers' salaries in Maryland that would have equal significance throughout the South, where the practice was systemic. Heading the teacher salary equalization battle in the courts, Marshall, along with LEON A. RANSOM, another

NAACP attorney, in 1937 filed the case of *William B. Gibbs Jr. v. Edwin W. Broome et al.* in the Circuit Court for Montgomery County. Gibbs was being paid $612 per year, while whites with equal experience were earning $1,125 per year. Later that year Governor Harry W. Nice, upon being advised that the unequal salaries were unconstitutional, announced that he would end the practice. The following July, the board of education of Montgomery County agreed to settle the case out of court and to equalize the salaries for black and white teachers. Other county superintendents agreed to do the same.

Also in 1937, on behalf of the Reverend E. D. Meade, the NAACP branch filed one of the first lawsuits in the nation challenging the judicial enforcement of racial restrictive covenants in deeds. The following year the Baltimore branch lost the case in the Court of Appeals, but it nevertheless helped to lay the foundation for the national NAACP's challenges to the constitutionality of the covenants. In 1948, in *Shelly v. Kraemer* and two other cases, the Supreme Court ruled that the deeds could not be enforced in state courts.

Hardened by confrontation, Jackson led the NAACP in 1942 in creating an umbrella Citizen's Committee for Justice, which led a Citizen's March of two thousand people on Annapolis, the state capital, to protest the shooting of a black soldier by a policeman in Baltimore. Governor Herbert R. O'Conor responded by creating the Governor's Committee on Interracial Problems and initiating several reform steps, but it was the popularly called "Veney Raids" —the search for two accused murderers by the police throughout the black community—that climaxed this campaign. In 1966 the Fourth Circuit Court of Appeals, in a case led by Juanita, enjoined the Baltimore City Police Department from conducting mass searches of homes without a warrant. The opinion said the searches were "the most flagrant abuses to come before this court in its history."

In 1942, after the march on Annapolis, the NAACP, with the assistance of Carl Murphy, launched its register-and-vote campaign, centered in the local churches. The campaign changed somewhat after the war to focus on veterans. The Reverend John L. Tilley, upon joining the branch's staff in 1957, intensified the annual campaign. During services on Sundays, Jackson got the ministers to call on members to hold up their voter registration cards as inspiration to others to add their names to the rolls.

During World War II Jackson continued to fight for blacks in the private and public sectors. Public accommodations discrimination was another inescapable focus for Jackson and the Baltimore NAACP branch. In 1944 neither the Lyric Theater nor Ford's Theater was willing to serve as the venue for the branch's racially integrated membership meeting in May, even though Eleanor Roosevelt was the principal speaker. So the NAACP had to move the meeting to the Sharp Street Methodist Church, where Roosevelt's audience packed the sanctuary, with seven hundred more filling the basement and one thousand more standing outside on the streets to hear her.

Two years later Jackson launched a seven-year desegregation struggle with picket lines against Ford's, which for eighty-one years had been segregating blacks. Jackson, furthermore, urged Actors Equity Association, the players' union, to refuse to send its members to perform at the theater. The union cooperated, thus forcing Ford's to change its Jim Crow policy. But even though blacks were permitted to enter, they had to sit in the top balcony. Finally, after meeting with Jackson, Governor Theodore R. McKeldin, who as mayor of Baltimore had skipped the NAACP meeting when Roosevelt spoke, ended the segregation there.

In 1950 she led an NAACP picket line at City Hall protesting high taxes. In 1959, in conjunction with a group of ministers, she led another march on Annapolis to urge the passage of civil rights legislation. For six months in 1961 she led the picketing of the gas, electric, and telephone companies that won jobs in those companies for blacks. She also played a significant role in the appointment of Dennis Mello in 1966 as Baltimore City's first black police captain.

At the peak of the civil rights demonstrations, from 1960 to 1963, Jackson led the NAACP in providing bail for three hundred sit-in demonstrators who had been arrested or convicted on charges of criminal trespass. While Juanita enlisted lawyers to provide their services pro bono, Jackson got churches to pass the plate to obtain contributions for bail, which was substantial. The Supreme Court in 1965 reversed those convictions in the historic test case of *Robert Mack Bell et al. v. State of Maryland.*

Jackson launched campaigns against the proliferation of bars and pool halls in black neighborhoods, particularly because they were often placed next to churches and schools. She felt that those businesses undermined black communities. She believed in rehabilitating young men who had committed crimes, so she urged local judges to release them on parole, and then she helped to find jobs for them.

Much of her political influence came from her badgering of office holders, admonishing them to do right. Even though the NAACP was nonpartisan, Jackson did at times enter the political arena to support those who supported the NAACP's agenda, and she opposed those who did not.

Jackson was undeviating in her fight against segregation. In 1953 she resisted pleas by the all-white board of directors of the Baltimore Urban League, led by Sydney Hollander, not to file a lawsuit to desegregate Baltimore's public schools. The NAACP's militancy, according to the league's Parents and Citizens Committee, was hurting race relations in the city more than helping it because the desegregation lawsuits were demanding change for which the community was not prepared. The league wanted the NAACP to take a "separate but equal" approach to segregation but she rejected that course. Her legacy was that of transforming Maryland from a Jim Crow state to one complying with the Constitution.

FURTHER READING

Mitchell, Juanita Jackson. Oral History (OH) 8095, 25 July 1975; OH 8097, 10 Jan. 1976; OH 8183, 9 Dec. 1976; and Colloquium Proceedings, OH 8182, 16 Nov. 1976, all at Maryland Historical Society, Baltimore.

Callcott, George H. *Maryland and America, 1940 to 1980* (1985).

Watson, Denton L. *Lion in the Lobby, Clarence Mitchell, Jr.'s Struggle for the Passage of Civil Rights Laws* (2002).

Obituary: *Afro-American* (Baltimore), 8 July 1975.

DENTON L. WATSON

Jackson, Lisa P. (8 Feb. 1962–), politician and director of the Environmental Protection Agency, was born in Philadelphia. Two weeks after birth, she was adopted by Benjamin and Marie Perez and relocated to New Orleans. She was raised in the Lower Ninth Ward, near the Pontchartrain Park section of New Orleans. Her father, who died when she was in tenth grade, was a postal worker, and her mother occasionally did secretarial work. During high school Perez distinguished herself academically, graduating as valedictorian at Saint Mary's Dominican High School in 1979. Perez

Lisa P. Jackson, Environmental Protection Agency director, in an official photo.

subsequently took her talents to Tulane University, where she majored in chemical engineering. After earning her B.S. degree in 1983, Perez was admitted to Princeton University. There she continued her studies in chemical engineering and earned her M.S. degree in 1986, one of only two women in that year's engineering class. Following graduation Perez was hired by the Environmental Protection Agency, thus beginning her long association with not only the EPA but with environmental issues. She married Kenneth Jackson, with whom she has two sons, Marcus and Brian.

Jackson's decision to work for the Environmental Protection Agency in 1986 was fortuitous. In 1981, activist BEN CHAVIS had coined the term "environmental racism," to describe the propensity of local and state governments, as well as businesses and corporations, to release poisonous chemicals in economically depressed and, often, racial minority communities. The idea spurred a movement to clean up such areas, pressuring governments and businesses to take greater care of the environment and prevent any one area from being negatively impacted by such behavior. In 1986, Jackson went to work on the Superfund, a program created in 1980 to clean up places with hazardous waste. Centered in New Jersey, Jackson was so successful that she

was eventually promoted and served in a variety of positions, including acting director of the New Jersey enforcement division. Jackson spent sixteen years with the EPA before taking on a new challenge at the state level.

In March 2002, Jackson accepted a position as assistant commissioner of compliance and enforcement for the New Jersey Department of Environmental Protection. Demonstrating a keen understanding of the environment, politics, and the role of the law in protecting such precious resources, Jackson handled everything from water issues to land use management to regulatory issues. By the early 2000s, Jackson had caught of the eye of prominent Democrats and environmental interest groups, such as Jon Corzine and the Sierra Club. After then-U.S. Senator Corzine defeated the Republican Doug Forrester in the 2005 gubernatorial race in New Jersey, he nominated her for the position of Commissioner of Environmental Protection.

With a staff of three thousand, Jackson took an active role in protecting the environment of New Jersey. Moreover, she took an avid interest in environmental racism by involving local people in decision making and clean-up efforts in places such as Paterson and Camden. Through her work on environmental issues, Jackson became politically close with Governor Corzine; and he made her his chief of staff in 2008. Due to her new role, Jackson became very involved with the state legislature. However, fate, perhaps, intervened to prevent her from staying for very long. After supporting Senator Hillary Rodham Clinton in the Democratic primaries in 2008—even contributing money to her campaign—she was selected by then-president-elect Barack Obama to become administrator of the Environmental Protection Agency.

On 22 January 2009, Lisa Jackson became the first African American selected to head the premier environmental agency in the United States Government. Unlike her predecessors in the George W. Bush administration, Jackson, like Democratic predecessors, sought to reinvigorate the EPA and initiate stronger regulations, laws, and policies to protect America's natural resources. She has worked passionately on such issues as air and water quality, reducing greenhouse gases, and environmental racism. Furthermore, Jackson has been a supporter of the so-called cap-and-trade policies favored by America's most prominent scientists. However, she has not been without her critics, some of whom argue that she has been too easy on businesses who sought more flexibility from the state of New Jersey and the EPA. She has worked closely with the White House energy czar Carol Browner and the White House environmental adviser Nancy Sutley in coordinating policy and legislative strategy on environmental matters. Equally important, Jackson has vowed to base decisions, within her purview, on science and facts—arguably a counter to the previous administration of George W. Bush, which may be seen as favoring businesses and corporate profits over scientific and environmental concerns, and questioning the validity of the scientific community's assertions on climate change. As such, throughout the first two years of the Obama administration Jackson increasingly became the target of Republican opposition, with her push for increasing environmental regulation and support for climate change science making her a frequent target of conservatives.

FURTHER READING

Eilperin, Juliet. "EPA Head Lisa Jackson Is Prepared for Battle," *New York Times*, 2 Dec. 2010.

"Lisa P. Jackson," *Chemical & Engineering News*, 10 May 2010.

"Lisa P. Jackson, The New Team," *New York Times*, http://projects.nytimes.com/44th_president/new_team/show/lisa-jackson.

DARYL A. CARTER

Jackson, Luther Porter (11 July 1892–20 Apr. 1950), historian and activist, was born in Lexington, Kentucky, the son of Edward William Jackson, a dairy farmer, and Delilah Culverson, a schoolteacher. He was the ninth of twelve children of parents who had been slaves. Jackson attended Fisk University in Nashville, Tennessee, completing his AB in 1914 and his M.A. in 1916. Meanwhile, he began teaching in 1915 at Voorhees Industrial School in Denmark, South Carolina, where he was also director of the academic department. In 1918 he left South Carolina to become instructor of history and music at the Topeka Industrial Institute in Topeka, Kansas.

Jackson moved to New York in 1920, hoping to do graduate study at Columbia University, but Columbia would not accept his Fisk degrees as being up to Columbia's standards. Undaunted, he enrolled for a year at the City College of New York, where he studied history and education. He then spent a year at Columbia, receiving his second master's degree in 1922 from Columbia Teachers College.

That fall he joined the faculty of Virginia Normal and Industrial Institute (later Virginia State College and now Virginia State University) in Petersburg. Also in 1922 he married Johnella Frazer, a former classmate at Fisk, who had been employed at the institute since 1916 as instructor of music. Both spent the remainder of their careers on the Virginia State College faculty. The Jacksons had four children: a daughter and three sons.

From 1922 to 1928 Jackson served as director of the college's high school department. From 1930 to 1950 he was chairman of the department of history. He started as assistant professor of history and rose to associate professor in 1925 and professor in 1929. Meanwhile, he enrolled at Columbia University in the summer of 1923 but then transferred to the University of Chicago in 1928. On leave from Virginia State, he fulfilled the residence requirement at Chicago during 1928–1929 and 1932–1933. He received his Ph.D. in History from the University of Chicago in 1937.

Jackson became an authority on African American history, especially in Virginia. He wrote five books: four under 120 pages, one longer. The first of his five books, about a black teachers' group, was *The History of the Virginia State Teachers Association* (1937). His second book, *A Brief History of Gillfield Baptist Church of Petersburg, Virginia* (1941), documented 144 years of one of the nation's oldest black churches. His doctoral dissertation was selected for publication by the American Historical Association, in conjunction with the American Council of Learned Societies; it was titled *Free Negro Labor and Property Holding in Virginia, 1830–1860* (1942). Jackson traveled throughout the state visiting courthouses and unearthing birth and marriage records, estate records, property lists, tax records, and wills. He also used census findings. His other books include *Virginia Negro Soldiers and Seamen in the Revolutionary War* (1944) and *Negro Office Holders in Virginia, 1865–1895* (1945). His five scholarly books remain the standard accounts in each of these areas.

Jackson was more than an ivory-tower historian. He loved to interact with people off campus. Hence he became a social activist, throwing himself wholeheartedly into crusades. He was both a scholar and a man of the people. Jackson loved music, was very proficient at it, taught it at times, and played the cornet well. He formed a hundred-voice community choir, the Petersburg Community Chorus, and conducted its annual concerts from 1933 to 1941.

His major reform activity was a crusade for voting rights during the 1930s and 1940s when Virginia barred most African Americans from voting. In 1934 he organized the Petersburg League of Negro Voters, which became the Virginia Voters League, directing it until his death. Every year he compiled data on "The Voting Status of Negroes in Virginia." He preached to his students and to the masses that a voteless people is a hopeless people. He traveled throughout the state carrying this message. The Southern Regional Council asked Jackson in 1947 to conduct a study of black voting in the South. The study, "Race and Suffrage in the South since 1940," was published in a special issue of *New South* (June–July 1948).

Another area of his community service was fund-raising for two causes dear to his heart: the Association for the Study of Negro Life and History (ASNLH) and the NAACP. CARTER WOODSON's ASNLH had branches all over the nation. Woodson worked closely with Jackson and asked him to lead fund-raising efforts. Under Jackson's tutelage the Virginia chapter became one of the most productive of all state chapters. He did the same for W. E. B. DuBois's NAACP. Jackson spoke at rallies all over Virginia, promoting the NAACP and voting rights. The state conference of the NAACP honored him for his devoted work on behalf of voting rights. Jackson also formed the Petersburg Negro Business Association in 1937, expanding this in 1941 into the Virginia Trade Association. Furthermore, he wrote a column, "Rights and Duties in a Democracy," for the weekly *Norfolk Journal and Guide* from 1942 to 1948. He also served on many boards, including the Virginia World War II History Commission, the Southern Regional Council, and the Virginia Association of Elks.

To keep up with all these activities, he drove himself relentlessly, rising very early, walking to his office from his home on campus, taking a brief nap at midday, and returning to his office after dinner to work until midnight. He developed a heart condition, concealed it from his wife, and continued his frantic pace. He had a heart attack and died in Ettrick, Virginia.

FURTHER READING

Jackson's papers are in the archives at the James Hugo Johnston Memorial Library on the campus of Virginia State University.

Meier, August, and Elliott Rudwick. *Black History and the Historical Profession, 1915–1980* (1986).

This entry is taken from the *American National Biography* and is published here with the permission of the American Council of Learned Societies.

EDGAR ALLAN TOPPIN

Jackson, Mahalia (26 Oct. 1911–27 Jan. 1972), gospel singer, was born in New Orleans, the daughter of John Jackson, a dockworker, barber, and preacher, and Charity Clark, a maid. Her mother died when Jackson was five, and she moved in with her mother's sister, Mahalia Paul, also known as Aunt Duke. She worked both for her aunt and for a local white family from an early age, and during the eighth grade (the last grade she attended before quitting school), she also worked as a laundress for five hours after school. She began to sing as a young child, particularly at the Mount Moriah Baptist Church, but she was also profoundly influenced by the BESSIE SMITH recordings her more worldly cousin Fred owned. However, Jackson was most powerfully shaped by her experiences with the Sanctified Church that was next door to her house. As she later noted, the church had no organ or choir. Members played drums, cymbals, and tambourines, and "everybody in there sang and they clapped and stomped their feet and sang with their whole bodies. They had a beat, a powerful beat, a rhythm we held on to from slavery days, and their music was so strong and expressive it used to bring the tears to my eyes" (Jackson, 32–33).

In 1928 Jackson moved to Chicago, where her aunts Hannah and Alice already lived. For a decade she supported herself by doing laundry for white families and working as a hotel maid. She joined the choir of the Greater Salem Baptist Church, which became her second home, and cofounded the Johnson Gospel Singers with another woman and three of the minister's sons. The group sang in churches for $1.50 a night, often traveling throughout Indiana and Illinois. Jackson herself sang in churches as far away as Buffalo, New York, and at revivals, homes, and hospitals, already employing the down-home, deeply emotive style that created a powerful tie with her audience and accentuated a sense of community. The larger black churches wanted nothing to do with this style at first, so she sang most often for storefront and basement congregations. In 1935 Jackson met Isaac Hockenhull, a college-trained chemist who worked as a mail carrier. The two married in 1938; they had no children. For a time she traveled around the region selling cosmetics made from Hockenhull's own formulas, but by 1939 she had earned enough money from her singing to leave this and her other jobs and

Mahalia Jackson sings an impromptu "Just a Closer Walk with Thee" to the beat of the Eureka Brass Band at the New Orleans Jazz Festival on 23 April 1970. The gospel singer became a symbol of the civil rights movement during the March on Washington in 1963. (AP Images.)

open an enterprise she named Mahalia's Beauty Salon. The business thrived, and she soon attached a flower shop, generating business for the latter at the many funerals at which she was invited to sing. While her commitment to religious singing grew, her husband wanted her to take voice lessons and become a concert singer; he urged her to pursue a role in an all-black production of *The Mikado*, but she refused. The two grew apart and divorced in 1943, although they remained lifelong friends.

In 1937 Jackson began to work with gospel composer THOMAS A. DORSEY, and she made her recording debut that year with "God's Gonna Separate the Wheat from the Tares," a song already punctuated with her trademark moans and growls. Dorsey became her champion, and she traveled widely, singing his songs at churches; he wrote "Peace in the Valley" for her in 1937 and served as her accompanist from 1937 to 1946. Realizing the uniqueness of her style, Dorsey encouraged Jackson

to open her songs at a more tempered level, and to gradually build the excitement until the audience was ready for her uniquely celebratory climax: "In her deeply individualistic manner—running and skipping down the church and concert hall aisles, her eyes closed, hands tightly clasped, with feet tapping and body throbbing, all the while her voice soaring as if there were no walls to confine its spiritual journey—she was utterly possessed and possessing" (Schwerin, 62).

Jackson was a "stretch-out" singer who changed melody and meter as the spirit moved her. Her style borrowed from the "Baptist lining style," "a slow, languorous manner, without a regular pulse … that allowed the singer to execute each syllable by adding several extra tones, bending these added tones in myriad directions, and reshaping the melody into a personal testimony" (Boyer, 11). Thus her voice was at its most resonant and beautiful in slow hymns like "Just as I Am," sung with precise control and intense feeling. Her work with Dorsey also made Jackson a powerful presence in the city and raised the position of church singer to a new status; politicians frequently hired her to sing at funerals, an unprecedented "professionalization" of a sacred calling.

In 1945 the Chicago broadcaster Studs Terkel brought new attention to Jackson when he played one of her recordings, "I'm Goin' to Tell God All about It One of These Days," over and over again on the air. Deeply impressed, Bess Berman signed her to a contract with Apollo Records in 1946, guaranteeing her $10,000 a year. Her first four sides sold poorly, but her 1947 recording of "Move On Up a Little Higher" brought her royalties of $300,000 in the first year alone, earning her the title of "Gospel Queen." From 1946 to 1954 she recorded seventy songs for Apollo, and she commanded fees of $1,000 a night for appearances in New York and Chicago. Stung by dishonest promoters earlier in her career, she always insisted on being paid in cash on the day of her performance.

In 1950 the jazz historian and critic Marshall Stearns invited Jackson to perform at the Music Inn, near Tanglewood in Massachusetts, at a symposium on the history of jazz. Her appearance transformed her into an overnight national celebrity; she received dozens of offers to perform, appeared on *The Ed Sullivan Show*, and was appointed the official soloist for the National Baptist Convention. She also sang at the first of a series of Carnegie Hall concerts that broke all house records. Her 1952 recording of "I Can Put My Trust in Jesus" was awarded a prize by the French Academy of Music and led to her first European tour, with stops in England, Holland, Belgium, Denmark, and France. Although she collapsed in Paris six weeks after starting the tour, she received acclaim almost everywhere she sang, and her recording of "Silent Night" became a best-seller in Norway.

Courted by John Hammond, who was impressed by her rejection of the commercialization of gospel music, Jackson signed a lucrative contract with Columbia Records in 1953. She had her own radio show on a CBS station in Chicago in 1954, later converted to a half-hour television show. Although the reviews were excellent and the audience large, the network turned her down when she asked about taking the show national; they argued that they would never be able to get sponsors for the southern audience. And though she was often invited to appear on Chicago television, she found the experience frustrating, with arrangers trying to tone down her style and telling her how to sing her own songs. Even at Columbia, for which she recorded more than a dozen albums, producers filled her repertoire with "pop-gospel" songs like "A Rusty Old Halo," a "cute" crossover song, and burdened her with orchestras and choirs that only dampened the powerful impact of her impassioned voice. But Jackson enjoyed the popularity and the money, even as she complained that commercialization was compromising the music. And the results were not always disappointing; witness her 1955 recording of "Joshua Fit the Battle of Jericho," which clearly incorporates the battle against slavery into its meaning.

Jackson also toured widely during the 1950s, generally with her regular accompanist, Mildred Falls, and her cousin John Stevens. The three experienced the segregation that continued to curse the South, even while Jackson was enjoying huge commercial successes in the national white music market, and she soon immersed herself in the civil rights struggle. She appeared in Montgomery, Alabama, in 1956, for instance, when the Reverend RALPH ABERNATHY asked her to sing at a ceremony honoring ROSA PARKS. And she personally experienced the racial hypocrisy of the North in 1957, when she bought a house on Chicago's South Side in a white neighborhood. Someone fired air rifle pellets into her living-room windows, and once again she found herself a national figure. The journalist Edward R. Murrow interviewed her on his *Person to Person* television show at her house, and for days crowds of people gathered outside in sympathy. She developed a close relationship with MARTIN LUTHER KING JR. In May 1957, at the Lincoln Memorial, she sang "I Been 'Buked and I Been Scorned" as part of a Southern Christian Leadership Conference Prayer Pilgrimage for Freedom. In 1959 she recorded "Great Gettin' Up Morning," highlighting the song's implicit attack on slavery. She was most proud of her participation in the August 1963 March on Washington, where she again sang "I Been 'Buked and I Been Scorned," beginning soft and gentle, then shouting for joy and leading the crowd in singing and clapping.

Jackson's involvement in the civil rights movement enhanced her career. After the Murrow interview she appeared on *The Dinah Shore Show*, the two singing a duet of the antiwar gospel song "Down by the Riverside." She appeared as a guest star on most of the popular television variety shows of the decade, including those hosted by Bing Crosby, Perry Como, Steve Allen, Red Skelton, and

Ed Sullivan. She even made a movie appearance in 1958 (albeit a somewhat embarrassing one) as a happy "colored" servant in the film *Imitation of Life*; racist typecasting was all too typical of Hollywood in the 1950s. And, of course, her singing continued to garner approval. DUKE ELLINGTON featured her on his 1958 recording of the "Black, Brown, and Beige" suite; for the studio version of "Come Sunday," Ellington had the lights turned out while Jackson sang by herself in the dark. Her national reputation was enshrined when she sang "The Star-Spangled Banner" at President John F. Kennedy's inauguration eve gala. In 1961 she enjoyed huge popular success on a European tour and made one of her very greatest recordings, "Elijah Rock," at a concert in Stockholm, Sweden, accompanied only by Falls on the piano.

Jackson's health began to deteriorate in 1963, and she was periodically hospitalized over the last years of her life for exhaustion and heart problems. Yet in 1964 she embarked on a hugely successful European tour that ended with a private papal audience in Rome and a longed-for visit to Jerusalem. That same year she married Sigmund Galloway; they had no children and divorced in 1967. Also in 1967 she starred at the first-ever gospel concert at Lincoln Center. She appeared at the Newport Jazz Festival in 1970 and began another European tour in 1971, cut short by her last illness. She sang "Take My Hand, Precious Lord" at King's funeral, and sang at Robert F. Kennedy's funeral. She also expanded her business operations, establishing the Mahalia Jackson Chicken System, eventually a chain of 135 stores, and continued to pursue her little-publicized charitable efforts through the Mahalia Jackson Scholarship Foundation, using her own money to send students to college. Jackson died in Evergreen Park, a Chicago suburb. She was buried in New Orleans and was commemorated at funerals both there and in Chicago, the latter attended by scores of dignitaries and marked by ARETHA FRANKLIN singing "Precious Lord."

By the end of her life, Jackson had immersed herself in business and real estate deals, and she seemed to spend more and more of her time meeting with accountants and lawyers. Her appearance fees were far beyond the reach of even prosperous churches to pay. But though purists attacked her commercial concessions, she remained a regal, matriarchal presence in gospel and in American music in general. As the writer Anthony Heilbut noted, "All by herself, Mahalia was the vocal, physical, spiritual symbol of gospel music" (Heilbut, 57).

Jazz, blues, and gospel enthusiasts found a common bond in her rhythmic energy and spiritual intensity. She was the first to carry gospel music beyond the black community, and she affected lives in an unparalleled personal way. Ellington noted that his encounter with Jackson "had a strong influence on me and my sacred music, and also made me a much handsomer kid in the Right Light." As Jackson herself stated in her autobiography: "There's something about music that is so penetrating that your soul gets the message. No matter what trouble comes to a person, music can help him face it" (184).

FURTHER READING

Jackson, Mahalia, with Evan McLeod Wylie. *Movin' On Up* (1966).

Boyer, Horace Clarence. Notes accompanying *Gospels, Hymns, and Spirituals* (Columbia Records, 1991).

Goreau, Laurraine. *Just Mahalia, Baby* (1975)

Heilbut, Anthony. *The Gospel Sound: Good News and Bad Times*, rev. ed. (1992).

Schwerin, Jules. *Got to Tell It: Mahalia Jackson, Queen of Gospel* (1992)

Obituary: *New York Times*, 28 Jan. 1972.

DISCOGRAPHY

Jackson's most important recordings include her early sessions for Apollo Records.

Gospels, Spirituals, and Hymns (Columbia Records).

How I Got Over (Columbia Records).

Live at Newport 1958 (Columbia Records).

This entry is taken from the *American National Biography* and is published here with the permission of the American Council of Learned Societies.

RONALD P. DUFOUR

Jackson, Mattie J. (Jan. 1847–5 Feb. 1910), slave narrative author, was born in St. Louis, Missouri, on the Charles Canory plantation. She was the second of three daughters born to Ellen Turner and Westly Jackson, a married couple with different slavemasters. Mattie's sisters were Esther or Hester (married surname: Diggs) and Sarah Ann, who died as a small child. Mattie's great grandfather was born in Africa, kidnapped, and sold to a slavemaster in New York State. Her grandfather was born into slavery there, but lived as a free man and property owner for thirty years, only to be tricked into reenslavement in Missouri. Westly was his only child with another slave he married.

Although she last saw him when she was three, Mattie remembered her father's "little kindnesses" and "deep affection" (Jackson, p. 5) and her parents' struggles as slaves to continue their loving relationship. Finally Westly felt his only choice was escape to Chicago, where he became a preacher. The family fought unsuccessfully to reunite. In 1853 Ellen, Mattie, and Esther escaped to Illinois, but were all caught and sold to William Lewis in St. Louis. Mattie describes Lewis and his wife as violent toward their slaves, in contrast to the Canorys. Ellen intervened to protect her daughters from the Lewises' abuse.

Believing that Westly had died, Ellen married George Brown, an enslaved foreman of the Lewises' tobacco factory. They had two sons, one also named George. Their other boy died by age two because of Mrs. Lewis's abuse. After protesting the insufficient food he was fed, George Brown was sold. But he escaped to Canada, renamed himself John G. Thompson, and worked as a barber in Lawrence, Massachusetts. He heard and believed the false rumor that Ellen and the children died during an escape attempt. In 1860 he married Dr. Lucy Prophet Schuyler, an African American herbalist physician and Underground Railway conductor.

Much to the Lewises' chagrin, Ellen and Mattie both became literate enough to follow newspaper reports about the Civil War. After the Lewises switched and beat her severely, Mattie sought help from Union troops stationed nearby. After the Union General whipped William Lewis, his violence against Ellen, Esther, Mattie, and the younger George escalated. In 1862 the family again escaped, but Lewis rounded them up and sold them to a "Captain Tirrell," a Confederate slavetrader who masqueraded as a kindly Union officer. "Tirrell" sold all four family members to different masters in Kentucky, the very day Ellen planned to wed Samuel Adams, an old friend and a freed slave.

In 1863 Mattie fled to Indianapolis, Indiana. There she attended school, viewed the assassinated Lincoln's casket, and reunited, by 1865, with her mother and two surviving siblings. Returning to St. Louis, Ellen married Samuel Adams, and Mattie worked for the Canorys. John G. Thompson, hearing news of the family, called George and Mattie north to Lawrence. The two siblings arrived on 11 April 1866. Mattie enjoyed the kind, welcoming spirit of her stepparents and the almost entirely white townspeople, but missed her mother. With her stepmother's aid, Mattie penned her life story and published it through the office of Lawrence's *Sentinel* newspaper. The narrative was intended to play "some humble part in removing doubts indulged by the prejudices against the natural genius and talent of our race" (Jackson, p. 2) and provide Jackson "aid towards completing my studies" (Jackson, p. 29).

Jackson's slave narrative was once the only known source of information about her and her family. The public records research of DoVeanna Fulton Minor has uncovered more information. According to the 1870 Census, Mattie lived in St. Louis with Esther and Ellen and Samuel Adams. The younger George changed his name to George Brown Thompson and lived in Lawrence with his stepmother and father. On 27 July 1869 Mattie J. Jackson wed the Mississippi River steamboat porter and Missouri native William Reed Dyer. Five of their nine children lived to adulthood. By 1895 the couple was prosperous enough to own properties in O'Fallon and Dardenne, Missouri.

Mattie Jackson Dyer lived to age sixty-three. It is unclear whether she completed as much schooling as she wished. However, her narrative still boldly communicates, in her voice of firsthand experience, the all too often denied ill effects of slavery on both African and European Americans, along with the healing power of education. Most of all, she offers a vivid, multigenerational portrait of black family relationships and their deep strengths despite the repeated traumas of enforced separation.

FURTHER READING

Jackson, Mattie J. *The Story of Mattie J. Jackson; Her Parentage—Experience of Eighteen Years in Slavery—Incidents during the War—Her Escape from Slavery. A True Story* (1866).

Minor, DoVeanna S. Fulton. *Speaking Lives, Authoring Texts: Three African American Women's Oral Slave Narratives* (2010).

Minor, DoVeanna S. Fulton. *Speaking Power: Black Feminist Orality in Women's Narratives of Slavery* (2006).

Moody, Joycelyn. *Sentimental Confessions: Spiritual Narratives of Nineteenth-Century African American Women* (2003).

MARY KRANE DERR

Jackson, Maynard Holbrook, Jr. (23 Mar. 1938–23 June 2003), attorney and mayor of Atlanta, was born in Dallas, Texas, the third of six children of Irene Dobbs, a university professor, and Maynard Jackson Sr., a Baptist minister. His mother came from a prominent Atlanta family; she was the daughter of John Wesley Dobbs, an early-twentieth-century African American civic leader who coined the name Sweet Auburn for Atlanta's historic black business district and a founder of the Atlanta Negro Voters League in the 1940s. In 1945 the Jackson family moved to Atlanta, where Maynard Jackson Sr. became the pastor of the Friendship Baptist Church. A precocious student, Maynard Jackson Jr. was eighteen years old in 1956, when he graduated from Morehouse College with a B.A. in Political Science and History. He worked for a short time in Ohio and then returned to school, earning a law degree in 1964 from North Carolina Central University in Durham. He married Burnella "Bunnie" Hayes Burke; they had three children. The couple moved to Atlanta, where Jackson worked as an attorney for the National Labor Relations Board and later for a public interest firm that provided legal services for low-income Atlantans.

Jackson's political career began in 1968 with an improbable U.S. Senate run against the segregationist incumbent and former Georgia governor Herman E. Talmadge. Although he lost badly to Talmadge, Jackson carried Atlanta and received considerable media attention (including the *New York Times*). He soon began planning a run for vice mayor. In 1969 he defeated the alderman Milton G. Farris in the same election in which Atlanta chose its first Jewish mayor, Sam Massell, a moderate Democrat and vice mayor since 1962. During the late 1960s and early 1970s, Atlanta was in the midst of rapid population growth (to outlying counties, not the city itself) and suburban expansion. However, as economic and business opportunities increased, the metro area (especially the city) faced all of the challenges affecting many major American cities during this period, including soaring crime rates, poverty, white flight, and a looming transportation crisis.

Massell proved unable to substantively address any of Atlanta's problems during his four years as mayor. Meanwhile Jackson became a well-liked figure in city politics, and he decided the time was right to run against Massell in 1973. For the first time Atlanta's black population exceeded 50 percent. Massell had lost some of his appeal with black voters when he crushed a sanitation workers' strike in 1970, and Jackson stood to pick up substantial numbers of white liberal voters. But his path was not entirely smooth. Also tossing their hats into the ring that year were the liberal Democrat and former congressman Charles Weltner and the black state legislator Leroy Johnson. The field of candidates also included Hosea Williams, former executive director of the Southern Christian Leadership Conference (SCLC) and aide to MARTIN LUTHER KING JR. After winning 47 percent of the vote (but significantly only 6 percent of the white vote), Jackson faced a runoff with Mayor Massell. Jackson triumphed by a wide margin, becoming the first African American mayor of a large southern city and ushering in a new era of black political power in Atlanta. Nationally Jackson was one of a handful of black mayors in major cities, including Cleveland, Detroit, and Los Angeles, in the early to mid-1970s, which marked a significant shift in urban politics and one tangible result of the 1965 Voting Rights Act.

Jackson's first year in office stirred whites' fears that he would place the interests of black Atlantans over those of the city as a whole. First, he removed the white police chief John Inman and replaced him with Reginald Eaves, an old Morehouse friend. Second, with the recently revised city charter granting more power to the mayor and changing the board of aldermen to an eighteen-member city council, Jackson initiated an affirmative action program mandating that one-third of city construction contracts be given to minority-owned businesses. He opened doors previously closed to African Americans through generations of brutal segregation in Atlanta, but he was also acutely aware of the need to maintain Atlanta's status as a vital regional financial capital. During his first term, the city's economy improved, he made no drastic tax increases, and he generally kept white as well as black constituents happy. Although Atlanta's white business elites, which until his administration had been accustomed to sharing power with the city government, had been largely cut out of their usual political avenues, they were pleased with Jackson's quick firing of hundreds of striking sanitation workers in 1975.

Jackson's popularity translated into nearly 65 percent of the vote when he ran for reelection. In his private life, he and his first wife divorced in 1976, and the following year he married Valerie Richardson, an advertising executive. The couple had two children. One of the great triumphs of his second term was overseeing the construction and operation of the opening phase of the Southeast's first rapid transit system, the Metropolitan Atlanta Rapid Transit Authority (MARTA). Like most things in Atlanta, the new rail and bus system was marked by simmering racial hostility underlying a decade-old opposition to any rail line that connected the inner city to the northern suburbs. In fact, as it expanded over the years, MARTA's geographic routes and primary users made it a potent symbol of Atlanta's race and class divisions—as well as the subject of a well-known racist joke about the true meaning of the acronym. But in the face of rising gas prices and tensions in the Middle East, in 1979 many hailed MARTA as an important ingredient in making Atlanta a truly great city. During his second term Jackson also had to grapple with a string of vicious child murders that stumped the police department as well as the FBI and other agencies for two years before an African American man, Wayne Williams, was convicted of two of the killings.

Because he was legally unable to serve a third consecutive term, Jackson convinced his friend, Congressman ANDREW YOUNG, to run in 1981. Young served two terms, and Jackson jumped back into the fray in 1989. Ever popular, he won easily and played a pivotal role in helping Atlanta secure a bid to host the 1996 Summer Olympic Games. He is best remembered for overseeing a $400 million expansion of Hartsfield Airport, again insisting on strict affirmative action policies. The airport was later renamed Hartsfield-Jackson in his honor. After leaving city politics, he became active in the national Democratic Party. In the summer of 2003 Jackson collapsed at a Washington, D.C., airport, and on 23 June he died of heart failure in Arlington, Virginia.

FURTHER READING

Kruse, Kevin M. *White Flight: Atlanta and the Making of Modern Conservatism* (2005).

Pomerantz, Gary B. *Where Peachtree Meets Sweet Auburn: The Saga of Two Families and the Making of Atlanta* (1996).

Stone, Clarence N. *Regime Politics: Governing Atlanta, 1946–1988* (1989).

STACY BRAUKMAN

Jackson, Michael (29 Aug. 1958–25 June 2009), singer, dancer, songwriter, and pop and tabloid superstar, was born Michael Joseph Jackson in Gary, Indiana, a blue-collar town dominated by steel mills. His father, Joseph S. Jackson, a steelworker, and his mother, Katherine, were strict Jehovah's Witnesses. The couple had nine children—Maureen ("Rebbie"), Sigmund ("Jackie"), Toriano ("Tito"), Jermaine, Marlon, La Toya, Michael, Steven ("Randy"), and Janet—who grew up in poverty. The prohibitions of their religion were pushed aside in 1962 when Joseph, a frustrated singer, gathered Jackie, Tito, and Jermaine into a rhythm and blues act. The next year he added Michael, who was five.

The boys loved to sing, but Joseph became a demanding and controlling stage father who beat his children when they did not perform to his satisfaction. He pushed them mercilessly—especially Michael, the most talented. Even as a child Michael could dance like JAMES BROWN and sing with a soulful passion that quickly distinguished him from his brothers. Soon the boys were playing talent shows, nightclubs, and even strip joints. By 1966 Marlon had joined them. The next year they were signed to an Indiana label, Steeltown, as the Jackson Five. Michael soloed in a childlike voice on their first single, "Big Boy." The record was a local sensation that helped win them a deal with Motown in 1968. Their first four singles—"I Want You Back," "ABC," "The Love You Save," and "I'll Be There"—all made number one, an unprecedented coup. The Jackson 5 became the hottest pop-soul-R&B group in show business. BERRY GORDY JR., Motown's owner, recognized that Michael had real star quality. Although the group continued to record together, Gordy began grooming Michael as a headliner, and throughout the 1970s Michael met and surpassed all expectations. In 1971 Jackson's first solo single, "Got to Be There," shot to number four. A 1972 follow-up, "Rockin' Robin," made number two. That summer Jackson scored his first of twelve number 1 singles, "Ben," the title song of a horror film about an introverted boy whose best friend is his pet rat. In retrospect, the song, sung with a moving sensitivity, seems an ominous portent of the lonely and confused fantasy world that Michael would later find himself inhabiting.

In 1975 the Jackson 5 began to break up when Jermaine refused to leave Motown after his brothers signed with Epic Records as the Jacksons. Michael's appearance as the Scarecrow in a lavish film version of *The Wiz* in 1978 starring DIANA ROSS became a springboard to his solo career. Although the film flopped, Michael formed a close relationship with the musical director, QUINCY JONES, who went on to produce the singer's fifth solo album, *Off the Wall* (1979). Where Jackson's previous albums had been weighted down by sappy love songs, *Off the Wall* was a glitzy blending of dance tracks, funk, and a higher grade of pop-soul ballads. It yielded four Top Ten hits, two of-which—the Grammy-winning "Don't Stop 'Til You Get Enough" and "Rock with You"—reached number 1.

At his peak Jackson recorded *Thriller*, then the biggest-selling album in history, and made the

Michael Jackson at age thirteen, in his home in Encino, California, 1972. (AP Images.)

cover of *Time*. His videos turned the MTV cable television channel into a worldwide phenomenon. Fred Astaire raved about his dancing. Black pop had never had a higher profile. Jackson had "taken us right up there where we belong," said his producer, Quincy Jones. "Black music had to play second fiddle for a long time, but its spirit is the whole motor of pop" (*Time*, "Why He's a Thriller," 19 Mar. 1984). Yet the so-called King of Pop would become as famous for his bizarre behavior as he was for his talent. The world saw a man-child so fragile that he seemed ever in danger of snapping.

Jackson had continued singing with his brothers until the release of *Thriller* in December 1982. The album was inspired by one of his fixations, the occult. Jackson wrote most of the songs; several had spooky themes, sweetened by irresistible dance rhythms and flashy production. The guest musicians Paul McCartney and Eddie Van Halen added extra star glitter. Seven of *Thriller*'s nine tracks made the Top Ten. "Billie Jean" and "Beat It" hit number one.

The album's success owed much to the videos that accompanied it, at a time when the genre was still new. The title song featured a conglomeration of dancing zombies. "Beat It," a statement against gang violence, recalled the schoolyard ballets of *West Side Story*. "Billie Jean," a tale of accused paternity, looked like a surreal horror film, with Jackson as a sinister, lurking presence. Jackson's innovations in promoting the *Thriller* album were so frequently emulated that he could be regarded as the most important pioneer of the modern music video. In 1983 Jackson performed on Motown's twenty-fifth-anniversary TV special where he introduced his famous strutting-on-tiptoe "moonwalk" to an estimated 47 million viewers.

On 28 February 1984 *Thriller* won eight Grammy awards. The next year Jackson and LIONEL RICHIE teamed to write "We Are the World," an anthem for *USA for Africa*, an all-star hunger-relief album. Produced by Jones, the single raised $50 million and won three Grammy awards. Pepsi went on to offer Jackson a $10 million endorsement deal. Jackson, it seemed, had the magic touch—a notion perhaps reinforced by the single white sequined glove he wore in public.

But scandal soon began to overwhelm him. Jackson's skin was growing whiter, and rumors circulated that he was having his blackness bleached away, though the singer claimed he had vitiligo, a skin disease that leaves white blotches. Numerous attempts to alter his appearance through plastic surgery gave him a pale, gaunt, and strangely androgynous look. He started wearing surgical masks in public, ostensibly to keep out germs. Jackson seemed obsessed with staying a child. His best friends were either maternal figures—Jane Fonda, Diana Ross, Elizabeth Taylor—or children. He bought a huge ranch in Santa Ynez, California, and called it Neverland, after the magical place in *Peter Pan* where children never grow up. Jackson filled Neverland with amusement park rides and preadolescents. The press gave him a new nickname: "Wacko Jacko."

In September 1987 he released a new album, *Bad*. It debuted at number 1 and yielded five number 1 singles, "I Just Can't Stop Loving You," "Bad," "The Way You Make Me Feel," "Man in the Mirror," and "Dirty Diana." Jackson promoted *Bad* with the highest-grossing world tour of all time. *Bad*'s sales—an estimated 8 million copies—seemed a letdown after the reported 50 million-plus of *Thriller*. But that did not stop Sony from signing him, in March 1991, to a new contract—six more albums plus film projects and TV specials—for a reported $890 million.

A new album, *Dangerous* (1991), debuted at number 1, as did its first single, "Black or White." But overall his sales were declining, even as his tabloid allure zoomed. In 1993, during the *Dangerous* tour, the family of a thirteen-year-old Neverland regular charged Jackson with molesting the boy, who told his story in a deposition. Jackson countersued for extortion, while defending himself on TV; his only fault, he claimed, was "enjoying through [children] the childhood that I missed myself" (live interview, 22 Dec. 1993). He ended up settling out of court, paying the family an estimated $18 to $20 million. Subsequently Pepsi dropped him. A nineteen-month marriage (1994–1996) to Lisa Marie Presley, Elvis's daughter, was seen as a desperate scheme to save his image.

In 1994 Jackson released a double compact disc of old and new material: *HIStory: Past, Present and Future, Book I*. The album and a single, "You Are Not Alone," premiered at number 1. In keeping with the biblical grandiosity of the album's title, Jackson performed at the 1996 Brit Awards dressed as the Messiah and surrounded by worshipful children. The rock singer Jarvis Cocker stormed onstage in the middle of the song to protest the spectacle. More scandal erupted that year with the announcement that Debbie Rowe, his dermatologist's assistant, was carrying Jackson's baby. She married him on 14 November, and the couple had two children, Prince Michael Jackson Jr. and Paris Katherine Jackson. The couple divorced in October 1999. Jackson retained custody of Prince and Paris.

In 2001 Jackson was inducted into the Rock and Roll Hall of Fame. An all-star concert, televised from Madison Square Garden, celebrated the thirtieth anniversary of his first solo record. From there he returned to the front pages of the tabloids. A new solo album, *Invincible* (2001), debuted at number 1 but sank quickly, producing no hits. Blaming Sony for bad marketing, Jackson branded chairman Tommy Mottola a racist and the "devil." December 2002 found Jackson back in court, sued by a promoter for backing out of two millennium concerts. The singer gave near incoherent testimony, during which he revealed a nose caved in from a botched surgery. He was ordered to pay $5.3 million in damages.

Prince Michael II, his third child, had been born that year to an unnamed surrogate mother. Jackson nicknamed the boy "Blanket." On 19 November he stepped onto the terrace of his Berlin hotel suite to greet throngs of fans below. With TV cameras running, he dangled Blanket over the edge of the balcony, shocking people worldwide.

The most damaging exposé of all appeared in February 2003: the TV documentary *Living with Michael Jackson*, produced by the journalist Martin Bashir, who had gained Jackson's cooperation. Twenty-seven million American viewers got a hair-raising glimpse inside Neverland and heard Jackson admit that underage boys slept in his bed—platonically, he swore. Feeling betrayed, Jackson sold Fox TV a "rebuttal" documentary filled with home-movie footage that showed him in a highly favorable light. But the musical legend he had started building at age five seemed tainted beyond repair. In November 2003 further criminal charges of child molestation, made on the very day his latest recording was released, renewed the scandal and created another frenzy of criticism, commentary, and news-mongering. Jackson's trial finally began in Santa Maria, California, on 31 January 2005. After four months of controversy, salacious details, and media hysteria, Jackson was acquitted of all charges on 13 June 2005.

In March 2009, Jackson announced plans for a run of 10 concerts to be held exclusively at London's O2 arena, one of Europe's largest music venues. Dubbed "This Is It," the series claimed to be Jackson's final run of performances ever. Tickets to each concert sold out within an hour of going on sale, and 40 more shows were quickly scheduled. Two months later, Jackson hired Dr. Conrad Murray to be his full-time personal physician. Jackson had suffered a miscellany of health ailments in his later years, and the hiring of Murray was an attempt to ensure his fitness for the concerts, an enterprise estimated by some to generate over a billion pounds for the United Kingdom economy. A high-powered playboy who had founded boutique cardiology clinics in Las Vegas and Houston, Murray was contracted for $150,000 a month.

Within a few months, however, Jackson's health seemed to be deteriorating. At a rehearsal on 19 June, only weeks before the scheduled kickoff of "This Is It," Jackson appeared alarmingly ill. Shaken by his behavior, Jackson's tour manager and close friend Kenny Ortega questioned Murray, who insisted that Jackson was fine. Six days later, after a dose of the anesthetic propofol, Jackson was taken to the emergency room in Los Angeles; according to later court testimony, he had gone 20 minutes without breathing before Murray called an ambulance. A few hours later, on 25 June, Jackson was pronounced dead.

After an investigation lasting less than a month, Jackson's death was classified as a homicide by the

Los Angeles County District Attorney's office. The county's medical examiner cited "acute propofol intoxication" as the cause of death, and the following February Murray was charged with involuntary manslaughter. On 27 September 2011, Murray's trial commenced. Even in death Jackson couldn't escape from the intense scrutiny that had dogged him his entire life, as yet another media mob descended upon Los Angeles to beam intimate reports of his final days to fans across the world.

The trial lasted approximately six weeks. Murray's defense team, while admitting that Murray had regularly provided Jackson with propofol to help him sleep (according to Murray, Jackson referred to the substance as his "milk"), insisted that Murray had not administered the final, lethal dose. The prosecution argued that whether or not Murray had physically injected Jackson was irrelevant, and that merely allowing the singer unfettered access to the narcotic constituted "bizarre, unethical, unconscionable behavior" worthy of conviction. On 7 November 2011, Murray was found guilty. Called "a demonstrable risk to the safety of the public" by judge Michael Pastor (Gumbel), Murray was imprisoned without bail until his sentencing on 28 November, when he was sentenced to four years in prison.

Personal scandal and controversy diminished much of Jackson's popularity, but the eccentricity of his life cannot erase the unparalleled influence he had on the music industry—and thereby on American and even global culture—during the first twenty years of his career. He produced one of the best-selling albums and music videos of all time in *Thriller*, he garnered the most number one hits during the 1980s, and he holds the *Billboard* records for the most number one hits by a male artist (thirteen) and the highest number of singles to enter at the top position.

FURTHER READING

Andersen, Christopher P. *Michael Jackson: Unauthorized* (1994).

Bishop, Nick. *Freak: Inside the Twisted World of Michael Jackson (from the Files of the National Enquirer)* (2003).

Gumbel, Andrew. "Michael Jackson's Doctor Found Guilty of Involuntary Manslaughter." *The Guardian*, 7 Nov. 2011.

Taraborelli, J. Randy. *Michael Jackson: The Magic and the Madness* (1991).

Obituary: *New York Times*, 25 June 2009.

JAMES GAVIN

Jackson, Milt (1 Jan. 1923–9 Oct. 1999), musician, was born in Detroit, Michigan, the son of Manley Jackson and Lillie Beaty. His parents' occupations are unknown. Milt was surrounded by music from an early age, and his strongest influence came from the music he heard during weekly religious meetings: "Everyone wants to know where I got that funky style. Well, it came from church. The music I heard was open, relaxed, impromptu soul music" (quoted in Hentoff). Inspired by the music he heard in church, Milt began playing the guitar when he was seven years old. Four years later he began studying the piano, and while attending Miller High School, he focused on the drums in addition to playing timpani and violin and singing in the school's choir. At sixteen he sang in a local gospel quartet called the Evangelist Singers. Milt eventually took up the vibraharp, or vibraphone, after hearing LIONEL HAMPTON play the instrument in Benny Goodman's band.

In 1941 Jackson began his professional career, playing the vibraharp in two local groups led by Clarence Ringo and GEORGE E. LEE. His career was interrupted by a two-year stint in the U.S. Army from 1942 to 1944. In 1944 he started the Four Sharps, his first group. There would always remain a special place in Jackson's heart for the Detroit music scene that nurtured him: "[Detroit] was a beautiful environment then. I wish they could have kept that environment and enhanced it. The environment of the 40's in Detroit was very similar to the environment of 52nd Street when I first came to New York.... In Detroit we had Al McKibbon, HOWARD McGHEE, Teddy Edwards, who actually moved to the West Coast, the Jones brothers" (quoted in Rusch, 4).

In 1945 the visiting jazz giant trumpeter DIZZY GILLESPIE discovered Jackson and asked him to come to New York. While working in Gillespie's band, Jackson was introduced to CHARLIE PARKER, who was chiefly responsible for forging the musical revolution known as "bebop." Jackson was overwhelmed by the experience of playing with Parker: "I remember one night we were playing 'Hot House' and Bird was playing so fantastic that I came in four bars late in my solo" (quoted in De Micheal, 19).

Playing with Gillespie proved to be a springboard for Jackson's career, and within his first few years in New York he played with a veritable who's who of jazz. On 2 July 1948 he recorded with the pianist and composer THELONIOUS MONK for the seminal Blue Note label. Jackson also worked with the clarinetist Woody Herman and his orchestra in

1949. Upon returning to the Gillespie band in 1950, Jackson played alongside the tenor saxophonist JOHN COLTRANE. In addition to playing the vibraharp, he doubled as pianist and, on occasion, as vocalist for the Gillespie band. While playing with Gillespie, Jackson met the pianist JOHN LEWIS, with whom he would be associated musically for the next forty years. Lewis had served as the pianist in Gillespie's big band between the years 1946 and 1948, and it was in that band that the nucleus of the Modern Jazz Quartet was born.

Around 1951–1952 Jackson made his first album under his own name, *The Milt Jackson Quartet* (reissued on compact disc in 1991). Rounding out the group were Lewis on piano; the bassists Ray Brown, who became a mainstay in the pianist OSCAR PETERSON's group, and PERCY HEATH; the father of bebop drumming, KENNY CLARKE; and the drummer Al Johns. The group made public appearances as the Milt Jackson Quartet, but between 1953 and 1954 Heath became the MJQ's full-time bassist, and the initials of the group came to stand for the Modern Jazz Quartet. The Modern Jazz Quartet became one of the longest-running small groups in jazz, and with the exception of Clarke being replaced by Connie Kay in 1955, the lineup of the group remained intact until Kay's death.

Mixing blues with Lewis's more classically aimed compositions and wearing tuxedos at all of their live appearances, the MJQ took jazz music to venues normally not associated with jazz, including concert halls and theaters. Critical responses were favorable, and the term "chamber jazz" was used to describe their music. Some musicians, however, felt that the group was "pretentious," but that did not hinder its popularity. Jackson's vibes provided the perfect foil for Lewis's stoic compositions.

Jackson married Sandra Kaye Whittington in 1959; they had one daughter. In the 1960s Jackson recorded albums with Coltrane and RAY CHARLES. In 1974 the MJQ disbanded, leaving Jackson free to pursue a solo career, although the quartet reunited in 1981 and performed on a few tours. Jackson recorded albums for Pablo and for the producer Creed Taylor's CTI label, and he remained a vital and active jazz musician until his death in Manhattan. His improvisational skill and unique sound made him a true original in jazz, and he has influenced countless other musicians.

FURTHER READING
De Micheal, Don. "Jackson of the MJQ," *Down Beat* (6 July 1961).

Rusch, Bob. "Milt Jackson Interview," *Cadence* (May 1977).
Obituary: *New York Times,* 11 Oct. 1999.

DISCOGRAPHY
Hentoff, Nat. Liner notes, *Plenty, Plenty Soul* (Atlantic 1269-2).
This entry is taken from the *American National Biography* and is published here with the permission of the American Council of Learned Societies.

P. J. COTRONEO

Jackson, O'Shea. *See* Ice Cube.

Jackson, Peter (3 July 1861–13 July 1901), boxer, was born in Frederiksted on the island of St. Croix, Virgin Islands, the son of a fisherman. His parents' names are unknown. His father became weary of fishing the waters of the Caribbean and, seeking better opportunities in the South Pacific, moved the family to Australia in 1873. Three years later, however, Jackson's parents tired of life in Australia and returned to the Virgin Islands. An adventurous youth, Peter stayed behind and became a boatman and sailor in the area around Sydney. He never saw his parents again.

A natural athlete, Jackson developed a marvelous physique competing in sculling matches and became an excellent swimmer. He got his start in boxing while working as a sailor for a shipping firm owned by Clay Callahan. A successful American businessman and local boxer, Callahan saw in Jackson a quiet, polite young man who had the athletic skills and heart to become a first-rate boxer. He introduced Jackson to Larry Foley, a prominent boxing instructor and former pugilist. Foley took Jackson on as a pupil and brought him along slowly at his White Horse Saloon in Sydney. At a little over six feet tall and close to two hundred pounds, Jackson appeared to Foley as a promising candidate to contend for the world heavyweight championship.

For two years Jackson trained under Foley's supervision in the gymnasium in the basement of the saloon. During this period Jackson sparred with outstanding boxers such as the future heavyweight champion Bob Fitzsimmons, Frank Slavin, and Jim Hall, all of whom were also training with Foley. Beginning in 1882 Foley arranged a series of fights for Jackson. After earning a string of victories in these fights, Jackson was knocked out by Bill Farnan in 1884 and managed only a draw in a rematch later that year. Disappointed by his lack of success against Farnan, Jackson continued to develop his techniques at Foley's saloon. As a result he became heavyweight champion of Australia on 25 September 1886, when he defeated Tom Lees from Victoria in a thirty-round fight in Foley's saloon.

As Australia's first black heavyweight champion, Jackson quickly found it difficult to fight worthy opponents both because he outclassed most competitors and because some boxers, such as Jack Burke, simply would not fight against black opponents. In 1888 Jackson set sail for San Francisco in search of profitable matches and perhaps an opportunity to fight the world heavyweight champion, John L. Sullivan. He soon became associated with the California Athletic Club, where he was appointed as a professor of boxing. In the United States, Jackson again found it difficult to schedule matches because of racial prejudice. By the end of the nineteenth century segregation, either legal or informal, was becoming more common in American sports. While there was no categorical racial barrier in boxing, certain white boxers observed the color line. Jackson did defeat the African American boxer George Godfrey in 1888 to claim the "colored heavyweight championship of the world" and followed that victory with a knockout of Joe McAuliffe, considered the best heavyweight on the West Coast.

Jackson left California in 1889 and headed for New York, where he hoped to engage in more lucrative bouts, but he quickly moved on to London when a chance came to fight the former heavyweight champion of England, Jem Smith. Jackson soundly defeated Smith in two rounds in November 1889, and the sporting public began to clamor for a match between Jackson and Sullivan. Despite receiving several attractive offers, Sullivan refused to fight Jackson because he was black. Jackson's extreme disappointment and frustration at Sullivan's stance made him melancholy and adversely affected his performance in the ring during 1890. His spirits were revived in 1891 when he was able to arrange a match with James J. Corbett in San Francisco. In a rather slow-moving bout, the two boxers fought to a sixty-one-round draw. The match improved Corbett's chance for a title bout with Sullivan and convinced many boxing authorities that Jackson had reached the end of his career.

In early 1892 Jackson returned to England, where he was embraced by the sporting public and polite society, to fight against an old rival, fellow Australian Frank Slavin. Jackson knocked out Slavin in the tenth round in one of the most exciting fights ever held in England. He returned to the United States in late 1892 in hopes of getting another match with Corbett, who recently had won the heavyweight championship from Sullivan. For the next two years Jackson and his manager "Parson" Davies attempted unsuccessfully to arrange a title match with Corbett. The two boxers could not agree on terms and exchanged insults with one another. In the end Jackson's pride prevented him from accepting a match with Corbett under unfavorable conditions. Discouraged, in 1894 he returned to England, where his health deteriorated partly because of excessive drinking. Jackson fought his last boxing match in San Francisco in 1898 against the future heavyweight champion Jim Jeffries. Badly out of condition, Jackson lost the contest by a technical knockout when he failed to answer the bell for the fourth round. After suffering a near-fatal case of viral pneumonia, Jackson returned to Australia in 1900. He died of tuberculosis in Roma, Australia. One of the most noted athletes of his time, Jackson enjoyed a following among sports enthusiasts, both black and white.

FURTHER READING

Hales, A. G. *Black Prince Peter: The Romantic Career of Peter Jackson* (1931).

Langley, Tom. *The Life of Peter Jackson: Champion of Australia* (1974).

Wiggins, David K. "Peter Jackson and the Elusive Heavyweight Championship: A Black Athlete's Struggle against the Late Nineteenth Century Color-Line," *Journal of Sport History* 12 (Summer 1985).

Obituary: *Cleveland Gazette*, 24 Aug. 1901.

This entry is taken from the *American National Biography* and is published here with the permission of the American Council of Learned Societies.

JOHN M. CARROLL

Jackson, Rebecca Cox (15 Feb. 1795–24 May 1871), itinerant preacher, religious writer, and Shaker eldress, was born a free African American in Horntown, Pennsylvania. According to sketchy autobiographical information, she was the daughter of Jane Cox (maiden name unknown). No reference is made in her writings to her father, who probably died shortly after her birth. Rebecca Cox lived with her grandmother (never named) until she was between three and four years old, but by age six she was again living with her mother, who had remarried and was now called Jane Wisson or Wilson. Her stepfather, a sailor, died at sea the next year. At age ten, she was in Philadelphia with her mother and a younger sister and infant brother, the offspring, it seems, of a third marriage of her mother. Responsibility for caring for her younger siblings seems to have deprived Rebecca of the schooling her mother was somehow able to provide for the other children. Her mother died when she was thirteen, whereupon she probably moved into the household of her older brother Joseph Cox (1778?–1843), a tanner and clergyman eighteen years her senior.

The exact date of Rebecca Cox's marriage to Samuel S. Jackson is unknown, but it must have occurred before 1830, the year of her spiritual awakening and the year her autobiographical narrative begins. Apparently childless, she and her husband were living with Joseph Cox. She cared for her brother's four children and also worked as a seamstress, a relatively highly skilled and respected occupation for African American women at that time. Jackson had been brought up as a Methodist, presumably in the African Methodist Episcopal (AME) Church. Her brother Joseph was an influential preacher at the Bethel AME Church in Philadelphia, but Rebecca and her husband apparently were not active church members prior to her spiritual awakening, which occurred during a violent thunderstorm. Her career as an independent preacher began shortly thereafter.

Carried on the waves of a religious revival, she soon moved from leading a small praying band to public preaching. She stirred up controversy within AME circles not only as a woman preacher, but also because she had come to believe that celibacy was a necessary precondition of a holy life. She insisted that she be guided entirely by the dictates of an inner voice, which she identified as the authentic voice of God. In her incomplete spiritual autobiography, which she began to write in the 1840s, perhaps using earlier journal entries as a source, Jackson recorded a wide variety of visionary experiences, dreams, and supernatural gifts, including a remarkable "gift of reading," or literacy, in direct response to prayer in 1831. This "gift" gave her independent access to the divine word and allowed Jackson to free herself from what she believed was censorship in the letters she dictated to her clergyman brother. She also recorded instances of healing, the gift of foresight, and the more mysterious "gifts of power," spiritual means of protecting herself from threats, both natural and human.

By the late 1830s Jackson had separated from her husband, broken with the AME Church, and successfully launched a career of itinerant preaching that took her throughout Pennsylvania, northern Delaware, New Jersey, southern New England, and New York State. Her first experience with religious communal life occurred during this period, when she became involved with a group of religious Perfectionists organized near Albany, New York, by a man named Allen Pierce in 1837. This group valued visions and revelations and acknowledged Jackson's gifts in this realm. In 1843, when the community dissolved, sixteen of its members joined the nearby Shaker community at Watervliet.

Jackson visited the Shakers (the United Society of Believers in Christ's Second Coming) at this time and was attracted by their religious celibacy, their emphasis on spiritualistic experience, and their dual-gender concept of deity. In 1835 she had had a vision, which she believed was a "revelation of the mother spirit," and clearly was impressed by the sect's acknowledgment of the Holy Mother Wisdom as a "co-eternal" partner with the Almighty Father. With her younger disciple and lifelong companion, Rebecca Perot, Jackson lived in the Watervliet Shaker community from June 1847 until July 1851. The two women then returned to Philadelphia on an unauthorized mission to bring the truths of Shakerism to the African American community. In Philadelphia they experimented with seance spiritualism. In 1857 they returned to Watervliet, and after a brief second residence Jackson won the right to found and head a new Shaker "outfamily" in Philadelphia.

Little is known of the small Philadelphia Shaker family during the remainder of Jackson's life. Over the next twenty-five years the family varied in size and was located at several different Philadelphia sites. There was always a core group of African American women, some living together in a single house. They supported themselves by daywork as laundresses and seamstresses and held religious meetings at night. In 1878 the Shaker historian Alonzo G. Hollister visited with his copy of the collected writings of Rebecca Jackson—based on manuscripts entrusted to the Shakers by Perot after Jackson's death—and at that time, the core group comprised about a dozen women, including at least one Jewish sister. A smaller number of men, including one or two white spiritualists, also were associated with the community. Perot and several other aging Philadelphia sisters retired to the Watervliet community by 1896, but Shaker records indicate that the community still existed in some form as late as 1908.

Jackson was one of a surprisingly large number of African American women preachers in the nineteenth century who mounted significant challenges to the exclusionary practices of established churches, using their claim to extraordinary, direct experience of the divine to carve out careers as religious leaders despite the patriarchal biases of their churches. More theologically radical than most, Jackson sought a perfectionist religion that would acknowledge a "mother divinity," at first using only her own religious experience as her guide but later incorporating the dual-gender godhead theology developed by Shakerism. Her permanent legacy, however, was not a new religious sect, but a remarkable body of visionary writing that the writer ALICE WALKER has said "tells us much more about the spirituality of human beings, especially of the interior spiritual resources of our mothers, and, because of this, makes an invaluable contribution to what we know of ourselves" (Walker, 78).

FURTHER READING

Jackson's manuscript writings are in the Shaker collections of the Western Reserve Historical Society in Cleveland, Ohio, the Library of Congress, and the Berkshire Athenaeum at the Public Library in Pittsfield, Massachusetts.

Braxton, Joanne. *Black Women Writing Autobiography* (1989).

McMahon Humez, Jean. *Gifts of Power: The Writings of Rebecca Jackson, Black Visionary, Shaker Eldress* (1981).

Sasson, Diane. *The Shaker Spiritual Narrative* (1983).

Walker, Alice. *In Search of Our Mothers' Gardens* (1983).

This entry is taken from the *American National Biography* and is published here with the permission of the American Council of Learned Societies.

JEAN MCMAHON HUMEZ

Jackson, Reggie (18 Mar. 1946–), baseball player, was born Reginald Martinez Jackson in Wyncote, Pennsylvania, the first of two children born to Martinez Clarence Jackson, a tailor. Reggie's mother, whose name is unknown, had four children from a previous marriage. Said Jackson, "I was a black kid with Spanish, Indian, and Irish blood who lived in a white, Jewish suburb of Philadelphia" (Jackson, 12).

When Jackson was six years old his parents divorced. His mother moved to Maryland with three of his half siblings, while an older half sister and a brother stayed with Martinez. As a youngster

Jackson idolized his disciplinarian father. Martinez Jackson, who played semipro baseball and barnstormed with the Negro League's Newark Eagles in the 1920s and 1930s, taught his son to play baseball at the age of seven. Jackson had his first encounter with racism when his youth baseball team traveled to Fort Lauderdale, Florida. As the team's only African American member, he was not allowed to play against its all-white opponents. At Cheltenham Township High School Jackson excelled at football, track, basketball, and baseball. During his senior year his father was jailed for six months for bootlegging corn liquor out of his basement. With Martinez Jackson absent, Jackson had to juggle school, athletics, and running the family business. Nevertheless the six-foot, 195-pound left-hander hit .550 and pitched three no-hitters that year, attracting the attention of baseball scouts from across the United States. On his father's advice, however, he entered Arizona State University in the fall of 1964 on a football scholarship.

At Arizona State Jackson played both football and baseball, playing baseball well enough to be named the 1966 *Sporting News* College Player of the Year. But in that year's amateur draft the New York Mets, with the number one overall pick, passed on Jackson because, said the Arizona State manager Bobby Winkles, "They're concerned that you have a white girlfriend" (Jackson, 43). Jackson was then selected second overall by the Kansas City Athletics. In fact, Jackson's girlfriend, Jennie Campos, was a Mexican American. They married on 8 July 1968, only to divorce in February 1972.

In 1966 Reggie and Martinez Jackson negotiated a signing bonus of $95,000 from the notoriously tightfisted Kansas City Athletics' owner Charlie Finley. Jackson was assigned to Lewiston, Idaho, before moving on to Modesto in the Class A California League. Jackson hit .297 that season, with 23 home runs and 71 runs batted in more than 68 games, earning a promotion to Kansas City's top minor league team in Birmingham, Alabama, in 1967. Jackson's first extended experience in the South was often an unpleasant one, filled with racial insults and segregated dining and housing. His white teammates Joe Rudi and Rollie Fingers regularly invited Jackson to dine in their apartments to avoid public discrimination, until their apartment managers threatened the two with eviction. Jackson overcame all this to lead the Southern League in runs (84) and triples (17), earning recognition as the Southern League Player of the Year.

On 9 June 1967 Jackson made his major league debut with the A's, and he returned to the team intermittently throughout the season before joining the newly relocated Oakland A's as their regular right fielder in 1968. Jackson immediately impressed opponents and teammates alike. The Red Sox great and Washington Senators manager Ted Williams said, "Reggie Jackson is the most natural hitter I've ever seen." Joe DiMaggio, then an A's coach, accurately predicted, "He'll strike out a lot, but he'll hit a lot of homers." Indeed, Jackson struck out a record 2,597 times during his career, because, he believed, "You don't have a chance if you don't swing" (Vass, 25). This philosophy paid off in 1968 when Jackson slugged 29 home runs and drove in 74 RBIs, despite whiffing a career-high 171 times. The next year, with 37 home runs by the All-Star break, Jackson seemed poised to break Roger Maris's single-season record of 61, but he slumped in September and finished with career highs of 47 home runs and 118 RBIs.

After the 1969 season Jackson asked for a substantial raise, only to be denied by Finley. Jackson held out through spring training in four of his eight seasons with the A's, and he went to salary arbitration two other times. Jackson eventually earned $140,000 a year with the A's, on top of money generated by United Development, an Arizona-based real estate firm started by Jackson and his friend Gary Walker in 1968. Jackson's notoriously flashy lifestyle reflected his substantial earnings, with fine dining, fine clothing, and a stunning collection of antique cars.

After a lackluster 1970 season Jackson came back with thirty-two home runs in 1971 and again in 1973 to lead the league, winning the MVP award; in 1975 he led the American League with thirty-six home runs. Of these "dingers," as Jackson liked to call them, the most memorable was a towering shot that hit the transformer atop Detroit's Tiger Stadium during the 1971 All-Star game, one of twelve All-Star games that he played in during his twenty-one-year career. Meanwhile he helped the A's win five straight division titles from 1971 to 1975, despite persistent clubhouse turmoil that included a fight between Jackson and his teammate Bill North in 1974 and the circus atmosphere provoked by Finley's insistence on gaudy uniforms and maximum player facial hair. After losing to the Baltimore Orioles in the 1971 American League Championship Series (ALCS), the A's went on to win the World Series for the next three years, defeating the Cincinnati

Reggie Jackson, smiling broadly, talks with reporters before the third game of the World Series at Yankee Stadium in New York, 13 October 1978. (AP Images.)

Reds, the New York Mets, and the Los Angeles Dodgers. In 1973 Jackson won the World Series MVP, demonstrating for the first time his legendary postseason prowess. Over 27 career World Series games Jackson hit .357, with 10 home runs and 24 RBIs, and he won a second MVP in 1977.

After the 1975 season, in which the A's lost to the Boston Red Sox in the ALCS, many players, including Jackson, were anxious to test the newly introduced free-agent market. Preemptively Finley traded Jackson to the Baltimore Orioles on 2 April 1976. Jackson signed with the Orioles for one year at $190,000 but admitted, "I [thought] of myself as an interim Baltimore Oriole" (Jackson, 105). After a second-place finish that year, in which he hit 27 home runs with a league-leading .502 slugging percentage, Jackson entered the free-agent market, where thirteen teams vied for his services. The New York Yankees owner George Steinbrenner won out with a record offer of $2.9 million over five years, plus a $60,000 Rolls-Royce to clinch the deal.

With an implied comparison between himself and Babe Ruth, Jackson said in 1973, "If I played in New York, they'd name a candy bar after me." Sure enough, the Reggie Bar appeared in April 1978 and was given out as a promotional item at Yankee Stadium. To Jackson's dismay fans showered him with the chocolate bars when he returned to right field after a home run in his first at bat that day. It was one of many hopes that would sour in New York.

Jackson came to New York in 1977 to rescue a team that had been swept in the World Series the previous October by the Cincinnati Reds. Statements like "I didn't come to New York to be a star; I brought my star with me" did not endear him to his teammates, many of whom regarded him as conceited and arrogant. Their response to Jackson was fueled by a series of controversies, the first an article in May's *Sport* magazine in which the writer Robert Ward quoted—or misquoted, according to Jackson—the newcomer referring to himself as "the straw that stirs the drink," a direct affront to the team captain Thurman Munson. After a home run the night the article appeared, Jackson purposely avoided shaking hands with his teammates, compounding the team's tension. Four weeks later, on 18 June 1977, the team manager Billy Martin replaced Jackson in right field during the middle of an inning because he felt that Jackson had lazily pursued a fly ball. The two nearly came to blows in the dugout before they were restrained by teammates. Despite such turmoil Jackson hit 32 home runs and drove in 110 runs that year, helping New York to reach and win the World Series over the Dodgers. In the sixth and final game Jackson had his most memorable career performance. Having hit a home run in the last at bat of game five, he hit three home runs on only three pitches in game six, validating the nickname by which Munson had sarcastically referred to him: "Mr. October."

In July 1978 Jackson was again embroiled in controversy when he ignored the on-field instructions of manager Martin, earning himself a five-game suspension and spurring the firing of Martin soon after. The former pitcher Bob Lemon took over the troubled team and helped it rally from a fourteen-game deficit to overcome the Red Sox in a special play-off game on 2 October in which Jackson homered to provide the margin for New York's 5-4 win. The Yankees went on to defeat the Dodgers once again in the World Series. The team won the division again in 1980 but lost in the play-offs. In 1981

the Yankees returned to the World Series with a six-game loss to the Dodgers. Jackson continued to excel during these years, hitting .300 for the first time in 1980, with 41 home runs.

After the 1981 season, exhausted from his New York experience and sensing that Steinbrenner did not want him back anyway, Jackson joined the California Angels with a four-year, $900,000 contract. After topping 100 RBIs and tying Gorman Thomas for the American League lead with 39 home runs in 1982, Jackson slowed considerably in the ensuing four seasons. In that time his team made the play-offs only once, losing a heartbreaking five-game series to the Milwaukee Brewers in 1982. In 1987 Jackson returned to Oakland for his last season, batting a meager .220 with 15 home runs in 115 games.

Jackson left baseball with 563 home runs, 1,702 RBIs, and a career .262 batting average. His uniform number was retired by both the New York Yankees and the Oakland A's. In 1993 Jackson was the only inductee to the Baseball Hall of Fame, and that same year, to the surprise of many, he joined the New York Yankees as a special assistant to George Steinbrenner. During the latter part of his playing days and into his retirement Jackson was also a broadcaster for ABC Sports and host of the 1983 *Greatest Sports Legends* television series. Jackson is both a legendary and a controversial figure whose place in baseball is summed up in his own dictum: "Fans don't boo nobodies."

FURTHER READING

Jackson, Reggie. *Reggie: The Autobiography of Reggie Jackson* (1984).
Devine, Christopher. *Thurman Munson: A Baseball Biography* (2001).
O'Connor, Dick. *Reggie Jackson: Superstar* (1975).
Owens, Tom. *Greatest Baseball Players of All Time* (1990).
Thorn, John, and Pete Palmer, eds. *Total Baseball* (1989).
Vass, George. *Reggie Jackson: From Superstar to Candy Bar* (1979).

CHRISTOPHER DEVINE

Jackson, Robert R. (1 Sept. 1870–12 June 1942), politician, was born in Malta, Illinois, the son of William Jackson and Sarah Cooper. He spent most of his childhood in Chicago. At age nine he began selling newspapers and shining shoes in Chicago's central business district; he left school in the eighth grade to work full-time. By age eighteen Robert had garnered an appointment as a clerk in the post office, a position coveted by African Americans in this era because of its security compared to that of most other occupations open to them. He left the postal service as an assistant superintendent in 1909 to devote himself full-time to his printing and publishing business, the Fraternal Press. In partnership with Beauregard F. Mosely, in 1910 he cofounded the Leland Giants, Chicago's first African American baseball team. In 1912 Jackson won election as a Republican to the state legislature. From there he moved to the Chicago City Council, where he served as an alderman from 1918 through 1939. After leaving politics, Jackson returned to baseball, where he served a two-year stint as commissioner of the Negro American League.

Jackson built both his printing business and his political success on a remarkable level of participation in fraternal organizations, apparently bounded only by racial exclusion. A 1923 city directory describes him as "a member of nearly all the Fraternal orders in Chicago." These included the American Wood, the Appomattox Club, the Dramatic Order of Knights of Omar, the Elks, the Knights of Pythias, the Masons, the Odd Fellows, and the Royal Arch. He also participated actively in the establishment of the first cooperative grocery in black Chicago, joined the Musicians Union, and volunteered with the Boy Scouts and the Young Men's Christian Association. Estimates of his membership in voluntary organizations have run as high as twenty-five, a political asset that assured him continued visibility in the community.

Jackson's military career represented one particularly important aspect of his role as a joiner and a leader. Rising from a drummer to a major in what came to be known in black America as the "Famous Eighth Illinois" Infantry (notable for having an African American commanding officer, and ceaselessly promoted by the *Chicago Defender*), Jackson took advantage of his National Guard career by identifying himself as Major R. R. Jackson whenever he ran for office. His most notable service came during the Spanish-American War when the unit, then known as the Eighth Regiment of Illinois Volunteers, fought in Cuba. Characteristically, while in Cuba he organized the Mañana Club, dedicated to improving relations between Cubans and African American officers.

Jackson ranked among the foremost African American politicians of his generation. At a time when no African Americans could win election to federal office, and extremely few to state legislatures, his career epitomized the limitations imposed by racial discrimination. His route through business and fraternal organizations was one of the few paths to office for black politicians. As a state legislator he was most vocal on issues related to racial discrimination, most notably opposing an attempt to prohibit intermarriage and helping to block legislation that would have reduced African American employment on railroads. Jackson's most significant accomplishment was his role in securing state funding for Chicago's Emancipation Golden Jubilee in 1913. He exercised little influence on issues unconnected to race relations.

In the Chicago City Council, Jackson's nonconfrontational style endeared him to white power brokers, helping him to secure for his constituents such major capital projects as a large park, a library, and a playground, in addition to minor improvements and standard services. As a loyal member of a Republican organization dominated by Mayor William Hale Thompson (1915–1923, 1927–1931), however, Jackson compiled a record that did not endear him to reformers opposed to Thompson's renowned tolerance of vice and corruption. Jackson sponsored little major legislation other than an ordinance providing for a system of milk inspection.

Along with Edward H. Wright and OSCAR DE PRIEST, Jackson helped to establish the foundation of an approach to African American political leadership that remained influential in Chicago until the 1950s. This approach was characterized by loyalty to a white-dominated organization in return for recognition, patronage, and occasional (though highly visible) public works projects. Jackson's approach was made possible by the residential segregation—and therefore political consolidation—of a black population that increased dramatically during and immediately after World War I. These newcomers from the South identified Democrats with southern politics and Republicans with Abraham Lincoln, providing a base that not only elected first De Priest and then Jackson and others to the city council but also provided the margin of victory for Thompson in both primary and general elections.

As African American voters began moving into the Democratic Party in the 1930s, in many cases followed by their elected officials, Jackson remained a Republican. During his last eight years as alderman, a Democratic mayor and city council pushed him to the margins; his influence already diminished, he finally lost his seat to a Democrat in 1939. The emerging alliance between African American Democrats and the "Kelly-Nash" Democratic machine, however, was characterized by the familiar exchange of votes for recognition and power within the ghetto. Like Jackson and his peers, WILLIAM DAWSON, the dominating figure in Chicago black politics in the 1940s and 1950s, exercised little power on issues unrelated to race. Eventually he came to symbolize what African American activists in the 1960s called "plantation politics."

Jackson, his colleagues, and their successors had only minimal impact on public policy at the city or state level. They did, however, mobilize African Americans into a political force capable of electing black candidates and demanding recognition as legitimate participants in the urban polity. Jackson, in particular, stands out not only for his honesty amid a Chicago City Council notorious for corruption but also for his skill as a legislator who worked the system successfully within the considerable limits imposed by the exclusion of African Americans from the corridors of power. He died in Chicago, survived by his wife, Hattie Ball Lewis, and a son.

FURTHER READING

Drake, St. Clair, and Horace Cayton. *Black Metropolis: A Study of Negro Life in a Northern City* (1945).

Gosnell, Harold. *Negro Politicians: The Rise of Negro Politics in Chicago* (1935).

Grossman, James R. *Land of Hope: Chicago, Black Southerners, and the Great Migration* (1989).

Spear, Allan H. *Black Chicago: The Making of a Negro Ghetto, 1890–1920* (1967).

Obituaries: *Chicago Sun*, 14 June 1942; *Chicago Defender*, 20 June 1942.

This entry is taken from the *American National Biography* and is published here with the permission of the American Council of Learned Societies.

JAMES R. GROSSMAN

Jackson, Samuel L. (21 Dec. 1948–), actor, was born in Washington, D.C., the only child of Elizabeth (maiden name unknown), a clothing buyer, and an estranged father who moved to Kansas City, Missouri, when Jackson was young. Jackson was raised in Chattanooga, Tennessee, by his mother, grandmother, and grandfather, a maintenance man at a whites-only hotel. As a child Jackson was an avid film fan who frequented the local segregated movie house, delighting in the horror films of the 1950s and the serial adventures of actors such as Lash LaRue and Gene Autry. Little has been written about Jackson's childhood, but he was plagued by a debilitating stutter, and he may well have sought escape by going to the movies. He later overcame the problem; indeed his smooth, rich baritone voice became a hallmark of Jackson's acting style.

In 1966 Jackson headed south to attend Morehouse College as an architecture major. He soon became immersed in the politics of the day, attending lectures by MARTIN LUTHER KING JR., STOKELY CARMICHAEL, H. RAP BROWN, JULIAN BOND, and LERONE BENNETT. The day after King's assassination, Jackson participated in a march in Memphis and, upon his return to Atlanta, served as an usher at King's funeral service on the Morehouse campus. In 1969 several Morehouse students, including Jackson, demanded the establishment of a black studies department and greater African American representation on the board of trustees. To gain attention for their cause, they locked the board members in a building for two days. Although the students achieved their goal, Jackson was expelled for his participation. Instead of heading home to Chattanooga, he spent the summer in Atlanta, where he became involved in the Black Power movement. Working alongside Carmichael and Brown, the former cheerleader for the Morehouse pep squad was now stockpiling weapons for the coming revolution, a long way from the humiliations of a childhood in the segregated South. "I was in that radical faction," Jackson recalled. "All of a sudden, I felt I had a voice. I-was somebody. I could make a difference" (*Parade*, 9-Jan. 2005, 4–5).

Jackson's foray into radical activism was cut short by his mother. FBI agents visited Elizabeth Jackson in Chattanooga with the warning that her son's activities could endanger his life. She arrived in a panic in Atlanta, urging her son to abandon radical politics. Heeding his mother's pleas, Jackson moved to Los Angeles, where he worked in social services. In early 1971, after two unsatisfying years, he returned to Morehouse as a drama major. "I had done a play and fallen in love with acting," he said. "I decided that theater would now be my politics" (*Parade*, 9 Jan. 2005, 4–5).

Jackson's experience in college theater taught him a wide range of skills, including set design and construction, costumes, and lighting. He met his future wife, LaTanya Richardson, during an audition for a college musical. Richardson, who was studying theater arts at Spelman College, founded a local theater group with Jackson, staging political plays whose themes Jackson described as "Die, whitey, die—so black folks can take over!" (Rochlin, 28).

Samuel L. Jackson at an interview before the preview of his film "Changing Lanes" in Los Angeles, 7 April 2002. (AP Images.)

During his last year in college, Jackson made his film debut in Michael Schultz's *Together for Days* (1972).

After graduating in 1972 with a B.A. in Dramatic Arts, Jackson moved with Richardson to Harlem. Other than a brief six-month stint as a security guard, Jackson made a living in the theater; however, he also appeared in two television movies during the 1970s, *The Displaced Person* (1977) and *The Trial of the Moke* (1978). In the 1980s he performed in numerous stage productions, including several performances with the Negro Ensemble Company and the New York Shakespeare Festival. Jackson and Richardson married in 1980, and the couple had one daughter. His involvement in the 1981 Off-Broadway show *A Soldier's Play*, by CHARLES FULLER, proved pivotal in his career. During the production Jackson met MORGAN FREEMAN, who became Jackson's mentor, convincing him that he had the talent to be successful. In addition an unknown yet self-confident New York University film student, SPIKE LEE, caught Jackson's performance and, with a keen eye to Jackson's and his own future success, offered the actor a part in an

as-yet-unrealized film. Jackson became one of several Morehouse alumni in Lee's ensemble of actors, a group that included Giancarlo Esposito and Bill Nunn.

Jackson continued his affiliation with the Negro Ensemble Company, performing in numerous plays over the next decade, including *Home* (1981), Joseph A. Walker's play *District Line* (1984), *Burners Frolic* (1990), and *Jonquil* (1990). In 1990 Jackson costarred in AUGUST WILSON's *Two Trains Running* at the Yale Repertory Theatre. He also originated the role of Boy Willie in Wilson's *The Piano Lesson*, with the agreement that CHARLES S. DUTTON would replace him when the show debuted on Broadway. Jackson's disheartening role as Dutton's understudy, watching the lead actor take the spotlight, fueled what had become a serious alcohol and cocaine addiction. Once during this period, his wife found him unconscious, gripping a glass pipe, in their Harlem brownstone. After a stay in a rehabilitation clinic, he returned to acting with a renewed spirit, jumpstarting his film career in the supporting role of Gator in Lee's *Jungle Fever*. Jackson's performance as the down-and-out crackhead garnered him a special Jury Prize at the Cannes Film Festival and the New York Film Critics Circle Award for Best Supporting Actor.

During the 1990s Jackson earned a reputation as the hardest working man in Hollywood, averaging five movies a year. His role as Jules Winnfield, the Bible-quoting hit man in Quentin Tarantino's *Pulp Fiction*, earned him an Academy Award nomination for best supporting actor and catapulted him from a low-profile character actor into one of Hollywood's leading men. He earned acclaim as the Jedi Mace Windu in the *Star Wars* prequel trilogy. In 1996 he won an NAACP Image Award for Best Supporting Actor in a Motion Picture for his performance in *A Time to Kill*. In 2006 he became only the seventh African American to be honored with a hand and footprint ceremony at Grauman's Chinese Theater. That year he lent his trademark voice to the all-black cast audio version of the Bible as the voice of God.

Jackson was one of a handful of black actors who broke through the glass ceiling of Hollywood that limited black actors to supporting roles and bit parts. He actively worked to increase the types of roles available to African American actors. Applauding the industry's efforts to move beyond the restrictive themes and roles that presented only a narrow slice of African American life, he declared in 1995, "I would assume studios are accepting the fact that there's a greater diversity to our lives than kids in the 'hood, than the drug and violence stories and we are taking a prominent place in our society and our films are reflecting that" (Weinraub, C11).

Between 2006 and 2011 Jackson appeared in more than twenty feature films, including *Snakes on A Plane* (2006), *1408* (2007) *Iron Man 2* (2010), and *Captain America: The First Avenger* (2011). In 2011 the Guinness Book of World Records declared Jackson to be the highest grossing film actor of all time, noting a combined gross of $7.2 billion for all the movies he had appeared in up to that year.

FURTHER READING

Gabbard, Krin. *Black Magic: White Hollywood and African American Culture* (2004).

Rochlin, Margy. "Tough Guy Finds His Warm and Fuzzy Side," *New York Times*, 2 Nov. 1997.

Weinraub, Bernard. "Black Film Makers Are Looking beyond Ghetto Violence," *New York Times*, 11 Sept. 2005.

ELIZABETH MAULDIN

Jackson, Shirley Ann (5 Aug. 1946–), physicist, chair of the U.S. Nuclear Regulatory Commission, and educator was born in Washington, D.C., the second of four children to George Jackson, a post office employee, and Beatrice Cosby, a social worker. In elementary school Shirley was bused from the Jacksons' largely white neighborhood in northwest Washington to a black school across town. After the 1954 *Brown v. Board of Education* desegregation ruling and several years of "white flight" transformed the area into a predominantly black neighborhood, she attended the local Roosevelt High School, where she participated in an accelerated program in math and science. Jackson took college-level classes in her senior year, after completing the high school curriculum early, and she graduated as valedictorian in 1964. "As I was growing up," she recalled, "I became fascinated with the notion that the physical world around me was a world of secrets, and that science, as applied in direct experimentation, was the key that could unlock those secrets … experimentation was like a good mystery novel, a tangible, unfolding narrative of what made nature click" (Rensselaer Polytechnic Institute inaugural address, 11 Dec. 1998). Jackson was supported in her educational pursuits by her parents and teachers, and when she left for the Massachusetts Institute of Technology (MIT) in 1964, she was sustained in part by a modest scholarship from her local church, the Vermont Avenue Baptist Church. More substantial financial aid came from the Martin Marietta Aircraft Company, the PRINCE HALL Masons, and later the National Science Foundation and the Ford Foundation.

When she entered MIT, Jackson was one of forty-three women in her freshman class of nine hundred, and one of fewer than a dozen African Americans in a university of more than eight thousand students. She excelled despite her isolation—some students refused to eat with her or let her join their study groups—and the specious "advice" of a professor who counseled, "Colored girls should learn a trade." "I chose a 'trade,'" Jackson reminisced in a 1997 keynote address to the National Technical Association; "I chose physics!" While at MIT she volunteered at Boston City Hospital and tutored students at the Roxbury YMCA. Back on campus she served at the behest of the president of MIT on the Task Force on Educational Opportunity, helped found the university's Black Student Union, and lobbied successfully for the increased admission of African American students. Her student activism drew attacks, some of which were violent, mostly from outside MIT. In South Boston she was shot at, spit on, and chased by whites.

Jackson's highest priority, however, was physics, and in 1968 she received a B.S. for her innovative work in solid-state physics. Although she was wooed by several prominent physics departments for graduate research, she remained at MIT, in part to encourage more African Americans to attend the school. Under the direction of James Young, the first black tenured physics professor at MIT, her research culminated in a dissertation, "The Study of a Multiperipheral Model with Continued Cross-Channel Unitarity," subsequently published in the *Annals of Physics* (1975). When Jackson received her Ph.D. in Theoretical Elemental Particle Physics in 1973, she became the first African American woman to receive a Ph.D. at MIT and the second African American woman to earn a Ph.D. in Physics in the United States. Two years later she joined MIT's board of trustees, and in 1992 she became a lifetime trustee.

Jackson worked with a number of prestigious labs in the United States and Europe in the 1970s. As a research associate at the Fermi National Accelerator Laboratory in Batavia, Illinois, she studied hadrons (subatomic particles, including baryons and mesons, made up of quarks and gluons). As a visiting scientist at the accelerator lab at the European Center for Nuclear Research in Geneva, Switzerland, she researched theories of strongly interacting elementary particles. In 1976 she was a visiting scientist at the Aspen Center for Physics in Colorado and lecturer in physics at the Stanford Linear Accelerator Center in Menlo Park, California.

From 1976 to 1991 Jackson conducted research for AT&T Bell Laboratories in Murray Hill, New Jersey, in theoretical physics, solid-state and quantum physics, and optical physics, focusing on polaron physics. Her explorations yielded improvements in the signal-handling capabilities of semiconductor devices, keeping Bell Labs in the forefront of electronic communications. While at Bell Labs, she served as president of the National Society of Black Physicists (1980–1982) and met the physicist Morris Washington. The couple married in 1980, and a son, Alan, was born the next year. In 1991 Jackson joined the department of physics and astronomy at Rutgers University, where she also served on the board of trustees. During her four years at Rutgers, she consulted for AT&T and continued serving on the New Jersey Commission on Science and Technology, to which she had been appointed in 1985.

In the mid-1990s Jackson served on advisory committees at the Department of Energy (DOE) and the National Nuclear Security Administration (NNSA), and in 1994 she was appointed to a task force to determine the future of the DOE National Laboratories. In 1995, when President Bill Clinton appointed her to chair the Nuclear Regulatory Commission (NRC), Jackson became the first woman and the first African American to head the federal agency. Jackson's introduction of risk-informed, performance-based regulations within the NRC and her crackdowns on nuclear-power industry violations restored the NRC's credibility as a watchdog for nuclear safety while garnering respect from both environmentalists and nuclear energy proponents. Nicknamed the "Energizer Bunny," she served on two binational commissions led by Vice President Al Gore and spearheaded the formation of the eight-nation International Nuclear Regulators Association, for which she served as chair from 1997 to 1999.

In 1999 Jackson became the first black woman to head a major American research university when she was unanimously selected by the board of trustees as the new president of Rensselaer Polytechnic Institute (RPI) in Troy, New York, the nation's first degree-granting technological university. Hoping to transform RPI into a research and technology powerhouse, Jackson secured a $360 million gift,

Shirley Ann Jackson before the press conference at Rensselaer Polytechnic Institute in Troy, NY, pronouncing her the next president of the oldest engineering school in the United States, 11 December 1998. (AP Images.)

built a new leadership team, and oversaw extensive campus renovations, including plans for an $80 million biotechnology and interdisciplinary studies center and a $142 million electronic media and performing arts center. Some in the RPI community, however, balked at what they described as Jackson's inaccessibility and her autocratic leadership style.

Jackson continued to play a significant role in shaping public policy for science and technology by sitting on the advisory council of the Institute of the Nuclear Power Operations, on numerous committees at the National Science Foundation, and on the boards and on various committees of the National Research Council and National Academy of Sciences. Jackson also became a member of the National Advisory Council for Biomedical Imaging and Bioengineering, a research institute established in 2000 as part of the National Institutes of Health that advises the Department of Health and Human Services.

A proponent of public-private partnerships and of uniting research universities and corporate laboratories, Jackson has sat on the board of directors of FedEx, AT&T, Marathon Oil Corporation, Medtronic, and BEST (Building Engineering and Science Talent), and she has served as a trustee of Lincoln University, Georgetown University, Rockefeller University, Associated Universities, Inc., and the Brookings Institution. Jackson was also elected a member of the American Physical Society, the American Academy of Arts and Sciences, and the National Academy of Engineering, of which she was the first black woman member. She has received eighteen honorary degrees and numerous awards, including the New Jersey Governor's Award in Science, the Thomas Alva Edison Award, and induction into the National Women's Hall of Fame in Seneca Falls, New York, and the Women in Technology International Foundation Hall of Fame.

From 2004 to 2006 Jackson served as president of the American Association for the Advancement of Science (AAAS), the world's largest general scientific society. "Today's rapid scientific and technological advances are posing 'knife-edge' questions," she told the AAAS in April 2003. "How can we derive maximum benefit from scientific discovery, for example, without unleashing maximum danger? It is up to the science and engineering community to lead us through these critical times."

FURTHER READING

Current Biography (1999).

Jackson, Shirley Ann. Envisioning a 21st Century Science and Engineering Workforce for the United States (2003).

Jenkins, Edward Sidney. To Fathom More: African American Scientists and Inventors (1996).

LISA E. RIVO

Jackson, William (16 Aug. 1818–19 May 1900), the first officially designated black chaplain in the Union army, was born free in Norfolk, Virginia. His father and grandfather, Henry Jackson Sr. and Jr., had been vessel pilots on the rivers flowing into Chesapeake Bay; Jackson's father had been freed in 1811 and during the War of 1812 ran the British blockade. According to an unpublished 1848 autobiography William Jackson "learned all the arts of steamboating from the kitchen to the cabins from there to the machinery," and until NAT TURNER's 1831 insurrection Jackson worked in the barrooms of the steamers and freighters that traveled between Norfolk and both Baltimore and Charleston. Jackson's father, stung by laws curtailing the assembly of free blacks after the Turner revolt, went to Philadelphia to find shelter for the family, and his son followed in 1832.

From 1834 to 1835 Jackson served in the U.S. Navy onboard the sloop Vandalia. In Philadelphia, Jackson worked on merchant vessels and began to attend Baptist services, where he met and married Jane Majors in 1837. He was ordained a Baptist minister on 16 September 1842 and became pastor at Oak Street Baptist Church in West Philadelphia. Though he served in various short-term pastorates in Newbury, New York, and Wilmington, Delaware, he returned to Oak Street and remained through December 1851. Sometime that month he removed to New Bedford, where he became involved with the Underground Railroad. His documented antislavery activism began shortly after the passage of the Fugitive Slave Act in late September 1850. On 1 October 1850 he wrote in his journal, "More truble owing to the late act of Congress alowing the slave holder the privelege of taking his slave where ever he can find him—And in giveing one his freedom I have the honour of being the first martyr by going to Prison" (Journal of William Jackson, private collection, n.d.). In his unpublished memoir Jackson revealed that in Philadelphia he led the group to rescue the fugitive William Taylor "from the clutches of the Marshall," dressed him as a woman, and conveyed him somehow to Toronto; he was arrested because he was "leader of the rescuing party" (Jackson, "A Memoir of Rev. William Jackson"). Jackson's entry refers to his involvement in the case of William Henry Taylor, whom he and three other African American men had somehow conveyed to an "unknown quarter," the 24 October issue of the National Anti-Slavery Standard reported, "without the consent or knowledge of those who claimed his legal custody." Jackson stated he was "soon released by a writ of habeas corpus." Records of the case are scant and confusing. In any event, by 5-December 1851 he had accepted a pastorate at Second (Salem) Baptist Church in New Bedford, Massachusetts.

New Bedford, then the nation's principal whaling port and wealthiest city, also had a large African American population. As a proportion of total population, more blacks lived there than in either Boston or Philadelphia. Many had come from Norfolk and Portsmouth, Virginia, and by 1850 fugitives from slavery made up a significant portion of the local black-populace. Here Jackson's antebellum churches—Second Baptist and its 1858 offshoot, Salem Baptist—became at least in part havens for the fugitives. Names mentioned in several fugitive narratives and fugitive assistant accounts appear nowhere else except in Jackson's church records, including James Pritlow and Anthony Loney. In New Bedford the fugitive George Teamoh met James Pritlow, an enslaved man whom he had known by a different name in Norfolk; the Philadelphia fugitive assistant William Still, whom Jackson knew, related the escape of Anthony Loney in his 1871 study Underground Railroad. Jackson was also a member of the local Vigilant Aid Society, a small, all-black organization formed to help fugitives, which itself included two men who are documented to have escaped slavery and settled in New Bedford.

In February 1863 William Jackson presided over a meeting of the city's African Americans that aimed to raise recruits for all-black regiments then being formed in Massachusetts—ultimately known as the Fifty-fourth and Fifty-fifth Massachusetts Volunteer Infantry and the Fifth Massachusetts Cavalry. Governor John Andrew appointed Jackson on 10 March 1863—no doubt owing at least in part to his active recruiting efforts—as a post chaplain at Camp Meigs near Boston, the commonwealth's largest army training camp and where black recruits reported. Finally, under pressure from influential abolitionists, the federal government permitted Andrew to commission Jackson officially as chaplain of the Fifty-fifth Massachusetts, on 14 July 1863. About a week before the regiment left Camp Meigs for South Carolina on 21 July 1863 Jackson was in New Bedford when a draft riot similar to the one that had occurred in New York on 13–16 July of that same year was rumored to be imminent in the city. Jackson raised money among city residents on the streets to buy a revolver. He was among a group of armed African Americans who, with city militia, kept watch against a mob who intended to "burn the Negro houses in the west part of town," as one local abolitionist wrote. The riot never took place in New Bedford, although a small one did occur in Boston.

Jackson resigned on 14 January 1864 and remained with the Fifty-fifth Massachusetts Regiment until 30 May, when he resumed his pastorate in New Bedford. On 1 June 1870 he became minister of a Baptist church in Providence, Rhode Island. Toward the end of his life he spent summers in Oak Bluffs on the island of Martha's Vineyard, where he was a town crier. In that capacity he used a bell made from the remains of a bell melted in a fire at New Bedford's Liberty Hall in 1854. In February 1851 the bell at Liberty Hall, the site of many anti-slavery meetings, had been rung as a warning to fugitives during a rumored federal raid on that population. Two miniatures of the Liberty Hall bell were fashioned, one for Rodney French, mayor and fugitive champion, and the other for Jackson.

Jackson was buried in New Bedford. His bell has long since been lost, but his house, built in 1858, still stands on Smith Street in that city as of 2007.

FURTHER READING
Most of Jackson's papers are held privately, though some are on indefinite loan to Old Dartmouth Historical Society/New Bedford Whaling Museum, New Bedford. He is also mentioned in letters from New Bedford's Joseph Ricketson in the papers of the Weston Sisters, Rare Books and Manuscript Collections, Boston Public Library.

Boney, F. N., Richard L. Hume, and Rafia Zafar. *God Made Man, Man Made the Slave: The Autobiography of George Tekamah* (1990).

Fox, Charles. *Record of the Service of the Fifty-Fifth Regiment of Massachusetts Volunteer Infantry* (1868)

Redkey, Edwin S. "Black Chaplains in the Union Army," *Civil War History* 32.4 (1987).

Still, William. *The Underground Railroad: A Record of Facts, Authentic Narratives, Letters, &c.* 1871 (1970).

KATHRYN GROVER

Jackson, William Tecumseh Sherman (18 Nov. 1865–10 Nov. 1943), athlete and educator, was born in Glencairn, Virginia, to Lindsay Jackson, a plumber, and Mary Jane (Smith) Jackson, a domestic worker. The family moved to nearby Alexandria, and while in high school Jackson worked as a barber's apprentice. In 1883 he entered the Virginia Normal and Collegiate Institute (now Virginia State University) in Petersburg, a segregated public college. While at school he became good friends with fellow Virginian WILLIAM HENRY LEWIS. Jackson and Lewis were heavily involved in campus politics, and both left the school in 1887 after Democratic state legislators forced the school's president, the civil rights activist JOHN MERCER LANGSTON, to resign.

The following year, probably with Langston's help, Lewis and Jackson, who was known to his contemporaries simply as "Sherman Jackson," entered Amherst College in central Massachusetts. George Washington Forbes, another African American, entered Amherst that year, and the three young men were among the school's first black students since the 1820s. Jackson immediately took part in campus life, playing on his class baseball team and serving as the director of his class football team for four years.

As a sophomore he made Amherst's varsity football and track teams, becoming one of the first black athletes to represent an integrated college in both sports. On the gridiron he played halfback and frequently won praise for his skill. After a game against Harvard in 1891 the *New York Times* enthused: "Jackson, a young colored fellow, played half back for Amherst and was by all odds the best man on the field. His tackling was clean and pure; [and] he made some phenomenal runs" (11 Oct. 1891). He played three seasons of football for Amherst, and during his senior year the team elected his classmate Lewis to the captaincy, making him the first African American to be so honored at an integrated college. Jackson also had success on the track team, which won the New England Intercollegiate Athletic Association (NEIAA) team championship in each of his three seasons on the squad. In 1890 and 1892 Jackson won first place in the half-mile run at the NEIAA annual tournament.

In June 1892 he graduated with his class, and a contingent of Boston's young black community—including W. E. B. DuBois and WILLIAM MONROE TROTTER—trekked west to see Jackson, Lewis, and Forbes receive their diplomas. At the ceremonies, Lewis represented his peers with the class oration, and Jackson, who always held his alma mater in high esteem, must have agreed with Lewis's assessment of their undergraduate years: "The principles of true democracy which they teach have been incorporated into the life of the College…. [Here] is no snobbery, no caste, no invidious social distinctions. Every man is a fellow, a member of the true college fraternity" (Wade, 118).

After college Jackson taught Greek and Latin for two years at Virginia Seminary (now Virginia University of Lynchburg), an all-black school founded by the state's Baptist Convention. In 1893 the celebrated M Street High School of Washington, D.C., a public high school with a college preparatory curriculum strongly supported by the city's black middle class, hired Jackson to teach mathematics. He would remain at the school for the rest of his professional career.

While at M Street he continued his own education, studying social sciences at Catholic University of America. In 1896 he became the first African American to receive a degree (bachelor of social sciences) from the school. During his time at Catholic he played football, reclaiming his old position of halfback for the school's first organized squad. He remained involved with Catholic after his graduation, winning election to the executive council of the Alumni Association in 1901. The university, however, could not resist the rising tide of segregation, and about 1915 the school ceased admitting black students.

Soon after graduating from Catholic Jackson split time between the M Street School and Howard University, where he lectured for two years at the Law School. In 1897 he completed a thesis on the constitutional history of England and received a master's degree from Amherst, becoming the first African

American to receive a higher degree from the school. In 1902 Jackson married May Howard, a renowned artist and sculptor, who had been the first black student to receive a scholarship to Philadelphia's Pennsylvania Academy of Fine Arts. The couple had no children, but they helped raise the son and daughter of Jackson's sister, who died in 1902.

After the turn of the century Jackson focused his energies on the M Street School. He was an early booster of sports and encouraged the development and institutionalization of its athletics program. He continued to teach mathematics until 1906 when he assumed the principalship of the school. He held the position, one of the premier jobs in black Washington, until 1909. He stepped down to head the department of Business Practice for nine years, until that section was spun off into its own school, the Cardozo Business High School. In 1916 a state-of-the-art facility replaced M Street, and the school was renamed PAUL LAURENCE DUNBAR High School. Jackson returned to his old job of teaching mathematics at Dunbar from 1918 until his retirement in 1930.

Jackson remained loyal to his undergraduate alma mater and directed numerous gifted black scholars to Amherst during his thirty-eight-year career. Among the students he sent to Massachusetts were John Randolph Pinkett, CHARLES HAMILTON HOUSTON, WILLIAM MONTAGUE COBB, WILLIAM HENRY HASTIE, and CHARLES RICHARD DREW.

Amherst recognized his years of service to Washington's African American community with an honorary master's degree in 1942. In presenting the award to Jackson, the president of the school remarked:You have devoted a life-time to teaching and administration in the public high schools of our nation's capital. In admiration of your contribution to the cause of education and in recognition of your influence on students who have come from your classroom, many of them to this College, your alma mater recalls you today to receive your third Amherst degree. (Wade, 25)Jackson died in Washington, D.C., a little more than a year later.

FURTHER READING

"Colored College Men," *Boston Globe*, 6 Dec. 1891.

"Former Dunbar Head to Retire as Teacher," *Washington Post*, 25 Dec. 1930.

Mather, Frank Lincoln, ed. "Jackson, William Tecumseh Sherman," in *Who's Who of the Colored* (1915).

Nuesse, C. Joseph. "Segregation and Desegregation at the Catholic University of America," *Washington History* (Spring–Summer 1997).

Toppin, Edgar, and Lucious Edwards, Jr. *Virginia State University 1882 to 1992* (1993).

Wade, Harold, Jr. *Black Men of Amherst* (1976).

Obituary: *Washington Post*, 12 Nov. 1943.

GREGORY BOND

Jackson Lee, Sheila (12 Jan. 1950–   ), United States Congresswoman, was born Sheila Jackson in New York City, to working-class parents. She grew up in the borough of Queens, where she attended public schools and graduated from Jamaica High School. Jackson excelled in her studies and earned a scholarship to attend New York University, where she spent one year before being selected to be among the first class of women to integrate Yale University. In 1972 Jackson graduated from Yale with honors and a Bachelor of Arts degree in Political Science; she went directly into law school at the University of Virginia. While a student a UVA she married Dr. Elwyn Cornelius Lee and in 1975 graduated with a Juris Doctorate. Jackson Lee and her husband have two children; a daughter, Erica Shelwyn, and a son, Jason Cornelius Bennett.

Jackson-Lee moved with her husband to Houston, Texas, and was admitted to the Texas Bar in 1975. She worked as an attorney in Houston and in 1977 and 1978 served as staff counsel to the U.S. House Select Committee on Assassinations. In 1980 she became chairperson for the Black Women Lawyers Association. In 1983 Jackson Lee ran for Harris County Judge and was appointed to the City of Houston Municipal Court from 1987 to 1990. During her first year in office she also served as president of the Houston Lawyers Association. In 1989 she ran and won the at-large seat on the Houston City Council, becoming among the first African American women to serve in an at-large seat in Houston. During her tenure on the city council, Jackson Lee was adamant about initiatives to protect children from guns and increased recreational resources to deter gang activity. In 1994 Jackson-Lee campaigned for the 18th Congressional District of Texas, and defeated the incumbent CRAIG A. WASHINGTON 63 to 37 percent. Previously the 18th Congressional District has been served by one of her role models; the legislator and famed orator, BARBARA JORDAN, the first African American woman from a Southern state to assume a Congressional seat. Jackson Lee was appointed president of the 1994 freshman class of democrats and whip of the Congressional Black Caucus (CBC). During her second term, in 1998, Jackson Lee was appointed to the Judiciary Committee and became part of the commission to investigate impeachment charges against President Bill Clinton. Jackson-Lee has served the House Committees on Homeland Security, Foreign Affairs, Science, and the subcommittee that regulates NASA policy in space. In the 110th Congress, she was named Chairwoman of the Homeland Security Subcommittee on Transportation Security and Infrastructure Protection.

Jackson Lee has a record in the House demonstrating her strong support of civil rights, women's rights, immigrant rights, abortion rights, and other liberal causes, including her stance in opposition to the "Defense of Marriage Act," which would restrict recognition of homosexual marriages in Texas. She authored H.R. 254, the David Ray Hate Crimes Prevention of 2007 bill to enhance federal enforcement of hate crimes. In 2007 she also introduced the Save America Comprehensive Immigration Act, to address challenges from immigration. Jackson Lee participated in the introduction of the 2007 Assault Weapons Ban and Law Enforcement Protection Act. She has actively sought to eradicate the crime of racial cleansing through genocide in Darfur; on 28 April 2006, she was among five members of Congress and six activists protesting against the genocidal participation of Sudan's government in Darfur who were arrested for disorderly conduct in front of the Sudanese embassy Washington. Jackson Lee is a founder, cochair, and member of the Algerian Caucus, Afghan Caucus, Congressional Children's Caucus, and the Pakistan Caucus. Jackson Lee is also a member of Alpha Kappa Alpha Sorority, Inc., the first African American female sorority in the United States. In the Democratic primary of 2008 she endorsed Senator Hillary Rodham Clinton (D-NY), wife of Bill Clinton, for president of the United States. Following Clinton's primary defeat to Senator BARACK OBAMA (D-NY), Jackson Lee, like other Clinton supporters in the CBC, shifted her allegiance to the Democratic Party's first African American nominee. In 2010 Jackson-Lee voted with the majority in Congress in favor of the historic Health Care Reform Legislation proposed by President Barack Obama.

FURTHER READING

Barone, Michael, and Grant Ujifusa. *The Almanac of American Politics* (1998).

Ifill, Gwen. *The Breakthrough: Politics and Race in the Age of Obama* (2009).

Higginbotham, A. Leon. *Shades of Freedom: Racial Politics and Presumptions of the American Legal Process Race and the American Legal Process*, vol. 2 (1998).

SAFIYA DALILAH HOSKINS

Jackson McCabe, Jewell (2 Aug. 1945–), businesswoman and civil leader, was born in Washington, D.C., the daughter of Harold "Hal" B. Jackson, a radio personality, and Julia (Hawkins) Jackson, a businesswoman. Her father was a pioneer in the broadcasting industry, whose work in radio and television eventually took the family to New York City.

As a child, Jackson was drawn to the performing arts, especially dance. She studied classical ballet and jazz and was eventually admitted to New York City's High School of the Performing Arts. She continued her dance studies at Bard College from 1961 until 1963. She left the college in 1964 prior to her graduation to get married at age nineteen to Frederick Ward, an advertising copywriter. The marriage ended in divorce in 1967. Jackson McCabe later married Eugene McCabe, president of North General Hospital in New York City, in 1974. That marriage ended in divorce in 1992; however, she kept her husband's name for her professional career.

Prior to entering into the professional arena, Jackson McCabe was a dance instructor in an inner-city program that sought to curb antisocial behavior by exposing teens to culture and the arts. Her career consisted of various professional positions in the New-York City area, beginning in 1979 when she worked with the New York Urban Coalition as the director of public affairs. In 1973 she took a position as a public relations officer for New York City's Special Services for Children, which ceased operations in 1975. Jackson McCabe then worked for the State of New York's Governor's Office in the Women's Division, where she served as associate director for public information from 1975 to 1977. Following that post, from 1977 to 1982, she served as the director of government and community affairs for WNET-TV in New-York City

Jackson McCabe spent her entire adult life advancing the interests of her race and gender. She served as chairperson of the National Coalition of 100 Black Women. Years earlier, Jackson McCabe's mother, Julia Hawkins Jackson, had founded the New York Coalition of 100 Black Women with just two dozen individuals. However, after assuming the presidency of that organization in 1978, Jackson McCabe became the founder and chair of the National Coalition of 100 Black Women (NCBW) in 1981. With over seven thousand members and sixty-two chapters, NCBW was founded as a leadership forum that engages professional black women in a network to meet their career needs and the needs of their communities, and to facilitate their access to mainstream America.

Jackson McCabe also served on the boards of many civic organizations, including the New York Urban League, the NAACP, New York City Planned Parenthood, and the New York City Commission on the Status of Women. Jackson McCabe was widely recognized for her commitment to community service as early as 1980, when she served as deputy grand marshal of the annual MARTIN LUTHER KING JR. parade in New York City. She was a leader in numerous civil rights and women's rights causes, including service on the board of overseers for the Wharton School at the University of Pennsylvania, and the board of trustees for Bard College.

Jackson McCabe's community activism was recognized with citations from the YWCA and Malcolm/King College. In addition, she was honored with two honorary doctorates and a number of other awards for her accomplishments. She has also received awards from the Eastern Region Urban League Guild Award (1979), a Seagram's Civic Award (1980), a Links, Inc. Civic Award (1980), and an Outstanding Community Leadership Award from Malcolm/King College (1980).

Jackson McCabe's primary business interest from 1991 was as president of Jewell Jackson-McCabe Associates, a New York City bilingual (Spanish) management consulting firm that specialized in strategic communications, government/community/public relations, marketing to minorities, executive coaching, and training. As president, she advised a wide range of corporations in the private and public sector, including: American Express; Time Warner; The Coca-Cola Company; Matsushita Electric Corporation of America (Panasonic); International Business Machines Corporation (IBM); Council for Opportunity in Education (COE); NAACP Legal Defense and Educational Fund, Inc.; Metropolitan Museum of Modern Art; Solomon R. Guggenheim Museum; and The College Board.

FURTHER READING

Lanker, B. *I Dream a World* (1989).

Smith, Jessie Carney, ed. *Notable Black American Women* (1990).

ELIZABETH K. DAVENPORT

Jacobs, Harriet (c. 1813–7 Mar. 1897), autobiographer and reformer, was born into slavery in Edenton, North Carolina, the daughter of Elijah, a skilled slave carpenter, and Delilah, a house slave. In her slave narrative *Incidents in the Life of a Slave Girl: Written by Herself* (1861), published under the pseudonym Linda Brent, Jacobs explained that although it was illegal, she learned to read and to spell at six, when after her mother's death she was taken in by her mistress. When Jacobs reached puberty this mistress died, and she was willed to the woman's niece and sent into that child's home, where her new mistress's father subjected her to unrelenting sexual harassment. To save herself from concubinage, at sixteen she began a sexual liaison with a young white neighbor. (Called Mr. Sands in *Incidents*, he was Samuel Tredwell Sawyer, later a member of Congress.) This union produced a son and daughter. When she was twenty-one, her young mistress's father again threatened her with concubinage and, after she defied him, vowed to make her children plantation slaves. In June 1835 she ran away, hoping that instead of raising the children he would sell them and that their father would buy and free them. Her hopes were partially realized: the children were bought by their father, who permitted them to live with her grandmother, now a freedwoman, but he did not free them. As a fugitive slave in the South, Jacobs hid for almost seven years in a tiny space under the roof of her grandmother's home. In June 1842 she escaped to Philadelphia. She was eventually reunited with her children in the North. In 1849 she joined an abolitionist circle in Rochester, New York. Jacobs wrote that after passage of the 1850 Fugitive Slave Law, she was sought by her North Carolina mistress but rejected an offer to buy her freedom: "The more my mind had become enlightened, the more difficult it was for me to consider myself an article of property; and to pay money to those who had so grievously oppressed me seemed like taking from my sufferings the glory of triumph" (*Incidents*, 199).

Despite her protest, in 1853 Jacobs was purchased from Mary Matilda Norcom Messmore by her New York employer, Cornelia Grinnell Willis, and she and her children were free from the threat of reenslavement. Persuaded to tell her story by Amy Post,

INCIDENTS

IN THE

LIFE OF A SLAVE GIRL.

WRITTEN BY HERSELF.

"Northerners know nothing at all about Slavery. They think it is perpetual bondage only. They have no conception of the depth of *degradation* involved in that word, SLAVERY; if they had, they would never cease their efforts until so horrible a system was overthrown."
A WOMAN OF NORTH CAROLINA.

"Rise up, ye women that are at ease! Hear my voice, ye careless daughters! Give ear unto my speech."
ISAIAH xxxii. 9.

EDITED BY L. MARIA CHILD.

BOSTON:
PUBLISHED FOR THE AUTHOR.
1861.

Incidents in the Life of a Slave Girl. Title page of Harriet Jacob's autobiography, published in 1861. (Courtesy of Documenting the American South, The University of North Carolina at Chapel Hill Libraries.)

a Rochester abolitionist and feminist friend, and after a futile attempt to enlist best-selling author Harriet Beecher Stowe as her amanuensis, Jacobs spent years writing her book. When she finished, the black writer and activist WILLIAM COOPER NELL introduced her to the white antislavery writer and activist Lydia Maria Child, who edited the manuscript and helped obtain financial backing from Boston abolitionists.

With the publication of *Incidents* in January 1861, Jacobs entered public life as "Linda, the slave girl." Praised in the black and reform press for its vivid dramatic power, her book appeared the following year in two London editions, one pirated. Renamed *The Deeper Wrong: Incidents in the Life of a Slave Girl, Written by Herself*, Jacobs's book won excellent reviews in mainstream newspapers such as the *Morning Star and Dial* (London), which heralded it as "the first personal narrative in which one of that sex upon whom chattel servitude falls with the deepest and darkest shadow described her own bitter experience" (10 Mar. 1862).

Had the Civil War not broken out, Jacobs might have followed other slave narrators onto the lecture platform. Instead, throughout the war and early postwar years she aided the "contraband," black refugees crowding behind the Union lines, by using her celebrity to raise money and supplies from northern sympathizers and to publish a series of newspaper reports on the condition of the refugees. In 1862 she did relief work in Washington, D.C.; the following year she and her daughter Louisa moved to Alexandria, Virginia, where with the help of the New England Freedman's Aid Society they established the Jacobs Free School.

Jacobs's philanthropic and reform efforts were acknowledged in 1864, when she was named to the executive committee of the Women's Loyal National League, headed by Elizabeth Cady Stanton and Susan B. Anthony. Jacobs and Louisa later continued their philanthropic work in Savannah, Georgia. In 1868 she sailed to London to raise money for an orphanage and old people's home. Welcomed by British reformers familiar with her *Deeper Wrong* and her newspaper reports from the South, Jacobs was successful at fund-raising. Nevertheless, she recommended to her Quaker sponsors that the asylum not be built in Georgia, where the Ku Klux Klan was riding and burning.

When Jacobs returned to the United States with her daughter later in 1868 she retreated from public life. She moved first to Massachusetts and in 1877 to Washington, D.C., where, her health failing, she privately continued her work for the freedwomen and children.

Jacobs died of nephritis at her Washington home. She was eulogized by her longtime friend, the Reverend FRANCIS J. GRIMKÉ, as "no reed shaken by the wind, vacillating, easily moved from a position. She did her own thinking; had opinions of her own, and held to them with great tenacity."

Incidents in the Life of a Slave Girl is the most important antebellum autobiography written by an African American woman. Although nineteenth-century readers recognized Harriet Jacobs as the pseudonymous "Linda," before the Harvard edition appeared in 1987 many twentieth-century scholars thought the book was white-authored fiction. Since then, it has been recognized as black-authored autobiography. Jacobs's pseudonymous slave narrative, which centers on her struggle against sexual oppression in slavery and on her efforts to win freedom, defied nineteenth-century taboos against women discussing their sexual experiences. Jacobs's public letters, published during the Civil War and Reconstruction, present a unique first-person account of the black war refugees and the freed people in the South.

FURTHER READING

Jacobs's papers are scattered in several collections. The most important are the Isaac and Amy Post Family Papers, University of Rochester, and the Dr. J. Norcom Papers, North Carolina State Archives. Other sources include the Lydia Maria Child Papers (on microfilm); the Rochester Ladies' Anti-Slavery Society Papers, Clements Memorial Library, the University of Michigan; and the Julia Wilbur Papers, Haverford College.

Jacobs, Harriet. *Incidents in the Life of a Slave Girl*, ed. Jean Fagan Yellin (1987).

Andrews, William C. *To Tell a Free Story: The First Century of Afro-American Autobiography* (1986).

Foster, Frances Smith. *Written by Herself: Literary Production of African American Women, 1746–1892* (1993).

Garfield, Deborah M., and Rafia Zafar, eds. *Harriet Jacobs and Incidents in the Life of a Slave Girl* (1996).

Sterling, Dorothy, ed. *We Are Your Sisters: Black Women in the Nineteenth Century* (1984).

Yellin, Jean Fagan. *Women and Sisters* (1989).

This entry is taken from the *American National Biography* and is published here with the permission of the American Council of Learned Societies.

JEAN FAGAN YELLIN

Jacobs, John S. (1815–19 Dec. 1873), fugitive and abolitionist, like his more famous sister HARRIET A. JACOBS, was the child of slaves and born in Edenton, North Carolina. Their father, Elijah, was a carpenter; their mother, Delilah Horniblow, was the daughter of a woman who had been freed but re-enslaved around the time of the American Revolution.

In his 1861 "A True Tale of Slavery," published anonymously in four installments in the English serial the *Leisure Hour*, Jacobs stated that he had four masters in his first eighteen years. Jailed late in 1833 after his sister's escape from their owner, Dr. James Norcom, John Jacobs and the children were later purchased by the Edenton lawyer Samuel Tredwell Sawyer, the father of Harriet's two children. Aware that Norcom recognized his loathing of slavery, Jacobs effectively engineered the sale. "My mind was made up," he wrote, "that I must, in order to effect my escape, hide as much as possible my hatred to slavery, and affect a respect to my master, whoever he might be.... I must change owners in order to do that" (108).

John Jacobs became Sawyer's body servant, and when Sawyer was elected as a Whig to the U.S. Congress in March 1837, Jacobs went with him to Washington, D.C. Jacobs accompanied Sawyer on his wedding trip to Chicago and back through Canada, but rather than effect his escape Jacobs returned with Sawyer to New York because he wished to help his sister, still in hiding in Edenton. Consulting with friends in New York, however, persuaded Jacobs that returning to Washington with Sawyer would not serve Harriet's cause. He spirited his clothes and then his trunk away from the Astor House, left a note for Sawyer signed "no longer yours," and took a boat to Providence, Rhode Island.

From Providence, Jacobs went to New Bedford, Massachusetts. In his autobiography he stated that he was introduced in that city to "Mr. William P—, a very fatherly old man, who had been a slave in Alexandria" (126). Most likely Jacobs had met William Piper, a hostler in his early fifties who had been born in Alexandria and had come to New Bedford sometime between 1825 and 1830. At that time Piper worked for the whaling merchant William Rotch Rodman, whose mansion was the finest on the city's finest street. In 1838 a city assessor's document places Jacobs too in Rodman's household, suggesting that Piper had helped place him there. On 1 August 1839 Jacobs took out a seaman's protection paper at the U.S. Custom House in New Bedford and three days later joined the crew of the whaling ship *Frances Henrietta*, bound for the Pacific. (William Rotch Rodman's son and brother-in-law together owned one-half of the *Frances Henrietta*.) Jacobs vowed that whatever he earned "would be an inducement to any one to bring my sister off from the south" (126). Yet when he returned from the highly successful cruise more than three-and-a-half years later, he learned that Harriet Jacobs had escaped slavery, had come to New Bedford seeking him, and was then in New York City. John Jacobs immediately effected a reunion with the sister he had not seen in a decade.

In 1843 John and Harriet Jacobs moved to Boston, and for the next several years he worked to keep his sister's whereabouts a secret from the Norcom family. In an 1846 letter to the New York City abolitionist Sydney Howard Gay, Jacobs wrote that the Norcom family's wish to restore Harriet "to her former happiness" was in fact a desire to return her to "hell ... as my sister ... finds these cold regons [*sic*] more healthy than the suny [*sic*] South they will have to love each other at a distance the sweetest love that can exist between master and slave."

By 1846 John Jacobs had begun to work for "the oppressed the world over," as he wrote to Gay. He assisted fugitives in Boston, and in the late fall of 1847 he began an antislavery lecture tour with Jonathan Walker, whose attempt to help seven men escape slavery in Pensacola, Florida, ended in the branding of his hand with the initials "S.S.," for "slave stealer." For the Massachusetts and New England Anti-Slavery Societies, the two toured extensively in New England and New York State through May 1848. Jacobs, according to the *National Anti-Slavery Standard*, was a speaker "scarcely excelled by any of his predecessors." Jacobs spoke on the circuit by himself in the summer and fall of 1848, and early in 1849 he became the manager of the Anti-Slavery Office and Reading Room in Rochester, New York. After the Fugitive Slave Act became law in September 1850, Jacobs told a meeting at New York's Zion Chapel to "arm yourselves; aye, and I would advise the women to have their knives too.... I advise you to trample on this bill" (*National Anti-Slavery Standard*, 10 Oct. 1850).

Jacobs left soon afterward for California, just admitted to the Union as a free state, and by 1852 he was seeking gold in Australia. By 1857 he was in England working as a mariner, and four years later he published his serialized autobiography. When the Civil War began, Jacobs wrote to his sister that he would offer himself "on the altar of freedom ... if I am wanted" if the North intended to place the American flag on that altar. But "if it must wave over the slave, with his chains and fetters clanking, let me breathe the free air of another land, and die a man and not a chattel" (*National Anti-Slavery Standard*, 19 June 1861).

Jacobs married in London, and early in 1873 he returned to the United States. He lived near his sister Harriet and niece Louisa in Cambridge, Massachusetts, until his death in December that same year. He is buried with his sister and niece at Cambridge's Mount Auburn Cemetery.

FURTHER READING
Jacobs, John S. "A True Tale of Slavery," *Leisure Hour: A Family Journal of Instruction and Recreation* (28 Feb. 1861).

Fleischner, Jennifer. *Mastering Slavery: Memory, Family, and Identity in Women's Slave Narratives* (1996).

Jacobs, Harriet A. *Incidents in the Life of a Slave Girl, Written by Herself* (1987).

Yellin, Jean Fagan. *Harriet Jacobs: A Life* (2004).

KATHRYN GROVER

Jacobs, Little Walter (1 May 1930–15 Feb. 1968), blues singer and instrumentalist, was born Marion Walter Jacobs in Marksville, Louisiana, the son of Adam Jacobs and Beatrice Leviege, sharecroppers. Soon after Walter's birth, the family moved to Alexandria, Louisiana, where he grew up, and at age eight he began playing the harmonica, absorbing the sounds of both the white harmonica player Lonnie Glosson and Cajun music. At age eleven or twelve Walter ran away from home, his destination New Orleans, where he played on the streets and perhaps in some clubs in 1942; he also played at the Liberty Inn Club in Monroe, Louisiana, in 1943. By 1944 he was in Helena, Arkansas, learning a few pointers from Rice Miller (also known as "Sonny Boy") and appearing on radio on *King Biscuit Time* and *Mother's Best Flour Hour* in 1945–1946. Jacobs married Pearl Lee around 1945; they moved to East St. Louis and St. Louis before arriving in Chicago by 1946.

Although Jacobs had played in clubs in St. Louis, in Chicago he faced the tough Maxwell Street Market area, where hustling musicians battled for spare change on street corners. Maxwell Street became his home base, although he may have played some club dates in 1946 with established Chicago artists such as BIG BILL BROONZY, TAMPA RED, and MEMPHIS SLIM. Most important, he met his idol and major influence, JOHN LEE "SONNY BOY" WILLIAMSON, whom Jacobs rated as the best blues harmonica player that he had ever heard. In 1947 Bernard Abrams, owner of a Maxwell Street radio store, recorded Jacobs for his Ora Nelle label, cutting two takes each of "I Just Keep Loving Her" (with Jacobs singing and playing the harmonica and Othum Brown on guitar), "Ora Nelle Blues" (with Brown taking over the vocals), and a reworking of SLEEPY JOHN ESTES's "Liquor Store Blues," retitled "Little Store Blues" (with JIMMY ROGERS on vocals and guitar). Sales were limited, but the recordings revealed a brash, raucous sound that clearly pushed the limits of Williamson's Bluebird label sound and foretold the new wave of tough Chicago blues to come.

Williamson's influence was further revealed in Jacobs's recording as part of a group for the Tempotone label in 1948, with Sunnyland Slim on piano. But the most important feature of this session was the presence of the guitarist MUDDY WATERS—the first of many studio collaborations between Waters and Jacobs; together they forged the emergent Chicago blues sound. Waters began experiencing success with his recordings on the Aristocrat (later Chess) label, and Jacobs joined his band, touring extensively through the South but not yet appearing on Waters's recordings for Aristocrat. However, Monroe Passis signed Jacobs, Waters, and Baby Face Leroy for trio sessions in January 1950 for the Parkway label. These sessions yielded eight sides, four with lead vocals by Jacobs and all featuring his developing harmonica work or expressive guitar, with the interplay among Waters's slide guitar, Jacobs's harmonica, and moaning group vocals being particularly ferocious on "Rollin' and Tumblin' (part 2)."

Jacobs and Waters finally recorded together for Chess in August 1950, establishing a record label relationship that lasted the rest of Jacobs's life. In addition, he was Waters's harmonica player on other recording sessions for the next decade. Jacobs also recorded accompaniments for Jimmy Rogers, Johnny Shines, Floyd Jones, John Brim, the Coronets, and BO DIDDLEY, but it was his recordings as leader of his own group that best established his reputation. At an 11 July 1951 session Jacobs finally played amplified harmonica on record, accompanying Waters on "Country Boy." Other harmonica players had experimented with amplification previously, among them Williamson, Miller, and Snooky Pryor, but Jacobs forged a sound that explored the possibilities of amplification most successfully.

A 12 May 1952 session designed to provide Jacobs with his Chess label debut as a leader featured Waters's band and introduced Jacobs's mature style—a unique hybrid of Williamson, LOUIS JORDAN, and EARL BOSTIC, often awash in distortion and reverberation, and riding over tight, intricate, swinging band arrangements. His jazzy, melodic, and powerful yet controlled playing, often heavily amplified, demonstrated his imaginative flair and set the standard for amplified harmonica players. The band's first recording, "Juke," had been its signature tune, but when released under the name "Little Walter and His Night Cats" it went to number one on the rhythm and blues (R&B) charts, prompting Jacobs to leave Waters's band and trade places with JUNIOR WELLS. Wells joined Waters, and Jacobs took over Wells's band, the Aces, which was renamed the Jukes.

Over the next eleven years Jacobs recorded more than eighty songs as a leader for Chess, from the moody ("Blue Midnight") to the sensitive ("Everybody Needs Somebody") and the desperate ("Blue and Lonesome"), from lightly swinging ("Off the Wall") to pounding boogie ("Back Track"), and from the traditional ("Key to the Highway") to the startlingly new ("Roller Coaster"). On both diatonic and chromatic harmonicas he fashioned an approach that was unique and influential. He was an expressive, but never flashy, vocalist whose tunes—both instrumental and vocal—found favor with a wide audience. Fifteen of Jacobs's recordings, including "Juke," "Sad Hours," "Tell Me Mama," "Off the Wall," "You're So Fine," "Oh Baby," and "My Babe," were R&B chart hits between 1952 and 1959. Disagreements about money caused a falling-out between Jacobs and his band members in 1954, but the replacements, particularly ROBERT LOCKWOOD JR. and Luther Tucker on guitars, helped create an even more distinctive, jazzy sound, unlike any other in the blues genre.

In addition to his chart successes Jacobs not only played in Chicago but also toured widely all over the country, performing at the Apollo in New York City (1952 and 1953), at the Hippodrome Ballroom in Memphis (1954), with Alan Freed's Diddley Daddy Package Show in Boston (1955), and at the Regal Theatre in Chicago (c. 1957). In addition to more than 150 recordings on which he appeared while at Chess, Jacobs also accompanied OTIS RUSH for the Cobra label in 1957. In 1959 Jacobs recorded the blues classic "Everything's Going to Be Alright," and though he continued to record a number of other exciting songs, it was his last R&B hit to reach the top 25. Still, the blues revival in England and Europe provided Jacobs with another venue, and he was greeted as a star and genius when he arrived in Britain in September 1964 and began touring as a single or with the Rolling Stones. His final recording session as a leader for Chess in 1966 revealed a man who was literally sick and tired. His supersession recording with Waters and Diddley in 1967 was little better. Back in England and Europe with the American Folk Blues Festival Tour in 1967, however, Jacobs recaptured his earlier successes. Always a volatile person, he got into a street fight with a gang of drunks in Chicago, and his resultant injuries caused his death there.

Speaking of Jacobs, Waters told the researcher Peter Guralnick, "I'll tell you, I had the best harmonica player in the business, man." It was a sentiment echoed over and over by musicians and fans alike. Little Walter Jacobs helped establish the harmonica—often thought of as a mere toy—as a legitimate instrument, one capable of infinite expressiveness, and he himself became the major proponent and standard setter in the blues and rock idioms. His use of amplification and effects was distinctive and lustrous, but it was his ideas, his ability to improvise imaginatively and seemingly endlessly and to astonish and to move that made him a major voice. And even as he spoke through his instrument, Jacobs's singing also moved his audiences. JOHN LEE HOOKER called Jacobs his "favorite singer" (Leadbetter, 123). Singer, harmonica player, and composer, Jacobs was a consummate blues artist, pivotal for his imagination, his daring, and his honest and heartfelt delivery, as well as for his ability to so reshape the playing of the harmonica that virtually no harmonica player after him in blues or rock could deny his influence.

FURTHER READING

Guralnick, Peter. *Feel Like Going Home: Portraits in Blues and Rock and Roll.* (1971).
Leadbetter, Mike. *Nothing but the Blues* (1971).

DISCOGRAPHY

The Complete Muddy Waters 1947–1967.
The Essential Little Walter.
Little Walter: The Chess Years 1952–1963.
This entry is taken from the *American National Biography* and is published here with the permission of the American Council of Learned Societies.

STEVEN C. TRACY

Jacobs, Louisa (11 Oct. 1833–1917), slave and educator, was born Louisa Matilda Jacobs in Edenton, North Carolina, the daughter of HARRIET JACOBS, a slave, and Samuel Treadwell Sawyer, a prominent white lawyer. Louisa was the second child and only daughter born to this relationship; she had an older brother, Joseph. Louisa was given the nickname "Lulu" by her mother and was the namesake of her godmother, a slave named Louisa Matilda. Louisa's mother refused to give her children the last name of their slave owner, Norcom. To honor her father, Harriet gave Louisa and Joseph the last name Jacobs, the name denied Harriet's father, who was fathered by a white man. Harriet adopted the name Jacobs for herself too.

In 1835, when Louisa was two years old, Harriet Jacobs went into hiding due to continuous sexual advances from her slave owner Norcom and her desire for a better life. Louisa was left in the custody of Harriet's grandmother, Molly Horniblow, a free woman who ran a local bakery. Horniblow had been emancipated after the death of her mistress Margaret Horniblow. Although Harriet watched over her children from her hiding place in the attic of Molly Horniblow's house, she longed to touch and be with them. Fearing for the safety of her children, Harriet collaborated secretly through Horniblow with Sawyer, asking him for assistance in emancipating their children. In an effort to appease Harriet, Sawyer told his wife about Louisa and Joseph but said that the children's mother was dead. Sawyer and his wife purchased the children from Norcom anonymously in 1840, during a time when Norcom desperately needed the money.

After purchasing Louisa and Joseph, Sawyer was elected to the U.S. Congress and moved his family to Washington, D.C. Louisa was seven years old at the time, and Harriet had been in hiding for five years. Although Harriet remained fearful that her children could still be sold back to their previous owner, she was pleased that they had a good home. Harriet desperately wanted to see Louisa and Joseph before they left with the Sawyers. Horniblow and Sawyer arranged for her to spend time with the children on the eve of their departure. During the visit Harriet revealed herself to her children, who vowed to keep their mother's hiding a secret. Weeping, Harriet promised Louisa and Joseph that they would somehow be reunited.

While in Washington, Louisa served as nursemaid to her half sister Laura. Although these were temporary arrangements, Harriet was upset that Louisa was serving in this capacity. Within months Louisa was sent to Brooklyn, New York, supposedly to be raised and educated by Sawyer's cousin. Harriet heard no news of her daughter for six months, then a letter arrived from the young daughter of Sawyer's cousin reporting that Louisa had arrived safely in Brooklyn and was a gift to the young girl. Joseph remained in Washington with the Sawyers. Harriet again feared for the well-being of her children. Although things were better for them than in Edenton, they were still living as servants to their father and his family.

In 1842, after seven years in hiding, Harriet escaped from Edenton to the North and was reunited with Louisa, who was then nine years old. Harriet and Louisa moved to Rochester, New York, to escape Norcom, who was still actively looking for his fugitive slave. While in Rochester, Harriet and Louisa joined a circle of abolitionists working for the *North Star*, a newspaper owned by FREDERICK DOUGLASS. Worried that Harriet would be captured and returned to North Carolina, Harriet and Louisa

in 1844 moved to Boston, where they were reunited with Joseph, who had been sent to Boston earlier to live with Harriet's brother John. Harriet enrolled Joseph in the segregated Smith School. Louisa, who was ten years old, was embarrassed by her illiteracy and was tutored at home by her mother. Harriet had been taught to read and sew during her childhood by her previous mistress Margaret Horniblow (when Margaret Horniblow died, Harriet, then eleven years old, was willed to Norcom's three-year-old daughter Mary Mitilda Norcom). Once she had learned to read and write, Louisa continued her education in the Boston schools. Harriet worked as a housemaid to support herself and the children.

In 1846, when Louisa was twelve years old, she enrolled in Hiram Huntington Kellogg's Young Ladies Domestic Seminary in Clinton, New York, which focused on educating young women to become mothers and teachers. Her tuition was paid through a work-study program and contributions from wealthy reformers. Louisa studied reading, spelling, writing, music, and foreign languages. After completing her studies in Clinton, she was unable to find a teaching job. In 1853 Harriet's employer, Cornelia Grinnell Willis, bought her freedom from Norcom, thus ending her status as a fugitive. Louisa was twenty years old when her mother was emancipated. In 1863 Louisa and Harriet moved to Alexandria, Virginia, where they organized medical care for victims of the Civil War and established the Jacobs Free School, a refuge for both black teachers and displaced African Americans.

In 1865 Louisa and Harriet relocated to Savannah, Georgia, where Louisa continued relief work and started the Lincoln School behind a set of partitions in a ward in the Hospital for Freedmen and Refugees. She taught children in the mornings and adults in the afternoons. She enjoyed teaching and often wrote about the successful progress of her students for the *Freedmen's Record*, the newsletter of the New England branch of the Freedmen's Union Commission that documented the classroom experiences of black teachers at newly established schools. In March 1866 she reported that she had 130 students. However, she expressed great concern that many freed people and southerners were uninterested in the education of the freed black children. She was also disheartened by what she felt was the inability of newly freed slaves to break away from the attitudes of the old slave system.

Louisa continued her service work for a short time in Cambridge, Massachusetts, and in England, until she and her mother made their final move to Washington, D.C., in 1877. Louisa, then forty-four years old, found it impossible to find employment that was appropriate to her education. She secured several temporary jobs and in 1891, at the age of fifty-eight, took a job with the Census Bureau and the Treasury Department. She was underpaid, and work conditions were unpleasant. She handled dirty and potentially contaminated currency in the basement of the building, but the job allowed her to support her mother. She was forced to quit when her mother required full-time nursing.

Harriet's grandmother had managed to buy property in Edenton that was awarded to her heirs at her death in 1867. In 1889 Ann Ramsey, the widow of Harriet's brother Mark, died, leaving her property to Harriet and Louisa. But in 1892 the financial hardships of caring for her mother forced Louisa to sell their property in Edenton. This was a bittersweet decision because the sale broke all ties with their lives in Edenton. Louisa continued to nurse her mother until Harriet's death in 1897.

In 1898 Louisa went to work at the National Home for the Relief of Destitute Colored Women and Children. The home was organized during the Civil War by activist women who supported the kind of work Louisa and Harriet had done in Savannah. Joining a staff that included the superintendent, teachers, and physicians, Louisa, sixty-five years old, was appointed assistant matron and the next year was promoted to matron. She sponsored numerous activities for the women and children until her resignation in 1903. At the age of seventy she accepted a position at Howard University as matron of Miner Hall, a position that included room and board. She excelled in this capacity until her resignation in 1908 at the age of seventy-five. Howard University's president Wilber P. Thirkield praised her performance and the caring nature she exhibited with students. Louisa spent the last years of her life as a companion to the descendants of her mother's lifelong friends. She died in Brooklyn, New York, in the home of Edith Willis Grinnell.

FURTHER READING

Jacobs, Louisa. *Freedmen's Record* (Mar. 1866; July 1866).

Jacobs, Harriet A. *Incidents in the Life of a Slave Girl* (1973).

Yellin, Jean Fagan. *Harriet Jacobs: A Life* (2004).

LINDA WILSON-JONES

Jacobs, Phebe Ann (July 1785–28 Feb. 1850), religious figure, was born a slave in Morris County, New Jersey. Nothing is known of her family, but as a child she became the property of the Wheelock family of Hanover, New Hampshire. She served as a personal attendant to Maria Malleville, the stepdaughter of President Wheelock of Dartmouth College. When Malleville married William Allen in 1812, Jacobs continued as her servant, eventually moving with the Allens to Brunswick, Maine, when Allen became the president of Bowdoin College. After Mrs. Allen's death in 1828, Jacobs lived on her own and supported herself as a laundress for the students of Bowdoin College until her death.

According to the *Narrative of Phebe Ann Jacobs*, written by Mrs. T. C. Upham after Jacobs's death, Jacobs became a devout Christian while living with the Wheelock family. Upham, the wife of the theologian and Bowdoin professor Thomas C. Upham, was a friend of Jacobs's and a fellow church member. The *Narrative*, a short religious biography published by the American Tract Society, presented Jacobs as an exemplar of religious devotion, well known and respected in the Christian community of Brunswick. "Happy Phebe" is depicted in constant prayer, and the people she prays for sometimes reap mysterious benefits. Upham's account focused primarily on Jacobs's life as a free woman, contentedly living alone "with Christ," spending long hours at church and religious meetings, in addition to washing and ironing for the students of Bowdoin.

Of interest to literary scholars is the probability that Jacobs was the inspiration, in part, for the character of Uncle Tom in Harriet Beecher Stowe's 1852 novel *Uncle Tom's Cabin* (Stowe also based her character on JOSIAH HENSON, a man who was once enslaved in Maryland and Kentucky). In defending her characterization of Uncle Tom, which offended radical abolitionists of the time in its depiction of Tom as a servile, loyal slave of an undeserving master, Stowe refers to "'a small religious tract' on the life of a 'coloured woman named Phebe' which had been prepared by 'a lady of Brunswick'" (Hovet, 267). Stowe lived with the Uphams for a brief period in 1850 before moving to her own home in Brunswick. The critic Theodore R. Hovet traced parallels between Jacobs's extreme religious devotion and apparent contentment with her lot and Uncle Tom's humility and religious piety. Hovet also noted similarities between Upham's description of Jacobs's well-marked Bible with Stowe's depiction of Tom's Bible as "marked through" with pencil strokes noting favorite passages. In addition,

Hovet noted that an illustration of Jacobs's home at the beginning of the *Narrative*, with the caption "my little house has become a palace," may have served as inspiration for Stowe's portrayal of Tom's cabin. Upham described Jacobs's home as a haven for Christians of all classes in Brunswick; similarly, Tom's cabin was a frequent meeting place for enslaved African American Christians in Stowe's novel.

Little is known about Jacobs beyond Upham's account. Since slavery was not legal in Maine after the 1780s, Jacobs's status as a servant to the Allen family once they left New Hampshire was technically one of choice. Whether she was as content with her lot as Upham asserts is impossible to determine. Upham's only reference to possible discontent in Jacobs's character is when Jacobs is quoted as saying on occasion that "Satan is busy with me … but my Lord is stronger than he" (Upham, 6). Upham follows this tiny glimpse of Jacobs's struggle against sin with a prolonged description of how Jacobs "literally and truly sought out the *lowest seat*" (Upham, 6). Upham's description of Jacobs's "peculiar lowly attitude of spirit and manner which sat on her with a natural grace and beauty" (Upham, 6) belies the desire on the part of whites to believe that African Americans and former slaves chose and indeed preferred their "lowly" status. In Upham's account, Jacobs's voice is not heard; readers hear only the voice of a humble servant, content with her lot: a perfect slave.

Although she had no local family ties, Jacobs was certainly loved and revered in the Brunswick community. Her funeral was attended by many of the luminaries of Bowdoin College, as well as the retired president Allen and his family, who traveled from nearly two hundred miles away to be present. Interestingly, included with the manuscript collection of President Allen's tenure as president of Bowdoin is a thimble that once belonged to Jacobs. This thimble and Upham's account are fitting symbols of how the white community of Brunswick viewed Jacobs, through her labor and her acceptance of that "*lowest seat.*"

FURTHER READING

Upham, Mrs. T. C. *Narrative of Phebe Ann Jacobs.* (1850; repr. 2000). Available online at http://docsouth.unc.edu/neh/upham/upham.html

Hovet, Theodore R. "Mrs. Thomas C. Upham's 'Happy Phebe': A Feminine Source of Uncle Tom," *American Literature* 51.2 (May 1979).

ALICE KNOX EATON

Jacquet, Illinois (31 Oct. 1922–22 July 2004), tenor saxophonist, was born Jean-Baptiste Jacquet (pronounced "zha-KAY") in Broussard, Louisiana, near Lafayette, to Gilbert Jacquet, a French-Creole railroad worker, and a Sioux mother. He adopted the name *Illinois*, derived from the Sioux Indian word *Illiniwek* ("superior man"). When Jacquet was about a year old, his family moved to Houston, Texas, where his father worked as a part-time swing musician and bandleader, as did Jacquet's three older brothers.

Jacquet began performing professionally when he was three years old, singing on Galveston's GULF radio to promote his brothers' vaudeville show and also tap-dancing with his father's big band. His brother Lentham, a drummer, gave Jacquet, still a child, his first music lessons. Jacquet played soprano saxophone in his high school band and drums in the orchestra. Throughout the late 1930s Jacquet, who had switched to alto sax while in high school, played in various bands around Houston. During his final two years of high school, he played with the Milton Larkin Orchestra, a territory band based in the Midwest, that included Eddie "Cleanhead" Vinson and Arnett Cobb. Although Jacquet's career was thriving, unpleasant racial incidents prompted him, along with his older brother Russell, to leave Houston for Los Angeles in September 1940.

During the early 1940s Jacquet played tenor sax in top Los Angeles swing bands. In Los Angeles, Russell joined Floyd Ray's band, and Jacquet sat in briefly. During a Labor Day jam session with NAT "KING" COLE, CHARLIE CHRISTIAN, and JIMMY BLANTON, Cole introduced Jacquet to LIONEL HAMPTON, who hired him on the condition that he switch from alto to tenor sax (one of Jacquet's new bandmates would be DEXTER GORDON). Prevented from recording by an American Federation of Musicians ban that banned all union musicians from recording in a dispute over royalty income from recording sales, Hampton toured constantly and honed his band to precision.

Jacquet's tenor solos on "Flying Home," written by Benny Goodman, went over well with audiences. His approach to the tenor saxophone ushered in the "Texas tenor" style, consisting of a full, rich tone and use of the instrument's extreme upper register. The "Texas tenor" style also had characteristic rhythmic—sometimes "honking"—riffing, or a shouting quality akin to the approach of blues and R&B singers. Cobb and Vinson were also pioneers of this style.

After the recording ban ended Hampton's band went into the studio in 1942, and Jacquet made his first recordings, including "Flying Home" for Decca, which catapulted him to international fame. Jazz saxophone enthusiasts—particularly those in Great Britain—frequently transcribed in musical notation this solo, lending it legendary status. Jacquet's style was later imitated not only by jazz saxophonists, but also by R&B and soul players such as KING CURTIS and rock-and-roll saxophonists of the 1950s. The solo was transcribed for the Hampton band's saxophone section shortly after the 1942 release, becoming Hampton's theme.

Jacquet left Hampton to join CAB CALLOWAY from 1943 to 1944, alternating on alto and tenor. During this time he appeared in the film *Stormy Weather* as a member of Calloway's band. After leaving Calloway in 1944, he began jamming regularly with fellow saxophonist LESTER YOUNG and others. That year producer Norman Granz rented the Philharmonic Hall in Los Angeles for an all-star jazz benefit concert to raise funds for Mexican youths arrested in the Zoot Suit Riots, which occurred in Los Angeles beginning 31 May and continuing into early June involving Mexican American youths (who dressed fashionably in "zoot suits") and white servicemen and civilians. A group of youths were attacked after leaving a dance at a Venice ballroom. Jacquet played another solo that astonished audiences and critics on the hit "Philharmonic Blues, Pt. 2" (1944). The success of this benefit ushered in the Jazz at the Philharmonic (JATP) concerts. Granz organized a touring ensemble of musicians from this series, with Jacquet featured as a major soloist. Jacquet also appeared with other JATP musicians in director Gjon Mili's Academy Award-nominated short film *Jammin' the Blues* (1944).

After Granz moved to Geneva, Switzerland, by 1956, the ensemble disbanded. Remaining in Los Angeles, Jacquet formed his own small ensemble with his brother Russell and bassist CHARLES MINGUS. This group performed at clubs on Hollywood Boulevard, including an extended engagement at Billy Berg's Swing Club. Jacquet's early small-group recordings dated from this period.

In the fall of 1945 Jacquet received an offer to play with COUNT BASIE and moved to New York, settling in Queens. After a year and a half of touring and recording with Basie, Jacquet left to perform as the primary soloist with the Jazz at the Philharmonic orchestra (1946–1947) and to lead his own small ensembles. During this time he recorded his hits "Black Velvet," "Robbins' Nest," and "Port of Rico."

He recorded the classic "Bluesitis" in 1952 for small, independent record labels. In March 1947 he recorded with an ensemble that included a trumpet section staffed by MILES DAVIS and FATS NAVARRO. From 1950 to 1952 he recorded for a label, Verve, which specialized in jazz. He toured Europe for the first time in 1954 as part of the "Jazz Parade" show, along with his big band, the Illinois Jacquet Big Band, and guest soloists SARAH VAUGHAN and COLEMAN HAWKINS, a tenor saxophonist. Throughout the 1960s and 1970s Jacquet would continue to appear at jazz festivals in the United States and Europe, both as a leader of his own groups and with all-star ensembles, including periodic appearances with Hampton, MILT BUCKNER, JO JONES, and SLAM STEWART.

During the 1980s Jacquet formed the Texas Tenors, who were named by Kool Jazz Festival promoter George Wein, and included Cobb, Buddy Tate, and Herschel Evans. In 1983 Jacquet was the first jazz musician to be named artist-in-residence at Harvard University for a three-year period. While at Harvard he formed the Illinois Jacquet Big Band, which he led for the next twenty years. He recorded his last album, *Jacquet's Got It!*, for Atlantic Records in 1987.

In 1991 Jacquet was the subject of Arthur Elgort's documentary *Texas Tenor: The Illinois Jacquet Story*. Two years later he performed "C-Jam Blues" to acclaim with amateur saxophonist President Bill Clinton at the 1993 inaugural ball. Jacquet had also performed for Presidents Jimmy Carter and Ronald Reagan. He held an extended engagement at New York's Tavern on the Green in 1994 and in September performed at Carnegie Hall. In 2000 Jacquet received the Jazz at Lincoln Center Award for Artistic Excellence. In May 2004, only two months before his death, he received an honorary doctorate from Juilliard School of Music.

An important figure in the development of the tenor saxophone, Jacquet influenced jazz, R&B, and rock-and-roll saxophonists. Not only did he define swing and R&B tenor saxophone styles for the latter half of the twentieth century, but also his influence was heard in subsequent bop tenor saxophonists, such as JOHN COLTRANE and Curtis. Along with his contemporaries Young and Hawkins, he established the tenor saxophone as a major solo instrument in jazz. During his eighty-year career he recorded more than three hundred original compositions and played with such major jazz figures as LOUIS ARMSTRONG, DIZZY GILLESPIE, CHARLIE PARKER, and ELLA FITZGERALD.

FURTHER READING

Cook, Eddie. "Illinois Jacquet: The Texas Tenor Talks to Eddie Cook about His Life and Career," *Jazz Journal International* (Feb. 1994).

Deffaa, Chip. "Illinois Jacquet," *Down Beat* (Feb. 1989).

Deffaa, Chip. "Illinois Jacquet: He's Got It!" *Jazz Times* (Sept. 1988).

Feather, Leonard. "Before and After," *Jazz Times* (Sept. 1989).

McCord, Jeff. "The State of Illinois," *Texas Monthly* (Nov. 2002).

McDonough, John. "Illinois Jacquet: 'If You Can't Tap Your Feet, Something's Wrong,'" *Down Beat* (Oct. 1998).

GAYLE MURCHISON

Jafa, Arthur (30 Nov. 1960–), visual artist, filmmaker, and cinematographer, was born in Tupelo, Mississippi, and grew up in Clarksdale, Mississippi, the son of Rowena and Arthur Fielder. He studied architecture and film at Howard University from 1978 to 1982. While there, he worked with the filmmaker Haile Gerima, who became a mentor and an influential friend. Jafa's concerns with the centrality of the Middle Passage and slavery in the African Diaspora led him to rethink the political and aesthetic importance of defining "blackness," and how what Jafa called "primal sites" are crucial to any project concerned with the liberation of people of African descent.

Renowned for his cinematography on Julie Dash's path-breaking film *Daughters of the Dust* (1992), Jafa put into practice techniques he had long been theorizing. "Black Visual Intonation" was a radical aesthetic notion about the mechanics of filmmaking. Jafa won Sundance Film Festival's Cinematography Award (1991). He was the lead cinematographer on John Akomfrah's *Seven Songs for Malcolm X* (1993), SPIKE LEE's *Crooklyn* (1994), Isaac Julien's *Darker Shade of Black* (1994), *A Litany for Survival* (1995), Ada Gay Griffin and Michelle Parkerson's biographical film on AUDRE LORDE, and Louis J. Massiah's film *W. E. B. DuBois: A Biography in Four Voices* (1995).

Jafa also shot a series of films by Manthia Diawara, including *In Search of Africa* (1997), *Diaspora Conversations: From Goree to London* (2000), *Rouch in Reverse* (2000), *Bamako Sigi-Kan* (2002), and *Conakry Kas* (2003). Additionally, he was cinematographer on numerous films, including Stanley Nelson's *Marcus Garvey: Look for Me in the Whirlwind* (2001) and *Flag Wars*, about the gentrification of a black neighborhood in Baltimore. The latter was shown as part of the *POV* series on public television. His film *Slowly This* (1995) aired on PBS in 1998, part of WNET's "Reel NY" series. He directed music videos for Tricky, CASSANDRA WILSON, Dionne Farris, Mood, Alana Davis, and Low Keys.

Although Jafa's work was nearly always associated with his cinematography, he did, for some time, explore other dimensions of the visual arts, from installations to conceptual pieces. Jafa first showed work in 1999, at Artists Space in New York. He subsequently exhibited in Okwui Enwezor's "Mirror's Edge," which opened at the BildMusset, University of Umeå in Sweden and traveled to the Vancouver Art Gallery, Canada; Castello di Rivoli, Turin, Italy; and Tramway, Glasgow, Scotland (1999). Curatorial interest in his work led to a number of other exhibitions, including Bitstreams, Whitney Museum of American Art, New York (2001); 2000 Biennial Exhibition, Whitney Museum of American Art, New York; Media City, Seoul, Korea (2000), and Black Box, CCAC Institute, Oakland, California (2000). Jafa's work was shown in Social Formal, Westfälischer Kunstveren, Münster, Germany (2002). In the same year, as artist-in-residence at Artpace in San Antonio, Texas, Jafa created an installation called "My Black Death." This motif was explored further in an essay of the same name, written for an anthology edited by Greg Tate, *Everything but the Burden: What White People Are Taking from Black Culture* (2003). In 2005 Jafa's work was part of a large exhibition at the Contemporary Arts Museum Houston, entitled "Double Consciousness: Black Conceptual Art Since 1970."

FURTHER READING

Hooks, Bell. "Critical Contestations: A Conversation with A.J. (Arthur Jaffa [sic])," in *Reel to Real: Race, Sex, and Class at the Movies* (1996).

TIM HASLETT

Jai, Anna Madgigine (1793–1870?), slave, plantation mistress, and refugee, was born Anta Majigeen Ndiaye in Senegal during years of intense warfare and slave raids. While there is no conclusive evidence of Jai's lineage, legends in both Florida and Senegal suggest that she was a princess in Africa who was captured and sold into slavery after her father led an unsuccessful bid for power in the Wolof states of Senegal. While little is known of Jai's life before her arrival in Spanish Florida, historian Daniel Schafer suggests that she was one of the 120 Africans who survived the nightmarish Middle Passage from Africa to Cuba on board the *Sally*. In 1806 Jai was purchased by Zephaniah Kingsley, a slave trader and planter from Florida. From Cuba,

Jai sailed with Kingsley to his Laurel Grove plantation near what would later become Jacksonville, Florida. As the nineteenth century progressed, Jai's life was characterized by upheaval within the changing racial landscape in Florida.

Under early nineteenth-century Spanish rule, the racial codes in Florida were generally less restrictive than in the American states. Slave women were entitled to legal protection against harsh masters and were allowed to own and manage property. Slavery was not always assumed to be a permanent state, and slaves often purchased themselves out of slavery or were manumitted. In addition, relationships between people of different races were accepted, and many of Florida's prominent citizens acknowledged and provided for African wives and mulatto children. So even though Jai was purchased by Kingsley as a slave, it was not unusual that she lived with him in the main house as his wife and gave birth to three children—a son George and two daughters, Martha and Mary—within five years of her arrival in Florida. Although Jai and Kingsley were never legally married (she used both Jai and Kingsley as surnames after her marriage), she became the senior wife among Kingsley's various slave wives in what was in effect a polygamous family structure. He wrote of her in his will that "she has always been respected as my wife and such I acknowledge her, nor do I think that her truth, honor, integrity, moral conduct, and good sense will lose in comparison with anyone"(Schafer, 33). Drawing on her African heritage during her first years in Florida, Jai would have been familiar with the work accomplished at Laurel Grove and able to manage other slaves.

Jai's time as a slave was short. On 1 March 1811, five years after he purchased her, Kingsley freed Anna and their three children. One year after gaining her freedom, Jai petitioned the Spanish government for land and was granted five acres on the eastern shore of the St. John's River. Despite her relocation across the river, Jai continued her relationship with Kingsley and retained her duties as plantation manager at Laurel Grove. She also opened a store similar to one at her husband's plantation and began a successful business providing goods to local plantations and traders. Jai also assumed ownership of twelve slaves. Schafer argues that because of her roots in an African culture, where slavery was part of the social structure, her status—as a former slave who had become a slave owner—would not have seemed unusual. Jai would own slaves until 1860.

Just as it had in Africa, politics threatened Jai's way of life in Florida. The Patriot War erupted in 1812 when insurgent American migrants tried to seize East Florida. As American forces moved through the region, they looted and occupied local plantations. The Patriot War created an additional threat for Jai and her family. If East Florida became American territory, the liberal racial policies of Spanish Florida would probably be replaced by the more stringent black codes that were common in the Southern United States. More immediately, if Jai and her children were captured, they would be sold as slaves in Georgia. When the rebels reached her plantation, Jai set fire to the house and the outbuildings and then escaped with her children on a Spanish boat to the fortified town of San Nicolas to the town of Fernandina where they remained under the protection of Spanish forces. Jai's heroic exploits at Laurel Grove were not forgotten by the Spanish government, however. After the insurrection failed, Jai received 350 acres of land from the Spanish government to reward her loyalty.

In 1814 the Kingsleys sailed back to Fort George Island to rebuild their plantation. This time the "Ma'am Anna House" was built on the same grounds as Zephaniah's home. In 1824 Jai gave birth to John Maxwell Kingsley, and as she had with her other children, raised him within the Catholic Church. This decision was most likely pragmatic as well as spiritual. The Catholic Church afforded free blacks in Florida the protection of the godparents system where bonds of obligation joined two families together. If chosen correctly, freed black children could thus be protected by powerful godparents. More than likely, this fact entered into Jai and Kingsley's minds when they chose Zephaniah C. Gibbs, Kingsley's nephew, to be John Maxwell's godfather.

In truth Jai and Kingsley had cause for concern when thinking about their children's future. Florida became an American territory in the 1820s, and the new American government replaced the liberal manumission laws of Spanish Florida with ideas that more completely established black racial inferiority before the law. Interracial marriages were considered illegal, and the children of mixed-race couples were not entitled to inherit their parents' estates. Because they were residents of Spanish Florida, the Kingsleys should have been immune to some of these laws (except for John Maxwell, who was born after Florida became an American territory). Eventually however, white fears of a black uprising in Florida, which peaked at the time of the Second Seminole War (1835–1842), created a dangerous climate for free people of color. Kingsley resolved to move his family to Haiti, where free, skilled American blacks were needed as a foundation for financial prosperity to rebuild Haiti's commercial economy after the Haitian slave rebellion (Schafer, 63).

Jai lived in Haiti from 1838 to 1846 when, three years after Kingsley's death and shortly after her son's death, she returned to Florida and successfully battled Kingsley's sister, who tried to have his black family excluded from his estate. As the Civil War drew closer and racist sentiment continued to escalate in Florida, Jai became the center of a thriving community of freed blacks in Duval County. Kinship ties with Kingsley's powerful white family were valuable, as they protected Jai's legal and economic rights. Jai and her family lived in relative security on the St. John's River until 1862 when overextended Union forces withdrew from the area and left Jai's Unionist family vulnerable to Confederate sympathizers. Thus Florida's decision to secede from the Union forced Jai to leave her home once again. Many free African Americans in southern states feared that they would be sold into slavery under Confederate rule. Jai and her family likely went to New York City to wait out the war. It is not known when Jai returned to Florida. At that point, however, she had lost most of her financial resources to the war, including four slaves who were listed in her 1860 will, and she lived with her daughter until her death. Although the exact date of her death is not known, her will was delivered to the Duval County Court of Probate on 18 June 1870 (Schafer, 118).

FURTHER READING

Kingsley Plantation, on Fort George Island, is a National Historic Site that is open for tours. Papers concerning the will of Zephaniah Kingsley, 1844, 1846 can be found in Record Group 900,000; Series/Collection no. M87-20. Florida State Archives.

Kingsley, Zephaniah. "Address to the Legislative Council of Florida on the Subject of its Colored Population, by Z. Kingsley, A Planter of That Territory," Florida State Archives (c. 1832).

Landers, Jane. *Black Society in Spanish Florida* (1999).

Schafer, Daniel L. *Anna Madgigine Jai Kingsley: African Princess, Florida Slave, Plantation Slaveowner* (2003)

Tilford, Kathy. "Anna Kingsley: A Free Woman," *OAH Magazine of History* (Fall 1997).

BETHANY WAYWELL JAY

Jakes, T. D. (9 June 1957–), pastor, evangelist, and writer, was born Thomas Dexter Jakes in Vandalia, West Virginia, the third and youngest child of Ernest Jakes Sr. and Odith Jakes. Jakes's father owned a fifty-two-employee janitorial service and instilled in his son an appreciation for entrepreneurship and economic empowerment. Jakes's mother taught home economics. As a child "Tommy" Jakes followed in his parents' footsteps by working a paper route and selling vegetables grown by his mother. He grew up in his parents' Baptist church and as an adolescent served as its part-time choir director.

When Jakes was ten his father was diagnosed with a terminal kidney disease. Alongside his mother, Jakes cared for his father and helped with the business. When his father died five years later Jakes searched for a deeper religious experience and underwent a conversion at a storefront apostolic church that belonged to a small Pentecostal denomination. He began carrying his Bible to school and earned the moniker "Bible boy." Two months before he was supposed to graduate from high school Jakes dropped out to care for his-hospitalized mother. Jakes wanted to become a preacher but temporarily shelved that ambition because of a speech impediment. Instead he earned his GED and took classes in psychology at West Virginia State College.

In 1976 Jakes left college before obtaining his degree and pursued his dream of becoming a preacher. He began filling in at small churches in and around Charleston, West Virginia. While guest-preaching at a church in Beckley, West Virginia, Jakes met his future wife, Serita Ann Jamison, whom he married after a brief courtship in 1980. The couple eventually had five children. Jakes supported his family by working the swing shift in the local Union Carbide chemical plant.

In 1980, moving beyond his Baptist roots, Jakes began preaching regularly at the Greater Emmanuel Temple of Faith, a small Pentecostal church in Montgomery, West Virginia. Jakes's work with the Temple of Faith introduced him to Oneness Pentecostalism, a branch of Pentecostalism that baptizes only in Jesus' name rather than with the traditional Trinitarian formulation. The Union Carbide plant closed in 1982, forcing Jakes to work odd jobs to make ends meet. By 1986 Greater Emmanuel had grown to the point that it could pay Jakes a salary sufficient for him to devote himself fully to the church. Jakes was ordained as the bishop of the Greater Emmanuel Assembly of Churches in 1987. In 1990 Jakes founded a new Temple of Faith church in Charleston.

In the early 1990s Jakes's career suddenly exploded. After years of counseling women suffering through failed marriages and parenting difficulties, Jakes began teaching a Sunday school class for hurting women. The class grew rapidly—Jakes had touched a nerve. He published a series of tapes based on the class and wrote a best-seller, *Woman, Thou Art Loosed* (1994). Still a capable singer and composer, Jakes received a Grammy nomination for the companion CD to his book. Jakes began to receive speaking invitations and launched a cable TV show. In 1993 he launched a conference for men entitled *ManPower*, which became an annual event. The 2003 *ManPower* conference in Atlanta drew 44,000 men. In the mid-1990s Jakes enthusiastically supported Promise Keepers, an interracial evangelical movement that encouraged men to take spiritual leadership of their families.

By the mid-1990s Jakes envisioned relocating his church to a city that would provide him with a base from which he could reach mass audiences. In 1996 he purchased a vacant church in South Dallas, Texas, persuaded fifty core families from the Charleston Temple of Faith to join him, and established a new church, which he named the Potter's House. In large measure because of Jakes's fame, 1,500 people joined the church on its first Sunday. The Potter's House, although nondenominational, reflected Jakes's Pentecostal background through its charismatic worship and by upholding the validity of speaking in tongues. Within four years the church's membership skyrocketed to 26,000, and the Potter's House built an 80,000-seat sanctuary. In 1997 Jakes gained publicity when he baptized four members of the Dallas Cowboys football team, including EMMITT SMITH and DEION SANDERS.

Jakes continued to write best-selling books and spoke to huge crowds at the men's and women's conferences that in many ways defined evangelical and Pentecostal Christianity in the late 1990s. Although African Americans constituted the majority of his local congregation, Jakes reached predominantly white audiences at many of his conferences. Jakes became one of a small number of Christians in the United States able to draw crowds rivaling those of Billy Graham, and he reached even larger audiences through programs on the Trinity Broadcasting Network, Black Entertainment Television, and the Daystar Network. In the wake of the 11 September 2001 attacks Jakes collaborated with the gospel and R&B artist Kirk Franklin on a critically acclaimed song emphasizing the need for faith and hope. In 2004 Jakes starred in a movie version of *Woman, Thou Art Loosed*, which featured a candid portrayal of child molestation and became a modest success at the box office. Jakes spoke regularly about the threat that domestic violence and drug use posed to families, especially African American families.

After his move to Dallas, Jakes focused his attention on helping inner-city communities both spiritually and economically. The Potter's House developed literacy programs, a domestic-violence ministry, and an AIDS ministry. Jakes started his own prison ministry because he felt that African American inmates would respond more readily to black than to white evangelicals. Jakes also founded what he called the City of Refuge, a comprehensive urban ministry to provide spiritual and economic resources to South Dallas. The City of Refuge included everything from a preschool to a nursing home. Aspiring entrepreneurs—sometimes former drug dealers—could apply for loans to start their own legitimate businesses.

Other black ministers and activists criticized Jakes for his openly affluent lifestyle. Jakes purchased a $1.7 million home in Dallas far from the troubles of the communities surrounding the Potter's House. Jakes used his seven-figure publishing deal to decorate his home elegantly, purchase fine clothes, and drive a Mercedes-Benz. Jakes brushed off his critics by noting that his income derives from his own enterprises rather than from his church. He contended, too, that economically struggling African Americans benefited from his being a role model of entrepreneurial success.

By 2000 Jakes had gained recognition as one of the most influential Christian leaders in the United States. Both George W. Bush and Al Gore visited the Potter's House in advance of the 2000 presidential election. *Time* magazine dubbed Jakes "the next Billy Graham" on a 2001 cover. Theologically flexible, culturally sensitive, and always tapping into the this-worldly concerns of a broad spectrum of Christians, Jakes appealed to a diverse array of Christian audiences.

FURTHER READING

Lee, Shayne. *T. D. Jakes: America's New Preacher* (2005)
Starling, Kelly. "Why People, Especially Black Women, Are Talking about Bishop T. D. Jakes," *Ebony* (Jan. 2001).
Van Biema, David. "Spirit Raiser," *Time* (17 Sept. 2001).
Wellman, Sam. *T. D. Jakes* (2000).
Winner, Lauren F. "T. D. Jakes Feels Your Pain," *Christianity Today* (7 Feb. 2000).

JOHN G. TURNER

Jallo, Job ben Solomon (1702?–1773), rising member of a leading Muslim family in Senegal, a captive in Gambia, and later a slave in Maryland, was born Ayuba ibn Suleiman Diallo in Bondu, West Africa, to a prosperous family. Though little information about Job's early years is available, it is known that by the age of fifteen he was, his amanuensis wrote, well on his way to becoming an Alfa—following his father and grandfather—one of the religious leaders in an area of eastern Senegal renowned then and at the time of the explorer Mungo Park's 1775 visit as a territory where Muslims, at least, need not fear enslavement. Job not only advanced positively in his koranic and Arabic studies but he also proved to be a brave and resourceful trader. His growing wealth and respectability led to a marriage with the daughter of a neighboring Alfa of gold-exporting Tombut (Bambuk). After three children, he married a second wife, the daughter of the Alfa of the nearby Tomga (Damga), with whom he had a daughter.

In February 1730, with two servants, Job—as he was commonly called by later memoirists and thereafter into our own era—went to the Gambia River, a two-week journey, in search of paper and other goods in trade for two men his father wanted sold. Not agreeing with the English Captain Pike's offer instead he traded his captives for some cows. On his way home Mandingo kidnappers captured and sold him and his translator to the same Captain Pike Job had met earlier. His father attempted to ransom him but before the several slaves his father sent as trade could reach the ship, Job was carried off to Annapolis, Maryland. Such was Job's importance that Samba Geladio Jegi, one of his student peers—and himself the subject of popular local epics and later a prince in neighboring Futa Toro—sent an army to punish his captors.

Job was purchased by a Kent Island tobacco grower but proved to be a poor laborer, and within a year Job (there called Simon) took flight. Soon captured, however, he was imprisoned until June 1731, when he was visited by local clergy and his eventual amanuensis Thomas Bluett. Stories of his praying, of refusing pork and alcohol, his writing on the prison wall, and his calm manner led to favorable treatment. He was returned to his purchaser and to a life made easier, including a place to peacefully pray, but Job's discomfort and desire for freedom continued. He wrote a letter in Arabic to his father and gave it to Annapolis shipping agents. It came to the attention of the philanthropist James Oglethorpe, the future founder of slave-free Savannah, Georgia, who was impressed and set about securing Job's release. For some months Job remained in the care of several members of the Annapolis clergy until at last he set sail for England with Bluett in March 1733.

During the crossing, despite seasickness, Job prayed regularly, adhered to his dietary obligations, pleased all with his grace and manners, wrote the Koran from memory, and was taught enough English to roughly converse. Not yet legally emancipated, Job spent some time in limbo. In England Bluett introduced him to prominent ministers, scholars, philanthropists, antiquarians, nobility, and royalty. George Sale, the eventual translator of the earliest respectable English translation of the Koran brought Christian texts in Arabic to Job to encourage his conversion. Sale was not alone in this effort, but Job went no further than admitting Jesus was a prophet—consistent with conventional Muslim thinking. He found nothing about the Trinity in his New Testament and argued so sensibly and sensitively for his own faith that he gained universal respect.

His memory astounded many as he wrote out three Korans without reference to any outside copies. The antiquarians Joseph Ames and Sir Hans Sloane, physician to the queen, who sought his help in translating Arabic writings in their artifacts, became helpful allies. Other Royal African Company directors—with some thought about possible uses of Job back in Bondu—were also admirers. Sloane introduced Job to their majesties King George II and Queen Caroline and their families who repaid the visit with valuable gifts. The wealthy duke of Montagu became a patron, beguiled by Job's tireless interest in various mechanical tools and objects. Despite Job's Muslim unease over images, the painter William Hoare produced a sensitive portrait of the man Bluett described as being "five Feet ten Inches high, straight-limb'd, … His Countenance … exceedingly pleasant, yet grave and composed; his Hair long, black, and curled" (Bluett, 51). The Gentleman's Society of Spalding, which counted Isaac Newton and Alexander Pope among its members, made Job any honorary member. By January 1734 enough money had been raised by his new friends to buy his freedom, and shortly thereafter enough money to send him back to Africa without requiring a ransom.

Job, it had been concluded by friends of the Royal African Company, might be useful in enlarging English and lessening rival French trade in Senegambia. Before going Job carefully prepared.

Aware that his homeland was within shouting distance of a French fort and that his connection to the rival English would put him in danger, Job urged Sloane to obtain a French passport for him. By the end of July, accompanied by many good wishes, insistent orders on Job's behalf in royal and RAC letters, gifts both gaudy and useful (such as farming tools, a grist mill, clocks, candles, and lamps), Job was on his way. Seven weeks later he arrived at the Gambia. Almost simultaneously Bluett's book, written at Job's request, appeared. It gives its subject a positive character, a glimpse of Job's Africa, nothing about his Atlantic passage, something of his enslavement in Maryland, and his redemption in England. The role of providence and generous Englishmen in the latter are praised. Slavery is not criticized. As the first nonfiction narrative by a freed African enslaved in the New World, it offers another perspective on its age.

Job's post-emancipation history opened brightly, but dimmed quickly. The English factor on the Gambia, Francis Moore, who welcomed Job, liked him. He recorded commendable instances of Job's trading skills and philosophical and religious responses to his captivity and redemption. He and Job, via dictation or translation from Arabic, wrote to England about Job's meetings with messengers and friends relative to Bondu who told him that Job's father had died, that one wife had remarried, that civil war had disrupted the area, but that Job and his important Fula trader friends believed they could revive trade and bring it to the English on the Gambia.

By July 1735, however, Moore, carrying ivory, beeswax, and letters and gifts from Job to friends, had returned to England. One of his letters reminded the duke of Montagu about Job's translator still enslaved in Maryland. Bluett would eventually arrange for his freedom and his return to Africa. Moore also wrote a remarkably fair and sympathetic book about his African travels and about Job, further enhancing the latter's already sterling reputation. Still Moore's absence undoubtedly lessened the chances of Job having the effect on Senegambia that he and his English supporters might have hoped.

As Moore left Africa, Job and the nephew of the governor of Gambia were heading toward Bondu. Job was welcomed back and for six months strove to turn trade toward the Gambia and away from the French. His companion Thomas Hull kept a dull, only occasionally informative journal of the trip. Upon their return Job wrote again of promised trade. He and Hull soon left again for Bondu, nearby gum forests, and goldfields only slightly farther east. But Anglo-French disagreements and weather frustrated what might have arisen had Job been able to introduce to his countrymen some of the mechanical implements he had brought from England that so fascinated him. For some time in 1737 Job was either in a French prison or under their control while many of his gifts were destroyed on a ship off Senegal or by fire back in Gambia. Still French African records indicate something about Job's prestige as they describe a kind of blockade by Marabout (Muslim) traders against the French until Job was released.

Later in 1737 the Royal African Company sent Melchior de Jaspas, an Armenian fluent in Arabic, to explore and advance their trade from the Gambia. Trouble with the local RAC officers kept Jaspas on the river for a year before he, Job, and Job's redeemed translator could go again to Bondu. No records have been found on the two years Jaspas spent there. Something had gone wrong. Job asked the RAC for passage to England. Letters from the governor and the RAC denied Job's request but money was sent to Job already on another trip to Bondu. Only two more notices have been found. In 1744 Job sought RAC compensation on a bad deal and was again rebuffed. By then the RAC was failing in trade, exploration, and the utilization of Job. The last note on this remarkable man appears in the records of the Gentlemen's Society of Spalding noting his death.

FURTHER READING

Austin, Allan D. *African Muslims in Antebellum America: A Sourcebook* (1984).

Bluett, Thomas. *Some Memoirs of the Life of Job, the Son of Solomon the High Priest of Boonda in Africa* (1734).

Curtin, Philip D. "Ayuba Suleiman Diallo of Bondu," in *Africa Remembered: Narratives by West Africans from the Era of the Slave Trade* (1967).

Grant, Douglas. *The Fortunate Slave* (1968).

Moore, Francis. *Travels into the Inland Parts of Africa … with a Particular Account of Job Ben Solomon* (1738).

ALLAN D. AUSTIN

Jam Master Jay (21 Jan. 1965–30 Oct. 2002), hip-hop and DJ pioneer, was born Jason William Mizell, the youngest of Connie and Jessie Mizell's three children. The family lived in Brooklyn, New York, where his mother Connie was a teacher and his father Jessie was a social worker. Moving to the Hollis neighborhood of Queens from Brooklyn in 1975, Mizell quickly became a respected and powerful force in that small neighborhood. While Mizell was a student at Andrew Jackson High School, teachers and students alike would ask him to stop altercations between students because of his dominating presence and amiable nature. Mizell dropped out of high school but eventually obtained his equivalency diploma. Drumming, playing the guitar, and socializing with friends took up most of Mizell's free time. Mizell credited a desire to be "part of the hottest thing" as one of the main reasons for becoming a DJ in an interview with *DJ Times* in 2000. With inspiration from the style of Kurtis Blow's DJ Davey D, Mizell set out to be part of the party scene as a DJ. In 1980, going by the name of DJ Jazzy Jase, he formed the hip-hop group Two Fifths Down, after the Two Fifths Park where MC battles and parties took place, with Jeff "King Ruler" Fluud, a childhood friend, as the group's MC. Two Fifths Down dominated the hip-hop scene in Hollis, and Mizell became a sought-after DJ for local MCs. Two other childhood friends, Joseph "Run" Simmons and DARRYL "D.M.C." McDANIELS, invited Mizell to DJ for them several times before Mizell accepted the offer after his father's death in 1982. Mizell's stage name, Jam Master Jay, was given to him by McDaniels, reportedly because he was the "master of the record and master of the party."

Already signed to Profile Records before Mizell joined, the group named itself Run-D.M.C. and released its first single, "It's Like That," in May 1983. The self-titled album was released in 1984. Mizell's distinct DJ-ing style and his experimentations in fusing rap and other genres to make a new sound made Run-D.M.C.'s sound different because of its hybridity and edge. The 1985 album *King of Rock* illustrated Mizell's genius as a DJ who used a seamless mixture of electronics, hip-hop scratching, and heavy metal—an unusual yet bold mixture of his music. Run-D.M.C.'s album *Raising Hell* skyrocketed the group to widespread acclaim and stardom. Released in 1986, the top-selling single "Walk This Way," which involved a collaboration with rock group Aerosmith, thrust both Run-D.M.C. and rap music into mainstream American culture. The group's legendary style—Adidas sneakers with no laces, thick gold rope chains, and leather jackets—was Mizell's signature look from high school. During an interview with *DJ Times* magazine in 2000, Mizell stated, "How I dressed is how we dressed. My vibe is our vibe."

The 1988 successor to *Raising Hell*, *Tougher than Leather*, reached double platinum status, but the group's popularity soon began to wane. Personal problems—Simmons was accused of rape and McDaniel was drinking excessively—detracted from the group's reputation. The group would nonetheless go on to record several more albums, including *Back from Hell* in 1990, which was not well received.

In 1989 Mizell started J[am] M[aster] J[ay] Records, signing successful hip-hop group The Afros in 1990 and releasing their first album *Kickin' Afrolistics* the same year. He married Terri Coley in 1990 and fathered three children—Jason (from a previous relationship), and two with Coley, Terry and Jesse.

In 1993, while working with newly signed artists Onyx on their *Bacdafucup* album, Mizell also recorded *Down with the King* with Run-D.M.C. The album attempted to show the group's lasting power and grittier, "gangsta" side with help from newer artists like Q-Tip from the group A Tribe Called Quest and Naughty by Nature. *Down with the King* also marked Mizell's debut as a producer for the group. By 1996, Mizell was working with a relatively unknown rapper Curtis "50 Cent" Jackson. Mizell mentored Jackson, teaching him the fundamentals of recording and music production. Run-D.M.C.'s last record, *Crown Royal*, was released in 2001.

Mizell continued working on Jam Master Jay Records, and made numerous solo public appearances while remaining localized in his childhood neighborhood. To help give back to his community, Mizell helped initiate the Scratch DJ Academy in New York City in 2002. Tragically, on 30 October 2002 Mizell was murdered in his recording studio; a companion, Urieco Rincon also, was shot, but not killed. Five others were present. Speculation about the possible motive for Mizell's murder was everywhere. There were rumors of drug trafficking and unpaid debts. Mizell's murder was compared to the shooting deaths of NOTORIOUS B.I.G. and TUPAC SHAKUR. But Mizell, a pioneer of hip-hop music who was highly respected by peers and fans alike, had no known rivalries with any rappers at the time. Considerable speculation, however, did surround Mizell's willingness to work with 50 Cent after he had been blacklisted by the music industry because of his controversial music and criminal history. At the time of Mizell's death, 50 Cent had a fiery and widely known rivalry with Irv Gotti, record label The Inc.'s (formerly Murder Inc.) executive, as well as with the rapper Jeffrey "Ja Rule" Atkins, but the case has remained open and unsolved. Mizell was buried in Ferncliff Cemetery in Hartsdale, New York.

FURTHER READING

Adler, Bill. *Tougher than Leather: The Rise of Run-DMC* (2002).

Ro, Ronin. *Raising Hell: The Reign, Ruin, and Redemption of Run-D.M.C. and Jam Master Jay* (2006).

REGINA N. BARNETT

Jamal, Ahmad (2 July 1930–), pianist, composer, and bandleader, was born Frederick Russell Jones in Pittsburgh, Pennsylvania. He began playing the piano at the age of three; at seven he studied with Mary Caldwell Dawson, the founder of the first African American opera company in the United States; by the age of eleven he had performed Franz Liszt's piano etudes in classical competitions. Jamal also studied with local jazz pianists. He approached jazz and classical music with equal seriousness, and in later years he argued that jazz ought to be called "American classical music" (Brodacki, 40). In 1948 Jamal graduated from Westinghouse High School, an institution that produced many famous jazz pianists, including MARY LOU WILLIAMS, Dodo Marmarosa, and ERROLL GARNER.

Jamal was a full-time performer immediately after high school. He considered attending college, but by 1949 he was married with a family to support. He joined the violinist Joe Kennedy Jr.'s group the Four Strings, which was a drummerless quartet that included the guitarist Ray Crawford and the bassist Tommy Sewell. Kennedy left in 1950, and the group became the Three Strings. Following Jamal's conversion to Islam, he dropped the name Fritz Jones, and the trio changed its name one last time, becoming the Ahmad Jamal Trio.

The group relocated to Chicago, accepted a long engagement at the Blue Note in 1951, and remained a fixture on the city's jazz scene until 1962. Though based in Chicago, the group also performed around the county. During a brief engagement at the Embers in New York, John Hammond heard the trio, and he subsequently produced their first recordings for the Columbia/Okeh label. After Sewell left the trio, the bass chair was filled successively by Eddie Calhoun, Richard Davis, and Israel Crosby. By 1956 Crawford too had moved on; he was replaced by the drummer Vernel Fournier.

Jamal's trio, featuring Crosby and Fournier, played at Chicago's Pershing Hotel throughout the late 1950s. Jamal enjoyed many such long-term engagements, and following classical models he admired, he often referred to himself as an artist in residence. His residency at the Pershing led to one of the most popular jazz recordings of all time, *Ahmad Jamal at the Pershing/But Not for Me*. This 1958 Chess/Argo recording rose to number 3 on *Billboard* magazine's Hot 100 Albums chart and remained there for 107 weeks. Jamal's fame spread beyond the world of the jazz cognoscenti, and his performances at the Pershing soon began to draw prestigious audiences, including stars like BILLIE HOLIDAY and SAMMY DAVIS JR.

MILES DAVIS also heard Jamal at the Pershing. He incorporated Jamal's use of space into his own playing, and he brought his pianist RED GARLAND to the Pershing to study Jamal's style. Jamal's influence can also be heard in the arrangements Gil Evans composed for Davis's large ensemble recordings. "All of my inspiration," Davis said, "comes from Ahmad Jamal. I live until he makes another record" (Granat, 61).

The sound that so impressed Davis was Jamal's disciplined, orchestral approach to the jazz trio. Where earlier bebop pianists unleashed torrents of melody over repeating harmonic cycles, Jamal paused between phrases, allowing the rhythm section space to shine through, bringing new colors and textures to the venerable jazz-trio format. He constructed his solos slowly, developing a new idea, dynamic, or texture in each successive chorus, juxtaposing delicate riffs in the piano's highest register with rhythmic chordal figures and sweeping runs. Often he linked choruses with composed ensemble interludes that transformed jazz standards into multisectional works. Jamal's arrangements were complex, but they also swung with an often delicate but insistent rhythmic drive that invigorated even his drummerless trio recordings.

The success of *Live at the Pershing* enabled Jamal to pursue diverse artistic and commercial goals. He toured North Africa; he purchased a sixteen-room home in Chicago's Hyde Park; and he bought an office building in the South Loop, where he opened his alcohol-free nightclub the Alhambra. His management company ran Cross, Jamal, and AJP Records, and he produced recordings by SHIRLEY HORN, SONNY STITT, and others. But by the early 1960s Jamal had divorced, closed the Alhambra, disbanded the trio, and moved to New York, where he lived in semiretirement until 1965.

When Jamal resumed his career, he moved beyond the formulas that had led to his earlier success. He began working with larger ensembles or with trios augmented by strings and horns, and he expanded his rhythmic sensibility, adding Latin rhythms and sometimes brooding legato passages to the delicate yet propulsive swing of his early trio work. He also made several recordings featuring the electric piano. In 1974 Jamal became Twentieth Century–Fox's only jazz artist, and in the 1980s he made five recordings for Atlantic Records. Though he plays well on these recordings, they are not as highly regarded as his early work; sometimes the orchestrations overwhelm the piano, while at other times the strings and horns seem decorative and not fully integrated with the trio. Still, these recordings include many fine moments, and they demonstrate Jamal's ambitious conception of jazz.

In the 1990s Jamal again performed with trios, incorporating the rhythmic and harmonic vocabulary of his work from the 1970s and 1980s. Some recordings from this period, like the 1993 release *Chicago Revisited: Live at Joe Segal's Jazz Showcase*, feature many of the jazz standards that are staples of Jamal's repertoire. Others, like the exciting 2003 Dreyfus Jazz release *In Search Of: Momentum*, focus on original compositions. This recording found a seventy-two-year-old Jamal at the peak of his powers. Even as he continued to grow as an artist, in the 1990s a whole new generation of listeners discovered his early classic recordings, which were heard in popular films like *The Bridges of Madison County*.

Spanning seven decades, Jamal's career was one of long, continuous, and nationally recognized artistic growth. In 1994 the National Endowment for the Arts designated him an American Jazz Master, and Yale University appointed him a DUKE ELLINGTON Fellow. In 2007 the French government inducted him into its prestigious Order of the Arts and Letters, naming him Officier de L'Ordre des Arts et des Lettres (Officer, Order of Arts and Letters). Jamal ardently maintained that jazz is a serious art form worthy of the same consideration bestowed on European concert music; he composed and performed with a discipline and dignity that reflected this belief. At the same time he achieved great popular success, which led some critics to question his artistic integrity. Through it all, he forged a unique voice as a pianist, composer, and leader that continued to inspire jazz musicians in the early twenty-first century.

FURTHER READING

Brodacki, Krystian. "Ahmad Jamal: 'I Call It American Classical Music,'" *Jazz Forum* (1987).

Granat, Zbigniew. "Transforming the Influence: Miles-Ahmad Connections Revisited," *Jazz Research Papers* 16 (1996).

Haws, Pat. "Ahmad Jamal," *Jazz Journal International* (1997).

Khan, Ashlee. "Ahmad Jamal," *Jazz Times* (July 2003).

Lyons, Leonard. *The Great Jazz Pianists Speaking of Their Lives and Music* (1983).

Panken, Ted. "'I Hate the Word Trio': But Ahmad Jamal Has Made Some of His Most Inspired Work in Years," *Down Beat* (May 2003).

Tomkins, Les. "Ahmad Jamal Speaks His Mind," *Crescendo International* (Feb. 1982).

JOHN HARRIS-BEHLING

Jamerson, James (29 Jan. 1936–2 Aug. 1983), musician, was born James Lee Jamerson Jr. in Charleston, South Carolina, son of James Lee Jamerson Sr., a shipyard worker, and Elisabeth Jamerson, a domestic worker. Jamerson developed a deep sense of isolation early in life. As a fair-skinned, blue-eyed black child, he often felt alienated from his darker-skinned family and friends. At age nine, a traumatic bicycle accident required him to undergo reconstructive surgery and spend a year recovering in a wheelchair, leaving left him with a limp for the rest of his life. Feeling alone and unable to participate in sports activities, Jamerson had time to discover and develop his affinity for music.

He learned to play piano by the age of ten, and studied trombone in elementary school. His parents divorced while he was a young teenager, and in 1953 Jamerson and his mother relocated to Detroit, where she was able to find employment. The following year, while attending Northwestern High School, Jamerson spotted an acoustic bass in the school's music room and played it, immediately taking a liking to the instrument. He decided to study bass, and before long his musical ability grew by leaps and bounds. Jamerson jumped into the Detroit music scene by playing with local blues and jazz musicians, eventually earning a reputation as the new bass phenomenon in town. An astute local businessmen named BERRY GORDY JR., who at the time was getting his new company Motown Records off the ground, saw Jamerson play on a recording session and was eager to get him on Motown's recordings. Gordy, the first African American to run a record label, employed an overwhelmingly African American roster of artists and musicians, and asked Jamerson if he'd be interested in joining his company. Jamerson accepted the offer.

Although Jamerson's first instrument was the acoustic bass, he soon realized that music trends were changing and he would need to play the newly invented electric bass in order to keep his sound current. He bought his first electric bass, a Fender Precision model, in 1961, when the singer Jackie Wilson asked Jamerson to join him on tour. Jamerson continued to perform on the road with various Motown artists until 1964, when Gordy decided that Jamerson's bass was too essential an ingredient in Motown's hit-making studio formula to do without. In addition, Motown recording artists like SMOKEY ROBINSON and MARVIN GAYE insisted on using Jamerson on all their records, so Gordy kept Jamerson permanently off the road and in the studio as part of Motown's house band nicknamed "The Funk Brothers," paying him a weekly salary.

For the next fourteen years Jamerson's bass graced a long string of Motown hits, including "Dancing in the Streets," "How Sweet It Is," "My Girl," and "I Heard It through the Grapevine." With its huge success in record sales and on radio, Motown became the preeminent record label for black music, and people all over the world were hearing and dancing to recordings that Jamerson played on. By this time he had developed his own signature style on the electric bass, utilizing a unique combination of melody and syncopated rhythms, thereby liberating the instrument from the relatively simple bass lines of his predecessors. As a part of "The Motown Sound," Jamerson became one of the most influential bassists in music history, yet ironically his name was virtually unknown due to Berry Gordy's policy of not crediting the studio musicians on Motown's albums. Jamerson's name did not appear until 1971, when Gaye released his landmark album *What's Going On* and insisted that the bassist be credited.

In 1973 Motown moved its Detroit operations to Los Angeles. Suddenly finding himself in new surroundings and no longer playing with his Detroit studio mates, Jamerson often struggled. The lack of recognition for his work amid Motown's massive success was highly frustrating to him as well, and soon Jamerson began to suffer from alcoholism and personal problems. With the music scene changing, Jamerson's career slowed down, and his health deteriorated. In 1983 at age forty-seven, he died of cirrhosis of the liver and complications from a heart attack. He left the world in virtual anonymity, never knowing the level of fame he would eventually attain.

In the years following his death, various magazine articles and documentaries eventually shed light on Jamerson's enormous musical contributions. His name became well known in the music world, and he was inducted into the Rock & Roll Hall of Fame in 2000.

FURTHER READING

George, Nelson. *Buppies, B-Boys, and Bohos: Notes on Post-Soul Black Culture* (2001).
Slutsky, Allan. *Standing in the Shadows of Motown: The Life And Music of Legendary Bassist James Jamerson* (1989).

RICK SUCHOW

James, Anna Louise (19 Jan. 1886–12 Dec. 1977), the first African American woman licensed as a pharmacist in Connecticut, was born in Hartford, Connecticut, the eighth child of Anna (Houston) and Willis Samuel James. James's father escaped from a plantation in Virginia at the age of sixteen and ventured north with the help of the Underground Railroad. In 1874 he married Anna Houston and purchased a home in the North End of Hartford the following year. As suggested by professional portraits taken in the late nineteenth century, the James family identified with the self-sufficient black middle class of Hartford. While a tiny northern black elite existed there before the Civil War, the black middle class would expand during Anna Louise James's young adulthood, peaking during the Great Migration of 1915–1919.

James lost her mother in 1894 at the age of eight and was raised by her father with the help of relatives. She graduated from Arsenal Elementary School in Hartford in 1902 and then moved to Old Saybrook, Connecticut, where she was cared for by her sister, Bertha James Lane, and Bertha's husband, Peter Clark Lane. After graduating from Old Saybrook High School in 1905, Anna Louise James attended the Brooklyn College of Pharmacy in Brooklyn, New York. She graduated in 1908, the only woman in her class. In this year James's sister Bertha gave birth to a daughter, Ann Lane, who as ANN PETRY would become another family pioneer as the first best-selling African American woman author. Embarking on a career in medicine in the early twentieth century, James defied the burgeoning scientific racism and sexism of the day, which argued for innate differences between whites and non-whites, and between men and women. James was licensed as a pharmacist in 1909 but was initially rejected from the Connecticut Pharmaceutical Association (CPA) because of her sex. The CPA suggested she join the pharmacists' wives in the auxiliary. This was, in James's view, an absurd recommendation, considering that she had not only assumed a professional role but had also rejected a domestic one, claiming that "it never entered my mind to get married" (*Middletown (CT.) Press*, 16 Oct. 1967).

James operated her own drugstore in Hartford until 1911, when she moved back to Old Saybrook and went into business with her brother-in-law Peter Lane. In 1917 Lane returned to work in Hartford and James became the sole owner of the drugstore, renaming it the James Pharmacy. After the passage of the Nineteenth Amendment in 1920, James became one of the first registered women voters in the state of Connecticut. James would be active in Republican Party politics and town government throughout her life.

Upon her retirement James testified to the influence of her family on her professional life, recalling that "there were pharmacists in my family as long as I can remember" (*Middletown Press*, 16 Oct. 1967). James's older sister, Helen Evelyn James, served as a role model, and nurtured in Anna Louise the self-confidence crucial for a black woman to forge a successful professional career. Writing in October 1904 from Atlanta University where she was studying with W. E. B. DuBois, Helen instructed her younger sister Louise, as she was called, to "finish your schooling" and assured her that then she would be "ready for any school that you desire entering" (James papers, box 3, folder 90). Like DuBois, the James family supported higher education and cultural endeavor for African Americans, resisting the more conservative approach of BOOKER T. WASHINGTON and his call for industrial education for black people.

Anna Louise James would have to rely on her family's legacy of toughness and perseverance to maintain a business in a town that was less than 3 percent African American and was "an essentially hostile environment for a black family" (Petry, 257). James's nieces were forbidden to call her "Aunt Louise" in public for fear that the residents of the town would take the liberty of doing the same, in accordance with the racial tradition of whites addressing blacks by their first names. "She was always to be Miss James," remembered her niece Ann Lane Petry. "She felt she should have all the dignity of being called 'miss'" (*Hartford Courant*, 2 Feb. 1991). James retired in 1967 at age eighty-one, closing the pharmacy that had been family-owned for seventy-two years.

The town's public and private recollections of James emphasize her generosity, hospitality, and compassion. In 1974 the Old Saybrook Veterans of Foreign Wars honored James as Citizen of the Year and celebrated her role as a public servant, one who would cash checks and make small loans, a "keeper of keys" for the local Congregational Church and for summer residents during the off-season. James was honored a year later by the Republican town committee for her fifty-five years of party membership. After James's death in Old Saybrook in 1977 her nieces received a flood of condolences, many of which related personal stories of her kindness—a fee waived in a time of need, a parenting book given free of charge to an adoptive mother, her gentle guidance of young employees. The public memory of James, however, elides matters of race. In his recollections of working at James Pharmacy as a youth, a leading citizen of Old Saybrook averred that she never experienced racial discrimination or insults (*Hartford Courant*, 2 Feb. 1991). In recognition of Anna Louise James's legacy, James Pharmacy was added to the Register of Historic Places in 1994.

The novelist Ann Petry remembers her aunt as "a most remarkable woman—beautiful, brilliant, compassionate" (Petry, 261). Petry's tribute encapsulates the public memory of Anna Louise James, but the historical record presents many inconsistencies that make it difficult to distinguish between history and legend. In part these factual discrepancies reflect the efforts of African Americans to reinvent themselves in the wake of slavery and the ravages of Jim Crow. Although Anna Louise James lived most of her life quietly in a small New England town, her life story is remarkable in that it stands in opposition to the racial and gender injustices of the twentieth century.

FURTHER READING

The papers of Anna Louise James, which include diaries, correspondence, clippings, photographs, certificates, and financial records, are located at the Schlesinger Library, Radcliffe Institute for Advanced Study, Harvard University, Cambridge, MA.

Petry, Ann. "Ann Petry." *Contemporary Authors Autobiography Series* (1998).

Petry, Elisabeth. *Can Anything Beat White?: A Black Family's Letters* (2005)

Obituary: *Middletown Press*, 13 Dec. 1977.

ERIN ROYSTON BATTAT

James, C. L. R. (4 Jan. 1901–31 May 1989), revolutionary socialist writer, was born Cyril Lionel Robert James in the village of Caroni on the Caribbean island of Trinidad, a British colony, to Robert Alexander James, a schoolteacher and principal of modest means, and Ida Elizabeth ("Bessie") James, a devout Anglican and avid reader of English literature. His parents nicknamed him "Nello," a name later used among friends. His earliest education took place under his strict father in a tiny schoolhouse in North Trace. At age nine James won a scholarship to Queen's Royal College (QRC), the island's best school, in the capital, Port of Spain. At QRC between 1911 and 1918 James indulged his love for the game of cricket and English novels (Thackeray's *Vanity Fair* was a particular favorite), to the detriment of his grades. His teachers, as had his family, impressed upon him the importance of proper manners and fair play. In his celebrated autobiographical exploration of cricket, *Beyond a Boundary* (1963), James wrote,It was only long years after that I understood the limitation on spirit, vision and self-respect which was imposed on us by the fact that our masters, our curriculum, our code of morals, everything began from the basis that Britain was the source of all light and leading, and our business was to admire, wonder, imitate, learn; our criterion of success was to have succeeded in approaching that distant ideal—to attain it was, of course, impossible. (29–30)Be that as it may, an ethics of fair play informed James's subsequent objections to imperialism and Stalinism.

After graduating, James taught school and tutored students, among them Eric Williams, later the first prime minister of Trinidad and Tobago. He read MARCUS GARVEY's *Negro World*, but his primary interests were athletic and literary. In the 1920s he published several short stories and drafted his only novel, *Minty Alley*, published in 1936. James's political fires were kindled as he watched Arthur Andrew Cipriani, president of the Trinidad Workmen's Association, win election to the island's legislative council. In *The Life of Captain Cipriani: An Account of British Government in the West Indies* (1932), James hailed Cipriani's mobilization of the urban poor but passed beyond Cipriani in calling for West Indian self-government.

Sensing that in Trinidad he would be limited to civil service employment and attracted to the literary cornucopia of the metropolis, James departed for England in 1932. Initially he was the guest of Learie Constantine, a Trinidadian who had become an English cricket sensation, and he began to cover cricket for the Manchester *Guardian*. Discussions with trade unionists and members of the Independent Labour Party led James to read the left-wing classics. Like many others during the economic depression, with fascism on the march, he declared himself for Marxism. He preferred Trotsky to Stalin, and in 1934 he joined the Marxist Group, a small revolutionary socialist organization. He wrote *World Revolution, 1917–1936: The Rise and Fall of the Communist International* (1937), a lengthy assessment of the degeneration of the Soviet Union and its foreign policy, and was one of two British delegates at the founding of the Fourth International, an association of Trotskyist parties, in Paris in 1938. Simultaneously he became immersed in Pan-Africanism, associating with Jomo Kenyatta, T. Ras Makonnen, and GEORGE PADMORE (who as Malcolm Nurse had been his childhood friend) in opposing the Italian invasion of Abyssinia (later Ethiopia) in 1935. These diasporic intellectuals resented the Communist softening of anti-imperialist criticism of Britain and France because of the Soviet desire for collective security with liberal-democratic states against Nazism. Together they established the International African Service Bureau, a militant organization dedicated to African independence, to which only those of African descent could belong.

His anticolonial and revolutionary commitments informed James's research into the San Domingo revolution of 1791 led by Toussaint L'Ouverture. Inspired by the French revolution, San Domingo's revolution eventuated in the overthrow of slavery, the casting off of French colonialism, and the establishment of an independent state, Haiti, in 1804. James's play *Toussaint L'Ouverture* was performed in London with PAUL ROBESON as lead actor in 1936, and in 1938 James published *The Black Jacobins*, a history of the San Domingo events informed by Lenin's conception of revolutionary leadership and Trotsky's theory of permanent revolution, namely that in underdeveloped nations revolutions spill beyond their initial objectives and require both independence and international solidarity for their success.

"The race question is subsidiary to the class question in politics," James wrote in *The Black Jacobins*, "and to think of imperialism in terms of race is disastrous. But to neglect the racial factor as merely incidental is an error only less grave than to make it fundamental" (283). Trotsky, in exile in Mexico, desired James's counsel on precisely such matters and beckoned James to North America. In 1938 James departed for the United States to speak on behalf of the Socialist Workers Party (SWP), whose several thousand members made it the Fourth International's largest section. James intended merely to visit, but he would remain in the United States for fifteen years, mostly residing in New York City. His nationwide tour was a great success. James's lilting accent, elegant bearing, handsomeness, and ability to speak for hours without notes impressed his American comrades. James in turn found American culture, from the comics to the movies, absorbing, but he was disconcerted by a level of racism sharper than he had experienced in Trinidad or England.

After the tour James went into clandestine mode. He wrote under an array of pseudonyms, and his life centered ever more narrowly on the confined space of small socialist groups. In 1939 James visited Trotsky in Mexico to discuss "the Negro question," but when the SWP split apart in 1940 over a host of interrelated issues, James sided with the minority against Trotsky, and he helped form the breakaway Workers Party led by Max Shachtman. Within the new party James in turn formed a faction, joining with the Russian-born philosopher Raya Dunayevskaya to create the "Johnson-Forest Tendency" (an amalgam of their respective party names). This tendency, in which Grace Lee and JAMES BOGGS played significant roles, characterized the Soviet Union as state capitalist, was devoted to Hegelian dialectics, exuded revolutionary optimism, rejected top-down leadership (in theory if not practice), and perceived incipient resistance in popular culture. In 1947 the Johnson-Forest Tendency, which never numbered more than seventy members, returned to the SWP before breaking with Trotskyism altogether in 1951 and becoming independent, taking on the name Correspondence.

James was a charismatic leader. His devotees literally sat at his feet. With a few, however, he had less regal relations. He courted a young Los Angeles model and actress, Constance Webb, and they married in 1946 (and again in 1948, after legal affirmation of his divorce from Juanita Samuel Young, a Venezuelan whom he married in Trinidad in 1929 and left behind upon moving to England). His involvement with Webb was passionate, and in 1949 she gave birth to a son named after James, with the nickname "Nobby." The couple formed a close friendship with the novelist RICHARD WRIGHT and his wife.

Some of James's most important writings were produced in his American years. His article "The Revolutionary Answer to the Negro Problem in the United States" (1948) characterized independent black struggles as vital to American history and valid from a class perspective. *Notes on Dialectics* (1948) applied Hegelian reason to the internal debates of the revolutionary left. *State Capitalism and World Revolution* (1951) defended the proposition that bureaucratic communism and capitalism are exploitative class societies. *Mariners, Renegades, and Castaways* (1953) was a meditation on Herman Melville's novel *Moby-Dick*. During the 1950s James worked on a manuscript on American culture published posthumously as *American Civilization* (1993). Notwithstanding his enthusiasm for America, James was arrested in the McCarthy era, interned at Ellis Island, and deported back to Britain in 1953. By then his marriage to Webb had dissolved.

In London in 1956 James married Selma Weinstein, a Brooklyn native thirty years his junior, a marriage that lasted about a decade. He met MARTIN LUTHER KING JR. and CORETTA SCOTT KING in London in 1957, kept in contact with American followers like Martin Glaberman and George Rawick, and was able to visit the United States to teach and speak on occasion after 1967, exerting a limited but salient influence on the New Left of the 1960s and 1970s. An éminence grise at the height of Black Power and Third World national liberation movements, he advised the revolutionaries Walter Rodney of Guyana and Maurice Bishop of Grenada during their London phases in the 1960s, visited Cuba and Kwame Nkrumah's Ghana, and returned to Trinidad between 1958 and 1962, though his relations quickly soured with Eric Williams, whose government he judged increasingly authoritarian (a criticism he also made of Nkrumah). James experienced physical infirmity after a 1962 auto accident but was an active Marxist to the end, seeing events in Hungary in 1956, Czechoslovakia and France in 1968, and Poland in 1980–1981 as proof of the self-generating revolutionary creativity of the working class.

FURTHER READING

The C. L. R. James Collection is held at the University of the West Indies' Saint Augustine Campus in Trinidad and Tobago. James's correspondence with Constance Webb is held by the Schomburg Center for Research in Black Culture, New York.

James, C. L. R. *Beyond a Boundary* (1963).

Buhle, Paul. *C. L. R. James: The Artist as Revolutionary* (1988).

Buhle, Paul, ed. *C. L. R. James: His Life and Work* (1986).

Cudjoe, Selwyn R., and William Cain, eds. *C. L. R. James: His Intellectual Legacies* (1995).

Worcester, Kent. *C. L. R. James: A Political Biography* (1996).

Obituary: *New York Times*, 2 June 1989.

CHRISTOPHER PHELPS

James, Charles Edmund (17 July 1866–13 Sept. 1923), labor leader, was born in St. Paul, Minnesota, the eldest child of Maria Louisa (Griffin), a homemaker, and Edmund James, who was employed for twenty-five years as head porter at a St. Paul hotel. Both of James's parents came to Minnesota before the Civil War. Edmund James, who had arrived in St.-Paul in 1856, was one of the leaders of the successful struggle after the Civil War to extend the right to vote to African Americans in Minnesota. His wife Louisa arrived in Minnesota even earlier; her parents, James and Mary Griffin, were among the first settlers in Wright County, emigrating from Pennsylvania and homesteading near the town of Buffalo, Minnesota, in 1855.

Little is known of James's formal education. By 1881, fifteen-year-old James had begun work at the P. R. L. Hardenbergh Co. in St. Paul's manufacturing and warehouse district. Here James began, over several years, to master the craft of leather cutting. This was a skilled trade, and much in demand. Leather was utilized not only for virtually all footwear but also for the saddles and harnesses. In 1889 James married Celia Roberson; they had one daughter, Lucelia.

James worked at this trade for the next twenty years, until he was fired in retaliation for his role as a union organizer just after the turn of the century, while working at the North Star Shoe Company in Minneapolis. Yet in spite of his lengthy tenure in this industry, during which several shoe workers' unions came and went, the first documented evidence of James's participation in the labor movement comes after eighteen years as a shoe cutter. Existing records are too incomplete to tell whether James might have belonged to the early local assembly of the Knights of Labor, but in late 1899, after the previous shoe unions in Minneapolis and St. Paul had dissolved, a new effort was made to organize, centered at first on the North Star Shoe Company. The Boot and Shoe Workers Union Local (BSWU) 204 was quickly established, and Charles James was elected its first president. Shortly afterward he found work in St. Paul and helped to re-organize shoe workers there into three new locals.

In 1902 James was elected the union's district business agent and remained a full-time officer, traveling widely throughout the Midwest for the next twenty years. He organized shoe workers in cities and towns in Iowa, Wisconsin, and Illinois, as well as Minnesota. He delivered scores of speeches before national union conventions, farmers groups, city central bodies, and local unions, advocating organization and the union label.

In 1902 James was concurrently elected to the first of three six-month terms as the (unpaid) president of St. Paul Trades and Labor Assembly. He went on to serve seven more years as the assembly's recording secretary. The following year he was elected to the General Executive Board of the BSWU international union. James served continuously on this body until his death. For nearly a quarter-century he was one of the most prominent and recognizable figures the Minnesota labor movement had in the field.

From the time James burst onto the labor scene at age thirty-three in 1899, the labor movement seemed to heap every possible honor, office, and affection on him. The *Minnesota Union Advocate* editor Cornelius Guiney described him as "one of (the labor movement's) most capable, zealous and knowing representatives" (*Minnesota Union Advocate*, 13 Dec. 1907). He was, Guiney wrote, "in dead earnest, has ability to burn [and] is a strong, influential man among his fellow unionists" (*Minnesota Union Advocate*, 8 Feb. 1907).

In addition to labor organizing, James was a leading participant in the St. Paul African American community. Activists formed civil rights organizations throughout the 1880s and 1890s, held protest meetings, and solicited support from the white community. All this was written about in the daily newspapers and the black press, with numerous mentions of James's participation. Along with other leading members of the African American community, he was an active member of the Republican Party. They were a distinct and identifiable component of the city, county, and state conventions of the party. In April 1892 James was one of seven African American delegates to the Ramsey County convention of the Republican Party, which was attended by a total of 116 delegates.

In an era when most unions denied membership to African Americans, Charles James became one of the best-known and most-admired leaders of the Minnesota labor movement. Upon his death in 1923 the Boot and Shoe Workers Union noted, "Brother James joined this union in the early and struggling period of its existence, and has been one of the important individual factors in its growth.... He was a sterling trade union character, much loved and respected" (*Boot and Shoe Workers Journal*, Oct. 1923). James was buried in an unmarked grave in Forest Lawn Cemetery, St. Paul, along with his wife and daughter.

In the summer of 1997 the labor press reported on the election of Bridgette Williams as president of the Kansas City AFL-CIO. At the time she was identified as the first African American to head a major city labor council. With the rediscovery of Charles James we now know she was not the first.

FURTHER READING

The national records of the Boot and Shoe workers Union are held at the Wisconsin Historical Society, Madison, Wisconsin. Other major references to James are found in the microfilm collections of *The Appeal* and the *Minnesota Union Advocate* at the Minnesota Historical Society, St. Paul, Minnesota.

Riehle, David. "When Labor Knew a Man Named Charles James," *St. Paul Union Advocate*, Dec. 1997.

Obituaries: *Northwestern Bulletin*, 15 Sept. 1923; *The Appeal*, 22 Sept. 1923; and *Boot and Shoe Workers Journal*, Oct. 1923.

DAVID RIEHLE

James, Daniel, Jr. (11 Feb. 1920–25 Feb. 1978), U.S. Air Force officer, was born in Pensacola, Florida, the youngest child of Lillie Anna Brown, an educator, and Daniel James Sr., a laborer. Only six of the James's seventeen children were alive when Daniel was born. Considered "a gift" by his parents, James began his education under the tutelage of his mother, who, disenchanted with the segregated Pensacola schools, opened her own school, the Lillie Anna James Private School. While Lillie Anna taught him arithmetic, patriotism, religion, English, spelling, physical education, literature, "good, common sense," and public speaking, his father stressed hard work, academic excellence, and perseverance in the face of racism. Both parents provided homespun directives. According to his mother, there was an eleventh commandment: "Thou Shalt Not Quit. Prove that you can compete on an equal basis." James's parents gave him the desire to succeed, the ability to enjoy the humor in life, and an appreciation of freedom and fair play, attributes that served him well. The drone of navy aircraft flown from nearby Pensacola Naval Air Station helped mitigate the signs and realities of the Jim Crow South. The older he became, the more James watched the sky. As a teenager, he got to know the pilots at the local airfield, who took him up in old seaplanes and fighter aircraft in return for small chores.

At age thirteen James left his mother's school and enrolled in Pensacola's Washington High School. Soon after, in a nod to his older brother Charles—a football star, college graduate, and teacher—James

Daniel "Chappy" James Jr., U.S. Air Force General, announces his retirement at a news conference in Washington, D.C., 25 January 1978. (AP Images.)

announced that he would like to be called "Little Chappie—like my big brother!" (McGovern, 19).

Just before his high school graduation in 1937, James's plans to attend college were nearly derailed by the death of his father. His mother and siblings, however, assured him that they would help with his tuition, and in September 1937 he enrolled at the Tuskegee Institute in Alabama. Unsure of his career goal, James chose to major in physical education. Strong and more than six feet tall, he won acclaim as an athlete and student leader. His academic career, however, almost came to an end when he was expelled following a high-spirited escapade involving a few of his fellow students.

Luckily he was saved when an experimental civilian flying training program at the college was instituted, to determine the feasibility of training African American men as military pilots under the government-sponsored Civilian Pilot Training Program. James qualified for training and began the career he had dreamed about, not only learning to fly but also teaching others in the Army Air Corps Aviation Cadet Program, some of whom would become members of the Tuskegee Airmen. In March 1942 he received a B.S. in Physical Education and completed his pilot training under the Civilian Pilot Training Program. He fell in love with Dorothy Watkins of Tuskegee, Alabama, in 1938. They married on 3 November 1942 and had two sons, Daniel III and Claude, and a daughter, Danice.

James enlisted in the army air forces and was commissioned a second lieutenant in 1943. The military forces were rigidly segregated, and officers and enlisted men of color faced the tensions of racism in both civilian and military life. On one occasion James was arrested for staging a sit-in at a whites-only officers' club. As the emcee of a touring air force show called *Operation Happiness*, James managed to get each base to desegregate their base theaters temporarily. When President Harry Truman declared racial segregation in the military illegal in 1948, it was exactly what Chappie James wanted to hear.

James completed fighter pilot combat training at Selfridge Field, Michigan. Assigned within the United States until September 1949, he was then stationed in the Philippines as a flight leader in the Twelfth Fighter Bomber Wing at Clark Field. In 1950 he was sent to Korea, where he flew 101 combat missions in F-51 and F-101 aircraft. On one day he was shot down, returned to his base aboard a marine tank, and then flew another mission. Upon his return to the United States in 1951, he was assigned to an all-weather jet fighter squadron (the Fifty-eighth Fighter-Interceptor Squadron). Against the backdrop of his stellar military work, he shone in community relations, which in 1954 garnered him the Massachusetts Junior Chamber of Commerce Young Man of the Year Award. Promoted to major in 1955, he became the first black officer to command an integrated 437th Fighter-Interceptor Squadron.

In 1957 he graduated from the Air Command and Staff College at Maxwell Air Force Base, Alabama, and became a staff officer in the Air Staff Division of the deputy chief of staff for operations. Transferred in July 1960 to the Royal Air Force Station at Bentwaters, England, he served first as assistant director of operations and then as director of operations for the Eighty-first Tactical Fighter Wing. He soon became commander of the Ninety-second Tactical Fighter Squadron and, later, deputy commander for operations for the Eighty-first Wing. In 1964 he was transferred to Davis-Monthan Air Force Base, Arizona, as director of operations

with the 4453d Combat Crew Training Wing. These assignments significantly broadened his expertise and experience with air force operations.

In 1966 James entered the Vietnam War as deputy commander for operations of the Eighth Tactical Fighter Wing, becoming vice commander for the wing in June 1967. He flew seventy-eight combat missions into North Vietnam against the most stubborn and dangerous defenses and was one of the leaders of the now famous Bolo MiG sweep, destroying seven Communist MiG-21s, the highest kill of any mission in that war. James was transferred to Florida and Eglin Air Force Base in 1967 and to Wheelus Air Base in Libya in 1969, where he commanded the 7272d Fighter Training Wing. He became deputy assistant secretary of defense for public affairs in 1970 and principal deputy assistant secretary of defense in 1973.

Widely known for his speaking abilities, especially on the topics of Americanism and patriotism, James received notice both nationally and internationally. He was awarded the George Washington Freedom Foundation Medal twice in the 1960s and the Arnold Air Society Eugene M. Zuckert Award in 1970 for "outstanding contributions to Air Force professionalism" (quoted in Phelps, 345). The citation for this award recognizes him as a "fighter pilot with a magnificent record, public speaker, and eloquent spokesman for the American Dream we so rarely achieve" (Phelps, 345).

James was promoted to four-star general on 1 September 1975, becoming the first African American to hold the highest rank in the U.S. Air Force. In March 1977 he was assigned to the North American Air Defense Command as commander of the U.S. Air Force Aerospace Defense Command, with operational authority over American and Canadian strategic forces, a position that gave him the authority to initiate a nuclear attack. James retired from active service on 2 February 1978 and died less than one month later in the Air Force Academy Hospital, near Colorado Springs, Colorado.

FURTHER READING

Astor, Gerald. *The Right to Fight: A History of African Americans in the Military* (1998).

Dabbs, Henry E. *Black Brass: Black Generals and Admirals in the Armed Forces of the United States*, 2d ed. (1997).

McGovern, James R. *Black Eagle: General Daniel "Chappie" James, Jr.* (1985).

Phelps, Joseph A. *Chappie: America's First Black Four-star General* (1992).

Rose, Robert A. *Lonely Eagles: The Story of America's Black Air Force in World War II* (1980).

Obituary: *New York Times*, 26 Feb. 1978.

J. ALFRED PHELPS

James, Elmore (27 Jan. 1918–24 May 1963), blues singer and guitarist, was born Elmore Brooks in rural Holmes County, Mississippi, the son of Leola Brooks, a fifteen-year-old farmworker; the name of his father is not known. Elmore later took the surname of his stepfather, Joe Willie James. He showed an early interest in music, constructing such homemade instruments as a one-string guitar, or "diddley bow," before graduating to a regular guitar and performing locally while still in his teens.

In 1937 James's musical world broadened when his parents moved to the Turner Brothers Plantation in the Delta town of Belzoni, Mississippi. There he purchased a better guitar, entered a brief marriage to Josephine Harris, and met two musicians, the guitarist ROBERT JOHNSON and the harmonica wizard Aleck Miller (later known as SONNY BOY WILLIAMSON II), who would change his life. James was so impressed by Johnson's slide guitar technique that he added Johnson's "I Believe I'll Dust My Broom" to his repertoire. It became his signature song. Johnson and Miller eventually moved on (Johnson was murdered the next year), but James and Miller kept in touch and remained close for the rest of their lives.

Working with Miller and later with a combo that included saxophone, trumpet, and drums, James stayed relatively close to home for the next few years, alternating his music with seasonal farm work. Despite lifelong heart troubles, he entered the navy in 1943, serving in Guam. Discharged in 1945, he put together an electric band in Memphis, performing with a cousin, the guitarist Homesick James Williamson, or with the guitarist EDDIE TAYLOR. In 1947 he married Georgianna Crump and resumed performing around Belzoni. Periodically he visited his former partner Miller, who had become the South's foremost blues radio personality. The two of them teamed up briefly in 1947 to do a radio show pitching Talaho, an alcohol-based tonic made by a local drugstore. The show, broadcast across the heart of the Delta, brought new fame to James, allowing him to meet and work with other musicians, including Greenville pianist Willie Love and the guitarist ARTHUR CRUDUP.

In 1951 James traveled with Miller to Jackson, Mississippi, where Miller, by now performing as Sonny Boy Williamson, had a date to record for the Trumpet label. James was willing to play backup for Williamson but was reluctant to record his own tune, "Dust My Broom." According to legend, a surreptitious recording of the tune was made during a rehearsal in August 1951. With another artist on the flip side of the record, "Dust My Broom" was released in early 1952 and broke onto the rhythm and blues charts that April. The unexpected success drew interest from Trumpet's competitors, particularly Joe Bihari, who owned several West Coast labels in partnership with his two brothers. James was still under contract to Trumpet, however—although he never recorded another song for the label—so Bihari was leery of releasing any James material.

Finally, in 1952, Bihari lured James to Chicago to record; the resulting sides came out on Bihari's Meteor label. Other sessions for Bihari followed, as did an apparently illegal session for Checker. Over an eleven-year recording career, James had releases on Chess and Mel London's Chief label, both based in-Chicago, and on Bobby Robinson's New York-based Fire label and its subsidiaries. The backup group on many of these sides was tabbed the Broomdusters: Johnny Jones on piano, Odie Payne, drums, J. T. Brown, tenor sax, and, at times, Homesick James Williamson, second guitar.

James returned to Mississippi in 1958, working briefly as a radio disc jockey in Jackson, but soon returned to steady club dates in Chicago, where he often worked with Big Bill Hill, a club owner, promoter, and disc jockey. By 1961 James was again touring with his own band, but after trouble with the musicians' union he returned to Jackson. Despite failing health he continued to perform close to home for the next two years. In 1963 Big Bill Hill resolved the union problem and brought James to Chicago for a comeback. Before his appearance at Hill's Copacabana club, however, James suffered a fatal heart attack at the home of Homesick James. His body was returned to Mississippi and buried in the town of Durant. He was inducted into the Blues Foundation Hall of Fame in 1980 and the Rock and Roll Hall of Fame in 1992.

One could argue that Elmore James, like his mentor Robert Johnson, became more famous in death than he ever was in life. As one of the first artists to take Delta blues and electrify it, he was a clear link between down-home blues and world rock. His sound was emulated by rock artists, including Eric Clapton, Johnny Winter, George Thorogood, and the Allman Brothers. Possibly because of his failure to work with a single powerful record label or perhaps because of his down-home sound, James never achieved the stature of MUDDY WATERS or HOWLIN' WOLF. Still, his music was popular with audiences in rural juke joints and big-city clubs alike.

Although the body of his work has at times been judged repetitive—often the mark of a traditional artist who achieves a signature sound—James's best works were transcendent. On such songs as "Dust My Broom," "The Sky Is Crying," "Rollin' and Tumblin'," and "My Bleeding Heart," the combined force of his searing, driving slide technique and his hoarse, impassioned vocals could be breathtaking. Big Bill Hill put it this way: "No one touched me more than this man ... I mean blues-wise, because he did it from [his heart]. No imitation—originality.... An old timer, he played the blues because he felt the blues and he lived them." Fellow Delta blues artist Big Joe Williams echoed Hill: "Elmore, he had a way of playing and singing, nobody could get close to it. It come from his heart. And like he sung, he lived ... he sung it real hard."

FURTHER READING

Weinstock, Ron. "Elmore James: A BRQ Profile," *Blues Revue Quarterly* 12 (Spring 1994).

DISCOGRAPHY

Franz, Steve. *Elmore James: The Ultimate Guide to the Master of the Slide* (1994).

Leadbitter, Mike, and Neil Slaven, *Blues Records, January 1943 to December 1966* (1968).

This entry is taken from the *American National Biography* and is published here with the permission of the American Council of Learned Societies.

BARRY LEE PEARSON AND
BILL MCCULLOCH

James, Etta (25 Jan. 1938–20 Jan. 2012), blues, soul, jazz, and R&B singer, often referred to as the "Matriarch of the Blues," was born Jamesetta Hawkins in Los Angeles, California, to Dorothy Hawkins. Her mother, who was unmarried at the time of James's birth, said little about her father's identity, but occasionally dropped hints that he was a famous white man. Although it was never confirmed conclusively, James came to believe that her father was Rudolph Wanderone, better known as Minnesota Fats, the world-famous pool player; the two would not meet until 1987. Because of her mother's inability to care for her, James lived with Lula and Jesse Rogers, the proprietors of the rooming house where her mother was renting a room at the time. The Rogerses had no children of their own, and Lula Rogers raised James as her own daughter.

At the age of five, James began singing at the St. Paul Baptist Church in Los Angeles. She took voice lessons from James Earle Hines, her first musical mentor, and piano lessons from his wife. Years later in her autobiography she wrote that she "wasn't much on practicing" and that "singing was the only thing that suited my impatient nature" (James and Ritz, 19). Singing was her comfort, and it provided her with an emotional outlet. As an adolescent, she battled weight problems that she would continue struggling to overcome throughout her adult life. Furthermore, her fair complexion and straight hair often made her an outsider, both to blacks who accused her of "acting white," and to whites who accused her of trying to pass for white. "But once people got to know me and heard my raspy voice sounding like I came from way 'cross Georgia, they left me alone. They saw I wasn't putting on airs. And when I got older and started cursing bad as any jet-black nappy-headed man or woman, there was no mistaking me for white" (James and Ritz, 22).

After the death of her adoptive mother in 1950, James went to San Francisco to live with an aunt and uncle. But no matter where she lived, her birth mother, Dorothy, would come in and out of her life, creating an unstable home environment that led to a growing rebelliousness in James. Bouncing from one school to another, she eventually joined a female gang, which led to her receiving thirty days in juvenile detention for fighting. As her relationship with her mother worsened, she became more estranged from other family members as well.

It was during this time, in 1952, that she formed a singing trio with two sisters, Jean and Abysinia Mitchell, called the Creolettes. After the bandleader and promoter Johnny Otis auditioned them, he asked the girls (who were, he suspected, underage) to accompany him to Los Angeles to make records. Only fourteen at the time, James forged her mother's signature on a permission slip, quit the ninth grade, and headed to Los Angeles. Otis renamed the group the Peaches and inverted Jamesetta's first name, thus creating her stage name, Etta James. The R&B singer HANK BALLARD had just recorded a hit single "Work with Me, Annie;" as a reply to Ballard, James wrote and the Peaches performed "Roll with Me, Henry," which Otis recorded in 1954. Because the title was too suggestive for the times, the song was renamed "The Wallflower (Dance with Me, Henry)" and was released in 1955. James was only seventeen when the song reached number 1 on the R&B charts.

Shortly after the success of "The Wallflower (Dance with Me, Henry)," the Peaches and James split, and James would pursue a solo career. Her song, "Good Rockin' Daddy," reached number six on the R&B charts, but other James songs did not fare as well. In the 1950s James toured with such greats as Charles Brown, OTIS REDDING, and JOHNNY "GUITAR" WATSON; she would later cite Watson as the most significant influence on her style.

In 1960 James signed a recording contract with Chess Records, a musical relationship she maintained for fifteen years. She recorded some of her most memorable hits with Chess and reached the height of her stardom with that label. She released many successful duets, including "If I Can't Have You," (1960) with her then-boyfriend Harvey Fuqua, lead singer of the Moonglows.

James's greatest success, however, came as a solo performer. One of her first singles released by Chess in 1960, "All I Could Do Was Cry," reached number two on the R&B charts. Leonard Chess, one of the founders of Chess Records, viewed James as a classy ballad singer with pop crossover appeal. In 1961 she released one of her first pop-oriented songs, "At Last," which became her signature song. Defying easy categorization and displaying tremendous range and versatility, James never forgot her rough beginnings or her gospel roots, which would be reflected in later hits such as "Trust in Me" (1961) and "Something's Got a Hold on Me" (1962).

The mid-1960s were difficult for James. She endured troubled personal relationships and physical abuse, served time in Chicago's Cook County Jail for drug possession and writing bad checks, and she battled heroin and cocaine addiction. After a dry spell with almost no hits for four years, in 1967 James traveled to Rick Hall's Fame Studios in Muscle Shoals, Alabama, during which time she created some of her all-time classics—songs that would reflect the southern soul influence that Muscle Shoals had become famous for. "Tell Mama" became a top-10 hit on the R&B charts that year, and other songs, such as "Security" and "I'd Rather Go Blind" were just as successful. Her songs continued to chart during the 1970s, but her hits were becoming less frequent. Having become a mother, she tried to maintain a stable home environment for her two children. Her first son, Donto, was born in 1968; a second son, Sametto, was born in 1976. She married Artis Mills in 1969.

After several lean years (two of which she spent in a psychiatric hospital), James moved to Atlantic Records, and in 1988 she released *Seven Year Itch*, an album that was more soul-oriented than most of her previous recordings. Her 1992 album *The Right Time* was another R&B album produced by Elektra

Records. James was inducted into the Rock and Roll Hall of Fame in 1993. She continued to perform throughout the 1990s, the musical styles on her later albums ranging from pop to blues to soul. Her onstage performances have been described as sassy, sometimes gritty, and even sexually suggestive. James struggled with obesity for most of her life. At one point during the late 1990s she weighed more than 350 pounds, experienced problems with her knees and mobility, and sometimes performed in a wheelchair. In spite of her health problems, she continued to record and release albums, including *Matriarch of-the Blues* (2000) and *Burnin' Down the House* (2002). She was inducted into the Blues Hall of Fame in 2001.

In 2003 she underwent gastric bypass surgery and lost more than two hundred pounds. That same year, James received a star on the Hollywood Walk of Fame as well as a Grammy Lifetime Achievement Award. In 2004 *Rolling Stone* ranked her number 62 on their list of the One-Hundred Greatest Artists of All Time. Also in 2004 she released the album *Blues to the Bone*, and in 2006 RCA Records released her collection of pop standards, *All the Way*.

In 2012, James died in Riverside, California. The stated cause of death was complications of leukemia, although James at the time was undergoing treatment for a number of other health problems, including dementia.

In James's autobiography, *Rage to Survive*, coauthor David Ritz writes that Etta could "deliver her sultry jazz ballads and bone-chilling blues with an in-your-face ferocity, managing her great weight with grace or vulgarity, depending upon her mood.... She'd start by boasting how she felt like 'breakin' up somebody's home.' But an hour or two later she'd be singing *Take Me to the River*, a song of baptismal redemption, traveling from sin to salvation while expressing her sense of heartache, joy, defiance, sexual frustration and sexual satisfaction, celebration and loss, life and death" (James and Ritz, x). One of the twentieth century's most uniquely talented R&B and soul pioneers, Etta James was truly an American original.

FURTHER READING

James, Etta, and David Ritz. *Rage to Survive: The Etta James Story* (1995).
Welding, Pete, and Toby Byron, eds. *Bluesland: Portraits of Twelve Major American Blues Masters* (1991).
Obituary: *New York Times*, 20 January 2012.

ROBERT A. PRATT

James, Miles (1829–28 Aug. 1871), Civil War soldier and Medal of Honor winner, was born in Princess Anne County, Virginia. Likely a slave before the war, he listed his occupation as that of a farmer upon joining the Union army sometime in mid-1863 at Portsmouth, Virginia. The enlistment of Miles James, ALFRED HILTON, EDWARD RATCLIFF, and thousands of other blacks from the South in 1863 signaled a sea change in opinion in the federal government and the upper echelon of the Union army. For both political and racial reasons, Union generals such as George McClellan and William Tecumseh Sherman had vigorously opposed the idea of recruiting black troops; both men vociferously opposed the idea of racial equality and did not believe that African Americans could be effective soldiers. While the use of black troops would not gain full acceptance until mid-1863 with the establishment of the Colored Troop Bureau, some forward-thinking Union officers laid the groundwork by establishing such regiments even earlier. The first fully recognized black regiment raised in the war was the First South Carolina Volunteer Regiment, composed mainly of blacks from the area of Hilton Head, South Carolina, and the Sea Islands, and organized by General David Hunter in April 1862 and later commanded by the abolitionist minister, Colonel Thomas Wentworth Higginson. When questioned about the raising of this regiment by the House of Representatives, Hunter replied that he had not organized "fugitive slaves," but "a fine regiment of persons whose late masters are fugitive rebels" (Quarles, 111). This clever and apt description of the first black regiment was one that could later be applied to U.S. Colored Troop (USCT) regiments raised under Federal auspices in 1863.

James enlisted for service in the Second North Carolina Colored Volunteer Regiment on 16 November 1863. At age thirty-four and standing five-feet seven-inches tall, he listed his occupation as that of a farmer. He would be mustered in for duty at Fortress Monroe, Virginia, on 28 December 1863 after the Second North Carolina had moved northward. Among his fellow enlistees in Company B were Napoleon James (age forty-four), Early James (age twenty-two), and Horatio James (age twenty); all were from the same part of Virginia, and all were farmers. Though the surname James is not an uncommon one, in this case it is likely that Miles James, if not related to any of these men, surely knew them, and may have been a fellow slave on the same plantation. Interestingly, a number of men in the regiment that also had the surname James, but hailed from North Carolina, also served together, but in a different

company. After his training, Miles James must have quickly distinguished himself as a soldier as he was promoted to corporal on 15 February 1864. At the same time, his regiment was also accepted into the Union army and re-designated as the Thirty-sixth USCT Regiment. Stationed in the Department of Virginia and North Carolina, the men of the Thirty-sixth saw duty in North Carolina, at Point Lookout, Maryland (a prison camp), and in several minor expeditions in Virginia before its assignment to General. Benjamin F. Butler's Army of the James in July 1864. Stationed opposite the Confederate fortifications surrounding the capital city of Richmond, James and his regiment would soon be bloodied in battle.

By late September 1864, the stalemate in the trenches around Richmond was growing old; the Union army had tried to end the siege around Richmond once and for all when in June a mine shaft was carved out under the Confederate line at Petersburg and filled with explosives in an attempt to blow a gap in their defenses. The mine explosion and resulting Battle of the Crater, however, soon went wrong and Union losses were staggering. General Ulysses S. Grant was once again ready to break the Confederate line, and devised a two-pronged assault on both sides of the James River in an attempt to capture four key forts. Among his troops assigned to take the forts were the men of the Thirty-sixth USCT, stationed on the southerly part of the line; their objective would be to take Fort Harrison at New Market Heights in conjunction with three other USCT units, the Fourth, Sixth, and Thirty-eighth regiments. The battle began in earnest in the early morning hours of 29 September 1864 when James and his fellow USCT soldiers moved in for the assault. The battle was instantly joined by the Confederates, many of them hard-fighting Texans. Despite heavy losses, including that of many white officers whose places were unhesitatingly taken by black sergeants, Fort Harrison was captured after a fierce day's fighting. It was in the Battle of New Market Heights that the Union's black soldiers would again prove their ability and courage in battle to skeptical whites. Indeed, fourteen black soldiers would earn the Medal of Honor this day, among them Corporal James who, "After having his arm so badly mutilated that immediate amputation was necessary, loaded and discharged his piece with one hand and urged his men forward; this within thirty yards of the enemy's works" (*Official Records*, 169). For this gallant action while wounded, James not only received the Medal of Honor, awarded on 6 April 1865, and the

Butler Medal specially authorized for the battle, but was also promoted to the rank of sergeant.

Following this battle, in which he lost his left arm, Miles James was not done serving; most men so wounded would have gladly received their disability discharge and returned home. But not Miles James. Fearing such a discharge, he wrote to his brigade commander, Brigadier General Alonzo Draper, who was also in the fight at New Market Heights, and asked that he be allowed to stay in the army. Draper wholeheartedly supported James's request, writing to the hospital commander,I would most respectfully urge that his request be granted. He was made a Sergeant and awarded a silver medal by Major General Benjamin Butler, for gallant conduct. He is one of the bravest men I ever saw; and is in every respect a model soldier. He is worth more with a single arm, than half a dozen ordinary men. Being a Sergeant he will have very little occasion as a file closer to use a musket. He could be a Sergeant of my Provost-Guard…. If consistent with your views of duty, I would be greatly obliged if you can make it convenient for him to return to his Regiment. (North Carolina U.S. Colored Troops)James did indeed return to his regiment and was present when the Thirty-sixth USCT was transferred to Texas for duty in mid-1865. James completed his service there before receiving his certificate of discharge at Brazos Santiago, Texas, on 13 October 1865.

James subsequently returned to his native state and lived in Norfolk, Virginia. He is listed as a shoemaker in Norfolk's Third Ward in the 1870 federal census, along with his wife Sarah, and children John, Ella, and Edith. However, his time as a free man would be short. Likely still suffering the effects of his war wounds, and simply exhausted, James, a former slave turned soldier and Medal of Honor winner, died in 1871. He is buried in an unmarked grave somewhere in the city of Norfolk, a dishonor to one who had served his nation so well.

FURTHER READING

North Carolina U.S. Colored Troop Medal of Honor Recipients. "Corporal Miles James, Company C, 36th U.S. Colored Troops." Available online at http://www.rootsweb.com/~ncust/medals.htm.

Quarles, Benjamin. *The Negro in the Civil War* (1989).

United States Government Printing Office. *The War of the Rebellion: Official Records of the Union and Confederate Armies* (1893, Series I, vol. 42, Part III).

GLENN ALLEN KNOBLOCK

James, Rick (1 Feb. 1948–6 Aug. 2004), singer and performer, was born James Ambrose Johnson Jr. in Buffalo, New York, the third of eight children born to James and Mabel Johnson.

His youth was tumultuous, foreshadowing what would be a turbulent life and career. James's father was an autoworker, an abusive man who abandoned the family when James was eight years old. His mother had been a nightclub dancer who'd studied under KATHERINE DUNHAM, but soon she found herself running a numbers racket for the local organized crime syndicate. James was musically inclined (an uncle was a member of the Temptations), but he was also frequently in trouble with the law and began to use drugs. He attended local schools, including Buffalo's Bennett High, but dropped out and in 1963 enlisted in the Naval Reserve, apparently in a bid to avoid the draft.

Music became more and more his passion, however, one that soon brought him into conflict with his military superiors. He began to skip weekend duty in order to play gigs with his group, the Duprees, and after one such incident in 1964 he was declared AWOL. Now exposed to the draft, James fled to Ontario, Canada, where he continued to pursue his music. He soon formed a band, the Mynah Birds, with the Canadian rocker Neil Young and members of what would later become Steppenwolf, and performed under an assumed name. The group signed a record deal with the Motown label and were prepared to release an album when the project was scuttled due to James's status as a draft evader. James fled to England but soon turned himself in to the authorities and was jailed for a brief time. Once free, he returned to Ontario, where he again ran afoul of the law, this time on a charge of theft, and was eventually deported.

Throughout much of the 1970s, James performed and released songs under a variety of names. Bands were formed and dropped. It wasn't until 1978 that he finally found solo success, this time with Motown Records. His first album, *Come Get It*, was a hybrid of disco-funk and R&B that James had refined over the years. The single "You and I" went number one on the R&B charts and established James as a potential hit maker. Another single, "Mary Jane," also achieved notoriety, not least because it seemed to be about James's appetite for marijuana. The album eventually sold more than two million copies and hit double-platinum. Two more albums quickly followed—*Bustin' Out of L Seven* (1979) and *Fire It Up* (1980)—and James hit the road with what had become a massive and eye-catching stage show. Certainly James' on-stage appearance attracted attention, his beaded hair and

Rick James shown in Sept. 1982. (AP Images.)

outrageous and colorful style of dress (cribbed in part, he later admitted, from the rock band KISS) set him apart from many of the other R&B performers of the time. Among his early entourage was PRINCE, then just embarking on a musical career of his own.

Two years later, James released *Street Songs* (1981), the album that secured his place in funk and R&B history. *Street Songs* proved an enormous crossover success, climbing both the Billboard Pop and R&B charts. Among the album's singles was the Temptations-backed "Super Freak," a disco-pop dance smash that alone sold four million copies and made James a wealthy man. *Street Songs* itself sold three million copies, but "Super Freak" proved the highlight of James' career and was the hit for which he is most enduringly remembered. The song was later sampled by pop rapper MC Hammer for his own huge hit "U Can't Touch This" (1990).

Success, however, brought with it its own problems—or exacerbated James's existing problems. Flush with cash and now living the outrageous, hedonistic, and aggressively sexual life that his stage persona suggested, James fell deeper and

deeper into profligacy and drug abuse. He began to freebase cocaine and soon was spending away his fortune (by his own estimates, some $7,000 a week) on cocaine and wild living. Nevertheless, his work continued, both as a producer for Motown (in 1985 he wrote and produced a hit single for the comedian EDDIE MURPHY called "Party All the Time") and as a recording artist. The year 1982 saw the release of *Throwin' Down* and 1983 the release of *Cold Blooded*. In 1985 he was a popular enough figure that he appeared as himself on an episode of NBC's *A-Team*.

The early 1990s saw the collapse of James's career and personal life. James was now highly addicted to crack cocaine and had begun to exhibit dangerous and violent behaviors. In 1991, in Los Angeles, he and his girlfriend, Tanya Hijazi, kidnapped, assaulted, and tortured a record executive named Mary Sauger. James and Hijazi were released on bail, during which time they kidnapped and tortured a second woman, this time for several days, during which the young woman was beaten and burned with crack pipes. James was again arrested and tried, with a penalty of three life sentences hanging over him. In a bizarre circumstance, however, one of the prosecutors on the case was discovered to be a drug connection for a witness against James and Hijazi. James's defense team cut a deal with the DA's office and the singer was sentenced to a two-year sentence. He was released in 1996 and he and Hijazi were married the following year. The couple had a son and divorced in 2002.

In 1997 James mounted a comeback. In prison, he'd continued writing music and had attempted to come to grips with his past and his addictions. He embarked on a tour, but his health had become frail. He suffered from heart problems associated with drug use, and during a concert in 1997 he suffered a minor stroke. The tour was canceled, and James largely disappeared from public life. In 2002 he returned to public attention through a number of well-known comedic skits on the DAVE CHAPPELLE show in which Chappelle portrayed a drug-and-celebrity addled, violent, and out-of-control James.

James was found dead in his Burbank, California, home two years later. The subsequent autopsy revealed that he had resumed his drug use, including cocaine and methamphetamine, though the cause of death of was attributed to heart failure. His body was returned for burial to Buffalo, New York. A documentary about his life and career, *I'm Rick James*, was released in 2008.

FURTHER READING
James, Rick. *The Confessions of Rick James: Memoirs of a Super Freak* (2007).
Obituary: *Los Angeles Times*, 7 Aug. 2004.

                              JASON PHILIP MILLER

James, Sharpe (20 Feb. 1936–), politician, was born in Jacksonville, Florida, the son of Beulah Sharpe, a domestic worker, and Louis James, who died of pneumonia three months before his son's birth. In 1944 after a violent argument with her second husband, Willie Holmes, Beulah moved north with Sharpe and his older brother, Joseph. They stayed with relatives in Philadelphia for a short time before finally settling in Newark, New Jersey.

Every day Beulah James, a working mother rearing two sons on her own, would drop Sharpe off at school early in the morning on her way to work and pick him up afterward on her way home. Spending long hours in school and on the school's playground, Sharpe developed a special rapport with his teachers and a love for athletics. James played on the baseball team and ran track at South Side High School.

After graduating from high school with honors in 1954, he attended Panzer College of Physical Education and Hygiene in New Jersey (later part of Montclair State College). He received a B.S. in education in June 1958. Four months later he was drafted into the army and was shipped to Germany as part of the United States' peacekeeping mission during the cold war. While on temporary duty assignment James continued to compete athletically, playing on his company's basketball and flag football teams and excelling in track. He had hoped to represent the United States in track in the 1960 Olympics in Rome but dropped out of competition when he injured his foot during tryouts.

The army granted James an early out in the summer of 1960 so that he could attend graduate school at Springfield College in Massachusetts. After earning a master's degree in education he taught physical education from 1961 to 1962 at Newark's Broadway Junior High School. James began working toward a Ph.D. in sports medicine at Washington State University in Pullman, but in 1963 after the school's dean of physical education died he returned to Newark before completing the degree. Over the next five years he taught physical education and coached at four different Newark public schools. While teaching at Quitman Elementary School he met Mary Lou Mattison, another teacher. The two married in 1964 and took up residence in Newark's South Ward. The couple had three sons.

Around this time James started getting involved in politics by working on the campaigns of various black community leaders running for local office. African Americans were fast becoming the majority in Newark, and whites were fleeing the city. During the summer of 1967 Newark experienced five days of racial rioting, which left 26 people dead and 1,500 injured. Later that year James and other blacks in Newark's South Ward fought the white political establishment for control of the local board of the United Community Corporation (UCC), which administered federal funds for neighborhood antipoverty programs. In April 1968 James was elected president of the UCC's Area Board 9, a post he held for one year. Also in 1968 he was named director of athletics and department chairman at Essex County College, where he served on the faculty for eighteen years.

In November 1969 Newark's political activists held the Black and Puerto Rican Convention in direct response to the corrupt administration of Mayor Hugh Addonizio, who was, despite being under federal indictment for extortion and income-tax evasion, seeking reelection in 1970. At the convention James received the nomination for South Ward councilman on the Community Choice ticket. Kenneth Gibson, the Community Choice candidate for mayor, James, and two other Community Choice candidates for council won in runoff contests in June 1970. As a result Gibson became Newark's first black mayor.

James served as South Ward councilman for twelve years. In 1982 he was elected to one of the city council's four at-large seats. During his sixteen years as a councilman James was something of a maverick. At the outset he refused to take advantage of the council's many perks, eschewing a car, a private office, or travel at taxpayers' expense. He voted against the pay raises that council members tried to pass for themselves. To make city government more accessible to his constituents he opened a "Little City Hall" in the South Ward. Perhaps with his eye toward the future James began forging political alliances outside of Newark, working on the former New York Knicks basketball star Bill Bradley's New Jersey senatorial campaign in 1978 and on Edward Kennedy's presidential campaign in 1980.

In 1986 James opposed Gibson in his fifth mayoral bid. Declaring that Newark needed "A Sharpe Change," James beat Gibson 56 percent to 40 percent to become Newark's thirty-fifth mayor. Following the election former council president Louis Turco compared the two: "Gibson had a hands-off philosophy…. This guy is hands-on" (*Bergen Record*, 14

May 1986). Within months the new James administration commissioned an independent management productivity study led by the auditing firm Coopers & Lybrand. The report found areas of waste and mismanagement in the city's bureaucracy, which James promptly sought to remedy through sweeping government reorganization.

James established partnerships with Newark's power brokers in the business community, attracted new development projects to downtown Newark, built new housing in poor neighborhoods, and became a national spokesman for urban America. One of James's proudest moments was the opening in 1997 of the New Jersey Performing Arts Center, a collaboration between government and the private sector, and the model for downtown Newark's much-heralded renaissance.

In June 1999 James began to serve simultaneously as Newark's mayor and as a state senator from New Jersey's Twenty-ninth District, when he was chosen to fill out the term of WYNONA M. LIPMAN after her death. He won election to a full two-year term in 2001 and again in 2003 for a four-year term, in accordance with the New Jersey Senate's staggered 4-4-2 terms.

James remained a popular mayor, even after corruption convictions within his administration marred his third term. Although federal and state inspectors conducted investigations into James's campaign finances, he was never indicted on criminal charges. His police director and his chief of staff were convicted on corruption charges, but James was not implicated in those crimes. Arguably, the toughest mayoral election of his political career was that of 2002, in which he faced the first-term Central Ward councilman CORY BOOKER, a young African American who grew up in a mostly white middle-class New Jersey suburb and who had degrees from Stanford and Yale. The media portrayed the election as a contest between two styles of urban black leadership: the traditional civil rights–era leader who, in the words of the Rutgers historian Clement Price, "looks at most everything through the prism of race and racism" (*Newsweek*, 13 May 2002), and the new-generation black leader who has had little experience with America's more segregated past. Booker's supporters were largely in the white ethnic and Hispanic enclaves of Newark's North and East wards. In the end Newark voters decided to go with the incumbent. James squeaked by Booker to win an unprecedented fifth term as mayor.

In 2006 James decided to retire from city hall. Booker, who began campaigning for the mayor's office almost immediately after his 2002 defeat, won easily against New Jersey State Senator Ronald Rice, his leading opponent and a James ally. James completed his four-year term in New Jersey's senate, retiring his seat in 2007. In 2008 a federal jury convicted James on five counts of fraud and a judge sentenced him to two years in prison. He served eighteen months and was released in April 2010.

FURTHER READING

Colburn, David R., and Jeffrey S. Adler, eds. *African-American Mayors: Race, Politics, and the American City* (2001).

Cunningham, John T. *Newark*, 3d ed. (2002).

PATRICE D. JOHNSON

James, Skip (21 June 1902?–3 Oct. 1969), blues artist, was born Nehemiah James in Yazoo County, outside Bentonia, Mississippi, the son of Eddie James and Phyllis Jones. His father, reputed to be a musician and a bootlegger, moved north to Sidon, near Greenwood, to evade the law, leaving Skip with his mother on the Woodbine plantation, where she worked as a cook. After an attempt to reunite the family in Sidon failed, Skip and his mother returned to Bentonia, where he attended St. Paul School and Yazoo High School. At the age of eight or nine, inspired by local musicians—particularly the guitarist Henry Stuckey—Skip persuaded his mother to buy him a guitar. At the age of twelve he took one piano lesson from a cousin. Unable to pay for more lessons, he continued learning on an organ owned by an aunt.

After dropping out of high school at about age fifteen, James went to work at a sawmill near Marked Tree, Arkansas, just west of Memphis, Tennessee, where he met the pianist Will Crabtree, who became a teacher and role model. Crabtree introduced James to public performance, and from 1921 James worked at house parties and juke joints with his guitar mentor, Stuckey. During the 1920s James led the life of an itinerant musician, bootlegger, and hustler, roaming throughout the South. In the late 1920s he married sixteen-year-old Oscella Robinson. The couple organized their own house parties, with James providing music and whiskey. After a move to Dallas, Texas, they separated. James returned to Bentonia, working the barrelhouse circuit from Mississippi to Memphis. In 1931 he settled in Jackson, Mississippi, where he played the streets as a solo musician, worked parties with a protégé, Johnny Temple, and taught guitar at an informal music school.

In early 1931 James auditioned for H. C. Speir, a Paramount Records scout, and signed a two-year contract with Paramount, then located in Grafton, Wisconsin. A February 1931 recording session yielded eighteen sides, though James claimed that he recorded twenty-six selections—in either case, a remarkable number of sides for an untried artist during the Depression. The musicianship on these sides guaranteed James's reputation as a singular artist, but the records were not commercially successful because the ravages of the Depression and the looming demise of Paramount hampered sales. There are conflicting reports over just what James was paid—several hundred dollars, eight dollars in expense money, forty to sixty dollars in royalties. Whatever the amount, the failure of the records to sell so embittered the artist that he quit recording for more than three decades.

At the urging of his father, who had long since left the sporting life to become a well-known Baptist minister, James embraced the church and by 1932 was working with the Texas Jubilee Singers, a Dallas-based gospel group that traveled with his father. After religious study, James was ordained in both the Methodist and Baptist churches, and his religious activity continued through the 1940s. In the late 1940s he married Mabel (maiden name unknown), and by 1951 he was back in Mississippi, working in jobs unrelated to either music or the church.

Spurred by the blues revival, in which several artists who had recorded in the 1920s and 1930s were "rediscovered," blues researchers John Fahey, Bill Barth, and Henry Vestine tracked James to a Mississippi hospital in the summer of 1964. Although James had undergone surgery for cancer, a disease that he attributed to a hoodoo jinx, he was soon performing at the July 1964 Newport Folk Festival—a living legend launching a second career as a professional blues artist.

Following his dramatic Newport appearance, James began recording and touring once again. In contrast to fellow blues rediscoveries SON HOUSE and MISSISSIPPI JOHN HURT, however, James never caught on as a popular revival performer. The dark quality of his music made him inaccessible to mainstream audiences, and his aloof, egotistical personality made him difficult to work with. Despite moments of brilliance, his performances were erratic. Moreover, continuing health problems hampered his comeback. In 1965 he underwent more surgery for cancer in Washington, D.C.

Also in the mid-1960s he left his wife Mabel and began a common-law relationship with John Hurt's stepniece Lorenzo Meeks. Relocating to Philadelphia, Pennsylvania, he continued to try to make a living as a musician. He made several recordings for Vanguard, went to Europe in 1967, and attended the American Folklife Festival in 1968. In 1969 he entered the University of Pennsylvania Hospital in Philadelphia, where he died.

To a greater extent than most, James embodied the stereotype of the blues artist as outsider, loner, even misfit. Despite assertions that he was part of a broader, though lesser-known, regional Bentonia blues style shared by artists such as Henry Stuckey and Jack Owens, James's relation to tradition was more adversarial than accommodating. Whatever he chose to play bore his own idiosyncratic stamp: his piano style showed little affiliation with that of any other artist, he played guitar in open D-minor tuning, his vocal style made use of a striking falsetto, and his lyrics were often dark and brooding. A complex man, James was regarded as a genius by many of his blues revival fans. Yet he failed to make a satisfactory living from either of his dual callings—the blues or the church—and spent much of his life earning his keep in secular, nonmusical jobs, from bootlegger to miner to logger to overseer. But for his single, remarkable recording session for Paramount in 1931, his niche in blues history might have amounted to little more than a footnote. James was inducted into the Blues Foundation Hall of Fame in 1992.

FURTHER READING

Calt, Stephen. *I'd Rather Be the Devil: Skip James and the Blues* (1994).

Guralnick, Peter. *Feel Like Going Home: Portraits in Blues and Rock and Roll* (1971).

Obituary: *New York Times*, 4 Oct. 1969.

DISCOGRAPHY

Dixon, Robert M. W., and John Godrich. *Blues and Gospel Records: 1902–1943* (1982).

Leadbitter, Mike, and Neil Slaven. *Blues Records 1943–1970: A Selective Discography* (1987).

Oliver, Paul, ed. *The Blackwell Guide to Blues Records* (1989).

This entry is taken from the *American National Biography* and is published here with the permission of the American Council of Learned Societies.

BILL MCCULLOCH AND
BARRY PEARSON

James, Thomas (1804–1 Dec. 1891), minister and abolitionist, was born a slave in Canajoharie, New York. As he recounts in his *Life of Rev. Thomas*

James, by Himself, he was the third of four children, and at the tender age of eight he witnessed Asa Kimball, his owner, sell his mother, brother, and elder sister to slaveholders in Smithtown, New York. He never saw his mother and sister again, but he was reunited briefly many years later with his brother, who informed him that their mother had died in 1846. His youngest sister died when he was a youth, and he had never met or heard anything about his father. While living in Rochester he married a free slave in 1829 and had four children. After her death in 1841 he remarried in 1864, this time to a woman emancipated by General Sherman at the seizure of Atlanta.

His third master having whipped him, James fled under cover of darkness on the path carved out for the Erie Canal, finally reaching Lockport, New York, where a black man pointed the way to the Canadian border. He crossed the Niagara to Canada by ferryboat at Youngstown, New York, and immediately found work as a laborer on the Welland Canal. Several months later he returned to the United States, worked briefly as a woodchopper, and in 1823, at age nineteen, moved to Rochester, New York. James learned to read in a Sunday school for black youths. However, while he worked in the warehouse of the Hudson and Erie Line (i.e., Erie Canal), he strengthened his reading skills so dramatically that he was placed in charge of the freight business.

Also in 1823 James joined the African Methodist Episcopal (AME) Society in Rochester and soon started preparation for the ministry. In 1830 he preached his first formal sermon and was ordained in May 1833. Since he had been called "Tom" as a slave and "Jim" at the warehouse, he selected "Rev. Thomas James" as his name at his ordination. In 1831 Judge Sampson, vice president of the local branch of the African Colonization Society, gave James a large quantity of antislavery literature.

These documents became the catalyst for James's lifelong struggle in the antislavery movement for the freedom and equality of blacks across the world. With adamant support from abolitionists such as William Bloss and Dr. W. Smith, James organized Rochester's first antislavery society, created the antislavery journal *The Rights of Man*, purchased a printing press, and traveled the Rochester area in search of subscribers. These initiatives did not proceed without adversity, however. He frequently had to contend with angry mobs, frivolous arrests, and mock trials.

James founded and pastored a black church in Syracuse in 1835 while also promoting antislavery initiatives. After approximately three years' service in Syracuse, he transferred to Ithaca, buying land and building a church two years after arrival. Thenceforth the Anti-Slavery Society sent him to Sag Harbor, Long Island, and New Bedford, Massachusetts. In New Bedford he met FREDERICK DOUGLASS, who was new to freedom and public speaking. The AME Zion Church had granted Douglass permission to address publicly the slavery issue. Moreover, James licensed Douglass to preach, and he joined James's church momentarily, later becoming disillusioned with the church generically but not with Christianity.

After two years in New Bedford, James took charge of a black church in Boston. During this time he labored long and unrelentingly to free runaway slaves, including WILLIAM AND ELLEN CRAFT (1851), ANTHONY BURNS (1852), and the slave girl Lucy, whose master seized her in Boston, invoking the Fugitive Slave Law.

James returned to a pastorate in Rochester in 1856. During the Civil War the American Missionary Society summoned him in 1862 to pastor in Tennessee and Louisiana. However, he never reached either state, suddenly being redirected to Louisville, Kentucky, instead. James labored to free the homeless slaves interned within several camps on the periphery of the city. He established a Sunday and day school among the camps, meeting twice a week and on Sundays. Because Congress had legislated freedom to all black women and children of black soldiers and sailors who served the government, General William Jackson Palmer ordered James to marry every black woman in the camps to a black soldier. These marriages subverted the Fugitive Slave Law, which had no application in states like Kentucky that had not rebelled.

For several months after the close of the Civil War, James served the black camps, hospital, and government stores. In June 1868 the General Conference of the African Methodist Episcopal Congregation elected him general superintendent and missionary. In 1878 he became a missionary preacher for black churches in Cincinnati, Ohio. Suffering from cataracts and facing imminent blindness, James concluded his pastoral service in Lockport, New York, at the African Methodist Episcopal Church.

James finished his life and work where it had begun—Rochester. Though not as well known as Frederick Douglass, he arguably made Rochester one of the most important and successful pen-ultimate stops on the Underground Railroad to Canada. In addition, his struggles for equal access to public accommodations presaged Rosa Parks and others like her.

Perhaps his greatest role was that of sage; he observed that antislavery "agitation" had resulted in a peculiarly American civil rights phenomenon: "But now, that the end of the Anti-Slavery agitation has been fully accomplished, our white friends are inclined to leave us to our own resources, over-looking the fact that the social prejudices still close the trades against our youth, and that we are again as isolated as in the days before the wrongs of our race touched the heart of the American people" (James, 23).

FURTHER READING

James, Thomas. *Life of Rev. Thomas James, by Himself* (1886).

McKelvey, Blake. "Lights and Shadows in Local Negro History," *Rochester History* 22 (1959).

FLOYD OGBURN JR.

James, Willy F., Jr. (18 Mar. 1920–7 Apr. 1945), World War II soldier and Medal of Honor recipient, was born in Kansas City, Missouri. Little is known about James's life except for his military service during World War II.

Willy James Jr. enlisted in the U.S. Army on 11 September 1942 and was originally assigned to a noncombat unit, likely a transportation company. When he was sent overseas to Europe is unknown, but in early 1945 he was one of nearly three thousand African American soldiers serving in the European theater that volunteered and were selected for combat duty as infantry replacements. After receiving infantry training in France, Willy James was subsequently assigned to a black platoon of Company G, 413th Infantry Regiment, of the 104th Infantry Division, nicknamed the "Timberwolf Division."

During World War II over a million black men served in the army, mostly in ordnance, transportation, and quartermaster support units. Only a relatively small number of these men would be assigned to frontline combat units due to the army's racial policies that had been in force for years. Though unstated, army brass clearly operated under the old prejudicial notions that black soldiers could not perform in combat as well as their white counterparts, and even when they *were* allowed to go into combat, they were primarily assigned to serve in segregated units commanded by white officers.

Despite serving under difficult circumstances, African American soldiers were indeed vital to America's war effort. Those that did serve in support units, whether stateside or overseas, performed their duty capably and with honor. Those black soldiers, however, men like Willy James and EDWARD CARTER JR., who did get the opportunity to serve in combat proved that African American soldiers were every bit the equal of white soldiers. However, recognition in the form of combat-related decorations would be delayed for over fifty years.

The specific actions of Willy James during his first months of combat are unknown, but the fact that he was awarded the Bronze Star by March 1945 demonstrates both his capability and valor as a soldier. It was not until 3 April that Willy James was awarded the Combat Infantry Badge, signifying that he had undergone the proper training and was now a true combat soldier. Just four days later, on 7 April 1945 elements of the 104th Division were operating at Lippoldsberg, Germany, securing a bridgehead across the Weser River. James was serving as a lead scout for the 413th Infantry Regiment during the action when he came under heavy enemy fire and was pinned down for over an hour. However, during this time James carefully observed the German positions, and when he made it back to his platoon he helped to develop a new plan of attack. Private First Class Willy James Jr. subsequently led a renewed attack on the enemy positions, and though the Americans would ultimately prevail, he was killed by machine-gun fire while going to the aid of his wounded platoon leader. James was subsequently awarded the Distinguished Service Cross, based on the recommendation of his wounded platoon leader, who was white, and was buried at the Netherlands American Military Cemetery and Memorial in Margraten, survived by his wife Valcenie James (1914–2002).

The memory of Willy James was all but forgotten, except by his own family, until the early 1990s. By this time, historians and the public alike had begun to examine the army's awards policies during World War II, questioning why no African Americans were awarded the Medal of Honor, our nation's highest military decoration, during the war. Responding to public pressure, the army subsequently commissioned a study by Shaw University in Raleigh, North Carolina, to research the issue. After four years of exhaustive studies, the researchers at Shaw University, while not specifically citing the army's award practices as deliberately prejudicial, identified ten black soldiers, all but one of them Distinguished Service Cross recipients, including Willy James, as potential Medal of Honor candidates. While the army would later reduce this number to seven, James and six other men were subsequently posthumously approved for the award. On 13 January 1997 the Medal of Honor was presented to Valcenie James by President William Clinton in a historic White House Ceremony for all seven of the "new" African American Medal of Honor recipients.

Of all these black Medal of Honor recipients, only Willy James's award was met with either outright criticism or skepticism from soldiers that had served in his own division. This isolated criticism is likely due to the fact that James served in a black unit that was part of a division that was otherwise composed of white enlisted personnel, perhaps an example of the lingering racial tensions that had plagued the army during the war. In contrast, most of the other African American Medal of Honor recipients from World War II, including JOHN FOX, RUBEN RIVERS, CHARLES THOMAS, and VERNON BAKER, served in divisions that were composed of black enlisted personnel and junior officers. One veteran of the 104th Division went so far as to state that James did not even deserve the Distinguished Service Cross, let alone the Medal of Honor (Hanna, p. 131), while the National Timberwolf Association (TWA), the 104th Infantry Division veteran's organization, has stated in a letter to the author that it was their belief that the award was politically motivated. While James is mentioned briefly on their website as a Medal of Honor recipient, a TWA spokesman, when asked to comment about James's award, was careful not to say that James was not deserving of the award, but pointedly avoided specific commentary on the Medal of Honor, with the belief that the full details of James's actions were unverifiable. In fact, this statement is incorrect; the Shaw University study cites the names of two soldiers, both black men, who witnessed James's actions to confirm the upgraded award, with which the army concurred after their own subsequent review. Further, it should also be noted that Willy James's Distinguished Service Cross award was *not* a political award, but a contemporary award that, significantly, was recommended and forwarded up the chain of command by a white officer of the 104th Division in 1945.

FURTHER READING

Converse, Elliot V., Daniel K. Gibran, John A. Cash, Robert K. Griffith, and Richard H. Kohn. *The Exclusion of Black Soldiers from the Medal of Honor in World War II* (2008).

Hanna, Charles W. *African American Recipients of the Medal of Honor* (2002).

GLENN ALLEN KNOBLOCK

Jamison, Judith (10 May 1943–), dancer, educator, choreographer, and artistic director, was born in Philadelphia, Pennsylvania, the younger of two children of John Henry Jamison, a sheet-metal engineer, and Tessie Belle Brown. Jamison's parents had left the racially segregated South during the African American Great Migration of the 1920s in search of a better way of life. Jamison was born after the family had settled in the Germantown section of the city. The African American community in which she grew up built institutions that addressed the social, cultural, and political needs of its residents.

Jamison's parents held high aspirations for their daughter and their son, John Henry Jr., and attendance at Mother Bethel African Methodist Episcopal (AME) Church was an integral part of family life. Jamison's mother and father, who had met through their involvement in the church choir, made sure that their children were active in many youth groups. The Jamisons were a close-knit family with solid codes of behavior and a deep respect for critical thinking, education, and intellectual pursuits. Jamison's upbringing included exposure to all the cultural institutions of the city and family outings to the opera, symphony, theaters, and museums. The Jamisons took advantage of black Philadelphia's rich cultural arts tradition, attending performances of the Dra Mu Opera Company and the Philadelphia Concert Orchestra, and participating in Heritage House Cotillions. Because both of her parents had once dreamed of becoming concert musicians, Jamison studied piano and violin, and classical music filled the home. Jamison began formal dance classes at the age of six, when her mother enrolled her in the Judimar School of Dance, founded by MARION CUYJET, a master ballet teacher who was prominent in the African American community. Jamsion was inquisitive, energetic, agile, and tall for her age, and dance became the perfect physical outlet. Hailed by her teacher as a prodigy, Jamison displayed natural dance ability from the start. As a teenager, she studied ballet, tap, Caribbean, jazz, and modern dance and acrobatics with the teachers Delores Brown, John Hines, Joe Nash, Ernest Parham, and Anne Bernadino Hughes. Jamison progressed quickly and was given teaching responsibilities in addition to performing in numerous recitals. On occasion, she traveled with Cuyjet to study at professional dance studios in New York City. Jamison's ballet debut was in 1959, at the age of fifteen, when she danced the role of Myrtha in *Giselle*.

After graduating from Germantown High School in 1962, Jamison spent a year contemplating her future but never considered a dance career. In the early 1960s, at the suggestion of Cuyjet, she decided to attend Fisk University in Nashville, Tennessee. Jamison's desire to dance was stronger than her interest in her academic studies, and after a year she returned home to the Philadelphia Dance Academy (later the University of the Arts), with its dance curriculum that immersed students in ballet, modern dance, choreography, history, and notation. Jamison augmented her Horton technique at the studio of Joan Kerr, a noted Philadelphia modern dance teacher. She also attended a Philadelphia performance of the ALVIN AILEY American Dance Theater (AAADT) while at the academy. The concert made a strong impression on her because of the virtuosic performances of Alvin Ailey and one of his principal dancers, Minnie Marshall, and it was through this experience that she began to envision a career in dance.

In 1964 the choreographer Agnes de Mille discovered Jamison in a master class at the academy and invited her to come to New York to dance in American Ballet Theatre's (ABT) production of the *Four Marys*. She performed alongside the distinguished guest dancers CARMEN DE LAVALLADE, Cleo Quitman, and Glory van Scott. These black women were role models in a concert dance world slow to desegregate during a time of civil rights upheaval and the evolution of the Black Arts Movement. They followed in the path of KATHERINE DUNHAM and PEARL PRIMUS by creating their own performance outlets in addition to supporting the work of emerging black choreographers with newly formed dance companies.

After Jamison's work with ABT ended, she found a temporary job at the World's Fair and then auditioned for the choreographer Donald McKayle for a HARRY BELAFONTE television special. She was not chosen for the production, but Alvin Ailey was present, noticed her potential immediately, and was quite taken with her statuesque beauty. In 1965 he invited her to join the second generation of AAADT, and she soon became one of the most celebrated dancers of the twentieth century.

Ailey and Jamison developed a close personal and professional relationship. He created many

Judith Jamison, a principal performer of the Alvin Ailey dance company, May 1979. (AP Images.)

roles for her in major works, such as *Blues Suite* (1965), *Masekala Language* (1969), *Mary Lou's Mass* (1971), *Hidden Rites* (1973), and *The Mooche* (1975). She was known for her exquisite dancing style and majestic stage presence, with a performance delivery grounded in passion, lyricism, and spiritual fervor. In 1971 Ailey created his masterpiece *Cry*, which is dedicated to all black women, for Jamison to perform as a birthday present for his mother. The premiere was a definitive moment in Jamison's career, and the powerful performance and visual splendor moved the dance critic Clive Barnes to describe Jamison as "an African Goddess" (*New York Times*, 19 Nov. 1972). Her travels with AAADT took her throughout the United States and abroad, and the global exposure made her a sought-after guest performer with modern and ballet companies worldwide.

During the early years of her tenure with AAADT, Jamison met a fellow company member, the principal dancer Miguel Godreau. Born in Ponce, Puerto Rico, Godreau had attended New York's High School of Performing Arts and in 1967 joined Ailey's company. Four years later he and Jamison were married, but the union ended after nine months. In 1980, after fifteen years with

AAADT, Jamison left to star in the hit Broadway musical *Sophisticated Ladies*. She maintained her association with the Ailey company and school and began developing her skills as a choreographer. In 1984 AAADT performed her first work, *Divining*, and in 1988 she returned to Philadelphia to form her own company, the Jamison Project. Her choreography, like Ailey's, is rooted in an African American aesthetic and uses a dance language that speaks to the universality of the human spirit.

Shortly before his death in 1989, Alvin Ailey asked Jamison to assume his duties as artistic director of AAADT. She disbanded the Jamison Project, returned to New York, and graciously accepted her charge to lead the company into its fourth decade. She wanted to honor Ailey's mission to entertain, educate, and maintain a company dedicated to the preservation and enrichment of the American modern dance heritage.

Initially her leadership role was extremely challenging. She inherited a company with mounting debt, but with the help of a new board of directors, a progressive fiscal plan was established. She made the difficult decision to release several veteran dancers and then added younger dancers to the company. Jamison maintained classic Ailey works as a staple of the repertoire and, with her eyes on the future, began showcasing more works by contemporary choreographers, such as Dwight Rhoden, Lynn Taylor-Corbett, Ronald K. Brown, Alonzo King, JAWOLE WILLA JO ZOLLAR, ULYSSES DOVE, and Donald Byrd.

Jamison has evolved as a noted choreographer, adding several of her works to the AAADT repertoire, including *Hymn* (1993); *Riverside* (1995); *Sweet Release* (1996); *Echo: Far from Home* (1998); *Double Exposure*, for the Lincoln Center Festival (2000); and *HERE.... NOW*, commissioned for the 2002 Cultural Olympiad. She is the recipient of numerous awards and honorary doctorates; in 1999 she was chosen as a Kennedy Center honoree and in 2001 received the National Medal of Arts, the most prestigious award presented to artists in the United States.

Jamison's leadership has moved the AAADT organization to a position of financial stability and renewed artistic vitality. She has become a savvy businesswoman with adept public relations skills and an eloquent spokeswoman and ardent advocate for the arts in education. Affiliate programs that have flourished under Jamison's guidance include the AileyCamps for underserved youth, Arts-in-Education and Community Outreach, and the Ailey/Fordham University BFA degree program, which celebrated its first graduating class in 2002.

At the turn of the twenty-first century, Jamison spearheaded an ambitious campaign to build a permanent Manhattan home for AAADT that would serve as a testament to Ailey's vision of making dance accessible to all people. In 2004 it became the largest facility dedicated to dance in the United States. Jamison's journey from dancer, teacher, and choreographer to artistic director has allowed her to emerge as one of the most influential contemporary visionaries in the performing arts.

FURTHER READING

Jamison, Judith. *Dancing Spirit: An Autobiography* (1993).

Dunning, Jennifer, with Howard Kaplan. *Alvin Ailey: A Life in Dance* (1996).

Haskins, James. *Black Dance in America* (1990).

Maynard, Olga. *Judith Jamison: Aspects of a Dancer* (1982).

White Dixon, Melanye. "Black Women in Concert Dance: The Philadelphia Divas," in *Black Women in America*, ed. Kim Marie Vaz (1995).

MELANYE WHITE DIXON

Jarreau, Alwyn Lopez (Al Jarreau) (12 Mar. 1940–), jazz, R&B and popular music vocalist and songwriter, was born in Milwaukee, Wisconsin, the fifth of six children of Pearl and Emile Jarreau, a minister and welder.

Al came from a musical background. His mother, Pearl, was a piano teacher who taught her children to play that instrument, although Al was not fond of practicing. The family often performed as a group, the Jarreau Family, during fund-raising events at local churches. Al loved singing as a child. He would harmonize with his brothers and would perform in the local church choirs, at special events, and at school functions. He made his solo debut at four, singing "Jesus Wants Me for a Sunbeam" at a local church. Coming from a background in New Orleans jazz, Emile kept this style of music alive in his household. The children often listened to jazz and popular music on the radio, and Al was influenced at a young age by NAT KING COLE, BILLY ECKSTINE, ELLA FITZGERALD, JOHNNY MATHIS, and SARAH VAUGHAN. In junior high school Jarreau harmonized on doo-wop tunes with his friends on the street. In high school he was strongly drawn to jazz, including scatting and singing songs from Broadway musicals, and he performed with jazz bands at dances and at local bars. Jarreau was also a talented athlete. He received a basketball scholarship to Ripon College and sang with a group called the Indigos. He graduated with a B.S. degree in Psychology in 1962 and went on to obtain a master's degree in Vocational Rehabilitation from the University of Iowa in 1964. While in graduate school Jarreau was a member of a quartet, which performed at events at the university and played jazz gigs at local nightclubs and bars.

In 1965 Jarreau relocated to San Francisco and worked as a rehabilitation counselor for physically handicapped veterans at the California Division of Rehabilitation. His free time in the evenings and weekends was spent singing jazz. With George Duke he formed a jazz-club ensemble, the George Duke Jazz Trio, which frequently performed at the Half Note Club in San Francisco. He also worked with the John Herd Trio and formed a duo with Brazilian guitarist Julio Martinez. These experiences made Jarreau realize that singing professionally would be his life's mission. Jarreau resigned from his counseling job in 1968, confident he had what it took to make it in the music industry.

Searching for a record contract, Jarreau and Martinez moved to Los Angeles, where they performed at popular clubs such as Dino's and the Improv. They soon relocated to New York, becoming popular fixtures at many New York nightclubs. Jarreau also gained some fame with television appearances on television programs such as the *Merv Griffin Show*, the *Mike Douglas Show*, the *David Frost Show*, and the *Tonight Show with Johnny Carson*. He and Martinez moved to Minneapolis in 1971 and formed Jarreau, an eclectic band that performed a mixture of R&B, rock, and jazz, much of it composed by Jarreau. With his new eclectic jazz-fusion style, Jarreau returned to Los Angeles, but no record company was interested in him.

Jarreau and Martinez performed at many clubs in Los Angeles, such as the Bla Bla Café, Bitter End West, and at Hollywood's famous Troubadour club. Jarreau became well known for his scatting and vocal talents at mimicking a variety of musical instruments. In 1975, while performing at the Bla Bla Café, Jarreau caught the attention of Warner Brothers Records talent scouts who offered him a recording contract. His album *We Got By* was released that year and brought him international acclaim, earning an Echo award, the German equivalent of a Grammy for best new international soloist. His next album, *Glow* (1976), won the same award.

In 1977 Jarreau began a world tour that yielded the tracks for his double live album, *Look to the Rainbow*, for which he won his first Grammy for

Al Jarreau performs at the Bank of America Pavilion in Boston with the Hot Summer Nights Tour, 16 June 2005. (AP Images.)

best jazz vocal performance. The following year he released *All Fly Home*, an album that more insistently combined elements of jazz, pop, and R&B, for which he won another Grammy for best jazz vocalist. In spite of widespread critical acclaim that included top positions in readers' and critics' polls in *Down Beat, Stereo Review, Cashbox,* and *Record World*, it was not until *Breakin' Away* in 1981 that Jarreau achieved significant commercial success. The album again fused popular music idioms with jazz. Selling over a million copies, it was number one on both the R&B and jazz charts. Its first single, "We're in This Love Together," was to be Jarreau's biggest hit, reaching number six on the adult contemporary and black singles charts and number fifteen on the pop charts. The album also won two Grammy awards—for best male pop vocalist and best male jazz vocal vocalist for his rendition of Dave Brubeck's "Blue Rondo a la Turk." Jarreau received Ripon College's Distinguished Alumni Award in 1982.

In 1986 Jarreau worked with disco producer NILE RODGERS of Chic on *L Is for Lover*, but despite its mainstream R&B feel, the album did not sell well. Jarreau nevertheless continued to emphasize R&B influences in his work over the next few years. His 1988 album, *Heart's Horizon*, yielded a number two single on the R&B charts and a Grammy nomination for "So Good" as the best R&B album. Jarreau received an honorary doctorate in performing arts from Ripon College in 1988. In 1992 he became the first artist to win Grammys in the pop, jazz, and R&B categories with his album *Heaven and Earth*.

In addition to his prolific recording career, Jarreau also composed and performed music for television shows and movie soundtracks such as *Moonlighting* (1987) and *Touched by an Angel* (1996–97). In 1996 Jarreau was cast in the role of the teen angel in the Broadway musical *Grease*.

After several years of unremarkable recordings and compilation records in the late 1990s, Jarreau signed with Verve/GRP and once again began to work with Tommy LiPuma, who had produced his first Warner Brothers record. Together they produced a series of critically acclaimed records that again demonstrated Jarreau's versatility, beginning with *Tomorrow Today* (2000) and culminating with a collection of jazz standards titled *Accentuate the Positive* (2004), which won a Grammy nomination for best jazz vocal album. His comeback was perhaps cemented in May 2006 by a duet appearance with Paris Bennett on *American Idol*. His 2006 album with George Benson, *Givin' It Up*, received three Grammy nominations and won best traditional R&B performance for "God Bless the Child" in 2007. Jarreau was honored in March 2007 by the Kennedy Center for the Performing Arts as one of several extraordinary artists and living legends who has contributed to "Jazz in Our Time" and making jazz "America's greatest music."

For decades, Al Jarreau's music achieved international acclaim. His originality and talent as a vocalist and composer and his eclectic style—one that fused jazz with rock, pop, R&B, gospel, Latin and African music—made him one of the top artists in his field.

FURTHER READING

Carter, Kelley L. "Jarreau Frets About Aging of His Voice," *Newark Star-Ledger* (Feb. 2007).

Graham, Judith, ed. "Jarreau, Al," *Current Biography Yearbook* (1992).

"Jarreau, Al." *Encyclopedia of World Biography* (2006).

Watkins, Mel. "Al Jarreau: a Jazz Singer with Soul," *New York Times* (Apr. 1978).

BARBARA BONOUS-SMIT

Jarrett, Vernon D. (19 June 1918–23 May 2004), journalist, historian, and activist, was born in Saulsbury, Tennessee, the youngest son of Annie Sybil Thomas, a schoolteacher, and William Robert, a school principal. The grandson of slaves, from an early age he and his older brother Dr. Thomas Dunbar Jarrett, who were raised in Paris, Tennessee, were taught the importance of education. When he was in the first grade, his teacher assigned him to "be" ROBERT S. ABBOTT, the founder of the *Chicago Defender*, and instructed him to tell the class why they should read the newspaper. "My name is Robert S. Abbott and I am the editor of the *Chicago Defender* and you ought to read my newspaper because my newspaper's standing up for our race," Jarrett recalled in the 1999 documentary *The Black Press: Soldiers without Swords*. Jarrett went on to begin and end his journalism career at the newspaper.

A 1941 graduate of Knoxville College with a B.A. in History, Jarrett was the editor of the *Aurora*, the campus newspaper. Returning to Tennessee in 1946 following his discharge from the U.S. Navy after World War II, Jarrett became disillusioned with the Jim Crow laws that ruled the South. In the book *20th Century Chicago: 100 Years, 100 Voices*, Jarrett wrote, "I decided to tolerate a Jim Crow theater balcony so that my mother could see a Marx Brothers movie. The two of us were walking home when a car of drunken whites drove by and shouted that my mother was a 'nigger bitch' " (104). That experience prompted Jarrett to make a change.

Within days, Jarrett arrived in Chicago specifically to write for the *Chicago Defender*, with which he had already secured a position. Subsequently, from 1948 to 1951 Jarrett, along with the composer OSCAR BROWN JR., blazed the way for many future black broadcast journalists with *Negro Newsfront*, the first black daily radio newscast, which aired on WJJD-AM. In 1954 he moved to Kansas City and worked for a brief period in public relations. He was encouraged by supporters to return to Chicago and champion civil rights through his writing. Jarrett did postgraduate work at Northwestern University, studying journalism, and at the University of Kansas City, where he studied TV writing and producing.

In 1949 he married Fernetta Hobbs and they became parents of two sons, William Robert Jarrett, and Thomas S. Jarrett. William preceded his father in death in 1993. Thomas followed his father's journalistic footsteps and became a photojournalist for WLS-TV, Chicago.

In 1968 Jarrett branched into television, producing and hosting *For Blacks Only* for WLS-TV along with Warner Saunders and Holmes "Daddy-O" Daylie. Jarrett would go on to produce more than 2,000 public affairs shows at this ABC affiliate over the next thirty years including *Black on Black* and *Vernon Jarrett Face to Face*. It was not rare to find Jarrett uplifting youth on *Face to Face*, as he frequently invited high school and college journalists to co-host his Sunday morning show with him.

In 1970 Jarrett broke new ground when he became the first black syndicated columnist on the op-ed page of the *Chicago Tribune*. Just a few years later, in 1975, he was one of forty-four journalists who gathered on 12 December to establish the National Association of Black Journalists (NABJ). The founding of this organization was the catalyst for other professional groups for Hispanic, Asian, and Native American journalists. "The idea of these organizations was not for us to segregate ourselves from mainstream journalism … but to give us a better community foundation from which we could become involved in the mainstream more effectively" (Page, 27).

Jarrett went on to found one of the first local NABJ chapters in Chicago and became the organization's second national president in 1977. According to Chuck Stone, an NABJ founder and first national president, "As NABJ's second president, he guided the organization through an immediate increase in members." Les Payne, another founding member and the organization's fourth president said of Jarrett, "He gave the group its intellectual compass."

Concerned that black children too often saw only semiliterate sports stars and entertainers as role models, in 1977 Jarrett partnered with the NAACP to found ACT-SO, the Afro-Academic, Cultural, Technological, and Scientific Olympics. "Jarrett believed that when black people, particularly young blacks, saw their community at its best, they could imagine themselves doing great things. If they believed so, they would be able to 'act so'" (Trice, 1). As of 2004 this yearlong enrichment program for students of African descent in grades 9–12 had held competitions in over 400 cities and "awarded more than $1 million in cash, computers and scholarships to students" (NABJ obituary of Jarrett).

In 1983 Jarrett moved to the *Chicago Sun-Times*, where he wrote nearly 4,000 commentaries before his retirement in 1994. A staunch supporter of HAROLD WASHINGTON, Jarrett's "journalistic crusades helped elect Chicago's first black mayor in 1983" (Page, 27). In 1994 he initiated the Vernon Jarrett Oratorical Society for Kids. Jarrett taught journalism and black history at several Chicago area colleges and universities and was a senior fellow at the Great Cities Institute at the University of Illinois at Chicago from 1997 to 2004. After his retirement he returned to the *Chicago Defender*, where he wrote a weekly column until shortly before his death. At the time of his death he was the president of NABJ-Chicago and conducted a meeting from his hospital bed just weeks before he died of throat cancer.

In the course of his career Jarrett received more than one hundred awards and honors, including the 1988 American Civil Liberties Union James P. McGuire Award, 1990 NABJ Lifetime Achievement Award, 1993 National Association of Black School Educators President's Award, 1997 NABJ President's Award, and 1999 induction into the National Literary Hall of Fame for Writers of African Descent at Chicago State University's Gwendolyn Brooks Center. He was the first recipient of the NAACP JAMES WELDON JOHNSON Achievement Award and received the 2001 Silver Circle Award from the National Academy of Television Arts and Sciences Chicago/Midwest Chapter. In August 2004 at the UNITY: Journalists of Color Convention he was honored posthumously with the Legacy Award from the National Association of Black Journalists.

FURTHER READING

Dawkins, Wayne. *Black Journalists: The NABJ Story* (1997).

Dawkins, Wayne. *Rugged Waters: Black Journalists Swim the Mainstream* (2003).

Page, Clarence. "Farewell to an Old Friend: Journalist Vernon Jarrett Was Impatient with Those Who Squandered Golden Opportunities," *Chicago Tribune*, 26 May 2004.

Trice, Dawn Turner. "For Jarrett, Inspiring Blacks Was Part of Job," *Chicago Tribune*, 28 May 2004.

Obituaries: *Chicago Tribune* and *Chicago Sun-Times*, 24 May 2004; National Association of Black Journalists. "Obituary of Vernon Jarrett." Available at http://www. nabj.org/newsro\om/special_ reports/v_jarrett/v-print/story/427p-567c.html.

TREVY A. MCDONALD

Jasper, John (4 July 1812–30 Mar. 1901), Baptist preacher and orator, was born in Fluvanna County, Virginia, the son of slave parents, Philip Jasper, a slave preacher, and Nina, head servant of the Peachy family. (His father served as a preacher at slave funerals.) John worked as a cart boy accompanying the plantation oxcart and on errands around the Peachy "great house." In 1825 his master hired him out to Peter McHenry, for whom he worked one year in Richmond before returning to the Peachy plantation. He later labored in the coal mines of Chesterfield County. Jasper's master sent him to Richmond again to work at Samuel

Hargrove's tobacco warehouse. Jasper led a life he later confessed to have been irreligious and riotous. A fellow slave taught him to read and spell.

Jasper experienced conversion about mid-August 1837 while working in Hargrove's tobacco warehouse. Of his conversion, Jasper said, "I was as light as a feather; my feet was on de mount'n; salvation rol'd like a flood thru my soul, an' I felt as if I could 'nock off de fact'ry roof wid my shouts." Jasper began preaching in 1840, shortly after giving evidence of his conversion to members of the First African Baptist Church of Richmond, a large and stable organization. He quickly earned a reputation as an outstanding orator.

A man of imposing physical presence, Jasper impressed audiences, black and white alike, with his vivid imagery, command of the Bible (much of which he could recite from memory), and insight into human nature. Jasper made preaching funeral sermons his specialty, and white planters frequently called on his services as a preacher to their slaves. Two Sundays a month Jasper was allowed to go to Petersburg, Virginia, where the Third Baptist Church, a small black congregation, called him as pastor. During his travels he met and married Elvy Weaden, a slave woman of Williamsburg, Virginia. They had no children and separated when Jasper had to return to Richmond. Elvy later married another man, and Jasper, lacking formal divorce papers, went to the members of Richmond's African church to receive permission to marry again. He married his second wife, Candus Jordan, in 1844. They had nine children before they divorced. In 1863 he married Mary Anne Cole, who died in 1874. He married a fourth time, but his last wife's name is unknown.

Whites who attended his services, either out of curiosity or concern that he might be stirring black discontent, came away deeply impressed with his preaching abilities. His sermons focused on spiritual themes, and his style was part of the tradition later called "ol' time preaching." Jasper received even more public notoriety in the Richmond area when he began to preach his famous "The Sun Do Move" sermon. A contemporary estimated that Jasper delivered this sermon at least 250 times over a period of twenty years. Jasper interpreted Joshua 10:12–13 [AV] literally. He argued that the sun, which he believed rotated around the earth, stood still so that the Israelites could defeat the Canaanite confederacies. Jasper used this story to demonstrate the omnipotence of God, but many of his hearers were struck more by his antiquated cosmology, including his notion of a flat earth.

During the Civil War, Jasper worked as a factory hand in Richmond. He preached to the sick and wounded in the city's Confederate hospitals. After the fall of Richmond in 1865, Jasper joined the ranks of the freedmen and took charge of the Third Baptist Church of Petersburg. He also helped organize a black church at Weldon, North Carolina. In December 1866 Jasper gave up his ministry in Petersburg and returned to Richmond, where he did general missionary work. In 1867 he and nine other blacks organized a Baptist church that was housed in a wooden shanty opposite Richmond on Brown's Island in the James River. The congregation next rented a carpenter's shop at Fourth and Cary. Jasper's members eventually purchased an old brick church from the Presbyterians. The church was located at Duval and St. John's streets in the northwestern part of Richmond known as "Africa" and was called Sixth Mount Zion Baptist.

Sixth Mount Zion, which became an important Richmond landmark, was housed by 1887 in a large Norman-Gothic structure and reached a membership of two thousand during Jasper's lifetime. William Hatcher, a member of Richmond's First Baptist Church, was a frequent visitor to Jasper's church and wrote *John Jasper: The Unmatched Negro Philosopher and Preacher* (1908). Hatcher wrote of Jasper: "In the circle of Jasper's gifts his imagination was preeminent. It was the mammoth lamp in the tower of his being. A matchless painter was he." Jasper was known as "Father Abraham" among the black population of Richmond.

Jasper's style of preaching drew many of the curious to Richmond's First African Baptist Church. Some came to be amused by his shouting style and harsh words for what he called the "eddicated" preachers. Others sought him out because of his unique oratorical gifts and advocacy of a geocentric universe. Jasper was a Richmond sensation. Visitors to Richmond were taken to hear him, and a syndicate of investors sent him on a tour of the North. Jasper preached in Baltimore, Philadelphia, and Washington, D.C. French newspapers published his "The Sun Do Move" sermon, and his flat-earth and geocentric views were discussed in England. Jasper's literal interpretation of the Bible and the relentlessness of his advocacy of an outdated cosmology earned him considerable notoriety among whites, who were amused by his views, but drew opposition from several of Richmond's black clergy.

In the latter part of his life Jasper was known as something of a hermit. He lived alone in a small house at 1112 North St. James, contenting himself with reading the Bible and smoking a pipe. He continued to pastor Sixth Mount Zion until the end of his life. He supported missionary work in Africa and condemned the practice of "hoodoo-ism," or conjuring, among his members. He could often be seen walking the streets of Richmond with a top hat and cane or sitting on a bench in the Capitol Green gardens. Fifty years a slave, he had perhaps no more than six months of formal education, but he was a fluent speaker. At age eighty-nine he preached his last sermon. On his death in Richmond, the *Richmond Dispatch* described Jasper as a local institution. The *Dispatch* also commented, "Some people have the impression that John Jasper was famous simply because he flew in the face of the scientists and declared that the sun moved. In one sense, that is true, but it is also true that his fame was due, in great measure, to a strong personality, to a deep earnest conviction, as well as to a devout Christian character." Whatever Jasper's personal convictions or understanding of his role, many whites viewed him as a caricature of the slave exhorters from the days of plantation slavery when black preachers had to veil their hopes of a better life in the religious imagery of the Bible.

FURTHER READING

Jasper, John. *"The Sun Do Move!" The Celebrated Theory of the Sun's Rotation around the Earth, as Preached by Rev. John Jasper of Richmond, Virginia. With a Memoir of His Life* (1882).

Harlin, Howard. *John Jasper: A Case History in Leadership* (1936).

Hatcher, William E. *John Jasper: The Unmatched Negro Philosopher and Preacher* (1908).

Randolph, Edwin A. *The Life of Rev. John Jasper, Pastor of Sixth Mt. Zion Baptist Church, Richmond, Va.: From His Birth to the Present Time, with His Theory on the Rotation of the Sun* (1884).

Obituary: *New York Times*, 31 Mar. 1901.

This entry is taken from the *American National Biography* and is published here with the permission of the American Council of Learned Societies.

MILTON C. SERNETT

Jay-Z (4 Dec. 1969–), hip-hop artist and record executive, was born Shawn Corey Carter in Brooklyn, New York, the fourth child of Adnes Reeves and Gloria Carter, of whom little is known. Reeves abandoned the family when Shawn was eleven. It has been suggested that Reeves left because of despondency over the fatal stabbing of his younger

brother, though Carter himself did not learn this until he and his father reconciled, shortly before Reeves's death in 2003. A single mother, Gloria Carter raised Shawn and his siblings in the Marcy Houses housing project in the rough Bedford-Stuyvesant section of Brooklyn. At a young age, Carter demonstrated musical talent and became fascinated with hip-hop culture. He was given the nickname "Jazzy," which would eventually evolve into his stage name, Jay-Z. The name held two meanings: it was an homage to one of his early musical mentors, a smalltime rapper named the Jaz, as well as a reference to the J-Z subway line that runs through Brooklyn and Manhattan.

Carter attended George Westinghouse High School in downtown Brooklyn. Despite his obvious intelligence—Carter could read at the twelfth-grade level as a sixth-grader—he did not graduate. Instead, he pursued parallel careers in music and drug dealing. Cultivating a rapid-fire style of rapping, Jay-Z released a single with the group High Potent in 1986 and collaborated and toured with the Jaz. He also contributed guest verses to a group called Original Flavor. But Jay-Z's efforts to distinguish himself in the competitive New York hip-hop scene of the late 1980s and early 1990s—a period many refer to as rap's "Golden Era"—proved fruitless. Drug dealing ensured a steadier income. In some of his raps, Jay-Z claimed to have been so successful in the drug trade that he achieved the status of an outlaw celebrity in his neighborhood. Upon surviving a near-fatal shooting, Jay-Z decided to quit his illegal activities altogether and concentrate instead on his rap career. In 1993 he began recording a demo with the hope of securing a contract with a major record label. Other than a short-lived relationship with Payday Records, an independent label, he was unsuccessful. Undeterred—and inspired, partly, by the Jaz's brief and frustrating tenure with the Tommy Boy label—Jay-Z formed his own independent record label, Roc-A-Fella Records, with friends Damon "Dame" Dash, and Kareem "Biggs" Burke. It was an unusual strategy: most artists sought label deals for instant financial security and access to wide distribution networks, assurances that the trio's fledgling operation could not make. Roc-A-Fella agreed to a distribution deal with Priority Records and the label's first release was Jay-Z's debut album, *Reasonable Doubt* (1996). Even though he was working outside of the traditional label system, Jay-Z was able to collaborate with many established hip-hop artists, including the producers DJ Premier and Clark Kent, the

Jay-Z performs at Pier 54 in New York during a tour to celebrate his return to the music world, 18 November 2006. (AP Images.)

singer Mary J. Blige, and the rapper and fellow Westinghouse High alumnus NOTORIOUS B.I.G. Powered by Jay-Z's vivid gangland tales, the album was a critical success and achieved respectable, if not spectacular, sales.

Prior to the release of his second album, *In My Lifetime, Vol. 1* (1997), Carter, Dash, and Biggs signed a new, long-term distribution deal with Def Jam Records. The album sold remarkably well, thanks largely to the polished, pop-rap sound supervised by executive producer SEAN "PUFF DADDY" COMBS. It also represented a shift away from the grimy, autobiographical reflections of his debut and toward lighter, more populist lyricism. Jay-Z's next three albums—the Grammy Award–winning *Vol. 2: Hard Knock Life* (1998), *Vol. 3: Life and Times of S. Carter* (1999), and *The Dynasty: Roc La Familia* (2000)—cemented his status as a bankable pop star. The Roc-A-Fella label continued to grow, signing hip-hop artists such as Beanie Sigel, Memphis Bleek, and Amil. In 1999 Jay-Z and Dash founded Rocawear, a fashion line.

Despite his enormous financial successes, Jay-Z had yet to reclaim the critical praise of his early career. He returned to a more complex, confessional mode of writing with *The Blueprint* (2001), which was released at the height of his much-publicized squabble with fellow rapper Nas. The album, with its balance of breezy hits and grim, nostalgic raps about New York in the 1980s, allayed fears that Jay-Z had become the sole property of pop audiences. Importantly, the album also showcased the talents of two young, theretofore unknown, producers, Kanye West and Just Blaze, who would become highly influential in the 2000s. For his next release, *Jay-Z: Unplugged* (2001), he collaborated with the jazz-trained hip-hop band the Roots; the

album recapitulated Jay-Z's newfound image as an aesthete.

Strangely, Jay-Z's next two albums were wildly inconsistent: *The Blueprint 2: The Gift and the Curse* (2002) was an overstuffed double-album while *The Best of Both Worlds* (2002) was a lackluster collaboration with the singer R. Kelly. In 2003—fresh off the success of his guest verse on the singer Beyoncé Knowles's Grammy Award–winning single, "Crazy in Love"—Jay-Z announced his retirement. Many suspected the announcement to be a ruse but the mature introspection and weary penitence of *The Black Album* (2003) seemed to confirm his interest in leaving his recording career behind. That year he entered into a partnership with the shoe manufacturer Reebok, becoming the first-ever rapper to boast his own line of footwear. In 2004 he purchased a minority interest in the New Jersey Nets, a professional basketball franchise.

Jay-Z continued to contribute guest verses to other artists' work, including a collaboration with the rock band Linkin Park titled *Collision Course* (2004). But he focused most of his energies on financial pursuits. In late 2004 Jay-Z, Dash, and Biggs sold their remaining interests in Roc-A-Fella Records to Def Jam, which was now known as Island Def Jam. In a shrewd and controversial move, Jay-Z was appointed the new president and chief executive officer (CEO.) of Island Def Jam, thereby retaining control of Roc-A-Fella and becoming one of the few African American major label executives in the record industry. The move was the culmination of a long-simmering but civil feud between Jay-Z and his former partners, Dash and Biggs. In 2005 Jay-Z bought out Dash's remaining stake in Rocawear. As of 2005 Jay-Z was estimated to be worth around $320 million.

In October 2005 Jay-Z and Nas reconciled their differences, ending one of hip-hop's most historic feuds. While hip-hop had witnessed many intense, paradigm-shifting rivalries between rappers and producers, none had involved two artists with the artistic stature and commercial popularity of Jay-Z and Nas. Shortly thereafter, in one of the grandest moves of his early tenure heading Island Def Jam, Jay-Z signed Nas to a recording contract. In 2006 he ended his retirement and returned to the recording studio. That year he embarked on an ambitious world tour—the performances in Africa were cosponsored by the United Nations in order to highlight the world water crisis—and released *Kingdom Come* (2006), an uneven collection of flossy, party-oriented hits and middle-aged laments.

FURTHER READING

Bogdanov, Vladimir, ed. *The All Music Guide to Hip-Hop: The Definitive Guide to Rap and Hip-Hop* (2003).

Ogunnaike, Lola. "Meet the New Boss," *New York Times*, 28 Aug. 2005.

Touré. "The Book of Jay," *Rolling Stone* (5 Dec. 2005).

HUA HSU

Jea, John (1773–1817?), Methodist preacher and seaman, was born in the port town of Old Calabar, in Nigeria, West Africa, to Margaret and Hambleton Robert Jea. At age two Jea and his family were captured in Old Calabar and transported to America on a slave ship. With his parents and several siblings he was immediately sold to the family of Oliver and Angelika Tiehuen, members of the Dutch Reformed Church who owned land outside New York City. This knowledge comes from Jea's narrative, *The Life, History, and Sufferings of John Jea, the African Preacher*, written and published in 1815; it is the only source of information about most of Jea's life and travels.

The newly enslaved family was set to work as field hands and quickly felt the hardship of poor conditions and physical abuse. Jea found little comfort in the message of obedience and humility preached to him each Sabbath at Dutch Reformed services, and he resented his master's attempt to instill docility in him by sending him to a church school. "My hatred was so much against going to the chapel that I would rather have received one hundred lashes," Jea later recalled (Hodges, 21). Rejecting organized religion Jea found solace in private prayer and often meditated in secret. Discovery of his alternative practices of worship led to beatings, and his master, frustrated by Jea's rebellious nature, sold him. His subsequent masters were soon equally frustrated, and his third owner was furious to discover that Jea had been secretly baptized. Taking Jea to the magistrate the master demanded that the baptism be annulled. Yet Jea made a public testimony of his faith sufficient to convince the magistrate of the truth of his conversion and so was vindicated.

The fifteen-year-old Jea returned to fieldwork and prayed for guidance. Mistakenly believing that slaves who could read would be automatically freed, the illiterate Jea turned to the Bible and "held it up to my ears, to try whether the book would talk with me or not, but it proved all to be in vain" (22). Six weeks later a dream brought an angel to answer Jea's prayers. Imagining himself in a dungeon with a Bible beside him Jea heard the angel tell him,

"Thou hast desired to read and understand this book" (22). That wish was granted, and Jea awoke newly able to read the Gospel of John. The next day he repeated the feat before a Presbyterian minister who validated his abilities. Jea's miraculous story soon spread, and "people flocked from all parts to know whether it was true or not" (115). In 1789 a group of magistrates, apparently fearful that he might share his newfound literacy with fellow slaves, ordered his emancipation.

Liberated at last, Jea soon married Elizabeth, a Native American former slave, who bore him a child but soon fell into a deep depression under pressure from her employer to remain in near bondage as a domestic. Stress and anxiety led her to kill both her mother and her child, and she threatened to kill her husband. She was tried and hanged, events that Jea reported in his autobiography with the detachment of a man who would lose three wives and several children during his life.

In the aftermath Jea began to preach and travel, inaugurating a twenty-five-year itinerant ministry. Merging some elements of the Dutch Reformed tradition with some holdover African beliefs, Jea began identifying himself as a Methodist. Freedmen were flooding into Methodist ranks in the 1790s, drawn in by a rhetorical blend of antislavery, egalitarianism, and Loyalism. The denomination's acceptance of black members even propelled some, like Jea, into positions as itinerant preachers who traveled into rural areas to minister to enslaved populations. Thus Jea joined the first generation of black American preachers, alongside men such as ABSALOM JONES, RICHARD ALLEN, JOHN MARRANT, and George White, most of whom identified with evangelical denominations like Methodism.

The mushrooming growth of Methodism in the early nineteenth century did not preserve the denomination's early egalitarian principles for long. As organized Methodism grew, the church made increasing accommodations with pro-slavery power blocs. A schism soon emerged between black Methodists working to end slavery and white Methodists content to abandon abolition. This growing divide helps explain the degree to which John Jea eschewed formal church affiliation and any sort of Methodist sponsorship. Preferring the independence of transience and poverty Jea moved freely across borders and oceans preaching a personal gospel of salvation and individual liberty. His first preaching tour took him across New York State and eastern New Jersey. Every few miles he would hold a two-day outdoor revival similar to love feasts in order to reach the rural slave communities of which he had once been a part.

His calling first took him to sea in the early 1800s. As W. Jeffrey Bolster has shown, the life of a seaman was a popular and often profitable vocation for free blacks in the early republic; every year perhaps as many as 20,000 became so-called black jacks. Jea used his months aboard ship, often serving as cook, to preach the gospel to disbelieving crewmates, and he took every opportunity to discover providential signs in each storm and harbor that his vessels encountered.

Jea made landfall in 1805 and began the first of several European preaching tours, covering hundreds of miles in Ireland and England before returning to sea. Next came brief residences in Amsterdam, Rotterdam, and Helder near Hamburg before Jea returned to the United States. He spent more than two years in Boston before traveling south to New Orleans. There Jea met his greatest challenge, finding the city's residents distinctly uninterested in his message of moral rectitude and spiritual supplication. He departed after only three months, concluding that "all was in vain, for the people were like those [of] Sodom and Gomorrah, for it appeared that they neither feared God, nor regarded man" (137). He reached Liverpool, Boston, and the West Indies in quick succession before his ship was sent to aid in the failed British invasion of Buenos Aires in 1807.

His next destination was Ireland, by way of the West Indies, Virginia, Baltimore, and Boston. In Ireland he married his third wife, the second having died while Jea was away in the Netherlands. The fate of the third is unrecorded because Jea was soon back at sea, alone again. In 1810, while working as a cook aboard a British ship off the southern English coast, Jea was captured by a marauding French privateer and imprisoned in Brittany. His Loyalist sympathies were clearly discernible when he rejected the U.S. consul's offer of freedom in return for service aboard an American vessel in the War of 1812. Lambasting the American ship as a "floating hell" that was servant to a nation of tyrants, Jea refused to "ever fight against Old England, unless it be with the sword of the gospel, under the captain of our salvation, Jesus Christ" (29). His sojourn in prison did not last long, and Jea soon returned to England to begin a makeshift retirement in Portsea, a rough neighborhood of Portsmouth. The violent seaport community of Portsea was teeming with likely candidates for reform and rebirth, and Jea seems to have found some financial patronage for his foray into evangelical publishing. Between 1815 and 1817 Jea printed a collection of hymns and then his own autobiography, which he had dictated to a scribe.

Jea's autobiography marks a significant stage in the development of African American personal narratives. HENRY LOUIS GATES JR. called *The Life, History, and Sufferings of John Jea, the African Preacher* a "missing link of sorts" that continues the conventions of earlier generations of slave narratives while prefiguring the tropes of abolitionist-era autobiographies (Gates and Andrews, 23). Though Jea's text incorporated the convention of using animal metaphors to describe slave life, it also marks the literalization and apogee of the trope of the talking book.

Jea's narrative also stands at the cusp of two major transitions in the history of the autobiographies of former slaves. First, Jea is one of the last autobiographers to be born in Africa. Indeed, despite the brevity of his Nigerian childhood, his African origin looms large throughout the narrative: Jea continually refered to himself as a "poor African," a "black African," and an "African preacher." Second, the *Life, History, and Sufferings* is among the last slave narratives to place religion at the core of the story: the miraculous appearance of an angel would appear strangely anachronistic within the decade. Stylistically Jea's personal history also incorporated a new element that soon became standard in antebellum autobiography: the visual representation of the author. In profile and in silhouette the image of Jea featured on the title page draws attention to the African physiognomy and dark skin of the book's author.

As a piece of evangelical literature Jea's autobiography also established an important precedent. His voice, soon to be joined in chorus by other black preachers of the nineteenth century, was one of the first to mount a radical attack on slavery through personal evangelism. Stressing rebirth and often drawing comparisons between himself and the raised-again figure of Lazarus, Jea's gospel prefigured the radicalism of black Pentecostalists by several decades.

In recent years some historians have questioned the veracity of some elements of Jea's account. In particular John Salliant has cast doubt upon Jea's assertion that he was born a free man in Africa. Noting the certainty with which Jea declaims his year of birth and questioning the likelihood of a whole family being captured and sold together, Salliant provides a timely reminder of how little we know of Jea's life beyond the autobiography.

Indeed, after the publication of *Life, History, and Sufferings* the details of Jea's life are largely unknown. All that is known is that in 1816 he married Jemima Davis, his fourth wife, and a year later attended the baptism of their daughter Hephzabah at an Anglican chapel in Portsmouth. This is the last public record of John Jea, and it is likely that he returned to the sea, only to die soon afterward.

FURTHER READING

Hodges, Graham Russell, ed. *Black Itinerants of the Gospel: The Narratives of John Jea and George White* (1993).

Bolster, W. Jeffrey. *Black Jacks: African American Seamen in the Age of Sail* (1997).

Gates, Henry Louis, Jr., and William L. Andrews, eds. *Pioneers of the Black Atlantic: Five Slave Narratives from the Enlightenment, 1772–1815* (1998).

Salliant, John. "Traveling in Old and New Worlds with John Jea, the African Preacher, 1773–1816," *Journal of American Studies* 33.3 (1999).

RICHARD J. BELL

Jeffers, Lance (28 Nov. 1919–19 July 1985), novelist, poet, and short fiction writer, was born in Fremont, Nebraska, the only child of Henry Nelson and Dorothy May Flippin. From the age of one, he was raised primarily in Stromburg, Nebraska, by his grandfather, Dr. George Albert Flippin, the inspiration for Jeffers's volume of poetry, *Grandsire*. This arrangement largely separated the child from the African American community, as the majority of people around him, including his grandfather's wife, were white. Jeffers strove to reverse this cultural estrangement when, following his grandfather's death in 1929, he relocated to San Francisco to join his mother and stepfather, Forrest Jeffers. The tenants in the building where his stepfather worked as a janitor, however, were chiefly white, so Jeffers was encouraged to seek out African American companions among the poorer southerners who had migrated to the west coast.

Jeffers attended three high schools, including Continuations High School in San Francisco, and several colleges, among them Tuskegee, before joining the army in 1942 and serving in Europe. It was here, Jeffers attested, that he developed his ethos for militancy and an admiration for the African American recruits who were boldly defiant. He saw this as reckless rebelliousness, the result of having witnessed so much racial prejudice. Jeffers left the military in 1946 and married Camille Jones, whom he had met in England; the couple would have one son. He also completed his undergraduate (cum laude) and graduate degrees at Columbia University in 1951. As an English major, he found the works of Chaucer and Shakespeare particularly helpful in his development as a writer. A self-professed loner, he did not associate with other writers while living in New York, aside from a few casual ties to those in his creative writing class. In 1959 he divorced Camille, and married poet Trellie James, later a professor at Talladega College in Talladega, Alabama. They would have three daughters.

While developing his skills as a writer, Jeffers supported himself and his family by teaching at various colleges and universities across the nation, including California State College at Long Beach and North Carolina State University in Raleigh, the latter from 1974 until his death in 1985.

Jeffers published several volumes of poetry, including *My Blackness Is the Beauty of This Land* (1970), *When I Know the Power of My Black Hand* (1974), *O Africa, Where I Baked My Bread* (1977), and *Grandsire* (1979). Jeffers dedicated three of these volumes to his wife, Trellie, about whom he also wrote more than twenty poems, including the entire second section of *Grandsire*. His poems focused on surmounting racial injustice, honoring ethnic beauty, overcoming oppression, and celebrating ancestry and heritage, as well as the Holocaust, the civil rights movement, and the Vietnam War.

Jeffers's poetry was written in the decades that came to be identified with the Black Aesthetic, or Black Arts, Movement, a period of artistic and literary development in the 1960s and early 1970s that expressed African American experience in the United States. Yet, while his works were penned concurrently with the militant writers of the 1960s and dealt with some of the same black nationalistic themes, he was not grouped with the more combative artists associated with the times such as AMIRI BARAKA. A few of his volumes were printed by the Broadside Press, which published many of the era's radical writers, but his poetry focused positively on the splendor and potential of the African American race, in the tradition of LANGSTON HUGHES.

Despite a handful of critics who have shown critical attention to his work, Jeffers was counted among the lesser-known African American writers whose body of work has not been integrated into the mainstream analysis of American and African American letters. His work was frequently published, though, and his works appeared in such anthologies as *The Best Short Stories of 1948*, *Black Fire* (1969), *A Galaxy of Black Writing* (1970), *Burning Spear* (1971), and *New Black Voices* (1972), and such journals as *Phylon*, *Quarto*, and *The Tamarack Review*.

Witherspoon (1983) was Jeffers's only novel. Written as an act of passion, the manuscript was begun in 1963 and completed two decades later. The plot revolved around a black minister, Lucius Witherspoon, who lives vicariously through the execution of a convict, Willie Armstrong, a black man who has refused the clergyman's offer to ask for clemency from the governor on national television. Jeffers wrote the tale to describe black life as he had seen it, mingling actual events with composite versions of people he had known and fictional characters fashioned from his contact with African Americans in the South. Originally called *The Lord Is a Man of War*, the story was rechristened *Witherspoon* because Jeffers felt that, although the original title would be accepted by black readers, it would prove objectionable to white publishers. Jeffers's purpose in writing the novel was to make the readers "aware of what black people are" and that "there are heroes still among us, strong heroes" (Ward, 172).

Sounding much like the militant artists alongside whom he honed his literary voice, Jeffers once said,I find my deepest passion engaged by the conflict between blacks and whites. This is symbolic of the worldwide struggle between oppressor and oppressed. But I can't be parochial about this, and I can't imitate neurotic American elitism either. Humanity is evolving, and the world 200 years from now won't resemble the world of 1981. I simultaneously have to be as broad as humanity, and as intense and angry as the black man successfully fighting for his life against a pack of lynchers. (Ward, 173).

FURTHER READING

Dorsey, David. "Lance Jeffers," *DLB* 41, *Afro-American Poets since 1955*, eds. Trudier Harris and Thadious M. Davis (1985).

Harris, Trudier. "Lance Jeffers," in *The Concise Oxford Companion to African American Literature*, eds. William L. Andrews, Frances Smith Foster, and Trudier Harris (2001).

Laryea, Doris. "A Black Poet's Vision: An Interview with Lance Jeffers," *CLA Journal* 26 (June 1983).

Ward, Jerry W., Jr. "Lance Jeffers on the Art and Act of Fiction," *Black American Literature Forum* 18.4 (Winter 1984).

ROXANNE Y. SCHWAB

Jefferson, Blind Lemon (July 1897?–Dec. 1929), blues singer-guitarist, was born on a small farm near Wortham, Texas, the son of Alec Jefferson and Classie Banks, farmers. Because Jefferson was a poor, rural African American, few official documents exist to verify biographical details. Some researchers speculate that Jefferson, one of seven children, was born as early as 1880 (based on a studio portrait circa 1926 that reveals graying hair) and question the legend that he was blind from birth (printed in 1927 in *The Paramount Book of Blues*). Indeed, he may never have been totally blind, given stories about his ability to travel independently and to identify the denomination of paper money by its "feel."

One account dates Jefferson's performing career from around 1912, at parties and picnics and on the streets in Wortham, but he had moved to the streets, barrelhouses, and brothels of Waco and of the Deep Ellum area of Dallas by 1913. Around this time he may have worked as a wrestler and met singer-guitarist Huddie Ledbetter before LEAD BELLY, as the latter came to be known, went to prison in 1915. From that time into the 1920s Jefferson remained the itinerant blues singer, hopping freights and traveling extensively, especially in many southern states, and playing at various social functions and, eventually, at house rent parties in Chicago. Around 1922 Jefferson married a woman named Roberta (last name unknown), later fathering a son, Miles, who also became a musician. Jefferson's big career break came in 1925 when either the Dallas dealer R. J. Ashford or the pianist Sammy Price alerted J. Mayo Williams, manager of the Race Artist Series for Paramount Records, to Jefferson's talent. The peak years of the female vaudeville-blues artists were coming to an end by then. Paramount, seeking a followup to their success marketing male blues artist Papa Charlie Jackson, reaching the rural audience through their strong mail-order business, recorded Jefferson in Chicago in 1925. Though Jefferson was known as a blues performer, his first two recordings were spirituals, "Pure Religion" and "I Want to Be like Jesus in My Heart." These were not issued until Jefferson had had four releases, and then under the thinly disguised pseudonym L. J. Bates. The name was also used for the 1928 release of his two other recorded religious songs, presumably because of Christians' antipathy to singers of what they sometimes termed "devil's music," the blues.

Jefferson's second session, circa March 1926, yielded his first two Paramount releases, the second of which, "Got the Blues"/"Long Lonesome Blues," garnered six-figure sales. Altogether Jefferson had eight Paramount releases in 1926, recording every few months for the next four years, and was the company's premier blues artist for the rest of the decade. During those years Jefferson's ninety-four released sides (seven were unissued) on forty-three records reportedly sold in excess of 1 million copies. In 1927 his records were released at the rate of about one a month, and a special yellow and black label and photograph graced Paramount 12650, captioned "Blind Lemon's Birthday Record."

Jefferson's records enjoyed continuing popularity until and beyond the time of his death, despite his narrowing vocal range and the repetition of basic instrumental arrangements on many of his final recordings. Jefferson was officially listed as a porter living at Forty-fifth and State streets in Chicago in 1928–1929, despite his continued popularity recording and performing. For example, he sang with a medicine show and with the performer RUBIN LACY in Mississippi, where Jefferson reportedly refused twenty dollars to play a blues song because it was Sunday.

Jefferson died in Chicago under mysterious circumstances sometime in December 1929, possibly of a heart attack or exposure, or both, and perhaps abandoned by his chauffeur. There are various accounts left by various blues musicians. One story has an unknown woman cleaning out Jefferson's bank account and shipping his body to Mexia, Texas, while another has the pianist Will Ezell accompanying his body for burial in the Wortham Negro Cemetery, in Freestone County, Texas, on New Year's Day 1930. A grave marker was finally placed in the cemetery and dedicated on 15 October 1967.

Jefferson is indisputably one of the most influential American musicians of the twentieth century. The primary catalyst for the recording of male blues performers, he provided a vocal and instrumental model for generations of blues, country, jazz, rhythm and blues, and rock performers. Emerging from the same milieu as Texas Alexander and Henry Thomas, two probably older performers who reflected the field holler and folk song traditions of Texas, Jefferson melded traditional songs and themes with a highly original, idiosyncratic style that galvanized his listeners. He combined high vocals with a percussive and complex polyrhythmic guitar style consisting of interspersed bass runs and single-string treble riffs and arpeggios. His vast knowledge of traditional lyrics, increasingly modified by an original, poetic turn of mind, was so widely disseminated through recordings and appearances that his influence turns up in the work of blues performers of all styles and eras.

So great was Jefferson's popularity that many performers claim it a badge of honor to have seen, played with, or led him around on the streets. One who apparently did lead him, T-BONE WALKER, adapted Jefferson's guitar style to an urbanized, large-band format that made Walker a seminal blues figure in the 1940s and shaped the guitar playing of B. B. KING. King recorded Jefferson's "Bad Luck Blues" and in turn became a major blues figure who influenced countless musicians. One of Jefferson's compositions, "Match Box Blues," has been recorded by blues artists, country performer Larry Hensely (1934), rockabilly's Carl Perkins (1955), and the Beatles (1964), among many others.

Immediately upon his death, Jefferson became a figure of mythical status. The Reverend Emmet Dickinson's 1930 tribute compared him to Christ, while Walter Taylor and John Byrd's flip-side tribute also lamented his death, albeit in less grandiose terms. Roark Bradford's 1931 novel *John Henry* employed Jefferson as the archetypical blues singer/sage. But behind the mythologizing is the reality of his greatness—his originality, virtuosity, and intensity—recognized by literary artists such as LANGSTON HUGHES and STERLING BROWN, critics, and fans. He has entered the American consciousness to the extent that his face has appeared on T-shirts, sweatshirts, and matchbox covers. Jefferson is a member of the Blues Foundation's Blues Hall of Fame.

Blues performer Tom Shaw stated it simply: "He was the King."

FURTHER READING
Dixon, R. M. W., and John Godrich. *Blues and Gospel Records 1902–1942* (1982).
Evans, David. *Big Road Blues* (1982).
Groom, Bob. *Blind Lemon Jefferson* (1970).
Harris, Sheldon. *Blues Who's Who* (1979).

DISCOGRAPHY
Complete Recorded Works in Chronological Order (vols. 1–4, Document DOCD 5017–5020).

This entry is taken from the *American National Biography* and is published here with the permission of the American Council of Learned Societies.

STEVEN C. TRACY

Jefferson, Eddie (3 Aug. 1918–9 May 1979), jazz singer, lyricist, and tap dancer, was born Edgar Jefferson in Pittsburgh, Pennsylvania. Information about his parents is unknown. It is known that he started dancing around age eight. He also played tuba in a school band and taught himself guitar and drums, experience that later gave his singing a firm musical foundation. In Pittsburgh he was accompanied by the pianist ART BLAKEY, before Blakey took up drums, and he danced and sang with the Zephyrs at the Chicago World's Fair in 1933. In 1937 Jefferson danced in the Knockouts, a trio that included Dave Tate and Irv Taylor (Little Irv), and he worked in a dance team called Billy and Eddie in 1939. Around 1940 he performed with COLEMAN HAWKINS's big band at Dave's in Chicago. While in the army, around 1942, he was in charge of a drum and bugle corps.

Jefferson and Taylor are credited with the innovation of setting lyrics to recorded instrumental jazz improvisations, thus creating what has come to be known as "vocalese." This term describes a practice that stands in opposition to the similar-sounding French term *vocalise*, which applies to wordless singing (a highbrow cousin of jazz scat singing). Jefferson initially put the idea to work with melodies from big band recordings, such as the tenor saxophonist LESTER YOUNG's solos in COUNT BASIE's "Panassié Stomp" and "Taxi War Dance." In the late 1940s Jefferson set lyrics to Hawkins's famous solo from 1939, "Body and Soul." He had not intended these adaptations to be commercial projects: "It was just something for my wife [Tiny Brown, a singer] and I to do around the house" (Silsbee, 11). But in 1951, while Jefferson was working with the bassist Jack McDuff (later better known as an organist) at the Cotton Club in Cincinnati, Ohio, King Pleasure (Clarence Beeks) heard Jefferson sing his vocalese "Moody's Mood for Love," a setting of the tenor saxophonist JAMES MOODY's recorded improvisation on "I'm in the Mood for Love." In February 1952 King Pleasure recorded the tune for the Prestige label, and it became a hit. Prestige's Bob Weinstock asked King Pleasure for more such pieces, and he replied that this was not his work but Jefferson's.

Thus in July, Jefferson recorded four titles. Three were further examples of vocalese: "The Birdland Story," an outstanding tribute to Moody's bebop soloing when Jefferson heard the tenor saxophonist performing with the alto saxophonist CHARLIE PARKER, the trumpeter DIZZY GILLESPIE, the pianist BUD POWELL, an unnamed bassist, and the drummer SHADOW WILSON at Birdland in New York; "I Got the Blues," based on Young's solo in "Lester Leaps In"; and "Body and Soul," not from Hawkins's 1939 version, but from a less distinguished

improvised melody, again by Moody. The fourth title, "Honeysuckle Rose," showed Jefferson in another vein, delivering a swinging paraphrase of FATS WALLER and ANDY RAZAF's theme and then moving into a gritty-voiced adaptation of ELLA FITZGERALD's scat-singing style.

Jefferson continued dancing into 1953, when he met Moody after a performance with Taylor at the Apollo Theater in New York. Moody, having fallen out with his singer BABS GONZALES, initially hired Jefferson for a week. Jefferson stayed for sixteen years, both as Moody's singer and as his manager. During his first tenure, from 1953 to 1962, Jefferson recorded "Disappointed" on Moody's album *Hi-Fi Party* (1955), "I Got the Blues" on *Moody's Moods* (1955), and "I'm in the Mood for Love" on *Moody's Mood for Love* (1956). Jefferson also worked with King Pleasure at the Zebra Lounge in Los Angeles in 1957, and he sang with MILES DAVIS for two weeks in 1958 at Cafe Bohemia in New York while Moody was in the hospital. After Moody's mid-1960s membership in Gillespie's group—during at least a portion of which Jefferson worked once again as a tap dancer—Jefferson rejoined Moody from 1968 to late 1973 and under his own name recorded the album *Body and Soul*, which included the title track and a version of Miles Davis's "So What" (1968).

Jefferson joined Artistic Truth, the band of the drummer Roy Brooks, from 1974 to 1975. The next year he formed a partnership with the alto saxophonist Richie Cole that lasted until Jefferson's death. Jefferson's albums from this period include *Things Are Getting Better* (1974; with versions of Davis's "Bitches Brew"), EDDIE HARRIS's "Freedom Jazz Dance," and Parker's "Billie's Bounce" and *The Live-Liest* (1976), including "Parker's Mood." Jefferson's popularity was growing. He performed on the PBS television show *Sound Stage* with the singers Jon Hendricks, Annie Ross, and Leon Thomas; he sang in concert with SARAH VAUGHAN and BETTY CARTER at Carnegie Hall on 23 March 1979; and he made a film, *Eddie Jefferson: Live at the Showcase*, in May. But two days later he was murdered by a shotgun blast when he stepped out of the door at the end of an opening-night engagement at Baker's Keyboard Lounge in Detroit. He had been presented the key to the city by Mayor COLEMAN YOUNG the previous February.

Jazz is often said to tell a story. With Jefferson it literally did. A number of his lyrics presented typical fare about love; a few offered social commentary. His discussion of street violence, "Zap! Carnivorous," on his 1976 album *Still on the Planet*, was particularly ironic given his murder three years later. His most distinctive lyrics were the direct tributes to jazz musicians whose melodies Jefferson celebrated in vocalese. Although in some instances these settings have become badly dated (their mid-century hipsterisms sounding corny to later generations), Jefferson's finest reworkings of Moody, Hawkins, and Parker testify to his unusual and timeless feeling for jazz melody and his talent for transforming it into text.

FURTHER READING

Crawford, Carol. "Woodshed: Eddie Jefferson, Vocalese Giant," *Jazz Magazine* (U.S.) 3, no. 1 (1978).

Johnson, George Victor, Jr. "Eddie Jefferson the Innovator," *Jazz Spotlite News* 2, no. 3 (1981).

Silsbee, Kirk. "An Interview with Eddie Jefferson," *Coda* 174 (Aug. 1980).

Obituaries: *New York Times*, 10 May 1979; *Down Beat* 46 (21 June 1979).

This entry is taken from the *American National Biography* and is published here with the permission of the American Council of Learned Societies.

BARRY KERNFELD

Jefferson, Isaac (Dec. 1775–c. 1850), blacksmith and slave narrative author, was born a slave at Monticello, the Virginia plantation of future U.S. president Thomas Jefferson, to the slaves George, a foreman and overseer, and Ursula, a pastry cook and laundress. In 1773 Thomas Jefferson had purchased Isaac's parents from two different owners in Powhatan County. George rose from foreman of labor to become, in 1797, overseer of Monticello—the only slave to reach that position. Ursula, who had been a "favorite house woman" of Martha Jefferson's, was given charge of many of the domestic operations of the plantation.

The slave couple's third son, Isaac spent his childhood at Monticello near his mother. From an early age he performed simple tasks for the Jefferson household—lighting fires, carrying water and fuel, and opening gates. When Thomas Jefferson became governor of Virginia during the American Revolution, Isaac and his family accompanied their master to Williamsburg and Richmond. During Benedict Arnold's raid on Richmond in 1781, Isaac and other Jefferson slaves were captured by the British and taken to an internment camp near Yorktown, where they apparently remained until after the surrender. These experiences made a deep impression on the five-year-old slave. In 1847 the author and teacher Charles Campbell recorded Isaac's vivid memories of plundering soldiers and terrified slaves and the sights and sounds of battle. "Seemed like heaven and earth was come together," Isaac remembered almost seventy years later.

Isaac also recalled that his father "got his freedom" for saving Governor Jefferson's silver from Arnold's troops. Although there is no documentary evidence of such a release from servitude, there are indications of a special status for Isaac's parents. Jefferson's farm book reveals that George and Ursula received larger food rations than did other Monticello slaves. As overseer, George was paid a wage equivalent to almost half that of free white Monticello overseers. Whatever the status of his parents, Isaac and his brothers remained slaves.

About 1790 Isaac began his training in the metalworking trades. Jefferson took him to Philadelphia, Pennsylvania, where he was apprenticed for several years to a Quaker tinsmith. Isaac's recollections provide the only evidence of this apprenticeship and the unprofitable two-year tinsmithing operation that was established at Monticello. Isaac also trained as a blacksmith under his brother George and, after the opening of a nail factory in 1794, became a nailer as well, dividing his time between nail making and smith work. Jefferson's records indicate that Isaac was the most productive and efficient of his nailers, and that he was paid a threepenny premium for each pair of plow chains he made.

In 1797 Jefferson gave Isaac, his wife Iris, and their sons Squire and Joyce to his daughter Maria on her marriage to John Wayles Eppes. Jefferson's other son-in-law, Thomas Mann Randolph, then hired Isaac from the Eppeses, evidently purchasing him at a later date (Isaac and Iris's third child, Maria, was sold by Randolph to the Monticello overseer Edmund Bacon). Isaac continued to live and work at or near Monticello until a few years before Jefferson's death in 1826. When Campbell met Isaac in Petersburg, Virginia, in 1847, Isaac was apparently a freeman, still practicing blacksmithing at age seventy-one. He "bore a good character," said Campbell.

Thomas Jefferson, rather than Isaac Jefferson, is the central figure in Isaac's memoirs, as recorded by Campbell. "Nary man in this town walked so straight as my old master," the blacksmith recalled, and his observations of his master's domestic activities—reading, hunting, gardening, or lock making—are rare and authentic pieces of evidence. The recollections fail to mention, however, some of the most significant events of Isaac's own life. There is no reference to his wife and children, to the sudden deaths in 1799 and 1800 of his parents and brother, or to how he became free or acquired the Jefferson surname. Childhood memories preponderate in his recollections, and it is mainly a child's view of slavery that he shared with Campbell. He spoke of the kindness of both his masters, and tempered an account of the whippings doled out by Archibald Cary, a frequent Monticello visitor, with a grateful recollection of Cary's handsome tips. According to Jefferson's memorandum book, an Isaac belonging to Randolph tried to run away in 1812. If this was Isaac Jefferson, he chose neither to mention the event nor to recall the feelings that provoked it.

Isaac Jefferson's own account of his life, as taken down by Charles Campbell in 1847, is the only source for many of the details of his biography. Prepared for publication by Campbell in 1871, it did not appear in print until 1951, as *Memoirs of a Monticello Slave*, edited by Rayford W. Logan. A more extensively annotated edition appeared in 1967, as part of *Jefferson at Monticello*, edited by James A. Bear Jr. Isaac's account of life at Monticello has been a rich source for writers and scholars since its publication in 1951. Providing a rare perspective on historic events and a historic figure, it continues to inspire interpreters of the past with its vivid expressions and authentic testimony. Its immediacy is enhanced by a striking daguerreotype of Isaac in his blacksmith's apron in 1847. His image and memories have helped to give voice and substance to thousands of enslaved men, women, and children who were unable to leave records of their lives.

FURTHER READING
The daguerreotype of Isaac Jefferson and the most complete version of Campbell's manuscript of Jefferson's autobiography are in the University of Virginia Library.
Betts, Edmund Morris, ed. *Thomas Jefferson's Farm Book* (1953).
This entry is taken from the *American National Biography* and is published here with the permission of the American Council of Learned Societies.

LUCIA C. STANTON

Jefferson, Lewis (1866–26 Aug. 1946), real estate developer, general contractor, philanthropist, and shipping and excursion steamboat owner, was born in Orange, Virginia.

Jefferson spent his youth in Washington, D.C. In 1881, at the age of fifteen, Jefferson enlisted in the Navy after falsifying his age. He traveled around the world working as a coal heaver. During his service, Jefferson secured connections with wealthy, influential whites, including Canadian shipping magnate Sir Hugh Allen, from whom Jefferson received a significant bequest after his death in 1882. Following his service, Jefferson returned to Washington and started a small business that furnished manure and other fertilizers to city lawns and gardens and collected and shipped it out of town. His wealth grew as a result of real estate investments. Partnerships and friendships with influential whites in the city's business community helped to mitigate the effects of discrimination and protect him from the types of fraud and deceit that often befell ambitious black businessmen during this era. Jefferson became a millionaire by age thirty-five and the largest real estate owner in the city's southwest quadrant.

In the early 1900s, Jefferson invested his wealth in several excursion steamboats, including the *River Queen, Jane E. Moseley*, and *Angler*, which he chartered for African American parties on the Potomac River. He also managed the operations of several white-owned steamboat fleets. Later, with his business partner Samuel E. Bensinger, Jefferson purchased the Potomac riverside resort Notley Hall and opened Washington Park, a modern amusement park with rides, concessions, and a pavilion. Washington Park was located near Oxon Hill, Maryland, in Prince George's County, one mile south of the Washington, D.C.-Maryland border. Advertised as the "Coney Island of the South," the park catered to African Americans, who were excluded from the other resorts and amusement parks along the river and in the city. The park hosted social events for national black professional organizations that were in the city for meetings and conferences, excursion parties by local churches and fraternal clubs, and meetings and political speeches given by prominent black Washingtonians and national figures.

During a period when African Americans were excluded from many public amusements and accommodations, and forced into Jim Crow arrangements in others, Jefferson worked to provide first-class, dignified facilities for the city's black population. He was among the generation of black businessmen who came of age during what the historian RAYFORD W. LOGAN called "the nadir" of race relations in America, and who sought to capitalize on the segregation of the marketplace in entertainment. Jefferson appealed to African Americans' desire for respect and dignified treatment, and in advertisements for his excursion steamboats and Washington Park, he contrasted the indignities blacks suffered aboard white-owned boats and exclusion from white-owned resorts with the first-class treatment he provided. In the 1900s and 1910s, he penned several editorials in the city's black newspaper, the *Washington Bee*, which implored black readers to fight Jim Crow through supporting black-owned businesses. While Jefferson benefited from the exclusion of African Americans from other boats and resorts, his guests suffered routine harassment from the Harbor Patrol and police, and confrontations and arrests were frequent. By 1911, the *River Queen* was the only boat on the Potomac that ferried black parties. In 1913, the main structure at Washington Park burned down in a fire of "incendiary origins."

Jefferson became a well-known and beloved figure among African Americans in southwest D.C. During his lifetime, Jefferson donated a considerable amount of his wealth to individuals, groups, and charities in the neighborhood. He was a founding member of the South West Civic Association and served as its first president and was active in the Southwest Citizens' Neighborhood Improvement Association and the Southwest Social Settlement. Each summer he offered free trips to Washington Park aboard one of his ships for groups of impoverished children. On 10 June 1905, for example, he ferried 1,500 babies and mothers to Washington Park free of charge.

With the advent of the motion picture theater, and the rise of the dance hall, excursion steamers and riverside resorts quickly lost much of their appeal. In 1921, Suburban Gardens, a new, modern amusement park catering exclusively to African Americans, opened for business in the city's northeast quadrant, accessible via the trolley system. Moonlight excursions were quickly eclipsed by the vibrant nightlife to be found along U Street. Prohibition also played a role in the declining popularity of riverboat excursions and riverside resorts. Following the ratification of the Eighteenth Amendment in 1919, outdoor parties where alcohol flowed freely quickly dried up, replaced by clandestine affairs in speakeasies tucked away in the city's back alleys. Following a few dismal summers, in 1924, Jefferson closed Washington Park and sold the land. Other resort owners followed suit. By decade's end, few of the Potomac's riverside resorts remained in operation.

Jefferson remained active in community affairs during his final years, residing in a large mansion on 1st Street, Southwest. Following his death, Jefferson was buried in Arlington National Cemetery.

FURTHER READING

Kahrl, Andrew W. "'The Slightest Semblance of Unruliness': Steamboat Excursions, Pleasure Resorts, and the Emergence of Segregation Culture on the Potomac River, 1890–1920," *Journal of American History*, March 2008.

Obituary: *Washington Post*, 28 Aug. 1948.

ANDREW W. KAHRL

Jefferson, Mildred Fay (6 Apr. 1927–15 Oct. 2010), physician and political activist, was born in Carthage, Texas, the only child of Millard Jefferson, a Methodist minister, and his wife, a schoolteacher whose maiden name was Roberts. Many aspects of Jefferson's life, including her mother's name and her early history, are difficult to determine, as she has often guarded her privacy vigorously. However, a few sketchy details do emerge. In describing her childhood in Carthage, a small town in East Texas, Jefferson noted, "My family never had any money as such, but they represented the top of the limited social structure in which we lived" (Merton, 125). Her mother's family, the Robertses, owned property and donated the land for the Methodist church where Jefferson and her family worshipped. After graduating from the segregated schools of East Texas, Jefferson entered Texas College in Tyler, an institution established in 1894 by the Colored Methodist Episcopal Church. She received her B.A. in 1945.

Jefferson has stated that the motto "Decide what you want to do most, then set out to do it," has guided her life (Klemesrud, 44). This motto underscores the steely determination required for her to become a physician at a time when, according to the 1940 census, black women accounted for only 129 of the approximately 165,000 physicians in the United States. It is not known what prompted Jefferson's interest in medicine, but once she made her career choice, she pursued it passionately. After her graduation from Texas College, she moved to Boston to take premedical courses at Tufts University. In fall 1947 she became the first African American woman to enter Harvard Medical School, two years after it had admitted its first woman. In 1850 the medical school had admitted three black male students, including MARTIN R. DELANY, the black nationalist and later Civil War army officer. However, they were dismissed after just one semester after white students protested their admission.

When Jefferson entered Harvard Medical School, it was still uncommon for African Americans to receive their medical education outside of Howard University in Washington, D.C., or Meharry Medical

School in Nashville, Tennessee. In 1948, 84 percent of the first-year black medical students enrolled at a black medical school attended either Meharry or Howard. Little is known about Jefferson's years at Harvard except that she received financial assistance from a Boston synagogue and graduated in 1951, eighty-two years after Edwin C. J. T. Howard was the first African American male to graduate from Harvard Medical School, and 169 years after the first white male to do so. Upon graduation, Jefferson applied for a residency in surgery at Boston City Hospital. At the time it was rare for any woman to pursue a residency in the male-dominated specialty of surgery. Not until 1968 did the American Board of Surgery certify a black woman, Dr. Hughenna L. Gauntlett. Four years later, two more African American women physicians, including Mildred Jefferson, received their board certification.

After completing her residency, Jefferson accepted a position as assistant clinical professor of surgery at Boston University Medical Center. She later became the first black woman elected to membership in the prestigious Boston Surgical Society. In 1963 she married Shane Cunningham, a real estate manager whom she met on a skiing trip to New Hampshire. Up until 1970 Jefferson lived quietly in Boston with her husband, maintaining her clinical practice and fulfilling her teaching responsibilities.

In 1970, however, Jefferson moved from the operating theater to the political arena when the annual meeting of the American Medical Association passed a resolution liberalizing sanctions against members who performed abortions. Jefferson joined a group of physicians who unsuccessfully opposed the resolution, which held that it was not unethical for physicians to perform abortions if the procedure were legal in their state. Upon her return to Massachusetts, Jefferson began what became a lifelong campaign against abortion. She helped establish the Value of Life Committee, an organization whose objective was to provide educational materials against abortion. However, the organization learned that it would have to have to enter a political struggle against abortion when in a November 1972 election, seventeen communities in Massachusetts voted in favor of a nonbinding referendum that liberalized abortion. Leaders of the committee, including Jefferson, decided to form a more activist organization, the Massachusetts Citizens for Life, a coalition of local pro-life groups.

Roe v. Wade, the 1973 United States Supreme Court decision that legalized abortion, provided a call to arms for pro-life activists and marked the rapid ascendancy of Jefferson to the national spotlight. In 1973 she joined the board of the National Right to Life Committee (NRLC) and within the year was named chairperson of the board. The primary objective of the NRLC was to ban abortion, but it also saw its mission to protect life before and after birth, especially for vulnerable populations. In January 1975 Jefferson served as an expert prosecution witness during the trial of Dr. KENNETH EDELIN, an African American physician from Boston who had been charged with manslaughter for performing a third-trimester abortion. The jury found Edelin guilty, but his conviction was later reversed by the Massachusetts Supreme Judicial Court.

Jefferson stated her belief that life begins at conception and that abortions should not be performed under any conditions, including rape and incest. She attributed her pro-life activism in part to her belief that abortion was tantamount to genocide for African Americans, and claimed that "abortionists have done more to get rid of generations and cripple others than all of the years of slavery and lynching" (*Ebony*, Apr. 1978: 88). Jefferson also contended that it was her obligation as a physician to oppose abortion "because the Hippocratic oath represented a point at which the killing and curing function of the doctor was separated." Furthermore, she stated, "I know if I do not exercise my right as a physician to say 'no,' then maybe my silence will be interpreted as consent" (Timiraos). Jefferson described herself not as an antiabortion activist but as a pro-life one. "My objective is not to stop abortion," she argued. "My objective is to restore the right to live to the Constitution. I am a right to life activist. I am not an anti-abortionist" (Blenkinsopp, "Speaker Clarifies Right to Life Movement," Harvard *Crimson*, 29 Nov. 2001).

In June 1975, six months after her testimony in the Edelin trial, Jefferson was elected president of the NRLC, whose members were overwhelmingly white and Catholic. The election of Jefferson, a black Methodist woman, signaled the NRLC's intention to broaden its constituency and declare its autonomy from the Catholic Church. By 1978 the organization claimed approximately 2,800 chapters and 1 million members, but despite Jefferson's prominence, the organization remained predominantly white (Klemesrud, 44).

Jefferson emerged as an eloquent, politically astute, uncompromising, and formidable president. She crisscrossed the country advocating her views and did not hesitate to confront those who disagreed with them. Under her leadership the NRLC became a powerful political organization. It played a critical role in the 1976 passage through Congress of the Hyde Amendment, which prohibits federal Medicaid funding for abortion except when a woman's life is endangered. NRLC also launched its campaign for a Human Life Amendment to the U.S. Constitution that would prohibit all abortions. During Jefferson's presidency, the NRLC also established the NRLC Pro-Life Legal Action Project to fund legal strategies to reverse *Roe v. Wade*. Jefferson served three one-year terms as president of NRLC until political infighting forced her ouster in 1978 (Merton, 213).

Jefferson severed all her ties with the NRLC in 1980 but vigorously continued her activism in the pro-life movement, establishing her own organization, the Right-to-Life Crusade, of which she became president. She also has remained active with Massachusetts Citizens for Life, the organization that she helped to found, and the Americans United for Life Legal Defense Fund. Jefferson's husband shared her pro-life views and participated in NRLC activities. However, by 1981 the couple, who had no children, had ended their marriage.

Jefferson's political activism extended beyond the pro-life arena. She ran unsuccessfully in Massachusetts as a Republican candidate for the U.S. Senate in 1982, 1984, 1988, and 1990. In the 1990s she became chairman of the Citizens Select Committee on Public Health Oversight, which promotes moral education and abstinence. The committee grew out of Jefferson's opposition to the 1993 nomination of JOYCELYN ELDERS as surgeon general, who was pro-choice. Jefferson also became a popular speaker in conservative circles, speaking out against feminism, physician-assisted suicide, and secular humanism. *Conservative Digest* called her one of the ten most admired conservative women.

In 2002 Jefferson emerged as a possible candidate for a position on a federal advisory committee on the protection of human subjects. The nomination arose as part of an effort of President George W. Bush to include fetuses under federal guidelines for human research. Although Jefferson was ultimately not named to the committee, her nomination demonstrates that she continued to be an influential figure in conservative political circles.

Jefferson died at her home in Cambridge, Massachusetts at the age of 84.

FURTHER READING

Jefferson, Mildred F. "Introduction," in *Back to the Drawing Board: The Future of the Pro-Life Movement*, ed. Teresa R. Wagner (2003).

Klemesrud, Judy. "Abortion in the Campaign: Methodist Surgeon Leads the Opposition," *New York Times*, 1 Mar. 1976.

Merton, Andrew H. *Enemies of Choice: The Right-to-Life Movement and Its Threat to Abortion* (1981)

Sterling, Rosalyn P. "Female Surgeons: The Dawn of a New Era," in *A Century of Black Surgeons: The USA Experience*, eds. Claude H. Organ Jr. and Margaret M. Kosiba (1987).

Timiraos, Nick. "*Roe V. Wade* 30th Anniversary Prompts Conferences, Protests," *Hoya*, 24 Jan. 2003.

VANESSA NORTHINGTON GAMBLE

Jefferson, Roland M. (3 Sept. 1923–), research botanist and plant collector, was born in Washington, D.C., the second son of Edward Wilson Jefferson and Bernice Cornelia Bond, both U.S. government employees. Although his father held two jobs to support his family during the Depression, he found the time to carefully tend a flower garden, the pride of his neighborhood. A six-year-old Roland watched with interest as seeds his father planted sprouted and grew. When his family visited Potomac Park to see the famous Japanese cherry trees in bloom, Roland came to love the trees, not imagining that he would become an international authority on flowering cherries. After attending public schools in Washington, Jefferson served in the U.S. Army Air Corps during World War II. Following his discharge, he entered Howard University under the G.I. Bill of Rights and received his B.S. degree in Botany in 1950 and then pursued graduate study. Searching for employment as a botanist without success, he spent several years in clerical jobs.

In 1956 Jefferson would find employment making plant labels at the U.S. Department of Agriculture's National Arboretum. Soon the persistent problem of deteriorating plant display labels engaged his attention. After careful research, he found a solution by using a durable photosensitive metal, a design still used in many arboreta and parks. Promoted to junior agricultural assistant in 1957 and assigned to keeping records of plants at the arboretum, he developed a new recording system that the arboretum and many other botanical and horticultural institutions would adopt. While still responsible for the correct identification and labeling of plants, keeping plant accession records, and preparing plant location maps, Jefferson made an intensive study of the arboretum's new collection of crabapples. He published the results of his research in articles in the *American Horticultural Magazine* in 1966 and 1968. That year he was promoted to botanist, a title he held until retirement. The U.S. Department of Agriculture published his scholarly work, *History, Progeny, and Locations of Crabapples of Documented Authentic Origin*, in 1970.

In 1973 Jefferson began to compile extensive historical and scientific data about the cherry trees planted in 1912 in Washington's Potomac Park as a gift to the United States from Japan. After he had completed four years of meticulous research at the National Archives, the Library of Congress, and other repositories, the Department of Agriculture published his work in 1977. This piece, coauthored with Alan E. Fusonie, *The Japanese Flowering Cherry Trees of Washington, D.C.*, would become the definitive study on the subject. While recording data at Potomac Park, Jefferson observed that many of the original trees planted as a symbol of friendship in 1912 were dying. Between 1976 and 1979 he took cuttings from many survivors, including the commemorative tree planted by Mrs. William Howard Taft, and propagated over one hundred trees to avoid losing them forever. Japanese officials, who were concerned because they had lost the parent stock of many cherry trees they had given to the United States, dispatched a delegation to the National Arboretum in 1980 to ask Jefferson's assistance in restoring these lost trees. As a result of Jefferson's work, in January 1981 the National Arboretum presented Japanese officials with 3,000 cuttings from some of the original flowering cherries. At a White House ceremony, which Jefferson attended, First Lady Nancy Reagan presented to the Japanese Ambassador a three-foot cherry tree Jefferson had propagated from the commemorative tree that Mrs. Taft planted in 1912. Called the "President Reagan Cherry Tree," it would become a major attraction in Tokyo.

In addition to these activities, Jefferson published a comprehensive study, "Boxwood Round the Lincoln Memorial," in *American Horticulturist* in 1975. He also traced the source of century-old confusion about the names of two commercially important privets in "Differences between *Ligustrum Japonicum* and *Ligustrum Lucidum*" in the *American Nurseryman* in 1976. He was an instructor in plant materials from 1974 until 1987 at the George Washington University Continuing Education Center and from 1975 until 1987 at the U.S. Department of Agriculture Graduate School.

Jefferson accepted an invitation from Japanese officials to lecture about ornamental cherries and to study cherry trees with Japanese scientists in 1981. Beginning in the south, they followed blossoming cherries northward for five weeks, observing hundreds of wild and cultivated selections. Jefferson returned to Japan in 1982 and collected seeds and cuttings from superior ornamental cherry trees he had identified earlier. Like most of his research expeditions, this trip was privately funded. Beginning in the south at Kyushu in March, he reached northernmost Hokkaido in August, documenting trees that he would return to in 1983 for seeds that could supply disease-resistance, hardiness, and heavy-textured blooms. Jefferson was concerned about collecting enough seeds before the birds took them and suggested that Japanese children might collect cherry seeds in exchange for dogwood seeds from the United States. Adults and children in Japan collected many thousand cherry seeds that were presented to American children during a ceremony at the National Arboretum. Later Jefferson participated in a ceremony at the American Embassy in Tokyo where American children gave two million dogwood seeds to Japanese children.

While observing flowering cherries in Asia, America, and Europe, Jefferson noticed that horticulturists were using different names for the same trees. Since confusion about correct names made serious study impossible, he decided to organize available information about ornamental cherries. After surveying 728 scientific institutions for cherry holdings, he found a logical solution to the problem and wrote *Nomenclature of Cultivated Japanese Flowering Cherries: The Sato-zakura Group*, published by the National Arboretum in 1984. In 1986 Jefferson undertook plant exploration in northern Japan, the Republic of Korea, and Taiwan, collecting cherry seeds for research in the United States. He lectured at Youngnam University in South Korea and participated in a botanical garden symposium sponsored by the National Taiwan University. Collecting in mountains in Taiwan, he faced rough roads, steep cliffs, rock falls, and poisonous snakes. Dr. Frank N. Santamour, writing in the *Journal of the American Association of Botanical Gardens and Arboreta* in 1987, called Jefferson's work from 1982 to 1986 "perhaps the most extraordinary example of focusing in plant collecting." He cited the 400,000 seeds distributed to researchers throughout the United States and the 2,000 seedlings growing in test plots at the National Arboretum as evidence that Jefferson had gathered "the finest collection of germplasm ever."

By the time of his retirement in 1987, Jefferson had brought into the United States approximately half a million seeds. Yet his work continued. The Flower Association of Japan invited him to lecture and serve as a research panelist in 1989 and 1990 at international symposiums on flowering cherries. When he returned to Japan in 1998 to speak at a symposium, *Flower Friends* published his lecture. As guest lecturer at the Information and Culture Center, Embassy of Japan, Jefferson spoke about the dying Potomac Park cherry trees problem—only 200 of the original 3,020 remained. His "History of the Cherry Blossom Trees in Potomac Park" was published by the Center in its 1995 Lecture Series. In 1997 a *Washington Post* staff writer saw Jefferson's lecture and his photographs of the deplorable condition of the original trees and wrote a feature article urging the preservation of the genetic heritage of the Potomac Park trees. In response, the National Arboretum offered to take cuttings from the remaining original trees and grow seedlings for the Park Service. At a 1999 ceremony in Potomac Park attended by the secretary of the interior and representatives of the Japanese Embassy, the arboretum presented to Park Service officials 500 young cherry trees that could replace the dying ones. Jefferson's dream of reestablishing trees propagated from the original 1912 gift had become reality.

Although his early contributions to plant records and labeling and his study of crabapples are of great value, Jefferson will be remembered chiefly for his work with flowering cherries. His efforts revitalized interest in ornamental cherries and brought diversity to cherry breeding stock that will enable horticulturists to introduce trees of great beauty for varied landscapes throughout the United States. In addition, preservation of the historical lineage of the cherry trees in Potomac Park is largely the result of his efforts.

As of 2007, Jefferson was the first and only black botanist to work for the U.S. Department of Agriculture's National Arboretum. From his home in Honolulu, he and his wife traveled widely, observing flowering cherry trees in bloom wherever they grow.

FURTHER READING
Cunningham, Isabel Shipley. "Jefferson's Exploration in Japan," *Diversity* 14 (1988).

ISABEL SHIPLEY CUNNINGHAM

Jefferson, Roland Spratlin (16 May 1939–), forensic psychiatrist, novelist, and filmmaker, was born in Washington, D.C., to Devonia Jefferson, a teacher and playwright, and Bernard Jefferson, a judge. At an early age, Jefferson moved with his family to Los Angeles where he attended integrated public schools. Raised in a family that discouraged him from pursing a career as a writer, Jefferson studied anthropology in college, earning his B.A. from the University of Southern California in 1961. In 1965 Jefferson earned his MD from Howard University and became a practicing physician in Los Angeles. In 1966, he married a teacher named Melanie L. Moore, with whom he would eventually have four children, Roland Jr., Rodney, Shannon, and Royce. Between 1969 and 1971 he served as a captain and psychiatrist at Lockborne Air Force Base in Columbus, Ohio. It was during this time that he began writing film reviews for a variety of magazines and newspapers, an experience that would form the basis of his literary career.

Prompted by his interest in the media and the black film boom of the early 1970s, Jefferson wrote a series of academic articles about the cultural significance of urban graffiti, as well as the psychological effects on African Americans of blaxploitation films and the black press. It was also during this time that Jefferson became deeply involved in the formation of the Black Psychiatrists of America, whose focus was to bring mental health issues of minority populations into the collective consciousness of psychiatry. As a result of his efforts and the efforts of other black physicians, mandatory training in cultural competence on the issue of race was instituted for all psychiatrists. By the early 1990s, for instance, Cultural Bound Syndromes formally appeared in the Diagnostic and Statistical Manual of Mental Disorders.

Between 1972 and 1976 Jefferson worked at a health clinic in Watts, an African American neighborhood of Los Angeles. It was this experience that would inspire his first novel, the cult-classic *The School on 103rd Street*. The story of a black family practitioner who uncovers a secret government plot to house urban blacks in underground concentration camps in America's riot-torn cities, *School* was a timely political thriller in the spirit of John A Williams's *The Man Who Cried I Am* (1967), SAM GREENLEE's *The Spook Who Sat by the Door* (1969), and DONALD GOINES's Kenyatta series published between 1974–1975. The story behind *School's* publication was emblematic of the challenges faced by many African American writers during the black crime fiction boom of the 1960s and 1970s. Having first self-published the novel with Vantage Press in 1974, Jefferson re-released the novel in 1976 with Holloway House Publishing Company, the paperback press that discovered the ghetto crime novelists Goines, ROBERT BECK (Iceberg Slim), Odie Hawkins, Joe Nazel, and others. Fearing the novel did not fit the crime fiction genre, the chief executive officer of Holloway House, Bentley Morriss, changed the title from *The School on 103rd Street* to *The Secret Below 103rd Street* as a way of marketing it to a mass audience. Jefferson never approved of the name change, and when the novel was republished by Marc Gerald's Old School Books series in 1997, the original title was reinstated.

Throughout the 1970s and into the early 1980s, Jefferson divided his time between writing novels and working on a variety of films. Jefferson's novels combined hard-boiled plots, political critique, and sophisticated psychological character study. Jefferson's second novel, *A Card for the Players* (1978), came directly out of the American noir tradition of James M. Cain and Jim Thompson. A classic heist story, Jefferson's novel was a rich character sketch depicting the motivations, self-deceptions, and ultimate deadly consequences of addiction and greed. In his third novel, *559 to Damascus* (1985), Jefferson returned to the social commentary of *The School on 103rd Street*. Eerily prophetic of the global conflicts that would emerge in the late twentieth and early twenty-first century, using as its basis a fictionalization of the Palestinian-Israeli conflict, *559 to Damascus* examined the failure of America and Russia's cold war policies to contain the threat of terrorism and ideological extremism.

About the time Jefferson was publishing *A Card for the Players*, he also became interested in making films. In the late 1970s Jefferson wrote the screenplays for *Disco 9000* (1976), a black-themed drama about the recording industry, as well as *Pacific Inferno* (1979), a World War II film in which an American POW (played by former football player JIM BROWN) must negotiate the racial dynamics of war. For his work in film, Jefferson received the NAACP Image Award in 1980. In 1979 Jefferson served as the associate producer for the television drama *Angel Dust: The Whack Attack*, which explored drug abuse and which won best drama in the Black Filmmaker's Hall of Fame Film Festival. In 1991 he made his directorial debut with *Perfume*, the story of five wealthy black women who enter the cosmetics business. A film marketed specifically toward African American women, *Perfume* stages one of the recurring themes in Jefferson's work, the moral bankruptcy of certain portions of the black middle class.

Ultimately disenchanted by the amount of time and financing needed to make film, Jefferson went back to writing novels after a twenty-year absence. In 2005, Jefferson published *Damaged Goods*, a fast-paced story of a thief known as "The Motion Picture Bank Robber," who models his heists on those found in famous films. Jefferson followed *Damaged Goods* one year later with *One-Night Stand* (2006), the story of a gangster framed by the Los Angeles Police Department who must enlist the help of a white female public defender to rescue him from crooked cops. Although Jefferson's more recent work conceded to the conventions of mass market crime fiction, both *Damaged Goods* and *One Night Stand* subtly explored the motivations and loyalties of the criminal class operating in a racist society.

Infusing hard-boiled plots of crime and violence with psychological realism, Roland Jefferson's body of literature confronted issues of racism, class stratification, and social inequality with dark humor and political acuity. Jefferson's training as an academic and his eye as a filmmaker set his novels apart as uniquely conceived artistic narratives of satirical social protest.

FURTHER READING

Information for this article came from interviews conducted directly with the subject.

JUSTIN DAVID GIFFORD

Jefferson, William Jennings (14 Mar. 1947–), lawyer, politician, state senator, and U.S. congressman, was born one of nine children in Lake Providence, Louisiana, to Mose and Angelina Jefferson. His father worked for the Army Corps of Engineers and managed a sharecropping plot. After graduating from high school, Jefferson majored in political science and English at Southern University in Baton Rouge where he met his future wife, Andrea Green. There he became involved in campus politics. His activities included organizing a protest about campus living conditions; he was also elected student body president. In 1969 he received his B.A., and in 1972 he was awarded a J.D. degree from Harvard University. In 1996 he returned to school to complete a master of laws in Taxation from Georgetown University.

He married Green in 1970. Their union produced five daughters: Jamila, Jalila, Jelani, Nailah, and Akilah. His daughters attended prestigious New Orleans private schools and continued their education at schools such as Harvard University, Brown University, and Boston College. In 2003 Jalila won a seat in the Louisiana State House of Representatives.

William Jefferson, Democratic representative from Louisiana, questions former Federal Emergency Management Agency Director Michael Brown on Capitol Hill, 27 September 2005, during a hearing by a House select committee investigating FEMA's preparation and response to Hurricane Katrina. (AP Images.)

After finishing college Jefferson worked in a number of political support positions. In the 1970s he served as a law clerk for Judge Alvin Rubin and as a legislative assistant to Louisiana senator J. Bennett Johnston. Between 1979 and 1990 Jefferson served as a Louisiana state senator. While serving in the legislature, he made two unsuccessful bids for mayor of New Orleans in 1982 and 1986. In 1982 he was the third ranking candidate and lost to incumbent mayor ERNEST MORIAL. In 1986 he made it to the runoff with Sidney Barthelemy, who subsequently became mayor. When not holding political office, Jefferson worked as an attorney. He was a founding member and partner in the firm of Jefferson, Bryan, Jupiter, and Lewis in 1976. When no longer a partner, he continued to own a quarter stake in the law firm. Jefferson's bids for high-level Louisiana offices helped extend his local influence. In 1991 he won a seat in the U.S. House of Representatives for the second district of Louisiana. Winning a seat previously held by Ambassador Lindy Boggs, Jefferson was the first African American Congressman since Reconstruction to be elected from Louisiana.

Jefferson's domestic record highlighted his commitment to improving the lives of his constituents in the greater New Orleans metropolitan area. For example, he led a bipartisan effort to create and promote legislation to expand the U.S. free trade agreements. Signed by President George W. Bush in August 2002, the Trade Act of 2002 ensured future growth in Louisiana exports. In addition to this legislation, Jefferson supported tax relief for businesses, jobs creation, and flood prevention.

Through his leadership at the Congressional Black Caucus and his congressional office, he also supported issues in developing countries. Congressman Jefferson actively supported the 2000 Africa Growth and Opportunity Act, which provided incentives to encourage trade between the United States and a group of African countries. His committee and caucus appointments included the Ways and Means Committee, House Budget Committee, Africa Trade and Investment Caucus, Congressional Black Caucus Foundation, Congressional Caucuses on Brazil and Nigeria, and Congressional Travel and Tourism Caucus.

On 3 August 2005 a number of federal allegations targeted Jefferson's involvement in accepting and soliciting bribes, culminating in the search of his New Orleans home. In the raid $90,000 in marked bills was found in his family's freezer. On 29 August 2005 Hurricane Katrina struck New Orleans. The following day, after several flood levees broke, more than 80 percent of the city flooded. The substantial social, economic, and political ramifications of these events dominated national politics for weeks. As a result local media focus shifted from Jefferson's political affairs to the post-storm re-development. However, by 2006, federal officials began to revisit their investigation into Jefferson's activities. During this period a few of Jefferson's congressional aides and business associates pleaded guilty to aiding in the soliciting and abetting bribes. Another business partner, Lori Mody of the Win-Win Strategies Foundation, spurred the investigation into his activities. A number of developments surfaced, including a controversial search of his Washington, D.C., congressional office. After a difficult re-election bid, Jefferson successfully retained his congressional seat for a ninth term on 9 December 2006. Many political pundits, congressional watchers, and Louisiana citizens were surprised by the outcome. He triumphed in his re-election bid by defeating challenger Karen Carter in a run-off election. Although Carter received more funding and the support of many local and national political figures, including the filmmaker SPIKE LEE, Jefferson won the election.

Returning to Congress in 2007, Jefferson continued his support of post-hurricane legislation including funding, business support, and housing. In 2007 House Speaker Nancy Pelosi appointed him to the Homeland Security Panel.

On 4 June 2007 Jefferson was indicted on sixteen counts of racketeering, soliciting bribes, and money laundering. Although he proclaims his innocence, in 2009 a federal court found Jefferson guilty on 11 charges, including bribery, money laundering, and racketeering, and sentenced Jefferson to 13 years in prison. The lead prosecutor described his actions as "the most extensive and pervasive pattern of corruption in the history of Congress." (Tilove). It was the longest jail sentence imposed on a member of Congress for crimes in office.

FURTHER READING

Douze, Frank. "William Jefferson Undeterred by Allegations," *Times Picayune*, 18 Oct. 2006.

Fairclough, Adam. *Race and Democracy: The Civil Rights Struggle in Louisiana, 1915–1972* (1995).

Gordon, Russell. "In a Career Knotted with Family Ties, Rep. William Jefferson Has Long Been Hounded by Ethics Questions," *Times Picayune*, 19 Nov. 2006.

Lamis, Alexander P., ed. *Southern Politics in the 1990s* (1999).

Office of Honorable William Jefferson. "The Jefferson Report" (Aug. 2004).

Tilove, Jonathan. "William Jefferson sentenced to 13 years in prison," *Times-Picayune*, 13 Nov. 2009.

DONNA A. PATTERSON

Jeffrey, George S. (30 Nov. 1830–7 Dec. 1906), barber, orator, and activist, was born in Middletown, Connecticut, the son of Mary Ann (Campbell) and George W. Jeffrey. George's father was one of the first trustees of the Cross Street African Methodist Episcopal (AME) Zion Church of Middletown that was formed in 1828. Middletown's small black activist community shaped the life and work of George S. Jeffrey. There were several intermarriages between the Jeffrey family and the family of the Reverend JEHIEL C. BEMAN, Cross Street AME Zion's first minister. Jeffrey's maternal aunt Clarissa Marie Campbell Beman founded the Middletown Colored Female Anti-Slavery Society. Citizens of color of Middletown, including his grandparents, uncles, and father, petitioned the Connecticut state legislature seven times between 1838 and 1843 over such issues as repealing the "Canterbury Law" (which effectively restricted young women of color from attending the boarding school founded for them by Prudence Crandall in 1833 in Canterbury), trial by jury for accused fugitive slaves, and the right of people of color to vote.

Because educational opportunities were denied people of color in Middletown, Jeffrey was largely self-taught. His African and Native American roots included ancestors who had been enslaved in Connecticut and members of the Nehantic, Narragansett, and Montauk tribes. In his seventies he was a member of the Montauk council of administration that was engaged in a lawsuit with the Long Island Railroad for recovery of Montauk Point. Proud of his heritage, Jeffrey focused his life on the struggle for African American freedom. It was for this work that his former home in Meriden was placed on the Connecticut Freedom Trail in 2003.

By 1851 Jeffery settled in Meriden, Connecticut, and became a successful barber. Marrying Martha Agnes Williams in about 1860 enabled him to throw himself almost completely into the cause of civil rights by the late 1870s as she established a successful hairdressing emporium. They had six children, some dying young. Those who lived were successful high school graduates. Like Middletown's, Meriden's black community was small but vibrant. It reacted to the death of Reconstruction by forming an AME Zion Mission and by forming the Lincoln Club, an unabashedly Republican organization. George Jeffrey became an acknowledged leader on a local and statewide level. His temperance lecture "Sacrifice," given in Meriden in May 1879, drew a crowd of seven hundred people. He was known for his debating abilities, played Othello in a local play, and served as a county and city juror for more than thirty years.

The Lincoln Club of Meriden was formed in 1877. By the mid-1880s the club's integrated banquets drew two hundred to three hundred guests, including influential state Republican politicians and such luminaries as the former U.S. Senator JOSEPH RAINEY. Abraham Lincoln's memory and both black and white abolitionists were honored, and past and present issues of the color line were addressed. Jeffrey had been appointed president of the club at the close of the 1878 banquet and remained in that capacity. Lincoln Club membership was limited to men of color. Estimates from local newspaper accounts number thirty local members and at least seventy from out of town. Members ranged from leaders in their communities to men who worked as waiters and porters. Old New England families three generations out of slavery worked with those from the South whose experience of slavery had been more recent. By networking with the Republican Party in Connecticut, Lincoln Club members gained access through legislative caucus to doorkeeper and messenger posts at the state capitol. Jeffrey served as senate doorkeeper five times between the years 1881 and 1887. In 1884 he was an attaché of the state senate, representing the *Meriden Daily Republican*, presumably as their reporter.

The Lincoln Club played a role in the March 1879 formation of a black Connecticut National Guard regiment, named in honor of the Lincoln Club member Captain James H. Wilkins. Later that same year a white businessman who occupied the same building as Jeffrey publicly accused him of stealing his coal. Jeffrey confronted his accuser, who responded by making a racially derogatory remark. A fight between the two broke out when the owner shoved Jeffrey out of his store. The owner, Hervey Rogers Jr., had Jeffrey arrested on assault charges. Jeffrey was acquitted after defending himself in court and subsequently filed suit for slander. He won that case as well and was quoted in the *Meriden Daily Republican* as calling the judgment for a public retraction and his legal fees a "reparation."

In late May 1880 Jeffrey attended the Chicago Republican presidential convention expressly for the purpose of presenting a protest to delegates of color against the nomination of Ulysses S. Grant. Prominent leaders of color from Hartford, New Haven, Bridgeport, Middletown, and other Connecticut cities had met in Meriden and authorized Jeffrey to act as their representative. They did not think that Grant could win the presidency and would not risk Democrats, who represented to them the party of slavery, getting into power. In Chicago, Jeffrey made his appeal to delegates of color from North Carolina, South Carolina, and Virginia.

The 1883 Lincoln Club banquet was the club's last large banquet held on Lincoln's birthday. Later that year the Supreme Court struck down the Civil Rights Act of 1875. A suit brought to trial in Connecticut by Charles Cooper against the New Haven Steamboat Company for refusal of accommodations was abandoned because of this Supreme Court decision. A subsequent convention of men of color met in Norwich, sending a resolution to the state assembly asking that the Fourteenth Amendment be guaranteed in Connecticut. Jeffrey was present, representing Meriden. The 1884 Lincoln Club banquet was a small gathering limited to members only. Jeffrey issued a scathing press release on the election of the Democrat Grover Cleveland to the presidency.

In February of 1887 George Jeffrey went before the insurance committee at the state legislature and successfully advocated the passage of a bill to prevent discrimination by life insurance companies against people of color in Connecticut. Although prominent in his time, Jeffrey was omitted from the local and state historical records until nearly a century after his death.

FURTHER READING

Blight, David. *Race and Reunion: The Civil War in American Memory* (2001).

Cyr, Colleen. *Profiles in Meriden's Black History: George S. Jeffrey and the Insurance Bill of 1887* (People's Press, 2003).

Cyr, Colleen. *Profiles in Meriden's Black History: Richard Alonzo Jeffrey* (People's Press, July 2004).

COLLEEN CYR

Jemison, Mae (17 Oct. 1956–), astronaut and physician, was born Mae Carol Jemison in Decatur, Alabama, the daughter of Charlie Jemison, a carpenter and roofer, and Dorothy Jemison, a teacher whose maiden name is unknown. After living the first three and a half years of her life in Alabama near the Marshall Space Flight Center, Jemison moved to Chicago with her parents and older siblings, Rickey and Ada Sue. When her family experienced trouble with local gangs, they moved to another section of the city, where Jemison immersed herself in her schoolwork. An avid reader, she also was inspired by role models in the media, such as Lieutenant Uhura, a black woman astronaut portrayed by the actress NICHELLE NICHOLS in the 1960s television series *Star Trek*. At a time when all astronauts were white and male, even a-fictional character such as Lieutenant Uhura had a positive impact on Jemison. "A lot of times, fantasy is what gets us through to reality," Jemison later said (Katz, 38). An outstanding student, active in student government and arts organizations, Jemison excelled in science and graduated from Morgan Park High School in 1973.

She entered Stanford University at age sixteen, in part, she confessed, because of the renown of their football team. Unfortunately Jemison did not feel entirely welcomed by the Stanford science faculty, whom she believed underestimated or ignored her. "The majority of physical science professors pushed me away," she later recalled (Jemison, 123). These chilly rebuffs did not deter her, however, and Jemison continued to study science and engineering while also enrolling in many African and Afro-American studies classes. She-viewed her courses in the social sciences as vital, she recalled, "because I was unconsciously balancing the poor reception I often received in the science and engineering departments with the embrace of political science" (Jemison, 123). Jemison graduated in 1977 with a B.S. in Chemical Engineering.

After leaving Stanford, Jemison entered Cornell University Medical College (now Weill Cornell Medical College) in New York City. While in medical school, she also took modern dance classes in the city and became a great fan of the ALVIN AILEY dance troupe, particularly the dancer JUDITH JAMISON. During the summers between her second and third years in medical school, Jemison received a grant from the International Travelers Association and traveled to Cuba, Kenya, and Thailand, providing medical care. The experience deeply affected Jemison, whose attention to scientific and social concerns in the United States expanded to include international issues. She graduated with her medical degree in 1981 and returned to California as a medical intern at Los Angeles County/University of Southern California Medical Center in 1982. From 1983 to 1985 Jemison served as the area Peace Corps medical officer in Sierra Leone and Liberia. She supervised the pharmacy and laboratory and established guidelines for public health and safety issues. She also collaborated with the National Institutes for Health and the Centers for Disease Control in the United States, researching hepatitis B vaccines and conducting studies of rabies and infectious diseases such as schistosomiasis, which is widespread in rural areas of Africa. She returned to the United States in 1985 to work as a general practitioner in Los Angeles.

Always curious and eager to embark on new paths, Jemison continued to take graduate classes in engineering while practicing medicine, and eventually she became interested in applying to the astronaut program of the National Aeronautics and Space Administration (NASA). Jemison found NASA's early prohibition on women astronauts "nonsensical" (Jemison, 171) and first applied to the astronaut corps less than a decade after the space agency began accepting female candidates in 1978.

NASA accepted Jemison on her second application, and she became one of fifteen astronauts selected from more than two thousand applicants. She was the first woman of color and the fifth African American astronaut in NASA's history. Beginning her training in August 1987, Jemison was part of the first class of astronauts to be selected after the 1986 *Challenger* accident. She told reporters that she was not daunted by the prospect of danger, but remained committed to the challenges of space exploration for the unique knowledge it provides. Dr. Joseph D. Atkinson Jr., a member of the astronaut board that selected Jemison and chief of NASA's Equal Opportunity Programs Office, was struck not only by Jemison's commitment to science but also by her social awareness. He found her scientific skill and sensitivity "to the social needs of the community" a formidable combination of abilities (Marshall, 54).

On 12 September 1992 Jemison rocketed into space aboard the space shuttle *Endeavor*. Her mission, STS 47, was a joint project of the United States and Japan. Jemison's duties as a mission specialist involved life-science experiments focusing on bone cell research and other technical assignments, including verification of the shuttle computer software in the Shuttle Avionics Integration Laboratory

Mae C. Jemison aboard space shuttle *Endeavour* on the STS-47 NASA Space lab-J flight, a US/Japan joint mission, in September 1992. Dr. Jemison wears a headband and other monitoring gear that conducts physiological evaluations as part of the Autogenic Feedback Training Experiment (AFTE). (AP Images.)

(SAIL). Among the personal objects Jemison elected to take on board with her were an Alvin Ailey dance poster, a statue from Sierra Leone, a certificate from Chicago schoolchildren pledging to improve their math and science skills, and a MICHAEL JORDAN jersey from the Chicago Bulls basketball team. Jemison noted that the items she brought along suggested that "space is a birthright for all of us on this planet" (Katz, 40). During her eight-day mission, Jemison orbited the earth 127 times and logged 190 hours, 30 minutes, and 23 seconds in outer space. Her first mission in space was also her last. After six years with the space agency, Jemison resigned from NASA the following year to start her own technology companies and explore teaching interests.

In 1993 Jemison founded the Jemison Group, Inc., a business that focused on, in her words, "integrating social issues with technology designs" (Jemison, 172). The Jemison Group has been involved in projects involving thermal electricity and the use of satellite-based telecommunications to facilitate health care in West Africa. A year later Jemison established The Earth We Share, an annual science camp, which attracts children aged twelve to sixteen from around the world. She also served as professor of environmental studies at Dartmouth College from 1995 to 2002 and, while at Dartmouth, founded another scientific research company, BioSentient Corporation, which investigates the application of techniques for controlling motion sickness and other medical problems.

In 2001 Jemison wrote an autobiography for young adults, *Find Where the Wind Goes*, in which she highlights episodes in her life that inspired or changed her. She has been involved in other media projects, including science programs on PBS and the Discovery Channel. Fulfilling a childhood dream, she also appeared on *Star Trek: The Next Generation* during an episode titled "Second Chances." Until 2005, Jemison was the A. D. White Professor at Large at Cornell University, a position she held from 1999. She speaks on scientific literacy and the need to increase the numbers of women and minorities in science and technology.

Mae Jemison has been honored with awards from the National Women's Hall of Fame and the National Academy of Sciences Institute of Medicine. She holds honorary doctorates from Princeton University, Lincoln College (Pennsylvania), and Winston-Salem College (North Carolina). In 1999 she was selected as one of the seven most qualified women to be president of the United States by the White House Project, an organization that seeks to eliminate the glass ceiling for women in business and politics. As a resident of Houston, Texas, Jemison has continued to work toward the understanding that scientific progress and social equity are inextricably linked.

FURTHER READING

Jemison, Mae. *Find Where the Wind Goes: Moments from My Life* (2001).

Atkinson, Joseph D., and Jay M. Shafritz. *The Real Stuff: A History of NASA's Astronaut Recruitment Program* (1985).

Katz, Jesse. "Shooting Star." *Stanford Today* (July/Aug. 1996).

Marshall, Marilyn. "Child of the 60s Set to Become First Black Woman in Space," *Ebony* 44 (Aug. 1989).

MARTHA ACKMANN

Jemison, T. J. (1 Aug. 1918–), activist and denominational leader, was born Theodore Judson Jemison, the son of David Vivian Jemison, a Baptist minister, and Henrietta Hillips Jemison in Selma, Alabama. He earned a B.S. from Alabama State University (1940) and a B.D. from Virginia Union University (1945). He was later awarded the M.A. in Psychology by New York University. In August 1945 Jemison married Celestine Catlett, and from this union three children were born.

In 1945 Jemison took over the pastorate of Mount Zion Baptist Church in Staunton, Virginia. Four years later he transferred to Baton Rouge's Mount Zion First African Baptist Church, where he would remain for the rest of his career. One of his first acts was to drop "African" from the name of the church because it connoted racial exclusivism. At the time the church had only 300 members. The new pastor pioneered a prison ministry and offered legal assistance to those who could not afford a lawyer. Jemison was well regarded within the National Baptist Convention, U.S.A. (NBC) because his father had served as NBC president from 1940 to 1953. This connection served him well and in 1953 he was elected general secretary.

Jemison earned regional celebrity when he organized the nation's first bus boycott in Baton Rouge in 1953. The boycott started in June of that year when white bus drivers refused to follow a city ordinance that integrated ridership. Before the ordinance blacks were allowed to sit only in the back of the buses. As the city council debated what to do Jemison called for a boycott. He was helped by Willis Reed, a local organizer, who had held community meetings about integrating the bus system even before the boycott. Reed and Jemison organized the United Defense League to represent the black community in dealings with city authorities. A carpool was organized and blacks went to work without using public transportation. Black gas station owners sold fuel at cost to the drivers who volunteered their vehicles to the carpool. The boycott cost the bus company $1,600 in lost fares. After eight days the city council enacted a modified ordinance that allowed blacks to sit from the back to the front seats, with the first two front seats being reserved for whites. Appeased by the council's actions, Jemison made another speech at a meeting in Memorial Stadium and called off the boycott on 23 June 1953. Other black communities used this boycott as a model in Tallahassee, Florida, and Montgomery, Alabama, in 1956 and in New Orleans in 1957. The success of the bus boycott led others to integrate lunch counters and public facilities and triggered an increase in black voter registrations in Baton Rouge, Louisiana. Throughout the years Jemison remained a key player in local civil rights activities and his church hosted several community meetings for desegregation. He also worked on local race relations by inviting white Baptists to worship at Mount Zion.

In 1957 Jemison became the founding secretary of the Southern Christian Leadership Conference (SCLC) founded by a group of civil rights advocates including MARTIN LUTHER KING JR. Four years later he observed with pain the splitting of the NBC. A group of ministers and thousand of constituents, including King and his father, left the NBC because it did not support strong civil rights tactics such as marches and protests and limited tenure for elected leaders. Joseph H. Jackson, president of the NBC from 1953 to 1982, advocated gradualism—the use of lawsuits and less-threatening techniques to fight segregation. Jemison disagreed with Jackson but chose to remain loyal to him and the NBC. In 1965 he was appointed to the governor's interracial commission on race relations. In 1982 Jemison replaced Jackson as NBC president by winning the presidential elections. The following year he was elected president of the Louisiana Baptist State Convention. As the president of two Baptist groups Jemison was one of the most influential religious leaders in America. He increased denominational participation in the ecumenical movement by sending strong delegations to the sessions of both the National Council of Churches and the World Council of Churches. In 1983 he organized the National Baptist Benefits Society, a retirement plan for Baptist ministers that also sold life insurance. In 1984 he voted for a church law that limited presidential tenures to two five-year terms.

The new president also set about recruiting three million new members for the NBC, who would be encouraged to become registered voters. Traditionally, black church leaders took upon themselves the responsibility to educate their constituency about their political rights and duties. In national politics Jemison supported JESSE JACKSON's two presidential runs (1984 and 1988) and proposed a nuclear arms freeze to the Reagan administration. In 1989 Jemison earned for himself great fame in black Baptist history for building the new Baptist World Center (BWC) in Nashville, Tennessee, at the cost of $10 million. Previously the church office of the NBC president had also served as national headquarters for the denomination. The BWC complex also housed the Sunday School Publishing Board. As leader of the Louisiana Convention, Jemison sponsored the construction of the Baptist Student Center at Southern University at the cost of $1 million.

Jemison left the NBC presidency because of tenure restrictions in 1994. His successor, Rev. Henry Lyons, claimed that Jemison left only $38,000 in the NBC treasury and that financial records had disappeared. The state of Louisiana shut down the benefits society for insolvency in 1995, suggesting that Jemison may have been a poor financial manager. In 1995 he resigned the presidency of the Louisiana Baptist State Convention and eight years later retired from the Mount Zion pastorate, which had grown to 1,800 members.

FURTHER READING

Franklin, Katrice. "Baptist Leader Blames Jemison for Church's Problems," (Baton Rouge) *Advocate*, 14 Jan. 1995.

McMickle, Marvin A. *Encyclopedia of African American Christian Heritage* (2002).

Millhollon, Michelle. "Pastor's 54 Years Treasured: Jemison Honored for Civil-Rights Stance," (Baton Rouge) *Advocate*, 30 Jan. 2004.

Nunnally, Derrick. "Bus Boycott Portrait Missing Key Facet," (Baton Rouge) *Advocate*, 30 July 2003.

DAVID MICHEL

Jemmy (fl. 1730s), leader of the 1739 Stono slave rebellion, was born in central Africa, most likely in the Kingdom of Kongo, now part of Angola, and brought as a slave to the British colony of South Carolina in the 1730s. A majority of the African slaves sold by the British Royal African Company to South Carolina in the early eighteenth century originated in Kongo, an independent kingdom that had converted to Christianity more than two hundred years earlier. If typical of Kongolese slaves brought to South Carolina, Jemmy would have worshipped a combination of Roman Catholicism and older African faiths and may well have had knowledge of Portuguese, or some Creolized variant of that language, which was the *lingua franca* of the slave trade and of the Kongo elite. Jemmy's ability as a military leader and the fighting skills of his fellow rebels had probably been acquired through service in a series of wars fought in the Kongo region in the early eighteenth century. By the 1720s and 1730s those wars—in which Jemmy was most likely captured and enslaved—were increasingly fought using pistols and muskets. Thus knowledge of modern military tactics and weaponry, much like knowledge of rice cultivation, was something that African slaves such as Jemmy brought with them to South Carolina.

It is uncertain how long Jemmy had been living in South Carolina at the time he led the Stono rebellion. What is known is that between 1700 and 1739 South Carolina had been transformed from a relatively backward part of the British Empire to a dynamic, rapidly expanding plantation society. The slave population increased dramatically during that time period; and as a result of the labors of a predominantly young, male, and African-born labor force in the rice fields, the volume of rice exports increased as did the profits of South Carolina's planter elite. Many of the recent male arrivals resisted the long hours and back-breaking labor of rice cultivation, and they may have particularly resented having to perform agricultural tasks generally reserved for women in their native lands. Between 1732 and 1739 more than 250 South Carolina slaves—disproportionately male recent arrivals from Africa—escaped the rice fields. Many of them attempted to flee to nearby Florida, where Spanish colonial rulers offered them land and freedom, partly to undermine the British colonial presence in the Carolinas, but also because many of these slaves were fellow Catholics. In August 1739 the imminent possibility of a full-scale war between Britain and Spain persuaded South Carolina's colonial legislature to enact a Security Act requiring that all white men carry firearms to church on Sundays. Fearing that "our Negroes ... are more dreadfull [*sic*] to our safety than any Spanish invaders," Governor Thomas Broughton doubled the number of slave patrollers and strengthened the militia (Pearson, 581).

In the early morning of Sunday, 9 September 1739, two weeks after the announcement of the Security Act, Jemmy was working with around twenty fellow slaves on a public road gang near a bridge over the Stono River, twelve miles south of Charles Town (now Charleston). Preparations for the raid may have begun earlier, at least on the evening of Saturday, September 8, if not before. The Kongolese slaves may have chosen that date to launch a revolt because it coincided with a religious holiday—the Nativity of the Virgin Mary—which was one of the most important in the Catholic calendar. Despite the prevailing climate of fear among the slaveholders, this particular road gang, working on a day when slaves traditionally worked for themselves, appears to have been inadequately guarded.

Sometime before dawn, Jemmy led his men to a nearby store, where they stole guns and gunpowder and then killed the two white men occupying the building. The rebels decapitated the two men, leaving their severed heads on the steps of the store, perhaps in retaliation for similar beheadings of runaway slaves by the South Carolina authorities or perhaps as part of a traditional African martial ritual. Jemmy then led the men immediately to the house of a man named Godfrey; they burned down the house after plundering it for supplies and killed Godfrey, his son, and his daughter. Heading south, they reached Wallace's Tavern at daybreak, but did not kill the innkeeper apparently because he was kind to his slaves. The rebels did, however, kill Wallace's neighbors and more than twenty other whites. They acquired more firearms, powder, provisions, and alcohol as they progressed south of the Stono River, headed, most scholars assume, for Florida. At least thirty and perhaps as many as eighty slaves joined the rebels as they proceeded with drums and banners, one allegedly bearing the slogan "Liberty," through the South Carolina countryside. Historians have speculated that slaves recently arrived from the Kongo, in particular, would have been drawn to the beating of drums and the use of banners. Those who followed Jemmy may have been emboldened by the apparent ease with which the rebels overcame their masters, their growing arsenal of weaponry, and by what appeared to be a strong possibility of reaching friendly territory.

Other slaves resisted Jemmy's forces, however, and the colonial authorities later rewarded thirty of them for doing so. A slave named July was given his freedom and a suit of clothes for killing one of the rebels. Others hid their masters and helped raise the alarm that brought a posse of between twenty and one hundred heavily armed militia men and planters to a large field near the Edisto River by late Sunday afternoon. More importantly, the lieutenant governor of South Carolina, William Bull, witnessed the gathering of the rebels, turned his horse around, and sounded the alarm to local whites and the authorities. Although the rebels had traveled only ten miles from the Stono River Bridge, and were still a long way from Florida, they gathered to celebrate their victory and planned to cross the river the following morning. Again, the nature of their celebrations, which involved ceremonial dancing, drinking, and feasting, resembled Kongo martial traditions. On seeing the militia approach, the rebels ended their celebrations and began

firing, but they immediately received a volley of rifle fire that killed fourteen slaves. Within a few hours, thirty of the rebels were dead, while thirty or more escaped into the woods. Over the following month, most of those who made their escape were captured, killed, and in some cases beheaded. It is not known whether Jemmy was among those killed at Edisto Bridge, or whether he was one of several slaves who apparently reached St. Augustine.

The Stono rebellion proved to be the most serious and deadly slave revolt in colonial North America. The death toll among whites was not exceeded in a U.S. slave revolt until the NAT TURNER slave rebellion in Virginia in 1831. Though not as deadly as similar revolts in Jamaica and other British colonies in the Caribbean, the events in the South Carolina low country in September 1739 persuaded colonial authorities to take swift action to avoid a repeat of Jemmy's uprising. In 1740, for the first time in South Carolina's history, the legislature enacted a rigid slave code so that potential rebels such as Jemmy would be "kept in due subjection and obedience." This slave code gave slaveholders more power to regulate, control, and punish their slaves. It also prohibited slaves from assembling in groups, learning to read, or even earning their own money. Such measures largely succeeded in preventing further large-scale slave revolts in South Carolina during the colonial period.

For more than two centuries black South Carolinians kept alive a memory of the Stono rebellion and celebrated the revolt as a symbol of slave resistance. Jemmy, identified in the colonial records as the captain of this raid, is the only rebel whose name was recorded by the South Carolina authorities at the time of the Stono uprising. In 1937, however, George Cato, a fifty-year-old black laborer in Columbia, South Carolina, told interviewers for the Works Progress Administration's Slave Narrative Project that his great-great-grandfather, also named Cato, had been elected by his fellow slaves to lead the Stono uprising. The first Cato was literate, having been taught to read and write by his master, and he had often written passes for fellow slaves to help them to escape. It is possible that Cato and Jemmy were the same person, though it is equally possible that both men helped direct the rebellion. George Cato's telling of the Stono rebellion, based on oral tradition passed down over two hundred years, confirms many of the details of the events of 9 September 1739 that historians have discovered. These details included the date, the number of whites and slaves killed, the slaves' celebration once they reached the Edisto River, and the goal of reaching St. Augustine. In George Cato's telling of events, the slave rebels at Stono were defiant to the last, as witnessed by the reported final words of Commander Cato: "We don't [like] slavery. We start to jine de Spanish in Florida. We surrender but we not whipped yet and we 'is not converted'" (Rawick, 100).

FURTHER READING

Pearson, Edward A. "'A Countryside Full of Flames': A Reconsideration of the Stono Rebellion and Slave Rebelliousness in the Early-Eighteenth-Century South Carolina Lowcountry," in *The Slavery Reader* (2003).

Rawick, George P., ed. *The American Slave: A Composite Autobiography, North Carolina and South Carolina Narratives* (1977).

Smith, Mark. M. "Remembering Mary, Shaping Revolt: Reconsidering the Stono Rebellion," *Journal of Southern History* (2001).

Thornton, John K. "African Dimensions of the Stono Rebellion," *American Historical Review* (Oct. 1991).

Wood, Peter H. *Black Majority: Negroes in Colonial South Carolina from 1670 through the Stono Rebellion* (1974).

STEVEN J. NIVEN

Jenkins, Clarence (Fats Jenkins) (19 Jan. 1898–6 Dec. 1968), baseball and basketball player, was born in New York City. Jenkins began playing baseball and basketball at a young age and exhibited exceptional talents in each. As a baseball player he was a left-handed outfielder who could cover much ground in the field and hit for average at the plate. As a basketball player he was a commanding point guard whose speed and ball-handling skills translated into dazzling fast breaks and easy lay-ups.

His professional baseball career began first. In 1920 he was signed by the New York Lincoln Giants at the age of twenty-two. No statistics were kept in these beginnings of organized Negro League baseball, but when Jenkins was traded to the Harrisburg Giants in 1923, records show that he hit a .319 average in 1924 and .307 in 1925.

Fats Jenkins was perhaps even better at basketball than baseball. Along with Caribbean-born manager Bob Douglas and players such as TARZAN COOPER and "Wee" Willie Smith, Jenkins established the New York Rens basketball team in 1923. So named because they played in the black-owned Renaissance Hotel in Harlem (their full name was the New York Renaissance Big Five), the Rens played their first game on 23 November 1923, beating the Collegiate Big Five 28-22. Jenkins and the Rens went 15-8 that season, but in 1924 the team began barnstorming the country, playing as many as one hundred games a season. Jenkins was immediately named the captain of the team, and in 1925 the Rens won the first of many Colored World Basketball Championships.

Surprisingly, Jenkins seemed to get better and faster with age in baseball. After his trade to the Bacharch Giants in 1927 he posted a monster .398 average and followed this performance with a .379 batting average in 1928 and .365 in 1929. He was traded again to the Lincoln Giants in 1930 and bounced around the league, playing for the New York Black Yankees (for which he is perhaps best known), Harlem Stars, Pittsburgh Crawfords, Brooklyn Eagles, Brooklyn Royal Giants, Toledo Crawfords, and Philadelphia Stars.

Unlike their biggest rival, the Harlem Globetrotters, the Rens played technically superb basketball rather than wowing the crowd with behind-the-back passes and crossover dribbles. They were, however, known to impress fans with their quick ball movement, a talent at which Fats Jenkins was particularly adept. After a two-year hiatus from 1930 until 1932 owing to the Great Depression, the Rens came back in 1932 to have their best season ever. They won an amazing eighty-eight straight games in eighty-six days and finished the season 112-8, beating the original Celtics for the World Basketball Championship.

In baseball, Jenkins was named to the East-West All-Star teams in 1933 and 1935 (at thirty-five and thirty-seven years of age, respectively). His lifetime batting average is difficult to determine given the roughness of Negro League records, particularly during the time in which Jenkins was playing. Some sources claimed that his career average was somewhere in the neighborhood of .320, while the Biographical Encyclopedia of Negro Baseball credited him with a lifetime average of .334. The truth probably lies more toward the latter projection, somewhere between .330 and .335. Jenkins also stole many bases in his career, though statistics for this category in Negro League ball were almost never faithfully kept.

However, 1939 provided the most significant success for the Rens, as they entered the first ever World Basketball Tournament. The Rens were one of only two black teams (along with the Harlem Globetrotters) invited to the tournament and the event marked the first time all-white professional teams would be pitted against African American teams. The Rens won their bracket easily; playing against the Oshkosh All-Stars of the racially segregated National Basketball League (later to become the NBA), the Rens emerged victorious, beating the All-Stars 34-25. This was Fats Jenkins's final game. He was forty-one.

Jenkins retired from basketball in 1939 and from baseball one year later. Jenkins also managed the Brooklyn Royal Giants in 1940 before his retirement in 1941 at the age of forty-three.

Fourteen years after his basketball retirement, in 1963, the entire 1939 New York Rens team was inducted into the Basketball Hall of Fame. Fats Jenkins thus became one of the few black athletes of the first half of the twentieth century to be fortunate enough to see his achievements recognized by the wider public. Fats Jenkins died in Philadelphia five years after his induction, at the age of seventy.

BAILEY THOMAS PLAYER

Jenkins, David (1811–5 Sept. 1877), editor and abolitionist, was born in Lynchburg, Virginia, the son of William Jenkins. It is not known whether his father was a white slaveholder or a free black, and his mother's name is unknown. Jenkins received a sound education at the hands of a private tutor hired by his father. In 1837 he took up residence in Columbus, Ohio, employing himself as a housepainter and glazier. Jenkins's business acumen led to real estate investment and capital accumulation. The 1850 census for Franklin County, Ohio, records that Jenkins owned real estate valued at $1,500. The census also shows that he was married to Lucy Ann (maiden name unknown), a native of Virginia, and that they had one child.

On 27 December 1843 Jenkins founded and edited the *Palladium of Liberty*, an antislavery weekly newspaper also dedicated to the advancement of the African American in the United States. Inspiration for the establishment of the newspaper evolved from the Ohio State Convention of Colored People held in August 1843. While primarily antislavery, the *Palladium* also provided editorial support for the education of African American children, temperance, moral reform, and suffrage. The paper drew readers from Ohio and the northeastern United States. Among its local and traveling subscription agents were CHARLES HENRY LANGSTON, HENRY HIGHLAND GARNET, WILLIAM WELLS BROWN, William P. Newman, and James Sharp. The *Palladium* ceased publication in the winter of 1844 because of limited financial resources; nevertheless, Jenkins continued his journalistic pursuits with contributions to FREDERICK DOUGLASS's *North Star*.

Jenkins advocated tireless agitation against slavery. From the time of his move to Columbus until the end of the Civil War, he aggressively pursued this position with numerous speeches and writings. He played a key role in the African American convention movement on both the national and state levels. He attended the 1843 National Convention of Colored Citizens in Buffalo, New York, the 1848 National Convention of Colored Freemen in Cleveland, and the 1853 Colored National Convention in Rochester, New York. At the 1848 national convention he coauthored with Douglass, HENRY BIBB, and WILLIAM HOWARD DAY "An Address to the Colored People of the United States," which urged blacks "to act with white antislavery societies wherever they could and where they could not set up societies for themselves without exclusiveness." During the 1850s Jenkins frequently participated in Ohio African American conventions; over the decade his services included the presidency in 1851 and membership on the state central committee. He contributed to the founding of the Ohio Anti-Slavery Society in 1858 at the State Convention of Colored Men. Associates at these meetings included African Americans of national prominence, such as Charles Henry Langston and JOHN MERCER LANGSTON of Oberlin and PETER HUMPHRIES CLARK of Cincinnati.

Throughout the 1840s and 1850s Jenkins corresponded with both white and African American abolitionists, including Cassius Clay, MARTIN ROBISON DELANY, Douglass, Horace Mann, Joshua Giddings, John Quincy Adams, and Benjamin F. Wade. He also regularly attended sessions of the Ohio General Assembly, presenting petitions and memorials on behalf of African American rights. These appearances in the legislative chambers earned Jenkins the nickname "Member at Large." He carried on his person a supply of handbills with blank spaces that could be filled in as needed to advertise meetings denouncing slavery.

Jenkins's abolitionist activities moved beyond his speeches and writings and included direct involvement with the Underground Railroad in central Ohio counties. He also joined the Masonic order, serving as worshipful master of St. Marks Lodge No. 7 in Cincinnati from 1858 to 1860 and in a variety of other posts throughout the 1860s and 1870s.

During the Civil War, Jenkins, a Union supporter, encouraged the enlistment of African

American volunteers. In 1863 he presided over a statewide committee appealing for funds to assist African American troops and the Union cause. Two years later, just prior to the termination of the war, Jenkins was selected vice president of the Ohio State Auxiliary Equal Rights League.

Following the war Jenkins was involved with local Republican Party activities but was thwarted in his efforts to gain political office and appointment. Frustrated, in 1873 he moved from Columbus to Canton, Mississippi, to teach for the Freedmen's Bureau. Two years later Jenkins was elected to the Mississippi legislature and served a single two-year term. He died two years later in Canton. Jenkins's role in the antislavery movement was a critical one, especially in Ohio. His indefatigable energy on behalf of African American rights nationwide over four decades was matched by only a handful of African American leaders of his era.

FURTHER READING

Bell, Howard H., ed. *Minutes of the Proceedings of the National Negro Conventions, 1830–1865* (1969).

Foner, Philip S., and George E. Walker, eds. *Proceedings of the Black State Conventions, 1840–1865*, vol. 1 (1979).

Parham, William H., and Jeremiah A. Brown. *An Official History of the Most Worshipful Grand Lodge Free and Accepted Masons for the State of Ohio* (1906).

Ripley, Peter C., and George C. Carter, eds. *Black Abolitionist Papers* (1981).

This entry is taken from the *American National Biography* and is published here with the permission of the American Council of Learned Societies.

FRANK R. LEVSTIK

Jenkins, David Martin (4 Sept. 1904–9 June 1978), educator and university president, was born in Terre Haute, Indiana, the only child of David W. and Josephine Miller Jenkins, the former a civil engineer. He attended Booker T. Washington elementary school, which was segregated, and graduated in 1917. He then attended Wiley High School, an integrated school, where he became captain of the track team. He then went to Howard University, where he earned a bachelor's degree in engineering in 1925.

Jenkins returned to Terre Haute to work with his father in highway contracting. Lack of success led him to take classes at Indiana State Normal School (now Indiana State University). In 1927 he married Elizabeth Lacy. With her encouragement

he completed his bachelor's degree in education at Indiana State in 1931.

Jenkins was hired to teach at Virginia State College from 1931 to 1933. Convinced that his career lay in education, he applied for and was accepted into the graduate program at Northwestern University with a fellowship. There under the direction of his mentor, Paul A. Witty, a professor of education, he earned a master's degree in 1935 and his doctorate 1937.

The title of Jenkins dissertation was "A Socio-Psychological Study of Negro Children of Superior Intelligence." His approach to the question of racial differences in intelligence was to study black gifted children. He found that black gifted children were different neither in their proportion in the population nor in their personality characteristics. They typically grew up in an upper-class family where they received the kind of environmental stimulation to encourage their intellectual development. "Given opportunity for development … the gifted Negro child will emerge" (Jenkins, p. 189).

Jenkins considered his discovery of B, a black girl with an IQ of 200, to be his important finding. B had the highest recorded IQ at that time. After the completion of his dissertation, follow-up studies were done on B by Witty and his student Viola Theman, who went on to become a professor of education at the University of Pennsylvania.

In addition to his continuing interest in black gifted children, Jenkins was interested in the state of higher education for blacks. From the late 1930s until the mid-1950s he wrote articles on this topic, particularly on historically black colleges and universities, in the *Journal of Negro Education*. In all Jenkins was the author of more than eighty articles.

After obtaining his doctorate, Jenkins was the registrar and professor of education at North Carolina A&T College from 1935 to 1937. He then became dean of instruction at Cheyney State (Pennsylvania) Teachers College from 1937 to 1938. In 1938 he took a position as a professor of education at Howard University, where he spent the next eleven years, except for a year as senior specialist with the U.S. Office of Higher Education.

In 1948 Jenkins was named president of Morgan State College. He remained in that position until his retirement in 1970. He then became director of the Office of Urban Affairs for the American Council of Education until he retired again in 1974.

During his lifetime Jenkins received many honors. He was awarded honorary doctorates from the seven universities including University of Liberia,

Howard University, Morgan State College, Johns Hopkins University, and Indiana State University. He also received the Andrew White Award from Loyola College (Baltimore, Maryland) and the Department of the Army Outstanding Civilian Service Medal. In 1974 Morgan State College dedicated the Martin David Jenkins Behavioral Science Center in his honor.

Jenkins spent his final years in Washington, DC, where he died in 1978.

FURTHER READING
Guthrie, Robert V. *Even the Rat Was White: A Historical View of Psychology*, 2d ed. (2003).
Jenkins, Martin D. "A Socio-Psychological Study of Negro Children of Superior Intelligence." *Journal of Negro Education* 5 (1936): 175–190.
Kearney, Katheryn, and Jene LeBlanc. "Forgotten Pioneers in the Study of Gifted African-Americans." *Roeper Review* 15 (1993): 192–199.
Obituary: *Washington Post*, 11 June 1978.

STEPHEN TRUHON

Jenkins, Edmund (c.Oct. 1845–26 Dec. 1930), law enforcement officer, was born in South Carolina and likely enslaved until he was a young man. Records are unclear as to Jenkins's native locale. Although it is possible he resided most or all of his life in the vicinity of Charleston, South Carolina, details of Jenkins's early life are unknown. The 1880 Federal Census reveals that an Edmund Jenkins was living in St. Stephen's Parish near Charleston, listed as being age thirty-five, a "mulatto," working as a minister. His wife was named Cinda, age thirty-two, and his children were Cuffee (age fourteen), Nelly (age sixteen), Lavinia (age seven), Lily (age three), and Grace (age six months). His wife's name here leads to some confusion; Jenkins's only known wife was Elizabeth (also called Lizzie), making it possible, if this were the same Edmund Jenkins, that he had at least two wives during his lifetime. No listing is found for Jenkins in the incomplete 1890 Census, but he is once again found in the 1900 Census. At the time this count was taken, Jenkins was living in Mount Pleasant, a village within Charleston, South Carolina. Listed as a black man, age fifty-five, with a birth date given as October 1845, Jenkins had a wife named Elizabeth, born in November 1859, whose occupation was listed as that of a midwife. Whereas Elizabeth could both read and write, Edmund Jenkins could not.

From 1900 to 1927 Jenkins served as a policeman, marshal, and assistant police chief in Mount Pleasant. The history of African Americans serving as city or town policemen in the United States is as varied as the locales they served. In the north, black policeman were serving in Philadelphia by 1881, but New York would not hire its first black policeman until Samuel Battle was appointed in 1911, over ten years after Edmund Jenkins's service began. In the South in areas where whites predominated, black policemen were hired as early as 1803, primarily to control the slave population, but by the 1870s black police officers were common throughout the south in small numbers in such cities as Montgomery, Alabama; Jackson, Mississippi; Chattanooga, Tennessee; and Charleston, South Carolina, to name just a few (Dulaney, p. 13). Indeed, during the violence that arose from South Carolina's hotly contested gubernatorial race in 1876, black policemen in Charleston even fought against white citizens. In small black communities in the south, African American policemen were even more common and surely a welcome sight to the citizens they were hired to protect, in stark contrast to white law enforcement officials in most cities and towns throughout the region that generally ignored the violence, lynchings, and disenfranchisement activities perpetrated by whites against blacks during the post-Reconstruction era through the 1930s.

Mount Pleasant, South Carolina, with a population of about six hundred, split evenly between black and white, was not immune from the racial conflict that enveloped the state and the entire south in the post-Reconstruction era. On 23 October 1876, a group of white and black Democrats in Mount Pleasant favoring the old-line white conservative gubernatorial candidate Wade Hampton reportedly barricaded themselves in a house in fear of an alleged mob of black Republicans from outside the town who supported the Reconstruction governor Daniel Chamberlain and threatened to kill the town's Democrats, white and black. Although this threat never came to pass, it does indicate the complexity and fluidity of interracial relations in Mount Pleasant at the end of Reconstruction and in its aftermath, when members of both races belonged to both main political parties. The hiring of Edmund Jenkins as a police officer likewise suggests the willingness of whites to accept some degree of African American policing even in the early 1900s, when most Jim Crow laws were being established.

Although popular accounts state that Jenkins was a World War I veteran and that his career as a law officer began in 1920, this is incorrect. Federal Census records for 1900 clearly indicate that Jenkins began his career as a law enforcement officer prior to 1900, succeeding another man, "also colored," named James Hopkins (McIver, p. 152). Because the 1900 Census was likely conducted by someone in Mount Pleasant who could easily verify Jenkins's listed occupation as a policeman, there is no reason to believe that Jenkins's occupation was otherwise or somehow incorrectly listed. With regard to a possible military career, draft card records give no indication that Edmund Jenkins Sr. was a soldier, and he was likely too old for such duty. Perhaps it was his namesake son who was a soldier, although this has not been documented.

Because crime was not rampant in Mount Pleasant, Jenkins probably spent his time walking a beat, conversing with local residents, helping to solve simple disputes, and arresting occasional petty offenders. Just how much power Jenkins had is unknown; could he, for example, arrest white citizens? The answer to this question as it relates to Jenkins is unknown. However, one historian asserts that even in the post-Reconstruction era, "In most cities … African-American police officers had the right to arrest all citizens who broke the law" (Dulaney, p. 14). Jenkins's power was such that he did have a deputy or "assistant" named Sam Stinney, who was also black. As with any local policeman or town sheriff, a portion of Jenkins's time was surely spent dealing with unruly youths. The town history relates that "the nurses sang to the children. Sam Stinney is the Bully of the wharf, there's a new moon in the sky. But Edmund Jenkins pushed him off, there's a new moon in the sky" (McIver, p. 151). As this rhyme demonstrates, Jenkins was a respected and moderating force in town, which is further supported by the comments of town resident Jervey Royall, who recalled that while he was a boy, Jenkins "was strict but fair. He was very well thought of" (Quick, p. 18). It is also stated that Jenkins "bridged race issues with dignity and wisdom. He was known to many as the voice of reason," a sure indication of the high esteem in which Jenkins was held by all of Mount Pleasant's citizens, white and black (*Post and Courier*, p. 22).

Many questions remain unanswered with regard to Jenkins's family; in the 1920 Census he is listed as being a policeman, age sixty-eight, and living in a boarding house alone, but in his 1930 funeral notice indications are given that his wife, Elizabeth, was still alive. After a period of service as a policeman that lasted at least twenty-seven years, Jenkins retired in 1927 and died three years later. He is buried in the Ocean View portion of the Ocean Grove Cemetery in Mount Pleasant. After his death, Jenkins was never fully forgotten; a public housing complex was named in his honor in 1952. Recent efforts have led to the erection of a historical marker in his honor by the Mount Pleasant Historical Commission on 11 August 2006.

FURTHER READING

Dulaney, W. Marvin. *Black Police in America* (1996).

McIver, Petrona Royall. *History of Mount Pleasant, South Carolina* (1994 reprint).

Post and Courier. "Jenkins Marker Will Be Unveiled" (Charleston, SC, 3 August 2006, p. 27D).

Quick, David. "Mount Pleasant family honors black marshal from 1920s" (*Post and Courier*, Charleston, SC, 10 August 2002, p. 18).

GLENN ALLEN KNOBLOCK

Jenkins, Edmund Thornton (9 Apr. 1894–12 Sept. 1926), clarinetist, composer, and conductor, was born in Charleston, South Carolina, the son of Daniel Jenkins, a former slave, minister, and founder-director of the Jenkins Orphanage Band, and Lena James. Jenkins attended the Avery Institute in Charleston. As a child he learned to play violin, clarinet, and piano. His first music teachers were his father and other instructors at the orphanage, which was founded in December 1891 and formally incorporated as the Orphan Aid Society in July 1892. By the time he was fourteen years old, Jenkins had learned to play all the instruments of his father's brass band. In 1908 he entered Atlanta Baptist College (now Morehouse College), where he studied violin with Kemper Harreld. Jenkins participated in the symphony orchestra, glee club, and other musical activities. During vacations he performed, directed, and toured with the orphanage band. Jenkins left college during the summer of 1914 to travel with the band to London for the Anglo-American Exposition, organized by the Hungarian Imre Kiralfy. The band's original ten-week engagement was cut short by the outbreak of World War I in early August. The exposition closed on 11 August, and the band returned to the United States at the end of October.

Jenkins remained in London to study music. In September 1914 he entered the Royal Academy of Music to study composition with Frederick Corder. He studied clarinet with Edward J. Augarde, and in his fourth year he studied organ with H. W. Richards. He also studied piano. While at the academy, he won several prizes, including a bronze medal in singing (spring 1915), the Oliviera Prescott Prize in composition, the Charles Lucas Prize for merit (July 1918), the Battisan Haynes Prize for composition (December 1918), and the Ross Scholarship (September 1919). Entering into the extracurricular life of the school, he edited the academy's student publication, the *Academite*, during the Lenten and midsummer terms of 1919. He also organized musical groups and performed as clarinetist, organist, and conductor.

In 1918 Jenkins became involved in black politics in Britain. He and a group of friends organized the African Progress Union, established to promote racial understanding. In March or April 1919 Jenkins organized the Coterie of Friends, a social club for young men of color residing permanently or temporarily in Great Britain, including African American soldiers stationed in London during World War I. He also participated in the Pan-African Congress held in London in 1921. That same year Jenkins completed his studies at the Royal Academy of Music and received a distinguished honor: he was elected an associate of the academy, a promotion from his previous position as a subprofessor of clarinet.

Jenkins was studying in England just as jazz spread to Europe. In April 1919 the Original Dixieland Jass [*sic*] Band toured Britain, and on 4 July WILL MARION COOK's Southern Syncopated Orchestra (with which he played briefly) appeared at London's Philharmonic Hall. Black musicians were hired by London hotels, cafés, restaurants, theaters, music halls, and dances to take the place of German musicians. Jenkins began to play regularly at Madame Henry's Dance Hall on Regent Street. In October 1920 Jenkins and Herbert Henry converted the rooftop chamber music hall of Queen's Hall in Langham Place into a nightclub run by their company, the QSH Syndicate, Limited. Jenkins led four other men in a small band. In May 1921 the band made its first recordings in Hayes, Middlesex, on His Master's Voice, the British associate of Victor. Jenkins gained further experience as a dance-band musician in Paris in early 1922, working as a saxophonist and clarinetist (and later conductor) in Art Hickman's Orchestra. A white band, Hickman's Orchestra was one of the leading dance orchestras of America, ranked with those of Vincent Lopez and Paul Whiteman. They played at the Ermitage de Longes Champs in the Bois de Boulogne, a chic Paris tea and night dancing place. Jenkins's contract expired in February 1923, and in the fall he returned to London, where he worked briefly with JAMES P. JOHNSON.

In 1923 Jenkins went to the United States hoping to organize a symphony orchestra of black musicians, establish a music academy, and found a music publishing company with Will Vodery and Robert Young. He vainly tried to find financial backing in New York, Washington, D.C., Boston, Charleston, Chicago, and Baltimore. Only with the financial assistance of his father was he able to found the Anglo-Continental-American Music Press (the elder Jenkins had founded the *Charleston Messenger*, which began circulation in October 1894). Based in Paris, Jenkins's firm published art music compositions as well as popular songs and dance music. Jenkins conducted Will Marion Cook's twenty-one-piece orchestra in a series of concerts at the Shubert Theatre in New York, beginning an engagement Sunday night, 27 January 1924. By October 1924 he had returned to Paris, and by the following spring he was directing a band of black musicians, the International Seven. He continued to compose, and he published some of his own works. He also traveled throughout Europe, often to hear performances of his works or to conduct his dance band. Admitted to the Hôpital Tenon in Paris on 15 July 1926, Jenkins died following an operation for appendicitis.

Jenkins ranks among the first generation of twentieth-century African American art music composers. Inspired by African American musical idioms, in 1919 he completed *Folk Rhapsody*. In 1925 his works *African War Dance* for full orchestra and *Sonata in A Minor* for violoncello won Holstein prizes in New York. Recognized internationally, his *Charlestoniana* was premiered by François Rasse in the Jursaal, Ostend, Belgium, in September 1925. His second *Rhapsody* was presented posthumously during the 1926 season by the Pasdeloup Concert Orchestra with Rhene Baton conducting. All but forgotten in favor of his contemporary SIDNEY BECHET, Jenkins was also important as a transmitter of an early style of jazz to Europe. His 1921 recordings are in a style current in the United States prior to 1914.

Jenkins composed nearly fifty works in various genres, large and small, for both instrumental and vocal ensembles. Among his other well-known and successful works were *Afram*, an opera in three acts (1924); *Rapsodie spirituelle*, for orchestra (1923); and *Rêverie phantasie*, for violin and piano (1919). Jenkins made a total of twenty-one recordings, including "Idol of Mine" (B-1237), "Turque" (B-1236), "The Wind in the Trees" (B-1237), and "I'm Wondering if It's Love" (B-1236) in 1921 on

His Master's Voice. The arrangements of the items recorded in 1921 were similar to those of Paul Whiteman.

FURTHER READING

Chilton, John. *A Jazz Nursery: The Story of the Jenkins' Orphanage Bands* (1980).

Greene, Jeffrey P. *Edmund Thornton Jenkins: The Life and Times of an American Black Composer, 1894–1926* (1982).

Hare, Maud Cuney. *Negro Musicians and Their Music* (1936).

Rye, Howard, and Jeffrey Green. "Black Music Internationalism in England in the 1920s," *Black Music Research Journal* 15 (1995): 93–107.

Obituaries: *New York Age*, 2 Oct. 1926; *New York Age*, 23 Oct. 1926; *The Black Perspective in Music* 14 (1986): 143–180.

This entry is taken from the *American National Biography* and is published here with the permission of the American Council of Learned Societies.

GAYLE MURCHISON

Jenkins, Elaine Brown (2 Apr. 1916–21 Sep. 1999), chair of the Council of 100 Black Republicans, business owner, the first teacher of African descent in the Denver, Colorado, public schools, was born in Butte, Montana, the daughter of Russell S. Brown Sr., a minister (and later general secretary) of the African Methodist Episcopal (AME) Church, and Floy Smith Brown. The example of her grandfather, Charles S. Smith, founder of the business school at Wilberforce University in Ohio, was a strong influence in her later life. There is no record of why the Brown family was in Butte; however, small but thriving African American communities to the northeast were centered around Union Bethel AME Church in Great Falls and St. James AME Church in Helena.

By the time Elaine Brown was three years old, the family had moved to Atlanta, Georgia, where her brother, Russell Brown Jr., was born. In 1933, the family moved to Denver, Colorado, where her father accepted a call as pastor of Shorter Community AME Church. Soon after, she entered Denver University. Receiving a bachelor's degree in 1937, Brown began her teaching career at Whittier Elementary School in Denver. On 24 June 1940, she married Howard Jenkins, whom she had met at the university in 1935. The following year, he was the first African American to pass the Colorado bar exam. In 1946, she moved with her husband to Washington, DC, where he closed out his work in Colorado for the wartime National Wage Stabilization Board, and accepted a position on the faculty of Howard University Law School.

Elaine Jenkins taught in Washington at Buchanan, Mott, and Parkview elementary schools, and served for a time as assistant superintendent of the National Training School for Girls (renamed in 1964 in honor of its first president, NANNIE BURROUGHS). She was chosen national director of the Just Folks for Nixon–Lodge Committee in the 1960 presidential election, and in the early 1960s as vice chairman of the DC Republican Central Committee. She remained active in the Republican Party for the remainder of her life, attending national conventions as a delegate during the next three decades. In 1963, Howard Jenkins was appointed to the National Labor Relations Board, where he served for twenty years. Elaine Jenkins was named in the early 1960s as community coordinator of the Amidon Tri-School Project, which sought to integrate the diverse classes and races of students at the Bowden, Syphax, and Amidon schools in southwest DC, an area targeted for urban renewal.

In 1970, Jenkins formed One America, a Washington, DC, firm specializing in rehabilitation programs for female offenders and in affirmative action planning, with several early contracts focused on the utilities industry. The company also offered program design and evaluation, technical and management assistance, and data processing services. In 1973 One America was named by *Black Enterprise* as one of the Top 100 Black Businesses in America. Jenkins considered 1975 a "comeback year" with sales of $800,000 and a staff of twenty-two employees. In 1976, the company opened a branch office in Houston, Texas. Large corporations, she reported, "have gained confidence in companies like ours. They've realized they can't do the black thing themselves but we can" (*Black Enterprise*, June 1976, pp. 210, 212).

Jenkins received a number of appointments during Richard Nixon's presidency, including membership on the Nelson Commission studying the efficiency of District of Columbia government, the Citizens Advisory Council on European Affairs, which aided the State Department, and in 1974, the National Advisory Council on Education of Disadvantaged Children. She was also a member of the Urban League and the United Givers Fund in Washington, DC, a founder of the Alpha Wives (a charitable endeavor by wives and widows of members of the Washington, DC, Alpha Phi Alpha Fraternity), and served as president of the Howard

University Faculty Wives, national vice president of the Black Women's Political Caucus, and a trustee of the District of Columbia Institute on Mental Health.

In 1982, Jenkins joined the black Republicans Art Fletcher and Clarence Pendleton in meeting with South Carolina Senator Strom Thurmond to advocate that he support renewal of the Voting Rights Act of 1965. When President Ronald Reagan's cabinet divided in 1985 over Attorney General Edwin Meese's proposal to water down affirmative action guidelines—contained in an executive order signed by President Lyndon B. Johnson—Jenkins put her support behind Labor Secretary William Brock, HUD Secretary Samuel Pierce, Transportation Secretary Elizabeth Dole, and HHS Secretary Margaret Heckler, writing to Meese that "striking out the executive order would be extremely politically unwise" (*Jet*, 11 Nov. 1985, p. 4).

In an interview with *Jet* magazine in 1986, Jenkins criticized many African American political leaders for "An unwillingness to accept the two-party system as a way of being involved at all points of decision making. And this is being perpetuated by the present core of predominantly Democratic leadership, sometimes for selfish future controls." She also lamented "a dearth of Black teachers and educators willing to introduce creative and non-traditional training such as foreign languages (Russian, Japanese, Arabic), understanding the stock market, banking and space technology as important learning areas," and the absence of any "concerted drive to help ourselves via our own private sector initiatives." (*Jet*, 17 Nov. 1986, p. 12). That year she again served as vice president of the District of Columbia Republican Committee.

A member and one-term national cochair of Delta Sigma Theta sorority, Jenkins worked at sorority conventions to encourage businesswomen of African descent to develop business plans or strengthen existing ventures. In 1996 she published a book, *Jumping Double Dutch*, pleading for racial diversity in the Republican Party, while advocating that more African Americans become involved in the party. Jenkins died of a heart ailment at her home in Kensington, Maryland, and was survived by her husband, brother, two children, Judith and Lawrence, and two grandchildren.

FURTHER READING

Smith, Jessie Carney. *Notable Black American Women: Book 2* (1996).

CHARLES ROSENBERG

Jenkins, Esau (3 July 1910–30 Oct. 1972), businessman, educator, and civil rights leader, was born on Johns Island off the coast of Charleston, South Carolina, the only child of Eva (Campbell) and Peter Jenkins, the latter a rice and cotton farmer. Growing up on Johns Island, Esau Jenkins experienced first-hand the plight of African Americans on the Sea Islands of South Carolina, which was one of hardship and impoverishment. Jenkins's early formal education—or lack thereof—was common for many African American children on Johns Island in the early twentieth century. Because of the death of his mother and in an effort to help with the family income, Jenkins was obligated to leave Legareville Elementary School in the fourth grade. He initially went to work on a boat in Charleston harbor but returned to Johns Island as a vegetable and cotton farmer in the early 1920s. However, his resolve to obtain an education did not waver. He went to night school, worked with tutors, and took correspondence courses to increase his knowledge. Jenkins also learned sufficient Greek to attempt to communicate with immigrant grocers in Charleston. In 1926 Jenkins married Janie Jones, also a Johns Islander. Together they had thirteen children, and of the seven who survived to adulthood, all went on to earn college degrees.

Jenkins's business savvy led him to establish a successful trucking business, carrying vegetables to stores in downtown Charleston. Prosperity from this business, as well as the booming economy during World War II, allowed Jenkins to invest in other ventures and he soon became the owner of a fruit store, the Hot Spot Record Shop, and the J&P Motel and Café, all in Charleston. As a successful business owner, Jenkins had gotten a taste of the benefits of education, participation in commerce, and the conveniences afforded by urban life. As a result, he committed himself to improve the condition of his fellow isolated African American islanders through the means of education and political activism.

In 1945, because of nonexistent secondary education for African Americans on Johns Island, Jenkins purchased a bus to transport island children to Burke High School in downtown Charleston. The county school board initially acknowledged a need for this service and paid the cost of transportation. However, the school board later conceded the need for a high school on Johns Island and Jenkins was instrumental in the organization of what became the Haut Gap School in 1953. In 1948 Jenkins purchased several more buses in order to help islanders commute to work on the Charleston peninsula. Jenkins himself would drive the buses. On the morning drives, Jenkins stressed the importance of voting and trained his passengers to recite sections from the South Carolina State Constitution, which was a requirement to vote in South Carolina in the 1940s. Later in 1948 Jenkins organized the Progressive Club, which met in the Moving Star Hall and was a center for various educational, political, economic, and cultural activities for the advancement of the people of Wadmalaw, Yonges, James, and Johns Island. The Progressive Club later became a center for citizenship schools and voter registration campaigns in the mid 1950s.

In 1954, through the advice of fellow educator and civil rights leader SEPTIMA CLARK, Jenkins attended the Highlander Folk School's United Nations Workshop on race relations. The Highlander Folk School, in Monteagle, Tennessee, was founded in 1932 by Myles Horton. It offered adult education and assisted in the establishment of citizenship schools throughout the South. After returning to South Carolina, Jenkins, Septima Clark, and Bernice Robinson worked with Myles Horton and the Highlander Folk School to set up a citizenship school on Johns Island, which officially opened on 7 January 1957. The school period was two hours a night for two months and included literacy instruction, lessons on voter registration, and training in practical concerns such as completing postal order forms. In the late 1950s Jenkins, along with other leaders of the Progressive Club and Citizenship Schools, met with Reverend MARTIN LUTHER KING JR. to develop plans for bringing schools to other rural communities of coastal South Carolina. The concept soon spread, and Jenkins's model for education was implemented on other Sea Islands and in Charleston. By 1964, through the work of Jenkins and his colleagues, over fourteen thousand African Americans had registered to vote. The schools helped to create a united and educated African American front in Charleston, which later proved to be critical in the civil rights struggles of the 1960s.

During that decade Jenkins played a pivotal role in the civil rights movement. He served on the boards for the Charleston chapter of the NAACP, the Southern Christian Leadership Conference (SCLC), and the Conference of Human Relations. In June of 1963, in an act of nonviolent resistance towards local discrimination in Charleston, Jenkins, along with other adults and teenagers, was arrested while trying to receive service at the Fort Sumter Hotel. Into the mid-1960s he continued to labor for enhanced voter education, health care, and the improved general social and economic conditions of African Americans on the Sea Islands. His efforts brought greater voter awareness as well as increased job opportunities for African Americans in Charleston. Perhaps the most prominent example of this is Jenkins's role on the Citizens Committee of Charleston. Through the Citizens Committee, Jenkins was able to initiate the employment of the first African American sanitation truck drivers and the first African American bus drivers in Charleston, and he began the first Head Start center for children in Charleston, which provided preschool and after school programs. Jenkins also established the C.O. Federal Credit Union in 1966, which assisted developing communities by approving loans to finance automobiles, homes, renovations, education, hospitalization, and the establishment of businesses.

Esau Jenkins met a premature death at the age of sixty-two in an automobile accident, leaving a void in the Charleston community. Just before his death, Jenkins was appointed to the state advisory committee for the U.S. Commission on Civil Rights. Jenkins's motto that "Love is Progress, Hate is Expense" influenced the work of his children, grandchildren, and others in the African American community in Charleston and the surrounding Sea Islands.

FURTHER READING

The bulk of Esau Jenkins's papers are contained in the archives at the Avery Research Center for African American History and Culture, College of Charleston, Charleston, South Carolina.

Carawan, Guy, and Candie Carawan. *Ain't You Got a Right to the Tree of Life? The People of Johns Island, South Carolina—Their Faces, Their Words, and Their Songs* (1989).

Drago, Edmund L. *Charleston's Avery Center: From Education and Civil Rights to Preserving the African American Experience* (2006).

Frazier, Herb. "Jenkins, Esau," *The South Carolina Encyclopedia*, ed. Walter Edgar (2006).

Woodruff, Nan. *Esau Jenkins (1910–1972): A Retrospective View of the Man and His Times* (1984).

OTIS WESTBROOK PICKETT

Jenkins, Ferguson "Fergie" Arthur, Jr. (13 Dec. 1943–), baseball player, was born in Chatham, Ontario, the only child of Ferguson Jenkins Sr., a chauffeur and chef, and Dolores Jenkins. Jenkins moved with his parents to a mostly white neighborhood when he was seven, but endured few incidents of racism growing up. Though his primary athletic interest was hockey, he also played basketball, and he began to field baseballs when he was eight years old with his father, a former semi-pro ballplayer. He started as a hard-hitting first baseman, but got his first taste of pitching when he was fifteen, filling in for a sore teammate on the Chatham Junior All-Stars team. Eight major league teams had already shown interest in the tall Jenkins—a Pittsburgh Pirates scout called his home when he was a sophomore at Chatham Vocational High School, mistaking him for a senior—but it was the Philadelphia Phillies that most interested him. Given special strength training by two Philadelphia scouts throughout high school, Jenkins ultimately signed with them following his graduation in 1962.

In his first season in rookie ball, Jenkins displayed the precision pitching that would mark his career, walking just nineteen batters in sixty-seven innings while posting a 0.97 ERA and seven wins. Another type of education came off the field, as he experienced southern racism and segregation for the first time. Racial epithets and segregated facilities in the minor league towns were a trial that many black and Latin athletes endured. For players born and raised in fully integrated towns outside of America, it was difficult to comprehend.

Jenkins pitched year-round, spending the regular season in Philadelphia's minor leagues and the winter in Nicaragua and Puerto Rico. On 6 September 1965 Jenkins made his major league debut, replacing the future Hall of Famer Jim Bunning in a tied game, and earning a win in extra innings. Three weeks into the following season, he was traded to the Chicago Cubs in what became one of the more lopsided trades in baseball history, as Jenkins, John Herrnstein, and Adolfo Phillips were traded to the Cubs for Larry Jackson and Bob Buhl. While Jackson put together three fairly good seasons for the Phillies, he retired after the 1968 season; Buhl had a mediocre 1966 season with the Phillies, and was out of baseball having pitched just three innings in 1967.

Jenkins made his debut for Chicago in April 1966, when he entered a game against the Los Angeles Dodgers in long relief in the third inning. He pitched effectively, but also hit a home run and single, driving in both Cubs runs. Jenkins made his first start three months later, and by the end of the season was a fixture in the Cubs' rotation, earning the favor of cantankerous manager Leo Durocher.

In 1967, his first full season with the Cubs, the twenty-three-year-old Jenkins won a spot on the All-Star Game roster and tied a record by striking out six batters in three innings of work. By the end of the year, Jenkins had won twenty games, broken the Cubs record for strikeouts in a season, and finished second in the Cy Young Award voting. His popularity increased as well; hearing of his high school basketball success, the Harlem Globetrotters' general manager George Gillette signed the six-foot five-inch pitcher to play with the barnstorming team that winter and the next.

Jenkins's 1968 was symptomatic of his career; despite losing 1-0 five times, he still won twenty games, and finished second in the league in strikeouts. Poor offensive support and bad luck seemed to follow him: he suffered forty-five shutouts in his career. Though he never pitched for a postseason team, he joined the Boston Red Sox a year after their 1975 World Series appearance, and he retired from the Cubs the spring before they made their first postseason appearance since 1945.

The 1970 season, though successful professionally for him, was emotionally difficult for Jenkins. His wife, Kathy, whom he had married in 1965, suffered a miscarriage; weeks later, his blind mother succumbed to a long bout with cancer. The day after his mother's funeral, Jenkins won his twentieth game of the season. In 1971 he became the first Cub to win a Cy Young Award, winning twenty-four games with a 2.77 ERA, and earning *The Sporting News* Player of the Year honor. From 1967 through 1972 Jenkins strung together six consecutive twenty-win seasons, a streak that saw him average twenty-one wins and 248 strikeouts over the span.

Following a subpar 1973 season, Jenkins was dealt by the Cubs to the Texas Rangers. He bounced back in grand fashion, won twenty-five games to become the franchise's first twenty-game winner, and was named *The Sporting News* Comeback Player of the Year. Traded at the end of 1975 to the Red Sox, Jenkins pitched adequately, but was shipped back to the Rangers following the 1977 season. Early in 1980 he won his hundredth American League game, becoming the sixth pitcher to record a hundred wins in both leagues. Jenkins appropriately finished his career with the Cubs, retiring in March 1984. After his retirement from Major League Baseball (MLB), Jenkins played two seasons with the London Majors of the Intercounty Major Baseball League (IBL), an amateur men's baseball league operating in central and southern Ontario, Canada.

Held in high regard for his moral fiber, Jenkins suffered a serious blow on 25 August 1980, when he was arrested for cocaine, marijuana, and hashish possession during a road game in Toronto. Though Jenkins denied ownership of the narcotics, the commissioner of Major League Baseball, Bowie Kuhn, suspended Jenkins indefinitely. A month later, arbitrator Raymond Goetz had the decision overturned. That winter Jenkins was convicted in a Canadian court of law, but a judge erased the verdict, acknowledging the pitcher's fine record of community service. Jenkins had associated himself with both cancer and blindness foundations following his mother's death. He later established the Fergie Jenkins Foundation, which hosted events to raise money for the Canadian Red Cross, the Canadian National Institute for the Blind, and a number of other charities.

Retirement dealt Jenkins significant personal tragedy. Named the Texas Rangers' Triple-A pitching coach, Jenkins and his new wife (his first marriage having ended in divorce), Mary-Anne, were living in Oklahoma; in 1991 she was seriously injured in a car accident, and died just four days after Jenkins was elected to the Baseball Hall of Fame. Jenkins persevered, raising horses on his ranch, and helping found the Oklahoma Sports Museum. A year and a half later, soon after he accepted a coaching job with the Cincinnati Reds' Double-A affiliate, Jenkins's new girlfriend, Cynthia Takkieddine, took her own life and that of Jenkins's three-year-old daughter by carbon monoxide poisoning. In 1993, Jenkins married his third wife, Lydia Farrington.

The first Canadian to gain entry to the Hall of Fame, Jenkins praised his country in his inauguration speech. Canada was proud of its homegrown hero; the nation's Film Board made a one-hour documentary about him in 1972, his sixth-straight twenty-win season. In 2002 he became the founding commissioner of the short-lived Canadian Baseball League, whose postseason classic was known as the "Jenkins Cup." Jenkins's status as a Canadian hero was acknowledged not only by his induction into the Canadian Baseball Hall of Fame in 1987, but also by his being named to the prestigious Order of Canada in 1979 (though the inauguration did not take place until 4 May 2007).

One of the first great black pitchers in the major leagues, Jenkins also extended the popularity of the sport to America's northern neighbor. When the forty-year-old Jenkins retired in 1983, he ranked sixth on the all-time strikeout list with 3,192, and nineteenth on the career wins list with 284. His win and strikeout total were the highest for any black pitcher in the Major Leagues.

FURTHER READING

Jenkins, Ferguson, with George Vass. *Like Nobody Else: The Fergie Jenkins Story* (1973).

Elliott, Bob. *The Northern Game: Baseball the Canadian Way* (2005).

Pashko, Stanley. *Ferguson Jenkins: The Quiet Winner* (1975).

Turcotte, Dorothy. *The Game Is Easy—Life Is Hard: The Story of Ferguson Jenkins Jr.* (2002).

ADAM W. GREEN

Jenkins, Howard, Jr. (16 June 1915–3 June 2003), one of the earlier attorneys of African descent admitted to the bar in Colorado, and the first to be appointed to the National Labor Relations Board, was born in Denver, the son of Missouri natives Howard Jenkins Sr., and Nellie Poage Jenkins. Both were schoolteachers, although in Denver, Jenkins Sr. took a job delivering mail for the postal service.

Jenkins attended public schools in Denver. Neither Whittier nor Mariah Mitchell elementary schools were segregated by race, but he was the only African American student at Mitchell. After being chosen for the lead role in an operetta because of his strong singing voice, he was removed from the role because the script called for male and female leads to hold hands, and the female lead was non-black. At Manual High School, there were separate proms for students of presumed entirely European descent and students of visible African descent. Jenkins and several friends chained the gym doors so the "white" couples could not get in for their prom.

Entering the University of Denver in 1932, Jenkins was the only student of African descent, but was not excluded from any part of campus life. Transferring after one year to the University of Colorado at Boulder, he found that in the absence of a separate dorm for "colored" students, he had to find housing off campus. He and three friends got a job hashing at a Chi Psi fraternity house, in exchange for room and board. Jenkins returned to the University of Denver for his final two years, graduating in 1936.

Working his way through law school, he got a job as a clerk at the Post Office. In 1940, one year before earning his bachelor of laws degree, he married fellow University of Denver graduate Elaine Brown, a teacher in Denver public schools, on 24 June 1940. He finished law school in 1941, and was admitted to the bar in Colorado. Some sources, including his alma mater, claim that he was the first African American to pass the Colorado bar exam, but J. Clay Smith Jr., in *Emancipation: The Making of the Black Lawyer, 1844–1944* lists several dating back to 1883, including Archie Willard McKinney, only a year before Jenkins (pp. 490–491).

Jenkins opened his first law practice in space rented for $50 a month from his godfather, the Denver dentist Clarence Holmes. He volunteered for the Army Judge Advocate General's Office when the United States entered World War II, but was turned down, a colonel later telling him explicitly, "The Army has no place for Negroes in the JAG corps." He was employed by the Office of Price Administration in Denver, then at the War Production Board, which appointed him as regional attorney in 1943.

An appointment as Chief Regional Enforcement Officer of the National Wage Stabilization Board in 1945 lasted only a few months. On assignment in Washington, DC, to file a closing report for the board, he was invited to join the faculty of Howard University Law School, where he taught labor and administrative law from 1946 to 1956.

Jenkins worked for the building laborers local union in the District of Columbia, and the National Alliance of Postal Workers to curtail what he termed a sinister threat to the security of federal employees. In 1949 he charged that "prejudiced officials were using the threat of Communist hysteria as a weapon with which to silence Negroes who demanded their rights as first-class citizens" (Rubio, p. 347, fn. 59). Jenkins participated in writing briefs for the landmark *Brown v. Board of Education* case in 1954; although not prominent in oral argument, he was one of nine attorneys who appeared before the United States Supreme Court in the case. In 1955 he pursued additional education in philosophy of law, constitutional history, and legal history, at New York University.

In March 1956 Jenkins was appointed legislative attorney in the Solicitor's Office of the Department of Labor. In this job, he participated in drafting proposed legislation that became the Landrum-Griffin Act in 1959. He was then appointed director of the Office of Regulations at the Bureau of Labor-Management Reports, a key department for enforcement of the act. In 1962 he became assistant commissioner of the bureau. During his tenure in all of these positions, he worked to eliminate racial discrimination in labor unions and to establish that discrimination on the basis of race or sex constitutes an unfair labor practice.

In July 1963 President Kennedy announced that he would nominate Jenkins for a vacancy on the National Labor Relations Board. With the support of Colorado representative Byron Rogers, and the state's Republican senators, Gordon Allot and Peter Dominick, he was confirmed, and sworn in on 29 August 1963. Jenkins took an active speaking role, to the extent that he could do so without creating a conflict of interest. At an educational meeting of the American Bar Association Section of Labor Relations Law in August 1967, Jenkins was the main speaker for a morning session, delivering a "provocative talk on the duties of the labor relations bar," which "generated a lively question period," according to the association's *Journal* (vol. 53, Nov. 1967, p. 1068).

In July 1968 he was nominated to a second 5-year term on the National Labor Relations Board by President Lyndon Johnson. Reappointment by President Richard Nixon in 1973 was not a foregone conclusion, despite the fact that Jenkins and his wife were both lifelong Republicans. In 1969 the Nixon administration maneuvered to avoid having Jenkins become NLRB chair, which would have been routine for the senior member of the board. (*Jet*, 14 Aug. 1969, p. 12). His renomination in 1973 was opposed by an informal group of management lawyers connected with the National Association of Manufacturers and the United States Chamber of Commerce.

In 1972 Nixon had told Douglas Soutar, former vice president of the American Smelting and Refining Company, a leading member of the committee, that he would reappoint John Fanning, strongly backed by the building trades unions, to a fourth term, because Nixon expected to take strong support from this constituency if George McGovern received the Democratic nomination for president. But, employers were promised a more acceptable promanagement nominee in place of Jenkins the following year, which was expected to tip the balance of power on the board (Gross, pp. 198, 219, 222). Nixon announced Jenkins's renomination for a third term on 27 August, only hours before his second term expired; he was not sworn in until November. He was nominated for a fourth term in 1978 by President James Earl Carter, and retired in 1983, recognizing that the Reagan administration was receptive to urging from the U.S. Chamber of Commerce not to reappoint him. A year later, no nomination had been made to fill the position.

Jenkins in later years assisted his wife's consulting business, One America, and served as president of the Brightwood Community Association in DC. He was a director of the Nation's Capitol Child and Family Development organization, a member of the Cosmos Club, and the Epsilon Boule fraternity. In 1997 he wrote to Senate Labor Committee Chair James Jeffords in support of President Clinton's nomination of Alexis M. Herman to be secretary of labor. "I am confident that she will perform admirably" wrote the longtime Republican. He died of a heart ailment at Providence Hospital, Washington, DC, preceded in death by his wife, Elaine Brown Jenkins, 21 September 1999, son Howard Jenkins III, in 1993. and2. He was survived by son Lawrence C. Jenkins and two grandsons.

FURTHER READING

The Howard Jenkins Jr. papers are housed at the Penrose Library, University of Denver, primarily covering his years at the National Labor Relations Board.

The most comprehensive biography of Jenkins's life, based on his papers and oral interviews at Penrose Library, is maintained by University of Denver Law School at http://law.du.edu/jenkins/ table.htm.

Gross, James A., *Broken Promise: The Subversion of U.S. Labor Relations Policy, 1947–1994* (2003).

Rubio, Philip F. *There's Always Work at the Post Office: African American Postal Workers and the Fight for Jobs, Justice, and Equality* (2010).

Obituary: *Washington Post,* 7 June 2003.

CHARLES ROSENBERG

Jenkins, Norman A. (10 June 1882–23 Dec. 1935), physician, hospital founder, and entrepreneur, was born in Anderson, South Carolina, to Green and Clara (Riley) Jenkins, the fourth child in a family of nine children. His father was a successful farmer who owned 319 acres of land and also owned and operated several businesses simultaneously, including a grocery store, a fish market, a theater, a dairy farm, and a wood farm. Green Jenkins had never attended school, but he was an articulate man who read exceptionally well and was also skilled in math. His wife Clara died a few months after the birth of her youngest child.

All the Jenkins children received their early education at the Taylor School in Anderson, South Carolina, and all pursued a college education. Whitner, the sixth child, died while attending the historically black Claflin College in Orangeburg, but Joseph Newton became a Baptist minister and lecturer at Baylor University in Waco, Texas; Green F. became a teacher and dean at the historically black Morris College in Sumter, South Carolina; and the three sisters Clara E., Ida C., and Daisy F. all became teachers. The other three brothers pursued careers in healthcare: Norman A. became a physician, Moses F. became a pharmacist, and Douglass K. became a dentist.

Norman A. Jenkins graduated from Benedict College in Columbia, South Carolina, in 1903. After graduation he decided to pursue a medical degree, but there were no medical schools for African Americans in the state of South Carolina. The following year he entered Leonard Medical School of Shaw University in Raleigh, North Carolina. Leonard offered a rigorous four-year program when the white medical schools in the state offered only two-year programs. At Leonard, Jenkins was trained by some of the finest white doctors in the state and received his degree in 1908.

The medical board in South Carolina was said to mistreat African American physicians who sat for the state examination by grading them more harshly than their white peers. Many African American physicians from South Carolina refused to return to their home state to practice medicine and sought opportunities in the more tolerant North. Despite the hostile racial climate Jenkins returned to his native South Carolina in 1908, passed the state exam, and received a license to practice medicine. Shortly thereafter he began his medical career in Anderson. Jenkins later completed postgraduate coursework at Brooklyn School and Hospital in New York and at Rush Medical College in Chicago.

Norman's father had stressed the importance of land ownership and entrepreneurship to his family. With a son-in-law he later invested in a grocery store that was located at 402 Main Street in Anderson, South Carolina. Green also built a three-story structure on the same street that housed offices and a drugstore named Jenkins Pharmacy #1. Several years later Norman Jenkins built a two-story business complex on Anderson's Church Street. There were businesses housed downstairs, including Jenkins Pharmacy #2, operated by his brother Moses, a pharmacist. The building was also home to a hotel that operated upstairs.

In 1921 Norman Jenkins helped to found the Victory Savings Bank and served as its secretary; despite segregation, both black and white customers had accounts there. The bank was housed in an office complex that Jenkins owned at 1105 Washington Street in Columbia. This same complex housed a medical office for Norman, and a dental office for Douglass. In 1945 Norman and Douglass's nephew Frederick G. Jenkins, DDS, who had been a major in the Army Dental Corps, joined Douglass's dental practice.

The Jenkins siblings then pooled their money and bought almost a block on Pine Street in the Waverly neighborhood of Columbia, an area where black professionals including doctors, lawyers, and nurses lived. Norman Jenkins then founded and built the Waverly Fraternal Hospital, which opened in 1924 and was South Carolina's first hospital founded exclusively by African Americans. Jenkins served as the hospital's surgeon-in-chief and superintendent, and because he was Waverly's resident doctor he was always on call. Waverly Fraternal improved access to health care for Columbia's black citizens and gave local black doctors practicing rights. All the hospital's nurses were black. The hospital continued to grow, and eventually the original structure was torn down, replaced by a more modern building.

In 1924 Jenkins married Joyce Elizabeth Jones of Charleston, South Carolina, the daughter of a prominent Baptist minister, the Reverend W. P. Jones, who was pastor of Central Baptist Church. Norman and Joyce had two children: Joyce Elise, who became a journalist with *Life* magazine, and Norman A. Jr., who was an attorney and judge in Philadelphia, Pennsylvania.

Throughout his life Jenkins held membership in a number of professional organizations, including the National Medical Association, an important organization for many of the nation's African American physicians. It was founded in 1895 when only white physicians were eligible for membership in the American Medical Association. Jenkins was elected president of both the Palmetto Medical Association and the Congaree Medical Society. Jenkins was also actively involved in a number of civic organizations, holding memberships in Omega Psi Phi fraternity, the Elks, the Knights of Pythias, and the Odd Fellows. An active member of the NAACP, Jenkins was also involved in politics and once was the secretary of the Sixth District Republican Convention. He worked tirelessly to improve health care for African Americans until his death on 23 December 1935. In 1968 the trustees of Benedict College voted to name the board room on campus in his honor.

FURTHER READING

Durham, Diana K. "Leonard Medical School: The Making of African American Physicians," *Carolina Peacemaker* (16 Feb. 2006).

Savitt, Todd K. "Walking the Color Line: Alonzo McClennan, *The Hospital Herald*, and Segregated Medicine in Turn-of-the-Twentieth-Century Charleston, South Carolina," *South Carolina Historical Magazine* 104, no. 4 (Oct. 2003).

DIANA KRISTINE DURHAM

Jenkins, Robert H., Jr. (1 June 1948–5 Mar. 1969), Vietnam War soldier and Medal of Honor recipient, was born in Interlachen, Florida, the son of Robert and Willie Mae Jenkins. He graduated from Central Academy High School in nearby Palatka, Florida, the state's first African American high school, in 1967 and joined the military the following year to serve in Vietnam.

Robert Jenkins Jr. enlisted in the Marine Corps on 2 July 1968 at Jacksonville, Florida, and completed his basic training at Parris Island, South Carolina. Assigned for subsequent training at the Marine Corps Expeditionary Forces base at Camp LeJeune, North Carolina, in July 1968, he was assigned to the 3rd Reconnaissance Battalion, 3rd Marine Division. After his unit was designated for service in Vietnam, Jenkins subsequently became a machine gunner in Company C of the 3rd Recon. Battalion.

During the Vietnam War era over 200,000 African American soldiers served in the U.S. Army, Marine Corps, and Navy; it was the first war since the American Revolution in which black soldiers served on an equal footing with their white counterparts. The service of these African American soldiers, however, was not without controversy; not only did racial tensions lead to incidents at a number of army bases and aboard several navy ships, but the fact that a disproportionately higher number of black men were drafted for the increasingly unpopular war than whites also raised concerns among African American civic leaders. Despite these problems, the heroics of soldiers like Jenkins, WILLIAM BRYANT, GARFIELD LANGHORN, RILEY PITTS, and sixteen other African American Medal of Honor recipients (five of them Marines) proved yet again, as they had done in Korea and World War II, that African American soldiers were vital to America's military efforts.

By late February 1969 Private First Class Robert Jenkins Jr. was stationed at Fire Support Base (FSB) Argonne, Quang Tri, in the Republic of Vietnam, just south of the demilitarized zone. On the morning of 5 March 1969 he was part of a twelve-man reconnaissance group occupying a defensive position at FSB Argonne when they came under attack from a North Vietnamese force using mortars, automatic rifles, and hand grenades. Serving as a machine gunner, Jenkins was delivering return fire as part of a two-man team when an enemy soldier threw a hand grenade into his position. Without hesitation or regard for his own personal safety, Jenkins threw his fellow marine to the ground and jumped on top of him to provide a shield for the blast that he knew was coming. Jenkins's body subsequently absorbed the grenade blast, and while he was severely wounded and later died from his wounds, he had saved another marine. For this action, Robert Jenkins Jr. was posthumously awarded the Medal of Honor, which was presented to his family at a White House ceremony on 20 April 1970. Jenkins, the last African American member of the Marine Corps to earn the Medal of Honor (as of 2011) was buried at the Sister Springs Baptist Cemetery in Interlachen, Florida.

FURTHER READING

Hanna, Charles W. *African American Recipients of the Medal of Honor* (2002).

Murphy, Mary E. "Robert Henry Jenkins, Jr." http://www.virtualwall.org/dj/JenkinsRH01a.htm. Several photos of Jenkins and his Medal of Honor citation can be found at this website.

GLENN ALLEN KNOBLOCK

Jennings, Darius T. (13 Nov. 1980–2 Nov. 2003), soldier, was born Darius Tomel Jennings in Orangeburg County, South Carolina, the son of Harriet Elaine Johnson (maiden name unknown), a florist who also worked in a medical tool plant. Information about his father is unknown; Darius and his younger sister, Latrese, were raised by their mother and stepfather, John Johnson.

Darius attended the Edisto High School in Cordova, South Carolina, before transferring to the larger Orangeburg-Wilkinson High School. His teachers saw him as a "quiet, clean-cut, well-mannered student who respected authority" and as a "good student who enjoyed drama and the arts" (*Columbia [South Carolina] State*, 5 Nov. 2003). Nearly everyone who knew him commented on his love of music and clothes and noted that he was a stylish dresser. Like many teenagers Jennings was uncertain about his future goals. Most often he expressed an interest in a career in photography, though at times he also considered owning a funeral home, where he could work with his sister and mother. After graduating from high school in 2000 he briefly attended Denmark Technical College in his home state, but he dropped out after a few months. Jennings's efforts to find a well-paid, full-time job were thwarted, however, by the economic recession that marked the first years of George W. Bush's presidency. Unemployment was particularly high in South Carolina, where more than a quarter of the state's black residents lived below the poverty line.

In order to help pay for college courses in photography Jennings enlisted in the U.S. Army in June 2001. He signed up for three years, a common move for young African Americans in his situation. Since the Vietnam War the army had worked harder than most American institutions to promote equal opportunities for racial minorities and women. The army's racially egalitarian ethos was exemplified by the career of COLIN POWELL, the son of Jamaican immigrants, who rose to the position of chairman of the joint chiefs of staff under President George H. W. Bush and who then became secretary of state under George W. Bush. While stationed at Fort Carson in Colorado Springs, Colorado, Jennings met Ari Young and fell in love with her. The couple married on 29 October 2002 and enjoyed a few months together at Fort Carson, where Darius was assigned to the Second Squadron, Third Armored Cavalry Regiment.

Following the U.S. invasion of Iraq in May 2003, Specialist Jennings was shipped to the Middle East. His mother later recalled that Darius "didn't see the reason for [the war], but he wanted to serve his country to the best of his ability" (*Columbia [South Carolina] State*, 5 Nov. 2003). Jennings's views reflected a stark but little commented upon racial divide on the eve of that conflict: though as many as 70 percent of white Americans supported the invasion, fewer than 20 percent of African Americans did, according to a poll by the Joint Center for Political and Economic Studies, a Washington, D.C., think tank.

The six months that Jennings served in Iraq were regarded, at least by the American media, as successful for the U.S. military and its small international coalition of allies. The brutal Baathist regime of Saddam Hussein was overthrown within a month of the invasion. By autumn 2003, however, rank-and-file GIs like Jennings began to voice their concerns about their presence in a nation increasingly hostile to its occupation. Although letters, phone calls, and e-mails home to his family revealed his growing unease, Jennings nonetheless continued to perform his duties with his usual respectful diligence, and he found time to visit and pray with hospitalized comrades injured by mortar and grenade attacks. His mother recalled that because her son was "not raised in violence," he was not accustomed to "the things he was seeing over there. And it was really getting to him." "You don't know what I'm going through over here. You don't see the things I see," Jennings told his mother in late October 2003 (Endey).

Darius and Ari Jennings spent their first wedding anniversary apart. He remained in Iraq, and she was serving as an airman at a U.S. Air Force base in Texas. Darius was scheduled for a "rest and recuperation leave" in time for his twenty-third birthday, but he never made it. On 2 November 2003 in the city of Fallujah, Iraqi insurgents armed with a shoulder-fired missile struck the CH-47 Chinook helicopter that was transporting Jennings and other soldiers to Baghdad Airport. Jennings was among the fifteen soldiers who died; twenty-one others were injured in what was at that time the single largest loss of American lives during the war.

Distraught and angry at the politicians whom she blamed for starting the war, Harriet Johnson told reporters that her son's death was "senseless." Speaking of the weapons of mass destruction that the Bush administration had cited as a primary reason for the invasion, Johnson commented bitterly that "whatever the leadership of our country said we'd find, they have not come up with. People are tired of the war, and they need to bring those boys back" (Jubera).

Darius Jennings's family was not alone in its grief. Two other Orangeburg High School graduates, Army Sergeant Anthony Thompson and Private First Class Vorn Mack, had already died in Iraq that fall. On 15 November 2003 two thousand people crammed into Edisto High School for Jennings's memorial service. At Harriet Johnson's request, the Reverend AL SHARPTON, then actively campaigning in South Carolina's Democratic Party presidential primary, delivered the eulogy. Another presidential candidate, the former NATO commander General Wesley Clark, had also visited the family, who received considerable media attention following Harriet Johnson's pointed criticisms of U.S. policy in Iraq. The press also gave significant coverage to her rebuke of President George W. Bush for not visiting her family's home a few days before the funeral, even though he found time that day to hold a reelection campaign fund-raiser and visit a nearby BMW car plant. "Evidently my son wasn't important enough to [President Bush]," Johnson remarked (Allen).

Johnson's criticisms fueled a flurry of articles and news reports questioning the Bush Administration's policy of not attending any of the funerals held for the more than four hundred U.S. military personnel who had been killed in Iraq. Despite the criticisms President Bush continued his policy of avoiding funerals, though he did eventually meet in late November 2003 at Fort Carson, Colorado, with Harriet Johnson and ninety-seven other family members of soldiers killed in Iraq. When Johnson asked him why he did not attend her son's funeral, the president replied that he did not know that Jennings was dead. The answer did not satisfy Johnson, who later told an antiwar rally near Fort Bragg, North Carolina, that she was still questioning the president. She was also still mourning the consequences of a foreign policy that required the ultimate sacrifice of Darius Jennings, "a fine respectable, young mama's boy who loved his country" (Foster).

FURTHER READING

Allen, Mike. "Bush Visits Army Post with Heavy Casualties in Iraq," *Washington Post*, 25 Nov. 2003.

Endey, Haze Trice. "Grieving Mother's Advice to Bush: 'Bring Our Boys Home,' " *Wilmington (North Carolina) Journal*, 20 Nov. 2003.

Foster, Dick. "Slain Soldier's Mother Critical of Bush; Grieving Parent Slams White House as Unappreciative," *Rocky Mountain News*, 19 Nov. 2003.

Jubera, Drew. "With 3 Lives Lost to War, S.C. Town Asks, 'Why?' " *Atlanta Journal-Constitution*, 16 Nov. 2003.

STEVEN J. NIVEN

Jeremiah, Thomas (?–18 Aug. 1775), fisherman, harbor pilot, and elite member of Charleston, South Carolina's, black population, was executed by the provincial government for purportedly fomenting a slave insurrection at the outset of the American War for Independence. Much of Jeremiah's life is shrouded in mystery. Born to unidentified slave parents, Jeremiah—or "Jerry" as he may also have been known—secured his freedom by some means in the 1750s or 1760s and was married, but the identity of his wife is not known. The marriage apparently produced no children.

Like many other young Low Country slaves and free blacks, Jeremiah became intimately familiar with South Carolina's river transport networks, and by 1760 had established himself as a capable pilot in and around Charleston Harbor. He parlayed the time spent on the water into a lucrative fishing business. He supplied the port city residents with his daily catches, and in time became arguably one of the wealthiest free blacks in the colonies. Jeremiah also built upon his reputation through his activities as a volunteer fireman, which may have insulated him from punishment for a 1771 assault upon a white ship captain. A sentence of one hour in the stocks and ten strokes of the lash was commuted by an executive pardon. Jeremiah attracted the notice of none other than Lord William Campbell, royal governor of South Carolina from 1775 to 1778, who, as he assumed office, commented that Jeremiah was a man "of considerable property, one of the most valuable and useful men in his way in this province" (Morgan, 213). Henry Laurens, a prominent planter and assemblyman, did not hold such a high opinion of Jeremiah, characterizing him as "a forward fellow, puffed up by prosperity, ruined by Luxury & debauchery & grown to an amazing pitch of vanity & ambition." Jeremiah was certainly not the average black entrepreneur, especially when one considers that he lived in South Carolina, in many ways the most repressive and anxiety-ridden slave colony on the North American mainland.

The political and economic conflicts between Britain and its mainland North American colonies in the 1760s and early 1770s led to increased calls for independence based on Parliament's repeated violations of basic English rights to life, liberty, and property. Libertarian rhetoric among the white elite and middle classes was not lost on the colonies' slave populations, and African Americans eagerly appropriated the language of liberty to demand emancipation. During the Stamp Act crisis of 1765–1766, an ad hoc group of Charleston's slaves marched through the streets chanting "Liberty! Liberty!" in emulation of the white mobs that gathered around the houses of royal officials. A group of Boston slaves drafted a petition to Governor Thomas Gage and the Massachusetts General Court in 1774, reminding them that "we were unjustly dragged by the cruel hand of power from our dearest friends and sum [sic] of us stolen from the bosoms of our tender Parents ... and Brought hither to be made slaves for Life in a Christian land." It quietly demanded that the legislature grant them "our Natural right[,] our freedoms" (Davis, 259).

As South Carolina became embroiled in the pre-revolutionary tumult in the summer of 1775, Jeremiah was brought before the Provincial Congress in August on charges of having plotted a loyalist slave insurrection designed to aid the Royal Navy in besieging the city. Much of what is known about the trial and execution of Thomas Jeremiah is provided by a letter written by Henry Laurens to his son, Henry Jr.

Laurens was the president of South Carolina's Committee of Safety, charged with ferreting out loyalist plots and extinguishing loyalist political activity. Rumors of slave insurrection remained a constant concern in South Carolina, particularly after the Stono Rebellion (1739), and the committee was aware that slaves might seize the opportunity afforded by armed conflict between whites to free themselves *en masse*. Jeremiah and others were arrested on the flimsiest of suspicions, so sensitive were the colony's whites to their tenuous grasp on control when they made up less than 40 percent of the total population. Three witnesses came forward to offer testimonial evidence against Jeremiah. One of them was "Sambo," who recounted how he overheard Jeremiah predicting the onset of a "great war" that would "help the poor negroes." Jeremiah's brother-in-law, Jemmy, declared that Jeremiah had asked him to deliver guns to an unidentified runaway slave. He later retracted his testimony and maintained Jeremiah's innocence, but Sambo insisted upon the truth of his statement, which was sufficient to find Jeremiah guilty and sentenced to be hanged and burned.

Jeremiah's death sentence generated enormous controversy. He had many friends and defenders within the colony's free black community, a number of whom tried to save him from the gallows. This friendship and support extended even into the upper echelons of the white community. Most notably, both Governor Campbell and his secretary, as well as Charleston's two Anglican clergymen, were powerful sympathizers. Campbell fruitlessly pardoned him—fruitlessly because Campbell was a royal governor in a revolutionary state. Meanwhile, his supporters tried various legal strategies to get him acquitted, questioning the validity of a free black man's trial under the Negro Act of 1740, which concerned itself only with slaves. Laurens, for his part, was absolutely convinced of Jeremiah's guilt and agreed with other whites that unless Jeremiah was executed, a racial war would certainly ensue.

Whether Jeremiah actually plotted an insurrection against the provincial government is unclear. The evidence is at best dubious. He maintained his innocence to the end, but there was incriminating slave testimony and alleged perjury from Jeremiah himself that sealed his fate. Jeremiah's undoing was due largely to his extraordinarily prominent and fundamentally insecure place in Charleston society. This may have inspired him to aspire to, as Jemmy claimed, some "Chief Command" in the imminent war between Britain and its American colonies (Wood, 285). In any case, it made him a perfect scapegoat for patriots, who wanted both to intimidate the colony's black population and raise martial spirits. Thomas Jeremiah is thus emblematic of what eighteenth-century free blacks were capable of achieving, as well as the inherent perils awaiting all African Americans.

FURTHER READING

Davis, Thomas J. "Emancipation Rhetoric, Natural Rights, and Revolutionary New England: A Note on Four Black Petitions in Massachusetts, 1773–1777," *The New England Quarterly* 62 (1989).

Frey, Sylvia R. *Water from the Rock: Black Resistance in a Revolutionary Age* (1991).

Morgan, Philip D. "Black Life in Eighteenth-Century Charleston," *Perspectives in American History* 1 (1984).

Weir, Robert W. *Colonial South Carolina: A History* (1983).

Wood, Peter H. "'Taking Care of Business' in Revolutionary South Carolina: Republicanism and the Slave Society," in *The Southern Experience in the American Revolution*, eds. Jeffrey J. Crow and Larry E. Tise (1978).

JOHN HOWARD SMITH

Jernigan, William H. (or William H. Jernagin) (13 Oct. 1869–Feb.1958), Baptist minister, and activist, was born in Mashulaville, Mississippi, to Allen and Julia (Ruth) Jernigan. He married Willie A. Stennis on 15 October 1889, with whom he had four children: Lottie R., Rosabell, Gertrude J., and Mattie. He married a second wife upon the death of the first. Jernigan attended school at Meridian Academy, and then taught in the public schools for five years. Jernigan received a B.A. degree from Jackson College in Mississippi.

In 1906, Jernigan became the pastor of Tabernacle Baptist Church in Oklahoma City, where he served until 1912. Jernigan actively opposed the institution of Jim Crow laws dictating segregation in the newly formed state of Oklahoma in 1907. As a result of Jernigan and others' efforts, the U.S. Supreme Court decided in the case of *Quinn v. United States* in 1915 to outlaw the "grandfather clause" of Jim Crow laws. The "grandfather clause" gave the right to vote to those whose ancestors could vote before 1866. This naturally excluded African Americans, because most of their grandfathers were enslaved before 1866, and therefore unable to vote.

In 1912 Jernigan moved to Washington, D.C., to begin his ministry at Mt. Carmel Baptist Church. During Jernigan's forty-six-year tenure at Mt. Carmel the church experienced one of its strongest periods of growth. Outside of his own congregation, Jernigan held prominent leadership roles in the Baptist denomination. He served for thirty years as president of the National Sunday School and Baptist Training Union of the National Baptist Convention, U.S.A, Inc. Jernigan also served for ten years on the executive board of the Baptist World Alliance, extending his influence not only in the United States but also internationally. Jernigan attended the international Pan-African Congress of 1919 in Paris and again in 1921, which united people of African descent across the world to discuss issues related to European colonization on the continent of Africa. Jernigan represented the National Race Congress at the Pan-African Congress, but traveled as a correspondent for the *Washington Bee* newspaper because of difficulties obtaining a passport. Jernigan ministered widely to soldiers during the two world wars. He ministered to black soldiers serving in World War I on the battlefields in France. During World War II, Jernigan served as an official U.S. Army chaplain.

The year 1934 heralded the formation of the Fraternal Council of Negro Churches (FCNC). Before the founding of this council, Jernigan worked with the Federation of Christian Churches, which organized both black and white Christian churches into an institution. However, black participants often found the interests of the black community excluded from the agenda of the predominantly white Federation. Therefore, African Methodist Episcopal Bishop REVERDY CASSIUS RANSOM and Baptist Jernigan led the foundation of the FCNC to serve the interests of black churches and unite black denominations. The FCNC held its first annual meeting at Jernigan's Mt. Carmel Baptist Church.

Jernigan and Ransom's vision was not to unite churches around unanimous doctrine or religious practice, but rather to do so around social issues affecting blacks in the 1930s. The FCNC offered a middle ground between the leading ideologies of African Americans at that time. On the one hand many African Americans leaned toward the strong Pan-African nationalism of the day offered by leaders such as MARCUS GARVEY. On the other hand, integrationists advocated a move toward an integrated society with equal rights and privileges. The FCNC provided an ideological middle ground that vehemently advocated for African Americans without moving to complete separation from the predominantly white society. Ransom served as the first president of the FCNC, followed shortly by Jernigan from 1938 to 1939.

After serving as president, Jernigan assumed the role of executive committee chairman of the FCNC from 1940 to 1945. In 1943 Jernigan commenced the second stage of the FCNC and one of his most notable accomplishments—the formation of the Washington Bureau of the FCNC. The Washington Bureau functioned as a lobbying institution to fight segregation in the nation's capitol. The Washington Bureau inaugurated the FCNC's shift from an organization of words and opinions to one of action. Under Jernigan's leadership, the bureau served as the voice of the black church in Washington, D.C. The activism and lobbying of Jernigan organized clergymen across the United States into "Committees of One Hundred," assembled to lobby their local governmental representatives. The bureau advised presidents, appeared before Congress, and provided a voice for the rights of the African American community until the civil rights movement. Jernigan continued to play a significant role in the workings of the FCNC until his death.

In 1950 the widow Mrs. William Jernigan formed a Women's Auxiliary Branch of the FCNC, partnering with her husband's efforts. Throughout the rest of the 1950s, Jernigan cooperated with the movements of MARY ELIZA CHURCH TERRELL, cofounder in 1896 of the National Association of Colored Women. Terrell formed the Coordinating Committee for the Enforcement of the D.C. Anti-Discrimination Laws (CCEAD), of which Jernigan served as vice president. In that role, Jernigan secured a promise and commitment from President Dwight D. Eisenhower to end segregation in Washington, D.C. Jernigan and Terrell worked to bring the *District of Columbia v. Thompson* case before the Supreme Court, regarding the enforcement of the Anti-Discrimination Acts of 1872 and 1873. The Court found in favor of Thompson and enforced desegregation in the District of Columbia in 1953.

Jernigan's noteworthy work with the FCNC and CCEAD paved the way for the subsequent civil rights movement. In 1956 Jernigan partnered with others to lead a movement to institute a nationwide day of prayer in support of the Montgomery Bus Boycott. This work came to fruition on 28 March 1956 as the National Deliverance Day of Prayer. The day of prayer also led to an outpouring of financial assistance for African Americans in Montgomery and other cities seeking to end segregation in public transport. This was one of Jernigan's final acts before his death at the age of eighty-nine in Miami due to a gallbladder obstruction.

FURTHER READING

Jernagin, William H. *Christ at the Battlefront: Servicemen Accept the Challenge* (1946).

Jones, Beverly. "Before Montgomery and Greensboro: The Desegregation Movement in the District of Columbia, 1950–1953," *Phylon (1960–)* 43.2 (1982).

Sawyer, Mark R. "The Fraternal Council of Negro Churches, 1934–1964," *Church History* 59.1 (1990).

Obituary: *Miami Herald*, 22 Feb. 1958.

SARA BAGBY

Jessup, Gentry (4 July 1914–26 Mar. 1998), pitcher in the Negro Baseball Leagues, was born Joseph Gentry Jessup in Mount Airy, North Carolina. Better known as Gentry Jessup or sometimes even as "Jeep," Jessup grew up in rural North Carolina and learned to play baseball there. He came from an athletic family. His brother Sherman pitched for the Winston-Salem Pond Giants, a semi-pro club. Another brother, Tom, became a boxer and even had a bout with Henry Armstrong (HENRY ARMSTRONG).

Jessup pitched for a number of ball clubs in his career and spent quite a few winters in Cuba. His pitching in Cuba earned him election to the Cuban Hall of Fame in 1998. Jessup got his start in 1940 with the Birmingham Black Barons and then moved up north to join the Giants.

While pitching for the Chicago American Giants (1941–1949), Jessup appeared in five East—West All Star games from 1944 to 1948 at Chicago's Comiskey Park. In his first All Star appearance he pitched three innings and gave up only one run to earn the victory. In the 1947 game Jessup retired all nine hitters he faced before being relieved by Chet Brewer. In all, Jessup pitched nearly fifteen innings with a 1.84 earned run average (ERA) and gave up only three runs on nine hits. Jessup barnstormed with SATCHEL PAIGE's All Stars against Dizzy Dean and his crew during the off season in 1946.

As a pitcher, Jessup developed a reputation for having great stamina although not always the best control. He pitched a twenty-inning game in 1946 against the Indianapolis Clowns that ended in a tie. If you did not get to Jessup early, it could be a long game. Batters also learned it did not pay to dig in against him because he threw a lot of wild pitches and hit a number of batters.

Jessup helped his own cause with the bat whenever he pitched. He was a solid hitter, reportedly hitting .300 in 1948 while posting a 6–9 record. In 1945 black papers reported his average as .267 by mid-season. He did not have a lot of power but made contact when he needed to. In a 1945 contest against the famed Monarchs, which Jessup won 6–3, he hit a triple and a single to knock in two runs.

As a mainstay of the Giants pitching staff, Jessup helped the Giants win with consistency. He held the Cincinnati Clowns to only five hits in a game his club won 3–1. In a 1945 game against the Black Yankees, Jessup threw a three-hit shutout and the Chicago squad won 1–0. He retired the first twenty-one batters he faced before the Black Yankees offered any real threat. When the Giants played the 1944 World Champion Grays late in the season, Jessup held them down and allowed the Giants to take a 4–3 victory. Two errors by the Grays late in the game made the difference in the score. Jessup won the 1946 season opener against the Kansas City Monarchs, 9–2.

Jessup's records in the mid-1940s included seasons at 8–7, 14–9, 15–10, and 7–8 in 1946. His ERA nearly always fell below 3.00 because he did not give up a lot of runs. He often walked batters but got the clutch outs when he needed them, giving his offense the chance to win.

Late in the 1946 season Jessup got the chance to pitch in the annual South—North game. This game was the Negro Southern Leagues' attempt to mirror the East—West classic held each year at Comiskey Park. Jessup's team beat the South 8–2 in Chicago. In addition to giving up five hits and no earned runs, Jessup got two hits and drove in four runs, helping his own cause. One of his hits came with the bases loaded.

During the winter, Jessup found opportunities to keep pitching. He barnstormed one fall with the Satchel Paige All Stars to earn extra money. He pitched in a contest against Bob Feller's Major League All Stars, losing 6–5. The All Stars tied the game with a bases-loaded triple by Jeff Heath of St. Louis and the winning run scored on a triple by Ken Keltner of the Indians. During the 1946–1947 winter season Jessup twirled for Almendares in Cuba. In sixteen games Jessup compiled a 5–3 record, with four complete games.

One of the highlights of Jessup's career came in 1947 when he pitched a one-hitter against Indianapolis. A total of 7,500 fans watched the Giants win 9–0 as Jessup took a no-hitter into the eighth inning before giving up the only hit of the game to Ray Neil. He struck out four batters. Another highlight came in 1949 when the Giants won the second-half title by beating the Indianapolis Clowns in a double header. Eugene Smith pitched a shutout in the first game while Jessup mopped up in the second with another shutout, 2–0. Jessup gave up only five hits while Smith held the Clowns batters to only six hits in ten innings.

Jessup played some semi-pro ball from 1950 to 1952 and then minor league ball in the Man-Dak League along with a number of other former Negro Leaguers. JACKIE ROBINSON's integrating the majors in 1947 opened doors, but some, like Jessup, only got a chance to play in the minors and not the majors. In 1950 Jessup joined the staff of the Benton Harbor Cubs for the early part of the season. He pitched against the House of David in one contest. He pitched for the Carman team in the Man-Dak League, compiling 10–4 and 9–6 marks in his first two seasons. He also hit .278 and .298, respectively.

Jessup remained involved in the game for many years. In 1957 he pitched in an All Star game against the Skokie Indians. He appeared in the lineup for the Chicago Vets in 1961, pitching against the Skokie Indians in the Greater Chicago Semi-Pro League.

FURTHER READING

"Gentry, Jessup." In *The Biographical Encyclopedia of the Negro Baseball Leagues* (1994).

Smith, Wendell. "Jessup's Three-Hit Hurling Silences Red Sox' Big Guns." *Pittsburgh Courier*, 8 July 1944.

LESLIE HEAPHY

Jessye, Eva Alberta (20 Jan. 1895–21 Feb. 1992), choral conductor, composer, and actress, was born in Coffeyville, Kansas, to Albert Jesey, a chicken picker, and Julia (Buckner) Jesey. Eva changed the spelling of her surname to Jessye in the 1920s. Jessye later said that she received her life's directive in a speech she heard delivered by BOOKER T. WASHINGTON, wherein he declared: "I hope the time will never come when we neglect and scorn the songs of our fathers" (*Atlanta Constitution*, 6 Feb. 1978). That time never came for Eva Jessye, who dedicated herself to preserving the folk repertoire and performance practices of African Americans. Having ancestors born into slavery, she was uniquely exposed to their songs, with their inherent drama, during her youth.

Eva's mother struggled to purchase for her daughter the first black-owned piano in Coffeyville, which she learned to play by ear. A piano teacher was acquired when she demonstrated talent for composing, singing, and playing. Eva organized a girls' quartet and performed with it at the large Odd Fellows Hall. This was not a small feat for a twelve-year-old.

The next year Eva enrolled in Quindaro State School for the Colored (now Western University) in Quindaro, Kansas, for her high school years. While there she was inspired to become a musician by the touring conductor and composer WILL MARION COOK, for whom she copied orchestral scores. In 1914 she graduated with honors, and received her B.A. and teaching certification from Oklahoma's Langston University four years later. An elementary-school teaching career ensued in the Oklahoma towns of Muskogee, Haskell, and Taft; thereafter she formed the first choir at Morgan College in Baltimore, Maryland, and subsequently taught at Claflin College in Orangeburg, South Carolina. She also became a music critic for the *Baltimore Afro-American* newspaper and was invited to direct the local Dixie Jubilee Singers. In time this group would become the Eva Jessye Choir.

This ensemble relocated to New York during the Harlem Renaissance of the 1920s, and Eva Jessye came of age as a choral conductor who promoted the Negro spiritual and folksong tradition. Further study was encouraged and directed by Will Marion Cook and the theorist Percy Goetschius. Her reputation advanced through the medium of radio on the Major Bowes Capitol Family Radio Hour, and both the CBS and NBC Artist Series. Later, in May 1942, Jessye worked with the famed conductor Leopold Stokowski for a performance of WILLIAM GRANT STILL's "And They Lynched Him on a Tree."

In 1929 she became the choral director of Metro-Goldwyn-Mayer's *Hallelujah*, the first talking motion picture with an all-black cast. Five years later she was the choral director for Virgil Thomson and Gertrude Stein's opera *Four Saints in Three Acts*. This production pioneered in showcasing blacks in an opera unrelated to black life.

Jessye's most noteworthy legacy resulted from George Gershwin's invitation to be the choral director of his folk opera *Porgy and Bess* in 1935. Her skills in choral and vocal solo training brought more authenticity to the production. She was the keeper of that flame for countless national and international performances for the next thirty-five years. In 1963 the Eva Jessye Choir became the official choral group for the March on Washington.

Jessye's extensive conducting career sometimes featured larger forms of her spiritual arrangements and original works, including *The Life of Christ in Negro Spirituals* (1931) and *The Chronicle of Job* (written in 1936 and premiered at Clark College in 1978). Her folk oratorio *Paradise Lost and Regained*, from Milton's epic, was written in 1934 and premiered on NBC Radio late in 1936; a staged version was first performed at the Washington Cathedral to critical acclaim in 1972. Her dramatic flair as an actress can also be seen in such films as *Cotton Comes to Harlem* (1970) in which she appeared briefly, *Black Like Me* (1964), and *The Slaves* (1969).

Eva Jessye received numerous awards and honors during her almost century-long life, including honorary doctorates from the University of Michigan, Eastern Michigan University, and Wilberforce University. She was also named among the six most outstanding women in the history of Kansas in 1980 by the local Wichita, Kansas, chapter of Women in Communications, Inc. Her photograph was included in Brian Lanker's historic collection *I Dream a World: Portraits of Black Women Who Changed America* (1989). Eva Jessye was one of the first black women in America to earn an international reputation as a choral director and blazed the trail for many men and women to follow.

FURTHER READING

Information on Jessye can be found in the Eva Jessye Collection at the University of Michigan, Ann Arbor, and in the Eva Jessye Collection at Pittsburg State University, Kansas.

Black, Donald Fisher. "The Life and Work of Eva Jessye and Her Contributions to American Music," Ph.D. diss., University of Michigan, Ann Arbor (1986).

Smith, Helen C. "Eva Jessye: Earth Mother Incarnate," *Atlanta Constitution*, 6 Feb. 1978.

Southern, Eileen. *Biographical Dictionary of Afro-American and African Musicians* (1982).

Wilson, Doris Louis Jones. "Eva Jessye: Afro-American Choral Director," Ed.D. diss., Washington University, St. Louis (1989).

MARVA GRIFFIN CARTER

Joans, Ted (4 July 1928–7 May 2003), poet, visual artist, performer, and bohemian citizen of the world, was born Theodore Jones in Cairo, Illinois, to parents who worked on Mississippi riverboats. While little is known about Joans's childhood, two stories circulate widely. The first is that he was born on a riverboat; the second is that his father, a riverboat entertainer, gave the twelve-year-old Joans a trumpet and dropped him off in Memphis, Tennessee, to make his own way in the world. It has been documented that Joans's father was murdered in the 1943 Detroit race riots, and various autobiographical writings indicate that Joans spent some of his childhood in Indiana and Kentucky.

After earning his BFA in painting from Indiana University in 1951, Joans moved to New York's Greenwich Village and became a central figure in the Beat scene. He associated with Jack Kerouac and Allen Ginsberg, who would first encourage Joans to perform his poems, as well as abstract expressionist painters and jazz musicians. Joans quickly developed his trademark jazz reading style; "I swing the words," he noted in a 2001 interview aired on National Public Radio. Joans also made performance a lifestyle. When the jazz great CHARLIE PARKER passed away in 1955, it was Joans who memorialized his former roommate by writing "Bird Lives!" all over New York. He became known for his birthday parties and his rhinoceros obsession, and he hired himself out as one of Fred McDarrah's Rent-A-Beatniks, a job requiring that he wear a black turtleneck and beret and read his poems for upper-middle-class partygoers. By the late 1950s Joans was able to support his wife, Joyce Smith, and their four young children primarily by his poetry and performance work, including the sale of his chapbooks *Beat Poems* (1957) and *Funky Jazz Poems* (1959).

Joans is often quoted as saying that "Jazz is my religion and surrealism is my point of view," and he developed close friendships with the jazz and blues poet LANGSTON HUGHES and the French surrealist painter André Breton. While Hughes was an important connection to earlier African American writers and to the New York literary world beyond lower Manhattan, Breton and the surrealist movement connected Joans to an international community of artists. In 1961 Joans published *All of Ted Joans and No More*, a collection of jazz-influenced spoken-word poems accompanied by his surrealist collages and illustrations, and left his family and New York for good: "I hate cold weather and they will not let me live democratically in warm states of the United States, so I'm splitting and letting America perish." He would spend the rest of his life traveling between Europe and Africa, settling in Paris and other European cities in the summer months and living in Africa in the winter, primarily Timbuktu, Mali. (Later in life his circuit would include the Americas again.) He never remarried after his divorce but would have a number of romantic relationships and six more children.

Breton famously acknowledged Joans as the only African American surrealist, and from 1962 to 1969 Joans attended many surrealist meetings in Paris, believing, like Aimé Césaire, that surrealism's emphasis on psychological liberation could be a tool for black liberation. In his unpublished autobiography "I, Black Surrealist," Joans tells of writing to Breton that:

> without surrealism I would have been incapable of surviving the abject vicissitudes and racial violence which the white man in America imposed upon me every day. Surrealism became the weapon I used to defend myself, and it has been and always will be my own style of life (Fabre, 313).

In addition to being a center for surrealist activity, Paris served as meeting place for African diaspora artists and intellectuals, and Joans participated in many major events. He met Césaire, Alioune Diop, and MALCOLM X at a 1964 gathering sponsored by the Society of African Culture, and he shared the stage at a similar 1967 meeting with JAMES FORMAN, Julia Wright Hervé, Daniel Guérin, Césaire, and Sartre. In 1966 he played trumpet at a Langston Hughes poetry reading and chanted poems from his forthcoming book *Black Pow-Wow: Jazz Poems* (1969) at an event featuring the Jamaican writer and singer Fritz Gore, the free jazz musician Arthur Peebles, and the poet-singer ABBEY LINCOLN. In 1969 Joans participated in the Algiers Pan-African Arts Festival along with the poet Don Lee, the playwright ED BULLINS, and the singers Miriam Makeba, Marion Williams, and NINA SIMONE.

Joans published actively from the 1970s until his death in Vancouver, Canada. His work continued to feature irreverent and celebratory explorations of jazz, sexuality, racial and class politics, Africa, and rhinos, and he often collaborated with visual artists and dedicated poems to people and places that moved him. Joans produced over thirty books during this time, including *Afrodisia: New Poems* (1970), *A Black Manifesto in Jazz Poetry and Prose* (1971), *Flying Piranha*, with Joyce Mansour (1978), *Spectrophilia: Poems, Collages* (1973), *The Aardvark-Watcher: Der Erdferkelforscher* (1980), *Merveilleux coup de foudre: Poetry of Jayne Cortez and Ted Joans* (1982), *Teducation: Selected Poems 1949–1999* (1999), *WOW*, with Laura Corsiglia (1999), and *Our Thang*, with Laura Corsiglia (2001). He also wrote for jazz periodicals and held the editorship of *Dies und Das*, a mid-1980s German surrealist magazine.

Given Joans's productivity as a writer and his involvement with major twentieth-century artistic movements, it is striking to note his exclusion from major anthologies, including those focusing on surrealist, Beat generation, and African American writers. There are a number of possible reasons for this exclusion. First, Joans's spoken-word style often works best heard live rather than read silently on the page. Second, Joans was so committed to poetry as a way of living that some of his work feels too occasional, or too dated linguistically and thematically. Third, Joans's saying "no bread, no Ted" indicated his refusal to work cheaply or for free, perhaps a barrier for editors seeking his work; his travels may also have served as an editorial barrier. But Joans's work and life, always intertwined, are surely worth studying for the way he traveled through movements, histories, and continents, creating crossroads, and illustrating his commitment to the truths he believed poetry could tell.

FURTHER READING

Ted Joans's papers, including unpublished work, are archived at the Bancroft Library, University of California at Berkeley.

Fabre, Michel. *From Harlem to Paris: Black American Writers in France, 1840–1980* (1991).

Fox, Robert Elliot. "Ted Joans and the (B)reach of the African American Literary Canon," *MELUS* 29.3–4 (Fall–Winter 2004).

Lee, A. Robert. "Black Beat: Performing Ted Joans," in *Reconstructing the Beats*, ed. Jennie Skerl (2004).

Obituary: *Village Voice*, 16 May 2003.

JENNIFER DRAKE

Joe (c. 1813–?), survivor of the battle of the Alamo, was a slave about whom little is known. He was living with his master in Harrisburg, Texas, in May 1833 and was sometimes rented out as a laborer. One man that rented him was a young lawyer named William Barret Travis. Having arrived in Texas in 1831, Travis was undoubtedly in need of hired help while establishing his law practice. He purchased Joe on 13 February 1834, while living in San Felipe. The time that Joe was owned by Travis, though short, came during the most legendary time in Texas history.

Joe's specific activities from 1834 to 1836 are unknown; that Joe would remain a slave he likely knew well, as his master was occupied during his first years in Texas working to gain the return of runaway slaves harbored at the Mexican garrison at Anahuac. However, Joe's master was more concerned with Texas independence. In light of later events, it is likely that Joe accompanied Travis in his travels as his personal servant in December 1835 when he became a lieutenant colonel in the Legion of Cavalry. On 21 January 1836 Joe went with Travis and 29 men to the old mission at San Antonio de Bexar, known as the Alamo, in present-day San Antonio, arriving on 3 February. Travis would soon take command of the garrison under siege by Mexican forces. His force numbered approximately 250 men and included such legends as Davy Crockett and Jim Bowie. Joe was not the only African American at the Alamo; also present was a slave named John, Bowie's slave Sam, and an unidentified black woman. Although Travis requested reinforcements for his small garrison, only 32 men were able to join his force, arriving under cover of darkness on 1 March. Five days later, the battle of the Alamo began. Joe's account of this historic battle is one of the few reliable ones of the action. It was, however, never written down or published. Instead, it was told by him to an army officer after the battle, and related from memory by that officer in a private letter sent in May 1836. According to this letter, Joe related that the Alamo garrison was exhausted by hard work and the constant vigil they kept; the night before the attack all were up late working to repair and strengthen their fortifications. When the attack did come in the early morning hours of 6 March, Joe stated that everyone in the garrison, even the sentinels, was asleep except for Adjutant Baugh, the officer of the day. Joe was with Travis when Baugh came running into his quarters crying that the Mexicans were coming. Travis took up his gun and sword, called Joe to do the same, and headed out to the north wall of the mission. Travis mounted the wall and reportedly called to his men "Come on boys—the Mexicans are upon us, and we'll give them Hell." With that cry, Travis and Joe fired their weapons and were met with return fire; Travis was hit and fell off the wall. With Travis severely wounded and unable to get-up and Mexicans breaching the wall of the Alamo, Joe ran to a nearby house and fired through the loopholes several times before taking cover.

Opposed by 1,800 Mexican troops in the final assault, the fight was over quickly. Joe remained in hiding and only came out when a Mexican officer entered the house and asked in English if there were any blacks present. When Joe came out of hiding, two soldiers tried to kill him, but their officer stopped them and he was only slightly wounded. As for the rest of the Alamo defenders, nearly all were killed, including the slave John and the unidentified black woman. Sam, the slave of Jim Bowie, is thought to have survived. Upon his capture, Joe was brought before the Mexican commander, General Santa Anna (a fierce abolitionist), interrogated, and set free. Joe also witnessed a grand review of the Mexican Army, and later observed the burial of the Texan dead. While further accounts vary as to his movements, Joe later returned to Texas in the company of Susanna Dickinson and Ben, Santa Anna's black cook. On 20 March 1836 he appeared before the Texas Cabinet and "impressed those present with the modesty, candor, and clarity of his account" (Handbook of Texas) regarding the battle of the Alamo.

Joe's presence at the Alamo is illustrative of the larger African American experience in the South and of the frequent failure by earlier generations of historians to acknowledge their contributions. Not only is it a wonder that Joe's account of the Battle of the Alamo was never published, likely because of his race, but it is also even more incredible that legends persist that all of the Alamo's defenders were gallantly killed in battle. Joe's participation in the battle, no matter how small, is proof enough that the Alamo's African American defenders have been, at best, forgotten, and at worst ignored. Given the fact that the Texas Revolution was largely based on its citizens' rights to own slaves, an idea opposed by Mexican authorities, such historical bias is not surprising.

After his report to the Texas government, Joe later escaped from the man who purchased him from the Travis estate, John Jones, on 21 April 1836 with two horses and in the company of a Mexican man. Could it be that Joe's contact with Mexican authorities, and their sympathetic treatment of blacks, motivated his flight? Whatever the case, Joe was successful in his bid for freedom. Probably making a living as a laborer, perhaps also earning some money telling stories of the Alamo, Joe was still alive in 1877 when it was suggested he be brought to Austin, Texas, for a veterans' reunion. However, it is unknown whether Joe attended and he is thought to have died near Brewton, Alabama.

FURTHER READING

Cox, Mike. "*Joe: The Man Who Witnessed Travis' Death at the Alamo.*" Available online at http://www. texascapes. com/MikeCoxTexasTales/182-Joe-Slave-Alamo-Witness.htm.

Handbook of Texas Online. "*Joe.*" Available at http://www.tsha.utexas.edu/handbook/online/articles/JJ/fjol. html.

Lord, Walter. *A Time to Stand: The Epic of the Alamo* (1961).

GLENN ALLEN KNOBLOCK

Joel, Lawrence (22 Feb. 1928–4 Feb. 1984), Korean War and Vietnam War soldier and Medal of Honor recipient, was born in Winston-Salem, North Carolina, the son of Trenton and Mary Joel. The couple lived on the east side (Ward three) of Winston-Salem and had five children. Trenton Joel supported his family by working as a janitor in a theater. Later on in the 1930s, Lawrence Joel, "Larry" to family and friends, was raised by foster parents Clayton and Ethel Samuels after his parents separated due to the financial difficulties experienced during the Great Depression. Lawrence Joel attended Atkins High School in Winston-Salem but dropped out in 1945, his senior year, and soon joined the Merchant Marine, serving for one year.

Lawrence Joel enlisted in the U.S. Army in March 1946 at New York City and subsequently began a military career that would last nearly twenty-five years. He left the service in 1949 at the end of his first enlistment, and worked in a munitions factory in Baltimore, Maryland, for three years. He reenlisted in 1952 because he missed army life. While the specific details of Joel's early military career are unknown, he received specialized training as a combat medic and also became a paratrooper. Prior to his service in Vietnam, Joel would serve in such far-flung places as Italy and Germany, as well as posts in the United States. During the Vietnam War era, Joel was assigned to Headquarters Company, 1st Battalion (Airborne), 503rd Infantry, 173rd Airborne Brigade. In May 1965, Joel and his entire unit were sent from Okinawa to Vietnam for duty, the first major U.S. combat unit sent to Vietnam.

The service of African American soldiers in the Vietnam War, men like Lawrence Joel, EUGENE ASHLEY JR., and WEBSTER ANDERSON, marked a milestone in U.S. military history. For the first time since the Revolutionary War, black soldiers served on an equal basis with white soldiers in integrated units at both the enlisted man and officer level. No longer, as in World War II and even as recently as the Korean War, was the soldiering ability of African American servicemen in question. This newfound equality on the battlefield was demonstrated in circumstances that were both negative and positive; on one hand black draftees were selected for service during the Vietnam War at a proportionately higher rate than whites, and received far fewer educational deferments. This issue caused many problems, both politically on the home front and in the field at a number of military bases, and resulted in the widespread perception that the Vietnam War was a poor man's conflict whose burden was placed most heavily on the backs of black soldiers. Despite this perception, true only to a certain extent, positive developments for black servicemen did come out of the Vietnam War. For the first time since the Spanish-American War, African American servicemen were fully recognized for their valorous actions on the battlefield. Of the 244 Medal of Honor recipients during the Vietnam War, black soldiers accounted for twenty of them. In contrast, no contemporary award of the Medal of Honor was made to black soldiers serving in World War II, and only two in the Korean War.

Specialist Sixth Class Lawrence Joel was serving with his unit on 8–9 November 1965 about eighteen miles north of Bien Hoa, near Saigon in a mission that was called Operation Hump. The 173rd Airborne Brigade, along with members of the 1st Royal Australian Regiment, was tasked with finding and destroying Viet Cong elements that were occupying several important hills in the region. The operation began at 6am and was difficult from the start. When the Viet Cong launched heavy counterattacks, Joel's unit came under sustained fire and the fighting lasted for nearly twenty-four hours. He would subsequently treat the wounded men of the lead squad that suffered heavily from the initial enemy assault and continued to treat the wounded as the American force kept advancing. During the course of his actions, Joel was wounded in the leg by machine gun fire, but after bandaging himself and taking a dose of morphine to deaden his pain, he continued to treat the many wounded. As he was doing so, he continually encouraged the men around him, ignoring his wounds and the heavy fire that was all around him. He was subsequently wounded a second time, this time in the thigh, but still he dragged himself around the battlefield, treating over a dozen other wounded soldiers before he ran out of medical supplies. Undeterred, Joel replenished his supplies, and though twice wounded continued to treat the wounded men of the 173rd and offer words of encouragement. While the toll of the battle was severe, with 48 U.S. soldiers dead and many more wounded, it would have with certainty been greater were it not for Lawrence Joel.

After the battle ended, Joel stayed on the battlefield until he was ordered to evacuate for medical treatment of his wounds. For his actions that day, combat medic Lawrence Joel was awarded the Silver Star medal and was also nominated by the officers of his regiment for the Medal of Honor. He was thanked in person for his actions by General William Westmoreland while hospitalized. The nomination for our nation's highest military award was subsequently approved and Lawrence Joel was awarded the Medal of Honor by President Lyndon Johnson during a White House ceremony on 9 March 1967. Joel was the second African American soldier to earn the Medal of Honor in Vietnam, and the first African American soldier ever to have his award presented by a president. He was also the first living African American to receive the medal since the Spanish-American War. When he went home on leave to Winston-Salem, North Carolina soon thereafter, a parade was given in his honor on 8 April 1967, said to be one of the largest public events ever held in the city.

Following his Medal of Honor deeds, Lawrence Joel continued in the U.S. Army and did two more tours of duty in Vietnam. Upon recovering from his wounds in Japan, he returned to Vietnam in February 1966 and made patrols until he was sent home in April. After receiving the Medal of Honor, Joel made numerous public appearances for the Army, his long absence from home led to the breakup of his marriage to his wife, Dorothy, with whom he had two children, Deborah and Tremaine, who were nearly grown by this time. These personal troubles, combined with his difficulties coping with his public status as a Medal of Honor recipient, led Joel to return to Vietnam again for another combat tour in 1969. During his seventeen months of duty Joel earned the Bronze Star Medal for his actions during a mortar attack. Upon his return stateside, Lawrence Joel subsequently retired from the service in late 1973 as a specialist first class. He later resided in Bridgeport, Connecticut, and worked for the Veteran's Administration as a councilor in Hartford before moving back to his hometown of Winston-Salem, North Carolina.

Joel's death at age fifty-five was due to complications resulting from diabetes. He was subsequently interred at Arlington National Cemetery in Arlington, Virginia. A number of Army medical institutions around the country were named in honor of Lawrence Joel in the 1970s, including Joel Auditorium at the Walter Reed Army Medical Center, the service's flagship hospital, in Washington, D.C. His Medal of Honor heroics gained some media attention in 2011 after the Army announced it was closing the Walter Reed Medical Center in September 2011. A bust of Lawrence Joel, which had been on display in Joel Auditorium for many years, was given to his family, as the Army had no plans to carry the Joel name in the facilities of their new hospital.

FURTHER READING

Allen, Mel. "Larry Joel of Bridgeport, Connecticut," *Yankee Magazine*, March 1982, accessed at http://www.yankeemagazine.com/issues/2008-05/interact/10things/medals/larryjoel/1

Hanna, Charles W. *African American Recipients of the Medal of Honor* (2002).

GLENN ALLEN KNOBLOCK

John Hardy (c. 1867–19 Jan. 1894), an African American criminal whose fame lives in the ballad *John Hardy*, was hanged on the order of Judge T. L. Henritze in Welch, West Virginia, for the murder in January 1893 of Thomas Drews, also African American, at a camp of the Shawnee Coal Company near Eckman, McDowell County. He was convicted in Welch on 12 October 1893.

According to a 1925 statement by 67-year-old Lee Holley, a lifelong resident of Tazewell, Virginia, who claimed to have known Hardy well, he "was 27 or 8 when he was hung" (Chappell, 25). He may have been the John Hardy who was born in Virginia, was thirteen years old in 1880, and lived then in Glade Springs, Washington County, Virginia, with his parents, Miles and Malinda Hardy (U.S. Census, 1880). According to Holley, he was one of a "gang of gamblers," about a half dozen, who drifted around the coal camps. "They were all loafers and gamblers, and robbed the camps at night often after pay-day.... Most of the gang got killed sooner or later" (Chappell, 25).

Drews, about nineteen years old, is said to have beat out Hardy in a competition for a woman and to have won money from him shooting "craps" (dice). Hardy, who had been drinking heavily, retired from the game long enough to make plans, with his friend Webb Gudger (or Gudgin), to kill Drews. When they returned, Gudger was stationed behind a rock with a rifle and instructions to shoot Drews himself if the plan failed. Hardy laid his gun on the table and told it that he would kill any man who won his money. When Drews won, Hardy demanded his money back. Drews complied, but Hardy shot him anyway, saying, "Don't you know that I won't lie to my gun?" (Cox, 519)

Hardy hid out for a time, was apprehended, escaped, and fled with Gudger. They are said to have taken an eastbound train for a while and then to have come back westbound. Apparently acting on a tip, Sheriff John Effler (McDowell County) and Deputy Tom Campbell got on the westbound train in Mercer County, located Hardy and Gudger, and waited for the train to enter McDowell County at the Elkhorn Tunnel (Coaldale). One man was arrested without incident, but the other—some accounts say Hardy and some say Gudger—struggled with Effler, and both fell from the moving train. Despite a serious injury, Effler held onto his man long enough for help to arrive.

While imprisoned in Welch awaiting execution, Hardy could see and hear the building of the scaffold. He claimed that he would never hang there but was persuaded to change his mind and prepare to die. On the morning of his execution, he was led to the Tug River and baptized by Lex Evans, a white Baptist minister.

> John Hardy was a desperate little man,
> He carried two guns every day,
> He shot down a man in the Shawnee Camp,
> You ought to see John Hardy get away, poor boy,
> You ought to see John Hardy get away....
> "I've been to the east, I've been to the west,
> I've traveled this wide world around,
> I've been to the river and I've been baptized,
> And now I'm on my hanging ground," poor boy,
> "And now I'm on my hanging ground."
> (Ramella, 51)

Some of the three thousand to six thousand people present at the execution came by special excursion train. Good order was preserved by arresting the drunk and disorderly. Hardy's mother watched from a rocking chair.

Dressed in a new suit, shoes, and hat, the finest he had ever had, Hardy was led to the scaffold in the early afternoon. Speaking to the crowd, he said, "Don't live in sin as I have done, lest you fill your heart with sorrow" (Ramella, 50). He advised young men to avoid gambling and drink, sang "the purtiest song" (according to eyewitness Thursa Harris Mullins Belcher, quoted by Ramella, 48), sailed his hat into the crowd, and was hanged at 2:09 p.m. Seventeen and a half minutes later he was declared dead. When signs of life persisted after the initial fall, several deputies stationed under the gallows "wrenched his head backward until he was certainly dead" (Ramella, 48). This information is attributed to Mrs. Belcher, who obtained it from her husband, Ballard Belcher, who had been one of the deputies at the execution.

John Hardy has the same metrical structure as *John Henry* (*see* JOHN HENRY). The similarity of the names and ballad structure led some to the erroneous belief that John Hardy and John Henry were the same person. Governor W. A. MacCorkle, who served West Virginia in 1893–1897, expressed this view in 1916 (Ramella, 49). John Henry was a famous steel driver. He is often associated with Big Bend Tunnel, on the C & O railroad in Summers County, West Virginia. Lee Holley was definite in his denial that Hardy drove steel at Big Bend Tunnel or anywhere else. "I know John Hardy didn't drive steel in Big Bend Tunnel; he couldn't because he wasn't old enough when it was built, and he didn't work anyway. He got his living gambling and robbing 'round the camps" (Chappell, 25). Between 1924 and 1939, the ballad *John Hardy* was recorded commercially by at least seven white country artists. Today it is a bluegrass staple. Ironically, Stagolee is widely known among African Americans as the epitome of "bad" (SEE STAGOLEE). Yet, the historic person, "Stack" Lee Shelton, may have killed in self-defense only. John Hardy killed for trivial reasons but his story and ballad have had little currency among African Americans.

FURTHER READING

Cox, John Harrington. *Folk-Songs of the South* (1925).

Cox, John Harrington. "John Hardy," *Journal of American Folk-Lore* 32 (1919).

Chappell, Louis W. *John Henry: A Folk-Lore Study* (1933).

Ramella, Richard. "John Hardy: The Man and the Song," *Goldenseal* 18.1 (Spring 1992).

Wheeling Daily Register, 13 Oct. 1893; 20 Jan. 1894.

JOHN GARST

John Henry (c. 1850?–1887?), "steel-driving man" and legendary hero, may have been a historic person born a slave in Mississippi, Virginia, or some other Southern state. In ballad and legend he is simply "John Henry," but "John Henry" is a common combination of given names, so Henry may not have been his surname.

Songs about John Henry were collected as early as 1905. In 1916 the former West Virginia governor W.-A. MacCorkle confused him with JOHN HARDY, an African American gambler and murderer who was hanged in Welch, West Virginia, in 1894 and is the subject of his own ballad. By the mid-1920s the ballad "John Henry" was being recorded commercially by Riley Puckett (1924), Fiddlin' John Carson (1924), and other white "hillbilly" performers,

and shortly thereafter recordings by such African American bluesmen as Henry Thomas (1927) and MISSISSIPPI JOHN HURT (1928) began to appear. During the 1920s the folklorists Guy B. Johnson and Louis W. Chappell launched separate investigations into the John Henry tradition and published their results in 1929 and 1933, respectively. By the mid-twentieth century the John Henry ballad had distilled to an essentially stable form that names Polly Ann as John Henry's wife or "woman" and places his contest with a steam drill at "Big Bend Tunnel on the C&O [Chesapeake & Ohio] road" in Summers County, West Virginia.

Both Johnson and Chappell concluded that John Henry was probably a real person who worked on the Great Bend Tunnel at Talcott, West Virginia, informally known as Big Bend Tunnel, during its construction in 1870–1872. However, neither investigator was able to build a convincing case from testimonial and documentary evidence. Using somewhat circular reasoning, they cited the tradition itself as its own main evidence. In interviews with people who had been at Big Bend Tunnel during its construction, Johnson turned up a "mountain of negative evidence" (53). Four of seven informants did not believe that there had been a contest between a steam drill and a steel driver at Big Bend. One informant, Sam Wallace, flatly denied that there could have been such a contest—he would have heard about it. The brothers George and John Hedrick thought otherwise, but only on hearsay. C. S. "Neal" Miller, seventy-four, claimed to have witnessed the contest but said that he looked in only occasionally as he went about his chores. Miller gave different names for John Henry's shaker to Johnson and Chappell. In an interview published by Chappell, he did not mention witnessing the contest. Records have not revealed any steam drills at Big Bend Tunnel, though they were used in 1870–1871 at nearby Lewis Tunnel. At that time, when steam drills were just coming into use, it is plausible that there was a demonstration or contest at Big Bend.

Lewis Tunnel is on the C & O in Virginia, near the West Virginia border. Records found by Nelson detail the temporary use of steam drills there; the presence at the Virginia Penitentiary, Richmond, of a white workshop with an adjacent graveyard and railroad; the penitentiary's leasing of convict John William Henry for labor at Lewis Tunnel; and his subsequent disappearance. With the assumptions that Henry was the legendary steel driver, that he died at Lewis Tunnel, and that his body was brought back to the penitentiary for burial, these facts account for the following traditional stanza of the ballad.

> They took John Henry to the White House,
> And buried him in the san',
> And every locomotive come roarin' by,
> Says there lays that steel drivin' man.
> (Johnson, 99)

However, eyewitness L. W. Hill told Chappell that "Bob Jones was the best steel-driver in Lewis Tunnel" (44). In 1866 nineteen-year-old John W. Henry was 5' 1-¼" tall, an unlikely stature for a champion steel driver. There is no evidence that he was a steel driver at all, no evidence of a contest at Lewis Tunnel, and no John Henry tradition there.

Several other sites, including Dunnavant, Alabama, and the island of Jamaica, vie for the historical location of the legend. There is little support for Jamaica, but considerable circumstantial evidence boosts the Alabama claim. Giving many specific details, C. C. Spencer wrote Johnson that he had witnessed John Henry's contest with a steam drill in Alabama in the 1880s. His story is supported by letters from F. P. Barker and Glendora Cannon Cummings, who gave the year as 1887. Spencer said that John Henry was at "Cruzee" Mountain, Barker said "Cursey" Mountain, and Cummings said Oak Mountain. Tunnels through Coosa and Oak mountains, two miles apart, were put through in 1887–1888 as part of the construction of the C&W (Columbus & Western) railroad line between Goodwater, Alabama, and Birmingham.

A number of Spencer's details are wrong, such as the year (which he gives as 1882) and the railroad (which he names as the Alabama Great Southern), but many other of his details are confirmed by documentation. He said that John Henry was from Holly Springs, Mississippi, that his bosses included one named Dabner, and that he had been a slave to a Dabner. Cummings and a Chappell informant from Jamaica also gave Dabner or Dabney as the name of one of John Henry's bosses.

In fact Frederick Yeamans Dabney was chief engineer for the C&W and in charge of its construction. He was born in Virginia but was raised in Raymond, Mississippi, and he became a captain in the Civil War. After the war he lived in Crystal (not "Holly") Springs, in Copiah County. His father's slaves included Henry, a teenager during the war. On 4 November 1869 Henry Dabney, an African American, married Margaret Foston in Copiah County. The 1870 and 1880 census records for Copiah County indicate that this Henry

Dabney was born in 1850. Might he be the man now known as John Henry? Another African American named Henry Dabney, living in Copiah County in 1917–1918, was born 13 September 1879; this, too, is circumstantial, but some ballads do mention that John Henry had a son. The Marbury family of Leeds, Alabama, preserves memories from an ancestor, Ciscero Davis, who worked on the C&W. According to the Marburys, steel-driving contests were frequent and popular—and a man named John always won.

Ballads provide further evidence favoring the Alabama site. Rich Amerson's version places John Henry and "the Captain" (not "his Captain") "'tween them mountains." The title of "Captain" matches that used by Frederick Dabney, and according to local lore the contest took place outside the east portal of Oak Mountain Tunnel, which is between Oak and Coosa mountains, as is the town of Dunnavant. John Jacob Niles collected a version in Pigeon Forge, Tennessee, in which "A man in Chattanooga, two hundred miles away" heard the fall of John Henry's hammer. Chattanooga is about 135 miles from Dunnavant. In the same version they buried John Henry "And let two mountains be his grave-stones." According to the version of Harvey Hicks, "John Henry died on a Tuesday." Spencer wrote that John Henry died on 20 September, which in 1887 was a Tuesday.

The name of John Henry's wife also provides a circumstantial argument for identifying him. The Georgia bluesman Neal Pattman learned the song "John Henry" from his father and sang "John Henry had a little woman / Maggadee was her name." "Maggadee" could easily be "Maggie D." and refer to Margaret Foston Dabney. Furthermore, "Maggadee" or "Maggie D." could have been misheard as "Magdalene," suggesting "Mary Magdalene," which is found in the John Henry tradition. But "Magdalene" does not rhyme with "man"; it may have thus mutated to "Mary Ann," which is found also in some versions:

> John Henry had a little woman,
> Her name was Mary Ann,
> John Henry lay sick on his bed,
> Mary drove steel like a man.
> (Chappell, 120)

In the nineteenth century, "Polly" was a common nickname for "Mary." A substitution leads to the most popular name, "Polly Ann." Jamaican tradition preserves the name of John Henry's woman as "Marga." All of this points to (John) Henry Dabney as the original John Henry.

Johnson received letters identifying John Henry Martin, a Virginian, as a top steel driver at Big Bend Tunnel and as the legendary John Henry. According to Marie Boette, quoting a 1957 news article by Kyle McCormick, this is corroborated by records then possessed by James Twohig, a foreman at Big Bend. McCormick wrote that John Henry Martin died near Gap Mills, West Virginia, years after the completion of Big Bend Tunnel, that his father was from Africa, and that his son became a prominent educator. It could be that in about 1888, when a ballad about John Henry Dabney reached the Big Bend area, people there recalled John Henry Martin, assumed that he was the hero, and placed the contest at "Big Bend Tunnel on the C&O road." In this way the ballads may celebrate two John Henrys. Indeed, informants have named several other steel-driving John Henrys, and in a sense the tradition celebrates them all.

From the outset two kinds of songs about John Henry were recognized: hammer songs and ballads. The hammer song is a fluid work song, usually non-narrative and consisting of floating and improvised verses, only a few of which refer to John Henry. In the following selection "whop" is added to mark the fall of a hammer or pickaxe, perhaps accompanied or conveyed by a grunt on the part of a singer:

If I could drive steel (whop)
Like John Henry, (whop)
I'd go home, Baby, (whop)
I'd go home. (whop)
This ole hammer (whop)
Killed John Henry, (whop)
Drivin' steel, Baby, (whop)
Drivin' steel. (whop) (E. C. Perrow, *Journal of American Folklore* 26 [1913], 163)

This old hammer (whop)
Killed John Henry, (whop)
But it won't kill me, boys, (whop)
It won't kill me. (whop) (Johnson, 72)

Many ballad stanzas have been collected, but the following selection tells the essential story of how "this old hammer killed John Henry":

John Henry was a very small boy,
He sat on his daddy's knee,
He picked up a hammer, a little piece of steel,
Says, "This hammer'll be the death of me,"
(Lord, Lord)

"This hammer'll be the death of me." (Chappell, 104; the last line of each stanza is usually similarly repeated.)

John Henry said to his captain,
"A man, he ain't nothing but a man,
Before I'd let that steam drill beat me down,
I'd die with the hammer in my hand …"
(Johnson, 102)

John Henry told his shaker,
"Shaker, you better pray,
If I miss this piece of steel,
Tomorrow be your buryin' day …"
(Johnson, 107)

The man that owned that old steam drill,
Thought it was mighty fine,
But John Henry drove fourteen long feet,
While the steam drill only made nine …
(Chappell, 105)

John Henry made a steel-driving man,
They took him to the tunnel to drive,
He drove so hard that he broke his heart,
He laid down his hammer and he died …
(Chappell, 114)

A "steel driver" was a member of a work crew that removed rock. He was the "hammer man" of a "double-jack" team, the other being the "shaker" or "turner." In a rhythmic pattern often governed by the pace of an accompanying song, the driver swung a four-foot sledgehammer weighing at least eight pounds and struck the top of a "steel" held by the shaker, driving it into the solid rock. Steels were steel drills, chisel-like rods, usually one to one and a half inches in diameter, tempered at the sharpened end, and from two to eight feet long, perhaps more. Between hammer blows the shaker gave the steel a quarter turn and kept the hole clear of debris. When holes of the desired pattern and depth had been drilled, they were packed with explosives to blast away the rock. "Muckers" hauled away the debris. Steel driving was dangerous, especially for the shaker, and required great skill. For these reasons drivers were often the highest-paid laborers on the job.

Although "steel-driving man" represents the main tradition, songs and stories sometimes portray John Henry with other occupations. Children's literature and films frequently portray him as a spike driver on the railroad, perhaps from a misinterpretation of "steel driver." In other accounts he appears as a riveter, a longshoreman, or some other hard-working laborer. Some of John Henry's deeds are superhuman. As a little baby he talked and predicted his own death: "A hammer'll be the death of me." According to one story, "one day he drill all way from Rome, Georgia, to D'catur, mo' 'n a hundred miles drillin' in one day, an' I ain't sure dat was his bes' day" (Johnson, 145).

The legendary John Henry is particularly a hero to African Americans. In a letter to Guy Johnson, F. P. Barker, who claimed to have known John Henry in Alabama, quotes him as saying, "the steem Drill Beat men of every other Race down to the sand. Now Ill gaive my life before I let it beat the Negro man." John Henry died, but not before he had accomplished what most would think an impossible task, beating the machine that was intended to replace him. Whether John Henry was an actual person or purely fictional he has inspired generations, even beyond the African American community; indeed, labor movements claim him as a champion of all working people.

Not all of the John Henry tradition deals with his feats as a laborer. In some ballads he has several women. One informant allowed, "Lawd, I specs he had mo' 'n thousand wimmin" (Johnson, 146). Drilling and steel driving can be interpreted as sexual metaphors, and indeed "John Henry" has become a slang term for penis.

The legend and influence of John Henry now extend well beyond the ballads that made him famous. Roark Bradford published his novel *John Henry* in 1931 and his play of the same name in 1939. The next year the Broadway production of the play starred PAUL ROBESON as John Henry and featured JOSH WHITE as BLIND LEMON (JEFFERSON). In 1949, drawing on the image of John Henry, Lee Hays wrote the words and Pete Seeger the tune for "If I Had a Hammer," the hammer of justice. In 1972 an eight-foot bronze statue of John Henry by the sculptor Charles O. Cooper was placed in a park at Talcott, West Virginia, near the east portal of the now abandoned Great Bend or Big Bend Tunnel. A postage stamp commemorating John Henry was released in 1996, and an annual celebration, John Henry Days, was established that year in Talcott. The sledgehammer-carrying John Henry Irons, known as "Steel," was introduced in the *Superman* comic series in 1993. His niece Natasha Irons became "Steel" in 2003. Kenneth Johnson's 1997 film *Steel* stars the seven-foot-one-inch basketball player SHAQUILLE O'NEAL as John Henry Irons. In 2001 COLSON WHITEHEAD published *John Henry Days*, a novel that includes elaborated John Henry lore.

In the late 1970s the social psychologist Sherman A. James coined the term "John Henryism" to refer to a behavior pattern common among African Americans: "high-effort coping in the face of adversity," that is, trying harder and harder against difficult or even insurmountable odds. Clinical studies have explored the correlation between John Henryism and high blood pressure among African Americans.

The "John Henry effect" is another technical appropriation of the legend of hard-working John Henry by social scientists. In an experimental study of people, the performance of a study group may be compared with that of a control group. But if the members of the control group somehow learn that this comparison will be made, they may be inspired to an exceptionally high level of performance (the John Henry effect), thereby invalidating the study.

As one of the most enduring legends of humble strength and heroic determination, the story of John Henry will no doubt continue to provide inspiration especially to the workers, the poor, and the dispossessed who live and struggle within and against a system that seems to thwart their efforts and their dreams at every turn.

FURTHER READING

Chappell, Louis W. *John Henry: A Folk-Lore Study* (1933).

Garst, John. "Chasing John Henry in Alabama and Mississippi," *Tributaries: Journal of the Alabama Folklife Association* 5 (2002).

Johnson, Guy B. *John Henry: Tracking Down a Negro Legend* (1929).

Nelson, Scott. *Steel Drivin' Man: John Henry, the Untold Story of an American Legend* (2006).

Nelson, Scott. "Who Was John Henry," *Labor: Studies in Working-Class History of the Americas* 2 (2005).

Williams, Brett. *John Henry: A Bio-Bibliography* (1983).

JOHN GARST

Johns, Barbara (1935?–28 Sept. 1991), a student civil rights activist, was born Barbara Rose Johns in New York City, the eldest of five children born to Violet Johns and World War II veteran Robert Johns, who had been primarily a farm laborer.

Johns's ancestors worked as tobacco farmers in Prince Edward County, a rural area in southern Virginia still steeped in antebellum ideas of black inferiority. Before Johns's birth, her parents migrated north to New York. There, her mother worked as a domestic and her father held odd jobs; but soon, in search of better jobs, they relocated to Washington, D.C. After World War II erupted, Johns and her siblings were sent to Farmville, Prince Edward County, Virginia, to live with their maternal grandmother, Mary Croner. Johns tended the farm's tobacco crops and worked in the general store of her uncle the Reverend VERNON NAPOLEON JOHNS, whose powerful sermons challenged racial stereotypes. She first experienced blatant racism in Farmville; but, observing her uncle's outspoken example, she learned to question inequity.

Quiet, introspective, and a voracious reader, Johns excelled scholastically, despite the deplorable conditions of her school, the Robert R. Moton High School. Although it represented the first black high school in rural Virginia, the school's supplies and equipment were outdated and inadequate. The building lacked lockers, a cafeteria, and a gymnasium, and students rode dilapidated buses that had been discarded by white schools. Overcrowding represented the most pressing problem: constructed in 1939 to accommodate 180 students, when Johns entered school her sophomore year in 1949, Moton's enrollment had surpassed 450.

Elected to student council in her junior year, in 1950, Johns interacted with students from other schools, which experience heightened her frustration about Moton's conditions. Some outspoken blacks, including principal Boyd Jones and the Reverend L. Francis Griffin, pressed the school board for a new school based on the 1896 *Plessy v. Fergusson* decision that sanctioned segregation in public schools but required that facilities be equal. The board vaguely promised to construct a new school to accommodate the overflowing student population, but instead erected three haphazard wooden dwellings covered with tar paper.

The tar paper shacks were leaky and presented safety and health hazards: one small wood-burning stove provided the only heat. Appalled by the inadequacy, Johns complained to a teacher, Inez Davenport, who asked her why she did not try to change things. "Soon," Johns recalled, "the little wheels began turning in my mind" (Kluger, 468).

In the fall of 1950, Johns approached students Carrie and John Stokes with the idea of protesting the school's conditions by organizing a student strike. Over the next few months they planned the strike; and on 23 April 1951, having lured the principal away from the school, the entire student body was gathered into Moton's auditorium. Designated as spokesperson, Johns addressed her peers about the school's unacceptable conditions. She passionately insisted that the students needed to act to change conditions and urged them to walk out and remain on strike until a new school was under construction. Her rousing speech compelled the entire student body to quietly leave the school, and thus began the two-week strike.

Shortly afterward, she and John Stokes contacted the National Association for the Advancement of Colored People (NAACP) for assistance. Throughout the 1940s, the esteemed NAACP lawyers OLIVER W. HILL and SPOTTSWOOD ROBINSON fought to improve educational facilities for blacks in Virginia. Believing that equality would occur only in schools where whites and blacks had the same teachers and resources, they sought to bring a public school desegregation case before the Supreme Court. When they heard of the Farmville strike, both lawyers doubted that the majority of blacks in rural Prince Edward County would support the radical goal of desegregation. After meeting the students they agreed to accept the case on the condition that their parents support the idea. Johns was stunned at the pivotal effect of her strike: "it never entered my mind at the time that this would turn out to be a school desegregation suit" (Smith, 39).

On 3 May 1951 approximately one thousand community members crowded in the First Baptist Church in Farmville to listen to the NAACP's proposal to launch a desegregation suit. Some, including Moton's former principal, strongly opposed the idea, fearing that action would provoke violence from area whites. Robinson and Hill addressed the crowd, but it was sixteen-year-old Johns who spoke most eloquently and persuasively, imploring the adults to overcome fear and antebellum ideals of black subservience: "Don't let Mr. Charlie, Mr. Tommy, or Mr. Purval stop you from backing us. We are depending on you" (Smith, 59). Local newspapers publicized Johns's role in motivating the community, and to ensure her safety, she was sent to live with her uncle Vernon, then preaching in Montgomery, Alabama.

A few weeks after the strike, the NAACP filed a lawsuit on behalf of 117 Moton High School students. The case, *Davis v. Prince Edward*, became one of five included in the groundbreaking *Brown v. Board of Education* (1954) which outlawed segregation in public schools. Although Johns initiated the strike which altered the history of public education, ironically, her name did not appear on the lawsuit, and despite the victory of *Brown*, the county resisted integration, closing Moton High School from 1959 to 1964.

Davis v. Prince Edward, which began with the student strike Johns initiated, stands as one of the earliest civil rights protests at the grassroots level. The strike at Moton represented the only case included in the *Brown* desegregation suit initiated by students—and it provoked controversy. Many local whites believed that radical adults conceived of the idea and coerced students into taking action. Although Johns sought support from various adults after the strike began, she always maintained that the strike originated when she and the students empowered themselves to act.

After graduating from high school in Alabama in 1952, she attended Spelman College for two years, then left to marry the Reverend William R. Powell. The couple settled in Philadelphia and then enjoyed thirty-eight years of marriage, raising five children. As a sixteen-year-old student, Johns held a pivotal role in leading one black community to challenge racial discrimination and segregation. Although her action helped ignite the fight for civil rights, she did not partake in the civil rights movement as an adult, but earned a master's degree from Drexel University. As a librarian, she continued to promote equal education and access to resources. She died of cancer in Philadelphia at the age of fifty-five.

FURTHER READING

Irons, Peter. *Jim Crow's Children: The Broken Promise of the* Brown *Decision* (2002).

Kluger, Richard. *Simple Justice: The History of* Brown v. Board of Education *and Black America's Struggle for Equality* (2004).

Smith, Bob. *They Closed Their Schools: Prince Edward County, Virginia, 1951–1964* (1965).

MARILYN MORGAN

Johns, Moses (1815?–?), slave and religious leader, was born in Tennessee. The identity of his parents is not known. As a slave in Rutherford County, Tennessee, Moses was bequeathed to a son of John Johns. After Texas won its independence from Mexico and formed the Republic of Texas, Stephen B. Johns, with his brothers Edmund Johns and Clement R. Johns, migrated to the Republic of Texas with their slaves. The land grants they received in 1839 were in Red River County and what is now Bowie County, in the northeast area that borders Arkansas. Moses and the other Johns slaves probably worked clearing fields, building houses, and farming. East Texas was heavily populated by slave owners from the United States who raised cotton crops on large farms and plantations similar to those they left in the Deep South.

Just after entering Texas, Stephen B. Johns sold Moses and the other slaves to his brother Clement R. Johns. This recorded deed may have been for some tax purpose, since the will of Stephen B. Johns stated that his slaves be kept together. After his death in 1846, a year after the Republic of Texas became a state, the surviving family and slaves moved south to central Texas, where they joined friends who were early settlers of Hays County. This county was located just off the well-traveled main road between the major cities of San Antonio and Nacogdoches known as the Old San Antonio Road. The Johns party probably used this route from east Texas to reach Hays County.

The Civil War, from 1861 to 1865, affected the area when many settlers joined military units to serve in the Confederate army. Although few major battles were fought on Texas lands, on the farms the slaves were left with more responsibility and fewer resources as the war wore on. Meanwhile Moses Johns become a preacher to his fellow slaves. About 1864 under a brush arbor Rev. Johns organized the congregation, which became the Sweet Home Baptist Church. Usually religious services held in a "brush arbor" indicated a secret meeting. Later Moses deeded land for a church and school in this Elm Creek community, which was settled exclusively by former slave families and located in Guadalupe County, near the town of Seguin, Texas.

After the Civil War, in neighboring Hays County, this newly freed preacher led a small group and organized the Colored Baptist Church Zion in San Marcos. The name was later changed to First Baptist Church. Rev. Johns was its pastor from 1866 to 1873. After this building burned in 1873 the congregation rebuilt. Johns was one of the early ministers of the congregation that became Mount Zion First Baptist Church in San Antonio. He was probably an itinerant or circuit rider, which meant he traveled from one congregation to another, probably on horseback.

To be more effective, small Baptist churches often joined together to form an association. The churches in Seguin, San Marcos, New Providence, Capote, York's Creek, and perhaps a few others organized the Guadalupe Baptist District Association about 1873. This association cofounded Guadalupe College in Seguin, which was the only Baptist college for African Americans in south Texas at that time. For its first four years the association's moderator, or leader, was Rev. Johns.

The 1880 U.S. census shows Johns and his wife, Nancy, who was possibly also one of the Johns slaves, living in New Berlin, Guadalupe County. Four children with their families lived nearby. Rev. Johns performed the marriage ceremonies of his children and more than thirty other newly freed couples between

1868 and 1891. For the first national election after the Civil War, all men age twenty-one or older registered to vote. Moses Johns's name appears on the 1867–1869 voter registration list. He had been in Texas for thirty years when he registered on 16 July 1867. He also voted for the first time because his name appears on the Guadalupe County 1871 roster of voters. In addition to being a slave preacher, Moses was a farmer. Land was plentiful, and many former slaves, already skilled in agriculture, bought land as soon as they could. By 1880 the census shows that Moses Johns had a productive farm on Elm Creek. In one twelve-month period he reported hogs, poultry, and six milk cows. Sixteen acres were planted in Indian corn and ten acres were planted in cotton. In a deed Rev. Johns paid one seller "forty bales of cotton weighing five hundred lb. each, or two thousand dollars payable in four equal installments" for 598 acres of land. He then sold smaller land parcels to other freedmen. Before marrying Mrs. Jane Foster in 1887, Moses gave each of his children seventy-five acres.

His estate was partitioned in 1892, which indicates Moses died probably in early 1892. From a slave plantation in Middle Tennessee to the churches of south central Texas, Moses Johns, as a preacher, a mentor, a humanitarian, and a farmer, left a legacy.

FURTHER READING
Biographical Directory of the Texan Conventions and Congresses 1832–1845 (1942). *Memorial and Genealogical Record of Southwest Texas* (1894).
White, Gifford. *The First Settlers of Bowie and Cass Counties, Texas* (1983).
White, Gifford, ed. *The 1840 Census of the Republic of Texas* (1966).

JAMIE WALKER HARRIS

Johns, Vernon Napoleon (22 Apr. 1892–10 June 1965), Baptist pastor and civil rights pioneer, was born in Darlington Heights, near Farmville, Prince Edward County, Virginia, the son of Willie Johns, a Baptist preacher and farmer, and Sallie Branch Price. At age three, according to family tradition, young Vernon began preaching "on the doorstep or on a stump." Two years later he went with his older sister Jessie to a one-room school four miles from the Johnses' home. At seven, Vernon was kicked in the face by a mule. The injury scarred his left cheek, damaged his eyesight, and caused his left eyelid to twitch throughout his life. Johns later compensated for his weak eyesight by committing long passages of poetry and scripture to memory.

For several years after 1902, Jessie and Vernon Johns attended the Boydton Institute, a Presbyterian mission school near Boydton, Virginia, but the death of their father in 1907 brought Johns back to the family farm. Two years later he was nearly killed by the horns of a bull. Shortly thereafter Johns left the family home to study at Virginia Theological Seminary and College in Lynchburg, where he received an AB in 1915. Admitted to the Oberlin School of Religion, Johns became the student pastor of a small Congregational church in Painesville, Ohio. While at Oberlin, Johns was offered a scholarship to Western Reserve Law School, but he felt that the ministry was his vocation. After giving the annual student oration at Oberlin's Memorial Arch in 1918, Johns received a B.D. from the Oberlin School of Religion and was ordained in the Baptist ministry.

In 1918 Vernon Johns began teaching homiletics and New Testament at Virginia Theological Seminary and became a graduate student in theology at the University of Chicago. Continuing to teach at the seminary, he became the pastor of Lynchburg's Court Street Baptist Church, where he served from 1920 to 1926. Economic self-help in African American communities was a persistent theme in Johns's ministry, and, at Court Street Church, he persuaded the men's Bible class to launch a grocery store. In 1926 Vernon Johns preached for the first of many times at Howard University's Rankin Memorial Chapel, became the first African American preacher to have a sermon, "Transfigured Moments," published in Joseph Fort Newton's *Best Sermons* series, and was named director of the Baptist Educational Center of New York City. A year later he married Altona Trent, the daughter of William Johnson Trent, the president of Livingstone College in Salisbury, North Carolina. Vernon and Altona Trent Johns became the parents of six children.

In 1929 Johns left New York to become president of Virginia Theological Seminary and College. In that capacity he founded the Institute for Rural Preachers of Virginia, which he conducted for ten years, and the Farm and City Club, which promoted economic ties between urban and rural African Americans. In 1933 Johns was pastor of Holy Trinity Baptist Church in Philadelphia, Pennsylvania. He retired from the college presidency in September 1934 to his farm in Prince Edward County, where he lived until 1937. During those years Johns farmed, cut and sold pulpwood, operated a grocery store in Darlington Heights, and traveled, lecturing and preaching on the black church and college circuits. He launched the struggle to get school buses for African American students in Prince Edward County. Altona Trent Johns supplemented the family income by teaching public school in a one-room public school four miles from the family home.

In 1937 Johns became the pastor of First Baptist Church in Charleston, West Virginia. A former college president, the published pastor of an important African American congregation, and son-in-law of a college president, Vernon Johns seemed bound to a secure position in the African American elite. Yet he was rooted in the hard economic realities of Prince Edward County and grew contemptuous of the social pretense of the black bourgeoisie. As pastor of Charleston's First Baptist Church, he supplemented his income as a fishmonger. "I don't apologize for it," he later told students at Howard University, "because for every time I got one call about religion, I got forty calls about fish." It was a pattern Johns would repeat. In 1941 he returned to Lynchburg as pastor of Court Street Baptist Church.

In January 1948, months after Altona Trent Johns joined the faculty of Alabama State College in Montgomery, Vernon Johns was called as the pastor of that city's Dexter Avenue Baptist Church. He renewed his credentials as the publishing pastor of a leading African American congregation with an essay, "Civilized Interiors," in Herman Dreer's *American Literature by Negro Authors* in 1950, but he antagonized local white authorities with sermons such as "Segregation after Death," "It's Safe to Murder Negroes in Montgomery," and "When the Rapist Is White" and by summoning black passengers to join him in a protest of racial discrimination by walking off a bus in Montgomery.

In 1951, when his father-in-law became the first African American appointed to the Salisbury, North Carolina, school board, Vernon Johns's sixteen-year-old niece, BARBARA JOHNS, led African American students at R. R. Moton High School in Farmville, Virginia, in a boycott to protest conditions in Prince Edward County's schools. A month later attorneys for the National Association for the Advancement of Colored People filed suit to desegregate the county schools. That summer Barbara Johns left Prince Edward County to live with her aunt and uncle and spend her senior year of high school in Montgomery, Alabama. By then, however, Vernon Johns was antagonizing his own congregation's bourgeois sensibilities with sermons such as "Mud Is Basic" and by hawking

produce at church functions. After four stormy years at Dexter Avenue, the deacons accepted one of Vernon Johns's resignation threats in the summer of 1952. Altona Johns left Montgomery for a position at Virginia State College in Petersburg, but her husband thought the deacons would relent and sequestered himself in the parsonage. When the trustees cut off its electricity, gas, and water in December 1952, Johns finally left Montgomery. In 1954 MARTIN LUTHER KING JR. took charge of Dexter Avenue Baptist Church.

Vernon Johns was never the pastor of a church again. From 1953 to 1955 he shuttled between his Prince Edward County farm, where he raised livestock, and his wife's home in Petersburg, where he became a mentor to WYATT TEE WALKER, the pastor of Gillfield Baptist Church. Between 1955 and 1960 Johns was director of the Maryland Baptist Center, but he was asked to resign after a public rebuke to white Baptist clergymen in Baltimore for their failure of nerve in race relations. Briefly in 1961 Johns edited and published *Second Century Magazine*. After preaching his last sermon, "The Romance of Death," in Howard University's Rankin Chapel, Vernon Johns died in Washington, D.C.

FURTHER READING

Branch, Taylor. *Parting the Waters: America in the King Years, 1954–63* (1988).

Evans, Zelia S., with J. T. Alexander, eds. *Dexter Avenue Baptist Church, 1877–1977* (1977).

Gandy, Samuel L., ed. *Human Possibilities: A Vernon Johns Reader, Including an Unfinished Ms., Sermons, Essays, and Doggerel* (1977).

Smith, Robert Collins. *They Closed Their Schools: Prince Edward County, Virginia, 1951–1964* (1965).

Obituary: *Jet* (22 July 1965).

This entry is taken from the *American National Biography* and is published here with the permission of the American Council of Learned Societies.

RALPH E. LUKER

Johnson, Amelia Etta Hall (Jan. 1858–29 Mar. 1922), writer, was born Amelia Etta Hall in Canada to free black parents who had emigrated from Maryland. Little is known of her youth. Her death certificate puts her place of birth as Toronto; other sources say Montreal. Her father's name remains unknown, though there is evidence that he probably died before 1880. Her mother's given name was Eleanora, though she sometimes appears as Eleanor or Ellen; little is known of her other than a birth date of May 1828. Amelia was educated in Canada and settled in Baltimore, Maryland, with her family in the early 1870s. (Most sources agree that it was in 1874, though some documents suggest that it was as early as 1872.)

There Hall met the Reverend HARVEY JOHNSON, the son of an enslaved Virginia couple and an honors graduate of Wayland Theological Seminary who was appointed pastor of Baltimore's Union Baptist Church in November 1872. Hall and Johnson were married on 17 April 1877. The Johnsons had three children, a daughter, Jessie E., born in 1878, and two sons, Prentiss William, born in January 1883, and Harvey Jr., born in June 1884. Eleanora Hall also lived with the family between 1880 and 1900.

In the early years of their marriage Amelia Johnson undoubtedly focused on raising her children and helping her husband with his increasingly large congregation—which doubled between 1872 and 1874 and had risen to more than two thousand members by 1885. These were also years in which increasing tension between the white Maryland Baptist Union Association and black Baptists led Harvey Johnson to become more politicized both in his pulpit and beyond. In 1885 he and five other black Baptist clergymen formed the Mutual United Brotherhood of Liberty, which hosted a three-day conference on civil rights keynoted by FREDERICK DOUGLASS. Eventually Harvey Johnson called for a break with the Maryland Baptist Association, and in 1898 he organized a Colored Baptist Convention.

As the center of significant civil rights activism, the Johnson home saw not only national figures like Douglass but also important local figures like the Stewart sisters, whose successful suit over discriminatory steamship accommodations in 1884 and 1885 in the U.S. District Court of Maryland held a promise of hope that was later dashed by the infamous 1896 *Plessy v. Ferguson* decision that upheld the doctrine of "separate but equal."

In addition to keeping this home Amelia Johnson was also beginning to participate actively in area literary circles and to publish individual poems. She combined these interests to found a monthly magazine of religious literature for black youth, *The Joy*, in 1887. Even though the publication was short-lived, it received respectful notice, and Johnson's successes here led to publication in newspapers, to a regular column—entitled the "Children's Corner"—in Baltimore's *Sower and Reaper*, and to a short-story publication in the *National Baptist*.

More important, Johnson's successes led her to write *Clarence and Corinne, or God's Way* (1890). This short novel, which consciously downplays questions of race, centers on the poor and long-suffering, but also noble, title characters, who finally receive just treatment because they consistently choose to follow "God's way." Though far from a radical text, the novel represented an important breakthrough: Baptist newspapers noted that this was not only the first example of a black woman's "Sunday School fiction" being published by one of the largest publishing houses of the time, the American Baptist Publishing Society, but also the first example of a woman's text published by the society. The historian I. GARLAND PENN made much of this success in his book *The Afro-American Press* published the following year and awarded as a premium for securing new subscriptions to the *A.M.E. Church Review*. In addition to breaking new ground, publishing with the American Baptist Publishing Society meant that Johnson's book received wide distribution and notice in several Baptist periodicals. Further, it meant that the physical book was relatively well made and was illustrated.

The society also published Johnson's second and third novels in a similar format. Much like her first novel in theme and approach, *The Hazeley Family* (1894) focuses on religious subjects—seen mainly through the heroine Flora Hazeley's ultimately successful attempts to reunify her family and aid those around her in practicing Christian virtues. Johnson's final novel, *Martina Meriden, or What Is My Motive?* (1901), treats similar themes with similar approaches.

Johnson's first and second novels were republished as part of Oxford University Press's Schomburg Library of Nineteenth-Century Black Women Writers in 1988 and have enjoyed some critical attention since—much of it suggesting that there are nascent feminist themes played out in the tensions between the idealized Christian domesticity that Johnson preaches and the ways in which a world dominated by white men often attacks her characters. For most modern readers, though, Johnson's books can be perplexing in terms of the absence of discussions of race—especially given the author's clear and deep engagement in the civil rights struggle.

Little has been written about Johnson's later years, and the reasons that she stopped writing—or at least publishing—remain unclear. It is certainly likely that she turned more and more toward helping her husband run what had become a massive church; one of their sons remembered the Johnsons' marriage as a model of such support and friendship. She also devoted herself to her children—as least one of whom, Harvey Johnson Jr., went into teaching after graduating in 1904 from the Baltimore Normal School for the Education of Colored Teachers. Amelia Johnson died in Baltimore.

Though her novels remained out of print for close to a century, and though they arguably remain basic Sunday school stories—without really stretching the boundaries of the genre, as, for example, FRANCIS ELLEN WATKINS HARPER's work did—Johnson's work is important both for its relative prominence in religious circles and as material that crossed over into the white-owned religious popular sphere. Beyond her notable accomplishments as a writer and editor, Johnson was also an important force in her husband's public struggles for African American equality.

FURTHER READING

Primary source material on Johnson is limited. U.S. censuses, Baltimore death records, and various city directories help establish some of the basic facts of her life.

Majors, Monroe A. *Noted Negro Women: Their Triumphs and Activities* (1893)

Penn, I. Garland. *The Afro-American Press and Its Editors* (1891).

Spillers, Hortense J. Introduction to *Clarence and Corinne* (1988).

ERIC GARDNER

Johnson, Amy (c. 1784–6 Jan. 1849), free woman of color, property owner, and businesswoman in Natchez, Mississippi, was born into slavery. Little is known of her parents or early life. She was emancipated in 1814 at age thirty by her white owner, William Johnson, who was the likely father of her two young children, Adelia and William. He stated in the emancipation document executed in Concordia Parish, Louisiana, that in consideration of five dollars he had liberated Amy, who would be "able to work and gain a Sufficient Livilihood and maintenance" (Davis and Hogan, *Barber*, 15).

Amy was listed as a free Negro head of household in the Natchez, Mississippi, censuses of 1816, 1818, and 1820. Her children were also freed by William Johnson beginning with Adelia at age thirteen in 1818. Her son, WILLIAM JOHNSON (1809–1851), was emancipated two years after this, in 1820, at age eleven. The family helped constitute the free community of color in Natchez and surrounding Adams County, which was the largest of its kind

in Mississippi, numbering approximately 110 free black people in 1820. The people within this Deep South community occupied a stratum between slavery and complete freedom. Free people of color had to contend with many constraints that limited their rights, including restricted occupations, denial of voting rights, limited mobility, and inability to testify against whites. However, within this environment, free African Americans used their limited freedom to carve out niches for themselves and their families.

In 1819 Amy established her niche by procuring a license to retail within Natchez and probably peddled goods on the streets or maintained a small shop within the town by the Mississippi River. Throughout her life Amy was a dealer in small items and birds. No doubt she sold goods to the Natchez populace to support her two teenage children and experienced some measure of success in this pursuit. In later years she owned slaves of her own for profit, probably utilizing their labor to aid her in the management of her small business as well as leasing them out to others.

Besides maintaining a visible presence in the town's commerce, she at times had to answer to the public courts. Between 1816 and 1822 she sued and was in turn sued, mainly over payments of debt. In 1822 she sued Arthur Mitchum, a free barber of color, for assault. She charged that in 1819 Mitchum had caused her great bodily harm when he beat her with a brickbat and his fists, and he pulled out handfuls of her hair. For this substantial injury she asked the court for damages of $500. She was awarded damages in her case against Mitchum, but only in the amount of $27.50.

In 1820 the fortunes of the family began to change. At this time her daughter Adelia married a free barber of color from Philadelphia, James Miller, who apprenticed Adelia's eleven-year-old brother William to learn the trade. In 1830 William bought his brother-in-law's Natchez shop when James and Adelia moved to New Orleans. In 1835 William married Ann Battles, a free woman of color, and eventually they had ten children together. Amy was enfolded within the family, living with them.

All accounts of Amy Johnson paint a picture of an aggressive and outspoken woman who did not hesitate to voice her opinions and needs. William Johnson's diary entries from 1835 until Amy's death in 1849 are peppered with accounts testifying to her personal strength of character in her business dealings, slave transactions, and relations and suggesting a difficult personality. She regularly had verbal altercations with a great many people, and not exclusively people of color. For example, she brought one of William's tenants, a white fruit proprietor named Joseph Meshio, to tears by her insistence that he owed her $7.50, and even then Amy refused to relent.

On one particular occasion Amy fell victim to an act of violence emanating from her own child. In June 1837 William Johnson related how Amy had "commenced as usual to quarrel with Everything and Everybody" (Davis and Hogan, *Diary*, 183). A particularly ugly quarrel ensued, in which William took a whip to his own mother, giving her "a few cuts" as what seemed to him the most expedient way to quell her. After this humiliating incident Johnson refused to speak to his mother for a month and a half until his brother-in-law, James, intervened.

This diplomatic effort on the part of her son-in-law must have had an effect on Amy, for in a letter that William wrote to his sister a month later, he related that "she has quit running out in the streets to complete her quarrels—now she does pretty well—about 3 quarrells [sic] or three fusses a week will satisfy her very well—and before he [James Miller] came up here she used to have the bigest Kind of a fuss Every morning" (Davis and Hogan, *Diary*, 45). Unfortunately it was a short-lived period of relative peacefulness, as evidenced by a diary entry he made two months later: "The old woman is on a regular spree for quarrelling to day all day—oh Lord, was any One on this Earth So perpetually tormented as I am" (Davis and Hogan, *Diary*, 203). But in spite of her cantankerous personality, she was much loved by her family.

Amy Johnson died in 1849 of cholera. She almost outlived both of her children. Adelia had passed away of tuberculosis the previous year at age forty-two. William was murdered by a neighbor two years after Amy died. At the time of his mother's death, he related, "The remains of my poor mother was buried, oh my god. My loss is too great [sic]. Oh my poor belovd [sic] mother is losst [sic] to me forever in this world" (Davis and Hogan, *Diary*, 641).

FURTHER READING

Davis, Edwin Adams, and William Ransom Hogan. *The Barber of Natchez* (1954).

Davis, Edwin Adams, and William Ransom Hogan, eds. *William Johnson's Natchez: The Ante-bellum Diary of a Free Negro* (1951).

Davis, Ronald L.F. *The Black Experience in Natchez, 1720–1880* (1993).

Gould, Virginia Meacham. *Chained to the Rock of Adversity: To Be Free, Black & Female in the Old South* (1998).

NICOLE S. RIBIANSZKY

Johnson, Andrew N. (Apr. 1865–c. 1922), newspaper editor, businessman, and politician, was born in Marion, Alabama. Nothing is known of his parents. He was sent to a primary school, and he later attended the state normal school in his hometown and Talladega College in Talladega, Alabama. At age twenty he married Lillie A. Jones of Marion, and they had two children. At age twenty-six he became editor of the *Mobile State Republican*, and between 1894 and 1907 he edited the *Mobile Weekly Press*, described by BOOKER T. WASHINGTON as a "thoughtful Negro journal."

In his editorials, Johnson attempted to put the best cast on racial conditions and outwardly expressed optimism about the future for African Americans in the South. At other times, however, as when the Alabama Constitutional Convention of 1901 disfranchised blacks, he was less optimistic. Whites, he said then, had made a mockery of popular democracy. His editorials also opposed the "lily-white" faction in the Republican Party.

In business Johnson was a remarkable success. In 1896, while an editor, he opened a funeral home in Mobile for blacks. It took him a few years to build up his enterprise, but it became profitable. In 1904 Johnson boasted that he had "the most remarkable record in business of any young man, in my line in Alabama, White or Colored." Despite his bluster, the statement held truth.

As an editor and successful businessman, Johnson was a natural to enter politics. He was a member of the Republican state committee and was a delegate to the Republican National Conventions in 1896, 1900, and 1904. In his struggles with the "lily whites" in 1902 and 1904, he had already shown himself to be an adept politician. The "black and tans," as the Johnson Republicans were called, had effectively silenced the opposing faction, and in 1904 Johnson was selected as a state delegate at large to the Republican National Convention. However, in 1905 Johnson lost his fight with William Frye Tebbetts for the collectorship of the port of Mobile, an important and powerful patronage position. At Washington's urging, President Theodore Roosevelt received Johnson at the White House for an interview about the position. "I have just left the President," he wrote in 1905, "and I was never more sincerely or cordially greeted in my life." In the end, however, Roosevelt reappointed Tebbetts and further outraged Johnson by failing to speak to a black audience when he visited Mobile later that year.

The next year Mobile was the setting of a racial crisis when two black men were accused of raping a white woman. At first Johnson remained silent, but at the urging of others he spoke out, asserting that the men were guilty and had received their just punishment—they were lynched—but that "the white man makes and executes the law in the way that suits him." Unlike Atlanta in the same year, Mobile avoided a race riot, but in the aftermath of the episode rumors spread that Johnson was marked for assassination by blacks. Johnson thought that he was so marked because several of his enemies wanted to take over his prosperous undertaking business. Whatever the reality, he feared for his life and decided to leave Mobile.

In 1906 Johnson sold his business and moved to Nashville, Tennessee. The next year he opened an undertaking establishment there. It quickly became a financial success, and in 1909 Johnson was elected president of the black Embalmers and Undertakers Association of Tennessee. "I am very busy and my business is even more a brilliant success than Mobile," he wrote EMMETT SCOTT, Washington's private secretary. By 1913 Johnson had become the director of Nashville's black board of trade; a member of various black fraternal organizations, including Odd Fellows and Knights of Pythias; and a Congregationalist Church member, and he continued to participate actively in the National Negro Business League, an organization founded in 1900 by Washington.

Johnson had even reinvested in his old Mobile undertaking business, which had fallen on hard times, becoming a full partner in 1912 and sending his son Lorenzo back there to become the company's secretary. His one business failure was in 1912, when he opened the Majestic Theater in Nashville's black business district. Described as a magnificent playhouse, it drew few customers, in large measure because of the exorbitant one-dollar ticket price.

By the 1910s Johnson had moved away from politics, although he continued to offer advice on Republican patronage positions and was selected a delegate from Tennessee in 1916 to the Republican National Convention in Chicago. The location and cause of his death are unknown. Described as affable, polite, courteous, and refined, Johnson was a strikingly handsome man. Despite his political disappointments and his unfounded optimism about the possibilities for blacks in the South, his own life had made a mockery of racial stereotypes

of lazy, docile, and ignorant black men. Active, energetic, and intelligent, Johnson struggled and prospered in an era of extreme racial bitterness, hostility, and conflict. Like others of the black middle class, he espoused black self-help, solidarity, and civic betterment, but he also acquired a comfortable estate by taking advantage of the separation of the races.

FURTHER READING

Hartshorn, W. N., ed. *An Era of Progress and Promise, 1863–1910* (1910).

Mather, Frank Lincoln, ed. *Who's Who of the Colored Race: A General Biographical Dictionary of Men and Women of African Descent* (1915).

This entry is taken from the *American National Biography* and is published here with the permission of the American Council of Learned Societies.

LOREN SCHWENINGER

Johnson, Ann Battles (1815–20 Aug. 1866), free woman of color, property owner, and slaveholder in Natchez, Mississippi, was born enslaved. Her mother, Harriet Battles, was an enslaved mixed-race woman. It is not clear who Ann's father was, although presumably it was a white man due to Ann's racial classification as "mulatto." It is not readily evident, however, that it was Gabriel Tichenor, the white man who claimed ownership of mother and daughter. In 1822 Tichenor crossed the Mississippi River to Concordia Parish, Louisiana, and manumitted Harriet when she was thirty years old. Because of the laws of Louisiana, the children of freed people could not themselves be freed until they too reached age thirty. Four years after Harriet's manumission, Tichenor navigated around that issue by transporting Harriet and the eleven-year-old Ann to Cincinnati, Ohio, where he had their free papers duly recorded. The mother and daughter then returned to Mississippi as free people of color. Tichenor and his wife then sold Harriet a city lot in Natchez for two dollars.

In approximately 1829 fourteen-year-old Ann began a romantic involvement with the twenty-year-old free barber of color WILLIAM JOHNSON, whom she would eventually marry. After a five-year period of courtship punctuated by the two regularly attending the theater together as well as other public events, they were married on 21 April 1835. At the time of their nuptials William was the owner of Natchez's most popular barbershop, catering primarily to white patrons, including members of the wealthy and powerful plantocracy. He also held several thousand dollars in property as well as a few slaves.

Following the year of their marriage Ann and William became parents. Their first son, William Jr., was born on 10 January 1836. They would have nine additional surviving children, five boys and four girls: Richard, Byron, Anna, Alice, Catharine, Eugenia, Louis, Josephine, and Clarence. The family was a central component of Natchez's community of color, eventually integrating into the elite segment of that population.

In spite of the fact that both Ann and William were primarily white (perhaps as much as seven-eighths) they were recognized as free people of color and subject to the many constraints under which free blacks lived. For example, when Ann traveled to New Orleans in July 1842 the purpose of her trip was to baptize some of her children and have them formally recorded in that city as free people at St. Louis Cathedral. Although their children were recognized as free in Natchez, perhaps conditions necessitated one additional step for peace of mind. During this journey Ann, as a free woman of color, would have had to contend with second-class accommodations had it not been for the intervention of her husband. She would not have been able to take her meals with white women and would probably have had to sleep on the floor. But William persuaded the captain to provide a stateroom for Ann and the children she brought with her to New Orleans. The remaining children were all similarly baptized in 1856.

Education was an essential value that Ann inculcated within her family. Although her mother appears to have been illiterate, Ann Johnson obtained the ability to read and write at some point in her early life. She and William recognized that literacy was crucial to their placement within the community and afforded that opportunity to their children by personally teaching them, hiring private tutors, and sending some of the children to schools in New Orleans. The Johnson children studied reading, writing, mathematics, geography, and literature. Additionally the boys learned the barbering trade from their father and Ann instructed her daughters in music as well as domestic skills like sewing. Ann's daughters Anna and Catharine utilized this education by eventually becoming schoolteachers.

Typical of women in affluent households, Ann managed domestic duties and also tended to business matters. Early in her marriage, prior to experiencing the prosperity that eventually characterized

their household, Ann performed housekeeping chores. She also kept a garden stocked with fresh produce such as tomatoes, squash, beans, and okra. The cows, pigs, and chickens she maintained in pens and coops near the house allowed the family to produce their own meat, eggs, and dairy products. Ann sold the surplus to supplement the household income. She and her daughters were apt seamstresses and prolific producers of bonnets, scarves, hoods, caps, and the like, which they sold through the enslaved members of the household. Gradually she relegated most of her household tasks to the enslaved individuals and focused on the managerial aspects of the household.

The ownership of slaves guaranteed the family's hierarchical position within the free black community. During his lifetime William held at least thirty slaves; and after his murder in 1851 at age forty-two Ann inherited the remainder of them. These enslaved people performed a variety of tasks within the household: cooking, cleaning, working at the family's cotton plantation, Hard Scrabble, hawking Ann's handmade goods and produce on Natchez's streets, and hiring themselves out to others. Although the family engaged in slave ownership for economic reasons, there were other compelling reasons to enslave a few members of the household. In 1840 Ann purchased her cousin, Julia, and two daughters with the future plan to free them, which was difficult because of Mississippi's restrictive policy of manumission.

Ann Battles Johnson died in 1866 of intermittent fever. She had been the head of the family since William's murder in 1851 and had managed it well. She bequeathed to her children William's barbershop, their brick house on State Street, and some rental property, totaling thousands of dollars. After her death a friend writing to Ann's mother, Harriet, tried to comfort her by stating, "You know how much Anne leaned upon & looked up to you as her mainstay & had you been removed from her, how she would have suffered & how lost she would have been" (Gould, 41). No doubt Ann's death left a similar legacy to her own children.

FURTHER READING

Davis, Edwin Adams, and William Ransom Hogan. *The Barber of Natchez* (1954).

Davis, Edwin Adams, and William Ransom Hogan, eds. *William Johnson's Natchez: The Ante-bellum Diary of a Free Negro* (1951).

Davis, Ronald L.F. *The Black Experience in Natchez, 1720–1880* (1993).

Gould, Virginia Meacham. *Chained to the Rock of Adversity: To Be Free, Black & Female in the Old South* (1998).

NICOLE S. RIBIANSZKY

Johnson, Anthony (?–1670), a planter on Virginia's eastern shore, arrived in Virginia in 1621 aboard the *James* along with a handful of other Africans or Afro-Caribbeans listed as "servants." His place and date of birth are not known, though it is supposed that he was born a free man in Africa. He worked his way out of slavery, became a farmer in Northampton County, and later a slaveholding planter in neighboring Accomack County, Virginia. Between his arrival and 1635, he belonged to Richard Bennett of Warresquioake County, on the south side of the James River, at which time he apparently won his freedom and that of his wife, Mary, who was also a slave of the Bennetts. Anthony and Mary Johnson produced at least four children and were married until Anthony's death.

Known in 1621 simply as "Antonio," Johnson was listed in a 1625 census as a servant, though whether that meant an indentured servant or a slave remains unclear. While there were African Americans working as indentured servants throughout the English colonies by the mid-seventeenth century, there is no reason to presume that Johnson and his wife were not slaves. Sometime after 1635 the Johnsons acquired their freedom, presumably through self-purchase, and relocated to Northampton County. There Anthony acquired a small farm sometime around 1640, where he became a prosperous breeder of cattle and hogs, which were as vital to the Virginia economy as tobacco. Johnson did so well, in fact, that he was able in 1651 to purchase five headrights (50-acre allotments granted for each indentured servant transported from England) from neighboring planters, which garnered him a modest 250-acre estate on Pungoteague Creek in Accommack County. There he embarked on a career as a tobacco farmer, which was temporarily aborted by a fire that destroyed most of his property in February 1653.

This "unfortunate" event, as the Northampton Court termed it, forced Johnson to seek government relief in the form of a tax waiver, which the county granted, excusing Anthony and Mary from paying taxes on their two daughters for the remainder of "their naturall lives." A 1645 act of the legislature had explicitly stated "That *all negro men and women*, and al other men from the age of 16 to 60 shall be adjudged tithable," and it is significant that the Northampton Court made such an exception for the Johnsons. This extraordinary ruling, attributable at least in part to patronage from Bennett and possibly also the Scarboroughs, allowed Johnson to reestablish himself. More evidence of Johnson's rising status through patronage comes from another court case in October 1653 when Johnson and a white neighbor, Lieutenant John Neale, clashed over a matter that "concerned a cowe." The court ordered Captain Samuel Gouldsmith and Robert Parker, members of ambitious and influential Eastern Shore families, to investigate the matter rather than simply finding for Neale, as might have been the case with any other free black farmer in dire straits. They determined that Johnson's recent misfortunes left him vulnerable to harassment and attempted exploitation, and that Neale was trying to take advantage of him.

Gouldsmith frequently did business with Johnson, and on one occasion in 1654 "a Negro called John Casor" appealed to Goldsmith, claiming that Johnson held him illegally as a slave for the past seven years, when in fact he was an indentured servant (Breen and Innes, 13). Parker took up Casor's cause and sent him to work on his farm, while Johnson conferred with his family, which now included two sons with new families of their own. Johnson initially conceded Casor his freedom and paid appropriate freedom dues owed to a released servant, but changed his mind in 1655, accusing Parker of unlawful interference. Gouldsmith submitted a deposition to the Northampton Court in support of Johnson, and the court indeed ruled in Johnson's favor, compelling Casor's return and Parker to make restitution, including court costs.

Despite the fire that nearly destroyed his original estate, Johnson was able to recoup his losses and establish himself as a well-connected middling planter by 1660. He and his family formed the core of a vibrant, free black planter community in Northhampton, which included Anthony Payne and Emmanuel Driggus, whose careers closely resembled Johnson's. Anthony Johnson's son John patented 450 acres of land abutting his father's, and his other son Richard likewise established himself on 100 acres adjoining theirs. In 1665 the entire Johnson clan pulled up stakes and moved to Somerset County, Maryland, along with two wealthy white Eastern Shore planters, Ann Toft and Randall Revell, who claimed the Johnsons as headrights when they purchased their 2,350 acres. The Johnsons' free status was never in question in this unusual transaction, but it is clear that there were pecuniary benefits for all involved. Profits from land transfers and subsequent sales between Anthony Johnson and his sons allowed the latter to become formidable planters in their own rights. Anthony Johnson leased a 300-acre plantation that he named "Tonies Vineyard," where his wife lived until her death around 1675. His sons built on their initial prosperity and, after their father's death in 1670, passed property on to their sons, the most prominent of whom was John Johnson Jr., who purchased a plantation in Somerset County in 1677 that he named "Angola," perhaps in memory of his grandfather's homeland.

Anthony Johnson's life is but one thread in an intricate tapestry that constituted race relations in seventeenth-century Chesapeake society. T. H. Breen and Stephen Innes called him the "patriarch on Pungoteague Creek," and noted that in spite of his enslavement, upon emancipation he fully participated in the local planter culture, sharing his white neighbors' preconceptions about property rights and the legitimacy of slavery (Breen and Innes, 7). He moved easily as a peer within a planter-dominated society that—at a time when the differences in treatment of slaves and servants were narrow, and slavery was poorly defined by colonial law—conformed to no single pattern. The opportunities open to men and women like Anthony and Mary Johnson significantly narrowed after 1670, when race relations hardened as African and African American slaves became the preferred labor force and white planters gradually drove their black counterparts out of business.

FURTHER READING

Breen, T. H., and Stephen Innes. *"Myne Owne Ground": Race and Freedom on Virginia's Eastern Shore, 1640–1676* (1980).

Brewer, James H. "Negro Property Owners in Seventeenth-Century Virginia," *William and Mary Quarterly*, 3.12 (1955).

Morgan, Edmund S. *American Slavery, American Freedom: The Ordeal of Colonial Virginia* (1975).

JOHN HOWARD SMITH

Johnson, Bill (10 Aug. 1872 or 1874–3 Dec. 1972), jazz bassist and banjoist, was born William Manuel Johnson in Talladega, Alabama. Nothing is known of his parents, but he had five brothers, one of whom, Dink Johnson, played drums, piano, and clarinet, and a sister, Anita Gonzalez, who was an early paramour of the pianist and composer JELLY ROLL MORTON. At some point in the 1870s or 1880s the family moved to New Orleans, where Johnson started playing guitar at age fifteen. In 1900 he began doubling on bass and worked in a string trio at Tom Anderson's Annex in Storyville. Between 1901 and 1908 he played bass with the Peerless Orchestra and the trombonist Frankie Dusen's Eagle Band, doubling on tuba for work with the Excelsior and other marching bands.

After touring the Southwest with a trio in 1908, Johnson, the cornetist Ernest "Nenny" Coycault, and their trombonist, one H. Pattio (or Paddio), settled in Los Angeles in 1909. In 1913 the bassman added other New Orleanians to the group: the violinist and saxophonist Jimmy Palao, the guitarist Norwood "Giggy" Williams, and Johnson's brother Dink on piano and drums. But when he received an offer for a national tour on the flourishing Pantages circuit, Johnson sent to New Orleans for more skilled players—the cornetist FREDDIE KEPPARD, the trombonist Eddie Vincent, and the clarinetist GEORGE BAQUET—and with them he formed the Original Creole Band, although he may have used that name for the earlier group as well. Dink, however, chose to remain in Los Angeles when the band went on tour, and for some unknown reason a substitute was neither sought nor found.

Between 1914 and 1917 the now six-piece band of three horns and three strings toured extensively on the Pantages, Loew, and Orpheum vaudeville circuits, early on appearing regularly at the Grand Theater on Chicago's South State Street and the North American Restaurant on the Loop, thus making it the first jazz band of any sort to play for both black and white audiences in Chicago. In New York the band performed its "novelty" act—as jazz bands were billed in vaudeville houses—at the Winter Garden, the Columbia Theater, the American Theater, Loew's Orpheum, the Lexington Opera House, and the prestigious Palace Theater, all exclusively white venues. Legend has it that in 1916, when offered an opportunity to record for the Victor Talking Machine Company, then the leading producer of the new sound medium, Keppard turned it down in the belief that recordings would enable other musicians, particularly northerners, to steal his band's style, a product unique to New Orleans and one of which he was justifiably proud. After the group disbanded briefly in Boston in the spring of 1917, Keppard reassembled the group in the fall, replacing Vincent and Baquet with the trombonist George Filhe and the clarinetist Jimmie Noone. After a residency at the Logan Square Theater in Chicago and a long tour with the *Tan Town Topics*, a vaudeville revue, the group disbanded in April 1918.

After the band's breakup, Johnson settled in Chicago, where he was asked to assemble a band of New Orleans musicians for the opening of the Royal Gardens. Using the pianist Lottie Taylor and the drummer PAUL BARBARIN, who were already living in Chicago, Johnson sent to New Orleans for the cornetist JOE "KING" OLIVER, Vincent, and Noone to join him. However, another Original Creole Band, then under the leadership of the clarinetist Lawrence Duhé, was also working in Chicago and seeking to hire Oliver. The newly arrived cornetist quickly settled the problem by working with both bands, typically on the same night. At some point in late 1918 Johnson left for New York to form the Seven Kings of Ragtime for an Orpheum circuit tour, but he returned to the Royal Gardens in 1919 to rejoin the band he had since turned over to Oliver. During his four-year stay with Oliver's Creole Jazz Band, the personnel consisted of the trombonist HONORE DUTREY, the clarinetist JOHNNY DODDS, the pianist Lil Hardin (with Bertha Gonsoulin an occasional replacement), and the drummer Warren "BABY" DODDS. LOUIS ARMSTRONG was added as second cornetist in August 1922, more than a year after the club had been renamed the Lincoln Gardens.

Johnson most likely concentrated on bass when the Oliver band played for dancing at the Gardens, but because the limited recording technology of the period was not yet able to reproduce the lower frequencies of the instrument without distortion, when the Creole Jazz Band recorded its first session for Gennett on 6 April 1923, Johnson had to play banjo, but even on that instrument his presence is barely discernible. He did, however, have the opportunity to utter the first jazz vocal break on record when he shouted the high-pitched, exhortatory "Oh, play that thing!" following Oliver's three solo choruses on "Dipper Mouth Blues." To all indications Johnson remained with Oliver through mid-1924, but his role in the recording ensemble ended with the first session. On subsequent dates in June and October 1923, his place was taken by the banjoists Bud Scott and JOHNNY ST. CYR, respectively. When the Oliver band broke up in June 1924, Johnson, along with the Dodds brothers and Dutrey, joined Keppard and the pianist Charlie Alexander at Kelly's Stables. Throughout the remainder of the decade, Johnson worked with Johnny Dodds at Kelly's Stables, led his own small groups at various South Side clubs, and worked with the bandleaders Jimmy Wade and Clifford "Klarinet" King.

As a seminal New Orleans jazzman, Johnson was probably one of the first bassmen in history to alternate pizzicato rhythmic playing with conventional bowed techniques when playing dance music—whether traditional jigs, reels, and waltzes or the then new syncopated styles of ragtime and early jazz. Unfortunately, however, no recorded documentation exists of the music played in New Orleans during the formative 1890–1915 period. Similarly, because of Keppard's decision not to record in 1916, there exists no proof of the actual Original Creole Band sound, but later evidence, for example, the 1920s recordings of Keppard, suggests that the group probably played with a greater emphasis on blues intonation and a looser approach to ragtime rhythm than did the Original Dixieland Jass (later, Jazz) Band, the white New Orleans band that in 1917 became the first to record the new music.

Because the sound of Johnson's full-toned, resonant bass can be heard only on the records he made in 1928 and 1929, there are but a handful of citations, most notably Johnny Dodds's "Blue Piano Stomp," "Bull Fiddle Blues," "Blue Washboard Stomp," "Goober Dance," "Too Tight," and "Indigo Stomp." However, he was also present on some less well-known recordings by JIMMY BLYTHE, Junie Cobb, Frankie "Half Pint" Jaxon, his own Louisiana Jug Band, Banjo Ikey Robinson, the State Street Ramblers, TAMPA RED, and SIPPIE WALLACE. Although Johnson pioneered in creating the highly rhythmic style known as "slap bass," his contributions have been overshadowed by the more prominent work of other, younger, and more widely recorded New Orleans bassists, such as POPS FOSTER, WELLMAN BRAUD, Steve Brown, JOHN LINDSAY, and Al Morgan. However, Johnson is still credited for his early influence on Milt Hinton, a renowned swing-era bassist some forty years his junior. Nothing is known of Johnson's career during the 1930s except that he led his own small bands in Chicago and worked in a group called the Snizer Trio. His last known performances were in 1947, when he played in concerts with New Orleans-styled bands featuring the trumpeters BUNK JOHNSON and Lee Collins. In the 1950s Johnson retired from music and moved to Texas, where he died in New Braunfels, near San Antonio.

FURTHER READING

Charters, Samuel B. *Jazz New Orleans: 1885–1963* (1963)

Charters, Samuel B., and Leonard Kunstadt. *Jazz: A History of the New York Scene* (1962).

Lomax, Alan. *Mr. Jelly Roll* (1950).

Ramsey, Frederic, ed. *Jazzmen* (1939; repr. 1977).

Rose, Al, and Edmond Souchon. *New Orleans Jazz: A Family Album* (1978).

DISCOGRAPHY

Rust, Brian. *Jazz Records, 1897–1942* (1982).

This entry is taken from the *American National Biography* and is published here with the permission of the American Council of Learned Societies.

JACK SOHMER

Johnson, Blind Willie (1900?–1949?), gospel singer and guitarist, was born near Marlin, Texas, the son of George Johnson, a farmer, and a mother (name unknown) who died when Willie was quite young. Information about Johnson's life is sketchy and based largely on brief interviews with his two wives and a few friends and fellow musicians, who sometimes gave vague and contradictory information. The only tangible documents of his life are the thirty recordings that he made between 1927 and 1930.

When Willie was about five years old, his father remarried. Around the age of seven he was blinded, according to one report, by his stepmother throwing lye water in his face after an argument with his father, and in other reports, by wearing defective glasses or watching an eclipse of the sun through a piece of glass. Like many poor African Americans of the time, he took up music as a profession, learning initially on a cigar box guitar made by his father and modeling his singing on that of another local blind man named Madkin Butler. He soon graduated to a regular guitar, and his father would take him to Marlin and other nearby towns to play on the streets for tips. As far as is known, his repertoire consisted entirely of religious songs. In the 1920s he began to perform in Waco and Dallas on the streets as well as in church programs and revivals.

Johnson was first recorded by a mobile field unit of Columbia Records in Dallas on 3 December 1927, performing six songs alone with his guitar. On 5 December 1928 he recorded four more songs in Dallas for Columbia, this time with the help of female singer Willie B. Harris, who was from Marlin and a member of the Pentecostal Church of God in Christ; she claimed to have married Johnson around 1926 or 1927. By June 1929, or possibly a year or two earlier, Johnson had married another woman in Dallas named Angeline, who was of the Baptist faith. They moved briefly to Waco and Temple but soon settled in Beaumont, where they remained until Johnson's death about twenty years later.

From 10 to 11 December 1929 Johnson recorded ten songs for Columbia in New Orleans, accompanied on some by a local female singer whose identity is unknown. Johnson's final ten recordings were made for Columbia in Atlanta on 20 April 1930, with Willie B. Harris assisting in the singing.

Johnson's travels before his initial recording session appear to have been confined to the territory between Marlin and Dallas. The popularity of his recordings created a wider demand for his music, and in the late 1920s he apparently toured throughout much of eastern Texas and perhaps farther afield. His recording sessions in New Orleans and Atlanta allowed him to remain in those cities and to perform for up to a month. Atlanta musician BLIND WILLIE McTELL claimed to have traveled with Johnson "from Maine to the Mobile Bay," probably after the 1930 session in Atlanta in which both musicians recorded. McTell stated that he left Johnson in Union, Missouri, and later encountered him in Little Rock, Arkansas. Angeline Johnson, however, stated that her husband generally stayed close to their Beaumont home, particularly after she began having children. Johnson performed at church programs and conventions, sometimes with Angeline helping in the singing. They lived well in what were described as "fine homes," and Johnson bought a car and hired a driver. When his car was stolen at a Baptist convention in Houston, the delegates took up a collection and bought him another. In the winter of 1949 Johnson's house caught fire. Although the family escaped and the flames were extinguished, Johnson caught pneumonia from sleeping on a damp mattress. He was refused admittance to a hospital for some reason connected to his blindness, and he died a few days later.

Johnson's recordings are a rich cross section of African American religious music, including older spirituals and hymns and newer gospel songs. Several recounted stories from the Bible; others detailed recent historical events, such as the sinking of the *Titanic*, World War I, and the influenza epidemic of 1918. Although Johnson was raised a Baptist and worked mostly in Baptist circles following his marriage to Angeline, several of his songs contain references to doctrines of the then-emerging Pentecostal denominations, such as the Church of God in Christ. This influence is probably attributable to the period he spent with Willie B. Harris and in general to the encouragement of instrumental music by Pentecostal sects. Although the Baptists of the 1920s and 1930s were less tolerant of instrumental music, they too would have encouraged a blind performer who could make a living no other way. The themes of several of Johnson's songs likely had special meaning for him in respect to his blindness, the loss of his mother, and general feelings of helplessness. Among these songs are "Mother's Children Have a Hard Time," "If I Had My Way I'd Tear the Building Down," "Let Your Light Shine on Me," "Bye and Bye I'm Going to See the King," "Take Your Burden to the Lord and Leave It There," and "Everybody Ought to Treat a Stranger Right."

Frequently using a growling false bass voice derived from folk preaching technique, Johnson sang with a passion and sense of command seldom matched by other gospel singers of his day. On his duets a contrasting female voice, sweeter and higher pitched, was heard in an antiphonal or heterophonic relationship to Johnson's rough singing. On some of his pieces he played a simple repeated rhythmic phrase on the guitar, and on a few others he outlined rudimentary harmonic changes. On about half of his recordings, however, he used a metal ring on his finger or a pocketknife to play the guitar in a slide technique, outlining the song's melody up and down one of the guitar strings while at the same time creating a driving rhythm. Johnson is generally regarded as one of the masters of this folk guitar technique, which eerily recalls the human voice in its tonal and textural flexibility.

Johnson's singing and playing style and his repertoire were enormously influential on other gospel singers. Even many blues singers and guitarists performed versions of his songs. Eight of his recordings were reissued in 1935, and further reissues have occurred since the 1950s; his entire recorded work has remained in print since the 1970s. His "Dark Was the Night—Cold Was the Ground" has been used as background music in films, and popular recording artists since the 1960s have performed pieces from his repertoire.

FURTHER READING

Charters, Samuel. *The Country Blues* (1959).

Oliver, Paul. *Songsters and Saints: Vocal Traditions on Race Records* (1984).

DISCOGRAPHY

The Complete Blind Willie Johnson (Columbia/Legacy C2K 52835).

Sweeter as the Years Go By (Yazoo 1078).

This entry is taken from the *American National Biography* and is published here with the permission of the American Council of Learned Societies.

DAVID EVANS

Johnson, Budd (14 Dec. 1910–20 Oct. 1984), jazz saxophonist and arranger, was born Albert J. Johnson in Dallas, Texas, the son of Albert Johnson, an automobile mechanic, cornetist, and church organist. His mother's name is not known. His older brother Frederick H. "Keg" Johnson studied trombone with his father and also became a career professional. After having taught himself cornet by ear, Budd Johnson at age eight started taking piano lessons, but he soon switched to drums, which he played in the Moonlight Melody Six, a band formed by his brother Keg, the pianist Jesse Stone, and other school friends. In 1923 or 1924, when a better drummer joined the band, Johnson started teaching himself saxophone. Renaming their group the Blue Moon Chasers, the boys in 1925 traveled with the Gonzel White Show to Tulsa, but after becoming stranded, they returned home. Around 1926 Budd and Keg Johnson joined William Holloway's Music Makers (or Syncopators). In that traveling group Budd learned to read music from Holloway and the saxman Ben Smith, who in 1927 became the group's leader. In 1928 Johnson left Smith and joined Eugene Coy's Happy Black Aces in Oklahoma, staying with them until early 1929, when he joined Terrence Holder's Twelve Clouds of Joy in Dallas. It was while with Coy in Amarillo, Texas, that Johnson chanced to give the silent movie pianist BEN WEBSTER his first lessons on the saxophone. After Holder was ousted for stealing his sidemen's money, the band, now under the name of Jesse Stone's Blue Serenaders, worked in St. Joseph, Missouri; Kansas City, Missouri; and Iowa. When this group disbanded, Johnson and Stone joined GEORGE E. LEE's Orchestra in Kansas City, where they made their rather undistinguished debut recordings in November 1929.

In January 1932, at his brother's urging, Johnson moved to Chicago, where he found work in the bands of Ed Carry, Irene Wilson, the wife of TEDDY WILSON, Cassino Simpson, and Clarence Moore. Later that year Johnson and his brother played in Eddie Mallory's band before joining LOUIS ARMSTRONG's newly formed orchestra in January 1933. Johnson played promising solos on Armstrong's "Some Sweet Day," "Mahogany Hall Stomp," "Dusky Stevedore," "Mighty River," and "St. Louis Blues," and on "Sweet Sue, Just You" he sang an amusing scat chorus in duet with Armstrong. When Armstrong disbanded his orchestra in July, Johnson played briefly with Jimmie Noone at the Lido, worked for a while with Jesse Stone, and in 1934 began substituting regularly for the tenor saxophonist and arranger Cecil Irwin in EARL HINES's band at the Grand Terrace Ballroom. When Irwin was killed in a bus accident in May 1935, Johnson took his place. In 1936 the tenor saxophonist and arranger JIMMY MUNDY left Hines to join Benny Goodman's writing staff, at which time Johnson began turning out new arrangements of such older numbers as "Deep Forest," "Blue Because of You," and "Rosetta." Over the next six years he wrote scores on numbers such as "Grand Terrace Shuffle," "Father Steps In," "Piano Man," "Riff Medley," "XYZ," "Number 19," and "You Can Depend on Me" as well as perhaps dozens of others that were not recorded. With Hines's approval, in 1936 Johnson took some time off to join the writing staff of Gus Arnheim's revamped swing band for an opening at the Hotel New Yorker. When Arnheim disbanded the group, Johnson rejoined Hines in Chicago, recording four sessions with him between February 1937 and March 1938, out of which his CHU BERRY–influenced solo on "I Can't Believe That You're in Love with Me" was particularly notable. During a layoff from the Hines band in May 1938, Johnson accepted a job with FLETCHER HENDERSON as a replacement for the lead altoist Hilton Jefferson, leaving him in late July to remain in Chicago and work with his brother HORACE HENDERSON's band through October, when he rejoined Hines.

In October 1938 and again in February 1940, Johnson recorded two of his most fully realized solos to date on LIONEL HAMPTON's "Rock Hill Special" and "Till Tom Special," and these, along with the Hines recordings from July 1939 on, exemplify his by now thorough conversion to LESTER YOUNG's style, as is evidenced in his higher-pitched, alto-like tone; even, eighth note phrasing; and occasional use of offbeat rhythmic accents. He is heard to increasing advantage on Hines's "Grand Terrace Shuffle," "Father Steps In," "Riff Medley," "XYZ," "Gator Swing," "Call Me Happy," "Easy Rhythm," "In Swamp Lands," "Windy City Jive," "Yellow Fire," "I Never Dreamt," "Skylark," and "Second Balcony Jump." Johnson seems to have left Hines briefly in early 1940 to work for Johnny Long, probably as an arranger, but he returned in the spring and remained through December 1942, when he quit following an argument over salary. After leaving Hines, Johnson moved to New York, where he worked briefly in DON REDMAN's orchestra and with Al Sears's band at the Renaissance Ballroom in Harlem, later touring with a Sears-led USO band that also included Lester Young.

In 1943 Johnson became staff arranger for Georgie Auld's band and later freelanced as a writer for the modern big bands of Woody Herman, Buddy Rich, Gene Krupa, Charlie Barnet, and Boyd Raeburn. In February 1944 he replaced the tenor saxophonist DON BYAS in DIZZY GILLESPIE's bebop quintet at the Onyx Club on Fifty-second Street in New York, later writing for and occasionally playing in Gillespie's various big bands from 1946 through 1949. He also led his own modern jazz combo at the Three Deuces as well as organizing, writing for, and playing on two COLEMAN HAWKINS record dates, one in February 1944 and the other in December 1947, on which he played a remarkably bop-tinged alto solo on "Jumping for Jane." Although primarily a swing-era musician whose playing rarely deviated from the mainstream, Johnson was also one of the first arrangers to transcribe the sometimes convoluted, multinoted melodic themes, rhythmic accents, and altered harmonies of bebop, thereby making this then unconventional music more accessible to others. Beginning in April 1944 he served as BILLY ECKSTINE's musical director and chief arranger and was instrumental in organizing for him a bop-styled big band that between 1944 and 1947 included in its shifting personnel Gillespie, FATS NAVARRO, MILES DAVIS, CHARLIE PARKER, SONNY STITT, GENE AMMONS, DEXTER GORDON, WARDELL GRAY, Lucky Thompson, and ART BLAKEY.

In early 1945 Johnson worked for three months in John Kirby's sextet, playing alongside the swing veterans Emmett Berry, BUSTER BAILEY, and RUSSELL PROCOPE, and in 1946 he was with J. C. HEARD's sextet at Café Society Downtown in New York City on an engagement that also featured the former Hines and Eckstine vocalist SARAH VAUGHAN. In the mid-1940s Johnson was active on the freelance jazz combo recording scene as well, appearing on sessions led by COZY COLE, Clyde Hart, Coleman Hawkins, J.-C. Heard, PETE JOHNSON, Jimmy Jones, Walter "Foots" Thomas, and DICKY WELLS. From 1947 through the early 1950s he worked in the bands of SY OLIVER, MACHITO, Bennie Green, Snub Moseley, and CAB CALLOWAY in addition to leading his own groups, establishing a music publishing company, and continuing his busy career as freelance arranger and recording session saxman. Between February 1956 and spring 1957 he played tenor sax with Benny Goodman's new band, most importantly on a tour of the Far East, and from the mid-1950s through the early 1970s he participated in countless recording dates, including ones led by COUNT BASIE, Ray Brown, BUCK CLAYTON, Bill Coleman, ROY ELDRIDGE, Gil Evans, Gillespie, ILLINOIS JACQUET, QUINCY JONES, CHARLIE SHAVERS, CLARK TERRY, Ben Webster, and many others. Starting in the mid-1940s Johnson also appeared on recordings by such jazz, rhythm and blues, and pop singers as Mildred Bailey, LAVERN BAKER, Big Maybelle, RUTH BROWN, RAY CHARLES, Billy Eckstine, BILLIE HOLIDAY, Frankie Laine, CARMEN MCRAE, Anita O'Day, Carrie Smith, Dakota Staton, JOE TURNER, Vaughan, and at least three dozen others.

In 1960 he worked with Quincy Jones, and from mid-1961 through early 1962 he toured and recorded with Count Basie, later leading his own group at the Half Note in New York. He reunited with Hines for the latter's comeback in March 1964 and continued to record with him in small-band contexts through the 1960s, his last dates being in 1977 and 1982. After working briefly in New York with GERALD WILSON's Big Band in early 1966, Johnson visited Russia in the summer with Hines's septet, later playing with the Tommy Dorsey Orchestra under the direction of Urbie Green. In the spring of 1967, as a member of the Hines-led concert package called Jazz from a Swinging Era, Johnson toured Europe, also returning later that year as a featured soloist. After another European tour with Hines in 1968, he formed the JPJ Quartet in the summer of 1969, following that with a February 1970 European tour with Charlie Shavers. In 1974 he was appointed musical director of the New York Jazz Repertory Company's *Musical Life of Charlie Parker*. After disbanding the JPJ Quartet in 1975, he spent his later years freelancing as a soloist at festivals and recording with Benny Carter, Buck Clayton, Roy Eldridge, and Milt Hinton. He also appeared in the documentary film *Last of the Blue Devils* (1979). Johnson recorded his first leader date in June 1947 and after more than three prolific decades in the studio taped his last album in February 1984. He died in Kansas City, Missouri.

Although much has been made of the role that Johnson played as an arranger in the early years of bop, his contributions as an improvising jazzman appear to have been underrated. A technically fluent, strong-toned, inventive, and swinging soloist, Johnson played in a style that, though rooted in the swing era, came to reflect and in turn influence the work of such younger tenormen as Gene Ammons and Stitt and through them thousands of others.

FURTHER READING
Some oral history materials relating to Johnson are at Rutgers University, New Brunswick, New Jersey.
Bruyninckx, Walter. *Swing, 1920–1985*, 2 vols. (1985).
Dance, Stanley. *The World of Earl Hines* (1977).
Dance, Stanley. *The World of Swing* (1974).
Gitler, Ira. *Swing to Bop* (1985).
Rust, Brian. *Jazz Records, 1897–1942* (1982).
Schuller, Gunther. *The Swing Era* (1989).
Obituary: *Down Beat* (Jan. 1985).
This entry is taken from the *American National Biography* and is published here with the permission of the American Council of Learned Societies.

JACK SOHMER

Johnson, Bunk (27 Dec. 1889?–7 July 1949), trumpeter, was born William Geary Johnson in New Orleans, Louisiana, the son of William Johnson and Theresa (maiden name unknown), a cook, both former slaves. Though his early life remains shrouded in obscurity, Johnson claimed that he learned to play the cornet from Professor Wallace Cutchey, a music teacher at New Orleans University. His mother bought him an inexpensive cornet when he was about fourteen, and he played his first job with Adam Olivier's band in 1904 or 1905. Johnson also claimed that he played with BUDDY BOLDEN during this period, but this seems unlikely. He did play with the popular Eagle Band in parades, and in 1908 POPS FOSTER heard him playing with the Superior Orchestra, a ragtime band.

Johnson's tenure with the Superior Orchestra was cut short by the excessive drinking habits that plagued him his entire life. Over the next few years he played with several groups in New Orleans, and he may even have taught or influenced a very young LOUIS ARMSTRONG. He was recognized as one of the best players in New Orleans during this decade, praised for his beautiful tone and evocative blues playing. But Johnson left the city sometime around 1915, apparently burned out. He wandered around the region for several years, playing in sporting houses and similar venues in small towns west of New Orleans, including New Iberia. He seems to have spent some time in 1918 touring with circuses and minstrel shows, a common enough course for musicians at the time. In 1922 he was in Texas with a traveling carnival show. Sometime in the early 1920s he established his base in New Iberia and married Maude Fontenette, his second wife (there are no extant details concerning his first marriage, and he apparently had no children). During the 1920s he often played with a territory group called the Banner Band and traveled as a soloist as far afield as Houston, Texas, and, in 1931, Kansas City. He also played regularly with the Black Eagles, and he was present when the Eagles' leader was stabbed to death at a dance. In the melee that followed, Johnson's horn was destroyed. Already in some discomfort because of missing teeth, he put his musical career on the back burner, playing only occasional gigs with the Banner Band and retiring in 1932 to the life of a farmer in New Iberia.

For the next several years, Johnson essentially abandoned the jazz world. He occasionally taught children music under the auspices of the Works Progress Administration program and appeared as a whistler at local carnivals, but for the most part he worked as a laborer and truck driver. Then in 1938 Frederic Ramsey Jr. and Bill Russell, interviewing Chicago and New York musicians for a book on early jazz, "discovered" Johnson. They paid the dentist Leonard Bechet (SIDNEY BECHET's brother) to make him a new set of teeth, and the members of the revivalist Lu Watters Band raised enough money for him to buy a used trumpet and cornet.

In February 1942 an RCA employee interviewed Johnson and recorded him playing solo on a portable disc recorder. After Eugene Williams, record producer and editor of a new magazine called *Jazz Information*, heard the recordings, he and some enthusiasts from Los Angeles arranged to record Johnson in New Orleans for the Jazz Man label. These June 1942 sessions were the trumpeter's first commercial recordings; he made more than one hundred others during the next three years. Johnson played with apparently undiminished skill and authority in a group that included the legendary but then relatively unknown clarinetist GEORGE LEWIS. On various blues and tunes like "Moose March," Johnson's "lead is splendid in its supple invention of variations, his attack is direct and full of urgency" (Hillman, 51). Essential for their historic value, the sessions also show that Johnson was no New Orleans purist; he always preferred to play a wide variety of tunes, including popular songs.

Johnson recorded again in October, this time at the San Jacinto Hall in New Orleans; the session included ragtime numbers, a Hawaiian song, a piece by Louis Armstrong, and traditional blues and spirituals. These sides were picked up and distributed by Commodore Records. But though these recordings made him an instant celebrity among the rising number of jazz revivalists, Johnson returned to New Iberia, unaware of his growing fame.

In early 1943 the jazz historian Rudi Blesh gave a series of lectures on New Orleans jazz at the Museum of Art in San Francisco, and he arranged for Johnson to illustrate his talks. While there, Johnson made a series of recordings in May with the pianist Bertha Gonsoulin, later released on the American Music label. In pieces like "Pallet on the Floor," he revealed his continued mastery of the trumpet, with clean attacks and "a formal, almost precise, sense of variation" in his playing (Harrison et al., 36). Later in the year, prompted by the San Francisco Hot Jazz Society, Johnson played a series of dates with Lu Watters's Yerba Buena Jazz Band, one of the best known of the many groups promoting traditional jazz. From the beginning, Johnson's own musical diversity and difficult personality created considerable tension among the players; his drinking habits caused him frequently to miss dates. However, he did record with members of the group in early 1944, playing with freshness and intensity on pieces like "Careless Love." He also recorded some traditional hymns in duets with the gospel singer Sister Lottie Peavey. By the middle of the year he had his fill of life in the big city and returned to New Iberia, stopping off in Los Angeles to record some pieces for the World Transcription Service with a band that included Red Callender on bass and Lee Young on drums; he also played superlatively in a broadcast session with the KID ORY Band.

In late July Johnson traveled again to New Orleans to take part in a weeklong recording session at the San Jacinto Hall. These have become known as the "American Music" recordings (after the company that first released them on LP), and they are some of the best music of the revival years. A three-horn front line (including George Lewis) produced astonishingly flexible ensemble playing, the lead shifting constantly and unpredictably. Johnson shines, both in the ensembles and in solos, in pieces like "Careless Love" and "Sugarfoot Stomp."

In January 1945 Johnson was back in New Orleans, playing in a concert at the New Orleans Municipal Auditorium in a group headed by Armstrong that included Sidney Bechet, J. C. HIGGINBOTHAM, JAMES P. JOHNSON, and other luminaries. Johnson played well enough to arouse Bechet's interest, and before they left, the two agreed to play together in an engagement at the Savoy Cafe in Boston. After another less satisfying session with the American Music group, Johnson went first to New York City, recording a session for Blue Note Records with Bechet. The subsequent

Boston meeting was, however, a failure, undermined by Johnson's drinking and uneven playing.

After returning to New Iberia, he traveled again to New Orleans in May 1945 to make a series of recordings over three nights at George Lewis's house. He also recorded a session with a nine-piece band that produced a reasonable facsimile of a New Orleans marching band.

Meanwhile in New York City, Eugene Williams had decided to promote Johnson with a handpicked band. The group included Lewis on clarinet and BABY DODDS on drums. The engagement began less than propitiously; Johnson arrived a day late, and tension existed between him and the other musicians from the beginning. As always, he favored a wide variety of songs, while Lewis and the others played a more limited range of New Orleans traditional standards. At their first public session, on a Friday night in September 1945 at the Stuyvesant Casino, the hall was filled with four hundred fans, many of them musicians who subsequently told others of the exciting, "pure" New Orleans jazz they had heard. While the style was hardly pure, the impact of the music was indeed dramatic; few had ever heard such music played by its original practitioners. Record companies were just as interested, and the group recorded four sides for Decca and eight for Victor. Though the results were uneven, the performances on tunes like "One Sweet Letter" and "Franklin Street Blues" were excellent. The band was also featured in a New Year's Day concert at Town Hall, part of a celebration emceed by Orson Welles. They made their final appearance at the Casino on 12 January. A second New York engagement in May, with somewhat different personnel, was less productive. Lewis and the others were frustrated by Johnson's condescending attitude and lack of professionalism, and only a single recording session came from this later stay.

Johnson's day on center stage was all but over when he returned to New Iberia. He appeared in a 1946 concert at Orchestra Hall in Chicago in a group that included the guitarist LONNIE JOHNSON, but he played poorly. A concert at the University of Minnesota in the summer of 1947 was recorded, with Johnson playing strongly, and he subsequently toured the Midwest and played at a variety of dances and concerts. In September 1947 he played at the opening concert of the New York Jazz Club in New York City with a group that included EDMOND HALL, OMER SIMEON, and DANNY BARKER. While there he returned to the Stuyvesant Casino with a small group that included Barker, and the recorded

results show Johnson playing with drive and confidence, for once satisfied with the skills of his fellow band members. But the dances attracted little attention and were dropped after five shows. Johnson recorded only once more, at Carnegie Recital Hall in December 1947. Shortly thereafter he returned to New Iberia. He tried to get gigs in the North for the remainder of his life without success. He apparently died of a stroke in New Iberia.

Johnson was by all accounts a difficult person, opportunistic and often professionally irresponsible. Musically, his last recordings are perhaps the best representation of his art. They are not as adventurous or as sophisticated as the American Music efforts, but they clearly present him as a transitional figure, rooted in turn-of-the-century styles but willing to experiment with form and approach. His playing may have lacked the emotional magnetism of the early jazz stars, but he was an impressive, confident stylist and was more adventurous than most in incorporating a variety of tunes and styles into his repertoire. In the end he remains most important as the central figure in the revival of New Orleans–style jazz during the 1940s and early 1950s.

FURTHER READING

Harrison, Max, Charles Fox, and Eric Thacker. *The Essential Jazz Records*, vol. 1, *Ragtime to Swing* (1984).
Hillman, Christopher. *Bunk Johnson* (1988).
Porter, Lewis, and Michael Ullman. *Jazz: From Its Origins to the Present* (1993).
Sonnier, A. M., Jr. *William Geary "Bunk" Johnson: The New Iberia Years* (1977).
Tirro, Frank. *Jazz: A History* (1993).
Obituary: *New York Times*, 9 July 1949.
This entry is taken from the *American National Biography* and is published here with the permission of the American Council of Learned Societies.

RONALD P. DUFOUR

Johnson, Cernoria McGowan (10 Apr. 1909–19 May 1990), civil rights leader, was born Cernoria McGowan in Alto, Texas, a farming town east of Dallas, Texas, the oldest child of John McGowan, a construction worker, and Mollie. While McGowan was still a young child, she and her family moved to Tulsa, Oklahoma, in search of a better life. During the Tulsa race riot of 1921 McGowan and her siblings were hauled to safety in a truck to the state fairgrounds. In the aftermath of the riot, her family relocated to Oklahoma City, where McGowan attended Douglas High School. She graduated in May 1926 and was awarded a scholarship to attend Langston University in Oklahoma, where she received her undergraduate degree in sociology with honors. While at Langston she married William W. Johnson, a school teacher; the couple had two daughters, Judy and Janice.

After a brief period spent teaching, twenty-six-year-old Cernoria Johnson secured a job with the Oklahoma State Works Progress Administration (WPA) in 1935 and quickly advanced to a supervisory position. As director of one of the WPA programs she insisted that blacks be given the necessary skills for the job market. She worked tirelessly with this organization until it dissolved in 1942. Johnson's work with the WPA not only opened doors for those who learned from her but also brought new opportunities for herself as well. Bolstered by her faith, she returned to school at Atlanta University, where she earned a master's degree in Social Work.

LESTER GRANGER, the executive director of the National Urban League, chose Johnson to become the first executive director of the Oklahoma City chapter of the Urban League in 1946. The Urban League, which was one of the oldest and largest interracial and social service agencies in the United States, was an ideal match for Johnson. She already had gained extensive and valuable experience during her time with the WPA, building bridges between various racial, socioeconomic, and political groups. Johnson's dedicated work ethic was reflected in the following statement: "Once you really do the job, you have to cut across the line of racial, political, religious, and other divisions. You are just working with people and trying to help them with their problems" (Goddard). During her tenure with the Oklahoma City Urban League, she was instrumental in creating job opportunities for blacks. She found her calling as a voice for the disenfranchised, and she always championed economic justice. She served as a liaison for various national welfare agencies and other organizations devoted to improving interracial relations, including the regional and national boards of the National Association of Social Workers (NASW). She had a long-term relationship with the Oklahoma City YWCA, working as a consultant for their national board as a member of their bureau of research. She was also in high demand as a speaker at Urban League engagements and other civil rights engagements, and she spoke at the Social Action Forum of the 1966 National Conference on Social Welfare.

In the early 1960s WHITNEY M. YOUNG JR., executive director of the National Urban League, recognized Johnson's outstanding organizational skills and ability and asked her to join the staff of the National Urban League. As the first full-time director of the Washington bureau, she laid the groundwork for a productive working relationship between the National Urban League and the various agencies and departments of the federal government. She was known to be a tenacious negotiator on behalf of Urban League constituents and was the first female to serve as the president of the Council of the Urban League Executives. In 1973 she received the prestigious Ann Tanneyhill Award, the highest award given to a National Urban League employee, for excellence and extraordinary commitment to the Urban League movement. She was presented with the Whitney M. Young Jr. Medallion in 1988 by the National Urban League.

Johnson retired from the Urban League in 1974 and then served as a special consultant to the Commission on Aging under Arthur Fleming. She was responsible for developing policy based upon the guidelines of the Nursing Home Ombudsmen program under the Office of Aging. In a short period of time Johnson facilitated the establishment of Nursing Home Ombudsmen programs in every state in the country. After retiring from the Office of Aging in 1977, she continued to work on an informal basis as an advocate until her death in 1990. Starting out as a young black woman in a restricted, segregated society, Johnson moved beyond the traditional role of wife and mother into a career of activism and integration. With a passionate vision of life's possibilities, she was committed to improving the lives of the African Americans she served and encouraged positive relations among people of all races and cultures.

FURTHER READING

Goddard, Mary. "Cityan Lends Life to Build Racial Bridge," *Oklahoma City Times*, 28 Feb. 1956.

"Mrs. Cernoria Johnson to Give Address," *Oklahoma City Black Dispatch* (5 Apr. 1956).

"OC Urban League Director Is Chosen 'Alumna of Year,'" *Oklahoma City Black Dispatch*, 8 Nov. 1957.

MARY E. HUDDLESTON

Johnson, Charles Edward "Chas" (7 Feb. 1871–27 Dec. 1957), theatrical artist, tap and cakewalk dancer, and comedian, was born in St. Charles, Missouri (names and occupations of his parents are unknown). Johnson first appeared on stage in

1889 during an amateur performance at Brown's Theatre in Minneapolis. In St. Louis, Missouri, he joined Sam T. Jack's *The Creole Show*, where he met his wife and partner, DORA DEAN (maiden name Babbige; 1872–1949). After the couple had learned their routines, they left the show for vaudeville bookings and were an almost immediate success; in 1893 they were married and their son, Herman, was born in 1899 (up to 1914 he traveled with his parents on the same passport). Johnson and Dean claimed to have introduced the cakewalk on Broadway (Indianapolis *Freeman*, 23 April 1910, p. 6). Known as "Johnson & Dean, King & Queen of Colored Aristocracy," the couple were one of the best known vaudeville dance teams in the "gay '90s" and early 1900s. They were not only very talented but also considered the best dressed dance team on the American stage. They were the first black dance team to play Broadway in 1897 and the first dance team, white or black, to wear evening clothes on the stage. That was at Hammerstein's Roof Garden in 1901 (Sampson, p. 381). By 1901 their portraits were inserted on sheet music covers.

In October 1901 they were engaged by the prestigious Berlin Wintergarten. The enormous success of that show persuaded them to pursue their career in Europe. (The Wintergarten re-engaged them annually until World War I.) Johnson & Dean were the first to use the flicker Kinetoscope, a device that apparently produced a dazzling "crowd" of images, a sort of primitive strobe-light effect (Fletcher, p. 112). This dance caused a sensation at the Wintergarten, where it was called "The Living Biograph," and elsewhere in Europe. The years 1901 and 1902 saw them in Germany, Paris, and London, where the Oxford Theatre announced them as "America's Greatest Rag-Time Team" (*Referee*, 1 June 1902, p. 6). For the winter season they toured on the American Keith circuit in an "All Star Vaudeville Revue." The summer of 1903 saw them back in Berlin, where they embarked on an extended tour of the German cities, as well as London, Paris, Vienna, Budapest, Amsterdam, Strasbourg, and Moscow. When they returned to the United States in 1909 they discovered they had not been forgotten at home. The *Freeman*, noting their change of tasteful costumes, reviewed their performance at New York's American Theatre: "They finished the first part of their offering with soft-shoe dancing a la Charles Johnson, to good applause. Second part: … They sing 'Billy, I Love You,' while Johnson does some wing dancing that brought down the house. Third part: … they sing and dance, the song being 'I'm An English Coon.'

Mr. Johnson did some clever and original dancing at the finish of his act that won the team a great many encores" (Indianapolis *Freeman*, quoted in Sampson, p. 382).

A couple of months later, now known as "Johnson & Dean—Mulatto swells, singers and dancers," they returned to their sixth re-engagement at the Wintergarten, demonstrating "a new step-dance in wooden shoes." Once again, they crisscrossed Europe from Copenhagen to Rome. European papers report that they received the highest pay ever offered to a "colored" duet (*Das Programm*, p. 462, 12 Feb. 1911). The winter of 1911 saw them in Sydney, Australia. After touring the sixth continent, they returned to the United States, where they made preparations for yet another European adventure. In March 1913 they departed from New York with a "Ragtime Sextette," planning to tour fourteen European states and debuting at Vienna on 1 April 1913. The troupe included dancers Rufus Greenlee and Thaddeus Drayton, pianist Kid Coles, and drummer Peggie Holland—the former played and danced at the piano while the latter "handles an entire collection of percussion tools" (*Der Artist*, 8 Mar. 1914).

Despite their onstage success, the couple's marriage was failing. In January 1914 Dora Dean returned to the United States in the company of her son, Herman, and four entertainers (William Cole, Frank Vardon, Harry Perry, and Charles Holton); Charles Johnson added four new members to the company, which he continued to present in Paris and Berlin under the old name. One review noted that "Johnson and Dean's Ragtime Sextette is excellent. The comely Mulatto lady, Mrs. Dean, is no longer a member of the troupe … [but] The four boys, whom Mr. Charles Johnson contracted, dance quite extraordinary ragtime dances in rare precision" (*Der Artist*, 1531, 14 June 1914). After two months in Berlin, Johnson also returned home, with an intention to retire: "Mr. Johnson presently celebrates his 20th anniversary as a professional artist in Minneapolis … His pecuniary successes Mr. Johnson invested in property at home in Minneapolis where no less than six farm houses of absolutely identical design offer him a rest from his travels around the world" (*Moderne Kunst*, 1914). However, after his return to the United States, Johnson teamed up with Irving Jones, as "Johnson & Jones," and continued in vaudeville. Over the next few years, Johnson appeared on the same bill as leading performers of the day including BERT WILLIAMS, BESSIE SMITH, and FLORENCE

MILLS. In 1936, when both were in their fifties, Johnson and Dean reconciled and performed a comeback at Connie's Inn in Harlem; in 1940 they performed in Winnipeg, Manitoba. Dean died in 1949; Johnson survived her for several years and died at home in Minneapolis. An obituary noted, "Until a few years ago Johnson kept up his dance routines, performing occasionally for charity benefits" (Obituary, *Variety*, 2 Jan. 1957).

FURTHER READING

Fletcher, Tom. *100 Years of the Negro in Show Business* (1954).

Lotz, Rainer E. "Dora Dean and Charles Johnson, 1.deel & 2.deel," *Doctor Jazz*, Vol. 40, No. 178, 2002, pp. 4–8; No. 179, 2002, pp. 24–28.

Sampson, Edgar T. *Blacks in Blackface* (1980).

Stearns, Marshall, and Jean Stearns. *Jazz Dance—The Story of American Vernacular Dance* (1978).

Obituary: *Variety*, 2 Jan. 1957.

RAINER E. LOTZ

Johnson, Charles Richard (23 April 1948–), writer and educator, was born in Community Hospital, an all-black facility in Evanston, Illinois. He was the only child of Ruby Elizabeth and Benny Lee Johnson. While his father labored at a number of jobs to support his family (construction work, handyman, night watchman), his mother doted on their son by giving him books and sketchpads. Although Benny Johnson expressed occasional skepticism about his son's love for literature and drawing, Ruby Johnson encouraged his dream of becoming an artist.

Johnson excelled in academics while attending the nationally ranked and racially integrated Evanston Township High School. In addition to his schoolwork, he set for himself the goal of reading a minimum of one book a week. Furthermore, he began a two-year correspondence course in drawing with Lawrence Lariar, an influential cartoonist who edited the annual series *The Best Cartoons of the Year*. Johnson was soon publishing stories and cartoons in high-school publications, as well as working on commission to illustrate the catalog of a Chicago company that manufactured magic tricks. By the time he matriculated at Southern Illinois University Carbondale (SIU) in the fall of 1966, his career path seemed set.

At SIU, Johnson majored in journalism and furthered his drawing career by contributing cartoons to both the university's newspaper and the town's newspaper. In addition, he hosted a drawing program entitled *Charlie's Pad* on the local PBS station that was later broadcast nationally. He also published his first book, a collection of political cartoons entitled *Black Humor* (1970). Johnson spent his summers, however, living in his parent's house and working in Chicago. In June 1968, he met Joan New, a student at Evanston's National College of Education. They immediately fell in love and dated for two years. They married on 14 June 1970 and had two children: a son, Malik, born 1975; and a daughter, Elizabeth, born 1981. Elizabeth, an artist, later changed her name to Elisheba.

While completing his degree in journalism, Johnson took a number of courses in philosophy, and after graduation in 1971, enrolled in the master's program in philosophy at SIU. In addition to his coursework in philosophy and his drawing (he published a second book of cartoons entitled *Half-Past Nation Time* in 1972), Johnson began writing what he later called his "apprentice novels." Never intended for publication, these six works were exercises for him to experiment with different voices and literary styles. By the time he neared completion of his master's degree in philosophy, Johnson knew that he had fulfilled his self-imposed "apprenticeship" and felt ready to write his first novel for publication. Although he did not lack confidence in his own abilities, he still felt that he needed a tutor.

Johnson introduced himself to John Gardner, author of many distinguished novels and then professor of English at SIU, in the fall of 1972; the two formed a close and enduring friendship. Under his mentor's tutelage, Johnson immediately began writing his first published novel, *Faith and the Good Thing*. Between the time that he began the book and its publication in 1974, Johnson completed his master's thesis and enrolled as a doctoral student in the philosophy department at the State University of New York at Stony Brook. He intended to study phenomenology and literary theory, as well as write philosophical fiction.

After three years at Stony Brook, Johnson left the doctoral program to accept a professorship in the English Department at the University of Washington, where he taught creative writing until his retirement in 2009. He had completed all of his coursework, however, and following the 1988 publication of *Being and Race: Black Writing Since 1970*, a critique of the phenomenological aesthetics of contemporary African American fiction, Stony Brook awarded him the Ph.D. in philosophy.

As he struggled in 1981 to write his second novel, *Oxherding Tale*, Johnson's mother died. At this pivotal point in his life, Johnson committed himself to Buddhism. While he had long studied Eastern philosophy, yoga meditation, and kung fu martial arts (achieving the highest belts and becoming a master instructor himself), Johnson found a sense of purpose when, as he phrased the experience in an autobiographical essay, he "fully surrendered." His commitment to Buddhism only deepened through the years after he took Sanskrit lessons in order to read the sacred texts in their original language. He also began contributing short stories and essays to Buddhist periodicals such as *Tricycle: The Buddhist Review* and *Shambhala Sun*.

Following the well-reviewed *Oxherding Tale* (1982), Johnson wrote his masterpiece, *Middle Passage* (1990), which won the prestigious National Book Award (Johnson became just the second African American male to win the prize, following RALPH ELLISON in 1953 for *Invisible Man*). Moreover, the critical success of the novel turned it into a best seller. Since its initial publication, the novel has been translated into many languages and has been studied in high school and college classrooms. Although he had enjoyed a sterling reputation among his fellow writers for the challenging but clear prose and depth of plotting in his fiction, *Middle Passage* made Johnson a famous author.

Johnson published a fourth novel, *Dreamer* (1998), and three collections of short fiction: *The Sorcerer's Apprentice* (1986), *Soulcatcher and Other Stories* (2001), and *Dr. King's Refrigerator and Other Bedtime Stories* (2005). He published some of his essays about his spiritual growth and Buddhist philosophy in *Turning the Wheel: Essays on Buddhism and Writing* (2003). He has written more than twenty screenplays, including the script for the prize-winning PBS film of BOOKER T. WASHINGTON (*Booker*, 1985).

Moreover, Johnson has written or edited the text to such important non-fiction books as *Black Men Speaking* (1997), *Africans in America: America's Journey Through Slavery* (1998), *King: The Photobiography of Martin Luther King Jr.* (2000), and *Mine Eyes Have Seen: Bearing Witness to the Struggle for Civil Rights* (2007). His body of work has garnered many prizes, most notably a MacArthur Fellowship (1998), an American Academy of Arts and Letters Award for Literature (2002), and numerous honorary doctorates.

FURTHER READING

Byrd, Rudolph, ed. *I Call Myself an Artist: Writings by and about Charles Johnson* (1999).
Little, Jonathan. *Charles Johnson's Spiritual Imagination* (1997).
McWilliams, Jim, ed. *Passing the Three Gates: Interviews with Charles Johnson* (2004).
Nash, William R. *Charles Johnson's Fiction* (2003).
Storhoff, Gary. *Understanding Charles Johnson* (2004).

JIM MCWILLIAMS

Johnson, Charles Spurgeon (24 July 1893–27 Oct. 1956), sociologist and college president, was born in Bristol, Virginia, the eldest of six children of Charles Henry Johnson, a Baptist minister, and Winifred Branch. Because there was not a high school for blacks in Bristol, he moved to Richmond and attended the Wayland Academy. In 1913 Johnson entered college at Virginia Union in Richmond, and graduated in only three years. While at college, Johnson volunteered with the Richmond Welfare Association, and one incident there had a profound impact on his future career. During the holiday season, while delivering baskets to needy people, he came across a young woman lying on a pile of rags, groaning in labor. Although none of the doctors in the area would help the young woman, Johnson persuaded a midwife to deliver the baby. He then tried to locate a home for the young woman, but those he approached shut the door in his face. Some families rejected the young woman because she was black and others because, in their eyes, she had sinned. Edwin Embree, Johnson's longtime friend, once noted that Johnson could not get the image of the young woman out of his mind and could not "cease pondering the anger of people at human catastrophe while they calmly accept conditions that caused it" (*Thirteen against the Odds* [1944], 214).

In 1916 Johnson moved north to pursue a Ph.D. at the University of Chicago, which at that time employed some of the world's most prominent sociologists. It was there that he would meet his lifetime mentor, Robert E. Park. As a result of this relationship, many of Johnson's writings and approaches to race relations bear the mark of the eminent Chicago researcher. Johnson interrupted his studies to enlist in the military in 1918, but upon returning to Chicago a year later, he found himself in the middle of one of the most horrific race riots in U.S. history.

This incident sparked Johnson's involvement with the Chicago Race Relations Commission; as associate executive secretary for that body, he was largely responsible for the writing of *The Negro in Chicago: A Study of Race Relations and a Race*

Riot (1922). With this publication Johnson spearheaded a tradition of social science research that described changes in race relations as cycles of tension and resolution, largely caused by outside forces. Although partly based on the work of Park, Johnson's version of this sociological model envisioned a wider role for human intervention; in particular, he believed that government could influence this process. Johnson's work with the Chicago Race Relations Commission also introduced him to Julius Rosenwald, the Sears and Roebuck tycoon and creator of the Julius Rosenwald Fund (which assisted with the establishment of black schools in the South and provided scholarships to talented black intellectuals).

Johnson married Marie Antoinette Burgette on 6 November 1920. Johnson moved with his wife to New York City, where he became the director of research and investigations for the National Urban League. During this period he also edited the league's journal, *Opportunity*, and published short stories and poems by several prominent Harlem Renaissance authors, including LANGSTON HUGHES, COUNTÉE CULLEN, AARON DOUGLAS, and ZORA NEALE HURSTON. Johnson also used his well-established connections to white philanthropists to secure financial support for black literature and art. In his view, promoting culture was a way of combating racism.

The sociologist Blyden Jackson, Johnson's colleague while he was attending Fisk University in Nashville, Tennessee, credits him with helping to "ease the transformation of more than one neophyte in the arts, like a Zora Neale Hurston, from a nonentity into a luminary of the Renaissance" (*Southern Review* 25.4 [1990]: 753). Indeed, both Jackson and ALAIN LOCKE point to a 1924 dinner Johnson hosted in New York as one of the most important contributions to the Renaissance. With more than three hundred people from both the white and black worlds in attendance (including Locke, JAMES WELDON JOHNSON, William Baldwin III, JESSIE FAUSET, Countée Cullen, Albert Barnes, and W. E. B. DuBois), the event helped many black poets, artists, and writers find mainstream publishers and venues for their endeavors. For Johnson, events like this dinner were part of a carefully planned effort to improve opportunities for African Americans in the 1920s in ways that had not been possible during the nadir of race relations before World War I.

Near the close of the Renaissance in 1928, Charles Johnson returned south to Nashville to chair the department of social sciences at Fisk University. Supported by a grant from the Laura Spelman Rockefeller Memorial, the department was set up with the idea that Johnson would be its leader. Armed with solid connections and ample funding, he brought many important individuals to the Fisk campus, including STERLING BROWN, James Weldon Johnson, HORACE MANN BOND, Robert E. Park, E. FRANKLIN FRAZIER, ARNA BONTEMPS, and Aaron Douglas. Along with his colleagues in the social sciences, Johnson published widely. It was during this time that he produced some of his best known works, such as *Shadow of the Plantation* (1934), *Growing Up in the Black Belt* (1938), and *Patterns of Negro Segregation* (1942). Johnson also created an internationally renowned race relations institute at Fisk, which brought together leaders, scholars, and ordinary citizens from throughout the United States and the world to discuss race relations in an integrated setting. Despite suffering extensive criticism locally, especially from the segregationist *Nashville Banner*, the institute and Johnson's leadership drew great prominence to Fisk and to Johnson as an individual.

In 1946, at time when Fisk was experiencing a leadership crisis, its board of trustees considered selecting the first black candidate to lead the institution. Given his international stature and administrative skills, Johnson seemed like the most obvious candidate, but several of the alumni, including Fisk's most prominent graduate, DuBois, spoke out vehemently against his selection. Johnson's close ties to philanthropy, including the Whitney, Ford, and Rosenwald foundations, made him suspect in their minds. For this group, the foundations were forever tainted by their previous efforts to promote an industrial curriculum at black colleges. Despite this opposition, the financial needs of Fisk prevailed over ideology, and Johnson was inaugurated president in 1947; the board of trustees had recognized Johnson's success in advancing and improving Fisk's race relations institutes through his fund-raising efforts and believed that he might similarly ensure progress for the university as a whole.

In his role as president, Johnson created the Basic College Early Entry Program. Although Johnson was a proponent of integration, he doubted that it would occur quickly and thus was inspired to initiate a program to nurture young black minds within the black college setting. The Basic College offered students a cohesive learning environment in which they benefited from the knowledge and experience of literary, artistic, and political figures that Johnson invited to campus in the years before his death in 1956. The program produced such figures as the Pulitzer Prize–winning author DAVID LEVERING LEWIS; HAZEL O'LEARY, energy secretary during the administration of President Bill Clinton; and Spelman College president JOHNNETTA COLE.

In addition to his university-related service, Johnson served as a trustee for the Julius Rosenwald Fund from 1933 to 1948, working specifically as the codirector of the fund's race-relations program. From 1944 to 1950 he acted as the director of the race-relations division of the American Missionary Association. Concurrently with his foundation work, Johnson conducted research for the federal government and worked as a cultural ambassador. As a member of the New Deal's Committee on Farm Tenancy, Johnson supported President Franklin Roosevelt's efforts to end poverty and racism in the rural South. After World War II, under the direction of President Harry Truman, Johnson was one of ten U.S. delegates for the first United Nations Educational, Scientific, and Cultural Organization (UNESCO) conference in Paris. And he assisted President Dwight Eisenhower by serving on the Board of Foreign Scholarships under the Fulbright-Hays Act.

Johnson spent a lifetime cultivating black scholarship, creativity, and leadership and used research and culture as tools to fight racism. As he grew older, however, the pressure generated by his many obligations began to take its toll: his migraine headaches worsened, and he developed a heart condition. On 27 October 1956, on the way to a board meeting in New York, Johnson died of a heart attack on the train platform in Louisville, Kentucky, at age sixty-three.

Although Johnson's professional training and early practical experience in race relations were in the urban North, he chose to address race relations in the South, thereby differentiating himself from DuBois and other black intellectuals. He was not a radical, but rather a diplomat who, through his collaborations, realized many of the ideas of thinkers more radical than he.

FURTHER READING

Charles S. Johnson's personal and professional papers are located in the Special Collections at Fisk University, Nashville, Tennessee.

Gasman, Marybeth. "W. E. B. DuBois and Charles S. Johnson: Opposing Views on Philanthropic Support for Black Higher Education," *History of Education Quarterly* 42.4 (Winter 2002).

Gilpin, Patrick J., and Marybeth Gasman. *Charles S. Johnson: Leadership behind the Veil in the Age of Jim Crow* (2003).

Robbins, Richard. *Sidelines Activist: Charles S. Johnson and the Struggle for Civil Rights* (1996).

Obituary: *New York Times*, 28 Oct. 1956.

MARYBETH GASMAN

Johnson, Cornelius Cooper (21 Aug. 1913–15 Feb. 1946), track-and-field athlete, was born in Los Angeles, California, the son of Shadreak Johnson, a plasterer; his mother's name and occupation are not known. Shadreak Johnson had moved from Raleigh, North Carolina, to California in 1893 for better economic and social opportunities. Cornelius first competed in organized track-and-field events at Berendo Junior High School in Los Angeles. He achieved greater athletic success as a student at Los Angeles High School, competing statewide in the sprints and the high jump. His skill as a high jumper earned him a position on the 1932 U.S. Olympic team. While only a junior in high school, Johnson tied the veteran performers Robert van Osdel and George Spitz for first place at a height of 6 feet 65⁄8 inches at the 1932 Amateur Athletic Union (AAU) Championship, which also served as the Olympic trials.

One of four African Americans representing the United States in track and field in the 1932 Summer Olympic Games, Johnson performed admirably before a hometown crowd in Los Angeles, finishing in a four-way tie for first place at 6 feet 51⁄2 inches with van Osdel, Duncan McNaughton of Canada, and Simeon Toribo of the Philippines. Since all four athletes had failed to clear 6 feet 63⁄4 inches in regular competition, a jump-off was held to determine the gold, silver, and bronze medalists. As a result of the jump-off, Johnson finished in fourth place as McNaughton won the gold, van Osdel the silver, and Toribo the bronze.

In 1933 Johnson graduated from high school and entered Compton Junior College in Pasadena, California. That same year he captured the outdoor AAU high jump title, equaling the meet record of 6 feet 7-inches. In 1934 he shared the outdoor AAU championship with Walter Marty as both athletes topped a new meet record of 6 feet 85⁄8 inches. The following year Johnson soared above all American high jumpers, winning both the indoor and outdoor AAU titles with a mark of 6 feet 7 inches. In 1936 Johnson finished second in a jump-off against Ed Burke in the indoor AAU championship after both performers completed regular competition at 6 feet

8⁵⁄16 inches. In the outdoor AAU championship, which also served as the 1936 Olympic trials, both Johnson and Dave Albritton of Ohio State University set a world record with jumps of 6 feet 9¾ inches.

Berlin, Germany, then the capital of the National Socialist (Nazi) Third Reich, hosted the 1936 Summer Olympic Games. By that time anti-Semitic public policies had systematically removed Jews from nearly every aspect of German life. American participation in the "Nazi Olympics" was hotly debated in the United States; African Americans in particular were divided over sending athletes to Germany. While some maintained that a boycott of African American athletes would illuminate the racially discriminatory practices of the United States, others argued that a triumphant demonstration of African American athletic prowess would powerfully undermine both American and German racial insolence. The United States sent to the 1936 Olympics nineteen African Americans—twelve track-and-field performers, including two women, five boxers, and two weight lifters. Johnson won the gold medal in the high jump, setting an Olympic record performance of 6 feet 8 inches and leading an American sweep of the medals. Other African American trackmen, led by JESSE OWENS's quadruple gold medal feat, won every running event from the 100 to the 800 meters, the 400-meter relay, and the long jump. By capturing silver and bronze medals in many of the same events, they discredited Nazi racial theories but accomplished little in dispiriting American racism. Johnson, rather than Owens, was the victim of Adolf Hitler's most pointed snub. After honoring German and Finnish medal winners, in accordance with his belief in Aryan superiority, the Nazi leader left the stadium before the conclusion of the high jump and did not congratulate the African American medalists.

After the 1936 Olympics, Johnson's dominance over the high jump diminished rapidly. In 1937 he finished fourth in the 1937 indoor AAU championships, won by Burke, and he lost to Albritton in the outdoor AAU contest. Johnson, who later competed for the New York City Grand Street Boys Association, tied with Lloyd Thompson for the 1938 indoor AAU title at 6 feet 6 inches. After retiring from the high jump, Johnson became a letter carrier for the U.S. Post Office in Los Angeles, and in 1945 he joined the U.S. Merchant Marine and served as a baker on the *Santa Cruz*. The following year Johnson developed bronchial pneumonia aboard ship; he died before the ship reached the San Francisco harbor.

Although other aspects of his life may have been affected by discrimination and prejudice, Johnson was not denied opportunities to compete in track and field—except for the Nazi Olympics—because of his race. Unlike major league baseball and professional football, track-and-field had afforded African American performers the opportunity to participate since the late nineteenth century. Although African Americans were denied membership in exclusive amateur athletic organizations, such as the New York Athletic Club, they either formed their own athletic clubs, such as the New York City Grand Street Boys Association, or competed on the teams of predominantly white colleges and universities in the North, Midwest, and West. Only in the South, where the AAU recognized and upheld the region's discriminatory practices, were African Americans denied participation in track-and-field meets. Johnson and fellow African American trackmen made their first significant impact on the sport internationally in the-1936 Olympics, and African Americans have remained the mainstay of American track-and-field superiority.

FURTHER READING
Mandell, Richard D. *The Nazi Olympics* (1971).
Oates, Bob. "If Anybody Was Snubbed by Hitler, It Was Cornelius Johnson," *Los Angeles Times*, 22 July 1984.
Quercetani, Roberto L. *A World History of Track and Field Athletics* (1964).
Obituaries: *Baltimore Afro-American* and *Chicago Defender*, 23 Feb. 1946.
This entry is taken from the *American National Biography* and is published here with the permission of the American Council of Learned Societies.

ADAM R. HORNBUCKLE

Johnson, Dwight Hal (7 May 1947–30 Apr. 1971), Vietnam War soldier and Medal of Honor recipient, was born in Detroit, Michigan, the son of Joyce Alves. His family, including a younger brother, lived in the E. J. Jeffries housing project, and Johnson attended public school in Detroit prior to joining the military.

Dwight Johnson entered the U.S. Army at Detroit on 28 July 1966 and after completing his initial training served at Fort Knox, Kentucky, the army's main armored base. Here, Johnson was assigned to Company B, 1st Battalion, 69th Armor, 25th Infantry Division and received training as an M-48 Patton tank driver. Just prior to his deployment to Vietnam in February 1967, he was assigned to a new tank crew. While the army's armored units are seldom recognized for their role in the Vietnam War, units like Johnson's 69th Armor were critical in providing valuable infantry protection, support, and heavy firepower when needed. Upon arriving in Vietnam, the men of the 69th Armor were stationed near Pleiku and by October 1967 were attached to the 4th Infantry Division, which it had already been closely working with. By January 1968, Specialist Fifth Class Dwight Johnson was an experienced combat veteran.

The service of African American soldiers in the army during the Vietnam War, including enlisted men like Dwight Johnson, ROBERT JENKINS JR., and CLARENCE SASSER, was important for many reasons. First and foremost, the Vietnam War marked the first time since the Revolutionary War that black soldiers fought alongside white soldiers in integrated regiments. In fact, their role was even greater than in the previous wars of the twentieth century. In direct contrast to World War II, where few African Americans were sent into combat because of racial stereotypes that deemed them inferior soldiers, the role of black soldiers in the Vietnam War was disproportionately higher than that of white soldiers. While racism still existed in the army in the 1960s, the Selective Service System drafted nearly 60 percent of the eligible blacks, but only 30 percent of eligible whites were drafted, many of them given educational deferments not accorded to black draftees. This discrepancy caused many problems, political and otherwise, both on the home front and in the field, but one thing was certain; unlike in previous wars, black soldiers no longer had to prove their capabilities, and many, such as RILEY PITTS and CHARLES ROGERS, served in upper level leadership positions on the battlefield. One of the greatest indicators of this new status for African American servicemen was the award of combat decorations to those serving in Vietnam; the twenty black Medal of Honor recipients represent just over eight percent of all those that earned our nation's highest military award during the conflict.

On 15 January 1968, Specialist 5th Class Dwight Johnson and the four tanks of Company B, 69th Armor were en route to Dak To, Vietnam, when they were ambushed by a battalion of enemy North Vietnamese soldiers armed with rocket launchers and automatic weapons. Two of the unit's tanks were hit and set on fire, followed by enemy soldiers advancing on their position. Johnson's tank was also hit and disabled. One of the tanks hit and set afire was manned by Johnson's old tank crew, and Johnson quickly came to their aid. He pulled one man out before the tank's ammunition exploded, killing the remainder of the crew. Johnson subsequently battled back with a bravery and ferocity that killed many enemy soldiers and thwarted the ambush. He started by running to the scene of the ambush armed with only his .45 caliber pistol and killed as many of the enemy as he could. When he ran out of ammunition, he ran back to his tank through intense fire to retrieve a submachine gun. He then rushed back into battle, killing more enemy soldiers in close combat; when he again ran out of ammunition, Johnson killed one enemy soldier with the stock of his empty machine gun. Following this, Dwight Johnson returned to his platoon sergeant's tank and extricated a wounded crewman and carried him to the unit's armored personnel carrier. He then returned to the tank and helped man its machine gun until it jammed. Armed with only a .45 caliber pistol, Johnson fought his way back to his own disabled tank and manned its externally mounted machine gun until the battle had ended. When the battle was over, Johnson would have killed several enemy prisoners, so enraged was he at the death of his former tank crew, had he not been subdued by three of his fellow soldiers.

Not long after this battle, Dwight Johnson's tour of duty in Vietnam ended, and he returned stateside, subsequently receiving his discharge from the army at Fort Carson, Colorado, in July 1968. Upon returning to his home in Detroit, Dwight Johnson's experiences were typical of those of many returning veterans, white or black; employment was difficult to find, and an appreciation for their military service was decidedly lacking. Later events would also prove that Johnson was likely suffering from post-traumatic stress disorder. However, prospects for Dwight Johnson seemingly improved when it was announced that he would be awarded the Medal of Honor for his heroism at Dak To. The medal was subsequently presented to him on 19 November 1968 by President Lyndon Johnson at a White House ceremony. Following this, Sergeant Dwight Johnson accepted a job as an army recruiter and his future seemed bright. However, things in his life eventually spiraled downward, aggravated by his post-traumatic stress disorder, and he experienced severe financial difficulties. Desperate to solve his money problems, Johnson was shot and killed on 30 April 1971 while attempting to rob a Detroit liquor store. He was not yet twenty-four years old. Sergeant Dwight Johnson was subsequently interred at Arlington National Cemetery, Arlington, Virginia.

FURTHER READING

Hanna, Charles W. *African American Recipients of the Medal of Honor* (2002).

Schladweiler, Kief. "Congressional Medal of Honor: Dwight H. Johnson." Available at: http://www.aavw.org/served/homepage_djohnson.html.

GLENN ALLEN KNOBLOCK

Johnson, Earvin "Magic," Jr. (14 Aug. 1959–), Hall of Fame basketball player, businessman, broadcaster, and AIDS activist, was born in Lansing, Michigan, to Earvin Johnson Sr., a General Motors worker, and Christine, a school custodian. Johnson, often called "Junior" or "June Bug," was one of nine children and enjoyed playing and practicing basketball from an early age. He attended Everett High School, where he was nicknamed "Magic" by the sportswriter Fred Stabley Jr. after registering thirty-six points, sixteen rebounds, and sixteen assists in a game. In his senior year the team went 27-1 and captured the state title, with Johnson averaging 28.8 points and 16.8 rebounds for the season. He was selected to the McDonald's High School All-American team in 1976 and 1977. After graduation he attended Michigan State University in nearby East Lansing, where during his freshman year his varsity team captured the Big Ten Conference title. One year later the Spartans won the 1979 national championship game over the Indiana State team, which included the star forward and future NBA great Larry Bird. Afterward Johnson decided to enter the NBA draft two years before graduating from college.

The six-foot-nine Johnson was chosen as the number one draft pick by the Los Angeles Lakers, and the tallest point guard in NBA history quickly became popular with Lakers fans as the team powered its way to the 1980 NBA title. Never before had a rookie player compiled a record to match Johnson's 18 points, 7.7 rebounds, and 7.3 assists per game. Johnson, taking over at center for the injured superstar KAREEM ADBUL-JABBAR for game six of the finals, scored forty-two points and pulled down fifteen rebounds to finish off the Philadelphia Seventy-sixers. With this championship Johnson became one of an elite group to win basketball championships at every level: high school, college, and professional. He also joined an even smaller group of just three other men who won both NCAA and NBA titles back-to-back. He was the first rookie to win the NBA Finals Most Valuable Player (MVP) Award, but his rival Bird won the 1979–1980 season NBA Rookie of the Year Award with the Boston Celtics.

Johnson's prodigious scoring abilities, astonishing passing skills, and personal magnetism ushered in the "showtime" era at the LA Forum. Johnson was sidelined by a serious knee injury for forty-five games during the 1980–1981 season, and the Lakers lost in the play-offs. The following season was marred by friction. When Coach Paul Westhead announced plans to implement a slower half-court offense, Johnson, sensing a diminishment of his role, went into a locker room tirade. Westhead was fired the next day and replaced by the former assistant coach Pat Riley, who had a storied ten-season tenure at the helm of the Lakers. Fans around the league, who blamed Johnson for Westhead's firing, booed him and failed to select him as an All-Star Game starter that year. His play, however, did not suffer; the Lakers won another NBA championship, and Johnson was once again chosen the Finals MVP. A golden age was at hand. The "showtime" Lakers of the 1980s had every kind of offensive weapon at their disposal: fast breaks featuring Johnson's spectacular passing, James Worthy powering to the hoop for the dunk, the unstoppable hook shot of the Hall of Fame center Abdul-Jabbar, and the deadly accurate long-range shooting of Michael Cooper. The superb defense they played is not as well remembered but was equally crucial to their success. The nightly courtside presence of Jack Nicholson and other Hollywood stars woke up the historically reserved L.A. Forum crowd and lent the team an unprecedented mystique and glitz. Johnson signed a twenty-five-year contract with the Lakers worth $25 million in 1981, but during postseason play that year his team lost to the Celtics in the NBA Finals. Led by Robert Parish, Kevin McHale, and Bird, the Celtics were fiercely competitive rivals who consistently brought out the best in the Lakers and helped raise the profile of the NBA through the 1980s. Johnson's son Andre was born in February 1981 but grew up with his mother, a high school friend whom Johnson never married, in Michigan and Florida. Until Andre was in high school, he saw little of his father.

Over the next four years the Lakers won three more NBA titles, with Johnson's enthusiasm and outstanding play rallying the team. He reached a career high of 46 points in a game and averaged 23.9 points per game for the 1986–1987 season. After Abdul-Jabbar's retirement in 1987, Johnson took over leadership of the Lakers, adapting Abdul-Jabbar's trademark skyhook as his own. Johnson was not only the era's best all around player but was consistently able to make his own teammates better players. The Lakers beat the Celtics in the NBA Finals in 1987, and Johnson, who had worked hard to improve his outside shooting, was named NBA MVP for the first time. In 1988 Johnson married Earleatha "Cookie" Kelly.

In 1988 the Lakers became the first NBA team to win back-to-back championships in nineteen years. They won division titles in each of the next two seasons but failed to win another championship. The fading Lakers' last title run came in 1991, when they lost in the NBA Finals (Johnson's ninth appearance) in five games to MICHAEL JORDAN's Chicago Bulls, who were about to become the dynastic team of the 1990s, winning six titles throughout the decade.

On 7 November 1991 Johnson sent shockwaves through the sports world by announcing not only that he was HIV positive but also that he was immediately retiring from the NBA. He had not developed AIDS, and he began to manage his condition with medication. For a time his basketball playing days seemed over, and he did not play again until the 1992 NBA All-Star Game. There Johnson made a strong comeback and led the West to a 153-113 victory on his way to winning the All-Star MVP Award. His participation had not come without fear and criticism from some players, most notoriously Karl Malone of the Utah Jazz, who told a *New York Times* reporter: "Look at this, scabs and cuts all over me. I get these every night, every game. They can't tell you that you're not at risk, and you can't tell me there's one guy in the NBA who hasn't thought about it" (Harvey Araton, "Basketball Johnson's Return to League Isn't Welcomed by Some," *New York Times*, 1 Nov. 1992). Johnson joined the 1992 U.S. Olympic Basketball team—the original Dream Team—over protests that his participation could potentially infect other players. He nevertheless played, and the hypertalented team, made up almost entirely of future Hall of Fame players, cruised to the gold medal.

Johnson recorded public service commercials as part of an AIDS awareness campaign that earned him the J. Walter Kennedy Citizenship Award in 1991–1992. He also wrote a book about safe sex, *What You Can Do to Avoid AIDS* (1992), and worked as an NBA television commentator, and he and his wife had a son, Earvin "E.J." Johnson III, born on 4 June 1992. Johnson also hosted a short-lived talk show before taking over as the head coach of the Lakers near the end of the 1993–1994 season. He declined to continue coaching after the season and instead pursued his interests in business, which included the purchase of a share of the Lakers franchise in June 1994. He returned to the Lakers during

Earvin "Magic" Johnson of the Los Angeles Lakers leaps high over defenders Artis Gilmore and George Gervin of the San Antonio Spurs during their NBA game in Los Angeles, California, 25 March 1983. (AP Images.)

the 1995–1996 season but failed to recapture his past glory. Now playing in the unaccustomed power forward position, Johnson chafed at not having a point guard's control of the game, was fined for bumping a referee, and played only thirty-two games before retiring a second time in May 1996.

In 1995 Johnson began opening Magic Johnson Theaters in low-income neighborhoods of Los Angeles. While building his business empire, he continued to enjoy playing basketball on a traveling team composed of former NBA and college players that toured Asia and Australia. In 1995 Johnson and his wife adopted a daughter, Eliza Johnson.

Magic Johnson Enterprises (MJE) and Johnson Development Corporation included diverse real estate developments, partnerships, and commercial endorsements with a focus on development in urban neighborhoods often overlooked by large corporate development. The company became a sole franchisee of Starbucks Coffee stores and owned more than ninety stores in economically depressed neighborhoods. MJE partnered with Washington Mutual Home Loan Centers in twenty-seven locations. The corporation also opened a music and entertainment division that included animation, licensing, publishing, television, and film components. Their first music release by the solo artist Avant, distributed my MCA, certified platinum sales in 2000. The Magic Johnson Travel Group and SodexhoMagic, LLC, were established in 2006 to enhance minority business franchise and home-based travel agent ownership. Johnson has partnered with 24-Hour Fitness Centers and Loews Theaters across the country, and in June 2007 he penned a thirty-one-store, multiyear franchise agreement with Burger King Corporation to encourage minority ownership of the fast food restaurants. His son Andre joined him at the corporation. The Magic Johnson Foundation, founded in 1991, provided $20 million in educational scholarships, hosted charity basketball games and golf tournaments, and also supports AIDS research and education programs. Johnson continued to appear regularly as a television sports analyst and basketball commentator for the TNT channel throughout the first decade of the twenty-first century.

Johnson's basketball honors included five NBA championships, three NBA MVP Awards, three NBA Finals MVP Awards, twelve All-Star selections, and a place on the NBA's Fiftieth Anniversary All-Time Team. The Professional Basketball Writers Association created the Magic Johnson Award in 2001 to be given yearly to an outstanding NBA player who is available to both the press and the fans. He was inducted into the Naismith Memorial Hall of Fame in 2002. He broke OSCAR ROBERTSON's record of 9,887 career assists during the 1990–1991 season. Over 13 professional seasons, Johnson scored 17,707 points, grabbed 6,559 rebounds, dished out 10,141 assists, and stole the ball from opponents 1,724 times. The term *triple-double* (signifying double digits in points, rebounds, and assists in a game) was coined for Johnson, who achieved the feat 138 times—though Robertson had done it 181 times in an earlier era. Johnson was given a 2002 Robie Award by the Jackie Robinson Foundation for his humanitarian efforts and a 2007 Freedom Medal from the National Civil Rights Museum. Johnson stood out as one of the greatest champions in the history of basketball, and after his retirement he pioneered large-scale expansion of business opportunities for minorities and redevelopment of traditionally underserved communities.

FURTHER READING

Johnson, Earvin "Magic," and William Novack. *My Life* (1992).

Lazenby, Roland. *The Show: The Inside Story of the Spectacular Los Angeles Lakers in the Words of Those Who Lived It* (2005).

Nichols, John. *History of the Los Angeles Lakers* (2001).

Ross, Alan. *Lakers Glory: For the Love of Kobe, Magic, and Mikan* (2006).

PAMELA LEE GRAY

Johnson, Eddie Bernice (3 Dec. 1935–), nurse and U.S. Congresswoman, was born in Waco, Texas, the daughter of Edward Johnson, a Navy veteran and civil servant for the U.S. Department of Veterans Affairs, and Lillie Mae White Johnson, a homemaker and church organizer. Johnson was one of four children—sisters Ruth and Lee and brother Carl. The Johnsons were a tight-knit Christian family with a large extended family rooted in the Waco community. Johnson's parents instilled in their children a deep appreciation for education. Johnson's mother was an honor's graduate of AJ Moore High School in Waco, where Johnson would later attend and graduate in 1952.

By the early 1950s many segregationist laws had been enacted against African Americans and Hispanics. Texas maintained separatist policies related to education and public and residential areas and few opportunities existed for Johnson to pursue higher education locally. After graduation from high school, she attended St. Mary's College at the University of Notre Dame in South Bend, Indiana. In 1955 she obtained her nursing certificate and returned to Texas.

In 1956 Johnson married Lacey Kirk Johnson, with whom she had one son, Dawrence Kirk Johnson. The couple resided in Dallas, Texas, where Johnson began her career as a psychiatric nurse at the Veteran's Administration Hospital. Inspired by the civil rights movement, Johnson became active in her local community and focused on local politics, health, and education issues. In 1967 Johnson earned a Bachelor in Nursing degree from Texas Christian University in Forth Worth, Texas, and became chief psychiatric nurse at the Veteran's Administration Hospital. In 1970 Johnson and her husband divorced.

In 1972 Johnson began her political career with election to the Texas State Legislature, where she served in the House of Representatives representing District 33-D in the Dallas area. She was the first black woman elected to public office from the Dallas area since 1935. In the State Legislature Johnson worked on the Labor Committee, where she was the first woman chair, and the Constitutional Amendments Committee. Johnson was active in the national Democratic Party, serving on the Democratic National Committee and as vice-chairwoman of the State Democratic Convention.

In 1976 Johnson obtained her Master of Public Administration degree from Southern Methodist University in Dallas. In 1977 Johnson left the State Legislature when Democratic President Jimmy Carter appointed her regional director of the Department of Health, Education, and Welfare. With the election of Republican Ronald Reagan in 1980, Johnson left her post and public service. She served as a consultant between 1979 and 1981 for Sammons Corporation, a large private company. In 1981 she launched the venture Eddie Bernice Johnson and Associates, which focused on attracting business to the Dallas area and later expanded to manage concessionary business in the Dallas— Fort Worth Airport.

In 1986 Johnson re-entered politics and returned to the State Legislature, with a successful election to the State Senate representing District 23. In the State Senate Johnson served on the Finance Committee, where she chaired the subcommittees on Health and Human Services and Education. Johnson was influential in shaping legislation focused on fair housing, health care, and discrimination.

In 1991 Johnson chaired the Senate Redistricting Committee. The committee was responsible for defining the three new congressional districts Texas gained as a result of the 1990 Census. Johnson proposed controversial plans for all three districts to be majority African American and Hispanic, with District 30 representing downtown Dallas and composed of 50 percent African Americans and 17 percent Hispanic. When Johnson announced her candidacy to represent the newly defined District 30, she was widely criticized for gerrymandering for personal political gain. Despite negative local and national media attention, she was elected with 74 percent of the vote to the U.S. Congress House of Representatives, representing District 30, becoming the first African American since Barbara Jordan to represent the state of Texas and the first nurse elected to congress.

Johnson served on the Transportation and Infrastructure Committee and the Science and Technology Committee. Johnson's arrival in Congress accompanied dramatic change with the arrival of Democratic President William Clinton. The Clinton Administration energized the Democratic Party base, especially among African Americans, and raised expectations of change in American politics. Many of the administration's policy goals were ambitious and highly controversial. Johnson saw an opportunity to be a strong advocate for her district. She continued her advocacy of health care and housing-related issues and was an early proponent of the North American Free Trade Agreement (NAFTA). Johnson's support of NAFTA met controversy in 1993 when she was accused of trading votes on legislation in exchange for the production of aircrafts in her district. NAFTA was signed into law later that year and Johnson's popularity in her district remained intact.

The Clinton Administration's attempts to reform health care early in the term met with failure and proved costly for Democrats in the House of Representatives. The 1994 elections saw Republicans retake control and Democrats try to regain public confidence. In Texas, Johnson faced her own challenges—a court-ordered redistricting of District 30 that would reduce the number of minorities. Although the changes made victory less certain, Johnson would win reelection in 1996 with 55 percent of the vote. Johnson's control of her district continued to raise her profile in Congress and in the Congressional Black Caucus, where she served as chair between 2001 and 2003. In each succeeding election Johnson's percent of the vote increased. In 2008 Johnson was re-elected to Congress with 83 percent of the vote. Johnson was a "superdelegate" and supported Barack Obama in the 2008 election; however, her district heavily favored Hillary Rodham Clinton in the primary. In 2009, she was the Senior Democratic Deputy Whip.

Johnson's advocacy and public service earned her numerous awards and honorary degrees. She was recognized for her ability to build broad coalitions and draw attention to issues related to jobs, education, health care, and a strong economy.

FURTHER READING

Gale Research. *Eddie Bernice Johnson* (1996).

Kilpatrick, Carolyn. *Tribute to Lillie Mae White Johnson*, 17 Oct. 2007, pp. E2169–E2170.

"Johnson, Eddie Bernice," *Biographical Directory of the U.S. Congress, 1774–Present*.

"Eddie Bernice Johnson," *Black Americans in Congress, 1870–1907* (2008).

MICHAELJULIUS IDANI

Johnson, Edward Austin (23 Nov. 1860–24 July 1944), educator, lawyer, and politician, was born near Raleigh, North Carolina, the son of Columbus Johnson and Eliza A. Smith, slaves. He was taught to read and write by Nancy Walton, a free African American, and later attended the Washington School, an establishment founded by philanthropic northerners in Raleigh. There he was introduced to the Congregational Church and became a lifelong member. Johnson completed his education at Atlanta University in Georgia, graduating in 1883. To pay his way through college, he worked as a barber and taught in the summers. After graduation he worked as a teacher and principal, first in Atlanta at the Mitchell Street Public School from 1883 to 1885 and then in Raleigh at the Washington School from 1885 to 1891. While teaching in Raleigh, he studied at Shaw University, obtaining a law degree in 1891. He joined the faculty shortly after graduation and became dean of the law school at Shaw two years later. He acquired a reputation as a highly capable lawyer, successfully arguing many cases before the North Carolina Supreme Court.

Johnson was concerned that African American history was not being taught in schools, so he wrote *A School History of the Negro Race in America from 1619 to 1890* (1891). This account, which sought to inform African American schoolchildren of the "many brave deeds and noble characters of their own race," was the first textbook by an African American author approved by the North Carolina State Board of Education for use in public schools. In 1899 he published another text, *History of Negro Soldiers in the Spanish-American War*. In 1894 Johnson married Lena Allen Kennedy; they had one child.

While he was dean at Shaw, Johnson became involved in Raleigh city politics. He chaired the Republican Party in the Fourth Congressional District and was a delegate at the 1892, 1896, and 1900 Republican National Conventions. He served on the Raleigh Board of Aldermen for two years, and he was the assistant to the U.S. attorney for the Eastern District of North Carolina from 1899 to 1907. He helped found the National Negro Business League in 1900 and helped organize the National Bar Association in 1903. He experimented with several business ventures and was vice president and later president of the Coleman Manufacturing Company, a cotton mill jointly owned by African American investors. With six others he founded the North Carolina Mutual and Provident Association, which became the largest African American–owned insurance company in the world. By 1902 Johnson was one of only two African American citizens of Raleigh with an income large enough to necessitate paying the state income tax. His novel *Light Ahead for the Negro* (1904), set in the year 2006, portrays an ideal society, free from racial discrimination.

Racial prejudice and a continuing lack of opportunities for African Americans in the South prompted Johnson to leave North Carolina in 1907 and settle in New York City, where he set up a law practice. He continued his political and civic involvement on the Republican committee for the Nineteenth Assembly District and as a member of the Harlem Board of Trade and Commerce and the Upper Harlem Taxpayers Association. In 1917 Johnson became the first African American to win a seat in the New York legislature. While in office, he advocated bills to create free state employment bureaus and prevent racial discrimination in public hospitals. He also voted for an amendment to the Levy Civil Rights Act that outlawed racial or ethnic discrimination in public employment or public facilities. Largely because of a reorganization of political districts, Johnson was not reelected for a second term, so he returned to his law practice. In 1925 he became legally blind, although he retained some sight for at least ten years. He ran again in 1928 as the Republican candidate for the U.S. House of Representatives in the predominantly white and Democratic Twenty-first District. His candidacy, he later acknowledged, was not a serious bid to win office but a tool to encourage African Americans to register and vote. Johnson's final book, *Adam vs. Ape-Man in Ethiopia* (1931), contends that the first civilization emerged in Ethiopia at a time when Europe "had yet to emerge from the reindeer age and the apeman type." He also maintained that Egyptian culture, created by black Africans, had been corrupted and finally destroyed by the invasion of white "injustice and greed." Johnson died in New York City.

Johnson was one of the first African Americans to rise to social and political importance despite the climate of continuing racism and racial disfranchisement following the Civil War. He was a successful businessman, a Raleigh politician, an author of an early African American history text, and mostly notably, the first African American legislator in the New York House. Owing to the range of his achievements, Johnson provided an early model of African American success.

FURTHER READING

Johnson, Edward Austin. "A Congressional Campaign," *Crisis* 40 (Apr. 1929).

Johnson, Edward Austin. "A Student at Atlanta University," *Phylon* 3 (2d quarter 1942).

Lawson, Edwin R. "Edward Austin Johnson," in *Dictionary of North Carolina Biography*, ed. William S. Powell, vol. 3 (1988).

Obituary: *New York Times*, 25 July 1944.

This entry is taken from the *American National Biography* and is published here with the permission of the American Council of Learned Societies.

ELIZABETH ZOE VICARY

Johnson, Ellsworth "Bumpy" (1906–1968), Harlem gangster, was born Ellsworth Raymond Johnson in Charleston, South Carolina. He acquired the nickname "Bumpy" as a boy when his parents discovered a small marble-sized bump on the back of his head. This bump was simply an accident of birth, but it would provide Ellsworth with the nickname by which he would be known throughout his life. Little is known of Johnson's parents or childhood; however, by the age of fifteen he had moved to Brooklyn, New York, to live with an aunt. He finished high school and at sixteen he moved to Harlem to live on his own. He was soon involved in a life of petty crime. By sixteen he could already be described as a stickup gunman and a second-story burglar.

At the age of seventeen, Johnson was sent to a reformatory in Elmira, New York. This stay would serve as the beginning of nearly half a lifetime spent behind bars. Johnson used his time in prison to engage in cultural pursuits. He became an avid reader, a writer of poetry and prose, as well as a master chess player.

His life in Harlem in the 1920s and 1930s exposed Johnson to many famous and infamous personalities. Around the age of twenty he went to work for BILL "BOJANGLES" ROBINSON, one of the most famous African American dancers and actors of the day. Johnson worked as a bodyguard for Robinson, and performed other duties. On the street Johnson became a well-respected hustler. Always immaculately groomed and dressed, to the underworld he was known as an honest and generous man with a fiery temper. Despite his intelligence and cunning, his regular stays in prison continued.

Upon his release from a prison stay in 1932, he was recruited by STEPHANIE ST. CLAIR, known in the Harlem underworld as Madame Queen. Madam Queen was one of the most powerful bankers for the illegal lottery, called the "policy racket"

or "the numbers." Until then, Johnson had been engaged in other types of crime, such as enforcement, but the policy racket had slowly become the dominant and most profitable form of criminal enterprise in Harlem. Things were about to change. In the late 1920s members of the organized Italian and Irish mobs, including Dutch Schultz's, became gradually aware of the large profits being made by uptown Harlem bankers. By the early 1930s the black bankers in Harlem were under constant siege by the Bronx-based and downtown mobs, which were attempting to take over the lucrative business. This collection of ambitious and heartless mobsters, who were normally at war with one another, combined forces and engaged black middlemen to violently persuade Harlem bankers and numbers runners to join their organization. This alliance of mobsters would be known as "the Combination" (Lawrenson, 175). The "membership" in the group, of course, was limited those who "agreed" to turn over of 90 percent of their profits and hard-won territory to the downtown whites. In exchange the Combination would spare the lives of the kings and queens of Harlem policy. Neither Madame Queen nor Johnson viewed this as a fair trade.

Acting on behalf of Madame Queen, Johnson brazenly fought the Combination and their black henchmen until the early 1930s. White mobsters were unaccustomed to resistance uptown and were surprised by the fierceness of the response. In one of the bloodiest gang wars in Harlem's history, Johnson was successful in turning back the mob and returning the policy racket to black Harlem. As a result of this legendary fight Johnson became a folk hero to most black Harlemites. There were those, however, who viewed him as a reckless and dangerous criminal. Some saw him as the cause of unwarranted bloodshed on the streets of Harlem. In any case, his victory would be short-lived, as black bankers and gangsters lacked the political and economic clout of the mobsters who composed the Combination. The mob retook control of the policy racket in Harlem by 1935. Sensing defeat, Johnson urged Madame Queen to cooperate with the mob. She did so, and he went on to become the highest-ranking black in the Combination. Ironically, Johnson was put in charge of the enforcement of the white mob's policy in Harlem, the very presence he had fought against before he became involved with the Combination.

Johnson went on to become the most important black middleman for the mob in the period from 1940 to 1968. Despite his relationship to the mob he remained a well-respected member of the community. He would often be seen saving a poor family from eviction or supplying neighborhood children with Christmas presents. He donated to charities and was generous with his earnings. During this time period Johnson continued to serve intermittent, short terms in jail. In the early 1950s he was indicted for allegedly selling narcotics to undercover federal agents. He claimed that it was a setup. Proof of this is lost to history. However, after taking his case to the U.S. Court of Appeals, and losing, he was sent to prison in 1954. Because selling narcotics was a federal crime, Johnson was sent to Alcatraz to serve out the majority of his nine-year sentence. This would be his final prison term. He was released in 1963, and much of Harlem welcomed him back with open arms. Johnson never lost his rebellious spirit. In 1965 he staged a sit-in a police station because of what he deemed continuous surveillance and harassment (of himself). He was charged with refusing to leave a police station, but he was later acquitted. In 1967 Johnson was once again indicted on a federal narcotics charge, but he died of a heart attack in July 1968 at a well-known Harlem restaurant while out on a fifty-thousand-dollar bond.

Many have stated that the 1971-movie icon *Shaft*, an inner-city Robin Hood of sorts, was based on the real-life Johnson (Johnson, 118). Johnson has become a folk hero in the black community and in 1980 he was played by John Amos in the miniseries *Alcatraz: The Whole Shocking Story*. He was also played by LAURENCE FISHBURNE in both the *Cotton Club* (1984) and, more recently, *Hoodlum* (1997). Gangster, pimp, poet, and philanthropist are only a few of the words that were used to describe Johnson throughout his life. He was an unconventional hero at a time when the avenues to black success were few and exceedingly difficult to navigate. Within these constraints he cut his own extraordinary path.

FURTHER READING
Johnson, John H. *Fact Not Fiction in Harlem* (1980).
Lawrenson, Helen. *Stranger at the Party: A Memoir* (1975).
Schatzberg, Rufus. *African-American Organized Crime: A Social History* (1996).

H. ZAHRA CALDWELL

Johnson, Francis (1792–6 Apr. 1844), bandleader, composer, multi-instrumentalist, and teacher, was probably born in Martinique, West Indies, to parents whose names are unknown. He settled in Philadelphia in 1809. While there is little historical record of Francis "Frank" Johnson's early life, it is known that three key figures helped young Francis hone his prodigious music skills: Matt Black, an African American bandleader from Philadelphia; P. S. Gilmore, "the father of the American band"; and Richard Willis, the director of the West Point military band.

That Johnson played many instruments is clear from a student's observations of his studio, which housed "instruments of all kinds.... Bass drum, bass viol, bugles and trombones" (*A Gentleman of Much Promise: The Diary of Isaac Mickle, 1837–1845*, 196). While Johnson was an accomplished French horn player, he is best known as a virtuoso on both the violin and the Kent, or keyed bugle, which was used in orchestras and for martial music. The keyed bugle is much like a traditional bugle, but curved and with six keys that enable the instrument to cover a wide scale. Much American music in the antebellum period centered around military bands, with brigades often contracting their own ensembles. The War of 1812, in which African Americans fought, allowed blacks greater access to military bands. Johnson reportedly played in Matthew Black's band following the war and studied with Richard Willis before leading Philadelphia's Third Company of Washington Guards in 1815. By 1818, when Johnson was only twenty-six, he published *Six Setts of Cotillions*. These classical marches were the first music pieces ever to be published by an African American. Johnson's stature grew in Philadelphia—the burgeoning nation's cultural center—and he quickly became the city's best-known musician, playing concerts, balls, celebrations, and other social events for both the elite white society and the black community. A passage from Robert Waln's *The Hermit in America* (1819) attests to Johnson's popularity: "[Johnson is the] leader of the band at all balls public and private, sole director of all serenades, acceptable and not acceptable; inventor-general of cotillions; to which add, a remarkable taste in distorting a sentimental, simple, and beautiful song into a reel, jig, or country-dance" quoted in (Southern, 108). The historian EILEEN SOUTHERN explains that the word "distorting" in this context is one of the first examples of "infusing the music with rhythmic complexities ... and the transference of musical scores into actual sound" (113). That Johnson could change cotillions, waltzes, and quadrilles into popular music vernaculars such as reels, jigs, and country dances makes plain his virtuosity. Taking such great liberties with genres suggests

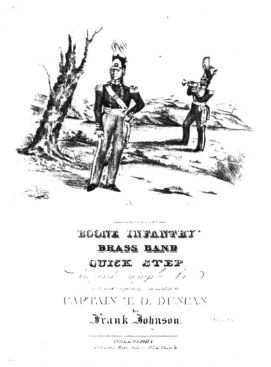

"Boone Infantry Brass Band Quick Step." Cover of one of Francis Johnson's compositions from 1844. (Library of Congress.)

that Johnson may have been the first American musician to employ improvisational techniques, a practice that fomented future music revolutions.

By the 1820s Johnson became affiliated with several regiment bands, including the Washington Grays, the Philadelphia State Fencibles, and the First Troop Philadelphia City Cavalry. During marches and parades, however, Johnson added drums and fife players to these bands, which consisted primarily of woodwinds, a French horn, and percussion. For dances, the band became Johnson's Celebrated Cotillion Band or Johnson's Fine Quadrille Band, employing woodwinds. In the 1830s, when brass instruments came to prominence in the United States, Johnson's band became a brass band.

When General Lafayette, the enormously popular Revolutionary War hero from France, returned to Philadelphia in 1824, Johnson received the honor of leading bands for the parades, balls, and celebrations. For the occasion, Johnson composed "Honour to the Brave" and "La Fayett's Welcome," as well as songs honoring Lafayette's battles, such as "Monmouth," "German Town," and "Yorktown."

It is known that Johnson was politically minded from at least two of his compositions. The first—"Recognition March on the Independence of Hayti, for the piano forte & flute. Composed expressly for the occasion and dedicated to President J. P. Boyer by his humble servant with every sentiment of respect"—was written in 1825 as a tribute to Haiti's independence from France, which stemmed from Toussaint-Louverture's slave revolt. Johnson's support for Boyer, the president of Haiti, makes it clear that Johnson, who was himself from the French colonial territory of Martinique, supported independence for the colonies. Johnson announced his abolitionist politics by composing music to accompany the popular antislavery poem "The Grave of the Slave," written by the white Philadelphia socialite Sarah Forten.

In addition to playing for white patrons, Johnson played for numerous African American social functions, including balls, festivals, funerals, and church concerts in cities up and down the East Coast. During one of these trips in 1841, Johnson led a sacred music concert at the First African Presbyterian Church in Philadelphia, conducting Haydn's *Creation* with a fifty-piece orchestra. In the autumn of 1837 Johnson and four band members traveled to Europe, where they played a series of concerts in the major English cities. These performances are the very first record of any American touring Europe. The varied program included pieces by Mozart, arias by Rossini, and patriotic songs, all arranged by Johnson. During his six-month stay, Johnson was invited to perform for Queen Victoria, who allegedly presented Johnson with a silver bugle and for whom he later penned "Victoria Gallop."

On his travels Johnson was greatly influenced by European music. In addition to hearing Johann Strauss, he attended his first promenade concert in the tradition of Philippe Musard, who combined classical music with promenade in 1833. Upon returning to the United States in 1938, Johnson presented his own Concerts a la Musard, in Philadelphia. This was the first time such music had been performed in the United States. The concerts were enormously successful, attracting thousands of spectators. As an article in the *Detroit Free Press* declared, "It may be said without fear of contradiction that as a composer or musician, [Johnson] stands without peer" (23 Sept. 1893).

Johnson's most popular compositions included "Voice Quadrilles," "Philadelphia Grays' Quicksteps," and "Bird Waltz." Many of the songs used inventive methods, such as onomatopoeic devices. In "Voice Quadrilles" he instructed his band to laugh out loud and sing, and in "Bird Waltz" tweeting birds could be heard. "Sleigh Waltzes" featured the sounds of a blacksmith forging nails, a gleeful sleighing party, horses galloping, the cracking of whips, and the jingling of bells. Johnson taught students, and an informal Philadelphia school of music began to develop around him, which included the musicians William Appo, William Brady, Aaron J. R. Conner, James Hemmenway, Isaac Hazzard, and Joseph G. Anderson.

Although Johnson was successful, he encountered racial discrimination throughout his career. Johnson, who was never able to perform in the American South, was once arrested and fined ten dollars "for being a free Negro with no license to be in Missouri." In 1821, despite Philadelphia's relatively tolerant reputation, white musicians in the Philadelphia Fencibles resigned over the inclusion of black musicians. Twenty years later, an 1843 *New York Tribune* story reported that one of Johnson's concerts in Pittsburgh had ended with an angry mob shouting "opprobrious epithets and hurling brick-bats, stones and rotten eggs."

Despite these indignities, Johnson held the first racially integrated concert on American soil in Philadelphia on 29 December 1843. He continued the practice until the spring of 1844, when he fell ill and died at the age of fifty-two. Johnson was buried with full honors at the St. Thomas African Church in Philadelphia. An editorial in the *Public Ledger* on 6 April 1844 lamented the great loss, stating, "It will be a long time before his place can be similarly filled."

Francis Johnson's trailblazing contributions to the American music canon are undeniable. He was the most popular musician in antebellum America, composing more than two hundred pieces of music and playing before some of the world's greatest dignitaries. He introduced new music styles to America and was the first African American to publish music and to hold public formal band concerts. He was as well the first American of any color to tour Europe and to perform integrated musical concerts. That he was able to accomplish these extraordinary feats in the face of unbridled discrimination, while millions of his fellow African Americans were enslaved, is miraculous.

FURTHER READING
Southern, Eileen. *The Music of Black Americans: A History* (1997).

DISCOGRAPHY
Hail to the Chief! American Political Marches, Songs, and Dirges of the 1880s (Sony Classical SFK 62485).
The Music of Francis Johnson & His Contemporaries: Early 19th Century Black Composer (Musicmasters 7029-2-C).

ANDY GENSLER

Johnson, George "Chappie" (1876–17 Aug. 1949), Negro League Baseball player and manager, was born in Bellaire, Ohio. Almost nothing is known of his early childhood.

Baseball came naturally to Johnson in the sandlots of Bellaire, Ohio. When he was twenty years old, he signed his first baseball contract. He played two years with the Page Fence Giants, playing left field and first base. The Page Fence club, though, was financially insecure, and in 1899 Johnson signed with the Columbia Giants.

The Columbia Giants became one of the dominant teams in the Midwest. With the Giants, Johnson gradually assumed catching duties. Lefty Wilson, an outstanding Negro League pitcher of the period, and Johnson formed one of the best batteries in baseball.

The Columbia Giants merged with the Union Giants in 1901. Johnson played with the Giants until the following year, when he signed with the Algona Iowa Brownies. While he was with that club, Johnson made a name for himself and he was able to parlay that into a contract with the Philadelphia Giants, one of the top Negro League teams, in 1904. Johnson excelled with the Giants and led the team to a championship. He hit .352 versus the Cuban X-Giants in the championship series. He would play one more year with the Giants.

In the off-season Johnson played in Cuba, where he developed a reputation as a smart baseball player. Owners took notice, and Johnson became a player/coach with the St. Paul Colored Gophers in 1907. There Johnson signed on with the white St. Paul Saints of the American Association as a trainer and coach. He was in charge of the team from the start of spring training until the beginning of the season. Johnson worked with the white St. Paul team until 1912. He had previous experience working with white baseball clubs. In 1906 he was the head trainer for the Boston Braves of the National League.

Besides his duties as a trainer with the St. Paul Saints, Johnson remained a highly productive player for the St. Paul Gophers. In 1909 he led the team to a Western Championship. The next year Johnson signed with the Leland Giants in the Florida Hotel League. While in Florida he developed a reputation for his sharp style of dress, as well as his jovial personality. He signed on with the Chicago Giants in 1910. In the years that followed, Johnson made two pioneering equipment changes to the catching position.

Previously catchers had not worn shin guards. Whether Johnson invented shin guards or whether he simply popularized them remains unclear. Within a decade, though, shin guards would be seen as absolutely necessary for catchers, and Johnson is generally credited with pioneering the practice. While playing for the Schenectady Mohawks, he used an oversized catcher's mitt. This allowed him to catch the ball with one hand and saved his throwing hand from being nicked by foul balls. This, too, permanently reshaped the catching position.

In 1911 Johnson signed with the St. Louis Giants. He continued to develop a reputation as a skilled defensive catcher. His offensive numbers lagged during the following years, and he hit in the bottom of the order. In 1917 he moved more into a managerial role. He became manager and part owner of the Dayton Chappies. He dressed impeccably, hired a valet to take his bags to the park, and developed a reputation as a gentleman.

In 1921 Johnson, while managing the Norfolk Stars, officially retired from playing baseball. In 1924 he formed "Chappie Johnson's All Stars." The team traveled throughout the Northeast and Midwest, playing against both white and black professional teams. As was typical in the day, the team combined skillful play on the field with high entertainment. Before games, the All Stars would play shadowball. Players would act out the game, with no ball in play, imitating spectacular diving plays. The team was so skillful at their art that they often pretended that multiple balls were in play at once. Fans showed up in large numbers wherever they traveled. As many as 9,000 fans turned out to see the All Stars play the Florence Braves in Saratoga, New York. Players who signed on with the All Stars often turned their careers around. Negro League players Nip Winters, Scrip Lee, DICK SEAY, and Ted Page all met success under the tutelage of Johnson.

While Johnson was never a dominant hitter, his defensive abilities were unquestionably strong. He pioneered the catching position, making innovations that would permanently affect the position. A cerebral player, Johnson proved to be one of the finest coaches and owners in Negro League history.

Johnson died in Clemson, South Carolina.

FURTHER READING
Riley, James A. *The Biographical Encyclopedia of the Negro Baseball Leagues* (1994).

LOU MANZO

Johnson, George W. (Oct. 1846–23 Jan. 1914), singer, composer, minstrel performer, street musician, and one of the world's first recording stars and the first African American to make any recording, was born in Wheatland, Loudon County, Virginia, though possibly in Fluvanna County, Virginia. It is unclear as to whether he was born free or as a slave. His father, Samuel Johnson, was listed as free soon after George's birth. His mother was known as Druanna, or "Ann Pretty." While still a small child Johnson was hired as the "bodyservant" for a young white boy his same age, Samuel Moore. Johnson grew up in the prosperous Moore household and was taught to read and write. He is thought to have spent the Civil War working as a laborer for one or both armies.

Johnson moved to New York sometime around 1873 and began performing on ferry boats. In 1890 he was discovered at the Hudson River Ferry Terminal by Victor H. Emerson of the New Jersey Recording Company. Johnson immediately began recording minstrel songs for Emerson's company. Johnson's biggest hits, both nationally and internationally, by far, became "The Whistling Coon," "The Laughing Song," and "The Laughing Coon." Johnson actually became known by the nickname "The Whistling Coon" and was billed as such, becoming somewhat famous for what early record company executive Gaisberg called his "low pitched and fruity whistle" (Kenney, 39).

He made many cylinder recordings and records for prominent labels of the time, including Thomas Edison's and the Columbia Phonograph Company. He was one of the most popular stars of the period from 1890 until about 1908. Johnson was universally reported to have a jovial, good-humored, and much-adored nature and is said to have had a knack for putting people at ease with his big, hearty laugh.

He possessed a rather unusual and hard-to-place accent; it is as if the songs could have been sung by anyone, white or black.

Although he is often called a "minstrel" performer, that is perhaps a bit of a misnomer, because his recordings often employ nonsense lyrics and do not often engage in the mocking of or exploitation of African Americans.

According to William Howland Kenney, a professor of history at Kent State University and a leading scholar on the history of early-twentieth-century American music, Johnson was able to "produce an entertainment commodity that fit the general expectations of minstrel show and coon song traditions without actually requiring that he sing lyrics that would be humiliating to either himself or African Americans in general. In this, Johnson became the first of many black performers in the long history of the phonograph to creatively adapt and transform minstrel traditions" (Kenney, 39). Like DAVE CHAPELLE or EDDIE MURPHY a hundred years or so later, Johnson's repertoire included the mocking of whites, as can be heard on his "The Merry Mailman," in which he impersonates a stodgy, old New England doctor, an Irishman, and a Russian Jew (several of Johnson's songs, including "The Merry Mailman," can be heard on the double-CD *Lost Sounds*, Archeophone Records, 2005).

Johnson found a certain amount of high society patronage. There was an 1899 report that Levi P. Morton, a prominent local and national politician who had been a congressman, diplomat, vice president of the United States (under Benjamin Harrison, 1889–1893), and governor of New York (1895–1897), was a fan and patron of Johnson's. After hearing Johnson sing at a party, Morton supposedly raised $100 for him to get on his feet in show business. It was also reported in 1890 that Alva Vanderbilt (Mrs. William K. Vanderbilt) wanted Johnson to perform privately for her, as she would not attend theaters.

Johnson had controversial relationships with women. He had at least two common law wives, each of whom he was accused of beating, and each of whom died under mysterious circumstances. In the first instance, in either late 1894 or early 1895, Johnson was arrested but not charged. In the second, in 1899, he was arrested, put on trial for murder, and acquitted. There is an unsubstantiated claim that Johnson married a white woman in Vienna, Austria, in about 1872 while he was traveling and performing with a minstrel troupe called the Georgia Minstrels. Neither the marriage nor the trip abroad is confirmed, and no census shows him to be married, yet the first common law wife of Johnson's who was found dead was purported to be a "German woman" (Brooks, 46). It seems unusual that an African American man could be suspected of killing a white woman and not be charged (could the hand of then-governor of New York Morton have been involved?). In both cases, the women were found dead in their apartments, after months of tumultuous relations

with Johnson. The second woman, Roskin Stuart, an alcoholic with a great temper, was African American. A year before her death in 1899 she fell, or was pushed, out a window during an altercation with Johnson.

The Columbia Phonograph Company came to Johnson's aid in his 1899 murder trial. Emerson, then a Columbia executive, raised $1,000 for his defense and Columbia's lawyer, Rollin C. Wooster, provided legal advice. The prominent sports and entertainment lawyer Emanuel M. Friend represented Johnson in the trial, which was covered widely in the New York press. Many character witnesses for the defense were said to be eager and available. Moore, who was by then a highly respected businessman and church deacon in Virginia, traveled to New York to support Johnson. Meanwhile, all the evidence against Johnson was circumstantial, and he was acquitted. Wooster, relieved that the label's star was saved, was quoted on the day of the acquittal as calling Johnson a "good coon" (Brooks, 57) and that he and Emerson planned to "give him a good dinner, sitting right down at the same table with him" that night (57).

In the early days of recording, a song had to be sung many times over and over in order to produce multiple copies. Only a few copies could be made from each performance, and performers were paid each time a song was sung in the studio. The change in technology that enabled many copies to be made from one take coincided with Johnson's aging and decline in health. Thus he found much less work in his later years and worked as a doorman for Len Spencer, another recording artist and music industry gadfly (who also played the mailman on "The Merry Mailman"). Spencer, a well-to-do southern white man, let Johnson live in his New York offices. At some point Spencer had to fire Johnson owing to his excessive alcohol consumption. Johnson then moved to Harlem, where he was residing at the time of his death.

FURTHER READING

Some of Johnson's early cylinder recordings are housed in the Department of Special Collections at the Donald C. Davidson Library, University of California at Santa Barbara.

Brooks, Tim. *Lost Sounds: Blacks and the Birth of the Recording Industry* (2005).

Kenney, William Howland. *Recorded Music in American Life: The Phonograph and Popular Memory, 1890–1945* (1999).

PAUL DEVLIN

Johnson, Georgia Douglas (10 Sept. 1886?–14 May 1966), poet and dramatist, was born Georgia Blanche Douglas Camp in Atlanta, Georgia, the daughter of George Camp and Laura Jackson, a maid. Her birth date has traditionally been recorded as 10 September 1886, but recent biographies—based on obituary notices and school sources—alternatively list her year of birth as 1880 or 1877. Georgia's paternal grandfather was a wealthy Englishman, her maternal grandmother was a Native American, and her maternal grandfather was an African American. Her early years were spent in Rome, Georgia, and she graduated from Atlanta University's Normal School in 1893. In 1902–1903 she continued her schooling at the Oberlin Conservatory of Music, where she studied piano, violin, harmony, and voice. Her interest in music was reflected in her literary work.

She taught school in Marietta, Georgia, and later became an assistant principal in Atlanta. In September 1903 she married Henry Lincoln "Link" Johnson, an Atlanta lawyer and Georgia delegate at large to the Republican National Convention since 1896. They had two children. In 1910 the family moved to Washington, D.C., and in 1912 Link was appointed recorder of deeds by President William Howard Taft.

Johnson's first poems, "Omnipresence" and "Beautiful Eyes," were published in the Atlanta-based *Voice of the Negro* in June 1905. After the move to Washington, W. E. B. DuBois selected three of her poems, "Gossamer," "Fame," and "My Little One," for *Crisis* (1916). Her first book of poetry was *The Heart of a Woman and Other Poems* (1918). Characteristic of Johnson's verse, it contained short, introspective lyrics written in traditional forms. The book was criticized in some quarters because it did not contain enough "racially conscious" poems. Perhaps in response to such criticism, Johnson's next book, *Bronze: A Book of Verse* (1922), was much concerned with issues of race as well as gender. In his foreword, DuBois noted somewhat condescendingly that Johnson's "word is simple, sometimes trite, but it is sincere and true." ALICE DUNBAR-NELSON, in her review in the *Messenger* (May 1923), called *Bronze* "a contribution to the poetry of America as well as to the race, that is well worth while."

In 1925 Link Johnson died. In appreciation of his services to the Republican Party, Georgia Johnson was appointed commissioner of conciliation in the Department of Labor by President Calvin Coolidge. Often beleaguered by professional, financial, and family pressures, Johnson lamented the lack of time to pursue her writing. She said, "If I might ask of some fairy godmother special favors, one would sure be for a clearing space, elbow room in which to think and write and live beyond the reach of the Wolf's fingers" (*Opportunity*, July 1927).

Despite these demands, in 1928 Johnson published *An Autumn Love Cycle*. The book contained what may be her most famous poem, "I Want to Die While You Love Me," later set to music by Johnson and sung by HENRY T. BURLEIGH. The poems of this book, like much of Johnson's verse, were in the "genteel" tradition of "raceless" literature advocated by fellow African American writers like WILLIAM STANLEY BRAITHWAITE and COUNTÉE CULLEN. However, when reread from a feminist perspective, the book contains some of Johnson's best work.

In addition to her poetry, Johnson wrote more than thirty one-act plays. Only about a dozen have survived, and few have been produced. The focus of her plays, more than her poetry, was on racial issues. Plays such as *Blue Blood* (1926), *Safe* (c. 1930), and *Blue-Eyed Black Boy* (c. 1930) discuss such subjects as lynching and miscegenation. *Frederick Douglass* (1935) and *William and Ellen Craft* (1935) treat of black heroes. Johnson's folk drama *Plumes*, which deals with the plight of a mother who must decide on spending her fifty dollars either on a dubious operation or on a splendid funeral for her daughter, won first prize in a 1927 *Opportunity* competition. *A Sunday Morning in the South* (c. 1925) concerns an innocent African American man who is lynched for the rape of a white woman. The use of hymns ironically adds to the chilling horror that unfolds throughout the work. Johnson submitted several plays to the Federal Theatre Project, but all were rejected by the readers, some of whom undoubtedly felt uncomfortable with her themes.

The need for money became an increasing burden in Johnson's life. She applied for many awards but was invariably rejected. Still, her poems were published in scores of periodicals, and she wrote a column of practical advice called "Homely Philosophy," which was carried in many newspapers from 1926 to 1932. She also published several short stories under the pseudonym Paul Tremaine.

Over the years, Johnson became increasingly important as a literary hostess. She called her house at 1461 S Street in northwest Washington "Half Way House" because "I'm half-way between everybody and everything and I bring them together."

Johnson's home was a popular haven for such writers as Jessie Fauset, Langston Hughes, Cullen, and Jean Toomer.

Johnson published her final book of poetry, *Share My World*, in 1962. This slim volume contained many previously published poems. The work was reflective, generally optimistic, and displayed her belief in the common bond of humanity. In 1965 Johnson was awarded an honorary doctorate of literature degree from Atlanta University. She died in Washington, D.C.

During her long life Johnson was frequently praised. James Weldon Johnson said that "[s]he was the first colored woman after Frances Harper to gain general recognition as a poet." DuBois described her as being "the leading colored woman in poetry and one of our leading poets." Only late in the twentieth century did she begin to receive more critical attention, and several of her surviving plays were published for the first time.

FURTHER READING

Manuscript material is scattered in various locations, including the Schomburg Center for Research in Black Culture (New York Public Library), the Moorland-Spingarn Research Center at Howard University, the Federal Theatre Project Research Division at George Mason University, and the Robert W. Woodruff Library at Clark Atlanta University.

Fletcher, Winona. "Gloria Douglas Johnson," in Trudier Harris, ed. *Afro-American Writers from the Harlem Renaissance to 1940* (1987).

Hull, Gloria T. *Color, Sex, and Poetry: Three Women Writers of the Harlem Renaissance* (1987).

Randolph, Ruth Elizabeth. *Harlem Renaissance and Beyond: Literary Biographies of 100 Black Women Writers, 1900–1945* (1990).

Shockley, Ann Allen. *Afro-American Women Writers 1746–1933* (1988).

This entry is taken from the *American National Biography* and is published here with the permission of the American Council of Learned Societies.

LOUIS J. PARASCANDOLA

Johnson, Gilbert (30 Oct. 1905–5 Aug. 1972), Marine Corps drill sergeant, was born in Mt. Hebron, Greene County, Alabama. At the age of seventeen he enrolled in Stillman College in Tuscaloosa, a Presbyterian institution founded for the training of black ministers. However, the life of a minister was not for Johnson, and in 1923 he joined the U.S. Army. He served for seven years as part of the segregated 25th Infantry Division and was stationed near the Mexican border before he was discharged as a corporal in October 1929. His occupation for the next four years is unknown, but he took the opportunity once again to serve his country when, in 1933, he joined the U.S. Navy, possibly due to financial difficulties as a result of the Great Depression. His enlistment came at a time when the navy had resumed enlisting African Americans after ceasing to do so in 1920. With the navy now in need of men to serve in the Steward's Branch, men like Johnson took advantage of this limited opportunity. While the prospect of a steady job with steady pay and housing accommodations was surely attractive during the Depression, they came at a price; blacks were only accepted in the service as mess attendants, their job—men like Johnson, Doris "Dorie" Miller, and Leonard Harmon—was to serve the officer corps primarily as food handlers, waiters, and sometimes as personal servants. This Johnson did, attending boot camp in Norfolk, Virginia, before being assigned to the old battleship *Wyoming*.

When Japanese forces attacked Pearl Harbor on 7 December 1941, Johnson was on board the *Wyoming* off the coast of Newport, Rhode Island, performing a gunnery training exercise. Shortly thereafter the ship was assigned to the Operational Training Command of the Atlantic Fleet and operated in Chesapeake Bay. When the navy announced in April 1942 that the Marine Corps would begin accepting blacks in its ranks, with plans to enlist 1,000 men a month beginning in June, Johnson saw an opportunity and asked for a transfer to the Corps. No doubt because of his lengthy service and fine record, his transfer request was granted, and by 31 August 1942 Johnson was officially a Marine Corps recruit.

The Marine Corps that Johnson entered in 1942 was, perhaps, the most conservative of all the branches of the armed forces. An entirely white organization with no tradition of black service beyond the Revolutionary War, the Marine Corps did not even have a segregated Steward's Branch like the navy. The Marine's highest ranking officer, Major General Thomas Holcomb, declared in early 1942 that "there would be a definite loss of efficiency in the Corps if we had to take Negroes … and their desire to enter the naval service is largely, I think, to break into a club that does not want them" (deClouet, 2). Even after the enlistment of blacks in the Marine Corps in 1942, many marine officers opposed the policy, with one stating that "we are just scared to death; we've never had any in; we don't know how to handle them." In response to this, Lt. Colonel Campbell Johnson, an African American Army Reserve officer serving as an administrator in the Selective Service system, replied that "I'll get the word around that if you want to die young, join the Marines. So anybody that joins has got to be pretty good" (deClouet, 3).

Upon being accepted as a marine, Johnson was assigned to the 51st Composite Defense Battalion and sent to Montford Point Camp in North Carolina, located on the New River near Jacksonville. With seventeen years of military experience to his credit, Johnson was one of the "old-timers" amongst the new recruits and quickly gained the nickname "Hashmark" for the four stripes on his uniform sleeve, one for every four years of his military service. The first drill instructors to train Johnson and his fellow recruits in the ways of the Marine Corps were white and were, as he would later recall, "the type of individuals who were not against the Negro being a Marine, and had it been otherwise, why I'm afraid that we would have all left the first week" (Shaw and Donnelly, 6). While the regimen was grueling, as only Marine Corps training can be, the new black marines excelled as soldiers, and by late November 1942 the first class with Johnson and 197 other men had graduated from Montford Point. The reaction of white civilians in the area of Jacksonville to black marines on liberty was anything but friendly, however, and often downright hostile; in some cases, black marines wearing their uniforms in public were arrested because they were thought to be impersonating marines.

With the expansion of Montford Point in 1943 as draftees arrived in increasingly greater numbers, all of the original white drill instructors were replaced by black non-commissioned officers; among them were two men, Johnson and EDGAR HUFF, who would make Marine Corps history and prove to be the foundation for blacks serving the marines during World War II and beyond. Johnson, named to head the 19th Platoon in May 1943, replaced the last white drill instructor at Montford Point. He was also named the recruit battalion's field sergeant major in charge of all drill instructors, and later became the sergeant major of the Recruit Depot Battalion. Though a tough drill instructor, Johnson was widely regarded as a fair-minded man who cared about his men; years later he would tell some of his former recruits that "I was an ogre to some of you that met me on the drill field.... I was a stern instructor, but I was fair. I was an exacting instructor, but with some understanding

of the many problems involved.... You were untried. The objectives were to qualify you with loyalty, with a devotion to duty, and with a determination equal to all, transcended by none" (Shaw and Donnelly, 12). The importance of these first black marine drill instructors, men like Johnson, cannot be overemphasized; it was their training that transformed raw, black recruits into the first black marines to go into combat, and by all accounts they succeeded brilliantly; after their first action in the Marianas on Saipan in June 1944, Marine Corps Commandant General Alexander Vandegrift announced that "The Negro Marines are no longer on trial. They are Marines, period" (deClouet, 20).

Johnson was not just a drill instructor in World War II; he was also a combat soldier. As sergeant major in the 52nd Defense Battalion, he went with his unit overseas, first to the Marshall Islands, and then to Guam. While blacks were at first denied the right to participate in combat patrols on the island, Johnson asked that they be allowed to do so and would eventually lead twenty-five patrols over the island's jungle terrain. Though conquered, small, isolated pockets of Japanese troops remained on Guam and carried out deadly ambushes from time to time, a number of which were likely prevented by the patrols of Johnson and his black marines. Following World War II, Johnson would later serve in Korea and retired from the service in 1959. In 1974, two years after his death, the camp at Montford Point was rededicated as Camp Gilbert H. Johnson in memory of this pioneer Marine Corps drill instructor and sergeant major.

FURTHER READING

deClouet, Fred. *First Black Marines; Vanguard of a Legacy* (1995).

Nalty, Bernard C. *The Right to Fight: African-American Marines in World War II* (1995).

Shaw, Henry, Jr., and Ralph Donnelly. *Blacks in the Marine Corps* (2002).

GLENN ALLEN KNOBLOCK

Johnson, Grant (21 Sept. 1874–4 Sept. 1963), baseball player also known as "Home Run Johnson," was born in Findlay, Ohio, to Edward Johnson, a laborer, and Sarah Johnson, a housekeeper. His formal education is unknown.

Despite playing in the dubbed "Deadball Era," characterized by loosely wrapped balls, and overused, the softer balls resulted in low-scoring games with fewer home runs. Johnson reportedly received his moniker playing for the 1894 Findlay

(Ohio) Sluggers and the Cuban Giants, hitting sixty home runs against various levels of competition. Although the Cuban club was all black, the traditionally white Findlay team included one other black player, JOHN "BUD" FOWLER.

The following season, in 1895, Johnson and Fowler entered into a partnership with two companies, the Page Woven Fence Company and the Monarch Bicycle Company of Chicago, Illinois.

The Monarch Bicycle Company was a prominent sponsor because it capitalized on the nation's cycling craze, led by African American cyclist MAJOR TAYLOR of Worcester, Massachusetts. The fence company was nationally known for building fences and cages for livestock on farms and exotic animals in zoos.

Together, in exchange for advertising opportunities, these prominent benefactors enabled Johnson and Fowler to entice some of the best black players in the country to form one of the country's first salaried African American baseball teams, the Page Fence Giants.

In an effort to avoid racially restricted public accommodations, the Giants traveled in a custom-made sixty-foot-long Louis XVI Pullman coach, which slept twenty men and employed a porter/barber and cook. As a perennial road team, press coverage was inconsistent and sparse, but Captain Johnson's team was reported to have won more than 100 games each season (1895–1898), and claimed 82 consecutive victories in 1897, en route to a 125–12 win—loss record. The team lasted four years, folding in 1898, and served as the blueprint for quality independent, professional black teams.

Johnson and several teammates relocated to Chicago in 1899 to form the Columbia Giants. Over the next few seasons, Johnson played for other Chicago-based teams; W. S. Peters' Chicago Unions and Frank Leland's Union Giants, before going to Philadelphia in 1903 to join RUBE FOSTER and Charlie Grant with the Cuban X-Giants. Johnson stayed with the X-Giants through the 1904 season before joining Sol White's Philadelphia Giants for one season, hitting eleven home runs and averaging one run batted in per game in eighty-eight games.

When Sol White published his *Official Base Ball Guide: A History of Colored Base Ball* in 1907, he chose Andrew "Rube" Foster to write a section on the science of pitching. Of equal importance was his selection of Grant "Home Run" Johnson to write his formula for successful hitting. The section entitled "Art and Science of Hitting" instructed in part as follows:

There are a number of requisites that a player should possess to be a first-class hitter, but in my opinion, two of the greatest and most essential ones are confidence and fearlessness. If, because of the reputation of the pitcher opposing you, your confidence in your ability to hit him is lacking, or you fear being hit by this wonderful speed or have the least fear in your heart at all, your success at such a time is indeed doubtful. If you possess both of these essentials, then it is an easy matter for the earnest student of hitting to acquire the science and judgment ...My advice to young players is secure a bat which you can handle perfectly, catch well upon it and in taking your position at the plate, be sure and stand firmly and face the pitcher, thinking you are going to hit without the least atom of fear about you. Seldom strike at the first ball pitched, as in letting it pass you get a line on the speed or curve of the pitcher. As he delivers one of our likings, try to meet it fairly, and when successful you will be surprised, and gratified, at the distance of the hit, with only ordinary force behind the swing. (pp. 100–102).

After departing the Philadelphia Giants, Johnson played for J. W. Connor's Brooklyn Royal Giants from 1905 to 1909. Unhappy, he left the team for Chicago's Leland Giants, now managed by Rube Foster. Johnson spent one season with the Leland team before dividing play between the 1911 Philadelphia Giants and the Chicago Giants.

In speaking of his difficulties with Johnson, owner/manager Connor gave his side of Grant's departure in T. THOMAS FORTUNE's *New York Age* of 14 April 1910: "Johnson is doing everything to get my players to leave me, but he has failed in every instance, the majority of my men are loyal and also know it will not do them any good to be contract breakers. The trouble with Johnson is that he got angry because I refused to give him an interest in the Royal Giants. For the last two years I have spent thousands of dollars trying to furnish New York with a championship team, and did not think that I should give anyone an interest at this time."

Johnson had ventured to Cuba for the 1910/1911 winter season to play for the Havana Reds. When the Detroit Tigers came for a tour of island baseball, Johnson greeted Tigers hurlers George Mullin, Ed Willett, and Ed Summers with a .429 average. That was a higher average than Hall of Famers Sam Crawford and Ty Cobb would attain against his Cuban teammates. Later that winter, the

Philadelphia A's came to Cuba with Cooperstown-bound pitchers "Chief" Bender and Eddie Plank. Johnson spanked them with a .375 paddling.

Jorge S. Figueredo, in his book *Who's Who in Cuban Baseball*, said Johnson played five seasons in Cuba, 1907, 1908, 1908/1909, 1910/1911, and 1912. Career-wise, in 156 games, he got 175 hits in 549 at bats, with eleven doubles, eight triples, and four home runs, for an overall .319 batting average. He twice led the leagues in hits and became the first American, in 1912, to win a Cuban winter league batting title with a .410 average.

An aging Johnson, thirty-seven, returned to Connor's Royal Giants in 1912, playing mostly at second base. His days as a regular shortstop ended with two seasons, 1913 and 1914, with the Lincoln Giants. Afterward he played sparingly with the Pittsburgh Giants, Buffalo Colored Giants, Pittsburgh Colored Stars, and Phoebe Snows of Buffalo, New York.

In 1917 Johnson, along with John Emory, broke the color barrier in Buffalo's Municipal Baseball Association, playing for the Phoebe Snows. Fielding objections from their patrons, the association printed their stand on the controversial issue of integrated play in the *New York Age*, 12 July 1917, stating:

> The Buffalo Municipal Baseball Association has not as yet drawn the color line and does not intend to do so as long as the present board of directors is running the affairs of the association for its good and welfare. We have no more right to bar a colored player from playing in a Municipal game than the city authorities have to prohibit colored people from using the public parks of this city for the purpose of enjoying themselves. The team that play Emory and Johnson was perfectly within their rights as neither player had played with or jumped from any team in our association and they were eligible to play and still are until they break any of our playing rules, and, furthermore, both men have worked a number of years for the Lackawanna Railroad, which the Phoebe Snows represent.

The last mention of Johnson's alliance with baseball came in an article on 17 April 1920 by the *New York Age*, reporting on the Bacharach Giants' spring training in Jacksonville, Florida. Johnson, at age forty-five, was filling in for the team's hotshot shortstop, Dick Lundy, who had failed to report, holding out for more pay. The article mentioned Johnson's influence in getting his teammates to regularly attend Jacksonville's Second Baptist Church. Upon Lundy's return to the team, Captain Dick Redding allowed Johnson to return to his Buffalo Stars.

Johnson continued to reside in Buffalo and reportedly played and/or managed part-time until age fifty-eight in 1932. His post-baseball career included working for the Lackawanna and New York Central Railroad Companies. Sketchy reports claim he became blind and died in Buffalo at ninety years old.

Pioneer Johnson is remembered not only as an innovator and a barrier breaker, but also as a fine vocalist. In the mode of smooth jazz singer Billy Eckstine, he had a luxuriously baritone voice. Only now, decades later, can we sing him the praise he so richly deserves.

FURTHER READING
Riley, James A. "Johnson, Grant 'Homerun'" in *Biographical Dictionary of American Sports, Baseball*, edited by David L. Porter (2000).

LARRY LESTER

Johnson, Hall (12 Mar. 1888–30 Apr. 1970), composer, arranger, and choral conductor, was born Francis Hall Johnson in Athens, Georgia, the son of William Decker Johnson, an African Methodist Episcopal (AME) minister, and Alice (maiden name unknown). Music was an important part of Hall Johnson's childhood. He heard his grandmother and other former slaves as they sang the old spirituals in his father's Methodist church. This grounding in the original performance of Negro spirituals was to represent a significant influence on his later life. Johnson, exhibiting an early interest in music, received solfeggio lessons from his father and piano lessons from an older sister. As a teenager he developed an interest in the violin and taught himself to play.

Johnson was educated in the South at the Knox Institute, at Atlanta University, and at Allen University in Columbia, South Carolina, where his father was president. Frustrated by his inability to find a violin instructor in the segregated South, Johnson left his southern roots and went to the Hahn School of Music in Philadelphia, where he could study his instrument. In 1910 he transferred to the University of Pennsylvania, where he received a bachelor of music degree in Composition and won the Simon Haessler Prize for outstanding composition.

Johnson married Polly Copening in 1914, and the young couple settled in New York City, where Johnson opened a violin studio. He taught during the day and freelanced at night in various dance and theater orchestras, playing violin or viola. He played with WILL MARION COOK's Southern

Syncopated Orchestra in 1918 and with Vernon Castle's Orchestra in NOBLE SISSLE and EUBIE BLAKE's 1921 Negro musical *Shuffle Along*. In 1923 he organized the Negro String Quartet, which included the violinists Arthur Boyd and Felix Weir, the cellist MARION CUMBO, and himself as violist.

From 1923 to 1924 Johnson did graduate study at the New York Institute of Musical Arts (later combined with the Juilliard School of Music). He studied music theory, violin, and composition with his favorite teacher, Percy W. Goetschius. During his three-year stint as a pit musician for *Shuffle Along*, Johnson became disenchanted with the manner in which a quartet sang spirituals. The barbershop treatment of Negro spirituals seemed a mockery of the rich choral style sung by former-slaves during his childhood. In an article for *The Crisis* (November 1966), Charles Hobson wrote about Johnson's feelings toward the spiritual and quoted him as saying, "It is serious music and should be performed seriously in the spirit of its original conception" (483).

This experience served as a catalyst for Johnson's true contribution to America's musical history. Johnson became a man with a mission. He resolved to forsake his instrumental career and devote his life to the preservation of an authentic performance style for Negro spirituals. Though his musical background was strictly instrumental, he decided to organize a choir that would realize his dream. In September 1925 he organized the Hall Johnson Choir—one of the first professional African American choirs to earn international acclaim. The choir was started with only eight members, but by the time of its debut in February 1926, its size had increased to twenty members because Johnson realized he needed more singers to achieve the traditional stylistic effect.

Johnson achieved worldwide fame for his arrangements of spirituals and for his original spirituals. During his career he composed and arranged over forty choral selections and twenty solo spirituals—all with authentic African American dialect and accurate rhythmic patterns. He arranged and directed music for Marc Connelly's production of *Green Pastures* (featuring the Hall Johnson Choir), which premiered on Broadway in 1930. Johnson received the 1931 Harmon Award for his role in the tremendous success of this Pulitzer Prize–winning musical.

In 1933 Johnson's own *Run, Little Chillun*, a Negro folk drama, was produced on Broadway for a run of 126 performances. He wrote both the lyrics and the music (twenty-five spirituals) for this successful production, which was his first dramatic attempt.

Johnson took his choir to Hollywood in 1936 to film *Green Pastures*. He made Hollywood his base over the next eight years as he wrote musical scores and conducted choirs for nine films. They included *Dimples* with Shirley Temple; *Lost Horizons*, which won two Academy Awards; *Swanee River* with Al Jolson; and *Cabin in the Sky* with LENA HORNE, ETHEL WATERS, LOUIS ARMSTRONG, and DUKE ELLINGTON. He also organized a two-hundred-voice Festival Negro Chorus in Los Angeles whose performances provided scholarships for talented students. While in Los Angeles, Johnson's *Run, Little Chillun* was staged as a WPA Negro Theatre Project. Its Broadway success was matched in Los Angeles and later in San Francisco as the show played to many enthusiastic audiences.

Johnson returned to New York in 1943 for a revival of *Run, Little Chillun*. His *Son of Man*, an Easter cantata (never published), was performed by the three-hundred-voice Festival Negro Chorus at the New York City Center in April 1946. It was presented again at Carnegie Hall on Good Friday of 1948. Johnson inaugurated an annual concert series titled New Artists to give visibility to young African American performers such as Kermit Moore, a cellist, and Robert McFerrin, a baritone singer.

In 1951 the Hall Johnson Choir was selected by the U.S. State Department to represent the nation at the International Festival of Fine Arts in Berlin. The choir won international acclaim as it toured Germany and other European countries. After the European tour Johnson alternated his career between Los Angeles and New York. A stroke in 1962 slowed his pace, but he soon recovered and resumed an active schedule of composing, teaching, and conducting. During that same year he was presented a citation by New York mayor Robert F. Wagner for thirty-five years of significant contributions to the world of music.

In 1965 Johnson was asked by MARIAN ANDERSON to arrange some solo spirituals for an RCA album she was doing. He also collaborated with Anderson and the Metropolitan Opera orchestra in arranging music for a concert production. He was honored again in March 1970 by Mayor John Lindsay, who presented him with New York's most prestigious citation, the George Frederic Handel Award.

Just over a month later Johnson died of smoke inhalation from a fire in his New York apartment. Anderson, in a *New York Times* (1 May 1970) tribute, wrote, "Hall Johnson's music was a gift of inestimable value that brought to all people a greater understanding of the depth of the Negro spiritual."

His outstanding legacy to the world lives on in his collections of spirituals that were published, in the few recordings that are still extant, and in his memoirs, which are at Rowan University (formerly Glassboro State College) in Glassboro, New Jersey.

FURTHER READING

Hall Johnson's papers are at Rowan University, Glassboro, New Jersey.

Floyd, Samuel A. *Black Music in the Harlem Renaissance* (1990).

Johnson, Francis Hall. "Notes on the Negro Spiritual," in *Readings in Black American Music*, ed. Eileen Southern (1983).

Lovell, John. *Black Song: The Forge and the Flame* (1972).

Roach, Hildred. *Black American Music: Past and Present* (1985).

Obituaries: *New York Times* and *New York Post*, 1 May 1970; *Jet* (21 May 1970).

This entry is taken from the *American National Biography* and is published here with the permission of the American Council of Learned Societies.

MARY FRANCES EARLY

Johnson, Halle Tanner Dillon (17 Oct. 1864–26 Apr. 1901), physician, was born in Pittsburgh, Pennsylvania, the daughter of BENJAMIN TUCKER TANNER, a successful minister and bishop in the African Methodist Episcopal (AME) Church and editor of the *Christian Recorder*, and Sarah Elizabeth Miller. Among the nine Tanner children was HENRY OSSAWA TANNER, the first African American artist to be celebrated internationally.

Halle Tanner married Charles E. Dillon of Trenton, New Jersey, in 1886, and the next year their only child was born. While the circumstances and date of Charles; Dillon's death are unknown, afterward Dillon returned to the Tanner family home in Philadelphia with her daughter, and then, at age twenty-four, she enrolled in the Woman's Medical College of Pennsylvania, the only black student in her class, and graduated with an MD in a class of thirty-six on 7 May 1891, with high honors.

Halle Tanner Dillon responded to BOOKER T. WASHINGTON's letter to the dean of the Woman's Medical College in search of a black woman to become resident physician at his Tuskegee Institute in Alabama. Although local white physicians had offered satisfactory school health services, Washington was determined to hire a black physician for the rural, black institution; he had led an unsuccessful four-year search. Washington wrote to Dillon on 16 April 1891 and described the town

as one with three thousand residents, half of whom were black. He said that the school was a "little colony" in the town, where 450 students were enrolled and thirty administrators and faculty were employed. Since the institution was supported by charity, Washington expected those who joined the staff to have "a broad missionary spirit" and to accept the modest salary that the school offered.

Dillon accepted Washington's offer as resident physician and arrived in Tuskegee on 3 August 1891. She received a salary of six hundred dollars for twelve months plus board and one month's vacation. She agreed to teach two classes a day, head the health department, and compound medicine for the school's needs.

As Dillon knew, physicians were required to pass either a local or state examination before practicing in Alabama. She left Tuskegee for Montgomery on 8 August and took temporary quarters in a quiet place so that she might study for the examinations. Washington did what he could to ease Bishop Tanner's anxiety over the gender and racial bias that his daughter might encounter in the examinations. To aid in the preparation, Washington arranged for study sessions with CORNELIUS NATHANIEL DORSETTE, a black physician practicing in Montgomery and the first black physician to pass the Alabama medical examinations. But racial discrimination was an established practice in Alabama. Anna M. Longshore, a white woman physician, was permitted to practice after failing the examination earlier. On 17 August Washington accompanied Dillon to the capitol building—the examination site—and introduced her to the supervisor. Both the supervisor and a white male candidate for the examination were startled. They told Dillon that they had never seen "a woman doctor before or a diploma from a Woman's Medical College" (Halle Dillon to Clara Marshall, 3 Oct. 1891, in Sterling). That she was a black woman probably aroused their curiosity even more. The ten-day testing period occurred without incident, with each day devoted to a different medical subject. The local press watched the event curiously and questioned what Dillon looked like and why she dared sit for the test. At the end the board supervisor complimented Dillon on the neatness and cleanliness of her work, but she was to return to Tuskegee and wait nearly three weeks before receiving the examination results.

Dillon passed the examination with an average of 78.81—a score lower than she had expected. But she did not dismiss the possibility of racial and gender bias, noting that "the critical medical pen has been too rigorously applied" (*Atlanta University Bulletin*, n.p.). She described the examination in a letter to her former dean at the Woman's Medical College of Pennsylvania: "Taking the examination as a whole is rather hard because there were so many questions, or rather a few questions which were technical in character. One question in Hygiene occurs to me now & it certainly was to my mind incomprehensible, 'Discuss the *hygiene* of the reproductive organs of the female'" (3 Oct. 1891, in Sterling). By this time, too, the major newspapers had lauded her achievement.

Dillon became the first woman of any race to pass the medical examination and to practice medicine in Alabama with a license. She was resident physician at Tuskegee Institute from 1891 to 1894. In addition to the duties that Washington initially defined for her, she established a Nurses Training School and the Lafayette Dispensary.

In 1894 she married John Quincy Johnson, an AME minister who taught mathematics at Tuskegee in the 1893–1894 school year. The next year he became president of Allen University, an AME college in Columbia, South Carolina. The Johnsons lived in Princeton, New Jersey, while John Quincy did postgraduate work at Princeton Theological Seminary. Then they moved to Nashville, Tennessee, where he pastored St. Paul AME Church, and Johnson became the mother of their three sons. No additional information on her professional life is known. She died at home, 1010 South Cherry Street, during childbirth complicated by dysentery.

While Halle Tanner Dillon Johnson was born into prominence, she achieved it later in her own right. She overcame the racial and gender bias of the period in which she lived to become a physician. In her work as resident physician at the Tuskegee Institute and as founder of a nurses' training program, she contributed to the health of rural black residents in Alabama and to the training of those who would later become health care professionals.

FURTHER READING

Johnson's papers are in the University of Pennsylvania Archives and the Archives and Special Collections on Women in Medicine, Black Women Physicians Project, the Medical College of Pennsylvania.

"Color and Sex No Barrier," *Atlanta University Bulletin* (Nov. 1891).

Hine, Darlene Clark, ed. *Black Women in America: An Historical Encyclopedia* (1993).

Smith, Jessie Carney, ed. *Notable Black American Women* (1992).

Sterling, Dorothy, ed. *We Are Your Sisters: Black Women in the Nineteenth Century* (1984).

This entry is taken from the *American National Biography* and is published here with the permission of the American Council of Learned Societies.

JESSIE CARNEY SMITH

Johnson, Harvey (4 Aug. 1843–Jan. 1923), minister and activist, was born to the slaves Thomas and Harriet Johnson in Fauquier County, Virginia. Little is known of his youth, though when Harvey was in his teen years—at the end of the Civil War—the Johnson family, like many newly free Virginians, moved to Alexandria. There Johnson became a congregant of the Alfred Street Baptist Church, was baptized, and when he received his own calling to preach was aided by Alfred Street's pastor, the Reverend Samuel W. Madden. Johnson attended one of the many schools that sprung up for freedmen in Alexandria, and then apparently went to a Quaker school in Philadelphia for a time. Ultimately Madden helped secure a place for Johnson at the new Wayland Seminary in Washington, D.C., which was fast becoming a key training ground for black clergy.

Johnson entered Wayland in 1868 and took his degree in 1872, but he was already preaching—both in Alexandria and in rural towns in Maryland and Virginia—sometimes under the auspices of the Baptist Home Mission Society. At the end of 1872 Baltimore's Union Baptist Church called on him to fill its pulpit; the young minister began to build a larger and stronger church and to have a growing voice in the community. On 17 April 1877 he married Amelia E. Hall, the nineteen-year-old daughter of former Marylanders who had moved to Canada. The Johnsons eventually had three children, a daughter Jessie E. in 1878 and two sons, Prentiss William and Harvey Jr., born in 1883 and 1884, respectively.

Johnson was both a stirring speaker and a skillful manager, and his congregation of about 250 doubled within his first two years with the church. Such growth gave him the confidence to separate the church from the funding of the white-run Union Association—and so from some of their control. By 1885 Union Baptist had more than two thousand members. Indeed, Union grew so much that it spawned other, new congregations—usually with Johnson's full blessing—including Macedonia Baptist in 1874 and Perkins Square Baptist in 1879.

Johnson's role as head of such a growing cluster of churches gave him some localized political power; as early as 1881 he joined with several other pastors and community leaders to call for fuller recognition of blacks' civil rights—and to push the Republican Party to remember its black constituents. By 1884 when he gave the dedication sermon at New York City's Mount Olive Baptist Church, Johnson had already attained the beginnings of a national reputation.

Both Johnson's sway in Baltimore and his skill led to increased scrutiny from white Baptists, who throughout the 1870s had maintained jurisdictional authority over all Baptist undertakings (including Baptist colleges and the Home Mission Society). In a three-party split among black Baptists—integrationists, moderates, and separatists—Johnson quickly emerged as a radical who demanded equal treatment and voice for black Baptists and who was often convinced that the way to achieve such was through maintaining separate black churches. Change was slow to come, but he repeatedly called for more autonomy for black churches and for more economic and political equality. He also gained some grudging respect from his white colleagues. In addition to his growing (if critical) voice in the Home Mission Society, Johnson served as a vice president of the mainly white Baptist Minister's Conference and was active in the Maryland Baptist state conventions.

Dissatisfied with the slow pace of change—and with the regressive and racist nature of some white Baptists' opinion of black churches—he formed the Colored Baptist Convention of Maryland in 1898, a year after delivering a fiery published speech that offered "A Plea for Our Work as Colored Baptists, Apart from the Whites." These concerns also led to an active stance against the pending merger of the Richmond Theological Seminary (which had given him a doctor of divinity degree in 1888) and his alma mater Wayland Seminary—which did eventually form two of the key building blocks of what became Virginia Union University. Throughout the 1890s in both speeches and a handful of published arguments (including letters to the *Richmond Planet*) Johnson repeatedly called for self-determination and economic independence for black Baptist colleges— just as he had for black churches. Later Johnson helped set up a school through the Colored Baptist Convention to train black ministers; the Clayton-Williams Academy worked for two decades to help the next generation of black Baptist clergy.

Johnson's church activism led naturally to community work; when he organized the Mutual United Brotherhood of Liberty (MUBL) in 1885, he did so with five other Baptist ministers. It is likely that the idea for the organization came in part from Johnson's support of the suit of his parishioners the Stewart sisters against the steamer *Sue* for their segregated accommodations, which ended in the Stewarts' victory in district court in February 1885. The MUBL was dedicated to the struggle for civil rights and was integral to securing the admission of the black attorney and Howard University graduate Everett J. Waring to the Maryland bar and to later legal fights for black education, including hiring black teachers. The MUBL gained some national prominence—FREDERICK DOUGLASS keynoted its first formal convention—and aided in Johnson's eventual work with the Colored Baptist Convention.

During these years Johnson's wife, AMELIA ETTA HALL JOHNSON, won some note as a writer and editor—eventually authoring three novels and several brief pieces for periodicals—and the Johnsons prospered economically. Their children were educated well, and in 1906 Harvey Jr. was one of the early graduates of the Baltimore Normal School for the Education of Colored Teachers. Johnson continued both preaching and activism well into the twentieth century. He eventually published at least half a dozen sermons in pamphlet form. His magnum opus, *The Nations from a New Point of View*, was published in book form by the National Baptist Publishing Board in 1903; it is a discussion of race and an extension of his earlier ideas. The book has generally been ignored by contemporary historians, who focus on the binaristic debate between BOOKER T. WASHINGTON and W. E. B. DuBOIS and deemphasize Johnson's brand of radical egalitarian Christianity.

In April 1912 Johnson was instrumental in founding the Baltimore branch of the National Association for the Advancement of Colored People (NAACP). He continued to pastor at Union Baptist, which celebrated his fifty-year anniversary in the pulpit in 1922, just a few months before his death.

FURTHER READING

The Daniel A. P. Murray Collection at the Library of Congress includes six of Johnson's sermons.

Grundman, Adolph H. "Northern Baptists and the Founding of Virginia Union University: The Perils of Paternalism," *Journal of Negro History* 63.1 (Jan. 1978).

Koger, A. Briscoe. *Negro Baptists of Maryland* (1946).

Simmons, William J. *Men of Mark: Eminent, Progressive, and Rising* (1887).

ERIC GARDNER

Johnson, Helene V. (7 July 1906–6 July 1995), writer, was born in Boston, Massachusetts, the daughter of Ella (Benson) Johnson and George William Johnson. Johnson was an only child and her parents separated shortly after her birth, resulting in her never knowing her father or her paternal grandparents. Johnson's maternal grandparents, Benjamin Benson and Helen Pease Benson (after whom Johnson was named), were born in slavery in South Carolina. Johnson's first cousin was the novelist and short story writer DOROTHY WEST and the pair grew up together in the Brookline section of Boston, spending most of their summers in Oak Bluffs, Massachusetts, on a Martha's Vineyard Island property owned by Benjamin Benson. From an early age both Johnson and West showed an interest in writing, which their families helped to foster by sending them to prestigious schools, as well as by providing them with a supplemental literary education. Together, the pair attended Boston's Lafayette School, the Martin School, and the Boston Girls' Latin School. Additionally, Johnson and West sought to further their literary skills by taking writing courses at Boston University and by joining a Boston organization called the Saturday Evening Quill Club, composed of aspiring black writers.

In 1924 Johnson submitted "Trees at Night," a poem composed of dark, evocative, nature images, to *Opportunity*—a magazine published by the Urban League that offered a venue for young black writers routinely excluded from white publications—which was accepted for publication. When the league held its first annual literary awards ceremony in May 1925, Johnson's poem won honorable mention. The July 1925 issue of *Opportunity* contained another Johnson poem, "My Race," and was followed by a third poem, "Metamorphism," in March 1926. These early poems by Johnson represent the themes of nature, racial oppression, black cultural pride, and female sexual awakening that would define her poetic work. Her use of these themes caused contemporary critics such as Verner D. Mitchell to hail her poetics as-"radical," both in her use of themes that defied the-genteel conventions of early-twentieth-century women writers and in her use of free verse as opposed to more traditional forms (Mitchell, 12).

Encouraged by her initial success, Johnson submitted three poems—"Fulfillment," "Magula," and "The Road"—to the magazine's 1926 contest. At Johnson's suggestion, West also submitted one of her short stories, and the pair persuaded their parents to let them attend the awards ceremony on 1 May 1926. In the competition Johnson's poems won first, fourth, and seventh levels of honorable mention, respectively, and West's story "The Typewriter" shared the second place prize for fiction with ZORA NEALE HURSTON for her story "Muttsy." In October and November 1926 Johnson also published poems in the *Messenger* and in the only issue of WALLACE THURMAN's journal *Fire!!*

One year later, still filled with awe for what West described as "the magical city of New York" (Mitchell, 6), the cousins decided to return, continuing their education at Columbia University's Extension Division, studying with the novelist John Erskine. With the help of Hurston, a lifelong friend to Johnson and West, the cousins were ushered into Harlem's literary renaissance, a period ranging from roughly 1920 until 1935 that represented an explosion of black literary, artistic, intellectual, and cultural production. The arrival of young female talents such as Johnson and West onto Harlem's literary scene was so noteworthy that it was later parodied by Wallace Thurman in his satiric novel *Infants of Spring* through the characters Hazel Jamison (Johnson) and Doris Westmore (West).

Shortly after arriving in New York, Johnson sold a poem—"Bottled"—to *Vanity Fair* magazine, which published it in the May 1927 issue. In June 1927, at the request of Hurston, who had received a grant and was going south to conduct research, Johnson and West moved from the Harlem YWCA on 137th Street to Hurston's 43 West 66th Street apartment, which was the only apartment building in mid-Manhattan that accepted black residents. When *Opportunity* held its third literary contest in 1927, Johnson's poems "Summer Matures" and "Sonnet to a Negro in Harlem" were awarded second and fourth place prizes, respectively. COUNTÉE CULLEN included a poem by Johnson in an all-black issue of the journal *Psalms* he was asked to guest-edit, as well as including eight of Johnson's poems in his *Caroling Dusk: An Anthology of Verse by Negro Poets* (1927). It was Cullen's inclusion of Johnson in his anthology that helped to cement her reputation as a promising Harlem Renaissance poet. In November 1928 Johnson published "A Missionary Brings a Young Native to America" in *Harlem* magazine, and between 1928 and 1931 five of Johnson's poems appeared in the *Saturday Evening Quill*, the annual publication of Boston's Quill Club. Additionally, JAMES WELDON JOHNSON included Johnson in the revised edition of his 1922 anthology *The Book of American Negro Poetry* (1931).

The stock market crash of 1929, which signaled the beginning of the end of the Harlem Renaissance, also signaled the end of Johnson's career as a poet. While West went on to be a more well-known figure from the Harlem Renaissance period with the publication of her novels *The Living Is Easy* (1948), *The Wedding* (1995), and her memoir *The Richer, The Poorer: Stories, Sketches, and Reminiscences* (1995), Johnson remained outside of the literary spotlight, publishing only about two dozen poems between 1925 and 1935, and is considered one of the minor poets of the period. Known for her shyness and desire to stay outside of the public eye, little is known of Johnson's life following the end of the Harlem Renaissance. In 1933 she married William Warner Hubbell III, a New York City motorman. In 1934 when West founded and released the first issue of the journal *Challenge: A Literary Quarterly*, she included a poem by Johnson. The third issue of *Challenge*, published in May 1935, included Johnson's last published poem "Let Me Sing My Song." On 18 September 1940 Johnson gave birth to her only child, Abigail Calachaly Hubbell (McGrath), in New York City, subsequently taking an extended hiatus from writing so that she could support her family, working outside the home as a civil service employee. Commenting upon Johnson's talent, the Pulitzer prize–winning poet YUSEF KOMUNYAKAA remarked that it is a shame "that she was unable to reconcile the demands of working nine to five and writing" (Mitchell, 9). From the 1960s to the early 1980s Johnson lived in an apartment at 210 Thompson Street in Greenwich Village. Johnson lived her entire adult life in New York City with the exception of several years spent in Cape Cod during the 1980s.

Although Johnson ceased publishing in 1935, she did continue to write. In 2000, a complete collection of Johnson's poems—entitled *This Waiting for Love: Helene Johnson, Poet of the Harlem Renaissance* (edited by Verner D. Mitchell)—was published and includes thirteen previously unpublished pieces, as well as photographs and selected letters. The publication of such a collection signals Johnson's importance as a poet who continues to affect writers with, as she wrote in her poem "Magula," her "Chromatic words, / Seraphic symphonies" (Mitchell, 34). Johnson died the day

before her eighty-ninth birthday at her daughter's home in Manhattan.

FURTHER READING
Boxwell, David A. "Helene Johnson," in *The Greenwood Encyclopedia of African American Literature*, vol. III, eds. Hans Ostrom and J. David Macey Jr. (2005): 874–875.
Ferguson, Sally Ann H. "Helene Johnson," *The Oxford Companion to African American Literature*, eds. William L. Andrews, Frances Smith Foster, and Trudier Harris (1997): 404.
Mitchell, Verner D., ed. *This Waiting for Love: Helene Johnson, Poet of the Harlem Renaissance* (2000).
Patterson, Raymond R. "Helene Johnson," *Dictionary of Literary Biography*, vol. 51, eds. Thadious Davis and Trudier Harris (1987): 164–167.
Wagner, Jean. *Black Poets of the United States* (1973): 184.
Obituary: *New York Times*, 11 July 1995.

J. JAMES IOVANNONE

Johnson, Henry (1897–5 July 1929), soldier honored for his heroic actions in France during World War I while fighting against the Germans, was born Henry Lincoln Johnson to a poor family in Alexandria, Virginia. Small in stature, weighing only 130 pounds and standing five feet four, Johnson traveled north when in his teens. He worked in a coal yard, as a soda mixer in a pharmacy, and as a redcap porter at the Union Station on Broadway in Albany, New York. He met his wife Minnie at church and they later moved to downtown Albany, close to his train station job.

On 5 June 1917 Johnson enlisted in the army, becoming part of the all black Company C, 15th New York Infantry, later renamed the 369th United States Infantry. Known as the "Harlem Hellfighters," this infantry spent most of its time on the front lines and built a reputation for never retreating and never leaving a soldier behind for capture. During his first months in the army Private Johnson completed guard duty in Albany and Rotterdam, New York, before attending combat training in South Carolina. On New Year's Day 1918 he arrived in France, where the 369th Infantry received materials, weapons, and clothing from the French command. The unit also trained in French military tactics and strategies. After only a few weeks of special training and an assignment unloading ships and digging trenches, Johnson was ordered to guard Outpost 29 in the Argonne Forest.

A fierce battle began on 15 May 1918 when German troops tossed grenades at Johnson and Private NEEDHAM ROBERTS. Suffering injuries to his lower body, Roberts was unable to continue fighting. When the Germans attempted to capture his comrade, Johnson attacked the advancing troops with his rifle butt and a nine-inch double-edged bolo knife, killing several of them. Though he was badly wounded, Roberts managed to hand grenades one by one to Johnson, who lobbed them at the Germans as they retreated. The German unit that attacked Johnson and Roberts was estimated to have consisted of at least twenty-four men.

Following the attack a stunned, wounded, and barely conscious Johnson was taken to a field hospital for treatment. He had sustained injuries, mostly cuts, to his arms, back, feet, and face. One of his twenty-one wounds required that a silver plate be placed inside his left foot. Johnson later described his battlefield heroics as a natural response, saying, "I just fought for my life. A rabbit would have done that." His own personal modesty notwithstanding, Johnson was awarded the Croix de Guerre, with star and golden palm, France's highest citation for bravery. Johnson's white American counterparts, however, were not so congratulatory. Johnson was promoted to sergeant before his discharge from the army on 14 February 1919, but because his injuries were not documented, he would not be eligible to receive disability benefits once he returned home.

Johnson participated in a Manhattan homecoming parade as a celebrated soldier days after he returned to the United States. In later years he traveled across the United States assisting the army with its recruiting efforts and marketing Liberty Bonds (his likeness was even used in advertising for Victory War Stamps). Despite returning as a hero, Johnson was unable to go back to his previous job at the Albany train station because of the extent of the injuries he had sustained in France. Racism too continued to dog him and other returning black veterans who watched as racial tensions escalated during the period known as the Red Summer of 1919. Not seeing an end to his struggle, Johnson soon succumbed to alcohol. In 1924 his wife Minnie left him and took their children to Schenectady, New York, where they were raised by their paternal grandfather, Herman Johnson, though they continued to see their father on rare occasions.

Henry Johnson died in 1929, in poverty and obscurity, having had no support from the government and nation he had served. On 25 June1996 Johnson was posthumously awarded the Purple Heart. A statue in Washington Park and a street, both in Albany, have since been named in his honor. His image is also emblazoned on the Liberty Memorial mural in Kansas City, Missouri. Though rumored to have been buried in an abandoned cemetery in Albany, Johnson was actually buried in Arlington National Cemetery. Johnson's son, Herman, campaigned for thirty years to see his father recognized by the U.S. government. On 11 April 2003 Johnson was awarded the U.S. Army's Distinguished Service Cross for bravery. During the ceremony Herman Johnson presented the medal to the Albany chapter of New York's Army National Guard 369th Infantry Regiment, the all-black unit in which his father had served.

FURTHER READING

Reasons, George, and Sam Patrick. *They Had a Dream: 53 Outstanding Black Americans Vividly Portrayed in Words & Drawings* (1971).

TIFFANI MURRAY

Johnson, Henry (11 June 1850–21 Jan. 1904), Indian Wars soldier and Medal of Honor recipient, was born in Boydton, Virginia. Nothing is known of his early life, except that he was likely enslaved until the end of the Civil War in 1865.

Henry Johnson enlisted in the U.S. Army in 1867, having previously worked as a laborer. He joined the 9th Cavalry Regiment, which was one of just six all-black regiments (soon consolidated to four) authorized by Congress the previous year. While many volunteer all-black regiments were formed during the Civil War and were vital to the Union Army, all these regiments were disbanded soon after the war ended. However, it was soon recognized that African Americans had a part to play in the army in the immediate postwar years, and Congress acted accordingly. Not only were these new professional soldiers loyal to the Union, they were also capable soldiers. Indeed, men like Johnson, THOMAS BOYNE, and GEORGE JORDAN are important just for the fact that they were among the first group of black professional soldiers ever to serve in the army during times of peace and war.

Henry Johnson and the men of the 9th Cavalry, as well as the black soldiers that served in the other newly designated regiments for African Americans, the 10th Cavalry and the 24th and 25th Infantry regiments, soon became collectively known as "Buffalo Soldiers" for their outstanding service in the west. Manned by black enlisted personnel and junior officers and commanded by white officers, the buffalo soldier regiments, in conjunction with white army regiments, helped open the American west by fighting the Native American warriors who resisted the heavy influx of settlers into their tribal lands, protecting new settlements and mining outposts, as well as performing a whole host of other duties. These arduous duties were not only dangerous, but were also performed under the most extreme weather conditions, including the desert heat of the Arizona and New Mexico territories, or the extreme winter conditions found in the Dakotas or Montana territory. However, despite these conditions, the Buffalo Soldiers were known as excellent fighters and gained the grudging admiration of both their fellow soldiers who were white and the Native American warriors they battled.

As for the career of Henry Johnson, he spent the first eight years of his career with the 9th Cavalry in Troop D on the Texas frontier and stationed at Fort Davis. However, the men of the 9th spent a lot of time in the saddle, patrolling the area between the Rio Grande River and El Paso for many continuous months. In 1875 the men of the 9th were sent further west to fight the Apache and Ute tribes in Texas, the territory of New Mexico, and Colorado. On 1 October 1879, Sergeant Henry Johnson and the men of Troop D, commanded by Captain Francis Dodge, departed their post and marched over 100 miles in less than a day to provide reinforcement for a detachment of the 5th Cavalry, which had been battling a force of Ute warriors at Milk River, Colorado, since 25 September. During the action, the cavalry and infantry forces and a large wagon train they were escorting took heavy casualties and sent for help. When Dodge and his black troopers arrived on 2 October, the situation and morale of the embattled soldiers improved; one of Sergeant Johnson's many duties was to supervise the digging of rifle pits in exposed forward positions and direct the fire of his men. It was later said of Johnson that his "coolness and bravery under fire steadied and inspired the buffalo soldiers, as well as the other besieged troopers" (Hanna, p. 70). Two days later, when his men were taking heavy fire and running out of water, Johnson crawled down to the river to get water, and once back among his men continually exposed himself to hostile fire while distributing it to wounded soldiers, both black and white. The battle finally ended on 5 October, when further reinforcements arrived and the Utes were driven off, leaving behind twenty-three dead and forty-four wounded army soldiers.

After the battle at Milk River, Sergeant Johnson continued his cavalry service, with only several brief interruptions between enlistments, until his retirement in July 1898. While brilliant under fire, Johnson, like many peacetime soldiers, was not always a model citizen. He was reduced in rank several times during the course of his later career, and in March 1881, while serving with the 10th Cavalry, was court-martialed and incarcerated for a time in the army prison at Fort Leavenworth, Kansas. In 1890, eleven years after taking part in the battle at Milk River, Private Henry Johnson applied for the Medal of Honor (an acceptable practice at this time), which was supported by his old commander, Francis Dodge. Henry Johnson was subsequently awarded the Medal of Honor on 22 September 1890. After his retirement, Johnson moved to Washington, DC, and at his death, being poor and in ill health for many years, was living at the Washington Asylum. As befitting his distinguished military service, Sergeant Henry Johnson was buried at Arlington National Cemetery with full military honors.

FURTHER READING

Hanna, Charles W. *African American Recipients of the Medal of Honor* (2002).

Schubert, Frank N. *Black Valor: Buffalo Soldiers and the Medal of Honor, 1870–1898* (1997).

GLENN ALLEN KNOBLOCK

Johnson, Henry "Hank" (1897?–24 Oct. 1944), activist, founding member of the National Negro Congress and the International Workers Order, and organizer for the Congress of Industrial Organizations (CIO), was best known as assistant national director of the Packinghouse Workers Organizing Committee, centered in Chicago.

Accounts of Johnson's life prior to 1932 rely on the transcript of a 1937 Works Progress Administration interview. He was born and lived until the age of nine in a rural area of Texas between the Colorado and Brazos rivers. The WPA account records his birthplace as Siblo, which may be phonetic for Cibolo, at the time an isolated rural town outside of San Antonio. Johnson recalled being closer to the Gulf of Mexico and "seventy five miles from the Louisiana state line," but both rivers reach the Gulf about 150 miles from Port Arthur. Even the year he was born is unknown.

He recalled being one of eight boys with three sisters; his father grew cotton and corn on his own land, did plastering and bricklaying during the winter to obtain sufficient cash to pay debts, sometimes driving wild horses and cattle across the border from Mexico to sell, and worked in logging camps and sawmills. Known as a "bad nigger" for his membership in the militant Industrial Workers of the World, Johnson's father was an expert marksman with a six-shooter. Between 1906 and 1908, the family had to flee the area to escape lynching, after an altercation that began when a white man kicked the Johnson's family dog. The family hid in a pond for eight hours, warned by a neighbor and a white IWW union brother, who had worked with Henry's father in the oil fields and logging camps. The neighbor took them by wagon to Columbus, Texas (a good distance from either the Gulf coast or Cibolo), to catch a train to San Antonio. The neighbor's "white" skin didn't save him from being killed by his own brother-in-law when it became known he had helped the Johnsons to escape (Cullen, p. 167; Brier, pp. 418–419).

In San Antonio, Johnson worked with his father doing bricklaying and plastering. At about the age of thirteen, he went out on his own. Living in Houston in 1917, he narrowly escaped being beaten during the Camp Logan Riot, and soon after left for Huntsville, Alabama, attending a Seventh Day Adventist school, and organizing a singing quartet. Moving to Oklahoma City, Johnson recalled that he witnessed another race riot, and soon after moved to Detroit. He worked six months in a Ford plant, was fired when a foreman discovered his old plasterers' union card, then did plastering and worked as a mechanic for an auto dealer. Moving on to New York, he finished high school, then earned a bachelor's degree from City College in 1934. The same year he married the sister of a classmate.

In 1932 he joined the Communist Party and became an organizer for the International Workers Order, a communist-inspired fraternal benefit and insurance association, organizing longshoremen in Baltimore, Norfolk, and Richmond, then moved on to Chicago, where in 1935 he plunged into building the local branch of the National Negro Congress, one of the more influential NNC branches, commonly referred to as the "Chicago Council" (Tompkins, p. 138). The NNC organizer Ishmael P. Flory recalled that Johnson "could work a crowd, both black and white, like few others" (Tompkins, p. 140). The following year, the Committee on Industrial Organization (CIO) was launching an organizing drive in the steel industry. Industrial relations managers were hoping black workers would be loyal to the company, as many had been during the 1919 steel strike. In July, the CIO regional organizer Van Bittner accepted the assistance of Johnson, James McDonald, and Eleanor Rye from the NNC for the new Steel Workers Organizing Committee (SWOC) (Bates, pp. 138–140).

George Kimbley, who claimed to have signed the first SWOC card in Gary, recalled Johnson as "an outstanding speaker and organizer. He was black and well educated," and "under his leadership we set up a volunteer organizing committee, and we just raked the town" (Needleman, p. 28). By October, workers in Chicago's stockyards demanded "When is the CIO coming to the yards?" After several thousand signed cards were delivered to Bittner, he convened the Packinghouse Workers Organizing Committee in 1937, with Johnson as assistant director.

Thoroughly familiar with workers' legal rights under the newly passed National Labor Relations Act, Johnson worked with two rank-and-file leaders at the Armour Soap Works, Richard Saunders and Burrette King, to develop effective strategy and tactics. Johnson becoming known as the "Negro orator of the yards," for his powerful lunch-hour speeches. PWOC signed its first written contract at one of the smaller meatpacking plants, Roberts and Oakes, after "Johnson took us by the hand, told us how to do it," recalled the PWOC member Jesse Vaughn. By the end of 1938, five out of six of the smaller plants had signed union contracts. But the main target was Armour and Company, the largest meatpacker, with plants in several states.

In 1939 Johnson told the *Chicago Defender*, "The present conflict at Armour & Company is more than a battle between a corporation and a union. It is also another chapter in the long epic of the Negro people. The PWOC has not only protected workers in their rights as workers but in their rights as citizens. Since the coming of the PWOC, Negroes entitled to promotion have a better chance of getting it because the union feels that every man has the right to advance according to his ability, whatever his color" (Street, p. 16). Around the same time, the *Defender* editorialized, "because the PWOC planted the seed of unity in the stony soil of Packingtown, Negroes walk freely and in safety. Any public place which refused them service would be quickly put out of business by a boycott of the white union members. On the very streets where danger once lurked for Negroes, colored men stop for long chats about baseball with Polish or Irish workers" (Street, p. 11).

Johnson demonstrated another face of interracial unity when he negotiated a contract between the Union Stockyards Transit Company and livestock handlers, still mostly Irish-American, in 1938. At other companies, with a large number of Polish and Lithuanian first- or second-generation immigrants, African Americans often filled leadership positions because they understood English better, and were more articulate, with higher rates of elementary and high school attendance and graduation (Street, p. 14).

In 1938 Johnson made a brief but important visit to Fort Worth, where the Armour plant was considered a potential weak link in national PWOC organizing. Johnson's presence and oratory inspired African American workers, about one third of employees at the plant, many of whom were first hired during a 1921–1922 strike. His oratory and polished manner of speaking also reassured workers who thought of themselves as "white," including the strategically placed livestock handlers (Zieger, pp. 161–163).

Rising to a position in the district political bureau of the Communist Party, Johnson removed himself from party work when it became a threat to his role in the labor movement. In 1939, on the eve of National Labor Relations Board representation elections in the Armour company plants, the Texas Democratic representative Martin Dies scheduled hearings in Chicago by the House Un-American Activities Committee (HUAC) on communist influence in the meatpacking industry. At the hearing, Johnson exposed criminal records of local officials for the rival AFL Amalgamated Meatcutters union, and suggested that Dies return to his home state of Texas, to investigate the Un-American activities of the Ku Klux Klan and lynch mobs. Four thousand Armour workers then voted for CIO representation, with only one thousand for the Amalgamated, and another thousand for no union. Contracts were signed early in 1940, ending an era described by PWOC member Sophie Kosciolowski: "the only difference between an outright slave and us was that we could go home" (Halpern, p. 166).

In 1940 Johnson sided with the CIO founder John L. Lewis, president of the United Mine Workers of America, who supported Republican presidential candidate Wendell Wilkie. CIO leadership and membership both remained loyal to Democratic president Franklin D. Roosevelt. In a complex interplay with local grassroots demand for a fully constituted union, opposed by increasingly bureaucratic CIO leadership, Johnson was dismissed from his post as assistant national director in 1941. He sought to bring

PWOC locals into United Mine Workers District 50, established as an alternative to CIO affiliation. Ironically, the CIO relied on Johnson's former comrades in the Communist Party to defeat this disruption, as the United Packinghouse Workers of America organized by constitutional convention in 1943.

Johnson became assistant director, midwest region, of District 50, until his death in 1944. He and another black organizer expelled from PWOC, Arthel Shelton—a beef butcher who had led a strike in Sioux City, Iowa, in 1938–1939—had a bitter argument over an organizing drive at a utility company in northern Indiana. During a formal inquiry convened by the UMWA, Shelton pulled out a pistol, wounded two others, and shot Johnson several times, killing him.

FURTHER READING

Barrett, James R. *Work and Community in the Jungle: Chicago's Packinghouse Workers 1894–1922* (1987).

Bates, Beth Tompkins. *Pullman Porters and the Rise of Protest Politics in Black America, 1925–1945* (2001).

Cohen, Lizabeth. *Making a New Deal: Industrial Workers in Chicago, 1919–1939* (1999).

Cullen, David O'Donald. *The Texas Left: The Radical Roots of Lone Star Liberalism* (2010).

Halpern, Rick. *Down on the Killing Floor: Black and White Workers in Chicago's Packinghouses, 1904–54* (1997).

Halpern, Rick, and Roger Horowitz. *Meatpackers: An Oral History of Black Packinghouse Workers and Their Struggle for Racial and Economic Equality* (1996).

Needleman, Ruth. *Black Freedom Fighters in Steel: The Struggle for Democratic Unionism* (2003).

Newell, Barbara Warne. *Chicago and the Labor Movement: Metropolitan Unionism in the 1930s* (1961).

Street, Paul. "The Backbone of the Union." *Chicago History* 29, no. 1, (Summer 2000): 4–21.

Zieger, Robert H. *Organized Labor in the Twentieth Century South* (1991).

CHARLES ROSENBERG

Johnson, Herman A. (19 Dec. 1916–17 Feb. 2004), civil rights and community activist, business leader, state legislator, and Tuskegee Airman, was born in New York state to HENRY JOHNSON, a World War I hero and recipient of the American Distinguished Service Cross. His maternal grandfather, Herman Phoenix, was in the early 1900s a leader in organizing the Niagara, New York, branch of the NAACP.

Johnson himself was thirteen when he joined the NAACP. Although he lived and worked in several cities, he was most connected with Kansas City, Missouri. He earned a bachelor's degree in economics from Cornell University in 1938 and a master's degree in business administration from the University of Chicago in 1940.

Soon after earning his master's degree, Johnson was a statistician for the War Production Board. During World War II, he enlisted and fought with the 332nd Fighter Group, known as the Tuskegee Airmen. Attaining the rank of major, he was the group's executive officer, working with General BENJAMIN O. DAVIS, JR. After the war, Johnson continued as an aide to Davis until he was appointed a director of the Freedman's Hospital in Washington, D.C., a teaching hospital for Howard University's medical school.

Stepping down from his post at Freedman's Hospital, Johnson entered the insurance and realty profession. He was made executive vice president as well as board member of the Gross-Robbins Realty Company. He later managed the offices of the North Carolina Mutual Life Insurance Company, Dunbar Life Insurance Company, and from 1954 to 1957 was vice president of the James E. Scott Realty Company, where he supervised a sales staff of twenty people. He went on to run the district offices of the Supreme Life Insurance Company in Washington, Cleveland, and Toledo, Ohio. In 1959 he was transferred to Kansas City, where he met Dorothy Hodge Davis. After a brief courtship, they were married in 1960. Soon after the marriage, however, his company decided to transfer him again to another city. But Johnson had found a home in Kansas City, working hard to become one of its civic leaders. Not wanting to move again, he resigned and opened his own business, the Herman Johnson Company, specializing in real estate, insurance and appraisals. Johnson built his company into one of Kansas City's leading businesses.

Looking back on Johnson's success, the president of Kansas City's Freedom, Inc., a black political club, noted that Johnson was an "astute businessman who demonstrated to the broader community that African Americans possessed business acumen." In fact, Johnson argued persuasively and effectively that Missouri's businesses and trade unions hire more of the state's black citizens. He then took on a much larger role in championing civil rights as president of the local chapter of NAACP. During the 1960s he campaigned against police brutality, fought to increase minority employment in local schools, and had a hand in persuading the University of Missouri-Kansas City law school to accept its first black student. "We're here. We want to live. We're not going to lay down and die," he informed Kansas City about its African American community. "If you close all the doors, you're going to have a bunch of hoodlums. You'll have things you don't want: welfare, crime and dope. It's as much a civic thing as anything." While marching with student protesters in the 1960s, Johnson was tear gassed three times in one day.

But it was in the boardroom that he felt he could best effect change. He worked hard with the white establishment, even though that strategy angered some in the black community who called him a "white man's Negro." After Johnson's death, one of his successors as president of Kansas City's NAACP said that he had "a lot of wisdom and could see beyond all the criticism. He saw that it would take all of us [blacks and whites] working together, and that's what everybody's doing today."

Johnson served on and chaired numerous boards throughout his active life, including the National NAACP Legal Defense Fund, American Red Cross, Chamber of Commerce of Greater Kansas City, the Civic Council of Kansas City, the Kansas City Commission on Human Relations, the University of Kansas City, the Missouri Association for Social Welfare, Missouri's Division of Youth Services, the Jackson County Land Trust and the Douglass National Bank. He also served two terms in the Missouri House of Representatives, from 1968 to 1972. He was then appointed by the governor to the State Capitol Restoration and Sesquicentennial Commission, Citizens Committee for State Reorganization, Lewis and Clark Trail Committee, and the Committee for Children and Youth.

Bridging that racial divide took on symbolic meaning in 2006 when Kansas City renovated a ninety-year-old bridge and, in a citywide ceremony, renamed it the Herman Johnson Bridge. The renaming of the bridge was the last in a long list of honors bestowed on Johnson over the years. Among those honors were the National Conference of Christians and Jews Protestant Award (1987), Urban League Image Award in Business (1990), William Jewell College's William F. Yates Distinguished Service Medallion (1999), Bank of America Small Business Lifetime Achievement Award (1999), Kansas City Economic Development Corporation's James C. Denneny Spirit Award (2001), and Truman Heartland Foundation Outstanding Citizens Award (2001). In 1998 the University of Missouri-Kansas City renamed its Black Scholarship Fund after Johnson, and in 2001 the Greater Kansas City Chamber of Commerce established in his honor the Herman A. Johnson Mentor Program for Minorities.

Johnson and his wife left the bulk of their estate for the education of minorities. They established the Dorothy H. Johnson Multicultural Scholarship in Journalism or Social Work at the University of Missouri-Kansas City and the Herman Johnson Minority Scholarship at the University of Kansas.

"My dad was ahead of his time," recalled his daughter, Tara, who has followed in his footsteps as a civil rights and business and civic leader. "He was our living example of how you can pick up your talent and your wisdom and sit at the table."

FURTHER READING

Some of the information for this entry was gathered through interviews with Tara Johnson, daughter of Herman Johnson, on 17 and 29 Nov. 2006 and Joe Mattox, a Kansas City historian, on 14 Nov. 2006.

Adofo, Adjoa. "Ceremonial Naming Honors the Life of a Civic Bridge Builder," *Kansas City Star*, 20 Nov. 2006.

Penn, Steve. "Bridge Name Is a Truly Fitting Honor," *Kansas City Star*, 12 Sept. 2006.

Uhlenhuth, Karen. "Working Adversity: To Herman Johnson, a Job Can Transform a Life. And He Wants to Make Sure Everyone Has a Chance," *Kansas City Star Magazine*, 15 Jan. 1995.

Obituary: *Kansas City Star*, 18 Feb. 2004.

STEPHEN L. HARRIS

Johnson, Isaac (1844–5 Dec. 1905), escaped slave, soldier, stonemason, and autobiographer, was born on a farm in Elizabethtown, Nelson County, Kentucky, in 1844. Four years earlier his mother, JANE JOHNSON, had been kidnapped in Madagascar by the slave traders Griffin Yeager and his brothers. She was brought to the United States and served as Yeager's slave until his death. Richard Yeager inherited his father's farm and Jane Johnson. The couple, who lived as husband and wife, had four sons, and Isaac Johnson was the second oldest. In 1851, when Johnson was seven years old, Yeager sold the farm and told Jane and their sons that he had to travel to New Orleans in order to sell his horses. Yeager's family waited in vain for approximately two months for his return until a sheriff took Johnson, his mother, and brothers to Bardstown, Kentucky, where they were sold to different buyers. Johnson later learned that his father had arranged for them to be sold at the slave auction.

During the next decade, Johnson worked for several masters in Kentucky, and he tried unsuccessfully to escape twice. In 1861, when Johnson was eighteen, he met Union soldiers and was hired by Captain Smith. The officer gave Johnson a revolver and twenty rounds of cartridges and ordered him to shoot any man who attempted to deny him liberty. Johnson went to Detroit with Smith, and on 3 February 1864, Johnson enlisted in the First Michigan Colored Infantry (later designated as the 102nd United States Colored Troops). Although he was wounded during several battles, including the battle of Honey Hill, South Carolina, Johnson remained with the regiment until the Civil War ended.

After the war, Johnson moved to Ontario, Canada, where he was employed as a stonemason. In 1874 Johnson, at the age of thirty, married twenty-year-old Theadocia Allen, who was born in Chateaugay, New York, and they became the parents of seven children. In 1883 Johnson built the now extant Chamberlin Crossing Bridge, which was a four-arch stone structure between two St. Lawrence County, New York, towns: Madrid and Waddington. In 1884 Johnson and his family moved to Waddington, where Johnson built the Town Hall, which was placed on the National Historic Register in 1992. Johnson built other stone structures in St. Lawrence County, including buildings in Ogdensburg, the town where the Johnson family moved in 1890. Johnson's autobiography, *Slavery Days in Old Kentucky. A True Story of a Father Who Sold His Wife and Four Children; By One of the Children*, published in 1901, ends with Johnson providing his Ogdensburg address. He lacked knowledge of what happened to his mother and brothers after the slave auction, and he included his address hoping that *Slavery Days* would enable his relatives to find him. Four years later on 5 December, Isaac Johnson suffered a heart attack and died at his home.

FURTHER READING

Johnson, Isaac. *Slavery Days in Old Kentucky. A True Story of a Father Who Sold His Wife and Four Children. By One of the Children.* 1901. (2009).

Marston, Hope Irvin. *Isaac Johnson: From Slave to Stonecutter* (2003).

LINDA M. CARTER

Johnson, J. J. (22 Jan. 1924–4 Feb. 2001), trombonist, composer, and arranger, was born James Louis Johnson in Indianapolis, Indiana, the son of

James Horace Johnson and Nina Geiger Johnson. The church was a dominant influence in the lives of Johnson and his two younger sisters when they were young. Johnson's mother and father, who worshiped at a Baptist church and at a Methodist church, respectively, on the same street, insisted on bringing up their children in the traditions of both denominations. Johnson's mother hired the church organist to teach him the piano at the age of nine. Later, at Crispus Attucks High School, the only African American public high school in Indianapolis, Johnson became passionate about music. Initially he was forced to-play the baritone saxophone, but by the time that-he was fourteen he was appearing in the high school band and the YMCA marching brass band as a trombonist.

In the spring of 1942, against his father's wishes, Johnson joined a local band, the Snookum Russell Orchestra, of which the trumpeter FATS NAVARRO was also a member. The group disbanded shortly thereafter, but Johnson's apprenticeship as a professional musician took off when, in October 1942, the visiting Benny Carter asked him to stand in for his absent trombonist. Carter and Johnson's musical relationship continued for another two and a half years as the band traveled extensively throughout the country; Johnson's earliest recordings are with the Benny Carter Orchestra, although Johnson was featured only as a sideman. His first recorded solo appears in a performance with Benny Carter of Cole Porter's "Love for Sale." During this time, Johnson was also asked to play at the very first Jazz at the Philharmonic concert.

By the mid-1940s Johnson felt confined and underutilized in Carter's big band format. He left the band to participate in the bebop revolution that was taking place on New York's Fifty-second Street. Johnson, whose fluid style and rapid-fire technique caught the attention of CHARLIE PARKER and DIZZY GILLESPIE, pioneered the playing of the trombone in a bebop arrangement. His recording debut was on 26 June 1946 as leader of a quintet called Jay Jay Johnson and His Beboppers, which included COUNT BASIE's Orchestra, a group that he had been playing with sporadically.

On 23 September 1947, Johnson married Vivian Elora Freeman, a high school sweetheart; they had two sons. In December of that year he sat in on recording sessions with the COLEMAN HAWKINS, ILLINOIS JACQUET, and Charlie Parker groups, as well as with his own quintet. By the early 1950s studio work for Johnson became less frequent, so he joined an all-star sextet led by OSCAR PETTIFORD on a USO tour through Korea, Japan, and the South Pacific. He left the tour early—probably because of a drug habit. Like many jazz musicians in New York at the time, Johnson had his bout with drug addiction, but by all accounts he never developed a heroin problem as serious or prolonged as Charlie Parker's, MILES DAVIS's, or Stan Getz's. Nevertheless, in August 1952 Johnson left the jazz scene in New York and took a job as a blueprint inspector for Sperry Gyroscope in Long Island. This "self-prescribed rehabilitation" lasted for two years, and Johnson was seldom seen performing. He did manage to sit in with Davis's sextet in a 1953 Blue Note recording session that included the titles "Tempus Fugit," "Ray's Idea," "C.T.A.," and Johnson's own compositions "Kelo" and "Enigma." In 1954, after leaving his job at Sperry Gyroscope, Johnson began playing with fellow trombonist Kai Winding. The collaboration marked the beginning of the most commercially and critically successful phase of Johnson's career. The Jay & Kai Group, as they became known, recorded several albums that featured a unique duetting of trombone instrumentation.

Partly because of the influence of conductor/ composer Gunther Schuller, Johnson's career began to move in other directions. Commissioned by the New York Classical Jazz and Classical Music Society to compose a piece for solo brass instruments and brass ensemble, Johnson recorded *Poem for Brass* in October 1956. The result of Johnson's growing familiarity with Central European modern classical music, especially the work of Paul Hindemith, *Poem for Brass* combined jazz and classical idioms and became a significant example of what Schuller called "third-stream music."

In June 1957 Johnson embarked on his first European tour, with concerts in Sweden, France, Belgium, Germany, and Holland. Back in New York in 1959, he was called as a key witness in one of the early "police card" cases. Since Prohibition, musicians in New York had been required by law to obtain a cabaret license from the New York Police Department before performing. The enforcement of the law by the NYPD was a grossly unfair and capricious use of power. Because of a 1946 conviction involving possession of a hypodermic needle, Johnson's card was revoked, and he was forced to apply for renewal every few months. Although the case did not overturn the licensing policy, Johnson's powerful testimony helped him get his card back and struck a heavy blow against the legality of the policy.

Later that year Johnson added the trumpeter Freddie Hubbard and the bassist Arthur Harper to his sextet, which went on to record one of Johnson's finest albums, *J.J. Inc.* The album contained some of Johnson's best-known compositions: "Shutterbug," "Fatback," "Aquarius," "In Walked Horace," "Minor Mist," "Mohawk," and "Turnpike," which was not issued on the original vinyl album but was included in the 1998 CD rerelease. The following year, 1960, Johnson disbanded the sextet to devote more time to composing. The fruit of this labor was the thirty-five-minute *Perceptions*. Commissioned by Gillespie, the six-part work was recorded on 22 May 1961 with a large orchestra under the direction of Gunther Schuller. Of *Perceptions*, which was Johnson's most ambitious and extended composition ever, Schuller said: "Beyond all externals of form and technique, this music combines an eloquent musical imagination with a strongly disciplined mind, producing an enjoyable music of depth, pulsating warmth and infectious spirit."

In early 1965 Johnson's career again took a turn when he received an offer to play in QUINCY JONES's soundtrack for the Sidney Lumet film *The Pawnbroker*. Emboldened by this experience, Johnson moved to Los Angeles in 1970 and worked on the music for several television shows, including *Mayberry R.F.D.*, *The Danny Thomas Show*, *That Girl*, *Mod Squad*, *Starsky and Hutch*, *The Six Million Dollar Man*, and *Mike Hammer*. His movie credits, either orchestrating or composing, include *Man and Boy*, *Top of the Heap*, *Across 110th Street*, *Cleopatra Jones*, and *Shaft*.

In the late 1980s Johnson and his wife returned to Indianapolis. There he received an honorary doctor of music degree from Indiana University and the Indiana Governor's Art Award in 1989. In 1991 his wife died of a stroke, and Johnson recorded a dedicatory album entitled *Vivian*. On 11 September 1992 he married Carolyn Reid, who acted as his business manager until his retirement in 1996. Up until then, Johnson continued to perform and record actively. He died in Indianapolis.

Arguably the greatest of all jazz trombonists, Johnson will always be remembered, first and foremost, as the man who modernized the instrument. Through his virtuosity and technical innovations, Johnson made it possible for the trombone to assume as important a position in bebop and other subsequent jazz movements as the saxophone and trumpet. Johnson is also duly esteemed for his prolific and diverse body of compositions; over a span of fifty years, he recorded everything from big band to experimental post-bebop works, and from hit musical arrangements for blaxploitation films to third-stream music.

FURTHER READING
Berrett, Joshua, and Louis G. Bourgois III. *The Musical World of J. J. Johnson* (1999).
Carter, Don. *J. J. Johnson Collection* (1996).
This entry is taken from the *American National Biography* and is published here with the permission of the American Council of Learned Societies.

STEFAN VRANKA

Johnson, Jack (31 Mar. 1878–10 June 1946), world boxing champion, was born Arthur John Johnson in Galveston, Texas, the eldest son of Henry Johnson, a janitor and former slave, and Tiny (maiden name unknown). Johnson landed in many-schoolyard fights, usually returning home beaten, bruised, and crying unless his sister came to his defense. Only when his mother, the more dominant of his parents, threatened him with a worse whipping did he begin to fight back. After attending public school for six years, he assisted his invalid father and then drifted from one job to another, working as a horse trainer, a baker, and a dockworker, usually near Galveston, although his autobiography lists more exotic, far-flung locations. That memoir contains serial exaggerations and embellishments, many of which are repeated in the Tony- and Pulitzer Prize–winning stage play (1969) and later movie (1970), *The Great White Hope*.

Johnson also participated in "battle royals," in which he and eight or more black youths, often blindfolded, fought each other. The last youth standing won only a few coins. Such fights, staged for the amusement of whites, were intended to strip young African Americans of self-respect; for Johnson, however, they instilled a strong sense of grievance against a white power structure that tried to confine him. These bouts also led him into the realm of professional boxing. After several fights in Texas and Chicago, most of which he won, Johnson was matched in Galveston in 1901 against Joe Choynski, a veteran heavyweight from the golden era of Jewish American boxing. Although Choynski was much slower than his nimble-footed challenger, he knocked the black fighter to the canvas with a right cross. Johnson remained there after a count of ten, at which point five Texas Rangers climbed into the ring to arrest both boxers under a state law that prohibited prizefighting. The two men shared a cell for three weeks, during which time Johnson

Jack Johnson, the first African-American world heavyweight boxing champion, 31 March 1915. (Library of Congress/ George Grantham Bain Collection.)

learned much about the art of boxing from his fellow prisoner. After his release, Johnson fought several bouts, mostly against black opponents, and in 1903 he defeated "Denver" Ed Martin on points to win the black heavyweight title. The conventions of boxing did not prohibit fights across the color line, but following the lead of John L. Sullivan in 1885, all world heavyweight champions had refused to defend their title against blacks. Johnson was determined to end that restriction. Between 1905 and 1908 he defeated several white former champions with ease, approaching those bouts with an uncharacteristic savagery. A Philadelphia newspaper reported in 1905 that Johnson, at six feet two inches and two hundred pounds, rendered Jack Monroe a "mass of palpitating gelatine" (Roberts, 43). Against black opponents Johnson emphasized speed, defensive counterpunching, and showmanship. However, he quickly tired of defeating black no-hopers and white has-beens, and in late 1906 he hired an ambitious white manager, Sam Fitzpatrick. With Fitzpatrick's backing, Johnson toured Britain and Australia in 1907, defeating several fighters and

enhancing his reputation as a world heavyweight contender. The next year he followed the reigning champion Tommy Burns to England and Australia, trying to goad him into a contest. Burns initially tried to avoid Johnson but was willing to abandon the principle of Jim Crow pugilism if the price was right. Thirty-five thousand dollars win, lose, or draw proved to be the right price.

On 26 December 1908 in Sydney, Australia, Johnson defeated Burns with a fourteenth-round knockout to become the first-ever black world heavyweight champion. In each round he taunted the short, hard-punching Canadian, calling him "white as the flag of surrender," and inflicted a series of punishing right-hand uppercuts. Even the novelist and white supremacist Jack London reported from the ringside that it had been a contest between a grown man and a naughty child. "The Fight!—There was no fight!" London famously wrote (Ashe, 34).

White commentators took up London's call for the undefeated former champion Jim Jeffries to come out of retirement to restore the title to its rightful Anglo-Saxon provenance. After lengthy negotiations, Johnson faced Jeffries in what was billed as the "fight of the century" in Reno, Nevada, on 4 July 1910. Global interest was such that the fighters would share $100,000 in movie rights, ushering in a new era in boxing. Again, Johnson dominated the contest. His merciless uppercuts and jabs exposed the once-invincible Jeffries for what he now was: an overweight, aging alfalfa farmer. The fight ended, mercifully for Jeffries, with a fifteenth-round knockdown. Johnson became the undisputed world champion and $110,000 richer, and Jeffries earned $90,000 for his considerable pains.

The full significance of the fight became clear the next morning, when newspapers reported a national wave of violence in which thirteen African Americans died and hundreds were injured. In some cases blacks had fired guns and attacked whites, but most of the clashes involved whites exacting revenge for Johnson's victory. The violence reflected the rancorous, indeed rancid, atmosphere of the early twentieth-century nadir in race relations, a time of white-on-black race riots and hundreds of lynchings of African Americans. In that respect, Johnson was merely a catalyst for preexisting white fears, though he took great pleasure in stoking and provoking those anxieties. He dressed flamboyantly, drank heavily, drove cars recklessly, taunted white boxers and spectators, and—most incendiary of all—flaunted a series of white lovers. In 1911 he married Etta Terry Duryea, a white woman. One year later, ostracized by her white friends and humiliated by beatings and what one biographer has called Johnson's "heroic infidelity," Duryea committed suicide, shooting herself in a room above his Chicago nightclub, the Café de Champion (Roberts, 140).

Like many famous and wealthy men, Johnson acted as though his money and celebrity placed him above the law. However, the world champion's skin color also attracted the attention of policemen, who arrested him for a string of offenses, usually involving reckless driving but most often for petty transgressions. After being arrested for having Chicago license plates while driving in New York, Johnson complained, "Next thing somebody'll arrest me for bein' a brunette in a blond town" (Roberts, 126).

The champion's arrest in October 1912 was much more serious. He was charged under the Mann Act, a 1910 federal law that prohibited the transportation of women across state or national borders "for the purpose of prostitution, debauchery, or for any other immoral purpose." The Bureau of Investigation, forerunner of the FBI, charged that Johnson had abducted Lucille Cameron, a white woman who had worked as his secretary, as part of an interstate prostitution ring. The vigor with which the federal authorities pursued their case against Johnson was in inverse proportion to the evidence they gathered. Cameron refused to testify and married Johnson in 1912 or 1913, but that did not deter the bureau, which found another white mistress, Belle Schreiber, to testify against him. The authors of the Mann Act had never intended to prosecute consensual sexual relations between an unmarried couple. Johnson's relationship with Schreiber may have been many things—tawdry, abusive, and maybe even "debauched" and "immoral" to some—but it did not violate the letter or the spirit of the law. Regardless of its flimsy evidence, the bureau pursued the case and secured a conviction in May 1913, when twelve white male jurors found Johnson guilty and a judge sentenced him to one year in prison. Released on bond, he fled to Europe.

Johnson defended his world title three times in Paris and proved even more successful in maintaining his reputation as the world's most notorious carouser. Financial problems and the onset of World War I encouraged Johnson to sail for Central America, and in April 1915 he arrived in Havana, Cuba, to defend his title against Jess Willard. The 250-pound white Kansan absorbed heavy punishment in the early rounds but remained standing; in the twenty-sixth round he knocked out the champion. White commentators celebrated what they saw as the return of the natural racial order. Johnson, for his part, claimed—indeed, he swore to God and to his mother—that he had been promised fifty thousand dollars to throw the fight. If so, he never received that payoff. Newsreel of the fight suggests a more prosaic explanation: the fitter, harder-hitting Willard had defeated the aging, poorly prepared Johnson.

After four years in Spain and Mexico, boxing, bullfighting, and squandering his fortune, Johnson surrendered to American authorities, serving one year in the federal penitentiary in Leavenworth, Kansas. Three years after his release in 1921, he divorced Lucille Cameron and married Irene Pineau. He briefly opened a nightclub, the Club De Lux, in Harlem in 1920, but money problems forced him to sell it to the New York gangster Owney Madden, who reopened it as the Cotton Club in 1923. After that, Johnson continued to box and perform in vaudeville shows, though the distinction between these activities became increasingly fine. In 1946 he lost control of his car near Raleigh, North Carolina, and died from his injuries.

Jack Johnson's life and legacy go far beyond the boxing ring. He was not only one of the greatest fighters ever but also a symbol of modernity, a movie-age celebrity who was at once renowned and reviled in his native land and beyond. He embodied the greatest fears of early twentieth-century whites; namely, that a hypersexualized "black beast" threatened the purity of white womanhood. For African Americans, Johnson presented more of a problem. Leaders like BOOKER T. WASHINGTON urged him to display more humility, fearing that the boxer's exuberant racial transgressions reflected badly on his race and might lead to even more violence against blacks. Yet for many blacks, Jack Johnson was a hero, a defiant forerunner of the assertive "New Negro" who emerged in the 1920s.

FURTHER READING
Johnson, Jack. *Jack Johnson—In the Ring—and Out* (1927); reprinted as *Jack Johnson Is a Dandy* (1969).
Ashe, Arthur R., Jr. *A Hard Road to Glory: A History of the African-American Athlete, 1619–1918* (1988).
Roberts, Randy. *Papa Jack: Jack Johnson and the Era of White Hopes* (1983).
Sammons, Jeffrey T. *Beyond the Ring: The Role of Boxing in American Society* (1988).
Obituary: *New York Times*, 11 June 1946.

STEVEN J. NIVEN

Johnson, James Alloyd (8 Nov. 1908–2 Aug. 1979), inventor, educator, author, race driver, musician, and community leader, was born in Portland, Cumberland County, Maine, the son of Frank M. Johnson and Eva M. Deering. His father died when he was three years old and his mother remarried James Verra, a widower. Johnson, called both Jim and, in his early years, Lloyd, was raised along with Mr. Verra's five children.

After graduating from Portland High School in 1928, Johnson enrolled at the Franklin Institute, a technical school in Boston, Massachusetts. His interest in automobiles had begun early and he became a mechanic and a machinist. His teaching ability was first noticed while he was serving in the U.S. Navy during World War II, where Johnson was praised by Naval officials. He instructed ordinance trainees and helped research a new technique for indexing all destroyer gun batteries and director-radar systems. At the same time he held the position of Ordnance Planner and Expediter at the Navy facility in Boston, becoming one of very few people to hold the engineering job without having earned a college degree.

Johnson was given a special award by the U.S. government for inventing a device to fire forty-millimeter guns by air, which proved to be instrumental in removing the element of danger in testing the guns.

Once he was out of the military Johnson became a service manager in Gardiner, Maine, before turning to his new love, teaching. He was one of the founding fathers of a new school, Maine Vocational Institute.

"Out of frustrations for veterans returning from World War II without means of employment or a vocation in order to care for themselves, and in some cases their families, Dad became very concerned," Johnson's daughter, Janet P. Johnson, said. "He then decided he could share his vocation and would train vets how to be auto mechanics. He then realized more than just one vocation was essential and sought others with practical skills and who would be interested in teaching. He came up with a carpenter, an electrician and a plumber. This is when Maine Vocational Technical Institute (MVTI) was born."

The school was established in 1946 in Augusta, Maine, not far from Johnson's home in Gardiner. Six years later in 1952 the school, which had continued to grow, was moved to the state's largest population center, taking over the buildings at Fort Preble, an old military base in South Portland, Maine. The school was renamed the Southern Maine Vocational Technical Institute (SMVTI) and later was renamed again, becoming Southern Maine Community College (SMCC).

While teaching Johnson designed and built several experimental automobiles, one of which won the first-place award at Autorama, an international competition held annually in Hartford, Connecticut. He began racing automobiles and won a first-place trophy. He also built a unique vehicle known as a "Hovercraft."

He invented and patented an automotive exhaust emission device, a helicopter toy, a golf putter, an electrical continuity tester, and a wheel balancer for passenger cars and trucks. When he invented the wheel balancer in 1959, known as the Trig Stato-DiNamic Wheel Balancer, it was so revolutionary and accurate that it cut the costs to one sixth of that charged by the electronic wheel balancers that were then in use. He invented the Truck-Trig balancer in 1976, which instructed mechanics where to put the wheel weights and how much weight was required. It, too, cut the cost of previous balancers by one sixth.

A Portland-area company field tested the Trig Stato-DiNamic Wheel Balancer and on the first one thousand wheels checked found there was complete accuracy within three minutes testing time per tire.

Johnson also established his own company in South Portland, which marketed another of his inventions, the "ACD Tester" (alternator diode circuit), an electronic testing device used in automotive troubleshooting.

In 1969 Johnson was named "Maine's Outstanding Teacher of the Year" by the New England Regional Conference of the American Technical Educational Association at a conference held in Providence, Rhode Island. Criteria for the selection included classroom teaching technique, contributions for welfare of the school and community, published books or technical reports, and contributions in technical education.

Beside his wheel balancer, Johnson was known internationally for his textbook, *Automotive Tune-up and Diagnosis*, published in 1972 by McGraw—Hill Book Co. and used in technical schools around the world. He also authored several educational guidelines, most notable of which was developed at the University of Maine for automotive instruction at SMVTI.

As a lecturer, Johnson received recognition from several service clubs, the Society of Automotive Engineers, and the National Association of College

Automotive Teachers. He served as a consultant for various industries and also received the Governor's Distinguished Service Award as "recognition for service excellence to SMVTI and its faculty."

He was a recipient of the national Jefferson Award, presented by the American Public Service Institute, was cited by former U.S. Senator William D. Hathaway (D-Maine) for an "excellent record of service," and received awards and citations from the Ford Motor Co.

Johnson built his first car at his home in 1948. Later, he made designing and building experimental cars from the ground up a hands-on class project at SMVTI. One of the vehicles was a low-slung, purple and white convertible that Johnson called the "JAJ Special." The car was 138 inches long and 72 inches wide. The eighty-five-horsepower engine, "souped" up to ninety-eight horsepower, allowed the eye-catching, head-turning vehicle to cruise at sixty miles per hour.

In 1974 Johnson was named Grand Knight of the two-hundred-member Msgr. Houlihan Council in Portland, becoming the first African American to head a Knights of Columbus group in Maine. At the time, he had been a member of the Knights of Columbus for only four years.

Johnson wrote an auto column for the *Sunday Telegram* newspaper and also was noted as a jazz musician.

Always interested in education, Johnson returned to school himself, earning his B.S. in Trade and Industrial Education from the University of Southern Maine in 1976. Two years later Johnson retired from SMVTI after a thirty-two-year career.

He had nine children.

FURTHER READING

Price, H.H., and Gerald E. Talbot. *Maine's Visible Black History* (2006).

BOB GREENE

Johnson, James P. (1 Feb. 1894–17 Nov. 1955), jazz and popular pianist, composer, and songwriter, was born James Price Johnson in New Brunswick, New Jersey, the son of William H. Johnson, a store helper and mechanic, and Josephine Harrison, a maid. Johnson's mother sang in a Methodist church choir and was a self-taught pianist. Johnson later cited popular songs and African American ring-shout dances at home and local brass bands in the streets as early influences. When his mother's piano was sold to help pay for their move to Jersey City in 1902, Johnson turned to singing, dancing, and

playing the guitar, but he played piano whenever possible. In 1908 the family moved to Manhattan, at which point he enrolled at P.S. 69, and in 1911 the family moved uptown.

Johnson got his first job as a pianist in Far Rockaway, New York, in the summer of 1912. He so enjoyed the work that he decided not to return to school, and in the fall he got other engagements in Jersey City and then in Manhattan. He studied the European piano tradition with Bruto Giannini from about 1913 to 1916 while also absorbing the skills of the finest ragtime pianists, among whom he singled out Abba Labba (Richard McLean), LUCKEY ROBERTS, and—in the summer of 1914—EUBIE BLAKE, who recalled that Johnson was able to play "Troublesome Ivories" perfectly after he had heard it only twice. Johnson was also composing rags that helped him win a piano contest in Egg Harbor, New Jersey, and he may have already developed a version of "Carolina Shout." He had certain advantages over his rivals, as he recalled in an interview with Tom Davin:I was born with absolute pitch.... I played rags very accurately and brilliantly.... I did ... glissandos in sixths and double tremolos. These would run other ticklers out of the place at cutting sessions. They wouldn't play after me.... To develop clear touch and the feel of the piano, I'd put a bed sheet over the keyboard and play difficult pieces through it.... I was considered one of the best in New York—if not the best. In the fall of 1914, while performing in Newark with the singer and dancer Lillie Mae Wright, Johnson met WILLIE "THE LION" SMITH. Both Johnson and Smith were formidable pianists and shared the belief that entertainers must be elegantly attired and have a dramatic stage presence. They became best friends; their personalities were complementary, Johnson as deferential as Smith was outspoken. That same year Johnson formed a songwriting and publishing partnership with William Farrell, who taught him to write music. Johnson began touring and writing for shows and dances.

From 1916 to 1927 Johnson made piano rolls, initially documenting many of his own ragtime compositions. He punched an as-yet-unperfected "Carolina Shout" for a roll issued in February 1918. Johnson married Wright in 1917; later they had two children and adopted a third, but initially Wright continued her career as an entertainer. In 1918 they toured in the *Smart Set Revue*. While performing regularly at a nightclub in Toledo, Ohio, Johnson studied composition at the local conservatory of music. He returned to New York late in 1919. Further piano rolls included a polished version of "Carolina Shout," issued in May 1921, and in September and October he made definitive early recordings in the stride piano style: "The Harlem Strut," "Keep Off the Grass," and, again, "Carolina Shout."

Stride piano has often been described as an orchestral style, and indeed, in contrast to boogie-woogie blues piano playing, it requires a fabulous conceptual independence; the individual player must play as though he were an orchestra, the left hand differentiating bass and mid-range lines while the right supplies melodic lines. Nevertheless, the overriding characteristic of Johnson's playing was his percussive attack. For all his harmonic subtlety and melodic invention, and for all his aspirations to become an arty orchestral composer, he was at his finest when he attacked the piano as if it were a drum set. By comparison with classic ragtime piano, Johnson's stride playing on these early recordings was vigorously faster and far more abrasive melodically; open to improvisation, his playing leaned rhythmically toward the uneven and propulsive feeling that later came to be called "swing." Denser and purposefully irregular, the left-hand patterns would "stride" between wide intervals in the piano's bass range; chords in the middle range were more dissonant harmonically, especially when Johnson "crushed" adjacent notes.

"Carolina Shout" became the test piece for aspiring pianists in the stride style. Those who copied it included Smith, DUKE ELLINGTON, Cliff Jackson, Joe Turner, CLAUDE HOPKINS, and FATS WALLER, who became Johnson's student after learning "Carolina Shout" from the piano roll. Smith and Waller subsequently were Johnson's closest colleagues and rivals as pianists at the rent parties that Harlem featured through the 1920s. By many accounts Johnson won the majority of these informal contests on the strength of his originality and keyboard technique, but surviving recordings give the honors to Waller.

Toward the end of 1922 Johnson became the musical director for the revue *Plantation Days*, a little-known touring show that took him to England from March to June 1923. In the summer he and lyricist CECIL MACK wrote the hit revue *Runnin' Wild*, which ran for more than five years on tour and on Broadway. *Runnin' Wild* presented Johnson's "Old Fashioned Love" and "Charleston," the latter perhaps the defining song of America in the 1920s.

In 1926 Johnson wrote "If I Could Be with You (One Hour Tonight)" with lyricist HENRY CREAMER; it became a hit song in 1930. From late 1927 into 1928

Johnson collaborated with Fats Waller, the lyricists ANDY RAZAF and Creamer, and others in the creation of the revue *Keep Shufflin'*, for which Johnson coauthored the song "'Sippi," directed the pit orchestra, and served as intermission pianist in duets with Waller. With Razaf in 1930 Johnson wrote "A Porter's Love Song to a Chambermaid" for the *Kitchen Mechanic's Revue* at Smalls' Paradise in Harlem.

During this period Johnson recorded regularly in jazz bands and as a soloist. His solo work yielded interpretations of his compositions "Riffs" (1929), "You've Got to Be Modernistic" (1930), and "Jingles" (1930), all carrying his playing to a new level of frenetically syncopated zaniness. He also accompanied recordings by singers as diverse as ETHEL WATERS ("Guess Who's in Town," 1928) and BESSIE SMITH. In "Preachin' the Blues" and "Backwater Blues" from his first session with Smith in 1927, Johnson somewhat toned down his busy pianistic style to conform to the musical aesthetics of the blues. In "Backwater Blues" he discarded the jagged and fast-changing oompahs of stride playing in favor of a loping, repeated boogie-woogie bass pattern. Johnson is the pianist on the soundtrack and on screen in Bessie Smith's movie *St. Louis Blues*, made in late June 1929.

Johnson also sought to create an African American version of European classical music, which proved to be the least successful of his many endeavors. Like most popular and jazz musicians of his era, he was a miniaturist whose great talent lay in the subtle manipulation of nuances of surface detail, not in the construction of grand architectural schemes characteristic of European classical masterpieces. *Yamekraw: Negro Rhapsody*, composed in 1927, was performed at Carnegie Hall for a 1928 concert organized by W.-C. HANDY, but Johnson's commitment as music director of *Keep Shufflin'* prevented him from participating. Portions of the rhapsody were recorded and in 1930 were made into a movie short, again without Johnson's participation.

Although careless living and hard drinking began to catch up with him in the 1930s, Johnson continued working. Unfortunately, like JELLY ROLL MORTON, Johnson was so rigidly tied to early jazz and popular styles that he could not adapt when the swing era arrived, and many of his efforts were unpopular. Johnson wrote for musical revues as the genre grew stale, and he composed largely forgotten pieces whose titles used words testifying to his European classical aspirations: "symphony," "concerto," "ballet," "opera." Many scores have been lost.

With the revival of interest in traditional jazz that began in the late 1930s, Johnson was sought out once again. He figured prominently in the Spirituals to Swing concerts that John Hammond produced and recorded at Carnegie Hall in December 1938 and December 1939. He also recorded in a trio with the clarinetist Pee Wee Russell and the drummer ZUTTY SINGLETON in 1938; for the trumpeter FRANKIE NEWTON's mixed swing and Dixieland group in January 1939; and with his own group, including the trumpeter HENRY "RED" ALLEN and the trombonist J. C. HIGGINBOTHAM, in March. In a few titles from these sessions, and particularly in "Blueberry Rhyme," recorded in June, Johnson plays with a lyricism and introspection quite different from his norm. In 1940 he led a band briefly, but in August he suffered the first of eight strokes.

Johnson's return to activity began in 1942, when the Brooklyn Civic Orchestra gave a concert of his "serious" works. He resumed playing in 1943, initially as a member of the trumpeter Wild Bill Davison's band in Boston and New York and then as a freelance bandleader and pianist. After Waller's death in December 1943, Johnson joined the guitarist Eddie Condon at New York Town Hall to perform Waller's tunes and his own music in a series of concerts extending into 1944. From August 1944 he engaged in stride piano contests with Willie "the Lion" Smith at the Pied Piper in Greenwich Village, but in December Johnson suffered a stroke, ending this now-legendary association.

Johnson recorded prolifically during the period 1942–1944, and discs such as "Arkansaw Blues," "Carolina Balmoral," and "Mule Walk—Stomp" (all from late 1943) give no indication that the stroke affected his playing. He also recorded as a bandleader and as a sideman, including beautifully melodic performances on Waller's song "Squeeze Me" and the slow blues "Too Many Times," both from the trumpeter Yank Lawson's session of December 1943.

In 1945 Johnson performed with LOUIS ARMSTRONG, and he heard performances of his concert works at Carnegie Hall and Town Hall. He worked occasionally the next year but became chronically ill. In 1947 he became a regular on Rudi Blesh's radio show *This Is Jazz*, which was broadcast nationally and recorded. Johnson held assorted freelance jobs, including participation in Friday night jam sessions at Stuyvesant Casino and Central Plaza in downtown Manhattan from June 1948 to February 1949. Johnson suffered a massive stroke in 1951. Paralyzed, he survived financially on songwriting royalties. He died in New York City.

Apart from his tremendously important contributions to American stage and song of the 1920s—in particular, *Runnin' Wild* and "Charleston"—Johnson's significance lies in his stature as the creator of a jazz piano style, stride, and as one of the greatest practitioners and composers in that style. During his lifetime, Johnson's stride piano style was further developed along original and highly personalized paths by Waller, ART TATUM, and THELONIOUS MONK, and it made its way into the jazz mainstream in, for example, numerous moments of stride playing that the pianists and bandleaders Duke Ellington and COUNT BASIE introduced into their performances.

FURTHER READING

Brown, Scott E., and Robert Hilbert. *James P. Johnson: A Case of Mistaken Identity* (1986).
Hasse, John, ed. *Ragtime: Its History, Composers, and Music* (1985).
Schuller, Gunther. *Early Jazz: Its Roots and Musical Development* (1968).
Smith, Willie "the Lion," and George Hoefer. *Music on My Mind* (1964; repr. 1975).
Obituaries: *New York Times*, 18 Nov. 1955; *Down Beat*, 28 Dec. 1955.

DISCOGRAPHY

Kappler, Frank. Liner notes in the Time-Life boxed LP set *Giants of Jazz: James P. Johnson* (1981).

This entry is taken from the *American National Biography* and is published here with the permission of the American Council of Learned Societies.

BARRY KERNFELD

Johnson, James Weldon (17 June 1871–26 June 1938), civil rights leader, poet, and novelist, was born in Jacksonville, Florida, the son of James Johnson, a resort hotel headwaiter, and Helen Dillet, a schoolteacher. He grew up in a secure, middle-class home in an era, Johnson recalled in *Along This Way* (1933), when "Jacksonville was known far and wide as a good town for Negroes" because of the jobs provided by its winter resorts. After completing the eighth grade at Stanton Grammar School, the only school open to African Americans in his hometown, Johnson attended the preparatory school and then the college division of Atlanta University, where he developed skills as a writer and a public speaker. Following his graduation in 1894 Johnson returned to his hometown and became principal of Stanton School.

James Weldon Johnson, diplomat, poet, novelist, critic, and composer, 3 December 1932. (Library of Congress/Carl Van Vechten, photographer.)

School teaching, however, did not satisfy his ambitions. While continuing as principal Johnson started a short-lived newspaper and then read law in a local attorney's office well enough to pass the exam for admission to the Florida state bar. He also continued to write poetry, a practice he had started in college. In early 1900 he and his brother JOHN ROSAMOND JOHNSON collaborated on "Lift Every Voice and Sing," an anthem commemorating Abraham Lincoln's birthday. African American groups around the country found the song inspirational, and within fifteen years it had acquired a subtitle: "The Negro National Anthem."

"Lift Every Voice and Sing" was not the only song on which the brothers collaborated. In 1899 the two spent the summer in New York City, where they sold their first popular song, "Louisiana Lize." In 1902 they left Jacksonville to join BOB COLE, a young songwriter they had met early on in New York, in the quickly successful Broadway songwriting team of Cole and Johnson Brothers. Over the next few years Johnson was largely responsible for the lyrics of such hit songs as "Nobody's Lookin' but de Owl and de Moon" (1901), "Under the Bamboo Tree" (1902), and "Congo Love Song" (1903). In 1906 Johnson's life took another turn when, through the influence of BOOKER T. WASHINGTON, Theodore Roosevelt appointed him U.S. consul to Puerto Cabello, Venezuela. In 1909 he moved to a more significant post as consul in Corinto, Nicaragua. A year later he returned to the United States for a brief stay in New York City, where he married Grace Nail, a member of a well-established African American family. They did not have children. In 1912 revolution broke out in Nicaragua. Johnson's role in aiding U.S. Marines in defeating the rebels drew high praise from Washington. He left the Consular Service in 1913; there would be, he felt, little opportunity for an African American in the newly elected Democratic administration of Woodrow Wilson.

Johnson maintained his literary efforts during this period. Several of his poems (including "Fifty Years," commemorating the anniversary of the Emancipation Proclamation) appeared in nationally circulated publications. In 1912 he published *The Autobiography of an Ex-Colored Man*, a novel whose central character, unlike Johnson, was light enough to "pass" as a white man; the book explores the young man's struggles to find his place in American society. Johnson returned to New York City in 1914, and he soon began a weekly column on current affairs for the *New York Age*, a widely distributed African American newspaper.

In 1917 Johnson joined the staff of the NAACP. He worked as field secretary, largely responsible for establishing local branches throughout the South and for increasing overall membership from 10,000 to 44,000 by the end of 1918. In 1920 Johnson became the NAACP's first African American secretary (its chief operating officer), a position he held throughout the 1920s.

Johnson was deeply committed to exposing the injustice and brutality imposed on African Americans throughout the United States, especially in the Jim Crow South. He labored with considerable success to put the NAACP on secure financial ground. He spent much time in Washington unsuccessfully lobbying to have Congress pass the Dyer Anti-Lynching Bill, legislation that would have made lynching a federal crime. Finally, Johnson was a key figure in making the NAACP a clearinghouse for civil rights court cases; he collaborated closely with such noted attorneys as Moorfield Storey, Louis Marshall, and Arthur Garfield Hayes in a series of cases defending African American civil rights and attacking the legal structure of segregation. In all these efforts he worked closely with WALTER WHITE, whom he brought into the NAACP as his assistant and who succeeded him as secretary, and W. E. B. DuBois, the editor of *The Crisis*, the NAACP monthly journal.

Johnson was probably better known in the 1920s for his literary efforts than for his leadership of the NAACP. He played an active role, as an author and as a supporter of young talent, in what has come to be called the Harlem Renaissance. Johnson urged writers and other artists to draw on everyday life in African American communities for their creative inspiration. He played the role of a father figure to a number of young writers, including CLAUDE MCKAY and LANGSTON HUGHES, whose often blunt prose and poetry drew condemnation from more genteel critics.

His own work during this period included a widely praised anthology, *The Book of American Negro Poetry* (1922), a volume that helped to give an identity to the "New Negro" movement. His continued interest in the African American musical tradition found expression in two collections of spirituals that he and Rosamond brought out: *The Book of American Negro Spirituals* in 1925 and *The Second Book of American Negro Spirituals* in 1926. A year later Johnson published his poetic interpretation of African American religion in *God's Trombones: Seven Negro Sermons in Verse*, a theme he first developed in "O Black and Unknown Bards" (1908). The year 1927 also saw the reissuing of *The Autobiography of an Ex-Colored Man*. Finally, Johnson published *Black Manhattan* (1930), the first history of African Americans in New York City.

In 1931 Johnson stepped down as secretary of the NAACP (though he remained on the association's board of directors) to become a professor at Fisk University. For the remainder of his life he spent the winter and spring terms in Nashville teaching creative writing and classes in American and African American literature. The rest of the year the Johnsons largely spent in New York City. He remained active as a writer, publishing *Along This Way*, his autobiography, in 1933 and *Negro Americans, What Now?*, a work of social criticism, a year later. Johnson's unexpected death was the result of an automobile accident near Wiscasset, Maine.

Johnson took deserved pride in his accomplishments across a wide variety of careers: teacher, Broadway lyricist, poet, diplomat, novelist, and civil rights leader. Though he suffered most of the indignities forced on African Americans during the Jim Crow era, Johnson retained his sense of self-worth; he proclaimed forcefully in *Negro Americans, What Now?* that "My inner life is mine, and I shall defend and maintain its integrity against all the powers of hell." The defense of his "inner life" did not mean withdrawal, but active engagement. Thus Johnson was a key figure, perhaps the key figure, in making the NAACP a truly national organization capable of mounting the attack that eventually led to the dismantling of the system of segregation by law.

Maintaining his "inner life" also led Johnson to write both prose and poetry that has endured over the decades. "Lift Every Voice and Sing," written a century ago, can still be heard at African American gatherings, and the title phrase appears on the U.S. postage stamp issued in 1988 to honor Johnson. *The Autobiography of an Ex-Colored Man* has remained in print since its reissue in the 1920s, and it holds a significant place in the history of African American fiction. *Along This Way*, also still in print after more than sixty years, is acknowledged as a classic American autobiography. Finally, *God's Trombones*, Johnson's celebration of the creativity found in African American religion, has been adapted for the stage several times, most notably by VINNETTE CARROLL (as *Trumpets of the Lord*) in 1963.

FURTHER READING

The bulk of Johnson's papers are held at the Beinecke Library, Yale University.

Johnson, James Weldon. *Along This Way: The Autobiography of James Weldon Johnson*, introd. Sondra K. Wilson (2002).

Fleming, Robert E. *James Weldon Johnson* (1987).

Levy, Eugene. *James Weldon Johnson: Black Leader, Black Voice* (1973).

Price, Kenneth M., and Lawrence J. Oliver, eds. *Critical Essays on James Weldon Johnson* (1997).

Wilson, Sondra K., ed. *In Search of Democracy: The NAACP Writings of James Weldon Johnson, Walter White, and Roy Wilkins, 1920–1977* (1999).

Wilson, Sondra K., ed. *The Selected Writings of James Weldon Johnson*, 2 vols. (1995).

This entry is taken from the *American National Biography* and is published here with the permission of the American Council of Learned Societies.

EUGENE LEVY

Johnson, Jane (1814?–2 Aug. 1872), fugitive slave and Underground Railroad participant, was born Jane Williams in Washington, D.C., the daughter of John and Jane Williams. Little is known of her life before freedom. Her marriage, probably by slave rites, in about 1840 to a man named Johnson produced at least three sons. Eventually, Johnson and her sons were sold to Cornelius Crew, a prominent businessman and plantation owner in Richmond, Virginia. Johnson suffered the heartbreak of having one of her sons sold far away and of being separated from her husband. Crew sold Johnson and her remaining two sons, Daniel and Isaiah, in January 1854 to John Hill Wheeler, an ambitious civil servant from North Carolina.

Wheeler had recently become the assistant secretary to President Franklin Pierce, and he brought Johnson to the nation's capital as his wife's personal maid. A reporter later wrote, "Jane is a fine specimen of the best class of Virginia housemaids, with a certain lady-like air, propriety of language and timidity of manner that prepossesses the audience in her favor.… She was very polite in her manners and spoke of 'colored gentlemen,' 'white gentlemen,' and 'colored ladies,' as though ladies and gentlemen had been her associates all her lifetime" (*Liberator*, 7 Sept. 1855, 143).

Avidly seeking higher office, Wheeler received a presidential appointment as resident minister to Nicaragua in August 1854. When the Wheeler family moved there two months later, they apparently did not take Johnson and her sons with them. However, when Wheeler returned the following summer to deliver treaties to the president, he made plans to return to Nicaragua via New York with Johnson and her sons. On 18 July 1855 Wheeler stopped en route briefly in Philadelphia to collect a trunk, causing him to miss the early afternoon boat for New York. Johnson knew this was her last chance for freedom. Perhaps fearing that the Southerners who wanted to expand slavery to Nicaragua would succeed, she had planned to flee in New York, which would have been her only opportunity on free soil, but the delay in Philadelphia presented a better opportunity. While Wheeler ate dinner at Bloodgood's Hotel, Johnson surreptitiously sought help from the black staff. They sent for WILLIAM STILL, a renowned black leader of the Underground Railroad, who notified Passmore Williamson, a white abolitionist in the Pennsylvania Anti-Slavery Society. Still and Williamson arrived at the hotel too late and just barely caught up with Johnson on the boat's deck. They informed her that all she had to do to be free was leave the boat. After a minor scuffle with Wheeler, Johnson and her young sons broke free and fled with Still.

That same day Wheeler sued Williamson, asserting that his slaves had been kidnapped and demanding their return. When Williamson denied any knowledge of their whereabouts, he was imprisoned without bail. Johnson risked her newly won freedom by appearing at the 30 August 1855 court hearing for Williamson. Wheeler had come to court armed with his pistol. The courtroom gasped as Johnson rose and courageously testified, "Nobody forced me away; nobody pulled me, and nobody led me; I went away of my own free will; I always wished to be free … I had rather die than go back" (Still, 95). She then hurriedly left under the protection of Lucretia Mott, other abolitionists, and state authorities. Her carriage raced through the streets to evade federal marshals attempting to enforce Wheeler's federal rights under the Fugitive Slave Law. She ran in the front door of Mott's house and directly out the back as Mott ran after her, tossing food supplies into the fleeing carriage.

In September 1855 Johnson arrived in Boston and settled her family in the Beacon Hill neighborhood. With the assistance of WILLIAM COOPER NELL and the Boston Vigilance Committee, she set about getting an education for her sons and employment for herself. After her marriage to Lawrence Woodfork in August 1856, the family moved several times within Beacon Hill, amid the vibrant community of some of the most educated and influential African Americans of that time, such as Nell, JOHN STEWART ROCK, the first black attorney to practice before the U.S. Supreme Court, LEWIS HAYDEN, another fugitive slave and a leader of the Boston Vigilance Society, and BENJAMIN FRANKLIN ROBERTS, who took the City of Boston to court and won desegregation of Boston public schools in 1850. Despite their own struggles, Jane and Lawrence Woodfork sheltered fugitive slaves fleeing to Canada on at least two occasions in 1857 and 1859. Heartbreak and insecurity returned to Woodfork's life when her husband died on 6 December 1861, after two years of illness, leaving her alone to support her family once again. One joy was Williamson's visit during the Civil War. She married again on 20 July 1864 to a William Harris, but he apparently died shortly afterward, as she is listed as a widow in the 1865 city directory.

Jane Harris watched with pride and agony as fifteen-year-old Isaiah, claiming to be eighteen, enlisted as a drummer in June 1863 in the Fifty-fifth Massachusetts Volunteer Infantry, a unit formed from the overflow of recruits for the famous Fifty-fourth Massachusetts. This created financial hardship for the family as well since both black

Massachusetts units refused to accept any pay for eighteen months until they were retroactively paid the same amounts that had been accorded to the white regiments. Fortunately Isaiah survived the war and returned to Boston when his unit mustered out in August 1865.

Harris and her sons disappear from Boston records after 1865—they may have returned to the South to look for her third son and other relatives—but she and Isaiah resurfaced in Boston in 1871. The following year Jane Harris died suddenly of dysentery amid a citywide epidemic that fetid August. Only a cheap metal plot marker identifies the grave of Jane (Williams) Johnson Woodfork Harris in Woodlawn Cemetery in Everett, Massachusetts. Almost one hundred and thirty years after her death, an unpublished manuscript dating to 1853–1859 titled *The Bondwoman's Narrative* came to light. The author, HANNAH CRAFTS, claimed to have been a slave owned by a Mr. Wheeler in Washington, D.C. She wrote that she had worked for him after one of his other slaves, a woman named Jane, escaped. Crafts's definite identity remains unknown, but a circumstantial case can be made that she may have been Jane Harris, writing under a pseudonym to protect herself from Wheeler. Jane Harris was a woman of innate intelligence, driven by a clear purpose and the will to gain freedom for herself and her children. That she faced down an incensed and armed Wheeler in a courtroom in 1855 speaks of incredible courage.

FURTHER READING

Brandt, Nat, and Yanna Kroyt Brandt. *In the Shadow of the Civil War: Passmore Williamson and the Rescue of Jane Johnson* (2007).

Flynn, Katherine E. "Jane Johnson, Found! but Is She 'Hannah Crafts'? The Search for the Author of *The Bondwoman's Narrative*," in *In Search of Hannah Crafts: Critical Essays on The Bondwoman's Narrative*, eds. Henry Louis Gates Jr. and Hollis Robbins, (2004).

Still, William. *The Underground Rail Road: A Record of Facts, Authentic Narratives, Letters, &c.* (1872, 2005).

KATHERINE E. FLYNN

Johnson, John (19 Jan. 1918–8 Aug. 2005), entrepreneur and publisher, was born Johnny Johnson in Arkansas City, Arkansas, the only child of Leroy Johnson, a sawmill worker, and Gertrude Jenkins, who worked odd jobs. He had a half sister named Beulah from Gertrude Johnson's previous marriage. Johnson's mother was his main source of encouragement. When he was eight years old, his father died in a sawmill accident. A year later his mother married James Williams.

The family lived in a caring but poor neighborhood, and Johnson attended the Arkansas City Colored School, which did not provide education beyond the eighth grade. Opportunities were limited for almost all African Americans; the adults were relegated to low-paying jobs. In his autobiography, *Succeeding against the Odds*, Johnson says that he noticed that the poor people worked in dirty overalls and sweated for a living, while the rich people wore suits, so he decided that his goal would be to work wearing a suit (Johnson and Bennett Jr., 45). His family saw a better chance to accomplish this goal in the North. In July 1933 the family moved to Chicago, Illinois, one of the many black families that moved from the rural South to the industrial North as part of the Great Migration.

For the family the economic promise of the big city faded fast. They had moved during the Great Depression, and soon after arriving Johnson's stepfather, mother, and sister were all unemployed. The family was forced to depend on welfare. While they struggled for money, Johnson, still a young teenager, enrolled in Wendell Phillips, an almost all-black high school. Because of a clerical error on his first day, he was designated a sophomore and thus skipped a year of school.

Chicago offered Johnson resources and new cultural opportunities. He spent hours at the public library reading about self-improvement and African American history. At school he got involved in a variety of extracurricular activities: he was elected class president of his junior and senior classes, he joined the French club, and was editor of the school newspaper. Because of his excellent school performance, he was the only student asked to speak at his commencement. Before the ceremony his teacher suggested that it was time for him to change his name as he entered adulthood. From then on, he decided he was to be known as John Harold Johnson. He graduated in 1936 and soon met an executive named HARRY PACE who would change his life.

Harry Pace was the head of Supreme Liberty Life Insurance, a prominent company in Chicago. Johnson had admired the business executive and heard Pace speak at an Urban League luncheon. Johnson approached Pace and was soon working part-time at Supreme Life. He began as an office worker making twenty-five dollars a month. Although the pay was low, it helped him accomplish two objectives. It allowed him to attend college at the University of Chicago with a partial scholarship, and it gave him his first exposure to African American businessmen. He loved the atmosphere so much that he dropped out of school in 1939 to work full-time.

In 1941 Johnson married Eunice Walker, the daughter of a physician from Selma, Alabama. The couple would later have two children, John Jr., and Linda. Shortly after the wedding, Johnson came up with an idea for a business. This idea took shape when Harry Pace assigned Johnson to edit the company's employee magazine. The experience was so inspiring that Johnson decided to start his own magazine.

Johnson wanted to publish a black version of *Reader's Digest* and went to the First National Bank for a loan to fund his project. Within minutes he was escorted out by two security guards, who referred to him as "boy" (Dingle, 10). Johnson then went to wealthy members of the black community and even to ROY WILKINS, head of the NAACP. All of them advised Johnson to put his energies toward more promising ventures. Undeterred, he persuaded his mother to put up her new furniture as collateral for a five-hundred-dollar loan from the Citizens Loan Corporation. He then formed the Negro Digest Publishing Company, and in November 1942 *Negro Digest* was born.

Johnson built his initial subscriber base by writing letters to Supreme Life policyholders. These efforts led to three thousand orders, but that was not enough to make a profit. To make more money, Johnson had to increase demand for his product. He went to distributing companies but was rebuffed because of their common belief that black products did not sell. To circumvent this obstacle, he told friends to go to newsstands and stores and ask for *Negro Digest*. Soon he received calls from dealers who were hearing about his magazine, and they ordered copies. With the help of word of mouth on the streets and advertisements in other outlets, circulation grew. Within a few months, the magazine was known throughout the nation. In 1943 Johnson persuaded First Lady Eleanor Roosevelt to contribute a column to one issue. After it was published, circulation doubled overnight to one hundred thousand copies.

Johnson decided to expand his empire. Because a large number of African Americans were buying *Life* magazine, he decided to create a black picture magazine. The result of this idea was *Ebony*, which first hit the newsstands in November 1945. The magazine was successful immediately. In a strange way, however, it was too successful, because his magazines did not have enough corporate advertising to make them profitable. The more magazines he sold, the more he had to print, which meant more costs. So Johnson used tenacity, charm, and creativity to convince mainstream corporations that black consumers were worth their advertisements. It worked, and *Ebony* became extraordinarily profitable in a short time.

Eventually *Negro Digest* outwore its welcome, and it was discontinued in 1951. After a few efforts to bring it back, publication ended in 1976. With *Ebony* as its foundation, the business was renamed Johnson Publishing Company in 1949, and it developed a number of other products to diversify its offerings. The most significant of these creations was *Jet*, a pocket-sized weekly magazine, and the Ebony Fashion Fair. Other offerings, such as *Tan Confessions* and *Ebony, Jr.*, were short-lived. Despite those occasional failures, Johnson Publishing has remained one of the nation's largest black-owned businesses for decades.

By 2002 *Ebony* had more than 12 million monthly readers, and *Jet* had 9 million readers. Johnson turned over the titles of chief executive officer and president to his daughter, LINDA RICE JOHNSON, who had graduated with an MBA from Northwestern University and worked in a number of roles for Johnson Publishing. (John Jr. had died in 1981 after a long bout with sickle-cell anemia.) Johnson remained the company's chairman until his death from cancer in Chicago's Northwestern Memorial Hospital on 8 August 2005.

In his autobiography Johnson wrote that he hopes his example will stand as proof that "the Dream is still alive and well and working in America" (Johnson, 356). He will be remembered as one of the fathers of modern black capitalism. His publishing empire is the largest and most influential in African American history, and its success helped to make the corporate world aware of the power of the African American market.

FURTHER READING
Johnson, John, and Lerone Bennett, Jr. *Succeeding against the Odds* (1989).
Dingle, Derek. *Black Enterprise Titans of the BE 100's: Black CEOs Who Redefined and Conquered American Business* (1999).

GREGORY S. BELL

Johnson, John (?–25 Dec. 1812), a sailor during the War of 1812, was a crewman on the privateer *Governor Tompkins*, a fourteen-gun schooner owned by principals from Baltimore, Maryland. The schooner departed New York in July 1812 under Captain Nathaniel Shaler, and among his crew were at least two black men, Johnson and JOHN DAVIS. While little is known about either man, it is likely that both were freemen and skilled sailors. Given the fact that the *Governor Tompkins* sailed from New York, it may be reasonably inferred that Johnson, if not from that city, had previously been employed there.

The action in which Johnson gained acclaim began on 25 December 1812 when Captain Shaler and his crew spied three ships at sunrise. Believing one of them to be a large and valuable British transport, the men of the *Governor Tompkins* worked their ship toward the enemy. A transport was considered a great prize; its capture would disrupt enemy supply lines and commerce. When a sudden squall drove the *Governor Tompkins* closer to the British ship, Shaler discovered that the ship was not a transport at all, but the forty-four-gun frigate *Laurel*, one of the newest in the British navy, and reputed to be the fastest. The fighting began when the *Governor Tompkins* closed on the same course and the British frigate fired. The first broadside from the *Laurel* struck the hardy schooner and caused a number of crew casualties, including John Johnson (his last name is also given in one account as Thompson), as well as John Davis. Johnson was struck in the hip by a twenty-four-pound cannonball, and it took away most of his lower body. Captain Shaler later reported that although Johnson was mortally wounded, "[i]n this state the poor, brave fellow lay on the deck, and several times exclaimed to his shipmates, 'fire away boys, neber haul de color down'" (Coggeshall, 143). In the end the fire from the British frigate caused no mortal damage to the ship, and the *Governor Tompkins* escaped with five wounded and three dead: Johnson, Davis, and a white crewman.

Though the actions of John Johnson were small, and one of many such instances of heroism on the high seas by sailors both black and white, they nonetheless symbolize the importance of African American seamen during the War of 1812. African American sailors played a significant role in manning American merchant ships prior to the war, serving in any capacity, from lowly cabin boy to able-bodied seaman. They continued this service with great enthusiasm and national pride when war with Britain became a reality. Thousands of such men served in either the regular American navy or in privately owned men-of-war, and they made great sacrifices; untold numbers of African American sailors died during the war, and more than a thousand more became prisoners of war.

John Johnson's heroism and patriotism, even when he surely knew that death was imminent, was recognized by the words of his own captain, who declared that Johnson's sacrifice "ought to be registered on the book of fame, and remembered with reverence as long as bravery is considered a virtue" (Coggeshall, 143).

FURTHER READING

Bolster, W. Jeffrey. *Black Jacks: African American Seamen in the Age of Sail* (1997).

Brown, William Wells. *The Negro in the American Rebellion: His Heroism and His Fidelity* (1867; repr. 1971).

Coggeshall, George. *History of the American Privateers, and Letters-of-Marque, During Our War with England in the Years 1812, '13 and '14* (1861).

GLENN ALLEN KNOBLOCK

Johnson, John (1839–?), U.S. Navy sailor and Medal of Honor recipient, was a native of Philadelphia, Pennsylvania. Little is known about his life, but he is probably the same man that enlisted in the navy at Philadelphia during the Civil War, serving as a landsman aboard the *U.S.S. Suwanee* for three years from 10 February 1865 to 31 March 1867. At the time of his enlistment in 1865, his occupation was listed as that of a waiter and barber. Johnson's activities after the war are uncertain; he may have returned to his peacetime occupation, but it seems likely that he continued serving in the navy, rising from landsman, to ordinary seaman, and thence to the rating of seaman.

Johnson was serving aboard the gunboat *U.S.S. Kansas* when it departed New York for Cuba on 29 November 1871, arriving in Havana early in December. The *Kansas*, with about one hundred crewmen aboard, departed Cuba on 25 February 1872 with the mission of transporting Commander Alexander F. Crosman and his team on a surveying expedition to Nicaragua. Their job was to survey the country in search of a possible location for the building of a ship canal to reach the Pacific Ocean, the second such expedition in which the *Kansas* was employed in as many years. The *Kansas* arrived off Greytown, Nicaragua, on 3 April but could not land the surveying party due to heavy weather. The ship then proceeded southward to the mouth of the Rio Colorado River, near the border with Costa Rica, on 6 April and here landed some of the men and the supplies of the survey expedition before stormy seas once again forced a halt to operations. The ship subsequently proceeded back to Greytown, and here once again attempted to land supplies for the expedition. On 12 April Commander Crosman departed the *Kansas* in the ship's whaleboat with some of his crew. During the attempt to cross the bar, the steering oar of the boat broke, and the whaleboat broached to and then capsized. Part of the crew of the whaleboat was in the water, while others, Crosman among them, clung to the bottom of the overturned boat. The commander then attempted to bring the boat to shallow water, but was washed away by strong waves and was never seen again. Meanwhile, the accident was seen by the crewmen of the *Kansas* and they quickly sent the ship's cutter, rubber boat, and gig to aid the men in peril. The first to arrive on the scene was the cutter, which was swamped and capsized; this same fate was met with by the ship's other rescue craft, and now the water was filled with men struggling to survive. Among these men was John Johnson, though it is unknown which boat took him to the scene. Through his actions, as well as that of fellow sailors Austin Denham and George Hill, many men were rescued and brought ashore after several hours of fighting the waves. In the end, six men, including Commander Crosman and five men from the cutter coming to his aid lost their lives in the accident. However, the loss of life could have been much greater were it not for the efforts of John Johnson, Denham, and Austin, and as a result they were subsequently awarded the Medal of Honor.

The heroic actions of men like John Johnson, ALPHONSE GIRANDY, and JOHN SMITH that resulted in the Medal of Honor are important for several reasons; not only are they part of a largely forgotten group of Medal of Honor recipients who earned the medal for actions during peacetime operations, but they are also representative of the fine service rendered by African American sailors in the post–Civil War period. This was a time in which the era of Jim Crow was taking hold ashore in the South, and yet black enlisted sailors still, at least for several decades, maintained a degree of equality at sea while serving in the navy as they had done since the days of the American Revolution.

After his heroic actions off the coast of Nicaragua in 1872, nothing certain is known of John Johnson and he disappears from the historical record.

FURTHER READING

Hanna, Charles W. *African American Recipients of the Medal of Honor* (2002).

"The Late Commander Crosman—Particulars of the Accident at Greytown, by which the Chief of the Nicaragua Surveying Expedition Lost His Life," *New York Times*, 20 May 1872.

GLENN ALLEN KNOBLOCK

Johnson, John Henry (24 Nov. 1929–3 June 2011), college athlete and professional football player, was born the son of Foster, a Pullman porter, and Ella Johnson in Waterproof, Louisiana. In the early 1930s the Johnson family moved to Pittsburg, California, near Oakland, where John Henry emerged as an exceptional athlete at Pittsburg High School. He earned varsity letters in baseball, football, basketball, wrestling, and track. In 1949 he set a California schoolboy discus throwing record. Three years running he was an All-Contra Costa County Athletic League all-star in football, basketball, and track. His legendary athletic performances resulted in numerous awards. Johnson married Barbara Flood in 1950, and they had five children together before their divorce. He later married Leona Johnson.

Johnson enrolled at California's St. Mary's College in 1950, where he developed the football playing style that would mark the rest of this athletic career. At 6'2" and 225 pounds, Johnson helped define the modern fullback position on offense. He was a devastating blocker and a relentless, punishing ball carrier whose exceptional quickness allowed him to dart to the outside of the line and whose superior strength allowed him to run up the middle. In 1951 the St. Mary's Gaels played an overwhelmingly favored University of Georgia squad that had never competed against an African American player. In a game filled with racial tension, Johnson outplayed his opponents and secured a 7–7 tie for his team with a spectacular ninety-one-yard kickoff return. Referees, however, ejected Johnson in the third quarter for alleged disorderly conduct.

St. Mary's subsequently dropped its football program, and Johnson transferred to Modesto Junior College, California, and then to Arizona State University. At Arizona State he led the nation in punt returns, participated in the 1952 Olympic track decathlon trials, and in 1955 earned a bachelor's degree in Education.

In 1953 Johnson was chosen by the Pittsburgh Steelers in the National Football League (NFL) player draft. Instead he signed, for $11,000, with the Calgary Stampeders of the Canadian Football League. He played only one season with the Stampeders but was awarded the Jeff Nicklin Memorial Trophy as the Western Division's most valuable player. The next season he left Canada to join the NFL's San Francisco 49ers, where he was part of the celebrated "Million Dollar Backfield" of JOE PERRY, Hugh McElhenny, and quarterback Y. A. Tittle. Their versatility, improvisational ability, and on-field creativity marked them as one of the most accomplished offensive units in NFL history.

Johnson was traded in 1957 to the Detroit Lions, whom he helped lead to a world championship. In 1960 he joined the Pittsburgh Steelers and in 1962 rushed for 1,141 yards, becoming the first Steeler and only the ninth professional back to rush for 1,000 yards in a regular season. He also was the first on the team to gain 200 rushing yards in a single game when he rushed for 200 yards versus the Cleveland Browns on 10 October 1964.

After being released in 1965 by the Steelers, Johnson spent the 1966 season with the Houston Oilers of the American Football League. When he retired the next year at age thirty-seven, he ranked as the fourth leading rusher in NFL history. In 143 games over thirteen seasons, he gained 6,803 yards rushing on 1,571 carries for a 4.3-yard rushing average, caught 186 passes, and scored forty-eight touchdowns. He was selected to the Pro Bowl in 1954, 1962, 1963, and 1964. In 1972 the *Oakland Tribune* named him Eastbay Area High School's Athlete of the Century and the Alameda Newspaper Group selected him as one of the Fifty Most Significant Bay Area Sports Figures of the twentieth century. In 1987 he was elected to the Pro Football Hall of Fame.

In retirement, Johnson worked for several years in public relations and urban affairs for a Pittsburgh utility company. He founded the Johnson Henry Johnson Foundation, an organization that worked with disadvantaged children. He later moved to Cleveland, Ohio, and, after the death of his second wife in 2002 and after recurring health problems associated with his professional playing career, to Fremont, California, to live with his daughter, Kathy Moppin. He died in Tracy, California, at the age of 81.

FURTHER READING

The John Henry Johnson File is kept at the Pro Football Hall of Fame in Canton, Ohio.

Faraudo, Jeff. "Johnson, St. Mary's Stun All-White Georgia," *Oakland Tribune*, 22 Jan. 2004.

Pattak, Evan. "In Recognition of John Henry Johnson," *Pittsburgh Steelers Weekly*, 9 Aug. 1980.

Scott, Jim. "Yesterday's Hero: John Henry Johnson," *Pro Quarterback* (Jan. 1971).

Smith, Myron J. *Professional Football: The Official Pro Football Hall of Fame Bibliography* (1993).

JOHN HANNERS

Johnson, John Howard (1897–24 May 1995), Negro National League commissioner, longtime Harlem community activist, and ordained Episcopalian minister was born in Richmond, Virginia, to John Wesley and Harriet Howard Johnson.

Although Johnson was known primarily for his role as the last president of the Negro National League (NNL), he actually had little baseball acumen. In fact his sport of choice was basketball, and as a student-athlete at Columbia University in the early 1920s, he was one of the best basketball players of his day.

After graduating with a bachelor's degree and a master's degree in Anthropology from Columbia College, Johnson studied at Union Theological and General Theological seminaries in Manhattan. Then in 1923 he became an ordained minister in the Episcopal Church, beginning a career of service in Harlem that spanned seven decades. In 1928 he founded St. Martin's Parish in Harlem and by the late 1940s had overseen the congregation's growth to more than three thousand people at its 122nd Street location.

Meanwhile his community service work took him on a rather circuitous route toward baseball. In 1935 Johnson became the first African American on the Depression-era Emergency Relief Bureau; four years later, New York City Mayor Fiorello LaGuardia named Johnson the city's first African American police chaplain.

Near the end of World War II, in 1945, LaGuardia invited Johnson to join a newly established special commission called the Committee on Unity, which would examine the question of integration in baseball and study its potential ramifications. In the fall of the previous year, Major League Baseball Commissioner Judge Kenesaw Mountain Landis died; he had been a vehement detractor of integration in professional baseball. Although Landis claimed no written rule existed barring black athletes, he never supported their signing either.

LaGuardia invited ten citizens to form the Committee on Unity under the direction of Daniel Dodson, a professor of sociology at New York

University. The committee members involved had a common interest in avoiding anything that might bring negative publicity to Major League Baseball. One of the committee members was Branch Rickey, who would eventually sign JACKIE ROBINSON to a major league contract with the Brooklyn Dodgers in 1947.

The final report of the committee placed the responsibility for ending the color barrier on the team owners. The committee also received assistance from the new baseball commissioner, Senator A. B. "Happy" Chandler, who supported Rickey's move to sign Robinson by simply not preventing it from happening. The LaGuardia committee, however, was not able to accomplish much more than to contain mounting pressure, allowing Rickey additional time to complete his integration plans for the 1946 season.

Meanwhile, in the NNL, the strong attendance and modest administrative improvements in 1946 seemingly provided the league with a firm foundation for continued progress. Yet additional gains, including affiliation with organized baseball, appeared unlikely without the introduction of new leadership. By late 1946 several New York–based individuals, including Johnson, surfaced as potential candidates for the presidency of the NNL.

Johnson's appointment to NNL president in 1947 represented a bold stroke certain to bolster the NNL's legitimacy among both blacks and whites. Despite impressive academic, civic, and religious credentials, Johnson had little formal experience in sports except as a college basketball player years earlier. While supporting integration, Johnson was equally concerned with the plight of the Negro League, and as early as December 1945 he openly recommended affiliation with organized baseball, Major League Baseball.

In his new position Johnson sought to encode and enforce morality at the ballpark, but these efforts achieved only limited success. National Association for the Advancement of Colored People executive secretary Walter White stopped attending league games in New York after tiring of the drinking, loud-mouthed profanity, vulgarity, and fighting among black fans. In reaction to White's disappointment, Johnson announced plans to cultivate better behavior at Negro League parks.

Although some observers welcomed Johnson's outsider status and his attempted reforms, most remained uncertain of Johnson's chances of success. After several seasons of financial stability, the NNL and the Negro American League found themselves in a vulnerable position. With the signing of Robinson to the Brooklyn Dodgers, blacks seemed to value the success of individuals within an integrated setting more than the preservation of their own institutions. Separate institutions, including black baseball leagues, seemed increasingly irrelevant once successful integration had occurred.

As the financial conditions of the Negro Leagues deteriorated, Johnson made no attempt to conceal the infrastructural problems that these leagues faced. He openly admitted that since the color barrier had been broken, there was no hope of competing with Major League Baseball. Johnson recognized that in the changing postwar environment, affiliation offered the best opportunity to delay the inevitable collapse of segregated baseball. Incorporated within the structure of organized baseball, black franchises might have created renewed interest and gained much needed credibility among both blacks and white fans.

Finally, it would be the most venerated of the black major leaguers whose criticisms would prove most damaging to the waning Negro Leagues. After commenting to a reporter in February 1948 that Negro baseball needed a thorough housecleaning, Robinson articulated his views more formally in a June article in *Ebony*. Robinson cited obvious administrative deficiencies, including the Kansas City Monarchs' failure to sign him to a formal contract, the often unpleasant lifestyle for players, the poor quality of play, the lack of player discipline, and the inadequacy of the league governments. However, Robinson did reserve some praise for Johnson as a capable leader.

By September 1948 a desperate Johnson appeared unable to formulate alternative strategies to address the Negro National Leagues' financial crisis, and after the initial attempts at cost reduction and affiliation with organized baseball failed, the league folded.

In 1953, Johnson married Faith Pullar Johnson. They had three sons: Reverend Johan Johnson, Dr. Michael Johnson, and Reverend David Johnson.

Over his seven-plus-decade career in the ministry, one of the things Johnson fought for most was to eradicate the notion of a "black church"; he encouraged whites, blacks, and foreign-born Americans to enter the Episcopal Church and reached out to New York's ethnic communities, including Jews and Irish.

FURTHER READING

Heaphy, Leslie A. *The Negro Leagues, 1869–1960* (2003).

Lanctot, Neil. *Negro League Baseball: The Rise and Ruin of a Black Institution* (2004).

LUKE NICHTER

Johnson, John Rosamond (11 Aug. 1873–11 Nov. 1954), composer, performer, and anthologist, was born in Jacksonville, Florida, to Helen Dillet, the first black public schoolteacher in Florida, and James Johnson, the headwaiter at a local restaurant. He and his younger brother, JAMES WELDON JOHNSON, were raised in a cultured and economically secure home, a rarity for African Americans in the South in this era. Their mother read Dickens novels to them every night before bed, and they received music lessons from an early age. Indeed, John began playing the piano as a toddler. He went on to attend Atlanta University in Georgia, and his brother followed eight years later.

When Johnson graduated in 1899 from the New England Conservatory in Boston, where he had studied classical music, he realized that he wanted to explore the realm of musical comedy. He became a vocalist with Oriental America, an African American opera company whose productions differed from the pejorative, stereotypical representations of African Americans present in most theater at the time, often described as "coon" songs. Johnson retuned to Jacksonville to teach music lessons and assume the position of musical director in the public schools. He and his brother, who would become a prominent social activist, novelist, and diplomat, then left for New York to attempt to have their comic opera, *Toloso*, produced; this work satirized the sense of American imperialism after the Spanish-American War. While *Toloso* was never performed on Broadway, the Johnsons did meet a number of prominent people in the musical and theatrical industry in the process of trying to have their work brought to the stage.

Indeed, it was then that they met BOB COLE. The three men went on to collaborate as Cole and Johnson Brothers and created hundreds of popular songs, most notably "Under the Bamboo Tree" (1902) and "Congo Love Song" (1903). The team's first collaboration was "Louisiana Lize," a love song written in a new lyrical fashion, for which they earned fifty dollars. This song and the ones to follow marked a shift away from the burlesque and minstrel styles. Some of their songs (which featured titles like "I'll Love You, Honey, When the Money's Gone, but I'll Not Be with You" and "Ain't Dat Scan'lous") became best-sellers and were featured in numerous Broadway productions. The Johnson brothers' most famous collaboration, "Lift Every Voice and Sing," was created in 1900 to mark the anniversary of Abraham Lincoln's birthday. James wrote the lyrics and Rosamond wrote the music. The NAACP adopted it as the organization's official song, and it soon became known as "The Negro National Anthem."

Rosamond Johnson often set poetry to music, particularly the poetry of PAUL LAURENCE DUNBAR. The Johnsons also created musical comedies such as *The Shoo Fly Regiment* in 1906 and *The Red Moon* in 1908. Johnson also composed "The Belle of Bridgeport" (1900), "Humpty Dumpty" (1904), and "In Newport" (1904). He then collaborated with BERT WILLIAMS in "Mr. Load of Koal" and soon found that the musical collaborations created by Cole and Johnson Brothers were being sung by such popular entertainers as Lillian Russell and George Primrose. Johnson studied with Samuel Coleridge-Taylor in London in the early 1900s, and when he toured Europe in the 1910s, he became one of the first African Americans to conduct a white orchestra when he directed the revue *Hello Paris*. He then returned to the United States to perform in vaudeville productions with Cole.

After Cole's death in 1911, Johnson became the musical director of the Hammerstein Opera House in London. Upon his return to the United States in 1914, he and his wife started a music school known as the Music School Settlement for Colored People. He had married Nora Ethel Floyd, one of his former piano students in Jacksonville, in 1913 in London. They had two children. Johnson toured across the country, singing spirituals with Taylor Gordon and covering the vaudeville circuit in the early 1920s. The Johnson brothers also edited collections of spirituals (*The Book of American Negro Spirituals* in 1925 and *The Second Book of American Negro Spirituals* in 1926). He performed on stage in the role of Lawrence Frasier in *Porgy and Bess* in 1935 and in *Mamba's Daughter* in 1939 and served as the musical director of *Emperor Jones*, starring PAUL ROBESON, in 1933, and *Cabin in the Sky* in 1935. Johnson spent the 1930s and 1940s as a music arranger and editor at a few publishing houses in New York and published hundreds of songs. He died at the age of eighty-one in New York City.

Johnson was an influential composer and performer who had a deep impact on the music and theater of New York from the beginning to the middle of the twentieth century. He and his brother will forever be remembered for giving the world "Lift Every Voice and Sing," but he should also be remembered as a prolific songwriter, singer, and anthologist. As talented as he was innovative, Johnson established new directions in both music and theater featuring African Americans, moving away from minstrelsy and toward productions that reflected his passion for musical comedy and his classical training in opera.

FURTHER READING

Johnson's papers are part of the Irving S. Gilmore Music Library at Yale University, a collection of music, correspondence, and photographs that resides across the street from the archive of his brother, James.

Floyd, Samuel A., Jr., ed. *International Dictionary of Black Composers* (1999).

Johnson, James Weldon. *Along This Way* (1933).

Perry, Frank, Jr. "John Rosamond Johnson," in *Afro-American Vocal Music: A Select Guide to Fifteen Composers* (1991).

Woll, Allen. "The End of the Coon Song: Bob Cole and the Johnson Brothers," in *Black Musical Theatre: From Coontown to Dreamgirls* (1989).

JENNIFER WOOD

Johnson, Johnnie (8 July 1924–13 Apr. 2005), musician, was born Johnnie Clyde Johnson in Fairmont, West Virginia, to Priscilla Banks Johnson and Johnnie "Buddy" Johnson, a coalminer. After Priscilla's death, Buddy's sister Cora and her husband Ernest Williams took in the infant Johnnie. Cora later purchased an upright piano, and a young Johnnie took to the instrument immediately. He quickly learned big band, R&B, and country tunes by listening to late-night radio broadcasts. One of Johnson's favorite artists was MEADE "LUX" LEWIS. Lewis's boogie-woogie style, in which the left hand plays a heavy, steady rhythm, would influence Johnson's piano technique. Johnson moved to Detroit at seventeen and there found work on a Ford Motor Company assembly line. Johnson served in the Marines in the South Pacific in World War II. He joined the Barracudas, a twenty-two piece orchestra that included servicemen from such bands as COUNT BASIE, Tommy Dorsey, and Glenn Miller. Johnson could not read music so he created a storehouse of musical snippets in his mind in order to keep up with the other musicians. His tenure with the Barracudas convinced him to pursue a career in music after the war. After returning to Detroit in 1946, he married Marguerite Rolls.

Three years later Johnson moved to Chicago. He worked during the day for Ford and received a valuable musical education in the Windy City's vibrant blues club scene. Johnson saw such performers as MUDDY WATERS, MEMPHIS SLIM, and BIG JOE TURNER perform on a nightly basis. He began to devote himself to music and formed a jazz and blues group, the Johnnie Johnson Quartet, in 1951, one year after separating from Marguerite, whom he would eventually divorce. The band had some local success, but with a severe drinking problem, Johnson could not hold jobs, and he decided to relocate to East St. Louis, Illinois, at his oldest brother Pless's urging.

In East St. Louis, Johnson put together the R&B-based Sir John's Trio. Before a New Year's Eve 1952 gig at the Cosmopolitan Club, the band's saxophone player took ill, and Johnson hired a flashy twenty-six year-old guitarist named CHUCK BERRY to fill in. Here began one of the most important collaborations in the history of rock 'n' roll. Berry's charisma and ambition led Johnson to cede control of the band. Local success led to a recording contract with Chicago's Chess Records, a blues label that featured on its roster such luminaries as Waters and BO DIDDLEY. Berry was one of the most successful of the early rock 'n' roll artists, churning out hit after hit beginning in the mid-1950s, including "Maybellene," "Roll Over Beethoven," "Carol," "School Day," and "Brown Eyed Handsome Man." Although Berry denied it, Johnson is generally credited as the inspiration for "Johnny B. Goode." Berry occasionally recorded without Johnson, but the piano player provided the driving rhythm and much of the joyful sound of his songs, although recording engineers kept the sound of Johnson's instrument low. During these good times, Johnson married Rose Hill in 1955. The marriage lasted approximately five years. Berry and Johnson performed together intermittently during the 1960s, due in part to Berry's imprisonment under the Mann Act. Berry was convicted after a fourteen-year-old Apache waitress he had hired to work in his St. Louis club was arrested for prostitution. Berry rarely paid Johnson more than the standard scale fee, even when they performed in the 1990s. Berry got rich from royalties and performance fees while his sideman struggled to earn a living.

Johnson played on many of Berry's post-prison 1960s sides and served a brief stint in ALBERT KING's blues band, but the following two decades were not kind to him. In 1973, he parted ways with Berry. The following year his wife Maudell Powell (m. 1968) died. In the early 1980s he performed in St. Louis clubs by night and drove a bus for senior citizens by day. His heavy drinking left him bloated and disheveled. Johnson's luck changed in 1986. The Rolling Stones guitarist Keith Richards was entrusted with finding a good band to back Berry for two performances that would be featured in the film *Hail! Hail! Rock 'n' Roll* (1987). Richards selected Johnson to play piano. The shows celebrated Berry's sixtieth birthday, but they also served as a rebirth for the sixty-two-year-old Johnson, who recorded his first solo album, *Blue Hand Johnnie*, in 1988. It would be followed by four more releases over the next seven years. His CD *Johnnie Be Bad*, featuring Richards, Eric Clapton, and JOHN LEE HOOKER, received a 1992 Grammy nomination for Best Traditional Blues Album. During this period Johnson cut back on his drinking with the help of his fourth wife, Frances Miller, whom he married in 1991. This, along with his securing of better management, enabled him to tour the world and to make more money than ever before.

In 2000, the year before he was inducted into the Rock and Roll Hall of Fame, Johnson filed a lawsuit against Berry, claiming that he had co-written over fifty songs for which Berry had failed to give him credit. A federal judge dismissed the case in 2002, stating that the statute of limitations had expired years before. The question of Johnson's contribution to Berry's catalog is contentious. Several rock legends, including Richards, Diddley, and Clapton, lent support to Johnson's side. Berry biographer Bruce Pegg asserted, however, that Johnson's comments on the matter have been inconsistent. It appears that Johnson help to arrange and write some of Berry's tunes, but the assertion, made by Richards and Johnson's biographer Travis Fitzpatrick, that Johnson contributed the music and Berry added the words lacks evidence. Johnson's drinking problems during the period and the difficulty in determining Berry's truthfulness make it nearly impossible to rule conclusively on the songwriting claim. However, the pianist's lack of public recognition and Berry's failure to pay him more than a standard sideman's wage lends moral, if not legal, support to his and his supporters' claims. Johnson died in St. Louis at the age of eighty. He was survived by Frances, ten children, and several grandchildren.

Johnson's contributions to popular music mark him as one of the most influential black musicians of the last fifty years of the twentieth century. Johnson borrowed from blues and jazz to create his own immediately recognizable style, which set the standard for rock piano. Most important, his collaborations with Berry formed the basis for the dominant style of rock 'n' roll to follow.

FURTHER READING
Fitzpatrick, Travis. *Father of Rock & Roll: The Story of Johnnie "B. Goode" Johnson* (1999).
Fricke, David. "Keith Remembers Johnnie," *Rolling Stone.com* (15 Apr. 2005).
Pegg, Bruce. *Brown Eyed Handsome Man: The Life and Hard Times of Chuck Berry* (2002).
Obituary: *St. Louis Post-Dispatch*, 13 Apr. 2005.

ZACHARY J. LECHNER

Johnson, Joshua (fl. 1795–1824), painter, was probably born in the West Indies. It is now generally believed by scholars of American art and history that Johnson was black and may have come to this country as a young man, probably as a slave. Johnson might be identified as the "negro boy" mentioned in the 1777 will of Captain Robert Polk of Maryland. This boy is thought to have been purchased by Polk's brother-in-law, the noted artist Charles Willson Peale. Stylistic resemblances between the work of Charles Willson Peale and Joshua Johnson are apparent. Unfortunately, very little documentation on Johnson exists, and identification of his works is accomplished through provenance (mostly oral family tradition), and connoisseurship—observation of technique, subject matter, iconography, and style.

Johnson's artistic career spanned nearly thirty years, during which he worked only in Baltimore, painting portraits of many of its citizens. Like many artists of the period he more than likely also worked in a related field, such as sign painting or carriage painting, in order to make a living. It is likely that for most of his professional life he was a freeman. If he had ever been a slave, he was evidently free by 19 December 1798, when he placed an advertisement for his services as a portrait artist in the *Baltimore Intelligencer*. A slave could not usually have advertised for clients in this manner, and in the advertisement he alluded to the difficulties of his life: "As a *self-taught genius*, deriving from nature and industry his knowledge of the Art; and having experienced many insufferable obstacles in the pursuit of his studies, it is highly gratifying to him to make assurances of his ability to execute all commands, with an effect, and in a style, which must give satisfaction." He is listed as a "Free Householder of Coulour" in the 1816–1817 Baltimore city directory, and an 1810 census lists a Josa. Johnston as a "free negro." "Johnson" was on occasion spelled with a "t," and there is some disagreement among scholars as to whether "Johnson" is the correct form of the artist's last name. The only signed painting attributed to him (*Sarah Ogden Gustin*, National Gallery of Art, Washington, D.C.) shows it as "Johnson," while his advertisement spells his name as "Johnston," as does his signature on a 1798 petition for the paving of German Lane, where he lived. Johnson was able to earn portrait commissions because of the growing wealth of Baltimore's citizenry. Colonial Baltimore attracted major capital investors in the 1780s; along with this growth came a certain cosmopolitan atmosphere. By 1800 a fifth of Baltimore's population was black, and nearly half of those persons were free, a very high percentage for the American South. The increasing popularity of Quakerism and Methodism in Maryland, both with strong antislavery stances, encouraged manumissions. Unfortunately, kidnapping for resale into slavery was a constant and real possibility, but safety in numbers helped somewhat, and Johnson, like many free blacks, initially chose to live in the poorer Fells Point area. However, he subsequently moved near the intersection of German and Hanover streets, a wealthier neighborhood that boasted a number of abolitionists and no doubt provided many more clients. All but two of his approximately eighty known portraits are of white subjects.

Johnson spent his entire career in Baltimore, the only artist of the first quarter of the nineteenth century to do so. He is listed as a limner at eight different Baltimore addresses between 1796 and 1824, apparently never moving to other cities or towns in search of new clients. This consistency may in part be attributable to the difficulties he faced as a free black in a slave-owning society. Johnson often painted likenesses of his near neighbors. The majority of his late images are of working- and middle-class Baltimoreans, while his early subjects reflect more upper-class individuals—members of prominent families, many of whom were also clients of the Peales (once again indicating an early connection to the Peale family).

Johnson probably did not maintain a painting studio, but like many artists of this period, he worked in his sitters' homes. Children constitute a particularly large percentage of his portrait subjects. He often posed them standing, and he used such decorative devices as fruit, books, and even butterflies. A painting of an unidentified girl shows the young subject holding a flower in one hand while she stands in front of greenery (Baltimore Museum of Art). Just under her other hand, an overlarge butterfly sits on a bush.

In another painting of a child, a young girl stands on a marble floor near a window with drapery pulled aside to reveal a hint of an exterior garden scene. (*Emma Van Name*, Whitney Museum of American Art, New York). Emma holds a strawberry in one hand and gestures to a wine glass nearly as big as she is filled with berries next to her. Johnson modeled the forms of the figure to indicate depth and created spatial relationships by using overlapping forms that moved back within the composition. His linear approach with thinly applied paint reflects knowledge of, if not training by, Charles Willson Peale and indicates some awareness of European styles, though Johnson's works remain within the American folk tradition.

There are only two known portraits by Johnson of black sitters. These probably depict Abner (Bowdoin College Museum of Art, Brunswick, Maine) and DANIEL COKER (American Museum in Britain, Bath, England), two dignitaries of the African Methodist Episcopal (AME) Church. The Daniel Coker identification is based on a comparison with a known portrait of him, while the identification of Abner Coker rests on its apparent pairing in size and composition with the other portrait and the professional relationship of the two men. There are few extant images of African Americans from this period, and these two portraits are respectful and dignified likenesses. A portrait of the Most Reverend John Carroll, first archbishop of Baltimore from 1808 to 1815, reflects Johnson's ties to the Catholic Church, supported by baptismal and death records for his children. Stylistically the elongated eyes, thin paint, and crossed hands with book are all characteristic of Johnson's style.

Johnson's technical approach to painting was distinctive, helping with the identification of his works. Johnson stretched his canvases onto strainers with fixed corners using plain weave fabric that was tightly woven and quite textured. He apparently liked a colored ground, which ranged from gray to buff, and he painted with thin paint, making very few revisions. He would apply small areas of intense color that contrasted with the surrounding, more limited palette. His subjects, always portraits of individuals, place him squarely within the colonial tradition of American Art. Johnson's career parallels the development of painting in the colonies, and he is significant within both African American history and the tradition of American art. The date of Johnson's death is unknown; he last appears in the Baltimore City Directory in 1824, in which he is listed as "Johnson, Joshua, portrait painter, Sleigh's Lane, S side E of Spring."

FURTHER READING

Very little archival documentation on Johnson exists, but both the Maryland Historical Society and the Abby Aldrich Rockefeller Folk Art Center have taken an interest in the artist.

Bearden, Romare, and Harry Henderson. *A History of African American Artists from 1792–Present* (1993).

Pleasants, Dr. J. Hall. "Joshua Johnston: The First American Negro Portrait Painter," *Maryland Historical Magazine* 37, no. 2 (June 1942): 121–149.

Weekley, Carolyn J., et al. *Joshua Johnson: Freeman and Early American Portrait Painter* (1987).

This entry is taken from the *American National Biography* and is published here with the permission of the American Council of Learned Societies.

J. SUSAN ISAACS

Johnson, Judy (26 Oct. 1899–15 June 1989), baseball player, manager, scout, and coach, was born William Julius Johnson in Snow Hill, Maryland, the son of William Henry Johnson, a seaman, boxing trainer, and athletic director, and Annie Lane. He was the youngest of three children, following his brother, Johnny, and his sister, Mary Emma. In 1905 or soon thereafter the Johnsons settled in Wilmington, Delaware, and William Henry secured a job as athletic director of the Negro Settlement House. He was skilled in the art of self-defense and taught the rudiments of boxing to both his youngest son and his daughter. Although Johnson hoped that his son would become a prizefighter, the youth preferred playing sandlot football and baseball.

Baseball became young Johnson's passion, and he played games in his neighborhood and the surrounding area, where his team would pass the hat and hope to get enough money to buy a couple of baseballs for the next game. His early equipment consisted of his father's hand-me-down glove that was falling apart from dry rot and street shoes with nailed-on metal spikes. He attended Frederick Douglass School and completed one year at Howard High School, both in Washington, D.C., before ending his formal education to take a job as a stevedore on the loading docks at Deepwater Port, across the Delaware River in New Jersey. He commuted to work and earned three dollars a week but continued to pursue the game he loved.

In 1918 he began playing semipro baseball with the Madison Stars of Chester, Pennsylvania. After the end of World War I he had a tryout with the Hilldale Daisies, a top black team in the Philadelphia suburb of Darby, Pennsylvania. (The team sometimes wore different uniforms and played as the Bacharach Giants in Atlantic City, New Jersey.) He played three games a week for five dollars per game, but it was clear that he was not yet ready to play at that level, and he soon returned to the Madison Stars, an unofficial farm team for Hilldale. Johnson was the Stars' shortstop until Hilldale, watching his progress, reacquired his contract in 1921 for $100. Johnson signed his first contract for $135 a month and acquired the nickname "Judy" because of his resemblance to an old-time baseball player named Jude Gans; he carried the name with him the rest of his life.

Hilldale's manager, Bill Francis, played third base, so Johnson was placed at shortstop, which was not his best position because of his restricted range. When JOHN HENRY LLOYD, a star shortstop himself, became Hilldale's manager in 1923, he moved Johnson to the hot corner (third base) and tutored him at the position, building his confidence. Johnson eventually became one of the best third basemen in the history of the Negro Leagues and always credited Lloyd with being instrumental in his success. He had good range, sure hands, and a strong and accurate arm. Although he was not fast afoot, Johnson was a smart, instinctive base runner. He batted right-handed and was a good line-drive hitter, with respectable extra-base power and an excellent batting eye. Having achieved professional success, he married Anita T. Irons, a schoolteacher, in 1923, and they had one daughter, Loretta, born in 1926. She would eventually marry Bill Bruton, a major league player.

In 1923 Hilldale became a charter member of the Eastern Colored League and won its first three pennants, with Johnson batting .391, .369, and .392 while playing a key role in the field. Johnson led the team in 1924 with a .341 batting average, but that year Hilldale lost in the first Negro World Series to the Negro National League champion, the Kansas City Monarchs, in a hard-fought ten-game series. The same two teams met again in the 1925 Negro World Series, but this time Hilldale emerged victorious, winning four games against a single loss to reign as the Negro Leagues champions. Johnson batted only .250 but contributed some clutch hits to the victory. That was Hilldale's last pennant, but Johnson remained with the franchise through the 1929 season, batting .390 that year.

In addition to his success with Hilldale, Johnson played in winter baseball leagues. In 1924–1925 he played at West Palm Beach in the Florida Hotel League before taking the first of four winter treks to Cuba in 1926–1927, when he hit .374 for Alacranes.

The next two winters Johnson played in Cuba, batting .331 and .341. He stayed home in the winter of 1929–1930 but returned for his last year in Cuba in 1930–1931 and finished with a lifetime Cuban batting average of .334.

Johnson left Hilldale in 1930 to become playing manager of a Pennsylvania team, the Homestead Grays. In July the Grays were playing the Kansas City Monarchs in Pittsburgh when the Grays' catcher suffered a split finger that forced him to leave the game. According to Johnson, he recruited a young JOSH GIBSON, who was sitting in the stands as a spectator, to catch the remainder of the game. After being pressed into service as a replacement, Gibson became the regular catcher for the balance of the season and went on to become the greatest slugger in Negro Leagues history. At the end of the regular season the Grays defeated the New York Lincoln Giants in a ten-game play-off for the eastern championship.

After only one season at the Homestead helm, Johnson returned to Hilldale as playing manager in 1931 until the team disbanded midseason in 1932. He then joined the Pittsburgh Crawfords, a dominant team in black baseball, and contributed batting averages of .332, .333, .367, and .315, respectively, from 1933 through 1936. During these years the Crawfords featured five future Hall of Famers: SATCHEL PAIGE, Josh Gibson, OSCAR CHARLESTON, COOL PAPA BELL, and Johnson himself. In 1933 the Crawfords' owner, GUS GREENLEE, who was also league president, claimed a disputed Negro National League pennant, but the Crawfords then defeated the New York Cubans in a play-off to win an undisputed 1935 championship; they repeated as champions in 1936. The 1935 team is considered by most baseball historians to be the greatest team in the history of the Negro Leagues.

During his tenure with the Crawfords, the inaugural East-West All-Star game was played in 1933. Johnson appeared in the game, getting a hit in his only time at bat, and made another appearance in the 1936 East-West classic. During his years with the Crawfords the team played several postseason exhibition games against teams that included white major leaguers. In 1932 the Crawfords defeated Casey Stengel's All-Stars in five of seven games played, and two years later beat the St. Louis Cardinals and their star pitcher Dizzy Dean in three exhibition games. Johnson also played exhibition ball in Mexico in 1936 against major leaguers Rogers Hornsby and Jimmie Foxx. Johnson's career batting average against major leaguers was .263.

In the spring of 1937 Gus Greenlee traded Johnson and Josh Gibson to the Homestead Grays for two mediocre players and $2,500, but Johnson chose to retire instead. He finished with a .309 career batting average in the Negro Leagues.

In retirement he lived near Wilmington in a two-story home in Marshalton, Delaware, that he had bought in 1934. He soon began coaching a local amateur baseball team, the Alco Flashes, and worked at a variety of jobs before returning to baseball. He was a supervisor for the Continental Can Company in Wilmington, operated a general store with his brother, drove a school bus, and worked in security at Mullins department store. In 1952 he was hired as a scout for the Philadelphia Athletics, and two years later he became the first black coach in the major leagues, when he went to spring training with the Athletics. His duties required that he also work with minor league clubs. While he was with the Athletics, the owner, Connie Mack, told Johnson that the reason he had not hired black players before JACKIE ROBINSON broke the color line was that "there were just too many of you to go in." Johnson scouted for the Milwaukee Braves in 1956 and for the Philadelphia Phillies in 1959.

Johnson finally retired in 1972 and was inducted into the National Baseball Hall of Fame in Cooperstown, New York, in 1975. Afterward, Wilmington's city government named the park where he had played in his youth in his honor, and a statue of Johnson was erected at the local minor league ballpark, home of the Wilmington Blues. After his wife, Anita, died in 1986, Johnson was never the same. The sadness of her death and the loneliness of her absence stayed with him until 1989, when he died of a stroke in Wilmington, Delaware.

During his career Johnson starred on several of the Negro Leagues' top teams and earned recognition as one of the greatest third basemen, black or white, of his generation. His affiliation with major league franchises after the color line was eradicated helped younger generations of African Americans to make the transition to organized baseball.

FURTHER READING
Holway, John. *Black Ball Stars: Negro League Pioneers* (1988).
Peterson, Robert. *Only the Ball Was White* (1970).
Rendle, Ellen. *Judy Johnson: Delaware's Invisible Hero* (1994).

JAMES A. RILEY

Johnson, Katherine G. (26 Aug. 1918–), physicist, space scientist, and mathematician, was born in White Sulphur Springs, West Virginia. Johnson started attending the local elementary school, but in the 1920s and 1930s, the public school system in White Sulphur Springs did not provide educational opportunities for black children beyond the eighth grade. In a 1997 interview with the *Richmond Post-Dispatch*, Johnson recalled that her parents were determined to give their children every educational opportunity and moved to Institute, West Virginia—120 miles away—in September of every year so that Johnson and her siblings could attend school. Johnson attended West Virginia State College, where she earned a B.S. in French and Mathematics and explored her interests in physics. Graduating summa cum laude in 1937, she taught high school and elementary school in southwest Virginia before going to work for NASA.

In 1953, Johnson joined NASA's Langley Research Center in Hampton, Virginia, as a pool mathematician, working with other women in racially segregated groups. Shortly after she arrived, Johnson began working as an aerospace technologist with the flight research division; she would continue to work there for the next thirty-three years. At Langley, Johnson distinguished herself as a scientist and mathematician when she helped develop mathematical techniques used in spacecraft navigation. In the *Richmond Times-Dispatch* interview, Johnson noted significant technological changes that occurred during her career with the space program. When she began as a mathematician, humans performed the complex numerical calculations. Johnson remembers doing "her early work with pencil and paper. It was a time when computers wore skirts" (Winston).

Johnson worked in NASA's Flight Dynamics and Control Division with the tracking team, which recorded the flight paths of both manned and unmanned orbital spacecrafts. In the late 1960s and 1970s, Johnson worked on many challenging mathematical problems, including those related to interplanetary trajectories, space navigation, and the orbits of spacecraft, problems that allowed NASA to pinpoint the exact location of the Apollo spacecrafts throughout their space missions. She also worked with the Earth Resources Satellite to locate Earth's underground mineral resources from outer space and, as a NASA mathematician, analyzed data gathered by tracking stations on Earth during the lunar orbital missions and the Apollo moon missions.

Among Johnson's most significant contributions was her collaborative work with the mathematician Ted Skopinski. Johnson and Skopinski devised the method that allowed NASA to project the position of spacecraft with respect to the earth, information needed to guide astronauts and their spacecrafts along a specific return path to Earth. The publication resulting from this work, "Determination of Azimuth Angle at Burnout for Placing a Satellite over a Selected Earth Position," was one of many technical reports to which Johnson contributed.

Johnson's calculations were instrumental in Alan B. Shepard Jr.'s first manned space flight in May 1961, John Glenn's circumvention of the earth in February 1962, and Neil Armstrong's moon walk in July 1969. In 1997, Johnson recalled that working on the flight path for Shepard's mission "was easy.... It was just a matter of shooting him up and having him come back down" (Winston). The major difficulty was making sure that he landed in the ocean and not on land. As NASA set increasingly ambitious goals, Johnson's work became more and more complex. For example, the *Apollo 11* mission, as compared to Shepherd's flight, required calculation of the trajectories to put the spacecraft into a lunar orbit, to send a lunar landing module to the moon's surface, to return the module to the spacecraft and to return the spacecraft to Earth.

Much of Johnson's work dealt with algebraic equations that allowed mathematicians to relate flight paths to the earth's rotation and the moon's movements. She calculated orbits around the earth, orbits farther into space and orbits around the moon and back. After mapping the stars the astronauts should see at each point in their orbit, Johnson developed emergency navigation systems for the early manned space flights. If navigation systems failed, her star maps would allow astronauts to determine their location in space, allowing them to stay on the correct course and, if necessary, to make corrections in the flight path. This type of map was particularly important to the successful return of the damaged *Apollo 13* capsule.

Johnson began her career with NASA at the height of the cold war. Fear of the Soviet Union's possible military aggression and technological superiority grew in 1949 when the Soviets successfully exploded a nuclear bomb, and again in 1957, when they launched *Sputnik 1*, the first craft to reach outer space. Fears were also heightened by the Apollo launching pad fire of 1969, which resulted in the deaths of the astronauts Virgil Grissom, Edward White II, and Roger Chaffe. All of these events brought more resources and urgency to NASA's space programs.

Throughout her career Johnson received numerous awards in recognition of her contributions to NASA and the fields of mathematics and physics. Along with other members of NASA's Lunar Spacecraft and Operations team, she received the Group Achievement Award for pioneering work in the field of navigation. In a single year, the Lunar Orbiter program produced five successful photographic flights, each returning to Earth with highly detailed images of the moon. These images increased NASA's understanding of the moon's geography and heightened the possibility of successful manned flights to the moon. NASA recognized Johnson with special achievement awards in 1970, 1980, and 1985. She received an honorary Doctor of Laws from the State University of New York at Farmingdale in 1998, and she was West Virginia State College's Outstanding Alumnus of the Year in 1999.

Johnson's career with NASA spanned more than three decades, beginning before the Mercury project and continuing until her retirement in 1986, during the earliest stages of the Space Shuttle program. She participated in almost every stage of America's twentieth-century space program. Johnson helped to make the American space program a success at a time when it seemed to many an essential component to U.S. national security and technological advancement. If her early career paralleled the expanding Cold War, it also encompassed the era of the civil rights and women's rights movements, which challenged the institutionalized racism and sexism of modern America. At a time when discrimination based on race and sex thwarted the ambitions of many, she attained the highest levels of excellence in her work, making significant contributions to NASA's manned and unmanned space flight programs.

FURTHER READING

"Katherine G. Johnson: Space Scientist." *Golden Legacy*, vol. 5 (1969).

Sluby, Patricia Carter. "Black Women and Inventions," *Sage: A Scholarly Journal on Black Women* 6, no. 2 (Fall 1989).

U.S. Department of Energy. *Black Contributors to Science and Energy Technology* (1979).

Winston, Bonnie V. "Katherine Johnson: Black History: Virginia Profiles," *Richmond Times-Dispatch*, 2 Feb. 1997.

PAMELA C. EDWARDS

Johnson, Kathryn Magnolia (15 Dec. 1878–13 Nov. 1954), educator, lecturer, journalist, and activist, was born in Darke County, Ohio. She was one of eight children of Lucinda Johnson. Her father, whose name has not been discovered, was dead by 1880.

Johnson grew up in Preble County, a rural area of Ohio in which African Americans made up less than 1 percent of the total population. In a community called New Paris, she attended public schools. Her stepfather, Harper Orchard, a former slave and a landowning farmer, was an active member of the African Methodist Episcopal (AME) Church. It was, in large measure, because of his encouragement and support that Johnson enrolled at Wilberforce University, the oldest, private, historically black college established by the Methodist Episcopal Church in 1856, and later operated by the AME Church. In an era when many doubted the intellectual capabilities of African Americans and wanted them restricted to menial employment, the school actively promoted the concept that African Americans were inferior to no one and capable of achieving any goal. At Wilberforce, Johnson was surrounded by and regularly interacted with living examples of this precept. She was influenced by educators and activists such as WILLIAM SANDERS SCARBOROUGH, probably the first African American classical scholar, HALLIE QUINN BROWN, who became the first dean of women at Tuskegee Institute and president of the National Association of Colored Women, and COLONEL CHARLES YOUNG, who distinguished himself as the third African American graduate of West Point and the first to attain the rank of colonel.

After completing the teacher training program in 1898, Johnson taught school in Ohio and Indiana. In 1901 she returned to Wilberforce and graduated with a B.S. degree in 1902. Subsequently she taught at the state normal school in Elizabeth City, North Carolina, and at Shorter College in Little Rock, Arkansas. Johnson was a student at the University of North Dakota in the summer of 1908.

By 1910 Johnson had relocated to Kansas City, Kansas, where she lived with her older brother, Jesse, and his family. She was teaching school and was likely a member of First AME Church, the oldest of that denomination in Kansas City. In 1911 the National Association for the Advancement of Colored People (NAACP) mounted a nationwide campaign against lynching. According to one of that organization's founders, Mary White Ovington, Johnson was hired as the first fieldworker for the southern and western portion of the

United States for the organization. In this capacity she sold subscriptions to *The Crisis*, the official NAACP journal founded by the scholar and activist W. E. B. DuBois as a vehicle for disseminating the group's message. Johnson also educated black southerners about their rights and recruited them as members. By 1913 her responsibilities included organizing branches throughout the southern and western United States. It was not until 1915 that she received a salary for her efforts; up to that time she was paid commissions based on sales and members recruited. In 1916 Johnson was terminated, allegedly due to her forceful personality and vocal opposition to the fact that whites held leadership roles in the organization. Ironically termination came six months after she had been commended for her success in organizing all-black branches.

During World War I, Johnson was employed by the YMCA and sent to France to observe the racial climate and protect the rights of African American soldiers. Along with Helen Noble Curtis and ADDIE W. HUNTON, both widowed, Johnson was among the first of fifteen African American women so employed. Johnson and Hunton co-authored a book published in 1920 entitled *Two Colored Women with the American Expeditionary Forces*. The book detailed discriminatory acts against African American soldiers, such as their having to wait for medical treatment until white soldiers were attended to more immediately. They reported that some canteens were racially restricted and that in others African American soldiers were served the food that remained after the white soldiers had eaten. They visually documented inequality of treatment by including photographs of "For Colored Only" signs. They also noted that the soldiers and welfare workers from the Salvation Army, YMCA, YWCA, and Knights of Columbus were segregated by race during the trans-Atlantic crossing, with African Americans confined to less desirable quarters.

In addition to exposing the demeaning conditions faced by African American soldiers, Johnson and her colleagues worked to uplift their morale by planning social activities. They met soldiers' spiritual needs through Bible study classes. In addition, the women established a lending library, conducted literacy classes, and wrote letters for the wounded. Johnson remained in France for fourteen months, returning to New York in August 1919.

Following her return to America, Johnson held a variety of positions. She was a sales representative for the Association for the Study of Negro Life and History and its publication arm, Associated Publishers. In this capacity she traveled throughout the nation in an effort to expose African Americans to the printed word and enhance their knowledge of the history and culture of people of African descent throughout the world.

By November 1919 Johnson was also serving as an associate editor of the *Half Century Magazine*, which was founded in 1916 and named to commemorate and celebrate the fiftieth anniversary of the Emancipation Proclamation. Its target audience was middle-class African Americans, particularly women. Most of the articles focused on fashion, etiquette, cooking, vacations, and news of importance to African Americans.

In the census of 1930 Johnson identified herself as an independent author and lecturer. For the remainder of her life, she continued to write and lecture on subjects related to the advancement of African Americans. She maintained her membership in the AME Church. She was a Republican and a member of the Independent Order of St. Luke, a fraternal organization, which aided the sick and aged, promoted charitable causes, and encouraged self-help among its members.

Johnson, who never married, died in Chicago's Provident Hospital. Her passing was briefly noted in the *Chicago Daily News*, where she was acknowledged as the first field agent for the NAACP.

FURTHER READING

Arnold, Thea. "Kathryn Magnolia Johnson," in *Black Women in America, An Historical Encyclopedia*, ed. Darlene Clark Hine (1993).

Bolden, Tonya. *The Book of African-American Women* (2004).

Obituary: *Chicago Daily Tribune*, 15 Nov. 1954.

DONNA TYLER HOLLIE

Johnson, Lonnie (8 Feb. 1889?–16 June 1970), singer and guitarist, was born Alonzo Johnson in New Orleans, Louisiana. His parents' names are not known. His father was a string-band musician, and Lonnie first learned to play the fiddle, then the six- and twelve-string guitars, mandolin, banjo, string bass, piano, and harmonium. Dropping out of school in about 1902, he performed regularly around New Orleans in the Storyville red-light district with his father, his brother James "Steady Roll" Johnson, and Punch Miller.

In 1917 he sailed to London with a (now unidentified) musical revue, returning in 1919 to find most of his family wiped out by the influenza epidemic.

From 1920 to 1922 Johnson was based in St. Louis, during which time he appeared with Charlie Creath's Jazz-O-Maniacs aboard the Mississippi riverboat SS *St. Paul* and with FATE MARABLE's band on SS *Capitol*. From 1922 to 1924 Johnson performed solo or with the comedic dancers Clenn and Jenkins on the Theater Owners' Booking Association circuit in the South, but he worked outside music in 1924 and 1925, save for some performances with his brother James in East St. Louis. In 1925 Johnson married the blues singer Mary Smith, with whom he had six children before their marriage ended in 1932.

By 1925 the blues craze of the 1920s had reached its peak, and the as-yet-unrecorded but remarkably original and versatile Johnson entered a blues singing contest at the Booker T. Washington Theatre in St. Louis as a means of securing a recording contract. Eight weeks later Johnson emerged victorious, signing with Okeh Records. He was amused to be cast as a blues singer since he had sung a blues song only because the contest called for it. On 2 November 1925 he sang and played fiddle on "Won't Don't Blues" with Creath's band, two days later recording his first sides under his own name and exposing his prodigious guitar technique on record for the first time.

Johnson recorded more than two hundred sides between 1925 and 1932, most of them under his own name and released on the Okeh, Gennett, and Columbia labels, including his groundbreaking and highly influential guitar duets with Eddie Lang and the Hokum recordings with Spencer Williams. In addition, Johnson answered Okeh's call to accompany a wide variety of performers, among them the field-holler-style vocalist Alger "Texas" Alexander, the vaudeville blues singers CHIPPIE HILL, CLARA SMITH, and VICTORIA SPIVEY, and the pop performer Martha Raye, as well as the jazz artists LOUIS ARMSTRONG, DUKE ELLINGTON, and the Chocolate Dandies. During this time Johnson traveled around the country, playing in Chicago, New York, Dallas, and Philadelphia, coming in second in a blues contest to Lillian Glinn in Dallas, and touring with BESSIE SMITH in the *Midnight Steppers Revue* in 1929. After performing in the *Lonnie Johnson Recording Guitarist* show in New York for about a year, he did some recordings for Okeh, and his first recording for Victor, from 1930 through 1932. However, by 1932 the Depression and "talkies" helped dry up opportunities for live theater shows, so Johnson relocated to Cleveland and returned to factory work, appearing occasionally with Putney Dandridge in clubs and on the radio.

A Decca recording contract in 1937 helped revive Johnson's career, precipitating club dates in Chicago and, following his signing with the Bluebird label in 1939, around the country. By this time Johnson was featuring fewer guitar pyrotechnics on recordings, generating a duet or small-band sound that was distinctive yet within the parameters of Lester Melrose's streamlined design, with Josh Altheimer, LIL ARMSTRONG, and BLIND JOHN DAVIS providing stellar accompaniment.

Following recordings for Disc in New York City in 1946 and for Aladdin in Chicago in 1947, Johnson reemerged as a rhythm and blues star in 1947. He had begun a five-year association with Cincinnati's King Records, scoring with pop hits "Tomorrow Night" and "Pleasing You" and mixing intimate small-group blues and ballads with blasting larger-band blues. Still, Johnson mixed performing dates at the Apollo Theater and Carnegie Hall (the latter with KID ORY) in New York and in England during the "Trad" jazz craze in 1952 with periods of working outside of music while he resided in Cincinnati in the late 1940s and early 1950s. Recordings for the Rama label, probably in New York City in 1956, signaled the end of this phase of Johnson's career.

In the late 1950s Johnson worked as a janitor at the Ben Franklin Hotel in Philadelphia. His coworkers were apparently unaware of his career as a musician. With help from the jazz aficionado Chris Albertson, Johnson made yet another comeback, this time as part of the burgeoning folk music scene. A series of albums for Prestige-Bluesville, recorded in the period 1960–1962, sparked club dates across the country and with the American Folk Blues Festival in Europe, where in 1963 he recorded for Fontana in Germany and for Storyville in Denmark. He finished out his career recording for Spivey in New York (1963 and 1965), for King in Cincinnati (1964), for HES in Canada (1965), and for Folkways in New York (1967). Around 1965 or 1966 Johnson settled in Toronto, owning and working at the Home of the Blues club and playing dates. After being struck by an automobile in 1969, he died in Toronto of a related stroke.

As a singer, Johnson was a notable exponent of the urbane city blues style, influenced by the vaudeville blues singers but providing a smoother, more relaxed delivery. As a guitarist, his influence on blues, rock, and jazz has been incalculable. His recordings influenced blues musicians performing a wide variety of styles: Chicago's BIG BILL BROONZY, Mississippi's ROBERT JOHNSON, Georgia's BLIND WILLIE MCTELL, and Texas's Ramblin' Thomas, as well as post–World War II stylists T-Bone Walker, B. B. King, Albert King, Freddie King, and Johnny Shines. Through the recordings of Walker and the three Kings, Johnson's melismatic single-string playing influenced virtually every modern blues and rock guitarist. In jazz, seminal guitarists Eddie Lang, Django Reinhardt, and Charlie Christian all acknowledged their debt to Johnson. During five decades of recording activity Johnson provided some of the most breathtaking, imaginative, and sensitive performances and compositions of the twentieth century.

FURTHER READING

Bogdanov, Vladimir, Chris Woodstra, and Stephen Erlewine. *All Music Guide to the Blues: The Definitive Guide to the Blues* (2003).

Cohn, Lawrence. *Nothing but the Blues: The Music and the Musicians* (1999).

Davis, Francis. *The History of the Blues: The Roots, the Music, the People* (2003).

Oakley, Giles. *The Devil's Music: A History of the Blues* (1997).

Oliver, Paul. *Conversation with the Blues* (1997).

Welding, Pete, and Toby Byron, eds. *Bluesland* (1991).

This entry is taken from the *American National Biography* and is published here with the permission of the American Council of Learned Societies.

STEVEN C. TRACY

Johnson, Lonnie G. (6 Oct. 1949–), inventor, entrepreneur, businessman, and nuclear engineer, was born and raised in Mobile, Alabama, the third of six children of David Johnson, a driver for the Air Force, and Arline Washington Johnson, a nurse's assistant. Johnson attended W. H. Council Elementary School and Williamson High School in his segregated hometown. Guided by tolerant and patient parents who encouraged him during his early creative years when he fiddled with junk, Johnson was painfully aware of racial inequities, but that did not deter his curiosity about how things worked. His mother ingrained in him and his siblings the importance of knowledge, emphasizing what one puts in the brain counts in life. Likened to a child prodigy, nosy young Johnson habitually tinkered with his siblings' toys to see how they functioned. In project after project he monkeyed with old jukeboxes, plastic pipes, compression motors, and explosive rocket fuel, occasionally getting himself in trouble. Thin and wearing eyeglasses, at an early age he was dubbed "the professor." When a senior in high school in 1968 at age 18, he won first place

in a national science competition for his ingenuity in making a remote controlled robot called "Linex" at the University of Alabama Junior Engineering Technical Society Exposition, an unprecedented honor for a student from his locale.

Johnson excelled on the SAT scores and won a mathematics scholarship to Tuskegee University where he continued his tinkering in between studying and college life. Loans, assorted employment, and an Air Force ROTC scholarship augmented his college welfare as he pursued a B.A. in Mechanical Engineering. He was elected to the Pi Tau Sigma National Engineering Honor Society, and graduated with distinction in 1973. Two years later at Tuskegee University Johnson received an M.S. in Nuclear Engineering, and had a short stint as a research engineer at the Oak Ridge National Laboratory in Tennessee in 1975 before joining the U.S. Air Force.

In 1978, by now married, Johnson was acting chief of the Space Nuclear Power Safety Section with the rank of captain at the Air Force Weapons Laboratory in Albuquerque, New Mexico. He left the Air Force in 1979, and accepted the post of Senior Systems Engineer at the Jet Propulsion Laboratory (JPL) of the National Aeronautics and Space Administration (NASA) in Pasadena, California, where he worked on the Galileo Project which sent an unmanned craft to Jupiter. In the spring of 1982, he returned to the Air Force at Omaha, Nebraska, as a managing officer of the Advanced Space Systems Requirements for Strategic Air Command (SAC) at Offett AFB. Then, from 1985 to 1987, he became Major Selectee and chief of the Data Management branch at SAC at Edwards Air Force Base in California.

His Air Force career netted him the Commander in Chief (CINC) Strategic Air Command nomination for astronaut training as a space shuttle mission specialist. Also he won an Air Force Achievement Medal in addition to two Air Force Commendation Medals. During his military life Johnson enjoyed seeking novel methods of providing power to satellite computer memories and delighted in finding new ways to detect enemy submarines. He found paperwork annoying, however, and was frustrated at efforts by the Air Force to honor people of higher rank for his work. Throughout his JPL career Johnson acquired numerous awards from NASA for his talent on spacecraft system design.

On his off-hours in military housing shared with his family, Johnson came up with a plethora of ideas. In 1977, fired with ambition, he decided to file for federal protection on his inventions so that, hopefully, he could reap some financial reward from them. He teamed up with inventor John M. Lederer on his first patent for a digital distance measuring instrument, which was granted on 6 March 1979. The following year he received two patents as sole inventor, the first for a variable-resistance type sensor-controlled switch, and the other for a smoke-detecting timer-controlled thermostat. He was well on his way to becoming a prolific creative genius. During these years Johnson, his wife, Thelma, and their children Aneka, David, and Kenya relocated several times, moving from state to state with boxes of his junk in tow.

Working on personal time in 1982, Johnson gave birth to the squirt gun, trademarked as the Super Soaker. He had been tinkering at home with a new heat pump that could use water instead of Freon as the cooling or heating medium. When he was experimenting with vinyl tubing and a self-made nozzle with a vacuum chamber, a powerful jet of water erupted across the bathroom, flinging the shower curtain aside and drenching the room. It was a breakthrough moment. He confided in his eldest, Aneka, then six years old, that he was going to make a great water gun. The sudden realization that kids could pressurize the water by forcing air into the gun mechanism that ejected water at a high velocity was inspiring. From that day forward, Johnson's creative juices flowed until he made his first powerful water gun. Much to the delight of his daughter and the neighborhood children, the prototype became an instant success. The history of the Super Soaker had begun.

To financially back his brainchild Johnson pursued investors at trade shows for venture capital, efforts which proved exhausting. He consistently corresponded with the U.S. Department of Energy about the efficiency of his heat pump, but was ignored for years, much to his distress. It took another seven laborious years for Johnson to get industry respect and recognition by any manufacturer. In the meantime his wife was feeling neglected, taking second place to his research. Nonetheless, Johnson began to file patent applications and was awarded his first squirt gun patent on 27 May 1986 (USP 4,591,071).

According to the *Washington Post*, "the lowest point [in his life] came in 1987, when Johnson left the Air Force with the understanding that an investment capital firm would contract to develop some of his ideas. At the last minute, the firm backed out, demanding that he first pay $8,000" (27 December 1991). This predicament left the family without income and a home, but more devastatingly, he was sued when he tried to retreat from an agreement.

The JPL rehired Johnson in 1987. Happy to have him back, supervisors described the inventor as "extremely innovative" and "very conscientious and hardworking … a team player." He was an employee with a winning personality who always had a fresh approach to a problem. Johnson worked on the Mars Observer projects and was significant in the early period of the Cassini (Saturn) Mission. He was liable for making certain that single point spacecraft failure would not cause a mission loss.

Privately continuing to produce new concepts from his inventive skills, Johnson in 1989 decided to establish a company, Lonnie G. Johnson Engineering, to promote his ideas. Finally setting his own path, he left the JPL in 1991, and moved his family to Atlanta, Georgia.

Johnson's fortitude, resilience, and perseverance paid off that year, when he renamed his firm Johnson Research and Development Company Incorporated, which produced and sold his successful toy gun invention. Johnson licensed the invention in 1991 to Larami Corporation (Philadelphia), one of the world's largest toy producers. An executive saw the Super Soaker at a New York Trade show. The first water gun, priced at ten dollars, sold very well at the beginning, and sales escalated after Johnny Carson experimented with it on his show, and a television commercial advertised it nationally. The phenomenal success of the Super Soaker allowed Johnson to devote himself full-time to his innovations. In 1991 ten million units of the Super Soaker were sold. The Cobb County, Georgia, Chamber of Commerce in that year gave Johnson's company the "Small Business of the Year" award. The sales figure doubled in 1992, generating more than $200 million in retail sales. For the next ten years sales reached close to one billion dollars.

In the mid-1990s Larami was purchased by Hasbro Corporation, a giant toy manufacturer. Due to Johnson's intellectual property rights, the Super Soaker maintained a competitive edge in the toy industry. From another license agreement with Hasbro, Johnson designed, engineered, and developed a soft foam dart gun, trademarked NERF, which has become a popular staple toy of the summer. Johnson Research also ventured into the field of toy rocketry and air power technology with Estes Air Rockets.

Capitalizing on the success of the Super Soaker, Johnson founded two other Atlanta-based companies, Excellatron Solid State LLC, and Johnson Electro-Mechanical Systems LLC, to develop leading edge technology from consumer products and toys to environmentally friendly alternative methods of power. The former company specializes in solid state thin film lithium rechargeable batteries—technology originating at Oak Ridge National Laboratory—while the latter company produces ideas that have the potential for changing the global energy market. Johnson's companies have been awarded contracts from NASA and the U.S. Department of Energy. Another of the Johnson group of companies, Johnson Real Estate Investments LLC, is involved with the community in outreach programs, and has a vested interest in stimulating economic growth in Atlanta's disadvantaged areas.

Johnson's phenomenal achievement did not go unnoticed. Many works chronicle Johnson's career. In addition to publishing in technical journals, Johnson made television appearances. He was on *The* OPRAH WINFREY *Show* and on a segment of *Science Times* viewed on the National Geographic channel. The Hasbro Corporation named him to their Inventor Hall of Fame in 2000, and the following year Tuskegee University bestowed upon Johnson, an adjunct professor there, an honorary Doctorate in Science. With his first marriage dissolved, Johnson in 2002 married Linda Moore who gave birth in the fall of the next year to a daughter, Jalelah.

In addition to the inventions already mentioned Johnson patented an electrochemical conversion system, a magnetic propulsion toy system, an automatic sprinkler control, a pinch-trigger pump water gun, a wet-diaper detector, a thin lithium film battery, and a hair-curler drying apparatus.

FURTHER READING

Babham, Vernon. "Accidental Invention Makes a Big Splash," *Inventor's Digest* (Mar./Apr. 1995).

Broad, William. "Rocket Science Served Up Soggy," *New York Times*, 31 July 2001.

Karlin, Susan. "From Squirts to Hertz," *IEEE Spectrum* (11 Mar. 2005).

Mathews, Jay. "Escaping the Office to Unlock Ideas," *Washington Post*, 27 Dec. 1991.

Roche, Timothy. "Soaking in Success," *Time* (4 Dec. 2000).

Sluby, Patricia Carter. *The Inventive Spirit of African Americans: Patented Ingenuity* (2004).

PATRICIA CARTER SLUBY

Johnson, Louis (19 Mar. 1931–), dancer, choreographer, and educator, was born in Statesville, North Carolina. The family moved to Washington, D.C., where Johnson, nimble in gymnastics and athletics, was noticed at the local YMCA. Recommended to the Jones-Haywood School of Ballet, which he attended on scholarship, the teenager was selected by the school's founders, Doris Jones and Clara Haywood, to apply to the prestigious School of American Ballet (SAB) in New York City. Along with classmate Chita Rivera, Johnson was accepted, again on scholarship, as one of the first African Americans and the first "black black" (Dunning, *New York Times*, 25 September 1975) to achieve this honor. He decided to first finish high school, where he was studying art, another talent that aided his professional career.

At SAB, Johnson was mentored by Jerome Robbins, co-director of the New York City Ballet, had a solo in the premiere of Robbins's *Ballade* in 1952, and was considered for the lead role in *Afternoon of a Faun*. A year later he made his choreographic debut with *Lament*, a ballet of love and longing, which premiered at the Third New York Ballet Club Annual Choreographers' Night. The performance was noteworthy for its integrated cast, made up of dancers like ARTHUR MITCHELL, later founder of the Dance Theatre of Harlem. Even though Johnson disproved the stereotype that "black bodies" (Dunning, *New York Times*, 25 September 1975) could not do classical ballet, he still was not accepted as a full member of a ballet company.

Turning to Broadway for work, Johnson appeared in such shows as *My Darlin Aida* (1952–1953), *House of Flowers* (1954–1955), *Hallelujah Baby* (1967–1968), and the longer playing *Damn Yankees* (1955–1957). In this last production he was lead dancer in a "non-ethnic" role and also appeared in the movie version in 1957. Johnson's other activities from this period include a 1952 Paris revival of *Four Saints in Three Acts* and performances at the 92nd Street YMHA in New York City, where he was hailed as choreographer, performer, and set and costume designer. Two of Johnson's works, *Folk Impressions* and *Waltze*, influenced by African dance and ballet techniques, were in the repertoire of the Negro Ballet's 1957 tour of Great Britain.

The 1960s brought more opportunities for black dancers, yet Johnson was succeeding as a choreographer where he combined his classical training, Broadway experience, modern dance elements from a short period at the KATHERINE DUNHAM School, social, and folk dancing. He used all styles of music as well, from classical to jazz, and frequently designed the costumes for his productions. Johnson established a number of small companies of his own, and choreographed for summer stock productions and the *Song of the Lusitainian Bogey*, which went to London and Rome (and won a 1968 Obie for its direction). He staged and choreographed works for the Modern Jazz Quartet and, in 1970, choreographed the musical *Purlie*, becoming the first African American choreographer to be nominated for a Tony. Johnson choreographed a revival of SCOTT JOPLIN's *Treemonisha* for the Houston Grand Opera Company (1975), and the films *Cotton Comes to Harlem* (1970) and *The Wiz* (1978). In 1975 he also choreographed *Aïda* (with LEONTYNE PRICE) and *La Giaconda* for the Metropolitan Opera Company, an indication of his long-overdue acceptance by the white, classical dance establishment.

Just as *Lament*, Johnson's debut piece, became a noted showpiece for the ALVIN AILEY Dance Theater Company, *Forces of Rhythm* (1972) became a signature work for the Dance Theatre of Harlem. Subtitled *A Fusion of Classical Ballet, Ethnic and Modern Dance Styles* and set to a variety of music from Tchaikovsky to rhythm and blues, it used white skirts, leotards, loin cloths, and bowler hats, while its separate suites exhibited an equally wide range of mood. This highly structured yet striking juxtaposition of styles and cultures, requiring well-trained dancers, became Johnson's hallmark. They appear also in *Fontessa and Friends*, another, later major piece, which, set to jazz, disco, and symphonic music, premiered at the Alvin Ailey Dance Theater Company in 1981. The same qualities of eclecticism, passion, precise technique, and humor that marked Johnson's choreography were mostly praised and sometimes criticized. Yet even when an individual piece was called a review, or rapid juxtapositions were not fully appreciated by the press, Johnson himself was praised for his dancing.

From 1980 through 2003 Johnson was the director of the Dance Department of the Henry Street Settlement on New York City's Lower East Side, where he taught, directed, choreographed, and produced dance performances, often with the children of the neighborhood. Two of his works at the Henry Street Settlement were *No Outlet* and *Harlem Swans*, drawing on Rachmaninolf and Sartre, Tchaikovsky and tap. Johnson also co-created *Go Down Moses* with Joanne Tucker of the multiethnic Avodah Dance Ensemble (1989). He choreographed for television and Broadway shows and stars; other works appear in the repertoires of Phildanco and the Cincinnati Ballet.

As an educator, Johnson promoted dance in classes and symposiums at Yale, Virginia State, Hampton Institute, Morehouse Dance Division, among other places, and he developed the Dance Division at Howard University. He was the recipient of a number of awards, including being one of the six honorees in *Men in Dance*, a 2002 event. Some of Johnson's other honors include the Katherine Dunham Legacy Award (2001) from the 651Arts organization, the Pioneer Award from the International Association of Blacks in Dance, and an Audelco Award for choreographing MELVIN VAN PEEBLES's play *Champeen* (1983).

Drawing on his African American cultural heritage, his own athleticism, classical ballet, modern dance, and many other sources, Johnson helped to break the barriers of race in dance to be accepted and praised as an African American ballet dancer. Overcoming stubbornly Eurocentric concepts of dance, he created works that celebrate both the African American experience and dance for all people. As Johnson himself said, "I love dance—any kind of dance."

FURTHER READING

DeFrantz, Thomas F. "Ballet in Black: Louis Johnson and African American Vernacular Humour in Ballet," in *Dancing Bodies, Living Histories; New Writings about Dance and Culture*, eds. Lisa Doolittle and Anne Flynn (2000).

Dunning, Jennifer. *New York Times*, 18 September 1975.

"Ballet," *Encyclopedia of African-American Culture and History. The Black Experience in the Americas* 2d ed. (1996).

The Encyclopedia of Dance & Ballet (1977).

RACHEL SHOR

Johnson, Lucy Bagby (c.1833–14 July 1906), believed to be the last fugitive slave returned to the South under the Fugitive Slave Act of 1850, was born Sara Lucy Bagby. Details about her ancestry, place of birth, and early years are unknown. At the time of her arrest in Cleveland, Ohio, on 19 January 1861, U.S. marshals identified Bagby as a slave of William S. Goshorn, a merchant from Wheeling, Virginia (now West Virginia). In 1852 Goshorn's father, John Goshorn, had purchased Bagby in Richmond, Virginia, and transported her to Wheeling. There she worked for John Goshorn until he sold her to his son William.

Bagby toiled for the Goshorns about eight years before seeking freedom. Shortly after federal marshals arrested and jailed her in Cleveland, she described her escape from slavery during an interview with a reporter from the *Cleveland Morning Leader*. Bagby identified herself as twenty-four-year-old Sara Lucy Bagby and asserted that she had gained her freedom when Isabella Goshorn, her owner's daughter, took her from Virginia to Pennsylvania, where she learned she was in a free state and therefore free. How she effected her escape is unknown, but Bagby soon exercised her freedom and traveled first to Pittsburgh and then Cleveland. William E. Ambush, chair of the Cleveland Fugitive Aid Society, helped her find employment as a domestic for Albert G. Riddle, a lawyer and recently elected Republican congressman. She obtained similar work with L. A. Benton, another Cleveland resident. Bagby was residing in the Benton home when the Goshorns and federal marshals arrived unexpectedly with a warrant for her arrest, only three months after she had first tasted freedom.

In their sworn affidavits, the Goshorns provided a very different account of Bagby's disappearance from Virginia. William Goshorn explained that he was in Minnesota from July through October 1860 and had not given anyone permission to take Bagby out of Virginia during his absence. John Goshorn asserted that Bagby ran away from Wheeling the night of 3 October 1860, and he insisted that Isabella and every member of his son's extended family were in Wheeling during the month of October when Bagby claimed Isabella took her on a trip to Pennsylvania. Therefore, Goshorn claimed, someone in Wheeling must have helped Bagby to escape to Pennsylvania.

About two months before the Goshorns located Lucy Bagby in Cleveland, Wheeling officials opened an investigation to determine if any members of the local black community had assisted her in her escape. Officials arrested Phillip Herbert, a freedman employed by a Wheeling lawyer, C. W. Russell, when they discovered that he had taken a trip to Pittsburgh around the time Bagby disappeared, and they believed he knew details about her escape and whereabouts. However, after interviewing Herbert thoroughly, they released him. Officials reportedly questioned thirty-one other African Americans, but none of them provided any information about Bagby's escape or the assistance Herbert may have provided in helping her run away.

Cleveland residents, in contrast, were not concerned with the method of Bagby's escape. Instead, they sought to ensure her freedom. By 1860, Cleveland had earned a national reputation as an abolitionist and Republican stronghold, particularly because of its citizens' work on the Underground Railroad. When slave states began seceding from the Union that year, their refusal to honor the Emancipation Proclamation incensed Cleveland residents. Secession complicated Cleveland's commitment to abolition by forcing residents to decide if they would uphold or defy the Fugitive Slave Act in assisting Bagby. After Benton informed Ambush of Bagby's arrest, Cleveland residents quickly learned of her plight and "all public sympathy [was] with the fugitive" (*Annals*, 513). Black and white abolitionists, along with many residents, gathered at the municipal courthouse where Bagby was being held. The prominent Cleveland law associates Rufus P. Spalding and Charles W. Palmer provided free legal service for Bagby. Spalding secured a writ of habeas corpus from Probate Judge Daniel R. Tilden, who also scheduled a hearing for that afternoon. With an increasingly belligerent crowd of men and women gathering outside the municipal building, Judge Tilden allowed Spalding to address the court without Bagby's being present because the judge deemed the large crowd to be potentially riotous. Spalding argued that Bagby should be released because an Ohio law passed in 1860 stipulated that local jails could only be used to detain individuals suspected of committing a crime. Judge Tilden, mindful of the volatile nature of the case, deferred his answer to Spalding's argument until one hour before Bagby's hearing in which the federal charges regarding the Fugitive Slave Law would be addressed in the U.S. court.

Early in the morning of 21 January 1861, Bagby's supporters gathered outside the municipal building and soon became an angry mob, many of whom were armed. Deputies transported Bagby from jail to the municipal building without incident, although a fight nearly broke out inside the courtroom when Ambush confronted William Goshorn, according to JOHN MALVIN (Malvin, 81). After reportedly drawing pistols, the two men were restrained (others have disputed Malvin's account, pointing out that none of the numerous newspapers covering the trial mentioned this confrontation). Judge Tilden ruled that local officials could not keep Bagby in jail, but he did not prohibit the marshals from detaining her elsewhere. One hundred and fifty local men, whom the *Cleveland Leader* described as "prison-rapscallions," were deputized to guard Bagby as she walked from the courthouse to the U.S. courtroom. Some members of the mob attempted to rescue her. Others tried forcefully to snatch her from the guards. An unidentified woman even threw hot pepper into the eyes of the U.S. marshal who was escorting Bagby.

Bagby's supporters were unsuccessful in liberating her, and the young fugitive appeared before Commissioner Bushnell White. Because the law prohibited the young woman from testifying in her own defense, Spalding entreated the court to allow him to seek testimony to support Bagby's version of events. Over Goshorn's objections of unnecessary delay, the commissioner granted Spalding two days to secure depositions from Wheeling residents to support Bagby's description of her escape. Commissioner White warned Bagby's lawyers that if they could not produce evidence in her favor, he was legally obligated to return Bagby to William Goshorn. Ultimately, the court ruled against Bagby's claim for liberty because she had entered the free state of Pennsylvania, following the precedent established by the U.S. Supreme Court's 1858 DRED SCOTT case in which justices ruled that slaves who traveled to free states with their masters could not emancipate themselves. The commissioner candidly addressed the court, informing them that the South was monitoring Bagby's case to see if Cleveland would uphold the Fugitive Slave Law. He remarked, "I want to show to the South that a law so distasteful to us, as a law against the slave trade is to them, can be carried out here; and that though they have mobbed and maltreated our citizens when found among them, that we are true and loyal to the Constitution" (Cleveland Leader, 22 Jan. 1861). Ohio Republicans were determined to remain faithful to the Union, even if that meant honoring legislation that violated the rights of enslaved African Americans whom they considered to be citizens. In so doing, they highlighted the seceding states' disloyalty through their insistence on maintaining slavery, a system that the federal government had outlawed in their region. Bagby was subject to the Fugitive Slave Law because she resided in Virginia, a state that had not seceded from the Union at the time of her escape.

Spalding traveled to Wheeling and obtained depositions from Isabella Goshorn, Amanda Virginia Goshorn, and two other Wheeling residents. All supported the male Goshorns' account of Bagby's escape. Spalding and his law partners reluctantly turned over their client to Goshorn as Spalding lamented, "While we do this, in the City of Cleveland, in the Connecticut Western Reserve, and permit this poor piece of humanity to be taken, peaceably, through our streets, and upon our railways, back to the land of bondage,

will not the frantic South stay its parricidal hand? Will not our compromising Legislature cry: Hold, enough!" (Cleveland Morning Leader, 24 Jan. 1861). Spalding's words did not dissuade Goshorn from taking Bagby back to Wheeling, however, and Commissioner White felt a responsibility to uphold the law. Administering the law did not prevent him from seeking other means to free Bagby, however. He pledged $100 to a fund collected by the Cleveland Leader to purchase Bagby's freedom for $1,200, double the figure Goshorn gave as her market value. Although Goshorn initially proposed to sell Bagby if the court permitted him to take her back to Wheeling, he reneged on his offer.

U.S. marshals and journalists accompanied Bagby and the Goshorns on the train ride to Wheeling. The conductor thwarted a final attempt to rescue Bagby: WILLIAM WHIPPER and W. A. Tyler had boarded the train, planning to overpower the marshals and liberate Bagby when the train reached the Lima, Ohio, station, but when the conductor saw an armed crowd waiting at the station, he refused to stop and continued on to Wheeling. Meanwhile, after Bagby left Cleveland, her supporters charged William R. Ambush with facilitating Bagby's capture by withholding the information that her freedom was in jeopardy. When the Fugitive Aid Society met to investigate the charges against Ambush, they discovered that he had received a letter from Pittsburgh indicating Goshorn was searching for Bagby. Ambush was exonerated when he convinced the society that he had informed Bagby that her master had discovered her hideaway, but she did not heed his warning.

When Bagby arrived in Wheeling in late January 1861 she was jailed and "severely punished" (Malvin, 81). About four months later William Goshorn joined a few other Wheeling residents in voting for secession from the Union. Rather than secure slavery and establish the South, however, Goshorn's actions helped lead to Bagby's emancipation. After the Civil War began, Union soldiers freed Bagby and arrested Goshorn. They imprisoned him in the same jail where he had placed Bagby when she returned to Wheeling. When the war ended, Bagby traveled to Athens, Ohio, and on to Pittsburgh, where she married George Johnson, a Union army veteran. They eventually settled in Cleveland.

Lucy Bagby Johnson attended Cleveland's Mt. Zion Congregational Church for more than thirty years. On 10 September 1904 members of the Early Settlers Association, an organization that promoted the spirit and memory of Ohio's early pioneers, introduced Johnson to the audience at their meeting. Two years later, at age seventy-two, Johnson was hospitalized after falling down some stairs. She never recovered from her injuries and spent about a year in City Hospital before she died. Her funeral was held at Mt. Zion Church. Johnson is buried in an unmarked grave in Woodland Cemetery in Cleveland.

FURTHER READING

Annals of Cleveland, 1818–1935, vol. 44, *1861* (1937).

Malvin, John. *North into Freedom: The Autobiography of John Malvin, Free Negro, 1795–1880*, ed. Allan Peskin (1966).

Vacha, John E. "The Case of Sara Lucy Bagby: A Late Gesture," *Ohio History* 76 (1967).

Obituary: *Cleveland Gazette*, 21 July 1906.

RHONDDA ROBINSON THOMAS

Johnson, Mamie "Peanut" (27 Sept. 1935–), baseball player, was born Mamie Belton in Ridgeway, South Carolina, the daughter of Della Belton, a hospital dietician, and Gentry Harrison, a construction worker about whom little else is known. Mamie spent her early years in Ridgeway, where she attended Thorntree School, a two-room schoolhouse. Part of a large family that included twelve half brothers and half sisters, Mamie lived with her maternal grandmother, Cendonia Belton, while her mother worked in Washington, D.C. Mamie's uncle, Leo "Bones" Belton, was so close to her in age that she regarded him more as a brother than as an uncle. Belton introduced her to baseball. Along with other children in the area, "Bones" and Mamie played baseball on a makeshift diamond, with a lid from a bucket of King Cane sugar serving as home plate and baseballs made of rocks wrapped in tape.

After her grandmother's death around 1945, Mamie moved to Long Branch, New Jersey, where she lived with an aunt and uncle and attended Liberty School. Her aunt and uncle urged their niece to shift her interest from baseball to softball, a sport that they considered more appropriate for girls. She did not find softball sufficiently challenging and quit after playing a few games. In place of softball Belton discovered a white boys' baseball team playing in the Police Athletic League (PAL). After convincing the coach that she was eager to play, she became the team's only female and only African American player.

In 1947 Belton moved to Washington, D.C., to live with her mother. On weekends she played with an African American recreational league on the Saint Cyprian's team and later joined the Alexandria All-Stars, a semipro squad. Hearing about the start of a women's professional baseball league, Belton traveled to nearby Virginia to try out with the AAGBL (All-American Girls Professional Baseball League). She was turned away by white officials who would not allow African American girls to play in the all-white league. She remembered in particular that none of the white women players spoke up in her behalf. Being denied a tryout was one of her first vivid encounters with racism. "It devastated me," she said, "because I didn't know what prejudice was" (*Washington Post*, 18 Feb. 2001).

In 1952 after marrying Charles Johnson and having a son, also named Charles, Mamie Johnson worked at a local ice cream soda fountain and played weekend baseball. During one of those weekend games Johnson attracted the notice of a scout for the Indianapolis Clowns of the Negro Leagues. McKinley "Bunny" Downs, business manager for the Clowns, came to watch Johnson play, and he signed her on the spot.

Johnson immediately left Washington for spring training in Virginia. Later she candidly explained that she was so thrilled to be offered a professional baseball contract that she left her infant son and mother behind. Talking with National Public Radio in 2003 she recalled, "Honestly, I'm going to be frank with you, I slipped away. I had a young son that particular time and when [my mother] found out I was playing baseball, you know, she took it in stride and I appreciate that so much" (NPR *Morning Edition*, 18 Feb. 2003).

When Johnson signed with the Clowns, the Negro Leagues were in decline. JACKIE ROBINSON had integrated baseball in 1947, joining the Brooklyn Dodgers. More and more African American baseball fans turned their attention away from the Negro Leagues and toward Major League Baseball as additional black players followed Robinson. The Negro Leagues looked for new ways to attract fans, and in 1953 TONI STONE became the first woman to play professional baseball on a men's team. Many observers looked upon Toni Stone's playing second base for the Clowns as merely a publicity stunt, but few could deny that she was a talented athlete.

Arriving in Portsmouth, Virginia, for spring training, Johnson followed in Stone's footsteps and was issued the same uniform used by men on the team, a blue flannel shirt with belted pants. Earlier Stone had refused to play in a skirt similar to those that women players wore in the AAGPBL. Johnson appreciated Stone's trailblazing efforts in demanding a suitable uniform and in dealing with players and fans who did not believe that women should play professional baseball. Like Stone, Johnson found a way to endure criticism by ignoring taunts and by associating herself with players who supported her efforts.

Johnson played for the Clowns during the 1953, 1954, and 1955 seasons. She pitched every sixth day and occasionally substituted as a utility infielder. Although official statistics for the Negro Leagues are often difficult to confirm, some reports indicate that Johnson's hitting ranged from .252 to .284 and that she could throw between eighty and eighty-five miles per hour. According to the Indianapolis Clowns' official program, Johnson weighed one hundred twenty pounds and stood five foot three. Although not large, Johnson always felt that she was strong and that good food made her healthy and competitive. "I didn't come up off sandwiches," she recalled. "I came up off greens and cornbread and buttermilk. I was just a strong person and where I got it, I don't know" (*Sports Connection Digest*, 22 Oct. 1999).

Playing in the Negro Leagues in the early 1950s was thrilling for Johnson because baseball was her passion, but she also experienced both racism and sexism. Jim Crow laws meant segregated accommodations and refusal to be served in restaurants. Fans often jeered at her, saying she should be home having babies. Long hours traveling on broken-down buses with little more than tasteless sandwiches to eat made one hundred fifty games from April to October a grueling experience.

Despite the hardships there were memorable highlights for Johnson. The great SATCHEL PAIGE helped her perfect the curveball. "Don't squeeze the ball so tight," Paige told her. "And let it break to the outside." According to Johnson one of her most unforgettable moments came in a game between the Clowns and the Kansas City Monarchs. Facing off against the third baseman Hank Bayliss with a runner on first, Johnson threw a called strike. The second pitch was high and outside. Johnson's third pitch was another strike. According to Johnson, Bayliss then yelled out to her with a voice so loud that the crowd could hear him, "You're nothing but a peanut." Johnson reared back and threw a third strike—gaining a strikeout and a nickname simultaneously; since that strikeout she has been known professionally as Mamie "Peanut" Johnson.

Johnson realized that as a woman she would never have a chance to play in the major leagues, and after three seasons she retired from the Clowns

in 1955 and returned to her son and mother. She later earned her LPN certificate by studying first at North Carolina A&T and finishing at New York University in 1958. She worked as a nurse in Washington, D.C., for thirty-five years.

Johnson divorced her first husband and married Eduardo Goodman in 1961. Eduardo Goodman died in 1978. Johnson continued to participate in Negro Leagues reunions and sports shows and to speak at schools and civic organizations about her career in baseball.

As one of only three women to play professional ball in the Negro Leagues, along with Toni Stone and CONNIE MORGAN—another female player for the Indianapolis Clowns—Mamie "Peanut" Johnson helped prove that women can compete successfully as professional athletes. With the death of both Stone and Morgan in 1996, Johnson became the sole surviving member of a remarkable trio. In 2001 she reminded a crowd assembled in Milwaukee for the rededication of the Negro Leagues Wall of Fame of the contributions that women made to baseball—and to the acceptance of the many professional women athletes who followed them in other sports. "I want it known all over the world," she said, "we were here too" (National Baseball Hall of Fame Library, Mamie "Peanut" Johnson file).

FURTHER READING

Berlage, Gai Ingham. *Women in Baseball: The Forgotten History* (1994).

Green, Michelle Y. *A Strong Right Arm: The Story of Mamie "Peanut" Johnson* (2002).

Lanctot, Neil. *Negro Leagues Baseball: The Rise and Ruin of a Black Institution* (2004).

MARTHA ACKMANN

Johnson, Marjorie Witt (18 Mar. 1910–19 July 2007), dancer, choreographer, educator, and social worker, was born in Cheyenne, Wyoming, to a racially mixed father, Hank Witt, who had been a buffalo soldier, and mother, Pearlie (Pryor) Witt, a black woman. Before settling in Cheyenne the family lived in Missouri, where Marjorie's older brother was born. It is not known what brought them to Cheyenne. Hank was a fair-skinned biracial man with a deep love for his dark-skinned wife. Marjorie Hayes Witt, their first daughter and the second-oldest of five children, took after her mother and was the only one of her siblings to have Pearlie's mocha coloring. Early on Marjorie learned that this legacy would be a burden. Her mother found that her own complexion was a handicap and went so far as to bathe her dark-skinned daughter in buttermilk in the belief it would lighten her. Marjorie also found that racial tension existed in her predominantly white school. But she met prejudice with charm, using her artistic talents to win people over. Marjorie acted in plays and was very good at impersonations. She found performing could be therapeutic and coveted the spotlight. The more she performed, the more self-confidence she gained. She learned that her uncle, Hayes Pryor, was a Broadway performer with the Lafayette Players, a black acting troupe that had begun in Harlem, New York; Marjorie decided to carry on that family tradition.

Still, she struggled in a school that did not nurture her ambition. School officials discouraged her when she wanted to do a portrayal of her white teacher on stage. They even visited her home to inform her parents that their child simply could not portray characters outside of her race. Marjorie's parents were insulted, and, after asking the school official to leave, they responded by encouraging their talented daughter to pursue higher education. Marjorie followed their advice and enrolled at Oberlin College, in Ohio, where her parents believed she would be judged by her abilities, not her race. Other members of her community, including fellow parishioners from the family church, friends, and neighbors, helped raise money for her to attend college.

Life at Oberlin, however, posed its own challenges. As one of the few African American students at the college, she encountered hatred unlike any she had ever experienced. Witt was verbally attacked, blatantly ignored, and even sat helplessly as a female student vomited on her lunch. But she persevered, and within the walls of hatred she found her first love, dance. Modern dance was a new form of self-expression, and Witt wanted to study for the art as her major at Oberlin, much to the dismay of her parents. Succumbing to parental pressure, she coupled her dance degree with a teaching certificate and earned her bachelor's degree in 1935.

During her last year at school Witt learned about the playhouse settlement movement in Cleveland that enabled blacks to use their artistic abilities to reach out to other African Americans in their poor and working-class neighborhoods. The discovery was a revelation for Witt, who decided to use dance as an educational tool. At a camp run by the Cleveland Playhouse settlement in Brecksville, Ohio, Witt spent a summer as a counselor, sharing the beauty of modern dance with the young campers, who were enchanted by her gift.

The connection Witt drew between spirit and body through dance inspired her to dedicate her life to the art. She returned to Cleveland as a dance counselor at the settlement, which later became the Karamu House, the oldest black theater company in the country. In Cleveland she witnessed firsthand the poverty of urban life, something she had never seen in her native Cheyenne. The close-knit family of artists at Karamu was shaped by these surroundings, where racism and poverty were inescapable. At the settlement house she found like-minded black people and met her husband, the stage actor Bill Johnson. She also befriended such artists as the lithographer William E. Smith and the legendary poet LANGSTON HUGHES.

Johnson became the Karamu choreographer and formed the Karamu dancers. She worked with twelve young women developing a new technique that married the spirit and body with the rhythm of the soul. One of the most famous dances, titled *The Sermon*, was at least partially inspired by a church on the western plain in Cheyenne. She choreographed movements that reflected life, and nothing was off-limits. The anguish of one neighborhood prostitute became the subject of a serenade for the Karamu Dancers. Another performer described, through elegant twists and turns, the pains of life brought on by her alcoholic mother. The Karamu Dancers gained popularity around Cleveland and were invited to perform at the 1939 New York World's Fair. Although the performance was a success, the dancers were disillusioned by their meager salaries and Johnson was fired. At about the same time, Johnson discovered she was pregnant. However, her husband Bill had dreamed of becoming a doctor, not a father, and eventually the couple split up.

Marjorie Witt Johnson remained in Cleveland, an unemployed, single, expectant mother, yet she found solace and success in education. She had returned to school and received her master's degree in Social Work from the Western Reserve University School of Applied Sciences in 1940. The following year her daughter Corrine was born. Shortly thereafter, Johnson moved to Chicago to continue her work at Hull House. Her friend William "Skinny" Smith followed her. He too had been criticized at Karamu because of his realistic artwork. Johnson remained a staunch supporter of his talent, while expanding her vision of "social group work" (Johnson described her methods as a blend of social group process and the creative arts). Johnson and her daughter lived in Chicago for nearly a decade. In 1949 Johnson took a teaching job at Atlanta University, where she became an advocate for the arts and a pioneer in social group work.

Johnson returned to Cleveland in 1978. By then she was approaching seventy years of age, yet she tirelessly continued her mission to help others use the arts as a tool for enlightenment through programs such as "Making History Dance." She used the stories she learned as the daughter of a buffalo soldier to reach the students in Cleveland's public schools.

Johnson's lifelong commitment to excellence in dance, education, storytelling, and social work was honored on many levels. In 1999 she received a Governor's Award for the Arts in Ohio for her pioneering work in dance education. She was also given the Sankofa Award by the National Black Storytellers Association and accolades from the National Association of Social Workers and the Cleveland Music Settlement. In the early twenty-first century students and professional dancers continued to re-create Marjorie Johnson's work in dance, inspiring generation after generation. Johnson died in 2007, at the age of 97.

FURTHER READING

Marjorie Witt Johnson's papers are kept in the Western Reserve Historical Society's African American Archive in Cleveland, Ohio.

Obituary: *Oberlin Alumni Magazine*, Fall/Winter 2007.

TARICE SIMS GRAY

Johnson, Mat (19 Aug. 1970–), novelist, was born in Philadelphia, and spent his early years in the diverse and progressive Germantown and Mount Airy neighborhoods of the city. His father was of Irish descent, and his mother was African American. Johnson attended a number of universities (including the local West Chester University and the University of Wales-Swansea) before graduating from Earlham College in Indiana in 1993. Subsequent to receiving his B.A. degree, he attended Columbia University's MFA program in creative writing, graduating in 1999.

Johnson's work transcends conventional genre categories, extending from novels and historical retellings to nonfiction accounts and graphic narratives. Much of Johnson's work has centered on the complexities of African American life in the United States—an interest that stems in part from his own experience growing up. In the prologue to *Incognegro*, his 2009 graphic novel, Johnson details the travails of growing up biracial in America (Johnson is primarily of African American and Irish descent), and remarks upon the complex racial legacy he has bequeathed to his twin sons—whose appearances differ greatly despite their shared genetic makeup. Johnson is particularly interested in the interstices of racial identity and the difficulties experienced by those who don't fit into America's binary racial system.

His first novel, *Drop* (2002), tells the semiautobiographical story of Chris Jones, a young African American man who escapes his stifling West Philadelphia home by taking a job in England. Jones's adventure abroad is short-lived, however, and he finds himself forced to return to the United States and the thorny neighborhood politics he had hoped to leave behind. *Hunting in Harlem* (2004), a thriller, looks at the dark underbelly of gentrification—satirizing the way in which landlords and realtors seek to remove poor, African American tenants in order to make way for more lucrative development projects.

Johnson's critically acclaimed novel *Pym* (2011) rewrites Edgar Allen Poe's only published novel, *The Narrative of Arthur Gordon Pym of Nantucket*. Poe's novel, published to much derision in 1838, narrated the exploits of Pym and the slave revolt that left him on the island of Tsalal, an isolated land where the native populace resembles the enslaved population he left behind in America. Johnson uses Poe's novel as an ur-text for his own exploration of race relations in the United States. *Pym* centers on the story of an African American academic who begins to take the nineteenth-century writer's story literally, eventually leaving in search of the mythical Tsalal.

His nonfiction work *The Great Negro Plot* (2007) also focuses on race in America—this time through the prism of paranoia and violence in eighteenth-century Manhattan. Employing extensive archival research and the published accounts of one of the judges involved in the case, Johnson recounts the story of how a series of fires and whispers of a potential slave revolt led to the trial and execution of a number of innocent people. Johnson's work follows in the footsteps of the historian Jill Lepore's *New York Burning* (2006)—a history of the same event. His work diverges from hers, however, in his insistence on the links between racism in the eighteenth century and in the contemporary period.

Johnson's many works shed light not only on the complexities of African American life, but also on the way in which whiteness and African American identity are often mutually constituted. As he puts it in an interview, "in the African American community, race is always in your consciousness, but the same isn't true if you're white. The point of distinguishing people as 'black' was used to define 'whiteness.' How else do you explain the idea of being civilized but by contrasting it to being a savage? That dichotomy of black/white is a myth, and they are dependent on one another. Black reinforces the idea of white and vice versa" (Pack and Craft). Johnson takes up this idea most explicitly in his graphic novel, *Incognegro*. The detailed black and white noir narrative focuses on the travails of Zane Pinchback, a journalist from Harlem who travels to the Jim Crow South to report on an epidemic of lynching. Pinchback's light skin and smooth hair make it possible for him to pass for white, allowing him to personally witness and record scenes of graphic racial violence. Johnson's story and the drawings of the artist Warren Pleece work in tandem to make the complexities of race in 1930s America visible. *Incognegro* also provides a meditation on both the possibilities and dangers of invisibility, a theme common in African American writing that culminated in Ralph Ellison's *Invisible Man*. Johnson and Pleece's depiction of lynching (and their suggestion that the reader is complicit in the violence as a witness and spectator), as well as their representation of Pinchback's canny ability to pass in and out of a deeply compromised whiteness, dramatize the intersection of race and reading in the novel.

Incognegro was not Johnson's only foray into comics and the graphic novel. In 2005, he contributed the story to a limited series in the popular *Hellblazer* comic. Johnson's contribution told the story of one of the central and most misunderstood characters in the *Hellblazer* series, Papa Midnite, a gangster and voodoo priest, who had been depicted since the beginning of the series as a racial caricature of sorts. Johnson intervened in this depiction of Midnite, providing a much-needed backstory to a character who had appeared as a crudely drawn racial stereotype. In Johnson's graphic novel, *Dark Rain: A New Orleans Story*, post-Katrina New Orleans becomes the setting for a thriller about race, criminality, and ethics in the aftermath of disaster.

Johnson has long received praise for his diverse body of work. In 2007, he was the first artist to receive the prestigious James Baldwin Fellowship from the United States Artists Foundation. A professor in the creative writing program at the University of Houston, this prolific artist, activist, and historian continues to produce work that illuminates the difficult history of race in America.

FURTHER READING
Pack, Jimmy J. and Craft, Sonja. "An Interview with Mat Johnson." *Tinge* Magazine. http://www. tingemagazine.org/an-interview-with-mat-johnson/

JENNIFER GLASER

Johnson, Mess (?–1840), Ohio frontier settler, was likely born a slave in Maryland. Though Johnson's life remains largely undocumented in official records, oral tradition regarding his life and that of his family members has been extensively recorded. The fragmentary details they reveal are a fascinating commentary both on the role African Americans played in settling the Northwest Territory and the lives they led afterward in what would soon become the state of Ohio.

According to the Zanesville, Ohio, historian Norris Schneider in his book *Y Bridge City*, based in part on the oral history newspaper columns written by Elijah Church for the *Zanesville Courier* in 1878, Johnson was a slave in Maryland in 1799 when he learned that his master was going to sell him. Perhaps afraid of being separated from his family, Johnson decided to flee and, with another slave named Sam, made his way north to Pittsburgh. On the way Johnson and Sam reportedly fell in with two horse thieves on the run, but confronted the men about their illegal activities when they overheard them scheme to capture and sell Johnson and Sam back into slavery, thus thwarting the plan. Once they had arrived in the bustling frontier town of Pittsburgh, Johnson and Sam were employed on one of the many flatboats carrying settlers and supplies down the busy Ohio River. Upon reaching Wheeling, the men were hired by the legendary Colonel Ebenezer Zane, the builder of one of the area's major overland routes, Zane's Trace, to work on his ferry-boat there during the winter. Later, in the spring of 1800, Johnson, called "Black Mess," and Sam were hired by either Zane, or his son-in-law, John McIntire, to carry Mrs. McIntire and her household goods by flatboat down the Ohio River to Marietta, and from there up the Muskingum River to her new home in Westbourne, soon renamed Zanesville in 1801. Once this work was done, so Schneider related, Johnson stayed in the area for the rest of his life, while Sam returned east to Philadelphia and was later recaptured and returned to slavery. Whether or not Johnson arrived in the Ohio country by design or chance is unknown. However, one tantalizing but undocumented possibility exists. Was he seeking out his own family, maybe even his own mother? Zane and his family had a number of slaves in their employ, including one, "Aunt Rachel" Johnson, born on 20 October 1736, who came with them when they moved to Wheeling on the Ohio River in 1769–1770. She was with the Zane family during the siege of Fort Henry by "Indian" and British forces during the Revolutionary War in September 1777 and was prominent "leading in this effort" to cook and carry food and water to the fort's defenders (Eckert, 133). Aunt Rachel had four children and lived to the age of 111 before her death in 1847. Her possible connection to Johnson based on their mutual last name and connection to the Zane family is as of yet unproven, but at the very least they must have became well acquainted with one another over the years in Zanesville.

The employment of slaves or former slaves such as EZRA and Mess Johnson along the Ohio River frontier as boatmen, baggage handlers, substitute militiamen, and servants had long been a practice since the area first saw extensive settlement in the 1770s but has been little recognized. In fact, men like Johnson may be considered part of the first wave of black pioneer settlers in America, succeeded generations later by others like the Kentuckian DANIEL HICKMAN and his followers, that would over the years continue to move westward in ever-increasing numbers and more organized fashion, settling in Kansas and beyond after the Civil War. While the westward expansion movement in American history has been primarily portrayed from the white perspective, blacks too were vital participants.

The status of Johnson as a freedman or slave is not fully known after his arrival in the Ohio country; while the Northwest Ordinance of 1787 forbade slavery in the territory, the means of enforcing such were another matter and, with many of the settlers arriving here from Virginia, the antislavery statute was often ignored. Significantly for Johnson, the ordinance did not prohibit the return of runaway slaves lawfully owned in the original thirteen states. Indeed Schneider recounts that Johnson's Maryland master learned of his arrival in Zanesville and came to reclaim him. However, Johnson was able to hide in the woods while McIntire stalled the slave master, and he was forced to pay room and board at McIntire's hotel. After several days McIntire pointed out to the master both the futility of trying to locate Johnson in the wild country, as well as his mounting hotel bill, stating that it "might eventually amount to as much as Mess was worth" (Schneider, "Mess Johnson") the longer he stayed.

Persuaded by this argument, the master accepted McIntire's offer of $150 for Mess's bill of sale and left for good. However, Johnson's legal status as a freeman is ambiguous; though McIntire purchased Johnson's freedom, Johnson referred to McIntire as his "Massah" and "liked to fiddle and he liked to please McIntire" (Schneider, 46). At the very least, it may be speculated that Johnson had to work off the amount of his bill of sale for McIntire before likely gaining his full freedom by 1808.

Whatever his status, be it slave or freeman, Johnson and descendants of his family became well-known citizens in Zanesville for over 100 years. Johnson always remained close to the McIntire family and was employed by them as a ferryman on the Muskingum River and perhaps at their hotel. Tradition states that he was a renowned fiddle player at local Fourth of July celebrations and, curiously, that he had fathered his first child, Silas, in December 1802 with a woman whose name is unknown. As an infant, Silas was abandoned by his mother and left with the McIntire family, who, tradition relates, raised him on their own. According to Muskingum County marriage records, Johnson wed Ann Thompson in November 1808. Together the couple lived in a log cabin on what is now Linden Street and had five children, Robert, George Washington, Samuel, Prudence, and Elizabeth. They were active about town and joined the Methodist Church in 1827 during a period of religious revival. At the time of his death, Johnson was one of the town's most respected citizens.

FURTHER READING
Eckert, Allan W. *That Dark and Bloody River: Chronicles of the Ohio River Valley* (1995).
Schneider, Norris F. "Mess Johnson," *Zanesville Times Signal*, 25 Feb. 1951.
Schneider, Norris F. *Y Bridge City: The Story of Zanesville and Muskingum County, Ohio* (1997).

GLENN ALLEN KNOBLOCK

Johnson, Mildred Louise (25 Mar. 1914–11 Aug. 2007), educator and founder of Harlem's The Modern School, was born in Jacksonville, Florida, the only daughter of Nora Ethel Floyd and J. ROSAMOND JOHNSON. Her father, a singer, composer, and musician, and her uncle, the lawyer and poet JAMES WELDON JOHNSON, cocreated the Black National Anthem, "Lift Every Voice and Sing." Her mother was a homemaker. Mildred Johnson was married once to Hedley Vivian Edwards, a wealthy Jamaican businessman and horticulturist with whom she had one daughter, K. Melanie Edwards, and whom she later divorced (1963).

When Mildred was very young, the family moved to New York City, settling in Harlem. Mildred was homeschooled through kindergarten by her Bahamian paternal grandmother, Helen Louise Billet, an educator herself. When Mildred was six, she began attending the School of Ethical Culture, an elite private school in New York City. She grew up in a house was filled with music, and she would often be asked to judge her father's new songs. She attended the Ethical Culture Fieldston School, where she became the first black student to graduate from Ethical Culture's teacher training department in 1932. Her formal education was continued at New York University, Columbia University, and the Bank Street Graduate College.

Upon graduating in 1934, Johnson could not get a teaching position at any of the private schools in New York City, which she needed to fill a student-teaching requirement. Since New York private schools excluded blacks from student teaching at the time, she decided to start a school of her own, the first black private school in Harlem, The Modern School. Housed in the basement of Saint Philip's Episcopal Church, and with just eight students, most of them children of her friends, Johnson founded a secular, independent school that served black children. Within a few years of the school's founding, Ms. Johnson was able to purchase a building in Harlem, and enrollment increased to two hundred pupils. The Modern School came to be respected as one of the best private schools in Manhattan for children from prekindergarten to the sixth grade until it closed its doors in 2007.

During the Great Depression of the 1930s, Ms. Johnson founded and ran Camp Dunroven. The camp operated from 1933 until 1965. Johnson's Camp Dunroven, a private, coed sleep-away summer institute on her parent's estate in Pine Bush, New York, gave black, middle-class children an experience that fostered a sense of heritage and pride. Each day of camp would begin with the singing of "Lift Every Voice and Sing."

Aside from her work with children, Ms. Johnson wrote and produced over fifty musicals and two books of poetry. She received a number of awards including special recognition from United States President Ronald Reagan. Mildred Johnson vacationed in Oaks Bluff, in Martha's Vineyard, Massachusetts, and was a longtime member of the Cottagers, a philanthropic organization of African American women homeowners on Martha's Vineyard founded in the mid-1950s. Mildred also supervised religious education at St. Philip's Episcopal Church for eight years and performed much volunteer work. She was an active member of the NAACP; the Girls Club; Jack and Jill of America, Inc.; the New York Chapter of Girl Friends, Inc.; and the American Society of Composers, Authors, and Publishers. Johnson served on the boards of the Urban League, the YWCA, and National Girl-Friends, Inc.

In 2005 she received an award from the Martha's Vineyard chapter of the National Association for the Advancement of Colored People. After a brief hospitalization following a stroke, Mildred Louise Johnson died Saturday, 11 August 2007 in New York City. She was ninety-three years old.

FURTHER READING
"Mildred Johnson Edwards Founded Harlem School." *Vineyard Gazette*, 24 Aug. 2007.
Siegal, Nina. "After a Sale, School's Future Is Uncertain." *New York Times*, 8 Aug. 1999.
Julian Bond, and Sondra K. Wilson. *Lift Every Voice and Sing: A Celebration of the Negro National Anthem* (2000).
Obituary: *New York Amsterdam News*, 6 Sept. 2007.

ALEXANDER J. CHENAULT

Johnson, Mordecai Wyatt (12 Jan. 1890–10 Sept. 1976), university president and clergyman, was born in Paris, Henry County, Tennessee, the son of the Reverend Wyatt Johnson, a stationary engine operator in a mill, and Caroline Freeman. Johnson received his grammar school education in Paris, but in 1903 he enrolled in the Academy of the Roger Williams University in Nashville, Tennessee. The school burned in 1905, so Johnson finished the semester at the Howe Institute in Memphis. In the fall of that year, he moved to Atlanta to finish high school in the preparatory department of Atlanta Baptist College (renamed Morehouse College in 1913). There he completed a bachelor's degree in 1911. While at Atlanta Baptist, Johnson played varsity football and tennis, sang in various groups, and began his long career as a public speaker on the debating team.

After graduating, Johnson became an English instructor at his alma mater. For the 1912–1913 school year he taught economics and history and served as acting dean of the college. During the summers he earned a second bachelor's degree in the social sciences from the University of Chicago (1913). Johnson decided that he wanted to be a minister and enrolled in Rochester Theological

Mordecai Wyatt Johnson, the first African American president of Howard University. (Schomburg Center.)

Seminary. In seminary he was greatly influenced by Walter Rauschenbusch's theory of the Social Gospel, in which Christianity was responsible for economic and social change. While studying at Rochester he was a student pastor at the Second Baptist Church in Mumford, New York. He was granted a bachelor's of divinity degree in 1921—with a thesis titled "The Rise of the Knights Templars." In December 1916 Johnson married Anna Ethelyn Gardner of Augusta, Georgia; they had five children. That year Johnson worked as a student secretary of the Young Men's Christian Association (YMCA). He traveled for one year in the Southwest, studying predominantly black schools and colleges. This effort resulted in the formation of the Southwestern Annual Student Conference.

Johnson was ordained in 1916 and received an assignment in 1917 to be the pastor of the First Baptist Church in Charleston, West Virginia. In his nine years in West Virginia, Johnson was responsible for organizing the Commercial Cooperative Society, the Rochdale Cooperative Cash Grocery, and the Charleston branch of the National Association for the Advancement of Colored People (NAACP). Under his leadership, the membership of the local branch of the NAACP increased to one thousand in nine years. He also became active in the Negro Baptist Convention. By the time he left in 1926,

Johnson was well known as a community activist and speaker. In 1921 he took a year of absence while he studied at Harvard. The following year Johnson received a master's degree in Sacred Theology and gave the commencement address on postwar racism, titled "The Faith of the American Negro."

On 30 June 1926 Johnson was elected the thirteenth president of Howard University in Washington, D.C. Howard was chartered in 1867 out of the Freedmen's Bureau and was originally intended to be a theological seminary for African Americans and a normal school. By 1917 Howard and Fisk University were considered the only traditionally black schools offering a college-level education. When Johnson assumed the presidency of Howard on 1 September 1926, he had a broad vision for improvements to the university.

Johnson was the first African American to hold the presidency of Howard and came to office at a time when all other presidents of traditionally black colleges were white. Further, Howard was currently undergoing a time of controversy: Johnson's predecessor had been asked to resign, and the administration and the faculty sharply disagreed on a number of issues. Johnson sought to elevate the position of the professors by raising their salaries and providing tenure and security. During his tenure he brought in professors with national reputations and a large number of African Americans with PhDs.

Johnson's priorities for improvements were explained in his Twenty-Year Plan, which called for educational and physical development. In 1926 the only two accredited schools at Howard were dentistry and liberal arts. During his years at Howard, Johnson doubled the number of faculty members, doubled the library resources, tripled the amount of laboratory equipment, and constructed twenty new buildings. Under Johnson, all of the schools and colleges became fully accredited. In addition, the university enrollment increased by 250 percent, and the budget grew from $700,000 to $8 million.

Johnson's most important contribution to Howard was fund-raising. He was not only successful at securing private donations and grants, but he also persuaded Congress to amend the charter of the university to provide annual appropriations on 13 December 1928. Between 1946 and 1960, Howard received an average of more than $1 million annually. This added funding gave Howard an advantage over similar schools. For his work in gaining Howard annual federal funds, Johnson received the Spingarn Medal for Public Service in 1929. (The Spingarn Medal is the highest award given by the NAACP.)

Johnson retired in June 1960 and became president emeritus. Howard had been remade in his thirty-four-year tenure. The school had students from more than ninety countries. The professional schools in particular were impressive. Howard's medical school was producing half of the nation's African American doctors, and the law school was in the vanguard of civil rights, providing 96 percent of the African American lawyers.

After leaving Howard, Johnson served on the District of Columbia's Board of Education in 1962. In his three-year tenure, he was a vocal critic of the disparity between funding of predominantly white schools and black schools in the district. Johnson was also a member of several charitable organizations. He was on the National Council of the United Negro College Fund; vice chairman of the National Council for the Prevention of War; director of the American Youth Committee; a member of the Advisory Council for the National Youth Administration; a member of the National Advisory Council on Education; a member of the National Religion and Labor Board; and director of the National Conference of Christians and Jews. In addition, he was a strong advocate for nations under colonial control by countries such as Great Britain and France, and he was a member of the advisory council for the Virgin Islands. He was an early proponent of India's independence from Great Britain and often spoke on the topic. In one such lecture, he spoke at MARTIN LUTHER KING JR.'s seminary, Crozer Theological Seminary in Philadelphia.

In 1969 Johnson's wife died. In April 1970 he married Alice Clinton Taylor King; they had no children. Howard University honored Johnson in 1973 by naming the administration building after him. His service was also recognized internationally: Ethiopia, Haiti, Liberia, and Panama all gave him awards for his achievements. Johnson died in Washington, D.C.

Johnson has been recognized for his excellent administrative skills and as "one of the great platform orators of his day." His involvement in civil rights and religious causes gained him notice. His organization and development of Howard University was remarkable. Johnson insisted on a quality faculty, high-caliber students, adequate funding, and sufficient facilities and laboratory equipment. These factors put Howard on a path for success. Johnson's contributions to Howard and his other causes have assured his legacy of improved educational opportunities for all.

FURTHER READING
Johnson's papers concerning Howard University are in the Moorland-Spingarn Research Center at Howard.
Logan, Rayford W. *Howard University: The First Hundred Years, 1867–1967* (1969).
McKinney, Richard I. *Mordecai—The Man and His Message: The Story of Mordecai Wyatt Johnson* (1998).
Winston, Michael R., ed. *Education for Freedom* (1976).
Obituaries: *New York Times* and *Washington Post*, 11 Sept. 1976.
This entry is taken from the *American National Biography* and is published here with the permission of the American Council of Learned Societies.
SARA GRAVES WHEELER

Johnson, Nathan (1797–11 Oct. 1880), abolitionist and entrepreneur, was born in circumstances that are unclear. One undocumented account states that he was born in Virginia; another, simply that he was born into slavery; a third, that he purchased his freedom. It is known that Johnson was in New Bedford on 24 October 1819, the day he married Mary (called Polly) Mingo Durfee Page, who was descended at least in part from the Fall River tribe of Wampanoag Indians.

In 1820 Polly Johnson was working in the home of Charles Waln Morgan, who in June 1819 had come from Philadelphia to New Bedford to marry Sarah Rodman and begin his career as a whaling industry merchant. Nathan Johnson's mother, Emily Brown, who lived with her son in 1850 and was buried with him in New Bedford, claimed to have been born in Philadelphia; so too did his brother Benjamin. A free black Nathan Johnson household—possibly including his mother, Polly, and one of Polly's three daughters from her first marriage, Mahala Durfee—is listed in the 1820 Philadelphia census. Two people of color—one adult male and one adult female—are listed in Morgan's New Bedford household in 1820, but their accounts do not indicate who among the numerous black domestics they hired in that decade lived in their household. It is possible that Johnson and Morgan had a prior relationship in Philadelphia, just as Polly Page and her daughters may have known the Rodmans in New Bedford.

By the late 1830s Nathan Johnson owned at least three large houses and was a bathing house operator, trader in exotic foods, and caterer, while his wife was probably the city's leading confectioner. The New Bedford author and historian Daniel Ricketson recalled the couple as "the *sine qua non* at all the fashionable parties of our places, as caterers and waiters" (New Bedford *Daily Mercury*, 6 Oct. 1880, 2). Nathan Johnson's long involvement in abolitionism and fugitive assistance appears to have begun in 1822, when Nantucketers and New Bedford residents thwarted the efforts of Virginia slave agents to return three fugitives to slavery. Five years later Johnson and some twenty other men of color stormed the residence of "a coloured man from New York or farther south whose object it was to get information of run-away slaves," according to the account of one local abolitionist (Zephaniah W. Pease, ed., *Diary of Samuel Rodman: A New Bedford Chronicle of Thirty-Seven Years, 1821–1859* [1927], 45).

Nathan Johnson attended nearly every early colored people's convention, was one of two vice presidents of the fifth annual meeting in 1835, and was president of the Troy, New York, meeting in 1847. By 1838 he was well known in abolitionist circles and in 1840 was one of five vice presidents of the Massachusetts Anti-Slavery Society. That he was working in fugitive assistance with DAVID RUGGLES of the New York Vigilance Committee is documented in FREDERICK DOUGLASS's account of his escape from slavery in *My Bondage and My Freedom* (1856). Though two white New Bedford abolitionists met the fugitive slave born Frederick Bailey and his wife, ANNA MURRAY DOUGLASS, in Newport, Rhode Island, in September 1838, once in the Massachusetts city Douglass and his wife were taken to the home of Johnson, "to whom we had a line from Mr. Ruggles." Johnson "was the owner of more books—the reader of more newspapers—was more conversant with the political and social condition of this nation and the world—than nine-tenths of all the slaveholders in Talbot county, Maryland," Douglass wrote (*My Bondage and My Freedom*, ed. William L. Andrews [1987], 210), and in casting about for Douglass's new name in freedom Johnson turned to the Scots chief in Sir Walter Scott's *Lady of the Lake*, the book he was then reading.

How long Douglass lived with Johnson is not clear; it was probably a matter of months before he moved on to rent other quarters in New Bedford. But Johnson's home was the documented shelter for other fugitives as well as for the two daughters of WILLIAM WELLS BROWN, who were schooled in New Bedford while their father was a lecturer for the Massachusetts Anti-Slavery Society between 1847 and 1850.

In early April 1849, leaving his wife his property and power of attorney, Nathan Johnson, his stepson

George Page, and his brother Benjamin took out seamen's protection papers and left New Bedford for California on the ship *America*. Johnson evidently did poorly there and moved on to Oregon, and in 1869 there is record of his presence in Caribou, British Columbia. On 19 November 1871 Polly Johnson died and left a will stipulating that her husband might have "a maintenance from my estate during his term of life, provided he comes home to New Bedford within two years from the date of my decease." By 27 February 1873 Nathan Johnson had acceded to these terms. In a letter he wrote from New Bedford on that day to the white New York abolitionist Gerrit Smith, he applauded the "much that you have done for the Race" and sought whatever funds Smith might spare him "to healp [*sic*] me through the present year; if I should tarry longer things will grow better for me" (Gerrit Smith Papers, Syracuse University).

There is no record of a response from Smith, but in Johnson's later years Douglass visited him several times, his last visit coming just a few weeks before Nathan Johnson's death. Johnson's "long sojourn on the Pacific coast" had kept their visits few and far between, but time had not diminished Douglass's estimation of him. "I do not remember to have met a man more courageous and less ostentatious, more self-respectful and yet more modest," he averred in the New Bedford *Mercury* a week after Johnson's passing. Nathan Johnson's New Bedford gravestone carries the inscription "Freedom to All Mankind."

FURTHER READING
No collection of Johnson's papers exist, but he and his wife are mentioned with some frequency in the Charles W. Morgan Papers, G. W. Blunt White Library, Mystic Seaport Museum, Mystic, Connecticut, and the Gibson Papers, New Bedford Free Public Library, New Bedford, Massachusetts.
Douglass, Frederick. *My Bondage and My Freedom* (1856; repr. 1987).
Grover, Kathryn. *The Fugitive's Gibraltar: Escaping Slaves and Abolitionism in New Bedford, Massachusetts* (2001).
Obituary: *New Bedford Evening Standard*, 13 Oct. 1880; *New Bedford Mercury*, 18 Oct. 1880.

KATHRYN GROVER

Johnson, Noble Mark (18 Apr. 1881–9 Jan. 1978), actor and film producer, was born Noble Mark Johnson in Marshall, Missouri, to Perry Johnson, a nationally renowned horse trainer, and Georgia Reed. Their first child, Virgel, was born in Indiana in 1879.

They had relocated to Missouri before Noble Mark was born, however they soon moved permanently to Ivywild, a suburb of Colorado Springs, Colorado, where Perry built his own facilities to train the horses of gold mining millionaires. Colorado Springs is often mistakenly listed as Johnson's birthplace but is, rather, the birthplace of his siblings Iris Hazel (1883) and George Perry (1885). Georgia Johnson died two days after George's birth. As a result the infant George was turned over to Mrs. Nancy Turner, a servant in the home of the Johnson's neighbors. Virgel largely took responsibility for Noble and Iris. The Johnson children attended public schools in Colorado Springs. Among their classmates was future actor Lon Chaney.

Johnson quit school at the age of fifteen and joined his father for two summers on the racing circuit. In 1898, the seventeen-year-old left home, intent on being a cowboy. Noble Johnson secured jobs as diverse as rancher, cook, and lumberjack throughout the Northwest, but returned often to Colorado Springs. During an extended trip to New York in 1905 he abandoned horsemanship, hoping to box professionally. However, breaking his hand in June of 1907 sent him west again. Amidst more fair weather ranching, he twice wintered in Los Angeles as an auto mechanic, not knowing he would later return for a very different profession.

In June 1914, Johnson returned to Colorado Springs to find Lubin Film Manufacturing Company of Philadelphia filming the Western *Eagle's Nest*. An actor portraying a Native American was injured in a horse stunt, and Johnson replaced him. Impressed by Johnson's excellent horse handling and overall performance, Lubin management asked him to join them as a player in Philadelphia. Johnson accepted and made at least four short films with them in a year, playing non-black characters. Noble Johnson was physically impressive at six feet two and 225 pounds. Moreover, strong features and an olive-toned complexion allowed him to portray many different ethnic types. Recognizing his own potential in the film industry, Johnson moved again to Los Angeles.

Johnson was signed by Universal Pictures for his ability as a stunt man and began appearing in their films in 1915. Quickly noticed by the black press, he was called "the race's daredevil movie star" and "America's premiere African American screen star," despite the fact that his small roles were rarely African Americans. In 1918 Johnson approached his friend Harry Gant (a white Universal cameraman), his brother George (a postal employee in Omaha, Nebraska), Dr. J. Thomas Smith (a well-to-do black druggist), and Clarence Brooks (an African American actor) and founded Lincoln Motion Picture Company to make black films for a black audience, with Johnson as president. Many prominent local businessmen, both black and white, invested in the project. The world's first black motion picture production and distribution company began with the respectable sum of $75,000. Lincoln released three movies, all starring a dashing Noble Johnson: *The Realization of a Negro's Ambition* (1916), *The Trooper of Company K* (1917), and *The Law of Nature* (1918). Advertisements alone show the company's historic social effect, like that in *The California Eagle* proclaiming "*The Trooper of Co. K* … Colored Persons Shown True to Life on the Screen."

Johnson was dedicated to Lincoln, even working without salary to combat costs, which left him reliant on his work at Universal. However it was rumored that Universal gave him an ultimatum. Large posters of Johnson at black movie houses caused African Americans to pass up Universal pictures at neighboring theaters—Johnson was competing against his employer. Accordingly he resigned from Lincoln in 1920. Clarence Brooks became the company's new star, but he did not have Johnson's glamour, and after two further films the company folded.

Johnson was again relegated to supporting parts, but he nonetheless gained notable roles such as Friday in *Robinson Crusoe* (1922) and Uncle Tom in *Topsy and Eva* (1927). He also played against some of the 1920s greatest talents in its largest spectacles, including Cecil B. DeMille's *The Ten Commandments* (1923), *The Four Horseman of the Apocalypse* (1921) with Rudolph Valentino, *The Thief of Baghdad* (1924) with Douglas Fairbanks, and MGM's *Ben-Hur* (1925). Working on another MGM film in 1928, *West of Zanzibar*, he got the chance to reminisce with Lon Chaney. Indeed, Johnson was cast anywhere he could fit, often uncredited, with great use made of his many skills. For example, he "fought" world champion boxers James J. Corbett and Jack Dempsey in silent serials, and is clearly masterful as a charioteer in *The King of Kings* (1927).

He transitioned to talkies, playing Queequoq to John Barrymore's Captain Ahab in *Moby Dick* (1930). He is best remembered as the Native Chief in *King Kong* (1933). His film career ended as it began, playing a Native American, in *North of the Great Divide* (1950).

Over the years Johnson stretched to a spectacular array of ethnic parts, including American Indians, Mexicans, Africans, Caucasians, Arabs, Indians (notably Chief Sitting Bull), South Sea Islanders, and Asians (including the original henchman of Dr. Fu Manchu). How he saw himself is less clear. On a 1936 application for a Social Security Number, he is "neither White, Black, nor Red, but have blood mixture of the three races, to what extent of each is undetermined."

Johnson was married at least two times, first in 1912 in Denver, Colorado, to Ruth Thornton, for an indeterminate period but without children. When he married Gladys Blackwell in the early 1940s, he called himself Mark Noble. They invested in real estate, traveling the Northwest until retiring in small Yucaipa, California. Noble Johnson died, as Mark Noble, at age 96. On his death certificate he is documented as racially white and thirty-five years a rancher. For unknown reasons he had been secretive about his film work with Mrs. Gladys Noble, and had destroyed all relevant papers and memorabilia shortly before his death—this despite appearances in over 167 movies during a forty-year career.

FURTHER READING

Bogle, Donald. *Bright Boulevards, Bold Dreams: The Story of Black Hollywood.* (2006.)

Cappello, Bill. "Noble Johnson—Part I." *Classic Images* 199. (1992.)

Cappello, Bill. "Noble Johnson—Part II." *Classic Images* 200. (1992.)

CARA GRACE PACIFICO

Johnson, Norma Holloway (28 July 1932–18 Sept. 2011), teacher, lawyer, and judge, was born Norma Holloway in Lake Charles, Louisiana, to H. Lee Holloway, a laborer, and Beatrice Williams Holloway, an elementary school teacher. Norma was the elder of two children; a son named Lionel was born later. The family left Lake Charles for Washington, D.C., when Norma was fourteen years old, during the Great Migration of blacks to Northern cities. H. Lee died shortly after the move. Beatrice continued to teach, although in Washington she began to teach adults, which offered better pay and was to her more personally rewarding. Beatrice Holloway believed strongly that a good education would be the salvation of African Americans, and she strongly encouraged academic achievement in her children.

The children thrived in the outstanding public schools of the District of Columbia, which at the time were renowned for their rigorous and academically excellent curricula. Norma attended Shaw Junior High School and then Dunbar Senior High School, graduating in 1950.

She was accepted by the Miner's Teachers College (later part of Howard University), where she majored in English and minored in history. She graduated magna cum laude and was the class valedictorian in 1955. At Miner's she met another aspiring lawyer, Julius A. Johnson; they courted, and two years after finishing after law school, on 18 June 1964, they were married.

Even before gaining her college degree to become a teacher, Johnson knew that she wanted to be a lawyer. She often declared that the turning point for her had come in 1954 when she was a junior at Miner's. The U.S. Supreme Court had made its decision in *Brown v. Board of Education*, and its pronouncements on justice and equal opportunity in America inspired her.

With little money to finance further education, Johnson took her first teaching assignment at Washington's Taft Junior High School, where she taught English and history and saved her money for law school. Soon she was able to enroll at Georgetown University's law school, from which she received her J.D. in 1962. She was Georgetown's first African American woman graduate.

Johnson's first job after law school was at the U.S. Department of Justice, where she became a regular trial attorney. After three years Johnson left the Department of Justice to become a trial attorney for the D.C. Office of Corporation Counsel, where she got even more exciting and useful trial experience.

It was in the Corporation Counsel's office—headed by the black legal superstar Charles Duncan—that Johnson began to recognize how the law really operated, and it was "a real eye-opener," she recalled in an interview. Duncan oversaw all the legal affairs of the District of Columbia and was second in line to be mayor of the city. Johnson thrived in that environment. She rose to become the section chief of the juvenile division, where her lifelong commitment to the youth of the city was nurtured.

While working at the Corporation Counsel's office Johnson was approached about a possible judgeship. In 1970 President Richard M. Nixon appointed her to the newly created Superior Court of the District of Columbia, the first court of general jurisdiction in the district and not long after its creation one of the busiest. During her tenure on that court Johnson served in all of the major divisions. It was during this time that she became active in the National Council of Juvenile and Family Court Judges and was a founding member of both the National Association of Black Women Attorneys and the National Association of Women Judges, for which she served as director from 1979 to 1981.

On 12 May 1980 President Jimmy Carter appointed Johnson to the U.S. District Court for the District of Columbia, making her the first African American woman appointed to a federal court in the District of Columbia. She was also an active member of the American Judicature Society, where she served on the executive committee from 1979 to 1981; of the National Institute for Citizen Education in the Law, where she was a director and was chairman of the board between 1975 and 1984; of the Council for Court Excellence; of the Judiciary Leadership Development Council; and of the American, national, and Washington bar associations. Her many awards and honors included the University of the District of Columbia's 1988 Outstanding Alumna Award.

Johnson became the chief judge on the district court in 1997 and gained even more prominence when she presided over the grand jury investigation of President Bill Clinton's affair with the White House intern Monica Lewinsky. At one point Johnson stunned the White House with her refusal to limit the scope of Kenneth Starr's grand jury investigation of the president. With the heightened scrutiny from the media and the public that came with the case, Judge Johnson kept one tenet at the forefront of her thinking: her first responsibility was always the matter before the court. No matter how they might try, the press and anyone else faced nearly insurmountable odds in reaching her for interviews or other matters. Access to her was strictly controlled to avoid anything that would impede her focus, and she worked the long hours required because she believed that a judge should work as long as necessary to fulfill the oath of office that he or she had taken for the position. In December 2003, as the senior and presiding judge, Judge Norma Johnson stepped down from the court. She died in Lake Charles, Louisiana, at the age of 79.

FURTHER READING

Cohen, Adam. "The Nonsense Stops Here," *Time* (16 Mar. 1998).

Hine, Darlene Clark, ed. *Black Women in America: An Historical Encyclopedia* (1993).

LUTHER BROWN JR.

Johnson, Pauline Byrd Taylor (5 Feb. 1904–2 Dec. 1988), educator, writer, and community activist, was born Pauline Byrd in Kalamazoo, Michigan, to Edith Belle Hill Byrd, a hairdresser, and Oscar Byrd, an accountant. Her ancestors descended from a Kentucky slave owner and his black mistress, who educated their children and sent them north with money and wagons before the Civil War broke out. Her family was well known as one of southwest Michigan's aristocratic black families. Her grandfather, Forrest Hill, owned numerous properties and, as a teamster and builder, constructed several roads and two buildings at Kalamazoo College. Her grandparents, with whom Pauline and her mother lived after her parents divorced in 1906, emphasized courage, responsibility, hard work, and, above all, education. Her family was clearly inspired by the principles of BOOKER T. WASHINGTON, the foremost black spokesman of the early twentieth century. His emphasis on industrial education and attainable goals for middle-class blacks that included property ownership, self-employment, and small business success spoke directly to the values of the Byrd family. Johnson's family always lived in white neighborhoods. These standards and sense of social responsibility led Johnson's family to enroll her not in the one largely black elementary school in town but rather in an all-white school close to their home, which was accomplished since Kalamazoo public schools were not legally, only geographically, segregated.

The emphasis on education continued as Johnson attended Kalamazoo Central High School as the only black student in her class of sixty. Many in the black community did not support Johnson as she pursued her education. According to Mrs. Johnson, "In those days Negroes did not go to high school. That was almost like going to college. They would say, 'There's no sense in going to high school—what do you want to go with those white folks for? You don't need a high school education to be a maid or a cook'" (Moerdyk, 224). According to her friend and contemporary Judge Charles Pratt, many blacks also considered her and her family "prideful of their position" (Moerdyk, 224). To make matters worse, members of the Allen Chapel African Methodist Church snubbed her, so she turned instead to the First Church of Christian Science, which she believed to have healed her of a serious childhood illness: leaky heart valves. She remained a member throughout her life. When she graduated from Central High School in 1922, she immediately went on to Kalamazoo College, a small, private, liberal arts college. In 1926 she became the first black to graduate from the college, with a degree in English. She obtained a teaching certificate and applied for a teaching position in the Kalamazoo public schools, but her application was ignored. She then spent one year at the University of Chicago pursuing a master's degree in Social Work. Deciding that teaching appealed to her more, she began her teaching career in an all-black, one-room schoolhouse in rural Cass County, a stop on the Underground Railroad in Clinton Township, southwestern Michigan, where many escaped slaves settled, in 1929.

In 1930 she received an offer to teach at Lincoln Ridge Junior College near Louisville, Kentucky. WHITNEY MOORE YOUNG JR., who went on to be executive director of the National Urban League from 1961 to 1971, was one of Johnson's students. He credited Johnson as the teacher who had been the greatest influence on him and kept in touch with her until his death in 1971.

Though her teaching experience was a success, the level of prejudice in the South made Johnson uncomfortable. She returned to Kalamazoo and married Chester Taylor whom she met while volunteering at the Frederick Douglass Community Center for Negroes, started during World War I for returning African American veterans. He was, according to Johnson, "a very fine fellow, … he was smart and hardworking…. He went to school at Western Michigan University for awhile and then he painted houses" (Moerdyk, 241). In 1933 she gave, birth to her only child, Edith Joanne. Johnson, however, felt constrained by marriage and motherhood, divorcing her husband in 1939. She then moved to Gary, Indiana, and took a teaching job at Roosevelt High School, a brand new all-black school. In the early 1940s Gary's school system experienced an influx of African American students due to wartime factory expansions that employed many blacks from the Deep South. Roosevelt High School employed professional African American teachers from all over the United States. During these years she visited Chicago regularly and wrote articles for the *Chicago Defender* and the *Pittsburgh Courier*, two top black newspapers.

In 1944 Johnson applied again to Kalamazoo public schools. This time she was hired. As the first African American schoolteacher in Kalamazoo, Johnson started teaching in 1945 at Lincoln Elementary, where most of the city's black students were concentrated. She also served as the first woman director of the Douglass Community

Association, a local community center. She was executive secretary for a Community Self-Survey titled *Negroes in Kalamazoo*, cosponsored by Fisk University in Nashville, Tennessee. She also served on a committee for the Michigan Board of Education that published a bulletin on intercultural education, a popular educational trend that sought to teach children about other cultures to reduce racial hostility and encourage desegregation. In July 1946 Johnson was invited to attend the Bureau of Intercultural Education, a nonprofit consulting institute in New York City. She received a Julius Rosenwald Fellowship in 1947 to attend New York University's School of Education to study the applications of intercultural education. The Rosenwald Fund, active from 1917 to 1949, funded blacks and whites in pursuit of racial equality through mostly educational means. When the experimental Center for Human Relations at NYU opened in 1947, Johnson had a prominent role in developing the curriculum designed to promote positive race relations within educational, social, governmental, and industrial agencies.

After a year in New York City, Johnson returned home to teach high school in Kalamazoo. In 1957 she married Clifford Johnson, a bail bondsman and rental property owner who died of a heart attack in 1967. Pauline Johnson had a difficult time during the civil rights movement of the mid- to late 1960s. African American students had become more militant and deplored her commitment to working within the system to correct its wrongs. Her commitment to the Republican Party, originally the party of racial equality, her adamant opposition to busing, and her fastidious adherence to middle-class morals gave her the reputation as an accommodationist. She bitterly denounced these attempts to portray her in an unfavorable light, as she had worked, in her own way, all her life to further positive race relations in her community. She retired in 1969 at the height of the controversy over busing in Kalamazoo, which she opposed on the grounds that it was not educationally sound for children to spend time riding the bus when they could be learning in school. After her retirement she was active in local politics in Kalamazoo and wrote for numerous local publications and the *Christian Science Monitor*. Though she was highly respected by many, until her death white liberals and most African Americans could never forgive her conservative political leanings and refusal to endorse the methods, though not the principles, of the civil rights movement.

FURTHER READING

Moerdyk, Ruth Ann. "'Lone Wolf': Pauline Byrd Johnson," in *Emancipated Spirits: Portraits of Kalamazoo College Women*, ed. Gail B. Griffin (1983).

Wilson, Benjamin C. *The Rural Black History between Chicago and Detroit, 1850–1929: A Photograph Album and Random Thoughts* (1985).

Obituary: *Kalamazoo Gazette*, 4 Dec. 1988.

CARSON GRATH. LEFTWICH

Johnson, Pete (24 Mar. 1904–23 Mar. 1967), blues and jazz pianist, was born in Kansas City, Missouri. His date of birth was given as 25 March in an interview with Johnny Simmen, but the date was corrected to 24 March in the reprint of Simmen's article in Hans Mauerer's book and was repeated as 24 March in Mauerer's reprint of a 1962 article by Johnson's wife; the *New York Times* obituary concurred, giving 24 March. His full given name was probably Kermit Holden Johnson. The names of his parents are unknown.

Johnson was raised by his mother alone, who worked as a domestic to support him. She placed him in an orphanage for a time because she could not care for him adequately, but she took him back home when she learned that he was being ill treated. As a child Johnson played homemade drums, and in ward school he first played a real drum. He also learned piano from local players, most significantly his uncle Charles Johnson, who taught him a fast rag, "Nickels and Dimes." Johnson started school late and dropped out of the fifth grade, at age twelve or thirteen, to work mainly as a laborer. He worked as a drummer from about 1922 to 1926, when he switched to piano permanently.

The chronology of Johnson's activities in Kansas City nightclubs from the late 1920s through the mid-1930s is unclear. Around 1927, while performing at the Backbiter's Club, he accompanied the singer JOE TURNER and thereby initiated one of the best matched partnerships in jazz and blues. At the Hole in the Wall he accompanied the singer Edna Taylor, whom he then followed to Jazzland for better pay. He also worked, often with Turner, at the Hawaiian Gardens in a small band led by Abie Price, the Black and Tan Club, El Trocadore, the Yellow Front, the Peacock Inn, the Grey Goose, and the Spinning Wheel with Herman Walder's Rockette Swing Unit.

In 1933 or 1935 Johnson began working at the Sunset Crystal Palace in a duo with the drummer Murl Johnson that gradually expanded to become a seven- or eight-piece band plus the singers Turner and Henry Lawson. The group also broadcast on radio. Johnson and Turner were discovered by the jazz impresario John Hammond, who brought them to New York City for a performance at the Apollo Theater in Harlem in 1936. Singing a pop song instead of their strength, the blues, the duo was quickly pulled off the stage. They are also reported to have performed at the Famous Door, but it may be that this event happened two years later. They returned home, and Johnson resumed his job at the Sunset, from which he made nightly broadcasts in 1938. In May of that year Hammond introduced the duo on Benny Goodman's NBC radio show *Camel Caravan*. Their breakthrough to success, however, began on 23 December 1938, when Hammond presented them at his From Spirituals to Swing concert at Carnegie Hall, where they performed the blues song "It's All Right Baby." This concert also marked the formation of a boogie-woogie piano trio with Johnson, ALBERT AMMONS, and MEADE LUX LEWIS, whose performances received considerable acclaim. (Recordings from this concert were first issued in 1958.) The next week Turner and Johnson recorded the blues classic "Roll 'em, Pete."

In 1939 the piano trio worked with Turner as their singer at Café Society in New York and the Hotel Sherman in Chicago and broadcast nationally from the latter. In New York, Johnson broadcast with Turner from the Chamber Music Society of Lower Basin Street (August 1940). He worked in a piano duo with Ammons at the uptown location of Café Society to 1942, when the two men began touring. Johnson's recordings from this period include "Pete's Blues" and "Let 'em Jump" as an unaccompanied pianist (April 1939), "Cherry Red" and "Baby, Look at You" with his Boogie Woogie Boys (June 1939), and "Vine Street Bustle" and "Some Day Blues" with his Blues Trio (December 1939). He also recorded "Piney Brown Blues" with a five-piece group that included the trumpeter HOT LIPS PAGE under Turner's nominal leadership (November 1940), "627 Stomp" from that same session of 1940 but with an eight-piece group and without Turner, and "Just for You" (1941) with his trio. He performed in the film short *Boogie Woogie Dream* (1941).

In the mid-1940s Johnson toured in duos with Ammons, Lewis, and Turner. He and Turner opened their own Blue Room Club in Los Angeles in 1945, and Johnson regularly appeared on Turner's recordings, including "Old Piney Brown Is Gone" (1948). From 1947 to 1948 Johnson worked in California both as a soloist and in duos with Ammons at the Streets of Paris in Hollywood or with Turner in Los Angeles and San Francisco. He then toured the Northeast.

From late 1948 onward Johnson's career declined severely. For more than a decade he had been pigeonholed as a boogie-woogie pianist, a label that raised expectations of relentlessly repetitious piano bass patterns, and he had difficulty finding work within this restricted and by now rather worn-out blues style, even though he was actually a versatile pianist fluent not only in other blues styles but in jazz and popular song as well.

In 1949 Johnson first played in Buffalo and met Margery (maiden name unknown). They married and had one daughter. Johnson decided to settle in Buffalo in 1950 but came to regret that decision because few places there offered him work. He toured the Northeast and Midwest in the Piano Parade with ERROLL GARNER, Lewis, and ART TATUM in 1952. That same year he worked with Lewis in Providence, Rhode Island, and Detroit, and he occasionally found jobs playing at little-known venues. But for most of the decade he worked by day, often doing heavy labor.

In 1955 Johnson recorded the album *Listen to the Blues* with the singer JIMMY RUSHING. The album *Joe Turner Sings Kansas City Jazz* (reissued as *Boss of the Blues*) included Johnson and a number of COUNT BASIE's sidemen and presented pop songs and reprises of Turner and Johnson's early blues recordings (1956). In 1958 Johnson joined Turner on tour with Jazz at the Philharmonic in Europe, at the Newport Jazz Festival, where he also accompanied the singer Big Maybelle and the singer-guitarist CHUCK BERRY, and at the Great South Bay Jazz Festival. Johnson had a heart condition and diabetes, and this same year, 1958, he suffered a stroke that left him partially paralyzed, ending his musical career. He died in Buffalo after suffering another stroke.

Wertheim said, "Pete Johnson was a complete jazz musician who could handle an extensive variety of music and pianistic technique. The only link[s] Pete Johnson had with the piano style of the 'primitive' [are] that he did not read music too well, although he knew chords, and his fast boogie woogie solos generated the same wild excitement" (quoted in Mauerer, 37). By way of example, Turner's "Roll 'em, Pete" offers Johnson's definitive boogie-woogie playing. The "627 Stomp" (1940) finds Johnson comfortably settled into a jazz band; this piece is a blues done in the style of Kansas City

swing, and here a boogie-woogie bass line comes in only at the end, for climactic effect.

On "Just for You" (1941) Johnson has the support of the bassist AL HALL and the drummer A. G. Godley, and he plays a relaxed, quiet, and elegant bass and chord pattern in the stride piano tradition while concentrating on the melody, ornamented by trills and cascading lines. "Pete's Lonesome Blues" (1946) finds him applying this elegant stride style to the unaccompanied blues, and in this setting his approach in its earthiness surpasses the work of the more famous practitioners of Harlem stride piano. On "Piney Brown Blues" and the duo "Little Bittie Gal's Blues" (1944), Johnson's focus is on trembly trills floating rhythmically across the beat. This sort of tuneful interplay between tinkling piano melodies and Turner's full-bodied voice, of which there are numerous additional examples, perhaps represents Johnson's finest work.

FURTHER READING

Hentoff, Nat, and Albert J. McCarthy, eds. *Jazz* (1959).

Mauerer, Hans J., ed. *The Pete Johnson Story* (1965).

Pease, Sharon. "Swing Piano Styles: Pete Johnson Got His Start Shining Shoes in Kaycee," *Down Beat* 6 (15 Dec. 1939): 22.

Schuller, Gunther. *The Swing Era: The Development of Jazz, 1930–1945* (1989).

Simmen, Johnny. "My Life, My Music," *Jazz Journal* 12 (Aug. 1959): 8–11.

Obituaries: *New York Times*, 24 Mar. 1967; *Down Beat* 34 (4 May 1967): 12.

This entry is taken from the *American National Biography* and is published here with the permission of the American Council of Learned Societies.

BARRY KERNFELD

Johnson, Peter August (17 June 1851–1 Jan. 1914), physician, was born near Eatontown, New Jersey, the son of Joseph Johnson and Martha A. Frazier. Before moving to New York, where he would spend his entire professional career, Peter attended Roger Smith High School in Newport, Rhode Island. After completing additional studies at Clark's Collegiate Institute in New York, Johnson enrolled at the Long Island College Hospital (a precursor to the College of Medicine of the State University of New York Health Science Center of Brooklyn), a reputable private institution. On his graduation from the Brooklyn medical school in 1882, Johnson became the fifth black graduate of the institution, forty-five years after the first African American to earn a professional degree in medicine, JAMES MCCUNE SMITH, had earned his degree in

Scotland. Johnson initially practiced medicine in New York under the guidance of David K. McDonough, a physician who had been born a slave, and Edward J. Messener, a former mentor from medical school. Messener invited the young medical graduate to work with him at New York's Mount Sinai Hospital, where Johnson spent seven years, four of which he also spent at the People's Dispensary. Johnson married Mary Elizabeth Whittle in 1882; they had two children.

Throughout his medical career, Johnson fought the discrimination and racism that constrained educational and clinical training opportunities for black physicians, who constituted less than 1 percent of all physicians when he graduated from medical school. Black Americans who aspired to enter medicine in the late nineteenth century and early twentieth century commonly found that racism—and in the case of black women, sexism as well—categorically excluded them from many medical schools. Even when some black applicants gained entrance and later graduated from medical school, they would confront, as graduates, discrimination and hostility while searching for training opportunities in hospitals and clinics. Prominent early twentieth-century black public figures, such as BOOKER T. WASHINGTON, told friends and colleagues that Johnson and other black physicians wrote to him about their difficulty in securing places for themselves on hospital staffs or rooms for their patients in some institutions. As cofounder of McDonough Memorial Hospital (named for his former colleague and friend), a voluntary institution that opened in 1898 at 439 West Forty-second Street, Johnson became active in this initiative to bring high-quality medical services to the urban poor in New York City. McDonough's admission policy disallowed discrimination against patients on the basis of race, ethnicity, or religious affiliation. Johnson served as the chief of attending staff and chief surgeon during a five-year affiliation with the facility.

Johnson spent the remainder of his career with the New York Milk Committee for the Prevention and Cure of Infant Diseases and as a staff member in the Division of Tuberculosis Prevention and Control at the New York City Board of Health. As a board member of the Committee for Improving the Industrial Condition of Negroes in New York and the National League on Urban Conditions among Negroes (later organized as the National Urban League), Johnson's concern for social reform extended beyond his medical practice environment in New York City. In 1909 Johnson was elected to serve as the tenth president of the National Medical Association, an organization founded in 1895 to redress the exclusion of black physicians from the American Medical Association and to address the unique challenges facing their members. Johnson also remained an active member of the Medico-Chirurgical Society of Greater New York, the New York County Medical Society, and the New York State Medical Society. He died in New York City.

FURTHER READING

Kenney, John A. *The Negro in Medicine* (1912).
Morais, Herbert M. *The History of the Negro in Medicine*, 2d ed. (1968).
"P. A. Johnson, M.D.," *Journal of the National Medical Association* 6 (Jan.–Mar. 1914).

This entry is taken from the *American National Biography* and is published here with the permission of the American Council of Learned Societies.

GERARD FERGERSON

Johnson, Rafer (18 Aug. 1935–), athlete, Olympian, and media personality, was born Rafer Lewis Johnson in Hillsboro, Texas, the son of Lewis Johnson, a laborer, and Alma Gibson, a domestic. Rafer had one brother, Jim, who later played in the National Football League, and two sisters, Emma and Dolores. When jobs became scarce during the Great Depression the family relocated to Oklahoma, only to return to Dallas a short time later where Lewis Johnson worked as a handyman for a company that manufactured drilling implements and Alma Johnson secured a position as a domestic for the proprietor's family. Texas acquainted Rafer Johnson with institutionalized segregation and racism. Like countless others, the Johnson family moved to California during World War II. Besides the promise of higher-paying jobs, the relocation also carried with it the hope of leaving Jim Crow permanently behind them. In 1945 when defense contractors began downsizing, the family moved to Kingsburg, California, a Swedish settlement of 2,500 people located in the San Joaquin Valley. Although Kingsburg had few black residents, Asians and Latinos added to the town's diversity.

A four-sport athlete, Johnson earned thirteen varsity letters at Kingsburg High School. A 1952 visit to nearby Tulare, California, the home of the Olympian Bob Mathias, inspired Johnson to dedicate himself to the decathlon. He was highly recruited and ultimately enrolled at the University of California at Los Angeles (UCLA), in large part because of the university's tradition of racial equality. Moreover, two of Johnson's heroes, RALPH BUNCHE and JACKIE ROBINSON, had also attended

UCLA. Johnson excelled at UCLA. In 1955 he set a new Pan American record of 6,994 points in the decathlon. Later that year he broke Bob Mathias's world record in the decathlon, the first of three world records that he would hold in the event. In spite of his rigorous training schedule Johnson was elected student body president and joined Pi Lambda Phi, a predominantly Jewish fraternity, becoming the first African American to pledge a national fraternity at the school. "It was then that I realized that trying to build bridges between people can bring resentment and heartache as well as respect and satisfaction," Johnson recalled in his autobiography (112).

In 1956 Johnson represented the United States at the Melbourne Olympics. During practice for the pole vault Johnson injured a knee, forcing him to withdraw from the long jump. During the two-day decathlon he tore an abdominal muscle. Despite the pain and injuries Johnson still secured a silver medal. As the cold war reached its zenith, in July 1958 Johnson participated in the Little Olympics, a dual track meet between the United States and the Soviet Union held in Moscow. An international audience eagerly awaited the showdown between Johnson and Vasily Kuznetsov, the new world record holder in the decathlon. Johnson later wrote, "I was fully aware of the irony that a black man was an emissary of a nation where discrimination raged and racists still got away with lynchings" (115). In the end Johnson defeated his rival and reclaimed the world record by 300 points. He later noted, "At a time when the superpowers were demonizing each other, here was the graphic proof of our common humanity and the power of human contact to heal the damage done by politicians and generals" (122). *Sports Illustrated* magazine recognized Johnson's record-setting performance by naming him the sportsman of the year in 1958.

After completing his collegiate eligibility Johnson began training with C. K. Yang (Yang Chuan-Kwang), a world-class decathlete from Taiwan who enrolled at UCLA. Although fierce rivals, the two men became friends, even taking the unusual step of helping one another improve in their weakest events. Johnson's dreams of Olympic gold, however, were nearly ruined by a car accident in 1959. Only a grueling rehabilitation schedule helped him secure a spot on the 1960 Olympic team. To compound matters Johnson also felt pressure to get more involved in the civil rights movement. Word of an Olympic boycott by black athletes troubled Johnson. Instead of boycotting the Olympics to protest racial conditions in the United States, Johnson believed that black athletes "could contribute more to the cause of equality by showing up, doing their best, and conducting themselves with dignity" (Johnson, 147).

During the 1960 Rome Olympics, Johnson was named captain of the U.S. Olympic team, marking the first time that a person of color carried the American flag during the opening ceremonies. In 1960 Johnson also achieved his gold medal aspirations, holding off a determined charge by C. K. Yang, his friend and training partner, in the decathlon's final event, the 1,500-meter run. Johnson's two-day total of 8,392 points also set a new Olympic record. A plethora of awards followed, including his selection as the 1960 Associated Press athlete of the year and as winner of the James E. Sullivan Memorial Award, presented to the amateur athlete whose influence most advanced the cause of good sportsmanship during the year. Johnson was subsequently inducted into the USA Track & Field, the Black Athletes, the U.S. Olympic, the National High School, and the World Sports Humanitarian halls of fame. In 1961 David L. Wolper and Mike Wallace produced the documentary *The Rafer Johnson Story*.

Rafer Johnson parlayed his 1960 gold medal into a movie contract with Twentieth Century–Fox and several television appearances. Although Johnson enjoyed his acting career, the glitter of Hollywood did not fulfill his desire to make a real effect on people's lives. His fame eventually helped him secure a position with People to People International, an organization launched by President Dwight D. Eisenhower to promote international goodwill. The flexible nature of the position also afforded Johnson the chance to make movies and volunteer his time with other worthy causes.

During the 1964 Tokyo Olympics, Johnson worked as a broadcaster covering track, weight lifting, and wrestling. Two years later he accepted a sports reporting job with KNBC in Los Angeles, California, and later became a weekend anchor. He also became politically active, largely because of his deep admiration for Robert F. Kennedy. His ties to the Kennedy family led to his involvement with the Peace Corps and the Special Olympics. Robert Kennedy, then the U.S. attorney general, frequently solicited Johnson's advice regarding race relations in the United States.

When the civil rights movement intensified during the 1960s Johnson pursued a moderate course, adhering to MARTIN LUTHER KING JR.'s strategy of nonviolent resistance. This nonconfrontational style sparked accusations that Johnson "was not black enough." For Johnson, however, the path of moderation enabled him to participate in the struggle without jeopardizing his career. "I was angry," noted Johnson, "but my anger was directed at ignorance, bigotry, and selfishness wherever I saw it, not at American society or white people as a whole" (Johnson, p. 189). Johnson felt that he could do the most good by maintaining a positive public image. He opposed a planned boycott of the 1968 Olympics by black athletes because the Olympics was, in his view, one institution that treated blacks and whites equally, as well as a platform to educate people and promote cultural understanding. Though the boycott never materialized, two black athletes, TOMMIE SMITH and John Carlos, generated controversy when they raised their fists in the Black Power salute while on the medal stand.

Rafer Johnson focused on issues close to home. During his stint as an actor he actively championed equal opportunity efforts in both the Screen Actors Guild and the American Federation of Television and Radio Artists. He was also actively involved with the NAACP, the Fair Housing Congress, and the Urban League, especially following the 1965 Watts riot. He worked on THOMAS BRADLEY's first campaign for mayor of Los Angeles. Johnson and several of his Hollywood friends, including Frank Sinatra, Marlon Brando, and SAMMY DAVIS JR., also attended JAMES MEREDITH's twenty-one-day march in June 1966 to help mobilize black voters in Mississippi. Johnson's activism turned political in 1968 when his friend Robert Kennedy launched his bid for the presidency. Besides hosting a "Hollywood for Kennedy" fund-raiser, Johnson spoke at press conferences and addressed rallies to persuade voters that Kennedy could heal a divided nation. Johnson was at Kennedy's side when the candidate was assassinated at the Ambassador Hotel in Los Angeles in June 1968. In fact, Johnson helped subdue the assailant.

Following the 1968 presidential election Johnson resumed his acting career, appearing in several films and numerous television shows. In 1971 he accepted a position as a part-time consultant with Continental Telephone. Within two years he was named a corporate vice president, and he remained affiliated with the company for fifteen years. In December 1971 Johnson married Elizabeth Thorsen. The couple had two children, Jenny, a future Olympian, and Josh. In 1978 Johnson signed on as the head coach for the Hershey Track and Field Youth Program. During this time he also remained actively involved with the Special Olympics and the Close-Up Foundation, a program designed to promote the study of government and politics among high school students. In 1984 Johnson found himself back in the spotlight when he was selected to light the Olympic flame during the opening ceremonies of the Los Angeles Olympics.

FURTHER READING

Johnson, Rafer, with Philip Goldberg. *The Best That I Can Be: An Autobiography* (1998).

Ammons, Ronald L. "Rafer Johnson," in *Great Athletes*, ed. Rafer Johnson (2001).

Cazeneuve, Brian. "Rafer Johnson, Olympic Hero," *Sports Illustrated* 93 (11 Sept. 2000).

JON L. BRUDVIG

Johnson, Ralph H. (11 Jan. 1949–5 Mar. 1968), U.S. Marine Corps soldier and Medal of Honor recipient, was born in Charleston, South Carolina, the son of Rebecca Johnson. He attended local public schools in Charleston and soon after reaching the age of eighteen enlisted in the Marine Corps Reserve at Oakland, California, on 23 March 1967. Though Johnson's military career lasted less than a year, he would nonetheless gain a place in the Marine Corps pantheon of heroes.

On 2 July 1967 Ralph Johnson was discharged from the Marine Reserve so that he could enlist in the regular Marine Corps, doing so immediately. He was assigned to Company A, 1st Reconnaissance Battalion, of the 1st Marine Division and completed further infantry and combat training at Camp Pendleton, California. Promoted to private first class in November 1967, Johnson subsequently was transferred for overseas duty, arriving in Vietnam in January 1968. Just two months later, Ralph Johnson was on patrol with the 1st Recon Battalion during the period of the Tet Counteroffensive, manning an observation post with fourteen other men on Hill 146 near the Quan Duc Valley, deep inside enemy held territory. The American patrol was subsequently attacked in the early morning hours of 5 March 1968 by an enemy force using satchel charges, hand grenades, and automatic rifles. When a live grenade landed in the foxhole of Johnson and two other marines, he shouted a warning and threw himself on the grenade. The blast that resulted killed Private First Class Ralph Johnson instantly, but by absorbing the blast he saved one of his fellow marines and, as his Medal of Honor citation would later state, "undoubtedly prevented the enemy from penetrating his sector of the patrol's perimeter" (Hanna, p. 163).

The service of African American Marine Corps soldiers, men like Ralph Johnson, OSCAR AUSTIN, and RODNEY DAVIS, was vital to the war effort in Vietnam. Nearly 41,000 African Americans served in the Marines during the war, and though racial conditions were far from ideal, the vast majority persevered and served with honor. Indeed, while the employment of fully integrated units in the American military began in the Korean War, albeit with some controversy, the valor and skill of these men, embodied in the deeds of black Medal of Honor recipients, during the Vietnam War truly ushered in a new era of race relations within the U.S. military, proving once and for all that the color of a man's skin had nothing to do with his performance as a soldier.

Following his death, Private First Class Ralph Johnson's body was returned stateside, and he was buried in the Beaufort National Cemetery in Beaufort, South Carolina. On 20 April 1970 Johnson's family received his Medal of Honor from Vice President Spiro Agnew during a White House ceremony. In 1991, the veteran's hospital in his hometown of Charleston, South Carolina, was renamed the Ralph H. Johnson Veteran's Administration Medical Center.

FURTHER READING

Hanna, Charles W. *African American Recipients of the Medal of Honor* (2002).

Shaw, Henry, Jr., and Ralph Donnelly. *Blacks in the Marine Corps* (2002).

GLENN ALLEN KNOBLOCK

Johnson, Robert (8 May 1911–16 Aug. 1938), musician, was born Robert Leroy Johnson in Hazelhurst, Mississippi, the son of Noah Johnson and Julia Major Dodds (occupations unknown). His mother was married at the time to another man, Charles Dodds Jr., who, because of an acquaintance's personal vendetta against him, had been forced to flee Mississippi for Memphis in 1907, changing his name to Charles Spencer. After his mother eked out a living for two years working in migrant labor camps supporting Robert and his sister Carrie, she and her children joined Spencer, his mistress, and their children in Memphis in 1914. Eventually Julia left her children. Around 1918 Robert, an unruly, strong-willed child, also left Memphis, joining his mother and new stepfather, Willie "Dusty" Willis, in Robinsonville, Mississippi. Although Robert went to the Indian Lake School at Commerce, Mississippi, through the mid-1920s, eyesight problems both plagued him and provided him with an excuse to quit school. Johnson's favored instruments of his early teen years, Jew's harp and harmonica, were supplanted around 1929 by an interest in what became his primary instrument, the guitar, though he continued to play harmonica in a neck rack.

Johnson next began absorbing the sounds of other guitarists, developing his technique by listening in houses and juke joints to little-known locals like Harvey "Hard Rock" Glenn, Myles Robson, and Ernest "Whiskey Red" Brown, as well as now-legendary bluesmen CHARLEY PATTON and Willie Brown. After Johnson's marriage to Virginia Travis in 1929 ended in tragedy—both she and their baby died in childbirth in April 1930—he intensified his musical efforts, benefiting from the arrival of SON HOUSE in June 1930. House had recorded with Patton and Louise Johnson for Paramount Records, and it was House's furiously emotional performances that helped inspire some of Robert Johnson's best recordings. At the time, though, House and Brown often ran off the younger Johnson, an inexperienced neophyte who House claimed "made such a mess outta everything he played" (Calt and Wardlow, 43).

When Johnson left behind sharecropping and Robinsonville in search of his birth father and a musical vocation, he returned around 1931 to Hazelhurst, performing with his mentor Ike Zinnerman in juke joints, writing down and practicing his songs in isolation in the woods, and playing on the courthouse steps during the day on Saturdays. In May 1931 Johnson married Calletta Craft, a woman ten years his senior, who showered him with attention, making his stay in southern Mississippi personally and musically fruitful, spurring a newly confident Johnson to seek greener musical pastures. Deserting his family a short time later in Clarksdale, he headed back to Robinsonville to visit his mother and kin as well as to astonish House and Brown with his progress. After a couple of months he left this farming community for a performing base centered around Helena, Arkansas, though he traveled widely, playing in joints and levee camps in Mississippi, Arkansas, Tennessee, New York, and even in Canada. While around Helena, Johnson not only met Estella Coleman, who became his common-law wife, but also became a primary musical influence on her son, future recording artist ROBERT LOCKWOOD JR. In this period he also played with and inspired some of the Delta's greatest blues musicians, SONNY BOY WILLIAMSON II, HOWLIN' WOLF (Chester Burnett), ROBERT NIGHTHAWK, and ELMORE JAMES among them.

By the middle 1930s Johnson was a popular Delta musician, albeit one with a reputation for drinking and womanizing. He was also ambitious, anxious to record as his old teachers Brown, Patton, and House had done. He auditioned for Jackson, Mississippi, music store owner and talent scout H. C. Speir, who passed Johnson's name on to ARC record label salesman/talent scout Ernie Oertle. Oertle took Johnson to radio station KONO facilities at the Blue Bonnet hotel in San Antonio, Texas, in 1936, recording two takes each of sixteen different songs on 23, 26, and 27 November. The success of Johnson's "Terraplane Blues," the title of which refers to a make of automobile, for the Vocalion label led to another session, in Dallas, where he recorded multiple takes of thirteen songs on 19 and 20 June 1937.

Riding the higher profile that "Terraplane Blues" brought him across the country, Johnson left the Delta with guitarists Calvin Frazier and Johnny Shines. They followed Highway 51 to St. Louis, Chicago, and Detroit and even played briefly in New York and New Jersey. Johnson proved to be an influential but elusive traveling partner, however, frequently departing unannounced, so the trio split, Frazier making a name for himself in Detroit, and Shines in Chicago. When Johnson produced no follow-up hits, ARC let his contract expire in June 1938 without recalling him to the studio. On 13 August 1938, at a club where Johnson was performing outside Greenwood, Mississippi, called Three Forks, he drank some whiskey reputedly poisoned at the direction of a husband jealous of the attention that his wife and Johnson were paying to each other. Three days later Johnson died of pneumonia, just months before the talent scout John Hammond intended to bring him to Carnegie Hall and probable acclaim at the Spirituals to Swing Concert in New York.

Johnson is a pivotal musician in the development of the blues. In many ways his work is a culmination of the work of Mississippi blues artists who preceded him and is a startling transformation of that material into a personal vision and style that defined the direction of post–World War II Chicago blues. The distinctive boogie figure that became his trademark, the famous bottleneck guitar intro to "I Believe I'll Dust My Broom," and the striking imagery of compositions such as "Cross Road Blues," "Sweet Home Chicago," "Love in Vain Blues," and "Hellbound on My Trail" influenced Williamson, Wolf, Nighthawk, James, and especially the young MUDDY WATERS (McKinley Morganfield), cementing his position as primary fountainhead of inspiration for artists whose work would lead blues and rock musicians like JIMI HENDRIX and the Rolling Stones back to Johnson's mesmerizing work. The sketchy nature of Johnson's biography before 1970 led to a good deal of mythologizing and misinformation, but his music has continued to startle listeners with its force and beauty. The Chicago blues pioneer Muddy Waters called Johnson "one of the greatest there's ever been." The British blues-rock performer Eric Clapton added reverently: "I have never found anything more deeply soulful than Robert Johnson. His music remains the most powerful cry that I think you can find in the human voice, really" (*Robert Johnson: The Complete Recordings*, 23). Longtime researcher Mack McCormick heard in Johnson's lyrics "a chilling confrontation with aspects of American consciousness. He is a visionary artist with a terrible kind of information about his time and place and personal experience." While Stephen Calt and Gayle Wardlow allow that among his contemporaries he was "conspicuous for his seediness, facial disfigurement … black derby," asserting that "only in his music did Johnson project anything but a prosaic figure," it is clear that, for many, Peter Guralnick's encomium—that Johnson was "certainly the most influential of all bluesmen"—is true (Guralnick, *Feel Like Going Home*, 54). He is a member of the Rock and Roll Hall of Fame and a recipient of the Blues Foundation's highest honor, the W. C. HANDY Award.

FURTHER READING

Calt, Stephen, and Gayle Dean Wardlow. "Robert Johnson," *78 Quarterly* 1, no. 4 (1989): 40–51.
Guralnick, Peter. *Feel Like Going Home* (1999).
Guralnick, Peter. *Searching for Robert Johnson* (1988, repr. 1998).
Pearson, Barry Lee, and Bill McCulloch. *Robert Johnson: Lost and Found* (2003).
Wald, Elijah. *Escaping the Delta: Robert Johnson and the Invention of the Blues* (2004).

DISCOGRAPHY

Robert Johnson: The Complete Recordings (Columbia C2K 46222).

This entry is taken from the *American National Biography* and is published here with the permission of the American Council of Learned Societies.

STEVEN TRACY

Johnson, Robert L. (8 April 1946–), founder, chairman, and chief executive officer of Black Entertainment Television (BET), was born in Hickory, Mississippi, the ninth of ten children of

Archie Johnson, a wood dealer, and Edna Johnson, a schoolteacher, respectively), but he spent most of his childhood in Freeport, Illinois. His father later became a factory worker and janitor. Robert Johnson, who is commonly known as Bob, was the only one of his siblings to attend college. He graduated with a B.A. degree in History from the University of Illinois in 1968. It was there that he met Sheila Crump, who would later become his wife. Johnson's interest in becoming an ambassador inspired him to earn an M.A. in Public Administration from the Woodrow Wilson School of Public and International Affairs at Princeton University in 1972. He then moved to Washington, D.C., and worked for both the Corporation for Public Broadcasting and the Urban League. He went on to become the press secretary for WALTER E. FAUNTROY, the congressional delegate for the District of Columbia. From 1976 to 1979 Johnson served as a lobbyist and then as the vice president of government relations for the National Cable and Telecommunication Association, the main trade association of the American cable television industry.

At this point in his life, Bob Johnson had a revolutionary idea and very little money. His dream was to create the first cable network aimed at attracting African American viewers. With a $15,000 bank loan, Johnson approached John Malone, who was then the chief operating officer of Tele-Communications Inc., the country's third-largest cable company at the time. Malone invested $500,000 in the project and enabled Johnson and his wife to start Black Entertainment Television in 1979. The channel first aired at midnight on 8 January 1980, initially featuring reruns of comedies, infomercials, and old films before including music videos, which became a staple of the network. In 1991, BET became the first black-led company to be listed on the New York Stock Exchange, before going private in 1998.

BET quickly became an African American icon. Johnson also created BET Holdings Inc., which entered the fields of publishing, film production, fashion design, and event production. BET expanded to include other channels such as BET International, BET Classic Soul, BET Hip Hop, BET Gospel, and BET Jazz, creating a cable empire of five channels reportedly reaching more than 75 million homes. The BET Web site, BET. com, was a joint venture created by Microsoft, USA Networks, News Corporation, and AT&T's Liberty Digital for $35 million in 1998. Through BET, Johnson created jobs for hundreds of African Americans in the television industry and provided a showcase for black artistic talent. Johnson sold BET in 1999, twenty years after its inception, to Viacom (the media conglomerate that owns CBS, Showtime, Nickelodeon, MTV, and Paramount Pictures) for nearly $3 billion in stock (more than five times Johnson's initial investment), but he remains the chairman and CEO, and he received $1.6 billion from the sale, making him the richest African American in the United States. Johnson has donated money to various charities and organizations, including the United Negro College Fund and Howard University.

Johnson went on to create RLJ Companies and to buy restaurants, casinos, motion picture rights, and hotels. Out of the proposed merger of United and U.S. Airways, Johnson's goal was to own D.C. Air, the first major black-controlled American airline, but the airline merger was prevented by governmental intervention. Johnson has been known as an ardent financial backer of the Democratic Party, but in 2002 he agreed to serve on the Social Security Commission under President George W. Bush. Johnson also initiated a million-dollar campaign to produce and air advertisements on BET to encourage viewers to vote. In 2003 he outbid the basketball great Larry Bird to purchase the Charlotte Bobcats of the NBA and the Charlotte Sting of the WNBA for $300 million, making Johnson the first African American owner of a major sports franchise. He also owns one of the nation's largest collections of African American art, the Barnett-Aden Collection. Johnson has served on the boards of U.S. Airways, General Mills, the American Film Institute, and Hilton Hotels, as well as on the board of governors for the Rock and Roll Hall of Fame in Cleveland and the Brookings Institution. Johnson is the recipient of the NAACP's Image Award and Princeton's Distinguished Alumni Award and is listed in *Sports Illustrated* magazine's list of the 101 Most Influential Minorities in Sports. He also received *Broadcasting & Cable* magazine's Hall of Fame Award. When he received *Cablevision Magazine*'s 20/20 Vision Award, the publication listed him as one of the twenty most influential people in the cable industry. Johnson and his former wife, Sheila, have two children.

Johnson's goal in creating BET was geared more toward economics than social policy, but his success in creating the network and using his financial power in such an impressive array of fields enabled him to break through numerous racial barriers and serve as a role model for many. Some critics fault

BET's misogynistic rap videos and lack of original programming, as well as Johnson's sale of the company to the global media giant Viacom and his firing of the popular BET personality, TAVIS SMILEY. It is Johnson's personal story, however, that merits acclaim. He went from a relatively humble background to amass unbelievable wealth by pursuing a dream. His life's accomplishments illustrate a remarkable example of perseverance, faith, and courage.

FURTHER READING

Dingle, Derek T. *Black Enterprise Titans of the B.E. 100s: Black CEOs Who Redefined and Conquered American Business* (1999).

Pulley, Brett. *The Billion Dollar BET: Robert Johnson and the Inside Story of Black Entertainment Television* (2004).

JENNIFER WOOD

Johnson, Sargent Claude (7 Oct. 1887–10 Oct. 1967), artist, was born in Boston, Massachusetts, the son of Anderson Johnson and Lizzie Jackson. When Johnson was ten years old, his father died of an unknown cause. Because his mother suffered from tuberculosis, the children were sent to relatives. Johnson lived with his maternal uncle, Sherman William Jackson, and his wife, the sculptor May Howard Jackson, for several years in Washington, D.C. Then he and his siblings stayed briefly with their maternal grandparents in Alexandria, Virginia. When their mother died in 1902, the girls went to a Catholic school in Pennsylvania and the boys went to a Sisters of Charity orphanage in Worcester, Massachusetts. Johnson attended public school and worked in the Sisters of Charity Hospital. He began painting as an adolescent while recovering from a long illness. After Johnson studied singing briefly at a music school in Boston, he lived with relatives in Chicago. Despite his tragic childhood, Johnson was a cheerful man. His friend, the painter Clay Spohn, described him as "perennially happy, joyous, exuberant in living."

In the early 1910s Johnson moved to San Francisco, where he married Pearl Lawson in 1915; they had one child before they separated in 1936. Lawson was hospitalized for mental illness in 1947 and remained at the Stockton State Hospital until her death in 1964. Johnson worked as a fitter for Schlusser Brothers from 1917 until about 1920, as a photographic retouch artist for Willard F. Worden in 1920, and as a framer for Valdespino Framers from about 1921 until 1931.

Johnson began studying drawing and painting at the A. W. Best School of Art, and then he studied at the California School of Fine Arts (1919 to 1923 and again from 1940 to 1942) under the sculptors Robert Stackpole and Beniamino Bufano. Johnson won first prize for his work there in 1921 and 1922. Much later, he studied metal sculpture with Claire Falkenstein. Upon leaving school, Johnson made his primary living as a framer. From 1925 to 1933 Johnson worked in wood, ceramics, oils, watercolors, and graphics in a backyard studio in Berkeley. In 1928 he won the Harmon Foundation's Otto Kahn Prize for *Sammy*, a terra-cotta head. Two years later he won the foundation's bronze award for fine arts, and in 1933 he received the Robert C. Ogden Prize for the most outstanding combination of materials for *Pearl*, a porcelain bust of his daughter, and two drawings, *Mother and Child* and *Defiant*. Johnson also exhibited several pieces with the foundation's traveling exhibitions, and thousands saw them in the Oakland Municipal Art Gallery in 1931 and 1933. Already recognized in the San Francisco Bay Area, Johnson was the only Californian in these national shows. *Chester* (1931), a terra-cotta portrait head of an African American boy resting his cheek in his right hand, was purchased by the German minister to Italy.

In 1935 the Harmon Foundation presented Johnson in a three-man exhibition at the Delphic Studios in New York. Included was a lacquered, redwood, polychrome sculpture of a woman, *Forever Free*. Incised on the skirt of her tubular body are two children playing under their mother's protective care. Covered with several coats of gesso and fine linen and highlighted in black and white paint, this is Johnson's best-known piece. "It is the pure American Negro I am concerned with," he said, "aiming to show the natural beauty and dignity … in that characteristic hair, bearing and manner; and I wish to show that beauty not so much to the White man as to the Negro himself" (*San Francisco Chronicle*, 6 Oct. 1935). Johnson, whose mother was of Cherokee and black ancestry, identified himself as African American. Among his memorable sculptures of the 1930s is a series of stylized bronze and copper heads and masks on art deco–like wooden bases. The stoic faces borrow certain qualities from West African, pre-Columbian (Maya and Aztec), and cubist art.

In the mid-1930s Johnson was employed by the Federal Art Project of the Works Progress Administration as artist, senior sculptor, assistant supervisor, assistant state supervisor, and unit supervisor. He produced several large-scale works, including an enormous carved redwood organ screen for the California School for the Blind (1937), semiabstract carvings of marine life in green Vermont slate, and a tile mural for San Francisco's Maritime Museum at Aquatic Park (c. 1938). He also completed statues at the Golden Gate International Exposition in San Francisco: two Inca—one a rich man, the other an intellectual—seated on llamas for the South American front of the Court of Pacifica, and three works symbolizing industry, home life, and agriculture for the Alameda-Contra Costa County Fair Building (1939). In 1939 he also created a series of six animals in green and gray cast terrazzo for a child care center playground in San Francisco.

Johnson had been elected to the San Francisco Art Association in May 1932 and to its council board in 1934. He served on the organization's annual juries (1936, 1938, 1940, 1942, 1947, and 1948) and received awards from the group in 1925 (for *Pearl*), in 1931 (for *Chester*, a terra-cotta head), in 1935 (for *Forever Free*), and in 1938 (for *Black and White*, a lithograph). At the same time, local museums acquired Johnson's work; in the mid-1930s the San Francisco Museum of Art received the collection of the local philanthropist Albert M. Bender, which included several of Johnson's pieces (such as *Forever Free*), and in 1939 the San Diego Fine Arts Gallery purchased *Esther*, a terra-cotta head. Various museums and collectors purchased a number of the 150 copies of the lithograph *Singing Saint* in 1940. The semiabstract work of two women, one playing a guitar, was widely reproduced in the 1940s.

Johnson's long friendship with Bufano, his principal mentor, ended because of a long and acrimonious competition between the men for a contract to produce a work of art for the San Francisco Art Commission in 1940. Johnson's best-known large-scale decorative work is a tremendous cast-stone frieze, which covers the entire retaining wall across the back of the George Washington High School athletic field in San Francisco (1942). It depicts young men and women diving, rowing, wrestling, and playing football, basketball, baseball, and tennis.

Travel provided Johnson with much artistic inspiration. An unknown benefactor and two Abraham Rosenberg scholarships (1944 and 1949) helped finance numerous trips between 1945 and 1965 to Mexico, where he visited renowned archeological sites and studied ancient art and Chelula polychrome pottery. Working with black clay found outside Oaxaca in the manner of Zapotec Indians and Mexicans, he produced many small, hollow forms, including a representation of a do-nothing politician (a type that annoyed Johnson during the Depression). Johnson's anonymous patron also sponsored a seven-month trip to Japan in 1958. There Johnson visited Shinto shrines and studied Japanese art. An avid reader and guitarist, Johnson also taught art to several private students in his studio over several years and offered classes for the Junior Workshop program of the San Francisco Housing Authority and Mills College in 1947.

From 1947 to 1967 Johnson produced about one hundred abstract, surrealist, and impressionist porcelain enamel panels and plates on steel, a technique that he learned at the Paine-Mahoney Company, which produced enameled signs on steel plates. The company invited Johnson to create aesthetic porcelain plates on steel in his spare time. He shaped the metal in his studio or at the Architectural Porcelain Company, exploring religious, multiracial, antiwar, and mother-and-child themes. Johnson produced several commissions in this medium, including a semiabstract mural of pots and pans for Nathan Dohrmann & Company, a crockery and glass shop (1948), and a decorative map of Richmond, California, for its city hall chambers (1949). In 1949 the Paine-Mahoney Company hired Johnson to complete the details of a commission of an enamel mural for Harold's Club in Reno, Nevada. Reportedly the largest mural in the United States ever created by that method, it is 38 feet high and 78 feet long and depicts wagon-train pioneers crossing the Sierras. Johnson finished a similar mural—25 feet long by 50 feet high—for the West Club Casino in Las Vegas.

Johnson also continued large-scale works in other media. The Matson Navigation Company of Honolulu commissioned two works for pleasure ships: a large mahogany panel depicting Hawaiian leaders and warriors for SS *Lurline* (1948), and two ceramic tile walls for SS *Monterey* (1956). Two years after Johnson moved to San Francisco in 1948, he began to bring color back to his sculpture, affirming his earlier artistic statement:

> The slogan for the Negro artist should be 'Go south, young man!' Too many Negro artists go to Europe and come back imitators of Cézanne, Matisse or Picasso, and this attitude is not only a weakness of the artists, but of their racial public. In all artistic circles I hear too much talking and too much theorizing. All their theories do not help me any, and I have but one technical hobby

to ride: I am interested in applying color to sculpture as the Egyptian, Greek, and other ancient people did (*San Francisco Chronicle*, 6 Oct. 1935).

In the late 1950s and 1960s the sculptor produced polychrome wood pieces with universal themes influenced by Asian, northwest Native American, and ancient Egyptian and Greek art. He also executed works in diorite rock, cast bronze, and forged enameled forms, and he collaborated with the ceramist John Magnani on glazes and clay bodies. During the 1960s Johnson also worked for the Flax Framing and Art Supply Company. Johnson died in San Francisco. Although somewhat isolated as one of the few African American artists consistently active in California from the 1920s through the 1960s, Johnson was nationally known for his stylistic pluralism, versatility, and daring innovation.

FURTHER READING

The whereabouts of Johnson's papers are not known. The Archives of American Art has a thirty-three-page transcription of an oral history interview from 1964.

Bearden, Romare, and Harry Henderson. *A History of African-American Artists from 1792 to the Present* (1993).

Montgomery, Evangeline J. *Sargent Johnson: Retrospective* (1971).

"Sargent Johnson," *International Review of African American Art* 6, no. 2 (1984).

Obituary: *Oakland Tribune*, 12 Oct. 1967.

This entry is taken from the *American National Biography* and is published here with the permission of the American Council of Learned Societies.

THERESA LEININGER-MILLER

Johnson, Thomas Lewis (7 Aug. 1836–11 Mar. 1921), missionary, evangelist, and author, was born into slavery in Rock Rayman, Virginia. Little is known of his parents, but his mother apparently told him about her sisters and brothers, all children of an African and all separated from their parents by slavery. She encouraged him to acquire literacy. Johnson became a house slave, had access to books, and by subterfuge learned to read as his owners moved about in Virginia and Washington, D.C.

Residing in Richmond, Virginia, at the beginning of the Civil War, Johnson became the cook for his owner's son in the Confederate army. In 1863 he married Henrietta Thompson, maid to the sister of General Robert E. Lee. The Johnsons witnessed the fall of the Confederacy in 1865, then moved to New York City, where Johnson worked as a waiter.

A committed Christian, Johnson sought others of the Baptist faith, moving first to Chicago and then to Denver, Colorado, where he was the pastor of a black church until 1872. How he became a pastor, and what course of education he followed, is unknown.

Contacts with a British family in Chicago encouraged the Johnsons to sail to England in September 1876, where they lived in Manchester with William Hind Smith, a leading member of the Young Men's Christian Association (YMCA). Johnson moved to London to study at the Pastor's College, established by the preacher Charles Haddon Spurgeon, who was famous on both sides of the Atlantic (his printed sermons had even reached Johnson's owner). Thomas and Henrietta Johnson were joined by her sister, whose first name is unknown, and her sister's husband, Calvin Harris Richardson, from Washington, D.C. Clement Bailhache and Alfred Baynes, who were officials of the Baptist Missionary Society, London, supported the two men in their college studies. Along with biblical subjects they studied English grammar and the language of the district of Cameroon, West Africa, where they were to work as missionaries.

The Baptist mission in Cameroon had been established in the 1840s, largely by black Jamaicans like Joseph Jackson Fuller (1825–1908), the Baptist leader there. The four Americans left for Africa in November 1878, but Thomas and Henrietta Johnson soon became very ill, and Henrietta died. While the Richardsons would remain for over a decade, Johnson soon returned to England, where he was welcomed back by Spurgeon and other Baptists. They encouraged him to return to the United States to recruit more black missionaries and to raise funds for their work.

Johnson married Sarah Artemico McGowan in Chicago on 28 July 1881. They moved back to Great Britain, speaking about and gathering money for black Christian missionaries in Africa. In 1882 his short autobiography *Africa for Christ: Twenty-eight Years a Slave* was published in London. In 1884 he spoke at an Anti-Slavery Society meeting in London chaired by Queen Victoria's heir, Edward, Prince of Wales. Johnson had become part of a network of individuals of African descent who were interested in conducting and supporting missionary work in Africa. For instance, Theophilus E. S. Scholes, a Scottish-trained physician from Jamaica, toured Ireland with Thomas and Sarah Johnson, her sister Ora McGowan, and a Jamaican carpenter named John Ricketts. In the following year,

1886, the two Jamaicans sailed for the Congo to be practical Christian workers in Africa. Meanwhile Johnson returned to the United States in 1887 for a tour promoting missionary efforts in Africa, the essential theme of his life after 1880.

Back in England, where he would live for the rest of his life with occasional visits to America, Johnson continued to be active in both the evangelization of Africa by New World blacks and in the education of the British, who learned about slavery in America and life in Africa. When the Baptist missionary William Hughes returned from the Congo with two African companions to establish a school for Africans in his native North Wales, Johnson supported his venture by appearing there, speaking, and allowing his picture to be published by them. News spread of the African Institute in Colwyn Bay and the publication of Hughes's *Dark Africa and the Way Out* (1892). The African Institute's students came from the Caribbean, South Carolina, the Congo, South Africa, Liberia, and British West Africa. Men and women were trained in practical skills including pharmacy, carpentry, tailoring, and printing (local supporters provided tuition); often the students were already able to speak the language and understand the mindset of the people of their mission field when they moved on from the African Institute. Some attended British universities. Dr. Scholes visited the school before working in Nigeria. After his return to London he would write four books attacking colonialism, inspiring younger generations including independent Kenya's first president, Jomo Kenyatta.

The death in 1892 of the Johnsons' six-year-old daughter Ruth, together with Thomas's inability to return to Africa because of his continued health problems (believed to be malaria), blighted the lives of Thomas and Sarah Johnson. By the end of the century the couple had settled in Bournemouth, a resort on England's south coast. Their house at 66 Paisley Road, Boscombe, was named Liberia. In 1900 he became a British citizen, his application supported by Bournemouth residents. Thomas Lewis Johnson continued to be a well-known figure in British Baptist circles, where his name was usually written Thos. L. Johnson. In that format it appears as the vice-chairman of the Pan-African Conference committee of 1900. Held in London in July 1900, the conference involved W. E. B. DuBois and Bishop ALEXANDER WALTERS. The conference organizer, the Trinidad-born lawyer HENRY SYLVESTER WILLIAMS, had associated with BOOKER T. WASHINGTON, WILLIAM SCARBOROUGH,

and Bishop HENRY MCNEAL TURNER when the American race leaders were in England in 1899.

Johnson's role in the conference is unknown. His autobiography, republished in Bournemouth in 1909, included a photograph of Henry Macpherson, a Briton he had known since the 1880s and the treasurer of the conference committee. That this extended version of his *Twenty-Eight Years a Slave* was the seventh edition suggests that the five earlier reprints were sold at meetings and by mail. A portrait photograph, published as a postcard, would have been sold at his lectures. In 1897 he published a hymn, republished in 1903, the same year that his *Consecration Thoughts for the New Year* appeared.

In the 1900s Johnson continued to travel around Britain, giving lectures at more than eighty locations. The titles of the lectures included "Twenty-eight Years a Slave," "The Underground Railroad; or, How the Slaves Escaped to Canada," "Africa: What It Was, What It Is, and May Become by Missionary Effort," "How Do You Do," and "The Progress of the Liberated Slaves in the Southern States of America since the Close of the War, 1865." He had written a hymn with Calvin Richardson titled "Ethiopia's Cry." Another of his hymns, "A Plea for Africa," included the line, "Has not English gold been the gain of tears and blood when the slaves were sold?" Collections at these lectures suggest that the public's generosity was substantial (an October 1907 collection totalled twelve pounds, equivalent to two months' income for a laborer).

Seventy years after his birth in Virginia, Thomas Lewis Johnson had been accepted in Britain. He was a citizen of the kingdom, he moved among the people of Bournemouth, and his face was familiar to readers of Baptist publications. His purple-bound autobiography sat on the shelves of associates including Arthur Acland Allen, the parliamentary member for nearby Christchurch. In a letter dated 30 November 1909 the former slave told Allen that he had cast his first vote for him "after being made a British subject." Allen tucked the letter into the book, which eventually made its way to the library of the Anti-Slavery Society in London.

Visitors recalled the frail old man in his house, with slave chains and whips on the wall, talking about his slave experience in Virginia. He was taken out in a wheelchair, his wife scolding him humorously: "Stand up, Thomas L., you're not an old man yet." At age eight this witness and his parents attended Johnson's funeral in 1921. The gravestone of the "African missionary" in Boscombe Cemetery marks a plot that has room for a second coffin. However, after two years Sarah Johnson's name disappeared from the town's street directories. She had inherited £1,000 (then $5,000) and she may have returned to Chicago. The remains of Thomas Johnson rest alone, in a town far removed from his early life—one spent in three continents, as his autobiography declares.

FURTHER READING

Johnson's autobiography was first published in 1882. The seventh edition (1909) appears to be two narratives.

Johnson, Thomas Lewis. *Twenty-eight Years a Slave: The Story of My Life in Three Continents* (1909).

Green, Jeffrey P. "Thomas Lewis Johnson (1836–1921): The Bournemouth Evangelist," in *Under the Imperial Carpet: Essays in Black History 1780–1950*, eds. Rainer E. Lotz and Ian Pegg (1986).

JEFFREY GREEN

Johnson, Toki Schalk (Gertrude) (1906–April 1977) best known for her many years as society columnist and women's editor for the nationally distributed *Pittsburgh Courier,* was born in Boston, Massachusetts, the daughter of Theodore O. Schalk and Mary Wilkerson Schalk, both of whom worked as waiters at a local hotel. Her father was a native of either North or South Carolina, and her mother born in Massachusetts to parents from Virginia.

Literary critics have inferred that Gertrude Schalk and her sister, Lillian, were the same person, using two different names, but census records show that they were members of the same family, born two years apart. Family life was a bit unstable. In 1910 their parents were lodgers in the home of in-laws Charles and Nora Harris at 240 West Canton Street, the children perhaps living elsewhere, or simply overlooked by the census. In 1920 the family was reunited in one of three flats at 63 Sawyer Street, with two brothers, George and Theodore. In 1930 Gertrude and Lillian were working respectively as a stenographer and a maid at a doctor's office, living, at the ages of twenty-four and twenty-two, with their widowed aunt, Nora Harris, one of four households at 80 West Rutland Square.

Schalk studied journalism at Boston University in 1924 and 1925, in subsequent years publishing four short stories in the *Saturday Evening Quill.* The best known of these is "Flower of the South," published in June 1930. She also had stories published in *Love Story Magazine,* the *New York Mirror,* and the *Boston Post.*

Schalk's work with Boston newspapers is not well documented, in part because the only comprehensive archives of Boston's African American papers were destroyed by flooding. She wrote a column called "Bean Town," possibly for the *Boston Post.* She was an organizer of the Girl Friends, Inc., chapter in Boston in January 1931. This was a relatively new social, civic, and charitable organization organized on a national basis; the Boston chapter was the fourth to be accepted and installed.

Schalk began writing as a Boston correspondent for the *Pittsburgh Courier* in the mid-1930s. When she came to visit Pittsburgh in 1938, her "Bean Town" byline was mirrored by reference to the steel production center as "Smoketown" in the pages of the *Courier.* She was invited to move to Pittsburgh and take up a full-time assignment with the *Courier* in 1943, as the longtime women's editor, Julia Bumry Jones, was in declining health. Later, she wrote, "When I was asked to come to Pittsburgh, it was the greatest dilemma I think I've ever encountered. I had the feeling that if I didn't accept the offer, I would live to regret it. In my poor way, I prayed for an answer, and it came in the deep of the night" (Johnson, "Faith Came When I Needed It Most," *Message Magazine,* Feb. 1954, p. 17).

The column that became her signature at the *Courier,* "Toki Types," appeared beginning in June 1943, while Jones's long-established "Talk O Town" continued to run. During the transition Jones was helped by Bessie M. Holloway as assistant women's editor, from February to July 1943. After suffering a stroke, Jones also had assistance in writing her column from Edna McKenzie. Schalk was listed in the paper's masthead as Gertrude von Schalk, Acting Women's Editor, beginning 10 July 1943. After 27 May 1944, she was women's editor, while Jones retained a position as contributing editor until her death.

In 1946 Schalk married John V. Johnson, thereafter being known personally and professionally as Toki Schalk Johnson. She soon organized the Pittsburgh chapter of Girlfriends, Inc., founded in 1946, and formally installed in 1947. It was the tenth chapter formed in the United States. Johnson was a charter member and served as vice president.

Schalk Johnson's embrace of the Seventh Day Adventist faith was not prominently reflected in her column, but she wrote several times for the denomination's *Message Magazine,* and expressed her faith at times in her *Courier* writing. After an illness, she began to put little sermonettes into "Toki Types." Uncertain of the response, she was amazed to receive fan mail "praising me for having the courage to put God in a social column" (*Message Magazine,* Feb. 1954, p. 33).

She became editor of the Lifestyles section of the *Courier,* along with Hazel Garland and Jean Farrish. Johnson handled most national social affairs, Garland more the local features. Johnson once observed, "To be a social editor, you must have a strong constitution, cast iron stomach, a private income, lots of good clothes, and the ability to say 'dahling'" (Major, p. 358).

Her writing was not all devoted to social events. In the 29 November 1958 *Courier,* she authored "Pittsburgh Neighborhood Units Coping with Urban Renewal Migrations." She is listed among the contributors to the *Dillard Women's Club Cookbook,* published in 1958 with acknowledgment to "teachers, graduates and some well-connected friends of national prominence." Not being a teacher or graduate of Dillard University, she was probably a well-connected friend.

One of the few staff from the old and original *Courier* who eventually went to work for the New Pittsburgh Courier Publishing Company after 1966, Johnson placed third in 1969 at the National Newspaper Publishers Association annual meeting, in the feature story category of the Merit Awards contest. First place went to Chester Higgins, senior editor of *Jet* magazine, and second place to Carole Malone of the *Milwaukee Courier.*

In December 1975, Toki Schalk Johnson was living in a convalescent home in Detroit, Michigan, where her sister had moved her. Johnson remained quite lucid, retaining the charm for which she had been known. Aside from Social Security records, there is little evidence that her death was noted, although she had been receiving visitors within the previous two years.

FURTHER READING

Roses, Lorraine Elena. *Harlem's Glory: Black Women Writing, 1900–1950* (1996).

Major, Gerri. *Black Society* (1976).

CHARLES ROSENBERG

Johnson, Tommy (c. 1896–1 Nov. 1956) singer, guitarist, and songwriter, was born near Terry, Mississippi, about twenty miles south of Jackson. He was the sixth of thirteen children born to Idell and Mary Ella Johnson, who farmed on the George Miller Plantation. Tommy's large family was musical and his uncles played various instruments. His older brothers played as well, and it was his brother Ledell who taught Tommy to play guitar when he was around fifteen years old, shortly after the family moved to Crystal Springs, Mississippi. Tommy ran off with a woman, and though the relationship was brief, he traveled to the Delta, where he worked on the Tom Sander Plantation, which was near Drew, Mississippi. There he met Delta bluesmen CHARLEY PATTON and Willie Brown, who would greatly inspire and influence him. He was already versed in the traditional music of southern Mississippi, and when he came back home to visit, his brother Ledell was impressed by the Delta blues he had learned farther north.

Johnson married Maggie Bidwell, considered by some to be the "Maggie Campbell" of his famous song of that name, around 1914. They moved back to the Drew area, which was rife with accomplished Delta blues musicians such as Dick Bankston and Ben Maree in addition to Patton and Brown. Johnson worked on and around the Dockery Plantation, which was frequented by Patton and "HOWLIN'" WOLF among other bluesmen, and he hoboed and played all over Mississippi, Arkansas, and Louisiana in juke joints and on street corners. When he again visited Ledell in Terry, Johnson was a changed man. He kept company with many women and had become a heavy drinker. He adopted a trickster personality and told of having sold his soul to the devil after visiting the crossroads (the crossroads, although literally an intersection of two main roads, signified a place where a man's soul could be traded for wealth, talent, or fame). Other famous bluesmen such as ROBERT JOHNSON and PEETIE WHEATSTRAW subsequently used similar stories, probably derived from African, Caribbean, and voodoo lore. Tommy Johnson carried a large rabbit's foot and developed a dramatic flair. He borrowed some of Charley Patton's guitar acrobatics as well as inventing a few of his own and was a riveting showman and storyteller.

Johnson frequently worked with Willie Brown and occasionally with Patton as well as the accomplished accompanists Charlie McCoy and Ishman Bracey. It was Bracey who brought Johnson to the attention of H. C. Speir, a white record store owner in Jackson who also served as a talent scout for various record companies. Johnson recorded eight songs in Memphis in 1928 for Victor records, and they are among the most poetic blues ever recorded. The quality of the recordings is remarkable, and Johnson had sympathetic guitar accompaniment from Charlie McCoy on four songs. McCoy wove high-pitched mandolin-style lines that blended perfectly with Johnson's steady rhythms. Fellow Mississippian, bluesman, and historian DAVID "HONEYBOY" EDWARDS lauded Johnson's guitar playing, having heard him in 1929 when Tommy and one of his brothers came to his vicinity to pick cotton and play music. Though influenced by Patton's and Brown's strong, driving, and unwavering rhythms and occasional string snapping, Johnson had his own style, which rolled evenly, almost serenely, revealing his traditional country roots.

It was his voice and songs, however, that made him the most important influence in Mississippi blues at that time. He used themes and phrases that were then prevalent but also contributed lyrics that have become classics in the genre. His "Big Road Blues" has been covered by countless blues artists who sing "I ain't going down that big road by myself." Another familiar lyric is "the sun's gonna shine on my back door someday" from "Maggie Campbell Blues," which also sported what may have been the first recorded reference to "See See Rider." Johnson's "Cool Drink of Water Blues" became the basis for "I Asked for Water," which was recorded by Howlin' Wolf in 1956. Wolf lifted the eerie, repetitious single-note guitar line while he sang of asking for water and getting gasoline. It was Johnson's vocal technique of slipping into a falsetto at the end of a vocal line that Wolf had turned into his "howl." Wolf admitted being influenced by the blues yodeling of Jimmie Rodgers, the famous early country music singer who himself had seen and heard Tommy Johnson in the 1920s and 1930s. Reputedly Rodgers had been influenced by Johnson's blues falsetto and adapted it to his yodel.

Johnson's voice had a smoothness that was starkly different from the harsher styles of many of the Delta and gospel singers of that time. Perhaps Johnson's most compelling and haunting song is "Canned Heat Blues," in which he confesses to (and decries) his addiction to drinking the Sterno-type product used for heating food. On top of an almost bucolic, easy, loping guitar figure, Johnson sings, "Crying canned heat, canned heat, mama, crying, sure, Lord, killing me." Johnson would heat the liquid, filter it through a cloth, and add it to orange soda or the like. Evidently its kick was something he could not resist, and he remained a severe alcoholic throughout his life. Canned Heat, a blues rock group of the 1960s, derived its name from his classic song.

Johnson recorded nine songs in Wisconsin for Paramount in 1929 and though the quality of these recordings is decidedly inferior to his Victor recordings, they offer new insights to his talent. He played a jazzy kazoo, accompanied by various jazz musicians and Ishman Bracey on guitar. He revealed a humorous side to his personality on "I Wonder to Myself," and "Lonesome Home Blues" has a uniquely minor tuning not unlike that of SKIP JAMES. In the late 1920s and throughout the 1930s no other Mississippi blues artist was as influential as Tommy Johnson. His blues were more accessible than Charley Patton's because of his smoother style and tighter song structure. Unlike so many other bluesmen of the Delta however, he did not play slide guitar.

Johnson lived and played in the Jackson and Crystal Springs area for the rest of his life, though he never recorded again. He frequently played house parties and on street corners, and he died of a heart attack at age sixty after performing at length at a birthday party for his niece. Tommy Johnson was portrayed by the musician and actor Chris Thomas King in the award-winning film *O Brother, Where Art Thou?* (2000). Tommy Johnson's influence on the foundation of blues music cannot be overstated.

FURTHER READING
Edwards, David Honeyboy, with Janis Martinson and Michael Robert Frank. *The World Don't Owe Me Nothing: The Life and Times of Delta Bluesman Honeybody Edwards* (1997).
Evans, David. "Goin' up the Country: Blues in Texas and the Deep South," in *Nothing But the Blues*, ed. Lawrence Cohn (1993).
Harris, Sheldon. *Blues Who's Who* (1979).
Oliver, Paul. Liner notes to *Tommy Johnson (1928–1929): Complete Recorded Works* (2000).
Palmer, Robert. *Deep Blues* (1981)
Russell, Tony. *Blacks, Whites, and Blues* (1970).

DISCOGRAPHY
Tommy Johnson (1928–1929): Complete Recorded Works (Document Records 5001).
MARK S. MAULUCCI

Johnson, W. Bishop (11 Dec. 1858–1917), Baptist minister and editor, was born in Toronto, Ontario, Canada, to John and Matilda Johnson. He graduated from public school in Buffalo, New York, in 1868, and he was baptized in Toronto four years later. After graduating from normal school in 1874, he became a minister the next year. He moved to Washington, D.C., to attend Wayland Seminary, a school named after a northern abolitionist and backed by the American Baptist Home Missionary

Society (ABHMS), a group of northern white Baptists intent on converting and ministering to the spiritual needs of freedmen. Johnson graduated with honors and won a prize for best orator in 1879. That year he was also ordained as a Baptist minister and became pastor at First Baptist Church in Frederick, Maryland. In 1881 the ABHMS appointed Johnson the General Missionary of an area that included Maryland, Virginia, West Virginia, and Washington, D.C. The next year he became professor of mathematics and political science at Wayland Seminary, a post he held until 1902. In 1884 he became pastor of Second Baptist Church in Washington, D.C., in what would be a long affiliation that would make him well known. While pastor, he successfully led fund-raising efforts that garnered $75,000 for a new building, and he began a Sunday School Lyceum that became widely respected for its literary discussions. The date of his marriage is not known, but in 1885 he and his wife, Gertrude, had one daughter, Helen Adele, who became an important educator in the South.

From 1886 to 1891 Johnson edited the *Baptist Companion*, a magazine published out of Virginia. In 1888 he received a Doctorate of Divinity (DD) from the State University of Louisville, Kentucky. According to one contemporary, I. GARLAND PENN, when Johnson received the DD he was the youngest man in the country to hold that degree. In 1891 he organized the National Baptist Educational Convention. Thanks to his influential articles, particularly "The Religious Status of the Negro," he became editor of the *National Baptist Magazine*, and he was appointed to the Education Board of the newly formed National Baptist Convention (NBC) in 1895. The NBC was an umbrella group for black Baptists that coordinated missions abroad, home missions, education, and fund-raising; it was the culmination of years of organizing. Many valued the NBC for its freedom from the white-controlled ABHMS.

Even though he was an established minister and well-published author, Johnson continued his education and received an LLD from Virginia Theological Seminary and College. In 1909 he founded the Afro-American School of Correspondence in Washington, D.C. In the 1913 book *The African Abroad*, William H. Ferris described Johnson as "a preacher of massive physique, towering intellect, ripe scholarship and indomitable will" (Ferris, 871). Ferris also claimed Johnson was the most sought-after black preacher to give speeches for important events. Johnson's life testifies to the tremendous work done to build up black churches in the postbellum period. Before the Civil War, most black Baptist slaves worshipped under circumstances carefully controlled by whites. After emancipation, African Americans flocked to form their own churches, despite white opposition. By 1880 most black Baptists in the South had entirely separated from white churches, although they still felt that they were a part of the same denomination. Johnson, a Canadian, deliberately chose to work in the South as part of a missionary effort to bring religion to former slaves. His many orations, published sermons, pamphlets, and books encouraged African Americans to take pride in their race, to celebrate their religion, and to honor their history. These endeavors, and the tremendous denominational growth of the black Baptists, helped African Americans assert their humanity during the stresses and setbacks of the Jim Crow era.

FURTHER READING

Ferris, William H., A.M. *The African Abroad, or, His Evolution in Western Civilization, Tracing His Development under Caucasian Milieu* (1913).

Mather, Frank Lincoln. *Who's Who of the Colored Race*, vol.1 (1915).

Pegues, A.W. *Our Baptist Ministers and Schools* (1892).

Penn, I. Garland. *The Afro-American Press and Its Editors* (1891).

MICHELLE KUHL

Johnson, William (1809–17 June 1851), diarist and entrepreneur, was born in Natchez, Mississippi, the son of William Johnson, a slaveholder, and AMY JOHNSON, a slave. When William was five years old his mother was emancipated and established her household in Natchez. In 1820 the eleven-year-old William was freed by the Mississippi legislature at the request of his owner. Once emancipated, he apprenticed with his brother-in-law, James Miller, in Miller's barber business in Natchez. Johnson became proprietor of the business—reportedly the most popular barbershop in Natchez—when Miller moved to New Orleans in 1830. Johnson and his African American staff ran the shop, which served a predominantly white clientele. Not only did Johnson's barbers offer haircuts and shaves, they also fitted wigs, sold fancy soaps and oils, and, beginning in 1834, operated a bathhouse at the Main Street location.

Between 1830 and 1835 Johnson frequently traveled to New Orleans and to St. Francisville, Louisiana, as well as to other towns in Mississippi, to vacation and to court potential marriage partners. Johnson traveled less after 1835, the year he married twenty-year-old ANN BATTLES JOHNSON of Natchez, a free black woman. They had ten children together.

Also in 1835 Johnson began to keep a diary, writing entries almost daily until his death. The initial purpose of the diary was to record business transactions, purchases he made, and debts paid to him, but in addition Johnson recorded town gossip, described events, and reported local political election results. Johnson's diary thus tells the unusual story of a free African American who lived in the antebellum South and successfully pushed the limits of his status. The barbering business was Johnson's primary source of revenue, but he was a true entrepreneur, acquiring additional income through money lending, property rentals, and agricultural endeavors. His other enterprises included a small toy shop, wallpaper sales, and buggy-and-cart rentals for the transportation of goods to the Natchez market. Johnson purchased and built several buildings, homes as well as commercial structures, and at the time of his death he owned more than 350 acres of land; he was purchasing land toward the development of a small farm or plantation. He hired a white overseer and owned as many as fifteen African American slaves, some of whom he periodically hired out for additional income. A few of his slaves became apprentices in his barbering business.

Because he recorded his wins and losses in his diary, it is known that Johnson competed against both blacks and whites in sports such as hunting, fishing, and horse racing and that he participated in lotteries and raffles and played cards, shuffleboard, and checkers. Johnson spent time reading each week, either the books he owned or the several newspapers and magazines to which he subscribed. Johnson contributed to philanthropic organizations and was a theatergoer. He also attended church but did not continuously belong to one religious denomination.

Although the law prohibited him from voting, Johnson was actively interested in politics and expressed sympathy for the Democratic Party. He was in favor of universal suffrage and education and opposed imprisonment for debt. In general, Johnson had unusual relationships with whites, renting property to them, lending them money, suing them in court, and even employing them as workers on his farm. Indeed, the level of Johnson's participation in commerce, politics, and social events was rare for free blacks in the antebellum South. For the most part, he was able to conduct business and financial matters on an equal basis with whites, but despite his status as one of the most respected members of Natchez society, Johnson was subject to segregation as it applied to all African Americans in his community. Thus he sat in the balcony at the theater and stood outside white churches in order to hear ministers speak. Exceptions were sometimes made for Johnson, but as the years passed, he became less satisfied with—and somewhat embittered by—the limitations placed on him because of his race.

At the age of forty-two Johnson was murdered in Natchez over a land dispute. His killer, Baylor Winn, was arrested, but after two years of public trials Winn was released from custody. The prosecution ultimately abandoned its case, in part because Winn was presumed to be white, while the three witnesses were African American and therefore, according to Mississippi law, were forbidden from testifying against Winn. Johnson's diary, which was preserved by his children and published a century after his death, comprises two thousand pages and fourteen volumes. It is an important and unique account of antebellum southern life, race relations, economic and social conditions, and political affairs.

FURTHER READING

In 1938 the Johnson family donated Johnson's diary, as well as 1,310 other items in his collection, to the Department of Archives at Louisiana State University in Baton Rouge.

Johnson, William. *William Johnson's Natchez: The Ante-Bellum Diary of a Free Negro*, eds. William Ransom Hogan and Edwin Adams Davis (1951).

Berlin, Ira. *Slaves without Masters: The Free Negro in the Antebellum South* (1975).

Davis, Edwin Adams, and William Ransom. *The Barber of Natchez* (1954).

This entry is taken from the *American National Biography* and is published here with the permission of the American Council of Learned Societies.

DEVORAH LISSEK

Johnson, William (1855–3 May 1903), a sailor in the U.S. Navy and Medal of Honor recipient, was a native of St. Vincent in the West Indies. Nothing is known of his personal life or background except the fact that he immigrated to the United States in 1870, making his arrival in New York at the young age of fifteen. When he enlisted in the navy is unknown.

By 1879 William Johnson was serving aboard the wooden steamer *U.S.S. Adams* as a cooper, an important skilled member of the crew whose job was to make and repair the barrels and casks that held the ship's stores and water supplies. Whether Johnson had learned the trade of cooper prior to his arrival in the United States is unknown. In the fall of 1879, the *Adams* and her crew arrived in San Francisco after having spent twenty-three months in Alaska keeping an eye of the sealing and whaling industry in the area while operating out of Sitka and serving as a moderator of disputes between the many foreign traders active in Alaskan waters and the native peoples that lived there. Upon arriving back in the states, the *Adams* was laid up at the Mare Island Navy Yard in San Francisco and was temporarily decommissioned on 20 September 1879. The ship was subsequently manned by a skeleton crew, William Johnson included, and was being overhauled by navy yard personnel on 14 November 1879 when workman Daniel W. Kloppen accidentally fell overboard. Without hesitation, William Johnson dove into the water and saved Kloppen from drowning. Five years later, on 18 October 1884, Johnson was awarded the Medal of Honor for his heroic actions. It is unknown how or why the five-year delay occurred in the award of the medal, the highest U.S. military decoration, and who recommended the award. The delayed award for the medal may have come from the *Adams*'s commanding officer, or may have been awarded based on a petition from Johnson himself, something permissible in the early years of the Medal of Honor.

William Johnson, along with men such as JOHN JOHNSON, JOHN SMITH, and ALPHONSE GIRANDY, is important as he belongs to an oft-forgotten group of Medal of Honor recipients that earned the award for acts of heroism in peacetime. Many naval officers and sailors, including eight African Americans, earned America's highest military decoration in such conditions until the practice was discontinued in 1916. Such awards as this to African Americans during this time are important because they are indicative of their status in the post–Civil War navy; while the era of Jim Crow was taking hold ashore in the south, black sailors at sea continued to serve in the same ratings as whites and maintained a degree of equality until the 1890s, when the navy abandoned its traditions and adopted racist policies that remained in place for nearly fifty years.

The subsequent details of William Johnson's career in the U.S. Navy are unknown, but he continued in the service for most, if not all, of the remainder of his life. By 1900 he was serving as an officer's cook 1st class at the Washington Navy Yard in Washington, DC. Interestingly, his change in rating from that of a cooper to cook probably came about when the rating of cooper was discontinued in the navy in 1884. After his death in 1903, William Johnson, as befits a Medal of Honor recipient, was buried in Arlington National Cemetery (grave number 23-16648-32).

FURTHER READING

U.S. Navy, "Dictionary of American Naval Fighting Ships, *Adams*," http://www.history.navy.mil/danfs/a2/adams-ii.htm.

GLENN ALLEN KNOBLOCK

Johnson, William H. (18 Mar. 1901–13 Apr. 1970), artist, was born William Henry Johnson in Florence, South Carolina, the first of five children of Henry Johnson and Alice Smoot. From the moment of William's birth, neighbors speculated whether this light-skinned, wavy-haired child was the offspring of Henry Johnson, a dark-skinned laborer, and his wife, a woman with dark mahogany skin who worked as a domestic in the home of a prominent white family.

As a child, Johnson attended Wilson School, an all-black elementary school, where he exhibited an early interest in sketching. A teacher encouraged his talent by giving him supplies, and Johnson thought of becoming a cartoonist. However, as a youth he devoted most of his time to supplementing the meager family income as a pinsetter at a bowling alley, shoveling coal, and working at a laundry. Realizing that his opportunities for professional and artistic development were severely limited in a small, segregated southern town, Johnson boarded a train for New York City in 1918.

Upon his arrival in New York, Johnson lived on 128th Street in Harlem with his uncle, Willie Smoot. He found menial work in hotels and restaurants until the fall of 1921, when his drawings earned him a place at the National Academy of Design (NAD). Johnson excelled in his early studies and won a prize in a student competition for one of his drawings. During his second year Johnson fell under the influence of Charles Hawthorne, a new instructor at the NAD, who fundamentally altered Johnson's perspective on art. Hawthorne urged his students to seek inspiration from their subjects, to experiment with form, and to abandon the more subdued conservative palette in favor of vivid color and bold expression. During the summers from 1924 to 1926 Johnson studied with Hawthorne at the Cape Cod School of Art, doing odd jobs around the school to earn his tuition. He was usually the only black student in these settings, and he had a reputation for being reticent, even aloof, preferring to let his work speak for him. Hawthorne recognized Johnson's exceptional talent and encouraged him to go to Europe, cautioning him that in America "there is bound to be prejudice against your race" (Powell, 37).

It is widely believed that Johnson was denied the NAD's most coveted award, the Pulitzer Traveling Scholarship, in 1926 because of class and race prejudice. Hawthorne and others were so incensed by this apparent act of discrimination that they privately raised the funds to support Johnson's study in France. Shortly after arriving in Paris, Johnson met the most renowned black painter of his generation, HENRY OSSAWA TANNER, who had long since made Paris his home. Johnson's European work from 1926 to 1932 focuses on the challenges of capturing landscapes and pastoral vistas rather than on human subjects. These paintings show an admiration for Paul Cézanne and the expressionist Chaim Soutine. Johnson often described what he was trying to express in his paintings as "primitivism." The art historian Richard Powell explains that Johnson's concept of primitivism "was not based on black culture itself, but rather on emotional and psychological interpretations of that culture" (Powell, 75).

In 1928 Johnson moved to Cagnes-sur-Mer in southern France. There he met the German expressionist sculptor Christoph Voll; Voll's wife, Erna; and her sister, Holcha Krake, a ceramic and textile artist. Together this group traveled to Corsica, France, Germany, Luxembourg, and Belgium, visiting museums and sharing their work.

Anxious to find an audience for his growing body of work and hoping to live on the proceeds of his art, Johnson returned to America in 1929 and entered six of his pieces in the William E. Harmon Foundation competition. He won the Gold Medal, which came with a four-hundred-dollar cash award, and four of his paintings were selected for an exhibit, where they received favorable reviews. Johnson returned for a brief visit to Florence, South Carolina, where the local YMCA arranged a one-day show featuring more than one hundred paintings by their up-and-coming native son. On his return trip to New York City, Johnson stopped in Washington, D.C., where he stayed at the home of ALAIN LOCKE, a leading spokesperson for the Negro arts movement during the Harlem Renaissance. Locke became a mentor to Johnson, finding buyers for some of his paintings and introducing him to luminaries in the art and literary world.

In May of 1930 Johnson returned to Europe, married Holcha in June, and settled in the small Danish fishing village of Kerteminde. Many of Johnson's Scandinavian paintings, such as *Lanskab fra Kerteminde* (c. 1930–1932, National Museum of American Art [NMAA]) and *Sun Setting, Denmark* (c. 1930, NMAA), use vibrant color, thick paint, and strong brushwork reminiscent of the work of Vincent van Gogh. By the age of thirty Johnson had tried a variety of aesthetic approaches, from Postimpressionism to European Expressionism, yet, in his words, he had not found the "the real me." As he put it, "Europe is so very superficial. Modern European art strives to be primitive, but it is too complicated" (Powell, 69). Like Pablo Picasso and Paul Gauguin, who had incorporated African and Tahitian imagery into their work to great acclaim, Johnson planned a trip to North Africa for the spring of 1932. There, as he put it, "I might be the first at the same time primitive and cultivated painter the world has ever seen" (Turner and Dailey, 24).

Johnson and Holcha spent three months in Tunisia. They traveled to Kairouan, where Johnson painted a series of watercolors depicting the bustling markets, the towering minarets, and the majestic mosque. When they returned to Denmark at the end of the summer, his paintings and her ceramics appeared in several local exhibitions, but Johnson sent the majority of his new work to the Harmon Foundation in New York, expecting that it would be exhibited and sold. The foundation managed to sell only two of Johnson's paintings in six years, owing both to its lack of effort and the contracting art market during the Depression. By the late 1930s the scourge of Nazi propaganda was spreading across Europe; Christoph Voll's work was discredited by the Nazis as "degenerate art," resulting in Voll's being fired from his teaching position in Germany. In November 1938, with these ominous clouds on the horizon, Johnson and Holcha sailed for New York.

Back in America, the Works Progress Administration had created the Federal Art Project (FAP). In May 1939 Johnson was hired by the FAP and assigned to teach art at the Harlem Community Art Center. Two important developments emerged from this experience: Johnson again became part of the Black Arts Movement, surrounded by contemporaries like JACOB LAWRENCE and GWENDOLYN KNIGHT, and African Americans reappeared as the primary subject of his paintings.

During this period Johnson's paintings began to take on an Egyptian-like flatness, as can be seen in

Jitterbug (I) (c. 1940–1941, NMAA), where the figures are animated on the canvas by bold colors and kinetic gestures. In addition, much of Johnson's American oeuvre contains explicit political messages, readily seen in *Chain Gang* (c. 1939, NMAA) and *Moon over Harlem* (c. 1943–1944, NMAA), which depicts acts of police brutality against blacks; and his Fighters for Freedom series, which pays homage to such significant figures as FREDERICK DOUGLASS, HARRIET TUBMAN, and NAT TURNER.

Following Holcha's death from cancer in 1944, religious themes appear in Johnson's work with greater frequency, though his interest in spiritual subject matter was already well established. Johnson's own physical and mental state began to deteriorate rapidly after 1945. In 1946 he returned to Denmark, hoping to find the peace and happiness of an earlier time. However, Johnson's behavior became increasingly erratic and confused, and he lived briefly as a vagrant on the streets of Copenhagen until it was determined that he suffered from an advanced case of syphilis-induced paresis. Johnson's European relatives sent him back to America, where he spent the rest of his life as an inmate at Central Islip State Hospital on Long Island. Johnson never painted again, and he died in 1970, oblivious to the growing critical acclaim of his work.

FURTHER READING

The papers of William H. Johnson are in two collections: William H. Johnson Papers, Archives of American Art, Smithsonian Institution, Washington, D.C., and William H. Johnson Papers, Smithsonian Institution Archives, Washington, D.C.

Breeskin, Adelyn D. *William H. Johnson* (1971).

Powell, Richard J. *Homecoming: The Art and Life of William H. Johnson* (1991).

Turner, Steve, and Victoria Dailey. *William H. Johnson: Truth Be Told* (1998).

SHOLOMO B. LEVY

Johnson, William Henry (4 Mar. 1833–1918), abolitionist, Union soldier, barber, politician, and journalist, was born to free parents near Alexandria, Virginia. His mother was Patsy Johnson, but his father's name is unknown. At twelve, Johnson left Virginia and ventured to Philadelphia, Pennsylvania, to learn the apothecary business, but instead he decided to be a hairdresser. He moved to Albany, New York, in 1851 and became interested in the abolitionist movement. After returning to Philadelphia in 1855 he joined the Banneker Literary Society to write and speak against slavery. Later, in 1859, he was caught helping fugitive slaves escape via the Underground Railroad, and he was forced to flee the city to avoid imprisonment.

Johnson was a Freesoiler in his younger days, having trained with the old antislavery party that included such notables as FREDERICK DOUGLASS, Bishop Logan, and OCTAVIUS CATTO. For many years a staunch Republican and a great admirer of Abraham Lincoln and Ulysses S. Grant, Johnson attended the first Republican National Convention in 1856 in Philadelphia, as well as several others throughout the years.

Johnson moved to Norwich, Connecticut, where he was residing in 1861 at the outbreak of the Civil War. He wanted to join the war movement but was refused muster into the Second Connecticut Volunteer Infantry because of his color. Johnson served as an "independent" in the Second Connecticut and became the war correspondent of James Redpath's Boston newspaper, the short-lived *Pine and Palm*. Nine of Johnson's letters appeared in the paper. He also served as a correspondent for Frederick Douglass's *North Star* and for the African Methodist Episcopal (AME) Church's *Christian Recorder*. In the 1890s Johnson published his own newspapers, the *Calcium Light* and the *Albany Capitol*.

After serving ninety days with the Second Connecticut he became part of the Eighth Connecticut, fighting at the First Battle of Bull Run (First Manassas), Virginia, on 21 July 1861, and participating in Burnside's expedition when Roanoke Island was captured on 9 February 1862. Because of failing health Johnson left the army four months later, returning to Albany, where he became a recruiting agent for the Fourteenth Congressional District and the Twentieth Regiment of the U.S. Colored Troops.

A successful businessman involved with local and state politics, Johnson served as a delegate to the Republican National Convention in 1864. Later he drew up the constitution of the New York State Equal Rights Committee, of which he was chairman from 1866 to 1873. He lobbied for numerous political issues, including drafting an amendment to the military code of the State of New York to strike the word "white" from the document that was passed in 1872. Johnson also fought in 1867 for legislation to eliminate the property clause that made real estate ownership a condition for allowing black citizens to vote. He lobbied for the civil rights bill that became a law on 9 April 1873 and drafted the bill passed by the New York legislature on 1 April 1891 to abolish the insurance law that allowed blacks to purchase insurance at the same cost as whites but at death to have one-third of the face value deducted on the pretense that whites lived a third longer than blacks. Johnson was most proud of his work on a bill adopted by the New York legislature on 18 April 1900 abolishing all laws that prohibited the free and equal accommodation of children of African descent in New York public schools. In recognition of his patriotism Johnson was presented with the pen used by Governor Theodore Roosevelt when he signed the antidiscrimination school bill.

A self-made man who established a successful barbering business at 27 Maiden Lane in Albany, Johnson also studied medicine and law. He became the first black elected to any official position in the State of New York, being elected in 1872 janitor of the state senate for two years. In 1887 he was elected a committeeman at large of the Republican state committee, and he was reelected the next year by the state convention held in Buffalo, a position never held before by a black in the state. After becoming disillusioned with the Republican Party over the civil rights bill, he switched to the Democratic Party. However, Johnson was an independent when it came to the concerns of his people, even to the extent of standing against his own party. An eloquent public speaker in great demand, Johnson was an aggressive and outspoken advocate of civil rights.

Johnson married Sarah A. F. Steward on 2 August 1852 at the Clinton Square Presbyterian Church in Albany. When he wrote his autobiography, published in 1900, he was a member of St. Peter's Episcopal Church. A thirty-third-degree Freemason, he was elected Grand Master of the Most Worshipful Grand Lodge (Colored) in 1882. He was also a member of the Knights of Labor, which was integrated, and therefore protested against the color line that existed in the Masonic fraternity.

FURTHER READING

Johnson, William Henry. *Autobiography of Dr. William Henry Johnson* (1900).

Moss, Juanita Patience. *The Forgotten Black Soldiers in White Regiments during the Civil War* (2004).

Redkey, Edwin A., ed. *A Grand Army of Black Men* (1992).

JUANITA PATIENCE MOSS

Johnson-Brown, Hazel (10 Oct. 1927–5 Aug. 2011), army general, nurse, and educator, was born Hazel Winifred Johnson, the daughter of Clarence L. and Garnett Johnson, in Malvern, Pennsylvania. One of seven children, she grew up in a close-knit family on a farm in West Chester, Pennsylvania. Although she was rejected from the local nursing program because of racial prejudice, Johnson persisted in her childhood dream of becoming a nurse and received a nursing diploma in 1950 from Harlem Hospital School of Nursing in New York City. Following graduation, she worked as a beginning-level staff nurse at Harlem Hospital's emergency ward and in 1953 went to the Veterans Administration Hospital in Philadelphia, quickly becoming the head nurse on a ward.

Two years later Johnson decided to join the army because, she said, "the Army had more variety to offer and more places to go" (Bombard, 65). She was commissioned as a second lieutenant in the U.S. Army Nurse Corps (ANC) and sent to Fort Sam Houston, Texas, for the medical Officer Basic Training Course. Johnson adjusted quickly to military life, saying, "All that drilling … it was fun, going to school, going to classes" (Bombard, 67).

As a reserve officer on active duty, her first assignment was to the women's ward at Walter Reed Army Hospital in Washington, D.C., followed by duty as an obstetrical nurse with the 8169 Hospital, Camp Zama, Japan. Having already accumulated almost eighty credits toward her bachelor's degree in nursing, in 1957 she left the active army to serve in the U.S. Army Reserve while studying part time at Villanova University and working at the Veterans Administration Hospital in Philadelphia. Johnson was subsequently accepted into the ANC RN Student program and completed her BSN degree in 1959. Receiving a direct commission as first lieutenant in the regular army, Johnson returned to active duty in 1960 and was assigned to Madigan General Hospital at Fort Lewis, Washington, to care for a patient on a respirator. Johnson, who said, "My love for the OR started as a student," then completed the Basic Operating Room Nurse course at Letterman Army Medical Center at the Presidio in San Francisco and returned to Walter Reed in the operating room. In the summer of 1963 Johnson, by then a captain, was selected to attend Columbia University Teachers College, and in 1963 she completed her M.A. in Nursing Education with a minor in Medical Surgical Nursing. She then went back to Letterman, where she taught the OR course from 1963 until 1966.

In 1966 Johnson was chosen to participate in a special project at the Forty-fifth Surgical Hospital in

Hazel Johnson-Brown, brigadier general and chief of the Army Nurse Corps. (Army Nurse Corps Historical Collection, Office of the Surgeon General.)

Texas, evaluating the first MUST (or Medical Unit, Self-contained Transportable) hospital. Illness prevented her from deploying to Vietnam as the unit's OR supervisor and she went instead to Valley Forge General Hospital in Pennsylvania in October 1966 as the supervisor of Central Material Services. Then, in 1967, Johnson was promoted to major and became the first nurse to be a member of the staff at the army's Medical Research and Development Command. There she served as a project director for the Field Sterilization Equipment Development Project, reviewing procedures for field sterilization and developing new surgical equipment for army field hospitals. In 1969 she was promoted to lieutenant colonel.

After completing a three-year course of study toward her doctorate at Catholic University in Washington, D.C., Johnson became director and assistant dean at Walter Reed Army Institute of Nursing (WRAIN), University of Maryland School of Nursing, overseeing the last two classes to graduate from WRAIN. In the meantime Johnson was working after hours on her dissertation, and in 1978 she was awarded her doctorate in Educational Administration from Catholic University.

That same year she went to Japan as assistant for nursing at the Eighth Army Command Office of the Surgeon and Chief, Department of Nursing, at the U.S. Army hospital in Seoul, Korea. There she worked closely with the Korean Army Nurse Corps and Ewaha University School of Nursing students and, as the head nurse, traveled extensively to visit military health facilities in South Korea.

In 1979 Johnson was selected to be the sixteenth chief of the ANC and was promoted to the rank of brigadier general. She was the first chief to hold a doctorate, fourth chief to hold the rank of a general officer, and first black woman general in the history of the U.S. Army. "This achievement was not a straight road from her native Malvern, Pa.," the surgeon general, Lieutenant General Charles C. Pixley, said, "but was a road beset with obstacles and difficulties that could be overcome by extraordinary dedication, enduring vitality and great moral courage." Johnson told newsmen, "For the nurse corps and my colleagues in nursing, I hope the criterion for selection didn't include race but competence" (*All Volunteer*, Feb. 1980). Competence, "integrity of purpose," and "honesty" in her job have been Johnson's lifelong goals. As chief of the ANC, Johnson initiated steps to include nursing in the Reserve Officers' Training Corps (ROTC) scholarship program, established a summer clinical experience opportunity for ROTC nursing students, and published the first documented Standards of Nursing Practice for army nursing. Seeing a need for "research, writing, and publishing by nurses," Johnson encouraged the writing of an ANC history and continued education for army nurses, including the first Nursing Research Symposium. She also initiated the publishing of graduate education and military education requirements for all major positions for ANC officers and laid the foundation for a strategic planning conference to plan for the future of the corps.

Johnson retired from active duty in the army in 1983 to become the director of the government affairs division of the American Nurses Association and an adjunct professor at Georgetown University School of Nursing. In the 1980s Johnson married David B. Brown and in 1986 joined the faculty at George Mason University in Virginia as a professor of nursing.

Among her many honors, Johnson-Brown received the Evangeline C. Bovard Army Nurse of the Year Award, the Army Nurse of the Year Award from Letterman General Hospital, and the Daughters of the American Revolution's Nurse of the Year, Dr. Anita Newcomb McGee Award. Her military decorations included the Distinguished Service Medal, Army Commendation Medal with

Oak Leaf Cluster, Meritorious Service Medal, and Legion of Merit. Johnson-Brown also held honorary degrees from Morgan State University, the University of Maryland, and Villanova University.

When asked how she would like people to remember her, Johnson-Brown said, "Probably as a good person, one who tries to do the best job possible for the Corps and for the profession of nursing, and that I did try" (Bombard, 155). She died in Wilmington, Delaware, at the age of 83.

FURTHER READING

The best account of Johnson-Brown's life is Lieutenant Colonel Charles F. Bombard's 1984 oral history of the Army Nurse Corps, at the Center for Military History, Washington, D.C., which includes her curriculum vitae.

Carnegie, Mary Elizabeth. *The Path We Tread: Blacks in Nursing Worldwide, 1954–1994* (1995).

Samecky, Mary T. *A History of the U.S. Army Nurse Corps* (1999).

BARBARA B. TOMBLIN

Johnston, Albert (17 Aug. 1900–23 June 1988), physician and radiologist, was born Albert Chandler Johnston Jr. in Chicago, Illinois, to Albert Chandler Johnston Sr. His mother's name is unknown. Nothing is known about his childhood or early schooling. It appears that he grew up with several brothers and that one of his brothers passed for white. Johnston married Thyra Baumann from Boston, and the couple had four children.

Johnston attended the University of Chicago from 1919 to 1923, graduating with a bachelor of science degree. While there he joined the black fraternity Kappa Alpha Psi. Johnston then studied at Rush Medical College in Chicago, where he was one of two black students in his class. He received his medical degree from Rush in 1925. In order to complete his medical training and earn an MD, which he received in 1929, Johnston was required to complete a medical internship. Numerous hospitals eagerly accepted his application, but the positions vanished or were given to other candidates when the hospitals learned his race. Married with a son and working as a porter and dining-car waiter to support his young family added to the pressures that Johnston was experiencing. After several years of applying for internships, he was finally accepted at Maine General Hospital (Portland), which never asked about his race.

While at Portland, Johnston learned of a vacancy for a general practitioner in Gorham, New Hampshire, and began his practice there in 1931 as a country doctor for the town's twenty-five hundred residents. The Johnstons' seventeen-room home in the wealthy Prospect Hill section quickly became popular for community events such as the Congregational Church's Christmas social and the couple's New Year's reception. Johnston was head of the school board, served as a selectman, coached basketball, and was chair of the local Republican Party. When locals inquired about his complexion, Johnston explained that he was one-eighth Cherokee, which was true. Johnston was thirty-seven when Harvard Medical School offered him a Graduate Voluntary Assistantship in Radiology. He eagerly accepted and became the first black physician to study radiology at the prestigious institution. He moved his family to Boston to serve a one-year residency at Peter Bent Bingham Hospital and to establish his medical specialty as a radiologist.

When World War II broke out Johnston was eager to serve his country. His credentials included a Diplomate of the American Board of Radiology and membership in the American Medical Association. Although the navy actively recruited and commissioned him as a lieutenant commander in its medical corps and even assigned him a ship, naval intelligence during a routine check discovered his membership in the black fraternity and rejected Johnston. They informed him that he did not meet their physical requirements, although they had not given him a physical examination. The rejection profoundly changed his life and the lives of his wife and children.

After more than two decades of living in all-white towns in Maine and New Hampshire and passing as white, Johnston had the difficult task of telling his children that they were actually black. To some people the idea of passing was cowardly. To others it was a practical way to deal with legal and de facto segregation and racial discrimination. It was Johnston's eldest son who prompted his family to discuss publicly their family history and the issue of passing. Albert Jr. met with a visiting New Hampshire filmmaker, Louis de Rochement, who was intrigued by the young man's story and asked for a written summary. The summary became a *Reader's Digest* article in 1947. In 1948 William L. White published *Lost Boundaries*, a biography of Albert Johnston that raised questions about what it meant to be black in the United States.

The following year de Rochement produced a fictionalized feature-film adaptation of the book, directed by Alfred L. Werker. The film *Lost*

Boundaries was marketed with the tagline "The true story of a family who lived a lie for twenty years!" and starred Mel Ferrer as Dr. Scott Carter, a black doctor who passes for white. Though the film's leads were, notably, not played by African American actors, the film did feature CANADA LEE and BILL GREAVES in smaller roles. The movie won the 1949 Best Screenplay Award at the Cannes Film Festival, and the *New York Times* cited it as one of the ten best films of 1949. Mel Ferrer later claimed that President Harry S. Truman's decision to desegregate the armed forces was accelerated after he viewed *Lost Boundaries*. Though the film was generally well received, several cities in the South banned it.

After the release of the *Lost Boundaries* book and film, the citizens of Keene, New Hampshire—the Johnstons' hometown—remained welcoming and accepting of the family. For several years Johnston became a speaker at NAACP events throughout the country. In 1966 Johnston and his wife relocated to Hawaii, where he worked as a radiologist at the G. N. Wilcox Memorial Hospital, Lihue, Kauai, until his retirement in the mid-1970s. A respected physician in Hawaii, Johnston served for eight years as councilor of the American College of Radiology and served in 1968 as president of the Kauai Medical Society. Johnston was a member of the New Hampshire Medical Society from 1929 to 1967, the Roentgen Ray Society of North America, the New England Roentgen Ray Society, the New Hampshire Pathology Society, the Cheshire County (New Hampshire) Medical Society, and the New Hampshire Roentgen Ray Society, which he served as president.

As for the controversy surrounding the Johnston family, Johnston's youngest son, Paul, summed it up: "My family wasn't unique for passing. They were unique for telling people about it" (Perry).

FURTHER READING

Kroeger, Brooke. *Passing: When People Can't Be Who They Are* (2003).

Perry, Amanda. "It Was about Time People Knew," *Concord Monitor*, 28 Dec. 2003.

United States Congress. *Congressional Record, Extension of Remarks*, 101st Congress, 1st session (1989).

White, William L. *Lost Boundaries* (1948).

PAUL WERMAGER

Joiner, Charlie (14 Oct. 1947–), Hall of Fame football player, was born Charles Joiner Jr., in Many, Louisiana, son of Charles Joiner Sr., a truck driver, and Effie Joiner. Joiner grew up watching Dallas Cowboys and Baltimore Colts football games and idolized Raymond Berry, the star wide receiver for the Colts. Joiner spent much time trying to emulate Berry's moves, especially when he played receiver for the W. O. Boston High School team in Lake Charles, Louisiana, coached by Wiley Stewart.

Stewart, who had played under legendary coach EDDIE ROBINSON, head football coach at Grambling State University, recommended Joiner to Grambling, and convinced Robinson to accept Joiner in spite of his relatively small size. Joiner became a star receiver for Grambling and lettered in all of his four years there. He was also a serious student, graduating in 1969 with a B.A. in Accounting.

Professional scouts considered Joiner too small (five feet eleven inches and 188 pounds) for the National Football League (NFL), and Joiner was not drafted until the fourth round of the 1969 NFL draft, when the Houston Oilers selected him. The Oilers originally planned on converting him to defensive back, and he spent his rookie season on defense and returning kicks. The Oilers converted him back to receiver for his second season, and Joiner became a "deep threat" receiver, with his average yardage per catch being among the league leaders. During the off-season, Joiner worked in the accounting department of the Gulf Oil Company, a job he would keep for thirteen years. Joiner played three seasons for the Oilers before being traded to the Cincinnati Bengals in 1972, where he played for four seasons. In 1973 he married Dianne, and they had two children.

Joiner served as the deep-threat receiver for Cincinnati, accumulating impressive yards-per-catch averages. After four seasons in Cincinnati, Joiner was traded to the San Diego Chargers. He continued as a deep-threat receiver his first two seasons in San Diego. Prior to the 1978 season, Joiner almost quit football. He had off-season knee surgery, would turn thirty-one in October, and was surrounded by the Chargers' bevy of new receivers. Joiner saw these events as signs that his career was over. Head coach Tom Prothro convinced him to stay.

The Chargers then underwent a major offensive philosophy change. In 1978 the team hired Don Coryell as head coach, and the following season they hired Joe Gibbs as offensive coordinator. These two coaches saw Joiner as an intelligent receiver who ran precise routes. They converted him to a possession-type receiver who became the cornerstone of the Chargers' new pass-oriented offense, dubbed "Air Coryell." Joiner, never known for high reception totals, had three consecutive seventy-plus catch seasons (1979–1981) and Pro Bowl appearances, a streak broken only by the 1982 players' strike. He had perhaps his best season in 1980, culminating in his six-catch, 130-yard, and two-touchdown performance in the American Football Conference title game. Joiner was named all-NFL in 1980.

During his time in San Diego, Joiner blossomed as a clutch receiver, becoming the so-called security blanket for his quarterback, Dan Fouts, who considered Joiner his third-down specialist; Joiner always seemed to find a way to make the important catch when the Chargers' offense needed it. Joiner also proved to be a highly durable receiver, rarely missing a game because of injuries. In fact, he missed only one game in his final thirteen seasons. There were times he even played with major injuries, including a broken rib on one occasion and a separated shoulder on another. In a 1979 game against the Denver Broncos he even continued playing after suffering a concussion—he had no recollection of catching the winning touchdown. His durability allowed him to play until he was thirty-nine, which was considered old for a wide receiver, before retiring after the 1986 season. For his career, Joiner had 750 receptions (an NFL record at the time of his retirement), 12,146 yards, 65 touchdowns, and ranked sixth on the all-time yards per catch list with 16.2. Joiner also set an NFL record for games played by a wide receiver with 239.

After he retired from playing, Joiner moved into coaching, taking over as the Chargers' receivers coach in 1987. As a coach Joiner was able to take his considerable skills and knowledge of the game and impart this to a new generation of wide receivers. After five seasons with the Chargers, he became the receivers' coach for the Buffalo Bills in 1992. In 2001 he became the receivers' coach for the Kansas City Chiefs, serving under his former coach, Al Saunders.

In 1990 Joiner was inducted into the Louisiana Hall of Fame. In 1996 he was inducted into the Pro Football Hall of Fame, voted in alongside his former coach Gibbs. It took five years of eligibility for Joiner to get into the Hall of Fame, not because of his talent but because of his style. Joiner played his entire career in the shadows, never being overly popular with fans or even the star of his own team. In Houston, Joiner played in the shadow of Jerry Levias; in Cincinnati, Isaac Curtis dominated; and in San Diego, J. J. Jefferson, Wes Chandler, and Kellen Winslow were the team's stars. When other receivers were doing back flips or performing other theatrics after making big plays, Joiner merely handed the ball to the officials and got ready for his next play. Though he was never flashy, he was one of the best receivers to ever play the game. Bill Walsh, who coached Joiner in Cincinnati, called him the most intelligent and calculating receiver the game had ever known.

FURTHER READING

DuFresne, Jim. *Take to the Air: Pro Football Pass Catchers* (1983).

O'Donnell, Chuck. "The Game I'll Never Forget," *Football Digest* (Nov. 1997).

Zimmerman, Paul. "He's Catching Up to the Catching Record," *Sports Illustrated* (Oct. 1984).

MICHAEL C. MILLER

Joiner, Philip (1837–1876?), radical Republican, labor leader, Georgia state representative, and carpenter, was born a slave in Mecklenburg County, Virginia. Little is known of Joiner's mother, Lucy Parker, except that she bore at least four other children (Lucy Ann Joiner, Betsey Gill, and Carter and George Murray). Even less is known of Joiner's father, a man Philip never met. One of an estimated 3 million enslaved men and women who were forcibly transported from the upper to the lower South between 1790 and 1860, Joiner was sold away from most of his Virginia kin in 1847. Accompanied by his mother, Joiner arrived as an eleven-year-old in southwest Georgia, an area of the cotton South later made famous by W. E. B. DuBois in *Souls of Black Folk* (1903). Most likely coming of age on one of the plantations that dominated the region's landscape, Joiner eventually met, married, and began a family with a Florida-born slave named Henrietta. The couple had five children.

Joiner also apparently acquired valuable training as a carpenter during his time as a slave. Although it is not known if his master permitted him to hire his own time, Joiner had accumulated sufficient funds by the spring of 1866 to pay $300 cash for a city lot in Albany, the seat of Dougherty County, Georgia, a property that he immediately deeded to Henrietta and their children. Four years later, Joiner added to his family's patrimony when he purchased a second Albany lot for $205; by the time of the first postwar federal census in 1870, he owned $2,000 worth of real estate. Securing his and his family's freedom with land was not enough, however, for the former slave. Joiner believed that black people more generally, especially those who had emerged from slavery with few material resources to call their own and who constituted the rank and file of the agricultural working class, deserved similar opportunities. Thus even as he made his own transition from property to propertyholder, Joiner played a leading role in a political insurgency that for a brief and exhilarating moment would illuminate a working-class vision of black freedom.

Black southwest Georgians wasted no time in articulating their own brand of political and productive order. Angered by planters who continued to insist that workers ought to behave like slaves, the region's black men and women had begun by January 1866 to mobilize in their own defense. As word of the newly formed Georgia Equal Rights Association (the GERA, which was not directly related to the similar-sounding Equal Rights League) spread throughout the region, raising funds for the indigent, establishing schools for black children, and promoting landownership by former slaves, mobilization quickened. By fall, the GERA chapter located in Dougherty County boasted a membership of nearly one thousand; six months later, it had reconfigured itself into a branch of the openly partisan Union League of America. The Union League of America (also known as the Loyal League) had originated in the North during the Civil War as a patriotic club. After the war, Republican leaders used the club's existing structure to "evangelize" among the newly freed slaves, and the local branch elected Joiner president. Eschewing the moderate position of many of Georgia's leading black Republicans, Joiner espoused a particularly radical brand of politics, one predicated on economic and political equity, and one that endeared him to a constitution almost wholly composed of impoverished agricultural wage workers. By November 1867, the man who had made his first recorded public appearance the previous April was on his way to Atlanta as a popularly elected representative to the state's constitutional convention. Four months later, he again headed for Atlanta, this time as the first person of African descent to represent Dougherty County in the Georgia House of Representatives. While Joiner kept a low profile at the constitutional convention, it became clear from his votes in favor of debtor relief and against restrictions on political participation that he had pledged his support to those who struggled to support themselves.

Fairness, however, found little favor among former slaveholders, who objected vehemently to Joiner's insistence that all workers—black or white—deserved equal access to plantation resources. Within a matter of months, the optimism that had swept

black men into state offices was dealt a series of crippling blows. On 3 September 1868 moderate and conservative lawmakers voted to expel all identifiably black members from the Georgia legislature. Sixteen days later, white Southerners opened fire on a crowd of nearly 150 former slaves who had gathered in Camilla, a diminutive Mitchell County village, for a Republican rally. Before the shooting was over, as many as a third lay injured or dead, and dozens of others fled for their lives as what Joiner later bitterly described as "mobbing crowds" of "southern so called democrats" (P. Joiner to J. E. Bryant, 30 Sept. 1868, J. E. Bryant Papers, Special Collections Department, Perkins Library, Duke University) combed the countryside for "every Colored man that is farming to his self or supporting the nominee of grant and Colfax" (P. Joiner to J. E. Bryant, 30 Sept. 1868). Joiner, who survived the massacre, struggled to rally his constituents, but the wave of violence produced the outcome that conservatives had intended. Black and Republican voter turnout for the 1868 presidential election plummeted. Only two radicals dared come forward to vote in Camilla; "scarcely a radical vote" was cast in nearby Cuthbert (George R. Ballou to O. H. Howard, 3 Nov. 1868, Letters Received, Records of the Bureau of Refugees, Freedmen, and Abandoned Lands, 1865–1870, National Archives, Record Group 105, microcopy 798: Records of the Assistant Commissioner for the State of Georgia, reel number 23); and in Dougherty County, where black voters outnumbered white by more than eight thousand, a lifelong Democrat won a seat in Congress. Despite continued threats to his life, some of which came from local organizations styled after the Ku Klux Klan, Joiner refused to concede defeat. Steadfast in his belief that former slaves were citizens and entitled to all the rights of citizens, he drafted a powerful memorandum to Congress outlining black people's grievances, chiding military authorities for failing to protect the nation's ex-slaves, and condemning an inequitable legal system that too often sent black workers away "cur[sing] the law and the white man who cheated him out of his honest" living (House Committee on Reconstruction, *Condition of Affairs in Georgia*, 41st Cong., 1st session, 1869, H. Misc. Doc. 34, 95). It was a refrain Joiner returned to a year later, when as a representative to the state's first black workers' convention, he predicted that "unless Dougherty County consented to give the colored man his 'rights,' she will find herself without labor after the first day of January next" (*Albany (Ga.) News*, 7 Oct. 1869). Such an exodus never came to pass, but in 1869 the county's Republican voters sent Joiner to the state legislature for a second term. It would, however, be his last. Despite having sponsored legislation directly beneficial to the county's small farmers, Joiner lost his bid for a third term in an election that saw the state "redeemed" by a conservative Democratic Party.

Joiner's public career came to an abrupt end following his 1872 defeat. Four years later, he disappeared from the public record, leaving his wife Henrietta and their children a small patrimony in the form of a city lot long paid for. He also left compelling evidence that an effective leader need not be affluent, educated, or a man of the cloth. None of those, Joiner nonetheless organized and led a radical insurgency that for a brief and brilliant moment, had threatened to topple traditional hierarchies of privilege and power.

FURTHER READING

O'Donovan, Susan Eva. *Becoming Free in the Cotton South* (2007).

O'Donovan, Susan Eva. "Philip Joiner: Southwest Georgia Black Republican Leader," *Journal of Southwest Georgia History* 4 (Fall 1986).

SUSAN E. O'DONOVAN

Jones, Absalom (6 Nov. 1746–13 Feb. 1818), first black Protestant Episcopal priest, was born in Sussex, Delaware, the son of slave parents. He was a small child when his master took him from the fields to wait on the master in the house. Jones was very fond of learning and was very careful to save the pennies that were given to him by ladies and gentlemen from time to time. He soon bought a primer and would beg people to teach him how to read. Before long he was able to purchase a spelling book, and as his funds increased he began to buy books, including a copy of the New Testament. "Fondness for books gave me little or no time for amusements that took up the leisure hours of my companions" (Bragg, 3).

When Jones was sixteen, his mother, five brothers, and a sister were sold, and he was taken to Philadelphia by his master. There he worked in his master's store, where he would pack and carry out to customers' carriages goods that had been purchased. Gradually he learned to write and was soon able to write to his brothers and mother "with my own hand." In 1766 he began attending a Quaker-operated night school for blacks. When he was twenty-four he married Mary (maiden name unknown), a slave woman. Shortly after the marriage, he arranged to purchase his wife's freedom. His wife's mistress agreed to a price of forty pounds, and Jones borrowed thirty pounds and the mistress forgave the remaining

Absalom Jones co-founded the St. Thomas African Episcopal Church in Philadelphia with Richard Allen in the early 1790s. When he was ordained in 1804, he became the first black priest in the United States. (Schomburg Center.)

ten pounds. For the next eight years Jones worked almost every night until 12:00 or 1:00 to raise money to repay what he had borrowed.

By 1778 he had paid off the loan with which he had purchased his wife's freedom and made application to his owner to purchase his own freedom with some additional money that he had saved. This was not granted. Jones then bought a lot with a sizable house and continued to work and save his money. Again he applied to his master to purchase his freedom, and on 1 October 1784 he was granted manumission.

At this time the city of Philadelphia was alive with the spirit of the revolution and the ideal of universal freedom. In 1780 a law was passed that called for the gradual emancipation of the slave population. Also at this time a new religious movement was developing in the emerging United States. The Methodists were evangelicals within the Church of England who met in small groups to enhance their religious life. They were particularly strong in New York, Baltimore, and Philadelphia. On 24–25 December 1784, under the leadership of Thomas Coke and Francis Asbury, members of these Methodist societies met at Lovely Lane Chapel in Baltimore and organized the Methodist Episcopal Church as a new denomination separate from the Church of England. In the three large cities previously mentioned, numerous blacks joined the Methodist Church. Many of the free blacks of Philadelphia attended the mostly white St. George's Methodist Episcopal Church, as did Jones. Also among them was RICHARD ALLEN, who became the founder and first bishop of the African Methodist Episcopal (AME) Church. For a while the blacks and whites got along well at St. George's Church. As Methodism spread among the whites, the space occupied by black Methodists in the church building was more and more in demand by the increasing number of white congregants. The blacks were moved from place to place in the building as circumstances required. One Sunday morning in 1787 a number of blacks were seated together and had knelt for prayer. Jones, the leader of the group, was pulled from his knees, and the blacks were told to move to another place in the building. The entire group of blacks arose and walked out of the church never to return. This unpleasant episode was the occasion that prompted the first organization among free blacks of which there is any record.

On 12 April 1787 some of these black Methodists met in a home in Philadelphia and organized the Free African Society. Jones was the leader of the group, and Allen was one of the overseers. It was a benevolent and social reform organization at first. The Episcopal bishop William White of Pennsylvania was a leader in the encouragement and support of the Free African Society. Gradually the Free African Society transformed itself into an "African Church" with no denominational ties. At a meeting held 21 July 1792, a resolution was adopted that appropriated money to purchase property on which to erect "a place of worship for this Society." The society erected a church building that was dedicated on 17 July 1794. Later in the year an election was held to determine with which denomination to unite. "There were two in favor of the Methodists, Absalom Jones and Richard Allen; and a large majority in favor of the Church of England. This majority carried" (Bragg, 9). Jones went with the majority, but Allen did not. On 12 August 1794 the African Church became St. Thomas Episcopal Church, the first black Episcopal church in the United States. It was formally received into the Diocese of Pennsylvania on 12 October 1794.

At that October diocesan convention Jones was received as a candidate for holy orders in the Episcopal Church and was licensed as a lay reader. On 21 October 1794 he formally accepted the position of pastor of St. Thomas Church. At the diocesan convention on 2 June 1795, it was stipulated that St. Thomas Church was not entitled to send a clergyman or any lay deputies to the convention, nor was it "to interfere with the general government of the Episcopal Church." Jones was ordained a deacon on 23 August 1795 and then priest on September 1804, the first black to become a deacon or a priest in the Episcopal Church. From 1795 until his death, Jones baptized 268 black adults and 927 black infants. His ministry among blacks was so significant that he was called the "Black Bishop of the Episcopal Church." Jones died in Philadelphia.

FURTHER READING

The few extant Jones papers are in the Archives of the Episcopal Church, Austin, Texas.

Bragg, George F. *The Story of the First of the Blacks, the Pathfinder, Absalom Jones, 1746–1818* (1929).

Lammers, Ann C. "The Rev. Absalom Jones and the Episcopal Church: Christian Theology and Black Consciousness in a New Alliance," *Historical Magazine of the Protestant Episcopal Church* (1982): 159–84.

Lewis, Harold T. *Yet with a Steady Beat: The African American Struggle for Recognition in the Episcopal Church* (1996).

This entry is taken from the *American National Biography* and is published here with the permission of the American Council of Learned Societies.

DONALD S. ARMENTROUT

Jones, Addison. *See* Nigger Add.

Jones, Amanda (16 Dec. 1898–18 Dec. 2008), centenarian and symbol of racial progress, was the daughter of Emmanuel Alfred Roberts, emancipated from slavery in 1865, and Moriah Josephine Washington, farmers on Alum Creek, east of Austin, Texas. Jones gained widespread recognition as a symbol of America's racial progress when, at age 109, she voted for Senator BARACK OBAMA (D-IL) for President in November 2008. She was one of the oldest registered active voters in Texas at the time.

Amanda Jones was a deeply religious woman who had for most of her life been a stay at home mother of ten in rural Central Texas. She resided along a rural highway in central Texas for most of her life. Her granddaughter, Brenda Baker, said she lived to be 110 because of her religious faith, which was evident in the scriptures and photographs of her in her Sunday best which decorated the walls of her home in Bastrop, Texas, thirty miles from Austin.

Her father, Emmanuel Alfred Roberts, took the name of his last master, a farmer and rancher named Abe Roberts. Emmanuel Roberts herded sheep and guarded Abe Roberts's flock from Central Texas mountain lions until he was emancipated at age twelve. Emmanuel Roberts married Moriah Josephine Washington and had thirteen children.

Amanda Jones, their middle child, became a local celebrity in October 2008 when her story ran in the *Austin American-Statesman* newspaper. She became symbolic, as did the small number of other surviving daughters of slaves in America, of the hope embodied in Barack Obama's candidacy and eventual election to the highest office in the country. Jones lived in three different centuries of very radical racial changes and had lived long enough to vote for America's first black president after voting consistently as a Democrat for seventy years. In the year that Jones was born no African Americans served in the Texas state legislature— the last black legislator left the Texas House in 1897. Violence against black voters, intimidation, and gerrymandering of election districts drastically reduced the number of eligible black voters in the state in the 1890s, a process that was furthered by the passage of a poll tax in 1902 and the adoption of an all white Democratic Primary in 1905. Her story eventually reached Good Morning America, ABC News, and National Public Radio, among other news outlets. She was one of several centenarians who voted in the election but she was part of a small percentage of active Central Texas voters above age 100 in the state and the country. A 106-year-old American nun living in Rome, Italy, Sister Cecilia Gaudette, was referred to as the nation's oldest voter, but there were others older than her. In Los Angeles, Gertrude Baines, 114, voted for Obama and was acknowledged as the oldest person of African descent in the world.

The sheer size of voter rolls in Texas made it impossible for the Secretary of State to confirm whether Jones was the state's oldest active voter. In Jones's home county, Bastrop, an elections administrator said that some counties automatically list voters who were born before the turn of the twentieth century with birth dates of January 1900. The oldest active voter in surrounding Central Texas at the time was 106, which made Jones the oldest-known active voter in Central Texas. She had been able to go with the help of her daughters, Eloise Baker

and Joyce Jones, to the polls to vote for President Barack Obama in the primary, but for the national elections she filled in an absentee ballot because of her failing health.

Jones grew up under Jim Crow segregation in Texas, during a time when women had not yet earned the right to vote and blacks had to pay poll taxes to vote until the practice was outlawed nationally by Amendment XXIV to the U.S. Constitution in 1964. She told reporters that she had to pick cotton to save up enough money to pay poll taxes. She remembered that she first voted during the Franklin D. Roosevelt administration but she could not recall the exact year. Small numbers of southern African Americans voted for FDR in the 1930s, but more likely she cast her first ballot in 1944, following the *Smith v. Allwright* 321 U.S. 649 (1944) U.S. Supreme Court decision, which invalidated Texas's all-white Democratic Primary. By 1946, 20 percent of eligible African Americans voted in the Democratic primary. Nevertheless, by the time of the passage of the 1965 Voting Rights Act, when Jones was sixty-six years old, only a handful of black Texans held any elective office. None sat in the Texas legislature and none in the U.S. Congress. The following year Democrat BARBARA JORDAN became the first ever African American woman and the first African American elected to the Texas Senate since 1883, while two other African Americans entered the Texas House for the first time since 1897. In January 1973, when Jones was seventy-four years old, Jordan and ANDREW YOUNG (D-GA) became the first southern African Americans elected to the U.S. Congress in the twentieth century.

She was married to C. L. Jones, Sr. for more than fifty years. She worked for a time as a maid making twenty dollars a month, then with her husband in his Bastrop grocery store before she dedicated herself to raising her children. The family has been a fixture in Cedar Creek and other parts of the county for at least five generations, even when its members had to eat at segregated restaurants and endure the indignities of walking through the back door while white customers came in through the front, according to Amanda Jones's sixty-eight-year-old daughter, Joyce Jones.

Jones was an active member of the Inspiration Pentecostal church in Bastrop. Her relatives said that she was a consistently positive woman, who enjoyed having visitors to her home and when someone would ask her how she was, she would always respond, "Blessed." Everyone who knew Jones referred to her respectfully as a "Woman of

God." Her relatives attributed her long life to her devout Christian faith. Her daughter, Eloise Baker, said that Amanda Jones was faithful and obedient to God and had taught her children to be the same. She liked to be dressed in her Sunday best—complete with a pretty Sunday hat and a suit—whenever she attended church.

More than 200 people signed an online petition to get Amanda Jones to Barack Obama's inauguration. She was feted with birthday cards and presidential t-shirts after news of her historic vote spread. In early December 2008, she was hospitalized with pneumonia, right before her 110th birthday. On Thursday, December 18, she passed away in her sleep. More than 100 of her family members from as far away as Washington and California came to honor her life at a downtown Austin hotel. They celebrated her with a dinner, cake and a slideshow of snapshots with her family throughout her life and remarks from relatives about how blessed they had been to know her. Brenda Baker said that there had been plans to present her with proclamations from the Governor of Texas, Rick Perry, and to give her the key to the city where she grew up. Amanda Jones had been the sole survivor of her siblings. She left behind thirty-three grand-children, sixty-five great-grandchildren and twenty great-great grandchildren.

FURTHER READING

Sanders, Joshunda. "Daughter of Slave Votes for Obama," *Austin American-Statesman*. Retrieved 27 October 2008 from: http://www.statesman.com/news/content/news/stories/local/10/27/1027jones.html

Obituaries: *Austin American-Statesman*, 20 Dec. 2008. Retrieved 20 December 2008 from: http://www.statesman.com/news/content/news/stories/local/12/20/1220jones.html; *San Antonio Express-News*, 21 Dec. 2008. Retrieved 21 December 2008 from: http://www.chron.com/disp/story.mpl/headline/metro/6174043.html

JOSHUNDA SANDERS

Jones, Bessie (8 Feb. 1902–4 Sept. 1984), folksinger, storyteller, and founder of the Georgia Sea Island Singers, was born in Smithville, Georgia, to Abby Lou Frances, a domestic, and Ronnie Smith, a farm worker (her stepfather was James Sampson). Originally named May Elizabeth after her grandmother and great-grandmother, she was raised largely by her grandparents who had been slaves and who taught her a large repertoire of song, children's games, and folktales. She came from a musical family: her grandfather played accordion; her uncles played guitar and banjo (the latter of which they made themselves); and her mother played autoharp. Her grandfather, who had been brought from Africa to a Virginia plantation, taught her games and songs such as "Jibber" (more commonly known as "Juba") and "Step It Down." During her childhood and young adult years, Jones moved with her family from one central Georgia farm town after another. Jones attended Hickory Level School in Bronwood, leaving at the age of nine to work as a domestic. Throughout her life, she worked variously as a sharecropper, domestic, and migrant farm laborer. Jones had her first child at the age of twelve, a daughter born 15 September 1914 in Osterfield, Georgia. She married the father, Cassius, after they moved to Fitzgerald, where Jones worked as a farmhand.

Born on the mainland, Jones made her first trip to the Sea Islands in early June 1919, to St. Simons Islands. After a three-month stay on the coast spent picking cotton, she and her husband returned to Brunswick, where Cassius died shortly thereafter. Jones returned to Fitzgerald and later moved to Osterfield. Her mother married Jasper Johnson and moved to Millen, Georgia, and Jones joined them there. In 1926 the family moved to Miami and then the Florida Keys, where Jones found work as a washerwoman. Returning to Miami, Jones met her companion Sam Sebourne. They found work as migrants at Caxambas on Marco Island on the Gulf Coast in 1928 but returned to Miami after a year. Following the end of their relationship, Jones met George Jones, her second husband, in August 1929. They spent the next years as migrant workers traveling from Florida to Connecticut. In 1932 she and her husband returned to his hometown, St. Simons. She gave birth to her second child, George Jr., on 25 August 1935. Her third child, Joseph, was born two years later, on 26 December 1937. Shortly thereafter Jones resumed work as a migrant, this time in Maryland at a canning factory. In 1939 she returned to St. Simons Island.

Through her marriage she joined Lydia Parrish's Spiritual Singers Society of Coastal Georgia in 1933 (her husband's uncle used to sing in the group). George Jones died on 6 May 1945 in Tampa, Florida. Shortly after joining John Davis, a singer and performer who led one group that performed songs and other Sea Island traditions, and the St. Simons group, Jones was "discovered" by the folklorist Alan Lomax in spring 1954 when he came to St. Simons to record Davis. She made her first recordings for Lomax.

Meeting Lomax launched her professional singing career. Jones became a lead singer and proponent of the Georgia Sea Islands tradition, performing songs that had been sung by slaves dating back to before the Civil War. Her repertoire included spirituals, jubilees, and ring shouts, play party songs and other children's games, folktales, and work songs. Over the next thirty years Jones would appear at folk festivals, concert halls, and universities throughout the United States. In 1954 she and others performed at New York's Carnegie Hall. Jones and other Sea Islanders traveled to Williamsburg, Virginia, to appear in a film produced by Lomax. He brought Jones to New York where he recorded an oral history that became the basis for *Step It Down* (completed by his sister, Bess Lomax Hawes). Lomax asked Jones what she and her group would like to call themselves, and Jones replied the Georgia Sea Island Singers. At this time the group's other members included John Davis, Mabel Hilary, Mr. and Mrs. George Chens, and Charlotte Reese (over the years the roster would change, including the addition of original members' children and grandchildren, including Jones's own). Jones continued to appear at folk festivals in the East. In the summer of 1956 she performed and taught at a camp in the Catskill Mountains, where she met folk singer Pete Seeger, who arranged for her to appear at Carnegie Hall in September 1961. In 1962 she was featured on *Southern Journey*, recorded by Lomax and released on the Prestige label. Over the next twenty years she would appear at festivals such as the Folk Life Festival in Washington, D.C., the Mariposa Festival in Toronto, and the Pavilion in Montreal. She made three records with the Georgia Island Singers, *Deep South* (1977), *Georgia Sea Islands, vol. I* (1975), and *Georgia Sea Islands, vol. II* (1975). In fall 1971 she sustained serious injuries in an automobile accident, but by April 1972 she had resumed performing regularly. In October of that year she was honored by Yale University and given the Ellington Medal. In 1976 she returned to Yale to teach a course in African American folk traditions. That year she performed at President Jimmy Carter's inauguration. Jones continued to perform in concert, on university campuses, at festivals, and in workshops at public schools around the country. In summer 1982 Jones received a National Heritage Fellowship from the National Endowment for the Arts. In 1982 Jones's book, *Step It Down: Games, Plays, Songs and Stories from the Afro-American Heritage*, cowritten with Hawes, was published. In 1983 Jones published her autobiography (cowritten with John Stewart), *For the Ancestors: Autobiographical Memories*.

A legendary folk performer, Jones was also a cultural steward, actively keeping alive the traditions that had been passed on to her by her parents and grandparents, former slaves on the mainland, and those of the Sea Islands community. As such, Jones educated audiences a century removed from slavery in her performances, and she preserved the music, songs, tales, and other folklore in her recordings and books. Jones died of complications from leukemia at Glynn-Brunswick Memorial Hospital in Brunswick, Georgia, at the age of eighty-two.

FURTHER READING
Jones, Bessie. *For Ancestors: Autobiographical Memories*, ed. John Stewart (1983; repr. 1989).

Jones, Bessie, and Bess Lomax Hawes. *Step It Down: Games, Plays, Songs and Stories from the Afro-American Heritage* (1972; repr. 1987).

Jones, Bessie, and John Stewart. *For the Ancestors: Autographical Memories* (1983).

Parrish, Lydia, comp. *Slave Songs of the Georgia Sea Islands* (1942; repr. 1992).

Obituary: *New York Times*, 8 Sept. 1984.

GAYLE MURCHISON

Jones, Bill T. (15 Feb. 1952–), dancer and choreographer, was born William Tass Jones in Bunnell, Florida, the tenth of twelve children of Ella and Augustus Jones, migrant farmworkers who traveled throughout the Southeast. The family became "stagnants" in 1959, when they settled in the predominantly white community of Wayland in the Finger Lakes region of upstate New York. There they harvested fruits and vegetables and also operated a restaurant and juke joint.

In childhood Jones navigated between the rural, southern black cultural values of his home life and the predominantly white middle-class world of his peers at school. Black English was spoken at home, white English in the classroom. That experience was not without its complications and, sometimes, pain, but Jones believed that it served him well as a performer by teaching him that the "world was a place of struggle that had to be negotiated" (Washington, 190). He did well at school, won awards for public speaking, directed a production of Arthur Miller's *The Crucible*, and starred on the track team. But Jones also cultivated an independent streak that one of his teachers, Mary Lee Shappee, encouraged. An outspoken atheist in a largely devout community, Shappee advised him, "There's something more than this" (Washington, 191).

Determined to find that "something," Jones entered the State University of New York at

Binghamton in 1970 to study drama and prepare for a career on Broadway. He found himself increasingly isolated from fellow black students, however, believing that they viewed him as an "unauthentic, white dependent Negro" (Jones, 81). Although he had been in relationships with women in high school, he was also sexually attracted to men and was intrigued by a student group poster with the invitation "Gay?? Come Out and Meet Your Brothers and Sisters!!" At the consciousness-raising meeting, Jones confessed that coming out was especially difficult for him, because he was convinced that African Americans felt that being gay was the "ultimate emasculation of the black man" (Jones, 82).

During his second semester Jones met Arnie Zane, a Jewish–Italian American photographer and drama student from Queens, New York. In 1971 Zane became Jones's first male lover, and the couple began a personal and professional partnership that would last for seventeen years. Jones had begun dance lessons shortly before meeting Zane, but it was Zane who inspired his passion for dance. Jones enrolled in Afro-Caribbean and West African dance classes at Binghamton with the Trinidadian choreographer PERCIVAL BORDE, participated in workshops on contact improvisation, and became grounded in the Cecchetti method of classical ballet. Martha Graham, who codified the language of modern dance, and Jerome Robbins, who choreographed *West Side Story*, were also influential in his development as a dancer.

During the early 1970s Jones and Zane lived a peripatetic, bohemian existence, first in Amsterdam and then in San Francisco, before returning to Binghamton in 1974. There the couple helped a fellow dancer, Lois Welk, revive her American Dance Asylum, supplementing their income with part-time jobs—Zane as a go-go dancer and Jones as a laundry worker. By 1976 Jones was beginning to achieve recognition in the dance world, receiving a Creative Artist Public Service Award for *Everybody Works/All Beasts Count*, a performance in which he spun around half naked in Central Park while shouting, "I love you," to the heavens in memory of two of his favorite aunts.

Determined to establish their own distinctive style, Jones and Zane rejected both the refined, regimented modernism that they believed characterized ALVIN AILEY's Dance Theater of Harlem and the cultural nationalist aesthetic of the Black Arts Movement. Instead, they developed an avant-garde approach influenced by Yvonne Rainier, a postmodernist choreographer and filmmaker known for her experiments with fragmented movements and for placing characters and narrative in radical

Bill T. Jones, the co-founder and artistic director of the Bill T. Jones/Arnie Zane Dance Company, poses in the spotlight during rehearsals in Chicago while on tour in December 1992. (AP Images.)

juxtapositions. From the beginning of Jones and Zane's collaboration, reviewers noted that the bodies, movements, and personalities of the two dancers provided the most dramatic juxtaposition of all. As one early review noted: "Mr. Jones is black, with a long, lithe body, a fine speaking voice and a look of leashed hostility. Mr. Zane is white, short and chunky, with a buoyant, strutting walk and the very funny look of an officious floorwalker in a second-rate department store" (*New York Times*, 5 Apr. 1981). The couple also experimented with innovative locations for their performances—including the Battery Park Landfill in lower Manhattan—and often employed dancers who had little in the way of professional dance training. Looking back at their work in the late 1970s and early 1980s, Jones recalled that he and Zane "used to turn up our nose at refined technique. We thought it made for dead art. Instead, we'd look for the beauty in falling, running or in watching a large person jump" (*People*, 31 July 1989).

Jones and Zane left the American Dance Asylum in 1980, and the following year Jones appeared in

Social Intercourse: Pilgrim's Progress, which was one of five pieces by promising newcomers selected for performance at the prestigious American Dance Festival in Durham, North Carolina. In that piece Jones improvised a solo with a monologue in which he paired seemingly paradoxical outbursts: "I love white people / I hate white people; Why didn't you leave us in Africa? / I'm so thankful for the opportunity to be here; and I love women / I hate women." Jones's provocative style also ensured plenty of detractors, notably the *New Yorker's* Arlene Croce, who described his work as narcissistic. In 1982 Jones and Zane founded Bill T. Jones/Arnie Zane and Company, with Zane focusing mainly on directing and managing and Jones starring as the primary dancer. The company debuted the following year at the Brooklyn Academy of Music with *Intuitive Momentum*, a performance that drew on the martial arts, vaudeville, and social dance and which received positive reviews for the dancers' frenzied, acrobatic movements. The company won its first New York Dance and Performance Award (known as "Bessies") for its 1986 season at New York's Joyce Theater, and soon emerged as among the most popular and challenging troupes in the world of modern dance. In March 1988, however, with Jones at his bedside, Zane died of AIDS-related lymphoma. Jones, too, was diagnosed as HIV positive in the 1980s but remained asymptomatic. The couple's last collaboration, *Body against Body* (1989), includes Zane's photos, Jones's poetry and prose, performance scripts, and commentaries by dancers, critics, composers, and others.

Jones's career continued to flourish after his partner's death, and the company—which retained Zane's name—remained true to its founders' vision of an inclusive troupe that embraced different races, sexual orientations, and body shapes. Jones received a second Bessie in 1989 for *D-Man in the Waters*, and the following year, along with his sister Rhodessa Jones, he won an Isadora Duncan Dance Award (Izzy) for *Perfect Courage*.

Despite his growing fame, Jones continued to infuriate some reviewers, notably for *Last Supper at Uncle Tom's Cabin/The Promised Land* (1990), a multimedia work that ended with audience members joining the dancers on stage in taking off all of their clothes. Jones responded to those critics by noting that the nudity was the entire point of the piece. "In this polarized, sexually very confused city," he told the *New York Times*, "can we stand up as a group and not be ashamed of our nakedness?" (4 Nov. 1990). Even more controversial was *Still/Here* (1994), a work that addressed the subject of death and dying. The

performance incorporated videotaped testimonies of a diverse range of people with terminal illnesses that Jones had collected at "Survival Workshops" that he had organized in several American cities. The *New Yorker's* Arlene Croce dismissed the work as "victim art" and refused to attend the performance, provoking a firestorm of debate among Jones's many admirers and detractors.

The clearest answer to Jones's critics has been the steady flow of awards that he and his company continue to receive. These honors include a MacArthur Foundation award in 1994, a Laurence Olivier Award for Outstanding Achievement in Dance and Best New Dance Production for *We Set Out Early … Visibility Was Poor* (1999), a second Izzy for *Fantasy in C-Major* (2001), and a third Bessie for *The Table Project* and *The Breathing Show* (2001). In addition to choreographing more than fifty works for his own company, Jones has also received commissions for works for, among others, the Boston Ballet, the Berlin Opera Ballet, the Houston Grand Opera, and the Glyndebourne Festival in England. In 1995 Jones teamed up with the legendary jazz drummer MAX ROACH and the Nobel Prize–winning author TONI MORRISON to produce *Degga*, a collaboration of dance, percussion, and spoken word at the Lincoln Center's Serious Fun Festival. Perhaps the most significant and fitting of Jones's awards came in 2002, however, when the Dance Heritage Coalition of America named him an "Irreplaceable Dance Treasure."

In 2007 Jones won a Tony award for choreography in *Spring Awakening*, a feat he repeated in 2010 with the musical *Fela!* about the Nigerian musician and political activist, Fela Kuti.

FURTHER READING
Jones, Bill T., and Peggy Gillespie. *Last Night on Earth* (1995).
Gates, Henry Louis, Jr. *Thirteen Ways of Looking at a Black Man* (1997).
Washington, Eric K. "Sculpture in Flight," *Transition* 62 (1993).

ELSHADAY GEBREYES AND
STEVEN J. NIVEN

Jones, Billy (1946–), the first African American to play college varsity basketball in the Atlantic Coast Conference, was born in Towson, Maryland, and raised by his mother, Ruth Jones, after her husband Ernest Jones was killed by the collapse of a trench he was working in. Jones, who always found the name William "so aristocratic and formal," grew up on the east side of Towson, near Baltimore, where his family had lived since 1903. While east Towson was overwhelmingly African American, the Towson Theater, six blocks from home, refused admission to anyone of dark skin color until 1969. Ruth Jones worked as a maid on the west side of Towson to support her four daughters and son. Towson High School, where Jones graduated, was described as "predominantly white" (Martin, p. 156).

The first African American signed to an Atlantic Coast Conference (ACC) team, Jones was little noticed in the media. Maryland coach Herman "Bud" Millikan gave Jones credit for the lack of drama. "Had I gone into detail about how mistreated the University of Maryland and/or Billy Jones were" said Millikan, "why there'd have been much, much written," but "because of Billy Jones being like he is, it was dropped. Had there been turmoil, it would have been news" (Jacobs, p. 2).

Jones and his teammate Pete Johnson, who started classes the same year, but joined the varsity squad a year later, said there had been many racial incidents that Millikan never knew about, because they chose not to tell him or make an issue of it. "I give Millikan credit," said Jones. "His moral fiber was operating correctly. He didn't understand the scenario. I *am* different. When somebody tells me, 'I never see you as a black person.' My message to them is 'Then you don't see me.' Because I *am* black" (Jacobs, p. 9). White teammates were protective during road trips to states further south, one making a point of assuring him "Don't worry about a thing."

One of the more dramatic incidents in the team's games with Jones on the squad came in 1965 when the Terrapins arrived in New Orleans to play in the Sugar Bowl Tournament. Jones thus became the first African American to appear on the varsity squad in a major postseason basketball game south of the Mason-Dixon line, for a historically white university.

When the team came into the dining room of their hotel, the chef, who was African American, came out of the kitchen to shake his hand, as did several others of the kitchen staff. "I knew what they were doing" Jones later recalled, "Other folks didn't. 'Do you know those people?' they asked. 'Nah, I don't know them.' They were acknowledging the fact that here's this black guy in uniform in a scenario that's not typically seen down here" (Jacobs, p. 1). The city was under a federal court order to register African Americans to vote at the time, highlighting racial tension.

Jones had no thought of a professional career in the National Basketball Association. "My whole point was, I'll swap my basketball for a degree" he later recalled. "I'll go down there and play my heart out for Coach Millkan, and in return I'll get a degree. That's my focus; I want to get a degree" (Jacobs, p. 8).

By the turn of the twenty-first century, college and professional basketball teams commonly had a majority of African American players, but it was not until the 1981–1982 season that more than half of ACC players were black. When North Carolina State took the NCAA title in 1982, all five starters were of African descent. Jones served as cocaptain his senior year. After graduation he earned a master's degree at California Polytechnic State University, San Luis Obispo, then worked as assistant coach at Stanford University. In June 1974 Jones left Stanford to take a job as head basketball coach at University of Maryland, Baltimore County, for twelve years.

He has since pursued a human resources career in private industry, focused on wellness and benefits, immigration policy, project management, and worker expertise. He worked as a college recruiter for Martin Marietta Aero and Naval Systems, 1987–1989, then manager of human resources and chief of college relations for the same company until 1993. After a year as manager of human resources for Tupperware in 1993, he began work as manager of segment benefits and wellness at Walt Disney World in Orlando, Florida, 1996–2009, then as health services manager for Walt Disney Parks and Resorts U.S. Jones is a member of Omicron Delta Kappa–National Leadership Society.

FURTHER READING

Jacobs, Barry. *Across the Line: Profiles in Basketball Courage; Tales of the First Black Players in the ACC and SEC* (2008).

Martin, Charles. *Benching Jim Crow: The Rise and Fall of the Color Line in Southern College Sports, 1890–1980* (2010).

Ungrady, Dave. *Legends of Maryland Basketball* (2004).

CHARLES ROSENBERG

Jones, Billy (17 Dec. 1912–20 Mar. 1987), attorney, civil rights pioneer, and Illinois circuit judge best known as "Judge Billy Jones," was born in St. Louis, Missouri, and formally named William Jones, the only child of Nathaniel (or Nathan) and Helen Jones. He grew up across the Mississippi River in East St. Louis, Illinois, where he attended Dunbar Elementary and Lincoln High School. His father, born in Mississippi, owned a pool hall. His mother, born in Illinois to parents from Alabama and Tennessee, generally did not work outside the home.

After graduation, he became a drummer, and served as director of a local music project sponsored during the Great Depression by the Works Progress Administration. He later enrolled at Tennessee Agricultural and Industrial State College (now Tennessee State University) in Nashville, where his teachers included Dr. Merle R. Eppse, chair of the History and Political Science Department. Graduating cum laude, he entered Howard University Law School, where he earned the LL.B degree.

Returning to East St. Louis in 1945, Jones established his own law practice. He was helped by the advice of David M. Grant, who had entered legal practice and civil rights advocacy in his native St. Louis, across the Mississippi River in Missouri, some ten years earlier. Grant advised Jones to open his office earlier, stay at work later, take every opportunity to speak to groups in the community, and every Sunday, go to Sunday School at one church, worship service at a second, and an afternoon gathering at another, every week. Above all, he advised "Get a cause and stick with it! And East St. Louis is *pregnant* with causes" (Grant, pp. 156–157).

Jones professed faith as a Roman Catholic at an early age, and for most of his adult life was a member of St. Joseph's Parish in East St. Louis. He married Mildred O. Mattison. Jones and the local NAACP president David Owens organized a group of adults on 31 January 1949 to bring children classified as "Negro" into nine half-empty East St. Louis schools reserved for students classified as "white." This was not only a protest against Jim Crow education, but a protest against busing—at that time, used to send students of African descent on long bus trips to racially segregated schools.

After three days, at Grant's urging, the sit-in at the schools ended, partly out of concern that children might be hurt or killed. Jones followed up the spectacular protest with litigation. Reference to a state law denying funds to school districts practicing discrimination threatened the school board with the loss of $677,898. *The Crisis* reported in April 1950, "Jim Crow schools no longer exist in East St. Louis Illinois. When 105 Negro students of that city took their rightful places in the classrooms of the formerly all-white schools on January 30, 1950, the fight of the local NAACP branch to break down segregation had been won." Public commercial facilities, such as theaters, restaurants, and drive-in movies, soon followed. Jones filed similar suits in Sparta and Cairo, Illinois.

In 1952 he was a consultant in school discrimination cases presented to the United States Supreme Court, which were joined with those decided as *Brown v. Board of Education*, 17 May 1954. Also in 1954, Jones joined in the investigation of the murder of George Lee, a Baptist minister in Belzoni, Mississippi, founder of the local NAACP branch, and one of only ninety-five Americans of African descent in the county registered to vote, long rumored to be first on the hit list of terrorists associated with the local White Citizens Council. Considerable effort had been made to avoid investigation of the killing in isolated Humphreys County, with a 1950 population of sixteen thousand "Negroes," and seven thousand "whites," of whom a total of two thousand were registered to vote. The night Lee was shot driving home from a dry cleaners, telephone operators told callers that all long-distance lines were "in use."

One of several witnesses to the murder, Alex Hudson, had fled to East St. Louis, where he was staying with his sister. He showed Jones a letter of recommendation from his employer, stating that Hudson had had to leave the state "due to circumstances beyond his or our control." Jones, serving at the time as president of the state conference of the NAACP in Illinois, and chair of the East St. Louis Legal Redress Committee, obtained an affidavit concerning the murder of Lee, and persuaded Hudson to talk to the Federal Bureau of Investigation. The FBI refused to allow Jones to be present during the interview. The FBI built a substantial case, but local prosecutors refused to present it to a grand jury (Mendelsohn, p. 9).

In 1955 Jones filed unsuccessfully for a writ of habeas corpus to release Artes Jones from custody in the St. Clair County jail, based on a request for extradition to Mississippi. The fugitive warrant charged Artes Jones with "obtaining money under false pretenses." His attorney argued that Artes had not committed any crime, and that if returned to Mississippi he would be imprisoned for debt, in violation of the federal constitution (*The Crisis* 62, no. 19, Dec 1955, p. 628). This was the same year that the murderers of EMMETT TILL had been acquitted and released by a Mississippi court. NAACP branches around the country were raising funds in response to a call by THURGOOD MARSHALL of the NAACP Legal Defense Fund to "help fight terrorism in Mississippi" (ibid., p. 587).

Jones was elected president of the Illinois NAACP in 1954, and became a life member of the NAACP at the organization's 1956 convention. In 1963 Jones was among the team of attorneys providing pro bono defense to a group of Congress on

Racial Equality (CORE) members who had blocked the entrance to Jefferson Bank in St. Louis, in defiance of a court injunction. CORE, after a careful study of hiring practices, had written to the bank demanding the immediate hiring of four Negroes; the bank's attorney, Wayne L. Millsap, responded that there were not "four blacks in the city" qualified for white-collar jobs, which triggered massive picket lines at the bank (Clay, William L., *Bill Clay: A Political Voice at the Grass Roots*, p. 111).

In 1965 Jones was appointed as an associate circuit judge of the Twentieth Judicial Circuit Court of Illinois, the first American of African descent to hold such a position. He was known as "Judge Billy Jones" for the rest of his life. In 1967 he was elected to a one-year term as president of the National Bar Association.

In 1981 Jones attracted the attention of *Car and Driver* magazine (vol. 27, p. 29) for dismissing Chicago traffic court cases at the rate of three hundred an hour, after requiring violators to raise their right hand and repeat, "I do hereby absolutely promise, now and in the future, not to park where I'm not supposed to."

By the end of his life, Jones had served as a lector of St. Joseph's parish; member of the board of St. Mary's Hospital, East St. Louis; a member of the Knights of Peter Claver, St. Augustine Council No. 268; president of the Howard University Alumni Association; Midwestern vice president of Alpha Phi Alpha fraternity; founder and first president of the fraternity's Delta Epsilon Lambda chapter; chair of the Economic Opportunity Commission of St. Clair County; commissioner of the Court of Claims for Illinois; and life member of the YMCA.

Jones died shortly after being hospitalized for an unexpected illness, and was received into the Omega Chapter of Alpha Phi Alpha. He was survived by his wife, three children (Lolita D'Jones, Billy Jones Jr., and Therese Helena Jones Johnson), and five grandchildren. In 1987 the former Monroe Elementary school was renamed for Judge Jones. An older building, it was closed in 2011 due to ongoing physical maintenance problems. The third Monday in September has been observed as Judge Billy Jones Day in East St. Louis, by proclamation of successive mayors. In 1992 Jones was inducted posthumously into the National Bar Association Hall of Fame.

FURTHER READING
Grant, Gail Milissa. *At the Elbows of My Elders* (2008).
Mendelsohn, Jack. *The Martyrs: Sixteen Who Gave Their Lives for Racial Justice* (1966).

Obituary: *The Sphinx* 73, no. 3 (Fall 1987): 58.

CHARLES ROSENBERG

Jones, Booker T. (12 Nov. 1944–), multi-instrumentalist, producer, and arranger, was born in Memphis, Tennessee, to Booker T. Jones Sr., a high school teacher, and his wife, a school secretary. His musical talent showed early on: at age five he learned to play ukulele and piano. Five years later his parents bought him a clarinet. He played oboe in his high school band and also mastered flute, saxophone, trombone, and baritone horn. Inspired by RAY CHARLES, Jones started playing club gigs at age fourteen. Two years later, in 1960, he began work as a session musician for Stax Records in Memphis.

In 1962 Jones formed the instrumental group Booker T. and the MGs with members of the Mar-Keys, the first house band of Stax who had scored a national hit in 1961 with "Last Night." Depending on the source, the band was either named after the British sports car or after an abbreviation for "Memphis Group." Unusually for the time, Booker T. and the MGs consisted of two black players—Jones on Hammond M-1 and later B-3 organ and AL JACKSON on drums—and two white players—Steve Cropper on electric guitar and Donald (Duck) Dunn on bass guitar. Their first and biggest hit "Green Onions" (1962) evolved out of a jam session and was originally released as the B side of the blues number "Behave Yourself." However, Jones's chopped-up organ riff, Cropper's staccato guitar licks, Dunn's rhythmic bass playing and Jackson's spare drum beats catapulted the song to number one on the R&B charts and number three on the pop charts.

In the following years Jones worked on his bachelor's degree in Music Education at Indiana University. Majoring in trombone, he made the dean's list and graduated in 1966. He married his first wife Wilette (Gigi) Armstrong when he was a freshman in college. In addition to his studies, Jones continued to work for Stax as a studio musician, arranger, and producer. The MGs served as the house band for the label, backing up OTIS REDDING, Sam & Dave, the Staple Singers, Eddie Floyd, and many others in the studio and occasionally on stage as well. Jones also produced many Stax musicians, including blues guitarist ALBERT KING. Between 1963 and 1968 Booker T. and the MGs appeared on more than 600 Stax/Volt recordings. Their groove-oriented, rhythmic style was called the "Memphis Sound" and employed a grittier and less polished approach than did Detroit's Motown records. As an instrumental group, Booker T. and the MGs had seven Top Forty hits in the 1960s, most notably "Time Is Tight," number six on the pop charts in 1968, and "Hang 'Em High," number nine on the pop charts in 1969, both of which highlighted Jones's floating organ lines.

In 1968 Jones began using string arrangements on Stax recordings, which set a trend for soul music in the 1970s. The MGs's soundtrack for Jules Dassin's movie *Uptight* about black militancy from 1968 predated both ISAAC HAYES's *Shaft* (1971) and CURTIS MAYFIELD's *Superfly* (1972). Despite his growing success, Jones, who had become vice president of Stax in 1968, became dissatisfied with the company's politics and left it as an employee in 1969. However, he continued to record with the MGs until they finally disbanded in 1972. Their last two records showcased the versatility of the group. *McLemore Avenue* (1970), named after the street where Stax was located, was a treatment of the Beatles' *Abbey Road*. *Melting Pot* (1971), on the other hand, contained all originals and saw the band experimenting with expanded jazz jams. The latter album was only released after some resistance from Stax co-owner Jim Stewart, who deemed it not commercial enough.

By 1969 Jones had moved to Hollywood, eventually joining A&M records as staff producer. He recorded with his second wife Priscilla, sister of the soul singer Rita Coolidge. Booker T. and the MGs reunited in 1974 and were working on another album when Jackson was fatally shot on 1 October 1975. In 1977 Jones joined Levon Helm's RCO All Stars for an album and a tour. Jones's credits as a producer included BILL WITHERS, Coolidge, and country singer Willie Nelson, whose 1978 effort *Stardust*, produced by Jones, went multiplatinum and remained on the pop charts for two years. Jones also worked as a session musician for Charles, Barbra Streisand, Bob Dylan, and various others. The music of Booker T. and the MGs appeared in many Hollywood movies such as *American Graffiti* (1973) and *Barfly* (1987). After Jones had tried his luck as a soul singer in the 1980s, he reunited with the MGs in 1990 for a tour of the United States and Europe. In 1992 Booker T. and the MGs were inducted into the Rock and Roll Hall of Fame. On 16 October 1992 they served as the house band for the four-hour Bob Dylan Tribute concert at Madison Square Garden. The following year they accompanied the Canadian rock star Neil Young on a tour and eventually recorded an album with Young in 2001. In 1994 Booker T. and the MGs released *That's the Way It Should Be*, their first album since 1977. The song "Cruisin'" won a Grammy as Best Pop Instrumental Performance in the same year. Jones continued to live and work as a musician in Los Angeles with his third wife Nan and three children.

Jones significantly shaped the "Memphis Sound" of Stax records and was involved with different areas of music production. With the MGs, Jones made soul music palpable for a larger audience, attracting the pop market as well as the R&B market. At the same time, the group did not compromise their spare and groove-oriented sound that set a contrast to Motown's orchestrated pop-soul. Jones's musical talents were diverse. He may have had his strongest effect as a popularizer of the Hammond B-3 organ.

FURTHER READING
Bowman, Rob. *Soulsville, U.S.A.: The Story of Stax Records* (1997).
Garland, Phyl. "Booker T. and the MGs," *Ebony* (April 1969).
Guralnick, Peter. *Sweet Soul Music* (1986).
ULRICH ADELT

Jones, Charles Price (9 Dec. 1865–19 Jan. 1949), pastor, holiness preacher, composer, and denominational leader, was born in Texas Valley, Georgia. He was born the son of Clifford Milner and a Baptist mother, Mary Jones Milner. The Milners gave birth to three children. Jones's father died and his mother remarried Berry Latimer with whom she had a daughter, Lucy. After his mother died in 1882, Jones moved to Cat Island, Arkansas, where he was saved in 1884. In May 1885 he was baptized and joined Locust Grove Baptist Church and that same year started preaching. He was licensed in 1887 by George W. Dickey, then pastor of Locust Grove. Three years later Jones left Cat Island, going to Helena, Arkansas, where he joined Centennial Baptist Church, pastored by ELIAS CAMP MORRIS, then president of the Arkansas Baptist Convention. Jones later moved to Little Rock in order to enroll at Arkansas Baptist College in 1888, the year he also entered the pastorate and was ordained by Charles Lewis Fisher, the academic dean of Arkansas Baptist College.

Several important events took place in Jones's life in the year 1891. He left Saint Paul Baptist Church, where he had been since November 1888, to take over Bethlehem Baptist Church in Searcy, Arkansas. Jones graduated from college and married Fannie

Brown of Little Rock. They had a daughter, Ola Mae, in 1893. Ola, the only child from this marriage, died three years later.

In 1892 Jones accepted the call to Tabernacle Baptist Church in Selma, Alabama, where he remained until 1895. While in Selma, Jones claimed the blessing of sanctification. The general belief was that without this subsequent experience, one was doomed to go to hell. Since 1866 the doctrine of sanctification, also called the doctrine of holiness, had been promoted in the entire country by the National Holiness Association through conventions and literature. In turn, black evangelists such as AMANDA BERRY SMITH and JULIA FOOTE disseminated the doctrine of holiness in black communities by preaching widely in settings mostly connected to Methodism. The entry of Jones into the holiness movement is significant because he was one of the few promoters of holiness among black Baptist communities in the South and beyond.

In 1895 Jones responded to the call of the Mount Helm Baptist Church in Jackson, Mississippi, which then became the base of his ministerial work for the next twenty-two years. Committed to holiness, Jones founded a newspaper, *The Truth*, and published a booklet, "The Work of the Holy Spirit in the Churches," in 1896. The following year he started organizing annual holiness conventions and later opened Christ's Holiness School. Though Jones's conventions were interracial, interdenominational, and interstate, he became the target of reprisals from Baptist associations in Mississippi and Arkansas. Black Baptists from the South had been strictly Calvinistic and influenced by Landmarkism, a doctrine inherited from the white Baptists James R. Graves and James M. Pendleton that held, among other things, that the believer was doomed to sin and therefore could not be perfected in this world and that only Baptists who had been baptized by a Baptist minister were true Christians. Jones's embrace of Landmarkism drew the ire of the Jackson Missionary Baptist Association (JMBA) and the local church elders because his movement was ecumenical. In 1900 he was expelled from the JMBA and two years later his elders forced him out of Mount Helm. Jones first tried to change the name of the congregation to Church of Christ; when this failed, he left Mount Helm with a large following, bought land, and in 1902 erected a new frame church, Christ's Tabernacle.

Jones was a prolific songwriter. He published several songbooks *Jesus Only* I (1899), *Jesus Only* II (1901), *Selected Songs* (1901), and *Fullness Songs* (1906). Jones was so prolific that he claimed to have written one thousand songs. As a black leader and with his new book, *An Appeal to the Sons of Africa* (1902), he encouraged black youths to get more education. Like most urban ministers of the era, Jones preached that the way to racial uplift was through religious, educational, and economic development and not through white politicians.

In 1903 he built a large complex that included a 1,200-seat sanctuary, a printing press, and a school building. The entire complex was burned in 1905 by a mob that he believed was sent by James Vardaman, the governor of Mississippi. Elected in 1903, Vardaman was well known as a racist, an advocate of lynching for rapes committed against white women by black men, and a critic of both black education and educated blacks. He believed that blacks should be employed only in menial jobs. Without any concrete proof, the mob alleged that a black man had molested a white woman and hidden in the church. Jones denied the presence of any criminal on his property. Nevertheless firemen were not allowed by the mob to extinguish the fire. Jones later claimed that he had attracted the attention of white racists who could not stand "the idea of a Nigger printing books" (Cobbins, 416). In the same vein, rapes and lynching were not common in the city of Jackson. Prior to 1902 only one lynching was reported in Jackson, in 1895, and that was for larceny. After 1895 the next reported lynching was in 1906, for killing a horse. Thus the mob's allegations behind the burning of Jones's church may be further questioned. In 1906 Jones rebuilt the church building, which now seated two thousand.

Through his paper, conventions, and wide preaching, Jones secured a large following among the black Baptist ministry and laity of Mississippi and beyond. When ministers and churches were removed from intolerant Baptist associations, they found in Jones a leader ready to provide whatever support they needed. Jones continued to host annual conventions, and it was only in 1906 that a new denomination was organized, with Jones as general overseer. The new denomination took up the name "the Church of God in Christ" (COGIC). CHARLES H. MASON, overseer of Tennessee and Jones's assistant, claimed that God gave him this name as he was walking down a street in Little Rock. Nevertheless, some local congregations still used other names such as "Church of God" or "Church of Christ" to designate themselves. Because of Baptist sectarianism, Jones's followers looked for local church names to identify affiliations.

Between 1902 and 1910, auxiliaries such as the Christian Women Willing Workers, the Foreign Missions Board, and the Holiness Young People's Union were organized. Meanwhile, the holiness school became Christ's Missionary and Industrial College (CMI), which transferred to a 142-acre farm. With more space CMI also became a coeducational boarding school whose graduates served as ministers and leaders of a growing denomination.

In 1907 the COGIC under Jones's leadership suffered a split over the issue of the Pentecostal baptism of the Holy Spirit. Two views emerged on the Holy Spirit within the COGIC. On the one hand, there were those like Jones who claimed that speaking in tongues was biblical but could not be the only evidence of the Holy Spirit. For this faction the essential evidences of the Holy Spirit were love, faith, and hope. On the other hand, Mason and others stood by the view that speaking in tongues was the initial evidence of the baptism of the Holy Spirit. Since Mason was not willing to change his position, Jones expelled him. Mason opened another organization and won a court judgment to keep the name "the Church of God in Christ." This forced Jones to choose "the Church of Christ (Holiness)" as the new name for his organization. In 1915 Arkansas Baptist College awarded Jones the honorific doctor of divinity degree.

In 1916 Fannie Brown died; two years later Jones married another woman, Pearl Reed, and the couple had three sons. In 1927 Jones assumed the title of senior bishop and consecrated four other junior bishops. For twenty-two years he pastored in Los Angeles, where he died. Following the death of its founder, the growth of the Church of Christ Holiness (U.S.A.)—it changed its name in 1915— was steady but not phenomenal. At the end of 1998 it reported 167 churches and more than 10,000 members in the United States. Its foreign missions program reached Liberia, Benin, Mali, and the Dominican Republic.

FURTHER READING

Beasley, Delilah L. *The Negro Trailblazers of California* (1919; repr.1997).

Clemmons, Ithiel. *Bishop C. H. Mason and the Roots of the Church of God in Christ* (1996).

Cobbins, Otho B., ed. *History of Church of Christ (Holiness)* (1966).

Crawford, Isaiah W., and Patrick H. Thompson. *Multum in Parvo: An Authenticated History of Progressive Negroes in Pleasing and Graphic Biographical Style* (1912).

Dayton, Donald W. *Theological Roots of Pentecostalism* (1987).

Goff, James R., Jr., and Grant Wacker. *Portraits of a Generation* (2002).

Holmes, William F. *The White Chief: James Kimble Vardaman* (1970).

Williams, Lawrence H. "Black Landmarkism: Sectarian Theology among the National Baptists," *Baptist History and Heritage* (Oct. 1993): 45–54.

DAVID MICHEL

Jones, Clara Stanton (14 May 1913–30 Sept. 2012), pioneering librarian and community advocate, was born in St. Louis, Missouri, the fourth of five children born to Etta James Stanton and Ralph Herbert Stanton. Ralph Stanton worked as an insurance supervisor with several African American insurance companies and was the son of a former slave and grandson of a slave owner in Natchez, Mississippi. Etta James, also the descendant of slaves, was born in St. Geneve, Missouri, and worked as a teacher and amateur pianist and organist. The Stanton family was very close-knit and placed a high priority on education and community involvement. Clara Stanton attended the segregated public schools of St. Louis and went on to attend Milwaukee State Teachers College for a year. She then transferred to Spelman College in Atlanta, Georgia, where she graduated with an A.B. degree in English and History in 1934. All five Stanton children graduated from college, and her younger sister also became a professional librarian.

From a very early age Clara had felt at home in libraries. She taught herself how to use the card catalog and became very adept at selecting her own reading materials. With her love of libraries well in place, it was not hard for several trusted adults to plant the seed in her mind that one day she should pursue librarianship as a career.

Her actual library career began as a paraprofessional at the Atlanta University library, where she was a clerk-typist in the cataloging department while still a student at Spelman. The professional librarians for whom she worked nurtured her interests and potential; it was a librarian at Atlanta University who guided her toward the University of Michigan at Ann Arbor as the best library school for Jones and played a role in getting her accepted into the program. Shortly after attaining her BLS degree in Library Science from Michigan in 1938, Stanton married Albert Jones, a social worker. The couple settled in New Orleans and eventually would have three children: Stanton William,

Vinetta Clair, and Kenneth Albert. In New Orleans she worked as a reference librarian for Dillard University and in 1940 became associate librarian at Southern University in Baton Rouge. In 1944 the family moved to Detroit, and it was here, at the Detroit Public Library, that Jones would make an indelible and legendary contribution over the next thirty-four years.

At the time Jones joined the Detroit Public Library she was one of only three African American librarians working in the citywide library system. During her lengthy tenure in Detroit she worked her way up in the ranks from librarian to library neighborhood consultant, which was a middle-management position that called on Jones to serve as a liaison between the library and the community at large. In this position she used her speaking, program development, outreach, public relations, and marketing skills to promote the library as a place of education open to everyone. She also played a key role in Detroit race relations following the riot of 1943. Jones became a volunteer speaker for the then-mayor's Interracial Commission (later the Commission on Community Relations); in this outreach position, Jones's task was to speak to predominantly white audiences and act as an ambassador for the black community. By relating the goals and culture of the black community to outside audiences, while simultaneously getting feedback from the white community, Jones was able to act as a bridge and facilitate race relations in the city of Detroit.

Despite issues of race and gender, Jones was encouraged and promoted by a determined member of the library's hiring commission who was steadfast in his belief that Jones was the most qualified person for the position of director and that the library system would benefit from her twenty-five years of expertise in the library system. After some controversy, in 1970 Jones was appointed as the director of the Detroit Public Library, the library's first female and first African American director. Her appointment also made her the first African American director of any major city public library.

As director, Jones stabilized the library financially and became a known and sought-after speaker locally, nationally, and internationally on the topics of public library financial health and survival and library services to disenfranchised populations. She ran for president of the American Library Association in 1974; she did not win her bid, but owing to the successful candidate's illness, Jones did become acting president and was then elected president in her own right in 1976,

becoming the first African American to lead the American Library Association. She continued to serve the organization as a councilor until 1978. Also in 1978 she retired from her position as director of the Detroit Public Library.

A powerful and dynamic speaker, Jones was well loved and respected by both the library and African American communities. She received nine honorary doctorate degrees; she was appointed by President Jimmy Carter to serve on the National Commission on Libraries and Information Science from 1978 to 1982; and the American Library Association awarded her its Honorary Lifetime Membership Award (the organization's highest honor) in 1983. For her contributions to the library profession and to the African American community, Clara Stanton Jones is revered as a pioneer. She died in Oakland, California, aged 99.

FURTHER READING

The personal papers of Clara Stanton Jones are housed in the library of the School of Library Science, North Carolina Central University. An oral history, conducted in 1972 by Ann Allen Shockley, is housed in the Black Oral History Collection at the Fisk University Library.

Josey, E. J. "Clara Stanton Jones," in *Notable Black American Women*, ed. Jessie Carney Smith (1992).

McCook, Kathleen de la Pena. "Clara Stanton Jones," in *Women of Color in Librarianship*, ed. Kathleen de la Pena McCook (1998).

NICOLE A. COOKE

Jones, Claudia (21 Dec. 1915–25 Dec. 1964), writer, activist, and newspaper editor was born in Port-of-Spain, Trinidad, the second eldest of four daughters. Jones's mother worked in a garment factory while her father held a series of jobs as a furrier, elevator operator, newspaper editor, janitor, and apartment building superintendent. During her early childhood, Port-of-Spain hosted vigorous labor and anti-colonial protests. In 1924, at the age of eight, Claudia sailed with her three sisters to the United States, joining her parents who had relocated to New York City's Harlem section. The Cumberbatches, the family surname, were part of two overlapping migrations: the Great Migration, an internal movement of African Americans that increased the Northern black population by 20 percent between 1910 and 1930, and the immigration of West Indians to the United States, which increased their numbers from 5,633 in 1907 to 12,243 in 1924. Seeking a better life, migrants often found that life was harsh up North.

Six years before the Great Depression, life for black Harlemites was already tough. Many employers barred African Americans, unions refused to represent them, and housing was segregated and often substandard. At the same time, Harlem was home to a vibrant political and cultural life where street corner preachers, artists, writers, entertainers, and activists intersected, eventually sparking the Harlem or New Negro Renaissance in the 1920s.

In Harlem, the Cumberbatches lived in abject poverty. In 1927, when Jones was about twelve years old, her mother collapsed at her sewing machine and died shortly thereafter. Jones later linked her mother's death to her interest in social change: "My mother, a machine worker in a garment factory, died when she was just the same age I am today—thirty-seven years old. I think I began then to develop an understanding of the sufferings of my people and my class and to look for a way to end them" (Jones, 33). Despite her family's worsening situation, the young Jones excelled at academics and sports, and belonged to several Harlem social clubs. In her junior year of high school, Jones contracted tuberculosis, an illness she attributed to living in a room with an open sewer line, and was forced to spend a year in the Sea View Sanitorium where she read avidly. After graduating from Wadleigh High School in 1934, Jones worked in a laundry, millinery, and lingerie shop before she began writing a column titled "Claudia's Comments" for an African American newspaper in 1932.

In 1936, Jones joined the Young Communist League (YCL), the Communist Party USA's (CPUSA's) youth section. She was inspired to do so by the CPUSA's vigorous defense of the SCOTTSBORO BOYS, nine African Americans falsely accused of raping two white women after an altercation erupted between white and black youth traveling as hobos on a train. Jones joined the YCL, the CPUSA's youth section. She quickly rose through the ranks, joining the editorial staff of the *Daily Worker* in 1937 and serving as associate editor of the *Weekly Review* from 1936 to 1938 and YCL's *Spotlight* between 1943 and 1945. During this period, she also served as the YCL's New York State chairperson. In 1940, Jones married Abraham Scholnick; however, little is known about the marriage, which ended in 1947.

In 1945, at the age of thirty, Jones formally joined the CPUSA. She was promptly elected to the National Committee, the party's highest council, and served as executive secretary to the National Negro Council from 1945 to 1946.

Jones also continued to write, serving as the editor for the *Daily Worker's* Negro Affairs Bureau from 1945 to 1946 and penning several influential pamphlets and articles, including "Jim Crow in Uniform" (1940), "Lift Every Voice—For Victory" (1942), "An End to the Neglect of the Problems of the Negro" (1949), "International Women's Day and the Struggle for Peace" (1952), and "BEN [JEFFERSON] DAVIS [JR.]: Fighter for Freedom" (1954). Although active in CPUSA circles, Jones was also a staunch advocate for gender and civil rights, agitating for greater equity within the CPUSA and embarking upon a forty-three-state speaking tour between 1947 and 1951 organized by the National Council of Negro Women. She also worked with the National Negro Congress and the Southern Negro Youth Congress, which were two early civil rights organizations.

Jones's activities drew the wrath of the federal government. Along with hundreds of Communists, Jones was harassed and arrested during the McCarthy era. Under the provisions of the 1940 Smith Act, which criminalized membership in any group that advocated the overthrow of the U.S. government, Jones received a deportation warrant on 19 January 1948. Other arrests and warrants followed in the ensuing years including one in June of 1951 accusing Jones and seventeen other CPUSA members of sedition. The government's case hinged upon an article Jones wrote urging black and white women to unite. The government's harassment of Jones and other CPUSA members sparked a defense movement sustained by the efforts of PAUL and ESLANDA ROBESON, Benjamin Davis Jr., and other close friends, which lasted from 1948 to 1955. Jones herself raised thousands of dollars, initiated dozens of appeals, and even petitioned the United Nations on behalf of herself and other CPUSA members. In July 1953, the trial of all eighteen CPUSA members ended, and Jones was sentenced to 366 days in Alderson Federal Prison for Women, a sentence she and fellow Communists Betty Gannett and Elizabeth Gurley Flynn began serving in January 1955. Prison life only further weakened Jones's already frail heart, which had been damaged by her childhood bout with tuberculosis. After serving ten months of her sentence, Jones was released and almost immediately deported to Britain.

The transition was a rough one, and Jones spent her first two months in Britain in a hospital. Upon her release, Jones continued to write and began working with the Communist Party of Great Britain and the Caribbean Labour Congress, championing the rights of black workers and African and Asian immigrants. During this period, she also began a relationship with Abhimanyu Manchanda (Manu), an immigrant from India and a fellow Communist.

In 1958 Jones and AMY ASHWOOD GARVEY launched the *West Indian Gazette*, a monthly newspaper influenced by the journal *Présence Africaine* and anticolonial writers Frantz Fanon, Kwame Nkrumah, W. E. B. DuBois, and Jomo Kenyatta. Committed to racial equality and Third World national liberation, the newspaper linked global struggles to the local lives of Caribbean immigrants. The newspaper quickly became a major vehicle for Caribbean immigrants in the U.K., particularly after white mobs attacked African, Caribbean, and Asian immigrants in the Notting Hill riots of 1958. In response, Jones began organizing an annual carnival to showcase Caribbean culture. The event, known as the Notting Hill Carnival, debuted in 1959 and became one of the largest street festivals in Europe. Despite her worsening heart disease, Jones visited Moscow, China, and Japan between 1962 and 1964. Shortly after her return to the U.K., Jones died of a massive heart attack while reading in bed. She is buried next to Karl Marx in London's Highgate Cemetery.

FURTHER READING

Some of Claudia Jones's papers have been deposited in the Communist Party Archive housed in Manchester's National Labour History Museum.

Johnson, Buzz. *'I Think of My Mother': Notes on the Life and Times of Claudia Jones* (1985).

Sherwood, Marika. *Claudia Jones: A Life in Exile* (1999).

CYNTHIA A. YOUNG

Jones, David "Deacon" (9 Dec. 1938–), football player, was born David Jones in Eatonville, Florida, five miles from Orlando. David's parents, Mattie and Ishmeal, who worked a variety of jobs including farm workers, had eight children, three boys and five girls. He was the seventh. The poverty-stricken family lived in an old, wooden house with no indoor plumbing until David attended high school. He was a three-sport star (baseball, basketball, and football) at all-black Hungerford High School.

However, all David dreamed about as a child was becoming a star professional football player. His father demanded that all three boys play the sport. But he noticed that David had the greatest potential for success in the pros. Jones said of his

father in *Pro Football Weekly*, "He used to watch me practice at 5:00 in the morning doing my running when nobody else did. He supported the hell out of me" (Arkush, 27 Jan. 2005).

Still, despite his success in high school, no college recruiters flagged him down with big scholarship offers. He spent one year at South Carolina State and then transferred to Mississippi Vocational College (later Mississippi Valley State). Regarded as an "unknown," the 6'5", 272-pound Jones was taken in 1961 in the fourteenth round of the National Football League (NFL) draft by the Los Angeles Rams. He might not have played pro football if the Rams' scout Eddie Kotal attending a South Carolina State game had not noticed that not only was he outrunning the back he scouted, but also he was all over the field playing both offensive and defensive tackle (Klawitter and Jones, 62). They recommended him as a "sleeper pick."

A lot of people in the NFL woke up quickly when Jones exploded into the backfield, knocking pass blockers facedown into the grass without their helmets and causing quarterbacks to scramble for their lives. Jones entered the pro game with raw skills but left as the epitome of a defensive end. The Rams head coach George Allen once said of Jones, "No one has ever had his combination of speed, instinct, intelligence, motivation, and drive" (Wiebusch, 1). Jones greatly respected Allen and was fiercely loyal to him throughout their association. He also credited Rams assistant coach Don Paul for helping him to develop into a great defensive player. Paul saw the killer instinct in Jones and switched him from offensive tackle to defensive end.

He adopted the moniker "Deacon" when he became a pro. He wanted a name that people would remember. *Deacon* had religious connotations, and he loved the way it contradicted the violence of pro football. When he listed it in a Rams media guide questionnaire, the name was printed and he permanently became Deacon Jones.

Jones also became one of the most dominating defensive linemen in NFL history. Among the plethora of special honors Jones received was being an NFL All-Pro (ten times), elected to the All-Star Pro Bowls (nine times), selected as the NFL Most Valuable Defensive Player in 1967 and 1968, and the *Los Angeles Times* heralded him as "Most valuable Ram of all time." In his career Jones recorded 752 solo tackles (727 regular season, 25 post-season). Jones had a sprinter's speed and roamed from sideline to sideline, delivering what he called "civilized violence." He explained, "It used to be that the big defensive linemen just sat in one place and waited for the play to come to them. But mobility is what makes a football player exciting, so I made myself exciting as hell" (Smith, 172).

One of Jones's most creative innovations was the head slap. The idea was that a pass rusher sharply slapped the blocker's helmet so that he could gain the extra steps needed to tackle the quarterback. Jones used the technique with such devastating effect that NFL officials banned it. But outlawing the head slap didn't prevent Jones from dismantling quarterbacks. "No legislation, nothing could slow me down. Man, I was a force! I was never mean.... I just tried to do my job the best I knew how" (Wiebusch, 1).

Jones was credited with coining the term "sack," which became a common part of the NFL lexicon. He was the first one to match the word with the action of hitting a quarterback like he was marked with a bull's eye. In an interview, he described it as, "You know, like you sack a city—you devastate it" (Smith, 172).

Jones had a team best 159.5 sacks with the Rams and an unofficial league best (the NFL did not start recording sacks until 1982). According to the statistics in his book, *Headslap*, Jones claimed (with a note stating it is verified by "official NFL team records and statistics") that he accumulated 180.5 sacks in his career. His career spanned fourteen seasons—eleven years with the Rams from 1961–1971, 1972–1973 with the San Diego Chargers, and 1974 with the Washington Redskins. He had an unofficial league record of twenty-six in 1967 in fourteen games. He was also the first defensive lineman to record one hundred solo tackles in a single season.

Teams tried to control Jones by double- and triple-teaming him, but that strategy rarely worked, particularly since Jones, also known as the "Secretary of Defense," anchored the "Fearsome Foursome," made up of the tackles Merlin Olsen and ROSEY GRIER and the end Lamar Lundy. This defensive unit averaged nearly 270 pounds. They terrorized the league and created havoc together for five years, 1963–1968. Olsen and Jones partnered for ten years, perfecting innovative stunting and looping maneuvers that confused defenders and established them as one of the best tackle/end combinations in the history of the NFL.

The partnership ended when Jones left the Rams to play for the San Diego Chargers in 1972 and 1973 in a multi-player trade with San Diego Chargers. He rejoined his old coach, Allen, for one last year in 1974, playing with the Washington Redskins. Jones never played in an NFL championship game or Super Bowl. But this obscure draft pick who missed only three games in his fourteen years was elected to the South Carolina Sports Hall of Fame (1978), a member of the NFL Hall of Fame (1980) in his first year of eligibility, elected to the Central Florida Sports Hall of Fame (1981), a recipient of the Vince Lombardi Award by the Boy Scouts of America (1991), elected to the Black Sports Hall of Fame (1995), awarded the Gale Sayers Lifetime Spirit Achievement Award (1999), given the highest honor by the NFL Alumni Organization "The Order of the Leather Helmet" (1999), and recipient of the Junior Seau Foundation "Legend of the Year Award" (2005). Jones was also ranked number 13 on the *Sporting News'* list of the "100 Greatest Football Players. He was the highest ranked defensive end and the second-ranked defensive lineman.

Among the honors he was most proud of was the 2005 Humane Award by the Christian Okoye Foundation, which he received for his outstanding work in the community. Jones was involved in charitable work involving the youth of inner-city communities. He was the founder and president of the Deacon Jones Foundation, which was established in 1997. Its expressed goal was to develop leaders in the community by offering underprivileged youth a comprehensive program that included education, mentorship, on-the-job training in corporate and business programs, and scholarships to four-year universities. His wife, Elizabeth, was the chief financial and operating officer of the foundation. He was also a chairman and spokesman for the AstraZeneca Pharmaceutical "State of the Heart" program and visited U.S. troops in Iraq in March 2004. He and Elizabeth invited soldiers undergoing rehab because of lost limbs to join them for their annual trip to the Hall of Fame in Canton, Ohio.

In the three decades after his retirement from playing, Jones was an actor, primarily appearing in cameo roles in numerous television programs, and a guest analyst on several sports television and radio shows. Many observers who watched him play believed that he would be a superstar in the speedier modern game. As Olsen once said, "There has never been a better football player than Deacon Jones" (Wiebusch, 16 June 2004).

FURTHER READING

Arkush, Dan. "Franchise Players: Q & A with Former Rams DE Deacon Jones," *Pro Football Weekly* (2005).

Klawitter, John, and Deacon Jones. *HEADSLAP: The Life and Times of Deacon Jones* (1996).

Smith, Ron. *Pro Football's Heroes Of The Hall* (2003).

Wiebusch, John. "The Very Frightening Secretary of Defense," *AOL Exclusive* (2004).

WAYNE L. WILSON

Jones, E. Edward, Sr. (1931–), religious leader and civil rights activist, was born in DeRidder, Louisiana, to the Reverend David Jesse Jones and Daisy Jones. The Reverend Jones was the pastor of two churches in Louisiana: Sweet Home Baptist and Mount Calvary Baptist. Daisy Jones was a homemaker. Growing up in a spiritual environment pointed young Edward toward the religious community, where he believed he was destined to accomplish great things. He attended elementary and secondary school in DeRidder and aspired to earn a college degree to prepare him for a career in teaching and religious service.

Edward Jones graduated from Grambling State University with a B.S. in Elementary Education in 1952. During his freshman year there, he met his future wife, Leslie M. Alexander. The couple dated through college and married on 31 August 1952. They went on to have two daughters, two sons, and nine grandchildren as of 2007.

After graduating from college, Jones taught upper elementary school and coached sports at Morehouse Parish School in Shreveport, Louisiana, from 1953 to 1959. Following in his father's footsteps, he then became the pastor of Galilee Baptist Church in Shreveport in 1959. Shortly after accepting his position as pastor, and while continuing to fulfill his pastor duties, Jones attended Bishop College and received a B.A. in Religion and Philosophy in 1961.

Soon after he moved to Shreveport, Jones became acquainted with MARTIN LUTHER KING JR. Shortly before Jones became pastor of Galilee Baptist Church, King gave a speech there that inspired Jones to become an advocate for civil rights—a passion that did not diminish over the years. His first accomplishment as a civil rights activist was to spearhead the desegregation of the Caddo Parish School District in Shreveport to provide more equality for black youth. This desegregation policy served as a model for others in the 1960s.

In 1985 Jones became president of the National Baptist Convention of America (NBCA) and served in this capacity for eighteen years until he stepped down in 2003. The mission of the NCBA was to provide teaching and evangelizing to the black community in order to ensure religious freedom and social justice, as well as economic development. As one of the largest black, Christian organizations in the country, the NCBA offered Jones an opportunity to channel his civil rights passions through a powerful medium. Those who voted Jones into the presidency viewed him as a progressive thinker who could move the organization forward.

With the NCBA corporate offices located in Shreveport, Louisiana, where he lived, Jones was able to contribute to the organization through the establishment of an in-house printing service for printing religious and educational publications. He also helped to incorporate the convention, which included establishing term limits, and helped to expand the organization's foreign missions involvement. He stepped down from his position in 2003 to devote more time to his expanding church community and his vision for Galilee City and to open the door for new blood into the NCBA. Some of the NCBA offices were located in Galilee City, a community surrounding Jones's church that provided housing and other services to underprivileged blacks.

In 1996, while still president of the NCBA, Jones developed an organization called Revelation, Inc., whose mission was to provide black consumers easier access to a number of goods and services, such as insurance, mortgages, and durable goods, providing increased economic power to the black community. In partnership with four other black religious groups, probably other Baptist groups, the organization's goal was to increase the economic power of the black community through churches by reaching their twenty million members with its services.

In 1975, after outgrowing its original church facility, Galilee Baptist purchased approximately forty acres of property in downtown Shreveport. The original church facility served as a historical site for one of King's first podium speeches on civil rights. A portion of Galilee Baptist's new property, once an elite neighborhood, included several run-down buildings. Over the years, and with Jones's vision as impetus, the property slowly evolved to what became known as Galilee City.

After building a new church facility, Jones secured funding in 1985 and again in 1990 from the U.S. Department of Housing and Urban Development to construct housing developments for the handicapped and elderly community, which he called Galilee Gardens and Galilee Majestic Arms. Following this the church built recreational facilities for youth that included computer labs, healthcare facilities, and educational programs.

In 2004 Jones partnered with the city and several financial institutions to build a seventy-six-unit apartment building that some considered one of the nicest in the city. By providing quality housing and healthcare to the black community's elderly, youth, and underprivileged, Jones hoped to meet some of the greatest needs of his people and create a promising future for youth. Galilee City grew to a city-church financial partnership that revitalized the city and offered hope to those in need.

Jones's vision continued to grow with plans to build service-centered businesses and training facilities for adults and youths. Additionally, plans to expand the ever-growing church building were in the works in 2007. Whatever project Jones envisioned seemed to come to fruition, and his energy seemed to tap from some endless well of passion, driven by his desire to care for the black community.

In addition to his church and community involvement, Jones was a member of several organizations, including the Baptist World Alliance, the National Association for the Advancement of Colored People, the Grambling State University Foundation, the Governor's Commission on Race Relations and Civil Rights, and the Board of Supervisors of Louisiana State University. He also received numerous awards, such as the National Award for Outstanding Service from his fraternity Alpha Phi Alpha. Grambling State University inducted him into their Hall of Fame in 1986, and in 1992 he was inducted into the Northwest Louisiana Hall of Fame. He was listed as one of the 100 most influential black Americans in *Ebony* from 1986 to 2003. He was also the recipient of more than eight honorary doctorate degrees, including a doctorate of sacred theology and a doctorate of humanities.

FURTHER READING

Difilippo, Dana. "Health, Housing Had List of Baptists' Concerns," *Cincinnati Enquirer*, 7 Sept. 1999.

"One Man's Vision." *Homes & Communities: U.S. Department of Housing and Urban Development.* Available at http://www.hud.gov/local/la/library/archives/2003-07-16.cfm.

CHERYL DUDLEY

Jones, Eddie (Guitar Slim) (10 Dec. 1926–7 Feb. 1959), singer, guitarist, and songwriter, was born in Greenwood, Mississippi. His mother died when he was five years old, and he moved to the L. C. Haves plantation in Hollindale, in southern Mississippi, to be reared by his grandmother. He never knew his father. Jones was interested in music and sang in the church choir. He made his living working in the cotton fields and visited the local juke joints to sing and dance with the bands passing through. His accomplished dancing skills would serve him well as he developed his stage act. Jones began working with fellow Greenwood native Willie Warren's band and started playing guitar at Warren's encouragement. He was deeply moved by the slide guitar playing of ROBERT NIGHTHAWK. Jones met his first wife, Virginia Dumas, when he was eighteen years old, but the marriage was short-lived, as he spent time in the army and served in Korea from 1951 to 1952.

Although he grew up in the Delta, Jones was smitten by the Texas guitar styles of T-BONE WALKER and Clarence "Gatemouth" Brown, which featured more jazzy and fluid lines than those found in early electric blues. He would use Brown's "Boogie Rambler" as his theme song for several years. He relocated to New Orleans, which had a long jazz and rhythm and blues music tradition and where the unique music fused with complex rhythms that harkened back to the former slave gatherings in Congo Square. Some bluesmen from the Delta would occasionally travel to New Orleans to play, but Jones was the only one of consequence to make the Crescent City his home.

Jones developed a wild stage act, and with his good looks, vocal ability, and dancer's physique adopted the name "Guitar Slim." Although there were at least two other bluesmen who had used the name, they are now relegated to obscurity, with Jones having indelibly branded the name as his own. He formed a trio with the future rock and roll star Huey "Piano" Smith and recorded four songs for Imperial Records in 1951. The records were not successful, and he recorded for the Bullet label in Nashville in 1952. The session yielded the modest but important hit "Feelin' Sad." Church singing inflections had always crept into blues music, but Guitar Slim took it a step further and used the actual eight-bar structure of the gospel song and fairly preached his secular lyrics—largely biographical ones. Using church music in this context shocked many who regarded it as blasphemous, and impressed others who recognized the heralding of a new age in modern music. One such musician was RAY CHARLES, who ended up playing piano and arranging the horns on Slim's 1954 recording debut for Specialty Records, which had signed Slim after competing with Atlantic Records. Ray Charles's career took off when he adapted this gospel style to his own "I Got a Woman."

Guitar Slim recorded "The Things I Used to Do," which became a million seller and spent twenty-one weeks on the rhythm and blues charts, ultimately reaching number 1 in January 1954. This brought Slim national attention, and he toured the United States playing major venues, such as the Howard Theatre in Washington, D.C., and the Apollo Theater in New York City, where he played a week-long engagement in 1954. Slim won over his audiences with his dynamism, wearing flashy clothes and sometimes dyeing his hair to match the color of his outfits. He would use a guitar cord measuring more than three hundred feet in length so that he could ride on the shoulders of an associate out into the audience and sometimes even out to the street to stop traffic.

Slim's guitar playing on "The Things I Used to Do" ushered in a new era for electric guitar. Although some Chicago and Memphis blues guitar players turned their small amplifiers up to produce distortion, never before had such searing, high-pitched sustain and distortion on an electric guitar been in the forefront on a hit record. Slim favored the new solid-body electric guitars, which could be played loudly without feedback. Although he used other guitars, his trademark was a Gibson Les Paul model, which was the loudest available. He was known to have played through the public address sound systems in venues so he could play at the highest volume possible. The New Orleans guitarist Earl King, who occasionally would substitute for an unavailable Guitar Slim, claimed that Slim was overdriving his guitar a full decade before JIMI HENDRIX, another flamboyant guitarist in the Slim tradition. The Louisiana-born BUDDY GUY was so impressed after seeing Guitar Slim that he decided to make music his livelihood and borrowed many of Slim's moves. In addition to his stage theatrics, incendiary guitar playing, and impassioned vocals, Slim was a provocative songwriter and lyricist. His "Done Got Over It" presaged Ray Charles's "Hit the Road Jack," and his "Twenty-five Lies" surely inspired Eddie Cochran's "Twenty Flight Rock," which a teenage Paul McCartney played for an impressed John Lennon. Slim's music would influence the rockabilly artists of the mid-1950s. Aided by the infectious drumming of Oscar Moore and other top New Orleans musicians, Guitar Slim helped usher in the age of rock and roll, and his licks can be heard in guitar players ranging from CHUCK BERRY to Stevie Ray Vaughan.

Slim drank heavily and was a notorious womanizer. After being released from Specialty, he was signed to Atlantic Records. Although he did not enjoy another hit record as successful as "The Things I Used to Do," Slim recorded many fine songs until he died of pneumonia in 1959 at the age of thirty-two. His influence on both soul and rock and roll music cannot be overstated. His total package of songs, vocals, guitar playing, and showmanship connect a straight line from T-Bone Walker to Jim Hendrix and beyond. One of Slim's children, Rodney Armstrong, carried on his father's tradition as Guitar Slim Jr.

FURTHER READING

Harris, Sheldon. *Blues Who's Who* (1979; repr. 1993).

Johnson, Greg. *Guitar Slim* (1999).

Marshall, Wolf. "Guitar Slim," *Vintage Guitar* (Mar. 2006).

Palmer, Robert. *Deep Blues* (1981).

DISCOGRAPHY

Guitar Slim 1951–1954 (Classics 5139).

MARK S. MAULUCCI

Jones, Edith Mae Irby (23 Dec. 1927–), physician and community leader, was born Edith Mae Irby in Conway, Arkansas, to Mattie Irby, a domestic worker, and her husband Robert, a sharecropper. Several childhood experiences—some traumatic—shaped Edith's early choice of medicine as her profession and the relief of racial health disparities as her special focus. When she was only five, an illness rendered her unable to walk for eighteen months. At six she lost her thirteen-year-old sister and almost lost an older brother in a typhoid fever epidemic. She noticed that people who could afford more medical care fared better with the disease. When she was eight a horse-riding accident fatally injured her father.

The year of her father's death a white doctor and his family hired Edith to help care for their eighteen-month-old child. They told Edith that she was highly intelligent and encouraged her to consider a medical career. Members of her Baptist church rallied around her, communicating through their words and deeds that she had unique gifts that she was meant to share with others. Before she started formal schooling at age ten, Edith read literary classics and an encyclopedia, all under her mother's tutelage at home. Irby grew up in Hot Springs, Arkansas, where the therapeutic baths attracted out-of-town visitors with many different infirmities. In high school Irby devised a way to aid them and support her family: she offered visitors her skills at shorthand, transcription, and 120-words-a-minute typing. Irby won a scholarship to the historically black Knoxville College in Tennessee. She worked as a typist for the school's president and graduated magna cum laude in 1948 with a B.S. in Biology, Chemistry, and Physics. That year she was accepted at the University of Arkansas Medical School, becoming its first African American student. According to the U.S. Supreme Court's rulings in *Missouri ex rel. Gaines v. Canada* (1938) and *Sipuel v. Board of Regents of the University of Oklahoma* (1948), black students had to be admitted to existing institutions if no "separate but equal" public university existed. Once she was in the door, however, the medical school banned Irby from the white students' dining room, housing facilities, and bathrooms. But the two white women in her class befriended her, and each day the black custodians placed a vase of fresh flowers on her table in the segregated staff dining room. Black Arkansans proudly gathered up their change to help pay for Irby's tuition and living expenses.

Her greatest moral support, Irby felt, came from the man she met during her second year of medical studies. Dr. James Beauregard (J. B.) Jones, a psychologist nine years her senior, was then head of the personnel and guidance department at Arkansas AM&N in Pine Bluff. They married in June 1950 and remained together until his death in 1990. They had three children: Gary Ivan Jones (1954–), Myra Jones (later Romain, 1956–), and Keith Irby Jones (1964–).

When Jones earned her MD in 1952, newspapers all over the United States carried the news. After interning at the University of Arkansas Hospital she launched a general medical practice. She worked with DR. MARTIN LUTHER KING JR. and joined the Freedom Four team of civil rights movement speakers and recruiters. A future U.S. surgeon general, M. JOCELYN ELDERS, decided to enter medicine after hearing a Jones speech. In 1959 Jones moved with her family to Houston, Texas, where she became the first black female medical resident at Baylor University Affiliated Hospitals and her husband continued his academic career.

In 1962 Jones established a private practice in inner-city Houston specializing in geriatrics. She and her secretary took turns caring for one another's small children in a back room of the practice, decades before anyone coined the term "onsite day care." Jones soon landed enduring clinical medicine faculty appointments at Baylor and at the University of Texas, as well as a position on the medical staff executive committee of Riverside General Hospital (formerly Houston Negro). She gained privileges at several other Houston-area facilities, co-founded the city's Mercy Hospital, and started clinics in Mexico, Uganda, and Haiti.

Over the decades Jones served countless organizations, including Physicians for Human Rights; the National Medical Association, of which she was the first woman president; Delta Research and Education Foundation, of which she was chair and first president; the Houston Council on Human Relations, of which she was a member of the board of directors; Knoxville College, of which she was chair of the board of trustees; Planned Parenthood of Houston, of which she was a member of the medical advisory board; the Houston Council on Alcoholism, of which she was an advisory board member; and the American Task Force for Health in Haiti, of which she was chair. Among her business ventures has been the first African American bookstore in Houston.

She received hundreds of honors, such as a lifetime membership in the National Council of Negro Women; the declaration of Edith Irby Jones Day in 1979 in the state of Arkansas; induction in 1985 into the National Black College Alumni Hall of Fame; the Certificate of Appreciation of the city of Houston in 1995; the United Negro College Fund Award for Contribution to the Health of Haiti, 2000; and induction into the University of Arkansas Alumni Hall of Fame, 2005.

In her seventies Jones helped establish a foundation to award scholarships to needy college students. In the lobby of the medical school at University of Arkansas, where she was once barred from the white students' cafeteria, her portrait remains on permanent view. The school's chapter of the Student National Medical Association, an advocacy group for medical students of color, is named for Jones.

FURTHER READING

The Black Women Physicians' Project, Drexel University School of Medicine, has a few clippings on Edith Irby Jones.

Pierce, Paula Jo. *"Let Me Tell You What I've Learned"*: *Texas Wisewomen Speak* (2002).

MARY KRANE DERR

Jones, Edward P., Sr. (1807 or 1808–1865), missionary, educator, journalist, and reformer, was born in Charleston, South Carolina, in either 1807 or 1808. Edward Jones was the son of Jehu Jones, who operated an inn in Charleston and held membership in the Brown Fellowship Society, a philanthropic and educational organization of free blacks in the city.

Jones's family had amassed a sizable fortune, made possible by Jehu's hotel, which the South Carolina elite often used while visiting Charleston. Jones's early educational experiences remain a mystery, though it is likely that he received his elementary education at schools operated by the Brown Fellowship Society.

This educational foundation enabled Jones to be admitted to the recently founded Amherst College in 1822. In this same year the South Carolina legislature, responding to the rumored DENMARK VESEY slave revolt, passed legislation barring free blacks who had migrated to the North from reentering the state. Thus Jones's sojourn as a student in New England became a form of permanent banishment from his home state.

After graduating from Amherst in 1826—the first African American to graduate from college—Jones enrolled at the equally conservative Andover Theological Seminary. Both Amherst and Andover were heavily involved in preparing students for careers as missionaries, and the faculty and students at each institution also supported the schemes for colonization of free blacks that had received increased attention beginning in 1817 with the formation of the American Colonization Society. Jones never completed his studies at Andover, instead leaving to enroll at the African Mission School in Hartford, Connecticut. Jones was one of only three graduates from this short-lived school, which aimed to prepare free blacks for the ministry, with the ultimate goal of sending graduates to the coast of West Africa as missionary colonists. Jones's decision to enroll in the African Mission School may have reflected his increasing interest in migrating to West Africa. However, the Episcopal-sponsored Mission School may have been a better religious fit for Jones, who had been raised an Episcopalian, than the more theologically conservative Andover. In 1830 Jones was ordained as a minister in the Episcopal Church, thus becoming one of only a handful of African Americans to be ordained in that church during the antebellum era.

In 1831 Jones migrated to West Africa, but he chose to establish himself in the British colony of Sierra Leone rather than in the American colony of Liberia. Several factors may have contributed to this decision: the strong affiliation of Sierra Leone with the Anglican-based Church Missionary Society of England made the English colony a close fit for Jones theologically; intensifying criticism of American schemes for colonization by immediate abolitionists in 1831 may also have tarnished

Liberia in Jones's mind, particularly when juxtaposed against the wholehearted opposition to the slave trade expressed by the government and populace of Great Britain; and finally, just as Jones was preparing to embark for West Africa, citizens in the free state of Connecticut were rallying against plans to create educational institutions for free blacks. Opposition to racial equality might be expected in the slaveholding South, but it would have been disheartening for Jones, who had left the South looking for better opportunities in the North. Jones's conflicted feelings toward the country of his birth become clear in his correspondence with the Episcopal hierarchy of Connecticut, to whom he wrote of his love for his nation, "however she may refuse to acknowledge me for her son, however she may deny me inheritance among her children" (quoted in Hawkins, "Edward Jones, Marginal Man").

In Sierra Leone, Jones soon found work as a schoolmaster in the Banana Islands. He also married the daughter of a German missionary and fathered several children, further cementing his links to the British colony. However, Jones's American citizenship created friction with the British governor, Major H.D. Campbell, who accused the American of sedition. Jones weathered this challenge and by 1841 had risen to the position of principal of the Fourah Bay Christian Institute. The Church Mission Society had established this school in 1827 as a center for the training of Christian African students for missionary service among their fellow Africans. Until Jones's arrival most of the graduating students, however, had taken jobs either in the colonial government or in private business rather than in evangelization. Jones attempted to reform the school, creating a grammar school to handle more elementary education and renaming the advanced school Fourah Bay College in 1848. Students and faculty at the college also began to create dictionaries and grammars and to translate religious texts into various languages of West Africa.

In 1845, in a sign of his increasing commitment to Sierra Leone, Jones traveled to England, where he petitioned for and received a special status as a naturalized citizen of Sierra Leone (though his citizenship would not transfer either to Great Britain itself or to any of the British Empire's other protectorates). Despite, or perhaps as a result of, Jones's reforms designed to bring Fourah Bay College more in line with its original evangelical intent, the college began to lose support among both the populace and various colonial agents. The grammar school enjoyed success among the residents of Freetown, however, who saw immediate benefits to the basic skills offered there. Meanwhile, attendance at the college declined, and by 1856 it had only eight students enrolled.

Jones twice spoke before Parliament (in 1841 and 1848) regarding the condition of Africans who had once been enslaved but who had now received their freedom and were settled in Sierra Leone. Jones testified that liberated Africans, many of whom had been rescued from ships illegally engaged in the international slave trade, were basically content. However, reflecting his broader interest in evangelization, Jones also advised that liberated Africans should receive a Christian education before being resettled in Sierra Leone. In addition to his work as an educator, Jones also edited the *Sierra Leone Weekly Times and African Record*. After leaving Africa, Jones resettled in London, where he died in 1865.

FURTHER READING

Blyden, Nemata. "Edward Jones: An African American in Sierra Leone," in *Moving On: Black Loyalists in the Afro-Atlantic World*, ed. John W. Pulis (1999).

Hawkins, Hugh. "Edward Jones: First American Negro College Graduate?" *School and Society*, 4 Nov. 1961.

Hawkins, Hugh. "Edward Jones, Marginal Man," in *Black Apostles at Home and Abroad*, eds. David W. Wills and Richard Newman (1982).

CHERYL DUDLEY

Jones, Edward Paul (5 Oct. 1950–), author, was born in Arlington, Virginia, the son of Jeanette S. M. Jones, a cleaning woman, and a father who disappeared when Jones was three. Among the writers of his generation, Edward P. Jones stands out not only for his prodigious storytelling gifts but for the marked deprivation of his early life. His mother was illiterate, and Jones lived with her and his sister in eighteen different apartments in Washington, D.C., in his youth. "Each place," he has said, "was worse than the place before" (Bookbrowse.com). His earliest reading matter was comic books, which he began to read at seven or eight. At thirteen, he read his first book without pictures, a mystery by Basil Thomson entitled *Who Killed Stella Pomeroy?* Visiting his aunt's home in Brooklyn, he discovered RICHARD WRIGHT's *Native Son* and *His Eye Is on the Sparrow*, the autobiography of ETHEL WATERS. A high school teacher gave him a copy of Wright's *Black Boy* and afterwards he moved on to JAMES BALDWIN, RALPH ELLISON, and Truman Capote. "I was quite struck by the Southern writers, white and

black," he recalled, and now counts white southerners William Faulkner, Eudora Welty, and Erskine Caldwell, as well as European authors Anton Chekov and James Joyce, among his most admired writers.

Jones's mother was a devout Roman Catholic and managed to send him to parochial school for kindergarten and first grade. Thereafter, he was educated in the public schools of the District of Columbia. As he approached his high school graduation, a local priest urged him to apply to Holy Cross, a Roman Catholic college in Massachusetts. He was accepted and graduated with a degree in English in 1972, although he did not consider writing as a career. He returned to Washington to care for his terminally ill mother and to work in a variety of short-term jobs. Eventually, he was hired by *Science*, the journal of the Association for the Advancement of Science, where he stayed for three years. While there, he read a short story in his sister's copy of *Essence* magazine and concluded he could do better. In 1975 he sold his first story to *Essence* for four hundred dollars. The acceptance arrived at a particularly painful moment in his life—his mother had died and he was living in a city mission.

In 1979, he enrolled in the MFA program in creative writing at the University of Virginia, finishing in 1981. After graduation, Jones took a position as proofreader and later as a writer summarizing tax cases for *Tax Notes*, a job he held for eighteen years. While there, he wrote many of the stories that were published in 1992 as *Lost in the City*, his first book, which was nominated for a National Book Award and received the Ernest Hemingway Foundation/PEN Award.

Lost in the City is a short story collection modeled on James Joyce's *Dubliners*. All of the stories in the Jones collection take place in the poor neighborhoods of Washington, away from the official buildings and monuments of the Capitol. As Wyatt Mason notes in *Harper's Magazine*, "The stories of *Lost in the City* (like *Dubliners*) are sequenced developmentally: early stories focus on children, and as the book moves forward, attention turns to young adults, the middle-aged, and, by the book's end, the elderly … Both books share a similar view of history—that of a nightmare from which the characters are unable to awaken." The works diverge, however, in the regard with which the writers hold their city. Joyce held Dublin in such contempt—"the city of failure, of rancour and unhappiness"—that he ultimately went into exile. Jones, however, has remained in Washington for nearly all of his fifty-eight years and the stories he tells in *Lost in the City* command the reader's compassion for the plight of the characters portrayed.

During this period, he also began to conceive of his masterpiece, the extraordinary novel *The Known World*. It took Jones ten years to work out the entire novel in his mind. When he was ready to write, he produced the first draft in two and a half months. *The Known World* was published in 2003 to widespread acclaim, receiving a number of awards, including the Pulitzer Prize for fiction in 2004. Set in an imaginary county in Virginia before the Civil War, it tells the story, as Mason describes, of "a community of people, black and white, whose lives intersect in some way with that of a black man named Henry Townsend. Townsend, though born in slavery, becomes free in his late teens, acquires land, builds a plantation, and turns slaveholder himself—overlord to thirty-three human beings at the time of his death—the event that provides the novel's springboard." It has been called "one of the best American novels of the last twenty years."

In 2006 Jones published *All Aunt Hagar's Children*, another collection of short stories set in Washington. Each revisits a tale in *Lost in the City*, bringing the latter stories into greater focus. As with *The Known World*, Jones weaves a community with his short stories composed of grandchildren, cousins and neighbors, each told plainly, beautifully, in the vernacular.

With only three works of fiction to his credit, Edward P. Jones has been compared to William Faulkner, TONI MORRISON, and Charles Dickens for his extraordinary ability to create a functioning literary world from his pen. In the words of Maria Guarnaschelli, editor of *Lost in the City*, "If there's such a thing as a born writer, [Jones] is one. There are a lot of wonderful writers, but when you hear his prose, you hear music."

As of 2009 Jones was living alone. He has never owned an automobile and has never married. In 2010 Jones received the PEN/Malamud Award for excellence in the art of the short story.

FURTHER READING

Birnbaum, Robert. "Interview, Edward Jones, Author of *The Known World*," *identity theory: an online magazine*, 21 January 2004. Online at http://www.identitytheory.com/interviews/birnbaum138.php.

"Edward P. Jones," Author Biography, updated 01 August 2006, online at http://www.bookbrowse.com/biographies/index.cfm?author_number=930.

"Edward P. Jones Biography," Notable Biographies, February, 2005, online at http://www.notablebiographies.com/newsmakers2/2005-Fo-La/Jones-Edward-P.html.

Eggers, Dave. "Still Lost in the City," *The New York Times*, 27 August 2006.

Mason, Wyatt. "Ballad for Americans: The Stories of Edward P. Jones," *Harpers Magazine*, September, 2006.

JULIAN HOUSTON

Jones, Edward Smyth (Mar. 1881–28 Sept. 1968), poet, was born in Natchez, Mississippi, to Hawk Jones and his wife, Rebecca, whose maiden name is unknown. Both of his parents had been born as slaves and neither had any formal schooling, but they encouraged young Edward's interest in reading and writing and his attendance of Natchez's black public schools. His grade school education coincided with the peak of public expenditures on Mississippi's black schools, but by the late 1890s and following the state's disfranchisement of all but a handful of African Americans, spending on black students plummeted to less than one-fifth the spending on whites. The state's superintendent of schools stated in 1899 that public education was only "incidentally" for blacks. That same year the future Mississippi governor James K. Vardaman offered the opinion that educating blacks was a "criminal folly … that spoils a good field hand and makes a shyster lawyer or a fourth-rate teacher" (McMillen, 72).

Such prevailing views did not deter Jones's desire to further his education, however, and in 1902 and 1903 he attended the nearby Alcorn Agricultural and Mechanical College for fourteen months, paying his way by working as a laborer. Although Alcorn was in the minds of its all-white board a vocational college only, many of Jones's teachers had been educated at Fisk and remained true to the liberal arts vision of its first president, HIRAM REVELS. It was probably at Alcorn that Jones's interest in becoming a poet was first encouraged and that he became acquainted with and influenced by the works of the ancient Greek poets, the British romantics, and the New England transcendentalists.

Around 1908 Jones moved to Louisville, Kentucky, where, under the pseudonym "Invincible Ned" he published his first book of poems, *The Rose That Bloometh in My Heart*, a collection of thirty verses written mainly after the style of Longfellow, Emerson, and other mid-nineteenth-century New England poets. One piece, "A Psalm of Love," parodied one of Longfellow's most famous poems, "A Psalm of Life," written while he was a professor of language at Harvard in 1839. Jones published a second volume of verse, *Our Greater Louisville: Souvenir Poems* in 1908, before leaving Kentucky for Indianapolis, where his poetry was well received.

Perhaps in the hope of emulating Longfellow, Jones set off in July 1910 for Cambridge, Massachusetts, to try to enter Harvard College. Armed with copies of his work and letters of recommendation from the mayor of Indianapolis, the governor of Indiana, and the former U.S. vice president Charles Fairbanks, the penniless poet walked, slept rough, and rode freight trains when possible, during his twelve-hundred-mile journey. When he arrived, starving and exhausted, at Harvard Yard several weeks later, Jones made immediately for the president's residence, hoping to personally press his case for admission. By the time he located University Hall, however, it was late, and he was met not by Harvard President Charles W. Eliot but by a printer working overtime who saw Jones's bedraggled state and black face and assumed that he was a vagrant. The printer promptly summoned the police, who arrested Jones and took him to cell number 40 of the East Cambridge Jail. While in prison Jones penned "Harvard Square," a poem about his journey from "the Sunny South," and his arrest in the "haunt of childhood dreams / more beauteous and fair / Than Nature's landscape and her streams / Historic Harvard Square." From "Deep in a ghastly cell," for three days, Jones kept his spirits high by summoning the words of his favorite poets, including Homer, Dante, Burns, Keats, Shelley, Poe, and PAUL LAURENCE DUNBAR. Indeed, it was Jones's much longer version of Dunbar's "Ode to Ethiopia," complete with references to black Harvard alumni, that most impressed Arthur P. Stone, the judge and Harvard graduate who presided at Jones's arraignment and secured his release.

Assisted by CLEMENT G. MORGAN, a Harvard-trained lawyer, and WILLIAM H. HOLTZCLAW, a fellow Mississippian and founder of the Utica Normal and Industrial Institute who was attending Harvard summer school, Jones found work as a janitor at the college. He also attended Boston Latin School for a year and published the *Sylvan Cabin, A Centenary Ode on the Birth of Lincoln and Other Verse* in 1911. Jones dedicated the volume to Judge Stone. Unable to save enough money to complete his studies at Boston Latin and enter Harvard, Jones left Cambridge for New York City around 1912. There he found work as a waiter at the faculty club of Columbia University and continued to write poetry. A 16 February 1913 *New York Times* feature described Jones as a "lyric poet of real promise" and praised the "coherency … sincerity … and imagination" of the *Sylvan Cabin*, particularly Jones's "Ode on the Birth of Lincoln." The same article viewed the poet's most recent, and at that time unpublished, work, "Sea-Queen: A Poem in Memory of the Ill-Starred Titanic," as his longest and most accomplished to date. The *Times* reporter also noted wryly, though perhaps with a touch of condescension, that Jones "may not be the best waiter that waits in the [Columbia] faculty club, but it would be interesting to know how many better poets eat there."

Despite other favorable reviews, Jones's career as a poet appears to have stalled after World War I, when he moved to Chicago. His Thanksgiving poem "A Song of Thanks," was, however, anthologized in several collections, notably JAMES WELDON JOHNSON's the *Book of American Negro Poetry* (1922). By then both Jones's Victorian lyricism—"A Song of Thanks" celebrates "the fish which swim in the babbling brooks / … the game which hide in the shady nooks"—and the stirring patriotism of poems like "Flag of the Free" had become deeply unfashionable in the wake of the race-conscious modernism of LANGSTON HUGHES, COUNTÉE CULLEN, and other Harlem Renaissance writers. Either unwilling or unable to adapt to these new forms, Jones lived out the rest of his life in relative obscurity, working as a manual laborer in Chicago, the city where he died of a cerebral thrombosis in 1968.

FURTHER READING

McMillen, Neil R. *Dark Journey: Black Mississippians in the Age of Jim Crow* (1990).

Sollors, Werner, Caldwell Titcomb, and Thomas A. Underwood, eds. *Blacks at Harvard: A Documentary History of African-American Experience at Harvard and Radcliffe* (1993).

STEVEN J. NIVEN

Jones, Etta (25 Nov. 1928–16 Oct. 2001), jazz singer, was born in Aiken, South Carolina, but moved to New York City with her family at age three. At age sixteen her rhythm-and-blues vocalizations led to a spot in a local talent competition and netted her a touring gig with pianist and bandleader Buddy Johnson. She made her recording debut that same year (1944) on the Black & White label with ALBANY "BARNEY" BIGARD's pickup band, singing four Leonard Feather songs, three of which were popularized by DINAH WASHINGTON, including "Evil Gal Blues," "Salty Papa Blues," and "Long Long Journey." During these early years in her career she also recorded for RCA and worked with leading boogie woogie player PETE JOHNSON; swing, bop, and blues drummer J. C. HEARD; and bandleader and piano virtuoso EARL HINES, the latter of whom she worked with for three years.

During the 1950s Jones worked as a soloist, performing only occasionally while laboring as an elevator operator, seamstress, and album stuffer to make ends meet. In 1960 she accepted the opportunity to record on one of the era's leading independent jazz labels, Prestige Records. That same year she recorded her hit "Don't Go with Strangers," which earned her a gold record and reportedly a million dollars for the record company. She cut several more albums for Prestige over the next five years, including a guest turn on one of the saxophonist GENE AMMON's numerous recordings.

In 1968 she met tenor saxophonist Houston Person, with whom she developed an engaging, intuitive style of musical response. The pair were jointly billed and married for a while, with Person serving as her manager and producer over the next three decades. Jones toured the Far East in 1970 with ART BLAKELY and the Jazz Messengers, suspending her recording career until 1976, when she cut the album *Ms. Jones to You* for Muse Records. She then moved to High Note, where she recorded eighteen records, as well as performing steadily in New York and on the jazz festival circuit. Jones was featured in Carnegie Hall with saxophonist ILLINOIS JACQUET and appeared at Town Hall with pianist Billy Taylor.

Influenced by BILLIE HOLIDAY, Dinah Washington, and Thelma Carpenter, Jones was noted for her sensitive phrasing mixed with a rich, bluesy approach. Her elegant interpretations resulted in Grammy nominations for "Save Your Love for Me" in 1980 and *My Buddy: The Songs of Buddy Johnson* in 1999. She also received the EUBIE BLAKE Jazz Award and the Lifetime Achievement Award from the International Women in Jazz Foundation.

Jones performed regularly until the end of her life, both as a solo artist and as a collaborator with young musicians, such as pianist Benny Green and bluesman Charles Brown. She succumbed to complications from cancer in Mount Vernon, New York, in 2001. Her last recording, a tribute to Holiday entitled *Etta Jones Sings Lady Day*, was released in the United States on the day of her death and was nominated for a Grammy Award in 2003. Jones enjoyed a successful music career, despite being little known outside of the jazz world, where she was regarded as a hidden treasure by her devoted fans and designated a "jazz musician's jazz singer."

FURTHER READING

Clark, William, Jim Cogan, and Quincy Jones. *Temples of Sound: Inside the Great Recording Studios* (2003).

"Etta Jones Remembered," *Westchester County Business Journal* (22 Oct. 2001).

ROXANNE Y. SCHWAB

Jones, Eugene Kinckle (30 July 1885–11 Jan. 1954), social welfare reformer, was the son of Joseph Endom Jones and Rosa Daniel Kinckle, a fairly comfortable and prominent middle-class black couple in Richmond, Virginia. Both his parents were college-educated. Jones grew to maturity at a period in American history when the federal government turned its back on providing full citizenship rights to African Americans. Although the Civil War had ended slavery and the Fourteenth and Fifteenth amendments to the U.S. Constitution had guaranteed blacks equal rights, state governments in the South began to erode those rights following the end of Reconstruction in 1877.

Jones grew up in Richmond at a time of racial polarization, and he watched as African American men and women struggled to hold on to the gains that some had acquired during Reconstruction. Like others in W. E. B. DuBois's "Talented Tenth," he saw education as the best means of improving his own life and of helping others, and he graduated from Richmond's Virginia Union University in 1905. He then moved to Ithaca, New York, to attend Cornell University, where, in 1906, he was a founding member of the nation's first black Greek-lettered fraternity, Alpha Phi Alpha. He later helped found two other chapters at Howard University and at his alma mater, Virginia Union. He graduated from Cornell with a master's degree in 1908 and taught high school in Louisville, Kentucky, until 1911. In 1909 he married Blanche Ruby Watson, with whom he went on to have two children.

In 1911 Jones began working as the first field secretary for the National Urban League (NUL), a social service agency for blacks that had been founded in New York City in 1910. By the 1920s he had superimposed the philosophy and organization of Alpha Phi Alpha upon the league, which was by that time dealing with the problems of poverty, poor housing, ill health, and crime that emerged during the first great black migration from the rural South to the urban North. He worked diligently to establish as many local branches as possible, believing that the concept of local branches would further the NUL's national agenda. Jones also placed key individuals in the directorships of local branches, which enabled him to be informed at all times of the conditions in black urban areas. In addition, he established fellowship programs to ensure that a larger pool of African American social workers would be available to tackle the problems that rural migrants faced in the burgeoning inner cities of the North. In 1923, along with the NUL's research director, the sociologist CHARLES S. JOHNSON, Jones helped launch *Opportunity*, a journal that addressed the problems faced by urban blacks but which also provided an outlet for a new generation of African American writers and artists, including AARON DOUGLAS and LANGSTON HUGHES.

In 1915 Jones and a group of other black social reformers founded the Social Work Club to address the concerns of African American social workers. This organization was short-lived, for by 1921 black social workers had become actively involved with the American Association of Social Workers. In 1925 the National Conference of Social Work elected Jones treasurer, making him the first African American on its executive board. Jones went on to serve the organization until 1933, by which time he had risen to the position of vice president of the National Conference of Social Work (NCSW). This post put him in a position of importance within the national structure of the social work profession. During Jones's tenure as an executive officer of the NCSW, he worked with other black social workers to make white reformers aware—often for the first time—of the urban problems particular to African Americans.

In 1933 Jones became one of the leading black figures in Washington, D.C., when he took a position with the Department of Commerce as an adviser on Negro Affairs. Perhaps no single person matched Jones's efforts in delivering to African American communities the opportunities that became available to them through the federal government's newly initiated relief programs. While in Washington, he also served as the voice of the black community through the NUL and its local branches. In so doing, Jones came to personify the NUL in the 1930s, while he served along with MARY MCLEOD BETHUNE, ROBERT WEAVER, and WILLIAM HENRY HASTIE as part of President Franklin Roosevelt's so-called black cabinet.

By the time of Jones's retirement in 1940, the NUL had become a relatively conservative organization. A younger generation was rising to prominence, and many African Americans were no longer willing to wait as patiently for justice and their full citizenship rights as Jones and his contemporaries had been willing to do. However, Jones's handpicked successor, LESTER B. GRANGER, continued in the more conservative style of leadership embraced by Jones. The NUL therefore did not engage in the direct methods of the modern civil rights movement until 1960, when WHITNEY YOUNG was appointed executive secretary. Jones died in New York after a short illness in January 1954.

Like other middle-class blacks, Jones felt a strong sense of responsibility for uplifting less fortunate members of his race. In that regard, his social views conformed with other turn-of-the-century African American social reformers, such as DuBois, CARTER G. WOODSON, JAMES WELDON JOHNSON, IDA B. WELLS-BARNETT, and MARY CHURCH TERRELL. The accomplishments of these progressive-era reformers have historically been ignored compared with those of their white counterparts, such as the settlement house leader Jane Addams. Scholars have recently begun to acknowledge, however, that African American middle-class activists like Jones led the early-twentieth-century social reform movement in black America, even though the middle-class ethos of these reformers did not exactly mirror that of the larger white society. Above all, Jones's tenure as executive secretary of the NUL showcases the achievements of early black social reformers. He also helped make the league an African American, and an American, institution.

FURTHER READING

Information on Jones can be found in the National Urban League Archives in the Manuscript Division of the Library of Congress, Washington, D.C.

Carlton-LaNey, Iris B., ed. *African American Leadership: An Empowerment Tradition in Social Welfare History* (2001).

Weiss, Nancy J. *The National Urban League, 1910–1940* (1974).

Wesley, Charles H. *The History of Alpha Phi Alpha: A Development in Negro College Life* (1929).

FELIX L. ARMFIELD

Jones, Frederick McKinley (17 May 1893–21 Feb. 1961), a self-taught mechanical genius, best known for inventing the refrigeration system used in long-haul trucking and rail shipment (under the Thermo King label), held over forty patents, including the first feasible two-cycle gas engine. He was most likely born in Ohio, in the vicinity of Cincinnati, but may have lived in West Covington, Kentucky, as well. There is little documentation for his life prior to arrival in Hallock, Minnesota, on Christmas Eve 1912. By appearance and social experience he was African American; his death certificate describes him as "Indian and Negro." For the rest of his life he called Hallock home, and Hallock followed the career of its beloved favorite son with affectionate pride.

Knowledge of his childhood comes from brief remarks Jones made to news writers and recollections shared with friends in Minnesota. His mother either died or abandoned him when he was very young. He recalled his father as an itinerant Irish railroad worker. At around the age of nine, his father left him in care of a Roman Catholic priest named Ryan, who may have been Father William B. Ryan at St. Ann's in West Covington or Father Edward A. Ryan at St. Mary's in Cincinnati. Jones recalled

doing yard work and other chores in exchange for room and board while attending school until about the sixth grade.

Around 1905 he obtained a job at Robert C. Crowthers's auto repair shop, located at 130 East Ninth Street, in Cincinnati. Within three years, his mechanical aptitude won him a promotion to foreman, as he improved the performance of cars Crowthers entered in local races. A disagreement over not being allowed to attend a race at Rising Sun, Indiana, when he was expected to be minding the shop, led to an indefinite suspension. "I was a touchy kid then," Jones recalled in 1949, "and I just up and quit and decided to take a trip to Chicago to see the sights" (Spencer).

He arrived in Hallock by way of a series of jobs, including one at the Cadillac Garage in Chicago and repairing the boiler of the Pacific House hotel in Effingham, Illinois. In December 1912 Jones arrived in Hallock, securing employment the following spring maintaining the extensive array of steam-powered tractors at the thirty-thousand-acre farm owned by

Frederick McKinley Jones, in front of a refrigerated truck, c. 1950. (Minnesota Historical Society.)

James J. Hill, managed by his son Walter. During his employment for Hill, Jones acquired the nickname "Casey," from a railroad engineer Jones accompanied to deliver a new tractor to the farm.

By June 1917 he was employed as a mechanic at Oscar Younggren's garage, also in high demand to repair farm equipment. Jones was inducted into the army 7 September 1918, assigned to Company E of the 809th Pioneer Infantry, and sent to France 23 September 1918. Promoted to corporal 4 November 1918, he was assigned to rewire an entire camp. He was honorably discharged 23 July 1919. In 1920 he was boarding with a family named Trempeleau in Hallock. He and Oscar Younggren became a well-known team on the dirt-racing circuit of the upper Midwest; if there was any question about his color when arranging motel accommodations, Oscar would rent the room for himself and his friend. Jones quit racing after 1925, when three drivers died at the Hawthorne racetrack near Chicago and Jones himself was injured.

His life in Hallock included building radios, playing saxophone in the town band, singing in a quartet, fishing, and hunting ducks. Jones rented a shop in the back of the Grand Theater. Together with local news publisher Clifford Bouvette, he built the town's first radio broadcast station and belatedly got a license when they learned one was needed. Jones installed the first X-ray unit at Hallock's hospital in 1923. The same year, he married Minnie B. Hagstrom, the daughter of Swedish immigrants, sometimes known as May; they divorced after 1930. Among his inventions during the 1920s in Hallock were an early transistor and what may have been the first condenser microphone, but because he had no connections for patents or distribution, these were reinvented and patented by others years later. He developed two sound systems for the theater, for soundtracks played on phonograph and then for the sound-on-film system, at a fraction of the cost of commercial equipment.

Jones's genius with movie theater equipment came to the attention of Joseph Numero in Minneapolis, owner of a company called Ultraphone, marketing sound equipment. He invited Jones to come work for him; on arrival, a receptionist told him the company was not hiring janitors. He had Numero's letter, however, and was soon impressing company engineers with solutions to problems they had grappled with for months. Because of patent infringement lawsuits by Western Electric, American Telephone and Telegraph, and

Electrical Research Products, Numero switched from the Ultraphone label to Cinema Supplies, Inc. Jones invented the first automatic system for movie theater tickets, patented in 1939.

In 1938 Numero's golfing buddy, Harry Werner, lost a truckload of poultry when the ice it was packed in melted. Numero teased a mutual friend in the air conditioning business that he could build a refrigeration system for trucks, but didn't expect Werner to take him up on it. Werner did, and before Numero could back out, Jones worked out a system nobody thought possible. Numero sold Cinema Supplies to RCA and started the company that became Thermo-King. Over the next fifteen years Jones patented one improvement after another, developing units that were lightweight, mounted on the top front of the trailer, and easily removable for maintenance or replacement.

With the advent of World War II Jones's design for refrigeration equipment was adopted as a national standard by the military. He was called to Washington for a conference of refrigeration experts, but housed in a run-down Negro hotel, whereas the other experts were put up at the finest hotels in the city. Preservation and delivery of food and medicine, air conditioning for planes evacuating wounded soldiers, and even delivery of ice cream to troops in the South Pacific relied on Jones's designs. Brigadier General Georges F. Doriot, director of military planning for the quartermaster corps, wrote in 1945, "we are especially grateful for the work of Mr. Fred Jones."

In 1945 some co-workers invited Jones to an Elks convention, where he met Louise Lucille Powell, the widowed daughter of a French—German mother and a Jewish father. The following year they married. Louise recalled in 1971 that her husband was "a strange, wonderful, stubborn, loveable, cantankerous, frighteningly brilliant eccentric, who made dreams come true" (*St. Paul Pioneer Press*, 6 June 1971, pp. 1–2). Jones routinely turned his paycheck over to his wife, telling her "Mama, save enough so I can get a new Packard." She did—he paid cash for a dark-green Packard Patrician sedan. Jones continued to work tirelessly, adding railroad refrigeration equipment to his list of patents in the early 1950s, aided by draftsman Stanley Grunewald.

Jones was inducted into the American Society of Refrigeration Engineers in 1944, continuing to serve as a consultant to the United States Bureau of Standards. He died 21 February 1961 and was buried at Ft. Snelling National Cemetery, where Lucille was buried at his side in 1998. He was posthumously inducted into the Minnesota Inventors Hall of Fame in 1977 and received the National Medal of Technology in 1991.

FURTHER READING

An archive of miscellaneous papers related to Frederick McKinley Jones is available at the Minnesota Historical Association Library, St. Paul, Minnesota, including some patent applications and final patents, local news clippings, and articles from *Saturday Evening Post* and *Ebony*.

"America's Greatest Negro Inventor." *Ebony*, Vol. 8, No. 2, 1952, pp. 41–44.

Kenny, Dave. *Minnesota Goes to War: The Home Front during World War II* (2005).

Spencer, Steven M. "Born Handy." *Saturday Evening Post*, Vol. 221, No. 45, 7 May 1949.

Swanson, Gloria, and Margaret V. Ott. *I've Got an Idea! The Story of Frederick McKinley Jones* (1994).

CHARLES ROSENBERG

Jones, Friday (1810–10 Aug. 1887), slave narrative author, was born in Wake County, North Carolina, to Barney and Cherry, two slaves of the High family. Jones's 1883 slave narrative lists his first owner as "Olser Hye," asserts that his father was "a desperate wicked man" and an alcoholic who died about 1820, and tells of how his "poor dear mother" who taught him to pray was "traded for a tract of land and sent to Alabama" (1). Jones and three of his eleven siblings were raised in the large High household; he says little about his childhood other than noting that "I had hard struggling to get bread and clothes" and "after I was ten years old I knew nothing about going to church" (6). When his master's daughter Emily High married planter Tignall Jones on 25 January 1825, Friday Jones seems to have been given to the new couple.

In about 1830, Friday Jones met his future wife Milly (sometimes Milley), a slave on a neighboring farm. However, when he approached his master about the possibility of marrying, Tignall Jones was resistant. Through subterfuge, Friday Jones was able to convince his wife's master, Dr. Benjamin Rogers, to allow the pair to go "together, like goose and gander—no wedding"; the marriage would last throughout the couple's lifetime (7). Jones reported that the couple later had eleven children and "raised all but two." Tignall Jones tried to separate the couple on several occasions, but seems to have tolerated their marriage for a time because of Friday Jones's value. Jones was hired out in the late 1830s and early 1840s to the state of North Carolina

and to the Raleigh and Gaston Railroad; he also seems to have worked for a succession of temporary masters as well as on his owner's large farms. Jones seems to have grown increasingly resistant, and finally Tignall Jones jailed him while attempting to sell him off.

Through circumstances that the narrative is hazy about, Calvin Rogers (sometimes Rodgers), a wealthy planter in Wake County and "the agent of my master" seems to have taken control of Jones in the early 1850s, and Jones reported hiring himself, his wife, and his elder children out in Raleigh. (5). Financial troubles forced Rogers to sell Jones's family, but Jones persuaded him to sell them to John O'Neil of Raleigh. O'Neil had promised to keep them for life, but quickly sold Milley Jones and one of their children. Jones was able to persuade Joshua James, a wealthy farmer and Baptist minister, to purchase them, but Jones increasingly had troubles finding viable places for himself and his large family. His narrative relates, for example, the story of how his eldest daughter—whose name may have been Lily—was purchased by a trader in 1853, "imprisoned in a corn crib," whipped, sold again, and "abused." (12). Still, Jones was able to relate in his 1883 narrative that "she professed religion" and "is now living in Raleigh, a sound and healthy woman." (15).

Jones himself was repeatedly threatened with whipping; Rogers even asserted at one point that he would shoot him; Jones, though, survived. While Jones seems to have struggled with alcohol during his early years, he attended a series of revivals beginning in 1853, "professed religion" in 1854, and was baptized in November of 1855. Most of his short narrative credits God for allowing him to live and to salvage his family in the midst of slavery.

Jones's narrative says little about the Civil War or Reconstruction. After the end of the war, he stayed in Raleigh, and was living with his wife and three youngest daughters (Mary, Cherry, and Katy) in 1870. His occupation was given as "watchman" in the Federal Census of Raleigh, and the family was listed with $500 in real estate and another $300 in personal property (p. 291). Jones and his wife were still listed together—along with youngest daughter Katy—in the 1880 Census of Raleigh. Friday Jones's occupation was listed as "laborer," and both his wife and daughter were listed as "washer" women (p. 311A). Friday Jones's obituary suggests that he was "quite prominent among his race as a politician," that he "was at one time watchman at the capitol" in Raleigh, and that he "had been both a democrat and a republican, and died a democrat."

It is thus likely that his place as a watchman was a minor patronage appointment, and that, as the Democrats moved into power in North Carolina, Jones shifted parties. His obituary noted that he was introduced in the U.S. House of Representatives by William Ruffin Cox, a Confederate General, three-term Democratic congressman from Raleigh, and Democratic Party boss of Wake County.

Jones's introduction to the House was likely one of the highlights of a three- or four-year period in the 1880s when he lived in Washington, D.C.—where, according to his obituary, he hoped to get a position as a janitor in the Federal buildings. Certainly the publication of his brief narrative *Day of Bondage: Autobiography of Friday Jones, Being a Brief Narrative of His Trials and Tribulations in Slavery* in 1883 was a similar highlight, although his choice of publishers (the Washington-based jobber the Commercial Publishing Company), makes it likely that Jones's narrative (like several postbellum slave narratives) was essentially self-published and designed for economic gain as well as historical remembrance. It was recovered and reissued in 1999. Jones died in Raleigh.

FURTHER READING

Jones, Friday. *Days of Bondage: Autobiography of Friday Jones, Being a Brief Narrative of His Trials and Tribulations in Slavery* (1883). William L. Andrews, ed. (1999).

Obituary: *Raleigh News and Observer*, 11 Aug. 1887.

ERIC GARDNER

Jones, Gayl (23 Nov. 1949–), writer, poet, and teacher, was born in Lexington, Kentucky, to Franklin Jones, a cook, and Lucille Wilson Jones, a fiction writer. Her maternal grandmother, Amanda Wilson, was also a writer and a playwright, whose work was performed in church productions. Jones was exposed to a literary tradition early in life, through stories written and read to her by her mother, and she began writing her own stories as early as the second grade. She and her brother Franklin Jr. attended public schools, which remained segregated until her tenth-grade year. After graduating from Lexington's Henry Clay High School, Jones left home for Connecticut College, where she earned her B.A. in English in 1971. She subsequently studied creative writing at Brown University, earning both an M.A. in English in 1973 and a doctor of arts in English in 1975.

While studying at Brown, Jones saw the production of her first play, *Chile Woman*, which was first produced at Brown in November of 1973 by Rites and Reason, a research and performing arts theater associated with Brown's Africana studies department. It won the new play award in the 1974 New England regional competition for the National American College Theatre Festival. In 1975, when she was only twenty-six years old, Random House published her first novel, *Corregidora*, which both established her as an accomplished novelist and introduced her trademark fascination with blues and jazz and African American oral tradition. In a 1982 interview with the *Callaloo* editor Charles H. Rowell, Jones said *Corregidora* marked the first time in her writing that her interest in the relationship between spoken language and literature "became a deliberate decision, a conscious working out" (Rowell, 33). She credited her knowledge of oral tradition to her mother's early influence as well as to the "speech community" in which she grew up (Tate, 144). Jones identified herself as a storyteller, and her characters were storytellers as well. The challenge for Ursa Corregidora, a blues singer in 1940s Kentucky, is to find a balance between her desire to tell the stories of her maternal ancestors and her need to overcome an inherited history of oppression and suffering. Through Ursa's narrative of generational memory, Jones explored America's legacy of slavery, particularly for African American women. Jones continued to explore the personal and collective histories of African Americans in her second novel, *Eva's Man*, published in 1976 and, like *Corregidora*, edited by the author TONI MORRISON. Eva, unlike Ursa, is a reluctant storyteller and an intentionally unreliable narrator who maintains control of her story through deliberately withholding or distorting information. The telling and retelling of Eva's story, along with Eva's refusal to divulge information at other times, reiterates Jones's preoccupation with language, memory, and interpretations of the past. *Eva's Man* also examines relationships between gender and sexuality, abuse and sexual violence, lesbian relationships, and public and private discourses. This novel contains an unforgettable scene in which Eva bites off her lover's penis, a method of castration also alluded to in *Corregidora*. Some critics charged that Jones's novels perpetuated stereotypes of African American men and women. Others praised her honesty and candor in depicting personal relationships. In a 1979 interview with the literary critic Claudia C. Tate, Jones explained that her African American female characters are more autonomous than traditionally heroic, more complex than unified in any

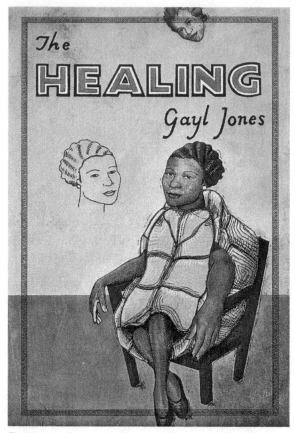

The Healing. Cover of Gayl Jones' 1999 novel that chronicles the life of Harlan Jane Eagleton, a beautician, photojournalist, and traveling faith healer. (Beacon Press, Boston.)

simplistic way: "I think it's important to be able to work with a range of personalities, as well as with a range of personalities within one personality" (Tate, "An Interview," 147).

As she was establishing herself as a creative writer, Jones was also beginning an academic career. She taught at Wellesley College before becoming, in 1975, an assistant professor of English at the University of Michigan, where she earned a Howard Foundation Award that same year and a National Endowment for the Arts Grant in 1976. While on the faculty at Michigan, she published *White Rat*, a collection of short stories, in 1977. She also published *Song for Anninho*, a long narrative poem, in 1981, and a collection of poems called *The Hermit-Woman* in 1983. During this time she met her husband, Robert ("Bob") Higgins, then a student at the University of Michigan.

Jones left the university abruptly in February 1985, following Higgins's indictment for brandishing a shotgun at a gay rights rally in Ann Arbor

in 1983, and disappeared from public view. She and Higgins, who eventually took her name in marriage, moved to Europe. *Xarque and Other Poems* was published in 1985, and while she was living abroad, her novel *Die Volgelfaengerin* ("The Birdwatcher"), was published in Germany. In 1988 Jones and her husband returned to the United States and to her hometown, Lexington, where the author attempted to live her life as privately as possible. She did not publish again in the United States until the release of her critical work, *Liberating Voices: Oral Tradition in African American Literature*, in 1991.

In 1998 Jones released *The Healing*, a novel focused on faith, hope, and forgiveness, to critical acclaim, including a nomination for the National Book Award. Like Ursa Corregidora and Eva Canada, *The Healing*'s protagonist, Harlan Jane Eagleton, faces the violence of her past. Yet Harlan's story is about overcoming and escaping the past—learning to heal. Jones's successful and optimistic return to the literary world was overshadowed by personal tragedy only a month after the publication of her novel. On 20 February 1998, Lexington police came to the Joneses' house following reports of bizarre behavior by her husband and to execute an old warrant dating back to his 1983 arrest. This led to a standoff during which the couple barricaded themselves in their home. The confrontation ended with Bob Jones's suicide and Gayl Jones's admission to Eastern State Hospital for psychiatric observation. Still, Jones continued writing and published another novel, *Mosquito*, in 1999.

Protective of her private life, Jones contends that "her work must live independently of its creator, that it must sustain its own character and artistic autonomy" (Tate, 142). Jones's fiction, poetry, and literary criticism satisfy this requirement, acting as dynamic testaments to the African American oral tradition, southern culture, the legacy of slavery, and the blues.

FURTHER READING
Bell, Bernard W. "The Liberating Literary and African American Vernacular Voices of Gayl Jones," *Comparative Literature Studies* 36.3 (1999).
Coser, Stelamaris. *Bridging the Americas: The Literature of Paule Marshall, Toni Morrison, and Gayl Jones* (1995).
Robinson, Sally. *Engendering the Subject: Gender and Self-Representation in Contemporary Women's Fiction* (1991).
Rowell, Charles H. "An Interview with Gayl Jones," *Callaloo* 16 (1982).

Tate, Claudia C. "An Interview with Gayl Jones," *Black American Literature Forum* 13.4 (1979).

Tate, Claudia C. ed. *Black Women Writers at Work* (1983).

REBECCA L. SKIDMORE

Jones, Gilbert Haven (23 Aug. 1883–24 June 1966), philosopher and educator, was born in Fort Mott, South Carolina, to Bishop Joshua H. Jones and Elizabeth Martin Jones. Joshua H. Jones, who was remarried in 1888 to Augusta E. Clark, was a president of Ohio's Wilberforce University (1900–1908), a preacher of the African Methodist Episcopal (AME) Church from age eighteen, and a bishop of the AME Church from 1912. The elder Jones was well educated, receiving a B.A. from Claflin University in South Carolina, studying at Howard University, and receiving both his bachelor of divinity and doctor of divinity degrees from Wilberforce University.

Gilbert Haven Jones was still young when his parents moved from South Carolina to Providence, Rhode Island, where he was educated in public schools. Later the family moved to Columbus, Ohio, where he graduated from Central High School at age fifteen. He then attended Ohio State University (College of Arts and Sciences) for three years, subsequently transferring to Wilberforce University, where he received his B.A. in 1902. He received his B.S. from Wilberforce just one year later. After graduating, Jones became principal of Lincoln High School in Carlisle, Pennsylvania, while also studying at Dickinson College, Carlisle, for a B.A. in Philosophy, which he received in 1905 or 1906. In 1907 he received an M.A. in Philosophy.

After working for one year as chair of classic languages at Langston University in Langston, Oklahoma, Jones completed his studies abroad: studying at the University of Göttingen, Berlin; the University of Leipzig; the University of Halle; the University of Toulouse; and the Sorbonne in Paris. In 1909 he received his Ph.D. in Philosophy from the University of Jena, Germany; his dissertation was called "*Lotze und Bowne: Eine Vergleichung ihrer philosophischen Arbeit*" ("Lotze and Bowne: A Comparison of Their Philosophical Work"). Over the course of his career he also received honorary degrees from Dickinson College (doctor of laws), Wilberforce University (doctor of laws and doctor of humanities), and Howard University (doctor of laws). Jones married Rachel Gladys Coverdale, who was born in Germantown, Pennsylvania, on 10 June 1910. They had four children: Gladys Havena, Gilbert Haven Jr., Ruth Inez, and Donald Coverdale.

Jones clearly was influenced by both his father's educational values and the AME Church's sensibilities in terms of its emphasis upon educational excellence; the AME Church is historically known for its activist social gospel. Indeed, as early as 1863 BISHOP DANIEL A. PAYNE was involved in the founding of Wilberforce University, which was one of many black colleges founded and financially supported by the AME Church. Jones was not only a member of the AME Church but also Ohio state superintendent of the church's Allen Endeavor Society, which was dedicated to Christian education in the form of youth fellowship.

Jones was dean of the College of Liberal Arts at Wilberforce University from 1914 to 1924 and then became the university's fourth president, serving from 1924 to 1932. During Jones's first four years as president, his father was president of the board of trustees and shared many of the challenges his son faced with the university administration. Such challenges involved not only perennial difficulties with funding and raising academic standards but also with bishops around issues of church politics and the distribution of institutional power. During the last four years, Jones's father was both a vice president of the board and a very active member of the executive committee. During this time Jones and his father maintained a very cooperative relationship.

As president, Jones worked hard to make salaries and academic requirements comparable to other educational institutions at the time. The Great Depression hit black people particularly hard. This had an adverse effect on Jones's efforts to raise the necessary funds to attract and retain capable teachers. At Wilberforce the Depression caused a reduction of about 14 percent in the number of faculty personnel and a salary reduction for those remaining. These reductions made it difficult for the university to become a member of the North Central Association of Colleges and Secondary Schools, which was the accrediting agency for colleges in that region. While president, however, Jones lessened the indebtedness of the university and created a greater operating surplus. Doubting the financial strength of the church to maintain its schools, Jones sought private funding. Never, however, did he abandon the centrality of the church's role at Wilberforce University.

Besides his dissertation, Jones wrote a number of magazine articles and other published works.

He was the author of *Education in Theory and Practice*, which was published in 1919, evidently making Jones the first black scholar to write a major treatise on educational theory. The myriad subjects explored in the book included discipline in the school, the importance of the field of psychology to education, and issues of hygiene, body comportment, manners, dress, social development, heredity, mnemonics, means of teaching patriotism, and religion. He examined the role of teachers within the community, length of school hours, rewards used in school, and dynamics of the physical and social environmental aspects of the school and classroom, as well as intellectual, cultural, and practical education and the arts and sciences. Most importantly, the text was structured by the theory that the self is dynamic and capable of growth, movement, progress, and change. This model challenged white myths that held that blacks were genetically inferior. As he put it in this book, "Great minds, 'men of genius,' are not so much born so (by nature) as they are made so (by nurture)" (38).

How could Jones, who was imbued with the spirit of the AME Church, argue otherwise? The aim of education, for Jones, was "to equalize the opportunity of all in their access to the accumulated knowledge of the race and to give to one and all alike equal opportunity to acquire skill in the use of its material achievement" (39). In more race-sensitive language, if one allows black people to gain an equal-quality education, then one also opens up possibilities for them to gain greater control over their circumstances. Jones's educational theory stressed the importance of black empowerment.

Jones was widely known as an exceptional administrator, an enthusiast for the maintenance of black institutional power, and as a scholar. He appeared in *Who's Who in Colored America, International Who's Who*, and *Leaders in Education*. He was a member of the American Academy of Political and Social Science and of the advisory board for the Northeastern Life Insurance Company, New York City, and served as treasurer of Kappa Alpha Psi Fraternity, which, as one of the earliest predominantly black fraternities, was founded in 1911 at Indiana University, Bloomington. Its organizing motif was achievement.

Gilbert Haven Jones died in 1966, in the midst of the Black Power movement. He knew the importance of economic and educational power for black people. In *Education in Theory and Practice* he noted, "Men [and women] afraid of opposition and criticism never turn the world upside down by their 'doughty deeds'" (247). Within the historical context of African American struggle, Jones knew what it meant, in JAMES MEREDITH's words, to "march against fear"; moreover, he knew the challenges involved in attempting "to turn the world upside down."

FURTHER READING

Gilbert Haven Jones's papers are in Archives and Special Collections, Rembert E. Stokes Learning Resources Center, Wilberforce University, Wilberforce, Ohio.

McGinnis, Frederick A. *A History and an Interpretation of Wilberforce University* (1941).

Robinson, George F. *History of Greene County, Ohio* (1902).

Yancy, George. "In the Spirit of the A.M.E. Church: Gilbert Haven Jones as an Early Black Philosopher and Educator," *A.M.E. Church Review* 118 (Oct.– Dec. 2002).

GEORGE YANCY

Jones, Grace (19 May 1952–), model, singer, performance artist, and actress, was born in Spanishtown, Jamaica, the daughter of Marjorie and Robert Jones. Her mother was a clothing maker whose design skills influenced her daughter's eventual reputation as a fashion trendsetter. Her father was a minister whose charismatic preaching influenced his daughter's sense of drama. Jones, a twin, was one of seven children, and the large family shared an enthusiasm for music that shaped her childhood ambition of becoming a singer.

Like thousands of people of African descent from the Caribbean, the family relocated to the United States to seek more opportunities. They settled in Syracuse, New York, in the 1960s, with the parents preceding their children to the United States and then reuniting the family in 1964 in their new home. Jones continued her education in Syracuse and enrolled in Syracuse University in 1968, where she focused on theater arts but left before graduating to pursue her interest in stage performance in New York City.

Jones developed her performing skills in clubs and theaters during the early 1970s, but recognized the importance of crafting an image that would catch the eye of promoters. Moving into the world of high-fashion modeling, she deliberately cultivated an exotic, androgynous appearance that emphasized her tall, sinuous body and dark skin coloring; to heighten the distinctiveness of this image, Jones cut her hair in a short, "masculine" manner and designed make-up to draw attention to her sculpted, expressive facial features. By the mid-1970s, major fashion magazines and designers, especially in Europe, were featuring photos of Jones in this gender-bending persona.

Concurrently remaining focused on her singing career, Jones continued to perform when possible, and in 1977 she accepted a recording contract with Island Records. In swift succession, she produced three disco-themed albums, *Portfolio* (1977), *Fame* (1978), and *Muse* (1979). She worked closely with the French photographer and artist Jean-Paul Goude, whom she met in 1977, to hone her transgressive approach to gender and sexuality. Goude, who became her lover and fathered her only child, Apollo (born in 1980), originally received credit for conceiving Jones's "macho" look, but his major contribution to her career was actually to develop her overall image by co-designing her elaborate stage sets, costumes, and performance poses. Playing with racially provocative images, Jones and Goude developed hallmark performances, including one in which Jones, naked and in the guise of a caged tiger, appeared to attack and devour an actual tiger. Such elaborate theatricality both pushed audiences to expect more from a singer than straightforward delivery of her songs and also commented ironically on Jones's status as a performer of African ancestry (linked stereotypically in white-directed popular culture to "darkest Africa" and jungle savagery). Building on the popularity of disco with many young gay men, Jones and Goude also had her perform as a boxer and dance with muscular male body-builders; Jones's appeal to gay male audiences established her as one of the first "disco divas" with record sales strongly boosted from heavy play in gay-centered nightclubs.

Her fourth and fifth albums, *Warm Leatherette* (1980) and *Nightclubbing* (1981), had diverse musical inspirations and crossed over into rock-and-roll; the single "Pull Up to the Bumper," from *Nightclubbing*, reached the Billboard Top 20. Jones parlayed these successes into several popular film appearances (including *Conan the Destroyer* in 1984 and *A View to a Kill* in 1985). At this point in her career, she also moved into avant-garde art, working with the painter Keith Haring and the photographer Robert Mapplethorpe.

Audience tastes shifted away from disco and performance-based "glam rock" in the 1980s, but Jones continued to record; she released five more albums over the decade. Her eight releases in the 1990s and early 2000s were primarily remixed compilations of earlier recordings. She garnered

Grace Jones spins records for the opening of Song Airlines' first airline concept store, titled *Song in the City*, 6 November 2003 in New York. (AP Images.)

negative publicity in the 1980s with drug-related charges and a much-publicized incident on a live British talk show that involved Jones slapping the host when he seemed to ignore her.

Given Jones's ability to pursue publicity to her own advantage, however, even controversial stories kept her in the spotlight. Throughout her career she seemed to understand both the superficiality and necessity of image-based media hype. Her penchant for manipulating journalists helped maintain her air of mystery as Jones, tongue in cheek, tended to provide contradictory dates, names, and other details about her life when interviewed. For example, although Jones had married a security guard named Atila Altaunbay in 1996, she was reported in 2003 to be engaged to Ivor Guest, a British viscount—even though she had not divorced Altaunbay. As Jones described the illusory and crafted nature of her identity in an interview in 2000, "I do change roles in life, I live that way" (Usborne, 1).

Although white performers like David Bowie and Annie Lennox received much attention for their androgynous stage personae and social critiques embedded in theatrical music, Grace Jones was among the first to "imprint a pop moment on mass consciousness" through working to "redefine images of race and gender on … a wide scale" (O'Brien, 260). Her "multilayered references to racial and sexual stereotypes associated with the African diaspora" and racism helped Jones intrigue, mock, and confound her mostly white audiences (Kershaw, 19).

FURTHER READING

Kershaw, Mariam. "Postcolonialism and Androgyny: The Performance Art of Grace Jones," *Art Journal* 56 (Winter 1997).

O'Brien, Lucy. *She Bop II: The Definitive History of Women in Rock, Pop and Soul* (2002).

Usborne, David. "Grace in Favour," *Independent* (London), 4 Sept. 2000.

BETH KRAIG

Jones, Grace Morris Allen (7 Jan. 1876–2 Mar. 1928), educator, was born Grace Morris Allen in Keokuk, Iowa, to James Addison Morris and Mary Ellen (Pyles) Morris, of whom little else is known. Grace grew up in Burlington, Iowa, was educated in the Burlington schools, and is believed to have graduated from the University of Iowa. She also studied public speaking at the Chicago Conservatory of Music.

Allen's primary concern was for oppressed blacks, especially women and children, and she spent most of her life working to improve their conditions. She established the first integrated kindergarten in Burlington and also founded the city's Grace M. Allen Industrial School in 1902. The school, which employed both black and white teachers, was intended for African Americans, but it proved so successful that white students began to attend.

Allen also worked as a solicitor for the Eckstein-Norton Institute, a college in Cane Springs, Kentucky. It was while in this position that she met the man who would become her husband, LAURENCE JONES, at a speech he gave in Iowa City when he was still a student at what was then known as the State University of Iowa. Allen was in the audience and responded to his speech with her observations, and she impressed Jones with her knowledge of the position of blacks in the South. The two exchanged letters occasionally and eventually met

again in Des Moines, Iowa. By this time Laurence Jones had graduated from the University of Iowa and had founded the Piney Woods Country Life School in 1909, located in impoverished Piney Woods, Mississippi. The school offered an education to poor black children that aimed at providing students with practical skills, so in addition to teaching reading, writing, and math, instruction was also given in laundry, sewing, weaving, and basket making. The students' days were rigorous: a typical day began at five in the morning, and students were expected to do manual labor in the morning and attend classes in the afternoon.

Naturally Jones and Allen bonded quickly through their shared interest in education, and they married and moved to Piney Woods in 1912. Grace Allen Jones was touched by the poverty of the area and the determination of its residents to obtain an education for their children; in fact, the school, which included day students and boarders, had many more students than it could accommodate comfortably and funds were always limited. Allen Jones immediately began to play a role in the duties at Piney Woods. Because her husband devoted much of his time to the necessary task of fund-raising, she and the other principals' wives had a prominent part in managing the school. Allen Jones taught English, was director of the handcrafts department, and played a significant role in the expansion of the school. As the school grew, local men and women were invited to attend the cooking, sewing, and handcraft classes, and they responded enthusiastically. During the summer months when she was not teaching, Allen Jones assisted her husband in raising funds for the school, traveling throughout the country. She was in fact an exceptional fund-raiser. Because so many of the students had impressive musical talents, she decided to take some of them with her during the summer as a strategy for raising money. The first year she traveled with a vocal quartet called the Cotton Blossoms, and they proved to be such a success at motivating their audiences to contribute to the school that they continued to tour each year.

In addition to her constant work at the school, Allen Jones was determined to do what she could to help those in the surrounding community. She advocated prison reform and, as a result, a reform school was built for black children. She also organized the Piney Woods Mothers' Club, which was affiliated with the Mississippi State Federation of Colored Women's Clubs. The organization had been launched at a national level in 1895 and was established in

Mississippi in 1903. The Mississippi federation was in decline until Allen Jones was elected president in 1920. Under Allen Jones's leadership the club thrived. Its members were taught sewing, cooking, and other useful skills that would improve the quality of their everyday lives. Its additional contributions to the community included operating retirement homes, providing education for handicapped children, establishing training schools, and placing libraries in elementary schools.

Allen Jones and her husband first resided in what had been a slave cabin in Piney Woods. They continued to move from building to building when their quarters were needed for students; they always lived in substandard conditions because the students were their priority. In 1912 they moved into a cottage that was built using funds from a donation meant for that purpose. Before long, though, a fire resulted in their sharing their home with other teachers. Finally, in 1922 they built a home in Piney Woods where they raised their two sons, Turner and Laurence Clifton Jr.

In 1928 Allen Jones returned from one of her long trips with the Cotton Blossoms and was diagnosed with pneumonia. She recovered briefly, but her determination to return to work caused her condition to decline. Her death was felt by all, and it "took half a dozen to absorb the jobs she had carried alone" at Piney Woods (Day, 152). She and her husband are buried at the Piney Woods School, where a log cabin was built in Allen Jones's honor.

FURTHER READING

Grace Morris Allen Jones's papers are housed in the Iowa Women's Archives, University of Iowa Libraries, Iowa City.

Day, Beth. *The Little Professor of Piney Woods: The Story of Professor Laurence Jones* (1955).

Harrison, Alferdteen B. *Piney Woods School: An Oral History* (1982).

DIANE TODD BUCCI

Jones, James Earl (17 Jan. 1931–), actor, was born in Arkabutla, Mississippi, the only child of Robert Earl Jones, a prizefighter and actor, and Ruth Williams Connoly, a seamstress. Jones's parents parted ways in search of work before their son was born, and he was raised by his mother's parents, John and Maggie Connoly. He grew up on their farm, alongside seven children and two other grandchildren. From an early age Jones was put to work beside his aunts, uncles, and cousins, tending the livestock, hunting, and helping with harvests.

At night Maggie Connoly would regale the family with lurid bedtime stories—tales of lynchings, hurricanes, and rapes. The Connolys knew that Mississippi schools offered their children little, and in 1936 they planned a move to Dublin, Michigan. Before the family left, John Connoly took Jones to his paternal grandmother's house in Memphis, but Jones refused to leave the car. He followed the family north later that year.

Soon after the move to Michigan, Jones began to stutter; he spoke only to his family, to the farm animals, and to himself. In grammar school he managed to get by on written work, and it was not until high school that someone sought to help him. An English teacher, Donald Crouch, pushed Jones to join the debate team. With practice, Jones proved a captivating orator and, by the end of high school, managed to overcome his stuttering in conversation, too. As he regained his powers of speech, he took to the classics Crouch taught and spent many an afternoon reading Shakespeare aloud in the fields.

At this time Jones's father was living in New York City and trying his hand at theater. When Jones announced to his uncle Randy that he, too, would be an actor, John Connoly pounced on his grandson and struck him in the back of the head. In 1949 Jones entered the University of Michigan on a Regents Scholarship and enrolled in premed classes, but the pull of the theater proved too strong; he began taking roles in school plays and spending his holidays in summer-stock productions. Jones had joined the Reserve Officers' Training Corps (ROTC) to help fund his education, and he abandoned school in 1953, just before graduation, convinced that he would shortly be killed in the Korean War. But the conflict cooled off that summer, and Jones spent his two years of service at the Cold Weather Training Command in Colorado. He enjoyed the strenuous work and the solitude of the Rockies, but when he told his commanding officer that he wanted to be an actor, he was urged to pursue theater before committing to military life. Jones finished his B.A. through an extension program and moved in with his father in New York. He enrolled in acting workshops at the American Theatre Wing, paying his way with funds from the GI Bill.

After twenty-four years of separation, Jones and his father did not get along well, and during one argument they nearly came to blows. But if the two did not bond as father and son, they came together over their shared passion. Late into the night they would recite scenes from *Othello*. After six months Jones moved to the Lower East Side and continued his austere routine of workshops, auditions, and menial jobs. In 1957 he landed his first Broadway role as an understudy to Lloyd Richards in *The Egghead*. That same year he found more substantial work in Ted Pollock's play *Wedding in Japan*.

In the early 1960s Off-Broadway theater offered a heady cocktail of new talent, edgy scripts, and run-down venues. Jones entered the fray as Deodatus Village in the 1961 production of Jean Genet's *The Blacks*, a savage and absurdist allegory of race relations written for an all-black cast. Critics at the *Village Voice* and the *New Yorker* swooned, and both singled Jones out for praise from a cast that included CICELY TYSON, ROSCOE LEE BROWNE, LOU GOSSETT, and MAYA ANGELOU. Given the charged political climate and the play's violent language, performances were hard on audiences and performers alike, and Jones left the cast, to recover, some six times during the play's two-year run. In 1962 Jones earned several awards for his performances in *Moon on a Rainbow Shawl* and won an Obie as Best Actor in Off-Broadway Theater for his work in *Clandestine on the Morning Line*. Throughout the 1960s Jones built a name for himself at the New York Shakespeare Festival and his 1964 appearance in the title role in *Othello* won a Drama Desk Award for Best Performance. The following year, he received two Obies for his work in *Othello* and in Bertolt Brecht's *Baal*.

No role propelled his career, however, like his 1967 portrayal of Jack Jefferson, a character based on JACK JOHNSON, the first black heavyweight boxing champion, in Howard Sackler's play *The Great White Hope*. To prepare for the audition he began a brutal exercise regimen. Six feet two inches tall, slimmed down to two hundred pounds, his head shaved and shiny, Jones landed the part, which earned him his first Tony Award and another Drama Desk Award. The play, which challenged and titillated audiences with its interracial love story, moved from the Arena Stage in Washington, D.C., to Broadway in 1968. Jones reprised the role two years later in Martin Ritt's film adaptation of the play, which costarred Jane Alexander and earned Jones an Oscar nomination.

SIDNEY POITIER urged Jones to avoid the stock parts film and television typically offered black actors. For several years Jones heeded the advice, but in 1964 he took a small part as a pilot in Stanley Kubrick's film *Dr. Strangelove*. Jones also began to make inroads into the small screen. A 1965 stint on *As the World Turns* made him the first African American with a continuing role in a daytime soap opera. In 1967 Jones married Julienne

James Earl Jones gives the keynote address during the 2002 Martin Luther King Day celebration, 19 January 2002, at the Lauderhill Boys and Girls Club in Lauderhill, Florida. (AP Images.)

Marie Hendricks, who had played Desdemona to his Othello in 1964. But Jones's growing success brought a new measure of instability to his life, and the marriage did not last.

On stage in 1970 Jones appeared in LORRAINE HANSBERRY's play *Les Blancs* and costarred with RUBY DEE in Athol Fugard's *Boesman and Lena*. He continued working in film and television throughout the early and mid-1970s. Highlights included appearing as the big screen's first African American president of the United States in *The Man* in 1972 and playing the title role in *King Lear* on television in 1974. In 1977 Jones was cast as PAUL ROBESON in the one-man show based on the life of the actor, singer, and activist who had once been feted for his magnetic stage presence but wound up blacklisted as a result of his politics. Robeson died in 1976, and the play was meant to honor his career, but it, too, fell victim to censorship. Rallied by the actor's son, Paul Robeson Jr., the Ad Hoc Committee to End the Crimes against Paul Robeson charged that the play distorted Robeson's life. Theater after theater was picketed. After one of the last performances, Jones delivered a blistering indictment of the committee's antics. In 1979 Jones starred in the play's film adaptation directed by Lloyd Richards.

Jones, who continued his stage work in such plays as Fugard's *Master Harold and the Boys* and

Of Mice and Men, has been known to stop mid-performance to shush members of the crew and the audience or to ask them in his round, resonant basso to "stop popping that fucking bubble gum!" (Jones, 334). His relationships with directors and writers have also been strained at times. In 1981, while preparing for a new production of *Othello*, Jones accused the director Peter Coe of turning Shakespeare's tragedy into a farce. In 1987's *Fences*, a father-son play about a poor black family, Jones butted heads with the playwright AUGUST WILSON. In spite of these clashes—or perhaps because of them—both plays won critical acclaim. *Othello* received a Tony for Best Revival, while *Fences* won Jones both a Tony and a Drama Desk Award for his performance.

In early 1982 Jones married Cecilia Hart. That December their son, Flynn Earl Jones, was born. To support his new family, Jones chose to spend more time in the unglamorous world of made-for-TV movies, bit parts, and voice-overs. The last came in droves after Jones lent his voice to the role of the archvillain Darth Vader in George Lucas's *Star Wars* films released in 1977, 1980, and 1983. Asked why he had agreed to provide the film's most evil character with a black voice, Jones replied that the work took two hours and paid seven thousand dollars.

Following *Fences*, Jones decided that he no longer had the energy for leading roles on the stage, which may account for his increased presence on the screen. In addition to his many featured roles on television, Jones appeared in a variety of films, including John Sayles's *Matewan* (1987), about coal miners struggling to form a union in Mingo County, West Virginia, in 1920. Jones worked in comedy as well, in such films as *Soul Man* (1986) and the EDDIE MURPHY vehicle *Coming to America* (1988). In 1989 he appeared as the reclusive, misanthropic writer in *Field of Dreams*, one the year's most popular films. Throughout the 1990s Jones appeared in films and on television at an astounding rate. He played Admiral Greer in the highly popular films *The Hunt for Red October*, *Patriot Games*, and *Clear and Present Danger*, based on the novels by Tom Clancy. Notable leading roles included the title role in the television series *Gabriel's Fire*, in which he starred for two seasons, and a priest accused of murder in the 1995 film version of Alan Paton's novel about South Africa, *Cry the Beloved Country*.

More and more, however, Jones has been in demand simply as himself, as a host, presenter, and narrator. He voiced the animated characters King Mufasa in Disney's *The Lion King* (1994) and the long-silent Maggie on *The Simpsons*. A popular commercial pitchman, Jones and his distinctive voice have become part of American daily life, telling television viewers that they are watching CNN or thanking callers for using a Verizon pay phone. Instead of asking for autographs, fans beg Jones to record their answering machine messages. Over the last half century Jones has appeared in more than two hundred films and television shows. For his work as an actor, Jones has won four Emmy awards, two Tony awards, two Obie awards, five Drama Desk awards, a Golden Globe Award, and a Grammy. A presidential appointee to the National Council on the Arts from 1970 to 1976, Jones has received five honorary doctorates and the NAACP Hall of Fame Image Award. In 1992 he was awarded the National Medal of Arts by President George H. W. Bush. While Jones's career displays a boundless range, depth, and energy, most of his fans see his legacy in more grandiose terms; he is, quite simply, the voice of America.

FURTHER READING

Jones, James Earl, and Penelope Niven. *James Earl Jones: Voices and Silences* (1993, 2002).

Bryer, Jackson R., and Richard A. Davison, eds. *The Actor's Art: Conversations with Contemporary American Stage Performers* (2001).

Gill, Glenda E. *No Surrender! No Retreat!: African American Pioneer Performers of Twentieth-Century American Theater* (2000).

CHRIS BEBENEK

Jones, James Francis (24 Nov. 1907–12 Aug. 1971), religious leader known as the "Prophet," was born in Birmingham, Alabama, the only son of Catherine and James Jones. He was consistently evasive about his youth, though he did speak of being raised by his devoted mother and not by his alcoholic, absentee father (from whom Jones always remained distant). He claimed also to have been called to God at a young age, and at age eighteen he was ordained a minister of Triumph, the Church and Kingdom of God in Christ, an unaffiliated Christian church. While Jones frequently said that the only book he ever touched was the Bible, he claimed to have a degree from Johnson C. Smith University, a black school in Charlotte, North Carolina (hence his fake "Doctor" title). In fact Jones had no degree.

Using Birmingham as a home base, he was an itinerant preacher until 1938. During that time Jones's following was racially mixed, though in an oddly segregated way. According to a member of his inner circle and, at one point, his organ player Ralph Boyd, Jones preached directly to black southerners, but outside the church or tent walls where Jones preached, whites often lingered to listen. "They would be all parked outside in their cars," he said. "They would come to listen but just wouldn't come in" (Boyd). Part of the draw may have been Jones's already flamboyant styling. Even in the Depression-era South, Jones arrived in town with an entourage, riding in a Cadillac. As much as a religious event, Jones was a peculiarity, a sideshow for those languishing in dying southern towns. He moved to Detroit in 1938 to serve as a "prince" of Triumph and leader of Band Number 2, a parish of sorts that included Detroit. He was promoted to "county prince" by Triumph the Church leadership in 1943, the year that the city was torn apart by race riots.

Detroit, like most other northern industrial cities, was adjusting to demographic shifts. Because Jones was serving a largely African American population, he stepped into a region with a displaced black population that looked toward its churches for reminders of home. Jones could relate to the new migrants. Paradoxically, though, it was his difference from those migrants that seems to have led to his rise. One of Jones's followers who knew him in his Birmingham days said, "The Prophet has always been a member of the 'third sex'—that is, on the 'feminine side.'" Jones himself talked up his difference from others. In a master's thesis written at Wayne State University in Detroit, H. F. McFadden quoted Jones as saying: "I have never played baseball; I have never had a baseball in my hands. I have never shot marbles. I have never had a marble in my hands. I have never been intoxicated; I have never tasted an intoxicating beverage. I have never had sexual intercourse with a woman" (McFadden). With the final negative in that quotation, Jones, inadvertently or not, hinted at his sexual orientation, which many of his followers assumed was homosexual. But if his orientation served as a differentiator, it too served as his downfall.

In 1944 *Life* magazine profiled "Prophet" Jones, as he was now widely known. The photo spread included a large photograph of Jones reclining on a couch, which was backed by ceiling-to-floor silk curtains. A grand piano appears on the edge of the frame. The article was less a study of Jones's theology than a fashion portrait. The material splendor soon became a legal issue when Triumph, the Church and Kingdom of God, sued Jones, along with members of his entourage, for taking as their personal property gifts to Jones while, Triumph argued, he served as a representative of their church. The parties eventually settled for a $5,000 payment from Jones to his now former church. But the case and Jones's defense signaled that he had become larger than the church that brought him to Detroit. Rather than a church representative, Jones was the sole charismatic leader of a flock. He did not receive the gifts—Cadillacs, the mansion in an elite Detroit neighborhood, the white mink fur coat—because he was a Triumph representative. His followers, many of them poor or blue-collar workers, gave him the gifts, they said, because he was different.

Jones offered a theology in which he placed himself at the center. He attempted to control members' sexual practices by telling them when "to mate," according to Boyd's recollections and McFadden's thesis. Owing to the combination of his charismatic leadership and, perhaps, his promise of eternal life on earth if the people followed his rules, according to Boyd, some members followed, though it is impossible to know how many. Three other points were central to membership: to be a member, one had to revoke any membership in other churches; if members followed his rules and they lived until the year 2000, they would never die; that subsequent eternity would be under Jones's dispensation, when Jones would lead the world. Boyd explained that these were all things followers "understood" rather than read in texts such as the Bible or the Koran. Because Jones never wrote a text such as the Bible, he possessed a malleability that allowed him to change rules as he saw fit.

Services at his new church, the Universal Triumph Church, similarly named to his old church, became marathon tests of devotion, usually lasting more than twelve hours. Jones did not appear until several hours had passed. Before he arrived, attendees danced to swinging jazz, listened to preaching by some of Jones's lieutenants, and perhaps most importantly, heard testimonies from members describing how Jones healed them of various ailments. Resplendent in a bejeweled gown, Jones finally danced down the center aisle to his seat on a golden throne. He never wore jewels on the right side of his body, better not to interfere with the breeze to his right ear, which flowed directly from God, he claimed.

The central part of the service was "the Expressions of Life," for which members paid $1 to participate. A person paid, approached Jones on stage, and then asked him for advice on a problem. Jones answered with advice that he said arrived through the holy breeze in his right ear, a breeze that helped him predict future events, such as the use of atomic bombs against Japan.

Jones often claimed to have millions of followers around the world, when in fact he more likely had thousands around the United States. The increased fame—he had a radio show that broadcast throughout the Midwest and a local late night television program—began to draw negative attention. One time a would-be assassin riddled one of Jones's cars with bullets, and in 1952 he was the victim of an extortion plot in a semiliterate note threatening his life. When the FBI interviewed Jones, he revealed that when he was a fourteen-year-old the Birmingham police had arrested him on charges of committing an "immoral act." No further definition was left in the FBI files, but the vague wording does hint toward Jones's possible homosexuality, which eventually helped end his reign.

On 29 December 1955 John Henry, a young undercover police, made a visit to Jones's home, the so-called French Castle, to investigate Jones's long-rumored numbers running, an underground sort of lottery. Henry's initial visit was to claim he had back pain and needed a cure. The final visit was to report that Jones had cured the back pain. Once Henry was inside Jones's private chambers, Jones attempted to seduce him, asking him to masturbate. Jones eventually blew on the officer's penis, and Henry pulled away. Jones was arraigned on "morals charges" on 21 February 1956. The local press mocked Jones and celebrated his arrest. Tim Retzloff, in his study of the case, quotes the *Detroit Tribune*. The paper's editorial feared that others—white Detroiters—would think African Americans had been under the leadership of "a sex deviant." There was no public support for Jones. While he was never convicted of a crime, his public outing proved too much for Jones to overcome and his followers to endure. While followers seemed to understand that Jones was homosexual, that he acted in any sexual way, especially when he held such tight control over followers' sexuality, was apparently too much. For them, it seems, his attitude was less immoral than hypocritical.

Jones's empire soon crumbled. While he still visited Detroit, he lived mostly in Chicago. The homes, cars, and jewels still drew attention, however. Jones was a financially broken man. He had no income other than the gifts his devoted followers gave. Once he lost his following, he lost his income. Convinced that he was still wealthy, federal investigators drilled into his safety deposit box in 1958.

The only things of value they found were 1,215 pennies. Jones had nothing, material at least, left.

After more than a decade of exile in Chicago, Jones died from a heart attack during a Detroit visit. Detroit newspapers carried pictures of lines of thousands of mourners snaking around the block, waiting to view his body one more time.

FURTHER READING
Boyd, Ralph J. Personal interview with author, 27 Feb. 2002.

Brean, Herbert. *Life* (27 Nov. 1944).

McFadden, H. F. "A Study of a Negro Cult: Thankful Center Number One, of the Religious Organization of 'Prophet' James Francis Jones," M.A. thesis, Wayne State University (1949).

Retzloff, Tim. "'Seer or Queer?' Postwar Fascination with Detroit's Prophet Jones," *GLQ: A Journal of Lesbian and Gay Studies* 8 (2002): 271–296.

Obituary: *New York Times*, 13 Aug. 1971.

PATRICK CLIFF

Jones, James Monroe "Gunsmith" (15 Jan. 1821–7 Nov. 1905), gunsmith and engraver, was born in Raleigh, North Carolina, the eldest son of Allen Jones, a slave and a blacksmith, and Temperance Jones, a slave. He was one of eight children, a daughter and seven sons, born into a long line of slavery. His paternal grandfather, Charles Jones, was born in Africa around 1770 and brought to America to be sold into slavery some years later. Although born a slave, Gunsmith Jones was freed in 1829, when his father purchased liberty for his entire family. Allen Jones was a skilled blacksmith who labored intensely for himself and his family while simultaneously performing his slave duties to earn the vast sum of money necessary to buy his family's freedom. After saving the extraordinary amount of $2,000, he was cheated out of the money by his master and left with nothing. With admirable determination, he worked harder still, persuading a local Quaker to use the money that he had saved to buy and then free him. Once a free man, Allen Jones bought his father, Charles, for $350. At the same time, he also petitioned for his family's freedom and eventually succeeded in emancipating them in 1829.

The Jones family suffered a great deal of persecution in Raleigh. Allen Jones and his associates were threatened and beaten, particularly after they set up a school for the children of freed slaves. This school was attacked by angry white residents and burned to the ground. In 1843, perhaps because of the particularly savage beating he had suffered a few months before, from which he almost did not recover, Allen Jones decided that his family would leave North Carolina for Ohio, where he had heard that his sons would be able to gain an education. James Monroe and his brothers, John Craven, William Allen, Elias Toussaint, and Charles Brougham, all attended Oberlin College, and James Monroe graduated A.B. in 1849. He became a skilled blacksmith and gunsmith like his father and until 1852 carried out his trade successfully in Cleveland. In that year he moved to Canada to become part of the burgeoning black population of Chatham County, a final stop on the Underground Railroad where many ex-slaves settled. In Chatham, Jones met Emily Francis, who had been born in 1829 in New Jersey to free parents. They were married on 16 November 1854 and bought a shop where Jones could practice his craft and where they would also reside. James became an established blacksmith and engraver in Chatham County, earning the name "Gunsmith" because of his outstanding craftsmanship of firearms.

Jones's skills as a rifle maker were nationally renowned, winning him multiple prizes, and in 1860 he received his highest honor yet. The Prince of Wales, the future King Edward VII, was to make an extensive tour of Canada, and Gunsmith was to have the chance to present him with a specially crafted pair of Derringer pistols. The Prince arrived in Chatham County expecting to receive a gift of beautiful pistols, made by one of Canada's finest gunsmiths. However, at the last moment, county officials discovered that the talented craftsman was, in fact, an African American. It was deemed impossible to present a member of the Royal Family with a gift made by black hands, and the Prince was sent away empty handed.

The feelings of Jones on this incident are unknown; in his alumni update to Oberlin College in 1905, the year of his death, it is omitted. The numerous other accolades he received, however, are mentioned, including two medals and three diplomas received "for fine work." A medal Jones won from the Montreal Manufacturing and Trade Fair was for a duplicate pair of Derringer pistols. The medal he won from the California State Agricultural Society in 1859 was also for a pair of Derringer pistols. In fact, James Gooding, publisher of *The Canadian Journal of Arms Collecting*, designates James Monroe Jones as "one of six Canadian gunsmiths who had the skill ... to be compared with the best in the world." It seems that the future king may have missed out on a very fine pair of pistols indeed.

The prejudice Jones experienced throughout his entire life clearly did not embitter him. He claimed in later life to belong to no religious denomination or church membership because he felt that "all men are my brethren." From the late 1880s there was a steady decline in the gun- and rifle-making industry, so Jones focused instead on his other great skill, engraving, to sustain his family. His children, six in total, were a source of great pride to him. In 1883 he sent them to Ann Arbor, Michigan, with the intention of educating his daughter in medicine. Dr. SOPHIA BETHENA JONES graduated as the first black female doctor from the University of Michigan in 1885 and later founded the first nurses' training course at Spelman College, Atlanta.

By 1875 Gunsmith Jones had become a Justice of the Peace in Chatham County, noting in his alumni record that he was "appointed for life by the Government and Governor-General," a highly respected position; Jones was clearly a valued community leader, entrusted with delivering fair and honest judgements, despite his harsh and decidedly unfair beginnings. He died in Ann Arbor, surrounded by his family, at the age of eighty-four.

FURTHER READING

Simser, Guy. "The Prince and the Pistols," *The Beaver: Canada's Historical Magazine*, February/March 2004.

VERITY J. HARDING

Jones, Jerrel, newspaper publisher and multimedia owner, was born in Milwaukee, Wisconsin, to Mary Ellen Shadd Jones, later Mary Ellen Shadd-Strong, a journalist. A descendant of MARY ANN SHADD CARY, the first female African American publisher, his mother was a correspondent for the *Chicago Defender* and *World* in an era of an only intermittent presence for the black press in Wisconsin after the loss of the legendary *Wisconsin Enterprise-Blade* in the 1940s under J. ANTHONY JOSEY.

Lacking a stable local black press, African Americans in Wisconsin seemed almost silent amid the civil rights movement for most of the next decade. Several attempts at a black press in the state failed until Shadd-Strong founded an affiliate of the *Defender* in 1956; she maintained her *Milwaukee Defender* until 1960 (McBride, 343–344). The silence was deceptive, however, as struggling publishers of the period were literally and figuratively fathers and mothers to the later, successful local black press. The *Milwaukee Star*, founded in 1960, came first and dominated most of that decade, but

Jerrel Jones's *Milwaukee Courier* brought the most stability to Milwaukee's black press for the rest of the millennium (McBride, 344–348).

After the demise of his mother's *Defender* and her local black business directory, Jones considered working for the *Star*, but instead he brought together a local group to again "bring a branch of a National Negro Weekly newspaper to Milwaukee" in June 1964. Almost all of the four cofounders brought extensive experience to the project. The least experienced in journalism was Jones, the advertising director. Soon Jones was the only one still on the paper, although his mother's influence helped to "steer advertising dollars the *Courier* way" (*Milwaukee Courier*, 9 July 1994).

Jones brought the paper through outside proprietorship when most pages came from the *Chicago Courier*, where the paper was printed, and he bought out his local competitors little more than a decade later (*Milwaukee Courier*, 9 July 1994). By 1966 the locally printed *Courier* had a larger staff than both the *Soul City Times*, also founded in 1964, and the *Star*; but the *Star* still led the local black press—if not for long—under an extraordinary editor, Walter Jones (no relation to Jerrel), formerly of the *Chicago Defender* (McBride, 342–343).

In the summer of 1967 a riot in Milwaukee proved a turning point for the *Courier*, its community, and the careers of both Jerrel Jones and Walter Jones. After three deaths, seventy injuries, and more than 1,700 arrests, the city closed down and called in five thousand National Guardsmen. The *Courier* provided comprehensive coverage, while the *Star* struggled to stay on top of the story. Within weeks, Walter Jones joined the *Courier* as editor and publisher, and he soon brought over many talented *Star* staffers (*Milwaukee Courier*, 19 Aug. and 7 Oct. 1967; McBride, 344–345).

Hiring his leading local competitor's talent freed Jerrel Jones to focus on advertising sales and forays into other media, including a news program on local minority radio. He was elected in 1968 to the National Newspaper Publishers Association board of directors, joining prestigious leaders in the black press nationwide, while *Courier* coverage for that year won NNPA merit awards for the first time in 1969 (*Milwaukee Courier*, 16 July 1994).

No competitor of the *Courier* could keep up with the Joneses, Jerrel and Walter, who fostered a level of excellence previously unseen in Wisconsin's black press. But their complicated working relationship soon caused Walter Jones to return briefly to the *Star*, and Jerrel Jones again resumed duties

as *Courier* publisher. In 1971, following a merger of the *Star* and *Soul City Times*, with production at the *Courier*, Jerrel Jones became publisher of both the *Courier* and *Star*, with Walter Jones returning as editor. Walter would resign many times in the coming decades, although he repeatedly returned as a consultant to the *Courier* until his death (*Milwaukee Courier*, 16 July 1994, 25 May 2002). However, even when Walter Jones worked for competitors, his presence in the local black press was a benefit to all, especially to Jerrel Jones's *Courier*.

For the duration of the 1970s, the *Courier* dominated the black press in Wisconsin, with increasing advertising sales and successful public service campaigns, such as voter-registration drives and Black History Month promotions. Consequently, Jerrel Jones began to expand his Courier Communications into a multimedia conglomerate. In 1973 he purchased the Milwaukee radio station WNOV from Chicago ownership for $385,000, appointing his mother as vice president and Milwaukee physician John Terry as treasurer. The cost of this venture, however, crippled the *Courier* and demoralized the staff. Two decades later, Jones recalled 1973 and 1974 as "two of the hardest years in his business career," and a time when "he considered 'throwing in the towel.'" His wife, mother, and others provided the "emotional wherewithal for him to persist," although he admitted that "he didn't know anything else but the newspaper business" (*Milwaukee Courier*, 16 July 1994).

Still, the *Courier* staff continued to win awards in 1974 from the NNPA and, in a first for the black press, from the Wisconsin Newspaper Association (*Milwaukee Courier*, 18 May 1974). The *Courier* did not report until decades later that its publisher, staff, "and Black people, generally, were insulted" at the WNA meeting, hosted by a pork growers' group, when a speaker "made a snide remark about Black people and pigs that was in very poor taste." Several publishers "appeared embarrassed" and apologized to Jones, but his compensation came in the coming years as the *Courier* staff continued to best their competitors statewide and at the national level, until the *Courier* led the NNPA in awards. Jones was elected vice president of the NNPA board in 1976 and later reelected to subsequent terms (*Milwaukee Courier*, 19 June 1976, 16 July 1994).

As the fiscal status of Courier Communications stabilized in the late 1970s and 1980s, Jones's stature steadily increased in both the African American community and the Milwaukee business community. The *Courier* was thus able to weather major changes, as associate publisher Roy Kemp left for the New York *National Scene*, partly owned by Jerrel Jones; and Walter Jones, by then the *Courier*'s general manager, left for the *Milwaukee Community Journal*, founded in 1976 by a former *Soul City Times* publisher (*Milwaukee Courier*, 16 July 1994). He was followed by *Courier* freelancer Nathan Conyers, who founded yet another competitor in 1981, the monthly *Milwaukee Christian Times* that went weekly in 1985, eventually expanding elsewhere in Wisconsin (McBride, 342).

By 1990, as competition and the economy began to negatively affect the *Courier*, Jones was hustling for advertising once again and battling with officials over radio signal rights. "There are no blacks who have made it in Milwaukee. Not one," he said. The leading local mainstream media called him "the closest thing Milwaukee has to a black media mogul," as he purchased part ownership in print and broadcast media across the country (*Milwaukee Journal*, 25 Sept. 1990).

By 2000 Jones had rebounded, looking beyond the news business and emerging from behind the political scenes as a powerbroker in his city and state. As fearless in politics as he was in business, he was "not afraid to step forward on controversial issues," as a colleague said. For example, when a leading legislator of color who was supported by the *Courier* for decades lost his seat in 2003, Jones funded a successful recall because he felt that that the legislator had betrayed *Courier* readers by forsaking the inner city for the suburbs. Jones "came out of the community and became successful, but never forget where he came from"—the community of color in Milwaukee that had made him by far the longest lasting publisher in the black press in Wisconsin history (*Milwaukee Journal*, 25 Sept. 1990, *Milwaukee Journal Sentinel*, 17 Apr. 2003).

FURTHER READING

Geib, Paul. "From Mississippi to Milwaukee: A Case Study of the Southern Black Migration to Milwaukee, 1940–1970," *Journal of Negro History* 83:4 (Autumn 1998).

McBride, Genevieve G. "The Progress of 'Race Men' and 'Colored Women' in the Black Press in Wisconsin, 1892–1985," in Henry Lewis Suggs, ed., *The Black Press in the Middle West, 1895–1985* (1996).

Trotter, Joe William, Jr. *Black Milwaukee: The Making of an Industrial Proletariat, 1915–1945* (1985).

GENEVIEVE G. MCBRIDE

Jones, Jo (17 Oct. 1911–3 Sept. 1985), jazz drummer, was born Jonathan David Samuel Jones in Chicago, the son of Samuel Jones, an artificer, and Elizabeth (maiden name unknown). Jones suffered severe burns as a young child, and during his long convalescence he turned to music. He was raised by relatives in Alabama, mainly in the Birmingham area. His aunt bought a snare drum for him when he was ten. Two or three years later he studied with the drummer Wilson Driver at the Famous Theater in Birmingham. Jones also played trumpet, saxophone, and piano, and he danced, sang, and acted, all of those talents put to use when he toured in shows and carnivals as a teenager. When not wrapped up in practice and performance, Jones attended the Tuggle Institute and in 1926 Lincoln Junior High School, both in Birmingham, and Alabama A&M near Huntsville.

By the late 1920s Jones was working as a drummer. In Omaha he joined Lloyd Hunter's Serenaders. He played with Hunter from 1931 to 1933 but also worked with Grant Moore in Milwaukee during some portion of this period. Hunter's group recorded in Kansas City in 1931. In 1933 Jones worked as a pianist and vibraphonist with the reed player Tommy Douglas in Joplin, Missouri, and Kansas City. The following year marked the beginning of Jones's association with COUNT BASIE, again as a drummer. After holding jobs with lesser-known bands in Minneapolis and Kansas City, he rejoined Basie in Topeka in late 1935, played briefly alongside WALTER PAGE with the Jeter-Pillars band in St. Louis in 1936, and then followed Page back into Basie's band at the Reno Club in Kansas City late that year. When in March 1937 the guitarist Freddie Green joined the pianist Basie, the bassist Page, and the drummer Jones in Basie's big band, the finest rhythm section of the swing era was in place. Jones's career paralleled Basie's until August 1948, apart from freelance recordings (including sessions with TEDDY WILSON and BILLIE HOLIDAY), absences because of illness, a feature role in the film short *Jammin' the Blues* (1944), a period of drafted army service (mid-September 1944–January 1946), a tour with Norman Granz's Jazz at the Philharmonic (1947), and another feature in the movie *The Unsuspected* (1947).

Jones joined the tenor saxophonist ILLINOIS JACQUET (1948–1950), and in 1948 he led his own trio. He worked with LESTER YOUNG at Birdland in New York in 1950, rejoined Jazz at the Philharmonic (1951), and then became a member of the pianist Joe Bushkin's quartet for two years. He led groups and recorded a session for the Vanguard label in 1955. For a few days in December 1957 Jones reunited with Basie to make the television show *The Sound of Jazz*. He accompanied the pianists Teddy Wilson, CLAUDE HOPKINS, RAY BRYANT, and Bushkin, among others. By this time he was sometimes called Papa Jo, and he was chagrined to be confused with the younger drummer PHILLY JOE JONES, a fiery and flamboyant hard-bop musician whose work with MILES DAVIS had perhaps made him more famous than Papa Jo in these years. Jones again toured with Jazz at the Philharmonic, and in 1969 he worked in Europe with the pianist-organist MILT BUCKNER. He figured prominently in the documentary films *Born to Swing* (1973) and *The Last of the Blue Devils* (c. 1979). After a long bout with cancer, he died in New York. His wife, Vivian, had died in 1946; details of the marriage are unknown. They had four children.

Jones exemplified the highest standards in responsibility and musicianship. He demanded the same and was rarely satisfied outside Basie's sphere, an attitude made legendary by his act of throwing a cymbal at the then inebriated CHARLIE PARKER at a jam session in Kansas City in 1937. Alternately sweet or abusive, he was outspoken on music and race, and perhaps he was excessively aware of his stature as one of the most important jazz drummers.

Jones may be heard as a soloist on "Shoe Shine Boy," recorded by a small group from Basie's band under the name Jones-Smith, Inc. (1936); "I Know That You Know," with a few of Basie's sidemen as the Kansas City Five (1938); and "Swingin' the Blues," with Basie's orchestra (also 1938). These solos emphasize drums rather than cymbals to heighten the contrast with his regular accompanying style. He was an innovator in developing a crisp technique for wire brushes (rather than wooden sticks), as heard on "I Know That You Know."

Jones's great contribution was as an accompanist playing swing rhythms. He softened the role of the bass drum. He played the high hat cymbals in a gentle manner, with the opposing cymbals struck while slightly open, so that a sizzling sound replaced the abrupt click or chomp of earlier drumming styles. He achieved extraordinary gradations in the tone and duration of cymbal sounds by varying the position and manner of striking with sticks, brushes, or mallets; he later demonstrated these techniques in detail on his album *The Drum* (1973). "Jo Jones discovered he could play the *flow* of the rhythm and not its demarcation. And he perceived that the rhythmic lead was passing to

the [string] bass, which he could complement with his cymbals," the jazz critic Martin Williams wrote. Any of Basie's classic recordings—such as "One O'Clock Jump" and "Jumpin' at the Woodside"— demonstrate his achievement.

FURTHER READING
Interviews with Jones are in the oral history collections at Yale University, New Haven, Connecticut, and the Institute of Jazz Studies, Newark, New Jersey.
Columbé, Graham. "Jo Jones Speaks Out," *Jazz Journal* (Dec. 1972).
Korall, Burt. *Drummin' Men: The Heartbeat of Jazz, The Swing Years* (1990).
Russell, Ross. *Jazz Style in Kansas City and the Southwest* (1971).
Shapiro, Nat, and Nat Hentoff, eds. *Hear Me Talkin' to Ya: The Story of Jazz as Told by the Men Who Made It* (1955).
Obituary: *New York Times*, 5 Sept. 1985.

DISCOGRAPHY
Sheridan, Chris. *Count Basie: A Bio-Discography* (1986).
This entry is taken from the *American National Biography* and is published here with the permission of the American Council of Learned Societies.
BARRY KERNFELD

Jones, John (3 Nov. 1816–21 May 1879), civil rights activist and Chicago county commissioner, was born on a plantation in Greene County, North Carolina, the son of John Bromfield (occupation unknown), of German ancestry, and a free woman of color, whose last name was Jones (first name unknown). Because of the legal status of his parents, John Jones was considered a free person. His mother, fearing that his father might attempt to reduce Jones to slavery, apprenticed Jones to learn a trade. It was in Tennessee that he received training as a tailor.

In 1841, while working for a tailor in Memphis, Jones fell in love with Mary Jane Richardson, the daughter of a free blacksmith. The Richardsons moved to Alton, Illinois, and Jones remained in Memphis to complete his apprenticeship. At age twenty-seven, after saving about one hundred dollars, he went north to Alton and married Richardson in 1844. Little is known of their life in Alton, but both Jones and his wife were compelled in 1844 to obtain certificates of freedom in accordance with Illinois law, which required all blacks to file a certificate of freedom, with bond, so that they would not become a charge of the county in which they resided.

Their freedom certified, the Jones family, including their only child, journeyed to Chicago in March 1845. Jones opened a downtown tailoring shop that was one of the first black business establishments in Chicago. Located at his home at 119 Dearborn, J. Jones, Clothes Dresser and Repairer became a thriving business. During the earliest days of Jones's residency in Chicago, the prominent Chicago abolitionist Lemanuel C. Paine Freer taught Jones the fundamentals of reading and writing. Not having any formal schooling because of his race, Jones realized that knowledge of such basic rudiments was essential to the operation of his business.

Jones worked actively with the abolitionist movement. His home became a major center of the Underground Railroad and the rendezvous site for escaped slaves. He frequently played host to abolitionists such as FREDERICK DOUGLASS, John Brown (1800–1859), and Wendell Phillips.

Jones particularly distinguished himself in the black convention movement and in his long but ultimately successful campaign for the repeal of the Illinois Black Laws. According to laws passed by the first General Assembly of Illinois in 1819, blacks had no legal rights. They could not sue or be sued, nor could they testify against whites. They had no right to an education, their oath was not binding, and they could not make a contract (*Laws of Illinois*, 143, 354–361). Jones's first attempt to repeal the Black Laws began in the heated debate surrounding the constitutional convention of 1847. In a series of articles in Chicago's *Western Citizen* (21 Sept. 1847, 2; 28 Sept. 1847, 2), Jones defended the rights of blacks. He stated that the enlightenment of the nineteenth century, the standards of republican government, and the record of blacks during the American Revolution were sufficient reasons for recognizing black citizenship. He insisted that blacks were entitled to equal representation and equality before the law.

On 7 August 1848, black Chicagoans meeting at a Baptist church selected Jones, who was already achieving a reputation as a spokesperson for black rights, and the Reverend Abraham T. Hall as delegates to the Colored National Convention of free black men to be held on 6 September in Cleveland, Ohio. Frederick Douglass, already prominent nationally, was named president, and Jones became vice president. The Cleveland delegates were primarily interested in improving the status of blacks in the United States. Jones believed that equality of persons could be achieved only by equality of attainments. For example, he felt that mechanical trades, business, farming, and the learned professions were honorable occupations that should be pursued by blacks. Jones demeaned menial labor, calling on delegates to "deem it our bounden duty to discountenance such pursuits, except where necessity compels the person to resort thereto as a means of livelihood" (*Liberator*, 20 Oct. 1848, 2).

After Jones returned to Chicago, he concentrated on the repeal of the Illinois Black Laws. On 11 September 1848, Jones and other prominent Chicago blacks, notably HENRY O. WAGONER, William Johnson, and the Reverend Abraham T. Hall, established a correspondence committee that had two functions: ascertaining the feasibility of circulating a petition for the repeal of the Black Laws, and canvassing the Fourth Congressional District (including Chicago) for the names of blacks. Their efforts provided a model for the establishment of repeal associations and petition drives throughout the state. In spite of Jones's efforts at repeal, the Illinois legislature passed a measure in 1853 banning the immigration of free blacks into the state.

The severity of the Fugitive Slave Act and the intensity of discrimination against blacks promoted the revival of the black national convention movement. Jones denounced the Fugitive Slave Act as "not only unconstitutional but also inconsistent with the view that all men are created equal; it was a measure dictated by the vested interests of the South, ignoring the rights of every party save those of the master" (*Western Citizen*, 24 Dec. 1850, 2). At the Rochester, New York, black convention of 6 July 1853 and as elected president of the first Black Illinois State Convention in Chicago from 6–8 October, Jones denounced any schemes for colonizing blacks. Jones was chairman of the colonization committee, and the delegates enthusiastically adopted his report that "we regard all schemes for colonizing the free people of color of the U.S. in Africa … as directly calculated to increase pro slavery prejudice, to depress moral energies, and to unsettle all our plans for improvement" (*Chicago Tribune*, 11 Oct. 1853, 3). As president of the convention, Jones was lauded for presiding "both with dignity and with truly surprising parliamentary accuracy" (*Chicago Tribune*, 11 Oct. 1853, 3).

On 4 November 1864, Jones published *The Black Laws of Illinois and a Few Reasons Why They Should Be Repealed*, a sixteen-page pamphlet that he himself financed. Basing his arguments on moral, economic, legal, and constitutional principles, Jones directed his comments to the people of Illinois and to newly elected members of the legislature.

Addressing individuals who did not consider blacks as citizens, Jones argued, "If being natives and born in the soil of parents belonging to no other nation or tribe, does not constitute a citizen in this country, under the theory and genius of our government, I am at a loss to know in what manner citizenship is acquired by birth." Jones's publication received generally favorable treatment in the press. An editorial in the *Chicago Tribune* (27 Nov. 1864, 2) urged the public to become informed about the Black Laws by reading Jones's pamphlet; the editorial also insisted on repeal of the laws. The *Chicago Evening Journal* (19 Nov. 1864, 4) also praised Jones for his efforts. Jones did not rely solely on his rhetoric. He continued to circulate petitions and to organize correspondence committees and repeal associations.

The climate generated by the Civil War and the ratification of the Thirteenth Amendment by Congress were additional factors that aided Jones in his fight for repeal. He supported wartime emancipation and black enlistment. The performance of black soldiers in battle earned the gratitude and respect of many midwesterners who had previously questioned the capabilities of blacks in battle. This war spirit began to break down some of the barriers against the blacks. With the arrival of the news of congressional adoption of the Thirteenth Amendment to the U.S. Constitution, the Illinois General Assembly on 1 February 1865 ratified the amendment, making Illinois the first state to approve the abolition of slavery. As a proper corollary toward black freedom, the Illinois legislature acted to repeal the Black Laws. The repeal became law on 7 February 1865.

Jones continued his civil rights work when he went to Washington in 1866 with a committee headed by Frederick Douglass to urge President Andrew Johnson to grant suffrage to the freed slaves. In 1869, when blacks were eligible for political office, Governor John M. Palmer appointed Jones as the state's first black notary public. Ratification of the Fifteenth Amendment on 30 March 1870 allowed blacks to participate for the first time in Illinois elections. In 1871 when the Republican and Democratic central committees selected fifteen Cook County commissioners to run on the Fire-Proof ticket, Jones was nominated by the Republicans and was unanimously accepted by the Democrats. He was elected for a one-year term, practically without opposition, and was the first black man elected to public office in Chicago. In 1872 he was renominated by the Republicans and

was reelected for a three-year term. Jones's election was politically unique since there was neither a separate black political organization nor a black community large enough to serve as a base for electoral support. In 1875 he was defeated with the other Republican candidates.

After a lengthy illness, Jones died in Chicago. Chicago's most prominent black citizen, he left an estate valued at sixty thousand dollars.

FURTHER READING

The John Jones Papers are on file in the Chicago Historical Society, including his significant work, *The Black Laws of Illinois and a Few Reasons Why They Should Be Repealed.*

Bell, Howard F. "Chicago Negroes in the Reform Movement, 1847–1853," *Negro History Bulletin* 21 (Apr. 1958): 153–155.

Cromwell, John W. *The Early Negro Convention Movement* (1904).

Gliozzo, Charles A. "John Jones and the Black Convention Movement, 1848–1856," *Journal of Black Studies* 3 (1972): 227–236.

"John Jones: A Study of a Black Chicagoan," *Illinois Historical Journal* 80 (Autumn 1987): 177–188.

Obituary: *Chicago Tribune,* 22 May 1879.

This entry is taken from the *American National Biography* and is published here with the permission of the American Council of Learned Societies.

CHARLES A. GLIOZZO

Jones, John W. (22 June 1817–26 Dec. 1900), a noted humanitarian in the fields of slavery and the Civil War, was born on the Ellzey Plantation called Mt. Middleton near Leesburg, Loudoun County, Virginia. His mother was named Hannah and he never knew his father, who was sold before John W. Jones was born. Other known family members included a sister, Alice; his stepfather Enoch; and two half-brothers, Charles and George. He also had two half-sisters whose names are unknown. Jones's grandmother on his mother's side was part Native American and was known as an herb doctor.

Jones was a favorite of his owner, Sarah (Sallie) Ellzey, and he was allowed to work around the house until he was twelve years old. Then he was sent to work in the fields under the care of William Rollins, the overseer of the plantation. Rollins had a young son named Johnny and he and Jones became friends.

One day as Jones and his grandmother were sitting together, a flock of geese flew overhead. She told Jones that the geese were flying north to a country where everyone was free. That gave Jones the first idea of becoming free someday.

Years later when Sarah Ellzey became elderly, Jones gave more thought to being free. He was worried that after she was gone, his new owner might not treat him so kindly. He spoke of it to his mother and she encouraged him by telling him that if he left he should take his brothers with him.

On 22 June 1844, Jones told his mother he was going to a party and asked her to lay out his best suit. This was his twenty-seventh birthday and as he kissed his mother goodbye, he knew he would never see her again. At a prearranged meeting place, he met up with his half-brothers, Charles and George, and two other friends from neighboring plantations, John D. Smith and Jefferson Brown. Each man had a change of clothing and a four-day supply of food and was armed with a pistol and a knife. By morning they were eighteen miles away and they hid in an old barn, waiting for nightfall to start out again. After they had reached Maryland, they became a bit bolder and started traveling in the daytime.

They outwitted slave catchers in Maryland and made their way into Pennsylvania. On 4 July 1844, they were in South Creek, Pennsylvania, at the farm of Dr. Nathaniel Smith and his wife, Sarah. They were warmly welcomed at the farm and given a wonderful meal. After spending the night in the barn, the fugitives left early in the morning and made their way to Elmira, New York, and a new life of freedom.

Jones and his companions were hard workers and they started working odd jobs immediately. They were also befriended by the abolitionists of the community who were some of the most prominent men in Elmira. Some of the abolitionists were Jervis Langdon, a lumber and coal dealer; Sylvester Andrus, a partner of Jervis Langdon; Ariel Thurston, a prominent judge; Simeon Benjamin, the founder and first president of Elmira College; and Nathan Reynolds, the wealthiest man in Big Flats, New York. Jervis Langdon is better known as the father-in-law of Mark Twain than he is for his own history.

Judge Ariel Thurston saw great potential in Jones and asked him why he did not learn to read and write. Jones told him that he wanted to learn but the two teachers in town had turned him down. Judge Thurston made arrangements for Jones to attend classes with Hugh Riddle, a teacher who boarded at his home. Jones said young Master Loop, a fourteen-year-old student who was a fellow classmate, actually taught him. Jones only received one year of schooling but he put it to good use.

Jones became the sexton at two cemeteries in Elmira and in 1847 he was appointed the sexton at the First Baptist Church, a position he held for forty-three years. In 1854 he bought a small house that was next to the church and in this house he sheltered over eight hundred individuals who were seeking freedom through the Underground Railroad. In 1856 Jones married Rachael Swales. Jones and Rachel had four children.

When the Civil War broke out, Elmira became a major training center for the Union soldiers. In 1864, one of the old barracks along the Chemung River was remodeled to become a stockade and Elmira became a prison camp for the Confederate soldiers. Nearly 3,000 men died at this prison camp and they were all buried at Woodlawn Cemetery by John W. Jones. He kept careful records of the name, rank, regiment number, and burial plot of each soldier. One of the soldiers he buried was young Johnny Rollins, his friend from Virginia. Jones contacted the Rollins family and after the war his body was sent to Virginia for burial.

In 1877, Woodlawn Cemetery was declared a national cemetery, all owing to the work of Jones, who had only one year of education. Jones died in 1900 and was buried in Woodlawn Cemetery. In 1997 a group of concerned citizens saved the last home Jones lived in on College Avenue. This home was purchased and moved to Davis Street across from Woodlawn Cemetery.

FURTHER READING
Civil War burial records, newspaper interviews, and other articles are housed in the John W. Jones Collection at the Chemung Valley History Museum, Elmira, New York.
Horigan, Michael. *Elmira Death Camp of the North* (2002).

CAROLE E. KNOWLTON

Jones, K. C. (25 May 1932–), basketball player and coach, was born K. C. Jones in Taylor, Texas, the son of K. C. Jones, a laborer, and Eula (maiden name unknown), a maid. In 1941 his parents separated and his mother took her five children to San Francisco, in search of new opportunities. The segregation of 1930s Texas was suffocating, and Jones left Texas with few expectations for his future. His family lived in a public-housing project and relied on welfare. Lacking confidence in his academic skills, Jones found sports one arena in which he was comfortable and successful. As a senior in 1951, Jones, who played at Commerce High, made the All-Northern California All-Star basketball and football teams. After the season Phil Woolpert, the coach of the University of San Francisco (USF) Dons, gave him a basketball scholarship.

In the summer before he started college, Jones grew four inches to stand six feet one inch tall. At the same time he mysteriously lost the touch on his jump shot and would remain a below-average shooter for the rest of his playing career. Woolpert, who took over the team in 1950, had his first winning season in 1953–1954, when BILL RUSSELL, as a sophomore, played his first varsity campaign. In that season Jones played only one game because of a ruptured appendix. But he and Russell were roommates and good friends, and they were about to put USF on the national basketball map.

In the 1954–1955 season Jones, Russell, and Hal Perry, the third African American starter, led the Dons to a 28–1 record and the NCAA championship. Because Jones had missed all but one game as a junior, the NCAA awarded him a fifth season of college eligibility during 1955–1956 but, in an unusual decision, would not allow him to play in the NCAA tournament that year. In the regular season the Dons were undefeated, but Jones had to watch as the Dons won their second consecutive NCAA tournament. In his final two seasons Jones averaged ten points and was an intimidating defender. He capped off his amateur career by playing on the 1956 U.S. Olympic team that won a gold medal in Melbourne, Australia. Although drafted by the NBA's Boston Celtics in the second round of the 1956 draft, Jones spent the next two years in the army, where he continued to play basketball. In March 1958 he led Fort Leonard Wood to the semifinals of the Amateur Athletic Union's prestigious national tournament in Denver and earned a place on the AAU All-American team.

In the fall of 1958 Jones signed his first contract with the Boston Celtics. Coached by the legendary Arnold "Red" Auerbach, the Celtics were the perfect team for Jones. He did not need to score because the Celtics had plenty of offensive weapons with Tom Heinsohn, SAM JONES (1933–), and John Havlicek. He would make himself into one of the NBA's best defensive players and fit into the team concept masterminded by Auerbach. In Boston Jones was also reunited with Russell, and the two became charter members of the Celtic dynasty that won eight consecutive titles between 1959 and 1966. At the end of the 1958–1959 season,

Jones married Beverly Cain, the sister of Carl Cain, an All-American at the University of Iowa and a member of the 1956 Olympic team. They had five children: Leslie, K. C. Jr., Kelly, Bryan, and Holly.

When Jones joined the Celtics, their guards were Bob Cousy and Bill Sharman, two NBA stars. In his first five years Jones was a role player, only becoming a starter in the 1963–1964 season, following Cousy's retirement. In the 1965–1966 season the Celtics made history when they became the first NBA team to start five black players. In that year and the next two, the Celtics would win the NBA championship. Their streak of eight straight titles ended when the Philadelphia 76ers and WILT CHAMBERLAIN defeated them in the 1967 Eastern Conference finals.

After the 1967 season Jones retired but remained in basketball as a coach. Coaching at Brandeis University for three years (1967–1970), he then put in a one-year stint as an assistant at Harvard and for the Los Angeles Lakers. Jones's first head coaching position in professional basketball was in 1972–1973 with the San Diego Conquistadors in the American Basketball Association and his team finished 30–54. The following year he became the fourth African American (Bill Russell, LENNY WILKINS, and Al Attles preceded him) to coach in the NBA when the Capital Bullets (later the Washington Bullets) hired him. He had three winning seasons, won two division titles, and lost to the San Francisco Warriors in the 1975 finals. In 1975–1976 the Bullets finished with a 48–34 record, but lost in their first playoff series and fired Jones. While he struggled to find a job, Jones's marriage ended in a divorce. In 1978 Celtics coach Tom "Satch" Sanders hired Jones as his assistant, a position he continued to hold when Bill Fitch replaced Sanders. The Celtics had suffered through three miserable seasons between 1977 and 1979, but their fortunes and Jones's were about to change when Boston made a series of drafts and trades that brought Larry Bird, Kevin McHale, Robert Parish, Dennis Johnson, and Danny Ainge on board. The Celtics won their fourteenth title in 1981, but after the 1982–1983 season Red Auerbach, the Celtic president since 1966, named Jones to replace Bill Fitch as the Celtic coach. In 1981 Jones married again, to Ellen (maiden name unknown), and they had a son, Kent Christopher.

Jones was a perfect fit for the Celtics. Whereas Fitch was intense and controlling, Jones was more relaxed and had the benefit of his connection to Boston's glory days. His first season with the Celtics culminated in a dramatic seven-game championship series against the Los Angeles Lakers, which the Celtics took to win their fifteenth NBA title. The following season Los Angeles defeated the Celtics for the first time in nine championship series between two rivals. In 1985–1986 Jones directed the Celtics to their sixteenth NBA crown by defeating the Houston Rockets, now coached by Bill Fitch. In 1987 the Lakers whipped the Celtics in a six-game NBA final. Jones won his fifth division title in 1988, but he announced his retirement before losing to the Detroit Pistons in the conferences finals. In five seasons Jones's Celtics compiled an impressive 308–102 record. Jones, in 1989, was inducted into the Naismith Memorial Basketball Hall of Fame. Three years earlier the Boston Celtics retired his number, 25.

In 1989–1990 Jones returned to coaching with the Seattle SuperSonics as an assistant coach. He was the head coach of the SuperSonics from 1990 to mid-1992. Afterward Jones served as an assistant with the Detroit Pistons (1994–1995) and the Celtics (1995–1997). His final coaching position was in the American Basketball League's New England Blizzard (1997–1999). Beginning in 2004 Jones worked as the special assistant for the University of Hartford, helping with fund-raising and analysis for the men's basketball program.

FURTHER READING

Jones, K. C., with Jack Warner. *Rebound* (1986).
Pluto, Terry. *Tall Tales* (1992).
Shaughnessy, Dan. *Ever Green: The Boston Celtics* (1990).
Thomas, Ron. *They Cleared the Lane: The NBA's Black Pioneers* (2002).

DOLPH GRUNDMAN

Jones, Laurence Clifton (21 Nov. 1884–18 July 1975), educator, was born in St. Joseph, Missouri, the oldest of four children and the only son of John Q. Jones, a hotel porter and barbershop owner, and Lydia Foster Jones, a seamstress and parlor room hostess. Laurence learned the value of hard work in his youth as he shined shoes, sold newspapers, and raised chickens. In 1898 he moved to Marshalltown, Iowa, where he worked for room and board at a hotel. In 1903 Jones became the first African American to graduate from Marshalltown High School. Local whites encouraged him to attend the University of Iowa (then the State University of Iowa) in Iowa City. Influenced by the ideas of BOOKER T. WASHINGTON, Jones decided to help educate poor blacks in the South when he graduated from the University of Iowa in 1907 with a bachelor of philosophy degree.

Jones joined the Utica Institute in Utica, Mississippi, that same year, and while visiting impoverished Rankin County during a Christmas vacation, he discovered that the blacks there had talked for years about establishing a school but never had possessed the needed funds. He offered his services to the county and, in 1909, with three illiterate students and a stump for a desk, he began to teach. He named his new school Piney Woods Country Life School.

While many local blacks and whites were initially skeptical of Jones, he soon received help from Edward Taylor and John Webster. Taylor, a former slave, gave Jones an old sheep shed, forty acres of land, and fifty dollars. Webster, a white businessman, gave Jones lumber and building tools. Students could supply food, materials, or labor in lieu of tuition. Later, white business leaders who accepted the idea of giving African American youth practical agricultural training offered support, and blacks from surrounding communities began to attend and provide resources. Piney Woods Country Life School was co-educational and offered reading, writing, arithmetic, agriculture, home economics, and industrial labor training. A devout Christian, Jones emphasized hard work, public service, and good character—attributes that would lead students to self reliance and personal advancement. Regardless of Jones's sincerity and drive, his school faced chronic financial problems. Like other entrepreneurial black educators, Jones looked to sympathetic northerners, especially acquaintances in Iowa, for donations. He began making speaking tours, especially to churches, soliciting aid.

In 1912 Jones married Grace Morris Allen of Burlington, Iowa, who joined in teaching and fundraising activities for the school, which received a charter from the state of Mississippi in 1913. By then Piney Woods had become a boarding school with several teachers and focused primarily on manual training and farming. Jones promoted diversified farming to students and community members alike. He hosted farm conferences and brought noted northern agriculturalists to speak, such as Asa Turner, president of the Iowa Corn Growers Association. His efforts were further enhanced when Iowa friends purchased eight hundred acres for the school to use for farm projects. Led by his wife, Grace, the school also offered free home extension service. Also in 1913 the Joneses contracted to go on the Chautauqua speaking circuit.

During World War I, Jones took charge of the Thrift Stamp Campaign, a government savings program using stamps instead of war bonds, among blacks, and he worked for Armenian Relief. In 1917 Piney Woods School served as a summer normal school for African American teachers, and the next year teacher training became a regular feature of the institution. Jones was named to the state committee to establish accreditation standards for black high schools.

GRACE ALLEN JONES organized the Cotton Blossom Singers in 1921 and, performing traditional black spirituals, they raised funds for the school as they traveled across the country and ultimately had their own radio program, which lasted until the 1970s. Grace, who accomplished much for the school as well as being noted for her efforts to improve health care, sanitation, and welfare in Mississippi, died in 1928. She left Laurence with two sons, and although he never remarried, Jones later adopted a daughter.

Mississippi did not offer any schooling for blind African American children, so Jones assumed that responsibility at Piney Woods School from 1929 until 1950, when the Mississippi School for the Blind was opened in Jackson. In 1931 he added a junior college, which continued at the school until the 1960s. Jones established a semiprofessional baseball team to play exhibition games, hoping the team would stimulate contributions to the school, and in 1939 he created the Sweethearts of Rhythm, an all-girl jazz band that performed widely into the 1940s.

By the 1950s the reputation of Piney Woods Country Life School was such that the U. S. State Department cited it as an example of American democracy and education. However, the biggest boost for Jones and the school came in 1954 when the television show *This Is Your Life* profiled Jones, and host Ralph Edwards enjoined viewers to send a dollar each to help the school. Within a few weeks $776,000 was raised. The next year Jones was designated "Mississippi's First Citizen" by Governor Hugh White. In 1974 Jones stepped down as the head of Piney Woods Country Life School. By then he had received awards and honorary degrees as well as having had much written about him and Piney Woods Country Life School. He also authored several books himself, including *Up through Difficulties* (1910), *Piney Woods and Its Story* (1923), *Spirit of Piney Woods* (1931), and *Bottom Rail* (1935). Jones died in 1975, ending a life inseparable from Piney Woods Country Life School. Hard work, dedication, faith, and an adroit understanding of

how an African American educator could succeed in the racist South created a heroic story and left a remarkable legacy. Jones assumed statewide leadership in civic and educational service, and in 1981 he became the first African American admitted to Mississippi's Hall of Fame.

FURTHER READING

Archival collections containing significant papers relating to Jones are the Piney Woods Country Life School Records at the Mississippi Department of History and Archives; Piney Wood Country Life School Archives at Piney Wood Country Life School; Laurence C. Jones Alumni Vertical File, University of Iowa; and Grace Morris Jones Papers, Iowa Women's Archives, University of Iowa. Much additional information on Jones and the Piney Woods Country Life School can be found in issues of the *Pine Torch*, the school newsletter that Jones began printing in 1911.

Apgar, Dorothy, ed. *The Continuing History of Marshall County Iowa* (1997).

Cooper, Arnold. *Between Struggle and Hope: Four Black Educators in the South, 1894–1915* (1989).

Day, Beth. *The Little Professor of Piney Woods: The Story of Professor Laurence Jones* (1955).

Harrison, Alferdteen. *Piney Woods School: An Oral History* (1982).

Martin, Lee. "Piney Woods Country Life School: An Educational Experience of African Americans," 1998 Proceedings of the Adult Education Research Conference. Available at http://www.edst.educ.ubc.ca/aerc/1998/98martin.htm

Purcell, Leslie Harper. *Miracle in Mississippi: Laurence C. Jones of Piney Woods* (1956).

THOMAS BURNELL COLBERT

Jones, LeRoi. *See* Baraka, Amiri.

Jones, Levi (c. 1802–?), former slave, slave owner, and pioneer for the legal rights of free blacks, was born a slave in 1802, probably in Virginia, although the precise place of his birth is unknown. Court records show that he was once owned by William Chenault Jr., a prominent lawyer and a member of the lower house of the Kentucky legislature. Prior to emancipation Jones resided on the Chenault family's farm, near Richmond, Kentucky, which was purchased in 1787 from the brother of Kentucky pioneer and settler Daniel Boone. Four years before Chenault died he emancipated Jones (31 May 1830). At the time Jones was married, although not legally, to Sally Ann, a slave woman, with whom he had four children. Although the date of Levi and Sally Ann's union is unknown, marriage between free blacks would not even become legal until 1825. Moreover, the law absolutely did not recognize marriages between slaves. Nonetheless, Sally Ann bore four children for her husband, all of whom resided with their mother. Historical records show that in 1830 Sally Ann's master, John Bennet, "though once an owner of slaves, seems to have been in principle opposed to slavery—liberated [the] female slave" (Court of Appeals of Kentucky, 1840). Because under Kentucky law the offspring of slaves assumed the status of their mother, the Jones' children were considered slaves. To secure the release of his children from the bondage of slavery, Jones verbally contracted with Bennet, who was moving to Missouri, to purchase the couple's four children for $300.00, payable on an installment agreement. The deal was mutually beneficial because Jones wanted his children and Bennet did not wish to take the Jones' children with him or to hold them any longer in slavery.

By the fall of 1831 Jones had defaulted on the agreement because he was not able to pay upon demand. In 1832 the son of John Bennet, Samuel, purporting to have been in possession of a bill of sale for the four children, abducted the Jones' three oldest children and held them as slaves and as collateral for the unpaid debt. It took four years for Jones to file a petition in the chancery court against Samuel Bennet. Jones prayed for a decree "upon equitable terms, which would return his children to him as restitution." However, Samuel Bennet argued that the case was being heard in the wrong court and the case was subsequently dismissed.

Jones appealed his case to the Court of Appeals of Kentucky with the assistance of two attorneys identified only as Mr. Owsley and Mr. J. T. Morehead. On this latter occasion, the court held that Jones, although a colored man, had a legal right to petition for his children, although they were born slaves, because they had been wrongfully taken from him. The Court heard his case and held that the abduction and detention of the children by Bennet were unauthorized and tortious, ordering that Bennet be required to pay damages.

This case clarified one of the fundamental rights of free persons of color in Kentucky—the right to stand in court and appeal for the return on one's children. The case also stood for the principle that a colored man who has acquired a right to his children, born slaves, by purchase or otherwise, may maintain a bill in chancery for a specific execution

of his contract of purchase or for their restoration when they have been wrongfully taken from him. The Chief Justice opined, "If a wrongdoer detain a family picture, or an ancient vase, or heirloom, or any other article … there can be no doubt that a bill in equity, for restitution of the specific thing, may be maintained …. Why then, in a case of abduction, may not the father appeal to a court of equity for securing the restitution of his own child?" (Court of Appeals of Kentucky, 1840). In 1840 Jones was reunited with his children and damages were scheduled to be awarded for their wrongful detention.

The Jones' were no strangers at the courthouse. In 1845, just five years after the court ordered his children returned to him, two of his children, Betsy, twenty-three, and Emily, nineteen, along with Betsy's two children, Spicy and Edmund, were in another Kentucky court suing for their freedom. According to the petition they asserted that Jones purchased Emily and Betsy "upon the express consideration that said Emily and Betsy were to be free whenever they should attain the age of twenty-one years as likewise all their children born before that time." Unfortunately Jones's children had been levied upon for debts and were about to be sold back into slavery to satisfy the debts owed to Robert Adams or Benjamin Bailey. The children prayed to the chancery court for an injunction and a declaration of freedom. Although Jones could have simply emancipated his children upon securing their initial release, it was common for purchased children and adults to work off their purchase price in exchange for their freedom. Although the exact outcome of this petition is unknown, census records show that by 1850 Emily and Betsy were still residing in the Jones household with their mother and father. In fact, Jones had managed to purchase more relatives. The records also list a seventy-three-year-old woman, Amy, residing with the Jones family. Jones, who was then forty-eight years old, worked as a farmer in Versailles, Kentucky. He did not own any land.

Jones and his family suffered from racial prejudice, even while considered free. It is not known why the Jones family chose not to flee to the North and its more lenient laws for free blacks. As free black residents of Kentucky, they stood their ground, fought for their legal rights, and made the best of their complicated existence. Jones is among a number of African Americans who lived in Kentucky as a free person of color during the first half of the nineteenth century. He is only one of a select few in Kentucky to own slaves. In 1830 black slave owners were only listed in less than one third of Kentucky counties.

FURTHER READING

Few primary materials on Levi Jones have survived or been discovered. Copies of the Jones's 1840 circuit court case and the 1845 chancery court petition of Mr. Jones's daughters are available in the Case Files and Records of the Circuit Court with the Kentucky Division of Libraries and Archives in Frankfort, Kentucky.

Chenault, Alexander. "Jones v. Bennet: The Bifurcated Legal Status of Early Nineteenth Century Free Blacks in Kentucky." *The Modern American* 5 (2009).

Johnson, E. Polk. *A History of Kentucky and Kentuckians* (1912).

ALEXANDER J. CHENAULT

Jones, Lewis Wade (13 Mar. 1910–19 Sept. 1979), sociologist and folklorist, was born in Cuero, DeWitt County, Texas, the eldest child of Wade E. Jones and Lucinthia Jones. His parents were literate and before Lewis's tenth birthday they were farming near Navasota in Grimes County, Texas. His upbringing would inform his later sociological and folkloric interests regarding the status of African Americans in the rural South.

Jones was admitted to Fisk University in 1927. In 1931 he received his AB degree. At Fisk he came under the influence of CHARLES SPURGEON JOHNSON, head of the Social Sciences Department. He did postgraduate work at the University of Chicago as a Social Science Research Council Fellow (1931–1932).

Upon his return to Fisk, Jones was an instructor in the Social Sciences Department and served as a research assistant and supervisor of field studies for Charles S. Johnson. In this capacity Jones collected data in the field for Johnson's *Shadow of the Plantation* (1934) and coauthored, with Johnson, *Statistical Atlas of Southern Counties* (1941). On 6 June 1939 Jones was awarded an M.A. in philosophy and pure science from Columbia University, where he was a Rosenwald Fellow. His thesis was titled "Occupational Stratification among Rural and Small Town Negroes before the Civil War and Today."

In 1941 Jones began supervising fieldwork for the most ambitious folklore study attempted to date. Fisk and the Library of Congress's Archive of Folk Culture cooperated in a two-year folklife survey in Coahoma County, Mississippi. Charles

Johnson and JOHN WESLEY WORK III of Fisk and Alan Lomax of the Library of Congress were the principal planners. A proposed book, including a sociological analysis by Jones, went unpublished after completion of the study. Sixty years later the original manuscripts, Jones's among them, were published as *Lost Delta Found: Rediscovering the Fisk University–Library of Congress Coahoma County Study, 1941–1942* (2005).

In 1943 Jones served on the summer faculty at Fort Valley (Georgia) State College, a historic black school that hosted an annual Negro Folk Festival. Jones recorded the music at the festival for deposit in the Library of Congress's Archive of Folk Culture. Later in 1943 Jones was inducted into the U.S. Army, where he served in the Office of War Information.

After completing his military service, Jones worked at Tuskegee Institute as a research associate for the Rural Life Council and in 1949 published *Shifts in Negro Populations in Alabama*. In the next two years he published *The Changing Status of the Negro in Southern Agriculture* and *The Cotton Community Changes* (with Professor Ernest E. Neal of Tuskegee). In 1954 Jones was appointed associate professor of sociology at Tuskegee and in 1955 he earned his Ph.D. at Columbia University. His dissertation was titled *Medical Care Practices in Four Rural Neighborhoods: A Study of the Choice of Alternatives*.

Two years later, still at Tuskegee, Jones became the acting director of the Rural Life Council. At this time he was also writing *Tithe for the Future*, a history of the first ten years of the United Negro College Fund. In 1958 Jones gained tenure and promotion to professor of sociology and acting director, social science research.

In 1962 Jones returned to Fisk as special project director of the Race Relations Institute. While at Fisk he published his most noteworthy book, *Cold Rebellion: The South's Oligarchy in Revolt*, a historical analysis of southern racial inequality as well as a current (1962) statement of improvements achieved despite obstruction by the white power structure. The book was unacceptable to American publishers; MacGibbon Co. in London, England, published the book. In 1965 Jones published another study of the civil rights movement, *The Negotiation of Desegregation in Ten Southern Cities*. Jones returned to Tuskegee in 1966 and that August he married Queen Esther Shootes. Jones served at Tuskegee for the next thirteen years, before his death there in 1979.

During a distinguished career as a fieldworker, educator, and administrator, Lewis Jones managed to write or edit nearly fifty books and articles. He received many accolades, among them the second W. E. B. DuBois award, in 1971, from the Association of Social and Behavioral Scientists. He served as a consultant to many national organizations including the U.S. Department of Labor.

Jones was a notable activist as well as academic. In 1942, as the first black on the Highlander Folk School executive council, Jones was instrumental in desegregating its residencies in New Market, Tennessee. Later in the 1960s during the time of civil rights demonstrations he led workshops for sympathetic white college students attending Highlander. As George Breathett of Bennett College and Daniel Williams of Tuskegee wrote in *The Journal of Negro History* (1981), "During his entire life, Jones was a 'renaissance man' without peer."

FURTHER READING

Papers of Lewis Wade Jones are in the John Hope and Aurelia E. Franklin Library Special Collections at Fisk University and in Tuskegee University Archives.

Lomax, Alan. *Land Where the Blues Began* (1993).

Work, John W., Lewis Wade Jones, and Samuel C. Adams Jr. *Lost Delta Found: Rediscovering the Fisk University–Library of Congress Coahoma County Study, 1941–1942*, ed. Robert Gordon and Bruce Nemerov (2005).

Obituary: *Journal of Negro History* 66, no. 1 (Spring 1981): 85.

BRUCE NEMEROV

Jones, Loïs Mailou (3 Nov. 1905–9 June 1998), artist and teacher, was born in Boston, Massachusetts, the second of two children of Carolyn Dorinda Adams, a beautician, and Thomas Vreeland Jones, a building superintendent. Jones's father became a lawyer at age forty, and she credited him with inspiring her by example: "Much of my drive surely comes from my father—wanting to be someone, to have an ambition" (Benjamin, 4). While majoring in art at the High School of Practical Arts, Jones spent afternoons in a drawing program at Boston's Museum of Fine Arts. On weekends she apprenticed with Grace Ripley, a prominent designer of theatrical masks and costumes. From 1923 to 1927 she studied design at the School of the Museum of Fine Arts and became one of the school's first African American graduates. Upon graduation, Jones, who had earned a teaching certificate from the Boston Normal Art School, received a one-year scholarship to the Designers Art School of Boston, where she studied with the internationally known textile designer Ludwig Frank. The following summer, while attending Harvard University, she designed textiles for companies in Boston and New York. She soon learned, however, that designers toiled in anonymity, and so, seeking recognition for her creations, she decided to pursue a career as a fine artist.

Jones's family spent summers on Martha's Vineyard, the beauty of which inspired her to paint as a child and where her first solo exhibitions, at ages seventeen and twenty-three, were held. A retreat for generations of African American intellectuals, Martha's Vineyard exposed the young artist to career encouragement from the sculptor META WARRICK FULLER, the composer HARRY BURLEIGH, and Jonas Lie, the president of the National Academy of Design. When she applied for a teaching job at the Museum of Fine Arts, administrators patronizingly told her to "go South and help your people." Jones did go to the South in 1928, but at the behest of CHARLOTTE HAWKINS BROWN, who offered her a position developing an art department at the Palmer Memorial Institute, an African American school in North Carolina. Two years later Jones was recruited by Howard University and remained on the faculty until her retirement in 1977. For forty-seven years she taught design and watercolor (which was considered more appropriate to her gender than oil painting) to generations of students, including ELIZABETH CATLETT. "I loved my students," Jones told the *Washington Post* when she was asked about teaching. "Also it gave me a certain prestige, a certain dignity. And it saved me from being trampled upon by the outside" (1 Mar. 1978). Jones emphasized craftsmanship and encouraged each student's choice of medium and mode of expression. As a former student, Akili Ron Anderson, recalled, "Loïs Jones would punish you like a parent ... but when you met her standards, when you progressed, she loved you like your mother" (*Washington Post*, 26 Dec. 1995).

Jones remained committed to her own work and education, and she received a B.A. in Art Education magna cum laude from Howard University in 1945. In the 1930s she was a regular exhibitor at the Harmon Foundation, and from 1936 to 1965 she illustrated books and periodicals, including *African Heroes and Heroines* (1938) and the *Journal of Negro History*, for her friend CARTER G. WOODSON. After receiving a scholarship to study in Paris in 1937, Jones took a studio overlooking the Eiffel Tower, enrolled at the Académie Julien, and switched her focus from design and illustration to painting. France also precipitated a shift in her attitude. Feeling self-confident and liberated for the first time, she adopted the plein air method of painting, taking her large canvases outdoors onto the streets of Paris and the hills of the French countryside. With the African American expatriate artist ALBERT SMITH and the French painter Emile Bernard as mentors, she produced more than forty paintings in just nine months. Jones's streetscapes, still lifes, portraits, and landscapes, typified by *Rue St. Michel* (1938) and *Les Pommes Vertes* (1938), illustrate a sophisticated interpretation of Impressionist and Postimpressionist style and sensibility.

African art and culture were all the rage during Jones's visit to Paris. Sketching African masks on display in Parisian galleries prepared her for what would become her best-known work, *Les Fétiches* (1938), a Cubist-inspired painting of African masks that foreshadowed Jones's embrace of African themes and styles in her later work. In 1990, when the National Museum of American Art in Washington, D.C., acquired *Les Fétiches*, Jones responded: "I am very pleased but it is long overdue.... I can't help but think this is an honor that is 45 years late" (*Washington Post*, 7 Oct. 1994).

Even while the Robert Vose Gallery in Boston exhibited her Parisian paintings shortly after her return to the United States, Jones longed for the racial tolerance she had experienced in France. When she met ALAIN LOCKE upon her return to Howard, he challenged her to concentrate on African American subjects. And so began what Jones later called her Locke period. Throughout the 1940s and early 1950s she continued to paint in a semi-Impressionist style but increasingly depicted African American subjects, as in the character studies *Jennie* (1943), a portrait of a black girl cleaning fish; *Mob Victim* (1944), a study of a man about to be lynched; and *The Pink Tablecloth* (1944).

Jones began exhibiting more extensively, primarily in African American venues such as the Chicago Negro Exposition of 1940 and the black-owned Barnett Aden Gallery, although traditionally white venues also included her work. On occasion, Jones masked her race by entering competitions by mail or by sending her white friend Céline Tabary to deliver her work. Such was the case in 1941 when her painting *Indian Shops, Gay Head* (1940) won the Corcoran Gallery's Robert Wood Bliss Award. It was several years before the Corcoran knew that the painting was the product of a black artist.

In 1953 Jones married Louis Vergniaud Pierre-Noel, a Haitian artist she had met at Columbia University summer school in 1934. The couple, who had no children, maintained homes in Washington, Martha's Vineyard, and Port-au-Prince, Haiti, until Pierre-Noel's death in 1982. Shortly after their wedding Jones taught briefly at Haiti's Centre d'Art and the Foyer des Arts Plastiques. Haiti proved to be the next great influence on Jones's work. "Going to Haiti changed my art, changed my feelings, changed me" (*Callaloo*, Spring 1989). Character studies and renderings of the picturesque elements of island life soon gave way to more expressive works that fused abstraction and decorative elements with naturalism. Drawing on the palette and the diverse religious life and culture of Haiti, Jones incorporated voodoo gods, abstract decorative patterns, bright colors, and African elements into her paintings. Throughout the 1950s and 1960s she used strong color and flat, abstract shapes in a diverse range of works, including *Bazar du Quai* (1961), *VeVe Voodou III* (1963), and *Paris Rooftops* (1965).

In 1970–1971 Jones took a sabbatical from Howard and traveled through eleven countries in Africa, interviewing artists, photographing their work, and lecturing on African American artists. Jones, who had spent the previous summer interviewing contemporary Haitian artists, used these materials to complete her documentary project "The Black Visual Arts." The bold, graphic beauty of African textiles, leatherwork, and masks resonated with her early fabric designs and provided a new vocabulary for her work, which now included collage as well as painting and watercolor. Once again, Jones visited museums and sketched African masks and fetishes, items increasingly significant in pieces like *Moon Masque* (1971) and *Guli Mask* (1972). Throughout the 1970s and 1980s, inspired by Haiti and Africa and by the Black Arts Movement in the United States, Jones's work centered on African themes and styles.

Jones, who finally returned to Boston's Museum of Fine Arts in 1973 for a retrospective exhibition, had more than fifty solo shows. She received numerous awards and honorary degrees, including citations from the Haitian government in 1955 and from U.S. president Jimmy Carter in 1980. In 1988 Jones's artistic life came full circle when she opened the Loïs Mailou Jones Studio Gallery in Edgartown, Massachusetts, on Martha's Vineyard. At age eighty-four Jones assessed the key influences on her work: "So now ... in the sixtieth year of my career, I can look back on my work and be inspired by France, Haiti, Africa, the Black experience, and Martha's Vineyard (where it all began) and admit:

There is no end to creative expression" (*Callaloo*, Spring 1989). Loïs Mailou Jones died at age ninety-two at her home in Washington, D.C.

FURTHER READING
Jones, Loïs Mailou. *Loïs Mailou Jones: Peintures 1937–1951* (1952).
Benjamin, Tritobia Hayes. *The Life and Art of Loïs Mailou Jones* (1994).
Howard University Gallery of Art. *Loïs Mailou Jones Retrospective Exhibition: Forty Years of Painting, 1932–72* (1972).
National Center of Afro-American Artists and Museum of Fine Arts, Boston. *Reflective Moments: Loïs Mailou Jones Retrospective, 1930–1972* (1973).
Obituaries: *Journal of Blacks in Higher Education* (Summer 1998); *Washington Post*, 12 June 1998.

LISA E. RIVO

Jones, Madame Sissieretta Joyner (5 Jan. 1869–24 June 1933), classical prima donna and musical comedy performer, was born Matilda Sissieretta Joyner in Portsmouth, Virginia, less than four years after the abolition of slavery. Jones was the only surviving child of Jeremiah Malachi Joyner, a former slave and pastor of the Afro-Methodist Church in Portsmouth, and Henrietta B. Joyner, a singer in the church choir. Thus, she was exposed to music during her formative years. When she was six years old her family moved to Rhode Island, where Jones began singing in the church choir, which her father directed. Her school classmates were mesmerized by her sweet, melodic, soprano voice and nicknamed her "Sissy."

She began studying voice as a teenager at the prestigious Providence Academy of Music with Ada, Baroness Lacombe, an Italian prima donna. Not long afterward, in 1883, when she was only fourteen, Sissieretta met and married David Richard Jones, a newspaperman who also served as her manager during her early years on stage. She also received more vocal training at both the New England Conservatory and the Boston Conservatory. After her first concert performance with the Academy of Music on 8 May 1888, the *New York Age* reported that Jones's "voice is sweet, sympathetic and clear, and her enunciation a positive charm. She was recalled after each number" (*Black Perspective in Music*, 192). In an attempt to make her more palatable to white audiences, David Jones, who was himself of a mixed-race background, took his wife to Europe to have her skin lightened and to have some of her features altered. Jones made her New York City debut in a private concert at the Wallack Theatre on 1 August 1888. She was already being compared to the Italian prima donna Adelina Patti, who was adored by audiences throughout the world. As a result, Jones was dubbed "Black Patti." She wanted her own identity but was forced to accept the nickname, which remained with her throughout her more-than-thirty-year career (Daughtry, 133).

In the early 1890s discussions ensued about possible appearances by Jones at the New York City Metropolitan Opera. She wanted very much to sing in a full-length opera at the Met. In the meantime, in 1891, she set out on a tour of the West Indies, where she was honored with numerous medals for her dynamic voice. After she returned to the United States, Jones appeared at Madison Square Garden in New York City in what was billed as an "African Jubilee Spectacle and Cakewalk." Thousands listened to Jones, who was fluent in both Italian and French, sing selections from grand operas like Meyerbeer's *Robert le Diable* as well as her popular signature piece, "Swanee River." By 1892 she had already appeared at the White House three times as well as before European royalty. After performances at the Pittsburgh Exposition in 1893 and 1894, Jones became the highest paid black performer of her day.

Jones emerged as a celebrity and wanted to control her career. However, when she made this groundbreaking attempt in 1892, her manager, Major Pond, took her to court. There the judge ruled that she was ungrateful because she failed to appreciate how Pond was largely responsible for her accomplishments on the concert stage.

In New York City, Jones joined the famed Czech composer Antonin Dvorak and his students from the National Conservatory of Music for a benefit concert in 1894. A *New York Herald* reporter said of the January concert, "Mme. Jones was an enormous success with the audience. To those who heard her for the first time she came in the light of a revelation, singing high C's with as little apparent effort as her namesake, the white Patti" (*Black Perspective in Music*, 199). Both the white and the black press continued to laud her as the "greatest singer of her race." Nevertheless, the opportunity to sing at the Metropolitan Opera was still denied to Jones because of her race. These restrictions inspired her to leave the concert stage behind.

At the turn of the century, black musical comedies, which were first called "coon shows," drew huge crowds into the theaters. Black female performers

THE BLACK PATTI

MME M SISSIERETTA JONES

THE GREATEST SINGER OF HER RACE·

Madame Sissieretta Joyner Jones was barred from singing at the Metropolitan Opera in New York because of her race. Instead, she became the star of her own musical comedy troupe. (Library of Congress.)

entered musical theater around 1885. During the height of popularity for musical comedies, managers were in control and dictated what performers would do. The managers Rudolph Voelckel and John J. Nolan, who are often credited along with David Jones for luring "Black Patti" to musical theater, planned to make the former concert stage prima donna the star of her own musical black touring company.

On 26 September 1896 Black Patti's Troubadours made their debut in a mini-musical called *At Jolly Coon-ey Island: A Merry Musical Farce*, cowritten by BOB COLE and William Johnson. *At Jolly Coon-ey Island* contained almost no plot. Rather, it was a revue that included classical music, vaudeville, burlesque, and skits performed by an enormous group of fifty dancers, singers, tumblers, and comedians. Black Patti's Troubadours were unique. Unlike other black companies, the Troubadours omitted the cakewalk, a popular, high-stepping

dance, from their finale. Instead, an operatic kaleidoscope featuring Black Patti concluded the show. The Troubadours placed the spotlight on Black Patti, who stylishly appeared in tiaras, long satin gowns, and white gloves to perform selections from the operatic composers Balfe, Verdi, Wagner, and Gounod.

Black Patti's Troubadours, billed as the "greatest colored show on earth," was based in New York City but toured throughout the United States and abroad. Advertisements claimed the group traveled thousands of miles in the United States in a train car called "Black Patti, America's Finest Show Car." Jones was the central attraction in productions like *A Ragtime Frolic at Rasbury Park* (1899–1900) and *A Darktown Frolic at the Rialto* (1900–1901). Although it is unclear how much of Jones's actual earnings went to Voelckel and Nolan, two years after the establishment of Black Patti's Troubadours, the *Colored American* reported that Jones commanded a salary of five hundred dollars per week. However, her husband was allegedly a gambler. His gambling, drinking, and misuse of their money led to the couple's divorce in 1899.

By 1900 Black Patti's Troubadours was solidly recognized as one of the most popular companies on the American stage. It helped to launch the careers of women like Ida Forsyne, AIDA OVERTON WALKER, and Stella Wiley. Many black performers who began their careers with Black Patti went on to experience success on their own. One might argue that their association with Jones, a highly respected, even revered performer, contributed to their later success.

As America's tastes began to change, the Troubadours adopted the name Black Patti Musical Comedy Company. Blacks began to view black musical comedies as negative depictions of their race, while whites began to turn their attention to other forms of entertainment. Some of the troupe's later productions were set in an African jungle. Jones played the queen in a 1907 production called *Trip to Africa*. She was included in the action of the comedy in a skit called "In the Jungles" for the first time in 1911. From 1914 to 1915 the operatic kaleidoscope no longer appeared in the Troubadours' program.

Jones made her final performance at New York City's Lafayette Theatre in 1915. As the mother of two adopted sons, she moved back to Providence, Rhode Island, where she also cared for her ailing mother. When Jones became ill and fell into obscurity, she was forced to rely on assistance from the National Association for the Advancement of Colored People (NAACP). Sissieretta Jones died on 24 June 1933 at Rhode Island Hospital. She remains one of the most celebrated black performers of the late nineteenth and early twentieth centuries.

FURTHER READING

A press scrapbook on Jones is housed in the Moorland-Spingarn Collection, Howard University, Washington, D.C.

Black Perspective in Music 4, no. 2 (July 1976).

Daughtry, Willia Estelle. "Sissieretta Jones: A Study of the Negro's Contribution to Nineteenth Century American Concert and Theatrical Life," Ph.D. diss., Syracuse University (1968).

Henricksen, Henry. "Madame Sissieretta Jones," *Record Research*, no. 165–166 (Aug. 1979).

Woll, Allen. *Black Musical Theatre: From Coontown to Dreamgirls* (1989).

MARTA J. EFFINGER-CRICHLOW

Jones, Marion (12 Oct. 1975–), Olympic track- and-field athlete, was born in Los Angeles, California, the first child of the American-born George Jones, a Laundromat owner, and the second child of the Belize-born Marion Hulse, a legal secretary. Jones held dual citizenship in the United States and Belize. Ira Toler, Jones's stepfather, contributed significantly to her upbringing. As Jones grew up, she tagged along with her older brother and often played against boys in her childhood games. A ferocious athletic competitor, she had little interest in anything except sports.

By the time she became a freshman in high school in 1989, Jones had drawn considerable attention in California interscholastic sports by beating many older and more mature women in the state 100- and 200-meter-dash championships. She won those events again during her next three years in school and added a ninth state title as a senior in the long jump. Her basketball talents were equally prodigious and earned Jones a scholarship to the University of North Carolina in 1993. In her first year, 1993–1994, the team won the NCAA championship. Injuries cut Jones's basketball career short, and she eventually turned her full attention to track and field.

After what amounted to a four-year absence from track and field and after only a few months of serious training, Jones won the 1997 U.S. championship in the 100 meters, becoming known as the fastest woman in the world. In the next season she participated in a world tour that was unprecedented for its ambition. She entered meets at a frenzied pace all over the world, returning home just long enough to become the first woman in fifty years to win three titles at the U.S. championships in New Orleans in 1998. In all she took part in thirty-seven different competitions in 1998 and won thirty-six of them. By the time the year was over, Jones held the number one position in the world in the 100-meter dash, the 200-meter dash, and the long jump. She capped the year by marrying the Olympic shot-putter C. J. Hunter on 3 October 1998.

A charismatic and attractive woman, Jones quickly became a media favorite and one of the most famous female athletes in the world. Reporters and fans speculated that Jones would win five gold medals—more than any other woman ever in track and field—at the 2000 Sydney Olympics. She came close. She won the 100-meter race by the second-largest margin in Olympic history, among men or women. She won the 200-meter race by the largest margin since WILMA RUDOLPH won it in 1960. Jones took a third gold medal as part of the U.S. 1,600-meter relay team. In the 400-meter relay, the U.S. team botched the handoff between the second and third legs; Jones made up some ground, but the Americans took the bronze for third place. The long jump, traditionally Jones's weakest event, left her with a fifth medal and a second bronze. In recognition of her achievements, Jones was named Associated Press Female Athlete of the Year.

The track-and-field world had long been dogged by allegations that athletes used performance-enhancing drugs. Jones stated repeatedly throughout her career that she wanted a drug-free sport and that she never used illegal drugs and never violated the drug ban. However, rumors of drug use swirled around her and effectively destroyed her career. The first major blow came on 26 September 2000, when her husband tested positive for steroid use. Suspended for two years, he retired from the sport, and the couple divorced in 2002. In the autumn of 2003 Jones was among several athletes to testify before a federal grand jury in San Francisco investigating steroid use.

In 2004 investigators looking at the Bay Area Laboratory Cooperative (BALCO) found a calendar with the initials "M J" written on it, appearing to indicate a schedule for steroid use in 2001. Hunter also reportedly told investigators that he had personally injected Jones with banned substances and had witnessed her doing the same. On 16 May 2004 Jones insisted she was drug free and said she would sue if the U.S. Anti-Doping Agency barred her from competing in the Athens Olympics without a positive drug test. In August 2004 Jones competed in the Athens Olympics but went home empty-handed. She finished fifth in the long jump, and her 4x100 relay team failed to finish after a bad handoff. Sponsors began to avoid her because of the drug-use rumors.

On 7 December 2004 the International Olympic Committee (IOC) opened an investigation into doping allegations against Jones after the BALCO founder Victor Conte alleged that he supplied her with an array of banned drugs before and after the Sydney Olympics. On 13 December 2005 the U.S. Olympic sprinter Tim Montgomery, Jones's boyfriend, was given a two-year ban from the sport based on evidence gathered in the BALCO investigation. Montgomery and Jones had produced a son in 2003. On 5 February 2006 Jones settled a $25 million federal defamation lawsuit against Conte for damaging her reputation by declaring on ABC's *20/20* that he supplied performance-enhancing drugs to Jones and Montgomery. Five days later the IOC announced that it would continue to investigate whether Jones took illegal substances at the 2000 Sydney Games. On 23 June 2006 Jones's "A" sample from the USA Track-and-Field Championships tested positive for the banned endurance-boosting hormone erythropoietin (EPO). She was faced with the possibility of a two-year ban from the sport. However, on 6 September 2006 Jones's backup, or "B" sample, was negative, clearing her of any wrongdoing and allowing her to return to competition. Observers noted that it was rare for a "B" sample to fail to conform to the "A" sample and speculated that the EPO in the sample may have deteriorated beyond recognition. The allegations of steroid usage prompted Jones to seriously consider withdrawing from athletic competition. On 24 February 2007 Jones married the sprinter Obadele Thompson. Jones continued to deny any allegations of drug usage, until 5 October 2007, when she pleaded guilty in federal court to lying to federal investigators in the BALCO steroid investigation. She announced her retirement the same day.

Following her admission of guilt, Jones was stripped of all her Olympic medals by the IOC. She was also sentenced to six months in federal prison in 2008. In 2010, she published an autobiography and mea culpa, *On the Right Track: From Olympic Downfall to Finding Forgiveness and the Strength to Overcome and Succeed.*

FURTHER READING

Jones, Marion, and Kate Sekules. *Marion Jones: Life in the Fast Lane* (2004).

Rapoport, Ron. *See How She Runs: Marion Jones and the Making of a Champion* (2000).

CARYN E. NEUMANN

Jones, Nancy (1860–?), missionary and teacher, was born in Christian County, Kentucky, but her family moved to Memphis, Tennessee, during her childhood. She discussed her family's relocation in her application for mission work, but there is no additional information about her parents, childhood, or life before she entered Fisk University. She also indicated in her missionary application that she decided at the age of twelve that she wanted to become a missionary. Jones graduated from the normal—or teaching—department course at Fisk University in 1886. Fisk University began in October 1865 as Fisk Free Colored School, one of several schools founded for freed people during the Union military occupation of Nashville, Tennessee.

With the reopening of the Nashville public schools, the institution was chartered as Fisk University on 22 August 1867. As a college, Fisk needed new quarters; and in 1871 the surplus Union Fort Gillem was purchased. A student choir under the leadership of George L. White was organized in 1867 and began touring the nation in 1871 to raise building funds. Known as the Fisk Jubilee Singers, the choir raised over $50,000 for the construction of Jubilee Hall. In January 1876 Fisk University opened its new campus.

Like other southern black schools of the late nineteenth century, Fisk University promoted the idea that it was the special mission of African Americans to help in the redemption of Africa. Jones recalled the words on a banner in the dining room at Fisk University: "Her Sons and Daughters are ever on the altar" (American Board of Commissioners for Foreign Missions Papers). She felt that she was included in that exclusive group. At Fisk, Jones was a friend of Henrietta Bailey Ousley, and the two later served as missionaries of the American Board of Commissioners for Foreign Missions (ABCFM) in Mozambique.

Although a Baptist, Jones applied to the Congregational ABCFM for a missionary appointment. Organized in 1810, the ABCFM was one of the earliest American Protestant missionary bodies. Initially interdenominational, the organization included Congregationalists, Presbyterians, and the Dutch Reformed and Associate Reformed denominations. In February 1812 the ABCFM sent its first foreign missionaries to India.

Two years later, in 1814, Baptists broke from the American Board and established their own separate missionary society. Subsequently other denominational missionary bodies were formed. With the rise of denominationalism, the inter-denominational makeup of the American Board ceased, and by the mid-nineteenth century the non-Congregationalists had all withdrawn.

On her application for mission service to the ABCFM, Jones was confronted with the following question: "When did you decide to go as a missionary and what led you to think of the subject?" She wrote that she believed God had directed her mind and heart to Africa. Jones served the ABCFM in Mozambique from 1888 to 1893 and later in eastern Southern Rhodesia (now Zimbabwe) from 1893 to 1897. The motivation for mission work among African American women missionaries in Africa probably did not differ much from other women who volunteered for mission service. Some were influenced through their experiences at churches or camps with missionaries who were on furloughs or those who had returned home permanently from overseas. A few were encouraged by family, friends, or local congregations to volunteer for missionary assignments. Others were influenced by church leaders or believed that they had received their calling directly from God. Jones was the first unmarried black woman commissioned by the American Board, and she joined Benjamin and Henrietta Ousley, both of whom she had met at Fisk, at the board's station in Kambini, Mozambique, in 1888 and worked with them for over five years. At the Kambini mission station, Jones began teaching and soon took charge of the school's primary department. She also visited nearby areas, working with the women there. Because of the great demand for schools from African children and adults, Jones eventually opened another school for area children, this one being a few miles from the mission station. Although she proposed to the American Board that a boarding school for African boys and girls be established, she was never successful in persuading the ABCFM of the necessity for such a school.

In 1893 the poor health of Benjamin Ousley forced the Ousleys to resign and return to the United States. Jones was left alone at the Kambini station, so the American Board decided to transfer its mission inland. Along with eight white missionaries, Jones joined the staff as the only black person in the new Gaza Mission, the ABCFM mission on the eastern border of Southern Rhodesia at Mount Silinda. There Jones initially worked as a teacher in the day school but was eventually relieved of that duty when a white teacher came and took over that task. Finally in 1897 she resigned from the East Central African Mission, stating she was "unable to work in harmony with the mission" (American Board of Commissioners for Foreign Missions Papers) because of the prejudice of some of her white co-workers. Although she asked the board to assign her to an area with other black missionaries, someplace where white missionaries would balk at the living conditions, she was never reassigned; eventually she returned to her home in Memphis. Nothing is known of Jones after she returned to Memphis.

FURTHER READING

The Nancy Jones Candidate File and Letters and the Henrietta Bailey Ousley and Benjamin Forsyth Ousley Biography File, American Board of Commissioners for Foreign Missions Papers, are at the Houghton Library of Harvard University.

Fisk University. *Catalogue of the Officers and Students of Fisk University* (1894–1895).

Goodsell, Fred Field. *You Shall Be My Witness: An Interpretation of the History of the American Board, 1810–1960* (1959).

Strong, William E. *The Story of the American Board: An Account of the First Hundred Years of the American Board of Commissioners for Foreign Missions* (1910).

Williams, Walter L. *Black Americans and the Evangelization of Africa, 1877–1900* (1982).

SYLVIA M. JACOBS

Jones, Nathaniel Raphael (12 May 1926–), federal judge, was born to Nathaniel B. and Lillian J. (Rafe) Jones in Youngstown, Ohio. His father worked at a mill and as a janitor, while his mother worked numerous domestic jobs to help support their family. Coming from humble beginnings, Jones used his circumstances of poverty and discrimination to motivate him through South High School in Youngstown, and through his service in the U.S. Air Force during World War II. In 1946 Jones returned home to attend Youngstown College (later Youngstown State University). As an undergraduate, he embarked on his lifelong association with the NAACP by joining the Youngstown College Chapter.

Jones had many positive influences in his life during his tenure at Youngstown, notably black community leaders such as the attorney Clarence Robinson and the businessman J. Maynard Dickerson. As an undergraduate, Jones worked as a reporter on the

Buckeye Review, an African American weekly in Youngstown. At twenty he became the editor of the *Review* and managed the Dickerson Printing Company for his mentor, Maynard Dickerson. Dickerson eventually encouraged Jones to attend law school. Jones agreed, but only if he could continue his work for the *Review*.

Jones received his AB in 1951 from Youngstown College, an LLB from Youngstown Law School in 1956, and was admitted to the Ohio bar the following year. Jones began his legal career in private practice for his first four years following law school. Later, he served as executive director of the Fair Employment Practices Commission.

The 1960s marked a major advance in Jones's legal career. In 1961 U.S. Attorney General Robert Kennedy appointed him as the first black Assistant U.S. Attorney for the Northern District of Ohio (Cleveland). Six years later he was appointed as assistant general counsel to President Lyndon Johnson's National Advisory Commission on Civil Disorders, which became popularly known as the "Kerner Commission." Afterward, Jones left government service for private practice, opting to return to Youngstown, where he accepted employment with the law firm of Goldberg and Jones.

Shortly after his return to private practice, Jones joined the NAACP legal department as general counsel under executive director ROY WILKINS in 1969. His addition to the NAACP's legal staff was a crucial appointment. The skills he had learned during his time in private practice placed him as one of the key strategists for several successful legal battles undertaken by the NAACP as it launched legal challenges against discrimination aimed at black servicemen in the military and at efforts to dismantle affirmative action. His most notable involvement in NAACP affairs was his work in the landmark school busing case *Milliken v. Bradley* (1974).

Nathaniel Jones's legal career reached another milestone on 15 October 1979. Jones took the oath to serve on the U.S. Court of Appeals for the Sixth Circuit; he became a senior judge in 1995. By 1983 Judge Jones became a member of the first all-black panel to sit in the Sixth Circuit Court of Appeals. Judge Jones was also active in a number of international civil and human rights causes. As a representative for the Lawyers' Committee for Civil Rights Under Law, he attended a trial of sixteen South Africans accused of terrorism in 1985. He later wrote of this experience in the article "Yearning to Breathe Free: A Report of the South African Treason Trial." In November 1986 Jones traveled to the Soviet Union as part of a four-person delegation to meet with Soviet officials and Jewish Refuseniks to discuss issues of human rights.

Judge Jones was able to observe several groundbreaking developments in South Africa. He monitored the election process that led to Namibia's independence from South Africa and the election that led to former political prisoner Nelson Mandela becoming the president of South Africa. Judge Jones played an important role in the development of South Africa's new constitution and laws.

Jones became a senior partner at Blank Rome LLP, a Philadelphia-based law firm with offices in Cincinnati, Washington, and New York. He was also an adjunct professor at the University of Cincinnati College of Law, Case Western Reserve School of Law, and Cleveland State University School of Law. Throughout Jones's legal career he contributed several notable scholarly works to legal journals, law reviews, and other legal periodicals, specifically addressing equal protection under the law. As a judge, an attorney, and an advocate for civil rights and diversity, Jones was recognized by numerous organizations and universities. He was a member of the National Bar Association's Hall of Fame, a recipient of the NAACP THURGOOD MARSHALL Lifetime Achievement Award and held seventeen honorary degrees. Most notably, the 106th Congress named the new federal courthouse in Youngstown, Ohio, the Nathaniel R. Jones Federal Building and U.S. Courthouse in honor of his dedication and service to the legal profession.

DONALD F. TIBBS

Jones, Paul R. (1 June 1928–26 Jan. 2010), a major collector of African American art, grew up as the son of the coal employment broker William "Will" Norfleet Jones and the homemaker Ella Reed Phillips Jones in the small mining camp of Muscoda on the edge of Bessemer, Alabama. The family enjoyed privileges that were not typical of other black mining families because of Will Jones's position with the Tennessee Coal, Mine, and Railroad Company. As a result, they straddled the line between the black working poor and the middle class. In 1938, at the age of ten, Jones went to New York City to receive a better education than he could get in the racially segregated schools of Alabama. He lived with an older brother, Joe, and returned home during the summer. On a class visit to a New York City art museum, Jones was captivated both by the art and by how it held the attention of people visiting. This experience would later prompt him to collect art.

Returning to Alabama, Jones graduated from Paul Laurence Dunbar High School in Bessemer. He subsequently earned a degree from Howard University in 1948. At Howard, Jones met the artist and art historian JAMES A. PORTER, who wrote the first history of African American art, *Modern Negro Art*, in 1943. Jones then spent most of his life in a range of government jobs including working as a probation officer, a community relations specialist, a director in the Model Cities Program, a deputy director in the Peace Corps, and as a White House staff assistant in the Nixon administration. He worked to achieve civil rights and to settle racial conflicts. As his work history indicates, Jones lived on a modest income for most of his life.

Jones began collecting African American art in the mid-1960s while living in southwest Atlanta. He wanted to decorate the walls of his apartment and decided to get original works of art and see what gaps existed in the art world. With a few exceptions, black artists were not getting into museums or private collections. By and large, galleries practiced the same exclusionary policies. Galleries would occasionally show a superstar of color but they usually did not keep the artist as part of their stable. He spotted this gap and thought that by collecting African American art, the work would not be lost to the art world. For Jones, art also became a means to show that the African American cultural tradition is part of American life and heritage.

Over forty years of collecting, Jones amassed more than two thousand works of art. The works overtook his home, consuming the existing wall space as well as his closets, dresser drawers, bookcases, and the spaces under beds and behind doors. Since 1968, Jones frequently lent work to more than one hundred exhibitions and has allowed more than thirty complete shows to be formed from his collection and seen in forty-two states. Meanwhile, Jones developed a relationship with the University of Delaware's Art History Department when it sought to mount an exhibit of African American art—a subject entirely missing from its curriculum at the time. Jones's wish had been to house his collection at a historically black college but he found that these institutions lacked the resources to preserve and protect the art works. Instead, he donated significant works from his collection to the University of Delaware in 2001, which in turn established a collaborative arrangement with the historically black Spelman College. The Paul R. Jones Collection of African American Art includes the works of James Little, Kofi Bailey, Ashanti Johnson, Leo Twiggs,

Bill Hutson, Howardena Pindell, Alvin Smith, Jack Whitten, Frank Bowling, and others. Jones's vision was that his collection would be preserved as a whole and used as a teaching and research collection that would transform the understanding of American art to include African American art. In 2008, however, Jones donated another vast part of his collection, chiefly photographs, to the University of Alabama to allow that school to showcase African American art. This collection includes works by ROY DeCARAVA, CARRIE MAE WEEMS, Bert Andrews, Frank Stewart, Ming Smith Murray, William Anderson, and ADGER W. COWANS. Paul R. Jones died in Atlanta on 26 January 2010.

FURTHER READING

Amaki, Amalia K., ed. *A Century of African American Art: The Paul R. Jones Collection* (2004).

Andersen, Margaret L., and Neil F. Thomas. *The Life of Paul R. Jones, African American Art Collector* (2009).

Obituary: *Atlanta Journal-Constitution*, 1 Feb. 2010.

CARYN E. NEUMANN

Jones, Philly Joe (15 July 1923–30 Aug. 1985), jazz drummer, was born Joseph Rudolph Jones in Philadelphia, Pennsylvania, the son of Amelia J. Abbott, a piano teacher and church organist. His father, whose name is unknown, died shortly after he was born. During his early childhood Joseph was featured as a tap dancer on a local Philadelphia radio program, *The Kiddie Show*. Interestingly, several other important jazz drummers, including JO JONES and Buddy Rich, were also tap dancers. Joseph's sisters studied violin and piano, and his first organized musical experience began in grade school, where he played drums. In 1941 he left high school and enlisted in the U.S. Army, where he served as a military policeman until his release in 1943. His wife's name was Eloise (maiden name and marriage date unknown), and they had one child.

After being discharged from the army, Jones played in local Philadelphia bands before moving in 1947 to New York City, where he came into contact with a number of important bebop musicians, including DIZZY GILLESPIE, DEXTER GORDON, and CHARLIE PARKER. In the late 1940s he worked with BEN WEBSTER in Washington, D.C., and toured with a rhythm and blues band led by the trumpeter Joe Morris. This ensemble at one time included the tenor saxophonist Johnny Griffin, the pianist ELMO HOPE, the trombonist Matthew Gee, and the string bassist Percy Heath, all of whom later became established bop musicians. After brief appearances with TINY GRIMES and LIONEL HAMPTON, Jones returned in 1952 to New York, where he worked with Zoot Sims, Lee Konitz, Tony Scott, and MILES DAVIS before playing and recording with TAD DAMERON's band in 1953.

In 1955 Jones became a member, along with PAUL CHAMBERS, RED GARLAND, and JOHN COLTRANE, of one of the most artistically successful Davis ensembles. This association gave Jones and the other members of the group popular recognition as the definitive bop ensemble of the 1950s. Jones worked in Davis-led small groups in 1958 and 1962 and was drummer on the memorable jazz orchestra recordings that Davis made with the pianist Gil Evans in 1957. Jones shared the drumming position with Jimmy Cobb in later Davis groups while appearing and recording with other well-known jazz figures in New York City, including DUKE ELLINGTON, Coltrane, Jimmy Oliver, and BILLIE HOLIDAY. Jones left Davis (along with Coltrane) when the trumpeter decided that Jones's substance abuse interfered with the success of the ensemble.

Jones led his own jazz groups starting in 1958 and toured from 1959 to 1962, during which time he played briefly with Gil Evans's band. In 1967 he joined the pianist Bill Evans before moving to London, where he taught percussion until 1969 and then moved to Paris. In Paris, Jones played in local jazz clubs, toured, and taught drums with expatriate and bop drummer KENNY CLARKE. He returned to Philadelphia in 1972, later forming (with Byard Lancaster) a jazz/rock group called Le Grand Prix. In the late 1970s Jones worked again with the pianists Evans and Garland and in 1981 formed Dameronia, a nine-piece ensemble dedicated to playing the music of the late Tad Dameron. He fronted this group until 1985, when he replaced Clarke as drummer with Pieces of Time. He died in Philadelphia.

Jones was primarily a self-taught drummer, but he credited COZY COLE, Charlie Wilcox, and James "Coatesville" Harris among his earliest teachers. Although anchored in swing drumming traditions, Jones displayed a unique style of playing that at times could be subtle, especially in his use of brushes, but was more often clean, precise, forceful, and commanding. He evolved a bop drumming style in which straight eighth note patterns formed the basis for his solos and fills that combined unusual phrase lengths, tight, controlled rhythmic patterns, and creative use of silence. A small-group player, Jones favored musicality and imaginative

rhythmic patterns over technique. This was demonstrated in his frequent use of cross-rhythmic solo and accompaniment patterns. He had few imitators in jazz, but perhaps because of his affinity to the even-note patterns so commonly found in rock, several rock drummers, including Blood, Sweat, and Tears drummer Bobby Colomby, incorporated Jones's concepts into their playing.

Jones's early playing can be heard on *Lou Donaldson with Clifford Brown* (1953) and on recordings that he made with his own band, including *Blues for Dracula* (1958). His work with Coltrane on *Blue Train*, recorded in 1957, was released in 1984. Jones's most important recordings, however, date from his association with Miles Davis and include *'Round Midnight* (1955–1956), *Workin'* (1956), and *Milestones* (1958). Jones allied himself with several major bop musicians during the 1960s, and his style is well documented on *The Complete Prestige Recordings of* SONNY ROLLINS (1992) and *The Complete Blue Note Recordings of the Tina Brooks Quintets* (1985). Here Jones demonstrates a mature bop drumming style that, in many cases, defines the genre during this era. Insights into his excellent brush technique can be found in a manual that he wrote, titled *Brush Artistry*.

FURTHER READING

Mattingly, Rick. "Philly Joe Jones," *Modern Drummer* 6, no. 1 (Jan. 1982): 10–13.

Taylor, Art. *Notes and Tones: Musician to Musician Interviews* (1979).

Obituaries: *New York Times*, 3 Sept. 1985; *Jazz Journal* 38, no. 11 (Nov. 1985); *Down Beat* 52, no. 1 (Dec. 1985).

This entry is taken from the *American National Biography* and is published here with the permission of the American Council of Learned Societies.

T. DENNIS BROWN

Jones, Quincy (14 Mar. 1933–), jazz musician, composer, and record, television, and film producer, was born Quincy Delight Jones Jr. on the South Side of Chicago, Illinois, the son of Sarah (maiden name unknown) and Quincy Jones Sr., a carpenter who worked for a black gangster ring that ran the Chicago ghetto. When Quincy Sr.'s mentally ill wife was institutionalized, he sent their sons, Quincy Jr. and Lloyd, to live in the South with their grandmother. In his autobiography Jones writes of growing up so poor that his grandmother served them fried rats to eat. By the age of ten he was living with Lloyd and their father in Seattle, Washington. "My stepbrother, my brother, and myself, and my cousin … we burned down stores, we stole, whatever you had to do," Jones said (*CNN Online*, "Q and A: A Talk with Quincy Jones," 11 Dec. 2001).

Modern jazz was Jones's way out. Inspired by the now legendary jazzmen who passed through Seattle in the 1940s, Jones began studying trumpet in junior high school. When COUNT BASIE brought a group to Seattle in 1950, Jones, then a teenager, approached one band member, CLARK TERRY, an acclaimed trumpeter, for lessons. "He's the type of cat, anything he wanted to do, he could've done," Terry said later in his autobiography.

Jones showed enough musical promise to win a scholarship to Schillinger House in Boston (now the Berklee School of Music), but he dropped out after a year to accept a place in the trumpet section of LIONEL HAMPTON's band. In 1951 Hampton made a record of Jones's "Kingfish" and gave the teenager his first recorded composition. Thereafter Jones settled in New York City, where he found work as an arranger for some of the biggest stars in jazz, including Count Basie, CANNONBALL ADDERLEY, and DINAH WASHINGTON. In 1956 he hired an array of top musicians for his first album, *This Is How I Feel about Jazz*. "His writing is not exploratory," writes jazz critic Leonard Feather. He wrote in his *New Encyclopedia of Jazz* about Jones's musical compositions, "Unlike many of the younger writers who have experimented with atonality and extended forms, he has remained within the classic jazz framework; his reputation rests mainly on brief compositions that combine the swinging big band feel of the better orchestras of the '30s with the harmonic developments of the '40s." In May 1956 Jones joined the DIZZY GILLESPIE Orchestra on a State Department–sponsored tour of the Middle East and South America. A year later he moved to Paris, where he studied with Nadia Boulanger, a conductor and composition teacher known for her illustrious expatriate pupils, including Aaron Copland and Virgil Thomson. Modern jazz was blossoming in Paris, and Jones became a producer-arranger for Disques Barclay, France's premier jazz label. In the fall of 1959 he became musical director of *Free and Easy*, a touring blues opera by Harold Arlen. Jones had assembled a big band for the show, and in September 1959 he took it on a European tour. The enterprise proved much too costly, and in 1960 it fell apart, leaving Jones deeply in debt.

Returning to New York, Jones was hired in May 1961 as an A&R (Artist and Repertory) man at Mercury Records. After producing a number-one hit—Lesley Gore's teenage pop lament "It's My Party"—and other artistic and creative successes, he became vice president of the company in November 1964. It was reportedly the first time a black man had held such a high position in the U.S. record business. In addition to arranging and conducting for Frank Sinatra, Basie, SARAH VAUGHAN, and Peggy Lee, Jones was writing and recording his own albums.

Beginning with Sidney Lumet's *The Pawnbroker* in 1964, Jones began composing film music, collaborating with many of the decade's seminal filmmakers, including Lumet, Sidney Pollack, Norman Jewison, Richard Brooks, and Paul Mazursky. He also teamed with the actor SIDNEY POITIER for six films during the 1960s and early 1970s. Jones's scores for such films as *The Pawnbroker, In Cold Blood* (1967), *In the Heat of the Night* (1967), *Cactus Flower* (1969), and *Bob & Carol & Ted & Alice* (1969) introduced jazz, soul, and, later, funk into films, contributing to the increased sophistication and interrelatedness of music to popular film. Jones also played a part in bringing a new sound to TV with his scores for *Ironside* (1967–1975); *The BILL COSBY Show* (1969); *Sanford and Son* (1972–1977), starring REDD FOXX; and the miniseries *Roots* (1977), based on the book by ALEX HALEY and for which Jones won an Emmy.

Jones's affairs with a string of women, including Dinah Washington and Peggy Lee, had put a severe strain on his marriage to Jeri Caldwell, his white high-school sweetheart and the mother of his first child, Jolie. Married in 1957, the couple divorced nine years later. Jones quickly entered into a brief marriage with Ulla Andersson, a blonde model. In 1974 he married Peggy Lipton, star of TV's *Mod Squad*. The couple had two children and divorced in 1989.

In 1969 Jones moved to A&M, by which time he had made a nearly full-time shift toward commercial pop. The trumpeter MILES DAVIS had plunged into fusion, a new style of electric jazz-rock, and Jones did the same in *Walking in Space* (1974), his first of several hit records that combined jazz, fusion, and funk. Jones continued his work as orchestrator, arranging the strings for Paul Simon's foray into pop-gospel and rhythm and blues, *There Goes Rhymin' Simon* (1973). But Jones remained loyal to the jazz musicians he loved and filled his orchestras with them. In 1973 he began a career in TV production with a gala-special on the CBS network called DUKE ELLINGTON … *We Love You Madly*, featuring a cast that included Vaughan,

Quincy Jones, jazz musician and composer, gestures in a New York hotel room overlooking New York's Central Park, 15 October 2001. (AP Images.)

Lee, Joe Williams, and Jones's boyhood friend RAY CHARLES, along with newer stars like ROBERTA FLACK and ARETHA FRANKLIN.

Jones, who had worked on behalf of MARTIN LUTHER KING JR.'s Operation Breadbasket, helped organize Chicago's Black EXPO, an offshoot of Operation PUSH, with JESSE JACKSON in 1972. He later served on the board of PUSH and, much later, produced a talk show with Jackson, *The Jesse Jackson Show* (1990). Jones, who had begun seriously educating himself about black and African music, became increasingly committed to the historical preservation of African American music. He helped establish the annual Black Arts Festival in Chicago and the Institute for Black American Music, which donated funds toward the establishment of a national library of African American art and music.

Jones's workaholic tendencies caught up with him in August 1974 when he suffered a near-fatal brain aneurysm and underwent two major neurological surgeries. Once recovered, he returned to his career with the same fervor. In 1979 he produced MICHAEL JACKSON's solo album *Off*

the Wall, which yielded four top ten hits. In 1981 Jones left A&M and established the Qwest label at Warner Bros. Although he made his initial mark as a jazz arranger, producer, and bandleader, Jones became a household name by producing Jackson's next album, 1982's *Thriller*, which sold 50 million albums and became the biggest-selling album of all time. Jackson and Jones remained a team for years, working on *Bad* (1987) and other projects.

Apart from his work with Michael Jackson, Jones's greatest commercial triumph came in 1985, with the slick all-star album *USA for Africa*, which featured the song "We Are the World." Written by Jackson and LIONEL RICHIE and performed by forty-six music stars, including Bruce Springsteen and DIANA ROSS, the single sold 7.5 million copies, raised $50 million for famine relief in Africa, and won Grammy awards for Song of the Year and Record of the Year.

Jones showed his ingenuity for mixing pop with traditional genres with *The Dude* (1980), a pop-soul extravaganza with Jackson, STEVIE WONDER, HERBIE HANCOCK, the jazz harmonica and guitar player Toots Thielemans, and two of Jones's protégés, the singers Patti Austin and James Ingram. He continued this pattern in 1989 with *Back on the Block*, an album that mingled Miles Davis, Dizzy Gillespie, ELLA FITZGERALD, and Sarah Vaughan with the rappers Kool Moe Dee and Big Daddy Kane. "I'll Be Good to You," a top twenty single from that album, paired Ray Charles with the pop-soul belter Chaka Khan.

After his successful turn in 1985 as coproducer of the Steven Spielberg film adaptation of ALICE WALKER's *The Color Purple*, Jones expanded his empire into film and television production. Through Quincy Jones Entertainment, Inc. (QJE), a joint enterprise with Time Warner formed in 1990, Jones created *The Fresh Prince of Bel Air* (1990–1996), the TV series that launched the career of the actor WILL SMITH, and the long-running comedy show *Mad TV*. Jones's other producing projects include the multipart *History of Rock and Roll* (1995) and the 2002 documentary TUPAC SHAKUR: *Thug Angel*. The founder of Quincy Jones Music Publishing, Jones also owns Qwest Broadcasting, which, with the Tribune Company, owns television stations in Atlanta and New Orleans. In 1990 Jones established a magazine, *Vibe*, which focused on black pop music. The next year he persuaded the ailing Miles Davis to revisit classic work of the 1950s in a concert at the Montreux Jazz Festival in Switzerland. Davis hated looking back; only

Jones could persuade him to do so. Davis died two months later.

The recipient of countless awards, Jones has earned seventy-seven Grammy nominations and won twenty-six times. He is a six-time Oscar nominee, and at the 1995 Academy Awards he won the Jean Hersholt Humanitarian Award. In 1990 Warner Bros. released a documentary based on his life, *Listen Up: The Lives of Quincy Jones*. Eleven years later he received a Kennedy Center Honor for lifetime achievement. As awards showered down on him in the 1980s and 1990s, some critics thought Jones outrageously overhyped. There is little disagreement, however, about his abilities in combining talent in the studio to dazzling effect. Throughout his career he showed a shrewd business sense, earning millions of dollars, riding almost every new musical trend, including fusion and rap. While he will not be remembered as an exceptional trumpeter, Jones remains one of the most celebrated and charismatic figures in the pop music business. He has also allied himself with the biggest names in jazz, pop, and film to a point where he has been absorbed into their ranks.

FURTHER READING

Jones, Quincy. *Q: The Autobiography of Quincy Jones* (2001).

Ross, Courtney, and Nelson George. *Listen Up: The Lives of Quincy Jones* (1990).

JAMES GAVIN

Jones, R. Wellington (18 Oct. 1940–), pianist, impresario, opera director, producer, television host, and educator, was born in Harlem, New York, to Walter Jones, born 1910, and Lucille Fairs, born 1908, a housewife from Wilmington, North Carolina. His father worked at the Capitol Theatre, which premiered the film version of *Gone with the Wind*. R. Wellington Jones had a sister, Jean Jones, now deceased. His maternal grandmother, Sukie Fairs, was a slave as a child and lived 106 years. His paternal grandfather was killed by the Ku Klux Klan in Scotland Neck, North Carolina, in the early 1920s. His great grandparents were slaves and part of the Cherokee Nation.

Wellington Jones graduated from New York's famed High School of Music and Art in 1958, and earned both his bachelor's degree (1962) and master of arts degree (1964) in Music and Music Education from New York University. At the age of seventeen, he had produced his first concert at Steinway Hall and was the first African American

usher at Carnegie Hall in 1959. He escorted First Lady Jacqueline Kennedy on opening night at Lincoln Center, Philharmonic Hall in 1962. He was also the first African American usher to open the Metropolitan Opera House at Lincoln Center in 1966. By the time Wellington was twenty-five, he was being hailed as the black Sol Hurok, for producing outstanding singers at Carnegie, Steinway, and Judson Halls. While still in college, he presented the soprano Martha Flowers at Carnegie Recital Hall in November 1969, on the recommendation of LEONTYNE PRICE. In the 1950s Ms. Flowers had traveled throughout Europe and the USSR in a U.S. State Department–sponsored production of Gershwin's *Porgy and Bess* with a touring company that also included Leontyne Price, soprano, and WILLIAM WARFIELD, bass.

After graduating from college, his first teaching job was with the New York State Corrections Department in Sullivan County. He also taught in School Districts 13, 5, 3, and 4 in Manhattan and Brooklyn over a period of twenty-eight years. A devout member of Rutgers Presbyterian Church, Jones has served on the Board of Deacons, the Session, the Board of Trustees, and since 1987 Chair of the Special Events Committee. He has directed and produced the annual concert to benefit the Christopher Roberts Homeless Shelter at Rutgers Church since its inception in 1987. Each performance has received rave reviews.

In 1964 Wellington presented the soprano Juanita King in a program of Bach and various composers, with instrumentalists accompanied by Kelly Wyatt, pianist, in a recital of which the *New York Times* wrote, "Ms. King has a bright, radiant voice, pure in quality and big enough to fill Carnegie Recital Hall twice over." In May 1971, Jones presented the soprano Victoria Villamel in a varied program. Peter Davis of the *Times* wrote, "She inflected Ravel's *Chansons Madecasses* with the art of an experienced diseuse." That same year, Wellington presented the soprano Hermine Bartee in Heitor Villa-Lobos's *Bachianas Brasileiras No. 5*, with eight cellos, a work not heard in New York in fourteen years. John Rockwell wrote in the *New York Times*, "Ms. Bartee did display an appealing spunk."

In 1973 Wellington's presentations included Joy Parks in J. S. Bach's Cantata BMV 51, *Jauchzet Gott in allen Landen,* with chamber orchestra including baroque trumpet. Peter Davis wrote in the *Times* of this recital that "Wellington Jones is one of the true producers of concert singers in New York City, and I look forward to seeing his other recitals."

Wellington was also one of the first African Americans to have his own cable television show in New York, which debuted in 1974. His show, *New Ventures,* remained on the air as of 2011, and also can be found on the Internet at www.mmn.org. His opera presentations are also videotaped for BBC European Networks.

He has received many honors including the Outstanding Achievement in the Arts and Music Award of the New York Black Caucus of the Music Educator's National Conference in 1988; the Mayor's Citation for Achievement in Art and Music from Mayor DAVID DINKINS, City of New York in 1991; Recognition for Directing the Annual Christopher Roberts Homeless Shelter Benefit Concert since 1987; Choral Directing at Junior High School 13; From the Cast of 2009 in Grateful Appreciation as Producer/Director of the Benefit Concerts at Rutgers Church.

On 1 May 2011 Wellington presented the *Cavalleria Rusticana* by Pietro Mascagni as the main attraction for the Benefit Concert at Rutgers Church. In the first half of the program, Wellington played the piano music of Edward McDowell, displaying virtuosity. Wellington was married once and has two children; Gavin Wellington Jones, an educator who lives in New York and Lia Jones Allen, a speech pathologist who lives in Lansdale, Pennsylvania. He has three grandsons: Connor, Hunter, and Samoa.

FURTHER READING

Abdul, Raoul. "Bronx Concert Singers Team with
Rutgers Choir," *Amsterdam News,* 10–16 May 2001.
Abdul, Raoul. "Wellington Jones' Anthology superb in
song," *Amsterdam News,* 12 May 2004.
Franklin, Roger. "Music from Rutgers." *Renewal* 27, no.
1 (August–September 2010).
Schrier, Janice. "New Ventures." *Cable TV World.*
November 1969.

LOIS BELLAMY

Jones, Rev. Thomas H. (1806–6 June 1890), Methodist minister, abolitionist lecturer, and self-emancipated slave, was born to slave parents, Grace and Tony Kirkwood, at the Hawes plantation in Hanover county near Wilmington, North Carolina. About 1815 he was sold to a storekeeper from whom he took his surname. After his escape to Massachusetts, Jones became a tireless speaker on the antislavery circuit in New England. The principal source of information for his early life is his widely circulated slave narrative, *The Experience of Thomas H. Jones, Who Was a Slave for Forty-Three Years.* First published in 1850, his book went through at least nine printings.

Thomas succeeded in learning to read despite the disapproval of Mr. Jones, the storekeeper. Thomas was converted to Christianity around 1824. He attended services at a neighboring plantation against the objections of his irreligious owner. Upon Mr. Jones's death in 1829 Thomas began to preach the Gospel informally to other slaves in the area with the encouragement of his new owner, Owen Holmes.

Thomas H. Jones's first wife, Lucilla Smith, was a slave at an adjoining farm. The couple had three children: Annie, Lizzie, and Charlie. When Smith's owners moved to Tuscaloosa, Alabama, Jones's family was separated and never reunited. Holmes helped him make several attempts to recover his family but with no success. Sometime in the mid-1830s he was married to Mary R. Moore, a slave, with whom he had four children, Edward, Mary, John, and Alexander. With Holmes's permission, Jones was able to earn money of his own, enough to purchase some land (held for him by a white man who later cheated him of it) and, with the help of a white friend, his family's freedom for $350. He later learned of a plot to re-enslave Mary and the children. In July 1849 a supportive lawyer failed to have passed a special legislative act that would ensure their freedom. Jones sent his family, except Edward, to safety in Brooklyn, New York, at the home of Robert H. Cousins, an African American porter with other contacts in North Carolina.

By September 1849 Jones himself took flight to join his family. He paid his last $8 to the steward of the New York-bound brig *Bell* and hid below deck. He was discovered by the captain, who threatened to have him returned to slavery. Desperate, Jones went overboard off New York City with a makeshift raft and was picked up by the sympathetic crew of a passing ship. They brought him to Robert Cousins, where he was briefly reunited with his wife and children. He took to the road preaching to provide for his family. In Hartford, Connecticut, he learned that he was being pursued by slave catchers. He traveled up the Connecticut River to Springfield and then east to Boston. There, he prepared the first edition of his narrative, with the help of an amanuensis. He earned enough money to bring his family on to Boston, finally settling in Salem by 1850.

With the passage of the Fugitive Slave Act in September 1850, many of the escaped slaves who had found refuge in the cities and towns of Massachusetts

578 JONES, RICHARD "DICK JONES" LEE

fled to Canada. Jones was among them. In his letter to the abolitionist minister Daniel Foster dated 5 May 1851, from St. John, New Brunswick, he wrote, "I know it will be a source of pleasure to you to be informed of my safe arrival here on British ground. Quite free from terror, I now feel that my bones are a property bequeathed to me for my own use, and not for the servitude or gratification of the white man, in that gloomy and sultry region, where the hue of the skin has left my race in thralldom and misery for ages" (Ripley, p. 135).

In Canada he developed the dramatic style of his lectures, displaying the instruments of bondage and torture used to enforce the slave system. Writing again to Foster on 15 July 1852 from Liverpool, Nova Scotia, Jones said, "I have frequently lectured on slavery, and exhibited the handcuffs, collar, chain, cowhide, and the paddle showing many friends in this country what constitutes the liberty of the United States of America" (Ripley, p. 213–214). He published the 1853 edition of his narrative in Saint John, New Brunswick.

The resistance of abolitionists in Massachusetts made enforcement of the Fugitive Slave Act very difficult. Feeling it was safe enough to return, Jones joined his family in Massachusetts in 1854. He immediately visited the offices of William Lloyd Garrison, who had written an early testimonial for the narrative. Jones relates how Garrison encouraged him to join Wendell Phillips, Samuel J. May, and himself at an antislavery convention in Western Massachusetts: "Accordingly, I took the cars and rode as far as Northampton, and then walked the rest of the way, a distance of eighteen miles. It was after dark when I reached Cummington … Mr. Phillips was speaking when I entered the door … After [he] ceased speaking, I was formally introduced to the audience. A perfect storm of applause followed, which lasted for several minutes" (Andrews, p. 265–266).

On his way from Northampton to Cummington, he passed through the village of Florence. His wife had already arranged to purchase a home near a cotton mill known for employing African Americans, especially former slaves. The modest house, built by former slave BASIL DORSEY, is listed on the National Register of Historic Places. With Florence as a base Jones lectured throughout Western Massachusetts, southern Vermont, and New Hampshire. SOJOURNER TRUTH was his neighbor and fellow speaker on the antislavery circuits.

In 1859 he and his family moved to Worcester, where he lived until around 1865. By 1867 he had moved to New Bedford, where he married Mrs. Anna

Campbell of that city, presumably after the death of his second wife. At the age of seventy-six he was married for the fourth time to Lavina Russell Leslie. He continued to preach and lecture. He kept his narrative in print, publishing the enlarged edition in 1885 in New Bedford, where he died on 6 June 1890.

FURTHER READING

Andrews, William L., General Editor. *North Carolina Slave Narratives: The Lives of Moses Roper, Lunsford Lane, Moses Grandy, & Thomas H. Jones* (2003).

Grover, Kathryn. *Dorsey-Jones House National Register of Historic Places Nomination* (2004).

Jones, Thomas H. *The Experience of Thomas H. Jones Who Was for Forty-Three Years A Slave* (1862 edition).

Ripley, C. Peter, Ed. *The Black Abolitionist Papers*, Volume II (1985).

STEVE STRIMER

Jones, Richard "Dick Jones" Lee (21 Dec. 1893–13 Oct. 1975), journalist, businessman, military leader, and diplomat, was born in Albany, Georgia, to Richard and Eliza (Brown) Jones. Richard Lee Jones, also known as Dick Jones, moved to Cincinnati, Ohio, with his family at fifteen saying:

> In the South, I was not the submissive kind, but I learned respect for authority. Many Negroes have not learned that yet. They come up here and try to run away with the town. I had no trouble in the South. I avoided trouble. If you see a nail, why sit on it? Much trouble could be avoided by Negroes in the South if they tried to. Get me straight! I am not for conditions down there. They are bad, but could be bettered (Wilson, "Interview with Dick Jones, Manager of South Center," *Negro in Illinois* papers).

He attended the University of Cincinnati from 1912 to 1915, and later abandoned his law studies at the University of Illinois to serve as a second lieutenant in World War I. Following the war, he worked as a cashier with the First Standard Bank in Louisville, Kentucky, before joining the staff of the *Chicago Defender* in 1926 as advertising and business manager, and then the *Chicago Bee* in 1927 as general manager. In 1928, he began a long association with the newly founded South Center Department Store, first as a floor walker, then as personnel director and eventually, vice president.

A small but vibrant black leisure class was emerging in Chicago's bustling African American neighborhood known as Bronzeville. Its financial center—the intersection of 47th Street and South Parkway—offered black Chicagoans a sense of freedom and purchasing power they could not find anywhere else in America at that time. Located in the heart of Bronzeville's shopping district, South Center was the "largest Negro-owned department store in America," attempting to challenge the older and more experienced white retail establishments (Drake and Cayton, p. 380–381).

The South Center Department Store was the first establishment that catered to the needs of Bronzeville residents, and where they could be helped by black salesmen and saleswomen. South Center opened in March 1928 with nine thousand square feet of floor space, an African American store doctor, and an African American law firm handling their business. It employed nearly four hundred people with a minimum salary of $15.00 a week. Sixty-nine percent of the women employed were African Americans and 31 percent were white, and fifty-one percent of the men were African American and forty-nine percent were white (Ardis Harris, "Negro Employees in Stores and Offices," Federal Writer's Project: Negro Studies Project).

Jones was conscious of his position as one of the race men on Chicago's South Side. In an interview conducted by the Federal Writer's Project he stated "I did not make myself. I make no speeches. I believe in fair play. When the final division comes I must be on the side of the Negro. I know that." As an attendee of Pilgrim Baptist Church he stated, "I hear them preach against the white man. But, I know that the Negro has no business. Were it not for stores like this, there would be no Negro business." He was well aware that South Center was more than just a store—one entire floor became the training ground for MADAME C. J. WALKER, whose school became a fixture in the community, helping many men and women become independent business owners—it was a fixture combating what Jones termed the African American's infancy: "We need more businesses like this. The Negro is an infant, and don't know it. He gets up every Sunday and cusses the white man. On Monday he asks the white man for bread" (Wilson).

During the mid-1930s and 1940s, Jones resumed his military career, balancing this with his commitments to South Center. He served with the Eighth Regiment as an officer. During World War II, he was with the Sixth Service Command as public relations officer and special service commissioner, earning a promotion to major. In May 1946, he was awarded the Legion of Merit for exceptional service on behalf of the black soldier. After World War II, Jones returned to business, first as vice president with an insurance company and, from 1949 to 1954, as vice president of the South Center Department Store. During this time, he was a reserve officer, carrying out recruiting assignments for the 99th Pursuit Squadron and the reactivated 178th Regimental Combat Team, a National Guard unit which he commanded as brigadier general until 1953 when he retired (Christmas, p. 45).

In 1954, President Dwight D. Eisenhower appointed Jones ambassador to Liberia, a post he held until 1959. He returned to the United States in 1955 to serve a year as an alternate delegate to the United Nations, then returned to Liberia for three more years before returning to Chicago to become executive vice president of the Victory Mutual Life Insurance Company.

In 1970, Illinois Governor Richard B. Ogilvie and Chicago Mayor Richard J. Daley proclaimed 19 October as General Richard L. Jones Day. A parade through Washington Park and a military review were held in his honor, followed by a reception in the armory which was renamed in his honor on that day.

Jones remained a bachelor until the age of 50 when he married Elgetha Ora Huffman, with whom he had son, Richard Lee III. He died in 1975 and was buried in his wife's hometown of Richmond, Indiana.

FURTHER READING

Christmas, Walter. *Negroes in Public Affairs and Government: Volume 1* (1966).

Green, Adam. *Selling the Race: Culture, Community, and Black Chicago, 1940–1955* (2007).

Drake, St. Clair and Horace Cayton. *Black Metropolis: A Study of Negro Life in a Northern City* (1945).

Stange, Maren. *Bronzeville: Black Chicago in Pictures, 1941–1943* (2002).

Obituary: Watson, Ted. "City Mourns Brig. Gen. Jones," *The Chicago Defender*, 15 October 1975.

ELIZABETH R. SCHROEDER

Jones, Robert Elijah (19 Feb. 1872–18 May 1960), clergyman and bishop, was born in Greensboro, North Carolina, to Sidney Dallas Jones and Jane Holley. He attended local schools and in 1895 received a Bachelor of Arts degree from Greensboro's Bennett College (years before it became an all-women's institution).

Jones wished to pursue a religious life, and in 1891 he took up a position as a preacher at a church in Leaksville, North Carolina. A year later, he was ordained as a minister in the Methodist Episcopal (ME) church, and was assigned to Reidsville, where in 1896 he rose to the rank of church Elder. Meanwhile, having taken his B.A. from Bennett, he continued his education, first attending Gammon Theological Seminary in Atlanta, where he received a Bachelor of Divinity degree in 1897. A year later, he was back at Bennett College, from which he earned a Master of Divinity degree in 1898.

After a four-year stint as assistant manager with the *Southeastern Christian Advocate* magazine, he received an appointment as field secretary of the ME Church's Sunday School Board. In 1901 he married Valena MacArthur. The couple would remain together until MacArthur died in 1917. In 1904, Jones accepted a position at the *Advocate*, this time as editor, and there he remained until 1920. Meanwhile, he became a noted lecturer and homilist.

In 1920 Jones was elected—with Matthew Wesley Clair—to be the first bishop of the ME Church. The church at the time essentially contained a separate black church within it (with many of its white constituents supporting a full and final separation), and Jones and Clair were only to preside over the African American part. He and Clair were, at least, full and equal members of the ME Church's Council of Bishops. In that same year, 1920, the widowed Jones married Elizabeth Brown.

In the 1930s, Jones led an unsuccessful effort to unify the black and white segments of the church, an attempt that ironically led to a more fully realized segregation. The strongest opposition came from churches in the South. For his part, Jones continued in his role of bishop and focused particularly on the crucial role of education for the black community. Among his many positions, honors, and activities, Jones served on the boards of trustees of a number of colleges and universities, including New Orleans University and Samuel Houston College. He was a trustee of his alma mater Bennett College and Atlanta's Gammon Theological Seminary. He served as the first vice president of the National Negro Press Association, which was formed in 1909 in Louisville, Kentucky, by HENRY ALLEN BOYD and others. In 1911 Howard University bestowed on him an honorary Bachelor of Law degree.

Jones remained active in his church throughout much of the twentieth century as an organizer and as a strong voice in support of the power and necessity of education for young black people. He died and was buried in Waveland, Mississippi.

FURTHER READING

Luker, Ralph E. *The Social Gospel in Black and White: American Racial Reform, 1885–1912* (1991).

Payne, Daniel A. *History of the African Methodist Episcopal Church* (1969).

JASON PHILIP MILLER

Jones, Robert Emmett, Sr. (15 June 1860–8 Dec. 1934), physician, hospital founder, educator, organizational leader, and civil rights activist, was born in Greensboro, Alabama, the only son of Alice Royal, a mixed-race woman, and an unidentified white father. Jones attended private school and later graduated from the Tullibody Academy for blacks at Greensboro in 1876. This well-respected school was founded and run by William Burns Paterson, who was later appointed principal of the Lincoln Normal School, the forerunner of Alabama State University.

Because Jones's youth precluded his acceptance into several medical schools, he taught for a couple of years before entering the University of Michigan at Ann Arbor's medical school in 1878 (*The Richmond Planet*, 5 Jan. 1895). Founded in 1850, the medical school had graduated its first black student, DR. WILLIAM HENRY FITZBUTLER, in 1872. Fitzbutler would gain renown by cofounding the Louisville National Medical College and Hospital in Louisville, Kentucky. Jones graduated from the medical school at the tender age of twenty-one in 1881 and practiced in the Detroit area before relocating with his mother, who was a native Virginian, to Richmond in 1882.

Jones (often referred to by his first two initials) quickly immersed himself in every facet of his community as one of the first few black physicians to establish a permanent practice in Richmond after the Civil War. In November 1884 Jones married Daisy McLinn of New Haven, Connecticut, and they had five sons. Jones practiced and resided in Jackson Ward, a historic district that housed the majority of the city's black population. Jackson Ward would become an epicenter of black achievement on the local, state, and national levels in areas as diverse as business, medicine, journalism, and politics. In 1885 Jones served as medical examiner for the Grand Fountain of the United Order of True Reformers, a black fraternal organization headed by Reverend WILLIAM WASHINGTON BROWNE. The True Reformers were inarguably the most powerful black fraternal organization in the country at the turn of the twentieth century, with nearly 100,000 members in at least twenty-two states. The True

Reformers made history in March 1888 by founding the first black-owned chartered bank in America.

To further serve his community, Jones won a seat on the city council from Jackson Ward and served from 1886 to 1888 on the council and as a member of the council's committee on health. Among the other noted black men who served on the city council during the period 1871–1896 were JOHN MITCHELL JR., the longtime editor and proprietor of the *Richmond Planet* newspaper, and Attorney Edwin Archer Randolph, the first black to graduate from Yale University's law school.

Dr. Jones was also a prolific organizational leader. In 1899 he served as Most Worshipful Grand Master of the Grand Lodge of Masons in Virginia. He also served as president of the Business League of Virginia, an affiliate of the National Negro Business League founded by BOOKER T. WASHINGTON in 1900 (Alexander, p. 138). Jones was also active at the local, state, and national levels in black medical organizations. Participating in the parallel organizations was essential then, because in the South, with few exceptions, black practitioners were systematically denied membership at all levels of majority medical organizations. Jones and a group of black physicians met in Arkansas in 1890 to discuss plans to form a national medical association for blacks five years before the founding of the National Medical Association in 1895 at the Cotton States and International Exposition in Atlanta. His demonstrated leadership and commitment culminated in his election to the presidency of the National Medical Association during its annual convention in Richmond, Virginia, in 1905.

Dr. Jones's commitment to enhancing educational opportunities and alleviating the high unemployment rates among black Richmonders was unwavering. As early as 1884 he espoused the need for industrial education. In 1898 he and a group of black women organized the Woman's Central League. This organization, which grew to over one thousand subscribers, purchased a large building and operated a training school that offered certificates in cooking, tailoring, domestic science, and nursing. When a hospital component was added in 1900, Jones served as surgeon-in-chief. The Woman's Central League Training School and Hospital was the first hospital staffed by blacks in Richmond. To gain further knowledge, Jones took a postgraduate course in medicine at the University of Vienna, Austria, during the summer of 1900. Dr. Jones and the Woman's Central League were the recipients of extraordinary interracial cooperation,

as the league's advisory board consisted of some of Richmond's best-known leaders and the school enjoyed the hearty support of both the city's government and the school board.

Dr. Jones also introduced scientific farming among the state's black farmers. To better facilitate the practical portion of agricultural education, Jones proposed establishing black farming settlements around the state. This proposal culminated in the 1902 establishment of the black settlement known as Jonesboro several miles outside of Richmond. Jones later moved to Jonesboro and sold his home in Jackson Ward to the black banking pioneer MAGGIE LENA WALKER.

Although Jones was affluent, he never hesitated to publically address social and racial injustices. One major affront that drew the ire of the black community was the decision of the Virginia Passenger and Power Company to enforce the segregation of black and white passengers on the trolleys in 1904 (Marlowe, pp. 93–94). At one of the mass meetings called to condemn the decision and mount a response, Jones delivered a passionate speech decrying the injustice (Alexander, p. 138).

After the death of his wife Daisy, Jones wed Lela Walker Bryan in 1920 and retired to Philadelphia, Pennsylvania. He died at his home at age seventy-four of a cerebral embolism and was eulogized at his beloved Third Street Bethel AME Church in Richmond, Virginia. Jones left an indelible mark upon the community in Richmond. His fostering of interracial cooperation, educational opportunities, and access to competent health care would serve to enhance the well-being of generations to come.

FURTHER READING
Alexander, Ann Field. *Race Man: The Rise and Fall of the "Fighting Editor," John Mitchell Jr.* (2002).
Marlowe, Gertrude Woodruff. *A Right Worthy Grand Mission: Maggie Lena Walker and the Quest for Black Economic Empowerment* (2003).
Obituaries: *Philadelphia Tribune*, 13 Dec.1934. *Richmond Planet*, 15 Dec. 1934.

ELVATRICE PARKER BELSCHES

Jones, Sam (12 Nov. 1924–15 Dec. 1981), jazz string bassist, was born Samuel Jones in Jacksonville, Florida. His parents' names are unknown. His father was a professional pianist. Sam was born with an infected kidney that led to a series of childhood illnesses, but by his adolescent years he was fully recovered. He was the only child of his mother's first marriage; he had eleven step-siblings from her second marriage, and evidently (his own accounts are contradictory) he was raised from age three in Tampa with his mother's sisters. This was a musical home with a piano available.

One of his uncles was a professional guitarist, and around age ten Sam taught himself to play that instrument. By the time he was in junior high school, he performed in church, and elsewhere he played blues. He joined the band at Middleton High School as a bass drummer, but when he heard the string bassist OSCAR PETTIFORD play a solo on a recording by the rhythm and blues singer WYNONIE HARRIS, Jones became fascinated by the sound and acquired his own instrument. He soon began to work professionally, and after graduating from Middleton in 1941, he toured Florida as a string bassist in popular groups. Around mid-decade he worked with the pianist RAY CHARLES in the Honeydrippers, a rhythm and blues band. In Miami Beach Jones led a bop group that copied DIZZY GILLESPIE and CHARLIE PARKER's recordings, with the trumpeter BLUE MITCHELL taking Gillespie's role. Jones also worked in Florida with the alto saxophonist CANNONBALL ADDERLEY.

Jones continued working alongside Mitchell in Paul Williams's rhythm and blues group, with which he toured. In December 1951 he made his first recording. He recorded "Powder Puff" and "Ping Pong" with TINY BRADSHAW's rhythm and blues group in 1953 and toured with Bradshaw until 1955 on the strength of these hit recordings. In 1956 he became a member of the trumpeter Kenny Dorham's Jazz Prophets, modeled after HORACE SILVER and ART BLAKEY's Jazz Messengers. After working in ILLINOIS JACQUET's band, Jones joined the Jazz Modes of the tenor saxophonist CHARLIE ROUSE and the french horn player JULIUS WATKINS. Jones played with Adderley from 1956 to 1957, and he was a soloist on "Tribute to Brownie" on Adderley's album *Sophisticated Swing* (1957).

While Adderley disbanded to work with MILES DAVIS, Jones joined the small groups of the tenor saxophonist Stan Getz in 1957–1958, the trumpeter Gillespie in 1958–1959, and the pianist THELONIOUS MONK in 1959. Among notable albums from this period with Jones as a performer are the pianist Bill Evans's *Everybody Digs Bill Evans* (1958), including a solo on "Night and Day," and the tenor saxophonist Johnny Griffin's album *The Little Giant*, including a solo on "63rd Street Theme" (1959).

By this time, if not many years earlier, Jones's nickname was "Home." He explained to the writer Chris Sheridan: "I used to call everyone that—and they called me 'Home' back. It just stuck." From November 1959 through 1965 Jones was a member of Adderley's group, for which he composed "Del Sasser," heard on *Them Dirty Blues* (1960), and "Unit 7," heard on *Nancy Wilson/Cannonball Adderley* (1962). "Unit 7" has a nicely crafted 44-bar structure, resulting from a fusion of blues and pop song forms. During this period Jones also recorded as a soloist on "Sam Sack" on *Bags Meets Wes*, a session co-led by the vibraphonist MILT JACKSON and the guitarist WES MONTGOMERY in 1961, and as both a string bass and a cello soloist on his own albums, including *The Soul Society* (1960).

In January 1966 Jones replaced RAY BROWN in the trio of the pianist OSCAR PETERSON, with whom he remained until 1970. In the early 1970s Jones held freelance jobs in New York, performing with the pianists BOBBY TIMMONS and WYNTON KELLY and with the THAD JONES–Mel Lewis quintet, but his career was disrupted by emphysema. He had formed a trio with the pianist Cedar Walton and the drummer BILLY HIGGINS by 1972, when they first recorded. The three men worked under the names of the Magic Triangle and Eastern Rebellion and toured Japan yearly. In 1978 they formed a quintet with the trumpeter Art Farmer and the alto saxophonist JACKIE MCLEAN. Jones also recorded further albums as a leader, including *Cello Again* (1976).

After performing regularly in Europe during the mid-1970s, Jones settled there temporarily. By 1978 he had returned to the United States, where he co-led groups with the trumpeter Tom Harrell, with whom he recorded the album *Something New* in 1979. Incapacitated by lung cancer, Jones stopped playing in the early 1980s. Obituaries give his place of death as New Jersey (the city unidentified) or New York City.

Although Jones could improvise fine melodies, he seemed uninterested in becoming a great jazz string bass soloist in the tradition of Pettiford, Brown, and CHARLES MINGUS. Except on his own albums, he was often content to play walking bass lines rather than to step into a melodic role. His special talent was as an accompanist, supplying an utterly reliable carpet of rhythm, harmony, and tone for a succession of notable instrumentalists.

FURTHER READING

Gardner, Barbara. "Along Came Jones," *Down Beat* 33 (10 Mar. 1966).

Gillespie, Dizzy, with Al Fraser. *To Be, or Not … to Bop: Memoirs* (1979).

Obituaries: *Melody Maker*, 16 Jan. 1982; *Cadence* 8, no. 2 (Feb. 1982); *Down Beat* 49 (Mar. 1982); *Jazz Journal International* 35 (Apr. 1982).

This entry is taken from the *American National Biography* and is published here with the permission of the American Council of Learned Societies.

BARRY KERNFELD

Jones, Sam (24 June 1933–), professional basketball player, was born in Wilmington, North Carolina. He attended high school at Laurinburg Institute from 1947 to 1951, where he was a four-year letter winner and an outstanding all-conference and all-state player in 1951. After he was drafted and served in the U.S. Army from 1954 to 1956, he graduated from North Carolina Central College in 1957, a historically black college in Durham. In college, Jones was again a four-year letter winner and was named all-conference three times. Jones was one of the few African American players on the National Collegiate Athletic Association list of outstanding players. After seven National Basketball Association (NBA) teams overlooked Jones, he was drafted by legendary Boston Celtics coach Arnold "Red" Auerbach in 1957. The Celtics had the last pick in the first round of the draft, and Auerbach chose Jones solely on the recommendation of Wake Forest University coach Bones McKinney, who had played for the Celtics. The quick, six-foot-four guard became famous for his rangy offensive game and an unorthodox but highly effective bank shot off either side of the glass—most notably over the outstretched arms of a frustrated WILT CHAMBERLAIN. His Celtics teammates nicknamed him "Square Eyes" because he watched television so often. In 1957 Jones married Gladys Chavis, a teacher, and they had five children, Aubre, born in 1958; Phyllis, born in 1959; Michael, born in 1960, Terri, born in 1964; and Ashley, born in 1965.

Jones had a solid rookie season, and by 1961 he had matured into a skilled starter and one of the outstanding shooters in the NBA. Replacing the retired star Bill Sharman, Jones averaged eighteen points per game. He soon developed a reputation as a clutch player. Considered one of the league's fastest guards with superb court vision and savvy, his perfect jump-shot form earned him the nickname "The Shooter." Teamed with the fast K. C. JONES in the backcourt, he contributed to the Celtics' mystique as the original dynasty in the NBA. The Celtic players and coaches were a tightly knit family. Jones's teammate Tommy Heinsohn recalled that when a restaurant in Lexington, Kentucky, refused to serve Jones

and Satch Sanders in 1961, the entire team walked out and woke up the mayor at 2 a.m. to complain. The next day Jones, Saunders, BILL RUSSELL, and K. C. Jones refused to play in the exhibition game against the Hawks. By the 1963–1964 season Jones was chosen for the Celtics' starting lineup, making Boston the first NBA team to not only recruit a black player but also put five black players on the court at the same time with Jones, K. C. Jones, Russell, Tom Sanders, and Willie Naulls.

The 1964 season was Jones's most successful; he averaged twenty-six points per game, shattering all the Celtics' scoring records. By the 1965–1966 season Jones was the key player on the NBA's first black starting lineup. A versatile and popular player, Jones was on the All-NBA Second Team in 1965–1967, a five-time NBA All-Star (1962, 1964 to 1966, 1968), and scored over fifteen thousand points in his remarkable career. With Jones playing on the famous Boston Garden parquet floor, the Celtics won an astonishing eight consecutive championships from 1959 to 1966. By the time of his retirement at age thirty-six, he held eleven Celtics records, leading the team in scoring for three seasons (1963, 1965, and 1966) and had the team's single-game scoring record of fifty-one points against the Detroit Pistons in 1965. He also had four consecutive seasons in which he averaged twenty points or more from 1965 to 1968 and helped win ten NBA championships in his twelve-year career with the Celtics. Boston's near invincibility ended when the self-effacing Jones retired at the end of the 1968–1969 championship season, and the next year the Celtics had a 34–48 record. No other team won two consecutive NBA championships for nineteen years. In his memoir, *Let Me Tell You a Story* (2004), Red Auerbach said he was not surprised when Jones and Russell both retired in the summer of 1969. He mentioned that although "they could both still play ... they were like me, burned out. The thing that comes with winning all the time is tremendous pressure."

Russell, Jones's teammate, recalled in his memoirs that Jones "was a master at laughing while playing his guts out. His humor was always therapy for us," especially when he taunted Chamberlain in close games and would then pass the ball to Russell for an easy basket. Russell said, whenever "the pressure was the greatest, Sam was eager for the ball. To me, that's one sign of a champion." Jones was the fastest player who could take over a game and "sometimes he gave off a feeling that he simply would not let us lose the game" (150).

Jones's family lived in Sharon, a suburb south of Boston, and moved to Silver Spring, Maryland, in 1969. Jones served as the athletic director and coach at Federal City College (1969–1972) in Washington, D.C., and coached basketball at his alma mater, North Carolina Central College (1972–1974). He also was an assistant coach for the New Orleans Jazz (1974–1975). In 1970 he was named to the NBA's Twenty-fifth Anniversary All-Time Team and was elected to the Naismith Memorial Basketball Hall of Fame in 1983. With typical humility in his speech at the induction ceremony in Springfield, Massachusetts, Jones gave credit to the Celtics as "a great team, not great individuals." From 1976 to 1989, he was a college representative for women's basketball with Nike, and later was the athletic director for the District of Columbia public school system (1989–1990) and a teacher in the Montgomery County public schools (1991–2004). In 1996 Jones was named to the NBA's Fiftieth Anniversary All-Time Team. In retirement Jones remained a close friend of Red Auerbach, often having lunch with the celebrated coach at a favorite restaurant in Washington, D.C., or Maryland, sometimes with his son Aubre Jones, who was an athletic director at George Washington University. When Auerbach died in 2006, the media recalled his uncanny skill in drafting unknown players who became stars for the Celtics. Jones was one name inevitably mentioned as an inspired Auerbach pick.

FURTHER READING

Auerbach, Red, and John Feinstein. *Let Me Tell You a Story: A Lifetime in the Game* (2004).

Fitzgerald, Ray. *Champions Remembered: Choice Picks from a Boston Sports Desk* (1982).

Heinsohn, Tommy. *Give 'Em the Hook* (1988).

Russell, Bill, and Taylor Branch. *Second Wind: The Memoirs of an Opinionated Man* (1979).

Shaughnessy, Dan. *Ever Green: The Boston Celtics: A History in the Words of Their Players, Coaches, Fans, and Foes, from 1946 to the Present* (1990).

PETER C. HOLLORAN

Jones, Sarah Emily Gibson (13 Apr. 1843 or 1845–21 Oct. 1938), writer and educator, was born in Alexandria, Virginia, to Daniel W. and Mary (sometimes listed as Margaret) Jane (Lewis) Gibson. Her father, who had been born in Virginia, and her mother, who had been born in the District of Columbia, were free African Americans who moved to the Cincinnati area in 1849 with their three children. Daniel Gibson worked as a barber and a porter in the years before the Civil War and was able to keep his growing family on the edges of the tiny black middle class in Cincinnati. In his *Noted Negro Woman* entry on Sarah Gibson, MONROE MAJORS wrote that her father was "a man of unusual strength of intellect and will … self-reliant and well read" and that her mother was "a quiet and practical woman, gentle, firm and efficient" (pp. 138–139). Sarah Gibson studied in a range of private schools—Majors lists a Mrs. Hallam and a Mrs. Corbin as her teachers—and later attended public schools. At some point, according to Majors, she was also a student of Black activist Peter H. Clark. In 1857, she joined Cincinnati's Union Baptist Church.

In late 1860, she took a job as a teacher in Newton, Ohio; later, she worked as a governess with an Oxford, Ohio, family, and operated a private school from her home in Cincinnati. The early 1860s also seem to have been the beginning of her writing career, as Majors notes that she "assisted J. P. Sampson, editor of *The Colored Citizen*"—an early Black Cincinnati newspaper—"writing articles on various subjects" (p. 139). Some have even speculated that she wrote on topics related to the Civil War, although none of this work has been found among the tiny handful of extant issues of the *Citizen*.

In September of 1863, she was hired by the Cincinnati public schools—most probably on the recommendation of her former teacher, Peter Clark, who had risen to a position of prominence in Cincinnati's then-segregated school system. She taught there for two years before marrying Marshall P. H. Jones, who was almost two decades her senior. The youngest son of a successful farmer and pioneering Black Baptist minister Samuel Jones, Marshall Jones was a spokesperson for Cincinnati's noted "Black Brigade" during the early Civil War and would continue to be a leader in the black community after the war's end. He invested successfully in Hamilton County real estate and listed himself as a photographer in the 1870 Federal Census. The couple had three children, but only Joseph Lawrence, born 12 June 1868, survived infancy.

Jones seems to have continued teaching in the Cincinnati public schools until 1868, when she took a position at the nearby Mt. Healthy schools. She worked there until 1870, and, after a two-year hiatus, taught for three years in Columbus. She returned to Cincinnati in 1875, when she took a position at what would become the Frederick Douglass School, long an anchor of the Walnut Hills section of the city. She held this post until retiring in 1911, and she emerged as a leading figure within Cincinnati's Black educational efforts. She continued to be active with Union Baptist but also crossed denominational lines—joining, for example, a scientific society founded in late 1875 through the Allen Temple African Methodist Episcopal Church and led by BENJAMIN W. ARNETT (*Christian Recorder*, 11 December 1875).

Majors noted that Sarah and Marshall Jones's marriage "was a congenial one," though the 1880 Federal Census shows them living apart—Sarah and their son Joseph in Cincinnati and Marshall in nearby Mt. Pleasant (pp. 139, 135B, 471B). Marshall Jones's health reportedly declined sharply, and he was nearly bedridden between 1886 and his death on 3 October 1891. Majors reported that Sarah Jones "nursed [him] with a tender patience that never even flagged for an instance" (p. 140).

Jones restarted her writing career in the 1880s. Majors describes a lecture tour including Dayton, Zanesville, and locations in and around Cincinnati, but notes that she was "forced to retire from the lecture field because it interfered with her school duties" (p. 140). However, she still occasionally lectured and regularly gave public readings—especially poetry readings—in Cincinnati during the next two decades. A lecture to Cincinnati's Allen Temple was also published in the 15 December 1887 *Christian Recorder* and declared that "I am sure that if every colored man felt toward every white man as I do towards every white woman, there would be no sense of humility while in their presence; many of them are my inferiors in every way, and I have never seen one who I acknowledge better than myself." While her comments on race were fairly radical, she was more conservative on questions of suffrage—asserting that "I am no politician—no Equal Rights woman either…." Majors reports other publications in the *Recorder* as well as in the *Indianapolis World*. The 1906 Ohio State Federation of the National Association of Colored Women's Clubs named Jones their "poet laureate." A 1915 entry in *Who's Who in the Colored Race* also noted public performances of her poem "Lincoln" at the 1909 Lincoln's birthday celebration in Cincinnati and "The Present Church" at Union Baptist's mortgage-burning ceremonies in July of 1912.

Jones also expanded her community activism. In 1884, she was named "lady manager" of the Cincinnati Colored Orphans Home, and she continued in this role until 1899. She helped found both the Home for Aged Colored Women and the Crawford Old Men's Home. She held leadership positions in the Cincinnati Federated Women's Clubs, the Ohio State Federation of Colored Women's Clubs, and the Cincinnati Progress Club, and even helped organized the World War I-era Soldiers Comfort Club.

After 1900, Jones often lived with her extended family—primarily in the home of her son Joseph, a successful entrepreneur who founded the Central Regalia Company and a well-known Cincinnati music teacher involved in local Republican politics. After his death in 1923, she lived with the family of a nephew, Houchell Ward. Her final years were marred by illness, and she died in Cincinnati.

FURTHER READING

Majors, Monroe. *Noted Negro Women* (1893).
Who's Who in the Colored Race for 1915.

ERIC GARDNER

Jones, Sarah Garland Boyd (Feb. 1866–11 May 1905), physician, surgeon, and hospital founder, was born Sallie Garland Boyd in Albemarle County, Virginia, the oldest of nine children born to George W. Boyd, a carpenter and general contractor, and Ellen D. Garland, a nurse. By 1868 the family had moved from Albemarle County to the Richmond area, where her father became the city's leading black contractor. He oversaw construction of such notable buildings as the Baker School, the Sixth Mount Zion Baptist Church—pastored by the nationally known JOHN JASPER—and other black-owned buildings. Sallie attended Richmond public schools and in 1883 graduated from Richmond Colored Normal and High School, an institution organized in October 1867 by the Freedmen's Bureau to prepare students to become educators. Courses in rhetoric, philosophy, geography, English classics, and the natural sciences provided a solid foundation that earned the school a reputation as one of the state's premier black educational institutions. Its graduates were in high demand, many achieving successful careers in education, law, the ministry, business, journalism, and medicine. The school produced such prominent alumni as Virginia E. Randolph, ROSA BOWSER, JOHN MITCHELL JR., WILLIAM P. BURRELL, and Sallie's classmates Maggie L. Mitchell (later MAGGIE L. WALKER) and WENDELL P. DABNEY.

After her graduation Boyd taught for five years at the Baker Elementary School, the first school built for blacks after the establishment of the Richmond public school system. On 4 July 1888 she married her fellow Richmond public school educator Miles

B. Jones; they had no children. As evidenced by her 1888 marriage record and her Howard University transcripts, Sallie changed her first name and became known as Sarah G. (Garland) Jones for unspecified reasons prior to finishing medical school. Her husband, a native of Amelia County, Virginia, graduated from Richmond Colored Normal in 1878 and attended Richmond Theological Seminary—a forerunner of Virginia Union University. He subsequently taught for ten years in the Richmond public schools before joining the Grand Fountain of the United Order of True Reformers, a fraternal order that broke away from the interracial Independent Order of Good Templars in 1876. Led by WILLIAM WASHINGTON BROWNE, a former slave and Union soldier, the all-black Grand Fountain temperance fraternity established its headquarters in Richmond, and by 1894 they had branches in twenty states with as many as 100,000 members. The order ran a weekly newspaper and had industrial, mercantile, insurance, and real estate divisions and a bank, which survived the panic of 1893 but failed in 1910. Sarah and Miles Jones's lives were inextricably linked to the True Reformers. The order's bank was housed in Browne's home until the erection of the True Reformers Hall in Richmond, constructed by Jones's father. Jones was a member of True Reformers Fountain No. 99, and her husband rose through the ranks to become the order's director and chief of finance and the grand worthy assistant secretary. In 1890 Sarah Jones enrolled in Howard University's medical department. She graduated in 1893 and that year passed the Virginia state medical boards. The Virginia Medical Examining Board records reveal that in 1890 C. Lee Haynes of Palmer, Massachusetts, became the first woman to pass the state's medical boards. There is no record, however, of her ever coming before the board to be sworn in to complete the licensure process. Thus Jones became the first female of any race to be licensed by the Virginia Medical Examining Board.

Jones immersed herself in her community's health care needs. To accommodate the many who needed medical care, she began to see patients at three different offices each day, driving her own horse and buggy. In addition she instituted a free clinic for women and children one day a week. In honor of her pioneering achievement, the Southern Aid and Insurance Company appointed her as a medical examiner for women.

By the beginning of the twentieth century Richmond had a burgeoning group of enterprising black physicians, dentists, and pharmacists.

Even Jones's husband decided to enroll in Howard University's medical department and earned his degree in 1901. Richmond blacks generally only received medical treatment in segregated hospital wards, where black physicians could not practice. Realizing the need for black physicians to provide medical care to black patients, on 19 February 1902 Sarah and Miles Jones and others founded the Medical and Chirurgical Society of Richmond. This group comprised black physicians, pharmacists, and dentists in the greater Richmond area. Core members of this group received a state charter in October 1902 to form the Richmond Hospital Association, a joint stock company organized to establish a hospital. The Richmond Hospital and Training School for Nurses opened in December 1902. The city's second hospital organized and operated by blacks began seeing patients in February 1903 and initiated a training program for nurses the next month. Jones's husband served as chief surgeon for over two decades.

Jones died of cerebral congestion at age thirty-nine. At her funeral throngs of her patients, both black and white, packed the black Second Baptist Church, with many attendees forced to stand outside. During the funeral George Ben Johnston, a leading white Richmond physician, complimented Jones's ability to accurately diagnose medical cases and praised her performance on the medical boards. Jones was further memorialized when the Richmond Hospital and Training School for Nurses was later renamed in her honor. A pioneering physician with remarkable dedication to serving her community, Jones proved to be an inspirational role model whose legacy endured in the hospital she helped found, which continued in the early twenty-first century as the Bon Secours Richmond Community Hospital.

FURTHER READING

Brown, Hallie Q., ed. *Homespun Heroines and Other Women of Distinction* (1926).

Burrell, W. P., and D. E. Johnson. *Twenty-Five Years History of the Grand Fountain of the United Order of True Reformers, 1881–1905* (1909).

Majors, Monroe. *Noted Negro Women: Their Triumphs and Activities* (1893).

Obituaries: *Richmond Planet*, 13 May 1905; *Richmond News Leader*, 17 May 1905.

ELVATRICE PARKER BELSCHES

Jones, Scipio Africanus (1863–28 Mar. 1943), lawyer, was born in Dallas County, Arkansas, the son of a white father, whose identity remains uncertain, and Jemmima, a slave who belonged to Dr. Sanford Reamey, a physician and landowner. After emancipation, Jemmima and her freedman husband, Horace, became farmers and adopted the surname of Jones, in memory of Dr. Adolphus Jones, a previous owner. Scipio Jones attended rural black schools in Tulip, Arkansas, and moved to Little Rock in 1881 to pursue a college preparatory course at Bethel University. He then entered Shorter College, from which he graduated in 1885 with a bachelor's degree in Education. When the University of Arkansas Law School denied him admission because of his race, he read law with several white attorneys in Little Rock and was admitted to the bar in 1889. His marriage to Carrie Edwards in 1896 ended in his wife's early death and left him with a daughter to raise. In 1917 he married Lillie M. Jackson of Pine Bluff, Arkansas.

By the turn of the century Jones had become the leading black practitioner in Little Rock. His clients, who were drawn exclusively from the African American community, included several large, fraternal organizations, such as the Mosaic Templars of America. He also played an active role in Republican politics, supporting the efforts of the black-and-tan faction to wrest control of the state party from the lily-whites. In 1902 he promoted a slate of black Republicans to challenge the party regulars and the Democrats in a local election, and in 1920 he made an unsuccessful bid for the post of Republican national committeeman. The struggle to secure equal treatment for African Americans within the party lasted from the late 1880s to the 1930s and resulted in a compromise that guaranteed black representation on the Republican state central committee. As a sign of changing times, Jones was elected as a delegate to the Republican National Conventions of 1928 and 1940. Despite the existence of poll taxes that disfranchised most black voters, he also won election as a special judge of the Little Rock municipal court in 1915, at a time when few African Americans held judicial office anywhere in the country.

Jones's lifelong commitment to protecting the civil rights of blacks led to his involvement in the greatest legal battle of his career: the defense of twelve tenant farmers who were sentenced to death for alleged murders committed during the bloody Elaine, Arkansas, race riot of October 1919. The violence grew out of black efforts to establish a farmers' union and white fears that a dangerous conspiracy was being plotted at their secret meetings. When two white men were reportedly shot near a black church, the white community engaged in murderous reprisals that left more than two hundred blacks and five whites dead. An all-white grand jury quickly indicted 122 blacks, and because most of the defendants were indigent, the court appointed defense counsel for them. These white lawyers did not interview their clients, request a change of venue, or object to all-white trial juries. The trials themselves lasted less than an hour, and it took juries only five or six minutes to return guilty verdicts. Several defendants and witnesses later claimed that they had been tortured, and an angry white mob surrounded the courthouse during the trials. Besides the twelve men who were sentenced to death, sixty-seven others received long prison terms.

The National Association for the Advancement of Colored People retained Jones and George W. Murphy, a white Little Rock attorney, to appeal the convictions. Jones became the senior defense counsel after Murphy died in October 1920, and he tirelessly pursued every avenue of relief under state law, risking his life on several occasions by his courtroom appearances in the hostile community of Helena. Jones's arguments impressed the Arkansas Supreme Court, which twice ordered new trials for six defendants. In the first instance Jones pointed to technical defects in the form of the verdicts. On the second appeal he contended that the trial judge's rejection of evidence pointing to racial discrimination in the selection of jurors had deprived his clients of their equal protection rights under the Fourteenth Amendment. To prevent the impending executions of the remaining six defendants, Jones turned to the federal courts. Arguing that the prisoners had been deprived of their constitutional right to a fair trial, he sought their release through a habeas corpus proceeding. Eventually the case reached the U.S. Supreme Court, where it resulted in a landmark decision, *Moore v. Dempsey* (1923). By looking behind the formal state record for the first time, the Court overturned the convictions and held that the defendants had been denied due process, since their original trial had been little more than a legalized lynching bee. Although Jones did not participate in the final argument of the case, his strategy had guided the litigation process from the beginning. In the aftermath of *Moore v. Dempsey*, he secured an order from the Arkansas Supreme Court for the discharge of six prisoners in June 1923. He then negotiated with state authorities to secure commutation of sentences and parole for all of the remaining Elaine "rioters" by January 1925.

In his later years Jones continued to attack racially discriminatory laws and practices in Arkansas. He was instrumental in obtaining legislation that granted out-of-state tuition payments to black students who could not enter the state's all-white professional schools. He died in Little Rock. To commemorate his community leadership, the all-white school board of North Little Rock named the black high school in his memory.

FURTHER READING

Letters from Jones are in the NAACP Papers in the Library of Congress and in the Republican Party State Central Committee Records in the University of Arkansas Library.

Cortner, Richard C. *A Mob Intent on Death* (1988).

Dillard, Tom. "Scipio A. Jones," *Arkansas Historical Quarterly* 31 (Autumn 1972): 201–219.

Ovington, Mary White. *Portraits in Color* (1927).

Waskow, Arthur I. *From Race Riot to Sit-in, 1919 and the 1960s* (1966).

This entry is taken from the *American National Biography* and is published here with the permission of the American Council of Learned Societies.

MAXWELL BLOOMFIELD

Jones, Sophia Bethena (16 May 1857–8 Sept. 1932), homeopathic physician, was born in Chatham, a hub of fugitive and free-black settlement in extreme southwestern Ontario, then known as Canada West. Little is known about Jones's early life. Her parents were James Monroe Jones and Emily Jones. Her father came from a family of manumitted slaves in North Carolina, and his father, James Madison Jones, had obtained the family's freedom in 1843 and moved to Oberlin, Ohio, where he graduated from Oberlin College with an AB degree in 1849; at least one of his brothers also graduated from Oberlin.

Sophia Jones had three sisters, Anna Holland Jones, Emma (or Emily) Jones, and Frederica Florence Jones, and two brothers, George and James. These children probably all attended one of the Chatham area's private schools for black students, and they excelled in their studies. As a young woman Sophia attended the Wilberforce Educational Institute, a secondary school for blacks and whites that opened at Chatham in 1872. The institute had been built using the proceeds of the defunct British-American Institute organized in the 1840s to aid black fugitives arriving from the United States. Having earned a diploma from the Wilberforce Educational Institute, Jones entered the University of Toronto as an undergraduate student in 1897.

Jones's chief interest was in studying medicine. Perhaps through the active network of well-educated black elites in southern Ontario, she learned that the University of Michigan at Ann Arbor had been admitting women to its prestigious medical school since 1870. In the autumn of 1880 Sophia left Toronto for Ann Arbor, where she enrolled in the medical school. The University of Michigan did not provide housing for its students, so Jones found accommodations with Mrs. Sarah M. Graham, the mother of the University of Michigan's first black female student, MARY HENRIETTA GRAHAM, who had just graduated in the spring of 1880. Sophia and her sisters Frederica and Emma were all social acquaintances of Mary Graham and her husband, Ferdinand Lee Barnett. Indeed, the Graham and Jones families probably knew each other in Chatham before each moved to Ann Arbor. Sophia Jones's medical studies culminated in her earning an MD from the University of Michigan in 1885. She has often been misidentified as the first black woman to earn a medical degree in Ann Arbor; GRACE ROBERTS earned an MD from the university's Homeopathic Medical College in 1878.

Sophia Jones was hired by the Atlanta Baptist Female Seminary, later known as the Spelman Seminary for Women and Girls (now Spelman College), in Atlanta, Georgia. This private postsecondary institution for black women had just received a large grant from the American industrialist John D. Rockefeller. Jones served as the school's resident physician, and while there she instituted a nurses' training program. She left Spelman in 1888, however, to become the resident physician at Wilberforce University in Xenia, Ohio.

In 1887 Frederica Jones had graduated from the University of Michigan with a bachelor of arts degree from the literary department, and she had accepted a position on the Wilberforce University faculty as an instructor in French and German language and literature as well as in the natural sciences. Sophia and Frederica both remained at Wilberforce until about 1892; their sister Anna Holland Jones, who had earned a degree at Oberlin College in 1875, was also briefly on the Wilberforce faculty during this period. Sophia Jones apparently remained at Wilberforce when Frederica accepted a position as lady principal and instructor in Greek and Latin at Paul Quinn College, a private postsecondary college for African Americans in Waco, Texas. By 1898 both Sophia and Frederica Jones had relocated again, this time to West Philadelphia, Pennsylvania, where Frederica taught at a private academy and Sophia opened a medical practice.

Some time after 1901 the two sisters moved to Kansas City, Missouri, apparently to live near their sister Anna Holland Jones, who had become a teacher at Kansas City High School and an integral member of W.E.B. DuBois's circle of political associates. Anna Jones was one of only two black women (the other was ANNA JULIA COOPER) to address the 1900 Pan-African Conference held in London under DuBois's leadership. Anna Jones was also active in the black women's club movement in Kansas City, and her sisters probably took up similar activities. Sophia Jones also opened a medical practice in Kansas City. Frederica Jones died in Kansas City on 4 March 1905 and was buried in Ann Arbor, Michigan. Also that year the women's father, James Monroe Jones, died in Ann Arbor, where their brother George was living. Sophia briefly maintained her Kansas City practice but later moved to live with family members in Monrovia, California, just north of Los Angeles.

In 1913 Jones was invited to return to the University of Michigan, where she presented a paper entitled "Fifty Years of Negro Health." In response to a questionnaire sent by the university to all alumni in 1920, Jones listed her occupation as orange rancher. She died in Monrovia, California, in September 1932, and twenty years later the University of Michigan honored her by creating the Sophia Jones Lectureship on Infectious Disease. In the 1990s a group of African American medical students at the University of Michigan formed the Fitzbutler-Jones Society, honoring the first black male and female graduates of the allopathic medical school, WILLIAM HENRY FITZBUTLER and Sophia Bethena Jones.

FURTHER READING

Information on and photographs of the Jones family in Chatham are held by the Chatham-Kent Black Historical Society, Chatham, Ontario. Biographical data on Sophia Bethena Jones and also on Frederica Florence Jones is available at the University of Michigan's Bentley Historical Library, in the alumni association's necrology file.

Cook, Myrtle Foster. "History of the Woman's League of Kansas City, MO," in *Lifting as They Climb*, ed. Elizabeth Lindsay Davis (1933).

Detroit Plaindealer, 1 July 1892.

LAURA M. CALKINS

Jones, Stephanie Tubbs (10 Sept. 1949–20 Aug. 2008), lawyer and politician, was born Stephanie Tubbs in Cleveland, Ohio. She was the youngest of three daughters born to Andrew Tubbs, a United Airlines skycap, and Mary Tubbs, a cook for a fraternity at Cleveland's Case Western Reserve University. The Baptist, church-going family lived in Glenville, a working-class black neighborhood. Stephanie excelled in the gifted program at Miles Standish Elementary. In 1967, she graduated from Collinwood High School with ten athletic and academic honors. On full scholarship, she attended Case Western, where she started the African American Students Association. After considering social work, she graduated (1971) with a B.A. in sociology and a minor in psychology. On another scholarship, she earned a J.D. at Case Western's law school (1974).

Her first job as a lawyer was as assistant general counsel to the northeast Ohio regional sewer district's equal opportunity administrator (1974–1976). In 1976, Stephanie Tubbs wed small business owner Mervyn L. Jones. After the couple started dating, Mervyn Jones had been convicted of voluntary manslaughter in the shooting death of his former girlfriend's cousin. According to Jones, he was pushed against a wall and his gun went off accidentally. He served three months in prison and was released on shock probation, a policy which gave defendants early probation in the hopes that exposure to prison life would "shock" him or her into not committing more offenses. In 1983 the couple had a son, Mervyn Jones II.

Stephanie Tubbs Jones served as assistant Cuyahoga County prosecutor (1976–1979) and trial attorney for the Equal Employment Opportunity Commission's Cleveland office (1979–1981). In 1982, she was elected a Cleveland municipal judge after a group of politically active black friends chose her to run. In 1983 Jones was appointed to a judgeship on the Cuyahoga County Court of Common Pleas and in 1990 elected Cuyahoga County prosecutor. The first African American chief prosecutor in Ohio history and the first woman to hold this particular office, she was re-elected twice. In 1998, Jones garnered national attention when she refused to reopen the famous 1954 Sam Sheppard murder case.

In 1998, Congressman LOUIS STOKES retired after three decades representing Ohio's Eleventh District, which covered both poor, majority-black, inner-city Cleveland neighborhoods and prosperous, majority-white suburbs. With 51 percent of the vote, Jones defeated four other candidates in the Democratic primary for the seat. She won 80 percent of the vote in the general election, becoming the first black Congresswoman from her state.

Looking back on getting elected and reaching her fiftieth year, Jones reflected that although she had accomplished a great deal, she did not "know whether there is something else after this or not. I am blessed never to have thought about the next step because before I had to think about it, God just swept me up …. This might be it. I don't want to be in public life until I am 70 or 80 years old …. But never say never. I am happy with this so far" (qtd. in *Washington Post* 2008).

Jones quickly emerged as a strong liberal voice in Congress, with an American Civil Liberties Union lifetime rating of 98 out of 100. She was the original sponsor of the 2000 Child Abuse Protection and Enforcement Act. She unsuccessfully advocated for several gun control measures, insisting, "We regulate cribs, food, and prescription drugs, we should regulate the manufacture and use of guns" (qtd. in Weitzman 2000). Jones was one of only eleven House members to vote against the 2003 U.S. invasion of Iraq. She raised awareness of uterine fibroids, a health problem affecting large numbers of black women, advocated for small businesses and credit unions and attacked predatory lending practices, and was active in the Congressional Black, Baltic, Census, and Women's Caucuses. Her committee memberships included Banking and Financial Services, Small Business, Ways and Means, and Standards of Official Conduct, or Ethics. In 2006, House Speaker Nancy Pelosi named Jones Ethics chair.

According to critics, Jones herself was ethically suspect. They cited trips she accepted from lobbyists and her use of campaign funds for personal expenses. However, other controversies surrounding Jones were political in nature. After the hotly disputed 2004 presidential election, Jones charged from the floor of the House that George W. Bush's victory was due to electoral manipulation and fraud. In the 2008 presidential race, she diverged from many black community leaders in campaigning for Senator Hillary Rodham Clinton (NY) in the Democratic primaries until Clinton's opponent BARACK OBAMA (IL) wrapped up the Democratic nomination. Jones explained that, while she was happy about Obama's successes, she had committed to support Clinton in late 2006 and did not want to be "a fair-weather friend" (2008).

Stephanie Tubbs Jones was elected a total of five times to represent Ohio's Eleventh Congressional District. During her last re-election in 2006, she won with 83 percent of the vote. She persisted in Congress despite the deaths of nine close family members, including her mother, father, sister, and, in 2003, her husband, while she was in office. Her hobbies of sailing and Southern cooking eased her stress. In 2008, yet another tragedy struck, just days before she was to attend the Democratic National Convention as a superdelegate and help to formally nominate Obama for president. A police officer found her driving erratically through the suburb of Cleveland Heights. When the car stopped, he found her slumped over the wheel, unconscious but still alive. At the Huron Hospital in East Cleveland, Jones was diagnosed with a ruptured brain aneurysm and severe brain hemorrhage. The next day, 20 August, she died at age 58 after being taken off life support. Her organs were donated.

Obama, who shortly afterwards became the nation's first black president, recalled, "It wasn't enough for her just to break barriers in her own life. She was also determined to bring opportunity to all those who had been overlooked and left behind—and in Stephanie, they had a fearless friend and unyielding advocate" (qtd. in *Cleveland Plain Dealer* 2008). Louis Stokes described her as a "beautiful, bubbling, charismatic woman … who was so highly talented [that she] lit the room up" (qtd. in *Cleveland Plain Dealer* 2008). Jones's former aide Marcia Fudge was elected to the Eleventh District seat. In 2009, the Congressional Black Caucus Foundation renamed its annual fundraiser for black college students the Mervyn L. & Stephanie Tubbs Jones Memorial Golf & Tennis Classic.

FURTHER READING

"Stephanie Tubbs Jones," Biographical Directory of the United States Congress, online at http://bioguide. congress.gov/.

"Stephanie Tubbs Jones," Black Americans in Congress, online at http://baic.house.gov.

Jones, Stephanie Tubbs, "Committed: Why I'm Sticking with Hillary," online at http://www.theroot.com/ views/committed-why-im-sticking-hillary 29 Feb 2008.

Mihaly, Mary, "Stephanie's Great Adventure," *Cleveland Magazine*, March 1993.

Weitzman, Lisa, "Stephanie Tubbs Jones," *Contemporary Black Biography* (2000).

Obituaries: *Cleveland Plain Dealer* (20 August 2008); *New York Times* (20 August 2008); *Washington Post* (21 August 2008).

MARY KRANE DERR

Jones, Thad (28 Mar. 1923–20 Aug. 1986), jazz horn player, composer, and bandleader, was born

Thaddeus Joseph Jones in Pontiac, Michigan. The names of his parents and details of his early childhood are unknown. However, it would seem that his was a musical family: his uncle William was a bandleader, and two of his four brothers were musicians.

Jones was inspired to play music by his older brother Hank Jones, who was an accomplished jazz pianist; his brother gave him his first job, at age sixteen, playing cornet in his band. During World War II, Thad Jones was employed as an entertainer with various midwestern bands playing United Service Organizations (USO) shows. After the war was over, he joined forces with his younger brother, the drummer Elvin Jones, working in a quintet led by Billy Mitchell in Detroit. Thad Jones worked for a year, from 1954 to 1955, with the composer and jazz bassist CHARLES MINGUS in his Jazz Composers' Workshop orchestra and then held a nine-year post with the COUNT BASIE Orchestra.

Discouraged by the lack of opportunity for performing in and composing for big bands in the 1960s, Jones settled in New York City in the mid-1960s. He formed a rehearsal band with the drummer Mel Lewis in 1965, specifically to highlight his own composing; the group had a regular Monday night engagement at New York's Village Vanguard for the next thirteen years. With this band Jones primarily played flügelhorn, developing a melodic style in his playing, arrangements, and compositions that separated his work from his more bop-oriented recordings of the 1950s. While working with the band, Jones wrote in a variety of styles, exploring waltz tempo in "The Waltz You Swang for Me" (1968), bossa nova in "It Only Happens Every Time" (1970), and jazz-rock in "Greetings and Salutations" (1975–1976) as well as traditional swing and bop, although even in traditional styles he experimented with new tonalities, voicings, and especially meters. The band became so successful that it toured and recorded extensively, becoming one of the few big bands to achieve success in the 1960s and the early 1970s and redefining the big-band style for a new generation. The Jones and Lewis orchestra recorded prolifically from 1966 through 1977 on the Blue Note, Solid State, and A&M Horizon labels.

Jones left the band in 1979, when an injury to his hip led him to change to a new instrument, the valve trombone. (Lewis continued to lead the Monday night group under his own name.) Jones moved to Europe that same year, settling in Denmark. He formed his own orchestra, Thad Jones Eclipse,

taught jazz at the Royal Conservatory, and worked as the leader of the Danish Radio Orchestra. In 1985 he returned to the United States to take over the helm of the revitalized Count Basie Orchestra. After a year he left the post, and six months later he died. Jones was married twice, fathering two children in his first marriage and one child in his second marriage to a Danish woman.

FURTHER READING

Hentoff, Nat. "They're All Talking about the Jones Boys," *Down Beat* 22, no. 23 (1955).

Tompkins, L. "The Thad Jones Story," *Crescendo International* 10, nos. 10–11 (1972).

Obituaries: *New York Times*, 21 Aug. 1986; *Down Beat* (Nov. 1986).

DISCOGRAPHY

Kirchner, Bill. *The Complete Solid State Recordings of the Thad Jones/Mel Lewis Orchestra* (1994).

This entry is taken from the *American National Biography* and is published here with the permission of the American Council of Learned Societies.

RICHARD CARLIN

Jones, Virginia Lacy (25 June 1912–Dec. 1984), librarian, library educator, administrator, and advocate for librarians, was born Virginia Lacy, the only child of Edward and Ellen Parker Lacy of Cincinnati, Ohio. Her father died when she was eighteen months old, and Jones spent her early years living with her mother and grandmother in a poor, racially mixed neighborhood in Clarksburg, West Virginia. Her mother took in boarders to help with expenses, and as Jones recalls of these additional residents, "They made a very good environment for me to grow up in because they were all rather accomplished people" (Anderson, 1978). In Clarksburg Lacy completed elementary school and her first two years of high school. There were also frequent trips with her mother to the Clarksburg Public Library as her mother worked to ensure that Lacy had an appreciation for the value of education, reading, and cultural arts. Under the guidance of her high school history and Latin teacher, Lacy employed the Dewey decimal system to help create and organize the Kelly Miller School's first library.

When Lacy began to think about college, her mother decided to send her off to St. Louis, Missouri, to live with Ellen Lacy's younger sister and her husband. Her aunt taught at Sumner High School, a well-known school for blacks, where Lacy enrolled in 1927. Visits to the St. Louis Public Library led to Lacy's participation in a citywide essay contest sponsored by the library, which she won. This event, coupled with a good impression of the St. Louis Public Library and its librarians, led her to choose librarianship as a career.

After she graduated from high school in the spring of 1929, Lacy went on to Hampton Institute (now Hampton University), completing a Bachelor of Science in Library Science degree in 1933. Hampton was, at that time, the only college in the South where African Americans could receive an education and training in library science. Lacy had many good memories of her years at Hampton, though she worked hard. "Those were some of the happiest years in my life," she recalled (Anderson, 1978). Lacy then went to Louisville, Kentucky, to work as the assistant librarian at Louisville Municipal College, the segregated branch of the University of Louisville. In 1935 she, along with Ann Rucker Anderson, librarian at Kentucky State College, organized the librarians' section of the Kentucky Negro Education Association. Librarians of color could not join the Kentucky Library Association.

Returning to Hampton in 1935, Lacy completed a second degree, a bachelor of science in Education—with honors. Upon graduation in summer of 1936, she was selected by Florence Rising Curtis, the director of Hampton's library school, to become one of four instructors in the Negro Teacher-Librarian Training Program (NTLTP), a program that provided coursework for more than two hundred African American school librarians in the South. In the fall of 1936, Lacy returned to Louisville Municipal College as the head librarian, though she continued to teach in the NTLTP each summer through 1939. Curtis encouraged her to pursue graduate-level education in library science at the University of Illinois in Urbana, and in 1937, Lacy was granted a leave of absence; with the aid of a scholarship from the General Education Board, she enrolled at the University of Illinois as the only African American student in the library school's master's program. In 1938, she received her master of science in library science degree.

In 1938 the former dean of Louisville Municipal College, Rufus Clement, had taken his new post as president of Atlanta University (AU) and while in Kentucky asked Lacy to work as cataloger at the Trevor Arnett Library on the Atlanta University campus. In 1939 she began her position as cataloger librarian. Clement had also implored Lacy to help with planning of the university's new library school, and to take a position on its inaugural faculty. Atlanta University's School of Library Service

opened in 1941. Also during this time, described as a milestone by Jones, on 27 November 1941, she married Edward Allen Jones, a professor of French and the chair of the Modern Language Department of Morehouse College. The couple did not have any children. Within a short period Lacy moved on from her earlier posts and in 1945 became the second dean of the Atlanta University School of Library Service, a position she held for thirty-nine years.

In September 1945, Virginia Jones received a Ph.D. in Library Science and became the second African American to receive a doctorate in the field. Her master's thesis and doctoral dissertation, respectively titled "United States Government Publications on the American Negro" and "Problems of Negro Public School Library Service in Selected Southern Cities," were hailed as groundbreaking work. Jones's survey of library services to African Americans and other minorities in the Southeast resulted in further development of libraries and librarians to provide access to information to all citizens in this geographical area.

Jones spent forty-three years (thirty-nine at AU) mentoring more than 1,800 librarians, mostly African Americans. During her tenure, the Atlanta University library school instituted outreach programs, such as lectures and film forums, to engage the local community and to immerse the students in the field of librarianship. Under Jones, the library school also hosted several professional conferences: The Role of the Library in Improving Education in the South, Seminar on Documentation, and Institute on Materials by and about Negroes. Jones authored more than twenty-five articles, reviews, and book chapters. She also served on numerous program panels and was in great demand as a consultant. Other notable positions she held included serving as councilor and member of the Executive Board of the American Library Association, 1971, and president of the American Association of Library Schools (now the Association of Library and Information Science Education) in 1967.

Jones was the recipient of numerous awards and honors including the American Library Association (ALA) Honorary Life Membership in 1976; ALA's prestigious Melville Dewey Award in 1973; the Joseph W. Lippincott Award in 1977; Beta Phi Mu Award in 1980; the ALA Black Caucus Centennial Award in 1976; the Mary Rothrock Award from the Southeastern Library Association in 1982; and two honorary doctoral degrees: Doctor of Human Letters, 1979, and Bishop College and Doctor of Letters, 1979, University of Michigan. President Lyndon B. Johnson appointed Jones to the President's Advisory Committee on Library Research and Training in 1967, and Georgia governor George Busbee appointed her to the state's Board of Certification for Librarians, on which she served from 1975–1980. In 1984, after retiring as dean of Atlanta University's library school, Jones was asked to serve as director of the newly built Woodruff Library, centrally located within the Atlanta University Center to provide shared library resources for five historically black colleges. Shortly after taking on this post, Jones became ill, and she died on 6 December 1984. No other library educator is believed to have affected the recruitment and education of African American librarians as much as Virginia Lacy Jones did during her career. As the former dean of the University of Michigan Library School, Russell E. Bidlack, wrote, "Dr. Jones is the personification of wise counsel, inspired teacher, patient mentor, and demanding scholar. In the library profession she is acknowledged as a courageous leader who has pointed the way to achievement and success against barriers most of us would have considered insurmountable" (*Reminiscences in Librarianship and Library Education* [1979]).

FURTHER READING
Anderson, Felicia Bowens, and Virginia Lacy Jones. Interview with Virginia Lacy Jones, June 19 and 20, 1978; October 10, 1978, *Black Women Oral History Project*, Schlesinger Library, Radcliffe College (1978).
Hunter, Julie V., and Samuel Morrison. "ALA Council Memorial Tribute to Virginia Lacy Jones," *The Georgian Librarian*, 22, 3 (1985).
Jones, Virginia Lacy. "A Dean's Career," in *The Black Librarian in America*, ed. E. J. Josey (1970).
Jordan, Casper LeRoy. "The Multifaceted Career of Virginia Lacy Jones," in *The Black Librarian in America Revisited*, ed. E. J. Josey, (1994).
Jordan, Casper LeRoy. "Virginia Lacy Jones," in *Notable Black American Women*, ed. Jessie Carney Smith, (1989).
Lundy, Kathryn Renford. "Women View Librarianship: Nine Perspectives," American Library Association, *Association of College and Research Libraries Publications in Librarianship*, 41 (1980).

ALLISON M. SUTTON

Jones, Vivan Malone. *See* Malone, Vivian.

Jones, Willa Saunders (22 Feb. 1904–15 Jan. 1979), playwright, musician, and choir director, was born Willa Saunders in Little Rock, Arkansas, the daughter of Ada Anderson and Atlas Saunders, a pastor. Her twin sister and only sibling, Jimmie, died in infancy. As a child Willa learned to play the piano by practicing on an image of a keyboard drawn with charcoal on cardboard. Unable to afford lessons, she sought instruction from a girl who lived next door. In 1920 she graduated from Arkansas Baptist College and married George W. Jones, who later became a pastor. Soon after, they fled to Chicago after George was wrongfully accused of raping a white woman. The couple had two sons and a daughter who died in infancy. Willa's mother, who worked as a maid in Arkansas, traveled to Chicago to help raise her grandsons.

In Chicago, Willa Jones joined St. John Church–Baptist, the first of many churches with which she had an affiliation. Establishing herself as a central figure in the sacred music community on the South Side, she served as choir director, vocal soloist, organist, and pianist for a variety of churches and at many church-related events. She studied voice with A. J. Offord, J. Wesley Jones, and George Garner and piano and organ with Charles Carleton of Columbia University, New York City. Her skills and reputation led to the invitation for her to direct thousand-voice choirs at the National Baptist Convention's annual meetings in Chicago, Cleveland, Detroit, New York City, Arkansas, and California and serve as assistant director for a five-thousand-voice chorus.

During the early 1920s Jones became seriously ill and promised to write a play in honor of God if she recovered. The resulting work, a Passion play that was first performed in April 1926, became her crowning cultural achievement. Entitled *The Resurrection*, by 1930 the play was performed annually during Easter in churches in and around Chicago. An early program describes the play as a "Sacred Pageant ... portraying the suffering and glorious triumph over death, hell and the grave" (Willa S. Jones Papers, box 1). The nature of the play and the fact that Jones was able to produce it regularly for nearly fifty years (except from 1959 to 1963 owing to illness) attests to her deep religious faith and her exceptional business, leadership, and artistic skills. She once described her most thrilling moment as the day "I accepted Christ as my personal savior" (box 1). Although the play's narrative grew over the years, all versions reenacted the final days of Christ's time on earth, his crucifixion, and resurrection. Later versions also included accounts of Christ's miracles.

The play, eventually titled *The Search for Christ*, developed into an elaborate spectacle that featured approximately three hundred cast members. In order to accommodate larger audiences and charge admission, Jones moved her play into the DuSable High School auditorium and, after a few seasons, the Civic Opera House in April 1946. Around this time, the play traveled to Brooklyn, New York. A feature on Jones's Passion play in *Ebony* magazine evoked some of its visual and aural attractions. The accompanying illustrations depict a multiracial, although predominantly black, cast in elaborate costumes provided by the opera company associated with the venue. Professional dance troupes, animals from the stockyards, and elaborate staging and technical equipment enhanced the event's splendor. Similar to medieval Passion plays that depicted Christ's ascension, cables hoisted the character of Christ, played for over thirty years by Jones's husband, up into "Heaven" above the stage.

Organ and vocal music, which included solos, choruses, and atmospheric hums, constituted another central component of the production. During Jones's lifetime the songs in the play were primarily Negro spirituals and European-American sacred music. Jones catered to the conservative tastes of middle-class audiences rather than to those of the working poor, who tended to gravitate toward gospel music. Jones's grandson, Rogers Jones, characterized his grandmother as a "cultured person" who considered the physical exuberance of gospel inappropriate for her play (interview with author, 8 Dec. 2004).

This attitude did not preclude Jones from capitalizing upon the popularity of famous gospel and secular performers. While the majority of the cast was made up of amateurs from all social stations in life, she marketed her play by including a few "stars." In the 1960s the gospel diva MAHALIA JACKSON, Jones's longtime friend, appeared in the play. Other well-known vocalists included DELOIS BARRETT CAMPBELL, Rev. Clay Evans, Rev. Maceo Woods, and the Norfleet Brothers. Jones also nurtured the talents of future musical celebrities, including Ruth Jones, who later changed her name to DINAH WASHINGTON, and sisters Sheila, Wanda, and Jeanette Hutchinson of the Emotions. She scouted Chicago-area churches and choirs for additional talent.

While comfortably positioned within Chicago's African American middle class, Jones did not get rich off of her play. Evidence suggests that she worked hard to secure the financial backing necessary to keep the play in production, especially once it entered commercial theaters. Sponsors included churches, Masonic orders, wealthy benefactors (primarily friends of Jones), the Church Federation of Greater Chicago, Southern Christian Leadership Conference (SCLC), and for a short period in the 1970s the *Chicago Tribune*. Jones typically donated any proceeds from the play to area churches.

Jones died at North Side hospital in Chicago, after which Rogers Jones took over as producer and director. In an effort to pull in larger and younger audiences, he infused the play with gospel music. The play was produced a few times in the early 1980s before closing permanently because of a lack of financial support. Willa Jones wrote and produced other plays, including *The Life Boat, Just One Hour to Live for the Dope Addict, The Call to Arms, Up from Slavery*, and *The Birth of Christ*, but none of these achieved the recognition garnered by *The Search for Christ*.

The Search for Christ became such a visible and important part of Chicago's cultural life that four mayors, including Richard J. Daley and HAROLD WASHINGTON, declared days in honor of Jones and her play. According to Earl Calloway, arts editor of the *Chicago Defender*, her play was "one of the great productions in Chicago every year" (interview with author, 13 Aug. 2006). In spite of this local recognition, however, neither has received broad critical attention. This is unfortunate considering that *The Search for Christ* is perhaps the first Passion play by an African American woman. It helped to establish Jones as a highly respected cultural authority in the black church. By integrating the casts, which was followed to some extent by integrated audiences, Jones demonstrated that the arts could foster progressive social relations, even in a city so glaringly divided by race. At the same time, it served for many as a beacon of black pride.

FURTHER READING

Programs, clippings, photographs, and other primary materials can be found in the Willa S. Jones Papers in the Vivian G. Harsh Research Collection of Afro-American History and Literature, Carter G. Woodson Regional Library, Chicago, and in the Willa Saunders Jones Papers [manuscript], c. 1964–1984 in the Chicago History Museum, Chicago.

"Operation Breadbasket Plans 40th Production of Passion Play," *Chicago Tribune*, 16 Mar. 1969.

"Passion Play: Annual Chicago Presentation of All-Negro Religious Play Proves Big Box Office Draw," *Ebony* (May 1950).

Smith, Patricia. "Passion Play: Vow Becomes a City Legacy," *Chicago Sun-Times*, 28 Apr. 1980.

                                    BRIAN HALLSTOOS

Jones, Willie "Suicide" (1908 or 1911–?), stunt parachutist, was born Willie Jones in either Memphis, Tennessee, or Mississippi to Rebecca Lang of Memphis. Nothing is known about his father or Willie's education. Little is known about Jones's early life, but published reports suggest he began to fly in his teens. Conflicting stories describe his first airborne stunts. According to the *Chicago Defender*, Jones joined the Orange Flying Circus in Fort Worth, Texas, in 1923, whereas an article published in *Ebony* magazine reports that Jones began to fly in Saint Louis at the age of fifteen and walked his first wing in 1927 at a Missouri county fair. Whatever the truth, all accounts agree that Jones took to flying right away, exhibiting the fearlessness that all the early stunt flyers had to have to do risky tricks with no safety equipment in the rickety wood, canvas, and wire World War I–surplus Jenny biplanes that were the barnstormers' preferred machine.

From the early 1920s until the 1950s Jones worked in over twenty air circuses and barnstorming tours, thrilling crowds with airborne stunts and parachute jumps. He performed a variety of airborne stunts, including hanging from a rope while the plane did loops and changing planes in midair, but his specialty became parachute jumping. According to the *Defender*, Jones joined the Hollywood Flying Circus, a group that did stunts in movies, and "averaged fifty leaps a day, going up with such expert stunt artists as Ace Corbin and Speed Schuman" (Gubert, Sawyer, and Fannin, 180). Throughout the 1930s Jones competed in U.S. Army air shows, becoming the most prolific African American jumper and one of the best, regardless of color. In 1936 he won first prize, competing against eleven white jumpers, at an army air show in Shreveport, Louisiana.

In 1938 Jones earned the nickname "Suicide" in Little Rock, Arkansas, in service to the military. A U.S. Coast Guard artillery unit needed to test its searchlights to locate potential enemy aircraft, and it needed someone to perform a night jump as a target. No jumper would make such a jump, declaring it to be suicide, but Jones volunteered. When the searchlights found him descending in the darkness, the intense lights blinded him, and he could not see the ground; he had to land by instinct. It took four days for him to regain his sight. From then on he was called Suicide.

Jones continued to expand his repertoire of daring jumps. He toured the country with Speed Schuman and became the featured attraction at several Chicago-area air shows after attracting the attention of Major Rupert A. Simmons, a Chicago entrepreneur who had promoted the first all-black air show in 1929. There was one stunt in particular that interested Jones, the delayed jump. This guaranteed crowd thriller required the parachutist to free-fall from as great a height and for as long as courage would allow (or in some cases, as high as the plane could go). A Russian parachutist held the unofficial record when he reportedly jumped at 26,500 feet and delayed opening his chute until 650 feet from the ground. Jones's first try at the record saw him free-fall for 27,000 feet, good enough for the record, but the official, government-issued barograph, a pressure-sensitive instrument used to measure altitude, was not properly sealed, and the jump was ruled unofficial.

On 16 November 1938 Jones's second attempt at the delayed jump almost took his life. Jumping from an altitude between 29,000 and 30,000 feet, Jones found himself in frigid air measuring 25 degrees below zero. He managed to open his chute at 2,500 feet before he landed unconscious in an empty lot in downtown Chicago, a victim of hypothermia. On 2 March 1939 Jones got his record. The event was described in the *Chicago Defender*:

> After soaring for three hours and ten minutes and gaining an altitude where the mercury registered a temperature of 45 degrees below zero, "Suicide" Jones was let out of the ship above the Dixie Airport near Harvey. He whirled through space four and one-half miles before opening the parachute. At 800 feet above the ground his trusted chute ballooned out and settled slowly to earth. He had set the world's record (Gubert, Sawyer, and Fannin, 181).

This time the barograph worked properly; it showed Jones had jumped from 24,468 feet, giving him the American record as well as the official world record. Five months later, on 25 August 1939, Jones married Ruthygale Griffin in Omaha, Nebraska.

World War II interrupted the barnstorming business. Not much is known about Jones's involvement in the war, although an article published in 1950 in *Ebony* magazine refers to him as an "ex-merchant seaman." After the war records show Jones was a regular attraction at Chicago-area air shows. His stunts got more daring but also safer, since he began to carry a second safety chute aloft. Still, a life full of risk has its drawbacks. Revealing the psychological toll of his chosen profession, he explained to a reporter that he was "not nervous at the jump or the fall before opening my chute.... [But] my plague is nightmares which come to me as long as a year after I've had a narrow escape" (Gubert, Sawyer, and Fannin, 182).

Jones also had an interest in long-distance flying records, although no evidence exists that he followed through with any attempts. Before the war he announced he was going to attempt to beat Howard Hughes's long-distance record by flying from New York to Seattle and back. In May 1947 he made the news again by announcing an attempt to beat the around-the-world record that had been set a month earlier by the aviator Milton Reynolds. "This will be the first time a Negro ever attempted to make such a flight around the world," he claimed, although at least two other African Americans—THOMAS COX ALLEN and HUBERT FAUNTLEROY JULIAN—had already announced similar plans. The newspaper account also noted that Jones's plane was more than one hundred miles per hour slower than the one used by Reynolds.

Jones continued to stunt jump well into his forties. At some point he also worked in a Chicago poultry house. The last press reference to Jones was in July 1980, when he appeared in a photograph taken in Chicago at a ceremony celebrating CORNELIUS R. COFFEY, a black aviation pioneer.

FURTHER READING

Gubert, Betty Kaplan, Miriam Sawyer, and Caroline M. Fannin. *Distinguished African Americans in Aviation and Space Science* (2002).

"'Suicide' Jones," *Ebony* (Feb. 1950).

DOUGLAS FLEMING ROOSA

Joplin, Scott (24 Nov. 1868?–1 Apr. 1917), ragtime composer and pianist, was born in or near Texarkana, Texas, one of six children of Giles Joplin, reportedly a former slave from North Carolina, and Florence Givens, a freewoman from Kentucky. Many aspects of Joplin's early life are shrouded in mystery. At a crucial time in his youth, Joplin's father left the family, and his mother was forced to raise him as a single parent. She made arrangements for her son to receive piano lessons in exchange for her domestic services, and he was allowed to practice piano where she worked. A precocious child whose talent was noticed by the time he was seven years old, Joplin had undoubtedly inherited talent from his parents, as Giles had played violin and Florence sang and played the banjo. His own experimentations at the piano and his basic music training with local teachers contributed to his advancement. Joplin attended Orr Elementary School in Texarkana and then traveled to Sedalia, Missouri, perhaps residing with relatives while studying at Lincoln High School.

Joplin built an early reputation as a pianist and gained fame as a composer of piano ragtime during the Gay Nineties, plying his trade concurrently with composers such as WILL MARION COOK and HARRY BURLEIGH. Joplin was essential in the articulation of a distinctly American style of music. Minstrelsy was still in vogue when Joplin was a teenager performing in vaudeville shows with the Texas Medley Quartette, a group he founded with his brothers. Joplin reportedly arrived in St. Louis by 1885, landing a job as a pianist at John Turpin's Silver Dollar Saloon. In 1894 he was hired at TOM TURPIN's Rosebud Cafe. As musicians flocked to the Chicago Columbian Exposition in 1893, Joplin was among them, playing at nightspots close to the fair. Afterward he returned to Sedalia, the "Cradle of Ragtime," accompanied by the pianist Otis Saunders.

Although he was playing piano in various cities, Joplin still found time to blow the cornet in Sedalia's Queen City Band. In 1895 he continued playing with the Quartette and toured as far as Syracuse, New York, where some businessmen were sufficiently impressed with his talents to publish his first vocal songs. Additionally, Joplin was hired as a pianist at Sedalia's famous Maple Leaf Club. He also taught piano, banjo, and mandolin, claiming among his students the pianists ARTHUR MARSHALL, SCOTT HAYDEN, and Sanford B. Campbell. By 1896 Joplin had settled in Sedalia and matriculated at the George Smith College for Negroes. With the confidence and ambition fostered by this formal training, he approached the Fuller-Smith and Carl Hoffman Companies, which published some of his piano rags. It was also in Sedalia that he met John Stark, who became his friend and the publisher of Joplin's celebrated "Maple Leaf Rag" (1899).

In 1900 Joplin began a three-year relationship with Belle Hayden, which produced a child who soon died. He then married Freddie Alexander in 1904, but her death that same year sent him wandering about for at least a year, returning at times to Sedalia and St. Louis. In 1905 he went to Chicago, and by 1907 he had followed John Stark to New York and married Lottie Stokes, who remained with him until his death. In the years after the turn of the century, the piano replaced the violin in popularity. Playing ragtime on the parlor piano became "all the rage" in both the United States and Europe. Although there were ragtime bands and ragtime songs, classic rag soon became defined as an instrumental form, especially for the piano. Many Joplin rags consist of a left-hand part that jumps registers in eighth note rhythms set against tricky syncopated sixteenths in the right hand. Joplin was both prolific and successful in writing rags for the piano, and he came to be billed as "the King of Ragtime." Ragtime or rag—from "ragged time"—is a genre that blends elements from marches, jigs, quadrilles, and bamboulas with blues, spirituals, minstrel ballads, and "coon songs." ("Coon songs" were highly stereotyped comic songs, popular from the 1880s to the 1920s, written in a pseudo-dialect purporting to record African American vernacular speech.) Ragtime is an infectious and stimulating music, usually in 2/4 meter, with a marchlike sway and a proud, sharp, in-your-face joviality. Its defining rhythm, based on the African bamboula dance pattern, renamed "cakewalk" in America, is a three-note figuration of sixteenth-eighth-sixteenth notes, which is also heard in earlier spirituals, such as "I Got a Home in-a That Kingdom" and "Ain-a That Good News!"

A predecessor of jazz, ragtime was correlated with the "African jig" because of its foot stamps, shuffles, and shouts, "where hands clap out intricate and varying rhythmic patterns ... and the foot is not marking straight time, but what Negroes call 'stop time,' or what the books call 'syncopation'" (JAMES WELDON JOHNSON, *The Book of American Spirituals* [1925], 31). Joplin alludes to these influences in his "Stoptime Rag," where the word "stamp" is marked on every quarter beat. Joplin admonished pianists to play ragtime slowly, even though his tempo for "Stoptime" is marked "Fast or slow." Campbell most revealingly wrote that rag was played variously in "march time, fast ragtime, slow, and the ragtime blues style" (Fisk University, Special Collections).

Vera Brodsky Lawrence's *Complete Works of Scott Joplin* lists forty-five rags, waltzes, marches, and other piano pieces that Joplin composed himself. In addition, he collaborated on a number of rags, including "Swipesy" with Arthur Marshall, "Sunflower Slow Drag," "Something Doing," "Felicity Rag," "Kismet Rag" with Scott Hayden, and "Heliotrope Bouquet" with LOUIS CHAUVIN. There are also various unpublished pieces and some that were stolen, lost, sold, or destroyed.

The most popular of Joplin's works, and one that brought continuous acclaim, is undoubtedly the "Maple Leaf Rag." No matter the studied care of "Gladiolus Rag" or the majesty of "Magnetic Rag," with its blue-note features, and no matter the catchiness of "The Entertainer," "Maple Leaf" beckons more. Over and above its engaging melodies and syncopations, the technical challenges alone are more than enough to induce an ambitious pianist to tackle "Maple Leaf." Whatever its ingredients, "Maple Leaf Rag" garnered a respect for ragtime that has lasted for decades. Numerous musicians have recorded it, and it has been arranged for instruments from guitar to oboe and for band and orchestra.

Joplin also composed small and large vocal forms, both original and arranged. A few of his nonsyncopated songs are related to the Tin Pan Alley types of the day, and at least two are influenced by "coon songs." He choreographed dance steps and wrote words for the "Ragtime Dance Song," and in a few cases he either wrote lyrics or arranged music for others. Joplin composed two operas, the first of which is lost. The second, *Treemonisha*, whose libretto Joplin also wrote, is an ambitious work containing twenty-seven numbers and requiring three sopranos, three tenors, one high baritone, four basses, and a chorus. Set "on a plantation somewhere in the State of Arkansas, Northeast of the Town of Texarkana and three or four miles from the Red River," the opera presents education as the key to success.

Throughout Joplin's preface to *Treemonisha*, one cannot help but note the parallelism of dates and geographic locations in the opera to those of his own past. The preface tells the tale of a young baby who was found under a tree, adopted, and named "Treemonisha" by Ned and Monisha. At age seven she is educated by a white family in return for Monisha's domestic services. The opera opens with eighteen-year-old Treemonisha touting the value of education and campaigning against two conjurers who earn their livelihoods promoting superstition. After various episodes with kidnappers, wasps, bears, and cotton pickers, who sing the brilliant "Aunt Dinah Has Blowed de Horn," Treemonisha is successful and joins the finale, singing "Marching Onward" to the tune of the "Real Slow Drag."

Compositionally, syncopated music is used in *Treemonisha* only when the plot calls for it, with the musical themes and harmonies employing "crossover" alternations between classical and popular styles. However, Joplin's intentions seem to have

Scott Joplin, "The King of Ragtime," c. 1911. (Schomburg Center.)

leaned more toward the classical. The basic harmonies are decorated with his favored diminished seventh chords and secondary dominants. Altered chords, chromatics, modulations, themes with mode changes, special effects to depict confusion, and even an example of seven key changes in "The Bag of Luck" all point toward Joplin's training and musical aspirations.

Joplin accompanied the first performance of *Treemonisha* on the piano. When he sought sponsors, and when he asked Stark to publish the opera, he was refused. Tackling these jobs himself proved to be his undoing. As a result of stress and illness, Joplin lost his mental balance in early 1917 and was admitted to the New York State Hospital. A diagnosis signed by Dr. Philip Smith states that Joplin succumbed to "dementia paralytica—cerebral form about 9:10 o'clock p.m.," that the duration of the mental illness was one year and six months, and that the "contributory causes were Syphilis [of an] unknown duration" (Bureau of Records, New York City).

Campbell wrote that Joplin's funeral carriage bore names of his rag hits. Sadly, only the *New York Age* and a notice by John Stark carried his obituary. High society from New York to Paris had strutted the cakewalk accompanied by his rags since the late 1890s, but now he was forgotten. Perhaps World War I diverted people's attention away from the exuberance of raggedy rags and thus from Joplin.

He received accolades for his piano rags, but his most difficult vocal music was not appreciated in his lifetime. Sixty years after his death he began to receive numerous honors, including the National Music Award, a Pulitzer Prize in 1976, and a U.S. postage stamp in 1983.

Several articles in the *Washington Post* and the *New York Times* inspired a revival of Joplin's music in the 1970s. Various films, especially *The Sting* (1973), and television productions have highlighted his work, and concerts and recordings by the finest of musicians have taken the music to new heights. Additionally, there have been several productions of *Treemonisha*. To be sure, rags were written before Joplin's *Original Rags* was published in 1899, but he must be credited with defining the classic concept and construction of ragtime and with rendering dignity and respectability to the style.

FURTHER READING

Selected repositories of music and other materials are at the New York Public Library; the Library of Congress, Washington, D.C.; the Fisk University Library, Nashville, Tennessee; the Center for Black Music Research, Chicago, Illinois; Indiana University Library, Terre Haute; and the Scott Joplin International Ragtime Foundation, Sedalia, Missouri.

Berlin, Edward A. *King of Ragtime: Scott Joplin and His Era* (1994).

Jasen, David, and Trebor J. Tichenor. *Rags and Ragtime: A Musical History* (1989).

Lawrence, Vera Brodsky. *The Complete Works of Scott Joplin* (1981).

Preston, Katherine. *Scott Joplin: Composer* (1988).

Obituary: *New York Age*, 5 Apr. 1917.

DISCOGRAPHY

Joplin, Scott. *Classic Ragtime from Rare Piano Rolls* (1989).

Rifkin, Joshua. *Scott Joplin: Piano Rags* (1987).

Zimmerman, Richard. *Complete Works of Scott Joplin* (1993).

HILDRED ROACH

Jordan, Barbara (21 Feb. 1936–17 Jan. 1996), lawyer, politician, and professor, was born Barbara Charline Jordan in Houston, Texas, the daughter of Benjamin M. Jordan and Arlyne Patten Jordan. Her father, a graduate of the Tuskegee Institute, was a warehouse employee until 1949 when he became a minister at Houston's Good Hope Missionary Baptist Church, in which his father's family had long been active. Arlyne Jordan also became a frequent speaker at the church. The Jordans were always poor, and for many years Barbara and her two older sisters shared a bed, but their lives improved somewhat after their father became a minister. Jordan attended local segregated public schools and received good grades with little effort. She gave scant thought to her future, beyond forming a vague desire to become a pharmacist, until her senior year at Phillis Wheatley High School, when a black female lawyer spoke at the school's career day assembly. Already a proficient orator who had won several competitions, she decided to put that skill to use as an attorney.

Restricted in her choice of colleges by her poverty as well as segregation, Jordan entered Texas Southern University, an all-black institution in Houston, on a small scholarship in the fall of 1952. Majoring in political science and history, she also became a champion debater, leading the college team to several championships. She graduated magna cum laude in 1956 and went on to Boston University School of Law, where she managed to excel despite rampant gender discrimination. Upon graduation she took the Massachusetts bar exam, intending to practice law in Boston, but ultimately decided to return to her parents' home in Houston. She used the dining room as her office for several years before setting up a downtown office, and she also worked as an administrative assistant to a county judge until 1966.

Jordan's first wholesale encounter with politics came during the 1960 national election campaign, when she became a volunteer for the Democratic presidential candidate John F. Kennedy and his running mate, the Texas senator Lyndon B. Johnson. She began at the Houston party headquarters by performing menial jobs but soon emerged as the head of a voting drive covering Houston's predominantly black precincts. The Democratic victory that fall changed Jordan's life in several ways: not only did it persuade her to enter politics, it also overturned her long-held sense that segregation was a way of life that had to be endured, and it convinced her that the lives of black people might be improved by political action. Jordan began her political career by running for a seat in the Texas House of Representatives in 1962 and again two years later. She lost both elections but received an impressive number of votes. In 1966, following a Supreme Court–mandated electoral redistricting to allow fair representation for blacks and other minorities, Jordan won election to the Texas Senate from the newly created Eleventh District

in Houston, becoming the first black state senator in Texas since 1883. Concerned that she might be branded a rabble-rousing liberal agitator, she determined to establish herself as a legislator working seriously for social change. She began by being an advocate for the ultimately successful passage of a bill establishing the state's first Fair Employment Practices Commission, to fight discrimination in the workplace. She also fought for passage of the state's first minimum wage law, for raises in workmen's compensation payments, and for the creation of a department of community affairs to deal with the problems of the state's rapidly growing urban areas. In addition, she blocked proposed legislation that would have made voter registration more difficult.

Named outstanding freshman senator during her first year in office, Jordan went on to reelection for two more terms, serving a total of six years and bringing to passage half of the bills she introduced. In March 1972 she became the first black woman in American history to preside over a legislative body when she was elected president pro tem of the Texas legislature. By that time she had decided to try for a seat in the U.S. House of Representatives from the state's new Eighteenth District, which was 50 percent black and 15 percent Mexican American. After winning a hard-fought primary against a black male state legislator, she ran for election that fall as the Democratic candidate and easily defeated her Republican opponent. Upon taking the oath of office in January 1973, she and another new representative, ANDREW YOUNG of Georgia, became the first two African Americans in modern times to sit as elected members of the U.S. House. Thanks to the assistance of former president Lyndon Johnson, who had become a friend during Jordan's years in the Texas legislature, she was appointed to a coveted seat on the House Judiciary Committee.

Jordan served three terms in the Congress, easily winning reelection in 1974 and 1976. She was a forceful presence, voting consistently for such liberal measures as increased federal aid to public schools and an extension of the guaranteed student loan program, legal aid for the poor, an increase in the minimum wage, and the continuation of the school lunch program. During her first term she also voted for several bills designed to limit U.S. involvement in the Vietnam War, and she voted against the construction of the Alaska oil pipeline because of concerns for the environment. But she first achieved a national presence in July 1974 as a member of the House Judiciary Committee.

Barbara Jordan, first southern woman to be elected to the House of Representatives, at an interview for *Family Circle* magazine, 18 October 1976. (Lyndon Baines Johnson Presidential Library.)

On the opening day of the televised hearings held by the committee to consider articles of impeachment against President Richard M. Nixon, Jordan delivered a preliminary statement that moved to their very bones almost all who heard it. Speaking slowly and deliberately in a powerful deep and solemn voice, Jordan declared that despite not having been considered among "We, the people" when the Constitution was adopted, "the process of amendment, interpretation, and court decisions" had now guaranteed her inclusion. "Today, I am an inquisitor," she continued. "I believe hyperbole would not be fictional and would not overstate the solemnness that I feel right now. My faith in the Constitution is whole, it is complete, it is total. I am not going to sit here and be an idle spectator to the diminution, the subversion, the destruction of the Constitution." Speaking with authority, Jordan then set forth her reasons for believing that Nixon should be impeached, concluding that if the committee did not vote to do so, then the Constitution was worthless and should be sent through a paper shredder. Although she projected great control, Jordan later revealed that she was shaking with nervousness throughout the proceedings, and after casting her vote she wept.

Following Nixon's resignation not long afterward, Jordan's opening remarks, as well as her penetrating questioning during the committee hearings, remained in the public mind, and she was talked about as a candidate for higher office. In 1976 she was called upon to be a keynote speaker at the Democratic National Convention, along with Senator John H. Glenn Jr. of Ohio. Following Glenn's unremarkable address, she electrified the convention with a speech delivered in a style part William Jennings Bryan and part hellfire Baptist preacher. Appealing for national unity, she declared that its achievement and the full realization of America's destiny lay only through the Democratic Party.

In the 1976 fall presidential campaign, Jordan traveled the country, making speeches in support of the Democratic candidate, Jimmy Carter. Upon his victory in November, Carter discussed appointing her to the cabinet, but she was only interested in becoming attorney general, a post Carter was not willing to offer her. A year later, in December 1977, she surprised supporters by announcing that she would not seek a fourth term in Congress the following year. Although she was rumored to have health problems, she denied this, saying only that she wanted to devote herself to other concerns back in Texas. After leaving the House in early 1979, she was appointed to the Lyndon B. Johnson Chair in National Policy at the Johnson School of Public Affairs, a part of the University of Texas in Austin. Teaching courses in policy development as well as political values and ethics, she became one of the university's most popular professors, and students had to participate in a lottery to gain admission to her classes.

Jordan returned to the national political stage in 1988, when she delivered a rousing speech at the Democratic National Convention seconding the nomination of Lloyd Bentsen as the vice presidential candidate. By this time, however, her physical ailment could not be denied: she was now confined to a wheelchair, the consequence, she said, of a "neuromuscular disorder." Later that summer she made national headlines again when she was found floating unconscious in the swimming pool at her home; she had gone into cardiac arrest while doing therapeutic exercises. She recovered, however, and by that fall was well enough to campaign for the national Democratic presidential ticket, headed by Michael Dukakis.

Jordan returned to the Democratic National Convention in 1992 as one of its keynote speakers, and again she riveted the audience with her call for support of presidential candidate Bill Clinton and his mandate for change. Although her health grew worse, she continued to teach at the university. She also served as chair of the Commission on Immigration Reform and in that capacity testified before Congress in 1995 on behalf of citizenship rights for children born in the United States to illegal immigrants.

Jordan, who never married, fiercely guarded her private life. Known to enjoy singing and playing the guitar, she was also a fan of the Lady Longhorns, the University of Texas women's basketball team, whose games she frequently attended. Following her death from viral pneumonia, which occurred at her home in Austin, it was disclosed that she had suffered from both multiple sclerosis and leukemia.

FURTHER READING

Jordan, Barbara, and Shelby Hearon. *Barbara Jordan: A Self-Portrait* (1978).

Haskins, James. *Barbara Jordan* (1977).

Rogers, Mary Beth. *Barbara Jordan: American Hero* (1998).

Obituary: *New York Times*, 18 Jan. 1996.

This entry is taken from the *American National Biography* and is published here with the permission of the American Council of Learned Societies.

ANN T. KEENE

Jordan, George (1847–24 Oct. 1904), Medal of Honor winner, was born a slave in Williamson County, Tennessee. Little is know about his early life. Like so many African Americans, he might have been hired to serve as a laborer, mechanic, or teamster for the massive Union army supply infrastructure operating out of Nashville, Tennessee, during the Civil War. On 28 July 1866 the U.S. Congress authorized the raising of six regiments of "Negro troops" that were broken down into two cavalry and four infantry regiments. The two cavalry regiments were numbered the Ninth and Tenth U.S. Cavalry Regiments. Jordan enlisted in the U.S. Army in Nashville in late 1866 and was assigned to the Ninth Regiment.

It was not uncommon to find a soldier who spent his entire military service with one regiment or company. This was the case with Private Jordan. He served with the Ninth through the regiment's initial service along the Rio Grande in Texas from 1867 to 1875 and remained with the unit during its transfer to the District of New Mexico to combat the growing menace of the Apaches and the Utes. The "Buffalo Soldiers," as these men became known, also dealt with civilian unrest, as in the Lincoln War of 1878–1881, which dealt with a power struggle for control of Lincoln County, New Mexico, by rival groups of cattlemen. This war became infamous due to the involvement of Billy the Kid on the side of the one of the rival groups. During this period Jordan was promoted to sergeant of Company K.

In late August 1879 the Warm Spring Apaches under the leadership of Victorio left the Fort Stanton reservation. This force of Apache warriors and Mescaleros raided on both sides of the U.S.-Mexican border and forced both governments to respond militarily. The Ninth and Tenth U.S. Cavalry Regiments were sent to the District of New Mexico. Both regiments attempted at various times to capture Victorio, but he and his warriors fled into the mountains or crossed the border into Mexico. In several cases cavalry detachments from both regiments drove themselves to the point of total collapse in pursuit of the raiding parties. Victorio's destructive raids continued against the civilian population throughout the winter of 1879 until 1880 despite the efforts of military forces on both sides of the border. Colonel Edward Hatch, commanding the Ninth U.S. Cavalry, marshaled his companies into several columns in an attempt to pin the marauding Apaches in the mountains during the spring of 1880.

As the different battalions of the Ninth U.S. Cavalry attempted to trap Victorio, Jordan was assigned a number of dismounted soldiers to escort a supply column and to occupy an abandoned post known as Fort Tularosa, New Mexico. It was not uncommon for cavalry units to go into action without horses, and in this case the men were assigned to miscellaneous duties. Jordan was to escort a supply column to the abandoned post to establish a resupply point for Colonel Hatch's columns as well as maintain security for the local settlers. By 13 May 1880 Jordan's column had reached a stage station, and the sergeant ordered his footsore men to rest. Soon a rider came in with news that Victorio and his Apaches had been seen near old Fort Tularosa, and the settlers were in danger of being attacked. Jordan gathered his men and began the overnight march to Fort Tularosa.

By the next morning Jordan and his troopers had reached the old post and found the civilian population safe. After a brief rest, he assigned his troopers to rebuild the stockade and to fortify the old corral. This work took nearly all day, and by nightfall it was nearly completed. Suddenly Victorio and his Apaches swooped down upon the small post, and Jordan and his troopers were forced to retreat to the stockade. Unfortunately the teamsters and two soldiers had to find cover in the corral and guard the horses and mules of the supply column. Under Jordan's direction, the soldiers and civilians repulsed a number of determined assaults by the Apaches. Realizing his inability to take the stockade, Victorio directed his warriors to focus on the fortified corral to seize the livestock. Jordan had wisely directed ten of his troopers to reinforce the corral while the Apaches were regrouping. Victorio met a reinforced corral and was forced to cease his attack. Hatch and elements of the Ninth U.S. Cavalry arrived on 15 May 1880.

When recommended for the Medal of Honor, Jordan was also being recognized for his leadership in the engagement at Carrizo Canyon, New Mexico, on 12 August 1881. In this fight Company K, Ninth U.S. Cavalry, was attempting to intercept Nana, an Apache warrior who had fought alongside Victorio. Captain H. K. Parker attempted to assault the Apaches, who were using the canyon for cover. Parker and Company K were soon outnumbered and were forced to pull back into a defensive

position. With a small platoon of nineteen men, Jordan was able to hold his exposed position and prevent the small detachment from being surrounded by the Apaches.

Jordan remained in the Company K, Ninth U.S. Cavalry until 1897, when he retired as first sergeant and settled near Fort Robinson, Nebraska, until his death in 1904. He was buried with full military honors at Fort Robinson, Nebraska, on 24 October 1904.

FURTHER READING

Amos, Preston E. *Above and beyond in the West: Black Medal of Honor Winners, 1870–1890* (1974).

Coffman, Edward M. *The Old Army: A Portrait of the American Army in Peacetime, 1784–1898* (1986).

Kenner, Charles L. *Buffalo Soldiers and Officers of the Ninth Cavalry, 1867–1898* (1999).

Leckie, William H. *The Buffalo Soldiers: A Narrative of the Negro Cavalry in the West* (1967).

Schubert, Frank N. *Black Valor: Buffalo Soldiers and the Medal of Honor, 1870–1898* (1997).

WILLIAM H. BROW

Jordan, June (9 July 1936–14 June 2002), poet, essayist, teacher, and activist, was born in Harlem, New York, the daughter of Jamaican-born parents Mildred Maud Fisher, a nurse, and Granville Ivanhoe Jordan, a postal clerk. Mildred, who was half East Indian, was a quiet and religious woman who had given up a career as an artist to marry; she struggled with depression and eventually committed suicide in 1966. Jordan's father, who was half Chinese and a follower of the black nationalist MARCUS GARVEY, made no apologies for his dissatisfaction with his only child's gender. He had wanted a boy and treated Jordan as such. Referring to her as "he" and "the boy," Granville subjected his young daughter to rigorous mental and physical training regimens that included camping, fishing, and boxing instruction; aggressive mathematical and literary testing; and often brutal physical beatings. Jordan describes her father's abuse in her memoir: "Like a growling beast, the roll-away mahogany doors rumble open, and the light snaps on and a fist smashes into the side of my head and I am screaming awake: 'Daddy! What did I do?!'" By her fifth birthday Jordan had endured, and excelled at, memorizing and reciting selections from the Bible and the works of PAUL LAURENCE DUNBAR, Edgar Allan Poe, Zane Grey, Sinclair Lewis, and Shakespeare. Jordan began writing poetry at age seven. When schoolmates started to buy her verses, she realized that poetry could be both powerful and useful in connecting people.

The Jordans moved to the Bedford-Stuyvesant neighborhood of Brooklyn when June was five years old. She was generally the only black student throughout her secondary school and college years. After one year at Midwood High School, she won a scholarship and transferred to the Northfield School for Girls, a private prep school in Massachusetts. Following graduation in 1953, she enrolled in Barnard College, where she met Michael Meyer, a white Columbia College student. The two married in 1955, and their son, Christopher, was born in 1958. Although she spent a year at the University of Chicago while her husband was in school there and another semester back at Barnard, she never received a college degree. Jordan later described her marriage, which at the time was illegal in forty-three states, as a "state criminalized relationship." In her "Letter to Michael," an essay in *Civil Wars: Selected Essays 1963–1980* (1982), Jordan illuminates the difficulties of interracial marriage, factors that contributed to the dissolution of her own marriage. The couple divorced in 1965. Considering a career in urban planning, Jordan studied urban design and architecture with Buckminster Fuller in the early 1960s. Her architectural redesign plan for Harlem was published in *Esquire* in 1965 and won the Prix de Rome in Environmental Design in 1970. Even though she ultimately decided against pursuing a career as an architect, space—literal and figurative—remained a significant theme in Jordan's work.

After her divorce, Jordan struggled to support herself and her son as a teacher and freelance writer. She published short stories and poems under the name of June Meyer in a number of top magazines and journals. While Jordan's artistic voice emerged as part of the civil rights, women's rights, and anti-war movements of the 1960s and early 1970s, they did not define her. Her political consciousness developed according to her own rules.

A dedicated and engaged teacher, Jordan began her professorial career in 1967 as an English instructor at City College and poet-in-residence at the Teachers and Writers Collaborative, both in New York City. She taught English and literature at Connecticut College, Sarah Lawrence College, Yale University, and SUNY Stony Brook, where she was awarded tenure in 1982. In 1989 she took a position at the University of California at Berkeley, teaching English, African American studies, and women's studies. An extremely popular teacher,

Jordan exhibited the same passion for teaching as she did for writing, challenging her students to be honest in their work and with themselves. While at Berkeley, Jordan founded Poetry for the People, a program that employs poetry as a tool of empowerment through workshops at high schools and prisons, marathon poetry readings, and the study of work by African Americans and Arabs that is generally overlooked in the classroom.

One of the nation's most published African American authors, Jordan's catalogue of work includes ten books of poetry, eight volumes of essays, children's books, four plays, two librettos, a spoken-word album, several edited anthologies, and a memoir. Jordan's writing career began in earnest with the 1969 publication of her first book of poetry, *Who Look at Me*, which ends with the plea, "Who see the roof and corners of my pride / to be (as you are) free? / WHO LOOK AT ME?" After the publication of *Some Changes* (1971), which, like *Who Look at Me*, focused on issues relating to African American identity, Jordan's poetry collections, including *Things I Do in the Dark: Selected Poems* (1977), *Passion: New Poems 1977–1980* (1980), *Living Room: New Poems 1980–1984* (1985), *Naming Our Destiny: New and Selected Poems* (1989), and *Haruko Love Poems* (1994), increasingly emphasized overtly political and international issues.

An early advocate of the use of Black English, Jordan wrote a novel for young adults, *His Own Where* (1971), entirely in black vernacular. The book was nominated for a National Book Award. Jordan's celebrated works for children and young adults began with *The Voice of the Children* (1970), an edited volume that grew out of a workshop for black and Hispanic readers, and continued with *New Life: New Room* (1975), *Kimako's Story* (1981), and the 1972 biography of FANNIE LOU HAMER. Jordan maintained a presence on the national stage as a regular columnist for the *Progressive* and a contributor to a host of specialized and mainstream publications. Seeking a collaborative medium and an alternate venue for her work, Jordan wrote and produced several plays, including *In the Spirit of* SOJOURNER TRUTH (1979) and *For the Arrow that Flies by Day* (1981), and a guide to writing and teaching poetry titled *June Jordan's Poetry for the People: A Revolutionary Blueprint* (1995).

At the core of these works Jordan battles injustice, repression, and oppression. "She is the bravest of us, the most outraged," ALICE WALKER contends. "She feels for all. She is the universal poet." From Oakland, California, to the Middle East and from

Nicaragua to South Africa, Jordan's work advocates for women, the poor, and the disenfranchised. According to TONI MORRISON, Jordan's career was shaped by "forty years of tireless activism coupled with and fuelled by flawless art" (*Guardian*, 20 June 2002). Affirmative action, war crimes in the Balkans, the situation of women in Afghanistan, black women's health, Palestinian rights—each of these topics and hundreds more made their way into Jordan's work and classroom. ISHMAEL REED characterizes Jordan's poetry as "straightforward, unadorned, in-your-face" (*San Francisco Chronicle*, 27 June 2002). This unflinching directness, always brave and sometimes heavy-handed, is exemplified by "Poem about Police Brutality":

Tell me something
what you think would happen if
everytime they kill a black boy
then we kill a cop
everytime they kill a black man
Then we kill a cop
you think the accident rate would lower
subsequently?

Autobiographical and interdisciplinary, Jordan's work chronicles a life intent on breaking down the barriers between poetry and prose, between politics and art, and between the personal and the political. Jordan resisted being labeled and pigeonholed with regard to her writing, her politics, or her sexuality. For Jordan, who was openly bisexual, each element of life and work was part of a larger commitment to the principles of freedom and equality. "If you are free, you are not predictable and you are not controllable," she wrote in the *Progressive*.

Petite, warm, and elegant, yet tough, tenacious, and controversial, Jordan had a distinctive laugh and a sardonic sense of humor. She was a dramatic and charismatic reader who presented her work at the United Nations and the U.S. Congress, at innumerable colleges and universities, and on radio, television, and film. A resolute political activist, she served on the executive board of the Center for Constitutional Rights and the Nicaraguan Culture Alliance. Jordan was the recipient of many fellowships, honors, and awards, including a Rockefeller grant in 1969; a PEN Center USA West Freedom to Write Award in 1991; and two journalism awards, one for international reporting from the National Association of Black Journalists in 1984 and a lifetime achievement award from the National Black Writers' Conference in 1988. A three-year award from the Lila Wallace–Reader's Digest Fund facilitated the expansion of the Poetry for the People program and the completion of several writing projects, among them Jordan's 1995 libretto for the opera director Peter Sellers, *I Was Looking at the Ceiling and Then I Saw the Sky*, and her poetry collection, *Kissing God Goodbye: Poems 1991–1997* (1997).

Jordan's last book, *Some of Us Did Not Die: New and Selected Essays of June Jordan* (2002), was published posthumously and includes pieces from two earlier volumes, *Affirmative Acts: Political Essays* (1998) and *Technical Difficulties: African American Notes on the State of the Union* (1992), along with new essays on Islam, the terrorist events of 11 September 2001, and her experience of having been raped twice. June Jordan died of breast cancer at her home in Berkeley, California, in June 2002.

FURTHER READING

The June Jordan Papers are located at the Schlesinger Library, Radcliffe College, Harvard University, Cambridge, Massachusetts.

Jordan, June. *Soldier: A Poet's Childhood* (2001).

Quiroz, Julie. "Poetry Is a Political Act: An Interview with June Jordan," *Colorlines* (Winter 1999).

Obituaries: *New York Times*, 18 June 2002; *Los Angeles Times*, 20 June 2002.

LISA E. RIVO

Jordan, Louis (8 July 1908–4 Feb. 1975), jazz musician, was born in Brinkley, Arkansas, the son of Jimmy Jordan, a bandleader and music teacher, and Lizzia Read. Louis was taught both clarinet and saxophone by his father, and while still in high school, he performed with his father's band, the Rabbit Foot Minstrels. Jordan's professional career began in 1929 with Jimmy Pryor's Imperial Serenaders. From 1930 to 1936 he performed with various bands, playing alto and soprano saxophones and occasionally singing. While in Arkansas he also worked with Ruby Williams between 1930 and 1936.

Jordan moved to Philadelphia, Pennsylvania, in 1932 and became a sideman in the band of the tuba player Jim Winters. Between 1933 and 1938 Jordan performed with Charlie Gaines (1933–1935), Leroy Smith (1935–1936), and CHICK WEBB (1936–1938), and he had brief stints with FATS WALLER and Tyler Marshall before forming the Tympany Five in 1938. The Tympany Five appeared in several films, including *Follow the Boys* (1944), *Meet Miss Bobby Sox* (1944), *Beware* (1946), *Swing Parade of 1946* (1946), *Reet, Petite and Gone* (1947), and *Look Out Sister* (1948). The group, which played a combination of rhythm and blues and jazz, achieved

Louis Jordan, jazz saxophonist, at the Paramount Theater in New York City, c. July 1946. (© William P. Gottlieb; www.jazzphotos.com.)

immense popularity throughout the 1940s. Jordan's role included his swinging alto saxophone style, his blues-inflected vocal style, and his engaging sense of humor. On his wide-ranging vocals he would croon and scat sing, with his lyrics occasionally focusing on problems confronting African Americans.

The Tympany Five recorded with Decca from 1939 to 1955. During this tenure Jordan produced more than two dozen recordings, many becoming hits, including "Five Guys Named Moe" (1943), "Is You Is or Is You Ain't My Baby" (1943)—which sold more than 1 million copies—"Buzz Me" (1945), "Caldonia" (1945), *Louis Jordan and His Tympany Five* (1945), "My Baby Said Yes" (1945; with Bing Crosby), "Beware" (1946), "Choo Choo Ch'Boogie" (1946), "Ain't That Just Like a Woman" (1946), "Let the Good Times Roll" (1946), "Open the Door Richard" (1947), "Baby It's Cold Outside" (1948; with ELLA FITZGERALD), "GI Jive" (1948), and "Saturday Night Fish Fry" (1949). Between 1942 and 1951 Jordan had fifty-seven singles released, fifty-five of which made the top ten on rhythm and blues charts. It was also during this period that he transformed African American popular music

by demonstrating that a big band could be paired down into a combo without losing its power.

After the breakup of the Tympany Five, Jordan signed as a soloist with Mercury. To capitalize on the fame that he achieved with Decca, Mercury had him rerecord some of his old hits, including "Caldonia," "I'm Gonna Move to the Outskirts of Town," "Is You Is or Is You Ain't My Baby," "Let the Good Times Roll," and "Choo Choo Ch'Boogie." To compensate for the end of the Tympany Five, Mercury hired QUINCY JONES to do the arrangements and hired sidemen such as Jimmy Cleveland, BUDD JOHNSON, Ernie Royal, and Sam "the Man" Taylor as accompanists. In 1951 Jordan organized a big band with which he recorded *Silver Star Series Presents Louis Jordan & His Orchestra* and toured for a couple of years. He also recorded with LOUIS ARMSTRONG, Bing Crosby, and Fitzgerald during the 1950s. Jordan moved to Phoenix, Arizona, in the early 1950s because of health problems, and then he moved to Los Angeles. From the early 1960s to 1968 he toured England, recorded a single low-sale album with Tangerine Records in 1964, and toured Asia in both 1967 and 1968.

Jordan returned to the big band format in 1968, recording the album *Santa Claus, Santa Claus/ Sakatumi* on his newly formed label, PZAZZ, with arranging and conducting by Teddy Edwards. He also recorded *Louis Jordan Swings* with the Chris Barber Band in the 1960s. His career experienced a revival with the help of a 1974 recording by the British pop musician Joe Jackson. The album, *Great Rhythm and Blues Oldies, Vol. 1*, introduced a new music generation to Jordan's style. After Jordan died in Los Angeles, this musical renaissance continued without him, when Jackson recorded *Jumpin' Five* in 1981, reviving songs by artists such as CAB CALLOWAY, King Pleasure, and Armstrong. Other groups, notably the Chevalier Brothers, Ian Stewart's Rocket 88, and the Big Town Playboys, carried Jordan's influence into the 1980s with covers of his music. Jordan's compositions also were recorded by CHUCK BERRY, B. B. KING, RAY CHARLES, FATS DOMINO, and LITTLE RICHARD. Both NAT KING COLE and DIZZY GILLESPIE admired Jordan for his inventiveness. Jordan's style, though rooted in blues and jazz, featured strong rhythms that drew on ballads, boogie-woogie, calypso, jump blues instrumentals and vocals, and rhumbas. Comedy and showmanship were integral to the way in which he performed; satirical lyrics were even aimed at the social and political ills to which African Americans were vulnerable. Charles and Berry, among others, noted Jordan's role as a pioneer of rock and roll, exemplified by the boogie beat on Bill Haley's "Rock around the Clock." Jordan was one of the most creative artists in the history of American popular music.

FURTHER READING

Chilton, John. *Let the Good Times Roll: The Story of Louis Jordan and His Music* (1992).

Shaw, Arnold. *Honkers and Shouters: The Golden Years of Rhythm and Blues* (1978).

Obituary: *New York Times*, 6 Feb. 1975.

This entry is taken from the *American National Biography* and is published here with the permission of the American Council of Learned Societies.

EDDIE S. MEADOWS

Jordan, Michael (17 Feb. 1963–), basketball player, was born Michael Jeffrey Jordan in Brooklyn, New York, the fourth of five children of James Jordan and Deloris Peoples. The family soon relocated to Wilmington in the parents' home state, North Carolina, where Jordan's father rose to supervisor in a General Electric plant and his mother worked as a bank teller. James Jordan's air force pension boosted the family into the middle class, and they instilled in their children a solid work ethic with an emphasis on loyalty and commitment.

Like his brothers and sisters, Jordan was a relatively short child—but exceptionally quick. He preferred baseball to basketball and pitched several no-hitters in Little League. Although he was initially a lazy child who bribed his siblings to do his chores, Jordan was invigorated by athletic competition. Regular one-on-one basketball games against his older brother Larry fueled a fiery competitiveness in him, since Larry was acknowledged to be more talented. When Michael entered Laney Wilmington High School in 1979 he was five feet eight inches tall and determined to play varsity basketball. Following a year on the freshman team, the varsity coaches encouraged him to try out as a sophomore and then cut him. He was devastated, cried in his bedroom that afternoon, and then averaged twenty-five points per game on the junior varsity team. He made varsity the next year, grew to six feet two inches tall, and during his senior season at Laney, Jordan led the Buccaneers to a 19-4 record before matriculating at Chapel Hill in the fall of 1981. He had previously earned an invitation to summer camps at the University of North Carolina at Chapel Hill and the prestigious Five-Star Camp in Pittsburgh. At Chapel Hill he got his first exposure to "the system," Coach Dean Smith's storied method of running a high-caliber basketball program; Smith and his assistants were immediately impressed not only with Jordan's athleticism but also with his determination to sneak into scrimmages when it was not his turn. Much of Smith's system involved teaching teamwork and humility. Although Jordan became increasingly cocky about his abilities, the system was the perfect antidote for his good-natured though occasionally abrasive attitude. The Tar Heel upperclassmen did not appreciate the fast-talking, bright-eyed freshman who detailed how he would dunk on them in practice—and they harbored no small amount of spite when he quickly made good on his word. But they could take some solace in seeing Jordan fetch loose balls during practice and lug the film projector on road trips—and in winning more games. The Tar Heels went 32-2 and won the Atlantic Coast Conference tournament; a few weeks later, Jordan hit a seventeen-foot jumper to clinch the National Collegiate Athletic Association championship. At his full height of six feet six inches, Jordan won Player of the Year honors for the next two seasons; after consulting his parents and Smith, he bypassed his senior year to enter the National Basketball Association (NBA) draft. In the interim, Jordan led the U.S. basketball team to the 1984 Olympic gold medal.

The ailing Chicago Bulls signed Jordan for five years at $800,000 per year. During his first two seasons Jordan became a phenomenon, boosting the Bulls' ticket sales by almost 90 percent and triggering a similar spike in attendance at road games. He played all eighty-two games and averaged 28.2 points, almost six assists, and more than six rebounds per contest, securing Rookie of the Year honors. During All-Star weekend, Jordan competed for the first time in the popular Slam Dunk Contest. Donning a gold chain and his trademark baggy shorts (which allowed him to wear his North Carolina shorts underneath), Jordan electrified the crowd with a combination of tremendous leaping ability and graceful aerial control.

Early in the 1985–1986 campaign, Jordan broke his foot. Doctors advised him to sacrifice the rest of the season for treatment, but he returned with more than a dozen games remaining and drove the Bulls into the play-offs against the powerful Boston Celtics. Although the Celtics swept the Bulls, Jordan averaged 43.7 points for the series, scoring a record 63 in the second game, and prompted the Celtic star Larry Bird to quip that he had played against "God disguised as Michael Jordan."

Jordan's dramatic performances—such as scoring more than fifty points in eight separate games during the 1986–1987 season—catapulted him into the NBA's highest echelon, and he signed lucrative endorsement deals for Wheaties cereal, McDonald's restaurants, and, most important, Nike sportswear. These companies quickly realized that Jordan's gracious public persona and clean-cut looks transcended the potential obstacle of his skin color; teenagers and children of all classes and races idolized him. Jordan hence became a crucial figure in the escalation of sports marketing into a multibillion-dollar industry. The only compensation he wanted when he originally signed with Nike was a car; in 1987 his contract guaranteed him $18 million over seven years, plus royalties from such products as the Air Jordan basketball shoe, thought to be more than $20 million per year by the mid-1990s. In 1998 *Forbes* magazine estimated that Jordan had generated more than $10 billion in overall revenue for the NBA during his career.

The quintessential slow-motion image of Jordan came from the clinching dunk in the 1987 Slam Dunk Contest. Jordan ran from beyond half-court, leaped from the free-throw line, and glided through the air in a seemingly effortless manner—lifting the ball and then lowering it, contracting his legs and then spreading and extending them—finally dunking the ball fifteen feet later. His rumored forty-four-inch vertical leap was impressive, though by no means unprecedented; the mythical quality of his dunks derived more from the way he seemed to hang in midair as if through sheer will. Primarily known for his offensive abilities, Jordan relied on his defense to catalyze the rest of his game; crowds would anxiously anticipate the inevitable moment when he would intercept a pass, streak downcourt, and take flight for a beautifully thunderous dunk.

Despite regular appearances in television and print advertisements, as well as his 1989 marriage to Juanita Vanoy (with whom he had three children), Jordan did not allow any distractions to hinder his and the Bulls' steady progress. For a half dozen seasons, Jordan had systematically improved every area of his game, becoming one of the most versatile players in the history of basketball. In 1988 Jordan won the first of five Most Valuable Player awards, as well as Defensive Player of the Year, becoming the first to win both in a single season. He would lead the NBA in scoring for ten seasons and was selected for the All-Defensive Team a record nine times. Originally considered a player who slashed toward the hoop and fired the occasional midrange jump shot, Jordan developed a deadly post game and extended his

Michael Jordan of the Chicago Bulls dunks during the slam-dunk competition at the NBA All-Star weekend in Chicago, Illinois, 6 February 1988. Jordan narrowly won the competition, edging out Dominique Wilkins of the Atlantic Hawks on the final dunk. He would go on to lead the Bulls to six championships in eight years during the 1990s, helping cement his status as the greatest basketball player of all time. (AP Images.)

shooting range, increasing his three-point percentage by .100 to .376 in 1990. The determination reflected in these accomplishments appeared finally to inspire his teammates, and the Bulls defeated MAGIC JOHNSON's Los Angeles Lakers for the 1991 NBA championship.

Later that year a Chicago sportswriter published *The Jordan Rules*, an exposé of the Bulls' championship season, which portrayed Jordan as being mean-spirited toward his teammates in order to elicit better play. Nevertheless, the Bulls won their second championship in 1992, and Jordan and his teammate Scottie Pippen traveled to Barcelona, Spain, to play on the first U.S. Olympic basketball team to include professional players. This Dream Team won the gold medal with unprecedented ease.

As the Bulls hurtled toward their third consecutive championship in 1993, hints surfaced that Jordan routinely gambled enormous sums of money. A year earlier Jordan had weathered the first of such murmurings when a murdered man was found in possession of three checks, all written by Jordan and totaling $108,000, one of them made out to a convicted cocaine dealer. Jordan claimed the checks were gambling debts from golfing, a longtime hobby. When another purported gambling golfer asserted that Jordan owed him more than $1 million, an NBA investigation ensued. Jordan was absolved of any violation, and on the heels of winning a third consecutive NBA title that spring, he decided to retire.

He was not, however, retiring from sports altogether; in 1994 he signed a free-agency baseball contract with the Chicago White Sox. The previous August, his father, James Jordan, had been found murdered in his car, and many reporters interpreted Jordan's actions as a means of realizing the childhood dreams he had shared with his father of someday playing major league baseball. After one lackluster season in Chicago's farm system with the AA Birmingham Barons (Jordan batted .202), and with a strike imminent for the 1995 baseball season, Jordan decided to rejoin the Bulls. He played a handful of games in the regular season and averaged more than thirty points in the play-offs before the Bulls lost in the second round. Again motivated by the sour taste of losing, he embarked upon a strict training regimen and bolstered his offensive arsenal with a fade-away jumper that he fired with amazing precision and that was nearly impossible to block.

The Bulls marched to three more consecutive NBA championships from 1996 to 1998, and Jordan never missed a game. His play-off performances were particularly memorable, as he continued to exhibit an uncanny ability to elevate his play during especially tense situations. He started every play-off game of his career, played more minutes in each game than in the regular season, grabbed more rebounds, gave more assists, and averaged 33.4 points per game—three points above his career regular season average. In the 1997 finals against the Utah Jazz, Jordan had a fever of one hundred degrees and severe nausea before the fifth game. But he scored thirty-eight points—fifteen in the final period—and the Bulls came from behind to win. The next year Jordan sparked another comeback and made the series-clinching shot from twenty feet away to win his final championship.

The next season, after an NBA labor dispute was settled in January 1999, Jordan again retired, cagily asserting that he was "99.9 percent certain" he was retiring permanently. He assumed an executive position with the Washington Wizards a year later. In November 2001 Jordan once again took to the court, playing for the Wizards against the New York Knicks. Jordan had a chance to tie the game with a three-point shot in the waning seconds, but he missed. Although he averaged more than twenty points with Washington and was twice voted to the All-Star team, the Wizards failed to make the play-offs both seasons.

In April 2003 Jordan was summarily dismissed from the Wizards' front office. After a short break from basketball, Jordan returned in 2006 as part owner of the Charlotte Bobcats. In 2009, he was inducted into the Basketball Hall of Fame. With his obsessive drive for personal success, Michael Jordan established himself as the most influential African American in athletics since MUHAMMAD ALI. Both men were unparalleled masters of their respective crafts; where Ali's career brought energy and a sense of pride to blacks during the civil rights era, Jordan's avoided politics but brought the world of sports to Wall Street.

FURTHER READING

Jordan, Michael. *For Love of the Game: My Story* (1998).

Greene, Bob. *Rebound: The Odyssey of Michael Jordan* (1995).

Halberstam, David. *Playing for Keeps: Michael Jordan and the World He Made* (1999).

Krugel, Mitchell. *One Last Shot: The Story of Michael Jordan's Comeback* (2002).

LaFeber, Walter. *Michael Jordan and the New Global Capitalism* (1999).

Patton, Jim. *Rookie: When Michael Jordan Came to the Minor Leagues* (1995).

DAVID F. SMYDRA JR.

Jordan, Vernon (8 Aug. 1935–), lawyer, civil rights leader, and corporate executive, was born Vernon Eulion Jordan Jr. in Atlanta, the eldest of two sons of Vernon Jordan Sr., a postal clerk at Fort McPherson, Georgia, and Mary Belle Griggs, proprietor of a catering business, who had a child from a previous union. Jordan was descended from Georgia sharecroppers who had their roots in slavery. His maternal grandfather told young Vernon, "If I could have anything in the world, I'd want to be able to go to the bathroom indoors, in a warm place, one time before I die" (Jordan, 23).

Until the age of thirteen Jordan lived in Atlanta's University Homes, the first public housing for black people built in the United States. His "project," as such low-income structures would come to be known, derived its name from the black college campuses that surrounded it and provided an abundance of positive role models for the residents. Jordan's success in school was strongly encouraged by his mother, who became president of the PTA at every school he attended from elementary to high school. As an adult, his tall, athletic build greatly contributed to his distinguished presence, but as a young boy, his dark complexion was not viewed so favorably; even his diligence was mockingly seen as "acting white," rather than as being black and highly motivated.

Jordan graduated from high school with honors in 1953 and opted to attend DePauw University in Greencastle, Indiana, where there were only four other black students and no black women. In retrospect he wrote that "never once in my youth did I go to a school with enough resources to help its students compete on an equal basis with the average white student" (Jordan, 47). Yet Jordan persevered in his studies at DePauw and won several public-speaking contests.

Given his deep faith and exceptional oratorical skills, Jordan seriously considered entering the ministry, but his mother, a devout member of the African Methodist Episcopal (AME) Church, would not hear of it. Instead, Jordan entered Howard University Law School in 1957 and spent his summers driving a bus for the Chicago Transit Authority to augment his finances. After his parents' divorce in 1958, Jordan decided to secure his relationship with Shirley Yarbrough, who had graduated from Howard the year before and returned to Atlanta, where she worked as a caseworker. The two were married during Jordan's second year in law school but continued to live in separate cities until Jordan received his J.D. degree in 1960 and relocated to Atlanta to be with his wife and infant daughter, Vickee.

Back in Atlanta, Jordan became a law clerk for the civil rights attorney Donald Hollowell and was paid the lowly sum of thirty-five dollars a week. Together they fought discrimination cases, defended death-row prisoners, and won a landmark decision in *Holmes v. Danner* that allowed CHARLAYNE HUNTER GAULT and HAMILTON HOLMES to become the first black students to attend the University of Georgia in 1961. Within a few months of this victory, Jordan came to the attention of the leadership of the National Association for the Advancement of Colored People (NAACP), who appointed him field director for the state of Georgia. In this position he set a new recruitment record; led a seven-month boycott in Augusta, Georgia, against discriminatory businesses; and became a colleague of A. LEON HIGGINBOTHAM, THURGOOD MARSHALL, ROY WILKINS, and MEDGAR EVERS, his counterpart in Mississippi.

In 1964 Jordan was recruited by the Southern Regional Council, the oldest interracial organization in the South, where he became the executive assistant and the director of the Voter Education Project. In these positions Jordan began to cultivate his legendary skills as a behind-the-scenes negotiator as he distributed funds to organizations such as the Southern Christian Leadership Conference (SCLC), Congress of Racial Equality (CORE), Student Nonviolent Coordinating Committee (SNCC), and the NAACP. As his reputation grew, invitations and opportunities multiplied. In 1965 he attended his first meeting at the White House when President Lyndon Johnson named him to serve along with MARTIN LUTHER KING JR., DOROTHY HEIGHT, and JOHN LEWIS on the White House Council to Fulfill These Rights. He also served on the Presidential Advisory Commission on Selective Service during the Vietnam War and became the first African American to hold a teaching fellowship at Harvard University's John F. Kennedy School of Government, during the 1969–1970 academic year. Jordan acquired foreign-policy experience during his visit to Israel shortly before the Six-Day War, and he was part of an American delegation sent to discuss economic and cold war issues at the Bilderberg conference in Denmark in 1969. He later served on the Council on Foreign Relations and the Trilateral Commission. Jordan planned to run for Congress in 1970 from the Fifth District of Georgia, but shortly after making his announcement he was offered the directorship of the United Negro College Fund. In his first year at the helm of that organization, previous fund-raising levels were surpassed by more than $10 million. Then, on 9 March 1971, WHITNEY YOUNG, the leader of the National Urban League, tragically drowned while in Lagos, Nigeria. Although he was only thirty-six years old, Jordan became Young's successor. As president he restructured the organization; promoted a young staffer, RON BROWN, who would later head the Democratic National Committee and become secretary of commerce, to the newly created office of general counsel; and began issuing an annual report called *The State of Black America*.

During Jimmy Carter's administration, Jordan attempted to mend the rift between African

Vernon Jordan, just named Executive Director of the National Urban League, addresses a news conference in New York City on 15 June 1971. (AP Images.)

Americans and American Jews caused when ANDREW YOUNG, the U.S. ambassador to the United Nations, and JESSE JACKSON met with representatives of the Palestinian Liberation Organization. Some black leaders welcomed the schism as representing the independence of black leadership; Jordan countered by saying that rather than moving apart, both groups needed to affirm a "Declaration of Interdependence" (Jordan, 265). On 29 May 1980, in Fort Wayne, Indiana, Jordan was shot in the back by an assailant using a hunting rifle. He recovered after a long convalescence, and Joseph Paul Franklin, a white supremacist and serial killer, later confessed to the shooting. In 1982 Robert Strauss invited Jordan to become a partner in the law firm of Akin, Gump, Strauss, Hauer, and Feld. Jordan, who had been one of the first African Americans to serve on the boards of such corporations as Xerox, American Express, and the Rockefeller Foundation, left the Urban League to accept this position because he believed that he had reached a point in his career where he could open more doors by working in the private sector.

In 1986 Jordan's wife, Shirley, died after a twenty-year battle with multiple sclerosis. The following year he married Ann Dibble Cook, a professor at the University of Chicago. In 1992 Jordan, who had known Bill and Hillary Clinton for two decades, became chairman of the transition team for President-elect Clinton. Jordan declined to be considered for the position of attorney general, but he actively coaxed COLIN POWELL and others into the administration. His role in securing employment for Webster Hubbell and Monica Lewinsky with Revlon Consumer Products Corporation, a company on whose board he served, brought his actions under harsh scrutiny during the wide-ranging Whitewater investigations of President Clinton's financial and personal affairs. Jordan subsequently took a position as senior managing director at the investment bank Lazard Frères. In 2006 he was appointed to the bipartisan Iraq Study Group.

Jordan's accomplishments in the public sector, in the corporate world, and as a Washington powerbroker firmly established him as a major player in the high-stakes game of power and politics.

FURTHER READING

Jordan, Vernon E. *Vernon Can Read!* (2001).

Current Biography (1993).

Gerth, Jeff. "Being Intimate with Power, Vernon Jordan Can Wield It," *New York Times*, 14 July 1996.

SHOLOMO B. LEVY

Joseph, Allison (18 Jan. 1967–), poet, university professor, and editor, was born Allison Elaine Joseph, in London, England, one of two children of Adella Dawkins, a nurse, and Everest Joseph, a nurse, electrician, and salesman, both of African Caribbean heritage. When Joseph was four months old, her family left London for Toronto, Canada, where they lived only briefly. In 1971 the family moved to the Bronx, New York, where Joseph spent the majority of her childhood. During her elementary school years, New York's Poets in the Schools program helped to cultivate her passion for writing. She then completed her secondary education at the Bronx High School of Science, graduating in 1984. Her childhood in the Bronx and her years at this high school allowed Joseph the opportunity to meet friends of diverse racial and socioeconomic backgrounds and provided for rich cultural experiences and lessons that would later influence her work.

After high school, her parents encouraged her to pursue a career in medicine, but Joseph was more interested in literary studies. She chose to attend Kenyon College, in Gambier, Ohio, because of its literary reputation, and embarked for college in 1984. Her arrival at this Midwestern college, where she was one of three black students in her freshman class, presented a bit of a culture shock for Joseph after her experiences in such a diverse city and high school. Despite her disappointment in the realization that Kenyon's literary tradition was largely white and male, Joseph embraced her studies there, and she emerged as a talented poet among her peers. When one of her poetry teachers expressed an interest in publishing her work in the school's literary journal, the *Kenyon Review*, Joseph became the only undergraduate student since Robert Lowell to have work published in this distinguished journal.

After graduating from Kenyon in 1988, with a B.A. in English and History, Joseph entered the MFA program at Indiana University in Bloomington. She earned her MFA in Creative Writing from Indiana in 1992. That same year Ampersand Press published her master's thesis, a collection of poetry entitled *What Keeps Us Here*. This first book deals primarily with her mother's struggle with cancer and is dedicated to her mother, who died during Joseph's sophomore year of college. She was awarded the John C. Zacharis First Book Prize and the Ampersand Press Women Poets Series Prize for this first collection. The training she received at Indiana was most significant in her development as a poet, and she flourished under the guidance of teacher and Pulitzer Prize–winning poet YUSEF KOMUNYAKAA, as well as under the encouragement of Maura Stanton and David Wojahn. While at Indiana she also served as associate editor and editor of the *Indiana Review*. Joseph met fellow poet Jon Tribble in their poetry workshops at Indiana, and the two were married in 1991.

Joseph began her teaching career at the University of Little Rock–Arkansas in 1992 before moving to Southern Illinois University Carbondale (SIUC), where she became an associate professor of creative writing under the Judge Williams Holmes Cook Endowed Professorship. She taught fiction writing, but primarily concentrated on teaching poetry at SIUC; she also edited the school's international literary journal, the *Crab Orchid Review*. In 1999 Joseph founded the Young Writer's Workshop at SIUC, an annual summer creative writing workshop for high school writers, seeing this project as an important opportunity to reach young writers at a crucial point and help them stay interested in writing throughout their lives.

In addition to *What Keeps Us Here*, Joseph is the author of four collections of poetry: *Soul Train* (1997), *In Every Seam* (1997), *Imitation of Life* (2003), and *Worldly Pleasures* (2004). Joseph is the recipient of numerous accolades, including an Illinois Arts Council Fellowship in Poetry; the Stanley P. Young Fellowship from the Bread Loaf Writer's Conference; the Tennessee Williams scholarship from the Sewanee Writers Conferences; and the World Press Poetry Prize for *Worldly Pleasures*.

Joseph finds the work of African American female writers most compelling, as "they are people who open up the trails for others" (Hamilton, 466). She is especially drawn to the work of the poet GWENDOLYN BROOKS, from whom she learned the importance of writing about that which is most familiar; that "you don't have to write about Mount Olympus. You can write about your neighborhood— what's happening on the corner" (Davis). This influence is apparent in many of Joseph's poems, which depict the experiences of African American girls growing up in an urban environment, revisiting episodes such as a Saturday afternoon in a beauty shop or the pains of adolescent gym class. Much of her work looks "at childhood events, to reveal what truths, challenges, and rewards a black girl finds in urban America as she grows to womanhood" (Balingit, *Magill Book Reviews*, 1 Nov. 1998). Joseph also counts writers as diverse as Sharon Olds, James Wright, Richard Hugo, and Dorothy Parker as important influences. She claims that in her work, she "always seeks to be a representative of my age, my race, and my gender" (Merrifield) and as such, Joseph's work continues along the trail that poets such as Gwendolyn Brooks helped to open for African American female poets.

FURTHER READING

Davis, Marilyn. "Unblinking," *Perspectives: Research and Creative Activities at Southern Illinois University-Carbondale* (Spring 2003). Available at http://www.siu.edu/%7Eperspect/03_sp/joseph.html

Hamilton, Kendra. "An Interview with Allison Joseph," in *Callaloo: Emerging Women Writers: A Special Issue* 19, no. 2 (Spring 1996).

Merrifield, Jennifer. "An Interview with Allison Joseph," in *Blackbird: An Online Journal of Literature and the Arts* 4, no.2 (Fall 2005). Available at http://www.blackbird.vcu.edu/v4n2/features/joseph_a_011306/joseph_a_text.htm.

CASEY KAYSER

Josey, E. J. (20 Jan. 1924–3 July 2009), librarian, was born Elonnie Junius Josey in Norfolk, Virginia, the son of Willie and Frances Josey. The eldest of five children, Josey attended a segregated school in Port Smith, Virginia. After studying the organ at the Hampton Institute, Josey attended Howard University's School of Music. Graduating with a bachelor's degree in 1949, he then went to Columbia University in New York and earned a master's degree in history. Unable to obtain a teaching job following graduation, Josey worked as a desk assistant in the Columbia University libraries. He developed a strong interest in libraries while working there and decided to pursue a master's degree in library science from the State University of New York at Albany.

Josey's first position was as a librarian in the Central Library of the Free Library of Philadelphia from 1953 to 1954. In 1954 Josey accepted a teaching position as an instructor in history and social science at Savannah State College in Savannah, Georgia. The following year he returned to librarianship as a librarian at Delaware State College in Dover, where he was also an assistant professor. In 1959 Josey returned to Savannah State College as a chief librarian and began his crusade to eradicate racial discrimination in the library profession.

Although the American Library Association (ALA) had allowed blacks in its membership for many years, state library associations remained segregated until 1954 when the Association approved the idea of a single affiliated library association in each state. Alabama, Georgia, Louisiana, and Mississippi continued to restrict membership to whites only. Josey was influential in the ALA's adoption of a resolution in 1962 declaring that state library associations must integrate or be denied national affiliation. He was elected the first black librarian member of the Georgia Library Association in 1965.

As an associate professor at Savannah State College, Josey was also active in civil liberties and intellectual pursuits at the institutional level. He was the faculty adviser for the first NAACP chapter established at a state-supported college in the South. He also served as the debate coach and leader of the Great Books Discussion Group. Under his leadership, the Savannah State College Library received the 1962 and 1964 John Cotton Dana awards for outstanding library public relations projects.

In 1966 Josey left Savannah State College for Albany, New York, to work in the Bureau of Academic and Research Libraries at the New York State Library. He started his career with the Division of Library Development and was promoted to chief of the bureau in 1968. As an administrator, he coordinated the development and improvement of cooperative services for the 216 academic libraries in the state of New York. Following the reorganization of the bureau in the 1970s, the scope of Josey's job was broadened to encompass all types of libraries in the state. He was instrumental in developing a coordinated state reference and resource library system to assist research and university scholars. Josey also helped to implement the statewide interlibrary loan program that was still widely used in 2007. In an article in *Ebony* in 1985, he summarized his career as "just happy to bring books and people together" (130).

During the 1970s Josey served as the chief advocate for the advancement of blacks and other minorities in the field of librarianship. He edited the book *The Black Librarian in America* (1970), which was the first to deal with the subject of black librarianship. At the 1970 conference of the American Library Association, he arranged the meeting of a group of black librarians that led to the formation of the Black Caucus. The aim of the group was to prepare a program for action to address the needs and concerns of black librarians. The "Statement of Concern" asserted that "black librarians are especially concerned about the effects of institutional racism, poverty, the continued lack of educational, employment, and promotional opportunities upon blacks and other minorities.... The library profession has been slow in responding to these problems" (Berry, 995–996). Josey was named the first chairman of the caucus.

The Black Caucus was active in helping blacks gain greater access to positions in the ALA and also emphasized issues and policies related to minorities. Josey's article "Coding Segregation" in the May 1971 issue of *School Library Journal* presented the findings of a joint study of the Black Caucus and NAACP regarding library services in private schools established to avoid desegregation. In 1971 the Council of the American Library Association adopted a resolution that opposed the creation of private schools that interfered with desegregation.

Through his work with the Black Caucus and the American Library Association Council, Josey became a prominent figure and boosted the status of black librarians within the ALA. His second edited work, *What Black Librarians Are Saying* (1972), filled the void of information on black librarians' views of society and librarianship. Josey also served as editor for other significant works on librarianship, including *New Dimensions for Academic Library Service* (1975) and *Handbook of Black Librarianship* (1977). Regarding the *Handbook*, one reviewer praised Josey and co-editor ANN ALLEN SHOCKLEY for "a landmark in library literature.... Even as it chronicles the involvement of America's largest minority group with books, libraries, and librarianship, it provides a wealth of hitherto obscure or uncompiled data on people, events, and resources" (Biddle, pp. 229, 251).

Josey was also prominent in the community of Albany, New York, serving as president of the local chapter of the NAACP from 1982 until 1986. Josey advocated for better living conditions and quality of education for communities of color. During his tenure, the NAACP chapter maintained a high visibility in the community as a result of its criticism that the proportion of African Americans employed by the city government was well below the city's 16 percent minority population. Josey also criticized the school district for being insensitive to minorities, especially for policies that labeled minorities as poor scholars and steered them toward vocational programs instead of academic programs. He received outstanding service awards from the local chapter in 1983 and 1986. In 1983 Josey was elected president of the American Library Association. He was the second black to be chosen for the position, Clara Stanton Jones being the first, following her inauguration in 1976. He chose "Forging Coalitions for the Public Good" as the theme for his presidency because of the disturbing trend of libraries beginning to charge fees for services, owing to budget cuts. He believed that working with other organizations that have similar responsibilities and goals to serve the public good would shed light on the effect of economics on the nature of library service. Moreover, Josey stated in his inauguration speech that by

working for the public good through coalitions representing large segments of the American people, we are directly pursuing three of ALA's priorities: access to information, legislation and funding, and public awareness—and indirectly serving the cause of intellectual freedom (Josey, 355).

During his presidency Josey established a program to educate libraries about efforts to state the case for supporting public goods, like libraries, through taxes rather than fees that undermine unlimited access to information. Josey also increased his advocacy efforts for services to minorities and the appointment of minorities to key leadership positions within the ALA. He established the President's Committee on Library Services to Minorities to study the disparities between libraries in minority and poor communities and libraries in white and affluent communities. Josey also led a delegation of approximately one hundred black librarians to the International Federation of Library Associations and Institutions (IFLA) Conference in Kenya (the first to be held in Africa) to convene the International African Librarians Seminar.

In 1986 Josey left the New York State Library to join the teaching faculty at the University of Pittsburgh School of Library and Information Sciences. As a teacher he made a strong effort to increase minority enrollment at the school. He retired from teaching in 1995 to pursue writing and research.

As a librarian, educator, and civil rights activist, Josey played a central role in attracting the attention of librarians and policy makers to the issue of library services for minorities. The Black Caucus of the American Library Association became an established institution to support African Americans and the communities they serve. In 1980 Josey was awarded the Joseph W. Lippincott Award for distinguished Service to the American Library Association. The citation praised Josey for giving "new strength, unity, purpose, and hope to many minorities of our profession." Josey continued to be a strong advocate for recruiting minorities into librarianship, as well as a mentor for many librarians, of all races. The Black Caucus of the American Library Association established the E. J. Josey Scholarship Award to be given annually to an African American citizen of Canada or the U.S. who is pursuing an accredited Master's of Library Science. Josey summarized his accomplishments in an interview in *American Libraries:* "While I began my fight for African Americans, I think that people who know me best will also say that I fought for all people who were disadvantaged, including minorities and women, not only in our profession but throughout the world" (Kniffel, 80–82). Josey died in Washington, NC at the age of 85.

FURTHER READING

Josey, E. J. *The Black Librarian in America Revisited* (1994).

Abdullahi, Ismail, ed. *E. J. Josey: An Activist Librarian* (1992).

"A Man Who Goes by the Books." *Ebony* 43 (July 1985).

Berry, John, III. "The Activism Gap," *Library Journal* 95 (Mar. 1970).

Biddle, Stanton. "Handbook of Black Librarianship," *Journal of Academic Librarianship* 4.4 (1978).

Kniffel, Leonard. "To Be Black and a Librarian: Talking with E. J. Josey," *American Libraries* (Jan. 2000).

Nicholas, Patti. "E. J. Josey," in *Contemporary Black Biography*, vol. 10, ed. L. Mpho Mabunda (1996).

Obituary: *Library Journal.* 6 July 2009.

MARK L. MCCALLON

Josey, J. Anthony (6 Jan. 1876–7 July 1957), journalist and activist, was born Jarius Anthony Josey to Anthony Josey and Patience (maiden name not known) in Augusta, Georgia. After completing high school there, Josey moved to Atlanta, where he coedited the *Atlanta Independent*, graduated from Atlanta University, and, in 1905, married Chestena M. Carmichael. They had migrated to the Midwest by 1910, when he attended the University of Wisconsin Law School in Madison for two years—which made them a rare couple of color in Madison, at a time when the census reported fewer than one thousand

African Americans even in their largest community in the state, in Milwaukee (Trotter, 4, 98).

Wisconsin was the last state in the Midwest without a black press, not having one until the 1890s in Milwaukee, where several newspapers had foundered for lack of fiscal support owing to the minuscule size of the African American community and the regional dominance of Chicago and its black press—especially the *Chicago Defender*, after 1905, and its "Milwaukee page." No matter how well out-of-state newspapers served racial progress, none could report the story of their neighbors to the north as well as an indigenous press, and the repeated reliance of local readers on newspapers published elsewhere also reinforced perceptions that readers of color and their press were outsiders in Wisconsin—until Josey turned to journalism (McBride, 325–335).

Based in Madison, the *Wisconsin Weekly Blade* debuted on 8 June 1916 under coeditors Josey, L. J. Quisely, and Z. P. Smith. Only Josey endured, owing to his news judgment as editor and his business acumen as publisher. From the first issue he established fiscal stability by positioning the *Blade* as the press organ in both Illinois and Wisconsin for both the Order of Odd Fellows and the Household of Ruth, African American social organizations with thousands on lodge rolls. In 1917 Josey combined his journalism and activism, and increased his circulation, by calling a "Great Gathering of Representative Negroes of the State" to start another organization, a Cooperative Development and Progressive Association, whose members served as subscribers as well as correspondents to the *Blade*. Its coverage from elsewhere in the state competed with the *Milwaukee Enterprise*, also founded in 1916 by S. H. Lane, which Josey would buy out within a decade (McBride, 336).

Both papers were more militant than previous and accommodationist attempts at a black press in Wisconsin, but Josey's new brand of black-press journalism established his editorial dominance early in his career. The *Blade* broke from the past with "a strong attack on [BOOKER T.] WASHINGTON's legacy of leadership and philosophy" that placed Josey in the forefront of "the emergent 'New Negro' movement," according to historian Joe William Trotter, who called his ideology the "most articulate and consistent focus" among press competitors for decades to come (Trotter, 106).

Josey took a courageous stance in World War I in Wisconsin, a state with a significant German American population. He initially wrote that he hoped that his "readers would be rewarded by enlistment in the armed forces" in World War I, "even in segregated regiments or lower ranks" (*Wisconsin Weekly Blade*, 22 June 1918). However, Josey eventually joined other editors in arguing against enlistment by men of color. The prevailing sentiment was against him: the *Milwaukee Journal* won a Pulitzer Prize for a "loyalty crusade," and the federal government closed down the country's Socialist organ, the *Milwaukee Leader*, and prosecuted its publisher, a congressman, for crusading for neutrality (Glad, 49); and, in Chicago the government investigated the *Defender* for its editorial campaign against enlistment. Even W. E. B. DuBois in his *Crisis* writings urged wartime caution by his readers of color (Simmons, 38–39).

Josey's journalistic crusades came closer to home in 1918, when he editorialized against exclusion of African Americans from Milwaukee juries. He won that campaign in 1919 and took up another cause against the increasingly dominant local newspaper, the *Journal*, for racial markers in its headlines about crimes. The *Journal* issued a public apology that appeared in both the *Journal* and the *Blade* (*Wisconsin Weekly Blade*, 27 Feb. 1919, 5 June 1919), although the *Journal* continued the practice for decades. Josey found success sooner, in the l920s, upon organization of the Ku Klux Klan in Milwaukee, when Josey campaigned for the mayor to close municipal facilities to the local Klavern, a battle won in 1922 (Trotter, 138).

Josey dominated the black press in Wisconsin despite circulation wars with the ever-encroaching *Chicago Defender*, which only weakened the *Blade*'s sole local competitor, the *Milwaukee Enterprise*, a paper that increasingly published irregularly until Josey bought it out in 1925. He became sole editor and publisher of the *Wisconsin Enterprise-Blade*, although attorney George DeReef of Milwaukee, coeditor of the former *Enterprise*, continued as "contributing editor" (McBride, 338). Josey also moved the paper to Milwaukee, where he foresaw a better community base and business climate as national curtailment of European immigration increased the manufacturing city's African American population from 2,200 to more than 7,500 by the end of the decade. However, local labor union practices had more of a dampening effect upon black migration to Milwaukee in comparison with other northern cities, and the city suffered less racial conflict than some of its neighbors, although it would become among the most segregated in the country (Trotter, 39–44).

In the late 1920s Josey continued his journalistic crusades against segregation, no matter the target. He attacked the city's policy of assigning African American social workers and probation officers solely to a clientele of color (Trotter, 107) and opposed an Urban League social center open only to African Americans as a "first step to segregation or Jim Crow in Wisconsin" (*Wisconsin Enterprise-Blade*, 13 Feb. 1932). He especially campaigned for municipal services in his community amid increasingly crowded housing conditions, even prior to the Great Depression at the end of the decade (McBride, 338).

Josey had proclaimed his loyalty to the Republican Party from his first issue and never wavered, proudly asserting decades later that he had attended every Republican convention since 1906 (*Milwaukee Journal*, 13 Nov. 1948) and attacked President Franklin D. Roosevelt and his New Deal throughout the 1930s. However, opportunities for editorial opposition became less frequent by the 1940s as his *Enterprise-Blade*, rarely more than four pages per week and with few advertisements, began publishing irregularly. In World War II Josey intermittently waged editorial warfare on discrimination against defense workers on the home front and segregation of soldiers overseas. But he would lose his own battle for the *Enterprise-Blade* (McBride, 338).

Even at the end, in the early 1940s, his paper was pivotal in several political campaigns, from the failure of his community's first attempt to elect an African American alderman to the premature success of a candidate of color for the state legislature, who was unseated in a recount (Trotter, 211–214). In 1944 the community at last sent one of its own to the state legislature, but the story was reported by the *Chicago Bee* (*Milwaukee Star*, 10 July 1965), because Wisconsin again was without a black press. Josey's *Enterprise-Blade* folded just as his city's African American population finally soared more than 250 percent in the 1940s to almost twenty-two thousand (McBride, 339).

The *Enterprise-Blade*, however, had established a sense of community that would serve African Americans in Wisconsin well amid Milwaukee's "late Great Migration" (Geib, 229). Even Josey's media foe, the *Journal*, hailed his postwar election as "mayor of Bronzeville" and community spokesman. Reelected by the community to the unofficial office twice, he remained active in "nearly every committee in the city that dealt with interracial affairs" until his death in Milwaukee (*Milwaukee Journal*, 13 Nov. 1945).

Not until 1992—the centennial of the state's black press—would another publisher, JERREL JONES, surpass Josey's journalistic longevity in Wisconsin (McBride, 339–348). In 1998, the oldest press club in the country posthumously honored the pioneer in Wisconsin's black press, Josey, as the first member of the African American media inducted into the Milwaukee Press Club's Milwaukee Media Hall of Fame.

FURTHER READING

J. Anthony Josey's papers are archived in the Milwaukee County (Wisconsin) Historical Society.

Geib, Paul. "From Mississippi to Milwaukee: A Case Study of the Southern Black Migration to Milwaukee 1940–1970," *Journal of Negro History* 83:4 (Autumn, 1998).

Glad, Paul W. *The History of Wisconsin, vol. V: War, a New Era, and Depression, 1914–1940* (1990).

McBride, Genevieve G. "The Progress of 'Race Men' and 'Colored Women' in the Black Press in Wisconsin, 1892–1985," in *The Black Press in the Middle West, 1865–1985*, ed. Henry Lewis Suggs (1996).

Simmons, Charles A. *The African American Press: A History of News Coverage during National Crises, 1827–1965* (1998).

Trotter, Joe William, Jr. *Black Milwaukee: The Making of an Industrial Proletariat, 1915–45* (1985).

Obituaries: *Milwaukee Journal*, 8 July 1957; *Madison Capital Times*, 10 July 1957; *Milwaukee Defender*, 11 July 1957.

GENEVIEVE G. MCBRIDE

Joyner Kersee, Jackie (3 Mar. 1962–), a multisport athlete ranked by *Sports Illustrated for Women* as the greatest female athlete of the twentieth century, was born Jacqueline Joyner in East St. Louis, Illinois, the second of four children of teenage housewife Mary Ruth Gaines Joyner and high school student Alfred Joyner. Joyner's father became an aircraft assembly and railway worker once he graduated. Her mother later became a nurse's aide. Joyner's brother Alfrederick Joyner won the 1984 men's Olympic triple jump. FLORENCE GRIFFITH-JOYNER, who won three Olympic gold medals in 1988 and set world records in the one-hundred-meter and two-hundred-meter dashes, was her sister-in-law.

Joyner's early interest was dance. After dancer-choreographer-anthropologist KATHERINE MARY DUNHAM opened her East St. Louis Performing Arts Training Center in 1967, the already long-legged Joyner took classes there, learned to stand tall and carry herself elegantly, and dreamed of a dancing career—until her dance teacher was killed during a drug-related argument. Violence surrounded the family. Before Joyner was twelve she had witnessed a nonfatal shooting, her grandmother's murder in Chicago, four people's murder inside a tavern across the street from the family home, and another man's murder leaving it.

As a child, Joyner's second home was the Mary E. Brown Community Center in East St. Louis' Lincoln Park, where she absorbed stories and lectures, created handicrafts, and worked at various other tasks. There, in 1972, she joined a team of girls training on the park's unusual 550-yard, circle-shaped cinder track and in its makeshift jumping pit. Joyner soon created her own pit at home, with sand she and her sisters brought home in empty potato-chip bags, and taught herself the basic long-jumping technique.

Despite difficulties with exercise-induced asthma, Joyner began competing in summer youth track meets in 1974 when she was twelve. Two years later, inspired by a television movie about Babe Didrikson and by Bruce Jenner's decathlon victory at the Montreal Games, Joyner added the pentathlon to her athletic repertoire and began dreaming of the Olympics.

Joyner's emergence as an elite track athlete came during her high school years. She first qualified for the Amateur Athletic Union's summer Junior Olympic Championships in 1977. There she won the pentathlon and set a national record for her age group. She won the pentathlon again in 1978, 1979, and 1980, each year increasing her point totals and setting new national age-group records, while also setting a new national age-group record in the long jump in 1979 and winning the Junior Olympic long jump in both 1979 and 1980. In 1980, at age eighteen, she went on to finish eighth in the long jump at the U.S. Olympic Trials.

Back home in East St. Louis, Joyner starred for Lincoln High's Tigerettes in volleyball, basketball, and track and field, and was the *St. Louis Globe-Democrat*'s Girl Athlete of the Year in 1978, 1979, and 1980. The Tigerettes won the Illinois girls track championship in 1978, 1979, and 1980, with Joyner setting state records in the 440-yard dash in 1978 and the long jump in 1979. She was an all-Illinois pick in basketball in 1980, when the Tigerettes also won the Illinois state basketball championship with a perfect 31–0 record. In September of 1980 Joyner entered the University of California at

Jackie Joyner-Kersee jumps during the qualifying round of the women's long jump at the World Track and Field Championships at Goteborg's Ullevi Stadium, 5 August 1995. (AP Images.)

Los Angeles (UCLA), where she promptly became a freshman All-American in both basketball and track despite losing her mother to a sudden attack of meningitis during the basketball season. She won the National Collegiate Athletic Association track heptathlon in 1982, and again in 1983 when she received the Broderick Award as the nation's best woman college track athlete. After forgoing the 1983–1984 school year to prepare for the Olympics, she returned for her senior year to become all-conference in basketball and win the Broderick Cup as the nation's best overall woman college athlete. She graduated from UCLA in the top 10 percent of her class in 1985.

Joyner began her Olympic career in 1984 at the Los Angeles Games, where she won the second-place silver medal in the new Olympic heptathlon, finishing just five points behind the gold medalist, and placed fifth in the long jump. The first of her many women's records followed in 1985, when Joyner set a new U.S. record of twenty-three feet, nine inches in the outdoor long jump.

In 1986, after marrying her coach Robert (Bobby) Kersee, Joyner began competing as Jackie Joyner-Kersee and received the James E. Sullivan Award as the nation's best male or female amateur athlete. That year she won the heptathlon at the Moscow Goodwill Games, setting a world record of 7,148 points, 202 points higher than the previous record, and becoming the first woman to score over 7,000 points. At the 1986 Olympic Festival, she raised that record to 7,158 points. She was also named the 1986 U.S. Olympic Committee Sportswoman of the Year and *Track & Field News* Athlete of the Year, and won the 1986 Jesse Owens Award as the top U.S. woman track athlete.

Another world record followed in 1987, when Joyner-Kersee tied the world long jump record of twenty-four feet, five-and-one-half inches at the Pan American Games, won the heptathlon and long jump at the World Championship Games, and again won the Jesse Owens Award. Two more world records came in 1988, when she raised her world heptathlon record to 7,251 points at the U.S. Olympic Trials, and then to 7,291 points in the Olympic Games at Seoul, South Korea. Joyner-Kersee won two gold medals at Seoul, in both the heptathlon and the long jump. She also set a new Olympic long jump record of twenty-four feet, three-and-one-half inches. She was named the 1988 Women's Sports Foundation Amateur Athlete of the Year.

Joyner-Kersee won the long jump at the World Championship Games again in 1991. In 1992 she again won the Olympic heptathlon at the Barcelona Games, together with the third-place bronze medal in the long jump. She won the heptathlon in the 1993 World Championship Games and was International Association of Athletics Federation Female Athlete of the Year in 1994.

Injuries forced Joyner-Kersee's withdrawal from the heptathlon at the Atlanta Games in 1996, but she was able to come from behind with a dramatic final jump to repeat as long jump bronze medalist. She retired from competition in 1998 at age thirty-six, after winning the heptathlon at the Goodwill Games for the fourth time.

Joyner-Kersee then returned to the St. Louis area, where she initiated a number of business and charitable ventures. In 2000 her Jackie Joyner-Kersee Foundation opened a youth center in East St. Louis bearing her name.

FURTHER READING

Joyner-Kersee, Jackie, with Sonja Steptoe. *A Kind of Grace: An Autobiography of the World's Greatest Female Athlete* (1997).

Woolum, Janet. *Outstanding Woman Athletes: Who They Are and How They Influenced Sports in America* (1992).

STEVEN B. JACOBSON

Joyner, Marjorie Stewart (24 Oct. 1896–27 Dec. 1994), entrepreneur, inventor, and activist, was born in Monterey, Virginia, to George Emmanuel Stewart, a teacher, and Annie Dougherty Stewart, a housewife. The couple had thirteen children, but only four daughters lived beyond infancy. After relocating their family to Dayton, Ohio, Stewart's parents divorced and, in 1912, she moved to Chicago to live with her mother. In Chicago, Stewart attended Edgewood High School, worked temporary jobs, and, on 4 April 1916, she married Dr. Robert Joyner, a podiatrist from Memphis, Tennessee. The couple had two daughters: Anne Joyner Fook and Barbara Joyner Powell, who both became educators. At some point during her early Chicago years, Stewart made the decision to become a beautician and that decision would shape her future.

Joyner became the first black graduate of the A.B. Molar Beauty School in 1916, and she opened her own beauty shop in Chicago, at 5448 South State Street, where she served a primarily white clientele. Joyner's mother-in-law encouraged and paid for her to enroll in MADAME C. J. WALKER's Beauty School; she wanted her daughter-in-law to learn how to work with black hair. Joyner graduated and became a Walker Agent, selling the company's products for black hair care door to door. As one of Walker's most trusted employees, she helped to develop the company's network of Walker agents, beauty schools, and shops throughout the Midwest. When Walker died in 1919, Joyner became vice president of the company and chief instructor for fifteen thousand Walker agents. This position allowed Joyner to advocate for the beauty industry. She helped to write the first Illinois law governing beauty schools and salons, and in 1926, was the first black woman licensed as a beauty culturist.

As an employee and administrator of the Walker Company, Joyner grew dissatisfied with the complex process and excessive time required for beauticians to complete a permanent wave, as well as the poor quality of results. In a 1993 interview, Joyner explained: "operators might put in a very nice hairdo, but it would never last very long" (Sullivan,

40). Having identified the problem, Joyner began looking for a way to speed up the procedure and produce a permanent that would last longer. Years later, she discussed the inventive process: "It all came to me in the kitchen when I was making a pot roast." At that time, "to speed up the cooking of a beef roast," cooks inserted "Thin rods … into the pot roast to hold it together and for cooking evenly." Joyner believed "you could use" similar rods "like hair rollers, then heat them up to cook a permanent curl into the hair" (Parker, 4). She tested her idea by linking pot roast rods to a hair dryer hood. She then joined the several rods together to draw electricity through a single electrical cord. Joyner's subsequent invention, the mechanical device known as the Permanent Waving Machine, "consisted of an electrically powered device with cords, metal curling irons, and clamping devices suspended from a dome" (Macdonald, 297–301). Using the new device, beauticians wrapped each one-inch square of the patron's hair in flannel, placed a special protector against the scalp, and when all curling irons were in position, attached the clamps, lifting them away from the patron's head for safety, and then turned on the electric current. In intensive courses, students practiced dividing, wrapping, and heating the curls, and unwrapping and setting newly permed hair. Joyner's invention worked on the hair of both blacks and whites, and looked better and lasted longer than any other method available at the time.

Because she was an employee of the Walker Company, the patent for Joyner's invention was assigned to the company on 17 November 1928. With the success of the Permanent Waving Machine, Joyner pursued other inventive ideas, receiving patents in the Walker Company name for a hair straightening comb and the "Satin Tress" formula, an early hair relaxer. While her corporate and creative efforts were exceptional, they also typified the experience of the highly educated corporate woman patentee, who qualified for positions in corporate research facilities in increasing numbers throughout the twentieth century. These women created new products, but like Joyner, their employers held all rights to the patented inventions and tended to reap the financial benefits.

Beyond her entrepreneurial and technological achievements, Joyner made significant contributions to the beautician's profession and as a civil rights advocate for blacks and women. She was an instructor in Walker's beauty schools by 1919, and in 1945, Joyner cofounded the United Beauty School Owners and Teachers Association and the Alpha Phi Omega sorority and fraternity, the two most important organizations for black beauty educators and practitioners. In 1954, when white beauty schools and professional organizations refused to admit blacks, Joyner organized a trip to Paris for 195 black cosmetologists; they would study cutting-edge stylistic techniques employed in the salons of Europe's capital of culture. In addition, Joyner carried the Walker Company's beauty secrets to the West Indies, West Africa, the Holy Land, and to other major urban centers of Europe, including London and Rome, because, she noted: "no one there ... was dressing colored people's hair" (Flug, 366–370).

Joyner had a long association with MARY McLEOD BETHUNE, the president and founder of Bethune-Cookman College in Daytona Beach, Florida. Bethune recruited Joyner as a speaker and fund-raiser for the college, and when Bethune organized the National Council of Negro Women in 1935, Joyner sat among the founding members. Joyner remembered: "Dr. Bethune was trying to reach black people for education; I was trying to reach black people for beauty culture.... There were few places for a black person to get higher education then.... Everything you were trying to do, you had to think up ways to beat this color line, this Jim Crow" (Flug, 366–370). Working closely with Eleanor Roosevelt and Nelson Rockefeller to raise funds for the college, Joyner went on numerous speaking tours, addressed segregated audiences, boarded Jim Crow trains to get to her next engagement, and, when the first lady attended a desegregated performance of the Bethune-Cookman choir, faced Ku Klux Klan harassment (Flug, 368). Continuing her association with the Roosevelt administration, during the Great Depression, Joyner worked with the New Deal's Works Progress Administration, Civilian Conservation Corps, and the National Youth Administration, and during World War II, she helped to lead the Women's Division of the Democratic National Committee. (Mcdonald, 297–301).

Back in Chicago, Joyner became an important figure in the city's Democratic Party, a party dominated by the powerful Daley political machine through much of the twentieth century. Joyner was a known entity, so much so that Mayor Edward Kelly asked for her help in 1943 when the United Service Organization (USO) refused black servicemen access to white USO clubs. While she raised funds to open a center for black servicemen in Chicago, Joyner protested the USO's policy of racial segregation. Not until 1983 did Joyner break with the Daley political machine to support HAROLD WASHINGTON in his successful bid to become the first black mayor of Chicago. Joyner also maintained a long association with ROBERT S. ABBOTT, founder of the *Chicago Defender*, and his successors at the head of the newspaper. Her association with this most important of African American newspapers took many forms. Beginning in 1929, she took charge of the *Defender*-sponsored Bud Billiken Parade; by 1945 she chaired the *Chicago Defender* Charities, organizing food and clothing drives for the poor. Always an active church member, Joyner fostered the establishment of the Cosmopolitan Community Church, which would augment Chicago's black community on the southside for years to come.

Marjorie Stewart Joyner's career as an entrepreneur, inventor, educator, philanthropist, and political activist brought her in contact with many influential women, including Madame C. J. Walker, Mary McLeod Bethune and Eleanor Roosevelt. She received many awards and honors during her life, including an honorary doctor of humanities degree from Bethune-Cookman College in 1961, the outstanding achievers award from The National Council of Negro Women in 1990, and in that same year, Mayor Richard M. Daley declared her birthday "Dr. Marjorie Stewart Joyner Day" in Chicago. At a time when African Americans and women faced discrimination on all fronts, she excelled, becoming an inspiration, mentor, and civil rights advocate. While working zealously to foster educational opportunities for others, she never stopped enhancing her own education. In addition to her beauty school degrees, Joyner received a music school certificate in 1924 and completed her high school education through the Chicago Christian High School in 1935. Returning to college late in life, she took courses at Northwestern University and the Illinois Institute of Technology, eventually completing her bachelor's degree at Bethune-Cookman College when she was seventy-seven years old. Her entrepreneurial and technological contributions have been the subject of exhibitions at the Smithsonian Institution, the DuSable Museum, the University of Illinois, and the Chicago Public Library. Known as the Grande Dame of Black Beauty Culture, the Godmother of Bethune-Cookman College, and the Matriarch of the Bud Billiken Parade, Joyner's greatest achievement may be the sheer breadth of her abilities. She was not only a skilled and creative entrepreneur and inventor; she was a community organizer, successful fund-raiser, demanding teacher, courageous civil rights advocate, lifelong student, and successful international businessperson.

FURTHER READING

Flug, Michael. "Marjorie Stewart Joyner (1896–1994) Entrepreneur, Educator, Philanthropist," in *Notable Black American Women, Book II* (1995).

Macdonald, Anne L. *Feminine Ingenuity: Women and Invention in America* (1992).

Parker, Christi. "Sixty-three Years Later, Inventor Glad She Made Waves," *Chicago Tribune*, 3 November 1989.

Smith, Jessie Carney. *Black Firsts: 4,000 Ground-Breaking and Pioneering Historical Events* (2003).

Sullivan, Otha Richard. *Black Stars: African American Women Scientists and Inventors* (2002).

PAMELA C. EDWARDS

Joyner, Tom (1949–), philanthropist, entrepreneur, syndicated radio and television talk show host, and activist was born Thomas Joyner in Tuskegee, Alabama, the second son of H. L. Joyner, an accountant, and Buddy Joyner, a secretary. He attended Tuskegee Institute and graduated with a degree in sociology in 1970. At Tuskegee he met and married Dora Chatmon in 1970 while both were in their senior year of college. The couple had two sons, Thomas Jr. and Oscar, and divorced in 1996.

During his time as a student at Tuskegee, Joyner developed both a social consciousness, born of his involvement in the civil rights movement, and a passionate sense of social responsibility, born of the mission and vision of historically black colleges and universities. These elements, when combined with his love for music, were instrumental in shaping his life into one of altruism and advocacy.

While growing up in Tuskegee, Joyner participated in a boycott in the early 1960s of the town's local radio station. Joyner and many of the children he grew up with in Tuskegee recognized that even though the town of Tuskegee was 99 percent black, the music played on the town's only radio station was 100 percent white. This caused them to lead a protest against the radio station and demand that it play music more representative of the town in which it was located. During the protest the radio station owner sensed the unrest of the crowd and offered to quell the turmoil by calling for a volunteer to play black music on the radio every Saturday. Joyner raised his hand to take advantage of the opportunity, and his career in radio took off from there.

Joyner's first official radio job in 1970 was in Montgomery, Alabama, at station WRMA-AM, where he worked in the news department. In the mid-1970s he was hired by the publishing mogul JOHN H. JOHNSON to revive station WJPC in Chicago. It was also agreed that if Joyner were successful in making WJPC radio a success in Chicago, an offer to host a television show would follow. Success in radio did ensue, and in the mid-1980s Joyner retired from radio briefly to become the first television host of the *Ebony/Jet Showcase*. Joyner returned to radio after the show failed.

In 1985 Joyner became famous when he was offered a morning radio show at KKDA-AM in Dallas, Texas, and an afternoon radio show at WGCI in Chicago and accepted both. He made history by being the first person to host two radio shows every day in two different cities, and from 1986 until 1993 he flew to Dallas every morning and to Chicago every afternoon to host his drive-time radio programs. This stint earned him the titles of the "Fly Jock" and, in homage to the funk star JAMES BROWN, the "Hardest Working Man in Radio."

Joyner's style of radio programming was similar to the format of AM soul stations created during the civil rights movement. A significant difference was that Joyner was successful at reaching a much larger audience. His radio format set out to target a primarily black audience by playing black music, offering entertainment by, for, and about black people, announcing job listings, giving sports wrap-ups and sports information, telling jokes, and offering snippets of the news—not from a mainstream perspective, but from a black perspective. This urban radio format was instantly successful, and in 1994 the ABC Radio Network offered Joyner a lucrative contract to put the *Tom Joyner Morning Show* (*TJMS*) into syndication. Joyner once again made history by becoming the first African American man to have a nationally syndicated morning radio program. By 2006 Joyner's audience had grown to more than 8 million listeners in more than 120 markets, estimated to be the largest audience of any African American urban radio program.

Among the prominent programming features created by Joyner for *TJMS* was the notion of what he referred to as advocacy radio. He made it a priority to spend valuable radio time advocating that companies across the nation advertise their products in a predominantly black market and with a black media entity. He also brought attention to controversial and unfair practices taking place in the black community, and he was successful at launching voter registration campaigns among his listening audience. In 2000 Joyner was able to leverage the participation of his listeners in successfully shutting down Christie's international auction house in New York when he learned that it was about to auction off items connected with America's slave trade. He had also been successful in 1999 in getting CompUSA, which had never before advertised on minority radio, to advertise on his show and to offer a discount on its products to members of his listening audience.

Because Joyner, his grandparents, his parents, and both his sons were all graduates of black colleges, Joyner developed a special passion for historically black colleges and universities, and in 1998 he founded the Tom Joyner Foundation, dedicated to providing financial assistance to students struggling to stay enrolled at them. In 2000 he started the Fantastic Voyage cruises, otherwise known as the cruises that "partied with a purpose," for the purpose of raising funds for the Tom Joyner Foundation. By 2006 the cruises had raised more than $30 million to help students stay in historically black colleges and universities. In 2005, in the aftermath of Hurricane Katrina, which devastated the city of New Orleans, Joyner learned of three historically black colleges, Dillard University, Xavier University, and Southern University, that were flooded and forced to close. Immediately he created a relief fund for which millions of dollars were raised, in order to give scholarships of one thousand dollars each to students who had been attending these three schools. The funds were earmarked to help students with tuition, fees, and the purchase of books in order that the students might transfer to other schools and continue their education uninterrupted.

In 2003 Tom Joyner founded Reach Media as an umbrella for his many companies. This included the *Tom Joyner Morning Show*, of which he took ownership in 2004; the *Southwest Airlines Sky Show*, which hosted a party about thirty times a year in cities where the *TJMS* was broadcast; BlackAmericaWeb.com, an Internet service founded in 2001 and dedicated to presenting news, sports, and other information from a black perspective; the Tom Joyner Family Reunion, which was dedicated to bringing families together for fun, entertainment, and fellowship; the *Tom Joyner Show*, a syndicated one-hour comedy and variety television show that launched in October 2005; and the Tom Joyner Foundation, which included the Fantastic Voyage cruise. In 2005 he sold 51 percent of Reach Media to Radio One for $56 million.

On his radio show Joyner has exhibited many acts of kindness and compassion. Through the *Tom Joyner Morning Show*, Joyner frequently gave away a gift of one thousand dollars to deserving parents. He has sold a twenty-five-dollar bag of groceries that included eggs, cereal, bread, and meat to struggling radio listeners for five dollars; and he has granted Christmas wishes to listeners that included items such as computers, hearing aids, and spa treatments for women who were worn out and could not afford them. After the terrorist attacks on the World Trade Center in New York on 11 September 2001, Joyner personally delivered monetary gifts to victims who had lost a family member or other loved one. On Valentine's Day he has been known to visit shelters for abused women to deliver gifts.

Joyner has received numerous awards throughout his lifetime. In 1998 he became the first African American to be inducted into the Radio Hall of Fame. Other awards include *Savoy* magazine's 2002 Person of the Year, the Marconi Radio Award in 2004 for Excellence in Radio, and the Good Samaritan Award in 2004 by the National Broadcasters Education Foundation (NABEF). He also won *Impact* magazine's Best DJ of the Year award so frequently that they finally renamed the award the Tom Joyner Award.

In 2008, Joyner was featured in scholar HENRY LOUIS GATES's PBS documentary, *African American Lives 2*, which revealed that two of Joyner's great-uncles, Thomas and Meeks Griffin, had been executed in South Carolina in 1915 for the alleged murder of a Confederate veteran. Even at the time, it was believed that the real perpetrator of the crime had framed Joyner's relatives, and some local whites appealed for clemency to the governor, albeit with no success. It was not until nearly a century later, with the airing of *African American Lives 2*, and the assembling of a legal team to seek exoneration for the Griffins, that the South Carolina Parole and Pardons Board gave the Griffins a posthumous pardon. In 2010 Joyner married fitness and lifestyle guru Donna Richardson.

FURTHER READING
Joyner, Tom, with Mary Flowers Boyce. *I'm Just a DJ but … It Makes Sense to Me* (2005).

KAREN BEASLEY YOUNG

Julian, Hubert F. (20 Sept. 1897–19 Feb. 1983), aviator, was born Hubert Fauntleroy Julian in Port-of-Spain, Trinidad, the son of Henry Julian, a cocoa plantation manager, and Silvina "Lily" Hilaire Julian. He was educated at the Eastern Boys' School, an excellent private school in Port-of-Spain. In 1909 he saw his first airplane; minutes later, he witnessed its pilot's fatal crash. Nevertheless, Julian was instilled with a passion for both the exotic and the mechanical aspects of aviation. In 1912 his parents, who wanted their only child to be a doctor, sent him to England for further education. When World War I broke out, he went to Canada and attended high school in Montreal. Late in the war he took flying lessons with the Canadian ace Billy Bishop. Julian earned his Canadian pilot's license at the age of nineteen and thus became one of the earliest black aviators. In 1921 he was awarded Canadian and American patents for an airplane safety device he called a *parachuttagravepreresistra*. Although it was never produced commercially, the invention operated on principles that later propelled helicopters and deployed the parachute system that returned space capsules to earth. When activated by the pilot of a plane in distress, a parachutelike umbrella would blow open and lower the disabled plane to the ground by a system of rotating blades.

In July 1921 Julian settled in Harlem, already cultivating the flamboyant elegance that would be his lifelong hallmark. He became active in MARCUS GARVEY's Universal Negro Improvement Association and an officer in its paramilitary unit. Under Garvey's influence, Julian became absorbed in African history, an interest that later led to an active role in the history of Ethiopia. He broke into the African American aviation scene as a parachutist, appearing at an August 1922 air show on Long Island headlined by the African American aviator BESSIE COLEMAN. Two highly publicized parachute jumps over Manhattan in 1923 inspired a New York journalist to dub him "the Black Eagle," a sobriquet that delighted Julian and that he retained for the rest of his life.

Invitations to lecture and perform air stunts poured in. Although many of Julian's exploits were greeted with skepticism and charges of self-promotion, he maintained that his activities were all intended to demonstrate that African Americans were as capable of extraordinary achievement as anyone else. Early in 1924 he announced plans for a solo flight from New York to Liberia and Ethiopia. On 4 July 1924 his overhauled World War I–era hydroplane *Ethiopia I* lifted off from the Harlem River. Within minutes a pontoon broke off. The plane plummeted two thousand feet into Flushing Bay. A solo transatlantic crossing would not be achieved until Charles Lindbergh's successful flight in 1927.

Over the next five years, Julian barnstormed all over the United States. In 1927 he married Essie Marie Gittens, a childhood friend from Port-of-Spain. She remained Julian's "constant advisor and companion" until her death in 1975; one daughter survived her (*New York Amsterdam News*, 11 Jan. 1975, A3). Julian subsequently married Doreen Thompson, with whom he had a son.

In 1930 Julian was recruited by the prince regent of Ethiopia, Ras Tafari Makonnen, to train the nascent Ethiopian air force. Soon after his arrival in Ethiopia, Julian's aerobatic prowess so impressed the prince regent that he awarded him Ethiopian citizenship and an air force colonelcy. The Ethiopian cadets and their entire air power—two German-made monoplanes and a British Gypsy Moth recently given to the future emperor—were to perform at the prince regent's November 1930 coronation as Emperor Haile Selassie I. During an air show rehearsal, Julian took up the untried Gypsy Moth. The engine failed, and the prized plane crashed. Whether or not the plane had been sabotaged, the Imperial Air Force had only two planes remaining; Julian was asked to leave the country.

On 30 July 1931 Julian received a U.S. Department of Commerce private pilot's license. On 6 December 1931 he took part in the Los Angeles air show, organized by the African American aviator William Powell, headlined "the Black Eagle and the Five Blackbirds." For the first time, six African American pilots appeared together. Throughout the early 1930s, Julian flew in capacities as varied as barnstormer, rum runner, and private pilot for the evangelist FATHER DIVINE. When the Italo-Ethiopian war became imminent in 1935, Julian returned to Ethiopia as a volunteer. He briefly commanded the air force, but a violent dispute with the Chicago aviator JOHN C. ROBINSON led to Robinson's appointment as air force commander in Julian's stead.

After the Italians overran Ethiopia in 1936, Julian publicly disavowed the Ethiopian cause—for which he was reviled in America. He traveled to Italy, ostensibly to offer his services to Benito Mussolini. He later wrote that his intent in fact was to assassinate Il Duce but that his loyalties became known and their meeting never took place. During the summer of 1939 he was the war correspondent for the *New York Amsterdam News* in France. Back in New York, Julian announced that he would prove that African Americans were as capable in the film industry as, he claimed, he had proved them to be in aviation. He assisted in producing two OSCAR MICHEAUX films, *Lying Lips* (1939) and *The Notorious Elinor Lee* (1940).

In Europe the war was escalating. In 1940 Julian served briefly with a Finnish air regiment, then publicly challenged Reichsmarschall Hermann Goering to an air duel over the English Channel to defend the honor of the black race, which Adolf Hitler and Goering had defamed. The challenge was not accepted. Volunteering to join the Royal Canadian Air Force, Julian found he could no longer pass the flying test. In July 1942 he enlisted in the U.S. Army as an alien infantryman and became an American citizen on 28 September 1942. In May 1943 he was honorably discharged at the age of forty-five. After the war he parlayed his international contacts into global businesses, founding first a short-lived air freight charter, Black Eagle Airlines. In 1949 Black Eagle Enterprises, Ltd., was registered as a munitions dealer with the U.S. Department of State. Over the next two decades, Julian supplied arms and materiel to clients in developing nations and diplomatic crisis spots around the globe.

A resident of the Bronx, New York, since the 1950s, Julian died there in the Veterans Administration Hospital. Although for fifty years he carried the honorific "Colonel" from his Ethiopian days, he was buried in Calverton National Cemetery, Long Island, courtesy of his service as a private in the U.S. infantry.

FURTHER READING

Julian, Hubert F., with John Bulloch. *Black Eagle* (1964).

Chamberlin, Clarence D. *Record Flights* (1928).

Nugent, John Peer. *The Black Eagle* (1971).

Powell, William A. *Black Wings* (1934; reprinted as *Black Aviator*, 1994).

Scott, William R. *The Sons of Sheba's Race: African Americans and the Italo-Ethiopian War, 1935–1941* (1993).

This entry is taken from the *American National Biography* and is published here with the permission of the American Council of Learned Societies.

CAROLINE M. FANNIN

Julian, Percy Lavon (11 Apr. 1899–19 Apr. 1975), chemist, was born in Montgomery, Alabama, the son of James Sumner Julian, a railway mail clerk, and Elizabeth Lena Adams, a teacher. He received his AB from DePauw University in 1920, and for the next two years he taught chemistry at Fisk University. In 1922 he was awarded Harvard University's Austin Fellowship in chemistry; he received his M.A. from

that school in 1923. He remained at Harvard for three more years as a research assistant in biophysics and organic chemistry. In 1926 he joined the faculty at West Virginia State College, and in 1928 he became associate professor and head of the chemistry department at Howard University. The following year he was awarded a fellowship from the Rockefeller Foundation's General Education Board to pursue his doctorate at the University of Vienna in Austria, where he earned that degree in organic chemistry in 1931. After graduating he returned to Howard, but he left in 1932 to accept a position as chemistry professor and research fellow at DePauw.

Julian's first major discovery involved physostigmine, a drug made from Calabar beans that is used to treat glaucoma and myasthenia gravis. In 1934, while he was preparing to publish his findings concerning d,1-eserethole, the penultimate step in synthesizing physostigmine, Sir Robert Robinson, the eminent Oxford chemist, made public the results of his work on the synthesis of eserethole. Much to Julian's surprise, the eserethole described in Robinson's paper bore no resemblance to the compound he had developed. Despite the professional stature of Robinson, Julian published his own findings and detailed the differences between his results and Robinson's. The next year, when Julian successfully synthesized physostigmine from his version of d,1-eserethole, he clearly demonstrated that he, not Robinson, had been correct. Julian's next project involved the extraction from soybean oil of stigmasterol, a sterol used in the production of sex hormones, which in turn were used to treat a variety of medical conditions. However, he abandoned this line of research in 1936 when he was invited to join the Glidden Company of Chicago, Illinois, as director of research of the soya products division. His first task was to oversee the completion of a modern plant for extracting oil from soybeans; his second was to develop uses for the oil that the plant would produce. He soon devised a method for extracting from the oil vegetable protein, which he then developed into an inexpensive coating for paper. After he learned how to adjust the size of the soya protein molecule, Julian was able to create soya derivatives for use in textiles, paints, livestock and poultry feed, candy, ink, cosmetics, food additives, and "Aero Foam," used by the U.S. Navy during World War II to put out oil and gasoline fires and known throughout the fleet as "bean soup." Serendipitously, in 1940, when a large tank of soybean oil became contaminated with water and turned into an oily paste, Julian discovered that the paste was an excellent

Percy Julian working in his laboratory, c. 1945. The holder of ninety-four patents, Julian made important discoveries in the extraction and production of progesterone, testosterone, and cortisone. (Schomburg Center.)

source from which to extract inexpensively sterols such as stigmasterol. Soon Glidden was producing in bulk quantity the female hormone progesterone, used to prevent miscarriages and to treat certain menstrual complications, and the male hormone testosterone, used in the therapy of certain types of breast cancer. In 1949 Julian developed a method for synthesizing cortisone—used to treat rheumatoid arthritis—from sterols.

In 1954 Julian, having become more interested in steroid research than in soybeans, left Glidden to start Julian Laboratories in Oak Park, Illinois, with a factory and farms in Mexico. The Mexican branch of the operation harvested and processed the roots of *Dioscorea*, a wild Mexican yam, which Julian had discovered was an even better source than soybeans from which to synthesize cortisone and the sex hormones. In 1961 he sold the business to Smith, Kline and French, a pharmaceutical firm that was one of his best customers, but he remained as president until 1964, when he began the Julian Research Institute and Julian Associates, both in Franklin Park, Illinois. He continued to experiment with the production of synthetic drugs until his death.

Julian also played an active role in the civil rights movement. In 1956 he chaired the Council for Social Action of the Congregational Christian Churches, and in 1967 he became cochairman of a group of forty-seven prominent blacks recruited by the Legal Defense and Educational Fund of the National Association for the Advancement of Colored People (NAACP) to raise a million dollars for the purpose of financing lawsuits to enforce civil rights legislation.

In 1935 Julian married Anna Johnson; they had two children. Julian received a number of honors and awards, including the NAACP's Spingarn Medal (1947) and nineteen honorary doctoral degrees. He was elected to membership in the American Association for the Advancement of Science, the National Academy of Sciences, and the National Inventors Hall of Fame. Classroom buildings at MacMurray College, Coppin State College, and Illinois State University bear his name, as do elementary schools in Arizona and Louisiana and a high school in Chicago. He held ninety-four U.S. patents for methods of producing vegetable protein, sterols, and steroids and published his research in more than fifty scholarly articles. He died in Waukegan, Illinois.

Julian contributed to the advance of science in two ways. His pioneering research into the synthesization of hormones and other chemical substances made it possible for people of average means to obtain relief from such maladies as glaucoma and arthritis. His work with soybeans led to the development of a number of new and valuable products for industrial and agricultural applications.

FURTHER READING
Julian's papers did not survive.

Sammons, Vivian O. *Blacks in Science and Medicine* (1990).

Witkop, Bernhard. "'Percy Lavon Julian,' National Academy of Sciences," in *Biographical Memoirs* 52 (1980): 223–66.

Obituary: *New York Times*, 21 Apr. 1975.

This entry is taken from the *American National Biography* and is published here with the permission of the American Council of Learned Societies.

CHARLES W. CAREY JR.

July, Johanna (1857?–1946?), a black Seminole, was born around 1857 or 1858 in Nacimiento de Los Negros, the settlement established in northern Mexico following the emigration of Indian and Black Seminoles from the United States Indian

Territory in 1849. In 1849 about two hundred Seminoles and blacks left the reserve without the permission of Indian agents or government officials and headed to Mexico. Nine months later they crossed into the Rio Grande at Eagle Pass. The Mexican government settled the new immigrants into two small military colonies at Muzquiz and Nacimiento de Los Negros. At its peak in 1850, this colony provided a home for more than seven hundred Black Seminole, men, women, and children. The tribes of Black Seminoles were a mixture of Seminole Indians and African American slaves fleeing from Florida after the Seminole War. This group became famous for their thorough clearing of marauders from their territory. Because of their familiarity with the geography and various dialects of the border country, the Seminoles were employed by the U.S. Army as scouts and translators.

Around 1870, in direct response to U.S. Army Captain Frank W. Perry's offers of scouting jobs and protection, the Black Seminoles under subchief John Kibbetts resettled in the United States at Fort Duncan near Eagle Pass, and Fort Clark at Brackettville. The mission of the scouts was to clear the Texas side of the Rio Grande of depredating Indians. During the summer and fall of 1871, JOHN HORSE brought more scouts from Mexico, bringing the total Black Seminole community to about 150. During this second immigration Johanna July, a cowgirl, joined the settlement. Unlike most girls of the time who learned to cook, sew, and take care of the family, Johanna learned from her father Elijah to fish, hunt, and take care of horses.

While her sisters and mother cooked and did the domestic chores, Johanna took care of horses. These skills she developed in Mexico were useful in Texas, where she herded livestock for her extended family. After her father's death, Johanna learned how to ride horses and mastered the basics of tracking that made scouts so successful. When she was eighteen she married a Seminole scout by the name of Lesley, who took her to Fort Clark to live. She was prepared to be a dutiful wife even though she didn't know how to cook, sew, or do laundry. Johanna's husband was apparently abusive, so one night she used a neighbor's horse to escape and rode home to Eagle Pass, where her mother lived. Her husband came to Eagle Pass several times to try and get Johanna to return. When she refused go back to Fort Clark, he shot at her twice and missed both times. He also tried to tie a rope around her but missed; she hid in the brush fearing for her life until he was gone.

After her first husband died, she married twice more, first to Ned Wilkes, with whom she had four children, John, Ned Jr., Lucinda, and Amanda. In 1900 Johanna was widowed and living with her four children in Eagle Pass. In 1920 Johanna was living with her third husband, Charles Lasley, and her grand-daughter Ora May Roach in Brackettville. Johanna was known as Joanna Lesley (Lasley) around the Eagle Pass area and among the Black Seminoles. Her nephew William Warrior believes she died after World War II, although no death record has been located. Johanna was buried in the Seminole cemetery at Brackettville, but her gravesite has not been located.

FURTHER READING

U.S. Progress Works Administration, Federal Writers Project, American Life Histories: Johanna July. Interview by Florence Angermiller. American Memories Collection, Library of Congress, 1936–1940. Online, August 2009. (http://www.lcweb.gov)

Blackpast.org, Johanna July (1857?–1946?). http://www.blackpast.org/?q=aaw/july-johanna-1857-1946

Massey, Sara R., ed. Black Cowboys of Texas (2000).

KENYATTA D. BERRY

Just, Ernest Everett (14 Aug. 1883–27 Oct. 1941), zoologist, was born in Charleston, South Carolina, the son of Charles Fraser Just, a carpenter and wharf builder, and Mary Mathews Cooper. Following his father's death in 1887, his mother moved the family to James Island, off the South Carolina coast. There she labored in phosphate mines, opened a church and a school, and mobilized farmers into a moss-curing enterprise. A dynamic community leader, she was the prime mover behind the establishment of a township—Maryville—named in her honor. Maryville served as a model for all-black town governments elsewhere.

Just attended his mother's school, the Frederick Deming Jr. Industrial School, until the age of twelve. Under her influence, he entered the teacher-training program of the Colored Normal, Industrial, Agricultural and Mechanical College (now South Carolina State College) in Orangeburg, South Carolina, in 1896. After graduating in 1899, he attended Kimball Union Academy in Meriden, New Hampshire (1900–1903), before proceeding to Dartmouth College. At Dartmouth he majored in biology and minored in Greek and history. Under the guidance of two eminent zoologists, William Patten and John H. Gerould, he developed a passion for scientific research. Some of his work, on oral arches in frogs, was included in Patten's classic book *The Evolution of the Vertebrates and Their Kin* (1912). Just graduated magna cum laude from Dartmouth in 1907. Essentially, there were two career options available at the time to an African American with Just's academic background: teaching in a black institution or preaching in a black church. Just chose the former, beginning his career in the fall of 1907 as an instructor in English and rhetoric at Howard University. In 1909 he taught English and biology and a year later assumed a permanent full-time commitment in zoology as part of a general revitalization of the science curriculum at Howard. He also taught physiology in the medical school. A devoted teacher, he served as faculty adviser to a group that was trying to establish a nationwide fraternity of black students. The Alpha chapter of Omega Psi Phi was organized at Howard in 1911, and Just became its first honorary member. In 1912 he married a fellow Howard faculty member, Ethel Highwarden, with whom he later had three children.

Meanwhile, Just laid plans to pursue scientific research. Patten had placed him in touch with Frank Rattray Lillie, head of the zoology department at the University of Chicago and director of the Marine Biological Laboratory (MBL) at Woods Hole, Massachusetts. Although both Patten and Lillie considered it impractical for a black to seek a scientific career (in the face of overwhelming odds against finding suitable employment), Just's persistence and determination won them over. Lillie invited Just to the MBL as his research assistant in 1909. Their teacher-student relationship quickly blossomed into a full and equal scientific collaboration. By the time Just earned a Ph.D. in Zoology at the University of Chicago in 1916, he had already coauthored a paper with Lillie and written several of his own.

The two worked on fertilization in marine animals. Just's first paper, "The Relation of the First Cleavage Plane to the Entrance Point of the Sperm," appeared in *Biological Bulletin* in 1912 and was cited frequently as a classic and authoritative study. Just went on to champion a theory—the fertilizin theory—first proposed by Lillie, who postulated the existence of a substance called fertilizin as the essential biochemical catalyst in the fertilization of the egg by the sperm. In 1915 Just was awarded the NAACP's first Spingarn Medal in recognition of his scientific contributions and "foremost service to his race."

Ernest E. Just, zoologist and researcher. (University of Massachusetts, Amherst.)

As Patten and Lillie had predicted, no scientific positions opened up for Just. Science was for him a deeply felt avocation, an activity that he looked forward to doing each summer at the MBL as a welcome respite from his heavy teaching and administrative responsibilities at Howard. Under the circumstances, his productivity was extraordinary. Between 1919 and 1928 he published thirty-five articles, mostly relating to his studies on fertilization. Though proud of his output, he yearned for a position or environment in which he could pursue his research full-time.

The MBL, while serving in some respects as a haven of opportunity for Just, generated thinly disguised, occasionally overt racial tensions. Just was excluded from certain social gatherings and subjected to verbal slurs. A few of the more liberal scientists cultivated his acquaintance, protecting him at times from confrontations and embarrassment, but to Just this behavior seemed paternalistic. Further, while many MBL scientists relied on his technical expertise, some showed little regard for the intellectual or theoretical side of Just's work.

Others, citing a special duty to his race, urged him to abandon science in favor of teaching and more practical pursuits.

In 1928 Just received a substantial grant from the Julius Rosenwald Fund, which allowed him a change of environment and longer stretches of time for his research. His first excursion, in 1929, took him to Italy, where he worked for seven months at the Stazione Zoologica in Naples. He traveled to Europe ten times over the course of the next decade, staying for periods ranging from three weeks to two years. He worked primarily at the Stazione Zoologica, the Kaiser-Wilhelm Institut für Biologie in Berlin, and the Station Biologique in Roscoff, France. As the political turmoil in Europe grew, Just remained relatively unaffected and continued to be productive in his research. That he felt more comfortable there amid the rise of Nazism and Fascism suggests how dismal his outlook on life in America had become.

In Europe, Just worked on what he considered his magnum opus: a book synthesizing many of the scientific theories, philosophical ideas, and experimental results of his career. The book was published in 1939 under the title *Biology of the Cell Surface*. Its thesis, that the ectoplasm or cell surface has a fundamental role in development, did not receive much attention at the time but later became a focus of serious scientific investigation. Just was assisted in this work by a German, Maid Hedwig Schnetzler, whom he married in 1939 after divorcing his first wife. Also in 1939 he published a compendium of experimental advice under the title *Basic Methods for Experiments on Eggs of Marine Animals*. In 1940 Just was interned briefly in France following the German invasion, then was released to return to America, where he died of pancreatic cancer a year later in Washington, D.C.

FURTHER READING

A collection of Just's papers is preserved in the Manuscript Division of the Moorland-Spingarn Research Center, Howard University, Washington, D.C.

Gilbert, Scott F. "Cellular Politics: Ernest Everett Just, Richard B. Goldschmidt, and the Attempt to Reconcile Embryology and Genetics," in *The American Development of Biology*, eds. Ronald Rainger, Keith R. Benson, and Jane Maienschein (1988).

Gould, Stephen Jay. "Just in the Middle: A Solution to the Mechanist-Vitalist Controversy," *Natural History* (Jan. 1984): 24–33.

Manning, Kenneth R. *Black Apollo of Science: The Life of Ernest Everett Just* (1983)

Obituary: *Science* 95 (2 Jan. 1942).

This entry is taken from the *American National Biography* and is published here with the permission of the American Council of Learned Societies.

KENNETH R. MANNING